T0189000

Lecture Notes in Artificial Intelligence   12084

Subseries of Lecture Notes in Computer Science

More information about this series at http://www.springer.com/series/1244

Hady W. Lauw · Raymond Chi-Wing Wong ·
Alexandros Ntoulas · Ee-Peng Lim ·
See-Kiong Ng · Sinno Jialin Pan (Eds.)

Advances in Knowledge Discovery and Data Mining

24th Pacific-Asia Conference, PAKDD 2020
Singapore, May 11–14, 2020
Proceedings, Part I

 Springer

Editors
Hady W. Lauw 🄳
School of Information Systems
Singapore Management University
Singapore, Singapore

Alexandros Ntoulas 🄳
Department of Informatics
and Telecommunications
National and Kapodistrian
University of Athens
Athens, Greece

See-Kiong Ng 🄳
Institute of Data Science
National University of Singapore
Singapore, Singapore

Raymond Chi-Wing Wong 🄳
Department of Computer Science
and Engineering
Hong Kong University of Science
and Technology
Hong Kong, Hong Kong

Ee-Peng Lim 🄳
School of Information Systems
Singapore Management University
Singapore, Singapore

Sinno Jialin Pan 🄳
School of Computer Science
and Engineering
Nanyang Technological University
Singapore, Singapore

ISSN 0302-9743   ISSN 1611-3349 (electronic)
Lecture Notes in Artificial Intelligence
ISBN 978-3-030-47425-6   ISBN 978-3-030-47426-3 (eBook)
https://doi.org/10.1007/978-3-030-47426-3

LNCS Sublibrary: SL7 – Artificial Intelligence

This Springer imprint is published by the registered company Springer Nature Switzerland AG
The registered company address is: Gewerbestrasse 11, 6330 Cham, Switzerland

PC Chairs' Preface

It is our great pleasure to introduce the proceedings of the 24th Pacific-Asia Conference on Knowledge Discovery and Data Mining (PAKDD 2020). The conference provides an international forum for researchers and industry practitioners to share their new ideas, original research results, and practical development experiences from all KDD-related areas, including data mining, data warehousing, machine learning, artificial intelligence, databases, statistics, knowledge engineering, visualization, decision-making systems, and the emerging applications.

We received 628 submissions to PAKDD 2020 from a variety of countries and regions all over the world, noticeably with submissions from China, Australia, USA, India, Germany, France, Japan, Singapore, Taiwan, South Korea, Bangladesh, New Zealand, and Indonesia. The large number of submissions and high diversity of submission demographics are testaments to the significant influence and reputation of PAKDD. A rigorous double-blind reviewing procedure was ensured via the joint efforts of the entire Program Committee consisting of 55 Senior Program Committee (SPC) members and 344 Program Committee (PC) members.

The PC co-chairs performed an initial screening of all the submissions, among which 60 submissions were desk rejected due to the violation of submission guidelines. For submissions entering the double-blind review process, each one received at least three quality reviews from PC members (with 79% of them receiving four or more reviews). Furthermore, each valid submission received one meta-review from the assigned SPC member who also led the discussion with the PC members. The PC co-chairs then considered the recommendations and meta-reviews from SPC members, and looked into each submission as well as its reviews and PC discussions to make the final decision. As a result, 135 out of 628 submissions were accepted, yielding an acceptance rate of 21.5%. All the accepted papers are presented in a total of 12 technical sessions. Due to the outbreak of COVID-19, PAKDD 2020 was conducted in an online environment. Each paper was allocated 13 minutes for pre-recorded video presentation and 4 minutes for live Q/A. The conference program also featured four keynote speeches from distinguished data mining researchers, one most influential paper talk, two invited industrial talks, five cutting-edge workshops, two comprehensive tutorials, and one dedicated data mining competition session. We wish to sincerely thank all SPC members, PC members, and external reviewers for their invaluable efforts in ensuring a timely, fair, and highly effective paper review and selection procedure. We hope that readers of the proceedings will find that the PAKDD 2020 technical program was both interesting and rewarding.

March 2020

Hady W. Lauw
Raymond Chi-Wing Wong
Alexandros Ntoulas

General Chairs' Preface

On behalf of the Organizing Committee, it is our great pleasure to welcome you to the 24th Pacific-Asia Conference on Knowledge Discovery and Data Mining (PAKDD 2020). Since its first edition in 1997, PAKDD has been well established as one of the leading international conferences in data mining and knowledge discovery. Held during May 11–14, 2020, PAKDD 2020 returned to Singapore for the second time, after a 14-year hiatus. Due to the unexpected COVID-19 epidemic, we made all the conference sessions accessible online to participants around the world, which was unprecedented in the PAKDD history.

Our gratitude goes first and foremost to the authors who submitted their work to the PAKDD 2020 main conference, workshops, and data mining contest. We thank them for the great efforts in preparing high-quality online presentations videos. It is also our honor that four eminent keynote speakers graced the conference: Professor Inderjit S. Dhillon from University of Texas at Austin, Professor Samuel Kaski from Aalto University, Professor Jure Leskovec from Stanford University, and Professor Bing Liu from University of Illinois at Chicago. Given the importance of data science not just to academia but also to industry, we were pleased to have two distinguished industry speakers: Dr. Usama Fayyad, Chairman & CEO of Open Insights and Co-Founder & Advisory CTO of OODA Health, Inc., as well as Dr. Ankur M. Teredesai, Founder & CTO of KenSci and Professor at the University of Washington Tacoma. The conference program was further enriched with two high-quality tutorials, five workshops on cutting-edge topics, and one data mining contest on prediction of disk failures.

We express our sincere gratitude to the contributions of the SPC members, PC members, and external reviewers, led by the PC co-chairs, Hady W. Lauw, Raymond Chi-Wing Wong, and Alexandros Ntoulas. We are also thankful to the other Organizing Committee members: industry co-chairs, Ying Li and Graham Williams; workshop co-chairs, Kenny Q. Zhu and Wei Lu; tutorial co-chairs, Huiping Cao and Gao Cong; publicity co-chairs, Evangelos E. Papalexakis and Aixin Sun; sponsorship co-chairs, Feida Zhu and Giuseppe Manai; competitions chair, Mengling Feng; proceedings chair, Sinno J. Pan; and registration/local arrangement co-chairs, Aloysius Lim and Bing-Tian Dai.

We appreciate the hosting organization Singapore Management University and our sponsor Singapore Tourism Board for their institutional and financial support of PAKDD 2020. We also appreciate Alibaba for sponsoring the data mining contest. We feel indebted to the PAKDD Steering Committee for its continuing guidance and sponsorship of the paper and student travel awards.

Finally, our sincere thanks go to all the participants and volunteers – there would be no conference without you. We hope all of you enjoyed PAKDD 2020.

March 2020

Ee-Peng Lim
See-Kiong Ng

Organization

Organization Committee

General Chairs

Ee-Peng Lim	Singapore Management University, Singapore
See-Kiong Ng	National University of Singapore, Singapore

Program Committee Chairs

Hady W. Lauw	Singapore Management University, Singapore
Raymond Wong	Hong Kong University of Science and Technology, Hong Kong
Alexandros Ntoulas	National and Kapodistrian University of Athens, Greece

Industry Co-chairs

Ying Li	Giving Tech Labs, USA
Graham Williams	The Australian National University, Australia

Workshop Co-chairs

Kenny Q. Zhu	Shanghai Jiao Tong University, China
Wei Lu	Singapore University of Technology and Design, Singapore

Tutorial Co-chairs

Huiping Cao	New Mexico State University, USA
Gao Cong	Nanyang Technological University, Singapore

Publicity Co-chairs

Evangelos E. Papalexakis	University of California, Riverside, USA
Sun Aixin	Nanyang Technological University, Singapore

Sponsorship Co-chairs

Feida Zhu	Singapore Management University, Singapore
Giuseppe Manai	ING, Singapore

Competitions Chair

Mengling Feng	National University of Singapore, Singapore

Proceedings Chair

Sinno J. Pan   Nanyang Technological University, Singapore

Registration/Local Arrangement Co-chairs

Aloysius Lim   KenSci, USA
Bing-Tian Dai   Singapore Management University, Singapore

Steering Committee

Co-chairs

Ee-Peng Lim (Chair)   Singapore Management University, Singapore
Vincent S. Tseng   National Chiao Tung University, Taiwan
  (Vice-chair)

Treasurer

Longbing Cao   Advanced Analytics Institute,
                                    University of Technology Sydney, Australia

Members

Min-Ling Zhang   Southeast University, China (Member since 2019)
Zhiguo Gong   University of Macau, Macau (Member since 2019)
Joao Gama   University of Porto, Portugal (Member since 2019)
Dinh Phung   Monash University, Australia (Member since 2018)
Geoff Webb   Monash University, Australia (Member since 2018)
Jae-Gil Lee   Korea Advanced Institute of Science and Technology,
                                    Korea (Member since 2018)
Longbing Cao   Advanced Analytics Institute, University
                                    of Technology Sydney, Australia
                                    (Member since 2013, Treasurer since 2018)
Jian Pei   School of Computing Science, Simon Fraser
                                    University, Canada (Member since 2013)
Vincent S. Tseng   National Chiao Tung University, Taiwan
                                    (Member since 2014, Vice-chair from 2019–2020)
Gill Dobbie   The University of Auckland, New Zealand
                                    (Member since 2016)
Kyuseok Shim   Seoul National University, Korea (Member since 2017)

Life Members

P. Krishna Reddy   International Institute of Information Technology
                                    Hyderabad (IIIT-H), India (Member since 2010,
                                    Life Member since 2018)

Joshua Z. Huang	Shenzhen Institutes of Advanced Technology, Chinese Academy of Sciences, China (Member since 2011, Life Member since 2018)
Ee-Peng Lim	Singapore Management University, Singapore (Member since 2006, Life Member since 2014, Co-chair 2015–2017, Chair 2018–2020)
Hiroshi Motoda	AFOSR/AOARD and Osaka University, Japan (Member since 1997, Co-chair 2001–2003, Chair 2004–2006, Life Member since 2006)
Rao Kotagiri	The University of Melbourne, Australia (Member since 1997, Co-chair 2006–2008, Chair 2009–2011, Life Member since 2007, Co-sign since 2006)
Huan Liu	Arizona State University, USA (Member since 1998, Treasurer 1998–2000, Life Member since 2012)
Ning Zhong	Maebashi Institute of Technology, Japan (Member since 1999, Life Member since 2008)
Masaru Kitsuregawa	Tokyo University, Japan (Member since 2000, Life Member since 2008)
David Cheung	University of Hong Kong, China (Member since 2001, Treasurer 2005–2006, Chair 2006–2008, Life Member since 2009)
Graham Williams	The Australian National University, Australia (Member since 2001, Treasurer 2006–2017, Co-sign since 2006, Co-chair 2009–2011, Chair 2012–2014, Life Member since 2009)
Ming-Syan Chen	National Taiwan University, Taiwan (Member since 2002, Life Member since 2010)
Kyu-Young Whang	Korea Advanced Institute of Science and Technology, Korea (Member since 2003, Life Member since 2011)
Chengqi Zhang	University of Technology Sydney, Australia (Member since 2004, Life Member since 2012)
Tu Bao Ho	Japan Advanced Institute of Science and Technology, Japan (Member since 2005, Co-chair 2012–2014, Chair 2015–2017, Life Member since 2013)
Zhi-Hua Zhou	Nanjing University, China (Member since 2007, Life Member since 2015)
Jaideep Srivastava	University of Minnesota, USA (Member since 2006, Life Member since 2015)
Takashi Washio	Institute of Scientific and Industrial Research, Osaka University, Japan (Member since 2008, Life Member since 2016, Vice-chair 2018–2019)
Thanaruk Theeramunkong	Thammasat University, Thailand (Member since 2009, Life Member since 2017)

Past Members

Hongjun Lu	Hong Kong University of Science and Technology, Hong Kong (Member 1997–2005)
Arbee L. P. Chen	National Chengchi University, Taiwan (Member 2002–2009)
Takao Terano	Tokyo Institute of Technology, Japan (Member 2000–2009)
Tru Hoang Cao	Eastern Washington University, USA, Ho Chi Minh City University of Technology, Vietnam (Member 2015–2017)
Myra Spiliopoulou	Information Systems, Otto-von-Guericke-University Magdeburg, Germany (Member 2013–2019)

Senior Program Committee

James Bailey	The University of Melbourne, Australia
Albert Bifet	Universite Paris-Saclay, France
Longbing Cao	University of Technology Sydney, Australia
Tru Cao	Ho Chi Minh City University of Technology, Vietnam
Peter Christen	The Australian National University, Australia
Gao Cong	Nanyang Technological University, Singapore
Peng Cui	Tsinghua University, China
Guozhu Dong	Wright State University, USA
Benjamin C. M. Fung	McGill University, Canada
Bart Goethals	Universiteit Antwerpen, Belgium
Dimitrios Gunopulos	University of Athens, Greece
Geoff Holmes	University of Waikato, New Zealand
Qinghua Hu	Tianjin University, China
Xia Hu	Texas A&M University, USA
Sheng-Jun Huang	Nanjing University of Aeronautics and Astronautics, China
Seungwon Hwang	Yonsei University, Korea
Shuiwang Ji	Texas A&M University, USA
Kamalakar Karlapalem	IIIT Hyderabad, India
Yoshinobu Kawahara	Kyushu University, RIKEN, Japan
Sang-Wook Kim	Hanyang University, Korea
Byung Suk Lee	University of Vermont, USA
Jae-Gil Lee	KAIST, Korea
Ying Li	Giving Tech Labs, USA
Gang Li	Deakin University, Australia
Jiuyong Li	University of South Australia, Australia
Ming Li	Nanjing University, China
Yufeng Li	Nanjing University, China
Shou-De Lin	National Taiwan University, Taiwan
Weiwei Liu	Wuhan University, China

Nikos Mamoulis   University of Ioannina, Greece
Wee Keong Ng   Nanyang Technological University, Singapore
Krishna Reddy P.   International Institute of Information Technology,
                                Hyderabad, India
Jian Pei   Simon Fraser University, Canada
Wen-Chih Peng   National Chiao Tung University, Taiwan
Vincenzo Piuri   Università degli Studi di Milano, Italy
Rajeev Raman   University of Leicester, UK
Chandan K. Reddy   Virginia Tech, USA
Masashi Sugiyama   RIKEN, The University of Tokyo, Japan
Kai Ming Ting   Federation University, Australia
Hanghang Tong   University of Illinois at Urbana-Champaign, USA
Panayiotis Tsaparas   University of Ioannina, Greece
Vincent Tseng   National Chiao Tung University, Taiwan
Jianyong Wang   Tsinghua University, China
Fei Wang   Cornell University, USA
Takashi Washio   The Institute of Scientific and Industrial Research,
                                Osaka University, Japan
Xintao Wu   University of Arkansas, USA
Jia Wu   Macquarie University, Australia
Xing Xie   Microsoft Research Asia, China
Xindong Wu   Mininglamp Academy of Sciences, China
Yue Xu   Queensland University of Technology, Australia
Jeffrey Xu Yu   Chinese University of Hong Kong, Hong Kong
Yanchun Zhang   Victoria University, Australia
Zhao Zhang   Soochow University, China
Xiaofang Zhou   The University of Queensland, Australia
Fuzhen Zhuang   Institute of Computing Technology, Chinese Academy
                                of Sciences, China

Program Committee

Swati Agarwal   BITS Pilani Goa, India
Karan Aggarwal   University of Minnesota, USA
David Anastasiu   Santa Clara University, USA
Xiang Ao   Institute of Computing Technology, CAS, China
Sunil Aryal   Deakin University, Australia
Jean Paul Barddal   PUCPR, Brazil
Leopoldo Bertossi   Universidad Adolfo Ibañez, Chile,
                                and RelationalAI Inc., USA
Raj K. Bhatnagar   University of Cincinnati, USA
Arnab Bhattacharya   IIT Kanpur, India
Kevin Bouchard   Université du Québec à Chicoutimi, Canada
Yingyi Bu   Google, USA
Krisztian Buza   Eotvos Lorand University, Hungary
Rui Camacho   Universidade do Porto, Portugal

K. Selçuk Candan	Arizona State University, USA
Huiping Cao	New Mexico State University, USA
Tanmoy Chakraborty	Indraprastha Institute of Information Technology Delhi (IIIT-D), India
Shama Chakravarthy	The University of Texas at Arlington, USA
Chun-Hao Chen	Tamkang University, Taiwan
Huiyuan Chen	Case Western Reserve University, USA
Lei Chen	Nanjing University of Posts and Telecommunications, China
Lu Chen	Aalborg University, Denmark
Meng Chang Chen	Academia Sinica, Taiwan
Rui Chen	Samsung Research, USA
Songcan Chen	Nanjing University of Aeronautics and Astronautics, China
Yi-Ping Phoebe Chen	La Trobe University, Australia
Yi-Shin Chen	National Tsing Hua University, Taiwan
Zhiyuan Chen	University of Maryland Baltimore County, USA
Jiefeng Cheng	Tencent, China
Meng-Fen Chiang	Singapore Management University, Singapore
Reynold Cheng	The University of Hong Kong, China
Silvia Chiusano	Politecnico di Torino, Italy
Byron Choi	Hong Kong Baptist University, China
Dong-Wan Choi	Inha University, Korea
Jaegul Choo	Korea University, Korea
Chi-Yin Chow	City University of Hong Kong, Hong Kong
Lingyang Chu	Huawei Technologies, Canada
Kun-Ta Chuang	National Cheng Kung University, Taiwan
Bruno Cremilleux	Université de Caen Normandie, France
Chaoran Cui	Shandong University of Finance and Economics, China
Boris Cule	University of Antwerp, Belgium
Bing Tian Dai	Singapore Management University, Singapore
Honghua Dai	Zhengzhou University, China
Wang-Zhou Dai	Imperial College London, UK
Dong Deng	Rutgers University, New Brunswick, USA
Jeremiah Deng	University of Otago, New Zealand
Xuan-Hong Dang	IBM T. J. Watson Research Center, USA
Zhaohong Deng	Jiangnan University, China
Pravallika Devineni	Oak Ridge National Laboratory, USA
Steven H. H. Ding	Queen's University, Canada
Trong Dinh Thac Do	University of Technology Sydney, Australia
Gillian Dobbie	University of Auckland, New Zealand
Dejing Dou	University of Oregon, USA
Lan Du	Monash University, Australia
Boxin Du	Arizona State University, USA
Lei Duan	Sichuan University, China
Vladimir Estivill-Castro	Griffith University, Australia

Xuhui Fan	University of Technology Sydney, Australia
Yuan Fang	Singapore Management University, Singapore
Kaiyu Feng	Nanyang Technological University, Singapore
Philippe Fournier-Viger	Harbin Institute of Technology, China
Yanjie Fu	University of Central Florida, USA
Ken-ichi Fukui	Osaka University, Japan
Sebastien Gaboury	Université du Québec à Chicoutimi, Canada
Dragan Gamberger	Rudjer Boskovic Institute, Croatia
Xiaoying Gao	Victoria University of Wellington, New Zealand
Yunjun Gao	Zhejiang University, China
Arnaud Giacometti	University Francois Rabelais of Tours, France
Heitor M. Gomes	Télécom ParisTech, France
Chen Gong	Nanjing University of Science and Technology, China
Maciej Grzenda	Warsaw University of Technology, Poland
Lei Gu	Nanjing University of Posts and Telecommunications, China
Yong Guan	Iowa State University, USA
Himanshu Gupta	IBM Research, India
Sunil Gupta	Deakin University, Australia
Yahong Han	Tianjin University, China
Choochart Haruechaiyasak	National Electronics and Computer Technology Center, Thailand
Shoji Hirano	Shimane University, Japan
Tuan-Anh Hoang	L3S Research Center, Leibniz University of Hanover, Germany
Jaakko Hollmén	Aalto University, Finland
Tzung-Pei Hong	National University of Kaohsiung, Taiwan
Chenping Hou	National University of Defense Technology, China
Haibo Hu	Hong Kong Polytechnic University, Hong Kong
Liang Hu	University of Technology Sydney, Australia
Chao Huang	University of Notre Dame, USA
David Tse Jung Huang	The University of Auckland, New Zealand
Guangyan Huang	Deakin University, Australia
Jen-Wei Huang	National Cheng Kung University, Taiwan
Xin Huang	Hong Kong Baptist University, Hong Kong
Nam Huynh	Japan Advanced Institute of Science and Technology, Japan
Akihiro Inokuchi	Kwansei Gakuin University, Japan
Divyesh Jadav	IBM Research, USA
Szymon Jaroszewicz	Polish Academy of Sciences, Poland
Przemyslaw Jeziorski	University of California, Berkeley, USA
Bo Jin	Dalian University of Technology, China
Xiaojie Jin	National University of Singapore, Singapore
Toshihiro Kamishima	National Institute of Advanced Industrial Science and Technology, Japan
Murat Kantarcioglu	UT Dallas, USA

Hung-Yu Kao	National Cheng Kung University, Taiwan
Shanika Karunasekera	The University of Melbourne, Australia
Makoto P. Kato	Kyoto University, Japan
Xiangyu Ke	Nanyang Technological University, Singapore
Jungeun Kim	ETRI, Korea
Kyoung-Sook Kim	National Institute of Advanced Industrial Science and Technology, Japan
Yun Sing Koh	The University of Auckland, New Zealand
Ravi Kothari	Ashoka University, India
Pigi Kouki	Relational AI, USA
P. Radha Krishna	National Institute of Technology Warangal, India
Marzena Kryszkiewicz	Warsaw University of Technology, Poland
Chao Lan	University of Wyoming, Canada
Dung D. Le	Singapore Management University, Singapore
Duc-Trong Le	University of Engineering and Technology, Vietnam National University, Vietnam
Tuan M. V. Le	New Mexico State University, USA
Dik Lee	HKUST, Hong Kong
Ickjai Lee	James Cook University, Australia
Jongwuk Lee	Sungkyunkwan University, Korea
Ki Yong Lee	Sookmyung Women's University, Korea
Ki-Hoon Lee	Kwangwoon University, Korea
Roy Ka-Wei Lee	University of Saskatchewan, Canada
SangKeun Lee	Korea University, Korea
Sunhwan Lee	Amazon, USA
Vincent C. S. Lee	Monash University, Australia
Wang-Chien Lee	Pennsylvania State University, USA
Yue-Shi Lee	Ming Chuan University, China
Zhang Lei	Anhui University, China
Carson K. Leung	University of Manitoba, Canada
Jianmin Li	Tsinghua University, China
Jianxin Li	Deakin University, Australia
Jundong Li	University of Virginia, USA
Peipei Li	Hefei University of Technology, China
Qi Li	Iowa State University, USA
Qian Li	University of Technology Sydney, Australia
Rong-Hua Li	Beijing Institute of Technology, China
Sheng Li	University of Georgia, USA
Wenyuan Li	University of California, Los Angeles, USA
Xiaoli Li	Institute for Infocomm Research, A*STAR, Singapore
Xiucheng Li	Nanyang Technological University, Singapore
Yidong Li	Beijing Jiaotong University, China
Yuchen Li	Singapore Management University, Singapore
Panagiotis Liakos	University of Athens, Greece
Sungsu Lim	Chungnam National University, Korea
Chunbin Lin	Amazon, USA

Hsuan-Tien Lin	National Taiwan University, Taiwan
Jerry Chun-Wei Lin	Western Norway University of Applied Sciences, Norway
Anqi Liu	California Institute of Technology, USA
Chenghao Liu	Singapore Management University, Singapore
Jiamou Liu	The University of Auckland, New Zealand
Jie Liu	Nankai University, China
Lian Liu	Roku Inc., USA
Lin Liu	University of South Australia, Australia
Qun Liu	Louisiana State University, USA
Shaowu Liu	University of Technology Sydney, Australia
Wei Liu	University of Western Australia, Australia
Yiding Liu	Nanyang Technological University, Singapore
Zemin Liu	Singapore Management University, Singapore
Zheng Liu	Nanjing University of Posts and Telecommunications, China
Wang Lizhen	Yunnan University, China
Cheng Long	Nanyang Technological University, Singapore
Hua Lu	Aalborg University, Denmark
Wenpeng Lu	Qilu University of Technology (Shandong Academy of Sciences), China
Jun Luo	Machine Intelligence Lab, Lenovo Group Limited, Hong Kong
Wei Luo	Deakin University, Australia
Huifang Ma	Northwest Normal University, China
Marco Maggini	University of Siena, Italy
Giuseppe Manco	ICAR-CNR, Italy
Silviu Maniu	Université Paris-Sud, France
Naresh Manwani	International Institute of Information Technology, Hyderabad, India
Florent Masseglia	Inria, France
Yasuko Matsubara	Osaka University, Japan
Alex Memory	Leidos, USA
Ernestina Menasalvas	Universidad Politecnica de Madrid, Spain
Jun-Ki Min	Korea University of Technology and Education, Korea
Nguyen Le Minh	JAIST, Japan
Leandro Minku	University of Birmingham, UK
Pabitra Mitra	Indian Institute of Technology Kharagpur, India
Anirban Mondal	Xerox Research Lab, India
Yang-Sae Moon	Kangwon National University, Korea
Animesh Mukherjee	IIT Kharagpur, India
Mirco Nanni	ISTI-CNR, Italy
Guruprasad Nayak	University of Minnesota, USA
Raymond Ng	UBC, Canada
Wilfred Ng	HKUST, Hong Kong
Cam-Tu Nguyen	Nanjing University, China

Canh Hao Nguyen	Kyoto University, Japan
Ngoc-Thanh Nguyen	Wroclaw University of Science and Technology, Poland
Quoc Viet Hung Nguyen	Griffith University, Australia
Thanh Nguyen	Deakin University, Australia
Thanh-Son Nguyen	Agency for Science, Technology and Research (A*STAR), Singapore
Athanasios Nikolakopoulos	University of Minnesota, USA
Yue Ning	Stevens Institute of Technology, USA
Tadashi Nomoto	National Institute of Japanese Literature, Japan
Kouzou Ohara	Aoyama Gakuin University, Japan
Kok-Leong Ong	La Trobe University, Australia
Yuangang Pan	University of Technology Sydney, Australia
Guansong Pang	The University of Adelaide, Australia
Dhaval Patel	IBM T. J. Watson Research Center, USA
Peng Peng	inspir.ai, China
Vikram Pudi	IIIT Hyderabad, India
Jianzhong Qi	The University of Melbourne, Australia
Qi Qian	Alibaba Group, China
Qiang Tang	Luxembourg Institute of Science and Technology, Luxembourg
Biao Qin	Renmin University of China, China
Jie Qin	ETH Zürich, Switzerland
Tho Quan	Ho Chi Minh City University of Technology, Vietnam
Uday Kiran Rage	University of Tokyo, Japan
Chedy Raissi	Inria, France
Santu Rana	Deakin University, Australia
Thilina N. Ranbaduge	The Australian National University, Australia
Arun Reddy	Arizona State University, USA
Chuan-Xian Ren	Sun Yat-sen University, China
Patricia Riddle	University of Auckland, New Zealand
Lee Sael	Seoul National University, Korea
Doyen Sahoo	Salesforce, Singapore
Aghiles Salah	Singapore Management University, Singapore
Jieming Shi	National University of Singapore, Singapore
Yu Shi	Facebook, USA
Navneet Potti	Google Research, USA
Huasong Shan	JD.com, USA
Wei Shen	Nankai University, China
Hong Shen	Adelaide University, Australia
Victor S. Sheng	Texas Tech University, USA
Chuan Shi	Beijing University of Posts and Telecommunications, China
Motoki Shiga	Gifu University, Japan
Hiroaki Shiokawa	University of Tsukuba, Japan
Andrzej Skowron	University of Warsaw, Poland

Yang Song	University of New South Wales, Australia
Arnaud Soulet	University of Tours, France
Srinath Srinivasa	IIIT Bangalore, India
Fabio Stella	University of Milano-Bicocca, Italy
Yuqing Sun	Shandong University, China
Guangzhong Sun	University of Science and Technology of China, China
Bo Tang	Southern University of Science and Technology, China
David Taniar	Monash University, Australia
Xiaohui Daniel	University of Southern Queensland, Australia
Vahid Taslimitehrani	realtor.com, USA
Maguelonne Teisseire	Irstea, France
Khoat Than	Hanoi University of Science and Technology, Vietnam
Maksim Tkachenko	Singapore Management University, Singapore
Hiroyuki Toda	NTT Data, Japan
Yongxin Tong	Beihang University, China
Leong Hou U	University of Macau, Macau
Jeffrey Ullman	Stanford University, USA
Dinusha Vatsalan	Data61, CSIRO, Australia
João Vinagre	LIAAD, INESC TEC, Portugal
Kitsana Waiyamai	Kasetsart University, Thailand
Fusheng Wang	Stony Brook University, USA
Hongtao Wang	North China Electric Power University, China
Peng Wang	Southeast University, China
Qing Wang	The Australian National University, Australia
Shoujin Wang	Macquarie University, Australia
Sibo Wang	The Chinese University of Hong Kong, Hong Kong
Suhang Wang	Pennsylvania State University, USA
Wei Wang	Nanjing University, China
Wei Wang	University of New South Wales, Australia
Wendy Hui Wang	Stevens Institute of Technology, USA
Wenya Wang	Nanyang Technological University, Singapore
Xiao Wang	Beijing University of Posts and Telecommunications, China
Xiaoyang Wang	Zhejiang Gongshang University, China
Xin Wang	University of Calgary, Canada
Xiting Wang	Microsoft Research Asia, China
Yang Wang	Dalian University of Technology, China
Yanhao Wang	National University of Singapore, Singapore
Yue Wang	AcuSys, USA
Yuxiang Wang	Hangzhou Dianzi University, China
Zhengyang Wang	Texas A&M University, USA
Victor Junqiu Wei	Huawei Technologies, Hong Kong
Zhewei Wei	Renmin University of China, China
Jörg Wicker	The University of Auckland, New Zealand
Kishan Wimalawarne	Kyoto University, Japan
Brendon J. Woodford	University of Otago, New Zealand

Fangzhao Wu	Microsoft Research Asia, China
Liang Wu	Airbnb, USA
Ou Wu	Tianjin University, China
Shu Wu	NLPR, China
Tianxing Wu	Southeast University, China
Yongkai Wu	University of Arkansas, USA
Xiaokui Xiao	National University of Singapore, Singapore
Min Xie	Shenzhen Institute of Computing Sciences, Shenzhen University, China
Guandong Xu	University of Technology Sydney, Australia
Jiajie Xu	Soochow University, China
Jingwei Xu	Nanjing University, China
Miao Xu	RIKEN, Japan
Tong Xu	University of Science and Technology of China, China
Bing Xue	Victoria University of Wellington, New Zealand
Hui Xue	Southeast University, China
Shan Xue	Macquarie University, Australia
Da Yan	University of Alabama at Birmingham, USA
Yu Yang	City University of Hong Kong, Hong Kong
De-Nian Yang	Academia Sinica, Taiwan
Guolei Yang	Facebook
Liu Yang	Beijing Jiaotong University, China
Shiyu Yang	East China Normal University, China
Yiyang Yang	Guangdong University of Technology, China
Lina Yao	University of New South Wales, Australia
Yuan Yao	Nanjing University, China
Mi-Yen Yeh	Academia Sinica, Taiwan
Hongzhi Yin	The University of Queensland, Australia
Jianhua Yin	Shandong University, China
Minghao Yin	Northeast Normal University, China
Tetsuya Yoshida	Nara Women's University, Japan
Guoxian Yu	Southwest University, China
Kui Yu	Hefei University of Technology, China
Yang Yu	Nanjing University, China
Long Yuan	Nanjing University of Science and Technology, China
Shuhan Yuan	University of Arkansas, USA
Xiaodong Yue	Shanghai University, China
Reza Zafarani	Syracuse University, USA
Nayyar Zaidi	Monash University, Australia
Yifeng Zeng	Teesside University, UK
Petros Zerfos	IBM T. J. Watson Research Center, USA
De-Chuan Zhan	Nanjing University, China
Dongxiang Zhang	Zhejiang University, China
Haijun Zhang	Harbin Institute of Technology, China
Ji Zhang	University of Southern Queensland, Australia
Jing Zhang	Nanjing University of Science and Technology, China

Lu Zhang	University of Arkansas, USA
Mengjie Zhang	Victoria University of Wellington, New Zealand
Quangui Zhang	Liaoning Technical University, China
Si Zhang	Arizona State University, USA
Wei Emma Zhang	The University of Adelaide, Australia
Wei Zhang	East China Normal University, China
Wenjie Zhang	University of New South Wales, Australia
Xiangliang Zhang	King Abdullah University of Science and Technology, Saudi Arabia
Xiuzhen Zhang	RMIT University, Australia
Yudong Zhang	University of Leicester, UK
Zheng Zhang	Harbin Institute of Technology, China
Zili Zhang	Southwest University, USA
Kaiqi Zhao	The University of Auckland, New Zealand
Mingbo Zhao	Donghua University, China
Peixiang Zhao	Florida State University, USA
Pengpeng Zhao	Soochow University, China
Yanchang Zhao	CSIRO, Australia
Zhongying Zhao	Shandong University of Science and Technology, China
Zhou Zhao	Zhejiang University, China
Kai Zheng	University of Electronic Science and Technology of China, China
Rui Zhou	Swinburne University of Technology, Australia
Shuigeng Zhou	Fudan University, China
Xiangmin Zhou	RMIT University, Australia
Yao Zhou	UIUC, USA
Chengzhang Zhu	University of Technology Sydney, Australia
Tianqing Zhu	University of Technology Sydney, Australia
Xingquan Zhu	Florida Atlantic University, USA
Ye Zhu	Deakin University, Australia
Yuanyuan Zhu	Wuhan University, China
Andreas Züfle	George Mason University, USA

External Reviewers

Isaac Ahern	University of Oregon, USA
Yasunori Akagi	NTT Data, Japan
Aleksandar Aleksandric	UT Arlington, USA
Diana Benavides Prado	The University of Auckland, New Zealand
Song Bian	The Chinese University of Hong Kong, Hong Kong
Tsz Nam Chan	The University of Hong Kong, Hong Kong
Yanchuan Chang	The University of Melbourne, Australia
Xiaocong Chen	University of New South Wales, Australia
Jinhyuck Choi	Towson University, USA

Duy Tai Dinh	Japan Advanced Institute of Science and Technology, Japan
Quynh Ngoc Thuy Do	University of Technology Sydney, Australia
Xinyu Dong	Stony Brook University, USA
Katharina Dost	The University of Auckland, New Zealand
Hongyi Duanmu	Stony Brook University, USA
Len Feremans	University of Antwerp, Belgium
Massimo Guarascio	ICAR-CNR, Italy
Guimu Guo	University of Alabama at Birmingham, USA
Jinjin Guo	University of Macau, Macau
Robert Hou	University of Otago, New Zealand
Chaoran Huang	University of New South Wales, Australia
Jinbin Huang	Hong Kong Baptist University, Hong Kong
Keke Huang	The Chinese University of Hong Kong, Hong Kong
Hussain Islam	Florida State University, USA
Seunghui Jang	Towson University, USA
Fan Jiang	UNBC, Canada
Enamul Karim	UT Arlington, USA
Wonjin Kim	Towson University, USA
Bowen Li	Florida State University, USA
Huan Li	Aalborg University, Denmark
Pengfei Li	Zhejiang University, China
Xiaomei Li	University of South Australia, Australia
Xuhong Li	Baidu Research, China
Yanbo Li	Hiretual, USA
Angelica Liguori	ICAR-CNR, Italy
Ray Lindsay	Australian Taxation Office, Australia
Guanli Liu	The University of Melbourne, Australia
Lihui Liu	University of Illinois at Urbana Champaign, USA
Chao Luo	Australian Government Department of Health, Australia
Khadidja Meguelati	Inria, France
Harshit Modi	UT Arlington, USA
Tanmoy Mondal	Inria, France
Ba Hung Nguyen	Japan Advanced Institute of Science and Technology, Japan
Thanh Tam Nguyen	EPFL, Switzerland
Adam Noack	University of Oregon, USA
Abdelkader Ouali	University of Caen Normandy, France
Hyun Park	Towson University, USA
Francesco Pisani	ICAR-CNR, Italy
Anish Rai	UT Arlington, USA
Sina Rashidian	Stony Brook University, USA
Saed Rezayi	University of Georgia, USA
Ettore Ritacco	ICAR-CNR, Italy
Mousumi Roy	Stony Brook University, USA

Abhishek Santra	UT Arlington, USA
Francesco Scicchitano	ICAR-CNR, Italy
Longxu Sun	Hong Kong Baptist University, Hong Kong
Wenya Sun	The University of Hong Kong, Hong Kong
Marcus Suresh	Australian Government Department of Industry, Innovation and Science, Australia
Katerina Taskova	The University of Auckland, New Zealand
Kai Tian	Fudan University, China
Bayu D. Trisedya	The University of Melbourne, Australia
Duc Vinh Vo	Japan Advanced Institute of Science and Technology, Japan
Kun Wang	Tencent, USA
Qinyong Wang	The University of Queensland, Australia
Yu Wang	Stony Brook University, USA
Shuhei Yamamoto	NTT Data, Japan
Shuai Yang	North Carolina State University, USA
Show-Jane Yen	Ming Chuan University, Taiwan
Fuqiang Yu	Shandong University, China
Gong Zhang	University of Oregon, USA
Liang Zhang	Dongbei University of Finance and Economics, China

Sponsoring Organization

Singapore Tourism Board

Contents – Part I

Classification

Clustering

Mining Social Networks

Representation Learning and Embedding

Mining Behavioral Data

Deep Learning

Feature Extraction and Selection

Human, Domain, Organizational and Social Factors in Data Mining

Contents – Part II

Novel Algorithms

Mining Multi-Media/Multi-Dimensional Data

Application

Mining Graph and Network Data

Mining Spatial, Temporal, Unstructured and Semi-structured Data

Sentiment Analysis

Statistical/Graphical Model

Multi-source/Distributed/Parallel/Cloud Computing

Recommender Systems

Fashion Recommendation with Multi-relational Representation Learning

Yang Li, Yadan Luo, and Zi Huang$^{(\boxtimes)}$

School of Information Technology and Electrical Engineering,
The University of Queensland, Brisbane, QLD 4072, Australia
yang.li@uq.edu.au, lyadanluol@gmail.com, huang@itee.uq.edu.au

Abstract. Driven by increasing demands of assisting users to dress and match clothing properly, fashion recommendation has attracted wide attention. Its core idea is to model the compatibility among fashion items by jointly projecting embedding into a unified space. However, modeling the item compatibility in such a category-agnostic manner could barely preserve intra-class variance, thus resulting in sub-optimal performance. In this paper, we propose a novel category-aware metric learning framework, which not only learns the cross-category compatibility notions but also preserves the intra-category diversity among items. Specifically, we define a category complementary relation representing a pair of category labels, e.g., tops-bottoms. Given a pair of item embeddings, we first project them to their corresponding relation space, then model the mutual relation of a pair of categories as a relation transition vector to capture compatibility amongst fashion items. We further derive a negative sampling strategy with non-trivial instances to enable the generation of expressive and discriminative item representations. Comprehensive experimental results conducted on two public datasets demonstrate the superiority and feasibility of our proposed approach.

Keywords: Fashion compatibility · Fashion recommendation · Representation learning

1 Introduction

With the proliferation of online fashion websites, such as Polyvore[1] and Farfetch[2], there are increasing demands on intelligent applications in the fashion domain for a better user shopping experience. This drives researchers to develop various machine learning techniques to meet such demands. Existing work is mainly conducted for three types of fashion applications: (1) clothing retrieval [1,1,8]: retrieving similar clothing items from the data collection based on the query clothing item; (2) fashion attribute detection [3,11,12]: identifying clothing attributes such as color, pattern and texture from the given clothing image;

---

[1] www.polyvore.com.
[2] www.farfetch.com.

© Springer Nature Switzerland AG 2020
H. W. Lauw et al. (Eds.): PAKDD 2020, LNAI 12084, pp. 3–15, 2020.
https://doi.org/10.1007/978-3-030-47426-3_1

(3) Complementary Clothing Recommendation [5,10,16,21,22]: recommending complementary clothes that match the query clothing item to the user. In this paper, we focus on the third application, which is more challenging and sophisticated due to the fashion data complexity and heterogeneity. It requires the model to infer compatibility among fashion items according to various complementary characteristics, which goes beyond visual similarity measurement.

The key point to tackle the above challenges is to derive an appropriate compatibility measurement for pairs of fashion items, which can effectively capture various fashion attributes (e.g., colors and patterns) from item images for comparison. The major stream of existing approaches for fashion compatibility modeling adopts metric learning techniques to extract effective fashion item representations. A typical fashion compatibility modeling strategy is to learn a latent style space, where matching item pairs stay closer than incompatible pairs. The compatibility of two given fashion items is computed by the pairwise Euclidean distance or inner product between fashion item embeddings. Nevertheless, the previous work has two main limitations that lead to sub-optimal performance. Firstly, some approaches consider fashion compatibility modeling as a single-relational task. However, this neglects the fact that people usually focus on different aspects of clothes from different categories. For example, people are more likely to focus on color and material for blouses and pants, while they may pay attention to shape and style for jeans and shoes. Moreover, using a single unified space is likely to result in incorrect similarity transitivity in fashion compatibility. For instance, if item A matches both B and C, while B and C may not be compatible, the embeddings of A, B and C will be forced to be close to each other in a single unified space, which degrades prediction performance because the compatibility essentially does not hold transitivity property. Therefore, such a category-independent approach will result in inaccurate item representations. Secondly, most existing approaches merely randomly sample negative instances from the training set. However, most of the randomly sampled triplets are trivial ones, which may fail to support the model to learn discriminative item representations.

In order to address the above mentioned limitations, we propose a novel **Category-Aware Fashion Metric Embedding** learning network (CA-FME), which models both instances and category-aware relation representations through a translation operation. Specifically, we formulate the fashion compatibility measurement as a multi-relational data modeling task. We treat fashion items as entities and define pairs of compatible categories as complementary relations, e.g., blouses-skirts. The overall flowchart of CA-FME is presented in Fig. 1: Item visual features are first extracted through a pre-trained CNN. Then, each pair of item embeddings is projected to their corresponding category-specific relation subspace. Finally, we model the compatibility based on a transition-based score function. Our main contributions can be summarized as below:

- We present a novel category-aware embedding learning framework for fashion compatibility modeling, which not only captures cross-categorical relationships but also preserves the diversity of intra-category fashion item representations.

- We devise a negative sampling strategy with non-trivial samples for discriminative item representations.
- Extensive experiments have been conducted on two real world datasets, Polyvore and FashionVC, to demonstrate the superior performance of our model over other state-of-the-art methods.

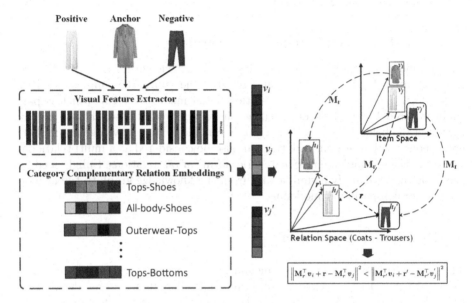

Fig. 1. The overview of proposed CA-FME model architecture for fashion compatibility modeling. The fashion clothing dataset consists of multiple categories, e.g., Hoodies, Skirts, Coats and Trousers. CA-FME mainly consists of three parts: (1) A pre-trained CNN for visual feature extraction; (2) A category complementary relation embedding space for modeling category-aware compatibility; (3) Multiple relation-specific projection spaces for preserving the intra-class diversity. The whole framework is finally optimized via a margin-based ranking objective function in end-to-end manner.

2 Related Work

2.1 Fashion Compatibility Modeling

The mainstream of work aims to map fashion items into a latent space where compatible item pairs are close to each other, while incompatible pairs lay in the opposite position. McAuley et al. [13] propose to use Low-rank Mahalanobis Transformation to learn a latent style space for minimizing the distance between matched items and maximizing that of mismatched ones. Following this work, Veit et al. [19] employ the Siamese CNNs to learn a metric for compatibility measurement in an end-to-end manner. Some researchers argue that the complex compatibility cannot be captured by directly learning a single latent space.

He et. al [6] propose to learn a mixture of multiple metrics with weight confidences to model the relationships between heterogeneous items. Veit et al. [18] propose Conditional Similarity Network, which learns disentangled item features whose dimensions can be used for separate similarity measurements. Following this work, Vasileva et al. [17] claim that respecting type information has important consequences. Thus, they first form type-type spaces from each pair of types and train these spaces with triplet loss.

2.2   Knowledge Graph Embedding Learning

The techniques of representation learning on the knowledge graph have attracted large attention in recent years. Different from the approaches implemented by tensor factorization, e.g., [14], translation-based models [2,7,20], which is partially inspired by the idea of word2vec, have achieved state-of-the-art performance in the field of the knowledge graph. Similar to the knowledge graph, heterogeneous fashion recommendation can also be considered as a multi-relational problem, where complementary categories form various relations. Enlightened by these findings, we apply a similar idea from the knowledge graph to the fashion domain for compatibility modeling.

3   Problem Formulation

The fashion complementary recommendation task we are tackling is formulated as follows. Suppose we have a collection of fashion item images denoted as $\mathcal{O} = \{o_1, o_2, o_3, ..., o_n\}$, where n is the number of items, and a set of category labels denoted as $\mathcal{C} = \{c_1, c_2, c_3, ..., c_m\}$, where m is the number of categories. Each fashion item $o_i \in \mathcal{O}$ has a corresponding k-dim visual feature vector $\boldsymbol{v}_i = g(o_i; \Theta_v), \boldsymbol{v}_i \in \mathbb{R}^k$ and a category label $c_i \in \mathcal{C}$. Here, $g(o; \Theta_v)$ represents a pre-trained CNN with trainable parameters Θ_v, which extracts visual features from a fashion item image $o \in \mathcal{O}$. We denote a set of category complementary relations as $\mathcal{R} = \{r^{c_i c_j}\}$, where $c_i, c_j \in \mathcal{C}$ represent a pair of complementary categories, such as *tops-bottoms*. We now use a triplet $(\boldsymbol{v}_i, \boldsymbol{v}_j, r^{c_i c_j}), s.t., \forall i, j, r^{c_i c_j} \in \mathcal{R}$ to represent embeddings of a pair of fashion items o_i and o_j and their corresponding category complementary relation $r^{c_i c_j}$. Each relation $r^{c_i c_j} \in \mathcal{R}$ corresponds to an embedding vector $\boldsymbol{r}^{c_i c_j} \in \mathbb{R}^d$ from the relation embedding space. Our target is to derive a fashion compatibility scoring function $f(\boldsymbol{v}_i, \boldsymbol{v}_j, r^{c_i c_j})$, which captures visual characteristics from the item embeddings for compatibility measurement.

4   Proposed Approach

In this section, we first present our CA-FME model for fashion compatibility modeling. Then, we introduce a novel negative sampling strategy for more effective training. Finally, we describe the optimization algorithm to train our model.

The overview of our proposed framework is shown in Fig. 1. We aim to build a model, which can (1) effectively model the notion of compatibility; (2) be easily generalized to unseen fashion item compatibility measurement; (3) focus on different aspects of item embeddings regarding different category complementary relations for the compatibility measurement. In particular, the framework consists of a pre-trained CNN for visual feature extraction and multiple category complementary relation subspaces for category-aware compatibility modeling.

4.1 Compatibility Modeling

To solve the above mentioned limitations, we assign each category complementary relation $r \in \mathcal{R}$ with a single d-dim transition vector $\boldsymbol{r} \in \mathbb{R}^d$. Intuitively, these relation vectors act as different fashion compatibility decision-makers who focus on different pairs of categories, which enables the model to concentrate on different aspects of fashion items from different categories. In particular, given a pair of fashion items o_i and o_j with their visual features $\boldsymbol{v}_i$ and $\boldsymbol{v}_j$, and their corresponding category complementary relation $r^{c_i c_j}$. If o_i is compatible with o_j, the compatibility relationship can be interpreted as:

$$\boldsymbol{v}_i + \boldsymbol{r}^{c_i c_j} \approx \boldsymbol{v}_j \tag{1}$$

which means o_j's embedding $\boldsymbol{v}_j$ should be the nearest neighbor to the resulting vector of $\boldsymbol{v}_i$ plus the relation vector $\boldsymbol{r}^{c_i c_j}$ in a specific latent space based on a certain distance metric, e.g., L1 or L2 distance.

However, there exists one issue in the above equation: in reality, items from a specific pair of categories share diverse fashion attributes such as material, style and pattern. Therefore, it is insufficient to preserve intra-category diversity by building only a single embedding vector for each category complementary relation. To address this issue, we propose to build multiple relation-specific subspaces, i.e., $\mathbf{M}_r \in \mathbb{R}^{k \times d}, r \in \mathcal{R}$, where k is the number of visual feature vector dimensions. Using such category-aware projection operations is twofold. Firstly, the relation-specific subspaces provide abundant trainable parameters to preserve intra-category diversity. Secondly, it also provides capability for handling unseen items through a projection operation. Thus, we define the projected item vectors of $\boldsymbol{v}_i$ and $\boldsymbol{v}_j$ as,

$$\boldsymbol{h}_i = \mathbf{M}_{r^{c_i c_j}}^{\top} \boldsymbol{v}_i, \quad \boldsymbol{h}_j = \mathbf{M}_{r^{c_i c_j}}^{\top} \boldsymbol{v}_j, \quad \boldsymbol{h}_i, \boldsymbol{h}_j \in \mathbb{R}^d \tag{2}$$

With the above defined compatibility relationship modeling rule and relation-specific projection, we now could perform compatibility score calculation within the corresponding relation space. Given a pair of fashion items denoted as o_i and o_j, and their corresponding category complementary relation $r^{c_i c_j}$, the compatibility score s_{ij} is calculated as,

$$s_{ij} = -\left\| \boldsymbol{h}_i + \boldsymbol{r}^{c_i c_j} - \boldsymbol{h}_j \right\|_2 \tag{3}$$

where L2 distance is used.

Algorithm 1: Negative Sampling

Input : $(v_i, v_j, r^{c_i c_j})$: a positive triplet,
$\hat{\mathcal{H}}_{(v_i, r^{c_i c_j})}$: negative candidate set,
$\bar{\mathcal{H}}_{(v_i, r^{c_i c_j})}$: selected negative triplet set,
N: size of negative candidate set,
M: size of selected negative triplet set, $M < N$
Output: The set of M negative training triplets $\bar{\mathcal{H}}_{(v_i, r^{c_i c_j})}$

1 Construct negative candidate set $\hat{\mathcal{H}}_{(v_i, r^{c_i c_j})} = \{v'_1, v'_2, ..., v'_N\}$, where $(v_i, v'_j, r^{c_i c_j}) \in \mathcal{N}$ and $c'_j = c_j$ by uniformly sampling.
2 Compute the score $f(v_i, v'_j, r^{c_i c_j})$ for all $v'_j \in \hat{\mathcal{H}}_{(v_i, r^{c_i c_j})}$ via Equation (3)
3 Construct the selected negative triplet set $\bar{\mathcal{H}}_{(v_i, r^{c_i c_j})}$ by multinomial sampling M items from $\hat{\mathcal{H}}_{(v_i, r^{c_i c_j})}$ with probability in Equation (6)
4 **Return:** $\bar{\mathcal{H}}_{(v_i, r^{c_i c_j})}$

4.2 Negative Sampling

Negative sampling has been proven to be an effective and helpful training strategy to learn discriminative item representations in various fields. We aim to derive a simple but effective negative sampling strategy to assist our model to identify more subtle style patterns from hard negative instances. Since a category complementary relation corresponds to two different categories, we want both sides of each training triplet can benefit from negative sampling. Therefore, we define the strategy should meet the following requirements:

1. The strategy should consider both sides of training triplets.
2. The strategy should identify hard negative instances effectively and efficiently.
3. The strategy should avoid false negative samples effectively.

Now we introduce the details regarding how our designed negative sampling strategy can meet the above-defined requirements. We also present the details of our strategy in Algorithm 1.

Requirement 1: We propose to sample negative instances from both sides of a given positive triplet $(v_i, v_j, r^{c_i c_j})$. In particular, we first fix v_i and category complementary relation $r^{c_i c_j}$, then replace v_j by randomly sampling an item embedding vector v'_j from category c_j. Similarly, we perform the same negative sampling for the other side item v_j.

Requirement 2: Given a positive triplet $(v_i, v_j, r^{c_i c_j})$, we first uniformly sample N negative candidates denoted as $\hat{\mathcal{H}}_{(v_i, r^{c_i c_j})}$ from category c_j's item set. Then, for each training triplet, we calculate scores for all negative triplets. This two steps correspond to the step 1–2 in Algorithm 1. Intuitively, the negative triplets with high compatibility scores can be regarded as hard negative samples.

Requirement 3: Despite the higher scores the harder negative samples are, these samples are likely to be false negative, which instead has destructive impact on the model performance. In order to avoid this issue, we propose to select

---

Algorithm 2: Training CA-FME

Data : Training set of positive triplets $\mathcal{P}$, negative triplets $\mathcal{N}$
Input: $g(o; \theta_v)$: pre-trained CNN with parameters θ_v for visual feature extraction,
$\qquad$ $\mathcal{R}$: category relation set,
$\qquad$ $\bar{\mathcal{H}}$: negative triplets,
$\qquad$ $\tilde{\mathcal{H}}$: 4-tuple training set,
$\qquad$ B: batch size

1 **initialize** r by Xavier initialization for each $r \in R$,
2 $\qquad$ $\mathbf{M}_r$ by Xavier initialization for each $r \in R$
3 **repeat**
4 $\quad$ Sample a training batch S_{batch} from $\mathcal{P}$ with batch size B
5 $\quad$ $T_{batch} \leftarrow \varnothing$
6 $\quad$ **for** $(o_i, o_j, r^{c_i c_j}) \in S_{batch}$ **do**
7 $\quad\quad$ $\boldsymbol{v}_i = g(o_i; \theta_v)$
8 $\quad\quad$ $\boldsymbol{v}_j = g(o_j; \theta_v)$
$\quad\quad$ // Get negative triplets with $\boldsymbol{v}_i$ and $r^{c_i c_j}$ fixed
9 $\quad\quad$ Construct negative triplets $\bar{\mathcal{H}}_{(\boldsymbol{v}_i, r^{c_i c_j})} = \{(\boldsymbol{v}_i, \boldsymbol{v}'_j, r^{c_i c_j})\}$ via Algo. 1
10 $\quad\quad$ Form the 4-tuple training set
$\quad\quad\quad$ $\tilde{\mathcal{H}}_{(\boldsymbol{v}_i, r^{c_i c_j})} = \{(\boldsymbol{v}_i, \boldsymbol{v}'_i, \boldsymbol{v}_j, r^{c_i c_j})\}, \boldsymbol{v}'_i \in \bar{\mathcal{H}}_{(\boldsymbol{v}_i, r^{c_i c_j})}$
$\quad\quad$ // Get negative triplets with $\boldsymbol{v}_j$ and $r^{c_i c_j}$ fixed
11 $\quad\quad$ Construct negative triplets $\bar{\mathcal{H}}_{(\boldsymbol{v}_j, r^{c_i c_j})} = \{(\boldsymbol{v}'_i, \boldsymbol{v}_j, r^{c_i c_j})\}$ via Algo. 1
12 $\quad\quad$ Form the 4-tuple training set
$\quad\quad\quad$ $\tilde{\mathcal{H}}_{(\boldsymbol{v}_j, r^{c_i c_j})} = \{(\boldsymbol{v}_i, \boldsymbol{v}_j, \boldsymbol{v}'_j, r^{c_i c_j})\}, \boldsymbol{v}'_j \in \bar{\mathcal{H}}_{(\boldsymbol{v}_i, r^{c_i c_j})}$
13 $\quad\quad$ $T_{batch} \leftarrow T_{batch} \cup \tilde{\mathcal{H}}_{(\boldsymbol{v}_i, r^{c_i c_j})} \cup \tilde{\mathcal{H}}_{(\boldsymbol{v}_j, r^{c_i c_j})}$
14 $\quad$ **endfor**
15 $\quad$ Update the whole network via Hinge loss function:
$\quad\quad$ $\sum_{T_{batch}} \nabla[\gamma + f(\boldsymbol{v}_i, \boldsymbol{v}_j, r^{c_i c_j}) - f(\boldsymbol{v}_i, \boldsymbol{v}'_j, r^{c_i c_j})]$
16 **until** *Convergence*;

M negative items from the above sampled N negative candidates with different probability by multinomial sampling, which corresponds to step 3 in Algorithm 1. In particular, we grant larger probability for harder negative samples according to their scores. Here, let $\mathcal{S} = \{s_1, s_2, ..., s_N\}$ be the set of calculated scores of N negative candidates. We first define the following normalization function $norm(s_{ij})$ to project all the scores into the range of $[0, 1]$,

$$norm(s_{ij}) = \frac{s_{ij} - s_{min}}{s_{max} - s_{min}}, s_{ij} \in \mathcal{S}, s_{min} = min(\mathcal{S}), \qquad (4)$$

$$s_{max} = max(\mathcal{S}) \qquad (5)$$

Finally, we could define the probability of sampling a negative item $\bar{v}$ by:

$$p(\bar{\boldsymbol{v}}_j | (\boldsymbol{v}_i, r^{c_i c_j})) = \frac{\exp(1 - norm(f(\boldsymbol{v}_i, \bar{\boldsymbol{v}}_j, r^{c_i c_j})))}{\sum_{(\boldsymbol{v}_i, \boldsymbol{v}'_j, r^{c_i c_j}) \in \hat{\mathcal{H}}_{(\boldsymbol{v}_i, r^{c_i c_j})}} \exp\left(1 - norm(f\left(\boldsymbol{v}_i, \boldsymbol{v}'_j, r^{c_i c_j}\right))\right)}$$
$$\qquad (6)$$

Margin-Based Optimization. With the above defined score function and negative sampling strategy, we present the whole training steps in Algorithm 16. Let $\hat{\mathcal{H}}_{(v_i, r^{c_i c_j})}$ and $\hat{\mathcal{H}}_{(v_j, r^{c_i c_j})}$ denote the 4-tuple training triplets constructed using the above defined negative sampling strategy. We could define the following margin-based loss function as our objective function for training:

$$
\mathcal{L} = \sum_{\left(v_i, v_j, v_j', r^{c_i c_j}\right) \in \hat{\mathcal{H}}_{(v_i, r^{c_i c_j})}} \left[f\left(v_i, v_j, r^{c_i c_j}\right) - f\left(v_i, v_j', r^{c_i c_j}\right) + \gamma \right]_+ +
$$
$$
\sum_{\left(v_i, v_i', v_j, r^{c_i c_j}\right) \in \hat{\mathcal{H}}_{(v_j, r^{c_i c_j})}} \left[f\left(v_i, v_j, r^{c_i c_j}\right) - f\left(v_i', v_j, r^{c_i c_j}\right) + \gamma \right]_+ \tag{7}
$$

where γ is the margin value and $[x]_+ \triangleq \max(0, x)$.

We adopt the stochastic gradient decent algorithm (SGD) for the model optimization. In each step, we sample a mini-batch of training triplets and update the parameters of the whole network.

5   Experiments

In this section, we first describe the experimental settings and then give comprehensive analysis based on the experimental results.

5.1   Dataset

We conduct our experiments on two public datasets, FashionVC and Polyvore-Maryland, provided by Song et al. [16] and Han et al. [5] respectively.

FashionVC [16]. This dataset consists of 14,871 top item images and 13,663 bottom item images, where each item has a corresponding image, a title and a category label. In this paper, we only consider the visual modality. Therefore, we use images for visual information extraction and category labels to determine which category complementary relation the item pairs belong to. We randomly split the data according to 80%;10%;10% for training, validation and test sets, respectively.

PolyvoreMaryland [5]. This dataset contains 21,799 outfits crawled from the online social community website Polyvore. We use the splits provided by Han et al. [5], which has 17,316, 3,076 and 1,407 outfits in training, testing and validation sets respectively. In this paper, we mainly study item-to-item compatibility, therefore, we keep four main groups of fashion items: tops, bottoms, bags and shoes from the outfit data. Each fashion item contains an image, a title and a category label. Note that each group of fashion items have several detailed category labels, e.g., there are hand bags and shoulder bags in the "bags" group.

5.2   Baseline Methods

We compare our model CA-FME with several state-of-the-art models for heterogeneous recommendation. For the fair comparison, we set the pre-trained Alexnet [9] as the visual feature extractor of all methods.

- **SiameseNet** [19]: The approach models compatibility by minimizing the Euclidean distance between compatible pairs and maximizing the distance between incompatible ones in a unified latent space through contrastive loss.
- **Monomer** [6]: The approach models fashion compatibility with a mixture of distances computed from multiple latent spaces.
- **BPR-DAE** [16]: The approach models compatibility through inner-product result of top's and bottom's embeddings and uses Bayesian Personalized Ranking (BPR) [15] as their optimization objective.
- **TripletNet** [4]: The approach models fashion compatibility in a unified latent space through triplet loss.
- **TransNFCM** [22]: The state-of-the-art method that learns item-item compatibility by modeling categorical relations among different fashion items.
- **TA-CSN** [17]: The state-of-the-art method that builds type-aware subspaces for fashion compatibility modeling.

5.3   Parameter Settings

In our experiment, all the hyper-parameters of our approach are tuned to perform the best on the validation set. For the fair comparison, we apply the Alexnet [9] as the visual feature extractor for all methods. In our model, we set margin γ as 1, learning rate $\alpha = 10^{-4}$ with momentum 0.9, batch size $B = 512$. Visual embedding dimension $k = 128$, with dropout rate 0.5 and relation embedding dimension is set to be 128.

5.4   Compatibility Prediction

Task Description. The compatibility prediction task aims to predict whether a given pair of items are compatible or not. In particular, we replace one item of each testing positive triplet with 100 randomly sampled negative items. Thus, for each testing instance, it requires to give ranking on 101 items based on the query image. We employ two widely-used evaluation metrics, Hit@k and Area Under the ROC curve (AUC) to evaluate the performance of our model and baseline methods based on the predicted compatibility scores. Hit@k is defined as follows, which indicates the proportion of the correct predicted item ranked in top k.

$$\text{Hits@}k = \frac{\#\text{hit@}k}{\|D_{\text{test}}\|} \tag{8}$$

where D_{test} denotes the collection of testing instances. The formula for AUC is defined as below,

$$AUC = \frac{\sum pred_{positive} > pred_{negative}}{|positiveInstances| \times |negativeInstances|} \tag{9}$$

where $\sum pred_{positive} > pred_{negative}$ indicates the number of cases that the predicted score of positive instance is larger than negative one, by comparing the predicted score of each positive instance with each negative instances in the testing set.

Table 1. Performance comparison between our proposed CA-FME and other baseline methods. CA-FME(Neg.) indicates the application of negative sampling training strategy.

FashionVC						PolyvoreMaryland				
Methods	AUC	Hit@5	Hit@10	Hit@20	Hit@40	AUC	Hit@5	Hit@10	Hit@20	Hit@40
SiameseNet	60.4	9.7	18.1	31.2	52.8	59.1	8.3	15.5	29.0	51.8
Monomer	70.2	16.9	28.6	45.8	69.1	70.5	17.6	28.9	45.7	69.0
BPR-DAE	70.9	16.7	27.3	46.7	70.4	69.5	17.3	28.2	43.9	67.5
Triplet Net	70.6	16.3	28.0	45.7	69.6	70.1	18.1	28.7	44.9	68.3
TA-CSN	71.6	16.7	28.4	46.7	70.8	70.2	17.3	28.4	45.1	68.4
TransNFCM	73.6	19.0	32.3	51.6	74.0	73.6	19.3	33.1	50.9	73.4
CA-FME	88.6	**26.6**	48.5	81.9	**99.9**	95.0	**59.8**	84.4	**97.7**	**99.7**
CA-FME (Neg.)	**88.9**	26.4	**49.9**	**83.2**	**99.9**	**96.2**	59.6	**88.4**	96.7	**99.7**

5.5   Performance Comparison

We evaluate our model with and without negative sampling strategy, i.e., CA-FME(Neg) and CA-FME. Table 1 shows the performance comparison on two datasets based on AUC and Hit@K evaluation metrics. From the table we have the following observations:

- Our model achieves the best performance on both datasets by significant margins compared with all the other state-of-the-art methods, which proves the effectiveness and superior performance of our method.
- The category-unaware models including SiameseNet and TripletNet, which merely learn fashion compatibility notions in a single latent space, perform worse than category-respected models including TA-CSN and TransNFCM. This proves that considering category label information is of great importance in fashion compatibility modeling, which can be helpful to avoid incorrect compatibility similarity transitivity. It also proves that items from different categories may have very different visual characteristics for compatibility.
- Compared with category-aware methods, TA-CSN and TransNFCM, our model obtains around 15% and 30% improvements on AUC and Hit@20 respectively. Although they build category-aware mask vectors to capture different fashion characteristics among different categories, it is still not sufficient to preserve the intra-category diversity among items. With the help of our relation-specific projection spaces, our model can capture much more specific information of compatibility from different categories. The improvements on PolyvoreMaryland dataset are even much better in terms of AUC and Hit@5. This is mainly because of the different number of relations in two

datasets. We define 146 category relations in the Polyvore dataset, while there are only 30 relations in the FashionVC dataset. It proves that more relational spaces can significantly contribute to the improvement of performance.
- The results of CA-FME(Neg.) show that our negative sampling strategy is helpful to improve our model's performance, which proves the effectiveness of our proposed training strategy.

5.6   Case Study

In this section, we conduct a case study, aiming to address a real-world fashion recommendation task: selecting the fashion item that matches the query one. As illustrated in Fig. 2, we conduct two query instances on the FashionVC dataset, where the items with a green box are ground-truths. In the first case, we give the model a woman blouse, the model successfully selects the ground-truth at first rank. It can be observed that the model identifies the color of the first ranked jeans matches the query blouse. Our model also successfully identifies that the 7th jeans are for men and thus gives it the lowest score. In the second case, the model gives a relatively high score to the ground-truth item. However, the main reason that our model gives a higher score to the first item probably due to the color attribute. For the latter items ranked at 5–7, we think our model successfully identifies that their shapes do not match the query skirt.

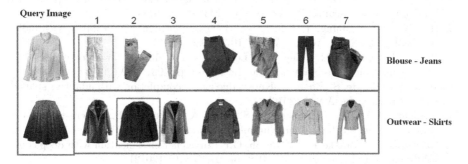

Fig. 2. Case study of fashion recommendation task by retrieving the most matching fashion items from a set of candidates based on the query fashion item. (Color figure online)

6   Conclusion

In this work, we introduced a novel category-aware neural model CA-FME to model the fashion compatibility notions. It not only captures cross-category compatibility by constructing category relation embeddings but also preserves intra-category diversity among items through build relation-specific projection spaces. To optimize our model, we further introduce a weighted negative sampling strategy to identify high-quality negative instances, which consequently assists our model to infer discriminative representations. In addition, although in our paper, we mainly study the compatibility of tops and bottoms, it can easily generalized to arbitrary types of clothing items. Extensive experiments were conducted on two public fashion datasets, which shows that our CA-FME model can significantly outperform all the state-of-the-art methods on fashion recommendation.

Acknowledgments. We would like to thank all reviewers for their comments. This work was partially supported by Australian Research Council Discovery Project (ARC DP190102353).

References

1. Ak, K.E., Kassim, A.A., Lim, J.H., Tham, J.Y.: Learning attribute representations with localization for flexible fashion search. In: CVPR (2018)
2. Bordes, A., Usunier, N., Garcia-Duran, A., Weston, J., Yakhnenko, O.: Translating embeddings for modeling multi-relational data. In: NIPS, pp. 2787–2795 (2013)
3. Chen, H., Gallagher, A., Girod, B.: Describing clothing by semantic attributes. In: Fitzgibbon, A., Lazebnik, S., Perona, P., Sato, Y., Schmid, C. (eds.) ECCV 2012, Part III. LNCS, vol. 7574, pp. 609–623. Springer, Heidelberg (2012). https://doi.org/10.1007/978-3-642-33712-3_44
4. Chen, L., He, Y.: Dress fashionably: learn fashion collocation with deep mixed-category metric learning. In: AAAI, pp. 2103–2110 (2018)
5. Han, X., Wu, Z., Jiang, Y., Davis, L.S.: Learning fashion compatibility with bidirectional LSTMS. In: ACM MM, pp. 1078–1086 (2017)
6. He, R., Packer, C., McAuley, J.J.: Learning compatibility across categories for heterogeneous item recommendation. In: ICDM, pp. 937–942 (2016)
7. Ji, G., Liu, K., He, S., Zhao, J.: Knowledge graph completion with adaptive sparse transfer matrix. In: AAAI (2016)
8. Kiapour, M.H., Han, X., Lazebnik, S., Berg, A.C., Berg, T.L.: Where to buy it: matching street clothing photos in online shops. In: ICCV (2015)
9. Krizhevsky, A., Sutskever, I., Hinton, G.E.: Imagenet classification with deep convolutional neural networks. In: NIPS, pp. 1097–1105 (2012)
10. Li, Y., Luo, Y., Huang, Z.: Graph-based relation-aware representation learning for clothing matching. In: Borovica-Gajic, R., Qi, J., Wang, W. (eds.) ADC 2020. LNCS, vol. 12008, pp. 189–197. Springer, Cham (2020). https://doi.org/10.1007/978-3-030-39469-1_15
11. Liu, Z., Luo, P., Qiu, S., Wang, X., Tang, X.: DeepFashion: powering robust clothes recognition and retrieval with rich annotations. In: CVPR. IEEE (2016)
12. Luo, Y., Wang, Z., Huang, Z., Yang, Y., Zhao, C.: Coarse-to-fine annotation enrichment for semantic segmentation learning. In: CIKM (2018)
13. McAuley, J.J., Targett, C., Shi, Q., van den Hengel, A.: Image-based recommendations on styles and substitutes. In: SIGIR, pp. 43–52 (2015)
14. Nickel, M., Tresp, V., Kriegel, H.: A three-way model for collective learning on multi-relational data. In: ICML, pp. 809–816 (2011)
15. Rendle, S., Freudenthaler, C., Gantner, Z., Schmidt-Thieme, L.: BPR: bayesian personalized ranking from implicit feedback. In: IJAI, pp. 452–461 (2009)

16. Song, X., Feng, F., Liu, J., Li, Z., Nie, L., Ma, J.: Neurostylist: neural compatibility modeling for clothing matching. In: ACM MM, pp. 753–761 (2017)
17. Vasileva, M.I., Plummer, B.A., Dusad, K., Rajpal, S., Kumar, R., Forsyth, D.: Learning type-aware embeddings for fashion compatibility. In: Ferrari, V., Hebert, M., Sminchisescu, C., Weiss, Y. (eds.) ECCV 2018, Part XVI. LNCS, vol. 11220, pp. 405–421. Springer, Cham (2018). https://doi.org/10.1007/978-3-030-01270-0_24
18. Veit, A., Belongie, S.J., Karaletsos, T.: Conditional similarity networks. In: CVPR, pp. 1781–1789 (2017)
19. Veit, A., Kovacs, B., Bell, S., McAuley, J.J., Bala, K., Belongie, S.J.: Learning visual clothing style with heterogeneous dyadic co-occurrences. In: ICCV, pp. 4642–4650 (2015)
20. Wang, Z., Zhang, J., Feng, J., Chen, Z.: Knowledge graph embedding by translating on hyperplanes. In: AAAI (2014)
21. Yang, X., et al.: Interpretable fashion matching with rich attributes. In: SIGIR (2019)
22. Yang, X., Ma, Y., Liao, L., Wang, M., Chua, T.: TransNFCM: translation-based neural fashion compatibility modeling. In: AAAI, pp. 403–410 (2019)

Off-Policy Recommendation System Without Exploration

Chengwei Wang[1,3], Tengfei Zhou[3], Chen Chen[1,3(✉)], Tianlei Hu[1,3],
and Gang Chen[2,3]

[1] The Key Laboratory of Big Data Intelligent Computing of Zhejiang Province,
Zhejiang University, Hangzhou, China
{rr,cc33,htl}@zju.edu.cn
[2] CAD and CG State Key Lab, Zhejiang University, Hangzhou, China
cg@zju.edu.cn
[3] College of Computer Science and Technology, Zhejiang University,
Hangzhou, China
zhoutengfei@zju.edu.cn

Abstract. Recommendation System (RS) can be treated as an intelligent agent which aims to generate policy maximizing customers' long term satisfaction. Off-policy reinforcement learning methods based on Q-learning and actor-critic methods are commonly used to train RS. Though these methods can leverage previously collected dataset for sampling efficient training, they are sensitive to the distribution of off-policy data and make limited progress unless more on-policy data are collected. However, allowing a badly-trained RS to interact with customers can result in unpredictable loss. Therefore, it is highly desirable that the off-policy method can stably train an RS when the off-policy data is fixed and there is no further interaction with the environment. To fulfill these requirements, we devise a novel method name Generator Constrained Q-learning (GCQ). GCQ additionally trains an action generator via supervised learning. The generator is used to mimic data distribution and stabilize the performance of recommendation policy. Empirical studies show that the proposed method outperforms state-of-the-art techniques on both offline and simulated online environments.

1 Introduction

Recommender System (RS) is one of the most important applications in artificial intelligence [15,20]. An intelligent RS can significantly reduce users' searching time, greatly enhance their shopping experience and bring considerable profits to vendors.

From the Reinforcement Learning (RL) perspective, RS is an autonomous agent that intelligently learns the optimal recommendation behavior over time to maximize each user's long term satisfaction through interacting with its environment. This offers us the opportunity to solve the recommendation task on top of

Supported by the National Key R&D Program of China (No. 2017YFB1201001).

H. W. Lauw et al. (Eds.): PAKDD 2020, LNAI 12084, pp. 16–27, 2020.
https://doi.org/10.1007/978-3-030-47426-3_2

the recent RL advancement. Considering that a previously collected customers' feedback dataset is often available for recommendation tasks, many researchers adopt the off-policy RL methods to extract patterns from the data [4,21,23].

Off-policy RL algorithms are often expected to fully exploit off-policy datasets. Nevertheless, these methods can break down when the datasets are not collected by learning agents. Theoretically, [2] points out that Bellman updates could diverge with off-policy data. The divergence issue would surely invalidate the performance of DQN agents. [12,16] find that in off-policy learning, the fix-point of Bellman updates may have poor quality even if the update converges. Empirically, [9] shows that off-policy agents perform dramatically worse than the behavioral agent when trained by the same numerical algorithm on the same dataset. Moreover, many researchers observe that these methods can still fail to learn the optimal strategy even when training data are deliberately selected by effective experts. All these observations suggest that off-policy methods are unstable to static datasets.

The instability of off-policy methods is highly undesirable in training an RS. One would hope that the RS has learned sound policies before deploying into a production environment. If its performance turns out to be unpredictable, deploying the RS would be risky. To stabilize off-policy methods, one can compensate for the performance of the RS by online feedbacks. That is, allow the off-policy agent to interact with customers and use the customers' feedbacks to stabilize its performance. In practice, collecting user's feedback is time-consuming, and deploying an unstable RS to interact with customers would greatly reduce their satisfaction. As a result, designing a stable off-policy RL method for RS which has reasonable performance for any static training set without further exploration, is a fundamental problem.

As indicated in [9,14], the instability issue of off-policy methods results from *exploration error* which is a fundamental problem with off-policy reinforcement learning. exploration error usually behaves as the value function is erroneously estimated on unseen state-action pairs. The exploration error can be unboundedly large, even if the value function can be perfectly approximated [9]. Moreover, it can accumulate during the training iterations [14]. It may misguide the training agent and make the agent take over-optimistic or over-pessimistic decisions. As a result, the training process becomes unstable and potentially diverging unless new data is collected to remedy those errors.

In this paper, we propose a novel off-policy RL method for RS to diminish the exploration error. Our method can learn recommendation policy successfully from large static datasets without further interacting with the environment. exploration error results from a mismatch in the distribution of data induced by the recommendation policy and the distribution of customers' feedback contained in the training data [9]. The proposed Generator Constrained deep Q-learning (GCQ) utilizes a neural generator to simulate customers' possible feedbacks. This generative model is combined with a Q-network which select the highest valued action to form recommendation policy. Furthermore, to reduce the decision time, we design the generator's architecture based on Huffman Tree. We show that with the generator pruning unlikely actions, the decision complexity can be reduced to $O(\log |A|)$ where $|A|$ is the number of actions, namely the number of items.

2   Off-Policy Recommendation Problem

A typical recommendation process can be formulated as a Markov Decision Process (MDP) $(\mathcal{S}, \mathcal{A}, r, P, \gamma)$ which is defined as follows.

- **State space** $\mathcal{S}$: The state $s_t^u = \{u, i_1, \ldots i_{c_t}\}$ contains the active user u and his/her chronological clicked items.
- **Action space** $\mathcal{A}$: The action space is the item set.
- **Reward** $r(s^u, a^u)$: Reward is the immediate gain of the RS after action a^u.

$$r(s^u, a^u) = \begin{cases} 1 & \text{if user } u \text{ clicks item } a^u \\ 0 & \text{otherwise} \end{cases} \tag{1}$$

- **Transition probability** $P(s_{t+1}^u | s_t^u, a_t^u)$: The state transits as follows.

$$s_{t+1}^u = \begin{cases} s_t^u \cup \{a_t^u\} & \text{if user } u \text{ clicks item } a_t^u \\ s_t^u & \text{otherwise} \end{cases}$$

- **Discount rate** γ: $\gamma \in [0, 1]$ is a hyperparameter. It is the tradeoff between the immediate reward and long term benefits.

The off-policy recommendation problem can be formulated as follows. Let $B = \{(s_t^u, a_t^u, s_{t+1}^u, r_t^u)\}$ be the dataset collected by a unknown *behavior policy*. Construct a recommendation policy $\pi : \mathcal{S} \to \mathcal{A}$ such that the accumulated reward is maximized. For notation simplicity, we may omit the superscript of s^u, r^u, a^u in the following section.

3   Preliminaries

3.1   Q-Learning

Q-learning learns the state-action Q-function $Q(s, a)$, which is the optimal expected cumulative reward when the RS starts in state s and takes action a. The optimal policy π can be recovered from the Q-function by choosing the maximizing action that is $\pi(s) = \arg\max_{a \in \mathcal{A}} Q(s, a)$. The Q-function is a fix point of the following Bellman iteration:

$$Q^{k+1}(s_t, a_t) = r_t + \gamma \max_a Q^k(s_{t+1}, a). \tag{2}$$

with (s_t, a_t, s_{t+1}, r_t) sampled from B. The above update formula is called Q-learning in reinforcement learning literature. According to [9,14], Q-learning may have unrealistic value on unobserved state-action pairs, which results in large exploration error and makes the performance of an RS unstable.

3.2   Batch Constrained Q-Learning

To cope with the exploration error, [14] proposes the Batch Constrained Q-Learning (BCQ) method. BCQ avoids exploration error by explicitly constraining an agent's candidate actions in the training set. Specifically, BCQ estimates the Q-function by the following batch constrained Bellman update.

$$Q^{k+1}(s_t, a_t) = r_t + \gamma \max_{(s_{t+1}, a) \in B} Q^k(s_{t+1}, a). \tag{3}$$

where "$(s_{t+1}, a) \in B$" means that there exist state s' and reward r' such that $(s_{t+1}, a, s', r') \in B$. Due to the sparsity of recommendation dataset, for most observed state s, there exists at most one action a such that $(s, a) \in B$. Thus, for most state-action pairs, the BCQ update (3) can be simplified to the following iteration

$$Q^{k+1}(s_t, a_t) = r_t + \gamma Q^k(s_{t+1}, a_{t+1}). \tag{4}$$

Such iteration implicitly assumes that the observed action a_{t+1} is optimal for state s_{t+1}, which is unrealistic because users' feedbacks are noisy.

4   Methodology

4.1   Generator Constrained Q-Learning

To prevent BCQ from overfitting into noisy data, we propose a new off-policy RL algorithm named Generator Constrained Q-learning (GCQ). GCQ utilizes a neural generator to recover the distribution of observed dataset. Then, the Q-function is updated on a candidate set sampled from the generator. Specifically, the main iteration of GCQ can be formulated as follows.

$$\begin{cases} A^k = \{a_i \sim g_{\theta_k}(a|s_{t+1})\}_{i=1}^c \\ Q^{k+1}(s_t, a_t) = r_t + \gamma \max \{Q^k(s_{t+1}, a)|a \in A^k\}. \end{cases} \tag{5}$$

where (s_t, a_t, s_{t+1}, r_t) is a randomly sampled tuple from B and $g_\theta(\cdot|s)$ is a neural generator which gives the conditional probability of actions. The size of candidate set c is a hyperparameter of GCQ method. When c is fixed to n, the number of items, GCQ becomes Q-Learning method.

Since the state space of RS is large, it is impossible to compute the Q-function of each state-action pairs. To handle the difficulty, we approximate the unknown Q-function by a deep neural network $Q_\theta(s, a)$ a.k.a deep Q-net where θ is its parameter.

4.2   Architecture of State Encoder

Obviously, both Q-net and generator need an encoder to extract features from a state $s = \{u, i_1, \ldots i_T\}$. According to [3], a shared encoder generalizes better than multiple task-specified encoders. Therefore, we use the same encoder for Q-net $Q_\theta(s, \cdot)$ and generator $g_\theta(\cdot|s)$. We depict the structure of encoder in Fig. 1(a).

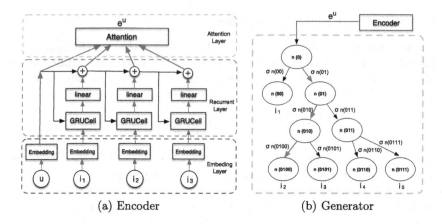

(a) Encoder   (b) Generator

Fig. 1. Neural architectures of proposed networks

Embedding Layer. The embedding layer maps a user or an item to correspondent semantic vector. Formally, Let $\mathbf{U} \in \mathbb{R}^{m \times d}$ and $\mathbf{V} \in \mathbb{R}^{n \times d}$ be the embedding matrix of user and item respectively. The embedding vector of user u and item i can be expressed as follows.

$$p_u = \mathbf{U}[u], \quad q_i = \mathbf{V}[i] \tag{6}$$

where we use $\mathbf{X}[k]$ to denote k-th row of matrix $\mathbf{X}$.

Residual Recurrent Layer. The layer transforms the sequence $s^u = \{u, i_1, \ldots i_T\}$ into hidden states. In the field of sequence modeling, GRU [6] and LSTM [10] are arguably the most powerful tools. However, both recurrent structures suffer from gradient vanishing/exploding issues for long sequences. Inspired by that residual network has stable gradients [19], we proposed a variant of GRU cell with residual structure. Specifically, we use the following recurrent to map the state s into hidden states $\{h_t\}_{t=0}^{t=T}$.

$$h_t = \begin{cases} p_u & \text{if } t = 0 \\ h_{t-1} + \mathbf{W} \cdot \text{GRUCell}(h_{t-1}, q_{i_t}) & \text{otherwise} \end{cases} \tag{7}$$

where p_u is the embedding vector of user u, q_{i_t} is the embedding vector of item i_t, and $\mathbf{W}$ is an alignment matrix.

Fast Attention Layer. The layer utilizes attention mechanism to aggregate hidden states $\{h_t\}_{t=0}^{t=T}$ into a feature vector e. For efficiency, we adopt a faster linear attention mechanism instead of the common tanh-based ones [7]. The linear attention has two stages. **Stage one:** compute the signal matrix $\mathbf{C}_t$ via the following recurrence.

$$\mathbf{C}_t = \begin{cases} h_0 h_0^\top & \text{if } t = 0 \\ (1 - \alpha_t)\mathbf{C}_{t-1} + \alpha_t h_t h_t^\top & \text{if } t > 0 \end{cases} \tag{8}$$

where $\alpha_t = \sigma(\mathbf{W}_\alpha h_t)$ is the forget gate and $\mathbf{W}_\alpha$ its parameter. **Stage two:** output encoding feature via

$$e = \mathbf{C}_T h_T. \tag{9}$$

The output vector e is the encoded feature vector of s.

4.3 Architecture of Q-Net

Considering that actions with high cumulative rewards shall have close correlations with the current state, we use the inner product of the two object's feature vectors to model the Q-function, that is

$$Q_\theta(s, a) = (e)^\top q_a \tag{10}$$

where $q_a = \mathbf{V}[a]$ is the embedding vector of action a.

4.4 Architecture of Generator

Since Huffman tree uses shorter codes for more frequent items, it results in a faster sampling process and is widely used in NLP tasks [17,18]. To reduce training time, we build a novel neural structure based on Huffman tree. The proposed structure is depicted in Fig. 1(b). The Huffman tree is built according to the popularity of items f which is defined by

$$f_i = \frac{\#\mathrm{ocurr}_i}{\sum_{i=1}^n \#\mathrm{ocurr}_i} \tag{11}$$

with $\#\mathrm{ocurr}_i$ being the occurrence number of item i. We assign Huffman code to each node of the tree by the following rules: (a) encode root node by $b_0 = 0$; (b) for a node with code $b_0 b_1 \ldots b_j$, encode its left child by $b_0 b_1 \ldots b_j 0$ and right child by $b_0 b_1 \ldots b_j 1$. Let $z_{b_{0:k}} \in \mathbb{R}^d$ be an embedding vector of a tree node with code $b_{0:k}$. For an item a with code $b_{0:j}$, its generating probability can be computed as follows.

$$g_\theta(a|s) = \prod_{k=0}^{j-1} \underbrace{\left(\sigma(z_{b_{0:k}}^\top e)\right)^{b_{k+1}} \left(1 - \sigma(z_{b_{0:k}}^\top e)\right)^{1-b_{k+1}}}_{\sigma_n(b_{0:k+1})} \tag{12}$$

According to above equation, computing $g_\theta(a|s)$ involves calculating $O(j)$ sigmoid functions where j is the length of a's Huffman code. Since the expected length of Huffman codes is $O(\log|A|)$, the time complexity for computing $g_\theta(a|s)$ is $O(d\log|A|)$. Similarly, sampling from $g_\theta(a|s)$ is equivalent to sample $O(j)$ sigmoids which has expected time complexity $O(d\log|A|)$.

Remark 1. The recommendation policy of GCQ can be derived by selecting an optimal action which has highest Q-value among a candidate set, that is

$$\pi(s) = \arg\max_{a \in A} Q_\theta(s, a) \text{ s.t. } A = \{a_i \sim g_\theta(a|s)\}_{i=1}^c \tag{13}$$

The recommendation policy can be executed in $O(d\log|A|)$ flops.

4.5   Parameter Inference

Loss Function of the Generator. We use the negative log-likelihood of the generator to evaluate the performance of the generator.

$$nll(\theta) = -\frac{1}{|B|} \sum_{(s,a)\in B} \log g_\theta(a|s). \tag{14}$$

Loss Function of the Q-Net. According to the framework of fitted Q-iteration [1], the loss function of Q-net is the mean square error between the Q-net and its bellman update, namely

$$qloss(\theta) = (Q_\theta(s,a) - r + \gamma \max\{Q_{\theta'}(s',a)|a \in A\})^2 \tag{15}$$

where $A = \{a_i \sim g_{\theta'}(a|s')\}_{i=1}^c$ is the candidate set and $(s,a,s',r) \in B$.

Algorithm 1: Generator Constrained Deep Q-Learning

---

    input : Replay Buffer B, size of candidate set c, regularizer λ, number of iterations K, discount rate γ, learning rate η

1   $tree = \text{BuildHoffmanTree}(\ B\ )$

2   $\theta_0 = \text{InitializeParameters}(\ tree\ )$

3 **for** $(\ k = 0;\ k < K;\ k++\ )$ **do**

4      $(s, a, s', r) = \text{GetRandomSample}(\ B\ )$

5      $A = \{a_i | a_i \sim g_{\theta_k}(a|s'), i \le c\}$

6      $\hat{Q} = r + \gamma \max\{Q_{\theta_k}(s', a_i) | a_i \in A\}$

7      $qloss = \frac{1}{2}\left(\hat{Q} - Q_\theta(s,a)\right)^2$

8      $nll = -\log g_\theta(a|s)$

9      $jointloss = qloss + \lambda nll$

10      $d\theta_k = (Q_{\theta_k}(s,a) - \hat{Q})\nabla Q_{\theta_k}(s,a) - \frac{\lambda}{g_{\theta_k}(a|s)}\nabla g_{\theta_k}(a|s)$

11      $\theta_{k+1} = \theta_k - \eta d\theta_k$

12 **end**

Joint Inference. Since the Q-net and the generator share the same encoder, We jointly train them via iteratively minimizing the following loss.

$$\min_\theta qloss(\theta) + \lambda nll(\theta) \tag{16}$$

where $\lambda > 0$ is a tuning parameter controlling the balance of mean square loss and log-likelihood. The joint loss can be optimized via stochastic gradient descent, as showed in Algorithm 1.

5   Experiments

In this section, we compare the performance of proposed GCQ method with state-of-the-art recommendation methods. We assess the performance of considered methods on both real-world offline datasets and simulated online environments. Besides, empirical studies on the hyperparameter sensitivities and computing time are conducted on several datasets. The baseline methods are listed as follows.

- **MF** [13]: It utilizes the latent factor model to predict the unknown ratings.
- **W&D** [5]: W&D uses wide & deep neural architecture to learn nonlinear latent factors.
- **GRU4Rec** [11]: It applies GRU to model click sequences.
- **DQN**: It recommends items by a deep Q-net. For fairness, We set the Q-net to the same one as the proposed method.
- **DDPG** [8]: DDPG utilizes deterministic policy gradient descent to update parameters.
- **DEERS** [22]: It tries to incorporate a user's negative feedback via sampling from the unclicked items.

5.1   Experiment Settings

We use three publicly available datasets: MovieLens 1M (M1M), MovieLens 10M (M10M) and Amazon 5-core grocery and gourmet food (AMZ) to compare the considered methods. These datasets contain historical ratings of items with scoring timestamps. Now according to timestamps, we can transform the datasets into replay buffers of the form $\{(s_t^u, a_t^u, s_{t+1}^u, r_t^u)\}$.

For simplicity, we set the dimension of user embedding, the dimension of item embedding, and the dimension of hidden states of the proposed neural architectures to the same value d. We call d the model dimension. We set the model dimension $d = 150$, the discount factor $\gamma = 0.9$, the size of sampling size $c = 50$, and the regularizer $\lambda = 0.1$ as default. All these hyperparameters are chosen by cross-validation. The hyperparameters of baseline methods are set to default values.

5.2   Offline Evaluation

According to the temporal order, we use the top 70% tuples in the derived replay buffers for training and hold out the remaining 30% for testing. In an offline environment, we cannot obtain the immediate reward of the recommendation policy. As a result, we cannot use the cumulative reward to evaluate the performance of the compared learning agents. Considering that a Q-net $Q_\theta(s, a)$ with high cumulative reward shall assign large value to clicked items and give small value the ignored ones, $Q_\theta(s, a)$ can be viewed as a scoring function which ranks the clicked items ahead of ignored ones. Thus, we can use the ranking metric such as Recall@k and Precision@k to evaluate the compared methods.

Table 1. Offline Recall@k of compared methods

	M1M			M10M			AMZ		
	Reca@1	Reca@5	Reca@10	Reca@1	Reca@5	Reca@10	Reca@1	Reca@5	Reca@10
DQN	0.0088	0.0416	0.0770	0.0052	0.0248	0.0429	0.0445	0.1877	0.3091
GRU4Rec	0.0079	0.0308	0.0540	0.0054	0.0235	0.0373	0.2735	0.4568	0.543
MF	0.0086	0.0324	0.0561	**0.0074**	0.0262	0.0439	0.2517	0.4359	0.5224
W& D	0.0069	0.0313	0.0519	0.0055	0.0238	0.0389	0.3734	0.5405	0.5982
DEERS	0.0048	0.0257	0.0461	0.0037	0.0193	0.0373	0.2926	0.6013	0.7176
DDPG	0.0083	0.0353	0.0596	0.0045	0.0210	0.0344	0.2359	0.4160	0.4743
GCQ	**0.0110**	**0.0495**	**0.0897**	0.0054	**0.0270**	**0.0539**	**0.3764**	**0.6015**	**0.6747**

Table 2. Offline Precision@k of compared methods

	M1M			M10M			AMZ		
	Prec@1	Prec@5	Prec@10	Prec@1	Prec@5	Prec@10	Prec@1	Prec@5	Prec@10
DQN	0.1543	0.1462	0.1396	0.0734	0.0754	0.0722	0.0523	0.0489	0.0432
GRU4Rec	0.1223	0.1043	0.0910	0.0922	0.0732	0.0588	0.3309	0.1263	0.0798
MF	0.1187	0.0920	0.0807	**0.1207**	0.0907	0.0695	0.3133	0.1220	0.0779
W& D	0.0992	0.0862	0.0740	0.1074	0.0836	0.0641	0.4539	0.1559	0.0920
DEERS	0.0770	0.0789	0.0757	0.0539	0.0582	0.0585	0.3414	0.1680	0.1110
DDPG	0.1598	0.1313	0.1155	0.0727	0.0679	0.0580	0.3016	0.1277	0.0791
GCQ	**0.1789**	**0.1658**	**0.1547**	0.0930	**0.0931**	**0.0930**	**0.4703**	**0.1829**	**0.1092**

To reduce randomness, we run each model five times and report their average performances in Table 1 and Table 2. From the tables, we can see that GCQ consistently outperforms DQN. Since the two methods share the same Q-net, such result shows that GCQ has a lower exploration error during the learning process. GCQ also has higher accuracy than DEERS. The reason is that the proposed encoder is more expressive than DEERS's GRU based one. Compared with DDPG, our GCQ consistently has better accuracy. This is because the policy-gradient-based method DDPG has higher variances during the learning process. Both Table 1 and Table 2 exhibit that GCQ outperforms non-RL methods, namely MF, W&D and GRU4Rec. These results demonstrate that taking the long term reward into consideration can improve the accuracy of recommendation.

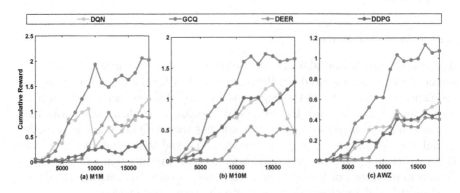

Fig. 2. Cumulative rewards of compared methods v.s. number of iterations

Table 3. Computational time of compared methods

	DQN	DDPG	DEER	GCQ
M1M	116.2 (s)	120.5	129.1	**86.1**
M10M	1175.7	1219.2	1306.3	**870.9**
AWZ	139.9	145.2	155.5	**103.7**

The computational time of compared RL methods is recorded in Table 3. The table exhibits that GCQ takes significantly less computational time in handling the benchmark datasets. This is because GCQ only takes $O(\log|A|)$ flops to make a recommendation decision while the decision complexities of other baseline methods are $O(|A|)$.

5.3   Online Evaluation

To simulate online environment, we train a GRU to model users' sequential decision processes. The GRU takes a user, the user's last clicked 20 items, and a candidate item as input. Then, it outputs the click probability of the candidate item. Such a simulation GRU is widely used in evaluating the online performance of RL-based recommender agent [22]. We split the datasets into the front 10%, the middle 80% and the tail 10% sub-datasets by temporal order. The front sub-dataset is used for initializing the learning agents. The middle sub-dataset is utilized for training the simulation GRU. The simulator will be validated on the tail sub-dataset. After training, we find that the simulator has classification accuracy greater than 75%. Therefore, the simulator quite precisely models a user's click decision. After the simulator is trained, we collect the simulated responses of users and then obtain cumulative reward.

The cumulative reward curves are reported in Fig. 2. From the figure, we find that GCQ yields much higher cumulative rewards than baseline methods. Its superior performance results from the smaller exploration error and better encoder structure. These figures also show that GCQ is more stable than the baseline methods. This confirms that GCQ has a lower exploration error during the learning process.

5.4   Model Stability

We find that the most important hyperparameters include: the model dimension parameter d which controls the model complexity of GCQ; and the size of candidate set c which controls exploration error.

We report Precision@10 of GCQ under different settings of d in Fig. 3(a). Figure 3(b) records Precision@10 of GCQ under different values of c. The experimental results in Fig. 3(a)(b) fluctuate within an acceptable range. This demonstrates the performance of our model is stable.

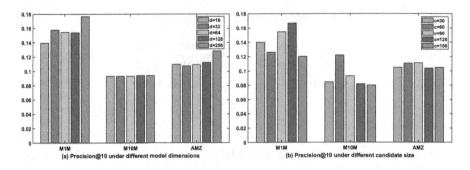

Fig. 3. Precision@10 of GCQ under different settings of hyperparameters

6   Conclusion

We proposed a novel Generator Constrained Q-learning technique for recommendation tasks. GCQ reduce the decision complexity of Q-net from $O(|A|)$ to $O(\log|A|)$. In addition, GCQ enjoys lower exploration error through better characterization of observed data. Further, GCQ employs a new multi-layer encoder to handle long sequences through attention mechanism and skip connection. Empirical studies demonstrate GCQ outperforms state-of-the-art methods both in efficiency and accuracy.

References

1. Antos, A., Szepesvári, C., Munos, R.: Fitted Q-iteration in continuous action-space MDPs. In: NeurIPS (2008)
2. Baird, L.: Residual algorithms: reinforcement learning with function approximation. In: Machine Learning Proceedings 1995, pp. 30–37. Elsevier (1995)
3. Bonadiman, D., Uva, A., Moschitti, A.: Effective shared representations with multitask learning for community question answering. In: ACL (2017)
4. Chen, M., Beutel, A., Covington, P., Jain, S., Belletti, F., Chi, E.: Top-k off-policy correction for a reinforce recommender system. In: WSDM (2019)
5. Cheng, H.-T., Levent Koc, H., et al.: Wide & deep learning for recommender systems. In: Proceedings of the 1st Workshop on Deep Learning for Recommender Systems, pp. 7–10. ACM (2016)
6. Chung, J., Gulcehre, C., Cho, K., Bengio, Y.: Empirical evaluation of gated recurrent neural networks on sequence modeling. arXiv preprint arXiv:1412.3555 (2014)
7. de Brebisson, A., Vincent, P.: A cheap linear attention mechanism with fast lookups and fixed-size representations. arXiv preprint arXiv:1609.05866 (2016)
8. Dulac-Arnold, G., et al.: Deep reinforcement learning in large discrete action spaces. arXiv preprint arXiv:1512.07679 (2015)
9. Fujimoto, S., Meger, D., Precup, D.: Off-policy deep reinforcement learning without exploration. arXiv preprint arXiv:1812.02900 (2018)
10. Gers, F.A., Schmidhuber, J., Cummins, F.: Learning to forget: Continual prediction with LSTM (1999)

11. Hidasi, B., Karatzoglou, A., et al.: Session-based recommendations with recurrent neural networks. arXiv:1511.06939 (2015)
12. Kolter, J.Z.: The fixed points of off-policy TD. In: Advances in Neural Information Processing Systems, pp. 2169–2177 (2011)
13. Koren, Y., Bell, R., Volinsky, C.: Matrix factorization techniques for recommender systems. Computer **42**(8), 30–37 (2009)
14. Kumar, A., Fu, J., et al.: Stabilizing off-policy Q-learning via bootstrapping error reduction. arXiv:1906.00949 (2019)
15. Linden, G., Smith, B., York, J.: Amazon.com recommendations: item-to-item collaborative filtering. IEEE Internet Comput. **1**, 76–80 (2003)
16. Munos, R.: Error bounds for approximate policy iteration. ICML **3**, 560–567 (2003)
17. Peng, H., Li, J., Song, Y., Liu, Y.: Incrementally learning the hierarchical softmax function for neural language models. In: AAAI (2017)
18. Rong, X.: word2vec parameter learning explained. arXiv:1411.2738 (2014)
19. Zaeemzadeh, A., Rahnavard, N., Shah, M.: Norm-preservation: why residual networks can become extremely deep? arXiv preprint arXiv:1805.07477 (2018)
20. Zhang, S., Yao, L., Sun, A., Tay, Y.: Deep learning based recommender system: a survey and new perspectives. CSUR **52**(1), 1–38 (2019)
21. Zhao, X., Zhang, L., Ding, Z., et al.: Deep reinforcement learning for list-wise recommendations. arXiv:1801.00209 (2017)
22. Zhao, X., Zhang, L., Ding, Z., et al.: Recommendations with negative feedback via pairwise deep reinforcement learning. In: SIGKDD (2018)
23. Zheng,G., Zhang, F., Zheng, Z., et al.: DRN: a deep reinforcement learning framework for news recommendation. In: WWW (2018)

GAMMA: A Graph and Multi-view Memory Attention Mechanism for Top-N Heterogeneous Recommendation

M. Vijaikumar[✉], Shirish Shevade, and M. Narasimha Murty

Department of Computer Science and Automation, Indian Institute of Science,
Bangalore, India
{vijaikumar,shirish,mnm}@iisc.ac.in

Abstract. Exploiting heterogeneous information networks (HIN) to top-N recommendation has been shown to alleviate the data sparsity problem present in recommendation systems. This requires careful effort in extracting relevant knowledge from HIN. However, existing models in this setting have the following shortcomings. Mainly, they are not end-to-end, which puts the burden on the system to first learn similarity or commuting matrix offline using some manually selected meta-paths before we train for the top-N recommendation objective. Further, they do not attentively extract user-specific information from HIN, which is essential for personalization. To address these challenges, we propose an end-to-end neural network model – GAMMA (Graph and Multi-view Memory Attention mechanism). We aim to replace the offline meta-path based similarity or commuting matrix computation with a graph attention mechanism. Besides, with different semantics of items in HIN, we propose a multi-view memory attention mechanism to learn more profound user-specific item views. Experiments on three real-world datasets demonstrate the effectiveness of our model for top-N recommendation setting.

Keywords: Heterogeneous information network · Recommendation systems · Memory attention network

1 Introduction

Due to exponential growth in the quantum of information available on the web, recommendation systems become inevitable in our day to day life. The objective of a top-N recommendation system is to come up with a ranked list of highly probable items that the user will interact in the future. Collaborative filtering (CF) techniques have been successful in modeling the top-N recommendation problem. Matrix factorization (MF) models [6,7,11] and the recently proposed neural network models such as [4,19] are a few instances of CF techniques.

However, a core strength of the CF models – *users' preferences are obtained from like-minded users' preferences through their historical records* – is also a

© Springer Nature Switzerland AG 2020
H. W. Lauw et al. (Eds.): PAKDD 2020, LNAI 12084, pp. 28–40, 2020.
https://doi.org/10.1007/978-3-030-47426-3_3

major drawback. This happens because the users interact with a very few items as compared to available items in the system. This phenomenon leads to *data sparsity problem* in recommendation systems.

Several works have been proposed to alleviate this data sparsity problem by exploiting information coming from external sources. In particular, leveraging knowledge coming from heterogeneous information networks is gaining more attention recently.

Definition 1. *Heterogeneous Information Network (HIN) [14]. An information network is defined by a directed graph $\mathcal{G}(\mathcal{V}, \mathcal{E})$ with an entity type function $f_e : \mathcal{V} \rightarrow \mathcal{O}$ and relation type function $f_r : \mathcal{E} \rightarrow \mathcal{R}$, where $\mathcal{O}$ and $\mathcal{R}$ denote entity (object) type and relation (edge) type, respectively. Here, $\mathcal{V}$ denotes the set of entities and $\mathcal{E}$ denotes the set of relations between the entities. This Graph $\mathcal{G}(\mathcal{V}, \mathcal{E})$ is called Heterogeneous Information Network (HIN) if $|\mathcal{O}| + |\mathcal{R}| > 2$.*

An example of a HIN is a network consisting of movies connected with 'actor' and 'genre' entities, and 'has' and 'belong to' relationships between them, respectively. In this work, we study top-N recommendation systems where items are involved in an external heterogeneous information network. We call the above setup top-N heterogeneous recommendation. Formally, we define this as

Problem Formulation: Top-N Heterogeneous Recommendation. Let $y_{(u,j)}$ be the rating that exists between user u and item j. Here, we consider the implicit rating setting, that is,

$$y_{(u,j)} = \begin{cases} 1, \text{ if } (u, j) \in \Omega \\ 0, \text{ otherwise} \end{cases}$$

where $\Omega = \{(u, j) : \text{user } u \text{ interacts with item } j\}$. In addition, a subset of items are involved in HIN, that is, $\mathcal{I} \cap \mathcal{V} \neq \phi$, where $\mathcal{I}$ denotes the set of items. The problem of top-N heterogeneous recommendation (short for top-N recommendation with heterogeneous information network) is to come up with a ranked list of highly probable items for each user by utilizing the associated HIN.

Recent advancements in deep neural networks have led to several models proposed for HIN based recommendation systems [3,5,12,22]. However, these models have the following shortcomings. First, they are not end-to-end – they rely on the tedious process of manual selection of meta-paths or meta-graphs, followed by offline embedding construction [12], similarity [3] or commuting matrix computation [22] for the entities in the HIN. Further, the proposed model in [3] uses similarity matrices which are inefficient in both memory and computation. Second, each user may look for different attributes of the items, for example, a user may decide to watch movies based on either the director or cast. We refer to subgraphs of a HIN associated with different attributes of items as different *views*. Therefore, the relevant information from the HIN should be extracted 'view-wise', according to each user's individual preferences. Third, users may look for more deeper characteristics such as *movies starring academy award-winning actors* (we call them *components*). In such cases, the model should not only be able to focus on the actors of the movie but also focus on whether they are academy award winners. This requires extraction of knowledge from the HIN 'component-wise' and such knowledge can potentially be used to explain why the recommendation system suggests a particular list of movies.

Contributions. To address the above challenges, we propose **GAMMA** – a Graph And Multi-view Memory Attention mechanism for the top-N heterogeneous recommendation problem. This is illustrated in Fig. 1. The novelty of our approach lies in making the model end-to-end – our approach does not require any offline similarity, commuting matrix computations or random-walk based embedding construction. Additionally, no manual selection of meta-paths is required. We achieve this by using graph attention networks – one for each view of the HIN. Further, we propose a multi-view multi-head memory attention layer, henceforth the *M3-layer*. The responsibility of this layer is to extract component-wise user-specific information. For example, it could extract information such as *actors who are academy-award winners*. Furthermore, we propose to use an attention mechanism to aggregate the knowledge coming from different views according to their influence. We conduct experiments on three real-world datasets and demonstrate the effectiveness of our model against several state-of-the-art models for top-N recommendation setting. Our implementation is available at https://github.com/mvijaikumar/GAMMA.

2 The Proposed Model

2.1 GAMMA

In this section, we persent our proposed model – GAMMA. The overall architecture is illustrated in Fig. 1. GAMMA has five building blocks. In what follows, we discuss them one by one in detail.

Embedding Construction from User-Item Interaction Matrix. This block is responsible for constructing embeddings for users and items from their interaction matrix. Let $P \in \mathbb{R}^{|\mathcal{U}| \times d}$ be the user embedding matrix and $Q \in \mathbb{R}^{|\mathcal{I}| \times d}$ be the item embedding matrix, where $|\mathcal{U}|$ and $|\mathcal{I}|$ denote number of users and items, and d denotes embedding dimension, respectively. Further, assume $x_u \in \mathbb{R}^{|\mathcal{U}|}$ and $z_j \in \mathbb{R}^{|\mathcal{I}|}$ be the one-hot encoding representations for user u and item j, respectively. We obtain the user embedding (p_u) and the item embedding (q_j) from P and Q as follows.

$$p_u = P^T x_u \text{ and } q_j = Q^T z_j. \tag{1}$$

In our proposed model, user embedding p_u has two roles to play. First, it learns the necessary user representations from user-item interactions. Second, it is used in further blocks as a query vector which extracts user-specific information from the HIN at both component- and view-levels.

Item-View Embedding Constructions via Graph Attention Mechanism (GAT Layers). This block is responsible for constructing initial view-wise embeddings for items from the HIN, each representing different views. To do this, we first extract different sub-graphs involving items with different entity types. For example, movies can be associated with both actors and genres. So, in this case, we construct two item-view sub-graphs – one with movie and actor nodes and the other with movie and genre nodes, as illustrated in Fig. 1.

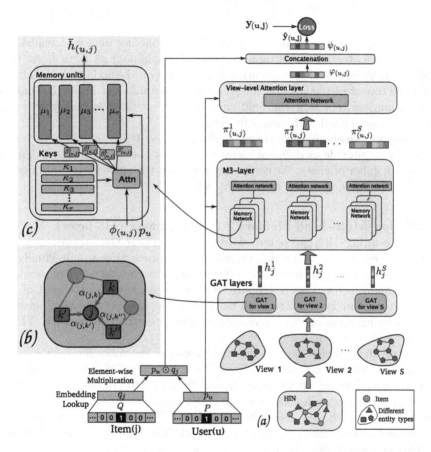

Fig. 1. The illustration of GAMMA architecture for top-N heterogeneous recommendation. Here, (a) provides overall architecture. The main components – (b) GAT layer, (c) memory network are given separately for more clarity. (Best viewed in colour.) (Color figure online)

Definition 2. *Item-view sub-graph. Formally, we define item-view sub-graph for each view (s) as* $\mathcal{G}_s(\mathcal{V}_s, \mathcal{E}_s)$ *where* $\mathcal{V}_s \subseteq \mathcal{V}$ *and* $\mathcal{E}_s \subseteq \mathcal{E}$. *Here,* $\mathcal{I} \cap \mathcal{V}_s \neq \phi, \forall s$.

Further, individually on these sub-graphs, we employ a multi-layer graph attention mechanism (GAT [16]) to construct first-level view-wise embeddings for the items. Let W_G^i and c_G^i be the weight matrix and vector associated with layer i and $\mathcal{N}(j)$ be a set of neighbors for the node j. The representations (f_j^i for item j at layer i) for the items involved in the sub-graphs are learned as follows.

$$f_j^i = \sum_{k \in \mathcal{N}(j)} \alpha_{(j,k)}^i W_G^i f_k^{i-1},$$

$$\text{where} \quad \alpha_{(j,k)}^i = \frac{\exp(a(c_G^i \cdot [W_G^i f_j^{i-1} \| W_G^i f_k^{i-1}]))}{\sum_{k' \in \mathcal{N}(j)} \exp(a(c_G^i \cdot [W_G^i f_j^{i-1} \| W_G^i f_{k'}^{i-1}]))}. \tag{2}$$

Here, $\|$ denotes concatenation operation, $f_k^0 = z_k$ (one-hot item representation), and $\alpha_{(j,k)}^i$ denotes influence value for node k on node j at layer i. At each GAT layer, we have multiple attention heads acting on the node representations. Then, we concatenate the embeddings coming from different heads. For ease of explanation, we represent the final embedding from GAT layers by h_j^s – the embedding associated with view s for item j.

Therefore, we obtain multiple embeddings for the items – one from each sub-graph. These provide us different views $\{h_j^s\}_{s=1}^S$ for the item j where S denotes the total number of views. We compactly represent the embeddings obtained for all the nodes for single view as $\mathbf{h}^s = [h_1^s, h_2^s, ..., h_n^s]$.

Multi-view Multi-head Memory Attention Layer (M3-layer). M3-layer takes embedding $\{\mathbf{h}^s\}_{s=1}^S$ obtained from the previous GAT layers as input, extracts attentively user specific components from each view s, individually. As we discussed earlier, the user may prefer to watch movies acted by an academy award-winning actor. Hence, keeping that into consideration, the goal of this layer is to capture such information using multiple memory attention networks followed by aggregating such information using the attention network. This is done for each view separately.

During this process, we use multiple memory networks for each view to capture the different notions of influential components. This can be intuitively thought of as different filters acting on the different parts of the input. Further, we utilize attention mechanisms to aggregate these constructed user-specific item embeddings for each view, as illustrated in Fig. 1. We first explain what happens in one view and one memory attention network. The same procedure is followed in other views and different memory attention heads, respectively.

Let $\mu = \{\mu_1, \mu_2, ..., \mu_\tau\}$, where $\mu_i \in \mathbb{R}^d$ and $\kappa = \{\kappa_1, \kappa_2, ..., \kappa_\tau\}$, where $\kappa_i \in \mathbb{R}^d$ be memory components and the corresponding keys, respectively. Here, τ denotes the total number of memory units. First, we get normalized user and item-view representation ($\phi_{(u,j)}$) as,

$$\phi_{(u,j)} = \frac{p_u \odot h_j}{\|p_u\| \|h_j\|}, \tag{3}$$

where $\phi_{(u,j)} \in \mathbb{R}^d$ and $\odot$ denotes Hadamard product. This is then combined with the keys (κ) to provide the required influential (attention) values,

$$\beta^t_{(u,j)} = \frac{\exp(\phi_{(u,j)} \cdot \kappa_t)}{\sum_{t'=1}^{\tau} \exp(\phi_{(u,j)} \cdot \kappa_{t'})}. \tag{4}$$

These influence values provide the influence score of how much each component contributes to the user's interest. They are then used along with the memory units that provide user-specific item views. This is done as follows. First, we extract the required information ($\bar{\mu}^t_j$) from item views using memory units and then we obtain the item representation ($\bar{h}_{(u,j)}$) as,

$$\bar{h}_{(u,j)} = \sum_{t=1}^{\tau} \beta^t_{(u,j)} \bar{\mu}^t_j, \text{ where } \bar{\mu}^t_j = \mu_t \odot h_j. \tag{5}$$

Here $\bar{h}_{(u,j)} \in \mathbb{R}^d$ denotes the user-specific item-view representation from a single memory network. We get multiple such representations from multiple views and multiple heads (indexed by γ) given as $\bar{h}^{(s,\gamma)}_{(u,j)}$. We then aggregate the representations view-wise (into $\pi^s_{(u,j)}$) as follows,

$$\pi^s_{(u,j)} = \mathcal{A}(\{\bar{h}^{(s,\gamma)}_{(u,j)}\}^{\Gamma}_{\gamma=1}, p_u), \tag{6}$$

where Γ denotes the total number of memory networks and $\mathcal{A}(\cdot)$ denotes attention network [9]. This is defined as,

$$\mathcal{A}(p_u, \{x^{\gamma}\}^{\Gamma}_{\gamma=1}) = \sum_{\gamma=1}^{\Gamma} \zeta_{u\gamma} x_{u\gamma}, \text{ where}$$

$$\zeta_{u\gamma} = \frac{\exp(\text{score}(p_u, x^{\gamma}))}{\sum_{\gamma'=1}^{\Gamma} \exp(\text{score}(x^{\gamma'}, p_u))} \text{ and } \text{score}(p_u, x^{\gamma}) = p_u^T W_{\mathcal{A}} x^{\gamma}. \tag{7}$$

Here, x^{γ} is a vector, $\zeta_{u\gamma}$ denotes influence value of γ on user u and $W_{\mathcal{A}}$ is weight matrix associated with the attention network. Note that, memory units and keys are initialized randomly and the weights are shared across the inputs.

View-Level Attention Layer. The previous layer provides the item embeddings ($\{\pi^s_{(u,j)}\}^S_{s=1}$) concerning different views, consisting of important user-specific information extracted, components-wise. The purpose of this layer is to aggregate the information present in item embeddings, view-wise. Different users get influenced by different views of items, for example, the genre of the movie or actors in the movie. Hence, we combine such different views attentively as follows,

$$\varphi_{(u,j)} = \mathcal{A}(p_u, \{\pi^s_{(u,j)}\}^S_{s=1}), \tag{8}$$

where $\varphi_{(u,j)}$ is a resultant item-view representation extracted from HIN.

Prediction Layer. This layer is responsible for gathering information coming from the interaction matrix and HIN network and provides the predicted probability that a user may interact with each item in the future. It first concatenates representations coming from the user-item interactions and the HIN. We then pass these representations through a sequence of fully connected layers and finally, we obtain the predictive probability as

$$
\hat{y}_{(u,j)} = g(\psi_{(u,j)}),
$$
$$
\text{where } \psi_{(u,j)} = (p_u \odot q_j) \| (p_u \odot \varphi_{(u,j)}).
$$

(9)

Here $g(x) = a(\cdots a(W_2 a(W_1 x + b_1) + b_2) \cdots)$ denotes a fully connected network, $a(\cdot)$ is an activation function and W_k and b_k are weight matrices and bias vectors, respectively.

2.2 Loss Function

Since our ratings are implicit (binary), one can use point-wise loss functions such as cross-entropy [3,4] or pair-wise loss functions such as BPR-loss [11]. In this work, we use cross-entropy loss function and the final optimization problem is,

$$
\min_{\mathcal{W}} \ \mathcal{L}(\mathcal{W}) = - \sum_{(u,j) \in \mathcal{D}} y_{(u,j)} \ln \hat{y}_{(u,j)} + (1 - y_{(u,j)}) \ln(1 - \hat{y}_{(u,j)}) + \lambda \, \mathcal{R}(\mathcal{W}),
$$

(10)

where $\mathcal{W}$ consists of all the model parameters, $\mathcal{R}(\cdot)$ is a regularizer and λ is a non-negative hyperparameter. We employ negative sampling strategy during training. Here, $\mathcal{D} = \mathcal{D}^+ \cup \mathcal{D}^-_{samp}$ where $\mathcal{D}^+ := \{(u,j) \in \Omega\}$ and $\mathcal{D}^-_{samp} \subset \{(u,j') \notin \Omega\}$, and $\mathcal{D}^-_{samp}$ is obtained using a negative sampling procedure [10].

3 Experiments

3.1 Experimental Settings

Datasets. We use three real-world datasets – Amazon, Yelp and MovieLens – for our experiments.[1] Besides the user-item interactions, the datasets contain HINs where items are involved. In particular, the HIN associated with the Amazon dataset has a co-viewed network, brand and category information for the products, the HIN associated with the Yelp dataset has category and city information for the businesses and the HIN associated with MovieLens dataset has actor, director, country and genre information for the movies, respectively. The MovieLens dataset has ratings in the range [0.5–5] and the other datasets have ratings in the range [1–5], respectively. We do the following pre-processing, as

---

[1] https://github.com/librahu/HIN-Datasets-for-Recommendation-and-Network-Embedding.

done in [3,4]. That is, (1) we retain the ratings more than 3 for the Amazon and Yelp datasets and 3.5 for the MovieLens dataset, and treat them as positive interactions, and (2) we retain users and items having more than 10 ratings for the Amazon and MovieLens datasets and more than 5 for the Yelp dataset, respectively. The statistics of the datasets are given in Table 1.

Metrics and Evaluation Procedure. We adopt two top-N recommendation metrics (ranking metrics) – hit ratio (HR@N) and normalized discounted cumulative gain (NDCG@N) for the performance comparison. Further, following [3,4], we split the dataset into train, validation and test sets where we hold-out one randomly selected item for each user for validation and test set, respectively. Since it is difficult to rank all the available items for each user during the evaluation, we sample 50 non-interacted items for each user to compare with the hold-out item in the validation and test set. We repeat this procedure five times and obtain five different splits. We report the mean and standard deviation of these five splits as the final result.

Table 1. Dataset statistics

Dataset	# Users	# Items	# Entities in HIN	# Connections in HIN	# Ratings
Amazon	4365	2617	5625	10324	131167
MovieLens	1761	1036	4301	13661	112616
Yelp	4511	3862	4406	15556	96356

Comparison Models. We evaluate our proposed model with the following models. Note that BPR, MF, GMF and NeuMF are rating-only models, and linear and non-linear variants of HERec and NeuACF are HIN based models for recommendation task.

- **NeuACF** [3] is a state-of-the-art model for top-N heterogeneous recommendation setting. NeuACF is a two-stage approach. In the first stage, it computes user-user and item-item similarity matrices offline using some manually selected meta-paths. In the second stage, it utilizes these similarity matrices along with the user-item rating matrix for prediction.
- **HERec** [12] is a recently proposed two-stage approach for heterogeneous recommendation setting. In the first stage, it computes user and item embeddings offline using a meta-path based random walk and skip-gram technique [10]. In the second stage, it leverages embeddings learned for users and items for the recommendation tasks. We include the two proposed variants of HERec – HERec (linear) and HERec (non-linear) for comparison.
- **NeuMF** [4] is one of the state-of-the-art models for rating-only top-N recommendation setting. NeuMF is a fusion between MF and a neural network approach. Further, **GMF** is proposed as a part of NeuMF.

- **MF** [6] is a standard and well-known baseline for the recommendation task.
- **BPR** [11] is a standard baseline for the top-N recommendation setting.

FMG [22] is another recently proposed model that utilizes commuting matrices learned from meta-graph based strategy. Since it has been shown in [3] that NeuACF outperforms FMG, we omit this from the comparison.

Hyperparameter Setting and Reproducibility. We implement our model using Python and TensorFlow 1.14. We tune the hyperparameters using the validation set and report the corresponding test set performance. From the validation set performance, we set the embedding dimension (d) to 32 for the Amazon and Yelp datasets, and 64 for the MovieLens dataset. We set the learning rate to 0.002, the number of negative samples to 3, the mini-batch size to 2048 with Xavier initialization, use an RMSprop optimizer, and a dropout of 0.5. We use a 2-layer GAT network with 6 and 4 attention heads in the first and second layers, respectively. Further, we set the number of heads (Γ) in M3-layer to 4, and the number of memory units (T) to 8, respectively. We tune and set the hyperparameters for the baselines according to the respective papers.

Table 2. Overall performance of different models on three real-world datasets – Amazon, MovieLens and Yelp (given in **HR@5**).

Model	Amazon	MovieLens	Yelp
MF [6]	0.4976 ± 0.0056	0.6579 ± 0.0045	0.5109 ± 0.0102
BPR [11]	0.5079 ± 0.0071	0.6516 ± 0.0046	0.5107 ± 0.0064
GMF [4]	0.5235 ± 0.0049	0.6757 ± 0.0078	0.5307 ± 0.0079
NeuMF [4]	0.5366 ± 0.0063	0.7025 ± 0.0056	0.5396 ± 0.0060
HERec (linear) [12]	0.5359 ± 0.0079	0.6927 ± 0.0040	0.5279 ± 0.0040
HERec (non-linear) [12]	0.5280 ± 0.0066	0.6947 ± 0.0072	0.5306 ± 0.0070
NeuACF [3]	0.5520 ± 0.0042	0.7054 ± 0.0108	**0.5678 ± 0.0124**
GAMMA (ours)	**0.5593 ± 0.0060**	**0.7171 ± 0.0117**	0.5579 ± 0.0067

Table 3. Overall performance of different models on three real-world datasets – Amazon, MovieLens and Yelp (given in **NDCG@5**).

Model	Amazon	MovieLens	Yelp
MF [6]	0.3467 ± 0.0052	0.4717 ± 0.0039	0.3568 ± 0.0073
BPR [11]	0.3585 ± 0.0022	0.4765 ± 0.0033	0.3565 ± 0.0035
GMF [4]	0.3664 ± 0.0040	0.5062 ± 0.0062	0.3768 ± 0.0056
NeuMF [4]	0.3782 ± 0.0057	0.5233 ± 0.0031	0.3808 ± 0.0028
HERec (linear) [12]	0.3816 ± 0.0071	0.5081 ± 0.0051	0.3741 ± 0.0013
HERec (non-linear) [12]	0.3760 ± 0.0054	0.5116 ± 0.0057	0.3764 ± 0.0049
NeuACF [3]	0.3992 ± 0.0041	0.5350 ± 0.0061	**0.4061 ± 0.0089**
GAMMA (ours)	**0.4049 ± 0.0028**	**0.5461 ± 0.0056**	0.3979 ± 0.0052

3.2   Experimental Results and Discussion

Overall Performance. We present the overall performance of our model – GAMMA in Table 2 and Table 3. Here, we conduct paired t-test and the improvements obtained here are statistically significant with $p < 0.01$. Note that HERec and NeuACF heavily utilize the embeddings constructed offline, while GAMMA does not use any such offline embeddings. As we can see from Table 2 and Table 3, our model outperforms the HIN based recommendation models as well as the rating-only models on the Amazon and the MovieLens datasets and performs comparably with NeuACF on the Yelp dataset. From this, we conclude that the GAT mechanism along with user-specific knowledge extraction from the HIN can effectively replace the tedious offline embedding construction strategies.

Performance Against Different Sparsity Levels. Here, we experiment to study the performance of the models for different sparsity levels. For this, we take

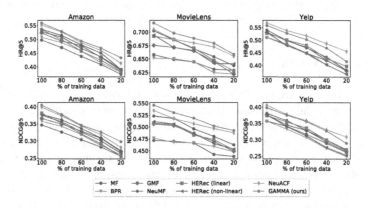

Fig. 2. Performance comparison of different models against different sparsity levels on the datasets: Amazon, MovieLens and Yelp. Here, the mean values obtained from the five different splits for each sparsity level are reported.

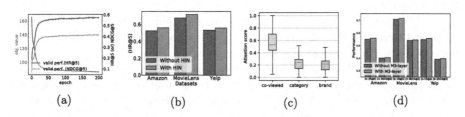

Fig. 3. (a) Objective function value, performance of GAMMA on validation set (in HR@5 and NDCG@5) against number of training epochs. (b) Performance comparison when HIN is ignored vs HIN is used. (c) Distribution of attention scores learned by GAMMA for different views on the Amazon dataset. Here, red-colored line inside the box signifies the median. (d) Performance comparison when M3-layer is not included vs M3-layer is included. (Best viewed in color.) (Color figure online)

the full training set, and at each level, we remove 20% of the interactions. This is illustrated in Fig. 2. Here, the x-axis denotes the percentage of the training data used, and the y-axis denotes the performance in HR@5 or NDCG@5. From this study, we observe that despite the varying sparsity levels, the performance of our model is consistent across different datasets.

Figure 3(a) shows the objective function value and the validation set performance (in HR@5 and NDCG@5) against the number of training epochs. Further, Fig. 3(b) illustrates the performance comparison of GAMMA when the HIN is ignored vs the HIN is included. The performance improvement shows that our proposed approach effectively utilizes the HIN to improve the top-N recommendations. Figure 3(c) demonstrates the attention score distribution for different views on the Amazon dataset. This indicates that the influence of different views on the recommendation tasks varies, and attentively selecting information coming from different views is essential. Further, Fig. 3(d) illustrates the performance of GAMMA when the M3-layer is not included vs the M3-layer is included. From this, we observe that incorporating the M3-layer indeed helps in improving the performance.

4   Related Work

Early CF techniques are mainly based on matrix factorization models – BPR [11] and MF [6] – and their extensions [7]. In recent years, due to their rich representation capabilities, several neural networks and deep learning models are developed for top-N recommendation settings [21]. For instance, NeuMF [4] combines MF with a multi-layer perceptron to learn better representations for users and items through MF as well as neural networks. Further, autoencoders and variational autoencoders [8] and graph neural network-based models [19] have also been proposed for recommendation systems. Nevertheless, since most of these models entirely rely on past interactions between users and items, their performance is mostly affected when sparsity increases. Recently, to mitigate the sparsity issues, there is an increasing interest in leveraging knowledge from the HIN. Our work falls under this category.

Early work on heterogeneous recommendation incorporate knowledge extracted from the HIN to MF models. For instance, HeteRec [20] uses meta-path based similarity construction followed by the Bayesian ranking optimization technique for the top-N recommendation. Besides, SemRec [13] employs weighted meta-paths to prioritize and personalize user preferences on different paths. Recently, due to its ability to effectively extract relevant information, employing attention mechanism [9,18] to recommendation systems is gaining ground [2,15]. Further, the memory attention network has been employed in the context of top-N social [1] and multi-media [2] recommendation tasks. In terms of utilizing multiple views (aspects) for the items from the HIN, our work is related to NeuACF [3], MCRec [5], HERec [12], KGAT [17] and FMG [22]. For instance, NeuACF [3] follows a two-stage approach – in the first stage, it constructs similarity matrices. In the second stage, these similarity matrices are used for learning deeper representations of the users and items. KGAT [17] incorporates information from the knowledge graph using graph neural networks. Further, Hu *et al.* [5] proposes a three-way neural interaction model with co-attention for the top-N heterogeneous recommendation. In place of meta-paths, FMG [22] proposes meta-graphs for extracting knowledge from HIN. Further, Shi *et al.* [12] propose HERec that fuses meta-path based embeddings into extended MF model.

5   Conclusion

In this work, we proposed a graph and memory attention-based neural network model – GAMMA for top-N recommendation systems. The proposed technique replaces the tedious process of computing similarity or commuting matrix offline with a graph attention mechanism. This makes the whole procedure end-to-end. Further, we proposed a multi-view multi-head memory attention layer to extract fine-grained user-specific information using a memory attention network. The proposed model is general, and it can easily be extended to scenarios where both users and items are involved in the HIN. Extensive experiments on three real-world datasets demonstrated the effectiveness of our model over state-of-the-art top-N recommendation models.

References

1. Chen, C., Zhang, M., Liu, Y., Ma, S.: Social attentional memory network: modeling aspect-and friend-level differences in recommendation. In: WSDM. ACM (2019)
2. Chen, J., Zhang, H., He, X., Nie, L., Liu, W., Chua, T.S.: Attentive collaborative filtering: multimedia recommendation with item-and component-level attention. In: SIGIR, pp. 335–344. ACM (2017)
3. Han, X., Shi, C., Wang, S., Philip, S.Y., Song, L.: Aspect-level deep collaborative filtering via heterogeneous information networks. In: IJCAI, pp. 3393–3399 (2018)
4. He, X., Liao, L., Zhang, H., Nie, L., Hu, X., Chua, T.S.: Neural collaborative filtering. In: WWW, pp. 173–182 (2017)
5. Hu, B., Shi, C., Zhao, W.X., Yu, P.S.: Leveraging meta-path based context for top-n recommendation with a neural co-attention model. In: SIGKDD. ACM (2018)
6. Hu, Y., Koren, Y., Volinsky, C.: Collaborative filtering for implicit feedback datasets. In: ICDM, pp. 263–272. IEEE (2008)
7. Koren, Y., Bell, R.: Advances in collaborative filtering. In: Ricci, F., Rokach, L., Shapira, B. (eds.) Recommender Systems Handbook, pp. 77–118. Springer, Boston (2015). https://doi.org/10.1007/978-1-4899-7637-6_3
8. Liang, D., Krishnan, R.G., Hoffman, M.D., Jebara, T.: Variational autoencoders for collaborative filtering. In: WWW, pp. 689–698 (2018)
9. Luong, M.T., Pham, H., Manning, C.D.: Effective approaches to attention-based neural machine translation. In: EMNLP, pp. 1412–1421. ACL (2015)
10. Mikolov, T., Sutskever, I., Chen, K., Corrado, G.S., Dean, J.: Distributed representations of words and phrases and their compositionality. In: Advances in neural information processing systems, pp. 3111–3119 (2013)

11. Rendle, S., Freudenthaler, C., Gantner, Z., Schmidt-Thieme, L.: Bpr: bayesian personalized ranking from implicit feedback. In: UAI, pp. 452–461. AUAI (2009)
12. Shi, C., Hu, B., Zhao, W.X., Philip, S.Y.: Heterogeneous information network embedding for recommendation. In: TKDE. vol. 31, pp. 357–370. IEEE (2018)
13. Shi, C., Zhang, Z., Luo, P., Yu, P.S., Yue, Y., Wu, B.: Semantic path based personalized recommendation on weighted heterogeneous information networks. In: CIKM, pp. 453–462. ACM (2015)
14. Sun, Y., Han, J.: Mining heterogeneous information networks: a structural analysis approach. ACM SIGKDD Explor. Newslett. **14**(2), 20–28 (2013)
15. Tay, Y., Luu, A.T., Hui, S.C.: Multi-pointer co-attention networks for recommendation. In: SIGKDD, pp. 2309–2318. ACM (2018)
16. Veličković, P., Cucurull, G., Casanova, A., Romero, A., Liò, P., Bengio, Y.: Graph attention networks. In: ICLR (2018)
17. Wang, X., He, X., Cao, Y., Liu, M., Chua, T.S.: Kgat: knowledge graph attention network for recommendation. In: SIGKDD, pp. 950–958 (2019)
18. Wang, X., et al.: Heterogeneous graph attention network. In: WWW, pp. 2022–2032 (2019)
19. XWang, X., He, X., Wang, M., Feng, F., Chua, T.: Neural graph collaborative filtering. In: SIGIR, pp. 165–174. ACM (2019)
20. Yu, X., et al.: Recommendation in heterogeneous information networks with implicit user feedback. In: RecSys, pp. 347–350. ACM (2013)
21. Zhang, S., Yao, L., Sun, A., Tay, Y.: Deep learning based recommender system: a survey and new perspectives. ACM Comput. Surv. (CSUR) **52**(1), 5 (2019)
22. Zhao, H., Yao, Q., Li, J., Song, Y., Lee, D.L.: Meta-graph based recommendation fusion over heterogeneous information networks. In: SIGKDD. ACM (2017)

Collaborative Recommendation of Temporally-Discounted Tag-Based Expertise for Community Question Answering

Gianni Costa and Riccardo Ortale$^{(\boxtimes)}$

ICAR-CNR, Via P. Bucci 8/9C, Rende, CS, Italy
{costa,ortale}@icar.cnr.it

Abstract. We propose an innovative approach to finding experts for community question answering (CQA). The idea is to recommend answerers, who are credited the highest expertise under question tags at routing time. The expertise of answerers under already replied question tags is intuitively discounted by accounting for the observed tags, votes and temporal information of their answers. Instead, the discounted expertise under not yet replied tags is predicted via a latent-factor representation of both answerers and tags. These representations are inferred by means of Gibbs sampling under a new Bayesian probabilistic model of discounted user expertise and asking-answering behavior. The devised model unprecedentedly explains the latter two CQA aspects as the result of a generative process, that seamlessly integrates probabilistic matrix factorization and network behavior characterization. An extensive comparative experimentation over real-world CQA data demonstrates that our approach outperforms several-state-of-the-art competitors in recommendation effectiveness.

1 Introduction

Expert recommendation [17] enables the timely sharing of high-quality knowledge for community question answering (CQA) [16]. Unfortunately, despite several previous research efforts, expert recommendation still remains problematic for various reasons. Firstly, question-answering (QA) communities are inherently time-evolving [21], with new users (both askers and answerers) joining daily and the existing users changing their interests and behavior (such as, e.g., long-term inactive users, who turn into active participants). Hitherto, expert recommendation has been studied, mostly by ignoring the temporal information of posts. Accordingly, the devised approaches are suitable neither to deal with the natural drift of users' interests over time, nor to promote short-term answerers (i.e., users with a limited recent answering history). This is a severe limitation, that lowers the effectiveness of expert recommendation, since the recommended experts may no more reply to questions matching initially-relevant and already-outdated

© Springer Nature Switzerland AG 2020
H. W. Lauw et al. (Eds.): PAKDD 2020, LNAI 12084, pp. 41–52, 2020.
https://doi.org/10.1007/978-3-030-47426-3_4

interests. In addition, short-term answerers would likely not be recommended at all, being their expertise gained in a far too short time period for such users to build a solid reputation as actual experts. Secondly, there is no common agreement on the choice of the discriminative content features to capture answerers' expertise. In most studies, the latter is inferred from the raw text of their answers, suitably weighted by the respective votes from the QA community. Tags are mainly ignored or, alternatively, incorporated into post contents as in [20]. However, tags are more insightful, concise and explicit user-generated explanations of both post meaning and topical expertise, with respect to the general topics inferrable from the textual post contents [19]. Thirdly, supplementing content features with further auxiliary data (e.g., networks of user interactions) for more effective expert recommendation involves devising a plausible joint processing of such information. Hitherto, both sources of information have been combined mainly through simplistic schemes such as, e.g., linear interpolation [17].

In this paper, we propose a new collaborative approach to recommending question-specific experts in QA communities. The expertise of answerers is determined from the tags, votes and temporal information of their answers as well as the asking-answering relationships in the targeted QA community. More precisely, answer tags are employed to capture and represent the topical expertise of answerers. Votes indicate the degree to which answerers are publicly acknowledged within the QA community as experts under the tags of the respective answers. Posting time allows for discounting [8] earlier answers of responders, so that to account for the natural drift of their interests over time, without penalizing short-term answerers. Besides, asking-answering interactions inform the identification of experts, since repliers to expert askers are likely to be expert as well. Essentially, for each posted question, the intuition behind the presented approach consists in recommending answerers, who are credited the highest degree of expertise under the tags of the particular question at routing time. In particular, the expertise of answerers under already replied tags is intuitively determined by means of the votes and temporal information of their answers to the questions labelled with such tags. Instead, the unknown expertise of answerers under not yet replied tags is predicted through a latent-factor generative model of temporally-discounted user expertise and asking-answering behavior. Under such a model, Bayesian probabilistic matrix factorization [15] and the statistical formalization of asking-answering are seamlessly integrated. This allows for explaining both the expertise of users and their behavioral patterns as the result of a generative process, that is governed by a certain number of latent factors. These are estimated via a MCMC algorithm, that implements the derived mathematical details of Gibbs sampling inference under the devised model.

Extensive tests over real-world CQA data show that our approach overcomes several state-of-the-art competitors in recommendation effectiveness.

This paper proceeds as follows. Notation and preliminaries are introduced in Sect. 2. The devised model is developed in Sect. 3. Expertise prediction for recommendation and posterior inference are covered in Sect. 4. The experimental evaluation of our approach is presented in Sect. 5. Finally, conclusions are drawn in Sect. 6, where future research is also previewed.

2   Preliminaries

A question-answering (QA) community D can be formalized as a triple $D \triangleq \langle U, T, G \rangle$, where

- $U = \{u_1, \ldots, u_N\}$ is a set of N users;
- $T = \{t_1, \ldots, t_M\}$ is a set of M tags;
- $G = \langle V, A \rangle$ is a directed communication network shaped by user interaction behavior, with $V \subseteq U$ and $A \subseteq U \times U$ being the set of nodes and edges, respectively.

The generic user $u \in U$ can ask questions and/or provide answers. In order to capture the expertise of u, we focus on her answering history $\boldsymbol{a}_u = \{a_{u,1}, \ldots, a_{u,N_u}\}$. $\boldsymbol{a}_u$ is the time sequence of N_u replies from u to as many questions posted by other users of D. The arbitrary answer $a_{u,h} \in \boldsymbol{a}_u$ (with $h = 1, \ldots, N_u$) is associated with a respective timestamp $ts_{u,h}$, an explicative set of tags $\boldsymbol{t}_{u,h} \subseteq T$ and a vote score $s_{u,h}$. $ts_{u,h}$ indicates when $a_{u,h}$ was posted. For any two answers $a_{u,h_i}, a_{u,h_j} \in \boldsymbol{a}_u$, $h_i < h_j$ iff $ts_{u,h_i} < ts_{u,h_j}$. Timestamps are useful for reasonably dealing with the drift of the interests and skills of u, across the respective answering history $\boldsymbol{a}_u$, by means of gradual forgetting [8]. The latter consists in estimating the expertise of u from the whole answering history $\boldsymbol{a}_u$, so that the earlier answers are realistically considered to be outdated and, thus, less informative of her current interests and skills. The tags in $\boldsymbol{t}_{u,h}$ are an insightful description of the actual themes covered by $a_{u,h}$[1]. In principle, $\boldsymbol{t}_{u,h}$ is a more accurate representation of the both the intended meaning of $a_{u,h}$ and the topical expertise of u, in comparison with the more general topics inferrable from the textual content of $a_{u,h}$ [19]. For this reason, the wording of $a_{u,h}$ is disregarded and, consequently, the computational burden of processing very large amounts of raw text is avoided. $s_{u,h}$ indicates the acknowledged degree of expertise gained by u with regard to the question answered through $a_{u,h}$ and, by extension, under each tag within $\boldsymbol{t}_{u,h}$.

At the current timestamp now, the expertise of all users in U under the tags of T is summarized by matrix $E^{(now)}$. Its generic entry $E_{ut}^{(now)}$ quantifies the expertise of user u under tag t at time now as the below weighted average

$$E_{ut}^{(now)} = \frac{\sum_{a_{u,h} \in \boldsymbol{a}_u} s_{u,h} \cdot \delta_{t,t_{u,h}} \cdot w_{u,h}^{(now)}}{\sum_{a_{u,h} \in \boldsymbol{a}_u} \delta_{t,t_{u,h}} \cdot w_{u,h}^{(now)}} \tag{1}$$

In Eq. 1, $\delta_{t,t_{u,h}}$ is 1 iff $t \in \boldsymbol{t}_{u,h}$ for some h (with $h = 1, \ldots, N_u$), and 0 otherwise. If $\delta_{t,t_{u,h}} = 0$ for each $h = 1, \ldots, N_u$, $E_{ut}^{(now)}$ is assumed to be 0, which corresponds to an unknown or missing value. Besides, $w_{u,h}^{(now)} = e^{-\lambda(now - ts_{u,h})}$ is a weighting scheme, that implements gradual forgetting by exponential ageing. Intuitively, the earlier answers are not ignored in the estimation of the current expertise of u under t. Rather, their contribution to $E_{ut}^{(now)}$ exponentially decays

---

[1] Answers retain the tags attached to the respective questions.

according to the respective timestamps. Remarkably, such a modeling choice does not penalizes the expertise of those users with a short replying history (such as new users or mostly inactive users with a recent answering history), without discarding the old answers of long-term answerers. Notice that $w_{u,h}^{(now)}$ is parameterized by the decay rate λ. The latter determines how rapidly the contribution of answers to user expertise decays over time. Essentially, larger values of λ imply a faster decay of earlier answers.

As a supplement to the information from the answering history of users, their asking-answering interactions are also captured as edges of G. More precisely, an edge $u_i \rightarrow u_j$ from a responder u_i to an asker u_j belongs to A, if u_i answered at least one question posted by u_j. By an abuse of notation, we also write G to denote the adjacency matrix associated with the asking-answering graph. The generic entry G_{ij} is 1 iff $u_i \rightarrow u_j \in A$ and 0 otherwise.

2.1 Problem Statement

Given a question q, let t_q be the set of tags attached to q by the asker. Also, assume that *now* is the time, when q is routed to the answerers. We aim to recommend q to targeted users, with the highest acknowledged expertise in the tags of t_q at time *now*, who are most likely to reply with high-quality answers.

Unfortunately, in the context of the generic QA community D, $E^{(now)}$ and G are generally very sparse. Consequently, the expertise of users under specific tags within t_q may not be known. In this paper, we exploit latent-factor modeling to predict the unknown values of $E^{(now)}$, that correspond to the current expertise of answerers under the various adopted tags. Thus, experts can be simply recommended from a list of answerers, ranked by their average expertise under the tags attached to q.

Hereinafter, to avoid cluttering notation, we will write E to mean $E^{(now)}$.

3 The ENGAGE Model

ENGAGE (*timE-evolviNG tAG-based Expertise*) is a Bayesian generative latent-factor model of temporally-discounted expertise and asking-answering behavior in QA communities. Under ENGAGE, the matrices E and G of a QA community D are the result of a probabilistic generative process, that is ruled by K latent factors. These are captured by embedding users and tags in a K-dimensional latent space, through the seamless integration of Bayesian probabilistic matrix factorization [15] and the statistical modeling of the asking-answering behavior.

Formally, each user $u \in U$ is associated with a column vector $L_u \in \mathbb{R}^K$ The k-th entry of L_u (with $k = 1, \ldots, K$) is a random variable representing the unknown degree to which the k-th latent factor explains the expertise of u. Analogously, each tag $t \in T$ is associated with a column vector $H_t \in \mathbb{R}^K$. The k-th entry of H_t (with $k = 1, \ldots, K$) is a random variable representing the unknown extent to which the k-th latent factor is inherently characteristic of t. The latent-factor representation of all users and tags is collectively denoted as $L \in \mathbb{R}^{K \times N}$ and $H \in \mathbb{R}^{K \times M}$, respectively. The data likelihood (i.e., the conditional distribution over the entries of E and G) is

$$\Pr(E|L, H, \alpha) = \prod_{u \in U} \prod_{t \in T} \mathcal{N}(E_{ut}; \mu_{u,t}, \alpha^{-1})^{\delta_{ut}} \tag{2}$$

$$\Pr(G|L, \beta) = \prod_{u_i \rightarrow u_j \in A} \mathcal{N}(G_{ij}; \mu_{u_i, u_j}, \beta^{-1}) \tag{3}$$

with

$$\mu_{u,t} = L_u^T \cdot H_t \text{ and } \mu_{u_i, u_j} = L_{u_i}^T L_{u_j}$$

In the above Eq. 2 and Eq. 3, $\mathcal{N}(\cdot|\mu, \alpha^{-1})$ is the Gaussian distribution having mean μ and precision α. In particular, according to Eq. 2, the current expertise of answerers under the adopted tags is centered around the intuitive explanation provided by the dot product of the respective latent-factor representations. δ_{ut} is 1 iff $E_{ut} > 0$ (i.e., if the expertise of u under t is actually acknowledged) and 0 otherwise. Equation 3 seamlessly incorporates the supplementary information regarding the asking-answering interactions of users. Specifically, according to Eq. 3, the asking-answering interactions are centered around the degree of agreement between the involved users. This provides a valuable contribution to the identification of experts, since those users, who answer questions from other users with a high expertise, are also likely to have gained a high expertise.

The latent-factor representations of users and tags stem from multivariate Gaussian prior distributions parameterized, respectively, by $\Theta_L = \{\mu_L, \Lambda_L\}$ and $\Theta_H = \{\mu_H, \Lambda_H\}$. In turn, such parameters are drawn from the below Gaussian-Wishart prior distributions (hereinafter indicated as $\mathcal{NW}$) [2]

$$\Pr(\Theta_X | \Theta_0) = \mathcal{N}\left(\mu_X; \mu_0, [\beta_0 \Lambda_X]^{-1}\right) \cdot \mathcal{W}(\Lambda_X; \nu_0, \mathbf{W}_0)$$

where $X \in \{L, H\}$, $\mathcal{W}(\Lambda_X; \nu_0, \mathbf{W}_0)$ denotes the Wishart distribution [2] and $\Theta_0 = \{\mu_0, \beta_0, \nu_0, \mathbf{W}_0\}$ is a set of hyperparameters.

The conditional (in)dependencies among the random variables under ENGAGE are shown by means of plate notation in Fig. 1a. Notice that unshaded nodes correspond to latent factors, whereas shaded nodes correspond to observed magnitudes. The generative process modeled by ENGAGE performs the realization of the observed random variables (i.e., the individual entries of E and G) according to the conditional (in)dependencies of Fig. 1a as detailed in Fig. 1b.

4   Model Inference

Under ENGAGE, the experts for a given question q are found by ranking users based on a recommendation score, that involves the latent-factor representations of users and tags. The recommendation score is introduced in Sect. 4.1. The inference of the latent-factor representations is discussed in Sect. 4.2.

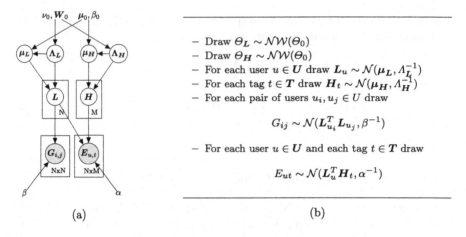

$$- \text{Draw } \Theta_L \sim \mathcal{NW}(\Theta_0)$$
$$- \text{Draw } \Theta_H \sim \mathcal{NW}(\Theta_0)$$
$$- \text{For each user } u \in U \text{ draw } \boldsymbol{L_u} \sim \mathcal{N}(\boldsymbol{\mu_L}, \Lambda_L^{-1})$$
$$- \text{For each tag } t \in T \text{ draw } \boldsymbol{H_t} \sim \mathcal{N}(\boldsymbol{\mu_H}, \Lambda_H^{-1})$$
$$- \text{For each pair of users } u_i, u_j \in U \text{ draw}$$

$$G_{ij} \sim \mathcal{N}(\boldsymbol{L}_{u_i}^T \boldsymbol{L}_{u_j}, \beta^{-1})$$

$$- \text{For each user } u \in U \text{ and each tag } t \in T \text{ draw}$$

$$E_{ut} \sim \mathcal{N}(\boldsymbol{L}_u^T \boldsymbol{H}_t, \alpha^{-1})$$

(a)   (b)

Fig. 1. Graphical representation of ENGAGE (a) and its generative process (b).

4.1 Answerer Ranking for Recommendation

The rank of an answerer $u \in U$ in the list of experts for q is determined by the score P_{uq} of her acknowledged/predicted expertise. P_{uq} is computed by averaging the current expertise of u under the individual tags of $\boldsymbol{t}_q$. This requires to distinguish between two alternative cases. Let t be an adopted tag of $\boldsymbol{t}_q$. If the expertise of u under t is acknowledged, E_{ut} can be directly used in the definition of P_{uq}. Otherwise, if the expertise of u under t is an unknown entry of $\boldsymbol{E}$, then E_{ut} is suitably predicted by resorting to the latent-factor representations of u and t under ENGAGE. Accordingly, $P_{uq} = \frac{1}{|t_q|} \sum_{t \in t_q} \hat{E}_{ut}$, where $\hat{E}_{ut}$ is defined in the below Eq. 4, so that to incorporate the current expertise of u under t according to the two above cases.

$$\hat{E}_{ut} = \begin{cases} E_{ut} & \text{if } E_{ut} > 0 \\ \frac{1}{S} \sum_{s=1}^{S} \left(\boldsymbol{L}_u^{(s)} \right)^T \cdot \boldsymbol{H}_t^{(s)} & \text{if } E_{ut} = 0 \end{cases} \tag{4}$$

In Eq. 4, S is the number of samples of both $\boldsymbol{L}_u$ and $\boldsymbol{H}_t$, which are respectively referred to as $\boldsymbol{L}_u^{(s)}$ and $\boldsymbol{H}_t^{(s)}$ (with $s = 1, \ldots, S$). Assume that $\Theta = \{L, H\} \cup \Theta_L \cup \Theta_H$. In principle, all samples $\boldsymbol{L}_u^{(s)}$ and $\boldsymbol{H}_t^{(s)}$ are to be drawn from the posterior distribution $\Pr(\Theta | \boldsymbol{E}, \boldsymbol{G}, \alpha, \beta, \Theta_0)$. However, the latter is analytically intractable. Therefore, the generic $\boldsymbol{L}_u^{(s)}$ and $\boldsymbol{H}_t^{(s)}$ are drawn through approximate posterior inference, as described in Sect. 4.2.

4.2 Approximate Posterior Inference

A well-known technique for approximate stochastic inference [14] is Gibbs sampling. The latter defines a (first-order) Markov chain, whose stationary distribution eventually approaches the true posterior distribution $\Pr(\Theta | \boldsymbol{E}, \boldsymbol{G}, \alpha, \beta, \Theta_0)$.

This is accomplished by means of reiterated transitions from the current sample of the model parameters $\boldsymbol{\Theta}$ to a new one. More precisely, at the generic transition, each parameter $\theta \in \boldsymbol{\Theta}$ is sequentially sampled from the respective full conditional $\Pr(\theta|\boldsymbol{\Theta} - \theta, \boldsymbol{E}, \boldsymbol{G}, \alpha, \beta, \boldsymbol{\Theta}_0)$. This is the conditional distribution over θ, given all other parameters $\boldsymbol{\Theta} - \theta$, the (hyper)parameters $\boldsymbol{\Theta}_0$ as well as the observations $\boldsymbol{E}$ and $\boldsymbol{G}$.

The derived full conditional distributions over the individual parameters of ENGAGE are reported next, along with the algorithm designed to perform Gibbs sampling inference.

Parameters $\boldsymbol{L}_u$ and $\boldsymbol{H}_t$. Due to the conjugacy between the multivariate Gaussian distribution on $\boldsymbol{L}_u$ (with unknown parameters $\boldsymbol{\Theta}_L$) and the Gaussian-Wishart prior on $\boldsymbol{\Theta}_L$, the full conditional on $\boldsymbol{L}_u$ is a multivariate Guassian distribution, i.e.,

$$\boldsymbol{L}_u \sim \mathcal{N}\left(\boldsymbol{\mu}_L^{*(u)}, \left[\Lambda_L^{*(u)}\right]^{-1}\right) \tag{5}$$

where

$$\Lambda_L^{*(u)} = \Lambda_L + \alpha \sum_{t \in T} \delta_{ut} \boldsymbol{H}_t \boldsymbol{H}_t^T + \beta \sum_{u \in U} \boldsymbol{L}_u \boldsymbol{L}_u^T$$

$$\boldsymbol{\mu}_L^{*(u)} = \left[\Lambda_L^{*(u)}\right]^{-1} \left[\alpha \sum_{t \in T} \delta_{ut} \boldsymbol{H}_t \boldsymbol{E}_{ut} + \beta \sum_{v \in U} \boldsymbol{L}_v \boldsymbol{G}_{uv} + \Lambda_L \boldsymbol{\mu}_L\right]$$

Likewise, because of the conjugacy between the multivariate Gaussian distribution on $\boldsymbol{H}_t$ (with unknown parameters $\boldsymbol{\Theta}_H$) and the Gaussian-Wishart prior on $\boldsymbol{\Theta}_H$, the full conditional on $\boldsymbol{H}_t$ is a multivariate Guassian distribution, i.e.,

$$\boldsymbol{H}_t \sim \mathcal{N}\left(\boldsymbol{\mu}_H^{*(t)}, \left[\Lambda_H^{*(t)}\right]^{-1}\right) \tag{6}$$

with

$$\Lambda_H^{*(t)} = \Lambda_H + \alpha \sum_{u \in U} \delta_{ut} \boldsymbol{L}_u \boldsymbol{L}_u^T$$

$$\boldsymbol{\mu}_H^{*(t)} = \left[\Lambda_H^{*(t)}\right]^{-1} \left[\alpha \sum_{u \in N} \boldsymbol{L}_u \delta_{ut} \boldsymbol{E}_{ut} + \Lambda_H \boldsymbol{\mu}_H\right]$$

Parameters $\boldsymbol{\Theta}_L$ and $\boldsymbol{\Theta}_H$. For each $\boldsymbol{X} \in \{\boldsymbol{L}, \boldsymbol{H}\}$, the conditional distribution over $\boldsymbol{\Theta}_X = \{\boldsymbol{\mu}_X, \Lambda_X\}$ is the below Gaussian-Wishart distribution [6, pp. 178]

$$\Pr(\boldsymbol{\mu}_X, \Lambda_X | \boldsymbol{X}, \boldsymbol{\Theta}_0) = \mathcal{N}(\boldsymbol{\mu}_X | \boldsymbol{\mu}_X^*, [(\beta_0 + c)\Lambda_X]^{-1})$$
$$\cdot \mathcal{W}(\Lambda_X | \nu_0 + c, \boldsymbol{W}_X^*) \tag{7}$$

where c is the number of columns within matrix $\boldsymbol{X}$ and

$$\boldsymbol{\mu}_X^* = \frac{\beta_0 \boldsymbol{\mu}_0 + c\overline{\boldsymbol{X}}}{\beta_0 + c}; \quad \boldsymbol{S}_X = \frac{1}{c} \sum_{i=1}^{c} (\boldsymbol{X}_i - \overline{\boldsymbol{X}})(\boldsymbol{X}_i - \overline{\boldsymbol{X}})^T; \quad \overline{\boldsymbol{X}} = \frac{1}{c} \sum_{i=1}^{c} \boldsymbol{X}_i$$

$$[\boldsymbol{W}_X^*]^{-1} = \boldsymbol{W}_0 c^{-1} + c\boldsymbol{S}_X + \frac{\beta_0 c}{\beta_0 + c}(\boldsymbol{\mu}_0 - \overline{\boldsymbol{X}})(\boldsymbol{\mu}_0 - \overline{\boldsymbol{X}})^T$$

Algorithm 1: Pseudo code of the Gibbs sampling algorithm

    Input: α, β, $\Theta_0 = \{\mu_0, \beta_0, \nu_0, W_0\}$ and H;

    Output: samples $L_u^{(s)}$, $H_t^{(s)}$ with $s = 1, \ldots, S$;

1 Initialize $L^{(0)}$ and $H^{(0)}$;

2 **for** $h = 1, \ldots, H$ **do**

3   Draw $\Theta_L^{(h)} \sim \Pr(\Theta_L^{(h)} | L, \Theta_0)$ through Eq. 7;

4   Draw $\Theta_H^{(h)} \sim \Pr(\Theta_H^{(h)} | H, \Theta_0)$ through Eq. 7;

5   **for** *each* $u \in U$ **do**

6   Draw $L_u^{(h)} \sim \mathcal{N}\left(\mu_P^{*(u)}, \left[\Lambda_P^{*(u)}\right]^{-1}\right)$ through Eq. 5;

7   **end**

8   **for** *each* $t \in T$ **do**

9   Draw $H_t^{(h)} \sim \mathcal{N}\left(\mu_H^{*(t)}, \left[\Lambda_H^{*(t)}\right]^{-1}\right)$ through Eq. 6;

10   **end**

11 **end**

Gibbs Sampling. Algorithm 1 sketches the pseudo code of the sampler, designed to implement approximate posterior inference under ENGAGE. After a preliminary initialization (line 1), the sampler enters a loop (lines 2–11), whose generic iteration h embraces two steps. $\Theta_L^{(h)}$ and $\Theta_H^{(h)}$ are drawn at the first step (lines 3–4), being functional to draw $L_u^{(h)}$ and $H_t^{(h)}$ at the second step (lines 5–10).

The maximum number H of iterations is established, by following the widely-adopted convergence-criterion in [12]. This allows the Markov chain behind the Gibbs sampler to reach its equilibrium after an initial burn-in period. As a consequence, the S samples used in Eq. 4, can be drawn when convergence is met (i.e., after the burn-in period, in which samples are instead still sensible to the preliminary initialization).

5   Experimental Evaluation

We comparatively investigated the recommendation effectiveness of ENGAGE.

5.1   Data Set

All experiments were conducted on *Stack Overflow*[2] [1,16], i.e., a real-world QA community for sharing knowledge on computer programming. More precisely, we formed our training and test sets from an anonymized and quarterly dump[3] of all *Stack Overflow* data, produced by its users within a time interval ranging from Jan 1, 2015 to July 31, 2015. Such a dump is publicly released by the *Stack Exchange* network under the *Creative Commons BY-SA 4.0* licence. More precisely, as far as the training set is concerned, we retained all those tags that were adopted at least 50 times in the time interval from Jan 1, 2015 to June 31, 2015. Further, we considered all those users, who provided more than 80

---

[2] https://stackoverflow.com/.

[3] https://archive.org/download/stackexchange.

posts [20] in the same period. The selected tags and users, along with their answers, the respective questions, timestamps and votes were included into the training set. Overall, the latter consists of $3,376$ users, $40,382$ questions, $60,968$ answers. Regarding the test set, we focused on a collection Q of questions (with $|Q| = 1,357$), that were posted by the users in the training set in a later time interval from July 1, 2015 to July 31, 2015. These questions are labelled with tags and answered by answerers in the training set. We chose such users, their answers to the questions of Q, the respective timestamps and votes as the test set. As a whole, the latter consists of $1,357$ questions, $3,376$ users, $3,771$ answers.

5.2 Competitors

We contrasted ENGAGE against a selection of various competitors.

Votes [17] ranks answerers based on the mean of the difference between the positive and negative votes of their answers as well as the average percentage of the positive votes.

InDegree [3] ranks answerers by their respective numbers of best answers.

The state-of-the art model in [19], hereinafter called TER (*Tag-based Expert Recommendation*), infers user expertise from the factorization of the user-tag matrix. The latter is built, so that the generic entry reflects the expertise of an answerer under a tag, as captured by averaging the votes of her answers marked by that tag. Unlike ENGAGE, TER ignores both the drift of users' interests over time and their asking-answering behavior.

TEM [20] is a state-of-the art joint model of topics and expertise. Essentially, under TEM, tags are incorporated into the textual content of posts, in order to infer the topical interests of users. The specific expertise of users under the different topics is explicitly captured.

CQARank [20] combines the user topical interests and expertise under TEM with the link analysis of the asking-answering interaction graph, in order to enhance the inference of user topical expertise.

Both TEM and CQARank disregard the drift of users' interests over time.

5.3 Recommendation Effectiveness

We comparatively assessed the recommendation performance of ENGAGE through several evaluation metrics. Let $q \in Q$ be a generic question of the test set. Assume that $\overline{R}^{(q)}$ and $R^{(q)}$ are, respectively, the ground-truth and the recommended list of experts for q. Essentially, $\overline{R}^{(q)}$ is the list of users, who actually answered q, ranked by the known scores of their answers. Instead, the users in $R^{(q)}$ are ranked by the recommendation score of Sect. 4.1. $R^{(q)} = |R^{(q)}|$ is the size of $R^{(q)}$. $R_i^{(q)}$ denotes the user at position i of $R^{(q)}$. $R_{best}^{(q)}$ indicates the rank of the best answerer. The adopted evaluation metrics are enumerated next.

- *Precision at top $R^{(q)}$* (*Precision$^{(q)}$@$R^{(q)}$*) [9] is the correctness of $R^{(q)}$, i.e., the fraction of top-$R^{(q)}$ recommended experts, who are ground-truth answerers. More precisely,

$$Precision^{(q)}@R^{(q)} = \frac{|\boldsymbol{R}^{(q)} \cap \overline{\boldsymbol{R}}^{(q)}|}{R^{(q)}}$$

- *Recall at top $R^{(q)}$ ($Recall^{(q)}@R^{(q)}$) [9] is the coverage of $\boldsymbol{R}^{(q)}$, i.e., the fraction of ground-truth answerers in the top-$R^{(q)}$ recommended experts. Specifically,*

$$Recall^{(q)}@R^{(q)} = \frac{|\boldsymbol{R}^{(q)} \cap \overline{\boldsymbol{R}}^{(q)}|}{|\overline{\boldsymbol{R}}^{(q)}|}$$

- *nDCG [10] (normalized Discounted Cumulative Gain) measures the goodness of the ranking of the recommended experts, based on their position in $\boldsymbol{R}^{(q)}$. This is accomplished by accumulating expert relevance to question q along $\boldsymbol{R}^{(q)}$, so that the relevance of higher-ranked experts is suitably discounted. Formally, $nDCG(q) = \frac{DCG(q)}{IDCG(q)}$, where*

$$DCG(q) = s_1^{(q)} + \sum_{i=2}^{R^{(q)}} \frac{s_i^{(q)}}{log_2 i}$$

In the above equation, $s_i^{(q)}$ represents the relevance of $R_i^{(q)}$ to q (according to thumbs-up/down). $IDCG(q)$ is the $DCG(q)$ value of the ideal ranking.

- *Accuracy ($Acc^{(q)}$) [22] measures the quality of the best-answer's rank, i.e.,*

$$Acc^{(q)} = \frac{R^{(q)} - R_{best}^{(q)}}{R^{(q)} - 1}$$

Larger values of the above measures denote a higher recommendation effectiveness. Table 1 summarizes the average values of such measures over the whole set $\boldsymbol{Q}$ of questions for all competitors. The reported results were found by adopting the following empirical settings. In all tests, the time decay factor λ was fixed to 0.2. The number K of latent factors was set to 15. The number S of samples used in Eq. 4 was set to 200. The overall number H of iterations for Algorithm 1 was fixed to 1,000, in compliance with the convergence-criterion in [12]. Additionally, for each $q \in \boldsymbol{Q}$, the number $R^{(q)}$ of recommended answerers for q was set to 10.

By looking at Table 1, it is evident that ENGAGE overcomes all tested competitors. In particular, the lower effectiveness of Votes and InDegree is due to the fact that both focus only on the importance of users, without accounting for their specific discounted expertise. TER is a state-of-the art competitor, that captures the tag-based expertise of answerers. Nonetheless, TER is still less effective than ENGAGE for two main reasons. Firstly, TER does not account for the drift of users' interests over time. Secondly, TER does not exploit any auxiliary information from the communication network, that is shaped by the asking-answering behavior. The latter is instead conveniently used, under ENGAGE, in order to more accurately inform the latent factor representation of users and tags. TEM and CQARank are two state-of-the-art competitors, that use tags to capture topical expertise. However, their effectiveness is penalized with respect to ENGAGE,

Table 1. Recommendation effectiveness of the compared approaches

Competitor	Precision@10	Recall@10	nDCG	Accuracy
Votes	0.2658	0.3880	0.7849	0.5618
InDegree	0.3379	0.4656	0.8235	0.5788
TER	0.3639	0.4803	0.8157	0.6161
TEM	0.3567	0.5066	0.8291	0.6548
CQARank	0.3896	0.5153	0.8348	0.6803
ENGAGE	0.4113	0.5379	0.8561	0.6952

since tags are mixed up with the textual content of posts, rather then being used as user-generated explanations of their topical expertise. Moreover, neither TEM nor CQARank discount the expertise of users, in order to account for the drift of their interests over time.

6 Conclusions and Further Research

We proposed a new latent-factor approach to expert recommendation in QA communities. The idea is to infer the time-evolving expertise of users from the tags of the answered questions, the votes and posting time of the respective answers as well as the asking-answering behavior of the CQA users. A thorough experimentation on real-world CQA data showed the overcoming recommendation effectiveness of our approach with respect to several state-of-the-art competitors.

It is interesting to explore the impact of alternative implementations of gradual forgetting on recommendation effectiveness. In this regard, temporal hyperbolic discounting [21] is a viable choice. Finally, three further lines of innovative research involve studying the incorporation of, respectively, user roles [5,7,13,18], exposure [11] to posted questions as well as the recent generative models of text corpora (such as, e.g., [4]) for more effective expert recommendation.

References

1. Anderson, A., et al.: Discovering value from community activity on focused question answering sites: a case study of stack overow. In: Proceedings of ACM SIGKDD International Conference on Knowledge Discovery and Data Mining, pp. 850–858 (2012)
2. Bishop, C.M.: Pattern Recognition and Machine Learning. Springer, New York (2006)
3. Bouguessa, M., Dumoulin, B., Wang, S.: Identifying authoritative actors in question-answering forums: the case of Yahoo! answers. In: Proceedings of ACM SIGKDD International Conference on Knowledge Discovery and Data Mining, pp. 866–874 (2008)

4. Costa, G., Ortale, R.: Document clustering meets topic modeling with word embeddings. In: Proceedings of SIAM International Conference on Data Mining (2020)
5. Costa, G., Ortale, R.: Mining overlapping communities and inner role assignments through Bayesian mixed-membership models of networks with context-dependent interactions. ACM Trans. Knowl. Disc. Data **12**(2), 18:1–18:32 (2018)
6. DeGroot, M.: Optimal Statistical Decisions. McGraw-Hill, New York (1970)
7. Fu, C.: Tracking user-role evolution via topic modeling in community question answering. Inf. Process. Manage. **56**(6), 102075 (2019)
8. Gama, J., et al.: A survey on concept drift adaptation. ACM Comput. Surv. **46**(4), 44:1–44:37 (2014)
9. Herlocker, J.L., et al.: Evaluating collaborative filtering recommender systems. ACM Trans. Inf. Syst. **22**(1), 5–53 (2004)
10. Järvelin, K., Kekäläinen, J.: Cumulated gain-based evaluation of IR techniques. ACM Trans. Inf. Syst. **20**(4), 422–446 (2002)
11. Liang, D., et al.: Modeling user exposure in recommendation. In: Proceedings of International Conference on World Wide Web, pp. 951–961 (2016)
12. Liu, J.S.: Monte Carlo Strategies in Scientific Computing. Springer, New York (2001). https://doi.org/10.1007/978-0-387-76371-2
13. Ma, Z., et al.: A tri-role topic model for domain-specific question answering. In: Proceedings of AAAI Conference on Artificial Intelligence, pp. 224–230 (2015)
14. Robert, C., Casella, G.: Monte Carlo Statistical Methods. Springer, New York (2004). https://doi.org/10.1007/978-1-4757-4145-2
15. Salakhutdinov, R., Mnih, A.: Bayesian probabilistic matrix factorization using Markov chain Monte Carlo. In: Proceedings of International Conference on Machine Learning, pp. 880–887 (2008)
16. Srba, I., Bielikova, M.: A comprehensive survey and classification of approaches for community question answering. ACM Trans. Web **10**(3), 18:1–18:63 (2016)
17. Wang, X., Huang, C., Yao, L., Benatallah, B., Dong, M.: A survey on expert recommendation in community question answering. J. Comput. Sci. Technol. **33**(4), 625–653 (2018). https://doi.org/10.1007/s11390-018-1845-0
18. Xu, F., Ji, Z., Wang, B.: Dual role model for question recommendation in community question answering. In: Proceedings of International ACM SIGIR Conference on Research and Development in Information Retrieval, pp. 771–780 (2012)
19. Yang, B., Manandhar, S.: Tag-based expert recommendation in community question answering. In: Proceedings of IEEE/ACM International Conference on Advances in Social Networks Analysis and Mining, pp. 960–963 (2014)
20. Yang, L. et al.: CQArank: jointly model topics and expertise in community question answering. In: Proceedings of ACM International Conference on Information and Knowledge Management, pp. 99–108 (2013)
21. Yeniterzi, R., Callan, J.: Moving from static to dynamic modeling of expertise for question routing in CQA sites. In: Proceedings of International AAAI Conference on Web and Social Media, pp. 702–705 (2015)
22. Zhao, Z., et al.: Expert finding for community-based question answering via ranking metric network learning. In: Proceedings of the International Joint Conference on Artificial Intelligence, pp. 3000–3006 (2016)

Relation Embedding for Personalised Translation-Based POI Recommendation

Xianjing Wang[1,2], Flora D. Salim[1(✉)] ⓘ, Yongli Ren[1] ⓘ, and Piotr Koniusz[2,3]

[1] RMIT University, Melbourne, Australia
{xianjing.wang,flora.salim,yongli.ren}@rmit.edu.au
[2] Data61/CSIRO, Canberra, Australia
piotr.koniusz@data61.csiro.au
[3] Australian National University, Canberra, Australia

Abstract. Point-of-Interest (POI) recommendation is one of the most important location-based services helping people discover interesting venues or services. However, the extreme user-POI matrix sparsity and the varying spatio-temporal context pose challenges for POI systems, which affects the quality of POI recommendations. To this end, we propose a translation-based relation embedding for POI recommendation. Our approach encodes the temporal and geographic information, as well as semantic contents effectively in a low-dimensional relation space by using Knowledge Graph Embedding techniques. To further alleviate the issue of user-POI matrix sparsity, a combined matrix factorization framework is built on a user-POI graph to enhance the inference of dynamic personal interests by exploiting the side-information. Experiments on two real-world datasets demonstrate the effectiveness of our proposed model.

Keywords: Knowledge Graph Embedding · Collaborative filtering · Matrix factorization · Recommender System · POI recommendation

1 Introduction

With the increase of mobile devices on the market and ubiquitous presence of wireless communication networks, people gain easy access to Point-of-Interest (POI) recommendation services. A great number of Location-based Social Networks (LBSNs) have consequently been established *e.g.*, Foursquare, Gowalla, Facebook Places, and Brightkite. The LBSNs often provide POI services that recommend users new POI venues that meet specific user criteria. In this paper, we develop a high quality personalized POI recommendation system by leveraging user check-in data. There are three technical challenges listed as follows:

Sparsity of User Check-in Data. One of the major challenges is to overcome the sparsity in the user check-in data. The user-POI matrix can be extremely sparse despite of millions of POIs and users in LBSNs.

Temporal Reasoning. Location-based POI recommendation systems utilize the temporal context [24] for the purpose of modeling personal preferences. The temporal information reflects users' needs and choices throughout the day.

© Springer Nature Switzerland AG 2020
H. W. Lauw et al. (Eds.): PAKDD 2020, LNAI 12084, pp. 53–64, 2020.
https://doi.org/10.1007/978-3-030-47426-3_5

Spatial Reasoning. A user's current geographical location limits their choice of check-in POIs [13]. Many approaches model relations between a user's current geographical location and their preferences with respect to the surrounding POIs.

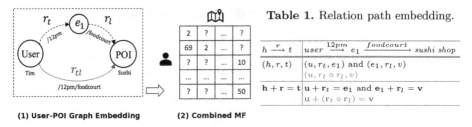

Table 1. Relation path embedding.

	$h \xrightarrow{r} t$	$user \xrightarrow{12pm} e_1 \xrightarrow{foodcourt} sushi\ shop$
(h, r, t)	(u, r_t, e_1) and (e_1, r_l, v)	$(u, r_l \circ r_l, v)$
$h + r = t$	$u + r_t = e_1$ and $e_1 + r_l = v$	$u + (r_l \circ r_l) = v$

(1) User-POI Graph Embedding   **(2) Combined MF**

Fig. 1. Overview of our GERec model.

The above issues are often addressed by the use of side information in traditional recommendation systems. Such a side information may be retrieved from social networks [9] and may include user demographic information, item attributes, and context information [26]. As the auxiliary data is useful for the recommendation systems [19], it is desirable to model and utilize heterogeneous and complex data types in recommendation systems. However, the traditional collaborative filtering techniques such as Matrix Factorization (MF) cannot deal with the above problems in a unified manner. Knowledge Graph Embedding (KGE) [1,21], also known as a translation-based embedding model, encodes the side-information to improve the performance of Recommender Systems (RS) [16,27]. He *et al.* [6] and Zhang *et al.* [27] employ the KGE model to represent users, movies, and movie attributes. The graph edges represent connections between users and movies in a knowledge base [6,27]. However, previous studies do not offer insights on the following challenges: (1) how to construct a user-POI graph that utilizes the user check-in data with side information, such as spatio-temporal data and semantic context information, to leverage data sparsity problem; (2) how to effectively integrate a translation-based embedding model with a traditional recommendation system to improve the quality of POI recommendation.

Problem Definition. Given an LBSN user check-in dataset, we aim to recommend each user with personalized top-k POIs they may be interested in visiting.

We build upon recent advances in graph embedding methods and propose *Graph Embedding for POI Recommendation*, a novel translation-based graph embedding approach specifically for POI recommendation, abbreviated as *GERec*. To overcome the challenge stemming from the spatio-temporal context, GERec encodes temporal and spatial information, as well as user dynamic check-in activities in a low-dimensional latent space. GERec addresses the issues of user check-in data sparsity by integrating user-POI graph embedding with a combined matrix factorization framework (Fig. 1).

Contributions

I. To deal with the data sparsity, we propose a novel translation-based POI recommendation model to effectively form a user-POI graph capturing the side information, such as spatial, temporal, and semantic contents.

II. We propose a spatio-temporal relation path embedding to model the temporal, spatial and semantic content information to improve the quality of POI recommendations.

III. We show our model outperforms the state-of-the-art POI recommendation techniques on two real-world LBSN datasets, Foursquare [2] and Gowalla [3].

2   Related Work

POI Recommendations. Making personalized POI recommendations is challenging due to the user dynamic check-in activities. Existing studies on MF-based POI recommendations either focus on aggregating spatially-wise personal preference or exploring temporal influences. Most aggregation-based POI recommendation approaches fail to capture jointly geographical and temporal influences with the semantic context while addressing the data sparsity in an unified framework. In [22,25], geographical locations are used to improve the performance of POI system which highlights that there is a strong correlation between user check-in activities and geographical distance. Geographical sparse additive generative model [22] for POI recommendations, Geo-SAGE, exploited co-occurrence patterns with contents of spatial items. A POI system [25] based on deep learning from heterogeneous features and hierarchically additive representation learning proposed spatially-aware model for personal preferences.

Knowledge Graph Embedding. KGE is well known for its use in recommendation systems. Zhang *et al.* [27] proposed a collaborative KG-integrated movie recommender framework to learn the latent and visual representations. Palumbo *et al.* [16] proposed *entity2rec* to capture a user-item relatedness from KGEs with the goal of generating top-k item recommendations. Qian *et al.* [18] adopts KGE to model the side information in POI recommendation system. Their work only focuses on embedding the user and POI entities, and mapping the spatio-temporal patterns as a translation matrix. Although their work explored KGEs and RS, it did not integrate graph embedding with the traditional MF model. Compared with our proposed model that combines the spatial and temporal information with semantic contents in a semantic relation embedding space, these KG embedding-based recommender models have limited expressive abilities as they model the key parameters (*e.g.*, spatial and temporal information) as a simple matrix. Finally, noteworthy is the family of Graph Convolutional Networks with models such as GCN [7], GraphSAGE [5], adversary GCN [20], kernel-based CKN [14] as well as generic graph embedding approaches such as DeepWalk [17] and Node2Vec [4] which all have the capacity to model graph-related tasks.

Difference with Existing Works. 1) To the best of our knowledge, this is the first work that investigates the joint modeling of temporal, geographical and semantic category information integrated with KG embedding POI recommendation system; 2) A novel embedding is proposed to bridge the gaps between embedding and traditional MF. Therefore, we propose a novel combined MF framework for dynamic user-POI preference modeling based on the learned embedding in a unified manner; 3) In contrast to the approach [24] based on the bipartite graph (homogeneous graph), our approach uses the translation-based graph (heterogeneous graph). Moreover, approach [24] does not apply MF while our model investigates MF for generating top-k proposals.

3   Proposed Approach

3.1   User-POI Graph Embedding

A heterogeneous graph admits two or more node types which can be then embedded by a symmetric function *e.g.*, one can use interchange *user type* and *POI type* input arguments. For the best recommendation performance, we develop an effective representation for the *user* and *POI* nodes. A user u and a POI v represent the *head* or *tail* of a triplet (*head, relation, tail*), denoted as (u, r, v), where $u, e, v \in \mathbb{R}^k$ are the vector representations of u, r and v.

Head-tail entity pairs usually exhibit diverse patterns in terms of relations [12]. Thus, a single relation vector cannot perform all translations between head and tail entities. For example, the relation path embedding has the diversity patterns, such as temporal, spatial and semantic contents patterns. The relation between user (head) and POI (tail) "user - sushi shop" exhibits many patterns: (i) Temporal pattern *i.e.*, a user visits a POI in a certain time slot <user, /time slot, POI>; (ii) Geographical pattern *i.e.*, a user visits a POI when she is in a particular area <user, /location, POI>; and (iii) Semantic content pattern *i.e.*, a user visits a specific POI that is associated with a category <user, /category, POI>. In our model, we embed spatio-temporal information as a relationship connecting users and POIs.

Take the 2-step path as an example. In Table 1, a user check-in activity (a user visits a POI) is associated with temporal and geographical patterns *i.e.*, $user \xrightarrow{12pm} e_1 \xrightarrow{foodcourt} sushi\ shop$ denotes a user visiting a sushi shop (POI) at 12pm (time slot) at food court (location). Instead of building triplets (u, r_t, e_1) and (e_1, r_l, v) for learning the graph representation, we form a triplet $(u, r_t \circ r_l, v)$, and optimize the objective $u + (r_t \circ r_l) = v$. The composition operator $\circ$ merges the temporal and spatial relations r_t and r_l into the spatio-temporal relation. Given a relation path $r = (r_1, \ldots, r_n)$, we obtain the relation path embedding $\mathbf{r}$ by composing multiple relations via the operator $\circ$, *i.e.*, $\mathbf{r} = \mathbf{r}_1 \circ \cdots \circ \mathbf{r}_n$. For the composition operator, we use the multiplication operation. Thus, the relation path vector is defined as $\mathbf{r} = \mathbf{r}_1 \times \cdots \times \mathbf{r}_n$. In our model, we embed temporal and geographical patterns, and semantic category contents into the relation path. For instance, $u \xrightarrow{r_t} e_1 \xrightarrow{r_l} e_2 \xrightarrow{r_c} v$ illustrates that a user visits a POI at a certain time slot t in location l, which has semantic category information c associated with the user's current location. We define a spatio-temporal and semantic-based relation path representation $\mathbf{r}_{tlc} = \mathbf{r}_t \circ \mathbf{r}_l \circ \mathbf{r}_c$, which consists of a temporal relation path $\mathbf{r}_t$, a geographical relation path $\mathbf{r}_l$, and a semantic relation path $\mathbf{r}_c$. The relation $\mathbf{r}_{tlc}$ is used as our default relation representation in our POI model. In what follows, we write $\mathbf{r}$ instead of $\mathbf{r}_{tlc}$ for simplicity.

TransR [12,21] is among the most representative translational distance models for a heterogeneous graphs. We apply TransR [12] to our POI recommendation model. For each triplet, including (u, r_{tl}, v) and (u, r_{tlc}, v) in the graph, entities are embedded into vectors $\mathbf{u}, \mathbf{v} \in \mathbb{R}^k$ and relation is embedding into $\mathbf{r} \in \mathbb{R}^d$. For each relation r, we set a projection matrix from the entity space to the relation space, denoted as $\boldsymbol{M}_r \in \mathbb{R}^{k \times d}$. TransR firstly maps entities u and v into the subspace of relation r by using matrix $\boldsymbol{M}_r$:

$$\mathbf{u}_r = \mathbf{u}\boldsymbol{M}_r \quad \text{and} \quad \mathbf{v}_r = \mathbf{v}\boldsymbol{M}_r, \tag{1}$$

and the TransR score function is defined as:

$$f_r(u,v) = \parallel \mathbf{u}_r + \mathbf{r} - \mathbf{v}_r \parallel_2^2. \tag{2}$$

The following margin-based ranking loss defined in [12] is used for training:

$$L = \sum_{(u,r,v) \in S} \sum_{(u',r,v') \in S'} max(0, f_r(u,v) + \gamma - f_r(u',v')), \tag{3}$$

where γ controls the margin between positive and negative samples, S and S' are the set of positive and negative triplets, respectively. The existing graphs that we construct from user-POI check-in datasets contain mostly correct triplets. Thus, we corrupt the correct triplet $(u, r, v) \in S$ to construct incorrect triplets (u', r, v') by replacing either head or tail entities with other entities from the same group so that:

$$S' = \{(h',r,t)\} \cup \{(h,r,t')\}. \tag{4}$$

We note that translation-based embedding provides a generic way for extracting a useful information from a graph. However, embedding cannot be applied directly to matrix factorization models. Thus, we propose a function $g(\cdot)$ that extracts the learnt entities. Given an entity u, v and a relation r, we obtain representation sets $\{\mathbf{e}_u^r\}$ and $\{\mathbf{e}_v^r\}$, where r denotes the set of relation paths, where $\mathbf{e}_u^r$ and $\mathbf{e}_v^r$ represent a user u and a POI v with respect to the specific relation path r. Thus, the entity extraction is denoted as:

$$\{\boldsymbol{\phi}_u\} \leftarrow g(\{\mathbf{e}_u^r\}), \qquad \{\boldsymbol{\phi}_v\} \leftarrow g(\{\mathbf{e}_v^r\}), \tag{5}$$

where $\{\boldsymbol{\phi}_u\}$ and $\{\boldsymbol{\phi}_v\}$ are sets of final representations for user and POI embedding, respectively. The function $g(\cdot)$ prepares the embedded user and POI information to become the entries for the matrix factorization by sorting the learnt user and POI embedding sets based on the distances from Eq. (2) sorted according to the descending order. Embedded pairs that are further from each other than some θ are pruned. When a user connects with a POI by a relation $(\mathbf{u} + \mathbf{r} \approx \mathbf{v})$, the smaller the score value, the lower distance between POI and user is. Hence, $(\mathbf{v} + \mathbf{r} \approx \mathbf{u})$ vice versa. Then, the sorted user and POI embedding sets are filtered according to the user's current location. In many cases, POIs may be outside of the user's home location and it may be not reasonable to recommend such POIs. Thus, we set a reasonable radius w.r.t. the geographical location by applying a threshold θ_d to filter the learnt POIs that are too far away from user's home location. Following [10,23], we assume a Gaussian distribution for user current location l, and we set the user's current check-in POI v_l so that $v_l \sim \mathcal{N}(\mu_l, \Sigma_l)$.

3.2   The Combined Matrix Factorization

We integrate the matrix factorization into our model by combining two parts: *1) spatio-temporal MF* and *2) User preference MF*. The spatio-temporal MF calculates the probability that a user will visit a POI. The user preference MF evaluates user's preference w.r.t. a POI. The combined probability determines the total probability of a user u visiting a POI v.

Spatio-Temporal MF. For each embedded user vector $\boldsymbol{\phi}_u$ and embedded POI vector $\boldsymbol{\phi}_v$, we apply the matrix factorization to predict a probability that a user u would visit a POI v based on her current location l and a particular time slot t. Given a frequency matrix $\boldsymbol{P}' \in \mathbb{R}^{|\{\phi_u\}| \times |\{\phi_v\}|}$, which represents the number of check-ins of the embedded users for the embedded POIs. MF is performed by finding two low-rank matrices: a user specific matrix $\boldsymbol{E} \in \mathbb{R}^{K \times |\{\phi_u\}|}$ and a POI specific matrix $\boldsymbol{O} \in \mathbb{R}^{K \times |\{\phi_v\}|}$, where K is the dimension of the latent vector that captures the corresponding user-POI preference transition. The probability of an embedded user u based on a particular spatio-temporal relation r_{tl} and embedded location v, is determined by:

$$P'_{uv} = \boldsymbol{E}_u{}^\top \boldsymbol{O}_v, \tag{6}$$

where $\boldsymbol{E}_u$ and $\boldsymbol{O}_v$ are vectors for the user u and the POI v from matrices $\boldsymbol{E}$ and $\boldsymbol{O}$, respectively, while P'_{uv} is a scalar frequency for u and v.

The goal of matrix factorization is to accurately approximate the probabilities for the user frequency data:

$$\min_{E,O} \ \alpha(\| \boldsymbol{E} \|_F^2 + \| \boldsymbol{O} \|_F^2) + \sum_{(u,v) \in \Omega} (P'_{uv} - \boldsymbol{E}_u{}^\top \boldsymbol{O}_v)^2, \tag{7}$$

where $(u, v) \in \Omega$ indicates the observed frequency of user u at POI v, $\| \cdot \|_F^2$ is the Frobenius norm, and $\alpha(\| \boldsymbol{E} \|_F^2 + \| \boldsymbol{O} \|_F^2)$ is a regularization term to prevent overfitting.

User Preference MF. The second part of the combined MF model is to predict the user preference given a POI. Based on the user historical check-in frequency, given an observed frequency matrix $\boldsymbol{F}$, MF factorizes users and POIs so that

$F \approx U^\top V$. Then, scalar P''_{uv} captures users' preference at a POI determined by the following equation:

$$P''_{uv} = U_u^\top V_v \tag{8}$$

The same objective as in Eq. (7) is applied to accurately approximate the probabilities for the user check-in frequencies.

Combined Matrix Factorization. We propose a combined MF model that is simply a product of probabilities that 1) a user is spatio-temporally compatible with a POI and 2) the user has a preference given the POI. The first term is the probability of an embedded user visiting an embedded POI given some spatio-geographic pattern, where P'_{uv} is defined by Eq. (6). The second term is the probability of the user's preference at a POI based on her historical records, where P''_{uv} is defined in Eq. (8). The combined model is denoted as:

$$P_{uv} = P'_{uv} \cdot P''_{uv}. \tag{9}$$

4   Experiments

4.1   Experimental Configuration

Datasets. We adopt two popular large-scale LBSN datasets: Foursquare [2] and Gowalla [3]. The experimental results for our approach and the baselines are compared in the same testbed. We selected the Foursquare dataset from Sep 2010 to Jan 2011 which contains 1,434,668 users' check-in activities in the USA. The Foursquare geographical area is divided into a set of 5846 locations/regions according to administrative divisions. There are $114,508$ user entities and $62,462$ POI entities connected with $46,768$ spatio-temporal relations. For Gowalla, another graph is built from $107,092$ user entities and $1,280,969$ POI entities connected with $1,633$ relations. We apply k-means [18,26] to form 200 region clusters for Gowalla geographical area.

Baselines. Two of the baseline models are translation-based models that are highly related work in RS [6,18]. **PMF** [15] is a classic probabilistic matrix factorization model that explicitly factorizes the rating matrix into two low-rank matrices. **GeoMF** [9] is a weighted matrix factorization model for POI recommendations. **Rank-GeoFM** [8] is a ranking-based geographical factorization model in which the check-in frequency characterizes users' visiting preference, and the factorization is learnt by ranking POIs. **GeoSoCa** model [28] extends the kernel density estimation by applying an adaptive bandwidth learnt from the user check-in data. **ST-LDA** [26] is a latent class probabilistic generative Spatio-Temporal LDA (Latent Dirichlet Allocation) model, which learns the region-dependent personal interests according to the contents of the checked-in POIs at each region. **TransRec** is the translation-based recommendation approach proposed in [6], which embeds items into a translation space and models users via a translation vector. Note that our proposed method is different from TransRec as we select both users and POIs as entities, and learn the embedding

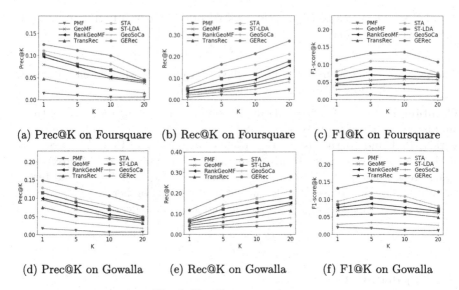

(a) Prec@K on Foursquare   (b) Rec@K on Foursquare   (c) F1@K on Foursquare

(d) Prec@K on Gowalla   (e) Rec@K on Gowalla   (f) F1@K on Gowalla

Fig. 2. Baseline comparisons.

representation for a different type of knowledge as well as the spatio-temporal relationships. **STA** [18] is a spatio-temporal context-aware and translation-based POI recommendation model. However, this solution does not consider the semantic relation embedding of spatial, temporal and category content information, and thus is incapable of leveraging the user-POI graph structure.

Evaluation Metrics. Following [8,9,28], we deploy the following evaluation methodology. The user-POI graph is built from historical user check-in activities in the training set. The spatio-temporal relations in the user-POI graph are composed based on each user's current time slot and the area from the given query $q = (u, l, t)$. We divide the time slot to different hour lengths $(1, 2, 4, 8, 12, 24)$. The user's current standing area before visiting v is selected for her location l. In the experiment, we first calculate the frequency for each user visiting ground-truth POIs. We use the 80% as the cut-off point so that check-ins before a particular date are used for training. The rest check-in data generated after this date is chosen for testing. We form a top-k recommendation list from the top k POI recommendations. We deploy measurement metrics such as Precision@k ($Prec@k$), Recall@k ($Rec@k$) and F1-score@k ($F@k$): $Prec@k = \frac{1}{M}\sum_{u=1}^{M} \frac{|V_u(k) \cap V_u|}{k}$ and $Rec@k = \frac{1}{M}\sum_{u=1}^{M} \frac{|V_u(k) \cap V_u|}{|V_u|}$.

4.2 Main Evaluations

Following [11,12], for translational distance model TransR, we set the learning rate $\lambda = 0.001$, the margin $\gamma = 1$, the dimensions of entity embedding and relation embedding $d = 100$, the batch size $B = 120$. We traverse all the training triplets for 1000 rounds on both Foursquare and Gowalla datasets.

Fig. 2 reports the performance of the POI recommendation models on Foursquare and Gowalla datasets, respectively. We present the performance for $k = \{1, 5, 10, 20\}$. Figure 2 presents the results of algorithms in terms of $Prec@k$, $Rec@k$ and $F1@k$ on Foursquare and Gowalla datasets. The figure show that the proposed GERec model outperforms all baseline models significantly for all metrics at different k values. Specifically, when comparing with the traditional MF models, GERec outperforms the Rank-GeoMF, which is the MF baseline with the best performance, by 50% and 47% in F1-score@10 on Foursquare and Gowalla, respectively. When comparing with translation-based models, our proposed model also improves the POI recommendation performance significantly. GERec outperforms STA, by 20% and 25% in F1-score@10 on both datasets. This demonstrates the capability of our graph-based GERec model to generate high quality POI recommendations. Although GeoSoCa exploits social influences, geographical locations and user interests, the simple kernel density estimation results in the poor performance. This validates the effectiveness of our GERec solution, especially our proposed step which exploits and integrates the user-POI interactions and spatio-temporal patterns to tackle the sparsity in the user-POI check-in data. The learned embeddings are well integrated into the combined matrix factorization model. Thus, GERec achieves the best performance among all compared baseline models. The user-POI graph constructed from Gowalla dataset has fewer relation edges than the Foursquare graph, as Gowalla relation patterns r_{tl} have fewer regions in the relation paths than Foursquare.

4.3 Impact of Data Sparsity

In Fig. 3, we conduct extensive experiments to evaluate the performance of the models under the data sparsity. Specifically, we create multiple datasets with various sparsity levels by reducing the amount of training data randomly by 10%, 20%, 30%, and 40% of the total amount of data (before the cut-off date), and at the same time keeping the test data the same. The results on both Foursquare and Gowalla are shown in the Fig. 3. Specifically, the 0 in the horizontal axis presents the experiment result without reducing the training data. We observe that the Precision@k and Recall@k value decrease for all baseline models. For example, the performance of these models in terms of Prec@10 decreases at least 40% on Foursquare when reducing 40% of the training data. Results of the ST-LDA drop significantly compared with the other baseline models with 37% drop in Rec@10 on both Foursquare and Gowalla, which indicates that the LDA-based model is sensitive to the sparse data. The PMF does not change much, however, it remains the least accurate result. The Rec@10 values of RankGeoMF, TransRec, and STA show a 42%, 41%, and 37% drop, respectively. The GERec drops by only 34%, which illustrates that our proposed model is more stable and robust under sparsity than the baselines.

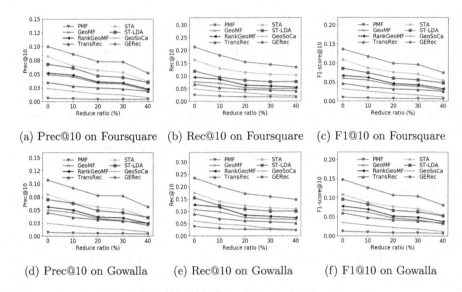

(a) Prec@10 on Foursquare   (b) Rec@10 on Foursquare   (c) F1@10 on Foursquare

(d) Prec@10 on Gowalla   (e) Rec@10 on Gowalla   (f) F1@10 on Gowalla

Fig. 3. Sensitivity to data sparsity.

4.4 Impact of Time Slot and Dimensionality

There are two parameters in the proposed GERec model: the time slot h and the embedding dimension d. Below, we investigate the effect of these two parameters. Table 2 shows the impact of the length of time slot on Precision@k and Recall@k. The length of the time slot affects the quality of POI recommendations. When the length of time slot changes, the relation paths change and the entire graph needs to be computed again. We split day activities into different lengths. The parameter h denotes the length of each time slot in hours. The larger length of time slot the less the time influence on recommendation results. We report the top-k recommendation precision and recall for each time slot on the Foursquare and Gowalla datasets. From the experimental results we observe that the POI recommendation accuracy improves when the time slot length increases. The recommendation accuracy reaches a peak point for 8 h long time slot. Then, it starts decreasing as the time slot keeps increasing. The reason for the improved accuracy is that the larger time length, the denser the data. Hence, there are more user check-in records at each time slot for generating recommendations. However, the recommendation accuracy decreases as the length of the time slot reaches 8 h. This is because when the length of the time slot is large enough, it may reduce the influence of temporal pattern. Moreover, we study the impact of varying dimension d of the relation embedding by setting it to $\{70, 80, 90, 100, 120\}$ (Table 3). The best parameter is determined according to the mean rank in the test set. The accuracy rate increases gradually when the dimension increases. Specifically, the accuracy keeps increasing until the dimension reaches 100, then it remains stable.

Table 2. Impact of the time slot length h.

Hours	Foursquare						Gowalla					
	Prec@1	Prec@10	Prec@20	Rec@1	Rec@10	Rec@20	Prec@1	Prec@10	Prec@20	Rec@1	Rec@10	Rec@20
1	0.075	0.061	0.041	0.062	0.128	0.163	0.089	0.064	0.047	0.071	0.141	0.169
2	0.100	0.083	0.054	0.082	0.170	0.218	0.119	0.086	0.062	0.094	0.150	0.225
4	0.113	0.090	0.060	0.092	0.192	0.245	0.134	0.096	0.070	0.106	0.168	0.253
8	**0.125**	**0.100**	**0.067**	**0.103**	**0.213**	**0.272**	**0.149**	**0.107**	**0.078**	**0.118**	**0.187**	**0.281**
12	0.119	0.095	0.064	0.098	0.202	0.258	0.142	0.102	0.074	0.112	0.178	0.267
24	0.115	0.092	0.062	0.094	0.196	0.250	0.137	0.098	0.072	0.108	0.172	0.259

Table 3. Impact of dimensionality d.

d	Foursquare						Gowalla					
	Prec@1	Prec@10	Prec@20	Rec@1	Rec@10	Rec@20	Prec@1	Prec@10	Prec@20	Rec@1	Rec@10	Rec@20
70	0.121	0.097	0.065	0.099	0.206	0.262	0.143	0.123	0.075	0.113	0.226	0.270
80	0.123	0.098	0.066	0.101	0.209	0.267	0.146	0.125	0.076	0.115	0.183	0.275
90	0.124	0.099	0.066	0.102	0.211	0.269	0.148	0.127	0.077	0.117	0.185	0.278
100	**0.125**	**0.100**	**0.067**	**0.103**	**0.213**	**0.272**	**0.149**	**0.128**	**0.078**	**0.118**	**0.187**	**0.281**
110	0.126	0.100	0.067	0.103	0.214	0.273	0.150	0.129	0.078	0.118	0.188	0.282
120	0.126	0.101	0.067	0.103	0.214	0.274	0.150	0.129	0.079	0.119	0.188	0.283

5   Conclusions

In this paper, we propose a novel translation-based POI recommendation model, which can effectively construct a user-POI graph and model the side information. To address time and geographical reasoning, we propose spatio-temporal relation path embedding to model the temporal, spatial and semantic contents to leverage the user-POI interaction and improve the quality of user embedding. To overcome the sparsity of the user-POI interaction data, we develop an embedding function which bridges gaps between the translation-based embedding model and traditional MF-based model. The user-POI graph is integrated with a combined MF model to improve the quality of POI recommendations.

Acknowledgments. We acknowledge the support of Australian Research Council Discovery *DP190101485*, Alexander von Humboldt Foundation, and CSIRO Data61 Scholarship program.

References

1. Cai, H., Zheng, V.W., Chang, K.C.C.: A comprehensive survey of graph embedding: problems, techniques, and applications. TKDE **30**(9), 1616–1637 (2018)
2. Cheng, Z., Caverlee, J., Lee, K., Sui, D.Z.: Exploring millions of footprints in location sharing services. In: AAAI (2011)
3. Cho, E., Myers, S.A., Leskovec, J.: Friendship and mobility: user movement in location-based social networks. In: SIGKDD, pp. 1082–1090 (2011)
4. Grover, A., Leskovec, J.: Node2Vec: scalable feature learning for networks. In: KDD, pp. 855–864 (2016)

5. Hamilton, W., Ying, Z., Leskovec, J.: Inductive representation learning on large graphs. In: NIPS, pp. 1024–1034. Curran Associates Inc., (2017)
6. He, R., Kang, W.C., McAuley, J.: Translation-based recommendation. In: RecSys, pp. 161–169 (2017)
7. Kipf, T.N., Welling, M.: Semi-supervised classification with graph convolutional networks. In: ICLR (2017)
8. Li, X., Cong, G., Li, X.L., Pham, T.A.N., Krishnaswamy, S.: Rank-geofm: a ranking based geographical factorization method for point of interest recommendation. In: SIGIR, pp. 433–442 (2015)
9. Lian, D., Zhao, C., Xie, X., Sun, G., Chen, E., Rui, Y.: Geomf: joint geographical modeling and matrix factorization for point-of-interest recommendation. In: KDD, pp. 831–840 (2014)
10. Lichman, M., Smyth, P.: Modeling human location data with mixtures of kernel densities. In: SIGKDD, pp. 35–44 (2014)
11. Lin, Y., Liu, Z., Luan, H., Sun, M., Rao, S., Liu, S.: Modeling relation paths for representation learning of knowledge bases. In: EMNLP, pp. 705–714 (2015)
12. Lin, Y., Liu, Z., Sun, M., Liu, Y., Zhu, X.: Learning entity and relation embeddings for knowledge graph completion. In: AAAI, pp. 2181–2187 (2015)
13. Liu, X., Liu, Y., Aberer, K., Miao, C.: Personalized point-of-interest recommendation by mining users' preference transition. In: CIKM, pp. 733–738 (2013)
14. Mairal, J., Koniusz, P., Harchaoui, Z., Schmid, C.: Convolutional kernel networks. In: NIPS, pp. 2627–2635. Curran Associates Inc., (2014)
15. Mnih, A., Salakhutdinov, R.R.: Probabilistic matrix factorization. In: NIPS, pp. 1257–1264 (2008)
16. Palumbo, E., Rizzo, G., Troncy, R.: Entity2rec: learning user-item relatedness from knowledge graphs for top-n item recommendation. In: RecSys (2017)
17. Perozzi, B., Al-Rfou, R., Skiena, S.: DeepWalk: online learning of social representations. In: KDD, pp. 701–710 (2014)
18. Qian, T., Liu, B., Nguyen, Q.V.H., Yin, H.: Spatiotemporal representation learning for translation-based poi recommendation. TOIS **37**(2), 18 (2019)
19. Shi, C., Hu, B., Zhao, W.X., Philip, S.Y.: Heterogeneous information network embedding for recommendation. TKDE **31**(2), 357–370 (2018)
20. Sun, K., Koniusz, P., Wang, Z.: Fisher-bures adversary graph convolutional networks. In: UAI (2019)
21. Wang, Q., Mao, Z., Wang, B., Guo, L.: Knowledge graph embedding: a survey of approaches and applications. TKDE **29**(12), 2724–2743 (2017)
22. Wang, W., Yin, H., Chen, L., Sun, Y., Sadiq, S., Zhou, X.: Geo-sage: a geographical sparse additive generative model for spatial item recommendation. In: KDD (2015)
23. Wang, W., Yin, H., Du, X., Nguyen, Q.V.H., Zhou, X.: Tpm: a temporal personalized model for spatial item recommendation. ACM TIST **9**(6), 61 (2018)
24. Xie, M., Yin, H., Wang, H., Xu, F., Chen, W., Wang, S.: Learning graph-based poi embedding for location-based recommendation. In: CIKM, pp. 15–24 (2016)
25. Yin, H., Wang, W., Wang, H., Chen, L., Zhou, X.: Spatial-aware hierarchical collaborative deep learning for poi recommendation. TKDE **29**(11), 2537–2551 (2017)
26. Yin, H., Zhou, X., Cui, B., Wang, H., Zheng, K., Nguyen, Q.V.H.: Adapting to user interest drift for poi recommendation. TKDE **28**(10), 2566–2581 (2016)
27. Zhang, F., Yuan, N.J., Lian, D., Xie, X., Ma, W.Y.: Collaborative knowledge base embedding for recommender systems. In: SIGKDD, pp. 353–362 (2016)
28. Zhang, J.D., Chow, C.Y.: Geosoca: exploiting geographical, social and categorical correlations for point-of-interest recommendations. In: SIGIR, pp. 443–452 (2015)

FlowRec: Prototyping Session-Based Recommender Systems in Streaming Mode

Dimitris Paraschakis$^{(\boxtimes)}$ and Bengt J. Nilsson

Malmö University, Nordenskiöldsgatan 1, 211 19 Malmö, Sweden
{dimitris.paraschakis,bengt.nilsson.TS}@mau.se

Abstract. Despite the increasing interest towards session-based and streaming recommender systems, there is still a lack of publicly available evaluation frameworks supporting both these paradigms. To address the gap, we propose `FlowRec` — an extension of the streaming framework `Scikit-Multiflow`, which opens plentiful possibilities for prototyping recommender systems operating on sessionized data streams, thanks to the underlying collection of incremental learners and support for real-time performance tracking. We describe the extended functionalities of the adapted prequential evaluation protocol, and develop a competitive recommendation algorithm on top of `Scikit-Multiflow`'s implementation of a Hoeffding Tree. We compare our algorithm to other known baselines for the next-item prediction task across three different domains.

Keywords: Streaming recommendations · Session-based recommendations · Prequential evaluation · Online learning · Hoeffding Tree

1 Introduction

In the past few years, the RecSys community has witnessed a paradigm shift from the traditional matrix completion problem to sequential *session-based* recommendations [9,15]. The latter approach is dominated by neural methods that are often evaluated in an online manner, i.e. when the events of a session are sequentially revealed and predicted one-by-one. However, these systems are still trained in batches on large chunks of recorded data [7,15,19]. To better approximate real-world scenarios with severe cold-start and concept drifts, *streaming* recommender systems [3,18,20] have been designed for incremental online learning from continuous data streams in the context of limited memory/runtime, and anytime prediction [17]. However, most of them address the conventional rather than session-based recommendation problem [6]. Bridging the gap between session-based and streaming recommender systems has been recently attempted [6,9], marking an emerging research direction of a high practical value.

© Springer Nature Switzerland AG 2020
H. W. Lauw et al. (Eds.): PAKDD 2020, LNAI 12084, pp. 65–77, 2020.
https://doi.org/10.1007/978-3-030-47426-3_6

Presently, only a few publicly available benchmarking frameworks for streaming recommendations exist. Some of them have been designed for a specific application domain [9,16], while others lack native support for session data [5,11]. Scikit-Multiflow [14] has recently been released as a general-purpose Python framework for stream mining, offering a variety of stream learners, change detectors, and evaluation methods. To facilitate the research on streaming session-based recommendations, we propose FlowRec[1] — an extension of Scikit-Multiflow for rapid prototyping of recommender systems. The proposed framework currently contains several stream-oriented recommenders and metrics for prequential evaluation. Additionally, we demonstrate a principled way of exposing a recommendation interface to an underlying stream learner class of Scikit-Multiflow (namely, a Hoeffding Tree). We show that the resulting recommender system has remarkable performance against established baselines. FlowRec's functionality is detailed in the next section.

2   FlowRec

The framework consists of three main entities: a stream, an evaluator, and a model. This section describes the interplay between these entities.

2.1   Problem Setting

Consider a stream D of (overlapping) user sessions $S = s_1, \ldots, s_{|S|}$ (Fig. 1). A session represents an ordered sequence of events of the form (X, y), where X is a feature vector describing the context for item y. As a bare minimum, X contains the session identifier for the item. Other common features are timestamp and event type (e.g. click, purchase, etc.). The scope of our study is limited to the context of collaborative filtering, which relaxes the assumption of item metadata in feature vectors (technically, any feature can be encoded as a part of X).

At each time step $t = 1, \ldots, T$, the stream provides a sample (X, y). Based on the information in X, the model is asked to generate a list of N predictions $\hat{Y} = (\hat{y}_1, \ldots, \hat{y}_N)$ in an attempt to correctly guess the hidden item y. This corresponds to the *next-item prediction task* in the RecSys literature [15]. In practice, only certain features of X are retained for the prediction part, such as the current session identifier, and possibly the timestamp of the event. After the prediction, the entire feature vector X together with the label y are revealed to the model, allowing it to make an incremental update. This iterative, supervised 'test-then-train' methodology is known as *prequential evaluation* [20] (Fig. 2).

In our framework, each processed sample (X, y) is added to the sliding window of the last n observations, which we refer to as *observation window* (depicted as the green box in Fig. 1). Although its use is not required in the ordinary stream learning, it can ease the development of session-based models by providing a snapshot of the recent session data on demand. The size of the window must be chosen in consideration of the system's memory and runtime constraints.

---

[1] https://git.io/flowrec.

2.2   Metrics

`FlowRec` implements several evaluation metrics, two of which are commonly used for next-item prediction [6,7,13,19], namely *recall* (a.k.a. hitrate) and *mean reciprocal rank* (MRR). Recall measures the average number of successful predictions, whereas MRR measures their average reciprocal ranking, i.e.:

$$Recall@N = \frac{1}{T}\sum_{t=1}^{T}\sum_{i=1}^{N}\mathbb{1}(y_t = \hat{y}_i) \qquad MRR@N = \frac{1}{T}\sum_{t=1}^{T}\sum_{i=1}^{N}\frac{1}{i}\mathbb{1}(y_t = \hat{y}_i) \quad (1)$$

The framework keeps two sets of measurements: (a) *global*, where the running average of each metric is calculated from all the past data; and (b) *sliding*, where the average is taken over a sliding window of recent events that we call the *evaluation window* (purple box in Fig. 1). The sizes of evaluation and observation windows are user-adjustable, offering flexibility in simulation setups.

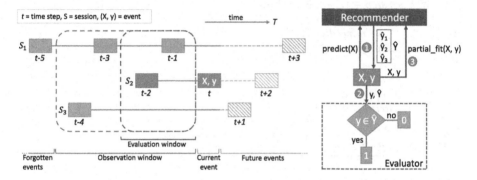

Fig. 1. Streaming sessions (Color figure online)   **Fig. 2.** Prequential protocol

2.3   Prequential Evaluation

The basic workflow for measuring recall using prequential evaluation is presented in Algorithm 1. The complete functionality of `Scikit-Multiflow`'s prequential evaluator is provided in its official documentation[2].

`FlowRec` introduces the following additional parameters[3] for the evaluator:

- Indices of data columns holding session, timestamp, and event type identifiers. The last two columns are optional, and allow for time-aware and event-specific training and/or evaluation.
- Stream-related configurations, such as the size of the observation window, and the number of events to skip from the start of the stream.

---

[2] https://scikit-multiflow.github.io/scikit-multiflow/documentation.html.
[3] https://flowrec.readthedocs.io/en/latest/eval_parameters.html.

– Recommendation-specific settings, such as the size of the recommendation list, and the event types that trigger recommendation requests. There are also flags for enabling/disabling *reminders* and *repeated* recommendations. Reminders are recommendations of items that were *visited* earlier by the user, whereas repeated recommendations are those that were already *given* earlier to the user.

Algorithm 1. Basic prequential protocol for measuring recall

Input: D: data stream, N: recommendation cutoff, n_{keep}: size of the observation window, M: set of recommendation models
Output: Recall@N of each model
1: $W \leftarrow create\_queue(n_{keep})$ $\triangleright$ observation window of n_{keep} latest events
2: $r_m \leftarrow 0, \forall m \in M$ $\triangleright$ reward counter
3: $n \leftarrow 0$ $\triangleright$ evaluation counter
4: **while** $D.has\_more\_samples()$ **do**
5:      $X, y \leftarrow D.next\_sample()$
6:      **if** $X.session \in W.sessions$ **then**
7:          **for all** $m \in M$ **do**
8:              $\hat{Y} \leftarrow m.predict(X)$
9:              **if** $y \in top\_N(\hat{Y})$ **then**
10:                 $r_m \leftarrow r_m + 1$
11:             $n \leftarrow n + 1$
12:         **for all** $m \in M$ **do**
13:             $m.partial\_fit(X, y)$
14:     $W.add(X, y)$
15: **return** $r_m/n, \forall m \in M$

The size of the evaluation window (as well as other settings) are covered by the original parameter list of the EvaluatePrequential class in `Scikit-Multiflow`. Note that the stream provides samples in the order as they appear in the dataset. The last column of the dataset should always contain the item identifiers.

3   Prototyping

Prototyping incremental session-based recommendation models in `FlowRec` is straightforward. First, a streaming model is built by extending the BaseSKMObject class of `Scikit-Multiflow` with the appropriate mixin. It is natural to treat the recommendation task as a multi-class classification problem, where each class corresponds to an item. Hence, the suitable mixin for this type of problems is ClassifierMixin[4]. What remains is to implement the following abstract methods:

---

[4] https://scikit-multiflow.github.io/scikit-multiflow/user-guide.core-concepts. architecture.html.

partial_fit(X, y) — Incrementally train a stream model.

predict(X) — Generate top-N predictions for the target's class.

predict_proba(X) — Calculate the probabilities of a sample pertaining to each of the available classes (implementing this method is optional).

Every stream model developed in `FlowRec` has access to useful shared resources, such as observation window, current session vector, and item catalog.

3.1   Session-Based Streaming Models

Presently, `FlowRec` contains the following streaming models for session-based recommendations:

Rule-Based Models. The first three models are rule-based recommenders that capture one-to-one relationships between items. These methods rely on the very last item of a session to make their predictions for the next item. Despite their simplicity, rule-based models have proven surprisingly effective in the domains of music and e-commerce [13], and have very low computational complexity. We briefly outline these methods below (refer to [13] for details).

Association Rules (AR). The rules are derived from co-occurrences of two items in a session (e.g. 'those-who-bought-also-bought'). A co-occurrence forms rules in both directions, i.e. $y_t \leftrightarrow y_{t'}, t \neq t'$.

Markov Chains (MC). The rules are derived from a first-order Markov Chain, describing the transition probability between items that appear in two *contiguous* events in a session, i.e. $y_t \rightarrow y_{t+1}$.

Sequential Rules (SR). The rules are derived from sequential patterns between two items in a session, but not necessarily in successive events, i.e. $y_t \rightarrow y_{t'}, t' > t$. The sequential association is assigned the weight $1/(t' - t)$.

In `FlowRec`, the above algorithms can be made event-specific by providing event_column_index. For instance, predictors of type *purchase* $\leftrightarrow$ *purchase*, *click* $\rightarrow$ *purchase*, etc. can be useful in e-commerce applications as components of an ensemble recommender [2].

Session kNN. This is a specialized version of the k-Nearest Neighbors (kNN) algorithm that operates on session data. It is a strong baseline with performance comparable to that of certain deep neural methods [8,13]. Being model-free, the algorithm is incremental by nature. S-kNN recommends items from other user sessions that are similar to the current session (a.k.a. neighbors). Given the active session S, the score of the candidate item $\hat{y}$ is calculated as follows:

$$score(\hat{y} \mid \hat{y} \notin S) = \sum_{S' \in \mathcal{N}(S)} sim(S, S') \cdot \mathbb{1}(\hat{y} \in S') \qquad (2)$$

where $\mathcal{N}(S)$ is the k-sized neighborhood of session S, and $sim(S, S')$ is a measure of similarity between two sessions.

FlowRec implements Cosine, Jaccard, Dice, and Tanimoto similarity. In the future, we plan to implement other kNN variants described in [13].

BEER[TS]. This is a bandit ensemble designed for streaming recommendations, which employs Thompson Sampling for the model selection. In [2], event-specific rule-based models were used as behavioral components of the ensemble. In FlowRec, any model implementing the predict_proba(X) method can be added as a component of BEER[TS]. For each recommendation slot, the ensemble picks a model m with the highest sample $\theta_m \sim Beta(\alpha_m + 1, \beta_m + 1)$, where α_m is the number of past successes, and β_m is the number of past failures. The method is adaptable to non-stationary data (e.g. occurring due to concept drift), which is achieved via exploration-exploitation. In addition, BEER[TS] supports component splitting into (relatively) stationary partitions (see [2] for details), which is achieved in FlowRec by setting the boundaries for probabilities returned by the predict_proba(X) method. Further, the components of the ensemble can complement each other in case of poor coverage, which helps to attack sparsity and cold-start issues.

Popularity Baseline. This is the traditional baseline that outputs the top-N most popular items in descending order.

The above methods can be incrementally trained either on the global scale, or within the observation window. The latter option acts as a forgetting mechanism for older data, which aids model scalability and adaptability to recent trends.

3.2 Hoeffding Tree Wrapper

Prototyping streaming session-based recommenders can be facilitated by employing the rich collection of incremental algorithms offered by Scikit-Multiflow, including Bayesian methods, lazy learners, ensembles, neural networks, tree-based methods, and more [14]. Utilizing any of these methods for recommendation tasks is achieved via a *wrapper*, which is a middle layer that handles the inputs and the outputs of an underlying learner. Some of the common tasks performed by wrappers include:

- transforming a sample to the desired input format accepted by a learner.
- calling the predict_proba(X) method of a learner, and manipulating its return values to generate top-N recommendations.

Using the above approach, we develop a recommender system by 'wrapping' the HoeffdingTree classifier provided by Scikit-Multiflow.

Hoeffding Tree (HT). Also known as a Very Fast Decision Tree (VFDT) [4], a HT is an incremental, anytime decision tree inducer designed for learning from data streams. Its key idea lies in the fact that only a small subset of samples passing through a node may be sufficient for deciding on the split attribute. For estimating the minimum number of samples needed, the method employs the Hoeffding bound, which offers sound theoretical guarantees of performance (see [4] for details), asymptotically comparable to that of a batch decision tree.

HT Wrapper Architecture. The `Scikit-Multiflow`'s implementation of a HT supports Naive Bayes prediction at the leaves of the tree, and the possibility of assigning a weight to each fitted sample. We take advantage of both capabilities in the proposed HT recommender. The core idea of our algorithm is to encode all item-to-item associations employed by rule-based methods (see above) in a unified learner. This allows HT to capture both sequential and co-occurrence patterns in a session. The idea is conceptually similar to the BEER[TS] framework [2], but instead of treating between-items associations as separate predictors explored by a bandit, we fit them to a single decision tree classifier using a specific weighting scheme, as explained below. We hence formulate the recommendation task as a multi-class classification problem. Due to the nature of the problem, HT is reduced to a *decision stump*, whose nodes represent input items, and the leaves contain item predictions obtained via Naive Bayes classification.

Training the Model. The incremental training of a HT in `Scikit-Multiflow` can be done by calling the method `partial_fit(X, y, sample_weight)`. The first two parameters specify the input feature vector and the output label, respectively, with an associated (optional) sample weight. We use these parameters to encode the sequential relation between two items, by letting the feature vector contain the antecedent item and the label represent the consequent item. For the ease of notation, we use the item in place of a feature vector in Algorithm 2 (y or y', lines 7 and 8). Internally, each antecedent is represented as a node of the tree.

Algorithm 2. HT Wrapper training procedure

Input: (X, y): sample from the stream; $w_{MC} \geq 1$: importance weight for Markov Chain sequences; $w_{inv} \in [0, 1]$: importance weight for inverse sequences.

1: $S \leftarrow (y'_1, \ldots, y'_{|S|})$ ▷ item vector (in time order) for the session id encoded in X
2: **for** $i \leftarrow 1, \ldots, |S|$ **do**
3:    **if** $i = |S|$ **then**
4:       $w \leftarrow w_{MC}$ ▷ weight for the 'next-item' sequence
5:    **else**
6:       $w \leftarrow 1/(|S| - i + 1)$ ▷ weight for a non-contiguous sequence
7:    ht.partial_fit(y'_i, y, w)   ▷ fit observed sequence
8:    ht.partial_fit($y, y'_i, w \cdot w_{inv}$)   ▷ fit inverse (unobserved) sequence

---

After fetching the current session vector S from the observation window, the wrapper learns all sequential patterns involving item y by fitting a series of samples $(y_i', y, w), \forall i = 1, \ldots, |S|$, where the sample weight is inversely proportional to the distance between two items. Clearly, these fits utilize the same patterns as captured in Sequential Rules (SR) described above. Among these patterns, $y_{|S|} \rightarrow y$ pertains to the Markov Chain (MC). The corresponding sample, $(y_{|S|}', y, w_{MC})$, uses a separate weight reflecting the perceived importance of the 'next-item' sequence. Finally, encoding co-occurrence patterns captured by Association Rules (AR) is achieved via a series of the so-called *inverse fits*, i.e. $(y, y_i', w \cdot w_{inv}), \forall i = 1, \ldots, |S|$, which complete the bidirectional associations. The fixed weight $w_{inv} \in [0, 1]$ is used to inform the influence of inverse (hence unobserved) sequential patterns on the classification.

Making Predictions. Unlike rule-based methods, where the predictions are made solely on the basis of the latest item in a session, our HT wrapper makes predictions in an ensemble-like manner by combining the responses of all the relevant nodes of the tree. The prediction procedure is detailed in Algorithm 3.

Algorithm 3. HT Wrapper prediction procedure

Input: X: feature vector containing session id; $w_{MC} \geq 1$: importance weight for
  Markov Chain sequences; $w_{inv} \in [0, 1]$: importance weight for inverse sequences;
  N: recommendation cutoff
Output: $\hat{Y}$: top-N recommendations
  1: $S \leftarrow (y_1', \ldots, y_{|S|}')$ ▷ fetch item vector for the current session id encoded in X
  2: $P \leftarrow (\mathbb{P}(y_1), \ldots, \mathbb{P}(y_{|P|}))$, set $\mathbb{P}(y_i) \leftarrow 0, \forall i, \ldots, |P|$ ▷ init class probabilities
  3: **for** $i \leftarrow 1, \ldots, |S|$ **do**
  4:     $P_i \leftarrow$ ht.predict_proba(y_i') ▷ predict class probabilities from item y_i'
  5:     **if** $i = |S|$ **then**
  6:         $P_i \leftarrow P_i \cdot w_{MC}$
  7:     **else**
  8:         $P_i \leftarrow P_i / (|S| - i + 1)$
  9:     $P \leftarrow P + P_i$
 10: **return** $\hat{Y} \leftarrow (y_1, \ldots, y_N), \forall \mathbb{P}(y_i) \in$ top-$N(P)$

For each item y_i' in the current session vector, the wrapper calls the predict_proba(y_i') method of a HT. This method returns a class probability vector that expresses the likelihood of each candidate item to follow item y_i'. The probability vectors P_i are then weighted with the recency of item y_i'. Predictions obtained from the most recent item, $y_{|S|}'$, receive the highest weight specified by w_{MC}. All weighted probability vectors are then added to produce the final scores for the candidate items, top-N of which are returned.

4   Simulation Results

4.1   Datasets

We use public datasets containing sessionized browsing logs. The datasets originate from three recommendation contests representing news, travel, and e-commerce domains. They are summarized in Table 1.

Table 1. Datasets summary (1M events each)

Dataset	Contest	Domain (Action)	Items	Sessions	Avg. session size
Clef	NewsReel'15 [10][a]	News (impressions)	109	305703	3.27 events
Yoochoose	RecSys'15 [1]	E-commerce (clicks)	21300	255166	3.92 events
Trivago	RecSys'19 [12]	Travel (clickouts)	243714	521677	1.92 events

[a]We use the subset of the dataset provided in [13].

4.2   Prequential Evaluation Setup

We consider the task of online *next-item recommendation*, where the goal is to suggest the list of most probable items to appear in the next session event. We track Recall@10 and MRR@10 during the entire run of the simulation using the real-time visualizer provided by the framework, which reports the global and the current (sliding) averages. Time horizon for each simulation is set to 1M events, with evaluation and observation window sizes of 10K and 50K events, respectively. The latter size was chosen in consideration of sufficient (sliding) session history and a reasonable memory/runtime overhead. We use a separate validation set of 100K events (preceding those of the simulation) for hyperparameter tuning. The evaluation itself is performed from pure cold-start, with no model pre-training involved. Sessions of size 1 are excluded from the evaluation. For our simulations, we use Intel Core i7 CPU @ 2.80 GHz and 16 Gb RAM.

4.3   Model Setup

We evaluate the models presented in Sect. 3, with an addition of a Random classifier that sets the lower bound for performance. Below we briefly outline the optimal model configurations after the hyperparameter tuning step.

Rule-based (AR, MC, SR) models operate on a global scale, whereas the popularity-based one (POP) works within a sliding window. S-kNN uses Cosine similarity, and $k = 100$ (Trivago), $k = 200$ (Clef), $k = 300$ (Yoochoose). We also use *recent session sub-sampling* [8], with sub-sample sizes of 500 (Clef), 1000 (Trivago), and 1500 (Yoochoose). BEER[TS] includes AR, MC, SR, POP, and S-kNN as components of the ensemble. The HT wrapper uses weights $w_{MC} = 3$ (Yoochoose), $w_{MC} = 5$ (Clef, Trivago), and $w_{inv} = 0.01$ (Clef), $w_{inv} = 0.9$ (Yoochoose, Trivago). The HoeffdingTree class of Scikit-Multiflow is instantiated with leaf_prediction='nb' to enable Naive Bayes prediction at the leaves. The pre-configured experiments are provided in FlowRec's code base for reproducibility.

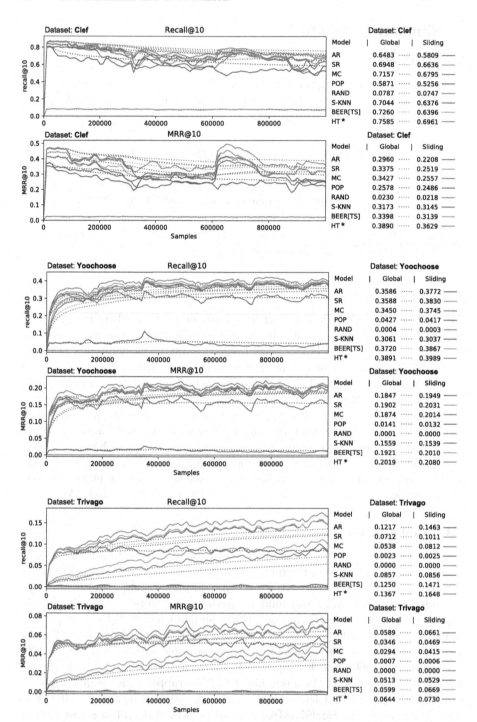

Fig. 3. Performance charts for Clef (top), Yoochoose (middle), and Trivago (bottom)

4.4 Results

The results of the simulation for the three datasets are presented in Fig. 3. The top performing model in each case is marked with an asterisk. Note that the column 'Sliding' contains the averages of the *very last* evaluation window.

The HT wrapper consistently achieves higher recall and MRR than the other baselines on all three datasets. This proves the effectiveness of combining item-to-item sequential patterns, and utilizing the entire user session at prediction time in an ensemble-like manner. The HT wrapper also happens to be noticeably faster than its main rival, BEER[TS] (in its current configuration). The total running times for each model are recorded by the framework. As a point of reference, we consider the upper limit of 100 ms per recommendation prescribed by the CLEF NewsReel challenge [10]. Table 2 reports average response times per recommendation request for each model. We observe that all runtimes fall within the recommended limit. The real-time visualization offers the possibility to diagnose potential issues at an early stage. For instance, the performance charts for Yoochoose and Trivago make it obvious that the inclusion of POP to BEER[TS] is not justified, and hence it can be dropped from the ensemble to gain speed. The live monitoring of model evolution helps to see how algorithms behave relative to each other on various segments of the dataset, as well as to better understand the peculiarities of the dataset itself. For example, the above two charts clearly show the stagnation of S-kNN after leaving the initial cold-start segment ($\approx$0–50K), while other models continue to learn. We also see that Clef exhibits a more dynamic domain (news) with more profound concept drift, which makes learning more challenging. It is the only dataset where the popularity recommender has decent performance, surpassing other models on certain data segments. The Clef chart also reveals the 'easy' portion of the dataset ($\approx$600K–800K), where most algorithms (but not POP) boost their performance.

Table 2. Average recommendation time (msec) per model

Dataset	Model							
	AR	SR	MC	POP	RAND	S-kNN	BEER[TS]	HT
Clef	0.270	0.213	0.204	0.187	0.204	26.543	27.858	2.542
Yoochoose	0.744	0.623	0.476	3.365	0.313	2.434	13.331	9.629
Trivago	4.276	4.093	4.082	11.380	1.150	5.675	85.163	23.036

5 Conclusion

We introduce `FlowRec` — a new recommendation framework for streaming session data developed on top of `Scikit-Multiflow`. It serves as a testbed for streaming recommendation models by offering prequential evaluation with real-time performance monitoring. One advantage of prototyping in `FlowRec` is the ability to 'wrap' various stream learners provided by Scikit-Multiflow, thus treating them as black boxes. We demonstrate how to develop such a wrapper for the HoeffdingTree class, capable of generating accurate session-based recommendations on evolving data streams. The framework will be further extended with additional evaluation protocols, metrics, and algorithms.

References

1. Ben-Shimon, D., Tsikinovsky, A., Friedmann, M., Shapira, B., Rfokach, L., Hoerle, J.: Recsys challenge 2015 and the yoochoose dataset. In: Proceedings of the 9th ACM Conference on Recommender Systems (RecSys 2015), pp. 357–358. ACM (2015)
2. Brodén, B., Hammar, M., Nilsson, B.J., Paraschakis, D.: A bandit-based ensemble framework for exploration/exploitation of diverse recommendation components: an experimental study within e-commerce. ACM Trans. Interact. Intell. Syst. **10**(1), 4:1–4:32 (2019)
3. Diaz-Aviles, E., Drumond, L., Schmidt-Thieme, L., Nejdl, W.: Real-time top-n recommendation in social streams. In: Proceedings of the Sixth ACM Conference on Recommender Systems (RecSys 2012), pp. 59–66. ACM (2012)
4. Domingos, P., Hulten, G.: Mining high-speed data streams. In: Proceedings of the Sixth ACM SIGKDD International Conference on Knowledge Discovery and Data Mining (KDD 2000), pp. 71–80. ACM (2000)
5. Frigó, E., Pálovics, R., Kelen, D., Kocsis, L., Benczúr, A.: Alpenglow: open source recommender framework with time-aware learning and evaluation. In: 2017 Poster Track of the 11th ACM Conference on Recommender Systems (Poster-Recsys 2017), pp. 1–2. CEUR-WS.org (2017)
6. Guo, L., Yin, H., Wang, Q., Chen, T., Zhou, A., Quoc Viet Hung, N.: Streaming session-based recommendation. In: Proceedings of the 25th ACM SIGKDD International Conference on Knowledge Discovery & Data Mining (KDD 2019), pp. 1569–1577. ACM (2019)
7. Hidasi, B., Karatzoglou, A., Baltrunas, L., Tikk, D.: Session-based recommendations with recurrent neural networks. CoRR abs/1511.06939 (2015)
8. Jannach, D., Ludewig, M.: When recurrent neural networks meet the neighborhood for session-based recommendation. In: Proceedings of the 11th ACM Conference on Recommender Systems (RecSys 2017), pp. 306–310. ACM (2017)
9. Jugovac, M., Jannach, D., Karimi, M.: Streamingrec: a framework for benchmarking stream-based news recommenders. In: Proceedings of the 12th ACM Conference on Recommender Systems (RecSys 2018), pp. 269–273. ACM (2018)
10. Kille, B., et al.: Stream-based recommendations: online and offline evaluation as a service. In: Mothe, J., et al. (eds.) CLEF 2015. LNCS, vol. 9283, pp. 497–517. Springer, Cham (2015). https://doi.org/10.1007/978-3-319-24027-5_48
11. Kitazawa, T.: Flurs: a python library for online item recommendation. https://takuti.me/note/flurs/ (2017). Accessed 03 November 2019
12. Knees, P., Deldjoo, Y., Moghaddam, F.B., Adamczak, J., Leyson, G.P., Monreal, P.: Recsys challenge 2019: session-based hotel recommendations. In: Proceedings of the 13th ACM Conference on Recommender Systems (RecSys 2019), pp. 570–571. ACM (2019)
13. Ludewig, M., Jannach, D.: Evaluation of session-based recommendation algorithms. User Model. User Adapt. Interact. **28**(4–5), 331–390 (2018). https://doi.org/10.1007/s11257-018-9209-6

14. Montiel, J., Read, J., Bifet, A., Abdessalem, T.: Scikit-multiflow: a multi-output streaming framework. J. Mach. Learn. Res. **19**(72), 1–5 (2018)
15. Quadrana, M.: Algorithms for sequence-aware recommender systems. Ph.D. Thesis, Politecnico di Milano (2017)
16. Scriminaci, M., et al.: Idomaar: a framework for multi-dimensional benchmarking of recommender algorithms. In: Guy, I., Sharma, A. (eds.) RecSys Posters. CEUR Workshop Proceedings, CEUR-WS.org (2016)
17. Srimani, P., Patil, M.M.: Performance analysis of hoeffding trees in data streams by using massive online analysis framework. Int. J. Data Min. Model. Manage. **7**(4), 293–313 (2015)
18. Subbian, K., Aggarwal, C., Hegde, K.: Recommendations for streaming data. In: Proceedings of the 25th ACM International on Conference on Information and Knowledge Management (CIKM 2016), pp. 2185–2190. ACM (2016)
19. Tan, Y.K., Xu, X., Liu, Y.: Improved recurrent neural networks for session-based recommendations. In: Proceedings of the 1st Workshop on Deep Learning for Recommender Systems (DLRS 2016), pp. 17–22. ACM (2016)
20. Vinagre, J., Jorge, A.M., Gama, J.: Evaluation of recommender systems in streaming environments. In: ACM RecSys Workshop on Recommender Systems Evaluation: Dimensions and Design (REDD 2014), pp. 393–394. ACM (2014)

Accurate News Recommendation Coalescing Personal and Global Temporal Preferences

Bonhun Koo, Hyunsik Jeon, and U Kang$^{(\boxtimes)}$

Seoul National University, Seoul, South Korea
{darkgs,jeon185,ukang}@snu.ac.kr

Abstract. Given session-based news watch history of users, how can we precisely recommend news articles? Unlike other items for recommendation, the worth of news articles decays quickly and various news sources publish fresh ones every second. Moreover, people frequently select news articles regardless of their personal preferences to understand popular topics at a specific time. Conventional recommendation methods, designed for other recommendation domains, give low performance because of these peculiarities of news articles.

In this paper, we propose PGT (News Recommendation Coalescing **P**ersonal and **G**lobal **T**emporal Preferences), an accurate news recommendation method designed with consideration of the above characteristics of news articles. PGT extracts latent features from both personal and global temporal preferences to sufficiently reflect users' behaviors. Furthermore, we propose an attention based architecture to extract adequate coalesced features from both of the preferences. Experimental results show that PGT provides the most accurate news recommendation, giving the state-of-the-art accuracy.

Keywords: News recommender systems · Personal and global temporal preferences · Attention · Recurrent neural network

1 Introduction

Given news articles and watch history of users, how can we accurately recommend news articles to users? Even though online news service has become a main source of news, a massive amount of news articles released everyday makes it difficult for users to search for articles of their interests. Thus, it is crucial for online news providers to recommend appropriate news articles for users to improve their experiences.

In online news services that provide news to customers, consumptions are extremely skewed to spotlighted news. Figure 1a shows the skewness of consumptions in Adressa dataset (see Sect. 4.1 for details), a real-world news service dataset; x-axis indicates the popularity ranks of news which could vary over time, and y-axis indicates the number of consumptions. As shown in the figure, interactions between users and news have *popularity pattern*, meaning that users

© Springer Nature Switzerland AG 2020
H. W. Lauw et al. (Eds.): PAKDD 2020, LNAI 12084, pp. 78–90, 2020.
https://doi.org/10.1007/978-3-030-47426-3_7

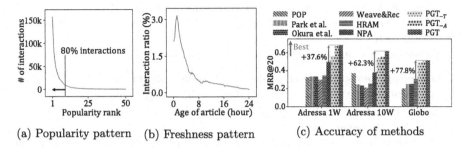

(a) Popularity pattern   (b) Freshness pattern   (c) Accuracy of methods

Fig. 1. (a) *popularity pattern*: users tend to prefer *popular* news. (b) *freshness pattern*: users prefer relatively *fresh* news. (c) Our proposed PGT gives the best accuracy, thanks to its consideration of both global and personal preferences.

mostly prefer popular news. For instance, the top-7 most popular articles account for 80% of total consumptions during the entire time. Figure 1b shows a *freshness pattern* in Adressa dataset, where the number of consumptions of each news rapidly decreases over its age. This indicates that customers prefer relatively fresh news since the novelty of news expires quickly over time. Thus, the challenge of designing an accurate news recommender systems is to consider the global temporal preference while taking into account each user's personal preference.

In this paper, we propose PGT (News Recommendation Coalescing **P**ersonal and **G**lobal **T**emporal Preferences), a novel approach for news recommendation considering both of personal and global temporal preferences. PGT gives a recommendation for each user at time t leveraging 1) the global temporal preference at time t, and 2) watch-history of the user before t.

1. **Global temporal preference.** Representing global temporal preference at time t as a low-rank latent vector is challenging since it has to involve both of popularity pattern and freshness pattern at that time. To deal with this challenge, PGT selects 1) document vectors of the most popular n articles at time t, which stand for popularity pattern, and 2) document vectors of the most fresh m articles at time t, which stand for freshness pattern. These vectors for the two different patterns are combined by the self-attention [15] with a scaled dot product (details in Sect. 3.2).

2. **Watch history.** A user's previous watch history epitomizes the user's personal preference. The goal of PGT is to extract a sequential pattern in the watch history with regard to the global temporal preference. For the purpose, PGT uses a bidirectional LSTM (BiLSTM) which has shown the best performance in encoding session-based sequential data [5] where a session is a set of consecutive behaviors of a user. PGT combines the hidden states of BiLSTM by an attention network using the global temporal preference as context (details in Sect. 3.3).

PGT then generates a prediction vector using a fully-connected neural network where information from both of personal preference and global temporal preference at time t is fed into. Lastly, PGT ranks candidate articles based on the similarity between the embedding vectors of the candidates and the generated prediction vector.

We summarize our main contributions as follows:

- **Modeling personal and global temporal preference.** We introduce *global temporal preference* which indicates the comprehensive pattern of all users in news services. PGT models how global temporal preference influences each user's personal preference.
- **Attention-based architecture coalescing preferences.** We propose an attention-based network architecture to dynamically control weights of features in 1) the representation of global temporal preference, and 2) the representation of personal preference. The global temporal preference vector is used as context in the attention network for the personal preference. Attention helps PGT effectively deal with a quick change of personal preference in the online news ecosystem.
- **Experiment.** Extensive experimental results show that PGT provides the best accuracy, outperforming competitors by significant margins (see Fig. 1c).

In the rest of paper, we review related works in Sect. 2, introduce our proposed method PGT in Sect. 3, evaluate PGT and competitors in Sect. 4, and conclude in Sect. 5.

2   Related Works

We review previous researches on news recommendation systems.

Early studies on recommendation systems use variants of recurrent neural network (RNN) to model input sequences [2,3]. However, these methods usually suffer from the cold-start problems. To deal with the cold-start problems, several studies enrich the embedding of newly published articles by utilizing the meta-information of articles [4]. Okura et al. [11] proposed a news recommender system based on variational autoencoder (VAE) and RNN. They used a method based on VAE to learn embedding vectors of articles, such that vectors in the same categories are made similar. After learning article embeddings, they used RNNs to predict the next article vector that a user is likely to watch. Park et al. [12] proposed a news recommendation system based on RNN to model each user's personal preference. They reranked the candidates by each user's long-term categorical preference which is the weighted sum of categories of news articles that the user has seen; this categorical preference improved the accuracy.

Recent studies proposed attention-based methods to model users' behaviors without RNNs. Wang et al. [16] proposed a deep news recommendation method with a CNN model [7] and a news-level attention network. They enhanced their method using the embeddings of the entities extracted from a knowledge graph. Chuhan et al. [17] proposed to use attention networks at both word-level and news-level to highlight informative words and news. They also proposed personalized attention by using the embedding of user ID as context to differentially attend to important words and news according to personal preference.

We note that none of the above methods consider the global temporal preference, and its coalesced relation to personal preference. Thus they show poor performance compared to our proposed PGT (see Sect. 4).

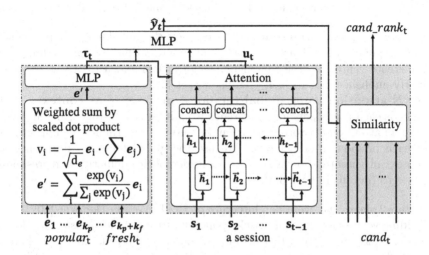

Fig. 2. Architecture of PGT. To recommend news articles to a user at time t, PGT generates a prediction vector $\hat{y}_t$ using previous article $s_1, \cdots, s_{t-1}$ in the session of the user, popular articles $popular_t$ at time t, and fresh articles $fresh_t$ at time t. PGT ranks candidate articles $cand_t$ based on their similarities to the prediction vector $\hat{y}_t$.

3   Proposed Method

We propose PGT, an accurate method for news recommendation. We first provide a brief overview of our method in Sect. 3.1. Then we describe how to generate 1) a representation for the global temporal preference in Sect. 3.2, and 2) a representation for the personal preference in Sect. 3.3. Finally, we introduce how to rank the candidate articles in Sect. 3.4.

3.1   Overview

We design PGT for balanced extraction of latent features from both of personal preference and global temporal preference. PGT reflects users' online news watch behaviors by accumulating these two preferences to provide an accurate recommendation. We concentrate on the following challenges to address in a news recommendation system.

1. **Cold-Start problem.** News recommendation systems need to recommend newly published articles which have no explicit user feedback. How can we provide accurate news recommendation for these fresh articles?

2. **Popularity and freshness patterns.** As shown in Fig. 1, the novelty of news expires quickly. How can we dynamically capture the personal and global temporal preferences to promptly trace changing trend of news?

We address the aforementioned challenges by the following ideas:

1. **Global temporal preference.** PGT extracts the global temporal preference from popular and fresh articles at recommendation time. The global temporal preference represents the time-dependent features and helps PGT consider newly published articles well (details in Sect. 3.2).
2. **RNN-attention using global temporal preference as context.** PGT embeds each user's personal preference from its watch history using an RNN with an attention network. The attention network determines the importance of each previous user behavior. We use the global temporal preference as context of the attention network to consider both popularity and freshness patterns (details in Sect. 3.3).

Figure 2 shows the overall architecture of PGT. We use Doc2Vec [10] to get embedding vectors for popular articles $popular_t$, fresh articles $fresh_t$, articles in a *session*, and candidate articles $cand_t$ at time t. PGT generates a prediction vector $\hat{y}_t$ from personal preference u_t and global temporal preference τ_t. Finally, PGT ranks candidate articles $cand_t$ by their similarities to $\hat{y}_t$.

3.2 Global Temporal Preference

Our goal is to generate a single vector of global temporal preference from several popular and fresh articles. The global temporal preference vector represents common interests shared by all users at a specific time. For the purpose, we adapt self-attention [15]; however, instead of generating vector representation for each key, we generate the single vector by computing the weighted average of article vectors using the attention weights. PGT generates the global temporal preference vector τ_t as follows:

$$v_{g_i} = \frac{1}{\sqrt{d_e}} e_i^T \sum_{e_j \in E} e_j$$

$$\tau_t = W_{g_a} \sum_{e_i \in E} \frac{exp(v_{g_i})}{\sum_j exp(v_{g_j})} e_i + b_{g_a}$$

where a linear layer, consisting of parameter W_{g_a} and b_{g_a}, calculates the global temporal preference vector $\tau_t \in \mathbb{R}^n$ at time t. The weighted average of popular and fresh article vectors $e_i \in E = \{popular_t \cup fresh_t\}$ passes through the linear layer where the weights come from the unnormalized attention score v_{g_i} for each article i.

3.3   Personal Preference

Considering individual user's personal preference is essential to make personalized news recommendations. We observe that each previous behavior of a user corresponds to a preference at that time. From this observation, we extract each user's personal preference from its previous watch history using an RNN model and aggregate them by an attention network to generate a vector representing the user's news preference. We use bi-directional LSTM (BiLSTM) in the RNN model since it is well known to summarize both the preceding and the following behaviors. Note that the hidden state h_i of BiLSTM represents the behavior of the user at time i. Then we aggregate all previous hidden states $h_1, \cdots, h_{t-1}$ with an attention network by utilizing the global temporal preference vector τ_t as context vector. The attention network traces the popularity and freshness patterns of online news services to highlight important previous hidden states.

PGT generates a personal preference vector u_t as follows:

$$h_i = f(s_i; \theta)$$
$$v_{u_i} = W_{u_a}[\tau_t, h_i] + b_{u_a}$$
$$u_t = \sum_i \frac{v_{u_i}}{\sum_j v_{u_j}} h_i$$

where f is a BiLSTM function, h_i is i-th hidden state vector in the session, and $s_i \in \mathbb{R}^{d_e}$ denotes the representation of the i-th selected article in the session. A linear layer, consisting of parameters W_{u_a} and b_{u_a}, takes a concatenated vector $[\tau_t, h_i]$ of τ_t and h_i as input, and then calculates the unnormalized attention score v_{u_i} for each hidden state. We generate the personal preference vector u_t at time t by calculating the weighted average of hidden states using attention scores.

3.4   Ranking Candidate Articles

To recommend news articles to a user, we rank candidate articles based on the user's interest at each time step. Ideally, candidate articles should include all of the existing news articles; however, in practice we need to narrow down candidates for scalability of recommender systems. We select candidate articles by removing unpopular articles at each time step. In the training process, we ensure that candidate articles contain the actually selected article at each time step by replacing the most unpopular candidate article with the actually selected article.

Given a session of a user, let $s_t \in \mathbb{R}^{d_e}$ denote the representation of the t-th selected article in the session. $\tau_t \in \mathbb{R}^n$ represents the global temporal preference at the t-th time step in the session. As discussed in Sect. 3.2, PGT generates τ_t utilizing both popular articles and fresh articles; this allows PGT to consider popularity and freshness as important factors for recommendation, which alleviates the cold-start problem. $u_t \in \mathbb{R}^n$ denotes a user's personal preference at the t-th time step in the session, allowing personalized news recommendation.

We generate the prediction vector $\hat{\boldsymbol{y}}_t$ as follows:

$$\hat{\boldsymbol{y}}_t = W_o[\boldsymbol{\tau}_t, \boldsymbol{u}_t] + \boldsymbol{b}_o$$

where the vector created by concatenating $\boldsymbol{\tau}_t$ and $\boldsymbol{u}_t$ is passed through a linear layer consisting of parameters W_o and $\boldsymbol{b}_o$. Then we rank candidate articles at the t-th time step based on the similarity to $\hat{\boldsymbol{y}}_t$.

We train PGT to minimize the L2 distance between the truly selected article vector $\boldsymbol{s}_t$ and the prediction vector $\hat{\boldsymbol{y}}_t$ as follows:

$$\mathcal{L}(\boldsymbol{s}_t, \hat{\boldsymbol{y}}_t) = \|\boldsymbol{s}_t - \hat{\boldsymbol{y}}_t\|_2.$$

We backpropagate gradients calculated from this loss function to the MLP, the RNN, and the attention network in PGT, while fixing the article embeddings. As a result, PGT is trained to reduce the distance between $\hat{\boldsymbol{y}}_t$ and $\boldsymbol{s}_t$, which leads to increasing the distance between $\hat{\boldsymbol{y}}_t$ and vectors of unselected articles.

4   Experiment

We run experiments to answer the following questions.

- **Q1. Accuracy (Sect. 4.2).** How well does PGT recommend news articles?
- **Q2. Effect of modeling global temporal preference (Sect. 4.3).** Does the modeling of global temporal preference help improve the accuracy?
- **Q3. Effect of attention network in personal preference (Sect. 4.4).** How well does the attention network for the personal preference help improve the accuracy?

4.1   Experimental Settings

Dataset. We use ADRESSA [1] and GLOBO [14] which are session-based datasets of news watch history (see Table 1). Adressa dataset[1] is generated from the behaviors of users in the Adresseavision, a newspaper media in Norway. The one week version ADRESSA 1W of the dataset contains news information from 1 to 7 January, 2017. The full version ADRESSA 10W of the dataset contains news information from 1 January to 31 March, 2017. The dataset contains URLs of all articles, and contents of a subset of the articles; articles with invalid URLs are removed. The second dataset GLOBO[2] [14] contains news information from a news portal G1 (G1.com) from 1 to 16 October, 2017. Instead of revealing the original news contents, it provides the embedding vector for each news article due to license restrictions.

---

[1] http://reclab.idi.ntnu.no/dataset.
[2] https://www.kaggle.com/gspmoreira/news-portal-user-interactions-by-globocom.

Table 1. Summary of news datasets.

Dataset	# Sessions	# Events	# Articles	Period
ADRESSA 1W[1]	112,405	487,961	11,069	7 days
ADRESSA 10W[1]	655,790	8,167,390	43,460	90 days
GLOBO[2]	296,332	2,994,717	46,577	16 days

Competitor. We compare the performance of our proposed PGT to the following competitors.

- **POP.** This method recommends the most popular items regardless of each user's personal preference.
- **Park et al.** [12]. To recommend the next article, this method ranks the candidate articles using a hidden vector generated from RNNs, and then reranks candidates by each user's long-term categorical preference. They also proposed a CNN model to infer missing categories of articles from their contents.
- **Okura et al.** [11]. This method recommends articles based on the similarity of articles using dot products of their vector representations. The method generates similar vector representations to articles with similar categories.
- **WEAVE&REC** [6]. This method utilizes the content of news articles as well as the sequence in which the articles were read by users. They use 3-dimensional CNN to embed both 1) the word embeddings of articles, and 2) the sequence of articles selected by users at the same time.
- **HRAM** [5]. This method aggregates outputs of two heterogeneous methods which are 1) user-item matrix factorization to model the interaction between users and items, and 2) attention-based recurrent network to trace the interest of each user.
- **NPA** [17]. This method uses personalized attention at both word-level and news-level to highlight informative words and news. The personalized attention uses the embedding of each user as context vector to differentially attend to important words and news according to personal preference.

Vectorized Representation of Article. For ADRESSA dataset, we train Doc2Vec model [10] with Gensim [13], which has shown a good performance on news recommendation [16]. We use sentences of each article if provided by the dataset, or use crawled sentences using the URL of it otherwise. We set the dimension of embedding vector to 1000, and the size of window to 10. We initialize α of Doc2Vec to 0.025, and decrease α by 0.001 for every 10 epochs. Note that these values are selected since they give the best result. For GLOBO dataset, we use the provided embedding vector for each article from it.

Evaluation Metrics. We evaluate the accuracy of methods using Hit Rate (HR) and Mean Reciprocal Rank (MRR). Given the probability ranks of truly seen news articles, we calculate HR@5 and MRR@20 as follows:

$$HR@5 = \frac{1}{|\mathcal{I}|} \sum_{i \in \mathcal{I}} |\{r_i | r_i <= 5\}|$$

$$MRR@20 = \frac{1}{|\mathcal{I}|} \sum_{i \in \mathcal{I}} c_i, \qquad c_i = \begin{cases} \frac{1}{r_i}, & \text{if } r_i \leq 20 \\ 0, & \text{otherwise} \end{cases}$$

where $i \in \mathcal{I}$ is an index of an article in the test data, and r_i is the estimated rank of i by a method. HR@5 is the proportion of predictions where the truth is within the top 5 articles with the highest scores. MRR@20 gives a higher score when r_i is more accurate but scores nothing if r_i is above 20.

Model Training. All of the competitors and our method are trained using the same hardware and early-stop policy. We divide our session data into training, validation [9], and test sets with ratio of 8:1:1 based on the user interaction time in a session. When a dataset consists of user interactions from 1 to 10 May, for example, data from 1 to 8 May is used as a training set, data on 9 May as a validation set, and data on the last day as a test set, respectively. This setting is useful to show the effect of the cold-start problem, since several fresh articles in the test set are not included in the training set.

Hyperparameters. We train methods to maximize the similarity between a prediction vector and the corresponding selected article vector for every time step. For PGT, we use the mean squared error (MSE) of the two vectors as a loss function, and Adam optimizer [8] as an optimizer. We use the hyperbolic tangent as a non-linear activation function, but omits it for the last MLP since it gives the best accuracy. For the competitors, we follow their best settings. We use mini-batched inputs of size 512 to feed models during training. When the validation loss keeps increasing for 10 epochs, we early stop training to prevent overfitting. All methods in our experiments early stopped before 200 epochs of training.

Table 2. Our proposed PGT shows the best performance for all of the datasets. This table shows the accuracy of PGT and competitors, measured with the hit rate (HR@5) and the mean reciprocal rank (MRR@20); higher values mean better performances.

Dataset	Metric	POP	Park et al. [12]	Okura et al. [11]	Weave&Rec [6]	HRAM [5]	NPA [17]	PGT
Adressa 1W	HR@5	0.4988	0.4714	0.4569	0.4377	0.5347	0.6512	**0.8668**
	MRR@20	0.3291	0.3361	0.3341	0.3013	0.3452	0.4983	**0.6857**
Adressa 10W	HR@5	0.5672	0.3677	0.3477	0.3007	0.3941	0.5819	**0.7106**
	MRR@20	0.3735	0.2461	0.2320	0.2101	0.2531	0.3818	**0.6197**
Globo	HR@5	0.2845	0.3551	0.3537	–	0.4474	–	**0.5663**
	MRR@20	0.2001	0.2483	0.2500	–	0.3101	–	**0.5116**

4.2   Recommendation Accuracy

Table 2 shows accuracies of PGT and competitors; WEAVE&REC and NPA, which require news contents, are not evaluated for GLOBO since it does not provide news contents. Note that PGT gives the highest accuracy compared to the competitors. We have the following observations from the results.

First, even though POP recommends news articles based only on the general popularity, the popularity pattern of news data (shown in Fig. 1) makes POP a strong baseline showing a good performance. Meanwhile, the performances of the other competitors (Park et al. [12], Okura et al. [11], HRAM, WEAVE&REC, and NPA) are less accurate especially in ADRESSA. It is because they consider only personal preference while users' behaviors in ADRESSA are more skewed toward the popularity pattern. Note that HR@5 of POP is the probability of watching one of the top 5 most popular articles. HR@5 of POP in ADRESSA 10W, ADRESSA 1W, and GLOBO are 0.5672, 0.4988, and 0.2845, respectively; this shows that users' interactions in ADRESSA are more skewed to popular articles which are more related to global temporal preference rather than personal preference. On the other hand, our proposed PGT shows the best performance even on ADRESSA compared to the other competitors by appropriately attending to personal and global temporal preferences.

Table 3. The global temporal preference and the attention network of PGT improve the accuracy of recommendation. PGT outperforms both 1) PGT$_{-T}$, a variant of PGT without the global temporal preference (Sect. 3.2), and 2) PGT$_{-A}$, a variant of PGT without the attention network of BiLSTM (Sect. 3.3).

Dataset	Metric	PGT$_{-T}$	PGT$_{-A}$	PGT
ADRESSA 1W	HR@5	0.6662	0.8497	**0.8668**
	MRR@20	0.5647	0.6756	**0.6857**
ADRESSA 10W	HR@5	0.6360	0.6946	**0.7106**
	MRR@20	0.5423	0.5610	**0.6197**
GLOBO	HR@5	0.5366	0.5562	**0.5663**
	MRR@20	0.4923	0.5035	**0.5116**

Second, the methods modeling each user's watch history by utilizing attention network (PGT, HRAM, and NPA) are more accurate compared to the other competitors (Park et al. [12], Okura et al. [11], and WEAVE&REC). The attention network dynamically attends to important previous behaviors, and thus increases recommendation accuracy. Meanwhile, due to the property of RNN, inference in RNN-based methods (Park et al. [12] and Okura et al. [11]) often neglects users' long-term behaviors. WEAVE&REC captures a temporal pattern of each user's watch history using 3-dimensional CNN, but provides poor recommendations to fresh users because of their insufficient watch histories.

Finally, HRAM and NPA, which train an embedding for each user, show poor performance compared to our proposed PGT. Note that we divide the dataset into training, validation, and test sets based on user interaction time (see Sect. 4.1), since such setting is more realistic for online news recommendation. However, this makes it very hard for HRAM and NPA to train the embeddings of fresh users well. On the other hand, PGT performs accurate news recommendation even in this case, by utilizing the global temporal preference.

4.3 Effect of Modeling Global Temporal Preference

PGT overcomes the cold-start problem by considering the global temporal preference. In Table 2, we compare the performances of PGT and other neural network based methods on ADRESSA 1W and ADRESSA 10W to show how well the global temporal preference helps preserve the accuracy from the cold-start problem, since the other methods neglect the global temporal preference. Note that all neural network based methods suffer from the cold-start problem more severely on ADRESSA 10W since the time gap between the train and the test set is the longest in it. MRR@20s of Park et al. [12], Okura et al. [11], WEAVE&REC, HRAM, and NPA decrease by 26.78%, 30.56%, 30.29%, 26.89%, and 21.42%, respectively, on ADRESSA 10W compared to those on ADRESSA 1W; on the other hand, MRR@20 of PGT decreases only by 9.12% on the same setting. This shows that PGT better handles the cold-start problem.

To further validate the effect of the global temporal preference in PGT, we evaluate the performance of PGT_{-T}, a variant of PGT, that does not use the global temporal preference, but keeps the attention network of BiLSTM by using the most recent hidden state vector as the context of attention. Columns PGT_{-T} and PGT of Table 3 show that 1) MRR@20 of PGT improves by 17.64%, 12.49%, and 3.77% on ADRESSA 1W, ADRESSA 10W, and GLOBO, respectively, and 2) HR@5 of PGT improves by 23.14%, 10.49%, and 5.24% on ADRESSA 1W, ADRESSA 10W, and GLOBO, respectively, compared to PGT_{-T} which does not use the global temporal preference. This result shows that the global temporal preference helps model popularity and freshness patterns well, leading to a better performance.

4.4 Effect of Attention Network in Modeling Personal Preference

We show the effect of the attention network in modeling personal preference, by evaluating the performance of PGT_{-A}, a variant of PGT, that gives uniform weights to all hidden states in the session RNN without utilizing the attention network. Columns PGT_{-A} and PGT of Table 3 show the accuracy improvements of PGT by the attention network. MRR@20 of PGT increases by 1.47%, 9.47%, and 1.58% on ADRESSA 1W, ADRESSA 10W, and GLOBO, respectively. HR@5 of PGT increases by 1.97%, 2.25%, and 1.78% on ADRESSA 1W, ADRESSA 10W, and GLOBO, respectively. This shows that the attention network highlights important previous hidden states, leading to a superior accuracy.

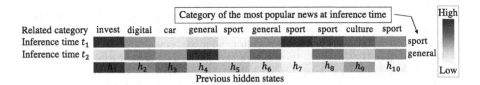

Fig. 3. Attention weights of previous hidden states derived from a sample news watch history. Note that the attention network reacts differently to the same news watch history when the inference time is changed. At times t_1 and t_2 where 'sport' and 'general' categories are popular, respectively, the attention network gives more weights to articles in the same categories.

We additionally perform a case study of the attention network to validate whether it effectively highlights important users' behaviors by considering popular topics. Figure 3 shows attention weights of a sample news watch history at two different inference times t_1 and t_2; a darker cell means a higher weight. At times t_1 and t_2 where 'sport' and 'general' categories are popular, respectively, the attention network gives more weights to articles in the same categories. This result illustrates that PGT dynamically models the personal preference by considering the popular topics at the inference time.

5   Conclusion

We propose PGT, a news recommender system which considers both personal and global temporal preferences to precisely reflect users' behaviors. We observe that the popularity and the freshness of articles, which decay quickly, play important roles in users' watch behaviors. Based on the observation, we introduce the concept of global temporal preference to news recommender system, to provide suitable recommendation results based on time. We also propose an attention based architecture to effectively deal with changes of users' personal preferences, with regard to the global temporal preference. Extensive experiments show that PGT provides the most accurate news recommendation, by considering both of personal and global temporal preferences. Future works include extending the method to handle multiple *heterogeneous* sessions.

Acknowledgments. The Institute of Engineering Research at Seoul National University provided research facilities for this work. The ICT at Seoul National University provides research facilities for this study.

References

1. Gulla, J.A., Zhang, L., Liu, P., Özgöbek, Ö., Su, X.: The Adressa dataset for news recommendation. In: WI (2017)
2. Hidasi, B., Karatzoglou, A., Baltrunas, L., Tikk, D.: Session-based recommendations with recurrent neural networks. In: ICLR (2016)

3. Hidasi, B., Quadrana, M., Karatzoglou, A., Tikk, D.: Parallel recurrent neural network architectures for feature-rich session-based recommendations. In: Proceedings of the 10th ACM Conference on Recommender Systems (2016)
4. Jeon, H., Koo, B., Kang, U.: Data context adaptation for accurate recommendation with additional information. In: IEEE BigData (2019)
5. Khattar, D., Kumar, V., Varma, V., Gupta, M.: HRAM: a hybrid recurrent attention machine for news recommendation. In: CIKM (2018)
6. Khattar, D., Kumar, V., Varma, V., Gupta, M.: Weave&rec: a word embedding based 3-D convolutional network for news recommendation. In: CIKM (2018)
7. Kim, Y.: Convolutional neural networks for sentence classification. In: EMNLP (2014)
8. Kingma, D.P., Ba, J.: Adam: a method for stochastic optimization. In: ICLR (2015)
9. Kohavi, R.: A study of cross-validation and bootstrap for accuracy estimation and model selection. In: IJCAI. Morgan Kaufmann Publishers Inc. (1995)
10. Le, Q.V., Mikolov, T.: Distributed representations of sentences and documents. In: ICML (2014)
11. Okura, S., Tagami, Y., Ono, S., Tajima, A.: Embedding-based news recommendation for millions of users. In: SIGKDD (2017)
12. Park, K., Lee, J., Choi, J.: Deep neural networks for news recommendations. In: CIKM (2017)
13. Řehůřek, R., Sojka, P.: Software framework for topic modelling with large corpora. In: LREC (2010)
14. de Souza Pereira Moreira, G., Ferreira, F., da Cunha, A.M.: News session-based recommendations using deep neural networks. In: DLRS@RecSys (2018)
15. Vaswani, A., et al.: Attention is all you need. In: Advances in Neural Information Processing Systems 30 (2017)
16. Wang, H., Zhang, F., Xie, X., Guo, M.: DKN: deep knowledge-aware network for news recommendation. In: WWW (2018)
17. Wu, C., Wu, F., An, M., Huang, J., Huang, Y., Xie, X.: NPA: neural news recommendation with personalized attention. In: SIGKDD (2019)

A Hybrid Recommendation for Music Based on Reinforcement Learning

Yu Wang[(✉)]

School of Electronics Engineering and Computer Science, Peking University, Beijing, China
wangyu18@pku.edu.cn

Abstract. The key to personalized recommendation system is the prediction of users' preferences. However, almost all existing music recommendation approaches only learn listeners' preferences based on their historical records or explicit feedback, without considering the simulation of interaction process which can capture the minor changes of listeners' preferences sensitively. In this paper, we propose a personalized hybrid recommendation algorithm for music based on reinforcement learning (PHRR) to recommend song sequences that match listeners' preferences better. We firstly use weighted matrix factorization (WMF) and convolutional neural network (CNN) to learn and extract the song feature vectors. In order to capture the changes of listeners' preferences sensitively, we innovatively enhance simulating interaction process of listeners and update the model continuously based on their preferences both for songs and song transitions. The extensive experiments on real-world datasets validate the effectiveness of the proposed PHRR on song sequence recommendation compared with the state-of-the-art recommendation approaches.

Keywords: Music recommendation · Hybrid recommendation · Reinforcement learning · Weighted matrix factorization · Markov decision process

1 Introduction

Recommendation systems have become indispensable for our daily life to help users navigate through the abundant data in the Internet. As the rapid expansion of the scale of music database, traditional music recommendation technology is difficult to help listeners to choose songs from such huge digital music resources. How to manage and recommend music effectively in the massive music library has become the main task of music recommendation system [1].

The mainstream recommendation algorithms can be classified as content-based [2, 3], collaborative filtering [5, 25], knowledge-based [6] and hybrid ones [7]. The collaborative filtering methods recommend items to users by exploiting the taste of other similar users. However, the cold-start and data sparse problem is very common in collaborative filtering. In knowledge-based approaches, users directly express their requirements and the recommendation system tries to retrieve items that are analogous to the users' specified requirements. The content-based recommendation approaches are to find items similar to the ones that the users once liked, and the content information or

H. W. Lauw et al. (Eds.): PAKDD 2020, LNAI 12084, pp. 91–103, 2020.
https://doi.org/10.1007/978-3-030-47426-3_8

expert label of items is also needed, but it does not require a large number of user-item rating records [4]. In order to improve performance, above methods can be combined into a hybrid recommendation system. The hybrid approach we use is feature augmentation, which takes the feature output from one method as input to another.

Nowadays, reinforcement learning [8] becomes one of the most important research hotspots. It mainly focuses on how to learn interactively, obtain feedback information in the action-evaluation environment, and then improve the choices of actions to adapt to the environment. In this paper, we propose a personalized hybrid recommendation algorithm for music based on reinforcement learning (PHRR). Based on the idea of hybrid recommendation, we utilize WMF-CNN model which uses content and collaborative filtering to learn and predict music features, and simulate listeners' decision-making behaviors by model-based reinforcement learning process. What's more, we establish a novel personalized music recommendation model to recommend song sequences which match listeners' preferences better. Our contributions are as follows:

- Our proposed PHRR algorithm combines the method of extracting music features based on WMF-CNN process with reinforcement learning model to recommend personalized song sequences to listeners.
- We make innovative improvements to the method of learning listeners' decision-making behaviors. And we promote the accuracy of model-learning by enhancing the simulation of interaction process in the reinforcement learning model.
- We conduct experiments in the real-world datasets. The experimental results show that the proposed PHRR algorithm has a better recommendation performance than other comparison algorithms in the experiments.

The rest of this paper is organized as follows. Section 2 reviews the related work. Section 3 presents details about the proposed PHRR algorithm. Section 4 introduces experimental results and analyses. In Sect. 5, we conclude our work.

2 Related Work

The recommendation system for music service differs from that for other service (such as movies or e-books), because the implicit user preferences on music are more difficult to track than the explicit rating of items in other applications. Besides, users are more likely to listen a song several times. In recent years, music recommendations have been widely studied in both academia and industry. Since music contains an appreciable amount of textual and acoustic information, several recommendation algorithms model users' preferences based on extracted textual and acoustic features [24].

What's more, the advanced recommendation approaches start to apply reinforcement learning [8] to the recommendation process, and consider the recommendation task as a decision problem to provide more accurate recommendations. Wang et al. [11] proposed a reinforcement learning framework based on Bayesian model to balance the exploration and exploitation of users' preferences for recommendation. To learn user preferences, it uses a Bayesian model that accounts for both audio content and the novelty of recommendations. Chen et al. [12] combined interest forgetting mechanism with Markov models because people's interest in earlier items will be lost from time to time. They believed that discrete random state was represented by random variables in Markov chain. Zhang et al. [15] took the social network and Markov chain into account, and proposed a PRCM recommendation algorithm based on collaborative filtering. Taking the influence of song transitions into account, Liebman et al. [13] added the listeners' preferences for the transitions between songs to the recommendation process and proposed a reinforcement learning model named DJ-MC. Hu et al. [14] integrated users' feedback into the recommendation model and proposed a Q-Learning based window list recommendation model called RLWRec based on greedy strategy, which traded off between the precision and recall of recommendation. It is a model-free reinforcement learning framework, and it has the data-inefficient problem without model.

Different from the previous research, we focus more on simulating interaction process of listeners based on their implicit preferences for songs and song transitions. Our main aim is to capture the changes of listeners' preferences sensitively in the recommendation process and promote the recommendation quality of music.

3 Our Approach

3.1 Music Feature Extraction

As the song transition dataset is not large enough to train a good model, we can do "transfer learning", i.e. the WMF-CNN process, from the larger Million Song Dataset [22]. To extract the music features, we use WMF [9, 17] to compute the feature vectors of some songs, which is an improved matrix factorization approach for implicit feedback datasets. The feature vectors calculated by WMF are used to train the CNN model [18] to learn the feature vectors of all other songs. Each song's feature vector only needs to be trained once, so it doesn't take a long time to train. Suppose that the play count for listener u listening to song i is r_{ui}, for each listener-song pair, we define a preference variable p_{ui} and a confidence variable c_{ui} (α and ϵ are hyper-parameters, and are set as 2.0 and 1e-6 respectively):

$$p_{ui} = \begin{cases} 1, r_{ui} > 0 \\ 0, r_{ui} = 0 \end{cases} \tag{1}$$

$$c_{ui} = 1 + \alpha log\left(1 + \epsilon^{-1} r_{ui}\right) \tag{2}$$

The preference variable p_{ui} indicates whether listener u has ever listened to song i or not. if it is 1, we assume that listener u may like song i. The confidence variable c_{ui} measures the extent to which listener u likes song i. The song with a higher play count is more likely to be preferred. The objective function of WMF contains a confidence weighted mean squared error term and an L2-regularization term, given by Eq. 3.

$$\min_{x^*y^*} \sum_{u,i} c_{ui}\left(p_{ui} - x_u^T y_i\right)^2 + \lambda\left(\sum_u ||x_u||^2 + \sum_i ||y_i||^2\right) \tag{3}$$

where λ is the regularization parameter set as 1e-5, x_u is the latent feature vector of listener u and y_i is the latent feature vector of song i.

In this paper, we use ResNet [26] as our CNN model, the input of the CNN model is mel-frequency cepstral coefficient spectrum (MFCC) [19] of songs, including 500 frames in the time dimension and 12 frequency-bins in the frequency dimension. The output vectors are the *20-dimensional* predicted latent feature vector of songs. The objective function of CNN is to minimize the mean squared error (MSE) and weighted predict error (WPE), given by Eq. 4 (θ representing the model parameters).

$$min_\theta \sum_i ||y_i - y_i'||^2 + \sum_{u,i} c_{ui}\left(p_{ui} - x_u^T y_i'\right)^2 \tag{4}$$

where y_i is the feature vector of song i calculated by WMF, and y_i' is the predicted vector of song i by the CNN model.

3.2 Problem Description

We model the reinforcement learning based music recommendation problem as an improved Markov decision process (MDP) [10], which is denoted as a five-tuple (S, A, P, R, T). And the framework is shown in Fig. 1. Given the song set $M = \{a_1, a_2, \ldots, a_n\}$, the length of song sequences to recommend is defined as k and the mathematical description of the MDP model for music recommendation is as follows.

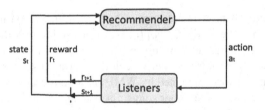

Fig. 1. Reinforcement learning framework for music recommendation.

State set S. The state set denoted as $S = \{(a_1, a_2, \ldots, a_i)|1 \le i \le k\}$ is the set of recommended song sequences including all intermediate states. A state $s \in S$ is a song sequence in the recommendation process.

Action set A. The action set A is the actions of listening to songs in M, denoted as $A = \{listening\ to\ song\ a_i|a_i \in M\}$. An action $a_i \in A$ means listening to song a_i.

State transition probability function P. We use abbreviated symbols $P(s, a, s') = 1$ to indicate that when we take action a in state s, the probability of transition to s' is 1, and 0 otherwise, i.e. $P((a_1, a_2, \ldots, a_i), a, (a_1, a_2, \ldots, a_i, a)) = 1$.

Reward function R. The reward function $R(s, a)$ obtains the reward value when listener takes action a in state s, and each listener has a unique reward function. One of our key problems is how to calculate the reward function of new listeners effectively.

Final state T. The final state denoted as $T = \{(a_1, a_2, \ldots, a_k)\}$ is the final recommended song sequence of length k.

Solving the MDP problem means to find a strategy $\pi : S \to A$, so that we can get an action $\pi(s)$ for a given state s. With the optimal strategy π^*, the highest expected total reward can be generated. However, the listener's reward function is unknown, so the basic challenge of song sequence recommendation is how to model R effectively.

3.3 Listener Reward Function Model

Towards our recommendation problem, the probability function P is already known, so the only unknown element is the reward function R. Most literatures about music recommendation only consider the listeners' preferences for songs, without considering their preferences for song transitions. The reward function R should consider the listeners' preferences both for songs and song transitions, as shown in Eq. 5.

$$R(s, a) = R_s(a) + R_t(s, a) \tag{5}$$

where $R_s : A \to R$ is the listener's preference reward for song a, and $R_t : S \times A \to R$ is the listener's preference reward for the song transition from song sequence s to song a.

Listener Reward for Songs. After extracting the features in Sect. 3.1, we obtain a *20-dimensional* song feature vector. Then we use the binarized feature vector by sparse coding of the feature vector to represent the song's features. As the feature vector is *20-dimensional*, it has 20 descriptors. Each descriptor can be represented as *m-bit* binarized feature factors, so the binarized feature vector of song a denoted as $\theta_s(a)$ is a *20 m-dimensional* vector. What's more, each listener has preference factors corresponding to binarized song feature factors respectively. For a *20 m-dimensional* binarized feature vector θ_s, listener u has a *20 m-dimensional* preference vector $\Phi_s(u)$. Therefore,

$$R_s(a) = \Phi_s(u) \cdot \theta_s(a) \tag{6}$$

Listener Reward for Song Transitions. When the listener listens to song a_j after song a_i, we note the reward function as $r_t(a_i, a_j)$. The song transition reward $R_t : S \times A \to R$ is based on a certain song sequence s and the next-song a to listen, as shown below.

$$R_t(s, a) = R_t((a_1, \ldots, a_{t-1}), a_t) = \sum_{i=1}^{t-1} \frac{1}{i^2} r_t(a_{t-i}, a_t) \tag{7}$$

In Eq. 7, the probability of the i-th song having influence on transition reward is $1/i$. And its influence is attenuated over time, so the i-th song's influence is reduced to $1/i$ times the original. As a result, the coefficient $1/i^2$ is the product of these two $1/i$ [13].

The calculation equation of $r_t(a_i, a_j)$ is similar to $R_s(a)$, as shown in Eq. 8. We use the sparse coding of song transition feature vector to generate the binarized feature vector $\theta_t(a_i, a_j)$. Each descriptor can be represented as m^2-bit binarized feature factors. Similar to $\Phi_s(u)$, listener u has a $20 m^2$-dimensional preference vector $\Phi_t(u)$ for the 20 m^2-dimensional binarized feature vector $\theta_t(a_i, a_j)$.

$$r_t(a_i, a_j) = \Phi_t(u) \cdot \theta_t(a_i, a_j) \tag{8}$$

Listener Preference for Songs. We keep the listener's historical song sequence whose length is longer than k_s. In order to make $\Phi_s(u)$ tend to be uniform, we initialize each factor of the vector $\Phi_s(u)$ to $1/(k_s + bins)$, where $bins$ indicates the discretization granularity of song feature and the value is same as m above. For each song a_i in the listener's historical song sequence, $\Phi_s(u)$ adds $1/(k_s + bins) * \theta_s(a_i)$ iteratively so the feature of song a_i can be learned. After $\Phi_s(u)$ is calculated, we normalize $\Phi_s(u)$ so that the weights of *m-bit* factors corresponding to each descriptor sum to 1 respectively.

Listener Preference for Song Transitions. Similar to the process of $\Phi_s(u)$, the length of song transition sequence is $k_s - 1$ noted as k_t. In order to make $\Phi_t(u)$ tend to be uniform, we also initialize each factor of the vector $\Phi_t(u)$ to $1/(k_t + bint)$, and the value of $bint$ is $bins * bins$. Obviously, the song transition pattern of historical song sequence is the best transition pattern that listener prefers. For each transition from a_i to a_j in historical song sequence, $\Phi_t(u)$ adds $1/(k_t + bint) * \theta_t(a_i, a_j)$ iteratively. After $\Phi_t(u)$ is calculated, we normalize $\Phi_t(u)$ in the same way as $\Phi_s(u)$.

3.4 Next-Song Recommendation Model

In order to reduce the time and space complexity of processing, we utilize the hierarchical searching heuristic method [20] to recommend next-song. And search is only performed from the search space where R_s is relatively high (line 1). Besides, we take the horizon problem similar to the Go algorithm into account, which chooses the first step of the path with highest total reward as the next step (lines 9-14).

Algorithm 1: *Recommend next-song by hierarchical searching*

Input: Song dataset M; the length of horizon h
Output: The next-song to recommend *recSong*
1. Select upper median of M as M^* based on R_s
2. $bestList \leftarrow []$, $highestReward \leftarrow -\infty$
3. **while** computational power not exhausted **do**
4. $list \leftarrow []$
5.   **for** $i = 1$ to h **do**
6. $songType \leftarrow$ select randomly from $songTypes(M^*)$ (avoid repetition)
7.   Add $songType$ *(noted as st_i)* to $list$
8.   **end for**
9. $allReward := R_s(st_1) + \sum_{i=2}^{h}(R_t((st_1, ..., st_{i-1}), st_i) + R_s(st_i))$
10.   **if** $allReward > highestReward$ **do**
11. $highestReward := allReward$
12. $bestList := list$
13. $songT :=$ first song type of $bestList$
14.   **end if**
15. **end while**
16. $recSong \leftarrow$ select the song with highest R_s from $songT$ (avoid repetition)
17. **return** $recSong$

Since the song space is too large, it is not feasible to select songs from the complete song dataset M. To alleviate this problem, we cluster songs by song type to reduce the complexity of searching (line 6). Clustering by song type is achieved by applying δ-medoids algorithm [21], which is a method for representative selection.

3.5 Song Sequence Recommendation and Update Model

To recommend song sequence, we define r_{adj} as $log(r_i/\bar{r})$, which determines the direction and size of update (lines 2-5). If r_{adj} is a positive value, it means that the listener likes the recommended song and the update direction is positive, and vice versa. And the relative contributions of the song reward R_s and the song transition reward r_t to their total reward are calculated as w_s and w_t respectively, as shown in Eq. 9 and Eq. 10.

$$w_s = \frac{R_s(a_i)}{R_s(a_i) + r_t(a_{i-1}, a_i)} \tag{9}$$

$$w_t = \frac{r_t(a_{i-1}, a_i)}{R_s(a_i) + r_t(a_{i-1}, a_i)} \tag{10}$$

$$\Phi_s = \frac{i}{i+1} \cdot \Phi_s + \frac{1}{i+1} \cdot \theta_s \cdot w_s \cdot r_{adj} \tag{11}$$

$$\Phi_t = \frac{i}{i+1} \cdot \Phi_t + \frac{1}{i+1} \cdot \theta_t \cdot w_t \cdot r_{adj} \tag{12}$$

Besides, the preference vector Φ_s and Φ_t are updated based on r_{adj}, w_s and w_t, and need to be normalized. This update process considers the changes of listener's interest over time and balances the degree of trusting history with new rewards (line 6-7).

Algorithm 2: *Song sequence recommendation*

Input: Song dataset M; length of song sequence to recommend K
Output: Recommended song sequence *songlist*
1. **for** $i = 1$ to K **do**
2.   Use Algorithm 1 to select song a_i
3.   The i-th song's total reward $r_i := R_s(a_i) + \sum_{j=1}^{i-1} \frac{1}{j^2} r_t(a_{i-j}, a_i)$
4. $\bar{r} :=$ average($\{r_1, ..., r_{i-1}\}$)
5. $r_{adj} := \log(r_i/\bar{r})$
6.   Update w_s, w_t, Φ_s, Φ_t using Eq.9 - Eq.12
7.   Per $f \in descriptors$, normalize Φ_s^f, Φ_t^f
8. **end for**
9. **return** *songlist* $= \{a_1, ..., a_K\}$

---

4 Experiment

4.1 Datasets

Million Song Dataset. Million Song Dataset (MSD) [22] is a dataset of audio feature for 1 million songs, providing powerful support for the CNN model to learn and extract music features. The dataset is available at http://labrosa.ee.columbia.edu/millionsong/.

Taste Profile Subset Dataset. Taste Profile Subset Dataset [22] as shown in Table 1 is in the form of *listener-song-play count* triple, providing a sufficient amount of dataset for WMF. The dataset is available at https://labrosa.ee.columbia.edu/millionsong/.

Historical Song Playlist Dataset. The dataset is collected from the music website Yes.com [23], which is available at http://lme.joachims.org/. As shown in Table 2, it contains 51,260 historical song sequences.

Table 1. A dataset of listener-song-playcount

#Listeners	#Songs	#Triplets
1000000	380000	48712660

Table 2. Listeners' historical song playlist dataset

#Playlists	#Songs	#Song Transitions
51260	85262	2840554

4.2 Comparison Algorithms and Evaluation Methods

Comparison Algorithms. We compare PHRR with baselines as below. For historical song playlist dataset, we use 90% of the dataset for training and the rest 10% for testing.

PHRR-S: PHRR-S algorithm is just the PHRR recommendation algorithm without taking song transitions into account.

DJ-MC [13]: DJ-MC algorithm is a reinforcement learning model added the listeners' preferences for the transitions between songs to the recommendation process.

PRCM [15]: PRCM algorithm is a collaborative filtering recommendation algorithm taking the social network and Markov chain into account.

PopRec [16]: PopRec algorithm recommends the most popular songs.

RandRec: RandRec algorithm recommends songs randomly.

Evaluation Methods. Our evaluation metrics include hit ratio of the recommended next-songs and F1-score of the recommended song sequences.

Hit Ratio (HR). We calculate hit ratio of the recommended next-songs for evaluation. In the historical song sequence dataset, the first n songs of each song sequence are used to recommend the n+1th songs. We compare the recommended n+1th song with the true n+1th song in the actual song sequence. If it is same, it is hit, otherwise it's not hit.

F1-Score (F1). The second evaluation indicator we use is F1-score. F1-score combines precision and recall of recommendation, and the *Score* calculated by Eq. 13 – Eq. 15 is used to evaluate the effect of song sequence recommendation.

$$Precision = \frac{|\{a \in S_p \cap a \in S_t\}|}{|S_p|} \tag{13}$$

$$Recall = \frac{|\{a \in S_p \cap a \in S_t\}|}{|S_t|} \tag{14}$$

$$Score = \frac{2 * Precision * Recall}{Precision + Recall} \tag{15}$$

where S_p represents the recommended song sequences, S_t represents the song sequences presented in the historical song sequence dataset and a indicates a song.

4.3 Experimental Results on Hit Ratio

The proposed PHRR algorithm is a recommendation algorithm to recommend song sequences. In this comparison experiment, the recommendation effects are measured by calculating the hit ratio of the recommended next-songs.

Performance Comparison on Hit Ratio. $HR@k$ is the hit rate of the most probable k songs of the recommended next-songs. The results of hit ratio of above recommendation algorithms are shown in Table 3, and the best results are boldfaced.

Table 3. Performance comparison on hit ratio

Algorithm	HR@10	HR@20	HR@30	HR@40	HR@50
PHRR	**0.1787**	**0.2394**	**0.2896**	**0.3302**	**0.3520**
PRCM	0.1255	0.1892	0.2356	0.2681	0.2897
DJ-MC	0.1232	0.1685	0.2110	0.2341	0.2462
PHRR-S	0.1016	0.1534	0.1965	0.2278	0.2619
PopRec	0.0651	0.0773	0.0916	0.1174	0.1289
RandRec	0.0060	0.0083	0.0101	0.0142	0.0186

Effect of Training Length of Song Sequence on Hit Ratio. Reinforcement learning process is based on the feedback of interactive information and simulates the decision behavior of listeners. The longer the length of training song sequence is, the more simulated interactions are in reinforcement learning process. The experimental results of the effect of training length on hit ratio are shown in Fig. 2(b).

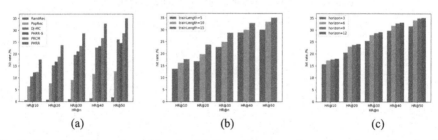

(a)   (b)   (c)

Fig. 2. Experimental results on hit ratio. (a) Comparison experimental results on hit ratio. (b) Effect of training length of song sequence on hit ratio. (c) Effect of horizon length on hit ratio.

Effect of Horizon Length on Hit Ratio. We consider the horizon problem similar to the Go algorithm when recommending next-song, that is, we choose the first song of the song sequence with highest total reward as the next-song (Algorithm 1). The experimental results of effect of horizon length on hit ratio are shown in Fig. 2(c).

Experimental Results and Analyses. The result of Fig. 2(a) shows that hit ratio of PHRR is 7% higher than PRCM, 10% higher than DJ-MC, 11% higher than PHRR-S, 20% higher than PopRec, and the hit ratio of RandRec is as low as 1%. The results of Fig. 2(b) indicates that when the training sequence length n is 15, the hit ratio is higher than when n is 10 or 5. The longer the training sequence length is, the higher the hit ratio of the recommended next-songs is, and the recommendation result will be more accurate. Figure 2(c) shows that, as the horizon length increasing, the hit ratio of the recommended next-songs also tends to be higher.

4.4 Experimental Results on F1-Score

In this section, we use F1-score as an evaluation indicator to measure the effect of above algorithms on song sequence recommendation.

Performance Comparison on F1-Score. The results of F1-score of above recommendation algorithms are shown in Table 4. F1@k represents the F1-score of the recommended song sequence whose length is k, and the best results are boldfaced.

Table 4. Performance comparison on F1-score

Algorithm	F1@3	F1@5	F1@10	F1@15	F1@20
PHRR	**0.2113**	**0.2472**	**0.2986**	**0.3432**	**0.3657**
DJ-MC	0.1738	0.1974	0.2610	0.3052	0.3374
PHRR-S	0.1640	0.1935	0.2421	0.2787	0.3068
PRCM	0.1365	0.1542	0.2098	0.2411	0.2576
PopRec	0.0354	0.0461	0.0697	0.1016	0.1262
RandRec	0.0042	0.0083	0.0186	0.0269	0.0325

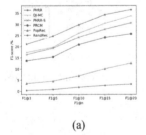
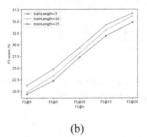
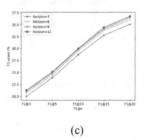

(a)   (b)   (c)

Fig. 3. Experimental results on F1-score. (a) Comparison experimental results on F1-score. (b) Effect of training length of song sequence on F1-score. (c) Effect of horizon length on F1-score.

Effect of Training Length of Song Sequence on F1-Score. Compared with other reinforcement learning based algorithms, the proposed PHRR promotes the precision by enhancing the simulation of interaction process. The experimental results of the effect of song sequence training length on F1-score are shown in Fig. 3(b).

Effect of Horizon Length on F1-Score. In the next-song recommendation stage (Algorithm 1), we only recommend the first song of the song sequence with highest total reward, instead of recommending this entire song sequence. Because as noise accumulating during the self-updating process, the variation of the model would be larger. The experimental results of the effect of horizon on F1-score are shown in Fig. 3(c).

Experimental Results and Analyses. As shown in Fig. 3(a), F1-score of PHRR is 4% higher than DJ-MC, 6% higher than PHRR-S, 11% higher than PRCM and 20% higher than PopRec on average. PHRR enhances simulating listener's interaction in the reinforcement learning process, while other algorithms don't consider it. Figure 3(b) presents that, when the song sequence training length n is 15, F1-score is higher than when n is 10 or 5. The longer training length can bring more chances to enhance the simulation of interaction. Figure 3(c) indicates that as the horizon length increasing, F1-score shows a slight higher. The horizon length shouldn't be too long, because too long horizon length is not significantly useful for improving the effect but increases the complexity.

5   Conclusion

In this paper, we propose a hybrid recommendation algorithm for music based on reinforcement learning (PHRR) to recommend higher quality song sequences. WMF and CNN are trained to learn song feature vectors from the songs' audio signals. Besides, we present a model-based reinforcement learning framework to simulate the decision-making behavior of listeners, and model the reinforcement learning problem as a Markov decision process based on listeners' preferences both for songs and song transitions. To capture the minor changes of listeners' preferences sensitively, we innovatively enhance the simulation of interaction process to update the model more data-efficiently. Experiments conducted on real-world datasets demonstrate that PHRR has a better effect of music recommendation than other comparison algorithms.

In the future, we will incorporate more human behavioral characteristics into the model. We also want to analyze the role of these characteristics for recommendation.

Acknowledgments. We would like to thank Kan Zhang and Qilong Zhao for valuable discussions. This work is supported by the National Key R&D Program of China (No. 2019YFA0706401), National Natural Science Foundation of China (No. 61672264, No. 61632002, No. 61872399, No. 61872166 and No. 61902005) and National Defense Technology Strategy Pilot Program of China (No. 19-ZLXD-04-12-03-200-02).

References

1. Bawden, D., Robinson, L.: The dark side of information: overload, anxiety and other paradoxes and pathologies. J. Inf. Sci. **35**(2), 180–191 (2008)
2. Pazzani, M.J., Billsus, D.: Content-based recommendation systems. In: Brusilovsky, P., Kobsa, A., Nejdl, W. (eds.) The Adaptive Web. LNCS, vol. 4321, pp. 325–341. Springer, Heidelberg (2007). https://doi.org/10.1007/978-3-540-72079-9_10
3. Aaron, V.D.O., Dieleman, S., Schrauwen, B.: Deep content-based music recommendation. In: NIPS, vol. 26, pp. 2643–2651 (2013)
4. Brunialti, L.F., Peres, S.M., Freire, V., et al.: Machine learning in textual content-based recommendation systems: a systematic review. In: SBSI (2015)
5. Fletcher, K.K., Liu, X.F.: A collaborative filtering method for personalized preference-based service recommendation. In: ICWS, pp. 400–407 (2015)
6. Koenigstein, N., Koren, Y.: Towards scalable and accurate item-oriented recommendations. In: RecSys, pp. 419–422 (2013)
7. Yao, L., Sheng, Q.Z., Segev, A., et al.: Recommending web services via combining collaborative filtering with content-based features. In: ICWS, pp. 42–49 (2013)
8. Francois-Lavet, V., Henderson, P., Islam, R., et al.: An introduction to deep reinforcement learning. Found. Trends Mach. Learn. **11**(3–4), 219–354 (2018)
9. Li, H., Chan, T.N., Yiu, M.L., et al.: FEXIPRO: fast and exact inner product retrieval in recommender systems. In: SIGMOD, pp. 835–850 (2017)
10. Puterman, M.L.: Markov Decision Processes: Discrete Stochastic Dynamic Programming. Wiley, Hoboken (2014)
11. Wang, X., Wang, Y., Hsu, D., et al.: Exploration in interactive personalized music recommendation: a reinforcement learning approach. In: TOMM, pp. 1–22 (2013)
12. Chen, J., Wang, C., Wang, J.: A personalized interest-forgetting markov model for recommendations. In: AAAI, pp. 16–22 (2015)
13. Liebman, E., Saartsechansky, M., Stone, P.: DJ-MC: A reinforcement-learning agent for music playlist recommendation. In: AAMAS, pp. 591–599 (2015)
14. Hu, B., Shi, C., Liu, J.: Playlist recommendation based on reinforcement learning. In: ICIS, pp. 172–182 (2017)
15. Zhang, K., Zhang, Z., Bian, K., et al.: A personalized next-song recommendation system using community detection and markov model. In: DSC, pp. 118–123 (2017)
16. Ashkan, A., Kveton, B., Berkovsky, S., et al.: Optimal greedy diversity for recommendation. In: IJCAI, pp. 1742–1748 (2015)
17. Hu, Y., Koren, Y., Volinsky, C.: Collaborative filtering for implicit feedback datasets. In: ICDM, pp. 263–272 (2008)
18. Kim, P.: Convolutional Neural Network. In: MATLAB Deep Learning, pp. 121–147 (2017)
19. On, C.K., Pandiyan, P.M., Yaacob, S., et al.: Mel-frequency cepstral coefficient analysis in speech recognition. In: Computing & Informatics, pp. 2–6 (2006)
20. Urieli, D., Stone, P.: A learning agent for heat-pump thermostat control. In: AAMAS, pp. 1093–1100 (2013)
21. Liebman, E., Chor, B., Stone, P.: Representative selection in nonmetric datasets. Appl. Artif. Intell. **29**(8), 807–838 (2015)
22. Bertin-Mahieux, T., Ellis, D.P.W., Whitman, B., et al.: The million song dataset challenge. In: ISMIR (2011)
23. Chen, S., Xu, J., Joachims, T.: Multi-space probabilistic sequence modeling. In: KDD, pp. 865–873 (2013)

24. Zhang, S., Yao, L., Sun, A., et al.: Deep learning based recommender system: a survey and new perspectives. ACM Comput. Surv. **52**(1), 1–38 (2019)
25. Wu, Y., Dubois, C., Zheng, A.X., Ester, M.: Collaborative denoising auto-encoders for top-n recommender systems. In: WSDM, pp. 153–162 (2016)
26. He, K., Zhang, X., Ren, S., et al.: Deep residual learning for image recognition. In: CVPR, pp. 770–778 (2016)

Relational Metric Learning with Dual Graph Attention Networks for Social Recommendation

Xiaodong Wang, Zhen Liu$^{(\boxtimes)}$, Nana Wang, and Wentao Fan

School of Computer and Information Technology, Beijing Jiaotong University,
Beijing 100044, China
jackwangsysu@gmail.com, {zhliu,nnwang,fwt.one}@bjtu.edu.cn

Abstract. Existing social recommenders typically incorporate all social relations into user preference modeling, while social connections are not always built on common interests. In addition, they often learn a single vector for each user involved in two domains, which is insufficient to reveal user's complex interests to both items and friends. To tackle the above issues, in this paper, we consider modeling the user-item interactions and social relations simultaneously and propose a novel metric learning-based model called RML-DGATs. Specifically, relations in two domains are modeled as two types of relation vectors, with which each user can be regarded as being translated to both multiple item-aware and social-aware representations. Then we model the relation vectors by neighborhood interactions with two carefully designed dual GATs to fully encode the neighborhood information. Finally, the two parts are jointly trained under a dual metric learning framework. Extensive experiments on two real-world datasets demonstrate that our model outperforms the best baseline by 1.91% to 4.74% on three metrics for top-N recommendation and the performance gains are more significant under the cold-start scenarios.

Keywords: Social recommendation · Metric learning · Graph attention networks · Neighborhood interactions

1 Introduction

Nowadays people are troubled by the information overload problem caused by the explosively growing online contents. Recommendation system, which aims at addressing this problem by providing personalized items to each user, has become an indispensable element of many web applications. Recently, top-N recommendation based on implicit feedback has attracted much research interest since implicit feedback is much more abundant and easier to collect in practice [10]. Among the various recommendation methods, collaborative filtering (CF) stands out to show good performance, with the assumption that similar users tend to share similar preferences [11,17]. However, the performance of CF models are often hindered by the data sparsity and cold-start issues [3].

© Springer Nature Switzerland AG 2020
H. W. Lauw et al. (Eds.): PAKDD 2020, LNAI 12084, pp. 104–117, 2020.
https://doi.org/10.1007/978-3-030-47426-3_9

With the prevalence of the online social platforms, social recommendation has emerged as a promising solution to address the above two issues. It assumes that people tend to spread their interests to their social connections and focuses on combing social information with user-item interactions for better item recommendations [19]. In conventional social recommenders [8,12], social relations are typically modeled as an ensemble term or a regularization based on the matrix factorization (MF). There also exists hybrid models which collectively factorize the user-item interaction matrix and trust matrix [4]. Recently, researchers also designed more advanced neural models for social recommendation and showed state-of-the-art performance [1,2,18]. E.g., [1] models both aspect-level and friend-level differences for social recommendation by attention mechanism and memory network. Although the above models are effective, we argue that they have three common limitations: Firstly, they typically incorporate all social relations into user preference modeling, ignoring the fact that users may have totally opposite tastes on specific items. Secondly, they often learn a single vectorized representation for each user, which is insufficient to reveal user's complex interests to both items and friends. Finally, none of them have fully considered the neighborhood information in both domains.

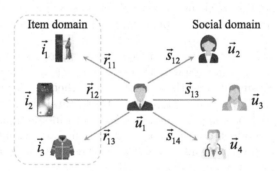

Fig. 1. The two kinds of relation vectors.

In this paper, we focus on implicit feedback and propose a dual metric learning framework to handle the above issues. As users involve in two heterogeneous graphs, we model the user-item interactions and social relations simultaneously instead of directly incorporating social information into user embeddings. Specifically, as shown in Fig. 1, we propose to model the two kinds of relations as interaction vector (e.g., r_{11}) and social vector (e.g., s_{12}) respectively. Then in the metric space, each user can be regarded as being translated to both mulitple item-aware points by the interaction vectors or to multiple social-aware points by the social vectors, which results in a much finer-grained model. In addition, from the perspective of CF, each user-item pair can be seen as being related by their respective neighboring items and users. Analogously, two users in the social domain are also connected by their neighboring friends. Therefore, we model the two kinds of relation vectors by neighborhood interactions, in which neighborhood-based representations in the two domains are generated by two carefully designed dual GATs [16]. Then they are fed into two corresponding MLPs to model the complex interactions between two neighborhoods as relation vectors. Finally, the two relation modeling parts are incorporated into a joint model to mutually enhance each other.

Our main contributions are summarized as followings:

- We propose a novel social recommendation model RML-DGATs which considers utilizing social information by simultaneously modeling the user-item interactions and social relations under a dual metric learning framework.
- Relations in two domains are modeled as relation vectors to translate each user to both multiple item-aware and social-aware representations. We model the two kinds of relation vectors by two carefully designed dual GATs, which could fully encode the neighborhood information in an explicit manner.
- Under extensive experiments conducted on two real-world datasets, our model consistently outperforms state-of-the-art baselines on three metrics for top-N recommendation tasks, especially in the cold-start scenarios.

2   Related Work

Top-N recommendation with implicit feedback has attracted more and more research interest due to its good applicability in practice [10]. However, traditional MF approaches are incapable of handling such a scenario for the absence of negative feedback. To address this issue, [14] first proposed a pairwise ranking assumption tailored for implicit feedback which states that user tend to rank items she consumed over those unobserved, then it optimizes MF with BPR-OPT criterion. [5] further extends MF to a neural architecture to model the implicit feedback as complex nonlinear user-item interactions. Recently, [7] argues that inner product used in most previous methods violates the import triangle inequality property and adopts the Euclidean distance as the relation modeling metric.

To alleviate the data sparsity and cold-start issues, many efforts has been devoted to incorporate social relations for better recommendation. These studies could be broadly categorized into two groups: MF-based and DNN-based. MF-based methods typically take social information as an ensemble term or a regularization. [22] extends BPR with the assumption that users tend to rank items consumed by their friends over those unobserved. [4] collectively factorizes the rating matrix and trust matrix to share the same user latent vectors. However, the above MF-based methods could only capture linear information encoded in social network, so several recent studies proposed to learn more complex features using deep neural networks [1,2,18]. Authors in [2] designed a NSCR model based on NCF [5] to model the social relations as a graph regularization. To learn non-linear features of each user from social relations, [18] presented a deep model which substitutes the user latent modelling part of PMF with DNN. A newly proposed method SAMN [1] leveraged attention-based memory network to model both aspect-level and friend-level differences for social recommendation.

3 The Proposed Model

In this section, we introduce the proposed RML-DGATs model and the overall architecture is shown in Fig. 2. We start with formulating the social recommendation problem concerned in this paper and then elaborate the three main components of the model: the ID Embedding part, the Relation Modeling part and the Joint Learning part.

3.1 Problem Formulation

Let $G = (U \cup I, Y)$ be the user-item interaction graph, where U is the user set with n users and I is the item set with m items. $Y \in R^{n \times m}$ is the user-item interaction matrix with $Y_{ui} = 1$ if user u has interacted with item i, otherwise $Y_{ui} = 0$. As social connections can be unilateral (e.g., followings on Twitter) or bilateral (e.g., friendships on Facebook), we describe the social network as a directed graph $S = (U, T)$. $T \in R^{n \times n}$ represents the social relations between users which satisfies $T_{uv} = 1$ if user v is in user u's trust list. Note that we term u as the truster and v as the trustee in T_{uv}. Then, the social recommendation problem can be described as:

Social Recommendation. Given an user-item interaction graph G and a social network S, the social recommendation aims to learn a mapping function f to predict users' preferences to items as: $\hat{R}_{ui} = f(G, S)$, where $\hat{R}_{ui} \in R^{n \times m}$ is the predicted preference scores.

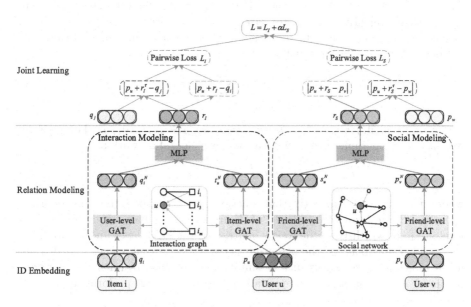

Fig. 2. The proposed RML-DGATs model.

3.2   ID Embedding Part

Let $P \in R^{n \times d}$ and $Q \in R^{m \times d}$ denote the low-dimensional embedding matrices of users and items, with d represents the dimension size of latent vectors. Given an user u, one of her interacted item i and an user v in her trust list, the ID Embedding part takes one-hot representation of triplet (u, i, v) as input and performs indexing operations from P and Q according to their one-hot IDs. Then it outputs the corresponding latent vectors p_u, q_i and p_v for u, i and v, respectively. Note that p_u could be regarded as the shared essential preference between the item and social domains.

3.3   Relation Modeling Part

The Relation Modeling part aims to model the user-item interaction relations and user-user social relations simultaneously. Next we will detail the user-item interaction modeling and social modeling respectively.

Interaction Modeling. In the user-item interaction graph, the items user has interacted form its neighborhood and they can reflect her preferences to some extent. Analogously, item's neighbors are the users who interacted with it and its attributes could be revealed by these users. We propose a dual GATs which consists of an user-level GAT and an item-level GAT to aggregate item's or user's neighborhood information.

User-Level GAT. Let $N(i)$ be the set of users who have interacted with item i. The user-level GAT aggregates latent vectors of item i and users in $N(i)$ attentively and then outputs the neighborhood-based item representation q_i^N. We define the aggregation function as:

$$q_i^N = \sigma(W \cdot \sum_{j \in N(i) \cup i} \alpha_{ij} h_{ij}) \tag{1}$$

where $h_{ij} = q_i$ if $j = i$, otherwise $h_{ij} = p_j$ for $j \in N(i)$. α_{ij} is the attention weight and we parameterize it with a two-layer neural network as:

$$\alpha_{ij} = Softmax(h^T \cdot \sigma(W' \cdot [q_i, h_{ij}] + b)) \tag{2}$$

where σ is the nonlinear activation function and $[,]$ denotes the concatenation operation. In addition, $\Theta_1 = [W, W', h, b]$ are the model parameters of the user-level GAT, in which W is the weight matrix for the GAT layer and W', h, b are the weights and bias for the attention network. Note that we also tried other forms of attention networks such as simple inner product or inner product with nonlinear activation, but we empirically found that Eq. (2) performs best.

Item-Level GAT. Latent vectors of user u and its neighboring items in $C(u)$, namely the set of items u has interacted, are aggregated to generate the neighborhood-based user representation t_u^N in item domain. Analogously, we define the aggregation function as:

$$t_u^N = \sigma(W \cdot \sum_{j \in C(u) \cup u} \beta_{uj} h_{uj}) \tag{3}$$

$$\beta_{uj} = Softmax(h^T \cdot \sigma(W' \cdot [p_u, h_{uj}] + b)) \tag{4}$$

where $h_{uj} = p_u$ if $j = u$, otherwise $h_{uj} = q_j$ for $j \in C(u)$.

Then a MLP which takes the two representations as input is designed to model the complex interactions between the two neighborhoods as the *interaction vector* r_I. Formally, we empirically design a two-layer tower structure as:

$$r_I = \sigma(W_2 \cdot \sigma(W_1 \cdot [q_i^N, t_u^N] + b_1) + b_2) \tag{5}$$

where W_1, W_2, b_1 and b_2 are the weights and biases of the MLP and we denote them as $\Theta_2 = [W_1, W_2, b_1, b_2]$.

Social Modeling. The social relation between two users can be seemed as related by their respective neighborhoods including themselves. Given user u and user v in her trust list, we propose another dual GATs which consists of two friend-level GATs to aggregate user's neighboring friends into neighborhood-based user representation.

Friend-Level GAT. For user u, the latent vectors of u and users in her trust list denoted as $v \in N(u)$ are aggregated into the neighborhood-based user representation s_u^N in social domain. We define the aggregation function as:

$$s_u^N = \sigma(W \cdot \sum_{j \in N(u) \cup u} \mu_{uj} h_{uj}) \tag{6}$$

$$\mu_{uj} = Softmax(h^T \cdot \sigma(W' \cdot [p_u, h_{uj}] + b)) \tag{7}$$

For user v, her neighborhood-based representation p_v^N is generated by the same friend-level GAT and we only need to replace p_u with p_v. Then we also model the *social vector* r_S by feeding s_u^N and p_v^N into a two-layer MLP as:

$$r_S = \sigma(W_2 \cdot \sigma(W_1 \cdot [s_u^N, p_v^N] + b_1) + b_2) \tag{8}$$

Note that we use the same parameters $\Theta_1 = [W, W', h, b]$ for the four different GATs and $\Theta_2 = [W_1, W_2, b_1, b_2]$ for the two MLPs, as we empirically found that it works the best. The rationale behind maybe that users and items share similar neighborhood structures and unifying them to train the same parameters booms the training process and reduce the risk of overfitting. In addition, as the number of users' or items' neighbors vary greatly, traversing all of them is time consuming and also may introduce too much noise. Therefore, we set a threshold K and for those nodes with more than K neighbors, we randomly sample K of them to aggregate their features.

3.4   Joint Learning Part

Scoring Functions. Since we consider the user-item interactions and social relations individually, we define the following two scoring functions to evaluate the qualities of interaction vector and social vector learned by the Relation Modeling part:

$$s_1(u,i) = \|p_u + r_I - q_i\|_2^2, \; s_2(u,v) = \|p_u + r_S - p_v\|_2^2 \tag{9}$$

Given latent vectors of user u, item i and their relation vector r_I, the interaction scoring function $s_1(u,i)$ penalizes any deviation of $p_u + r_I$ from q_i brought by the relation vector r_I. Analogously, the social scoring function $s_2(u,v)$ calculates the distance between user's translated vector $p_u + r_S$ and p_v. The smaller the scoring values s_1 and s_2 are, the higher preference user u will show to item i and the more user u will trust user v.

Loss Function. We adopt the widely-used pairwise hinge loss which was tailored for item-ranking task [7]. For each positive tuple (u,i) which satisfies $Y_{ui} = 1$, we pair it with t sampled negative tuples (u,j) to form the the pairwise training set in item domain as $D_I = \{(u,i,j)|Y_{ui} = 1 \wedge Y_{uj} = 0\}$, where t is the negative sampling ratio. Then we define the loss function in the item domain as:

$$L_I^p = \sum_u \sum_{(u,i,j)\in D_I} max(0, s_1(u,i) + \tau_I - s_1(u,j)) \tag{10}$$

τ_I works as the margin to ensure that the distance score between a positive user-item pair after translation is smaller than that between a negative pair, and a larger setting value of τ_I will push the two pairs far away from each other. Similarly, the loss function in the social domain is defined as:

$$L_S^p = \sum_u \sum_{(u,v,w)\in D_S} max(0, s_2(u,v) + \tau_S - s_2(u,w)) \tag{11}$$

where $D_S = \{(u,v,w)|T_{uv} = 1 \wedge T_{uw} = 0\}$ is the pairwise training set in social domain. Note that D_S is constructed in the same way as D_I and the margin τ_S functions similarly to τ_I.

Regularizations. Motivated by [13], we design two kinds of regularizers for our RML-DGATs model. As we translate each user u to her interacted item i (or user v in her trust list) by the interaction vector r_I (or social vector r_S), we define two distance regularizers to explicitly pull the translated user embedding closer to corresponding item or trustee embedding as:

$$reg_{dist}^I = \sum_u \sum_{i\in C(u)} s_1(u,i), \; reg_{dist}^S = \sum_u \sum_{v\in N(u)} s_2(u,v) \tag{12}$$

Furthermore, in order to explicitly encode the collaborative information in the user's (or item's) neighborhood, we design two neighborhood regularizers to guide users and items to be closer to their neighborhood representations as:

$$reg_{nbr}^I = \sum_u \|p_u - t_u^N\|_2^2 + \sum_i \|q_i - q_i^N\|_2^2, \; reg_{nbr}^S = \sum_u (\|p_u - s_u^N\|_2^2 + \|p_v - p_v^N\|_2^2)$$

(13)

Based on the pairwise loss functions and the two kinds of regularizers, the overall losses in two domains can be formulated as:

$$L_I = L_I^p + \lambda_1 reg_{dist}^I + \lambda_2 reg_{nbr}^I, \; L_S = L_S^p + \lambda_1 reg_{dist}^S + \lambda_2 reg_{nbr}^S$$

(14)

where λ_1 and λ_2 are the regularization coefficients for the distance regularizers and neighborhood regularizers respectively. Finally, we integrate the two relation modeling parts into a joint learning framework and the overall objective function to be minimized is:

$$L = L_I + \gamma L_S$$

(15)

Model Training. To optimize the above objective function, we implement the proposed model with Tensorflow and train it with mini-batch Adam [5]. At the end of each mini-batch, all the user and item latent factors are constrained within a unit sphere as $\|v\|_2^2 \le 1$, to prevent overfitting and ensure the robustness of the model [7].

Table 1. Statistics of the datasets.

	#Users	#Items	#Interactions	#Links	#R_density	#S_density
Ciao	7292	34840	192960	192960	0.0761%	0.4144%
Epinions	21121	92860	644316	353227	0.0329%	0.1584%

4 Experiments

In this section, we conduct experiments on two real-world datasets to evaluate the proposed RML-DGATs model. We first elaborate the experimental settings and then show the overall performance comparison, followed by detailed parameters analysis and cold-start testing. Finally, ablation studies are conducted to further evaluate different parts of the proposed model.

4.1 Experimental Settings

Datasets. In our experiments, we used two publicly accessible datasets: Ciao[1] and Epinions[2], to evaluate the performance of the proposed model. They both

---

[1] http://www.jiliang.xyz/trust.html.
[2] https://alchemy.cs.washington.edu/data/epinions/.

contain user-item ratings information which scale from 1 to 5 and social relations. As done in many previous works [5,6], we transformed the observed ratings to 1 indicating the interactions between corresponding user-item pairs, and all the unobserved ratings to 0. Then we filtered out users whose rating records or number of social relations are less than 2, and also removed items rated by less than 2 users. The statistics of the preprocessed datasets are summarized in Table 1, where #Links denotes the number of social relations, #R_density and #S_density denote the density of interactions and social relations respectively.

Baselines. We compared our proposed RML-DGATs model with following eight baselines:

- BPR [14]: A widely used pairwise ranking model tailored for implicit feedback recommendation and it optimizes MF with BPR optimization criterion.
- FISM [9]: An item-based CF model which generates user's embedding by the items she consumed and learn the item similarity matrix by a low-rank assumption.
- NeuMF [5]: A recently proposed DNN-based model which integrates MF and MLP into a unified model and achieves the state-of-the-art performance.
- CML [7]: By learning a joint metric space which satisfies the triangle inequality, this model can capture users' finer-grained preferences and show strong performance.
- LRML [15]: It also adopts the idea of translating users to items by translation vectors, while it relies on memory network to learn the relation vectors.
- SBPR [22]: It assumes that users tend to prefer items consumed by her friends than those unobserved and extends the preferences order in BPR to get a finer-grained model.
- CUNE-BPR [21]: It extracts latent semantic friends using random walks and graph embedding and then incorporates them into BPR for ranking task.
- SAMN [1]: A newly proposed DNN-based social recommender which leverages attention-based memory network to model both aspect-level and friend-level differences.

These baselines could be categorized into three groups: the first three belong to CF methods, the subsequent two are built on metric learning and the remainings are social-aware models.

Evaluation Protocols. We adopt the widely used leave-one-out evaluation protocol to evaluate the above methods [9]. Specifically, for each user, we keep her latest two consumed items for validation and testing and the remaining items for training. In line with many previous studies [5,15], we randomly sample 999 negative items that the user didn't interact with along with the last interacted one for testing, as it's too time consuming to rank all unobserved items. In addition, we use three widely used ranking-based metrics HR, MRR and NDCG to measure the recommendation quality [20]. Then we repeated each experiment 5 times and report the average performance.

Parameter Settings. We initialized all the baselines by the parameters declared in the original papers and carefully tuned them to achieve the optimal NDCG@10 on the validation set. Note that we also pretrained the NeuMF model with MF and MLP as the authors did in [5]. For our model, we empirically set the learning rate to 0.001, $d = 128$, the size of attention vectors to 32, $\lambda_1 = \lambda_2 = 0.01$, $t = 4$ on both datasets, and $\tau_I = 0.25$, $\tau_S = 0.5$. Moreover, we set K to 20 and 30, γ to 0.2 and 0.1 on Ciao and Epinions respectively. We also adopted ReLU as the nonlinear activation for all GATs and MLPs after the tuning process.

Table 2. Top-K recommendation performance of different methods on two datasets. The best performance is in boldface and the second is underlined. * denotes the significance p-value < 0.05 compared with the best baseline.

Dataset	Metric	BPR	FISM	NeuMF	CML	LRML	SBPR	CUNE-BPR	SAMN	RML-DGATs	Improv.
Ciao	HR@10	0.2286	0.2076	0.2328	0.2302	0.2471	0.2364	0.2823	0.2964*	**0.3108**	4.62%
	MRR@10	0.1101	0.0942	0.1196	0.1183	0.1232	0.1165	0.1292	0.1378*	**0.1405**	1.91%
	NDCG@10	0.1379	0.1207	0.1385	0.1365	0.1473	0.1446	0.1704	0.1732*	**0.1803**	4.74%
	HR@20	0.3074	0.2847	0.3147	0.3129	0.3184	0.3282	0.3729	0.4028*	**0.4157**	3.11%
	MRR@20	0.1154	0.0996	0.1219	0.1228	0.1289	0.1213	0.1441*	0.1425	**0.1478**	2.47%
	NDCG@20	0.1579	0.1403	0.1601	0.1563	0.1703	0.1625	0.1861	0.2009*	**0.2066**	2.75%
Epinions	HR@10	0.4104	0.3842	0.4017	0.4118	0.4327	0.3749	0.4377	0.4406*	**0.4625**	4.74%
	MRR@10	0.2123	0.1983	0.2142	0.2240	0.2209	0.1944	0.2295*	0.2284	**0.2348**	2.24%
	NDCG@10	0.2591	0.2421	0.2489	0.2562	0.2586	0.2436	0.2598	0.2623*	**0.2728**	3.83%
	HR@20	0.5087	0.4850	0.5023	0.5051	0.5319	0.4868	0.5583	0.5749*	**0.6018**	4.46%
	MRR@20	0.2191	0.2053	0.2178	0.2241	0.2353*	0.1903	0.2317	0.2334	**0.2414**	2.54%
	NDCG@20	0.2839	0.2676	0.2881	0.2972	0.3017	0.2653	0.2806	0.2981*	**0.3080**	3.20%

4.2 Overall Performances

The recommendation performances of different methods are shown in Table 2. We can make the following observations from the table:

- Our proposed model RML-DGATs consistently outperforms all the baselines in all cases, including the two state-of-the-art neural methods NeuMF and SAMN and also the competitive metric learning model LRML. The improvements could be attributed to the finer-grained modeling of each user and the two carefully designed dual GATs in neighborhood interactions.
- Methods incorporating social information generally perform better than those utilizing only user-item interactions in most cases. For example, social recommender CUNE-BPR is superior to non-social models like BPR, FISM and CML. In addition, all with neural architectures, SAMN and our model significantly outperform NeuMF and LRML.
- LRML consistently show superior performances to all other non-social methods as it also adopts the idea of translating users to multiple item-aware representations. However, we empirically found that it underperforms our model when both considering only user-item interactions. This further demonstrates

the effectiveness of our model in modeling the relation vectors by neighborhood interactions.

4.3 Parameters Analysis and Cold-Start Testing

Parameters Analysis. We also conduct experiments to investigate the impacts of the number of sampled neighbors K, the joint learning weight γ and the margin value τ on the two datasets. The results on NDCG@10 are shown in Fig. 3, from which we have the following findings:

- Performances on the two datasets both boost quickly first and then decrease when K varies from 5 to 100. This is reasonable since when neighbors are not enough, the larger K is, the more beneficial information will be incorporated. However, once K exceeds a certain value, the performance will be harmed by the noise introduced by neighbors.
- With the increase of γ, performance on the two datasets also improve first and then decrease. Furthermore, the optimal results on the two dataset are both achieved when γ is relatively small (0.1 and 0.2 respectively). It conforms to the reality since the interaction modeling part in item domain dominates the recommendation task.
- The margin value τ shows similar impact as K and γ. With a relative small τ, users and items would be squeezed tightly in the Euclidean space and results in the geometrical restriction issue as CML [16]. However, if τ exceeds certain value, the similarities among users and items may not retain as they need to meet the distance requirements first.

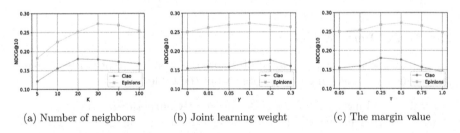

(a) Number of neighbors   (b) Joint learning weight   (c) The margin value

Fig. 3. Impacts of different parameters.

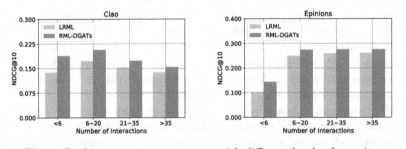

Fig. 4. Performances on user groups with different levels of sparsity.

Cold-Start Testing. In order to validate whether our proposed RML-DGATs model could mitigate the cold-start issue, we conduct experiments on different sparsity levels of user groups. Firstly, similar to [21], users are categorized into four groups according to the number of interacted items they have in the training set (i.e. <6, 6–20, 21–35, >35) and we term users in the first group as cold-start users. Then we take LRML as a baseline for its competitive performance as a non-social model. Results of the two methods on the two datasets w.r.t. NDCG@10 are shown in Fig. 4 (Results on HR@10 show similar trends). Compared with LRML, RML-DGATs achieves much better performance in all cases. Generally speaking, the sparser the training instances are, the more improvement will it obtain. For example, the relative improvements of our model on the four user groups are 6.32%, 4.15%, 3.76% and 2.43% respectively on Ciao. The rationale behind is that social information could work as the complement to user-item interactions and provide evidence to users' preferences. For users in the cold-start group which lack sufficient interactions, they will ask for more social relations to make up for the deficiency. In addition, Epinions achieves 3.71% of relative improvement in cold-start scenario, which is obviously smaller than on Ciao, this could be attributed to that interactions and social relations in Epinions are both much sparser than Ciao.

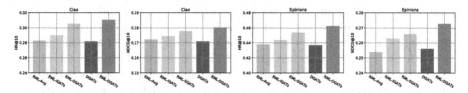

Fig. 5. Performances on different variants.

4.4   Ablation Study

The proposed RML-DGATs leverages two different relation vectors to model the complex relations between user-item in item domain and user-user in social domain. To investigate the effectiveness of the two dual GATs and the metric learning component, we compare our model with the following four variants:

- RML-Avg: This variant replaces the two dual GATs with mean operations, namely averaging neighbors' latent factors to obtain the corresponding neighborhood-based representations.
- RML-IGATs: The dual GATs in social domain are eliminated and mean aggregations are imposed.
- RML-SGATs: This variant is similar to RML-IGATs except that we remove the dual GATs in item domain instead.
- DGATs: It regards the inner product of two neighborhood-based representations in specific domain as the relation score and incorporates it into the log loss as NeuMF [15].

We report the results of all variants and the proposed model on two datasets w.r.t. HR@10 and NDCG@10 in Fig. 5. As shown in this figure, RML-IGATs and RML-SGATs both show better performances than RML-Avg, which demonstrates the importance of discriminating the contributions of different neighbors when aggregating their features. In addition, RML-SGATs performs better than RML-IGATs on the two metrics. The rationale behind may be that social connections does not necessary guarantee similar preferences while user's consumed items typically conform to her tastes. Therefore, considering the different contributions of social neighbors will bring more benefits. Furthermore, although all with two dual GATs, DGATs performs poorly than both RML-IGATs and RML-SGATs. This is not surprising since DGATs ignores the constructions of two relation vectors which could translate each user to both multiple item-aware and social-aware representations. Finally, our RML-DGATs consistently and significantly outperforms all the variants, which further verifies the effectiveness of the two carefully designed dual GATs in aggregating neighborhood information and also the metric learning framework for finer-grained user and item modeling.

5   Conclusions

In this paper, we propose a metric learning-based model named RML-DGATs for social recommendation. Specifically, user-item interaction and social relation in corresponding domains are modeled as interaction vector and social vector respectively. Then we model the two relation vectors by neighborhood interactions with two carefully designed dual GATs to fully encode the neighborhood information. Finally, the two domains are jointly trained to mutually enhance each other. Extensive experiments on two real-world datasets demonstrate the superiority of our model, especially in the cold-start scenarios. In the future, we are interested in exploring the dynamic diffusion of user's interests in social network.

Acknowledgement. This work was supported by the National Key R&D Program of China under grant No.2019YFB2102501.

References

1. Chen, C., Zhang, M., Liu, Y., Ma, S.: Social attentional memory network: modeling aspect-and friend-level differences in recommendation. In: WSDM, pp. 177–185 (2019)
2. Fan, W., Li, Q., et al.: Deep modeling of social relations for recommendation. In: AAAI (2018)
3. Guo, G., Zhang, J., Thalmann, D.: A simple but effective method to incorporate trusted neighbors in recommender systems. In: Masthoff, J., Mobasher, B., Desmarais, M.C., Nkambou, R. (eds.) UMAP 2012. LNCS, vol. 7379, pp. 114–125. Springer, Heidelberg (2012). https://doi.org/10.1007/978-3-642-31454-4_10
4. Guo, G., Zhang, J., Yorke-Smith, N.: TrustSVD: collaborative filtering with both the explicit and implicit influence of user trust and of item ratings. In: AAAI (2015)

5. He, X., Liao, L., et al.: Neural collaborative filtering. In: WWW, pp. 173–182 (2017)
6. He, X., Zhang, H., Kan, M.Y., Chua, T.S.: Fast matrix factorization for online recommendation with implicit feedback. In: SIGIR, pp. 549–558 (2016)
7. Hsieh, C.K., Yang, L., et al.: Collaborative metric learning. In: WWW, pp. 193–201 (2017)
8. Jamali, M., Ester, M.: A matrix factorization technique with trust propagation for recommendation in social networks. In: RecSys, pp. 135–142 (2010)
9. Kabbur, S., Ning, X., Karypis, G.: FISM: factored item similarity models for top-N recommender systems. In: KDD, pp. 659–667 (2013)
10. Koren, Y.: Factorization meets the neighborhood: a multifaceted collaborative filtering model. In: KDD, pp. 426–434 (2008)
11. Koren, Y., Bell, R., Volinsky, C.: Matrix factorization techniques for recommender systems. Computer 42(8), 30–37 (2009)
12. Ma, H., et al.: Learning to recommend with social trust ensemble. In: SIGIR, pp. 203–210 (2009)
13. Park, C., et al.: Collaborative translational metric learning. In: ICDM, pp. 367–376. IEEE (2018)
14. Rendle, S., Freudenthaler, C., et al.: BPR: Bayesian personalized ranking from implicit feedback. arXiv preprint arXiv:1205.2618 (2012)
15. Tay, Y., Anh Tuan, L., et al.: Latent relational metric learning via memory-based attention for collaborative ranking. In: WWW, pp. 729–739 (2018)
16. Veličković, P., et al.: Graph attention networks. arXiv preprint arXiv:1710.10903 (2017)
17. Wang, J., et al.: Unifying user-based and item-based collaborative filtering approaches by similarity fusion. In: SIGIR, pp. 501–508 (2006)
18. Wang, X., He, X., et al.: Item silk road: recommending items from information domains to social users. In: SIGIR, pp. 185–194 (2017)
19. Xu, G., et al.: Social networking meets recommender systems: survey. IJSNM 2(1), 64–100 (2015)
20. Yu, J., Gao, M., et al.: Adaptive implicit friends identification over heterogeneous network for social recommendation. In: CIKM, pp. 357–366 (2018)
21. Zhang, C., Lu, Y., et al.: Collaborative User Network Embedding for Social Recommender Systems (2017)
22. Zhao, T., McAuley, J., et al.: Leveraging social connections to improve personalized ranking for collaborative filtering. In: CIKM, pp. 261–270 (2014)

Modeling Users' Multifaceted Interest Correlation for Social Recommendation

Hao Wang[1(✉)], Huawei Shen[2], and Xueqi Cheng[2]

[1] Baidu Inc., Beijing, China
way_wh@yeah.net
[2] CAS Key Lab of Network Data Science and Technology,
Institute of Computing Technology, Chinese Academy of Sciences, Beijing, China
{shenhuawei,cxq}@ict.ac.cn

Abstract. Recommender systems suggest to users the items that are potentially of their interests, by mining users' feedback data on items. Social relations provide an independent source of information about users and can be exploited for improving recommendation performance. Most of existing recommendation methods exploit social influence by refining social relations into *a scalar indicator* to either directly recommend friends' visited items to users or constrain that friends' embeddings are similar. However, a scalar indicator cannot express the multifaceted interest correlations between users, since each user's interest is distributed across multiple dimensions. To address this issue, we propose a new embedding-based framework, which exploits users' multifaceted interest correlation for social recommendation. We design a *dimension-wise attention* mechanism to learn *a correlation vector* to characterize the interest correlation between a pair of friends, capturing the high variation of users' interest correlation on multiple dimensions. Moreover, we use friends' embeddings to smooth a user's own embedding with the correlation vector as weights, building the elaborate unstructured social influence between users. Experimental results on two real-world datasets demonstrate that modeling users' multifaceted interest correlations can significantly improve recommendation performance.

Keywords: Recommendation systems · Social influence · Interest correlation · Attention mechanism · POI recommendation

1 Introduction

Recommender systems suggest to users the items that are potentially of their interests [22] by mining users' feedback data on items [23]. Real-world recommender systems often allow users to build social relations [26], and such social relations provide an independent source of information about users beyond the

---

H. Wang—This work is done when Hao Wang was a Ph.D. candidate in Institute of Computing Technology, Chinese Academy of Sciences.

feedback information [13]. Social correlation theories [18], such as homophily and social influence, indicate that there are correlations between two socially connected users [2], which can potentially be used to exploit social relations for improving recommendation accuracy [25].

Many methods have been proposed for social recommendation in recent years, and these methods can be mainly grouped into two categories: (1) memory-based methods [1,12,14] use social relation as an indicator that filters relevant users and directly recommend friends' visited items to a user; (2) model-based methods [4,5,9,10,22,27,29,31] integrate social relation into factorization methods to constrain that friends share similar interest embeddings. Moreover, feedback-based similarities are utilized to weigh friends' interest relevance in memory-based methods [3] or embedding coherence in model-based methods [11,17]. In sum, existing methods refine two users' social relation into *a scalar indicator* to build their interest correlation.

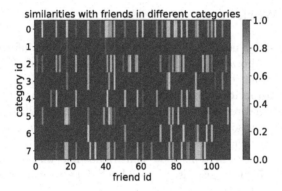

Fig. 1. Feedback-based similarities of 8 different categories between a random user and his 111 friends. We normalize similarities by the largest value in each category.

However, each user's interest is differently distributed across multiple dimensions, and the consistency in one dimension does not mean consistency in other dimensions. As Fig. 1 shows, a user's interest similarities with his friends vary greatly in different categories of items. When the user needs suggestions on one category, he may refer to friends with strong correlations on that category, and suggestions of friends with strong correlations on other categories are not useful. Therefore, a global scalar indicator used in existing methods cannot express the multifaceted interest correlations between friends. Unfortunately, there exists no explicit evidence to refine social networks into the elaborate correlation, and simply distinguishing items' categories would make the problem of data sparsity even more serious, which is not conducive to the learning of model parameters.

In this paper, we propose a new embedding-based social recommendation method (Fig. 2). We propose to use *a correlation vector*, instead of a scalar value, to characterize the interest correlation between each pair of friends, and design a dimension-wise attention mechanism with the social network as input to learn it. The correlation vector has the same dimension with user's embedding, thus can sufficiently capture the high variation in users' interest correlations on each fine-grained dimension. Moreover, we smooth a user's embedding by his friends' embeddings, with the correlation vector into consideration. The combination of the dimension-wise attention mechanism and the smoothing operation can impose strong and delicate unstructured correlations on users' embeddings while making interactions between users and items. Such an end-to-end framework allow the proposed method to learn the unstructured correlations in a fully data-driven manner.

We evaluate the proposed method by extensive experiments on two real-world datasets collected from Gowalla and Epinions respectively. Experimental results show that the proposed method outperforms the state-of-the-art social recommendation methods.

2   Related Work

Recommender systems normally utilize the user-item rating information for recommendation. Collaborative filtering [7] has become one of the most popular technologies, which achieves good recommendation results.

Social Recommender Systems leverage the social network information to enhance traditional recommendation methods [6,21,30,32]. According to the nature of the existing social recommendation techniques, we classify them into two main categories: memory-based methods [1,12,14] which normally directly or indirectly recommend users items that their friends like, and model-based methods [4,5,9–11,22,27,29,31] use users' social relations to constrain that friends share similar embeddings.

In sum, existing methods use a scalar value to build friends' interest correlation, which cannot sufficiently express their multifaceted interest correlations. Although Yang et al. [28] integrate items' category information to train a matrix factorization model for each category of items, they make data too sparse to learn parameters, and they cannot utilize correlations among different categories.

Attention Mechanism has recently been used in recommendation tasks [15, 16,24]. For example, Sun et al. [16] use attention to model the dynamic social influence for recommendation. However, they still express users' interest correlation by a scalar value, which cannot sufficiently capture the high variation of users' interest correlation.

3   Model

3.1   Problem Formulation

For ease of description, we first formalize variables used and the problem dealt with in this paper. We denote with U and I the set of users and the set of items respectively. For a user u and an item i, we denote with r_{ui} u's feedback to

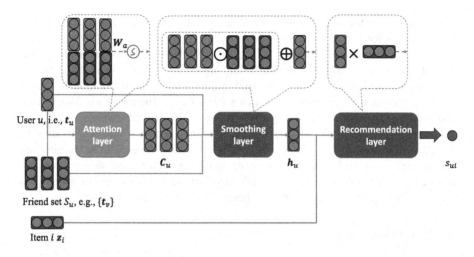

Fig. 2. Architecture of the proposed Dimension-wise Attention model for Social Recommendation, i.e., DASR. DASR infers a user u's preference to a candidate item i, with embeddings of the user u (t_u), user u's each friend v (t_v) and the item i (z_i) as the model input. DASR includes three parts, an attention layer for learning user u' correlation vectors with his friends, a smoothing layer for smoothing user u's embedding with embeddings of his friends, and a recommendation layer matching the preference between user u and item i.

item i. We use S to represent the social network over users in U. S_u represents user u's friend set and $S_{uv} = 1(0)$ indicates whether there exists social relation between user u and user v. In our model, we learn a preference vector t_u for each user u and a preference vector z_i for each item I.

Item Recommendation: Given a set of users U with social relations S, a set of items I and U's feedback over items I, item recommendation recommends for each target user $u \in U$ a list of items $\{i|i \in I\}$ consiting of items that the target user is potentially interested in and has not interacted with them up to the recommendation.

Next, we present the proposed Dimension-wise Attention model for Social Recommendation, i.e., DASR in Fig. 2.

3.2   Model Architecture

Users' interest is often differently distributed across multiple dimensions. To accurately capture friends' influence on user's preference, one needs to model the multi-dimensional interest correlation between users. Fortunately, attention mechanism seems to provide a feasible solution, since it can automatically models and selects pertinent piece of information with the attentive weights from a set of inputs, where higher (lower) weights indicate the corresponding inputs more informative to generate the outputs. To accommodate our problem, we further design a dimension-wise attention mechanism and use it to learn a correlation vector for each pair of friends, building their multi-dimensional interest correlation for social recommendation.

Figure 2 shows the architecture of DASR, which includes an attention layer, a smoothing layer and a recommendation layer. We learn a preference vector for each user and item, namely, t_u and z_i, and use DASR to infer a target user u's preference to a candidate item i with social influence of u's friends into consideration. Instead of directly performing inner product between t_u and z_i in the recommendation layer, we first use embeddings of user u's friends to smooth user u's own embedding in the smoothing layer, and the smoothing weights are the correlation vector learned in the attention layer. With these designs, we can learn strong and delicate unstructured correlations of users' embeddings in a fully data-driven manner and provide better item recommendation.

3.3   Attention Layer

We input the embeddings of the target user u and users in his friend set S_u to the attention layer, and compute the interest correlation vector between user u and each friend v.

We first use a weight matrix $\boldsymbol{W}_a$ to perform self-attention on user u and friend v as follows:

$$e_{uv} = LeakyReLU(\boldsymbol{W}_a^T(t_u\|t_v)), \tag{1}$$

where t_u and t_v are embeddings of user u and friend v. T represents transposition and $\|$ denotes the concatenation operation. $LeakyReLU(x) = max(0, x) + \beta min(0, x)$ acts as non-linear activation function with β as the negative slope. e_{uv} is the attention coefficient that indicates the importance of friend v's features to user u. To ensure that e_{uv} can express the correlation of each dimension in user's embeddings, we design $\boldsymbol{W}_a$ as a weight matrix with dimension $2d * d$.

For user u, we get an interest correlation matrix $\boldsymbol{C}_u$, and each column of $\boldsymbol{C}_u$ represents the correlation vector between user u and one of his friends. To make coefficients easily comparable across different friends, we normalize $\boldsymbol{C}_u$'s each row across all choices of v. We denote with $\boldsymbol{\alpha}_{uv}$ the normalized interest correlation vector between user u and friend v:

$$\boldsymbol{\alpha}_{uv} = \frac{exp(\boldsymbol{e}_{uv})}{\sum_{k\in S_u} exp(\boldsymbol{e}_{uk})}. \tag{2}$$

3.4   Smoothing Layer

For each friend v in user u's friend set S_u, we obtain a normalized correlation vector $\boldsymbol{\alpha}_{uv}$ to represent dimension-wise interest correlation between user u and user v.

We then smooth user u's embedding by adding each friend v's embedding with the correlation vector $\boldsymbol{\alpha}_{uv}$ serving as smoothing weight.

$$\boldsymbol{h}_u = \sigma(\sum_{k\in S_u} \boldsymbol{\alpha}_{uk} \odot \boldsymbol{t}_k + \boldsymbol{t}_u), \tag{3}$$

where h_u is user u's smoothing embedding. $\odot$ is the element-wise Hadamard product and $\sigma(z) = \frac{1}{1+e^{-z}}$ offers nonlinearity.

h_u consists of both user u's and his friends' embeddings, allowing the smoothing embedding not only to retain user u's own unique interest, but also to integrate his friends' interest. In this way, we can learn different patterns of each user's interest correlation, e.g., some users barely refer to their friends, while some users often refer to a few friends' suggestions, etc.

3.5 Recommendation Layer

In the recommendation layer, we use user's smoothing embedding, i.e., h_u, to make recommendation.

Denote p_{ui} as user u's preference to item i, and we compute p_{ui} as follows:

$$p_{ui} = h_u^T z_i, \tag{4}$$

where z_i denotes item i's embedding.

We define two types of objective functions according to the feedback type, including implicit feedback, e.g., users' check-in counts at POIs, and explicit feedback, e.g., users' rating scores to items. First, we define the objective function in a ranking manner. For each positive feedback (u, i), we randomly select c negative samples from item set I with item i excluded and denote the set of negative samples as $NEG(i)$. The objective function is defined as follows:

$$L(u, i) = - \sum_{j \in NEG(i)} \sigma(p_{ui} - p_{uj}). \tag{5}$$

The ranking-based objective function can be applied to both explicit feedback and implicit feedback.

Second, we define a square error-based objective function for explicit feedback only, in order to predict a user's rating score to an item:

$$L(u, i) = (p_{ui} - y_{ui})^2, \tag{6}$$

where y_{ui} is the user u's true rating score to item i.

Finally, for user u, we compute his preference to each item in I according to Eq. 4, and take top n items as the recommendation list.

4 Experiments

4.1 Datasets

We use two real-world datasets collected from Gowalla [20] and Epinions [12] respectively for evaluation.

Gowalla is a Location-Based Social Network (LBSN), and we utilize users' check-in at Point-of-Interests (POIs) and the social network to make POI recommendation [19]. There are 1,196,248 check-ins generated by 18,737 users over

32,510 POIs in the Gowalla dataset. The total number of users' friendship records is 86,985. Epinions is a general consumer review site where users can review items. Different from Gowalla with a two-way connetions between users, users' social relationship in Epinions is their Web of Trust, which is a one-way connection, like Twitter followings. We adapt our model to this different structure, and utilize users' rating histories and trust network to make item recommendation [12]. The Epinions dataset consists of 49, 290 users who rated a total of 139, 738 different items at least once. The total number of reviews is 664, 824. The total number of issued trust statements is 487, 181.

For each user u, we partition his feedback set into three parts, i.e., 70% as training data, 15% as validation data, and 15% as testing data.

4.2   Evaluation Metrics

To evaluate the recommendation performance, we use two widely-used metrics on both datasets, namely, $precision@n$ and $recall@n$, where n is the number of items in the recommendation list. They are computed as follows:

$$precision@n = \frac{1}{|U|} \sum_{u=1}^{|U|} \frac{|P_u^n \cap T_u|}{|P_u^n|}, \tag{7}$$

$$recall@n = \frac{1}{|U|} \sum_{u=1}^{|U|} \frac{|P_u^n \cap T_u|}{|T_u|}, \tag{8}$$

where P_u^n is the set of top n items in user u's recommendation list, and T_u is user u's ground truth set of items. $|x|$ denotes the cardinality of set x. For each metric, we consider 4 values (i.e., 1, 5, 10, 20) of n in our experiments.

For Epinions, we also evaluate the prediction on users' explicit rating scores with MAE, and it is computed as follows:

$$MAE = \frac{1}{|U|} \sum_{u=1}^{|U|} \frac{\sum_{i \in T_u} abs(p_{ui} - y_{ui})}{|T_u|}, \tag{9}$$

where y_{ui} is the true ratings given by user u for item i, and $abs(\cdot)$ is the absolute value function.

4.3   Baselines

Many existing methods are available for POI recommendation, and it is impossible to list all of them as baselines. Here, we select the baselines which serve as representative works of memory-based and model-based social recommendation methods. The baselines include:

- SoCF [3]: SoCF is a social-based collaborative filtering method, which recommend friends' visited items to users.

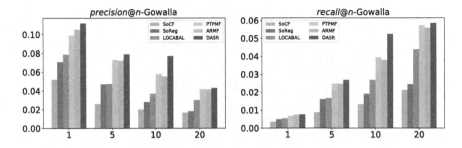

Fig. 3. *precision@n* and *recall@n* of DASR and baselines on the Gowalla dataset.

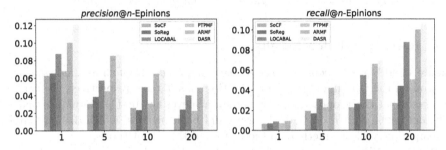

Fig. 4. *precision@n* and *recall@n* of DASR and baselines on the Epinions dataset.

- SoReg [11]: SoReg defines individual-based regularization with Pearson Correlation Coefficient (PCC) in traditional matrix factorization model. The PCC-version regularization achieves the best performance, compared with other variants, as reported in [11].
- LOCABAL [17]: LOCABAL takes advantage of both local friends and users with high reputations for social recommendation.
- PTPMF [22]: PTPMF is a probabilistic matrix factorization model that incorporates the distinction of strong and weak ties.
- ASMF/ARMF [8]: ASMF and ARMF argument user-item matrix using friends' visited as potential items. ASMF optimizes a square-loss based matrix factorization model with potential items being assigned a score lower than a user's own visited items. ARMF optimizes a ranking-based matrix factorization model which assumes that users' preference to different items are: visited items > friends' visited (potential) items > unvisited items.

4.4 Experimental Settings

In the experiments, we add a L_2 regularization term to the users' and items' embeddings when performing optimization, and the regularization coefficient is set as 0.001. We set the negative slope β of the *LeakyReLU* function as 0.2. For all latent vectors, we set their dimension as $n = 128$. We set the negative count c as 10. The learning rate decreases from an initial value of 1.0 with the increase of iterations, and the decay factor is set as 0.5.

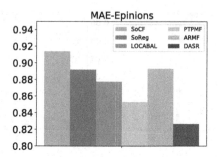

Fig. 5. *MAE* of DASR and baselines on the Epinions dataset.

4.5 Recommendation Results

Figure 3 and Fig. 4 present the *precision@n* and *recall@n* of all methods in comparison on the Gowalla dataset and the Epinions dataset respectively. It can be observed that the proposed DASR method achieves the best performance under different settings of n on both datasets and both metrics, which demonstrates the superiority of our method to these state-of-the-art methods.

We take Fig. 3 as an example to make a detailed discussion. Specifically, among these methods, SoCF is the only memory-based method, which directly recommend friends' items to users. Performance of SoCF is worse than other model-based methods, which learn users' and items' embeddings. SoReg integrates social relations as regularization term in matrix factorization model with feedback-based similarities as regularization coefficients, leading to that friends share similar embeddings. It achieves a good result. Besides social relations as local context, LOCABAL exploits extra social influence, i.e., users with high reputation as global social context. This makes LOCABAL outperform SoReg. PTPMF splits social relations as strong ties and weak ties, and distinguish the different influence of the two types of social ties. We can observe that the differentiation in PTPMF model benefit the recommendation performance. Since ARMF's performance is better than ASMF, we present ARMF only for comparison. It is observed ARMF is the best baseline method. This may profit from that ARMF introduce friends' visited items as potential items and it optimizes users' preference to items in a ranking manner. The proposed method, i.e., DASR, learns rich correlation patterns between users' interest by a correlation vector and finally beats these baselines.

Different from Fig. 3, we can observe that LOCABAL is better than PTPMF on the Epinions dataset in Fig. 4. This indicates that weak ties in Epinions dataset do not provide valuable suggestions for users.

4.6 Rating Prediction

Feedback in the Epinions dataset is users' rating scores for items. We also present rating prediction results of different methods in comparison, as shown in Fig. 5.

Note that, we use ASMF, rather than ARMF, since ASMF is a square loss-based method and ARMF focuses on item ranking.

It is observed that the proposed DASR achieves the best MAE metric on the Epinions dataset. By comparing all methods, we can find that the results of rating prediction is similar to those of recommendation results. The difference lies in that ARMF occupies the second best position in the comparison of recommendation results, while it is slightly better than SoCF only in the comparison of rating prediction. The reason may be: the value assigned to potential items cannot accurately express users' true preference and factorization on these potential values makes parameter learning deviate from a better direction.

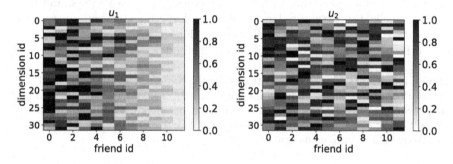

Fig. 6. The attention weights of user u_1 (left) and user u_2 (right).

4.7   Case Study: Correlation Vectors

We learn an interest correlation vector for each pair of users with social relations. Each dimension in the correlation vector represents the interest correlation in the same dimension of users' embeddings. In what follows, we study the interest correlation patterns between different pair of friends. For ease of exhibition, we set the dimension of users' embeddings as 32 and train a new DASR model to get the attention weights between each user and his friends. We select two users from our Gowalla dataset, and both them have 11 friends. Denote the two users as u_1 and u_2 respectively, we draw the heat map of the weights of attention vectors with their friends. Figure 6 shows u_1's (left) and u_2's (right) attention weights. For each user, we compute the norms of his correlation vectors with friends, and rearrange friend id in the descending order of the norm.

We have the following observations: (1) Most dimensions of the attention vector between u_1 and friend 0 are large values, which indicate that they are very similar and we can recommend friend 0's visited items to u_1. (2) Each dimension of the attention vector between u_1 and friend 11 is a small value, which indicates they have no similar interest and recommending friend 11's visited items to u_1 cannot achieve a good performance. (3) By comparing u_1 and u_2, we can find that each user's interest correlations with his friends have a specific patterns. u_1 may mainly refer to suggestions of several friends with very strong interest correlation, while u_2 may refer to suggestions of each friend dispersedly.

These observations demonstrate that the proposed method outperforms base-lines, and modeling users' multi-dimensional interest correlation can significantly improve recommendation performance.

5 Conclusions

In this paper, we propose a new embedding-based social recommendation method. We use a correlation vector to characterize the high variation of users' interest correlations on all dimensions, and design a dimension-wise attention mechanism to learn the correlation vector. Moreover, we use a user's friends' embeddings to smooth the user's embedding with the correlation vector as weights, and build strong and delicate unstructured social influence. Experimental results on two real-world datasets collected from Gowalla and Epinions respectively demonstrate the superiority of our method to state-of-the-art methods.

Acknowledgments. This work was funded by the National Key Research and Development Program of China under grant number 2017YFB0803302, and the National Natural Science Foundation of China under grant numbers 61425016 and 91746301. Huawei Shen is also funded by Beijing Academy of Artificial Intelligence (BAAI) and K.C. Wang Education Foundation.

References

1. Bedi, P., Kaur, H., Marwaha, S.: Trust based recommender system for the semantic web. In: IJCAI, pp. 2677–2682 (2007)
2. Chen, J., Feng, Y., Ester, M., Zhou, S., Chen, C., Wang, C.: Modeling users' exposure with social knowledge influence and consumption influence for recommendation. In: CIKM, pp. 953–962 (2018)
3. Guy, I., Zwerdling, N., Carmel, D., Ronen, I., Uziel, E., Yogev, S., Ofek-Koifman, S.: Personalized recommendation of social software items based on social relations. In: RecSys, pp. 53–60 (2009)
4. Huang, J., Cheng, X.Q., Guo, J., Shen, H.W., Yang, K.: Social recommendation with interpersonal influence. In: ECAI, pp. 601–606 (2010)
5. Jamali, M., Ester, M.: A matrix factorization technique with trust propagation for recommendation in social networks. In: RecSys, pp. 135–142 (2010)
6. Jiang, M., Cui, P., Chen, X., Wang, F., Zhu, W., Yang, S.: Social recommendation with cross-domain transferable knowledge. TKDE **27**(11), 3084–3097 (2015)
7. Jin, R., Chai, J.Y., Si, L.: An automatic weighting scheme for collaborative filtering. In: SIGIR, pp. 337–344 (2004)
8. Li, H., Ge, Y., Hong, R., Zhu, H.: Point-of-interest recommendations: learning potential check-ins from friends. In: KDD, pp. 975–984 (2016)
9. Ma, H., King, I., Lyu, M.R.: Learning to recommend with social trust ensemble. In: SIGIR, pp. 203–210 (2009)
10. Ma, H., Yang, H., Lyu, M.R., King, I.: SoRec: social recommendation using probabilistic matrix factorization. In: CIKM, pp. 931–940 (2008)
11. Ma, H., Zhou, D., Liu, C., Lyu, M.R., King, I.: Recommender systems with social regularization. In: WSDM, pp. 287–296 (2011)

12. Massa, P., Avesani, P.: Trust-aware recommender systems. In: RecSys, pp. 17–24 (2007)
13. Meng, Y., Chen, G., Li, J., Zhang, S.: PsRec: social recommendation with pseudo ratings. In: RecSys, pp. 397–401 (2018)
14. O'Donovan, J., Smyth, B.: Trust in recommender systems. In: IUI, pp. 167–174 (2005)
15. Song, W., Xiao, Z., Wang, Y., Charlin, L., Zhang, M., Tang, J.: Session-based social recommendation via dynamic graph attention networks. In: WSDM, pp. 555–563 (2019)
16. Sun, P., Wu, L., Wang, M.: Attentive recurrent social recommendation. In: SIGIR, pp. 185–194 (2018)
17. Tang, J., Hu, X., Gao, H., Liu, H.: Exploiting local and global social context for recommendation. In: IJCAI, pp. 2712–2718 (2013)
18. Tang, J., Hu, X., Liu, H.: Social recommendation: a review. SNAM 3(4), 1113–1133 (2013)
19. Wang, H., Ouyang, W., Shen, H., Cheng, X.: ULE: learning user and location embeddings for POI recommendation. In: DSC, pp. 99–106 (2018)
20. Wang, H., Shen, H., Ouyang, W., Cheng, X.: Exploiting POI-specific geographical influence for point-of-interest recommendation. In: IJCAI, pp. 3877–3883 (2018)
21. Wang, H., Wang, J., Zhao, M., Cao, J., Guo, M.: Joint topic-semantic-aware social recommendation for online voting. In: CIKM, pp. 347–356 (2017)
22. Wang, X., Hoi, S.C., Ester, M., Bu, J., Chen, C.: Learning personalized preference of strong and weak ties for social recommendation. In: WWW, pp. 1601–1610 (2017)
23. Wang, X., Lu, W., Ester, M., Wang, C., Chen, C.: Social recommendation with strong and weak ties. In: CIKM, pp. 5–14 (2016)
24. Wang, X., Zhu, W., Liu, C.: Social recommendation with optimal limited attention. In: KDD, pp. 1518–1527 (2019)
25. Wen, Y., Guo, L., Chen, Z., Ma, J.: Network embedding based recommendation method in social networks. In: WWW, pp. 11–12 (2018)
26. Wu, C., Wu, F., An, M., Huang, J., Huang, Y., Xie, X.: NPA: neural news recommendation with personalized attention. In: KDD, pp. 2576–2584 (2019)
27. Yang, B., Lei, Y., Liu, D., Liu, J.: Social collaborative filtering by trust. In: AAAI, pp. 2747–2753 (2013)
28. Yang, X., Steck, H., Liu, Y.: Circle-based recommendation in online social networks. In: KDD, pp. 1267–1275 (2012)
29. Yuan, Q., Chen, L., Zhao, S.: Factorization vs. regularization: fusing heterogeneous social relationships in top-n recommendation. In: RecSys, pp. 245–252 (2011)
30. Zhang, Q., Wu, J., Zhang, Q., Zhang, P., Long, G., Zhang, C.: Dual influence embedded social recommendation. WWW 21(4), 849–874 (2018)
31. Zhao, T., McAuley, J., King, I.: Leveraging social connections to improve personalized ranking for collaborative filtering. In: CIKM, pp. 261–270 (2014)
32. Zhao, Z., Lu, H., Cai, D., He, X., Zhuang, Y.: User preference learning for online social recommendation. TKDE 28(9), 2522–2534 (2016)

Modeling POI-Specific Spatial-Temporal Context for Point-of-Interest Recommendation

Hao Wang[1]([⊠]), Huawei Shen[2], and Xueqi Cheng[2]

[1] Baidu Inc., Beijing, China
way_wh@yeah.net
[2] CAS Key Lab of Network Data Science and Technology,
Institute of Computing Technology, Chinese Academy of Sciences,
Beijing, China
{shenhuawei,cxq}@ict.ac.cn

Abstract. Point-of-Interest (POI) recommendation is a fundamental task in location-based social networks. Different from traditional item recommendation, POI recommendation is highly context-dependent: (1) geographical influence, e.g., users prefer to visit POIs that are not far away; (2) time-sensitivity, e.g., restaurants are preferred in dinner time; (3) dependency in a user's check-in sequence, e.g., POIs planned in a trip. Yet, existing methods either partially leverage such context information or combine different types of contexts using a global weighting scheme, failing to capture the phenomenon that the importance of each context is also context-dependent rather than the same for all recommendation. In this paper, we propose a model to exploit spatial-temporal contexts in a POI-guided attention mechanism for POI recommendation. Such an attention mechanism offers us high flexibility to capture the POI-specific importance of each context. Experimental results on two real-world datasets collected from Foursquare and Gowalla demonstrate that the POI-specific context importance significantly improves the performance of POI recommendation.

Keywords: Point-of-Interest · Check-ins · Spatial-temporal context · Attention mechanism · Location-based social networks

1 Introduction

With the development of mobile Internet, location-based social networks (LBSNs) [6], such as Yelp and Foursquare, have emerged in recent years. In LBSNs, users can share their experiences and tips for Point-of-Interests (POIs) [2], e.g., restaurants and sightseeing sites, in the form of check-ins [14]. The rapid growth of LBSNs has attracted billions of users, promoting our urban

---

H. Wang—This work is done when Hao Wang was a Ph.D. candidate in Institute of Computing Technology, Chinese Academy of Sciences.

H. W. Lauw et al. (Eds.): PAKDD 2020, LNAI 12084, pp. 130–141, 2020.
https://doi.org/10.1007/978-3-030-47426-3_11

experience to a new stage [17]. To benefit LBSN users and promote location-based marketing, POI recommendation on LBSNs has become an essential task aiming to recommend new POIs to a user according to his personal preferences and to facilitate his exploration of the city [18].

Different from traditional item recommendation, e.g., movie recommendation, POI recommendation is highly context-dependent. First, locations of POIs are important factors for POI recommendations, since users prefer to visit POIs that are not far away. For example, in Gowalla and Foursquare, 90% of users' consecutive check-ins are within the distance less than 50km [15]. Second, users' preference over POIs exhibit salient temporal periodic patterns, e.g., restaurants are preferred in dinner time and theaters are visited more frequently in weekend than in weekdays. Finally, a user's check-in records form a POI sequence with continuous distance and time intervals, offering various sequential patterns [12], e.g., POIs planned in a trip. In sum, users' check-in records contain rich *spatial-temporal* context information that should be synthetically integrated to reflect the dynamics of the underlying check-in system.

Many methods have been proposed to exploit geographical influence [3,11, 18,20], temporal periodic patterns [5,22,25] and sequential dependency [1,4,12, 13,23,24] lying in users' check-ins for improving the performance of POI recommendation. However, these methods only partially leverage the spatial context and temporal context, and they integrate these contexts using a global weighting scheme [9,19,25], assuming that the importance of each context is unchanged for all POIs. These methods fail to capture the dynamic role of context, given that the importance of each context is POI-specific. Let's say we are going to make POI recommendation to a big foodie at 3 p.m. We may push a restaurant to him considering his long-term preference as a foodie. However, recommending a restaurant must happen at the right time, e.g., dinner time, rather than 3 p.m, at which restaurant cannot meet the user's current needs. In this scenario where restaurant is a candidate POI, we should inhibit the importance of user's long-term preference and let the temporal context play a more decisive role in user's check-in choice. That is to say, each context's importance to current recommendation should be POI-specific.

In this paper, we propose to model the spatial-temporal context for POI recommendation using an attention mechanism (Fig. 1). Temporal context is represented as a low-dimensional vector, capturing what type of POI is preferred for a specific temporal moment. For spatial context, due to the lack of location information of user, we infer the spatial context by exploiting users' check-in records, obtaining a low-dimensional representation through an attention enhanced recurrent neural network. Finally, a POI-guided attention mechanism is adopted to learn the importance of each context for each recommendation, offering high flexibility to capture the dynamic nature of context.

We evaluate the proposed POI recommendation method by extensive experiments on two real-world datasets collected from Foursquare and Gowalla respectively. Experimental results show that the POI-specific context importance can significantly improve the performance of POI recommendation, compared with state-of-the-art methods.

2   Related Work

In this section, we make a brief discussion on related works.

Check-in is the main inferential evidence for POI recommendation [3,20]. Due to its nature as implicit feedback, researchers utilize the weighted matrix factorization [10] or pairwise ranking methods [7,9] to model it.

Geographical Influence has been proved to be effective in improving POI recommendation accuracy, with a parameterized distribution to model the distance influence [3,10,16,20]. Moreover, Wang et al. [18] propose to model POI-specific geographical influence, which captures the asymmetry and high variation of geographical influence between POIs.

Periodic Pattern has attracted much attention from researchers. They split one day into multiple time slots and exploit the check-in pattern in each time slot in terms of temporal non-uniformness and consecutiveness [5,22].

Sequential Dependency has been exploited in recent years. Many methods based on matrix factorization [13], Markov models. [4,23,24], word2vec [14] or RNN [12] have been proposed to learn the transitive patterns between POIs.

However, the above methods only partially exploit the spatial-temporal context and integrate these contexts using a global weighting scheme [9,19,25] given that the importance of each context is POI-specific. Considering that the attention mechanism can automatically model and select pertinent piece of information from a set of inputs and achieve good performance in many neural network-based tasks [8]. In this paper, we design a POI-guided attention mechanism to address the above issue.

3   Problem Formulation

For ease of presentation, we first introduce the notations used in this paper. We denote U and V the user set and POI set, with u and i representing a user and a POI respectively. Each POI i's location is denoted by its longitude and latitude, i.e., (lon_i, lat_i). A check-in is a triple (u, i, t), which means user u visits POI i at time t. For each user u, a check-in profile D_u is provided, which is the set of check-ins generated by u in chronological order. We define a long-term preference vector P_u for each user u, a preference vector S_i and an influence vector I_i for each POI i, and a preference vector E_t for each time t.

POI Recommendation: given all users' check-in profiles $\{D_u\}$, we aim to provide a list of POIs which are not visited and potentially preferred by a target user u at a target time t.

4   Model

In this section, we describe the proposed framework for POI recommendation, which models the Spatial-Temporal context by an Attention enhanced Recurrent neural network (*STAR* in Fig. 1).

4.1   Model Architecture

Whether a POI will be chosen is sensitive to the spatial-temporal context, e.g., restaurant is popular at dinner time and the temporal context plays a more decisive role, compared with other factors in this scenario. Likewise, if user is on a food street, restaurant is also popular and the spatial context becomes more decisive. Therefore, we need a model that can automatically adjust the importance of the involved context to user's current preference, and the idea comes to fruition in the proposed STAR model by using a POI-guided attention mechanism.

STAR infers a target user u's preference to a candidate POI j at a target time t by capturing the dynamic influence of the spatial context and the temporal context, besides user u's long-term preference. To characterize the influence of each factor, we learn the following latent vectors in STAR:

- P_u: a n-dimension vector characterizes user u's long-term preference.
- S_j: a n-dimension vector characterizes POI j's preference distribution.
- E_t: a n-dimension vector characterizes time t's temporal periodic patterns.

Specifically, E_t contains two types of temporal information, including hour of a day, and day of a week, to capture which POIs are preferred at a specific time.

Figure 1(a) shows the architecture of the proposed STAR model. We input user u's long-term preference P_u, the temporal context E_t capturing temporal periodic patterns of the recommendation time t and the spatial context H_t capturing the geographical influence of user u's current location. An POI-guided attention layer is applied to distinguish the importance of each context. User u's instantaneous preference at time t, denoted as Q_u^t, is computed by integrating the involved contexts with their importance into consideration.

Note that, it is tricky to model the spatial context because the real location of user is usually not available. Therefore, we utilize the user's historical check-ins to simulate his current location and compute the spatial context as the geographical influence of historical check-ins. Figure 1(b) show the architecture of the generation of the spatial context, i.e., we use a recurrent neural network with user's historical check-in sequence as input to achieve this purpose, and we also take the influence of the geographical distance and time decay into consideration.

4.2   Model Specification

In what follows, we specify the details of the STAR model.

Spatial-Temporal Context-Aware Recommendation. To make context-aware recommendation, we first use a POI-guided attention mechanism to distinguish the importance of the involved contexts, including user u's long-term preference P_u, the temporal context E_t and the spatial context H_t. We introduce the generation of H_t in next part.

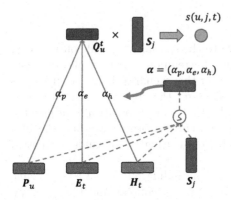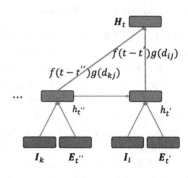

(a) Spatial-temporal context-aware recommendation   (b) Spatial context generation

Fig. 1. (a) Architecture of the proposed model which integrates the Spatial-Temporal context with an Attention-enhanced Recurrent neural network, i.e., STAR. STAR uses a POI-guided attention mechanism to distinguish the importance of user u's long-term preference $\boldsymbol{P}_u$, the temporal context $\boldsymbol{E}_t$ and the spatial-temporal context $\boldsymbol{H}_t$. α is the importance. (b) The spatial context refers to the geographical influence of user u's historical check-ins, e.g., POI $\{i\}$ at time t' ($t' < t$). $\boldsymbol{I}_i$ represents POI i's influence vector. $f(\cdot)$ and $g(\cdot)$ are the geographical influence function and the time decay function.

Specifically, we input not only $\boldsymbol{P}_u$, $\boldsymbol{E}_t$ and $\boldsymbol{H}_t$, but also the candidate POI j's preference vector $\boldsymbol{S}_j$, and compute the attention weights for the three factors based on the interaction between them:

$$
\begin{aligned}
\alpha_p &= \sigma(W^T(\boldsymbol{P}_u||\boldsymbol{S}_j)), \\
\alpha_e &= \sigma(W^T(\boldsymbol{E}_t||\boldsymbol{S}_j)), \\
\alpha_h &= \sigma(W^T(\boldsymbol{H}_t||\boldsymbol{S}_j)),
\end{aligned}
\tag{1}
$$

where α_p, α_e and α_h are attention weights of $\boldsymbol{P}_u$, $\boldsymbol{E}_t$ and $\boldsymbol{H}_t$ respectively and W is parameter. $||$ represents vectors' concatenation operation and $\sigma(z) = \frac{1}{1+e^{-z}}$ is the sigmoid function.

Then, a normalization on α_p, α_e and α_h is completed through a softmax function. Take α_p as an example:

$$
\alpha_p = \frac{exp(\alpha_p)}{exp(\alpha_p) + exp(\alpha_e) + exp(\alpha_h)}.
\tag{2}
$$

In this way, we can automatically determine the importance of each context guided by the candidate POI j. For example, when t is the time to eat and the POI j is a restaurant, α_e would be a large value to make the temporal context get more attention.

With the POI-specific attention weights pointing out the importance of different contexts, we compute user u's instantaneous preference at target time t, i.e., $\boldsymbol{Q}_u^t$, as follows:

$$
\boldsymbol{Q}_u^t = \alpha_p \boldsymbol{P}_u + \alpha_e \boldsymbol{E}_t + \alpha_h \boldsymbol{H}_t.
\tag{3}
$$

Denote the preference as $s(u, j, t)$ as the target user u's preference to candidate POI j at target time t. We compute $s(u, j, t)$ as the inner product between user u's instantaneous preference vector $\boldsymbol{Q}_u^t$ and candidate POI j's preference vector $\boldsymbol{S}_j$, like traditional matrix factorization does:

$$s(u, j, t) = \boldsymbol{Q}_u^{t\ T} \boldsymbol{S}_j. \tag{4}$$

Spatial Context Generation. Since we don't know user u's current location, we use the POIs in his check-in history to simulate the current location and model the spatial context $\boldsymbol{H}_t$ as the geographical influence from user u's historical check-ins.

We use a recurrent neural network to naturally line up user u's historical check-ins as a behavior sequence. In each recurrent unit, we input the check-in activity (u, i, t'), i.e., $\boldsymbol{I}_i$ as the influence vector of the visited POI i and $\boldsymbol{E}_{t'}$ as the preference vector of the check-in time t'. $\boldsymbol{I}_i$ is a n-dimension vector for characterizing historical POI i's influence on user's future check-in preference.

We use $h_{t'}$ to represent the hidden layer after visiting POI i at time t'. $h_{t'}$ is responsible for propagating past signals for future predictions, and it is computed as follows:

$$h_{t'} = a(W_i^T \boldsymbol{I}_i + W_e^T \boldsymbol{E}_{t'} + W_h^T h_{t''}), \tag{5}$$

where $h_{t''}$ denotes the hidden layer from the previous recurrent unit prior to time t'. W_i and W_e denote the weight matrices for input vectors. W_h denotes the recurrent connections among consecutive recurrent steps. $a(z) = \frac{1-e^{-2z}}{1+e^{-2z}}$ is the *tanh* function, which acts as non-linear transformation.

Instead of directly using h_t as the spatial context, we introduce another attention mechanism to build cross-dependency lying in user's check-in sequence. The spatial context $\boldsymbol{H}_t$ is regarded as the aggregation of the influence of all POIs that are visited prior to t, with the influence of geographical distance between historical POIs and the candidate POI j, and the time decay after historical check-in time serving as weights. Specifically, we compute $\boldsymbol{H}_t$ as follows:

$$\boldsymbol{H}_t = \sum_{(u,i,t'):t'<t} f(t - t')g(d_{ij})h_{t'}, \tag{6}$$

where $f(t - t')$ is the time decay function of the elapsed time from t' to t, and $g(d_{ij})$ is the geographical influence function, which is determined by the distance d_{ij} between historical POI i and candidate POI j. They are defined respectively by

$$f(t - t') = a * (t - t')^b, \tag{7}$$

$$g(d_{ij}) = c * d_{ij}^d, \tag{8}$$

where a, b, c, d are function parameters, controlling the initial scores and the steepness of time decay and geographical influence respectively.

Those two functions allow the influence of historical check-ins to decrease when the time interval becomes longer and the geographical distance becomes further, which fits intuitions and previous findings. Note that, existing methods have separately studied the time decay function [2] or the geographical influence function [20]. To our best knowledge, it is the first time to jointly integrate them for capturing the spatial-temporal attenuation effect.

4.3 Optimization

For each check-in activity (u, j, t), we randomly sample c negative POIs from POI set V with POI j being excluded and denote the set of negative samples as $NEG(j)$. The objective function is defined in a ranking manner as follows:

$$L(u, j, t) = - \sum_{l \in NEG(j)} \sigma(s(u, j, t) - s(u, l, t)). \qquad (9)$$

In the optimization, we learn four latent vectors, i.e., P_u, E_t, I_i and S_j, and four parameters in the time decay function and the geographical influence function, i.e., a, b, c and d.

We compute the score of each POI in V according to Eq. 4, and take top k POIs with highest scores as the final recommendation list.

5   Experiments

5.1   Datasets

We adopt two real-world datasets collected from Foursquare and Gowalla respectively for evaluation, which are also used in [15]. In the Foursquare dataset, there are 1,196,248 check-ins generated by 24,941 users over 28,593 POIs from April 3, 2012 to September 16, 2013, while in the Gowalla dataset there are 1,278,274 check-ins by 18,737 users over 32,510 POIs from February 4, 2009 to October 23, 2010. In both datasets, each POI is marked by its longitude and latitude, and each check-in is associated with a check-in time. For each user, we first sort her/his check-ins in chronological order, and then mark off the early 80% of her/his check-ins as training data, the next 10% as validation data, and the last 10% as testing data.

5.2   Evaluation Metrics

To evaluate the models, we adopt two widely-used metrics, i.e., $hit@k$ [21] and mean reciprocal rank ($MRR@k$).

Specifically, we denote the set of check-in time in user u's testing set as $T(u)$. For each check-in time in $T(u)$, we predict a recommendation list. Let $G_{u,t}$ denote the ground truth POI that user u visited at time t, and $P_{u,t}^k$ denotes the top k POIs recommended for user u at time t. Then, we calculate $hit@k$ as follows:

$$hit@k = \frac{1}{|U|} \sum_{u=1}^{|U|} \frac{\sum_{t \in T(u)} \delta(G_{u,t} \in P_{u,t}^k)}{|T(u)|}, \qquad (10)$$

where $\delta(z)$ is an indicator function which equals 1 if and only if boolean variable z is $True$, and otherwise 0. $|\cdot|$ denotes the cardinality of a set.

The $MRR@k$ is calculated as follows:

$$MRR@k = \frac{1}{|U|} \sum_{u=1}^{|U|} \frac{\sum_{t\in T(u)} 1/rank(G_{u,t}, P_{u,t}^k)}{|T(u)|}, \tag{11}$$

where $rank(G_{u,t}, P_{u,t}^k)$ represents the rank of POI $G_{u,t}$ in set $P_{u,t}^k$. If $G_{u,t}$ is not in $P_{u,t}$, $rank(G_{u,t}, P_{ut}) = \infty$.

We consider three values of k, i.e., 1, 5 and 10 in our experiments.

5.3 Baseline Methods

We first compare the proposed STAR model with its variants to demonstrate the effectiveness of the attention mechanism. Three variants are considered by respectively removing the attention layer in the generation of the spatial context ($STAR\text{-}sta$), the attention layer in the integration of different contexts ($STAR\text{-}ca$) and both the two attention layers ($STAR\text{-}sta\text{-}ca$).

Then, we compare the proposed STAR model with several baseline methods:

- UG [20]: UG combines a user-based collaborative filtering method and geographical influence. It uses a power-law function to characterize the relation between check-in probability and distance.
- UTG [22]: UTG improves the basic user-based collaborative filtering method to incorporate temporal periodic patterns, and then combines geographical influence.
- FPMC-LR [4]: FPMC-LR is a sequential prediction model, which embeds the personalized Markov chain and adds region localization constraint for next check-ins.
- ST-RNN [12]: ST-RNN extends RNN to model local temporal and spatial contexts with time-specific and distance-specific transition matrices.
- GE [19]: GE is a graph-based embedding model, which utilizes sequential dependency, geographical influence and temporal periodic patterns to constrain POI's representations.
- Geo-Teaser [25]: Geo-Teaser is the combination of a temporal POI embedding model and a geographically hierarchical pair-wise preference ranking model.

5.4 Experimental Setting

In the experiments, we add a L_2 regularization term to the parameters when performing optimization, and the regularization coefficient is set as 0.01. For all latent vectors, we set their dimension as $n = 128$. We set the negative count c as 10. The learning rate decreases from an initial value of 1.0 with the increase of iterations, and the decay factor is set as 0.5. Parameters learned for the time decay function and the geographical influence function, i.e., a, b, c, d, are $0.16, -0.35, 0.82, -0.27$ on the Foursquare dataset and $0.18, -0.24, 0.73, -0.32$ on the Gowalla dataset respectively.

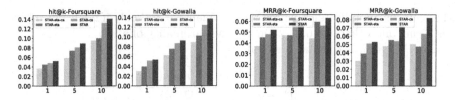

Fig. 2. hit@k and MRR@k of STAR and three variants.

5.5 Performance of STAR and Its Variants

Figure 2 present the *hit@k* and *MRR@k* of the proposed STAR model and its variants respectively. We can observe that removing any attention would cause performance degradation on both datasets. This phenomenon indicates that a global weighting scheme cannot effectively organize multiple heterogeneous contexts, and the attention mechanism plays a critical role while integrating the spatial-temporal contexts.

5.6 Performance of Methods in Comparison

Figure 3 and Fig. 4 present the *hit@k* and *MRR@k* of the STAR and baseline methods respectively. It can be observed that the proposed STAR method achieves the best performance under different settings of k on both datasets and both metrics, which demonstrates the superiority of our method to these state-of-the-art methods.

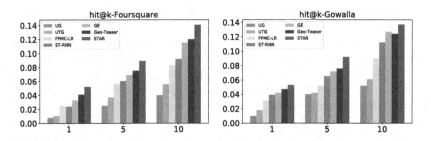

Fig. 3. hit@k of all methods on the Foursquare and the Gowalla dataset.

We take a detailed account of Fig. 3 as an example. Since UG considers only the geographical influence, it gets the worst performance. UTG further incorporates temporal periodic patterns (time slot in a day), resulting in a slightly better performance than UG. FPMF-LR and ST-RNN consider the sequential dependency and ignore the temporal periodic patterns, and its performance is better than that of UTG. This indicates that sequential dependence is crucial to POI recommendation. ST-RNN outperforms FPMC-LR in most cases except the

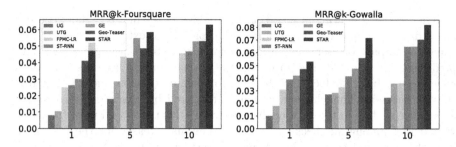

Fig. 4. MRR@k of all methods on the Foursquare and the Gowalla dataset.

case of $k = 1$ on the Foursquare dataset, this is due to the modeling of continuous distance and time intervals. GE and Geo-Teaser both consider all contexts, and thus perform better than the above methods. However, they just utilize these contexts to constrain POIs' representation learning, and combine the involved contexts using a global weighting scheme. STAR uses a POI-guided attention mechanism to distinguish the importance of different contexts, guaranteeing its superior performance against baseline methods.

5.7 Case Study: Importance of Different Contexts

In what follows, we study how important each recommendation context (user's long-term preference P_u, the temporal context E_t, the spatial context H_t) is over time. We directly compute the interactions between three types of factors and the true POI respectively, and compare the proportion of each part in the overall score. Specifically, we sample a user u from the Foursquare dataset for case study. u has 115 check-ins in total. We select her/his 10 consecutive check-ins from January 6, 2013 to April 6, 2013, and present the changes in proportions over time in Fig. 5.

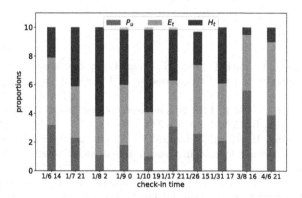

Fig. 5. Impact of different contexts for predicting a user's preference over time.

We have the following observations: (1) u visited the first 5 POIs in consecutive 5 days. As expected, the impact of the spatial context increases constantly, while the impact of user's long-term preference becomes negligible. (2) When predicting the 9th POI, the impact of the spatial context becomes very weak, which results from the fact that this check-in is more than one month away from the 8th check-in. This check-in is mainly triggered by user's long-term preference, since we find in the dataset that the 9th POI is the second most frequently visited POI among all check-ins of u. (3) The main reason for the last check-in is the temporal context, i.e., temporal periodic patterns (21:11). We guess that the last POI is a place for relax, as most check-ins at this POI occurred at non-working hours.

6   Conclusions

In this paper, we propose a new POI recommendation framework to dynamically integrate the spatial-temporal context. We use a low-dimensional vector to capture the temporal context and infer the spatial context by mining a user's check-in history through an attention enhanced recurrent neural network. We integrate the spatial-temporal context with user's long-term preference using another POI-guided attention, which can distinguish the importance of each context for recommendation. In this way, we can flexibly and accurately capture the dynamic nature of different contexts. We perform sufficient experiments on two real-world datasets and demonstrate that the proposed method consistently outperforms state-of-the-art methods for POI recommendation.

Acknowledgments. This work was funded by the National Key Research and Development Program of China under grant number 2017YFB0803302, and the National Natural Science Foundation of China under grant numbers 61433014 and 61472400. Huawei Shen is also funded by Beijing Academy of Artificial Intelligence (BAAI) and K.C. Wang Education Foundation. We thank Jinhua Gao at the Institute of Computing Technology for the valuable discussions and comments to this work.

References

1. Chang, B., Park, Y., Park, D., Kim, S., Kang, J.: Content-aware hierarchical point-of-interest embedding model for successive POI recommendation. In: IJCAI, p. 7 (2018)
2. Chen, J., Wang, C., Wang, J.: A personalized interest-forgetting Markov model for recommendations. In: AAAI, pp. 16–22 (2015)
3. Cheng, C., Yang, H., King, I., Lyu, M.R.: Fused matrix factorization with geographical and social influence in location-based social networks. In: AAAI, pp. 17–23 (2012)
4. Cheng, C., Yang, H., Lyu, M.R., King, I.: Where you like to go next: successive point-of-interest recommendation. In: IJCAI, pp. 2605–2611 (2013)
5. Gao, H., Tang, J., Hu, X., Liu, H.: Exploring temporal effects for location recommendation on location-based social networks. In: RecSys, pp. 93–100 (2013)

6. He, J., Li, X., Liao, L., Song, D., Cheung, W.K.: Inferring a personalized next point-of-interest recommendation model with latent behavior patterns. In: AAAI, pp. 137–143 (2016)
7. Li, H., Ge, Y., Hong, R., Zhu, H.: Point-of-interest recommendations: learning potential check-ins from friends. In: KDD, pp. 975–984 (2016)
8. Li, R., Shen, Y., Zhu, Y.: Next point-of-interest recommendation with temporal and multi-level context attention. In: ICDM, pp. 1110–1115 (2018)
9. Li, X., Cong, G., Li, X.L., Pham, T.A.N., Krishnaswamy, S.: Rank-GeoFM: a ranking based geographical factorization method for point of interest recommendation. In: SIGIR, pp. 433–442 (2015)
10. Lian, D., Zhao, C., Xie, X., Sun, G., Chen, E., Rui, Y.: GeoMF: joint geographical modeling and matrix factorization for point-of-interest recommendation. In: KDD, pp. 831–840 (2014)
11. Liu, B., Fu, Y., Yao, Z., Xiong, H.: Learning geographical preferences for point-of-interest recommendation. In: KDD, pp. 1043–1051 (2013)
12. Liu, Q., Wu, S., Wang, L., Tan, T.: Predicting the next location: a recurrent model with spatial and temporal contexts. In: AAAI, pp. 194–200 (2016)
13. Liu, X., Liu, Y., Aberer, K., Miao, C.: Personalized point-of-interest recommendation by mining users' preference transition. In: CIKM, pp. 733–738 (2013)
14. Liu, X., Liu, Y., Li, X.: Exploring the context of locations for personalized location recommendations. In: IJCAI, pp. 1188–1194 (2016)
15. Liu, Y., Pham, T.A.N., Cong, G., Yuan, Q.: An experimental evaluation of point-of-interest recommendation in location-based social networks. Proc. VLDB Endow. **10**(10), 1010–1021 (2017)
16. Liu, Y., Wei, W., Sun, A., Miao, C.: Exploiting geographical neighborhood characteristics for location recommendation. In: CIKM, pp. 739–748 (2014)
17. Wang, H., Ouyang, W., Shen, H., Cheng, X.: ULE: learning user and location embeddings for poi recommendation. In: DSC, pp. 99–106 (2018)
18. Wang, H., Shen, H., Ouyang, W., Cheng, X.: Exploiting POI-specific geographical influence for point-of-interest recommendation. In: IJCAI, pp. 3877–3883 (2018)
19. Xie, M., Yin, H., Wang, H., Xu, F., Chen, W., Wang, S.: Learning graph-based poi embedding for location-based recommendation. In: CIKM, pp. 15–24 (2016)
20. Ye, M., Yin, P., Lee, W.C., Lee, D.L.: Exploiting geographical influence for collaborative point-of-interest recommendation. In: SIGIR, pp. 325–334 (2011)
21. Yin, H., Cui, B., Huang, Z., Wang, W., Wu, X., Zhou, X.: Joint modeling of users' interests and mobility patterns for point-of-interest recommendation. In: MM, pp. 819–822. ACM (2015)
22. Yuan, Q., Cong, G., Ma, Z., Sun, A., Thalmann, N.M.: Time-aware point-of-interest recommendation. In: SIGIR, pp. 363–372 (2013)
23. Zhang, J.D., Chow, C.Y., Li, Y.: LORE: exploiting sequential influence for location recommendations. In: SIGSPATIAL, pp. 103–112 (2014)
24. Zhang, W., Wang, J.: Location and time aware social collaborative retrieval for new successive point-of-interest recommendation. In: CIKM, pp. 1221–1230. ACM (2015)
25. Zhao, S., Zhao, T., King, I., Lyu, M.R.: Geo-Teaser: geo-temporal sequential embedding rank for point-of-interest recommendation. In: WWW, pp. 153–162 (2017)

MsFcNET: Multi-scale Feature-Crossing Attention Network for Multi-field Sparse Data

Zhifeng Xie[1,2]([✉]), Wenling Zhang[1,2], Huiming Ding[1,2], and Lizhuang Ma[2,3]

[1] Department of Film and Television Engineering, Shanghai University,
Shanghai, China
{zhifeng_xie,Wxid7180a,huiming_shu}@shu.edu.cn
[2] Shanghai Engineering Research Center of Motion Picture Special Effects,
Shanghai, China
ma-lz@cs.sjtu.edu.cn
[3] Department of Computer Science and Engineering,
Shanghai Jiao Tong University, Shanghai, China

Abstract. Feature engineering usually needs to excavate dense-and-implicit cross features from multi-filed sparse data. Recently, many state-of-the-art models have been proposed to achieve low-order and high-order feature interactions. However, most of them ignore the importance of cross features and fail to suppress the negative impact of useless features. In this paper, a novel multi-scale feature-crossing attention network (MsFcNET) is proposed to extract dense-and-implicit cross features and learn their importance in the different scales. The model adopts the DIA-LSTM units to construct a new attention calibration architecture, which can adaptively adjust the weights of features in the process of feature interactions. On the other hand, it also integrates a multi-scale feature-crossing module to strengthen the representation ability of cross features from multi-field sparse data. The extensive experimental results on three real-world prediction datasets demonstrate that our proposed model yields superior performance compared with the other state-of-the-art models.

Keywords: Feature engineering · Feature interactions · Attention network · Factorization machines

1 Introduction

Feature engineering is the process of transforming the original data into features, which can better describe the potential characteristics of data, so as to further improve the accuracy of the predictive model. It has been considered to be a central task in a variety of machine learning applications, such as recommendation system, computational advertising, search ranking and so on. Unfortunately, multi-field sparse data often influence the effect of feature engineering because

H. W. Lauw et al. (Eds.): PAKDD 2020, LNAI 12084, pp. 142–154, 2020.
https://doi.org/10.1007/978-3-030-47426-3_12

it is very difficult to excavate the dense-and-implicit cross features among the different fields. Therefore, this paper mainly focuses on how to effectively extract and represent the cross features from high-dimensional incomplete data, in order to achieve higher-quality feature engineering and yield higher-accuracy predictive model.

In decade, a number of state-of-the-art models have been proposed to achieve the feature interactions of multi-field sparse data. FM (Factorization Machines) [11] and FFM (Field-aware FM) [6] use matrix factorization to finish low-order feature interactions. But these low-order operations can not produce valuable cross features, so they often fail to obtain higher accuracy for many complex prediction tasks. Recently, with the development of deep learning, Deep Neural Networks (DNN) are successfully applied into feature engineering, such as NFM (Neural FM) [4], Deep Crossing [12], Wide&Deep [1], DeepFM [2], xDeepFM [7], DIN [19], FNFM (Field-aware NFM) [18], AutoInt [13], and so on. But these DNN-based models still lack the powerful ability of extracting higher-dimensional cross features, especially the interaction of useless features may introduce noise and have a negative impact on the predictive model. In brief, for high-order feature interactions, the traditional methods need to be further improved.

Inspired by Attention Mechanism [5,15], we propose multi-scale feature-crossing attention network (MsFcNET) to significantly improve the quality of feature engineering in this paper. As shown in Fig. 1, our new network mainly contains six parts: input layer, embedding layer, multi-scale feature-crossing attention layer, hidden layers, combination layer and output layer. As a core component, our new attention layer can effectively extract dense-and-implicit cross features and dynamically learn their importance in the different scales. In this layer, we design a multi-scale feature-crossing module to better represent the cross features from multi-field sparse data. On the other hand, we also adopt the DIA-LSTM (Dense-and-Implicit Attention-Long Short Term Memory) units to construct a new attention calibration architecture, which can adjust the weights of features before and during feature interaction procedure adaptively. In a word, our MsFcNET model can strengthen the ability of feature interactions while avoiding the negative cross features.

Moreover, we build a new Tobacco dataset which contains static individual information of thousands of tobacco stores, their dynamic order and sales records, and their violation cases in the past four years. The Tobacco dataset has a small amount of data, a large number of feature fields, numerous null values, and a few of anomaly data. Thus it is difficult to predict the violations of tobacco stores. We conduct extensive experiments on the tobacco dataset and two public CTR prediction datasets (Avazu and Criteo). The experimental results demonstrate that our proposed MsFcNET model obtains superior performance compared with other state-of-the-art models.

2   Related Work

In feature engineering, FM (Factorization Machines) [11] is a very successful method, which uses the implicit inner product of features to compute the coefficients matrix of interaction term between features. Since FM considers feature interactions as the factorization problem of high-dimensional sparse matrix, many new cross features and hidden vectors can be efficiently extracted and represented. Later as an improvement of the FM model, FFM (Field-aware Factorization Machines) [6] further introduces the concept of fields to achieve higher-quality feature interactions. However, the feature dimension in many practical applications is very high, so the above models focusing on low-order feature interactions are hard to perfectly capture high-dimensional cross features.

Instead, a number of deep learning techniques have been proposed to effectively handle feature interactions in recent years. NFM (Neural Factorization Machines) [4] constructs deep neural network to improve the second-order feature interactions of FM. Wide&Deep [1] jointly trains linear model and deep neural network to integrate the advantage of memorization and generalization. DeepFM [2] integrates the architectures of FM and deep neural network by sharing the feature embedding, which is an end-to-end model without any manual feature engineering. Deep&Cross [16] replaces the wide component with a novel cross network that learn certain bounded-degree feature interactions. xDeepFM [7] learns explicit and implicit high-order feature interactions and cross features at the vector-wise level. FNFM (Field-Aware Neural Factorization Machine) [18] uses the second-order feature interactions of FFM as the input of deep neural network. In summary, those models based on deep learning can reduce or even get ride of manual feature engineering, and increase the strength of interaction between features. Unfortunately, most of them fail to learn the importance of cross features, and some negative feature interactions are easy to reduce the accuracy of predictive model.

Attention network [15] is motivated by human visual attention and it selectively focuses on the key part of information while ignoring the other perceivable parts. AFM (Attentional FM) [17] first introduces neural attention network to learn the significance of second-order feature interactions of FM. AutoInt [13] models feature interactions in the low-dimensional space by casting features into multiple subspaces and capturing different feature combinations in different subspaces. DIN [19] introduces attention mechanism to adaptively learn the representation of user interests from historical behaviors. Since the attention-based models learn the feature importance and avoid the negative feature interactions, we integrate multi-scale module and attention network into a new multi-scale feature-crossing attention model, which can further improve the quality of feature engineering.

3   Multi-scale Feature-Crossing Attention Network

In this section, we will introduce the neural network architecture of multi-scale feature-crossing attention model as shown in Fig. 1. Our proposed MsFcNET model is composed of the following six parts: input layer, embedding layer, multi-scale feature-crossing attention layer, hidden layers, combination layer and output layer.

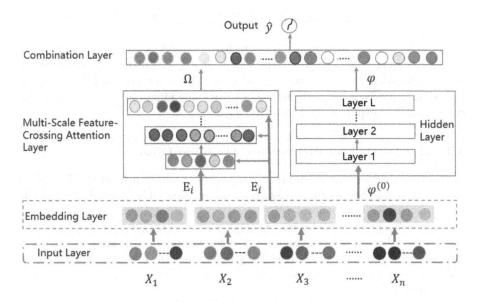

Fig. 1. The neural network architecture of proposed MsFcNET model.

3.1   Input Layer

In this layer, we first convert multi-field sparse data into initial feature vectors, which are composed of the categorical or numerical values in the different fields. The input layer is defined as followed:

$$X = [X_1, X_2, ..., X_i, ..., X_n]^T, X_i = [x_1, x_2, ..., x_t, ..., x_m] \qquad (1)$$

where X is the output matrix of the input layer; X_i the feature values of the i-th record; n is the number of total records; m is the number of fields; x_t is the value of the t-th field, which can be computed according to the following rules: if the field is categorical, then x_t is the one-hot encoding value; if the field is numerical, x_t is the normalized value.

3.2   Embedding Layer

The feature vectors of categorical fields are often extreme sparse and high dimensional, which must be compressed into low-dimensional feature space. Besides, we also need to convert the dense features of numerical fields into the same low-dimensional feature space in order to formalize a unified embedding output. Thus the embedding layer can integrate the different features and reduce their dimensions, which is defined as followed:

$$E = [E_1, E_2, ..., E_t, ..., E_m]^T, E_t = V_t Y_t \qquad (2)$$

where Y_t is a $n \times n$ feature matrix, which is denoted as $[X^t, X^t, ..., X^t]$; X^t is the feature vector of X in the t-th field, which is an one-hot encoding vector in the categorical field or a normalized vector in the numerical field; V_t is the embedding matrix in the t-th field; E_t is the embedding output of Y_t; E is the concatenation output of the embedding layer.

3.3   Multi-scale Feature-Crossing Attention Layer

In order to improve feature interactions, we get inspiration from DIANet [5] to construct multi-scale feature-crossing attention layer. The goal of the layer is to better extract and calibrate cross features by strengthening useful features and suppressing less useful ones. As illustrated in Fig. 2, it has two branches: attention calibration module and multi-scale feature-crossing module. The first module learns the importance of features and adjusts the feature weights dynamically; the second module extracts dense-and-implicit cross features among fields in different scales.

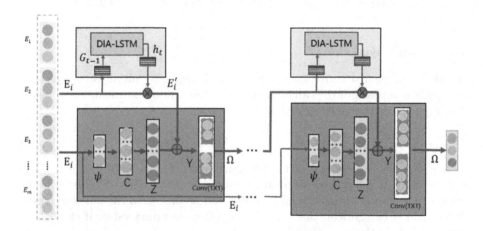

Fig. 2. The structure of multi-scale feature-crossing attention layer.

Attention Calibration Module. Lets $E_i = [e_{11}, e_{12}, .., e_{ti}, .., e_{mk}]^T$ denotes the 2-D $m \times k$ embedding matrix, where E_i represents the i-th embedding sample, $e_{ti} \in R^k$ is the i-th embedding vector of the t-th field , m is the size of fields and k is the embedding size of each embedding vector. First of all, we use mean pooling method to squeeze the embedding vectors of fields into one vector $G = [g_1, ..., g_t, ..., g_m]$ where $t \in [1, m]$. g_t represents the global information of the t-th field, which can be calculated as:

$$g_t = \frac{1}{k} \sum_{q=1}^{k} e_{tq} \tag{3}$$

Then we adopt DIA-LSTM [5] to dynamically capture feature information of different layers, and use the shared Fully Connected module (FC) to reduce the parameters in training process. The DIA-LSTM unit is shown in Fig. 3. The first FC layer is a compression layer with parameters W_1 which compresses the input dimension to the $1/4$ original size and uses σ_1 as nonlinear function; The second FC layer expands the dimension to 4 times of the original input with parameter W_2. Given the input vector G_{t-1} and the random initialization of hidden unit h_{t-1}, the output F is denoted as:

$$F = W_2 \sigma_1 (W_1 [G_{t-1}, h_{t-1}]) \tag{4}$$

where σ_1 is LeakyReLU activation function. The outputs of forget gate f_t, input gate i_t, cell state $\widetilde{C_t}$, and output gate O_t are denoted as:

$$f_t = \sigma(F); i_t = \sigma(F); \widetilde{C_t} = \sigma(F); O_t = \sigma(F). \tag{5}$$

where σ denotes sigmoid function. After obtaining these four internal units, we can further get the outputs C_t and h_t of LSTM:

$$C_t = C_{t-1} f_t + i_t \widetilde{C_t} \tag{6}$$

$$h_t = tanh(C_t) O_t \tag{7}$$

where we use tanh [8] function to replace sigmoid function.

Finally, the original embedding matrix E_i is calibrated to the new embedding matrix E_i', which can be defined as:

$$E_i' = h_t \odot E_i \tag{8}$$

where h_t is the weight vector, which represents the importance of features; $\odot$ denotes Hadamard product that is element-wise multiply.

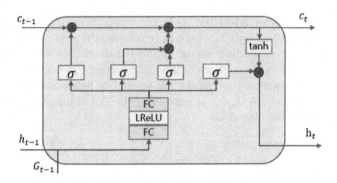

Fig. 3. The structure of DIA-LSTM unit.

Multi-scale Feature-Crossing Module. This module shares the same input with calibration module, and we use two Fully Connected layers (FC) to learn feature interactions from different fields. The first FC layer is a field dimension reduction layer with parameter U_1 and b_1 with reduction ration r that is a hyper-parameter. The second FC layer is a dimensional recovery layer with parameter U_2 and b_2. The cross feature can be calculated as follows:

$$C = U_2\psi + b_2; \psi = U_1E_i + b_1 \tag{9}$$

where $C \in R^{m \times k}$ is a 2-dimensional vector matrix; $\psi \in R^{k \times \frac{m}{r}}$ is the output of compress cross features; the hyper parameters are U_1, U_2, b_1, b_2; r is the reduction ratio.

Then we use a FC layer to transform dimension, and expand the embedding dimension from low dimension to higher dimension at different scales. The new cross feature is defined as:

$$Z = \tau C + b_3 \tag{10}$$

where $Z \in R^{m \times k'}$ denotes the matrix vectors in different layers; k' equals k in the first layer; τ and b_3 are the weight matrix and bias vectors in different layers.

Finally, in order to reinforce feature interactions, the cross features and calibration module can be fused as:

$$Y_i = [E'_{i1} \oplus Z_{i1}, E'_{i2} \oplus Z_{i2}, ..., E'_{im} \oplus Z_{im}] \tag{11}$$

where Y_i is a 2-dimensional $m \times k'$ matrix vectors; $\oplus$ denotes the element-wise addition; $E'_i \in R^{m \times k'}$ is the matrix vector of the attention calibration module; $Z \in R^{m \times k'}$ is the matrix vector of feature-crossing module.

1×1 convolution [3,14] has been widely applied to achieve dimensionality reduction and dimensionality upgrading. Thus we introduce the 1×1 convolution to upgrade the embedding dimension, which can be calculated as:

$$\Omega_i = conv1D(\omega Y_i) = LeakyReLU(\omega Y_i) \tag{12}$$

where $\Omega_i \in R^{m \times k'}$, k' is the expanded embedding dimension; ω is the convolution weight; the size of convolution kernel is 1×1; the number of filters are k'; the activation function is set to LeakyReLU.

3.4 Hidden Layers

The hidden layers are composed of several fully connected layers with same scale, which capture high-order and implicit feature interactions. Here, the embedding matrix includes different features which have various influence for the models, so we add a matrix parameter to adjust the embedding matrix. The input of this layer $\varphi^{(0)}$ is defined as:

$$\varphi^{(0)} = \zeta \odot E_i \tag{13}$$

where ζ denotes the matrix parameter; E_i is the embedding matrix.

Then, $\varphi^{(0)}$ is entered into the deep network and the forward process is defined as:

$$\varphi^{(l)} = \xi(W^{(l)}\varphi^{(0)} + \beta^{(l)}) \tag{14}$$

where l is the depth; ξ is the LeakyReLU function; $\varphi^{(l)}$ is the output of the l-th hidden layer; $w^{(l)}$ and $\beta^{(l)}$ is the hyper-parameter of the l-th deep layer.

3.5 Combination Layer

The combination layer concatenates interaction vector Ω and hidden vector φ and feeds the concatenated vector into a FC layer. It can be expressed as the following description:

$$\delta = F_{concat}(\Omega, \varphi) = [\Omega_1, ..., \Omega_n, \varphi_1, ..., \varphi_n]^T \tag{15}$$

where δ is the output of the combination layer; n is the number of samples.

3.6 Output Layer

We combine combination layer and linear part to make model stronger by capturing different feature interactions. The output unit is defined as:

$$\hat{y} = \sigma(\Theta\delta + \sum_{i=0}^{n} \beta_i E_i + b) \tag{16}$$

where $\hat{y} \in (0,1)$ is the predicted result of model; σ is sigmoid function; δ is the output of combination layer; n is the number of samples; E_i is the embedding vectors and β_i is the i-th weight of linear part; Θ and b are the weight and bias.

We introduce the Log loss as the loss function as the objective function, which is expressed as:

$$loss = -\frac{1}{N}\sum_{i=1}^{N}(y_i log(\hat{y}_i) + (1 - y_i)log(1 - \hat{y}_i)) \tag{17}$$

where N is the size of the training samples; y_i is the ground truth of the i-th training instance; $\hat{y}_i$ is the final output of the network.

4   Experiments

In this section, we will further evaluate our proposed model by replying the following questions:

RQ 1 How does our model perform compared with the state-of-the-art methods on multi-field sparse data? Is it efficient for CTR problems?

RQ 2 How do the implicit feature interactions affect performance?

RQ 3 How do the different configurations influence the performance of our model?

4.1   Experiment Setup

Datasets. Besides two public CTR evaluation datasets (Avazu[1] and Criteo[2]), we constuct a new Tobacco dataset with a small amount of data, a large number of feature fields, numerous null values, and a few of anomaly data. Their statistics are illustrated in Table 1. All of datasets are divided into 80% samples for training and 20% remaining ones for testing.

Table 1. Statistics of three evaluation datasets.

Dataset	Instances	Fields	Features (Sparse)
Tobacco	166,626	247	146,103
Avazu	40,428,967	23	1,544,488
Criteo	45,840,617	39	998,960

Evaluation Metrics. We use AUC and Logloss as our evaluation metrics. AUC is not sensitive to whether the samples are balanced and it reflects the sorting ability of the samples. Logloss measures the distance between two distributions and the smaller value indicates the better performance.

Model Comparison. We compare our proposed model with three classes of the traditional models: (i) shallow models, including LR [9], FM [11], AFM [17]. (ii) deep models, including Wide&Deep [1], Deep&Cross [16], DeepFM [2], xDeepFM [7]. (iii) high-order models, including NFM [4], PNN [10], CrossNet [16], CIN [7], AutoInt [13].

---

[1] Avazu:http://www.kaggle.com/c/avazu-ctr-prediction.
[2] Criteo:https://www.kaggle.com/c/criteo-display-ad-challenge.

Implementation Details. We implement all models with tensorflow. The embedding size is set to 40, 16 for Tobacco and two public datasets respectively. We use Adam as optimization method for all methods with the batch size of 256 for Tobacco and 1024 for other datasets. For Tobacco dataset, the depth of hidden layers is set to 4, the number of neurons per layer is 128, For Avazu and Criteo datasets, we use the same parameters with AutoInt [13] for baseline methods. We use three interaction layers for CrossNet and CIN. The hidden layer size of NFM is set to 200 which is recommended in the paper [4].

4.2   Effectiveness Comparison (RQ1)

Evaluation of Performance. We summarize the performance of different models on three datasets in Table 2. Compared with the shallow models, the deep models have a better performance on all datasets because cross features from deep models yield the higher predictive power. On the other hand, our MsFcNET model achieves an excellent performance over the three datasets. The results indicate that the feature interactions of our model are very effective on multi-field sparse datasets.

Table 2. The overall performance of different models on Tobacco, Avazu and Criteo datasets.

Model Class	Model	Tobacco		Avazu		Criteo	
		AUC	Logloss	AUC	Logloss	AUC	Logloss
Shallow model	LR	0.7240	0.4495	0.7560	0.3964	0.7820	0.4695
	FM	0.7883	0.4116	0.7706	0.3856	0.7836	0.4700
	AFM	0.7901	0.4102	0.7718	0.3854	0.7938	0.4584
deep model	Wide&Deep	0.8565	0.3657	0.7749	0.3824	0.8026	0.4494
	DeepFM	0.8655	0.3611	0.7751	0.3829	0.8066	0.4449
	Deep&Cross	0.8697	0.3588	0.7731	0.3836	0.8067	0.4447
	xDeepFM	0.8840	0.3403	**0.7768**	0.3823	0.8070	0.4447
	MsFcNET	**0.8872**	**0.3330**	0.7766	**0.3819**	**0.8081**	**0.4406**

Evaluation of Efficiency. We compare the runtime of different models on three datasets. Since most of shallow models have the simpler implementation, they are more efficient than the deep models. In the deep models, xDeepFM has an excellent performance, but due to the complexity of cross-layer computing, xDeepFM has much more time consumption. The runtimes for each epoch are 250s, 353100 s, 80145 s on three datasets respectively. MsFcNET's runtimes for each epoch are 171s, 78540 s, 20865 s on three datasets respectively, which has a great improvement in time consumption compared with xDeepFM.

4.3   Performance Comparison Without Deep Module (RQ2)

Table 3. The performance of different high-order models on three datasets.

	Tobacco		Avazu		Criteo	
Model	AUC	Logloss	AUC	Logloss	AUC	Logloss
NFM	0.7923	0.4089	0.7708	0.3864	0.7957	0.4562
CrossNet	0.8624	0.3590	0.7667	0.3868	0.7907	0.4591
PNN	0.8684	0.3520	0.7743	0.3834	0.7973	0.4523
CIN	0.8808	0.3396	0.7758	0.3829	0.8009	0.4517
AutoInt	0.8370	0.3952	0.7752	0.3824	0.8061	0.4455
MsFcNET-	**0.8863**	**0.3352**	**0.7764**	**0.3822**	**0.8068**	**0.4420**

Comparison with High-Order Models. Deep module improves implicit feature interactions and has been widely adopted in predictive models. Here, all of high-order models exclude the deep network layers. For a fair comparison, our MsFcNET model also gets rid of the part of the deep hidden layer, called as MsFcNET-. Table 3 shows the performance of high-order models on three datasets. Our MsFcNET model without deep module still has the outstanding performance on these datasets, which demonstrates the effectiveness of high-order feature interactions in our proposed model.

4.4   Hyper-parameter Analysis (RQ3)

Table 4. The performance of different embedding sizes on three datasets.

	Tobacco		Avazu		Criteo	
Embedding size	AUC	Logloss	AUC	Logloss	AUC	Logloss
10	0.8774	0.3491	0.7761	0.3821	**0.8083**	**0.4403**
20 (16)	0.8790	0.3491	0.7766	0.3819	0.8081	0.4406
30	0.8860	0.3378	0.7767	0.3816	0.8078	0.4412
40	**0.8872**	**0.3330**	**0.7770**	**0.3816**	0.8072	0.4416
50	0.8867	0.3357	0.7765	0.3822	0.8066	0.4424

Embedding Part. We analyze the effects of the embedding size from 10 to 50. As illustrated in Table 4, for Tobacco and Avazu datasets, when the embedding size is set to 40, our model can yield the best performance; for Criteo dataset, there is the best performance when the size is 10. Obviously, the appropriate embedding size can extract more valuable features while avoiding the difficult optimization of too many parameters.

Multi-scale Feature-Crossing Part. We compare the model performance in the number of multi-scale feature-crossing layers from 1 to 5. When the network depth increases from 1 to 3 on Avazu dataset, the AUC increases from 0.7745 to 0.7768 and Logloss decreases from 0.3830 to 0.3823.

However, when a number of layers continues to increase, the performance begins to decrease. Finally, the AUC decreases to 0.7756 and Logloss increases to 0.3828 on Avazu dataset. This is because too complicated models can easily lead to over-fitting. For Avazu dataset, it is more appropriate to set the layer number to 3. Furthermore, the size of reduction ratio can also lead to more complex models. We change the size of reduction ratio from 1 to 5 and get the similar results with the change of layer number. When we set 3 for Avazu dataset as the reduction ratio, our model gets the best performance.

5 Conclusion

In this paper, we propose a novel network named MsFcNET, which can not only dynamically adjust the weights of features, but also efficiently reinforce the extraction of cross features in the different scales. Our proposed model constructs a new attention network based on DIA-LSTM unit, which can learn the importance of features in the process of feature interactions. Moreover, our model also designs a multi-scale feature-crossing module to better extract and represent complex cross features. Experimental results on three real-world datasets demonstrate that our MsFcNET model can yield better performance than the state-of-the-art deep and shallow models.

References

1. Cheng, H.T., Koc, L., Harmsen, J., et al.: Wide & deep learning for recommender systems. In: The 1st Workshop on Recommender Systems, pp. 7–10 (2016)
2. Guo, H., Tang, R., Ye, Y., et al.: DeepFM: a factorization-machine based neural network for CTR prediction. arXiv preprint arXiv:1703.04247 (2017)
3. He, K., Zhang, X., Ren, S., Sun, J.: Deep residual learning for image recognition. In: Proceedings of the CVPR, pp. 770–778 (2016)
4. He, X., Chua, T.S.: Neural factorization machines for sparse predictive analytics. In: Proceedings of the 40th International ACM SIGIR, pp. 355–364 (2017)
5. Huang, Z., Liang, S., Liang, M., et al.: Dianet: dense-and-implicit attention network. arXiv preprint arXiv:1905.10671 (2019)
6. Juan, Y., Zhuang, Y., Chin, W.S., et al.: Field-aware factorization machines for CTR prediction. In: Proceedings of the 10th ACM. pp. 43–50. ACM (2016)
7. Lian, J., Zhou, X., Zhang, F., et al.: xDeepFM: combining explicit and implicit feature interactions for recommender systems. In: The 24th ACM SIGKDD, pp. 1754–1763. ACM (2018)
8. Malfliet, W., Hereman, W.: The tanh method: I. exact solutions of nonlinear evolution and wave equations. Physica Scripta **54**(6), 563 (1996)
9. McMahan, H.B., Holt, G., Sculley, D., et al.: Ad click prediction: a view from the trenches. In: The 19th ACM SIGKDD, pp. 1222–1230 (2013)

10. Qu, Y., Fang, B., Zhang, W., et al.: Product-based neural networks for user response prediction over multi-field categorical data. ACM TOIS **37**(1), 1–35 (2018)
11. Rendle, S., Gantner, Z., et al.: Fast context-aware recommendations with factorization machines. In: The 34th ACM SIGIR, pp. 635–644. ACM (2011)
12. Shan, Y., Hoens, T.R., Jiao, J., et al.: Deep crossing: Web-scale modeling without manually crafted combinatorial features. In: The 22th ACM SIGKDD, pp. 255–262 (2016)
13. Song, W., Shi, C., Xiao, Z., et al.: Autoint: automatic feature interaction learning via self-attentive neural networks. In: The 28th ACM CIKM, pp. 1161–1170 (2019)
14. Szegedy, C., Liu, W., Jia, Y., et al.: Going deeper with convolutions. In: Proceedings of the CVPR, pp. 1–9 (2015)
15. Wang, F., Jiang, M., Qian, C., et al.: Residual attention network for image classification. In: Proceedings of the IEEE CVPR, pp. 3156–3164 (2017)
16. Wang, R., Fu, B., Fu, G., et al.: Deep & cross network for ad click predictions. In: Proceedings of the ADKDD 2017, p. 12. ACM (2017)
17. Xiao, J., Ye, H., He, X., et al.: Attentional factorization machines: learning the weight of feature interactions via attention networks. arXiv preprint arXiv:1708.04617 (2017)
18. Zhang, L., Shen, W., Huang, J., et al.: Field-aware neural factorization machine for click-through rate prediction. IEEE Access **7**, 75032–75040 (2019)
19. Zhou, G., Zhu, X., Song, C., et al.: Deep interest network for click-through rate prediction. In: Proceedings of the 24th ACM SIGKDD, pp. 1059–1068. ACM (2018)

Balancing Between Accuracy and Fairness for Interactive Recommendation with Reinforcement Learning

Weiwen Liu[1], Feng Liu[2], Ruiming Tang[1,2,3(✉)], Ben Liao[1,2,3],
Guangyong Chen[3(✉)], and Pheng Ann Heng[1,3]

[1] The Chinese University of Hong Kong, Sha Tin, Hong Kong
tangruiming2015@163.com
[2] Harbin Institute of Technology, Harbin, China
[3] Guangdong Provincial Key Laboratory of Computer Vision and Virtual Reality
Technology, Shenzhen Institutes of Advanced Technology,
Chinese Academy of Sciences, Shenzhen, China
gychen@link.cuhk.edu.hk

Abstract. Fairness in recommendation has attracted increasing attention due to bias and discrimination possibly caused by traditional recommenders. In Interactive Recommender Systems (IRS), user preferences and the system's fairness status are constantly changing over time. Existing fairness-aware recommenders mainly consider fairness in static settings. Directly applying existing methods to IRS will result in poor recommendation. To resolve this problem, we propose a reinforcement learning based framework, *FairRec*, to dynamically maintain a long-term balance between accuracy and fairness in IRS. User preferences and the system's fairness status are jointly compressed into the state representation to generate recommendations. FairRec aims at maximizing our designed cumulative reward that combines accuracy and fairness. Extensive experiments validate that FairRec can improve fairness, while preserving good recommendation quality.

1 Introduction

Interactive Recommender Systems (IRS) have been widely implemented in various fields, *e.g.*, news, movies, and finance [20]. Different from the conventional recommendation settings [11], IRS consecutively recommend items to individual users and receive their feedback in interactive processes. IRS gradually refine the recommendation policy according to the obtained user feedback in an online manner. The goal of such a system is to maximize the total utility over the whole interaction period. A typical utility of IRS is user acceptance of recommendations. Conversion Rate (CVR) is one of the most commonly used measures of recommendation acceptance, computing the ratio of users *performing a system's desired activity* to users *having viewed recommended items*. A desired activity could be downloading from App stores, or making loans for microlending.

© Springer Nature Switzerland AG 2020
H. W. Lauw et al. (Eds.): PAKDD 2020, LNAI 12084, pp. 155–167, 2020.
https://doi.org/10.1007/978-3-030-47426-3_13

However, optimizing CVR solely may result in fairness issues, one of which is the unfair allocation of desired activities, like clicks or downloads, over different demographic groups. Under such unfair circumstances, majority (over-representing) groups may dominate recommendations, thereby holding a higher proportion of opportunities and resources, while minority groups are largely under-represented or even totally ignored. A fair allocation is a critical objective in recommendation due to the following benefits:

Legal. Recommendation in particular settings are explicitly mandated to guarantee fairness. In the setting of employment, education, housing, or public accommodation, a fair treatment with respect to race, color, religion, *etc.*, is required by the anti-discrimination laws [8]. For job recommendation, it is expected that jobs at minority-owned businesses are being recommended and applied at the same rate as jobs at white-owned businesses. In microlending, loan recommender systems must ensure borrowers of different races or regions have an equal chance of being recommended and funded.

Financial. Under-representing for some groups leads to the abandonment of the system. For instance, video sharing platforms like YouTube involve viewers and creators. It is desirable to ensure each creator has a fair chance of being recommended and promoted. Otherwise, if the new creators do not get adequate exposure and appreciation, they tend to leave the platform, resulting in less user-generated content. Consequently, users' satisfaction from both viewers and creators, as well as the platform's total income are affected in the long run.

The fairness concern in recommender systems is quite challenging, as accuracy and fairness are usually conflicting goals to be achieved to some extent. On the one hand, to obtain the ideal fairness, one could simply divide the recommendation opportunities equally to each item group, but users' satisfaction will be affected by being persistently presented with unattractive items. On the other hand, existing recommender systems have been demonstrated to favor popular items [5], resulting in extremely unbalanced recommendation results. Thus, our work aims to answer this question: *Can we achieve a fairer recommendation while preserving or just sacrificing a little recommendation accuracy?*

Most prior works consider fairness for the conventional recommender systems [1,2], where the recommendation is regarded as a static process at a certain time instant. A general framework that formulates fairness constraints on rankings in terms of exposure allocation is proposed in [19]. Individual attention fairness is discussed in [3]. [21] models re-ranking with fairness constraints in Multi-sided Recommender Systems (MRS) as an integer linear programming. The balanced neighborhoods method [4] balances protected and unprotected groups by reformulating the Sparse LInear Method (SLIM) with a new regularizer.

However, it is hard to directly apply those methods to IRS due to:

(i) It is infeasible to impose fairness constraints at every time instant. Forcing the system to be fair at any time and increasing fairness uniformly for all users will result in poor recommendations. In fact, IRS focus on the long-term cumulative utility over the whole interaction session, where the system could focus on improving accuracy for users with particular favor, and the lack of fairness at the time can later be compensated when recommending items to users with diversified interests. As such, we can achieve long-term system's fairness while preserving satisfying recommendation quality.

(ii) Existing work only considers the distribution of the number of recommendations (exposure) an item group received. Actually, the distribution of the desired activities that take place after an exposure like clicks or downloads has much larger commercial value and can be directly converted to revenue.

To resolve the problem, we design a **Fair**ness-aware **Rec**ommendation framework with reinforcement learning (FairRec) for IRS. FairRec jointly compresses the user preferences and the system's fairness status into the current state representation. A two-fold reward is designed to measure the system gain regarding accuracy and fairness. FairRec is trained to maximize the long-term cumulative reward to maintain an accuracy-fairness balance. The major contributions of this paper are as follows:

- We formulate a fairness objective for IRS. To the best of our knowledge, this is the first work that balances between accuracy and fairness in IRS.
- We propose a reinforcement learning based framework, FairRec, to dynamically maintain a balance between accuracy and fairness in IRS. In FairRec, user preferences and the system's fairness status are jointly compressed into the state representation to generate recommendations. We also design a two-fold reward to combine accuracy and fairness.
- We evaluate our proposed FairRec algorithm on both synthetic and real-world data. We show that FairRec can achieve a better balance between accuracy and fairness, compared to the state-of-the-art methods.

2 Problem Formulation

2.1 Markov Decision Process for IRS

In this paper, we model the fairness-aware recommendation for IRS as a finite time Markov Decision Process (MDP), with an action space $\mathcal{A}$, a state space $\mathcal{S}$, and a reward function $r : \mathcal{S} \times \mathcal{A} \rightarrow \mathcal{R}$. When a user u arrives at time step $t = 1, \ldots, T$, the system observes the current state $s_t \in \mathcal{S}$ of the user u and takes an action $a_t \in \mathcal{A}$ (e.g., recommending an item to the user).

The user views the item and provides feedback y_{a_t}, e.g., clicking or downloading on the recommended item, if she feels interested. Let $y_{a_t} \in \{0, 1\}$ denote the user's feedback, with $y_{a_t} = 1$ meaning the user performs desired activities, and 0 otherwise. The system then receives a reward r_t (a function of y_{a_t}), and updates the model. The problem formulation is formally presented as follows:

States $\mathcal{S}$: The state s_t is described by user preferences and the system's fairness status. We jointly embed them into the current state representation. The detailed design of the state representation is given in Sect. 3.2.

Transitions $\mathcal{P}$: The transition of states models the dynamic change of user preferences and the system's fairness. The successor state s_{t+1} is obtained once the user's feedback at time t is collected.

Action $\mathcal{A}$: An action a_t is recommending an item chosen from the available candidate item set $\mathcal{A}$. Our framework can be easily extended to the case of recommending a list of items. To simplify our presentations, we focus on recommending an item at a time in this paper.

Reward $\mathcal{R}$: The reward r_t is a scalar measuring the system's gain regarding accuracy and fairness after taking action a_t, elaborated in Sect. 3.3.

We aim to learn a policy π, mapping from states to actions $a_t = \pi(s_t)$, to generate recommendations that are both accurate and fair. The goal is to maximize the sum of discounted rewards (return) from time t onward, which is defined by $R_t^\gamma = \sum_{k=t}^{T} \gamma^{k-t} r_k$, and γ is the discount factor.

2.2 Weighted Proportional Fairness for IRS

Each item is associated with a categorical protected attribute $C \in \{c_1, \ldots, c_l\}$. Let $\mathcal{A}_c = \{a | C = c, a \in \mathcal{A}\}$ denote the group of items with an attribute value c. Take loan recommendation for instance, if the protected attribute is the geographical region, then $\mathcal{A}_c$ with $c = $ "Oceania" contains all the loans applied from Oceania. Denote by $x_t \in \mathbb{R}_+^l$ the *allocation vector*, where x_t^i represents the allocation proportion of group i up to time t,

$$x_t^i = \frac{\sum_{k=1}^{t} y_{a_k} \mathbb{1}_{\mathcal{A}_{c_i}}(a_k)}{\sum_{i'=1}^{l} \sum_{k=1}^{t} y_{a_k} \mathbb{1}_{\mathcal{A}_{c_{i'}}}(a_k)}. \tag{1}$$

where $\mathbb{1}_A(x)$ equals to 1 if $x \in A$, and 0 otherwise. Recall that y_{a_k} is the user's feedback on recommended item a_k. In loan recommendation, x_t^i denotes the rate of funded loans from the region i over all funded ones up to time t.

In this work, we focus on a well-accepted and axiomatically justified metric of fairness, the weighted proportional fairness [9]. Weighted proportional fairness is a generalized Nash solution for multiple groups.

Definition 1 (Weighted Proportional Fairness). *An allocation of desired activities x_t is weighted proportionally fair if it is the solution of the following optimization problem,*

$$\max_{x_t} \sum_{i=1}^{l} w_i \log(x_t^i), \quad s.t. \sum_{i=1}^{l} x_t^i = 1, x_t^i \geq 0, i = 1, \ldots, l. \tag{2}$$

The coefficient $w_i \in \mathbb{R}_+$ is a pre-defined parameter weighing the importance of each group. The optimal solution can be easily solved by standard Lagrangian multiplier methods, namely

$$x_*^i = \frac{w_i}{\sum_{i'=1}^{l} w_{i'}}. \tag{3}$$

We aim to improve the weighted proportional fairness $\sum_{i=1}^{l} w_i \log(x_T^i)$ while preserving high conversions $\sum_{t=1}^{T} y_{a_t}$ up to time T.

3   Proposed Model

This section begins with a brief overview of our proposed FairRec. After that, we introduce the components of FairRec and the learning algorithm in detail.

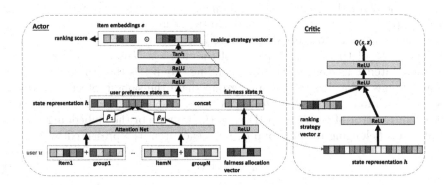

Fig. 1. The architecture of FairRec.

3.1   Overview

To balance between accuracy and fairness in the long run, we formulate IRS recommendation as an MDP, which is then solved by reinforcement learning.

The previously studied reinforcement learning models can be categorized as follows: *Value-based* methods approximate the value function, then the action with the largest value is selected [26,27]. Value-based methods are more sample-efficient and steady, but the computational cost is high when the action space is large. *Policy-based* methods directly learn a policy that takes as input of the current user state and outputs an action [6,24], which generally have a faster convergence. *Actor-critic* architectures take advantage of both value-based and policy-based methods [15,25]. Therefore, we design our model following the actor-critic framework.

The overall architecture of FairRec is illustrated in Fig. 1, which consists of an *actor* network and a *critic* network. The actor network performs time-varying recommendations according to the dynamic user preferences and the fairness status. The critic network estimates the value of the outputs associated with the actor network to encourage or discourage the recommended items.

3.2   Personalized Fairness-Aware State Representation

We propose a personalized fairness-aware state representation to jointly consider accuracy and fairness, which is composed of the the User Preference State (UPS) and the Fairness State (FS). State representation learns a non-linear transformation $h_t = f_s(s_t)$ that maps the current state s_t to a continuous vector h_t.

User Preference State (UPS). UPS represents personalized user preferences. We propose a two-level granularity representation: the item-level and the group-level. The item-level representation indicates the user's fine-grained preferences to each item, while the group-level representation shows the user's coarse-grained interests in each item group. Such two-level granularity representation provides more information on the propensity of different users towards diverse recommendation. Therefore, the agent could focus on accuracy for the users with particular favor, and the lack of fairness at a point in time can later be compensated when recommending items to users with diverse interests.

The input of UPS is the sequence of the user u's N most recent positively interacted items, as well as the corresponding group IDs that the items belong to at t. Items belonging to the same group share the same protected attribute value c. Each item a is mapped to a continuous embedding vector $e_a \in \mathbb{R}^d$. The embedding vector of each group ID e_g is the average of the embedding vectors of all items belonging to the group g. Then each item is represented by

$$\epsilon_a = e_a + e_g, \tag{4}$$

where $\epsilon_a \in \mathbb{R}^d$, and item a belongs to group g. The group embedding e_g is added to serve as a global bias (or a regularizer), allowing items belonging to the same group to share the same group information.

As for a specific user u, the affects of different historical interactions on her future interest may vary significantly. To capture this sequential dependencies among the historical interacted items, we apply an attention mechanism [23] to weigh each item in the interacted item sequence. The attention net learns a weight vector β of size N, $\beta = \text{Softmax}(\omega^1 \sigma(\omega^2 [\epsilon_{a_1}, \ldots, \epsilon_{a_N}] + b^2) + b^1)$, where $\omega^1, b^1, \omega^2, b^2$ are the network parameters and $\sigma(\cdot)$ is the ReLU activation function. The user preference state representation m_t is obtained by multiplying the attention weights with the corresponding item representations as $m_t = [\beta_1 \epsilon_{a_1}, \ldots, \beta_N \epsilon_{a_N}]$, where m_t is of dimension $N \times d$ and β_i denotes the i-th entry in the weight vector β. Therefore, the items currently contributing more to the outcome are assigned with higher weights.

Fairness State (FS). The input of FS is the current allocation distribution of the desired activities at time t. As a complementary for UPS, FS provides evidence of the current fairness status and helps the agent to promote items belonging to under-represented groups. In particular, we deploy a Multi-Layer Perceptron (MLP) to map the allocation vector x_t to a latent space, $n_t = \text{MLP}(x_t)$. Then we concatenate m_t and n_t to obtain the final state representation,

$$h_t = [m_t \| n_t], \tag{5}$$

with $\|$ denotes concatenation operation.

3.3   Reward Function Design

The reward is designed to measure the system's gain regarding accuracy and fairness. Existing reinforcement learning frameworks for recommendation only consider the recommendation accuracy, and one commonly used definition of reward is $r = 1$ if the user performs desired activities and -1 otherwise [15,25]. To incorporate the fairness measure into IRS, we propose a two-fold reward by first examining whether the user performs the desired activities on the recommended item, and then evaluating the fairness gain of performing such a desired activity.

As discussed in Sect. 2, to achieve the weighted proportional fairness, the optimal allocation vector is $x_*^i = \frac{w_i}{\sum_{i'=1}^l w_{i'}}$, with w_i the pre-defined target allocation proportion of group i. Therefore, we incorporate the deviation from the optimal solution $x_*^i - x_t^i$ into the reward as the fairness indicator:

$$r_t = \begin{cases} \sum_{i=1}^l \mathbb{1}_{\mathcal{A}_{c_i}}(a_t)\left(x_*^i - x_t^i + 1\right), & \text{if } y_{a_t} = 1 \\ -\lambda, & \text{if } y_{a_t} = 0 \end{cases}, \tag{6}$$

where $\mathbb{1}_A(x)$ is the indicator function and is 1 when $x \in A$, 0 otherwise, x_t^i is the allocation proportion of group i at time t. The constant $\lambda > 1$ is the penalty value for inaccurate recommendations and manages the accuracy-fairness tradeoff. A larger λ means that the agent focuses more on accuracy.

Since the fairness metric (Eq. (1) and Eq. (2)) is computed according to the number of the desired activities, only positive y_{a_t} influences fairness. Therefore, we simply give a negative reward $-\lambda$ for $y_{a_t} = 0$ to punish the undesired activities. When $y_{a_t} = 1$, we compute the fairness score $x_*^i - x_t^i$, which is the difference between the optimal distribution and current allocation. Suppose the user performs a desired activity on the item $a_t \in \mathcal{A}_{c_i}$. Then the fairness score $x_*^i - x_t^i$ is negative if the i-th group is over-representing ($x_t^i > x_*^i$), and is more negative if $\mathcal{A}_{c_i}$ already has a higher rate of the desired activity, indicating that the system should focus more on other groups. Similarly, the fairness score $x_*^i - x_t^i$ is positive if the i-th group is currently under-representing ($x_t^i < x_*^i$), and is more positive if $\mathcal{A}_{c_i}$ is more lacking in the desired activity. We add 1 to the fairness score to ensure the reward is positive if $y_{a_t} = 1$.

To sum up, the agent receives a large positive reward if the user performs a desired activity on the item and the item belongs to an under-representing group. Whereas the reward is a smaller positive number if the activity is desired, but the item belongs to an over-representing (majority) group. We punish the most severely with $y_{a_t} = 0$, as it neither contributes to accuracy nor fairness.

3.4   Model Update

Actor Network. The actor network extracts latent features from s_t and outputs a ranking strategy vector z_t. The recommendation is performed according to the ranking vector by $a_t = \arg\max_{a \in \mathcal{A}} e_a^\top z_t$. In particular, we first embed s_t to h_t following the architecture described in Sect. 3.2, then we stack fully-connected layers on top of h_t to learn the nonlinear transformation and generate z_t, as presented in Fig. 1.

Suppose the policy $\pi_\theta(s)$ learned by the actor is parameterized by θ. The actor is trained according to $Q_\eta(s_t, z_t)$ from the critic, and updated by the sampled policy gradient [18] with α_θ as the learning rate, B as the batch size,

$$\theta \leftarrow \theta + \alpha_\theta \frac{1}{B} \sum_t \nabla_z Q_\eta(s, z)|_{s=s_t, z=\pi_\theta(s_t)} \nabla_\theta \pi_\theta(s)|_{s=s_t}, \tag{7}$$

Critic Network. The critic adopts a deep neural network $Q_\eta(s_t, z_t)$, parameterized by η, to estimate the expected total discounted reward $\mathbb{E}[R_t^\gamma|s_t, z_t; \pi]$, given the state s_t and the ranking strategy vector z_t under the policy π. Specifically for this problem, the network structure is designed as follows

$$Q_\eta(s_t, z_t) = \text{MLP}([\sigma(W_h h_t + b_h)\|z_t]), \tag{8}$$

by first mapping h_t to the same space as z_t with a fully-connected layer and then concatenating it with z_t, while $\text{MLP}(\cdot)$ denotes a mutli-layer perceptron, and $h_t = f_s(s_t)$ is the state representation as presented in Sect. 3.2.

We use the temporal-difference (TD) learning [22] to update the critic. The loss function is the mean square error $L = \sum_t (\nu_t - Q_\eta(s_t, z_t))^2$, where $\nu_t = r_t + \gamma Q_{\eta'}(s_{t+1}, \pi_{\theta'}(s_{t+1}))$. The term $\nu_t - Q_\eta(s_t, z_t)$ is called time difference (TD), η' and θ' are the parameters of the target critic and actor network that are periodically copied from η, θ and kept constant for a number of iterations to ensure the stability of the training [14]. The parameter θ is updated by gradient descent, with α_η the learning rate and B the batch size:

$$\eta \leftarrow \eta + \alpha_\eta \frac{1}{B} \sum_t (\nu_t - Q_\eta(s_t, z_t)) \nabla_\eta Q_\eta(s_t, z_t). \tag{9}$$

4   Experiments

4.1   Experimental Settings

We evaluate the proposed FairRec algorithm on both synthetic and real-world data, comparing with the state-of-the-art recommendation methods in terms of fairness and accuracy.

Datasets. We use MovieLens[1] and Kiva.org datasets for evaluation. **Movie-Lens** is a public benchmark dataset for recommender systems, with 943 users, 1,602 items and 100,000 user-item interactions. Since the MovieLens data do not have protected attributes, we created 10 groups to represent differences among group inventories, and randomly assigned movies to each of such groups following a geometric distribution. An interaction with the rating (ranging from 1 to

---

[1] https://grouplens.org/datasets/movielens.

5) larger than 3 is defined as a desired activity in calculating CVR. **Kiva.org** is a proprietary dataset obtained from Kiva.org, consisting of lending transactions over a 6-month period. We followed the pre-processing technique used in [16] to densify the dataset. The retained dataset has 1,589 loans, 589 lenders and 43,976 ratings. The geographical region of loans is selected as the protected attribute, as Kiva.org has a stated mission of equalizing access to capital across different regions so that loans from each region have a fair chance to be funded. We define a transaction amount greater than USD25 as the desired activity for Kiva.

Evaluation Metrics. We evaluate the recommendation accuracy by the Conversion Rate (CVR):

$$\text{CVR} = \frac{\sum_{k=1}^{T} y_{a_k}}{T}, \tag{10}$$

and measure the fairness by Weighted Proportional Fairness (PropFair)[2]:

$$\text{PropFair} = \sum_{i=1}^{l} w_i \log(1 + x_T^i). \tag{11}$$

Table 1. Experimental results on MovieLens and Kiva.

	MovieLens			Kiva		
	CVR	PropFair	UFG	CVR	PropFair	UFG
NMF	0.7972	0.8592	4.2362	0.4211	0.8473	1.4635
SVD	0.8478	0.8337	5.4795	0.4870	0.8686	1.6931
DeepFM	<u>0.8612</u>	0.8098	5.8323	0.6349	0.8671	2.3752
LinUCB	0.8577	0.8464	5.9476	0.6517	0.8697	2.4970
DRR	0.8592	0.8470	<u>6.0177</u>	<u>0.6567</u>	0.8645	<u>2.5183</u>
MRPC	0.8361	<u>0.8608</u>	5.2508	0.4286	<u>0.8761</u>	1.5332
FairRec	**0.8702***	**0.8666***	**6.6776***	**0.6905***	**0.8838***	**2.8555***

We conduct a two-sided significant test [17] between FairRec and the strongest baseline DRR, where * means the p-value is smaller than 0.05.

Moreover, we propose a Unit Fairness Gain (UFG) to jointly consider accuracy and fairness,

$$\text{UFG} = \frac{\text{PropFair}}{\text{CVR}_{\max} - \text{CVR}} = \frac{\text{PropFair}}{1 - \text{CVR}}. \tag{12}$$

UFG indicates the fairness of the system under unit accuracy budget. For any recommendation system, the ideal maximum CVR, namely $\text{CVR}_{\max}$, equals to 1. Thus UFG can be interpreted as the slope of fairness versus accuracy—the fairness gain if we decrease a unit accuracy from $\text{CVR}_{\max}$. A larger UFG means a higher value of PropFair can be achieved with unit deviation from $\text{CVR}_{\max}$, namely, the larger, the better.

---

[2] The input of PropFair is shifted by one to avoid infinity results.

Reproducibility. We randomly sample 80% of the user with associated rating sequences for training, and 10% for validation, 10% for testing, so that the item dependencies within each session can be learned. We use grid search to select the hyper-parameters for all the methods to maximize the hybrid metric UFG: the embedding dimension in $\{10, 30, 50, 100\}$, the learning rate in $\{0.0001, 0.001, 0.01\}$. Embedding vectors are pre-trained using standard matrix factorization [11] following the traditional processing as in [15,25]. For the proposed FairRec, we set the number of recent interacted items $N = 5$, discount factor $\gamma = 0.9$, the width of each hidden layer of the actor-critic network is 1000. The batch size is set to 1024, and the optimization method is Adam. Without loss of generality, we set $w_i = 1, i = 1, \ldots, l$. All results are averaged from multiple independent runs.

4.2   Results and Analysis

Comparison with Existing Methods. We compare our proposed FairRec with six representative recommendation algorithms: **(i) NMF.** Non-negative Matrix Factorization (NMF) [12] estimates the rating matrix with positive user and item factors; **(ii) SVD.** Singular Value Decomposition (SVD) [10] is the classic matrix factorization based method that decomposes the rating matrix via a singular value decomposition; **(iii) DeepFM.** DeepFM [7] is the state-of-the-art deep learning model in recommendation that combines the factorization machines and deep neural networks; **(iv) LinUCB.** LinUCB [13] is the state-of-the-art contextual bandits algorithm that sequentially selects items and balances between exploitation and exploration in IRS; **(v) DRR.** DRR [15] is a deep reinforcement learning framework designed for IRS to maximize the long-term reward; **(vi) MRPC.** Multi-sided Recommendation with Provider Constraints (MRPC) [21] is the state-of-the-art fairness-aware method by formulating the fairness problem as an integer programming.

Table 1 shows the results. Bold numbers are the best results and underlined numbers are the strongest baselines. We have the following observations:

First, the deep learning based method (DeepFM) outperforms matrix factorization based methods (NMF and SVD) in CVR, while PropFair of DeepFM is lower. This is consistent with our expectation that DeepFM combines low-order and high-order feature interactions and has great fitting capability, yet it solely maximizes the accuracy, with fairness issues overlooked.

Second, LinUCB and DRR generally achieve better CVR than matrix factorization and deep learning methods. It is because LinUCB and DRR consider the IRS setting, and aims to maximize the long-term reward. Compared Lin-UCB to DRR, LinUCB underperforms DRR since LinUCB assumes states of the system remain unchanged and fails to tailor the recommendation to match the dynamic user preferences. DRR is the strongest baseline as it achieves the best tradeoff between accuracy and fairness, with UFG = 6.0177 on MovieLens and UFG = 2.5183 on Kiva, respectively.

Third, MRPC considers fairness by adding fairness constraints for static recommendation. Therefore, MRPC generates the fairest recommendation on both datasets, but the CVR significantly decreases as MRPC ignores the dynamic change of user preferences and the fairness status.

Fourth, FairRec consistently yields the best performance in terms of CVR, PropFair, and UFG on both datasets, demonstrating FairRec is effective in maintaining the accuracy-fairness tradeoff over time. FairRec outperforms the strongest baselines, DRR, by 1.3%, 2.3%, and 11% in CVR, PropFair, and UFG on MovieLens, and 5.1%, 2.2%, and 13.4% on Kiva. Considering UFG, with unit accuracy loss, FairRec achieves the most fairness gain. FairRec observes the current user preferences and the fairness status, and estimates the long-term discounted cumulative reward. Therefore, FairRec is capable of long-term planning to manage the balance between accuracy and fairness.

Influence of Embedding Dimension. Embedding dimension d is an important factor for FairRec. We study how the embedding dimension d influences the performance of FairRec. We vary d in $\{10, 30, 50\}$, and run 2500 epochs. The cumulative reward and the test performance are plotted in Fig. 2.

We observe that when d is large ($d = 30$ and $d = 50$), the algorithm benefits from sufficient expressive power and the reward converges at a high level. As for $d = 10$, the cumulative reward converges fast at a relatively low value, indicating that the model suffers from the limited fitting capability. In terms of UFG value, UFG $= 6.68$ when $d = 50$, which is slightly better than 6.6 as $d = 30$. Similar results can be found on Kiva, which is omitted for limited space. Therefore, we select $d = 50$ in FairRec for all the experiments.

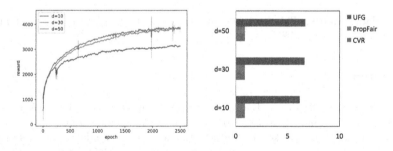

Fig. 2. Experimental results with embedding dimension d on MovieLens: cumulative reward (left) and CVR, PropFair, and UFG (right).

Table 2. Ablation study on MovieLens and Kiva.

	MovieLens			Kiva		
	CVR	PropFair	UFG	CVR	PropFair	UFG
FairRec(reward-)	0.8561	0.8053	5.5957	**0.6935**	0.8670	2.8290
FairRec(state-)	0.8194	**0.8758**	4.8494	0.6723	0.8746	2.6688
FairRec	**0.8702**	0.8666	**6.6776**	0.6905	**0.8838**	**2.8555**

Ablation Study. To evaluate the effectiveness of different components (*i.e.*, the state representation and the reward function) in FairRec, we replace a component of FairRec with the standard setting in RL at each time, and compare the performance with the full-fledged FairRec. Experimental results are presented in Table 2. We design two variants: **FairRec(reward-)** with standard reward as in [15, 25]; and **FairRec(state-)** with simple concatenation of item embeddings as the state representation as in [15].

Results show that FairRec(reward-) generally has high CVR, as no punishment on unfair recommendation. Moreover, the model simply optimizes accuracy, failing to balance between accuracy and fairness. As for FairRec(state-), CVR is downgraded significantly, validating the importance of our designed state representation. Overall, UFG of FairRec is the largest, confirming that all the components of FairRec work together yield the best results.

5   Conclusion

In this work, we propose a fairness-aware recommendation framework in IRS to dynamically balance between accuracy and fairness in the long run with reinforcement learning. In the proposed state representation component, UPS models both personalized preference and propensity to diversity; FS is utilized to describe the current fairness status of IRS. A two-fold reward is designed to combine accuracy and fairness. Experimental results demonstrate the effectiveness in the balance of accuracy and fairness of our proposed framework over the state-of-the-art models.

Acknowledgements. This work is supported by National Natural Science Foundation of China (No. U1813204).

References

1. Abdollahpouri, H., et al.: Beyond personalization: Research directions in multi-stakeholder recommendation. User Model. User Adap. Inter. (2020)
2. Abdollahpouri, H., Burke, R.: Multi-stakeholder recommendation and its connection to multi-sided fairness. arXiv preprint arXiv:1907.13158 (2019)
3. Biega, A.J., et al.: Equity of attention: amortizing individual fairness in rankings. In: SIGIR (2018)
4. Burke, R., et al.: Balanced neighborhoods for multi-sided fairness in recommendation. In: FAT* (2018)
5. Celma, Ò., Cano, P.: From hits to niches? Or how popular artists can bias music recommendation and discovery. In: Proceedings of the 2nd KDD Workshop on Large-Scale Recommender Systems and the Netflix Prize Competition (2008)
6. Chen, H., et al.: Large-scale interactive recommendation with tree-structured policy gradient. In: AAAI (2019)
7. Guo, H., et al.: DeepFM: a factorization-machine based neural network for CTR prediction. In: IJCAI (2017)
8. Holmes, E.: Antidiscrimination rights without equality. Mod. Law Rev. (2) (2005)

9. Kelly, F.P., et al.: Rate control for communication networks: shadow prices, proportional fairness and stability. JORS **49**, 237–252 (1998). https://doi.org/10.1057/palgrave.jors.2600523

10. Koren, Y.: Factor in the neighbors: Scalable and accurate collaborative filtering. TKDD **4**(1), 1:1–1:24 (2010)

11. Koren, Y., et al.: Matrix factorization techniques for recommender systems. Computer (2009)

12. Lee, D.D., et al.: Algorithms for non-negative matrix factorization. In: NIPS (2000)

13. Li, L., et al.: A contextual-bandit approach to personalized news article recommendation. In: WWW (2010)

14. Lillicrap, T.P., et al.: Continuous control with deep reinforcement learning. arXiv preprint arXiv:1509.02971 (2015)

15. Liu, F., et al.: Deep reinforcement learning based recommendation with explicit user-item interactions modeling. arXiv preprint arXiv:1810.12027 (2018)

16. Liu, W., Burke, R.: Personalizing fairness-aware re-ranking. arXiv preprint arXiv:1809.02921 (2018)

17. Ruxton, G.D.: The unequal variance t-test is an underused alternative to student's t-test and the mann–whitney u test. Behav. Ecol. (2006)

18. Silver, D., et al.: Deterministic policy gradient algorithms. In: ICML (2014)

19. Singh, A., Joachims, T.: Fairness of exposure in rankings. In: KDD (2018)

20. Steck, H., et al.: Interactive recommender systems: tutorial. In: RecSys (2015)

21. Sürer, Ö., et al.: Multistakeholder recommendation with provider constraints. In: RecSys (2018)

22. Sutton, R.S., et al.: Introduction to Reinforcement Learning (1998)

23. Vaswani, A., et al.: Attention is all you need. In: NeurIPS (2017)

24. Wang, X., et al.: A reinforcement learning framework for explainable recommendation. In: ICDM (2018)

25. Zhao, X., et al.: Deep reinforcement learning for page-wise recommendations. In: RecSys (2018)

26. Zhao, X., et al.: Recommendations with negative feedback via pairwise deep reinforcement learning. In: KDD (2018)

27. Zheng, G., et al.: DRN: a deep reinforcement learning framework for news recommendation. In: WWW (2018)

Joint Relational Dependency Learning for Sequential Recommendation

Xiangmeng Wang[1], Qian Li[2], Wu Zhang[1(✉)], Guandong Xu[2(✉)],
Shaowu Liu[2], and Wenhao Zhu[1]

[1] Shanghai University, Shanghai 200444, China
{chrystali,wzhang,whzhu}@shu.edu.cn
[2] University of Technology Sydney, Sydney, Australia
{qian.li,guandong.xu,shaowu.liu}@uts.edu.au

Abstract. Sequential recommendation leverages the temporal information of users' transactions as transition dependencies for better inferring user preference, which has become increasingly popular in academic
research and practical applications. Short-term transition dependencies
contain the information of partial item orders, while long-term transition dependencies infer long-range user preference, the two dependencies
are mutually restrictive and complementary. Although some work investigates unifying both long-term and short-term dependencies for better performance, they still neglect the fact that short-term interactions
are multi-folds, which are either individual-level interactions or union-
level interactions. Existing sequential recommendations mainly focus on
user's individual (i.e., individual-level) interactions but ignore the important collective influence at union-level. Since union-level interactions can
reflect that human decisions are made based on multiple items he/she has
already interacted, ignoring such interactions can result in the disability
of capturing the collective influence between items. To alleviate this issue,
we proposed a Joint Relational Dependency learning (JRD-L) for sequential recommendation that exploits both long-term and short-term preferences at individual-level and union-level. Specifically, JRD-L combines
long-term user preferences with short-term interests by measuring short-
term pair relations at individual-level and union-level. Moreover, JRD-L
can alleviate the sparsity problem of union-level interactions by adding
more descriptive details to each item, which is carried by individual-level
relations. Extensive numerical experiments demonstrate JRD-L outperforms state-of-the-art baselines for the sequential recommendation.

Keywords: Sequential recommendation · Long-term user preference ·
Short-term user preference · Multi-relational dependency

1 Introduction

Nowadays, abundant user-item interactions in recommender system (RS) are
recorded over time, which can be further used to discover the patterns of users'

© Springer Nature Switzerland AG 2020
H. W. Lauw et al. (Eds.): PAKDD 2020, LNAI 12084, pp. 168–180, 2020.
https://doi.org/10.1007/978-3-030-47426-3_14

behaviors [3,12]. Therefore, sequential recommendation is becoming a new trend in academic research and practical applications, because it is capable of leveraging temporal information among users' transactions for better inferring the user preference.

Dominant approaches aim to modeling long-term temporal information, capturing holistic dependencies of user-item sequence, while short-term temporal information which are essential in capturing partial dependencies are also significant. The long-term interaction is depicted in Fig. 1(a) where arrows indicate the dependency among a user-item interaction sequence. As a representative in long-term dependency modeling for general RS, factorization-based methods plays an important role in long-term dependency sequential recommendation for its remarkable efficiency [12]. Factorization-based methods model the entire user-item interaction matrix into two low-rank matrices. Such measure that aims to deal with the entire user-item interaction matrix is well-suited to train models that capture longer-term user preference profiles, however has limitations on capturing short-term user interests. Two main drawbacks exist in factorization-based methods for sequential recommendation: 1) they failed to fully exploit the rich information of transition dependencies of multiple items; 2) modeling the entire user-item dependencies causes enormous computing cost of growing size of user-item interaction matrix when user has new interactions [8,9].

As for modeling users' short-term interests, mainstream methods such as Markov chain-based approaches [3] leverage transition dependency of items from the individual-level. The short-term interaction at individual-level is shown as Fig. 1(b). Therefore, individual-level dependencies can capture individual influence between a pair of single item, but may neglect the collective influence [19] among three or more items denoted by union-level dependencies, as shown in Fig. 1(c). Namely, the collective influence is caused by the dependency of a group of items on a single item. To alleviate this issue, Yu et al. [19] leverages both individual and collective influence for better sequential recommendation performance. However, two main drawbacks exist in this methods: 1) the information of individual and collective influence is simply added to the output proximity score of a factorization-based model, leveraging none of the long-term information; 2) The union-level interaction requires a group of items to be joint modeled within a limit length of sequence, which may lead to sparsity problem.

In this paper, we propose a unified framework *joint relational dependency learning*(JRD-L), which exploits long-term temporal information and short-term temporal information from individual-level and union-level for improving sequential recommendation. In particular, a Long Short-Term Memory (LSTM) model [5] is used to encode long-term preferences, while short-term dependencies existing in pair relations among items are computed based on the intermedia hidden states of LSTM on both individual-level and union-level. LSTM hidden states can carry the long-term dependencies information and transmit them to short-term item pairs. Meanwhile, the individual-level relation and union-level relation are modeled together to fully exploit the collective influence among union-level pair relation and to address the sparsity problem. The framework of JRD-L is described in Fig. 3. Experiments on large-scale dataset demonstrate the effectiveness of the proposed JRD-L. The main contributions of our paper can be summarized as

- JRD-L considers user's long-term preferences along with short-term pair-wise item relations from multiple perspectives of individual-level and union-level. Specifically, JRD-L involves a novel multi-pair relational LSTM model that can capture both long-term dependency and multi-level temporal correlations for better inferring user preferences.
- A novel attention model is also combined with JRD-L that can augment individual-level and union-level pair relation by learning the contributions to the subsequent interactions between users and items. Meanwhile, the weighted outputs of attention model are fused together, contributing more individual-level information to alleviates the sparse problem in the union-level dependency.

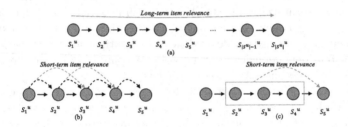

Fig. 1. (a) Long-term user-item interaction; (b) Individual-level item relevance; (3) Union-level item relevance. The dependencies of an item on its' subsequent item is represented as the transition arrows.

2   Related Works

Many methods consider long-term temporal information to mining the sequential patterns of the users' behaviors, including factorziation-based approaches [12,14] and Markov chains based approaches [2]. Recently, Deep learning (DL)-based models have achieved significant effectiveness in long-term temporal information modeling, including multi-layer perceptron-based (MLP-based) models [16,17], Convolutional neural network-based (CNN-based) models [6,15] and Recurrent neural network-based (RNN-based) models [1]. RNN-based models stand out among these models for its capacity of modeling sequential dependencies by transmiting long-term sequential information from the first hidden state to the last one. However, RNN can be difficult to trained due to the vanishing gradient problem [7], but advances such as Long Short-Term Memory (LSTM) [5] has enabled RNN to be successful. LSTM is considered one of the most successful variant of RNN, with the capability of capturing long-term relationships in a sequence and suffering from the vanishing gradient problem. So far, LSTM models have achieved tremendous success in sequence modelling tasks [20,21].

With respect to short-term temporal information modeling, existing works on modeling short-term temporal information mainly model pair relations between items. The representative work is Markov Chain (MC)-based models [3]. The objective of such model is to measure the average or weighted relevance values between a given item and its next-interaction item, this only captures dependencies between two single items. Tang et al. [15] propose a method capturing collective dependencies among three or more items. However, the model in [15] suffers from data sparsity problems. Therefore, in order to solve the sparsity problem when merely modeling collective dependencies, Yu et al. [19] add individual (i.e. individual-level) dependencies into collective (i.e. union-level) dependencies, but their work is still insufficient for it does not leverage long-term temporal information.

3   Joint Relational Dependency Learning

Before introducing the proposed method, we provide some useful notations as follows. Let U and I be the user and item set, as shown in Fig. 2. A sequence of interactions between U and I can be represented as $S = \{S_j^{u_i} : u_i \in U\}$, and u_i is associated with a interaction sequence $S_j^{u_i} = (S_1^{u_i}, S_2^{u_i}, ..., S_{|S_j^{u_i}|}^{u_i})$. The goal of JRD-L method is to predict the likelihood of the user preferred item $e_c^{u_i}$, based on the user's behavior sequences $S_j^{u_i}$.

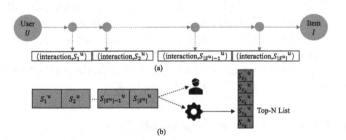

Fig. 2. (a) $S_j^{u_i} = (S_1^{u_i}, S_2^{u_i}, ..., S_{|S_j^{u_i}|}^{u_i})$ denotes a sequence of interactions between a user u_i and a given item set I. (b) Next-item recommendation aims to generate a ranking list exposed to users by modeling user-item interaction sequence.

The overall architecture of JRD-L is shown in Fig. 3. Generally, JRD-L first models long-term dependency over the whole user-item interaction data $S = \{S_j^{u_i} : u_i \in U\}$ in a LSTM layer. JRD-L takes the most recent n items before time point t of the whole sequence as the short-term interaction sequence. Then, JRD-L computes individual-level and union-level pair relations on the taken short sequence as short-term dependencies modeling. Specifically, with the input of u_i and $S_j^{u_i}$, JRD-L composes u_i and $S_j^{u_i}$ into a single user-item vector via an Embedding layer, and output $e_t^{u_i}$ as the user-item interaction embedding. A LSTM layer is then used to map

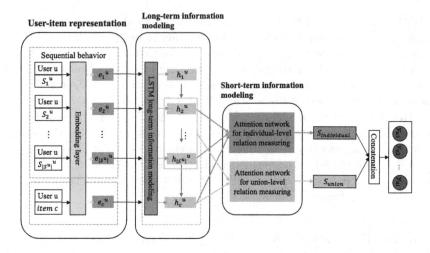

Fig. 3. The overall framework of Joint Relational Dependency Learning (JRD-L).

the whole interaction sequence of user-item vector $e_1^{u_i}, e_2^{u_i}, ..., e_{|S_j^{u_i}|}^{u_i}$ into a sequence of hidden vectors $h_1^{u_i}, h_2^{u_i}, ..., h_{|S_j^{u_i}|}^{u_i}$. More importantly, we take one further step from $h_{|S_j^{u_i}|}^{u_i}$ to derive hidden vector $h_{c_i}^{u_i}$ encoding $e_c^{u_i}$ to model long-term sequential information. Based on this, $h_{c_i}^{u_i}$ is paired with the most recent n items before time point t, i.e., $h^{u_i}_{t-1}, h^{u_i}_{t-2}, ..., h^{u_i}_{t-n}$ ($t - n < |S_j^{u_i}|$), individually. JRD-L then passes the corresponding hidden status pairs of the most recent items to an attention layer, output the correlation likelihood $S_{individual}$ and S_{union}, from which the short-term individual-level and union-level pair relation is modeled, respectively. At Last, $S_{individual}$ is concatenate with S_{union} to obtain the correlation of $e_c^{u_i}$ with the existing items for the next-item prediction task.

3.1   Skip-Gram Based Item Representation

By learning the item similarities from a large number of sequential behaviors over items, we apply skip-gram with negative sampling (SGNS) [10] to generate a unified representation for each item in an given user-item interaction sequence $S_j^{u_i} = (S_1^{u_i}, S_2^{u_i}, ..., S_{|S_j^{u_i}|}^{u_i})$. Before exploiting users' sequences dependencies, our prior problem is to represent items via embedding layer in a numerical way for subsequent calculations. In the embedding layer, the skip-gram with negative sampling is applied to directly learn high-quality item vectors from users' interaction sequences. The SGNS [10] generate item representations by exploiting the sequence of interactions between users and items. Specifically, given an item interaction sequence $S_j^{u_i} = (S_1^{u_i}, S_2^{u_i}, ..., S_{|S_j^{u_i}|}^{u_i})$ of user u_i from the user-item interaction sequence S, SGNS aims to solve the following objective function

$$\arg \max_{v_j, w_i} \frac{1}{K} \sum_{i=1}^{K} \sum_{j \neq i}^{K} \log(\sigma(w_i^T * v_j) \prod_{j=1}^{E} \sigma(-w_i^T * v_k)) \qquad (1)$$

K is the length of sequence $S_j^{u_i}$, and $\sigma(w_i^T * v_j) \prod_{j=1}^{E} \sigma(-w_i^T * v_k)$ is computed by negative sampling. $\sigma(x) = 1/(1 + \exp(-x))$, $w_i \in U(\subset \mathbb{R}^m)$ and $v_i \in V(\subset \mathbb{R}^m)$ are the latent vectors that correspond to the target and context representation for items in $S_j^{u_i}$, respectively. The parameter m is the dimension parameter that is defined empirically according to dataset size. E is the number of negative samples per a positive sample. Finally, matrices U and V are computed to generate representation of interaction sequences.

3.2 User Preference Modeling for Long-Term Pattern

To model the long-term temporal information in users' behaviors, we apply a standard LSTM [5] as in Fig. 3 to model the temporal information over the whole user-item interaction sequence. For each user u_i, we first generate an interaction sequence S_{u_i} with embedding items $x_j \in I$ based on U and V calculated by Eq. (1) from embedding layer in Fig. 3, represented as $P_u = e_1^{u_i}, e_2^{u_i}, ..., e_{|S_j^m|}^{u_i}$. We use $e_{|S_j^{u_i}|}^{u_i}$ as the d-dimensions latent vector of item x_j. Given the embedding of the user-item interaction sequence $e_1^{u_i}, e_2^{u_i}, ..., e_{|S_j^{u_i}|}^{u_i}$ and the candidate next-item $e_{c_i}^{u_i} \in e_c^{u_i}$, we generate a sequence of hidden vectors $h_1^{u_i}, h_2^{u_i}, ..., h_{|S_j^{u_i}|}^{u_i}$ by recurrently feeding $e_1^{u_i}, e_2^{u_i}, ..., e_{|S_j^{u_i}|}^{u_i}$ as inputs to the LSTM. The inner hidden states in LSTM hidden layer are updated at each time step, which can carry the long-term dependencies information and transmit them to item pairs. At each time step, the next output of computing last hidden status h_i^u is computed by

$$h_i^u = g(e_i^u, h_{i-1}^u, W_{LSTM}) \tag{2}$$

where g is the output function in LSTM and W_{LSTM} are network weights of e_i^u and h_{i-1}^u. Each $e_{c_i}^{u_i}$ is appended separately to $h_1^{u_i}, h_2^{u_i}, ..., h_{|S_j^{u_i}|}^{u_i}$ calculated by Eq. (2) to obtain the long-term-dependency-sensitive hidden states $h_{c_i}^{u_i}$.

$$h_{c_i}^u = g(e_{c_i}^u, h_{|S^u|}^u, W_{LSTM}) \tag{3}$$

Through *LSTM long-term information modeling* in Fig. 3, $h_{c_1}^{u_i}, h_{c_2}^{u_i}, ..., h_{|c_l|}^{u_i}$ is output by Eq. (3) and l is the total number of candidate next items. The sequence $h_1^{u_i}, h_2^{u_i}, ..., h_{|S_j^{u_i}|}^{u_i}$ is calculated by Eq. (2) for the following multi-relational dependency modeling stage.

3.3 Multi-relational Dependency Modeling for Short-Term Pattern

Long-term dependency models long-range user preferences but neglect important pairwise relations between items, which is insufficient in capturing pairwise relation from multiple level. Therefore our proposed method should unify both short-term sequential dependency (at both individual-level and union-level) and long-term sequential dependency. Inspired by [18], based on $h_{c_1}^{u_i}, h_{c_2}^{u_i}, ..., h_{|c_l|}^{u_i}$

and $h_1^{u_i}, h_2^{u_i}, ..., h_{|S_j^{u_i}|}^{u_i}$ output by *LSTM long-term information modeling* stage, we calculate pair relations on $h^{u_i}{}_{t-1}, h^{u_i}{}_{t-2}, ..., h^{u_i}{}_{t-n}$ $(t - n < |S_j^{u_i}|)$ selected from $h_1^{u_i}, h_2^{u_i}, ..., h_{|S_j^{u_i}|}^{u_i}$. The task is then to learn the correlation between the items in interaction sequence and candidate items. Rather than directly applying the work [18] for modeling the short-term dependency, we introduce an attention mechanism to calculate pair relations from individual-level and union-level to fully modeling the user preferences to different items. This is mainly because the work [18] implies that all vectors share the same weight, discarding an important fact that human naturally have different opinions on items. By introducing attention mechanism, our work can distribute high weights on these items user like more, thus improving recommendation performance.

Individual-Level Pairwise Relations. To capture the individual-level pairwise relations, the input of *attention network for individual-level relation measuring layer* is $h_1^{u_i}, h_2^{u_i}, ..., h_{|S_j^{u_i}|}^{u_i}$ and $h_{c_1}^{u_i}, h_{c_2}^{u_i}, ..., h_{|c_l|}^{u_i}$, which is the output vector of *LSTM long-term information modeling layer* in Fig. 3. Specifically, $h_{c_i}^u \in h^{(2)} = (h_{c_1}^{u_i}, h_{c_2}^{u_i}, ..., h_{|c_l|}^{u_i})$ (as indicated in Eq. 3) is paired with the hidden states of the most recent n items before time point t, which is $h^{u_i}{}_{t-1}, h^{u_i}{}_{t-2}, ..., h^{u_i}{}_{t-n}$ $(t - n < |S_j^{u_i}|)$ from $h_1^{u_i}, h_2^{u_i}, ..., h_{|S_j^{u_i}|}^{u_i}$ calculated by Eq. (2). An attention network is used for pairwise relation measuring. Let $H \in \mathbb{R}^{n \times l}$, $H_{ij} = h_i^{(1)} * h_j^{(2)}$ is a matrix consisting of output vectors of last LSTM layer, and n is the size of $h^{(1)} = (h_{t-1}^{u_i}, h^{u_i}{}_{t-2}, ..., h^{u_i}{}_{t-n})$ in Eq. (2) and l is the size of $h^{(2)} = (h_{c_1}^{u_i}, h_{c_2}^{u_i}, ..., h_{|c_l|}^{u_i})$ in Eq. (3). The attentive weights $\alpha = (\alpha_1, \alpha_2, ..., \alpha_{t-n})$ of the items in interaction sequence are defined by a weighted sum of these output vectors as $\alpha = \text{softmax}(\omega^T M)$ and $M = \tanh(H)$. We obtain M by a fully connection layer activated by *tanh* activation function. ω^T is a transpose vector of attention network's parameters. $\alpha_i \in [0, 1]$ is the weight of $h_{t-j}^{u_i}$ and $h_{t-j}^{u_i} \in h^{(1)}$. After obtaining the weight α_i of each existing item h_{t-j}^u, the likelihood S_{c_i}, which describe how likely the exiting items in user-item interaction sequence will interact with $e_{c_i}^{u_i}$ in candidate next-interact items set, can be calculated by

$$s_k = \text{softmax}(\beta_1 h_{t-j}^u + \beta_2 h_{c_i}^u + b)$$

$$S_{individual} = \sum_{i=1}^{n-1} \alpha_i \cdot s_k \tag{4}$$

where s_k is the correlation score of the pair of item $h_{t-j}^u \in h^{(1)}$ with $h_{c_i}^u \in h^{(2)}$, $S_{c_i} \in S_{individual}$ is the output of *attention network for individual-level relation measuring layer*. β_1, β_2 and b are LSTM parameters.

Union-Level Pairwise Relations. In order to model short-term union-level pair relation, we predefine a sliding window to determine the length of collective items set in existing user-item sequences. Based on the defined items set, collaborate influence in union-level pair relation can be learned in *attention network for union-level relation measuring layer*. Union-level pairwise relations learned by our method can capture collective dependencies among three or more items, which complements to the individual-level relation for improving recommendation performance. In the union-level pairwise relation modeling stage, the candidate length of collective items set is defined from $\theta = \{2, 4, 6, 8\}$. To learn the collaborate influence in union-level pair relation, we define a sequence $Q = \{Q_1, \cdots, Q_{n-\theta}\}$, $Q_i = (h_i^u, ..., h_{\theta+i}^u)$. For example, if $\theta = 2$, we have $Q = \{(h_1^u, h_2^u, h_3^u), \cdots, (h_{n-2}^u, h_{n-1}^u, h_n^u)\}$. Then each $Q_i \in Q$ is paired with $h^{(2)} = (h_{c_1}^{u_i}, h_{c_2}^{u_i}, ..., h_{|c_l|}^{u_i})$ as in Eq. (3). Then union-level pairs pass through the *attention network for union-level relation measuring layer* to obtain the weight α_i of each existing item h_{t-j}^u, and output the correlation likelihood S_{union} by

$$s_m = \text{softmax}(\beta_3 W_i + \beta_4 h_{c_i}^u + b)$$

$$S_{union} = \sum_{i=1}^{n-1} \alpha_i \cdot s_m \qquad (5)$$

$h_{c_i}^u \in h^{(2)}$, β_3, β_4 and b are model parameters. Then, S_{union} is output by *attention network for union-level pair relation measuring layer*. Finally, S_{union} is concatenated with $S_{individual}$ from *attention network for individual-level pair relation measuring layer* to calculate the correlation of $e_c^{u_i}$ with the existing items for the next-item prediction task.

3.4 Optimization

To effectively learn the parameters of the proposed JDR-L model, our training objective is to minimize the loss between the predicted labels and the true labels of candidate items. The optimization setup is, firstly, we define the item that has the latest timestamp among the user-item interaction sequence as the standard subsequent item, and define the rest of items as the non-subsequent items. Secondly, the loss function is therefore based on the assumption that an item (positive samples, i.e. standard subsequent item) this user liked will have a relative larger value than other items (negative samples) that he/she has no interest in. The loss function is then formulated as

$$\arg\min_{\Theta} \sum_{i=1}^{N} (\text{concatenate}(S_{individual}^{(i)}, S_{union}^{(i)}) - y_i)^2 + \frac{\lambda}{2}||\Theta||^2 \qquad (6)$$

where the parameter $\Theta = \{W_{LSTM}, \omega, \beta_1, \beta_2, \beta_3, \beta_4, b\}$. $S_{individual}^{(i)}$ in Eq. (4) represents the correlation likelihood output by *attention network for individual-level relation measuring layer*. $S_{union}^{(i)}$ in Eq. (5) represents the correlation likelihood output by *attention network for union-level relation measuring layer*. y_i is the label of the candidate item and λ is a parameter for l_2 regularization. Adaptive moment estimation (Adam) [11] is used to optimize parameters during the training process.

4   Experiments

4.1   Evaluation Setup

We conduct experiments to validate JDR-L for Top-N sequential recommendation task on the real-world dataset, i.e., Movie&TV dataset [19], that belongs
to Amazon data[1]. Since the original datasets are sparse, we firstly filter out
users with fewer than 10 interactions as in [19]. The statistical information of
the before-processing and after-processing of Movie&TV dataset is shown in
Table 1. Following the evaluation settings in [19], we set train/test with ratios
80/20.

Table 1. Statistical information of dataset.

Movies&TV	Users	Items	Interactions
Before-processing	40929	51510	1163413
After-processing	35168	51227	1070645

We compare JRD-L with three baselines: BPR-MF [12] is a widely used
matrix factorization method for sequential RS; TranRec [4] models users as
translation vectors operating on item sequences for sequential RS); RNN-based
model (i.e., GRU4Rec [6] uses basic Gated Recurrent Unit for sequential RS);
FPMC [13] is a typical Markov chain method modeling individiual item interactions; Multi-level item temporal dependency model (MARank) [19] models both
individual-level and union-level interactions with factorization model.

For fair comparisons, we set the dropout percentage as 0.5 [19]. The embedding size d of Embedding layer is chosen from $\{32, 64, 128, 256\}$, which should
be equal to the hidden size h of LSTM. The regularization hyper-parameter λ is
selected from $\{0.05, 0.01, 0.005, 0.001, 0.0005, 0.0001\}$. We set the learning rate
of Aadm as the default number 0.001 [11]. As n is the most recent items for
short-term dependency, we choose n from $\{10, 20, 40, 60\}$. The length l of the
sliding window of union-level interaction is chosen from $\{2, 4, 6, 8\}$. We define
the length N of ranked list as 20. For the hardware settings, JRD-L model is
trained on a Linux server with Tesla P100-PCIE GPU.

4.2   Effect of Parameter Selection for JDR-L

This section will discuss how the parameters influence the JRD-L model performance. We first explore the impact of n on the performance of JDR-L, the
comparison is set on different n chosen from $\{10, 20, 40, 60\}$. Secondly, we evaluate the influence of the length l, l is chosen from $\{2, 4, 6, 8\}$. We use two metrics

---

[1] https://www.amazon.com/.

to evaluate the model performance, which are MRR (Mean Reciprocal Rank) - the average of reciprocal ranks of the predicted candidate items, and NDCG (Normalized Discounted Cumulative Gain) - a normalized average of reciprocal ranks of the predicted candidate items with a discounting factor, the comparison results of different setups are shown in Fig. 4. Figure 4 show that when other hyperparameters are set equal, $n = 10$ achieves the best performance. These observations, presumably, because sequential pattern does not involve a very long sequence. Besides, $l = 4$ achieves the best performance, indicating that the collective influence of 4 items is informative for the Movie&TV dataset.

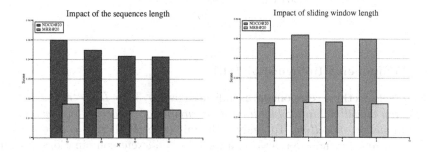

Fig. 4. Results of JDR-L under different settings.

4.3   Ranking Performance Comparison

Ranking performance evaluates how the predicted Top-N lists act on the recommendation system. Table 2 shows the comparison results of JDR-L with baselines. Encouragingly, we can find that JDR-L performs best with the highest MRR and NDCG scores. Besides, baselines may not perform well as JDR-L. Firstly, BPR-MF as matrix factorization-based method obtains less competitive performance when compared with GRU4Rec. This is mainly because BPR-MF considers user intrinsic preference over item while GRU4Rec models union-level item interaction along with users' overall preferences. Secondly, TranRec and FPMC are two state-of-the-art methods exploiting individual-level item temporal dependency. Both of them outperform the other baselines, since they consider individual-level item temporal dependency. This indicates that keeping directed interaction between a pair of items is essential for sequential recommendation. Thirdly, MARank considering individual-level and union-level interactions but neglecting long-term dependencies performs worse than JDR-L. Above all, BPR-MF performs the worst, this is mainly because BPR-MF models only intrinsic preferences within short sequences of user-item interactions, neglecting long-term user preferences and item interactions at individual-level and union-level.

Table 2. Ranking performance.

Methods	Movie&TV	
Measures@20	MRR	NDCG
BPR-MF	0.0089	0.0248
TranRec	0.0155	0.0392
GRU4Rec	0.0124	0.0344
FPMC	0.0162	0.0406
MARank	0.0170	0.0444
JDR-L	0.0179	0.0518
Improvement	5.2%	16.7%

4.4   Components Influence of JDR-L

JDR-L contains three components as indicated by Fig. 3, i.e. *Long-term user-item interaction modelling, individual-level item interaction modeling* and *union-level item interaction modelling.* To analyze the influence of different components to the overall recommendation performance, we set different combinations of components for evaluation, with the results been shown in Table 3. JDR-L with three components performs best compared with other combinations as shown in Table 3, verifying that our proposed JDR-L is optimal. As for other combinations, LSTM-only obtains the lower MRR and NDCG scores compared with JDR-L, this is because LSTM-only models long-term dependencies. LSTM+individual-level item interaction outperforms LSTM+union-level item interaction, the main reason is that union-level item interaction suffers from a sparsity problem as the length of item set increases. Besides, both of LSTM+individual-level item interaction and LSTM+union-level item interaction obtain lower scores compared with JDR-L model. This further indicates that the information in individual-level item interaction should be combined into union-level interaction modeling stage to solve the sparsity problem.

Table 3. Ranking performance on different components in JDR-L.

Methods	Movie&TV	
Measures@20	MRR	NDCG
LSTM-only	0.0154	0.0447
LSTM+ individual-level item interaction	0.0147	0.0442
LSTM+ union-level item interaction	0.0142	0.0423
JDR-L	0.0178	0.0518

5   Conclusions

In this paper, we design a Joint Relational Dependency learning (JRD-L) for sequential recommendation. JDR-L builds a novel model to unify both long-term dependencies and short-term dependencies from individual-level and union-level. Moreover, JDR-L can handle the sparsity problem when exploiting the individual-level relation information from the sequential behaviors. Extensive experiments on the benchmark dataset demonstrate the effectiveness of JRD-L.

Acknowledge. This work is supported by the National Key R&D Program of China (Nos: 2017YFB0701501) and Australian Research Council Linkage Projects under LP170100891.

References

1. Bogina, V., Kuflik, T.: Incorporating dwell time in session-based recommendations with recurrent neural networks, pp. 57–59 (2017)
2. Davidson, J., Liebald, B., Liu, J., Nandy, P., Van Vleet, T.: The YouTube video recommendation system. In: RecSys 2010 - Proceedings of the 4th ACM Conference on Recommender Systems, pp. 293–296 (2010). https://doi.org/10.1145/1864708.1864770
3. He, R., Kang, W.C., McAuley, J.: Translation-based recommendation. In: RecSys 2017 - Proceedings of the 11th ACM Conference on Recommender Systems, pp. 161–169. Association for Computing Machinery, Inc., August 2017. https://doi.org/10.1145/3109859.3109882
4. He, R., Kang, W.C., Mcauley, J.: Translation-based recommendation. In: Eleventh ACM Conference on Recommender Systems (2017)
5. Hochreiter, S., Schmidhuber, J.: Long short-term memory. Neural Comput. 9(8), 1735–1780 (1997). https://doi.org/10.1162/neco.1997.9.8.1735
6. Hsu, K., Chou, S., Yang, Y., Chi, T.: Neural network based next-song recommendation. arXiv: Information Retrieval (2016)
7. Krause, B., Lu, L., Murray, I., Renals, S.: Multiplicative LSTM for sequence modelling. arXiv preprint arXiv:1609.07959 (2016)
8. Li, Q., Niu, W., Li, G., Cao, Y., Tan, J., Guo, L.: Lingo: linearized grassmannian optimization for nuclear norm minimization (2015)
9. Li, Q., Wang, Z.: Riemannian submanifold tracking on low-rank algebraic variety. In: Thirty-First AAAI Conference on Artificial Intelligence (2017)
10. Mikolov, T., Sutskever, I., Chen, K., Corrado, G.S., Dean, J.: Distributed representations of words and phrases and their compositionality. arXiv: Computation and Language (2013)
11. Newey, W.K.: Adaptive estimation of regression models via moment restrictions. J. Econ. 38(3), 301–339 (1988)
12. Rendle, S., Freudenthaler, C., Gantner, Z., Schmidt-Thieme, L.: BPR: Bayesian personalized ranking from implicit Feedback, May 2012. http://arxiv.org/abs/1205.2618
13. Rendle, S., Freudenthaler, C., Schmidtthieme, L.: Factorizing personalized Markov chains for next-basket recommendation. In: The Web Conference, pp. 811–820 (2010)

14. Rendle, S., Gantner, Z., Freudenthaler, C., Schmidt-Thieme, L.: Fast context-aware recommendations with factorization machines. In: SIGIR 2011 - Proceedings of the 34th International ACM SIGIR Conference on Research and Development in Information Retrieval, pp. 635–644. Association for Computing Machinery (2011). https://doi.org/10.1145/2009916.2010002

15. Tang, J., Wang, K.: Personalized top-n sequential recommendation via convolutional sequence embedding, pp. 565–573 (2018)

16. Wan, S., Lan, Y., Wang, P., Guo, J., Xu, J., Cheng, X.: Next basket recommendation with neural networks (2015)

17. Wang, P., Guo, J., Lan, Y., Xu, J., Wan, S., Cheng, X.: Learning hierarchical representation model for nextbasket recommendation, pp. 403–412 (2015)

18. Wang, Z., Zhang, Y., Chang, C.Y.: Integrating order information and event relation for script event prediction, pp. 57–67. Association for Computational Linguistics (ACL), January 2018. https://doi.org/10.18653/v1/d17-1006

19. Yu, L., Zhang, C., Liang, S., Zhang, X.: Multi-order attentive ranking model for sequential recommendation. In: Proceedings of the AAAI Conference on Artificial Intelligence, vol. 33, pp. 5709–5716, July 2019. https://doi.org/10.1609/aaai.v33i01.33015709

20. Zhao, P., Zhu, H., Liu, Y., Li, Z., Xu, J., Sheng, V.S.: Where to go next: A Spatiotemporal LSTM model for next poi recommendation. arXiv: Information Retrieval (2018)

21. Zhou, Y., Huang, C., Hu, Q., Zhu, J., Tang, Y.: Personalized learning full-path recommendation model based on LSTM neural networks. Inf. Sci. **444**, 135–152 (2018)

Modelling Temporal Dynamics and Repeated Behaviors for Recommendation

Xin Zhou[1], Zhu Sun[2], Guibing Guo[1(✉)], and Yuan Liu[1]

[1] Department of Software Engineering, Northeastern University, Shenyang, China
xinzhou@stumail.neu.edu.cn, {guogb,liuyuan}@swc.neu.edu.cn
[2] Department of Computing, Macquarie University, Sydney, Australia
z.sun@mq.edu.au

Abstract. Personalized recommendation has yield immense success in predicting user preference with heterogeneous implicit feedback (HIF), i.e., various user behaviors. However, existing studies consider less about the temporal dynamics and repeated patterns of HIF. They simply suppose: (1) a hard rule among user behaviors (e.g., *add-to-cart* must come before *purchase* and after *view*); (2) merge repeated behaviors into one (e.g., *view* several times is considered as *view* once only), thus failing to unveil user preferences from their real behaviors. To ease these issues, we, therefore, propose a novel end-to-end neural framework – TDRB, which automatically models the *T*emporal *D*ynamics and *R*epeated *B*ehaviors to assist in capturing user preference, thus achieving more accurate recommendations. Empirical studies on three real-world datasets demonstrate the superiority of our proposed TDRB against other state-of-the-arts.

Keywords: Temporal dynamics · Repeated behaviors · Heterogeneous implicit feedback · Recommendation

1 Introduction

Recommender systems have recently become prominent tools to provide personalized services for customers, so as to alleviate the *information overload* problem [3]. A number of recommenders [2,3,10,11] have been proposed to help infer users' potential interests based on their heterogeneous implicit feedback (HIF). Taking e-commerce as an example, the recommenders mainly leverage users' historical behaviors of various types (e.g., *view, click, add-to-cart, purchase*) to help predict what product to *purchase* afterwards. In this scenario, *purchase* is the *target behavior*, which directly reflects users' preference towards products. In contrast, *view, click, add-to-cart* are *auxiliary behaviors* to indirectly suggest users' taste over products to some extent. Both target and auxiliary behaviors benefit for user preference inference, possibly with different degrees.

X. Zhou and Z. Sun—Contribute equally and share the co-first authorship.

© Springer Nature Switzerland AG 2020
H. W. Lauw et al. (Eds.): PAKDD 2020, LNAI 12084, pp. 181–193, 2020.
https://doi.org/10.1007/978-3-030-47426-3_15

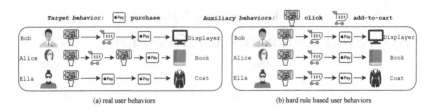

Fig. 1. Runing examples for sequential user behaviors on products in e-commerce, where (a) depicts the real sequential behaviors towards products; (b) illustrates the hard rule based sequential behaviors on products.

Running Example. To illustrate, Fig. 1(a) depicts real user behaviors on products in an e-commerce system (e.g. Amazon), where two essential characteristics are noted: (1) `Temporal dynamics`: users perform sequential behaviors over products with different orders, indicating different behavior patterns. For instance, Bob and Alice prefer *add-to-cart* before *purchase*, whilst Ella directly buys the 'Coat' after *click* without *add-to-cart*. (2) `Repeated behaviors`: users may perform certain behaviors several times over products, reflecting a reinforced preference to some degree. For example, Alice clicks twice to check details before she makes the purchase decision; Ella may be quite satisfied with the quality after purchasing the 'Coat' and directly buy another one for her friend.

The above examples highlight the presence of temporal dynamics and repeated behaviors in user-item interactions, which could potentially facilitate to model user preference, thus achieving better recommendations. They, however, are not well investigated by existing HIF based studies: (1) most methods [1,5,11–14] directly ignore the temporal dynamics. They only model the influence of limited types of user behaviors (e.g., only *view* and *purchase*) via a weighted combination, which heavily restricts the generability of these methods; (2) although several approaches [2,10] notice the temporal dynamics, they simply pre-define a hard rule to order various user behaviors, thus failing to capture the real temporal dynamics. For instance, they assume that *add-to-cart* must come before *purchase* and after *click*. In Fig. 1(b), all users share the same behavior pattern based on the hard rule: *click* → *add-to-cart* → *purchase* regardless of what their real behaviors are; and (3) none of them considers the repeated user behaviors. They merely merge the duplicated user-item interactions by keeping the earliest one. In Fig. 1, *click* twice is only treated as *click* once for Alice. In this sense, there's much room left to better exploit the temporal dynamics and repeated behaviors in HIF based recommendation.

In this paper, we, therefore, propose a novel end-to-end neural framework – TDRB, which exploits both *Temporal Dynamics and Repeated Behaviors* to truly uncover user behavior patterns, thus capturing user preference over items in a more accurate manner. Specifically, TDRB is composed of three modules, (1) `Target Module` employs outer product and a convolutional neural network to directly learn expressive and high-order user-item correlation (i.e., user preference over items) regarding to the target behavior (e.g., *purchase*); (2) `Auxiliary Module` aims to assist target module in predicting user preference over items. It uses gated recurrent units to accurately model the temporal dynamics and repeated patterns of auxiliary behaviors that happen before its corresponding target behavior; and (3) `Fusion Module` devises three strategies (i.e., MLP [6], Attention mechanism [9] and Outer product) to seamlessly integrate both target and auxiliary behaviors for a more accurate user preference estimation.

To conclude, our main contributions lie in three folds: (1) to the best of our knowledge, we are the first to exploit temporal dynamics and repeated behaviors in HIF based recommendation; (2) we propose a novel end-to-end neural framework – TDRB, which delicately models the temporal dynamics and repeated behaviors for user preference prediction, thus achieving high-quality recommendation; and (3) extensive experiments on three real-world datasets show the superiority of our proposed TDRB, which significantly beats state-of-the-arts with a lift of 27.91%, 61.32% w.r.t. HR and NDCG on average, respectively.

2 Related Work

The heterogenous implicit feedback (HIF)-based recommenders can be broadly classified into conventional recommenders and deep learning-based recommenders.

Conventional Recommenders. Early works solely leverage target behavior for the recommendation. For example, Rendle et al. proposed BPRMF [15] to maximize the difference of user preference over items with and without target behavior. After that, many variants have been proposed based upon BPRMF, such as GBPR [11], ABPR [12] and eALS [5]. However, they all fail to fully exploit the HIF by taking into account target behaviors only. Later, some researchers attempted to employ auxiliary behaviors (e.g., *view, click*) in addition to target behavior for the performance-enhanced recommendation. For instance, Qiu et al. designed TBPR/BPRH [13,14] to utilize *purchase, view* and *like* for trinity preference ranking. Ding et al. proposed VALS [1] by fusing *purchase* with *view* through manually pre-defined weights. GcBPR [3] resolved the data sparsity problem by generating target behavior from a linear regression of auxiliary behaviors. Yin et al. devised SPTF [18] to overcome the issue of heavy skewness of the interaction distribution w.r.t. different types of HIF. Nevertheless, these methods all ignore the temporal dynamics and repeated patterns of user behaviors for the recommendation. Furthermore, most of them only consider limited types of auxiliary behaviors, thus restricting their generability. Afterwards, Loni et al. proposed McBPR [10] to capture the temporal dynamics by a pre-defined hard rule (e.g., *add-to-cart* must occur before *purchase* and after *click*), as illustrated in Fig. 1(b). Undoubtedly, the proposed hard rule cannot truly express the temporal dynamics and repeated user behaviors.

Deep Learning-Based Recommenders. Deep learning has made great breakthroughs in various related areas, such as image recognition [4] and natural language processing [19]. Being capable of capturing the non-linearity of user-item interactions, they have been widely applied to the recommendation with HIF [6,7]. Similar to conventional recommenders, early deep learning-based recommenders only model user preference with target behavior, such as NCF [6]. Soon afterwards, He et al. further designed ConvNCF [7] to use an outer product and convolutional neural network (CNN) to learn high-order correlations among user-item interactions. Later, some studies turn to fuse both target and auxiliary behaviors. Wen et al. [17] devised a neural framework to capture both linearity and non-linearity of heterogeneous behaviors through. Recently, Gao et al. developed a neural model named NTMR [2] encoding a hard rule-based order for heterogeneous user behaviors, that is, *add-to-cart* must appear before *purchase* and after *view*. All of these methods mentioned above, however, fail to model the temporal dynamics and repeated behavior for a high-quality recommendation.

Note that, there are also some works model the temporal dynamics of item sequences, instead of user behavior sequences. For instance, GRU4rec [8], NARM [9] and SLRC [16] model the temporal dynamic of repeated purchased items for next item recommendation, which is out of our scope, i.e., exploiting temporal dynamics of repeated behaviors for general item recommendation.

3   The Proposed TDRB

This section presents the proposed neural framework – TDRB for heterogeneous implicit feedback (HIF)-based recommendation. It fully exploits the temporal dynamics and repeated behaviors to capture user preference in a more accurate fashion, thus achieving high-quality recommendation.

3.1   Problem Formulation

Notations. Let u, i, f, a denote user u, item i, target behavior f and auxiliary behavior a, respectively; $\mathbf{P}, \mathbf{Q}, \mathbf{O}$ are user, item and auxiliary behavior embedding matrices; $\mathbf{p}_u, \mathbf{q}_i, \mathbf{o}_a$ denote the corresponding embedding vectors for u, i, a. Throughout this paper, we use bold uppercase letter to denote a matrix (e.g., $\mathbf{P}$) and bold lowercase letter (e.g., $\mathbf{p}_u$) to denote a vector.

Data Segmentation. Most existing studies [1,6,7] consider less about the temporal dynamics of user behaviors, and always merge the repeated (both target and auxiliary) behaviors by remaining the earliest one. However, we contend that the temporal dynamics are capable of reflecting user behavior patterns, and the repeated behaviors may indicate a reinforced user preference. Hence, we conduct data segmentation to simulate the real scenario better. Given all behaviors between (u, i) pair ordered by time, for example, $B(u, i) = \{a_1, a_2, a_3, f, a_4, f, f\}$, we first split them into m sequences by target behavior, e.g., $S_1(u, i) = \{a_1, a_2, a_3, f\}$, $S_2(u, i) = \{a_4, f\}$ and $S_3(u, i) = \{f\}$, such that each sequence consists of one target behavior and all the auxiliary behaviors before it if available. m is the number of target behaviors in $B(u, i)$. We then feed all the segmented sequences, e.g., $S_1(u, i), S_2(u, i)$ and $S_3(u, i)$,

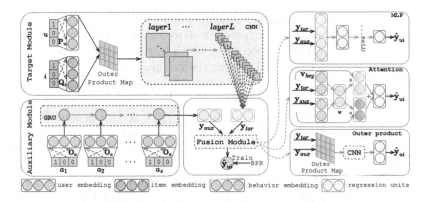

Fig. 2. The overall framework of our proposed TDRB, which is composed of three modules: (1) target module in the upper left corner; (2) auxilary module in the bottom left corner; and (3) fusion module in the bottom center. The three different fusion strategies (i.e., MLP, Attention and Outer product) are depicted on the right side.

between (u, i) pair for model training, to estimate the preference score of u over i, i.e., $\hat{y}_{ui}$, and generate a personalized ranking list with top-N items based on the preference scores. By doing so, the temporal dynamics and repeated (both target and auxiliary) behaviors can be preserved to the utmost.

3.2   Different Modules of TDRB

The overall framework of TDRB is illustrated by Fig. 2, mainly composed of three modules, namely (1) `Target Module` directly captures the high-order user-item correlation from the perspective of target behavior through the outer product and convolutional neural network (CNN) [7]; (2) `Auxiliary Module` utilizes gated recurrent units to encode temporal dynamics and repeated patterns of auxiliary behaviors, so as to enhance target module; and (3) `Fusion Module` unifies both target and auxiliary behaviors via three different strategies (i.e., MLP, Attention and Outer product) for high-quality recommendation. As mentioned in Data Segmentation, there are m segmented sequences for a (u, i) pair. For ease of presentation, we take one segmented sequence $S(u, i) = \{a_1, a_2, \ldots, a_s, f\}$ as an example to demonstrate different modules of TDRB. Note that $S(u, i)$ has and only has one target behavior, but may contain multiple auxiliary behaviors as well as repeated auxiliary behaviors.

Target Module. It aims to directly model u's preference over i regarding the target behavior f. We first project u and i into dense embedding space by,

$$\mathbf{p}_u = \mathbf{P}^T\mathbf{v}_u, \mathbf{q}_i = \mathbf{Q}^T\mathbf{v}_i \tag{1}$$

where $\mathbf{p_u}, \mathbf{q_i} \in \mathbb{R}^{1 \times 32}$ are dense embeddings for u, i; $\mathbf{v}_u, \mathbf{v}_i$ are one-hot sparse vectors for u, i. Different from existing neural recommenders [5,6] combining user and item embeddings via a simple concatenation or element-wise product, we are inspired by [7] to utilize outer product above the user and item embedding layers. It results in a 2D interaction map, which is more expressive and capable of capturing the high-order user-item correlation, given by,

$$\psi(\mathbf{p}_u, \mathbf{q}_i) = \mathbf{p}_u \otimes \mathbf{q}_i \tag{2}$$

where $\otimes$ denotes outer product operation; $\psi(\mathbf{p}_u, \mathbf{q}_i) \in \mathbb{R}^{32 \times 32}$ denotes the interaction map. Thanks to the superior capability of extracting local relations of graph features, we then apply a CNN on the interaction map, so as to fully capture the latent features of $\psi(\mathbf{p}_u, \mathbf{q}_i)$.

The structure of CNN is fine-tuned based on literature [7]. To be more specific, it has 5 hidden layers and 32 feature maps for each hidden layer. We set the kernel size as $2 * 2$ and the stride to be 2. Hence, the feature dimension is halved layer by layer. The input for the first layer is a 2D matrix, i.e., $\psi(\mathbf{p}_u, \mathbf{q}_i) \in \mathbb{R}^{32 \times 32}$, and its output is a 3D tensor. For the rest layers, both input and output are 3D tensors. The element $e^l_{x,y,k}$ of the xth row and y^{th} column of feature map in the kth filter $\mathbf{f}$ for layer l is defined as,

$$e^l_{x,y,k} = \varphi(\mathbf{b}_l + \sum\nolimits_{a=0}^{1} \sum\nolimits_{b=0}^{1} e_{2x+a,2y+b} \cdot \mathbf{f}^l_{1-a,1-b,k}) \tag{3}$$

where $\mathbf{f}^l_{1-a,1-b,k} \in \mathbb{R}^{2 \times 2 \times 32}$ if $l = 1$; otherwise $\mathbf{f}^l_{1-a,1-b,k} \in \mathbb{R}^{2 \times 2 \times 32 \times 32}$ when $1 < l \leq 5$; $\mathbf{b}_l$ denotes bias; k is the number of kernels; $\varphi(x)$ denotes the activation function (ReLU [8]). The final output of target module can be defined by Eq. (4), where g_θ denotes CNN with parameters $\theta = \{\mathbf{b}, \mathbf{f}\}$.

$$\mathbf{y}_{tar} = g_\theta(\psi(\mathbf{p}_u, \mathbf{q}_i)) \tag{4}$$

Auxiliary Module. Auxiliary behaviors (i.e., *view*, *click*) could indirectly reflect user inclination, thus benefiting for a better recommendation. Hence, the auxiliary module mainly takes advantage of auxiliary behaviors for a more fine-grained user preference inference. Existing studies either ignore the temporal dynamics of auxiliary behaviors [1,3,13,14], or pre-define a hard rule to order them [2,10]. Besides, all of them overlook the repeated behaviors. To ease this issue, we consider to accommodate the real auxiliary behavior sequence $S_a(u, i) = \{a_1, a_2, \ldots, a_s\}$, which can be obtained by removing the target behavior f from the segmented sequence $S(u, i)$. The gated recurrent units (GRU) [8] are applied to help model the temporal dynamics and repeated patterns encoded in the auxiliary behavior sequence $S_a(u, i)$, as GRU has proven to be more adaptive and stable with fewer parameters in comparison with recurrent neural network (RNN) and long short term memory (LSTM) [8].

Given $S_a(u, i) = \{a_1, a_2, \ldots, a_s\}$ as input, we project each auxiliary action a_t in the sequence into dense embedding space, given by,

$$\mathbf{o}_{a_t} = \mathbf{O}^T \mathbf{v}_{a_t} \tag{5}$$

where $\mathbf{o}_{a_t} \in \mathbb{R}^{1 \times 32}$ is the embedding vector of a_t; $\mathbf{v}_{a_t}$ is the one-hot vector for a_t. The embedding of each auxiliary behavior is then considered as the input of

GRU at each time step. In this case, if any duplicated auxiliary behaviors exist in $S_a(u,i)$, their embeddings will be fed into GRU repeatedly, so as to reinforce their influence automatically. Specifically, at time state t, the hidden state $\mathbf{h}_t$ of GRU is updated as follows,

$$\mathbf{h}_t = (1-z) \circ \mathbf{h}_{t-1} + z \circ \tau(\mathbf{o}_{at}\mathbf{U}_h + (\mathbf{h}_{t-1} \circ r)\mathbf{W}_h + b_h) \tag{6}$$

where $\tau(x)$ is the tanh activation function; $\circ$ is the multiplication between a vector and a scalar; $z = \sigma(\mathbf{o}_{at}\mathbf{U}_z + \mathbf{h}_{t-1}\mathbf{W}_z + b_z)$ and $r = \sigma(\mathbf{o}_{at}\mathbf{U}_r + \mathbf{h}_{t-1}\mathbf{W}_r + b_r)$ are the update gate and reset gate of GRU, respectively; $\delta = \{\mathbf{U}_z, \mathbf{W}_z, b_z, b_r, b_h\}$ is the parameter set of GRU. The last hidden state at time step s is supposed to be the output $\mathbf{y}_{aux}$, i.e., $\mathbf{y}_{aux} = \mathbf{h}_s$, which represents the influence of auxiliary behaviors on user preference. As the input sequence $S_a(u,i)$ is ordered by time and may contain repeated behaviors, the auxiliary module is capable of better capture temporal dynamics and repeated patterns of user behaviors. Note that, if there is only target behavior and no auxiliary behaviors between u and i, i.e., $S(u,i) = \{f\}$ and $S_a(u,i) = \emptyset$, we set $\mathbf{o}_{a_t}$ as an all-zero vector.

Fusion Module. It aims to automatically incorporate the influence of both target (i.e., $\mathbf{y}_{tar}$) and auxiliary (i.e., $\mathbf{y}_{aux}$) behaviors for a more comprehensive modeling on u's preference towards i, i.e., $\hat{\mathbf{y}}_{ui}$. Three different fusion strategies are thus devised for a better exploration as introduced below.

(1) MLP: a straightforward way is to adopt MLP on the concatenated $\mathbf{y}_{tar}$ and $\mathbf{y}_{aux}$, as shown in the upper right corner of Fig. 2. Following [6], we implement MLP with a tower structure, halving the layer size for each successive higher layer. Hence the estimated preference score $\hat{\mathbf{y}}_{ui}$ is,

$$\hat{\mathbf{y}}_{ui} = \zeta_{out}(\zeta_l(...\zeta_2(\zeta_1(\psi(\mathbf{y}_{tar}, \mathbf{y}_{aux})))...)) \tag{7}$$

where ζ_{out} and ζ_l denote the output layer and the lth layer in MLP.

(2) Attention: it fuses $\mathbf{y}_{tar}$ and $\mathbf{y}_{aux}$ by distinguishing their weights in an automatic fashion, as shown in the center right of Fig. 2. The attention weights $\mathbf{w} \in \mathbb{R}^{1\times2}$ and $\hat{\mathbf{y}}_{ui}$ are calculated by Eq. (8), where $\xi(x)$ is the softmax function; $\phi_\vartheta(x)$ is the regression function.

$$\begin{aligned} \mathbf{w} = [w_1, w_2] = \xi(\sum_x^k \mathbf{v}_{key}^x \cdot [\mathbf{y}_{aux}^x, \mathbf{y}_{tar}^x]), \\ \hat{\mathbf{y}}_{ui} = \phi_\vartheta(w_1 \circ \mathbf{y}_{tar} + w_2 \circ \mathbf{y}_{tar}) \end{aligned} \tag{8}$$

(3) Outer product: similar as described in the target module, it utilizes outer product with CNN to capture and extract more expressive and high-order correlation between $\mathbf{y}_{tar}$ and $\mathbf{y}_{aux}$, shown in the bottom right corner of Fig. 2. The user preference score $\hat{\mathbf{y}}_{ui}$ is re-defined as follows,

$$\hat{\mathbf{y}}_{ui} = \phi_\vartheta(g_{\theta_1}(\psi(\mathbf{y}_{tar}, \mathbf{y}_{aux}))) \tag{9}$$

Optimization. Following state-of-the-arts [3,7,15], we formulate top-N recommendation as a pair-wise ranking problem, where user u prefers positive item i (with target behavior) to negative item j (without target behavior). Hence, we sample triplet $\mathcal{D}_s = \{(u, i, j)\}$ for training and keep the sample ratio between items i, j as $1 : 1$. Finally, we minimize the objective function shown in Eq. (10), where Θ is the set of model parameters to update.

$$L = \sum_{(u,i,j)\in\mathcal{D}_s} -\ln \sigma(\widehat{y}_{ui} - \widehat{y}_{uj}) + \lambda_\Theta ||\Theta||^2 \qquad (10)$$

4 Experiments and Analysis

We conduct extensive experiments on three real-world datasets with the goal of answering four research questions: (RQ1) Does modeling temporal dynamics and repeated behaviors enhance the performance of TDRB? (RQ2) How do different fusion strategies affect the performance of TDRB? (RQ3) Does the proposed TDRB outperform state-of-the-art algorithms?

4.1 Experiment Setup

Datasets. Three real-world datasets are used for evaluation: Xing[1], Taobao2014[2] and Taobao2017[3]. In particular, Xing records the data from a job-hunting website and Taobao2014/2017 are obtained from Taobao (www. taobao.com.). They are different in three aspects: (1) Xing is much denser than

Table 1. Statistics of the two utilized datasets

Datasets	#Users	#Items	#Records	Density	#Behaviors	Behavior types
Xing	459	5,932	12,343	0.453%	4	click, bookmark, remove, reply
Taobao2014	1,569	811,063	1,052,488	0.082%	4	click, collect, add-to-cart, payment
Taobao2017	17,793	309,250	803,939	0.014%	4	click, favorite, add-to-cart, buy

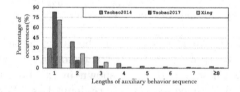

Fig. 3. Length distribution of the auxiliary behavior sequence.

[1] https://github.com/recsyschallenge/2016/.
[2] https://tianchi.aliyun.com/dataset/dataDetail?dataId=46.
[3] https://tianchi.aliyun.com/dataset/dataDetail?dataId=649.

Taobao2014/2017, as shown in Table 1; (2) in regard to the behavior types, in Xing *reply* is the target behavior; *click, bookmark* and *remove* are the auxiliary behaviors; and in Taobao2014, *payment* is the target behavior; *click, collect* and *add-to-cart* are the auxiliary behaviors; whilst in Taobao2017, the target behavior is *buy* and the auxiliary behaviors include *click, favorite, add-to-cart*; and (3) the distributions among the three datasets w.r.t. the length of auxiliary behavior sequences (i.e., $S_a(u, i)$) is quite different, as depicted in Fig. 3. The length of most sequences (above 90%) ranges from 1 to 4 on Taobao2014, whilst in Xing and Taobao2017, most sequences (90% or so) are shorter than 3. To balance the quantity and quality of each dataset, we filter out users with less than 3 target behaviors and items with less than 6, 2, 10 target behaviors for Xing, Taobao2014, and Taobao2017, respectively. The statistics of the processed datasets are summarized in Table 1.

Evaluation Protocols. We adopt the widely-used leave-one-out for evaluation [1,5–7]. For each user, we hold out her latest interaction as the test set; the second latest as validate set; and utilize the remaining data as the train set. In order to improve the test efficiency, we follow the common strategy [6,7], by randomly sampling 999 negative items that user has not performed target behavior on, and rank the test item among the 1000 items. HR@N and NDCG@N [6] are adopted to evaluate the ranking performance, where $N = \{5, 10, 20\}$.

Comparison Methods. We compare TDRB with the following state-of-the-arts, including (1) **MostPopular** is a non-personalized method that recommends the most popular items w.r.t. target behaviors to users; (2) **BPRMF** [15] is a pair-wise learning algorithm based on MF, which only considers the influence of target behavior on user preference prediction; (3) **McBPR** [10] is the multi-channel based BPR, which divides heterogeneous behaviors into different channels; (4) **ConvNCF** [7] is a deep learning-based recommender adopting outer product and CNN to learn high-order correlations among embedding dimensions; (5) **NMTR** [2] is a recently proposed deep learning-based recommender that utilizes a pre-defined hard rule to order different types of behaviors, that is, *add-to-cart/bookmark* shows before *purchase/reply* and after *click*.

Parameter Settings. The optimal parameter settings for all the comparison methods are achieved by the empirical study or suggested by the original papers. For a fair comparison, we set the embedding size and hidden state size to 32; a grid search in $[10^{-3}, 10^{-2}, 10^{-1}, 1, 10, 10^2]$ is applied to find out the best settings

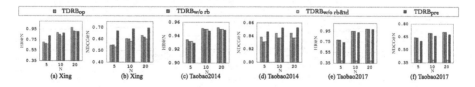

Fig. 4. Impacts of modeling temporal dynamics and repeated behaviors on TDRB.

for the regularization coefficient to avoid over-fitting; the learning rate for updating all embeddings (i.e., $\mathbf{P}, \mathbf{Q}, \mathbf{O}$) is tuned in the range of $[5^{-4}, 5^{-3}, 5^{-2}]$; and for other neural network parameters, it is tuned within $[10^{-4}, 10^{-3}, 10^{-2}, 10^{-1}]$. For all methods besides MostPop and BPRMF, we pretrain the user and item embeddings via BPRMF. For our proposed TDRB, it is implemented with Tensorflow and optimized with Adagrad optimizer.

4.2 Impacts of Temporal Dynamics and Repeated Patterns (RQ1)

To study the impacts of modeling temporal dynamics and repeated patterns, we compare three variants of TDRB: (1) $TDRB_{op}$ is our proposed TDRB adopting outer product with CNN as the fusion strategy; (2) $TDRB_{w/o\,rb}$ downgrades $TDRB_{op}$ by merging the repeated behaviors and only keeping the earliest one; (3) $TDRB_{w/o\,rb\&td}$ is the degraded version of $TDRB_{w/o\,rb}$, which utilizes a hard rule to order the non-repeated behaviors, that is, $click \rightarrow collect/favorite/bookmark \rightarrow add\text{-}to\text{-}cart/remove \rightarrow payment/buy/reply$.

The results are demonstrated in Fig. 4, where two major findings can be noted. First of all, the performance of $TDRB_{w/o\,rb}$ is generally worse than that of $TDRB_{op}$ on the three datasets, implying the benefit of modeling repeated behaviors for a more accurate recommendation. Note that the performance improvements on Taobao2014 and Xing are much larger than those on Taobao2017. This may be attributed to their different distributions w.r.t. the lengths of auxiliary behavior sequence. As shown in Fig. 3, the average length of sequences on Taobao2014 (10) and Xing (3) is longer than that on Taobao2017 (2), Second, by ordering various behaviors via a hard rule, $TDRB_{w/o\,rb\&td}$ is underperformed by $TDRB_{w/o\,rb}$ especially on Taobao2017, which validates the assumption that the hard rule cannot truly reflect user behaviors, thus failing to capture the real temporal dynamics. To sum up, the fact that $TDRB_{op}$ achieves the best performance firmly supports the effectiveness of modeling temporal dynamics and repeated behaviors on recommendations.

To further explore the effectiveness of our data segmentation (Sect. 3.1), that is, whether the segmentation will break the original temporal dynamics of the behavior sequences. This is because that a specific target behavior may be not only affected by the auxiliary behaviors in its corresponding segmented sequence $S(u, i)$, and also those behaviors far from it. Hence, we compare $TDRB_{op}$ with $TDRB_{pre}$, which utilizes all behaviors in previous sequences to help predict the target behavior in the current sequence; As shown in Fig. 5, $TDRB_{op}$ performs

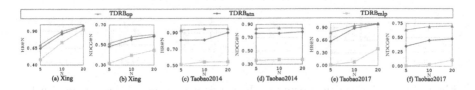

Fig. 5. Impacts of different fusion strategies on TDRB.

comparably to TDRB$_{pre}$ of the three datasets, and even achieves better performance on Taobao2017. This helps verify that: (1) the target behavior is highly affected by the auxiliary behaviors within the same sequence, whilst less influenced by those behaviors far from it; and (2) our data segmentation benefits for accurate recommendation by filtering out potential noise.

4.3   Impacts of Different Fusion Strategies (RQ2)

To further exam the impacts of different fusion strategies on TDRB, three variants are compared: (1) TDRB$_{mlp}$ uses MLP to fuse the influence of target and auxiliary behaviors; (2) TDRB$_{atn}$ employs the attention mechanism to distinguish the importance of target and auxiliary behaviors; (3) TDRB$_{op}$ adopts outer product (with CNN) to integrate target and auxiliary behaviors. Figure 5 depicts the performance on the three datasets. We can observe that TDRB$_{mlp}$ achieves the worst performance in comparison with the other two variants. By automatically distinguishing the saliency of target and auxiliary behaviors, the performance of TDRB$_{atn}$ far exceeds that of TDRB$_{mlp}$, suggesting the efficiency of attention mechanism. It, however, is outperformed by TDRB$_{op}$, validating the superiority of both (a) outer product on encoding expressive and high-order user-item correlation; and (b) CNN on capturing the abstract graph features.

4.4   Comparative Results (RQ3)

Table 2 reports the performance of all the comparison methods on the three datasets w.r.t. HR@N and NDCG@N, where $N = \{5, 10, 20\}$. We summarize the major findings as below.

(1) MostPop, as the only non-personalized recommender, performs the worst among all the comparisons across the three datasets, which indicates the essence of personalization in recommendation; (2) The deep learning-based recommenders (e.g., ConvNCF, TDRB) generally outperform the conventional recommenders (e.g., BPRMF, McBPR), demonstrating the superiority of deep learning advances over conventional methods; (3) Regarding to the conventional recommenders, McBPR with the incorporation of both target and auxiliary behaviors performs better than BPRMF on Xing, whilst it underperforms BPRMF on the two Taobao datasets. This might be explained as: the hard rule used to order heterogeneous behaviors in McBPR cannot truly reflect the temporal dynamics of user behaviors, thus introducing noises and hurting the performance. Similar trends can be observed on the performance comparison between the two deep learning-based recommenders: ConvNCF and NMTR. Only target behavior is exploited by ConvNCF; whilst NMTR adopts a hard rule to integrate both target and auxiliary behaviors; (4) Overall, our proposed TDRB achieves the best performance across the three datasets. The significant enhancements, with a lift of 27.91% and 61.32% w.r.t. HR and NDCG on average, demonstrate the effectiveness of modeling temporal dynamics and repeated behaviors.

Table 2. The performance of all comparison methods, where the best performance of the baselines is marked with '*'; the performance of TDRB (i.e., $TDRB_{op}$ that performs the best among all variants of TDRB) is highlighted in bold; 'Improve' indicates the improvements that TDRB achieves relative to the '*' results.

Datasets	Methods	HR@5	NDCG@5	HR@10	NDCG@10	HR@20	NDCG@20
Xing	MostPop	0.0021	0.0021	0.0065	0.0035	0.0065	0.0035
	BPRMF	0.4203	0.2603	0.6928	0.3483	0.8213	0.3824
	McBPR	0.4204*	0.2607*	0.7037*	0.3518*	0.8714*	0.3953*
	ConvNCF	0.4117	0.2545	0.6492	0.3309	0.8257	0.3766
	NMTR	0.4031	0.2546	0.4749	0.2777	0.5882	0.3063
	TDRB	**0.7058**	**0.5467**	**0.8845**	**0.6043**	**0.9825**	**0.6304**
	Improve	70.92%	109.70%	25.69%	71.77%	12.86%	59.47%
Taobao 2014	MostPop	0.0057	0.0031	0.0229	0.0081	0.0229	0.0081
	BPRMF	0.6533	0.4595	0.6832	0.4699	0.6851	0.4704
	McBPR	0.6564	0.4552	0.6908*	0.4670	0.6953*	0.4681
	ConvNCF	0.6596*	0.4782*	0.6838	0.4865*	0.6870	0.4873*
	NMTR	0.5876	0.4135	0.6195	0.4244	0.6214	0.4249
	TDRB	**0.9343**	**0.8385**	**0.9509**	**0.8441**	**0.9521**	**0.8444**
	Improve	41.64%	75.34%	27.35%	73.50%	36.93%	35.71%
Taobao 2017	MostPop	0.0233	0.0131	0.0425	0.0186	0.0425	0.0186
	BPRMF	0.5879	0.3951	0.8852	0.4914	0.9949*	0.5206
	McBPR	0.5772	0.3818	0.8859	0.4815	0.9947	0.5104
	ConvNCF	0.6066*	0.4127*	0.8863*	0.5033*	0.9944	0.5321*
	NMTR	0.4338	0.2660	0.6930	0.3499	0.8533	0.3910
	TDRB	**0.7826**	**0.6391**	**0.9520**	**0.6945**	**0.9944**	**0.7058**
	Improve	29.01%	55.85%	6.90%	37.98%	−0.05%	32.64%

5   Conclusions and Future Work

This paper proposes a novel neural framework TDRB, which exploits the temporal dynamics and repeated behaviors to further enhance the accuracy of heterogeneous implicit feedback based recommendation. Being equipped with three core modules (i.e., `Target`, `Auxilary` and `Fusion`), TDRB is capable of better modeling user preference, thus achieving superior recommendation performance. Extensive empirical studies on three real-world datasets validate the effectiveness of our proposed TDRB. For future work, we intend to explore more values of the repeated behaviors for the next item recommendation.

Acknowledgments. This work is partially supported by the National Natural Science Foundation of China under Grant No. 61972078 and 61702084, and the Fundamental Research Funds for the Central Universities under Grant No. N181705007.

References

1. Ding, J., et al.: Improving implicit recommender systems with view data (2018)
2. Gao, C., et al.: Neural multi-task recommendation from multi-behavior data (2019)
3. Guo, G., et al.: Resolving data sparsity by multi-type auxiliary implicit feedback for recommender systems. Knowl.-Based Syst. **138**, 202–207 (2017)
4. He, K., et al.: Deep residual learning for image recognition. In: CVPR (2016)
5. He, X., et al.: Fast matrix factorization for online recommendation with implicit feedback. In: SIGIR (2016)
6. He, X., et al.: Neural collaborative filtering (2017)
7. He, X., et al.: Outer product-based neural collaborative filtering (2018)
8. Hidasi, B., et al.: Session-based recommendations with recurrent neural networks. arXiv: Learning (2015)
9. Li, J., et al.: Neural attentive session-based recommendation. arXiv: Information Retrieval (2017)
10. Loni, B., et al.: Bayesian personalized ranking with multi-channel user feedback. In: RecSys (2016)
11. Pan, W., et al.: GBPR: group preference based Bayesian personalized ranking for one-class collaborative filtering. In: IJCAI (2013)
12. Pan, W., et al.: Adaptive Bayesian personalized ranking for heterogeneous implicit feedbacks. Knowl.-Based Syst. **73**, 173–180 (2015)
13. Qiu, H., et al.: BPRH: Bayesian personalized ranking for heterogeneous implicit feedback. Inf. Sci. **453**, 80–98 (2018)
14. Qiu, H., et al.: TBPR: trinity preference based Bayesian personalized ranking for multivariate implicit feedback. In: UMAP (2016)
15. Rendle, S., et al.: BPR: Bayesian personalized ranking from implicit feedback. In: UAI (2009)
16. Wang, C., et al.: Modeling item-specific temporal dynamics of repeat consumption for recommender systems. In: WWW (2019)
17. Wen, H., et al.: Leveraging multiple implicit feedback for personalized recommendation with neural network. In: AIAM (2019)
18. Yin, H., et al.: SPTF: a scalable probabilistic tensor factorization model for semantic-aware behavior prediction. In: ICDM (2017)
19. Young, T., et al.: Recent trends in deep learning based natural language processing (2018)

Classification

HIN: Hierarchical Inference Network
for Document-Level Relation Extraction

Hengzhu Tang[1,2], Yanan Cao[1], Zhenyu Zhang[1,2], Jiangxia Cao[1,2],
Fang Fang[1(✉)], Shi Wang[3], and Pengfei Yin[1]

[1] Institute of Information Engineering, Chinese Academy of Sciences, Beijing, China
{tanghengzhu,caoyanan,zhangzhenyu1996,caojiangxia,fangfang0703,
yinpengfei}@iie.ac.cn
[2] School of Cyber Security, University of Chinese Academy of Sciences,
Beijing, China
[3] Institute of Computing Technology, Chinese Academy of Sciences, Beijing, China
wangshi@ict.ac.cn

Abstract. Document-level RE requires reading, inferring and aggregating over multiple sentences. From our point of view, it is necessary for document-level RE to take advantage of multi-granularity inference information: entity level, sentence level and document level. Thus, how to obtain and aggregate the inference information with different granularity is challenging for document-level RE, which has not been considered by previous work. In this paper, we propose a Hierarchical Inference Network (HIN) to make full use of the abundant information from entity level, sentence level and document level. Translation constraint and bilinear transformation are applied to target entity pair in multiple subspaces to get entity-level inference information. Next, we model the inference between entity-level information and sentence representation to achieve sentence-level inference information. Finally, a hierarchical aggregation approach is adopted to obtain the document-level inference information. In this way, our model can effectively aggregate inference information from these three different granularities. Experimental results show that our method achieves state-of-the-art performance on the large-scale DocRED dataset. We also demonstrate that using BERT representations can further substantially boost the performance.

Keywords: Relation extraction · Hierarchical inference network · Multi granularity

1 Introduction

Relation extraction (RE) aims to detect the semantic relation between entities in plain text, which plays an important role in knowledge base population and natural language understanding. Most previous work focuses on sentence-level RE, i.e., extracting relational facts from a single sentence. In recent years, deep learning models have been widely applied to sentence-level RE and achieved remarkable success [4,16].

© Springer Nature Switzerland AG 2020
H. W. Lauw et al. (Eds.): PAKDD 2020, LNAI 12084, pp. 197–209, 2020.
https://doi.org/10.1007/978-3-030-47426-3_16

Input:
[1] "Nisei" is the ninth episode of the third season of the American science fiction television series The X-Files. [2] It premiered on the Fox network on November 24, 1995. [3] It was directed by David Nutter, and written by **Chris Carter**, Frank Spotnitz and Howard Gordon. [4] "Nisei" featured guest appearances by Steven Williams, Raymond J. Barry and Stephen McHattie ... [8] The show centers on FBI special agents **Fox Mulder** (David Duchovny) and Dana Scully (Gillian Anderson) who work on cases linked to the paranormal, called X-Files ...

Subject: *Chris Carter*
Object: *Fox Mulder*
Relation: *creator*   **Supporting Sentences: 1, 3, 8**

Fig. 1. An example from DocRED. Each document in DocRED is annotated with named entity mentions, coreference information, relations, and supporting sentences.

Despite the great success of previous work, sentence-level RE suffers from a serious restriction in practice: a large amount of relational facts are expressed in multiple sentences. Taking Fig. 1 as an example, in order to identify the relational fact (*Chris Carter, creator, Fox Mulder*), one should first identify the fact "Nisei" is an episode of the American science fiction television series from sentence 1, then identify the facts that *Fox Mulder* is a character in "Nisei" and *Chris Carter* is one of the writers of "Nisei" from sentence 8 and 3 respectively. To extract these relational facts, it is necessary to infer and aggregate over multiple sentences. Obviously, most traditional sentence-level RE models often fail to generalize extraction to this situation. To move RE forward from sentence level to document level, many efforts have been made [13,15], but most previous methods used only entity-level information and this is not adequate. Thus, there are still some deep-seated problems unsolved in document-level RE.

To predict the relation between two entities, we argue that the document-level RE model requires taking advantage of multi-granularity inference information: entity level, sentence level and document level. Let's go back to the former example, entity-level inference information is derived from the semantic of all mentions of *Chris Carter* and *Fox Mulder* in the document, sentence-level inference information represents the information related to relational facts in each sentence, document-level inference information aggregates all the necessary information in supporting sentences (sentence 1, 3 and 8) and discards information in noise sentences. Technically, it is clear that document-level RE faces two main challenges: (1) How to obtain the inference information with different granularity; (2) How to aggregate these different granularity inference information and make the final prediction.

In this paper, we propose a new neural architecture, Hierarchical Inference Network (HIN), to tackle above challenges. Specifically, inspired by translation constraint [1], which models a relational fact $r(e_h, e_t)$ with $e_h + r \approx e_t$, we apply this translation constraint to target entity pair. Besides, a bi-affine layer is also used to obtain bilinear representation for the target entity pair. To jointly attend to information from different representation subspaces, we implement the above two transformations in multiple subspaces in parallel, and acquire entity-level inference information. To obtain the sentence-level inference information, we first apply vanilla attention mechanism to calculate the vector representation for each sentence, which enables our model to pay more attention to the informative words. Then we adopt the semantic matching method [2] which is widely used in natural language inference (NLI) domain to compare the entity-level inference information with each sentence vector. Furthermore, in order to calculate the document-level inference information, we apply a hierarchical BiLSTM and again use attention mechanism to distinguish crucial sentence-level inference information for overall document-level inference representation. Finally, we aggregate inference information of different granularity, the entity-level and document-level inference representations are combined into a fixed-length vector, which is further fed into a classification layer for prediction.

To summarize, we make the following contributions:

1. We propose a Hierarchical Inference Network (HIN) for document-level RE, which is capable of aggregating inference information from entity level to sentence level and then to document level.
2. We conduct thorough evaluation on DocRED dataset. Results show that our model achieves the state-of-the-art performance. We further demonstrate that using BERT representations further substantially boosts the performance.
3. We analyze the effectiveness of our model on different number of supporting sentences and experimental results show that our model performs much better than previous work when the number of supporting sentences is large.

2   Task Description

For document-level RE, the input is a document with annotated entities, as well as multiple occurrences of each entity, i.e., entity mentions, the goal is to identify all the related entity pairs in the document. Following [15], we transform RE into a classification problem. We use upper case letters to represent entities $(E_1, \cdots, E_m)$ and lower case letters to represent mentions $(e_1, \cdots, e_m)$. The RE model is given a relation candidate (E_a, E_b, D) and expected to output the relations between E_a and E_b, where E_a and E_b are entities in the document D.

3   Proposed Approach

Figure 2 gives an illustration of our model. We describe the details of different components in the following sections.

3.1   Input Layer

– **Word Embeddings.** In order to capture the meaningful semantic information of words, we map each word into a low-dimensional word embedding vector. The dimension of word embeddings is d_w.

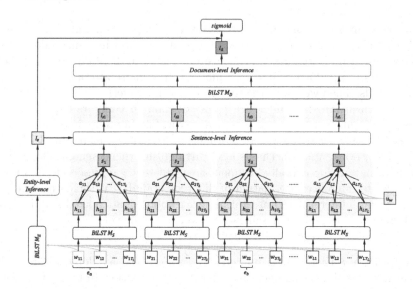

Fig. 2. The overall architecture of the Hierarchical Inference Network (HIN)

- **Entity Type Embeddings.** We utilize the entity type information to enrich
  the representation of the input. The entity type embedding is obtained by
  mapping the entity type (e.g., PER, LOC, ORG) into a vector. The dimension
  of entity type embeddings is d_t.
- **Coreference Embeddings.** Usually each entity may be mentioned many
  times in a document. Following previous work, we assign entity mentions
  corresponding to the same entity with the same entity id, which is determined
  by the order in which entities appear in the document. Then entity ids are
  embedded into vectors. The dimension of coreference embeddings is d_c.

We concatenate all three embeddings together for each word w_i, and a docu-
ment is transformed into a matrix $\mathbf{X} = [\mathbf{w}_1, \mathbf{w}_2, \ldots, \mathbf{w}_n]$, where each word vector
$\mathbf{w}_i \in \mathbb{R}^{d_w + d_t + d_c}$ and n is the length of the document.

3.2   Entity-Level Inference Module

In this section, we compute the entity-level inference information for target
entity pair. To represent each word in its context, we encode the document
$\mathbf{X} = \{\mathbf{w}_i\}_{i=1}^{n}$ into a hidden state vector sequence $\{\mathbf{h}_i\}_{i=1}^{n}$ with bi-directional
LSTM:

$$\mathbf{h}_i = \text{BiLSTM}_E(\mathbf{w}_i), i \in [1, n]. \tag{1}$$

where $\mathbf{h}_i \in \mathbb{R}^d$ is a contextualized representation of w_i, summarizing the context
information centered around w_i.

Considering that an entity may be mentioned many times in a document and
a mention may also contain more than one word, we represent each entity and

mention with the average of the embeddings of different elements. Correspondingly, the mention representation is formed as the average of the words that the mention contains, the entity representation is computed as the average of the mention representations associated with the entity:

$$\mathbf{e}_l = avg_{w_i \in e_l}(\mathbf{h}_i), \quad \mathbf{E}_a = avg_{e_l \in E_a}(\mathbf{e}_l) \tag{2}$$

We claim that it is beneficial to allow the model to jointly attend to information from different representation subspaces, thus, we use different learnable projection matrices to project entities into K subspaces:

$$\mathbf{E}_a^k = \mathbf{W}_k^{(1)}(ReLU(\mathbf{W}_k^{(0)} \mathbf{E}_a)) \tag{3}$$

where $\mathbf{E}_a^k \in \mathbb{R}^k$ corresponds to the representation of E_a in the k-th latent space, $\mathbf{W}_k^{(0)} \in \mathbb{R}^{d \times d}$ and $\mathbf{W}_k^{(1)} \in \mathbb{R}^{d \times k}$ are the learnable projection matrices corresponding to the k-th subspace. For each of these projected versions, we perform the entity-level inference in parallel. These are concatenated and once again projected, resulting in the final entity-level inference information.

Inspired by TransE [1] which modelled a triple $r(e_h, e_t)$ with $\mathbf{e}_h + \mathbf{r} \approx \mathbf{e}_t$, we argue that $(\mathbf{E}_b - \mathbf{E}_a)$ could represent the relation between E_a and E_b in the document to some extent. In addition, a bilinear representation can be obtained by a bi-affine layer to enhance the expression ability of model. We define the following formula as entity-level inference representation in the k-th latent space:

$$\mathbf{I}_e^k = Concat\left(\mathbf{E}_a^k \mathbf{R}^k \mathbf{E}_b^k; \mathbf{E}_b^k - \mathbf{E}_a^k; \mathbf{E}_a^k; \mathbf{E}_b^k\right) \tag{4}$$

where $\mathbf{R}^k \in \mathbb{R}^{k \times k \times k}$ is a learned bi-affine tensor, $Concat$ denotes concatenation.

Moreover, we believe that the relative distances between two target entities can help us better judge the relations. Empirically, we use the relative distances between the first mentions of the two entities as the relative distances between two target entities. Finally, all entity-level inference representations in different latent space and the relative distance embeddings are fed into a feed-forward neural network (FFNN) to form the final entity-level inference information:

$$\mathbf{I}_e = G_e\left(\left[\mathbf{I}_e^1; ...; \mathbf{I}_e^K; \mathbf{M}(d_{ba}) - \mathbf{M}(d_{ab})\right]\right) \tag{5}$$

here G_e is a FFNN with ReLU activation function, $\mathbf{M}$ is an embedding matrix, d_{ab} and d_{ba} are the relative distances between E_a and E_b in the document. $\mathbf{I}_e \in \mathbb{R}^d$ describes relation features between E_a and E_b at entity level.

3.3 Hierarchical Document-Level Inference Module

In this section, we propose a hierarchical inference mechanism, inference information is aggregated from entity level to sentence level and then to document level. In this way, our model can aggregate all useful information of the document.

Sentence-Level Inference. Assume that a document contains L sentences, and w_{jt} represent the t-th word in the j-th sentence. Given the j-th sentence S_j, to represent words in its context, the sentence is fed into a BiLSTM encoder:

$$\mathbf{h}_{jt} = \mathrm{BiLSTM}_S\left(\mathbf{w}_{jt}\right), t \in [1, T_j]. \tag{6}$$

Since different words in a sentence are differentially informative, inspired by [14], we introduce the vanilla attention mechanism to enable our model to selectively assign higher weights for the informative words and lower weights for the other words. Then we aggregate the representations of those informative words to form a sentence vector. Specifically,

$$\alpha_{jt} = \mathbf{u}_w^{\top} \tanh\left(\mathbf{W}_w \mathbf{h}_{jt} + \mathbf{b}_w\right) \tag{7}$$

$$a_{jt} = \frac{\exp\left(\alpha_{jt}\right)}{\sum_t \exp\left(\alpha_{jt}\right)} \tag{8}$$

$$\mathbf{S}_j = \sum_t a_{jt}\mathbf{h}_{jt} \tag{9}$$

where $\mathbf{u}_w, \mathbf{b}_w \in \mathbb{R}^d$ and $\mathbf{W}_w \in \mathbb{R}^{d \times d}$ are learnable parameters. Word hidden state $\mathbf{h}_{jt} \in \mathbb{R}^d$ is first fed through a one-layer MLP, then we obtain weights of words by measuring "which words are more related to the target entities". Finally, we compute the sentence vector $\mathbf{S}_j$ as a weighted sum of the word hidden states.

For obtaining the sentence-level inference information, we adopt a semantic matching method which is used in previous NLI model [2]. Through comparing sentence vector $\mathbf{S}_j$ with entity-level inference representation $\mathbf{I}_e$, we can derive sentence-level inference representation $\mathbf{I}_{sj}$ for the j-th sentence:

$$\mathbf{I}_{sj} = G_s\left([\mathbf{S}_j; \mathbf{I}_e; \mathbf{S}_j - \mathbf{I}_e; \mathbf{S}_j \circ \mathbf{I}_e]\right). \tag{10}$$

where G_s is FFNN with ReLU function, a matching trick with elementwise subtraction and multiplication is used for building better matching representations [10]. $\mathbf{I}_{sj}$ represents the inference information derived from the j-th sentence.

Document-Level Inference. In order to distinguish crucial sentence-level inference information for overall document-level inference representation, vanilla attention mechanism is again used. We build a BiLSTM followed by the attention network on top of the sentence-level inference vectors ($\mathbf{I}_s$) to aggregate all essential evidence information scattered in different sentences:

$$\mathbf{c}_{sj} = \mathrm{BiLSTM}_D\left(\mathbf{I}_{sj}\right), j \in [1, L] \tag{11}$$

$$\alpha_j = \mathbf{u}_s^{\top} \tanh\left(\mathbf{W}_s \mathbf{c}_{sj} + \mathbf{b}_s\right) \tag{12}$$

$$a_j = \frac{\exp\left(\alpha_j\right)}{\sum_j \exp\left(\alpha_j\right)} \tag{13}$$

$$\mathbf{I}_d = \sum_t a_j \mathbf{c}_{sj} \tag{14}$$

here $\mathbf{u}_s, \mathbf{b}_s \in \mathbb{R}^d$ and $\mathbf{W}_s \in \mathbb{R}^{d \times d}$ are learnable parameters, $\mathbf{I}_d \in \mathbb{R}^d$ is the document-level inference representation which represents all the inference information that we can obtain from the document.

3.4 Prediction Layer

To better integrate inference information of different granularity, we concatenate entity-level inference representation $\mathbf{I}_e$ and document-level inference representation $\mathbf{I}_d$ together to form the final inference representation. Since there are often multiple relations holding between an entity pair, we use a FFNN with the *sigmoid* function to calculate the probability of each relation:

$$P\left(r | E_a, E_b\right) = sigmoid\left(\mathbf{W}_r \begin{bmatrix} \mathbf{I}_e \\ \mathbf{I}_d \end{bmatrix} + \mathbf{b}_r\right). \tag{15}$$

where $\mathbf{W}_r$, $\mathbf{b}_r$ are the weight matrix and bias for the linear transformation.

A binary label vector $\mathbf{y}$ is set to indicate the set of true relations holding between the entity pair, where 1 means an relation is in the set, and 0 otherwise. In our experiments, we use the binary cross entropy (BCE) as training loss:

$$Loss = -\sum_{r=1}^{l} y_r \log\left(p_r\right) + \left(1 - y_r\right) \log\left(1 - p_r\right). \tag{16}$$

where $y_r \in \{0, 1\}$ is the true value on label r and l is the number of relations.

Given a document, we rank the predicted results by their confidence and traverse this list from top to bottom by F1 score on dev set, the probability value corresponding to the maximum F1 is picked as threshold δ. This threshold is used to control the number of extracted relational facts on test set.

4   Experiments

4.1   Dataset

To evaluate the effectiveness of our model, we use the DocRED dataset [15], which is the largest human-annotated document-level RE dataset constructed from Wikidata and Wikipedia. DocRED contains over 5,053 documents, 40,276 sentences, 132,375 entities and 96 frequent relation types. Entity types in DocRED are annotated. It is also introduced by the author of DocRED that about 40.7% of relational facts can only be extracted from multiple sentences and 61.1% relational instances require a variety of reasoning.

4.2   Comparison Models and Evaluation Metrics

We compare our model against the following document-level RE baselines:

CNN/LSTM/BiLSTM-RE: They first encode a document into a hidden state vector sequence with CNN/LSTM/BiLSTM as encoder, and then predict relations for each entity pair by feeding them into a bilinear function [15].

Table 1. Performance of different models on DocRED (%).

Model	Dev		Test	
	Ign F1	F1	Ign F1	F1
CNN-RE [15]	41.58	43.45	40.33	42.26
LSTM-RE [15]	48.44	50.68	47.71	50.07
BiLSTM-RE [15]	48.87	50.94	48.78	51.06
Context-Aware [12]	48.94	51.09	48.40	50.70
HIN-GloVe	**51.06**	**52.95**	**51.15**	**53.30**
BERT-RE [13]	-	54.16	-	53.20
BERT-Two-Step [13]	-	54.42	-	53.92
HIN-BERT	**54.29**	**56.31**	**53.70**	**55.60**

Context-Aware: It uses an LSTM-based encoder to jointly learn representations for all relations in the context, and then combines other context relations with target relation to make the final prediction [12].

BERT-RE: It uses BERT to encode the document, entities are represented by their average word embedding. A BiLinear layer is applied to predict the relation between entity pairs [13].

BERT-Two-Step: Based on BERT-RE, it models the document-level RE through a two-step process. The first step is to predict whether or not two entities have a relation, the second step is to predict the specific relation [13].

HIN: This is the main model of this paper. Multi-granularity inference information is used to better model complex interactions between entities.

The widely used metric F1 is used in our experiments. Moreover, since some relational facts present in both training and dev/test sets, we also report the F1 excluding those relational facts and denote it as Ign F1.

4.3   Implementation Details

We try two embedding methods in our experiments: 100-dimensional GloVe [11] embeddings and BERT representations [3]. For the BERT representations, the base uncased English model with dimension 768 is used, we map word representations into 100 dimensional vectors by a linear projection layer. Once the word representations are initialized, they are fixed during training. The embedding dimensions of coreference, distance and entity type are all set to be 20. For LSTM encoder, the dimension of the hidden units is 128. The number of latent space is 2. Furthermore, we regularize our network using dropout and the dropout ratio is 0.2. We optimized our model using Adam [5], with learning rate of 10^{-4}, $\beta_1 = 0.9$, $\beta_2 = 0.999$. The batch size is set to be 12 and the value of threshold δ is determined by the performance on the dev set.

4.4   Experimental Results and Analyses

Overall Performance. Experimental results are shown in Table 1. From the results, we can observe that: (1) Compared with BiLSTM-RE, the state-of-the-art model without BERT, our HIN-GloVe achieves significant improvements of 2.24% in F1, we claim that it is mainly due to the reasoning mechanism and hierarchical aggregation structure in HIN, which will be further discussed in ablation study. (2) Even though BERT based models provides strong prediction power, HIN-BERT consistently improves over them, which further proves the effectiveness of our hierarchical inference network. (3) Although Context-Aware model combines context relations with the target relation, it can't use the evidence information in document as effectively as HIN. Hence our model also outperforms it by 2.60% in F1. (4) BERT representations further boost the performance of our model, the HIN-BERT approach outperforms all these previous methods, which indicates the importance of prior knowledge.

Table 2. Results of ablation study (%).

Setting	Dev	
	Ign F1	F1
HIN-BERT	**54.29**	**56.31**
- Translation mechanism	53.09	55.10
- Bilinear transformation	52.15	54.29
- Multispace	52.44	54.59
- Sentence inference	52.82	55.06
- Hierarchical aggregation	51.36	53.50
- Above all	49.95	52.10

Ablation Study. To study the contribution of each component in HIN-BERT, we run an ablation study on DocRED dev set (see Table 2). From these ablations, we find that: (1) When we remove the translation mechanism and bilinear transformation, F1 score drops by 1.21% and 2.02% respectively, which indicates that these two transformations can enhance the expression ability of HIN at the entity level. (2) Removing the multi-space projection hurts the result by 1.72%, which proves that it is beneficial to allow the model to jointly attend to information from different representation subspaces. (3) F1 drops by 1.25% when we remove the sentence-level inference mechanism, i.e., replacing the sentence-level inference vector with sentence vector. (4) F1 drops by 2.81% when we discard the hierarchical aggregation approach. Instead, we run BiLSTM followed by mean-pooling layer over the whole document to get the document vector. (5) We also observe that F1 drops by 4.21% when we discard the above all factors together. In summary, all components play an important role in our model.

Analysis by the Number of Supporting Sentences. As we discussed before, it is challenging for document-level RE to reason from multiple sentences. To further prove the effectiveness of HIN, we analyze the recall on relational facts with different number of supporting sentences here.[1] As shown in Fig. 3, we find that our model always performs better than other baselines, especially when the number of supporting sentences increases gradually. More specifically, HIN-GloVe even outperforms BERT-RE when the number of supporting sentences exceeds 4, which fully proves the superiority of HIN. Note that when the number of supporting sentences exceeds 7, HIN-GloVe and other baselines behave the same. We think this is because there are very few samples with more than 7 supporting sentences in dev set. We believe when the number of relational facts with more supporting sentences increase our model will achieve better results.

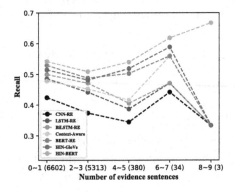

Fig. 3. Recall of models on relational facts with different number of supporting sentences. Numbers in parentheses represent the number of relational facts with different number of supporting sentences in dev set.

Case Study. We compare our model with BERT-RE on some cases from dev set, as shown in Table 3. (1) Example 1 represents the situation that logical reasoning is required. Specifically, in order to identify the relational fact, we have to first identify the fact that *Galaxy S* series is a line of *Samsung* from sentence 0 and 2, then identify the fact *Samsung Galaxy S9* is the latest smartphones in the Galaxy S series from sentence 4. We explain that our model uses a hierarchical aggregation approach to collect inference information from multiple sentences, so that it can better deal with this complex inter-sentence relationship. (2) Example 2 represents the case of coreference reasoning. In this situation, we claim that the attention and reasoning mechanisms in sentence-level inference module can help us to identify that "He" refers to *Robert Kingsbury Huntington* in sentence 3. In the end, our model can identify the right relation while BERT-RE mistakenly assumes that *Los Angeles* is the place where *Robert Kingsbury Huntington* died.

---

[1] Since there is no official code for BERT-Two-Step, its results are not counted.

Table 3. The results predicted by BERT-RE and HIN-BERT. The reasoning type of each example is different and the first row for each example is the input document. The *head*, *tail*, *relation* and supporting sentences are colored accordingly.

Logical reasoning	[0] The Galaxy S series is a line of Samsung Electronics, a division of *Samsung* [2] Galaxy S line has ... being *Samsung* 's flagship smartphones. [4] the latest smartphones in Galaxy S series are the **Samsung Galaxy S9** ...
Relation	**Lable:** *manufacturer* **BERT-RE:** *None* **HIN-BERT:** *manufacturer*
Coreference reasoning	[0] **Robert Kingsbury Huntington**, was a naval aircrewman and member of Torpedo Squadron 8. [2] ... **Huntington** was shot down during the Battle of Midway ... [3] <u>He</u> was born in *Los Angeles*, California ...
Relation	**Lable:** *birth place* **BERT-RE:** *death place* **HIN-BERT:** *birth place*
Common-sense reasoning	[0] IBM Research – Brazil is one of twelve research laboratories comprising IBM Research, its first in *South America*. [1] It was established in June 2010, with locations in **São Paulo** and Rio de Janeiro ...
Relation	**Lable:** *continent* **BERT-RE:** *country* **HIN-BERT:** *country*

(3) Example 3 is a case that needs to combine context information with common-sense knowledge. Through some external common-sense knowledge, we might know that *South America* is a continent and *São Paulo* is a city, which is the useful information to help judge their relation. We think the problem can be solved by adding some external knowledge and we leave it as our future work.

5 Related Work

In recent years, more and more neural models have been applied to RE. Zeng el al. [17] employed a one-dimensional CNN with additional lexical features to encode relations. Miwa et al. [9] used LSTM with tree structures for RE. Zhou el al. [18] showed that combining CNN/RNN with attention mechanism can further improve performance. And the emergence of various optimization algorithms [6–8] makes these neural models more effective. Most existing RE work focuses on modeling within a single sentence. However, usually documents provide more information than sentences. Moving research from sentence level to document level is necessary. Recently, there has been increasing interest in document-level RE. Yao et al. [15] proposed a large-scale human-annotated document-level RE dataset, DocRED, and first compute the representations for all entities then predict relations for each entity pair by feeding them into a bilinear function. Wang et al. [13] used BERT to encode the document, it also used bilinear layer to predict the relation between entity pairs, but it modelled the document-level RE through a two-step process. Most previous methods used only entity-level information and this is not adequate. In this paper, we propose to effectively aggregate the inference information of different granularity.

6 Conclusion

In this paper, we proposed a Hierarchical Inference Network (HIN) for document-level RE. It uses a hierarchical inference method to aggregate the inference information of different granularity: entity level, sentence level and document level. We show that our method achieves state-of-the-art performance on the largest human-annotated DocRED dataset. Experimental analysis shows that both the inference mechanism and hierarchical aggregation approach in our model play an important role. In the future, we plan to incorporate external knowledge to further improve the proposed model.

Acknowledgements. This research is supported by the National Key Research and Development Program of China (No. 2018YFB1004703).

References

1. Bordes, A., Usunier, N., Garcia-Duran, A., Weston, J., Yakhnenko, O.: Translating embeddings for modeling multi-relational data. In: NIPS (2013)
2. Chen, Q., Zhu, X., Ling, Z., Wei, S., Jiang, H., Inkpen, D.: Enhanced LSTM for natural language inference. arXiv preprint arXiv:1609.06038 (2016)
3. Devlin, J., Chang, M.W., Lee, K., Toutanova, K.: Bert: pre-training of deep bidirectional transformers for language understanding. In: NAACL-HLT (2019)
4. Han, X., Yu, P., Liu, Z., Sun, M., Li, P.: Hierarchical relation extraction with coarse-to-fine grained attention. In: EMNLP (2018)
5. Kingma, D.P., Ba, J.: Adam: a method for stochastic optimization. arXiv preprint arXiv:1412.6980 (2014)
6. Li, Q., Niu, W., Li, G., Cao, Y., Tan, J., Guo, L.: Lingo: linearized Grassmannian optimization for nuclear norm minimization. In: CIKM (2015)
7. Li, Q., Wang, Z.: Riemannian submanifold tracking on low-rank algebraic variety. In: Thirty-First AAAI Conference on Artificial Intelligence (2017)
8. Li, Q., Wang, Z., Li, G., Cao, Y., Xiong, G., Guo, L.: Learning robust low-rank approximation for crowdsourcing on Riemannian manifold. In: ICCS (2017)
9. Miwa, M., Bansal, M.: End-to-end relation extraction using LSTMS on sequences and tree structures. arXiv preprint arXiv:1601.00770 (2016)
10. Mou, L., et al.: Natural language inference by tree-based convolution and heuristic matching. In: ACL (2015)
11. Pennington, J., Socher, R., Manning, C.: Glove: global vectors for word representation. In: EMNLP (2014)
12. Sorokin, D., Gurevych, I.: Context-aware representations for knowledge base relation extraction. In: EMNLP (2017)
13. Wang, H., Focke, C., Sylvester, R., Mishra, N., Wang, W.: Fine-tune Bert for Docred with two-step process. arXiv preprint arXiv:1909.11898 (2019)
14. Yang, Z., Yang, D., Dyer, C., He, X., Smola, A., Hovy, E.: Hierarchical attention networks for document classification. In: NAACL (2016)
15. Yao, Y., et al.: Docred: a large-scale document-level relation extraction dataset. In: ACL (2019)
16. Yu, B., Zhang, Z., Liu, T., Wang, B., Li, S., Li, Q.: Beyond word attention: using segment attention in neural relation extraction. In: IJCAI (2019)

17. Zeng, D., Liu, K., Lai, S., Zhou, G., Zhao, J.: Relation classification via convolutional deep neural network. In: COLING (2014)
18. Zhou, P., et al.: Attention-based bidirectional long short-term memory networks for relation classification. In: ACL (2016)

Multi-Layer Cross Loss Model for Zero-Shot Human Activity Recognition

Tong Wu[1,2], Yiqiang Chen[1,2,3(✉)], Yang Gu[1,2,3], Jiwei Wang[1,2],
Siyu Zhang[1,2,3], and Zhanghu Zhechen[1,2]

[1] The Beijing Key Laboratory of Mobile Computing and Pervasive Device,
Institute of Computing Technology, Chinese Academy of Sciences,
Beijing 100190, China
{wutong17s,yqchen,guyang,wangjiwei}@ict.ac.cn, astro6974@gmail.com,
zhangzhanghuzhechen@outlook.com
[2] University of Chinese Academy of Sciences,
Beijing 100049, China
[3] Peng Cheng Laboratory, Shenzhen 518055, China

Abstract. Most existing methods of human activity recognition are based on supervised learning. These methods can only recognize classes which appear in the training dataset, but are out of work when the classes are not in the training dataset. Zero-shot learning aims at solving this problem. In this paper, we propose a novel model termed Multi-Layer Cross Loss Model (MLCLM). Our model has two novel ideas: (1) In the model, we design a multi-nonlinear layers model to project features to semantic space for that the deeper the network is, the better the network can fit the data's distribution. (2) A novel objective function combining mean square loss and cross entropy loss is designed for the zero-shot learning task. We have conduct sufficient experiments to evaluate the proposed model on three benchmark datasets. Experiments show that our model outperforms other state-of-the-art methods significantly in zero-shot human activity recognition.

Keywords: Human activity recognition · Zero-shot learning · Cross loss

1 Introduction

Human Activity Recognition (HAR) has appealed much attention in recent years because of its usage in many applications, such as fall detection [1], game consoles [2], etc. HAR mainly depends on 2 kinds of signals: video camera and inertial sensors integrated in wearable devices. With the developments of wearable devices, inertial sensors have been widely employed in the field of HAR. The main reasons are threefold: (1) The wearable devices with inertial sensors are convenient while the camera is usually fixed in a specific place. (2) The inertial sensors' data requires less storage while the camera usually needs large memory

H. W. Lauw et al. (Eds.): PAKDD 2020, LNAI 12084, pp. 210–221, 2020.
https://doi.org/10.1007/978-3-030-47426-3_17

for visual data. Besides the storage, processing the videos is also costly. (3) The inertial sensors just record the user's information, while the video camera contains information of others in the same place, so inertial sensors have inherent advantage of protecting user's privacy and are more target-specific.

Due to the fast developments in deep neural networks, the performance of human activity recognition has enhanced significantly in recent years. But most of the HAR methods are supervised learning methods [3–5]. They can just recognize the classes appeared in training dataset but are incapable of recognizing the classes not appeared in training dataset. Nevertheless, the training dataset can't contain all the activities, because on the one hand every individual can do plenty of activities, and we can't collect all the activities before training stage, on the other hand, it's extremely expensive to annotate an activity and label the training data. Recognizing the classes not appeared in training dataset is defined as zero-shot learning problem which is first proposed in [6]. This study provided a formal framework to solve the problem and a zero-shot learning example for the activity decoding task. In the setting of zero-shot learning, the classes in the training dataset (seen classes) and classes in the testing dataset (unseen classes) are disjoint. So in order to recognize the unseen classes, it needs extra information about the seen and unseen classes. The extra information can be defined as semantic space. After the model have captured the relations between the feature space and semantic space of the seen classes, it can transfer the relations to unseen classes. The main idea of zero-shot learning is to correlate the unseen classes with the seen classes via the semantic space. The semantic space can be divided into 2 categories. One is the text vector space, which includes the word-embedding of the classes' names and the text description of these classes. The other is the attribute space, where the attributes are defined by human beings.

In recent years, there are many zero-shot learning methods proposed in human activity recognition field. However, these methods have defects in different aspects. In [7], it used the Support Vector Machine (SVM) classifier as base classifier to detect attributes, and each attribute needed an SVM classifier. Once the attribute space became larger, the model would become extremely complex. In [8], the model needed to use the testing dataset during the training stage, so the model could just be used in a fixed number of unseen classes. Once a new instance which belonged to neither seen classes nor unseen classes appeared, it would be out of work. In this paper, we present a novel model for human activity recognition in the zero-shot learning task. It outperforms other state-of-the-art methods and is termed as **Multi-Layer Cross Loss Model** (MLCLM). In this model, it learns a multi-fully connected layers model to project features to the attribute space, and the instance is predicted through a similarity classifier (SC). What's more, our model is not sensitive to the number of unseen classes, for that it just learns the projection between the feature space and semantic space, and once the semantic representations of new classes are defined, our model can deal with these new classes. The major contributions of this paper are as follows:

- To the best of our knowledge, we are the first to introduce the word-embedding into zero-shot human activity recognition.

- We propose a novel model and split the problem into two sub-problems, which can optimize the model in two spaces.
- Sufficient experiments on three benchmark datasets show that the proposed model outperforms other state-of-the-art methods and through these results, we analyze how the attribute and word-embedding impact the performance of our model.

The rest of the paper is organized as follows: In Sect. 2, we review related work of the zero-shot learning and HAR. In Sect. 3, the proposed model is explained in detail. In Sect. 4, we evaluate the performance of our model. In Sect. 5, we summarize our work and discuss future work.

2   Related Works

Supervised human activity recognition has achieved great success in recent years. Many researches have been completed in this area [9–11]. Cao et al. [9] presented an integrated framework that used non-sequential machine learning tools to achieve high performance on activity recognition with multi-modal data. Wang et al. [10] constructed a decision tree to classify different walking patterns based on relations between gait phases. Shi et al. [11] proposed a dynamic coordinate transformation approach to recognize activity with valid recognition results. Most of these proposed methods based on supervised learning. They can only recognize the classes in the training dataset. An instance that does not belong to any classes in the training dataset will not be recognized. So these methods are limited to a fixed number of classes.

Zero-shot learning aims at figuring out the defects of supervised learning methods. In zero-shot learning methods, the methods are mainly divided into 2 categories. One category is inductive zero-shot learning [12–15], where the model has no information about the unseen classes except the semantic information. In other words, the unseen classes are uncertain. Kodirov et al. [12] proposed a semantic autoencoder model with a novel objective function to reconstruct the features after the projection from features to semantic space. Romeara et al. [13] applied the mean square loss and Frobenius norm as the objective function to learn a bilinear compatibility model. Liu et al. [14] employed the temperature calibration in the prediction probability and introduced an additional entropy loss to maximize the confidence of classifying the seen data to unseen classes. Another category is transductive zero-shot learning [16–18], where it can use the information of the unseen classes, including feature space and semantic space. The above methods are in the field of computer vision. In zero-shot learning for human activity recognition scenario, several methods have been proposed [7,15,19]. Chen et al. [7] proposed an inductive zero-shot learning method. In [7], for each attribute, it learned an attribute probability classifier (SVM). It then got the class representation in the semantic space and predicted label with the maximum a posteriori estimate (MAP). Cheng et al. [19] proposed an extended work following [7], it changed the SVM to CRF to improve the performance.

Wang et al. [15] proposed a model which learned a nonlinear compatibility function between the semantic space and feature space and classified an instance to the class with the highest score.

3   Proposed Method

In this section, we will explain the proposed zero-shot learning model for human activity recognition explicitly. We call it **Multi-Layer Cross Loss Model** (MLCLM). The input of our model is the features extracted from the inertial sensors' data.

3.1   Problem Definition

Unlike supervised human activity recognition methods, the problem of zero-shot learning is defined as follows: the training dataset $D_{train} = (x_i, y_i)_{i=1}^{N}$ contains N labeled training instances from the seen classes $S = \{S_1, S_2, S_3, ..., S_m\}$. The unseen classes are denoted by $U = \{U_1, U_2, U_3, ..., U_k\}$, whose instances are not in the training dataset. Seen classes and unseen classes are disjoint, $S \cap U = \emptyset$. Each class $c \in S \cup U$ owns a semantic representation, denoted by $a_c \in R^A$, where the dimension of semantic space is A.

3.2   Data Preprocessing

The data received by sensors can't be used directly in our model. It should be preprocessed first. To deal with the raw data from sensor readings, we adopt the sliding window mechanism which is commonly used in time series data to segment the data, as shown in Fig. 1. Each window of the time series data is defined as an instance.

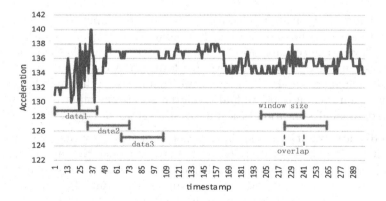

Fig. 1. Data segmentation

Then we collect statistical features from the segments, and the features are usually the mean value, standard deviation and time, etc. As the time series data in the window size may belong to different labels (for example, when the subject is changing activities), we discard these instances when labeling the instances after segmentation.

3.3 Proposed Model

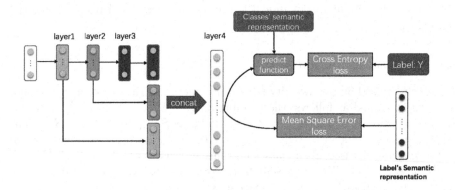

Fig. 2. The structure of the proposed MLCLM

In our model, we define four fully connected layers to project the features extracted from the sensor readings to the semantic space. As shown in Fig. 2. The model can be formulated as Eq. 1.

$$h_i = \begin{cases} \phi_1(f_1(x_j)) & i = 1 \\ \phi_i(f_i(h_{i-1})) & i = 2,3 \\ \phi_4(f_4([h_1, h_2, h_3]) & i = 4 \end{cases} \tag{1}$$

The input of the first fully connected layer is the input of the model, and the input of the second and the third fully connected layers is the output of the previous layer. The concatenation of the former three layers is the input of the forth fully connected layer. We believe that former fully connected layers' output can also contribute to classification as we conduct a traditional classification experiment on the datasets. we find that even we use the input of the layer1 to do a traditional classification task, we can still get good results.

Prediction function: The classification is predicted by the similarity classifier (SC). After the multi-fully connected layers' model, the input features x_i are projected to the semantic space, defined as $\phi(x_i)$. Then the similarities with all the classes T ($T = S$ during the training stage, while $T = U$ during the testing stage) are calculated, as shown in the equation (2).

$$SC(x_i, c_p) = \frac{\phi(x_i) \cdot a^p}{\sum_j^A a_j^p} \tag{2}$$

$c_p \in T$ and a^p is the semantic representation of the class c_p (a^p is a semantic vector), which can be obtained in many ways such as defined by human beings or pretrained word-embedding. The numerator is a dot product of the two vectors. After calculating the similarity with all the classes, we choose the most similar class as the prediction of input x_i:

$$\hat{y}(x_i) = argmax_{c_p} SC(x_i, c_p) \tag{3}$$

Cross loss: In our model, we consider the zero-shot learning problem as a regression problem and a classification problem. The regression problem occurs after projecting the input features to the semantic space. In this regression problem, the mean square loss is chosen as an objective function, defined as M:

$$M = \sum_{i=1}^{N} \sum_{j}^{A} (\phi(x_i)_j - a_j^i)^2 \tag{4}$$

$\phi(x_i)$ is the output of the multi-fully connected layers model and a^i is the semantic representation of x_i's true label. The classification problem is occurred after the prediction function. We choose the cross entropy loss as the objective function in this problem, for that the cross entropy loss is an effective solution for multi-class classification. Before we apply the cross entropy, we first transform the similarity to probability as:

$$p(c_p|x_i) = \frac{exp(SC(x_i, c_p)}{\sum_{c_j} exp(SC(x_i, c_j))} \tag{5}$$

where $c_p, c_j \in T$. Then we apply the cross entropy:

$$L = -\sum_{i=1}^{N} \sum_{c_p} y_{i,c_p} * log(p(c_p|x_i)) \tag{6}$$

So the optimization of the zero-shot learning problem can be formulated as:

$$\min_{\phi} M + L + \gamma\Omega(f) \tag{7}$$

where the $\Omega(f)$ is the regularization of the multi-fully connected layers model. In our code, we implemented the Ω regularization by weight decay.

4 Experiment

In order to evaluate the proposed model, we perform extensive experiments on three benchmark datasets. And we compare our model with other state-of-the-art methods. In this section, we will introduce the three benchmark datasets and experiments.

4.1   Datasets and Preprocessing

The three benchmark datasets are TU Darmstadt dataset (TUD) [20], Physical Activity Monitoring Data Set (PAMAP2) [21], and Opportunity Activity Recognition Data Set (OPP) [22]. When segmenting the datasets, we follow the sliding window strategy proposed in their papers. In TUD, we use a sliding window of 30 s with 15 s overlap between two adjacent windows. After the segmentation, we extract mean value and standard deviation as features in each dimension from the sensor readings in a window. Besides the 3 axies acceleration data from the sensors placed in the subjects, we add the time as another feature to the feature vector. In PAMAP2, we segment the dataset using a sliding window of 5.12 s with 1 s overlap between two adjacent windows. After the segmentation, we extract mean value, standard deviation as features in each dimension from the sensor readings in a window. In OPP, we follow the sliding window mechanism adopted by [23], where the window size is 1 s, and the overlap is 0.5 s. After the segmentation, we extract the mean and standard deviation as features from each dimension.

In the TUD, we discard the 'unlabeled' data, and in PAMAP2, we discard the data with label '0' (transient activities), while in the OPP dataset, we discard the data of 'drill's file.

To adopt zero-shot learning to HAR, the semantic space is essential for the three datasets. As presented in Sect. 2, there are two categories of semantic space: attribute space and text vector space, so we conduct experiments on the two categories.

4.2   Experimental Results

The evaluation metric in the experiments is the average accuracy of each class, defined as *average_acc_per_class* in Eq. (8) [24], which is commonly used in zero-shot learning. This is due to the fact that the activities are unbalanced in the dataset, e.g. Fig. 3 shows the amounts of classes in the PAMAP2. The amount of 'computer work' activity is extremely greater than in other activities. So if the model predicts all the testing instances as this class, the average accuracy on all the instances will be fine but the model has no robustness.

$$average\_acc\_per\_class = \frac{1}{k} * \sum_{i}^{k} \frac{N^i_{correct}}{N^i_{total}} \qquad (8)$$

where the $N^i_{correct}$ indicates the number of correct predictions of the class i, the N^i_{total} indicates the total instances of the class i, and the k indicates the number of unseen classes.

1) **Word-embedding experiments:** As presented in Sect. 2, there are two categories of semantic space: attribute space and text vector space. The attribute space is defined manually by experts with domain knowledge, which is costly. And once the activity classes change, it needs extra efforts to redefine the attributes for the new activity. So in this experiment, we firstly introduce the pretrained word2vec's [25] word-embedding on part of Google News

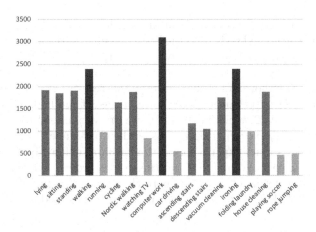

Fig. 3. The amounts of instances in each class of PAMAP2 dataset

dataset as the semantic space in the HAR field. In the word-embedding, every word has a 300-dimensional vector. But in the TUD and PAMAP2, each activity's name may contain several words, so we calculate the mean value of all words in the activity name as the word-embedding of the activity $w^{mean} = \{w_1^{mean}, w_2^{mean}, w_3^{mean}, ..., w_{300}^{mean}\}$ for the activity:

$$w_j^{mean} = \frac{\sum_i^I w_j^i}{I}, j = 1, 2, 3, ..., 300 \tag{9}$$

w_j indicates the jth word's word-embedding; I indicates the amount of the words in the activity name.

Table 1. Results of word-embedding experiments

Methods	TUD	PAMAP2	OPP
DCN [14]	27.42%	32.97%	46.03%
ESZSL [13]	20.57%	27.66%	**52.37%**
SAE [12]	17.71%	31.79%	44.55%
NCBM [15]	20.15%	27.49%	30.80%
MLCLM	**29.89%**	**54.93%**	**51.50%**

We compare the proposed model with the methods proposed in [12–15]. Wang et al. proposed a zero-shot learning method called **NCBM** [15] for HAR. Several representative methods of zero-shot learning in computer vision are also chosen: **DCN** [14], **ESZSL** [13], **SAE** [12] and we transfer them into HAR. In the experiments, we choose the class splitting strategy of the train and test datasets proposed in [15]. Here we adopt the 5-fold cross validation strategy to evaluate the performance of the methods and our model. Here we didn't choose the **DAP** [26] method, because the **DAP** used the SVM classifier as the attribute classifier, but the word-embedding is a continuous number, so the SVM classifier is not befitting.

The results are shown in Table 1. From the results, we can see that our method(**MLCLM**) outperforms other state-of-the-art methods significantly in the TUD and PAMAP2, while in the OPP, we are very closed to the best.

2) Attribute experiment: Besides using the word-embedding as the semantic space, we also conduct experiments with attributes defined by human beings. The results are shown in Table 2. From the results, we can see that our model (**MLCLM**) outperforms others over more than 23%–32% in PAMAP2 and is the best in OPP. While in the TUD, our method is also closed to the best in the table.

Table 2. Results of comparison experiments

Methods	TUD	PAMAP2	OPP
DAP [26]	16.08%	29.24%	30.93%
DCN [14]	24.69%	37.85%	47.52%
ESZSL [13]	27.36%	32.58%	60.55%
SAE [12]	34.73%	34.46%	61.41%
NCBM [15]	31.07%	38.06%	28.44%
MLCLM	**31.87%**	**61.28%**	**62.30%**

We analyze that the reason why the **MLCLM** outperforms the others is that in the **MLCLM**, the optimization has two constraints: On the one hand, the mean square loss can minimize the gap between the conversion of the features and the semantic space. On the other hand, the cross entropy loss can further optimize the results on classification. So combining with the two losses, our model can be optimized both on semantic space and the classification results.

In the **DCN**, there are two optimization functions in the **DCN**: the cross entropy loss of predicting seen data on seen classes and the entropy of predicting seen data on unseen classes. However, the second entropy loss can cause misclassification of seen data on unseen classes, which may cause an underfitting problem. The **SAE** uses an autoencoder model, and it reconstructs the features which are projected to the semantic space. However, even when the reconstruction is perfect, the classification results don't benefit from the reconstruction. In the **DAP**, it assigns an SVM classifier for each attribute. Assembling all results of SVM classifiers, the features are projected to the semantic space, and the prediction is made by the maximum a posteriori estimate (MAP). However, each SVM classifier only concentrates on its attribute and ignores the relations of the attributes and the truth label. In other words, it doesn't optimize directly on the classification results, which can cause overfitting on the attribute classification but underfitting on the class classification results. The **ESZSL** also has the problem that it is only optimized on the semantic space, but not on the class classification results. The **NCBM** learns a nonlinear compatibility function, which gives the compatibility scores of the input and all class prototypes, and the class with the highest score is the result of the input. The optimization of **NCBM** is the hinge loss, which is not sensitive to the outliers, however, the unseen classes are outliers to the seen classes, so this loss can not employ the outliers' information.

3) Comparison experiments: To evaluate how the attribute and word-embedding impact the performance of our **MLCLM**, we compare the performance when using them as semantic space, and Fig. 4. shows results. From the results, we can see that the performance of attribute outperforms the word-embedding. To find out why the attribute outperforms the word-embedding, we take the PAMAP2 dataset as a representative: we calculate the Pearson Product-Moment Correlation Coefficient (PPMCC) of these classes' semantic representations in attributes and word2vec. We find out that the PPMCC of attributes is larger than the PPMCC of word2vec. According to zero-shot learning, the model needs to learn the relations between the feature space and the semantic space in the seen classes, and then it transfers the relations to the unseen classes. So the more relevant between the seen classes and unseen classes in the semantic space, the better the model performs in the testing stage. This conclusion can guide us on how to define the attribute space better for the zero-shot learning task.

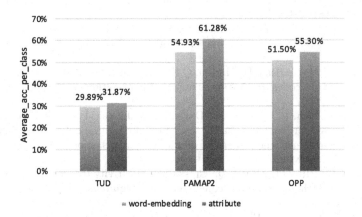

Fig. 4. Results of the word-embedding and attribute as semantic space

5   Conclusion and Future Work

In this paper, we propose a Multi-Layer Cross Loss Model for zero-shot learning in human activity recognition. Sufficient experiments validate that the proposed model is effective with both attributes and word-embedding as semantic space. In the future, we will upgrade our model for better performance in zero-shot learning, and apply our method to other fields like computer vision and natural language processing. As the results shown in Fig. 4, the results are not very ideal when using word-embedding as semantic space, so in the future, we will explore more researches on the employment of word-embedding as it needs fewer efforts of human beings.

Acknowledgement. This work is supported by National Key Research & Development Program of China No.2017YFC0803401; Natural Science Foundation of China No. 61902377; Beijing Natural Science Foundation No. 4194091; R & D Plan in Key Field of Guangdong Province No.2019B010109001; Alibaba Group through Alibaba Innovative Research (AIR) Program.

References

1. Khojasteh, S., Villar, J., Chira, C., González, V., de la Cal, E.: Improving fall detection using an on-wrist wearable accelerometer. Sensors **18**(5), 1350 (2018)
2. Direkoğlu, C., O'Connor, N.E.: Temporal segmentation and recognition of team activities in sports. Mach. Vis. Appl. **29**(5), 891–913 (2018). https://doi.org/10.1007/s00138-018-0944-9
3. Inoue, M., Inoue, S., Nishida, T.: Deep recurrent neural network for mobile human activity recognition with high throughput. Artif. Life Rob. **23**(2), 173–185 (2017). https://doi.org/10.1007/s10015-017-0422-x
4. Cao, L., Wang, Y., Zhang, B., Jin, Q., Vasilakos, A.V.: GCHAR: an efficient group-based context-aware human activity recognition on smartphone. J. Parallel Distrib. Comput. **118**, 67–80 (2018)
5. Asghari, P., Soelimani, E., Nazerfard, E.: Online human activity recognition employing hierarchical hidden markov models. arXiv preprint arXiv:1903.04820 (2019)
6. Palatucci, M., Pomerleau, D., Hinton, G.E., Mitchell, T.M.: Zero-shot learning with semantic output codes. In: Advances in neural information processing systems, pp. 1410–1418 (2009)
7. Cheng, H.T., Sun, F.T., Griss, M., Davis, P., Li, J., You, D.: Nuactiv: recognizing unseen new activities using semantic attribute-based learning. In: Proceeding of the 11th annual international conference on Mobile systems, applications, and services, pp. 361–374. ACM (2013)
8. Zheng, V.W., Hu, D.H., Yang, Q.: Cross-domain activity recognition. In: Proceedings of the 11th international conference on Ubiquitous computing, pp. 61–70. ACM (2009)
9. Cao, H., Nguyen, M.N., Phua, C., Krishnaswamy, S., Li, X.: An integrated framework for human activity classification. In: UbiComp, pp. 331–340 (2012)
10. Wang, J.S., Lin, C.W., Yang, Y.T.C., Ho, Y.J.: Walking pattern classification and walking distance estimation algorithms using gait phase information. IEEE Trans. Biomed. Eng. **59**(10), 2884–2892 (2012)
11. Shi, D., Wu, Y., Mo, X., Wang, R., Wei, J.: Activity recognition based on the dynamic coordinate transformation of inertial sensor data. In: 2016 Intl IEEE Conferences on Ubiquitous Intelligence & Computing, Advanced and Trusted Computing, Scalable Computing and Communications, Cloud and Big Data Computing, Internet of People, and Smart World Congress (UIC/ATC/ScalCom/CBDCom/IoP/SmartWorld), pp. 1–8. IEEE (2016)

12. Kodirov, E., Xiang, T., Gong, S.: Semantic autoencoder for zero-shot learning. In: Proceedings of the IEEE Conference on Computer Vision and Pattern Recognition, pp. 3174–3183 (2017)
13. Romera-Paredes, B., Torr, P.: An embarrassingly simple approach to zero-shot learning. In: International Conference on Machine Learning, pp. 2152–2161 (2015)
14. Liu, S., Long, M., Wang, J., Jordan., M.I.: Generalized zero-shot learning with deep calibration network. In: Advances in Neural Information Processing Systems, pp. 2005–2015 (2018)
15. Wang, W., Miao, C., Hao, S.: Zero-shot human activity recognition via nonlinear compatibility based method. In: Proceedings of the International Conference on Web Intelligence, pp. 322–330. ACM (2017)
16. Rohrbach, M., Ebert, S., Schiele, B.: Transfer learning in a transductive setting. In: Advances in neural information processing systems, pp. 46–54 (2013)
17. Kodirov, E., Xiang, T., Fu, Z., Gong, S.: Unsupervised domain adaptation for zero-shot learning. In: Proceedings of the IEEE International Conference on Computer Vision, pp. 2452–2460 (2015)
18. Fu, Y., Sigal, L.: Semi-supervised vocabulary-informed learning. In: Proceedings of the IEEE Conference on Computer Vision and Pattern Recognition, pp. 5337–5346 (2016)
19. Cheng, H.T., Griss, M., Davis, P., Li, J., You, D.: Towards zero-shot learning for human activity recognition using semantic attribute sequence model. In: Proceedings of the 2013 ACM International Joint Conference on Pervasive and Ubiquitous Computing, pp. 355–358. ACM (2013)
20. Huynh, T., Fritz, M., Schiele, B.: Discovery of activity patterns using topic models. UbiComp 8, 10–19 (2008)
21. Reiss, A., Stricker, D.: Introducing a new benchmarked dataset for activity monitoring. In: 2012 16th International Symposium on Wearable Computers, pp. 108–109. IEEE (2012)
22. Roggen, D., et al.: Collecting complex activity datasets in highly rich networked sensor environments. In: 2010 Seventh international conference on networked sensing systems (INSS), pp. 233–240. IEEE (2010)
23. Hammerla, N.Y., Halloran, S., Plötz, T.: Deep, convolutional, and recurrent models for human activity recognition using wearables. arXiv preprint arXiv:1604.08880 (2016)
24. Xian, Y., Lampert, C.H., Schiele, B., Akata, Z.: Zero-shot learning-a comprehensive evaluation of the good, the bad and the ugly. IEEE Trans. Pattern Anal. Mach. Intell. 41, 2251–2265 (2018)
25. Mikolov, T., Chen, K., Corrado, G., Dean, J.: Efficient estimation of word representations in vector space. arXiv preprint arXiv:1301.3781 (2013)
26. Lampert, C.H., Nickisch, H., Harmeling, S.: Attribute-based classification for zero-shot visual object categorization. IEEE Trans. Pattern Anal. Mach. Intell. 36(3), 453–465 (2013)

Hierarchical Gradient Smoothing
for Probability Estimation Trees

He Zhang$^{(\boxtimes)}$ [iD], François Petitjean [iD], and Wray Buntine [iD]

Faculty of Information Technology, Monash University, Melbourne, Australia
{he.zhang,francois.petitjean,wray.buntine}@monash.edu

Abstract. Decision trees are still seeing use in online, non-stationary and embedded contexts, as well as for interpretability. For applications like ranking and cost-sensitive classification, probability estimation trees (PETs) are used. These are built using smoothing or calibration techniques. Older smoothing techniques used counts local to a leaf node, but a few more recent techniques consider the broader context of a node when doing estimation. We apply a recent advanced smoothing method called Hierarchical Dirichlet Process (HDP) to PETs, and then propose a novel hierarchical smoothing approach called Hierarchical Gradient Smoothing (HGS) as an alternative. HGS smooths leaf nodes up to all the ancestors, instead of recursively smoothing to the parent used by HDP. HGS is made faster by efficiently optimizing the Leave-One-Out Cross-Validation (LOOCV) loss measure using gradient descent, instead of sampling used in HDP. An extensive set of experiments are conducted on 143 datasets showing that our HGS estimates are not only more accurate but also do so within a fraction of HDP time. Besides, HGS makes a single tree almost as good as a Random Forest with 10 trees. For applications that require more interpretability and efficiency, a single decision tree plus HGS is more preferred.

Keywords: Probability estimation trees · Class probability estimation · Hierarchical probability smoothing · Hierarchical Dirichlet Process

1 Introduction

Many critical classification tasks require accurate class probability estimates rather than class labels because probabilities can show people whether the prediction is reliable or not. For instance, the weather forecast not only predicts rain but also tells people how likely it is. In cost-sensitive learning, the misclassification cost could be significantly reduced if more accurate class probability estimates could be obtained [4].

This research was partially supported by the Australian Research Council's Discovery Projects funding schemes (project DP190100017 and DE170100037).

More recently, with the advent of many more learning tasks, such as online learning, or learning where the inference system have low computational resources, a single decision tree is seeing a resurgence. Extremely fast decision trees are one of the top performers for high-data-throughput contexts [11]. Random forests and gradient boosted trees have relatively high computational demands in inference, and thus may not be suitable for wearable or embedded IOT (Internet of Things) applications. So, the problem of making a single tree perform well in inference arises, and one can ask does a single decision tree beat a random forest with 10 trees. Moreover, trees also serve as one of the few global models considered to be interpretable, an increasingly important requirement in applications [12]. Thus, quality single decision tree built efficiently have many uses.

Probability Estimation Tree (PET) is a generalization of a single decision tree by taking the observed frequencies at a leaf node as the class probability estimates for any test examples that fall into this leaf. However, this method may lead to unreliable estimates when the number of training examples associated in a leaf is small [21]. Simple probability smoothing techniques, such as Laplace smoothing and M-estimation, have long been used to improve PETs' class probability estimates by making the estimates at leaves less extreme. However, they ignore the broader context of any leaf node, especially crucial in cases where the datasets are imbalanced.

Hierarchical smoothing has gained attention in the community in recent years. It assumes that the class probability of the leaf node depends on the probabilities of its parents in some hierarchy. To our knowledge, M-branch smoothing [5] is the first and only one hierarchical method for PETs. It smooths the leaf node to its direct parent using M-estimation, with the parent also been smoothed recursively until the root node reached. The results demonstrate that M-branch performs better than M-estimation. Hierarchical Dirichlet Process (HDP) [13] can also be used to smooth the probability at the leaves with its parent, partially mimicking what is done in M-branch, but it uses fully Bayesian inference. A decision tree can be turned into a HDP model tree with each node in the tree associated with a Dirichlet Process (DP). Similar HDP smoothing methods allow Bayesian network classifiers [13] and language models [17] to get state-of-the-art probability estimates but has not been applied to decision trees.

[14] believe that a thorough study of what are the best smoothing methods for PETs would be a successful contribution to machine learning research, which is also the main aim of this research. We first show that HDP can help PETs get better estimates compared with M-estimation. However, HDP is computationally intensive. A novel, more efficient hierarchical smoothing method called Hierarchical Gradient Smoothing (HGS) is proposed. Unlike HDP and M-branch, HGS smooths the leaf node to all the ancestor nodes at once, where each ancestor has a weight parameter to control the smoothness. We propose Leave-One-Out Cross-Validation (LOOCV) cost to PETs and conduct a gradient descent algorithm [16] on the cost to automatically obtain the parameters.

One time smoothing and gradient descent make HGS more efficient than recursive smoothing and sampling. A single PET With HGS makes more than 90/143 UCI datasets obtain the best probability estimates. Besides, HGS makes single tree superior to Random Forest with 7 trees and almost as good with 10 trees.

The remainder of this paper is organized as follows. The related works are reviewed in Sect. 2. M-branch and HDP are also introduced in this section. The HGS model is developed in Sect. 3. An extensive experiment results are reported in Sect. 4.

2   Related Work

There are some empirical studies [10, 23] of improving the class probability estimation of PETs, covering different tree learning algorithms, probability smoothing techniques and tree ensembles, among which we focus more on probability smoothing techniques.

C4.5, as a traditional decision tree learning algorithm [15], cannot produce accurate class probability estimates because it aims at building small trees with accurate class label predictions rather than accurate class probability estimates. Tree pruning technique is used in C4.5 to achieve this goal by removing the nodes and branches at the bottom of the tree that fitted to noise data. The pruned tree is more accurate on classification but less accurate on class probability estimation [22]. C4.4 is a variant of C4.5 with better class probability estimates by turning off pruning and applying Laplace smoothing method to leaf nodes [14].

Laplace and M-estimation as the two most simple smoothing methods have long been used on PETs [14, 22] and cost-sensitive learning [20]. Although more sophisticated smoothing methods such as Kneser-Ney [8] and Modified Kneser-Ney [2] have been used in language modelling for a long time, M-branch was the first hierarchical smoothing method for decision trees proposed in 2003 [6]. A recent smoothing method called Hierarchical Dirichlet Process (HDP) has had great success on language modelling [17] and Bayesian Network Classifiers [13], whereas it has not been used on decision trees. The following part introduces these methods in detail.

M-estimation Smoothing. M-estimation is more recommended by [22] for class-imbalanced data, which is defined as

$$\hat{\theta}_k^{M-esti} = \frac{n_k + M \times b}{n. + M} \tag{1}$$

where the base rate b is the expected probability without any additional knowledge, and it is usually considered uniform, i.e. $b = \frac{1}{K}$. M is a parameter that controls how much scores are shifted towards the base rate. When $m = K$ and $b = \frac{1}{K}$, it becomes Laplace smoothing.

M-branch Smoothing. M-branch is the first hierarchical smoothing method for PETs [5]. It considers each node in the tree is a subsample of the upper parent. This means that the sample used to obtain the probability estimates in a leaf is the result of many sampling steps, as many as the depth of the leaf. Then it is natural to consider all the history of samples when trying to obtain the probability estimates of a leaf.

Let $< v_1, v_2, ..., v_{l-1}, v_l >$ represents all the nodes on the branch that contains the leaf node v_l, where v_{l-1} is the parent of v_l and v_1 is the root. The class probability estimate for class k at node v_l is smoothed by M-estimation in the following way

$$\hat{\theta}_{l,k}^{Mbranch} = \frac{n_{l,k} + m_l \times \hat{\theta}_{l-1,k}^{Mbranch}}{n_{l,\cdot} + m_l} \tag{2}$$

where $n_{l,k}$ denote the observed count of class k and $n_{l,\cdot}$ is the total. The base rate b for M-estimation is the parent estimate $\hat{\theta}_{l-1,k}^{Mbranch}$, which also needs to be smoothed to the parent node at a higher level v_{l-2}. Repeat these steps recursively until the root node v_1 reached. The root node is smoothed to a uniform probability $\hat{\theta}_{0,k} = \frac{1}{K}$. The m parameter for each node has been defined as a function of the node height in the tree. Please refer to [5] for more detail.

HDP Smoothing. Unlike M-branch, HDP assumes that only leaf nodes have data and all the parent nodes are empty, instead of inheriting data from their children during the inference process. Each leaf passes some subset of its data to its parent, selected during the inference process. The subset passes higher and higher, thinning recursively until the root is reached. Suppose $t_{u,k}$ is the subset of data $n_{u,k}$ that node u passes up to its parent ϕ, the data for node ϕ is collected from all the children so that $n_{\phi,k} = \sum_{u \in \phi} t_{u,k}$ where $u \in \phi$ means u is the child of ϕ. The concentration c_ϕ controls how much data passes up to node ϕ, i.e. $t_{u,k}$. If we expect $\hat{\theta}_{u,k}$ to be very similar to $\hat{\theta}_{\phi,k}$, then choose a bigger c_ϕ that makes most of the data pass up, and the parent probability contribute more to the estimate. If c_ϕ is small, the parent probability contributes less to the estimate. The smoothing formula for node u and class k is defined as follows

$$\hat{\theta}_{u,k}^{HDP} = \frac{n_{u,k} + c_\phi \times \hat{\theta}_{\phi,k}^{HDP}}{n_{u,\cdot} + c_\phi} \tag{3}$$

Here $\hat{\theta}_{\phi,k}^{HDP}$ is the parent estimate which also needs to be smoothed. The class probabilities are calculated from the root to the leaves. Thus, when reaches the leaves, the probability estimates are already properly smoothed. Equation 3 can also be explained by the Hierarchical Chinese Restaurant Process (CRP) [19]. Please refer to [13] for more detail of HDP smoothing on Bayesian Network Classifiers.

Gibbs sampling is used in HDP to sample the concentration parameters. *iteration* is the number of iterations of Gibbs sampling. *tying* is used to tie some nodes together to share a single concentration in order to reduce the number of parameters. There are four types of tying. *SINGLE* means tying all the nodes together to share a single concentration parameter. *LEVEL* means the nodes on the same depth are tied together. *PARENT* means tying the sibling nodes under one parent. *NONE* means no tying.

3   HGS Algorithm

In this section, we propose a novel efficient hierarchical probability smoothing method for PETs called Hierarchical Gradient Smoothing (HGS). Like all other hierarchical smoothing methods, HGS considers that the class probability estimate of a leaf node is related to the probability estimates of all parent nodes on the branch that contains the leaf.

3.1   The Hierarchical Computation

HGS is different from HDP and M-branch. Figure 1 can more intuitively express the differences between them. It can be seen from this figure that HDP and M-branch both smooth the leaf node to an upper parent node, then the parent node also needs to be smoothed to a higher node until the root node is reached. Each node has a concentration parameter to control the smoothness, which is c for HDP and m for M-branch. However, unlike HDP and M-branch smoothing, HGS smooths the class probability estimate on a leaf node to all ancestor nodes on the branch at one time, instead of only to the nearest parent node recursively. Each parent node has a weight parameter α to control the degree to which the probability estimates are backed off to the parent. The one-time smoothing makes HGS faster than HDP and M-branch and also allows global optimization of hyper-parameters.

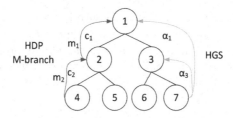

Fig. 1. The difference between HGS, HDP, and M-branch. HGS is represented by red, HDP and M-branch by blue and green, respectively. (Color figure online)

The probability smoothing formula for leaf l and class k using HGS is as follows,

$$\hat{\theta}_{l,k}^{HGS} = \frac{n_{l,k} + \sum_{p \in \text{anc}(l)} \alpha_p \hat{\theta}_{p,k}}{n_{l,\cdot} + \sum_{p \in \text{anc}(l)} \alpha_p}, \tag{4}$$

where $\text{anc}(l)$ represents all the ancestor nodes on the branch that containing the leaf node l. Each ancestor node $p \in \text{anc}(l)$ has a weight parameter α_p controls the degree of smoothness. The probability estimate of p is calculated by the Maximum Likelihood Estimation (MLE), which is defined as $\hat{\theta}_{p,k} = \frac{n_{p,k}}{n_{p,\cdot}}$. The term $\sum_{p \in \text{anc}(l)} \alpha_p \hat{\theta}_{p,k}$ is the weighted combined probability of all the ancestors. The term $\sum_{p \in \text{anc}(l)} \alpha_p$ is the sum of the weights.

3.2   Working with LOOCV

Let α denote the vector that contains all the weight parameter αs with the size being the number of internal nodes in the tree. How can one set the α properly, for instance, how should it be optimized?

Before going into the details of how to set α, it is worth briefly introducing LOOCV and incremental LOOCV. LOOCV is a special case of k fold cross-validation, where k equals to the number of training examples N. In each fold of the cross-validation, an example is treated as a test example while the others are the training examples. LOOCV could be sped up using incremental LOOCV [7,9]. The idea is instead of training a model during each fold of the cross-validation, first, train a model on the full dataset, then delete the one example that is left out, test on that example, then insert it into the model again. This delete-test-insert phase is repeated for each of the N folds. Incremental LOOCV can be conducted on any algorithm that supports incremental learning, allowing for dynamically adding or removing examples from the model. Decision tree learning is such an algorithm. Note incremental LOOCV means the model structure remains unchanged.

If one looks at a cross-validation in LOOCV, a test example at leaf l with true class k should be left out from the tree, which means the data count of both l and $\mathrm{anc}(l)$ should be reduced by 1. The total count becomes $n_{l,\cdot} - 1$. This Leave-One-Out (LOO) probability estimate for this test with class k becomes

$$\theta_{l,k}^{LOO} = \frac{n_{l,k} - 1 + \sum_{p\in\mathrm{anc}(l)} \alpha_p \theta_{p,k}^{LOO}}{n_{l,\cdot} - 1 + \sum_{p\in\mathrm{anc}(l)} \alpha_p} \tag{5}$$

Here $\theta_{p,k}^{LOO} = \frac{n_{p,k}-1}{n_{p,\cdot}-1}$. $n_{l,k} \geq 1$ must be satisfied so that there is at least one example to moved out. For other classes $c \in \mathcal{K}, c \neq k$, the probability estimate is formed without subtracting one in the renumerator.

If one performs an incremental LOOCV on the tree, the examples in every leaf $l \in \mathcal{L}$ with every class $k \in \mathcal{K}$ need to be left out once. The LOOCV measure using log loss of all the examples in the tree becomes

$$LOOCV(\alpha) = \frac{1}{N} \sum_{l\in\mathcal{L}} \sum_{k\in\mathcal{K}} n_{l,k} \cdot \log\left(\frac{1}{\theta_{l,k}^{LOO}}\right) \tag{6}$$

and note we have also tested a squared error loss $(1 - \theta_{l,k}^{LOO})^2$ yielding similar results. For more information about loss functions please refer to [18].

Now a Gradient Descent algorithm [16] can be performed on the $LOOCV(\alpha)$ cost to optimize the parameters α. The gradient of each α_p is

$$\frac{\partial}{\partial \alpha_p} LOOCV(\alpha) = \frac{1}{N \ln 2} \sum_{l\in\mathrm{des}(p)} \sum_{k\in\mathcal{K}} \beta_{l,k} \tag{7}$$

where $\beta_{l,k}$ is referred to

$$\beta_{l,k} = \frac{n_{l,k} \cdot \left(\theta_{l,k}^{LOO} - \theta_{p,k}^{LOO} \right)}{\left(n_{l,.} - 1 + \sum_{p \in \text{anc}(l)} \alpha_p \right) \cdot \theta_{l,k}^{LOO}} \qquad (8)$$

Here $\text{des}(p)$ represents the descendent leaves under p.

3.3   Algorithm Description

The HGS algorithm $HGS(T, b, v)$ takes a decision tree T, a learning rate b and a precision parameter ϵ as inputs, and a HGS smoothed tree as output. It has three steps in total. First, initialize $\boldsymbol{\alpha}$ to be the vector of parameters with the length to be the number of internal nodes and all the values to be 1. Second, conduct a standard gradient descent algorithm to get the optimized parameters $\boldsymbol{\alpha}$. Last, traverse the tree top-down in level-order to calculate the HGS smoothed probability estimates $\hat{\theta}_{l,k}^{HGS}$ for all the leaves. The top-down traverse method used here is the same as the first tree top-down traverse method in Algorithm 2 (line 1–9), except that the probability estimates are calculated using Eq. 4 in line 8.

The second step in the HGS algorithm uses a standard gradient descent algorithm to optimize the parameters, as shown in Algorithm 1. Gradient descent needs many iterations to reduce the cost until the cost difference between two iterations is less than a given ϵ. Algorithm 2 is called in every iteration to calculate the cost and gradients by going through the tree twice. First, traverse the tree top-down to calculate the LOO estimate $\theta_{p,k}^{LOO}$ using Eq. 5 and the cost $LOOCV(\boldsymbol{\alpha})$ using Eq. 6 (line 1–9). $\alpha_p^* = \sum_i \alpha_i$ and $\theta_{p,k}^* = \sum_i \alpha_i \theta_{i,k}^{LOO}$. Second, traverse the tree bottom-up to calculate the gradients for each internal node level by level (line 10–16). Last, return the cost.

The complexity of HGS smoothing on a PET is $O(I \cdot S \cdot K)$, where S is the total number of nodes and K is the number of classes. We call I the number of iterations for gradient descent. In practice, we use the standard stopping criterion corresponding to an improvement of less than ϵ. Each iteration of gradient descent has a complexity that is linear to the size of the tree S (total number of nodes).

Algorithm 1: $gradientDescent(T, \boldsymbol{\alpha}, b, \epsilon)$

    Input   : a decision tree T, an initialized vector $\boldsymbol{\alpha}$, a learning rate b, a learning
              rate b
    Output: an optimized vector $\boldsymbol{\alpha}$

1 $costDiff = Double.max;$
2 **while** $costDiff > \epsilon$ **do**
3      $cost \leftarrow calculateGradientsAndCost(T, \boldsymbol{\alpha});$
4   **for** *each node* $p \in T$ *and* $p \notin \mathcal{L}$ **do**
5   // internal nodes
6         $\alpha_p := \alpha_p - b\frac{\partial}{\partial \alpha_p} LOOCV(\boldsymbol{\alpha});$
7      $cost' \leftarrow calculateGradientsAndCost(T, \boldsymbol{\alpha}) ;$
8      $costDiff \leftarrow cost - cost';$
9 **return** $\boldsymbol{\alpha}$

Algorithm 2: *calculateGradientsAndCost*($\mathcal{T}, \boldsymbol{\alpha}$)

Input : a tree $\mathcal{T}$ with depth d and leaves $\mathcal{L}$
Input : a vector $\boldsymbol{\alpha}$
Output: *cost*

1 /* Traverse 1: Calculate cost top-down.   */
2 $cost \leftarrow 0$;
3 **for** $h \leftarrow 0$ *to* d **do**
4   **for** *each node* p *in level* h *and each class* $k \in \mathcal{K}$ **do**
5   **if** $p \notin \mathcal{L}$ **then**
6   calculate $\theta_{p,k}^{LOO}$, $\alpha_p \theta_{p,k}^{LOO}$, α_p^* and $\theta_{p,k}^*$;
7   **else**
8   calculate $\theta_{l,k}^{LOO}$ using Equ. 5;
9              $cost \leftarrow cost + n_{l,k} \cdot \log \frac{1}{\theta_{l,k}^{LOO}}$;
10 /* Traverse 2: update gradients bottom-up.   */
11 **for** $h \leftarrow d$ *to* 0 **do**
12   **for** *each node* p *in level* h *and each class* $k \in \mathcal{K}$ **do**
13   **if** $p \notin \mathcal{L}$ **then**
14   Calculate $\frac{\partial}{\partial \alpha_p} LOOCV(\boldsymbol{\alpha})$ using Equ. 7;
15   **else**
16   Calculate $\beta_{l,k}$ using Equ. 8;
17 **return** $cost \leftarrow \frac{1}{N \cdot In2} \cdot cost$

---

4 Experiments

The aim of this section is to show the performance of HGS smoothing compared with other existing smoothing methods for C4.5 trees. Section 4.1 gives the general experimental settings. The remaining sections then detail individual experiments.

4.1 Experiment Design and Setting

Design. An extensive set of experiments are conducted on 143 standard datasets from the UCI archive [3], where 20 have more than 10,000 instances, 52 have between 1,000 and 10,000, and 71 have less than 1,000 instances. A missing value is treated as a separate attribute value. The datasets The table that summarizes the characteristics of each dataset, including the number of instances, attributes and classes, can be found and downloaded from Github[1].

Evaluation Measure. The results are assessed by RMSE and 0–1 Loss. RMSE is the most important measure because it measures how well-calibrated the probability estimates are, and these better support tasks with unequal costs or imbalanced classes. 0–1 Loss refers to classification accuracy. For both RMSE and 0–1 Loss, the smaller, the better. Win-Draw-Loss (WDL) is reported when comparing

---

[1] https://github.com/icesky0125/DecisionTreeSmoothing.

two methods. A two-tail binomial sign test is used to determine the significance of the results. A difference is considered to be significant if $p \leq 0.05$.

Software. To ensure reproducibility of our work and allow other researchers to build on our research easily, we have made our source code for HGS smoothing on PETs available on Github (See foonote 1).

Compared Methods. Different smoothing methods are compared for the C4.4 decision tree (C4.5 without pruning), including Laplace smoothing, M-estimation, M-branch, HDP and HGS. The parameters of HDP are set to be *iteration* = 1,000 and *tying* = *SINGLE*, which are tested by us. All the methods are evaluated using 10-fold cross-validation.

4.2   HGS Parameter Tuning

HGS is basically a parameterless algorithm. The only two parameters are the learning rate b and the minimum cost difference threshold ϵ between two iterations needed in the gradient descent algorithm [16]. In this experiment, we tried different values $b = 0.01, 0.001$ and $\epsilon = 0.001, 0.0001$ and found that their results were all the same with only slight differences in training time. Based on these results, in the following experiment we choose standard values of $b = 0.01$ and $\epsilon = 0.0001$.

4.3   HGS vs. Existing Methods

This experiment evaluates the advantages of HGS compared with single-layer smoothing methods, including MLE, Laplace correction and M-estimation, and hierarchical smoothing methods, including M-branch and HDP. Table 1 and Table 2 are the table of WDL and the averaged value respectively. The error bars of all these models are 0.012 on RMSE and 0.015 on 0–1 Loss, respectively. It can be seen from these tables that HGS is significantly better than all of the existing methods on RMSE and better on 0/1 Loss.

The training time for HGS, as a hierarchical smoothing method, is similar to single-level methods, which is 1.1 s. While compared with the existing hierarchical methods, HGS is approximately 5 times faster than HDP and 9 times faster than M-branch on average. This indicates that HGS makes PET get both very accurate probability estimates and classification results efficiently.

Table 1. Win-Draw-Loss results (The boldface values are significant).

Method	RMSE	0–1 Loss
HGS vs. MLE	**108-2-33**	69-22-52
HGS vs. Laplace	**111-4-28**	68-22-53
HGS vs. M-esti	**98-4-41**	66-23-54
HGS vs. M-branch	**96-3-44**	59-32-52
HGS vs. HDP	**92-1-50**	64-21-58

Table 2. Averaged results

Methods	RMSE	0–1 Loss	Runtime
MLE	0.2596	0.2093	1.1
Laplace	0.2499	0.2093	1.1
M-estimation	0.2485	0.2068	1.1
HDP	0.2436	0.2078	4.9
M-branch	0.2428	0.2062	9.3
HGS	**0.2410**	**0.2059**	1.1

To compare the three hierarchical smoothing methods more intuitively, we take the RMSE of HGS as the benchmark for each dataset and subtract RMSE of M-branch and HDP, and drew Fig. 2. The X-axis represents the datasets arranged from large to small in terms of data size. The Y-axis represents the RMSE difference between HGS and each method, which is the lower, the better. The points in the grey area represent the datasets that perform better with HGS. The lower the point is, the stronger the advantage of HGS is. The following conclusions can be drawn. First, there are more points in the grey area, which indicates that HGS makes the majority of the datasets with better estimates. Second, the ∗ points are mostly centred around the line $y = 0$, while o points are more diffuse than ∗. This means HDP has high variance compared with M-branch. Last, among the top 20 largest datasets with more than 10,000 examples on the far left of the figure, HDP makes 14 out of them performs better than HGS and M-branch. This indicates that HDP is more helpful on large datasets.

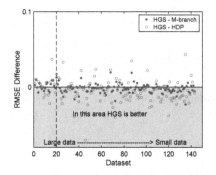

Fig. 2. Compare the probability estimates of HGS with HDP and M-branch.

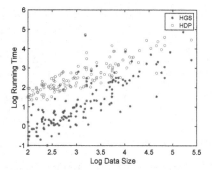

Fig. 3. Training time comparison according to log data size.

4.4 Running Time vs. Data Size

One of the most important motivations of HGS is its efficiency, i.e. running time. Table 1 only gives the averaged running time over all the datasets. Here it is also interesting to investigate the running times based on different data size. Figure 3 is the running time versus data sizes plot for HGS and HDP evaluated on all the datasets. We take the log of both the data sizes and the running times to make the figure more intuitive. It is evident that the blue ∗ are almost always lower than the red circles, which indicates that the training time of HGS on datasets of different sizes is basically shorter than that of HDP.

4.5 HGS on Random Forest

We sought to determine how many trees are needed in RF to beat HGS on a single tree, and the impact of smoothing with RF. Previously, [1] suggested that a non-corrected probability estimate should be used in RF. Figure 4 shows the RMSE changing with the forest size. RF_HGS represents random forest using HGS smoothing, while RF means no smoothing. C4.5 with HGS smoothing is represented by line $y = 0.24$. This figure shows that HGS makes RF worse after three trees because smoothing can reduce the diversity of RF. A single C4.5 tree using HGS yields RMSE better or close to RF with 7 trees and comparatively for 10 trees. While single trees with HGS smoothing cannot beat RF, a single tree is preferred if one is more interested in interpretability.

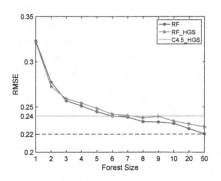

Fig. 4. HGS smoothing on random forest in RMSE.

4.6   Conclusions

It is well known that probability smoothing beats pruning, and M-branch showed us that hierarchical smoothing could further improve performance. This paper, however, develops a new hierarchical algorithm, HGS, and tests out a recent algorithm, HDP smoothing on trees for the first time. The originality of HGS is in removing recursive smoothing and efficient pre-computation of key statistics, which also allow better optimization of hyper-parameters. This experimental evaluation demonstrates three significant contributions.

- HDP smoothing developed in [13] is shown to be comparable to M-branch, and evidence suggests it is the superior algorithm for large data sets.
- HGS is an order of magnitude faster than M-branch and HDP smoothing, and significantly better in RMSE.
- HGS is generally superior to a random forest with 7 trees and almost as good with 10 trees, which makes HGS a single tree alternative to a random forest with 10 trees or less.

There has been a renewed interest in decision trees, and thus also PETS. For applications that require more interpretability and efficiency, such as online and embedded applications, a PET built using a single decision tree plus HGS is thus suitable for these.

References

1. Bostrom, H.: Estimating class probabilities in random forests. In: 2007 Sixth International Conference on Machine Learning and Applications (ICMLA 2007), pp. 211–216. IEEE (2007)
2. Chen, S.F., Goodman, J.: An empirical study of smoothing techniques for language modeling. Comput. Speech Lang. **13**(4), 359–394 (1999)
3. Dua, D., Graff, C.: UCI machine learning repository (2017)
4. Elkan, C.: The foundations of cost-sensitive learning. In: International Joint Conference on Artificial Intelligence, vol. 17, pp. 973–978. Lawrence Erlbaum Associates Ltd (2001)
5. Ferri, C., Flach, P., Hernández-Orallo, J.: Decision trees for ranking: effect of new smoothing methods, new splitting criteria and simple pruning methods. Technical report DSIC 2003 (2003)
6. Ferri, C., Flach, P.A., Hernández-Orallo, J.: Improving the AUC of probabilistic estimation trees. In: Lavrač, N., Gamberger, D., Blockeel, H., Todorovski, L. (eds.) ECML 2003. LNCS (LNAI), vol. 2837, pp. 121–132. Springer, Heidelberg (2003). https://doi.org/10.1007/978-3-540-39857-8_13
7. Joulani, P., Gyorgy, A., Szepesvári, C.: Fast cross-validation for incremental learning. In: Twenty-Fourth International Joint Conference on Artificial Intelligence (2015)
8. Kneser, R., Ney, H.: Improved backing-off for m-gram language modeling. In: ICASSP, vol. 1, p. 181e4 (1995)
9. Kohavi, R.: The power of decision tables. In: Lavrac, N., Wrobel, S. (eds.) ECML 1995. LNCS, vol. 912, pp. 174–189. Springer, Heidelberg (1995). https://doi.org/10.1007/3-540-59286-5_57
10. Liang, H., Zhang, H., Yan, Y.: Decision trees for probability estimation: an empirical study. In: 2006 18th IEEE International Conference on Tools with Artificial Intelligence (ICTAI 2006), pp. 756–764. IEEE (2006)
11. Manapragada, C., Webb, G.I., Salehi, M.: Extremely fast decision tree. In: Proceedings of the 24th ACM SIGKDD International Conference on Knowledge Discovery & Data Mining (KDD 2018), pp. 1953–1962. ACM, New York, (2018)
12. Murdoch, W.J., Singh, C., Kumbier, K., Abbasi-Asl, R., Yu, B.: Definitions, methods, and applications in interpretable machine learning. Proc. Nat. Acad. Sci. **116**(44), 22071–22080 (2019)
13. Petitjean, F., Buntine, W., Webb, G.I., Zaidi, N.: Accurate parameter estimation for Bayesian network classifiers using hierarchical Dirichlet processes. Mach. Learn. **107**, 1303–1331 (2018). https://doi.org/10.1007/s10994-018-5718-0
14. Provost, F., Domingos, P.: Tree induction for probability-based ranking. Mach. Learn. **52**(3), 199–215 (2003). https://doi.org/10.1023/A:1024099825458
15. Quinlan, J.R.: C4.5: Programs for Machine Learning. The Morgan Kaufmann Series in Machine Learning, San Mateo, Morgan Kaufmann, Burlington (1993)
16. Ruder, S.: An overview of gradient descent optimization algorithms. arXiv preprint arXiv:1609.04747 (2016)
17. Shareghi, E., Haffari, G., Cohn, T.: Compressed nonparametric language modelling. In: Proceedings of the Twenty-Sixth International Joint Conference on Artificial Intelligence, pp. 2701–2707 (2017)
18. Shen, Y.: Loss functions for binary classification and class probability estimation. Ph.D. thesis, University of Pennsylvania (2005)

19. Teh, Y.W., Jordan, M.I.: Hierarchical bayesian nonparametric models with applications. In: Bayesian Nonparametrics, vol. 1, pp. 158–207. Cambridge University Press, Cambridge (2010)
20. Wang, T., Qin, Z., Jin, Z., Zhang, S.: Handling over-fitting in test cost-sensitive decision tree learning by feature selection, smoothing and pruning. J. Syst. Softw. **83**(7), 1137–1147 (2010)
21. Zadrozny, B., Elkan, C.: Learning and making decisions when costs and probabilities are both unknown. In: Proceedings of the seventh ACM SIGKDD International Conference on Knowledge Discovery and Data Mining, pp. 204–213. ACM (2001)
22. Zadrozny, B., Elkan, C.: Obtaining calibrated probability estimates from decision trees and naive Bayesian classifiers. In: ICML, vol. 1, pp. 609–616. Citeseer (2001)
23. Zhang, K.: Probability estimation trees: empirical comparison, algorithm extension and applications. Ph.D. thesis, Tulane University (2006)

Optimized Transformer Models
for FAQ Answering

Sonam Damani$^{(\boxtimes)}$, Kedhar Nath Narahari, Ankush Chatterjee,
Manish Gupta, and Puneet Agrawal

Microsoft, Hyderabad, India
{sodamani,kedharn,anchatte,gmanish,punagr}@microsoft.com

Abstract. Informational chatbots provide a highly effective medium for improving operational efficiency in answering customer queries for any enterprise. Chatbots are also preferred by users/customers since unlike other alternatives like calling customer care or browsing over FAQ pages, chatbots provide instant responses, are easy to use, are less invasive and are always available. In this paper, we discuss the problem of FAQ answering which is central to designing a retrieval-based informational chatbot. Given a set of FAQ pages s for an enterprise, and a user query, we need to find the best matching question-answer pairs from s. Building such a semantic ranking system that works well across domains for large QA databases with low runtime and model size is challenging. Previous work based on feature engineering or recurrent neural models either provides low accuracy or incurs high runtime costs. We experiment with multiple transformer based deep learning models, and also propose a novel MT-DNN (Multi-task Deep Neural Network)-based architecture, which we call Masked MT-DNN (or MMT-DNN). MMT-DNN significantly outperforms other state-of-the-art transformer models for the FAQ answering task. Further, we propose an improved knowledge distillation component to achieve ∼2.4x reduction in model-size and ∼7x reduction in runtime while maintaining similar accuracy. On a small benchmark dataset from SemEval 2017 CQA Task 3, we show that our approach provides an NDCG@1 of 83.1. On another large dataset of ∼281K instances corresponding to ∼30K queries from diverse domains, our distilled 174 MB model provides an NDCG@1 of 75.08 with a CPU runtime of mere 31 ms establishing a new state-of-the-art for FAQ answering.

1 Introduction

Reducing agent costs in the call center is typically high on the list of priorities of call center managers in any enterprise. Enterprises put up frequently asked questions (FAQ) pages to satisfy users' frequent information needs so as to avoid such calls. But often such pages are too large and not very well structured for users to read. The difficulties faced by users in interacting with the FAQ pages are multi-fold – (1) User has to scan through a long list of QA pairs. (2) FAQs in a list may be poorly organized and not semantically grouped. (3) Multiple FAQs may answer the query, and the user must look out for a QA pair that answers

© Springer Nature Switzerland AG 2020
H. W. Lauw et al. (Eds.): PAKDD 2020, LNAI 12084, pp. 235–248, 2020.
https://doi.org/10.1007/978-3-030-47426-3_19

the question with the right level of specificity. (4) An FAQ list may sometimes be scattered over several documents.

In addition, a poorly managed call center or mismatching working hours for global customers, could lead to long wait times for customers who may then move over to other competitive businesses. Alternatively, users pose such queries on community question answering (cQA) forums, or contact businesses over slow media like emails or phone calls. In 2014, Quora, a popular cQA forum, claimed that 10% of U.S. population uses its service every month[1] contributing to a total of 61M questions with 108M answers[2]. Such popularity of cQA forums at least partially indicates the difficulty faced by users in interacting with FAQ pages to obtain answers.

To provide correct information instantly at much lower operating costs, retrieval-based chatbots that can match user queries with content on FAQ pages are highly desirable. In this paper, we discuss the problem of FAQ answering which is central to designing a retrieval-based information chatbot. Let D denote the set of question-answer pairs extracted from a set of FAQ pages s for an enterprise. Given D and a user query q, our goal is to rank question-answer pairs in D. Top K QA pairs with high scores are returned to the user. Figure 1 shows possible system snapshots using two user interfaces – web search as well as a chatbot. In case of web search interface (left of Fig. 1), K is set to 4, while $K = 1$ for the chatbot interface (right of Fig. 1).

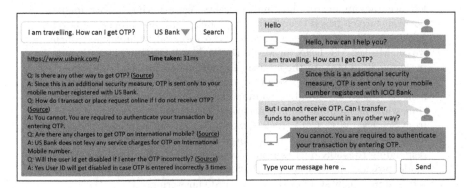

Fig. 1. Web Search interface (left), Chatbot interface (right);

Note that this problem is similar to the problem of automatically answering questions on cQA forums by matching existing question-answer pages. However, there are some major differences as follows: (1) Queries on cQA forums are much longer than queries and questions on FAQ pages. In fact, often times, cQA queries have a subject and a body [29]. (2) cQA forums have a user network. Thus every

---

[1] https://venturebeat.com/2015/12/21/quora-claims-10-of-u-s-population-uses-its-service-every-month/.

[2] https://www.quora.com/How-many-questions-have-been-asked-on-Quora-1.

QA pair is associated with a set of users. Unlike that, when ranking QA pairs from FAQ pages, we cannot exploit signals from any user network. (3) cQA pages typically have a question but multiple user-voted answers. FAQ pages have no user-voting, and only one answer per question. (4) On cQA forums, different answers may apply based on user context. On FAQ pages, every question has a unique answer.

FAQ answering is a challenging task. Solving the problem needs prediction of query-question semantic similarity and query-answer relevance, in a joint manner. Also, building a general system that works across domains implies that we cannot resort to any domain specific heuristics. Finally, although recent deep learning based systems provide high accuracy across multiple NLP tasks, building a deep learning based system for FAQ Answering for large QA databases with low runtimes and model size brings in more challenges.

Previous work on answering a question, given FAQ pages, was based on feature engineering (FAQ-Finder [8], Auto-FAQ [28], [11,22]) or typical attention-based recurrent neural network models (SymBiMPM [7]). Recently, transformer based networks [24] have shown significant gains across many natural language processing tasks. In this paper, we propose the use of transformer network based methods like Bidirectional Encoder Representations from Transformers (BERT) [6] and Multi-task Deep Neural Network (MT-DNN) [15]. Further, we propose a novel architecture, MMT-DNN, based on a masking trick specifically applicable to input in the form of (query, question, answer) triples. To make such models practically usable, we need to reduce the model size as well as the execution time. Hence, we propose an improved knowledge distillation method for our MMT-DNN model. Our experiments with two datasets show that the proposed model outperforms all the baselines by significant margins. Also, our distilled 174MB MT-DNN-3 model provides a runtime of mere 31 ms making it usable in real-time chatbot scenarios. We make the following main contributions in this paper.

- We propose the use of transformer based models like BERT and MT-DNN for solving the FAQ Answering task, and also present a novel architecture, MMT-DNN, that achieves better accuracy.
- We propose and experiment with an improved knowledge distillation method to reduce the model size and model runtime.
- On two real world datasets, our proposed MMT-DNN establishes a new state-of-the-art for FAQ answering.

2   Related Work

Data Mining for FAQ Web Pages. Research on FAQ web pages has focused on three sub-areas: (1) FAQ mining using list detection algorithms [11,14], (2) answering questions using FAQ web pages [8,11,22,28], (3) navigational interface for Frequently Asked Question (FAQ) pages [20], and (4) Completeness of FAQ pages [3]. In this paper, we focus on the FAQ answering task. Previous work on answering a question given FAQ pages (FAQ-Finder [8], Auto-FAQ [28], [2,11,13,21,23]) was based on traditional feature engineering for surfacing statistical/semantic similarities between query and questions. Most of these works considered similarity between query and questions, very few considered query-answer similarity. We use transformer based deep learning methods for jointly considering query-question and query-answer similarity.

Recently deep learning based methods have been proposed for FAQ Answering. Wu et al. [29] propose the attention-based Question Condensing Networks (QCN) to align a question-answer pair where the question is composed of a subject and a body. To suit our problem setting, we experiment by substituting query for the subject, and question for the body. Gupta et al. [7] propose SymBiMPM (BiLSTMs with multi-perspective matching blocks) for computing query-QA match. Recently, transformer network models have emerged as state-of-the-art across multiple NLP tasks. Hence, unlike previous deep learning works, we use transformer networks for FAQ answering.

Applications of Transformer Models. After the original Transformer work by Vaswani et al. [24], several architectures have been proposed like BERT [6], MT-DNN [15] etc. The GLUE [26] and the SuperGLUE [25] dashboards tell us that such models have outperformed previously proposed methods across complex NLP tasks like text classification, textual entailment, machine translation, word sense disambiguation, etc. We present the first work to investigate application of transformers to FAQ answering task.

Model Compression. Existing deep neural network models are computationally expensive and memory intensive, hindering their deployment in devices with low memory resources or in applications with strict latency requirements. Chatbots expect near realtime responses. Thus, transformer based models need to be compressed and accelerated. In the past few years, multiple techniques have been proposed for model optimization including pruning, quantization, knowledge distillation, and low rank factorization. Cheng et al. [5] provide a good survey of such methods. In this paper, we explore different variations of knowledge distillation and present a novel architecture that provides best results for the FAQ answering task.

3   Approach

Given a question-answer database, when a user query q arrives, we first compute a list of candidate QA pairs which have high BM25 score [19] with respect to the query. Given the latency constraints, we use computationally cheap BM25 match, however, understandably, BM25 may have missed semantically similar but syntactically different QA pairs. If q uses synonyms of the words in the ideal QA pair, it is possible that the pair would not be selected based on BM25 score. These candidate QA pairs, along with the original query, are scored using various methods described in this section. Top K QA pairs with high scores are returned to the user.

We first discuss baseline methods like BiLSTMs with attention and Sym-BiMPM [7]. Next, we discuss our proposed transformer based methods. All of these methods take query (q), question (Q), and answer (A) as input, and output one of the three classes: Good, Average or Bad indicating the degree of match between q and the (Q, A) pair. Figure 2 illustrates architectures of various methods discussed in this section.

3.1 Baselines

BiLSTMs. As illustrated in Fig. 2(A), in this approach, the query, question and answer are processed using three two-row bidirectional LSTMs [10]. The query and question BiLSTMs share weights. We use BiLSTMs with attention. The final output from the last hidden layer of each of the BiLSTMs is concatenated and fed into a fully connected neural network (MLP). The output layer has three neurons (one for each of the three classes) across all the architectures. The network is trained using Adam optimizer [12] with cross entropy loss.

SymBiMPM. Symmetric Bilateral Multi-Perspective Matching Block (Sym-BiMPM) is the method proposed by Gupta et al. [7]. This model uses a multi-perspective matching block [27] to compare two sequences and generate the matched representations for both these sequences. This block has four different matching mechanisms that are used on the input sequences. Matching is applied in both the directions, i.e. if P and Q are the two inputs, then the output is a matched representation of P obtained by attending to Q, and a matched representation of Q obtained by attending to P. All the BiLSTMs share weights. Also, both the match blocks share weights. As illustrated in Fig. 2(B), Multi-perspective matching blocks are used for query-question and query-answer matching followed by attention layer and fully connected layers to get the final class label.

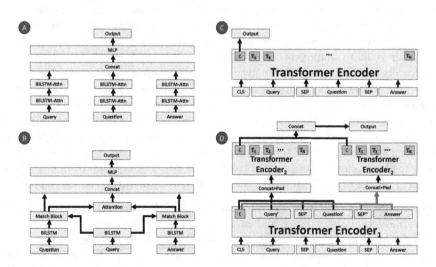

Fig. 2. Architectures of various methods: (A) BiLSTMs with attention (B) Sym-BiMPM (adapted from [7]) (C) BERT/MT-DNN (D) MMT-DNN

3.2   Proposed Methods

Transformer networks proposed by Vaswani et al. [24] follow a non-recurrent architecture with stacked self-attention and fully connected layers for both the encoder and decoder, each with 6 layers. BERT and MT-DNN are two most popular extensions of the Transformer encoder network. Broadly this architecture is illustrated in Fig. 2(C).

BERT. BERT [6] essentially is a transformer encoder with 12 layers. We used the pre-trained model which has been trained on Books Corpus and Wikipedia using the MLM (masked language model) and the next sentence prediction (NSP) loss functions. The query, question and answer are concatenated into a sequence and are separated with a special "SEP" token. The sequence is prepended with a "CLS" token. The representation C for the "CLS" token from the last encoder layer is used for classification by connecting it to an output softmax layer. Optionally, we can finetune the pre-trained model using labeled training data for the FAQ answering task.

MT-DNN. The MT-DNN architecture [15] extends BERT by further pre-training it with large amounts of cross-task data. Specifically, the MT-DNN is a 12 layer transformer encoder where the BERT model has been further pre-trained using single sentence classification, text similarity, pairwise text classification and relevance ranking tasks. The representation C for the "CLS" token from the last encoder layer is used for classification by connecting it to an output softmax layer. Optionally, we can finetune the pre-trained model using labeled training data for the FAQ answering task.

MMT-DNN. The proposed Masked MT-DNN method modifies the MT-DNN architecture, as illustrated in Fig. 2(D). The transformer encoder is divided into two parts: encoder$_1$ and encoder$_2$. Encoder$_1$ consists of l encoder layers, while encoder$_2$ contains 12-l layers. l is a hyper-parameter tuned on validation data. The input sequence (query, question, answer) is first processed by encoder$_1$ to get a transformed sequence (query', question', answer'). Intuitively, (query, question) pair is more homogeneous compared to (query, answer) pair. Hence, we explore disjoint encoding of the two pairs using separate encoder$_2$ blocks for query-question and query-answer matching. Both encoder$_2$ blocks share weights. Specifically, the first encoder$_2$ block receives the concatenated string of the CLS token, query and question as input, where the answer is masked by replacing answer tokens by zeros. Similarly, the second encoder$_2$ block receives the concatenated string of the CLS token, query and answer as input, where the question is masked by replacing the question tokens by zeros. The C token from both these encoder$_2$ blocks are concatenated and connected to an output softmax layer.

Knowledge Distillation. The proposed MMT-DNN model, like other Transformer models, is very large and also incurs a large number of computations at prediction time. Hence, we use knowledge distillation strategies [1] to compress the model and reduce latency while retaining accuracy. Figure 3 shows our improved knowledge distillation component.

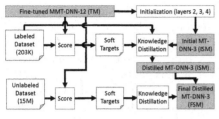

Fig. 3. Knowledge distillation for FAQ answering

Table 1. Dataset statistics (train/dev/test)

Dataset	SemEval-2017	FSD
#Queries	266/72/70	20242/1966/7478
#Question-Answer pairs	6711/1575/2313	1630/477/649
#Data points	9977/1851/2767	202969/22549/55751
Avg length of queries	41.2/37.9/43.7	7.2/9.3/9.5
Avg length of questions	50.4/47.2/49.1	7.7/9.8/7.9
Avg length of answers	48.9/45.1/46.3	61.4/55.3/57.9

We use student-teacher networks for knowledge distillation [9] by considering the fine-tuned MMT-DNN-12 model as a teacher model (TM) for knowledge distillation. Layers 2, 3, and 4 of the fine-tuned MMT-DNN-12 are used to initialize a MT-DNN-3 model which is the initial student model (ISM) for knowledge distillation. Note that the student model is a MT-DNN and not a MMT-DNN. A combination of hard targets from the labeled dataset and soft targets from the fine-tuned MMT-DNN-12 TM is used to define the loss for training the MT-DNN-3 model to obtain the distilled student model (DSM). Although not shown in the figure (due to lack of space), in order to facilitate gradual transfer of knowledge, the distillation from MMT-DNN-12 to MT-DNN-3 is done in a chain of steps where MMT-DNN-12 is first distilled to a MT-DNN-9, then to MT-DNN-6 and finally to an MT-DNN-3 student model (DSM) [17]. We also have access to a much larger (15 million sized) unlabeled dataset of queries which lead to clicks to FAQ pages. These are scored against the TM to generate soft targets. These soft targets are then used to further distill the DSM, followed by TVM compiler optimizations [4] to obtain the final distilled MT-DNN-3 student model (FSM).

4 Experiments

4.1 Datasets

Table 1 presents basic statistics about the two datasets.

SemEval-2017. This dataset[3] was intended for community question answering (cQA) originally, but the task 3 data had the QA pairs grouped by search query terms, which facilitated the transformation of this data into FAQ Retrieval format where FAQs are ranked for a query and are awarded ranks as Good, Average or Bad (as in original dataset). We used standard train, dev, test splits provided by the task organizers. Although this dataset is small, we experiment with it since this is the only publicly available dataset.

---

[3] http://alt.qcri.org/semeval2017/task3/.

FAQ Search Dataset (FSD). This dataset was created using ~30K queries (from a popular search engine's query log) leading to clicks to FAQ pages. We took only those queries which resulted into at least 5 clicks to some FAQ page. The query was then compared to all the QA pairs extracted from the clicked FAQ pages using BM25 score [19] to extract a max of top 15 QA pairs. We then got these (query, QA) instances judged into 3 classes (Good, Average or Bad) using a crowdsourcing platform with three-way redundancy. The queries and FAQ pages were carefully chosen such that (1) they belong to multiple domains like airports, banks, supermarkets, tourism and administrative bodies, (2) queries and QA pairs of various sizes are considered, and (3) FAQ pages with varying number of QA pairs are included. Note that this dataset is ~20x larger than the SemEval-2017 dataset.

4.2   Accuracy Comparison

The query, question and answer are all represented using GloVe [18] embeddings for all the baseline methods. Transformer based methods use WordPiece [30] embeddings. All experiments were done on a machine with 4 Tesla V100-SXM2-32GB GPUs. We use the popular ranking metric, Normal Discounted Cumulative Gain (NDCG)@K to compare various methods. For BiLSTMs in all baseline methods, the hidden layer size was 300. For transformer based methods, the embedding size was fixed to 30522 and the input sequence length was fixed to 512 tokens.

Table 2 shows accuracy comparison across various methods on both the datasets. Block A shows results for baseline methods. Surprisingly, Sym-BiMPM [7] performs worse than BiLSTMs. SemEval-2017 dataset has labels for query-question pair, for query-answer pair, as well as query-answer pair. For SymBiMPM [7], the authors used query-question label as the label for a (query, question, answer) triple. As a refinement, we first considered only those QA pairs where question-answer label is "good", and then used the label for query-answer similarity as the label for a (query, question, answer) triple. Also, queries in the SemEval-2017 set have a subject as well as a body. Gupta et al. [7] simply used the query subject and ignored the query body. We experiment with just the query subject as well as with query subject + body. Table 2 shows that using query subject + body usually provides better accuracy, sometimes with a large margin. We also experimented with QCN [29] but the results were worse than even BiLSTMs. This is expected due to mismatch in the problem setting, as discussed in Sect. 2. Further, Block B shows results for the proposed methods. As the table shows, our proposed methods outperform existing methods by a significant margin. All results are obtained as a median of 5 runs. Both BERT and MT-DNN benefit from finetuning across the two datasets. Also, MMT-DNN outperforms all other methods by a significant margin ($p < 0.05$ using McNemar Test [16]), establishing a new state-of-the-art for FAQ answering task.

Table 2. Accuracy comparison across various methods. For SemEval-2017 dataset, results are for two settings: (using just the query subject/using query subject + body).

	Model	SemEval-2017			FSD		
		NDCG@1	NDCG@5	NDCG@10	NDCG@1	NDCG@5	NDCG@10
A	BiLSTMs	36.62/38.83	38.43/43.17	41.76/46.3	55.70	63.02	69.34
	SymBiMPM [7]	34.21/34.00	38.55/38.59	40.86/44.71	54.03	61.21	68.11
B	BERT (pre-trained)	63.38/65.39	61.85/68.41	62.87/68.44	71.77	76.17	78.47
	MT-DNN (pre-trained)	68.01/60.97	64.92/61.85	64.67/62.83	70.29	75.08	77.65
	BERT (finetune)	68.01/69.22	65.19/68.61	67.46/71.12	73.97	78.29	79.79
	MT-DNN (finetune)	70.22/82.49	67.06/81.79	67.72/81.99	73.75	78.14	79.79
	MMT-DNN	71.03/84.71	70.67/82.59	71.51/82.18	75.38	78.59	80.24

Figure 4 shows NDCG@K for $K = 1$ to 10 for the MMT-DNN approach for both the datasets. With increase in K, while the accuracy improvement for the FSD is intuitive, the result is not very intuitive for the SemEval-2017 dataset. This is mainly because of the small size of the dataset because of which usually there are very few good answers matching any query.

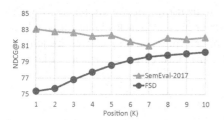

Fig. 4. NDCG@K for the MMT-DNN approach for both the datasets

Fig. 5. NDCG@5 with varying number of Encoder$_1$ layers (l) for MMT-DNN for the two datasets

q_1 **from SemEval-2017 dataset:** working permit ... 1- do i need working permit since i have residence visa in qatar n under husband sponsor? 2- without working permit expat's wife could not work in qatar? ...

   Q_1: Work permit for husband? I am thinking of sponsoring my husband to live in Qatar. I heard that if he gets a job; he will need to get a work permit. Are husbands able to get a work permit? ...

   A_1: If he is on a family visa he needs to find a job first so that the company who will hire him will be the one to process his work permit. ...

   Q_2: Work permit for husband? I am thinking of sponsoring my husband to live in Qatar. I heard that if he gets a job; he will need to get a work permit. Are husbands able to get a work permit? ...

   A_2: if you get over 7k you can sponser him with fam visa. once he is here and under your visa; ... he will still remain under your sponsorship. ...

   Q_3: Wife/Husband with family sponsorship to work. If your wife / husband under family sponsorship of your sponsor wants to work do they have to transfer the sponsorship to new sponsor or they can work without sponsorship change?

   A_3: they don't have to transfer their sponsorship under the Company; unless they either want to or the Company requires their transfer. ...

q_2 **from FSD:** i've paid for my parking but my flight is delayed

   Q_1: What happens if I exit the car park prior to my confirmed booking time?

   A_1: If for whatever reason you cannot exit the car park in your confirmed booking time (e.g., you haven't returned due a cancelled flight), the credit card or debit card that you use to exit the car park (i.e. your nominated card) will be debited with the cost of the additional time, based on the rates displayed at the entry to the car park.

   Q_2: What happens if I enter the car park prior to my confirmed booking time?

   A_2: If you enter the car park before your confirmed booking time, or exit the car park later than your confirmed booking time, the credit card or debit card that you use to exit the car park (i.e. your nominated card) will be debited with the cost of the additional time, based on the rates displayed at the entry to the car park.

   Q_3: How do I amend or cancel my booking?

   A_3: You may cancel your Booking, for any reason at any time up to 24 hours before the start of the Booking Period. To do this, ...

Fig. 6. Top 3 QA pairs returned by MMT-DNN for two queries (one from each dataset)

Figure 5 shows the NDCG@5 for MMT-DNN across the two datasets with varying number of Encoder$_1$ layers (l). As expected, the accuracy is better at larger values of l. This means that it is useful to allow attention across question and answer in the first few layers but let the query-question and query-answer attention be learned separately at higher layers. Note that $l = 0$ corresponds to not having Encoder$_1$ at all, and processing (query, question) and (query, answer) separately throughout the network.

Next, we show two queries with top three QA pairs ranked by our MMT-DNN system in Fig. 6. For query q_1, BiLSTMs had this question as the second result: "Work Permit How many days does it take to finish the processing of a Work Permit?". Similarly, SymBiMPM leads to unrelated questions within top 3 like "Hepatitis C (HCV) - Work permit I have Hepatitis C (HCV); Can i get work permit?".

Similarly, for q_2, baselines lead to the following unrelated question in top 3: "Can I get motorbike parking?", "What do I do if I take a ticket on arrival to the car park when I should have entered my credit card?".

4.3   Attention Visualization for MMT-DNN

In Fig. 7, we visualize the heads from the multi-head self attention module of the last encoder for our best approach. This visualization helps us understand what pairs of words in the (query, question, answer) have high self-attention weights. The results are very intuitive showing that query, question and answer are jointly enhancing each other's representations to contribute to high accuracy. Figure 7

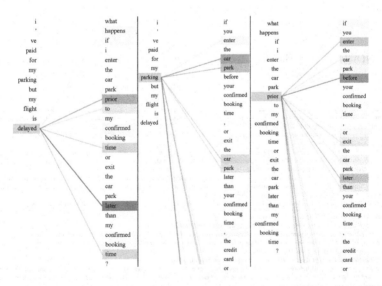

Fig. 7. Visualization of a few heads for various examples for the last encoder layer of our best approach. (left): query-question, (middle): query-answer, (right): question-answer

(left) shows the token "delayed" in the query has high attention weights for the tokens "prior", "time" and "later" in the question. Figure 7 (middle) shows the token "parking" in the query has high attention weights for the tokens "car" and "park" in the answer. Figure 7 (right) shows the token "prior" in the question has high attention weights for the tokens "before" and "later" in the answer.

4.4 Error Analysis

We analyzed error patterns for our best method (MMT-DNN). The most confusing category is the "Average class" with lowest precision and recall. Fortunately, this does not impact ranking significantly especially in cases where there are enough "good" QA pairs for a query. Further, we look at a few examples to do more detailed error analysis by manually assigning error categories to 60 (query, question, answer) triples incorrectly classified by MMT-DNN method. Table 3 shows percentages contributed by each error pattern and a few examples. Verbose Match errors accounted for more than half of the errors, which is in line with our expectations.

4.5 Knowledge Distillation (KD)

Table 4 shows the NDCG obtained using the proposed architectures for KD. Even with small labeled data, distilled MT-DNN-3 provides accuracy comparable to the teacher model. Further distillation using large unlabeled data leads to better results. Note that we fixed the hard versus soft loss balancing parameter α as 0.01. Overall, the final model TVM-optimized MT-DNN-3 provides NDCG@1 of 75.08 on FSD dataset with a model size of 174MB and a CPU/GPU runtime of 31.4/5.18 ms per instance.

Table 3. Analysis of various types of errors with examples

Category	Meaning	%	Examples
Entity mismatch	q and Q/A refer to a different main entity	29	q: "What is best mall in Doha to buy good **furniture**?", Q: "where to buy good **abhaya** in doha"
Generalization	q and Q/A have entities with "is a" relationship	7	q: "Any aquapark in **Doha**?", Q: "any water theme park in **qatar**?"
Intent mismatch	q and Q/A have different intents	5	q: "What is best mall in Doha to buy **good** furniture? ... showrooms ...", Q: "Where to buy **used** furniture? .. cheap ..."
Negation	q and Q/A have opposite intents	7	q: "Is there any Carrefour which is open?", Q: "any other good supermarkets **apart from** Carrefour"
Verbose match	q and Q/A match on unimportant parts	52	q: "Is it good offer? Hi Frds;i QA supervisor with 8 years exp in pharmaceutical have got job offer from Qatar pharma company; Salary which they have offered to me is 5000QAR...", Q: "Is it a good offer? Dear all; I need your help please:) ; i got an offer from Habtoor leighton group for Planning Engineer position. They are offering 10K ..."

Table 4. Accuracy vs size and runtime latency comparison across various models for the knowledge distillation experiments (on FSD)

Model	Size	CPU runtime	NDCG@1	NDCG@5	NDCG@10
MMT-DNN-12	417 MB	225 ms	75.38	78.59	80.24
MT-DNN-9	336 MB	210 ms	76.28	78.83	80.48
MT-DNN-6	255 MB	143 ms	74.55	77.88	79.76
MT-DNN-3	174 MB	68.9 ms	70.56	75.47	77.91
MT-DNN-3 (unlabeled data)	174 MB	68.9 ms	75.08	78.28	80.00
MT-DNN-3 (unlabeled data + TVM)	174 MB	31.4 ms	75.08	78.28	80.00

We tried various ways of initialization of the student model for knowledge distillation as shown in Table 5. Initialization using some layers of the teacher model (usually the first few layers) is clearly better than random initialization.

Table 5. Initialization for knowledge distillation for MT-DNN-3 model using MMT-DNN-12 layers or Random (on FSD)

Initialization	NDCG@1	NDCG@5	NDCG@10
Layers 1, 2, 3	69.20	74.76	77.24
Layers 2, 3, 4	70.56	75.47	77.91
Layers 4, 5, 6	65.83	71.35	75.03
Layers 7, 8, 9	68.57	73.87	76.66
Layers 10, 11, 12	59.83	67.16	71.87
Random	52.92	60.49	67.55

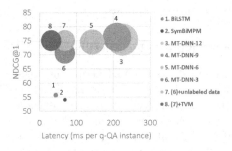

Fig. 8. Accuracy, runtime, model size comparison for various models (best viewed in color) (Color figure online)

Figure 8 shows the accuracy versus runtime trade-off for various models. The radius of the circle corresponds to the model size. Compared to all other approaches, the distilled MT-DNN-3 models are better than others, and among them the best one is the TVM-optimized MT-DNN-3 which also used unlabeled data during distillation.

5 Conclusion

We proposed the use of transformer based models like BERT and MT-DNN for solving the FAQ Answering task. We also proposed a novel MT-DNN architecture with masking, MMT-DNN, which establishes a new state-of-the-art for FAQ answering, as evaluated on two real world datasets. Further, we propose and experiment with an improved knowledge distillation strategy to reduce the model size and model runtime. Overall the proposed techniques lead to models with high accuracy, and small runtime and model size.

References

1. Ba, J., Caruana, R.: Do deep nets really need to be deep? In: NIPS, pp. 2654–2662 (2014)
2. Berger, A., Caruana, R., Cohn, D., Freitag, D., Mittal, V.: Bridging the lexical chasm: statistical approaches to answer-finding. In: SIGIR, pp. 192–199 (2000)
3. Chatterjee, A., Gupta, M., Agrawal, P.: FAQaugmenter: suggesting questions for enterprise FAQ pages. In: WSDM, pp. 829–832 (2020)
4. Chen, T., et al. *TVM*: an automated end-to-end optimizing compiler for deep learning. In: OSDI, pp. 578–594 (2018)
5. Cheng, Y., Wang, D., Zhou, P., Zhang, T.: A survey of model compression and acceleration for deep neural networks. arXiv preprint arXiv:1710.09282 (2017)
6. Devlin, J., Chang, M., Lee, K., Toutanova, K.: Bert: pre-training of deep bidirectional transformers for language understanding. arXiv preprint arXiv:1810.04805 (2018)
7. Gupta, S., Carvalho, V.: FAQ retrieval using attentive matching. In: SIGIR, pp. 929–932 (2019)
8. Hammond, K., Burke, R., Martin, C., Lytinen, S.: FAQ finder: a case-based approach to knowledge navigation. In: Conference on AI for applications, vol. 114 (1995)
9. Hinton, G., Vinyals, O., Dean, J.: Distilling the knowledge in a neural network. arXiv preprint arXiv:1503.02531 (2015)
10. Hochreiter, S., Schmidhuber, J.: Long short-term memory. Neural Comput. **9**(8), 1735–1780 (1997)
11. Jijkoun, V., de Rijke, M.: Retrieving answers from frequently asked questions pages on the web. In: CIKM, pp. 76–83 (2005)
12. Kingma, D.P., Ba, J.: Adam: a method for stochastic optimization. arXiv preprint arXiv:1412.6980 (2014)
13. Kothari, G., Negi, S., Faruquie, T.A., Chakaravarthy, V.T., Subramaniam, L.V.: SMS based interface for FAQ retrieval. In ACL, pp. 852–860 (2009)
14. Lai, Y., Fung, K., Wu, C.: FAQ mining via list detection. In: Multilingual Summarization and Question Answering, pp. 1–7 (2002)
15. Liu, X., He, P., Chen, W., Gao, J.: Multi-task deep neural networks for natural language understanding. arXiv preprint arXiv:1901.11504 (2019)
16. McNemar, Q.: Psychological Statistics. Wiley, New York (1969)
17. Mirzadeh, S., Farajtabar, M., Li, A., Ghasemzadeh, H.: Improved knowledge distillation via teacher assistant: bridging the gap between student and teacher. arXiv preprint arXiv:1902.03393 (2019)
18. Pennington, J., Socher, R., Manning, C.: Glove: global vectors for word representation. In: EMNLP, pp. 1532–1543 (2014)
19. Robertson, S., Zaragoza, H., et al.: The probabilistic relevance framework: BM25 and beyond. FnTIR **3**(4), 333–389 (2009)
20. Schmonsees, R.J.: Dynamic frequently asked questions (FAQ) system. US Patent 5,842,221, November 1998
21. Sneiders, E.: Automated FAQ answering: continued experience with shallow language understanding. In: Question Answering Systems. Papers from the 1999 AAAI Fall Symposium, pp. 97–107 (1999)
22. Sneiders, E.: Automated FAQ answering with question-specific knowledge representation for web self-service. In: Human System Interactions, pp. 298–305 (2009)

23. Song, W., Feng, M., Gu, N., Wenyin, L.: Question similarity calculation for FAQ answering. In: Semantics, Knowledge and Grid, pp. 298–301. IEEE (2007)
24. Vaswani, A., et al.: Attention is all you need. In: NIPS, pp. 5998–6008 (2017)
25. Wang, A., et al.:. SuperGLUE: a stickier benchmark for general-purpose language understanding systems. arXiv preprint arXiv:1905.00537 (2019)
26. Wang, A., Singh, A., Michael, J., Hill, F., Levy, O., Bowman, S.R.: GLUE: a multi-task benchmark and analysis platform for natural language understanding. In: ICLR (2019)
27. Wang, Z., Hamza, W., Florian, R.: Bilateral multi-perspective matching for natural language sentences. arXiv preprint arXiv:1702.03814 (2017)
28. Whitehead, S.D.: Auto-faq: an experiment in cyberspace leveraging. Comput. Netw. ISDN Syst. **28**(1–2), 137–146 (1995)
29. Wu, W., Sun, X., Wang, H.: Question condensing networks for answer selection in community question answering. In: ACL, pp. 1746–1755 (2018)
30. Wu, Y., et al.: Google's neural machine translation system: bridging the gap between human and machine translation. arXiv preprint arXiv:1609.08144 (2016)

Online Algorithms for Multiclass Classification Using Partial Labels

Rajarshi Bhattacharjee[1(✉)] and Naresh Manwani[2]

[1] IIT Madras, Chennai, India
brajarshi91@gmail.com
[2] IIIT Hyderabad, Hyderabad, India
naresh.manwani@iiit.ac.in

Abstract. In this paper, we propose online algorithms for multiclass classification using partial labels. We propose two variants of Perceptron called Avg Perceptron and Max Perceptron to deal with the partially labeled data. We also propose Avg Pegasos and Max Pegasos, which are extensions of the Pegasos algorithm. We also provide mistake bounds for Avg Perceptron and regret bound for Avg Pegasos. We show the effectiveness of the proposed approaches by experimenting on various datasets and comparing them with the standard Perceptron and Pegasos.

Keywords: Online learning · Pegasos · Perceptron

1 Introduction

Multiclass classification is a well-studied problem in machine learning. However, we assume that we know the true label for every example in the training data. In many applications, we don't have access to the true class label as labeling data is an expensive and time-consuming process. Instead, we get a set of candidate labels for every example. This setting is called multiclass learning with partial labels. The true or ground-truth label is assumed to be one of the instances in the partial label set. Partially labeled data is relatively easier to obtain and thus provides a cheap alternative to learning with exact labels.

Learning with partial labels is referred to as superset label learning [13], ambiguous label learning [2], and by other names in different papers. Many proposed models try to *disambiguate* the correct labels from the incorrect ones. One popular approach is to treat the unknown correct label in the candidate set as a latent variable and then use an Expectation-Maximization type algorithm to estimate the correct label as well the model parameters iteratively [2,9,11,13,18].

Electronic supplementary material The online version of this chapter (https://doi.org/10.1007/978-3-030-47426-3_20) contains supplementary material, which is available to authorized users.

© Springer Nature Switzerland AG 2020
H. W. Lauw et al. (Eds.): PAKDD 2020, LNAI 12084, pp. 249–260, 2020.
https://doi.org/10.1007/978-3-030-47426-3_20

Other approaches to label disambiguation include using a maximum margin formulation [20] which alternates between ground truth identification and maximizing the margin from the ground-truth label to all other labels. Regularization based approaches [8] for partial label learning have also been proposed. Another model assumes that the ground truth label is the one to which the maximum score is assigned in the candidate label set by the model [14]. Then the margin between this ground-truth label and all other labels not in the candidate set is maximized.

Some approaches try to predict the label of an unseen instance by averaging the candidate labeling information of its nearest neighbors in the training set [10,21]. Some formulations combine the partial label learning framework with other frameworks like multi-label learning [19]. There are also specific approaches that do not try to disambiguate the label set directly. For example, Zhang et al. [22] introduced an algorithm that works to utilize the entire candidate label set using a method involving error-correcting codes.

A general risk minimization framework for learning with partial labels is discussed in Cour et al. [3,4]. In this framework, any standard convex loss function can be modified to be used in the partial label setting. For a single instance, since the ground-truth label is not available, an average over the scores in the candidate label set is taken as a proxy to calculate the loss. Nguyen and Caruana [14] propose a risk minimization approach based on a non-convex max-margin loss for a partial label setting.

In this paper, we propose online algorithms for multiclass classification using partially labeled data. Perceptron [15] algorithm is one of the earliest online learning algorithms. Perceptron for multiclass classification is proposed in [7]. A unified framework for designing online update rules for multiclass classification was provided in [5]. An online variant of the support vector machine [17] called Pegasos is proposed in [16]. This algorithm is shown to achieve $O(\log T)$ *regret* (where T is the number of rounds). Once again, all these online approaches assume that we know the true label for each example.

Online multiclass learning with partial labels remained an unaddressed problem. In this paper, we propose several online multiclass algorithms using partial labels. Our key contributions in this paper are as follows.

1. We propose Avg Perceptron and Max Perceptron, which extensions of Perceptron to handle the partial labels. Similarly, we propose Avg Pagasos and Max Pegasos, which are extensions of the Pegasos algorithm.
2. We derive mistake bounds for Avg Perceptron in both separable and general cases. Similarly, we provide $\log(T)$ regret bound for Avg Pegasos.
3. We also provide thorough experimental validation of our algorithms using datasets of different dimensions and compare the performance of the proposed algorithms with standard multiclass Perceptron and Pegasos.

2 Multiclass Classification Using Partially Labeled Data

We now formally discuss the problem of multiclass classification given partially labeled training set. Let $\mathcal{X} \subseteq \mathbb{R}^d$ be the feature space from which the instances are drawn and let $\mathcal{Y} = \{1, \ldots, K\}$ be the output label space. Every instance $\mathbf{x} \in \mathcal{X}$ is associated with a candidate label set $Y \subseteq \mathcal{Y}$. The set of labels not present in the candidate label set is denoted by $\overline{Y}$. Obviously, $Y \cup \overline{Y} = [K]$.[1] The ground-truth label associated with $\mathbf{x}$ is denoted by lowercase y. It is assumed that the actual label lies within the set Y (i.e., $y \in Y$). The goal is to learn a classifier $h : \mathcal{X} \to \mathcal{Y}$. Let us assume that $h(\mathbf{x})$ is a linear classifier. Thus, $h(\mathbf{x})$ is parameterized by a matrix of weights $W \in \mathbb{R}^{d \times K}$ and is defined as $h(\mathbf{x}) = \arg\max_{i \in [K]} \mathbf{w}_i.\mathbf{x}$ where $\mathbf{w}_i$ (ith column vector of W) denotes the parameter vector corresponding to the ith class. Discrepancy between the true label and the predicted label is captured using 0–1 loss as $L_{0-1}(h(\mathbf{x}), y) = \mathbb{I}_{\{h(\mathbf{x}) \neq y\}}$. Here, $\mathbb{I}$ is the 0–1 indicator function, which evaluates to true when the condition mentioned is true and 0 otherwise. However, in the case of partial labels, we use partial (ambiguous) 0–1 loss [3] as follows.

$$L_A(h(\mathbf{x}), Y) = \mathbb{I}_{\{h(\mathbf{x}) \notin Y\}} \tag{1}$$

Minimizing L_A is difficult as it is not continuous. Thus, we use continuous surrogates for L_A. A convex surrogate of L_A is the *average prediction* hinge loss (APH) [3] which is defined as follows.

$$L_{APH}(h(\mathbf{x}), Y) = \left[1 - \frac{1}{|Y|} \sum_{i \in Y} \mathbf{w}_i.\mathbf{x} + \max_{j \notin Y} \mathbf{w}_j.\mathbf{x} \right]_+ \tag{2}$$

where $|Y|$ is the size of the candidate label set and $[a]_+ = \max(a, 0)$. L_{APH} is shown to be a convex surrogate of L_A in [4]. There is another non-convex surrogate loss function called the *max prediction* hinge loss (MPH) [14] that can be used for partial labels which is defined as follows:

$$L_{MPH}(h(\mathbf{x}), Y) = \left[1 - \max_{i \in Y} \mathbf{w}_i.\mathbf{x} + \max_{j \notin Y} \mathbf{w}_j.\mathbf{x} \right]_+ \tag{3}$$

In this paper, we present online algorithms based on stochastic gradient descent on L_{APH} and L_{MPH}.

3   Multiclass Perceptron Using Partial Labels

In this section, we propose two variants of multiclass Perceptron using partial labels. Let the instance observed at time t be $\mathbf{x}^t$ and its corresponding label set be Y^t. The weight matrix at time t is W^t and the ith column of W^t is denoted by $\mathbf{w}_i^t$. To update the weights, we propose two different schemes: (a) Avg Perceptron (using stochastic gradient descent on L_{APH}) and (b) Max Perceptron (using stochastic gradient descent on L_{MPH}). We use following sub-gradients of the L_{APH} and L_{MPH}.

---

[1] We denote the set $\{1, \ldots, K\}$ using $[K]$.

$$\nabla_{\mathbf{w}_k} L_{APH} = \begin{cases} 0, & \text{if } \frac{1}{|Y|} \sum_{i \in Y} \mathbf{w}_i.\mathbf{x} - \max_{j \in \overline{Y}} \mathbf{w}_j.\mathbf{x} \geq 1 \\ -\frac{\mathbf{x}}{|Y|}, & \text{if } \frac{1}{|Y|} \sum_{i \in Y} \mathbf{w}_i.\mathbf{x} - \max_{j \in \overline{Y}} \mathbf{w}_j.\mathbf{x} < 1 \\ & \text{and } k \in Y \\ \mathbf{x}, & \text{if } \frac{1}{|Y|} \sum_{i \in Y} \mathbf{w}_i.\mathbf{x} - \max_{j \in \overline{Y}} \mathbf{w}_j.\mathbf{x} < 1 \\ & \text{and } k = \arg\max_{j \in \overline{Y}} \mathbf{w}_j.\mathbf{x} \\ 0, & \text{if } \frac{1}{|Y|} \sum_{i \in Y} \mathbf{w}_i.\mathbf{x} - \max_{j \in \overline{Y}} \mathbf{w}_j.\mathbf{x} < 1 \\ & , k \in \overline{Y} \text{ and } k \neq \arg\max_{j \in \overline{Y}} \mathbf{w}_j.\mathbf{x} \end{cases} \quad (4)$$

$$\nabla_{\mathbf{w}_k} L_{MPH} = \begin{cases} 0, & \text{if } \max_{j \in Y} \mathbf{w}_j.\mathbf{x} - \max_{j \in \overline{Y}} \mathbf{w}_j.\mathbf{x} \geq 1 \\ -\mathbf{x}, & \text{if } \max_{j \in Y} \mathbf{w}_j.\mathbf{x} - \max_{j \in \overline{Y}} \mathbf{w}_j.\mathbf{x} < 1 \\ & \text{and } k = \arg\max_{i \in Y} \mathbf{w}_i.\mathbf{x} \\ \mathbf{x}, & \text{if } \max_{j \in Y} \mathbf{w}_j.\mathbf{x} - \max_{j \in \overline{Y}} \mathbf{w}_j.\mathbf{x} < 1 \\ & \text{and } k = \arg\max_{i \in \overline{Y}} \mathbf{w}_i.\mathbf{x} \end{cases} \quad (5)$$

We initialize the weight matrix as a matrix of zeros. At trial t, the update rule for $\mathbf{w}_i$ can be written as:

$$\mathbf{w}_i^{t+1} = \mathbf{w}_i^t - \eta \nabla_{\mathbf{w}_i} L(h^t(\mathbf{x}^t), Y^t)$$

where $\eta > 0$ is the step size and $\nabla_{\mathbf{w}_i} L(h^t(\mathbf{x}^t), Y^t)$ is found using Eq. (4) and (5). The complete description of Avg Perceptron and Max Perceptron is provided in Algorithm 1 and 2 respectively.

3.1   Mistake Bound Analysis

In the partial label setting, we say that mistake happens when the predicted class label for an example does not belong to its partial label set. We first define two variants of linear separability in a partial label setting as follows.

Definition 1 (Average Linear Separability in Partial Label Setting). Let $\{(\mathbf{x}^1, Y^1), \ldots, (\mathbf{x}^T, Y^T)\}$ be the training set for multiclass classification with partial labels. We say that the data is average linearly separable if there exist $\mathbf{w}_1, \ldots, \mathbf{w}_K \in \mathbb{R}^d$ such that

$$\frac{1}{|Y^t|} \sum_{i \in Y^t} \mathbf{w}_i.\mathbf{x}^t - \max_{j \in \overline{Y}^t} \mathbf{w}_j.\mathbf{x}^t \geq \gamma, \ \forall t \in [T].$$

Thus, average linear separability implies that $L_{APH}(h(\mathbf{x}^t), Y^t) = 0, \ \forall t \in [T]$.

Definition 2 (Max Linear Separability in Partial Label Setting). Let $\{(\mathbf{x}^1, Y^1), \ldots, (\mathbf{x}^T, Y^T)\}$ be the training set for multiclass classification with partial labels. We say that the data is max linearly separable if there exist $\mathbf{w}_1, \ldots, \mathbf{w}_K \in \mathbb{R}^d$ such that

$$\max_{i \in Y^t} \mathbf{w}_i.\mathbf{x}^t - \max_{j \in \overline{Y}^t} \mathbf{w}_j.\mathbf{x}^t \geq \gamma, \ \forall t \in [T].$$

Thus, max linear separability implies that $L_{MPH}(h(\mathbf{x}^t), Y^t) = 0, \ \forall t \in [T]$.

Algorithm 1. Avg Perceptron

Initialize $W^1 = 0$
for $t = 1$ to T **do**
    Get $\mathbf{x}^t$
    Predict $\hat{y}^t$ as $\hat{y}^t = \arg\max_{i \in [K]} \mathbf{w}_i^t.\mathbf{x}^t$
    Get the partial label set Y^t of $\mathbf{x}^t$
    Calculate loss $L_{APH}(h^t(\mathbf{x}^t), Y^t)$ using Eq. (2)
    if $L_{APH}(h^t(\mathbf{x}^t, Y^t) > 0$ **then**
        $\mathbf{w}_i^{t+1} = \mathbf{w}_i^t + \eta \tau_i^t \mathbf{x}^t$, $i \in [K]$ where

$$\tau_i^t = \begin{cases} \frac{1}{|Y^t|}, & i \in Y^t \\ -1, & i = \arg\max_{j \in \overline{Y}^t} \mathbf{w}_j^t.\mathbf{x}^t \\ 0, & \forall i \in \overline{Y}^t, i \neq \arg\max_{j \in \overline{Y}^t} \end{cases}$$

    else
        $\mathbf{w}_i^{t+1} = \mathbf{w}_i^t$, $\forall i \in [K]$
    end if
end for

We bound the number of mistakes made by Avg Perceptron (Algorithm 1) as follows.

Theorem 1 (Mistake Bound for Avg Perceptron Under Average Linear Separability). *Let* $(\mathbf{x}^1, Y^1), \ldots, (\mathbf{x}^T, Y^T)$ *be the examples presented to Avg Perceptron, where* $\mathbf{x}^t \in \mathbb{R}^d$ *and* $Y^t \subseteq [K]$. *Let* $W^* \in \mathbb{R}^{d \times K}$ ($\|W^*\| = 1$) *be such that* $\frac{1}{|Y^t|} \sum_{i \in Y^t} \mathbf{w}_i^*.\mathbf{x}^t - \max_{j \in \overline{Y}^t} \mathbf{w}_j^*.\mathbf{x}^t \geq \gamma$, $\forall t \in [T]$. *Then we get the following mistake bound for Avg Perceptron Algorithm.*

$$\sum_{t=1}^T L_A(h^t(\mathbf{x}^t), Y^t) \leq \frac{2}{\gamma^2} + \left[\frac{1}{c} + 1\right] \frac{R^2}{\gamma^2}$$

where $c = \min_t |Y^t|$, $R = \max_t \|\mathbf{x}^t\|$ *and* $\gamma \geq 0$ *is the margin of separation.*

The proof is given in Appendix A of [1]. We first notice that the bound is inversely proportional to the minimum label set size. This is intuitively obvious as the smaller the candidate label set size, the larger the chance of having a non-zero loss. When $c = 1$, the number of updates reduces to the normal multiclass Perceptron mistake bound for linearly separable data as given in [5]. Also, the number of mistakes is inversely proportional to γ^2. Linear separability (Definition 1) may not always hold for the training data. Thus, it is important to see how does the algorithm Avg Perceptron performs in such cases. We now bound the number of updates in T rounds for partially labeled data, which is linearly non-separable under L_{APH}.

Theorem 2 (Mistake Bound for Avg Perceptron in Non-Separable Case). *Let* $(\mathbf{x}^1, Y^1), \ldots, (\mathbf{x}^T, Y^T)$ *be an input sequence presented to Avg Perceptron. Let* W ($\|W\| = 1$) *be weight matrix corresponding to a multiclass*

Algorithm 2. Max Perceptron

Initialize $W^1 = 0$
for $t = 1$ to T **do**
    Get $\mathbf{x}^t$
    Predict $\hat{y}^t$ as $\hat{y}^t = \arg\max_{i \in [K]} \mathbf{w}_i^t.\mathbf{x}^t$
    Get the partial label set Y^t of $\mathbf{x}^t$
    Calculate loss $L_{MPH}(h^t(\mathbf{x}^t), Y^t)$ using Eq. (3)
    if $L_{MPH}(h^t(\mathbf{x}^t, Y^t) > 0$ **then**
       $\mathbf{w}_i^{t+1} = \mathbf{w}_i^t + \eta \tau_i^t \mathbf{x}^t$, $i \in [K]$ where

$$\tau_i^t = \begin{cases} 1, & \text{if } \max_{j \in Y} \mathbf{w}_j.\mathbf{x} - \max_{j \in \overline{Y}} \mathbf{w}_j.\mathbf{x} < 1 \\ & \text{and } i = \arg\max_{j \in Y} \mathbf{w}_j.\mathbf{x} \\ -1, & \text{if } \max_{j \in Y} \mathbf{w}_j.\mathbf{x} - \max_{j \in \overline{Y}} \mathbf{w}_j.\mathbf{x} < 1 \\ & \text{and } i = \arg\max_{j \in \overline{Y}} \mathbf{w}_j.\mathbf{x} \end{cases}$$

    else
       $\mathbf{w}_i^{t+1} = \mathbf{w}_i^t$, $\forall i \in [K]$
    end if
end for

---

classifier. Then for a fixed $\gamma > 0$, *let* $d^t = \max\left\{0, \gamma - [\frac{1}{|Y^t|}\sum_{i \in Y^t} \mathbf{w}_i.\mathbf{x}^t - \max_{j \in \overline{Y}^t} \mathbf{w}_j.\mathbf{x}^t]\right\}$. *Let* $D^2 = \sum_{t=1}^{T}(|Y^t|d^t)^2$ *and* $R = \max_{t \in [T]} ||\mathbf{x}^t||$ *and* $c = \min_{t \in [T]} |Y^t|$. *Then, mistakes bound for Avg Perceptron is as follows.*

$$\sum_{t=1}^{T} L_A(h^t(\mathbf{x}^t), Y^t) \le 2\frac{Z^2}{\gamma^2} + 2K\frac{R^2 + \Delta^2}{(\frac{\gamma}{Z})^2}$$

where $Z = \sqrt{1 + \frac{D^2}{\Delta^2}}$, $\Delta = \left[\frac{D^2 + KD^2R^2}{K}\right]^{\frac{1}{4}}$ *and* $K = [\frac{1}{c} + 1]$.

The proof is provided in the Appendix B of [1].

4   Online Multiclass Pegasos Using Partial Labels

Pegasos [16] is an online algorithm originally proposed for an exact label setting. In Pegasos, L_2 regularizer of the weights is minimized along with the hinge loss, making the overall objective function strongly convex. The strong convexity enables the algorithm to achieve a $O(\log T)$ regret in T trials. The objective function of the Pegasos at trial t is the following.

$$f(W, \mathbf{x}^t, Y^t) = \frac{\lambda}{2}||W||^2 + L(h(\mathbf{x}^t), Y^t)$$

Here, λ is a regularization constant and $||W||$ is Frobenius norm of the weight matrix. Let W^t be the weight matrix at the beginning of trial t. Then, W^{t+1} is found as $W^{t+1} = \Pi_B(W^t - \eta_t \nabla^t)$. Here $\nabla^t = \nabla_{W^t} f(W^t, \mathbf{x}^t, Y^t)$, η_t is the step size at trial t and Π_B is a projection operation onto the set B which is defined as $B = \{W : ||W|| \leq \frac{1}{\sqrt{\lambda}}\}$. Thus, $\Pi_B(W) = \min\{1, \frac{1}{(\lambda ||W||)}\}W$.

We now propose extension of Pegasos [16] for online multiclass learning using partially labeled data. We again propose two variants of Pegasos: (a) Avg Pegasos (using average prediction hinge loss (Eq. 2)) and (b) Max Pegasos (using max prediction hinge loss (Eq. (3)). We first note that ∇^t can be written as:

$$\nabla^t = \lambda W^t + \nabla_{W^t} L \tag{6}$$

where $\nabla_{W^t} L$ is given by Eq. (4) (for L_{APH}) and Eq. (5) (for L_{MPH}). Complete description of Avg Pegasos and Max Pegasos are given in Algorithm 3 and Algorithm 4 respectively.

Algorithm 3. Avg Pegasos

Input: λ, T
Initialize: W_1 s.t. $||W^1|| \leq \frac{1}{\sqrt{\lambda}}$
for $t = 1$ to T **do**
    Get $\mathbf{x}^t, Y^t$
    Set $\eta_t = \frac{1}{\lambda t}$
    Calculate loss $L_{APH}(h^t(\mathbf{x}^t), Y^t)$ using Eq. (2)
    if $L_{APH} > 0$ **then**
        $W^{t+\frac{1}{2}} = (1 - \eta_t \lambda)W^t - \eta_t \nabla_W L_{APH}$ where $\nabla_W L_{APH}$ is given by Eq. (4)
        $W^{t+1} = \min\{1, \frac{1/\sqrt{\lambda}}{||W^{t+\frac{1}{2}}||}\}W^{t+\frac{1}{2}}$
    else
        $W^{t+1} = W^t$
    end if
end for
Output: W^T

4.1 Regret Bound Analysis of Avg Pegasos

We now derive the regret bound for Avg Pegasos.

Theorem 3. *Let* $(\mathbf{x}^1, Y^1), (\mathbf{x}^2, Y^1), \ldots, (\mathbf{x}^T, Y^T)$ *be an input sequence where* $\mathbf{x}^t \in \mathbb{R}^d$ *and* $Y^t \subseteq [K]$. *Let* $R = \max_t ||\mathbf{x}^t||$. *Then the regret of Avg Pegasos is given as:*

$$\frac{1}{T} \sum_{t=1}^{T} f(W^t, \mathbf{x}^t, Y^t) - \min_W \frac{1}{T} \sum_{t=1}^{T} f(W, \mathbf{x}^t, Y^t) \leq \frac{G^2 \ln T}{\lambda T}$$

where $G = \sqrt{\lambda} + \sqrt{1 + \frac{1}{c}}R$ *and* $c = \min_t |Y^t|$

The proof is given in Appendix C of [1]. We again see the regret is inversely proportional to the size of the minimum candidate label set.

Algorithm 4. Max Pegasos

Input: λ, T
Initialize: W_1 s.t. $||W^1|| \leq \frac{1}{\sqrt{\lambda}}$
for $t = 1$ to T **do**
   Get $\mathbf{x}^t, Y^t$
   Set $\eta_t = \frac{1}{\lambda t}$
   Calculate loss $L_{MPH}(h^t(\mathbf{x}^t), Y^t)$ using Eq. (3)
   if $L_{APH} > 0$ **then**
      $W^{t+\frac{1}{2}} = (1 - \eta_t \lambda)W^t - \eta_t \nabla_W L_{MPH}$ where $\nabla_W L_{MPH}$ is given by Eq. (5)
      $W^{t+1} = \min\{1, \frac{1/\sqrt{\lambda}}{||W^{t+\frac{1}{2}}||}\}W^{t+\frac{1}{2}}$
   else
      $W^{t+1} = W^t$
   end if
end for
Output: W^T

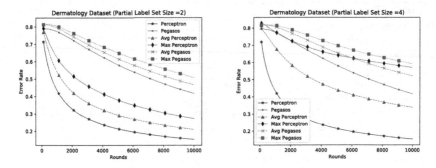

Fig. 1. Dermatology dataset results

5 Experiments

We now describe the experimental results. We perform experiments on Ecoli, Satimage, Dermatology, and USPS datasets (available on UCI repository [6]) and MNIST dataset [12]. We perform experiments using the proposed algorithms Avg Perceptron, Max Perceptron, Avg Pegasos, and Max Pegasos. For benchmarking, we use Perceptron and Pegasos based on exact labels.

For all the datasets, the candidate or partial label set for each instance contains the true label and some labels selected uniformly at random from the remaining labels. After every trial, we find the average mis-classification rate (average of L_{0-1} loss over examples seen till that trial) is calculated with respect to the true label. This sets a hard evaluation criteria for the algorithms. The number of rounds for each dataset is selected by observing when the error curves start to converge. For every dataset, we repeat the process of generating partial label sets and plotting the error curves 100 times and average the instantaneous error rates across the 100 runs. The final plots for each dataset have the average instantaneous error rate on the Y-axis and the number of rounds on the X-axis.

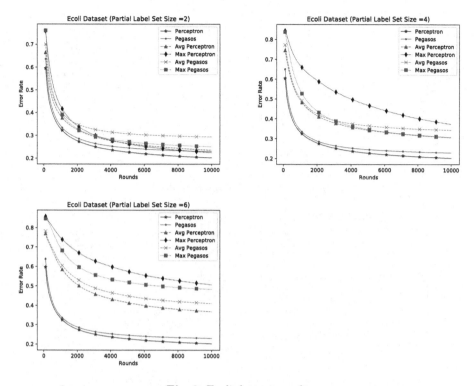

Fig. 2. Ecoli dataset results

For every dataset, we plot the error rate curves for all the algorithms for different candidate label set sizes. This helps us in understanding how the online algorithms behave as the candidate label set size increases. For the Dermatology dataset, which contains six classes, we take candidate labels sets of sizes 2 and 4, respectively, as shown in Fig. 1. We see that the average prediction loss based algorithms perform the better in both cases. The results for the Ecoli dataset for candidate label sets of size 2, 4 and 6 are shown in Fig. 2. Here, we find that the Max Pegasos algorithm performs comparably to the algorithms based on the Average Prediction Loss for candidate labels set sizes 2 and 4. But for candidate label set size 8, the Max Prediction Loss performs significantly worse than the Average Prediction Loss based algorithm. The results for Satimage and USPS datasets are shown in Fig. 3 and 4 respectively. For Satimage, the Max Pegasos performs the best for label set of size 2. But for label set size 4, the Average Prediction Loss based algorithms perform much better. For USPS, we see that though for candidate labels set sizes 2 and 4, the Max Perceptron and Max Pegasos perform better than our algorithms, for label set sizes 6 and 8, the Average Prediction Loss based algorithms perform much better. The results for MNIST are provided in Fig. 5. Here we observe the Max Perceptron and Max Pegasos performs much better than the other algorithms for label set sizes 2 and 4. However, for label set sizes 6 and 8, the Average Pegasos performs best.

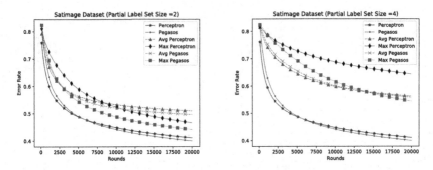

Fig. 3. Satimage dataset results

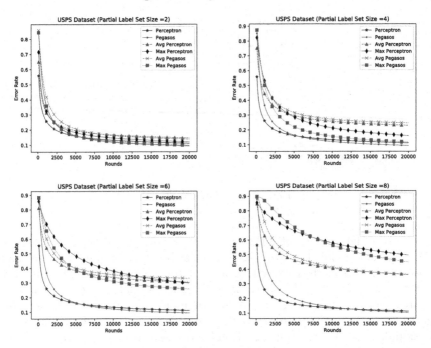

Fig. 4. USPS dataset results

Overall, we see that for smaller labels set sizes, the Max Prediction Loss performs quite well. However, the Average Prediction Loss shows the best for larger candidate label set sizes. Studying the convergence and theoretical properties of the non-convex Max Prediction Loss can be an exciting future direction for exploration.

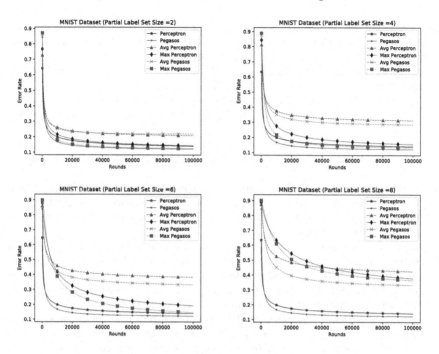

Fig. 5. MNIST dataset results

6   Conclusion

In this paper, we proposed online algorithms for classifying partially labeled data. This is very useful in real-life scenarios when multiple annotators give different labels for the same instance. We presented algorithms based on the Perceptron and Pegasos. We also provide mistake bounds for the Perceptron based algorithm and the regret bound for the Pegasos based algorithm. We also provide an experimental comparison of all the algorithms on various datasets. The results show that though the Average Prediction Loss is convex, the non-convex Max Prediction Loss can also be useful for small labels set sizes. Providing a theoretical analysis for the Max Prediction Loss can be a useful endeavor in the future.

References

1. Bhattacharjee, R., Manwani, N.: Online algorithms for multiclass classification using partial labels. arXiv e-prints arXiv:1912.11367, December 2019
2. Chen, Y., Patel, V.M., Chellappa, R., Phillips, P.J.: Ambiguously labeled learning using dictionaries. IEEE Trans. Inf. Forensics Secur. **9**(12), 2076–2088 (2014)
3. Cour, T., Sapp, B., Taskar, B.: Learning from partial labels. J. Mach. Learn. Res. **12**, 1501–1536 (2011)

4. Cour, T., Sapp, B., Jordan, C., Taskar, B.: Learning from ambiguously labeled images. In: Proceedings of the IEEE Computer Society Conference on Computing Vision and Pattern Recognition, pp. 919–926 (2009)
5. Crammer, K., Singer, Y.: Ultraconservative online algorithms for multiclass problems. J. Mach. Learn. Res. **3**, 951–991 (2003)
6. Dua, D., Graff, C.: UCI machine learning repository (2017)
7. Duda, R., Hart, P.: Pattern Classification and Scene Analysis. Wiley, New York (1973)
8. Feng, L., An, B.: Partial label learning with self-guided retraining. In: Proceedings of the 33rd AAAI Conference on Artificial Intelligence, pp. 3542–3549. AAAI Press (2019)
9. Grandvalet, Y., Bengio, Y.: Learning from partial labels with minimum entropy. Center for Interuniversity Research and Analysis of Organizations (2004)
10. Hüllermeier, E., Beringer, J.: Learning from ambiguously labeled examples. Intell. Data Anal. **10**(5), 419–439 (2006)
11. Jin, R., Ghahramani, Z.: Learning with multiple labels. In: Becker, S., Thrun, S., Obermayer, K. (eds.) Advances in Neural Information Processing Systems, pp. 921–928. MIT Press, Cambridge (2003)
12. LeCun, Y., Bottou, L., Bengio, Y., Haffner, P.: Gradient-based learning applied to document recognition. Proc. IEEE **86**(11), 2278–2324 (1998)
13. Liu, L., Dietterich, T.: A conditional multinomial mixture model for superset label learning. In: Bartlett, P., Pereira, F.C.N., Burges, C.J.C., Bottou, L., Weinberger, K.Q. (eds.) Advances in Neural Information Processing Systems, pp. 557–565. MIT Press, Cambridge (2012)
14. Nguyen, N., Caruana, R.: Classification with partial labels. In: Proceedings of the 14th ACM SIGKDD International Conference on Knowledge Discovery Data Mining, pp. 551–559 (2008)
15. Rosenblatt, F.: The perceptron: a probabilistic model for information storage and organization in the brain. Psychol. Rev. **65**, 386–407 (1958)
16. Shalev-Shwartz, S., Singer, Y., Srebro, N.: Pegasos: primal estimated sub-gradient solver for SVM. In: Proceedings of the International Conference on Machine Learning (ICML) (2007)
17. Smola, A.J., Schölkopf, B.: A tutorial on support vector regression. Stat. Comput. **14**(3), 199–222 (2004)
18. Vannoorenberghe, P., Smets, P.: Partially supervised learning by a **Credal EM** approach. In: Godo, L. (ed.) ECSQARU 2005. LNCS (LNAI), vol. 3571, pp. 956–967. Springer, Heidelberg (2005). https://doi.org/10.1007/11518655_80
19. Xie, M.K., Huang, S.J.: Partial multi-label learning. In: Thirty-Second AAAI Conference on Artificial Intelligence (AAAI 2018), pp. 1–8 (2018)
20. Yu, F., Zhang, M.-L.: Maximum margin partial label learning. Mach. Learn. **106**(4), 573–593 (2016). https://doi.org/10.1007/s10994-016-5606-4
21. Zhang, M.L., Yu, F.: Solving the partial label learning problem: an instance-based approach. In: Yang, Q., Wooldridge, M. (eds.) Proceedings of the 24th International Conference on Artificial Intelligence, pp. 4048–4054. AAAI Press (2015)
22. Zhang, M.L., Yu, F., Tang, C.Z.: Disambiguation-free partial label learning. IEEE Trans. Knowl. Data Eng. **29**(10), 2155–2167 (2017)

What's in a Gist? Towards an Unsupervised Gist Representation for Few-Shot Large Document Classification

Jaron Mar$^{(\boxtimes)}$ and Jiamou Liu

The University of Auckland, Auckland, New Zealand
{jaron.mar,jiamou.liu}@auckland.ac.nz

Abstract. The gist can be viewed as an abstract concept that represents only the quintessential meaning derived from a single or multiple sources of information. We live in an age where vast quantities of information are widely available and easily accessible. Identifying the gist contextualises information which facilitates the fast disambiguation and prediction of related concepts bringing about a set of natural relationships defined between information sources. In this paper, we investigate and introduce a novel unsupervised gist extraction and quantification framework that represents a computational form of the gist based on notions from fuzzy trace theory. To evaluate our purposed framework, we apply the gist to the task of semantic similarity, specifically to few-shot large document classification where documents on average have a large number of words. The results show our proposed gist representation can effectively capture the essential information from a text document while dramatically reducing the features used.

Keywords: Semantic representation · Few-shot learning · Unsupervised learning

1 Introduction

The gist can be viewed as an abstract concept that represents only the quintessential meaning derived from a single or multiple sources of information such as images or text. This brings into question how can an abstract concept such as the gist be computationally extracted and quantified? Due to this abstract nature, there does not exist a common formalism of the gist in psychology, computational linguistics or NLP. In computational linguistics the notion of gist appears in gist preservation for discourse [22] and gisting or summarisation [18]. Our view of the gist differs from these works in the sense that we view the gist as a very high level but low dimensional semantic representation of a text which can novelly be quantified as a real number known as the *gist score*. To evaluate the predictive capabilities of the gist score we experimentally applying our representation to few-shot document classification and compare

© Springer Nature Switzerland AG 2020
H. W. Lauw et al. (Eds.): PAKDD 2020, LNAI 12084, pp. 261–274, 2020.
https://doi.org/10.1007/978-3-030-47426-3_21

the results to existing classical and few-shot classifiers. In particular, we focus on the classification of large documents where documents on average are comprised of thousands of words. Standard datasets for document classification such as Yelp, IMDB, Reuters, etc. contain documents with only hundreds of words on average. As such, few works evaluate large document classification partly due to the fact that neural-based models have large memory requirements to train over documents with large numbers of words or are only trained using sections of the document. Intuition also tells us that extracting and quantifying the gist of a document should be more accurate in longer documents.

Few-shot or N-shot learning is a recent paradigm of learning originally applied in computer vision with high levels of success [7]. There has been recent interest in applying this methodology to NLP however the nature of language makes the complexity of few-shot learning more difficult. Many approaches to few-shot learning employ some form of transfer or meta-learning which requires supervised learning over related classes. However, in a real-world application where N-shot learning could be applied, it is also unlikely that suitable labelled training data of related classes will exist. Therefore, taking an unsupervised approach to few-shot learning is arguably more important and we show that few-shot learning in NLP can be approached in an unsupervised way by determining the semantic similarity based on our purposed method using the gist score. The fundamental difference in our approach compared to few-shot approaches in computer vision can be seen in the following problem formulations.

Typical Few-Shot Problem Formulation: Given a set of labelled training examples $\mathcal{X}^{train}$ with classes $\mathcal{Y}^{train}$. The goal is to create a model that acquires knowledge from the training examples such that the knowledge facilitates the prediction of the test set $\mathcal{X}^{test}$ using a few (N) labelled examples of each class in $\mathcal{Y}^{test}$ and classes in $\mathcal{Y}^{test}$ are disjoint but related to those in $\mathcal{Y}^{train}$.

Our Few-Shot Problem Formulation: In a more restrictive but more realistic scenario where given only the test set $\mathcal{X}^{test}$ to classify and N examples of each class from $\mathcal{Y}^{test}$ the goal is to predict the classes of $\mathcal{X}^{test}$ i.e. perform unsupervised N-shot learning.

Contributions and Paper Organisation: This paper presents two main contributions listed in the order they are described in the paper. (1) We propose an unsupervised gist representation that provides a link between psychology and computational linguistics which allows for the extraction and quantification of the gist from a text. This acts as a first step towards a possible computational model of FTT. (2) We apply the gist score to few-shot large document classification and experimentally show that our gist representation performs as well as centroid based similarity measures and better than traditional baseline algorithms while effectively only using a one-dimensional representation for each word. This has significant implications towards the dimensionality required for word embeddings by suggesting it is possible to train a greatly reduced embedding while still retaining high accuracy in downstream tasks.

2   Related Works

The concept of the gist is predominately found in cognitive and psychological contexts observing the manifestation of gist in human behaviour [15]. The concept of gist can also be found in artificial intelligence to explain norm emergence using gist information [10] and for summarising image information using gist descriptors [6], few works attempt to computationally quantify the gist in language. Many computational models were inspired by cognitive models which have been developed and studied in psychology. Our work is closely related to the psychological notion of fuzzy-trace theory (FTT), a well-founded theory that states that reasoning occurs on simple gists rather than exact details [4]. Underlying FTT are seven key principles, the first being gist extraction which is the task of reducing information to its essence. In FTT, it is hypothesised there are two cognitive systems of memory, the verbatim memory and the gist memory. The verbatim memory acts to retain detailed information whereas the gist memory acts to retain only the quintessential information. Therefore, assuming a sequential memory model the gist memory can be thought of as a compressed representation of the verbatim memory. In this paper, we explore a computational model for FTT that allows for the extraction and inference of the gist based on the underlying principles of FTT.

In NLP, gist extraction has previously been defined as a statistical problem where the goal is to infer $P(gist|words)$ using a generative model for language [9] where the gist is seen as a latent variable. In particular, latent Dirichlet allocation (LDA) [2] a generative topic model assumes that the distribution of the gist over topics is drawn from a Dirichlet distribution. The topic model presents a very structured representation that assumes there exists a strict predefined latent structure and dependencies on how the language was generated, our work differs from this as it assumes no such structure and no distribution over topics. Furthermore, the gist generated from these generative models have no direct application to other downstream tasks. In this paper, we apply our notion of the gist to document classification, the task of determining and assigning the classes of documents. This is an important and well-studied task in NLP with applications in information retrieval and spam identification with many different approaches from term frequency [12], state vector machines (SVM) [11], current state of the art neural-based methods [24] and recent few-shot learning approaches [8,23].

3   Gist Representation Framework

Intuitively, the gist of a text represents the singular most important semantic meaning that is representative of the overall text. We therefore define the *gist score* as a real number which encapsulates the above notion by condensing the semantic information of a text. The intuition behind such a compressed representation for the gist score is based on two psychological notions. The first notion being the *fuzzy-to-verbatim continua* [4] which states that the that people encode multiple representations at varying levels of precision along the fuzzy-to-verbatim continua, this suggests that information can be encoded as a real number. The second notion is a phenomenon displayed in humans known as *fuzzy processing preference* [5] which states that to make decisions they will use the least precise gist representation which allows for faster inferencing. If a human were to judge the similarity between two vectors of multiple dimensions or two real numbers, at a glance a human can easily determine the difference between two numbers.

This section will outline the intricacies around the seemingly simple gist representation framework proposed in Algorithm 1 motivated by an example to produce the gist embeddings in Fig. 1 using two chapters, C029 (red) and C002 (orange) from a medical textbook and the zebra Wikipedia page (purple) from datasets used in Sect. 5.1.

Algorithm 1. Gist Extraction Framework, GistEmbedding($T, size$)

Input: Text T, Segmentation size
Output: 1-Dimensional gist embedding of each word

1: $T \leftarrow preprocess(T)$
2: $embeddingArray \leftarrow embed(T)$
3: $segments \leftarrow segment(embeddingSet, size)$
4: $embeddingArray \leftarrow centroid(segments)$
5: $gist \leftarrow reduce1Dim(embeddingArray)$

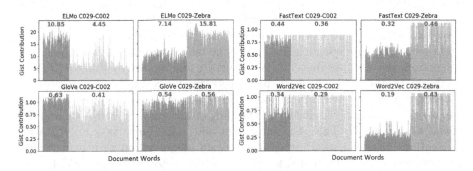

Fig. 1. Gist embeddings and scores with varying embedding methods for the verbatim memory. (Color figure online)

3.1 Modelling the Verbatim Memory via Semantic Embeddings

In FTT, verbatim representations are detailed and precise representations of complete and exact information. To model text as a verbatim representation, line 2 of the algorithm we use semantic embeddings, particularly word embeddings as it gives the highest level of granularity. In this paper we investigate popular word embedding models ELMo [20], FastText [3], GloVe [19] and Word2Vec [16] to determine which models are suitable for uncovering the gist using widely available pretrained models for each.

3.2 Verbatim to Gist Representation via Dimensionality Reduction

The gist only needs to represent the quintessential meaning, we aim to encapsulate only this essential semantic meaning by radically reducing the verbatim representation to one dimension using principal component analysis (PCA). Applying dimensionality reduction to embeddings is not uncommon and has been used as a post-processing step to reduce the size of the embeddings while still maintaining the quality of the embeddings when applied to downstream tasks [21] but the degree of reduction is not as radical.

It has long been known that the word frequency in language follows a power law distribution [25] which suggests that the embedding set generated from these words will also follow a power law distribution, especially in large documents. Given a centred word embedding set, a PCA to one dimension creates a linear projection such that the variance of the first principal component $\vec{p}$ is maximized for $\frac{1}{n}\sum_i^n (\vec{e_i} \cdot \vec{p})^2$ where e_i is the embedding for word i which in turn minimizes the mean squared error (MSE). Since PCA aims to minimize the MSE and the embedding set follows a power law distribution where a relatively small set of common words occur often, then intuitively p will be chosen such that the MSE is minimized for these common word embeddings. When p is chosen in this way the projected value for the common words will have a lower value as they contribute less to the variation on the first principal component. Conversely, the unique words that corroborate more closely to the gist will have a higher value in the resultant PCA. For example, when reducing the combined C002-C029 texts to 1-dimension via PCA using Word2Vec embeddings the words "patients", "physicians" and "clinicians" have the highest values in both the C002 and C029 segments. Figure 1 shows the result of a PCA on our example in which the global structure is preserved.

3.3 Quantifying and Extracting the Gist Score

Quantify the gist score from the gist embedding can be achieved simply by taking the average of the segment that corresponds to each document in the embedding as shown in bold red font in Fig. 1. To better understand what the average captures and how it can capture the gist, suppose we can treat the gist embeddings in Fig. 1 as values from a sample population that are drawn from a semantic distribution over words. Kernel density estimation (KDE), a non-parametric technique that estimates the probability density function (PDF) applied to the values of the gist embedding gives the probability of sampling a word or segment with a given gist contribution value. The KDE plot will uncover the underlying gist contribution distribution and thus the underlying semantic similarity of words from the original embedding set.

Evaluating the KDEs in Fig. 2 based on embeddings generated in Fig. 1 we see using ELMo embeddings it is obvious that the KDE based on C029-Zebra produces a bimodal distribution showing the existence of two classes, whereas C029-C002 is unimodal showing that these documents are highly similar. Therefore, when average and evaluating the distance been the gist scores the distance

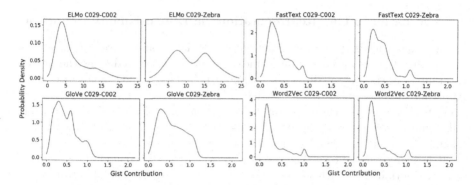

Fig. 2. Equivalent KDE plots with a Gaussian kernel and Scott's bandwidth selection for Fig. 1.

between C029-C002 and C029-Zebra should be lower because of the differences in the distributions, which is the case with values of 6.40 and 8.67. Comparing the gist embedding using Word2Vec and PCA we see that the distributions look almost identical due to the nature of having a single embedding for each word. The key difference is that the mode representing the highest values at $x = 1$ representing the unique words are spread across both documents in the C029-C002 gist embedding and only these values only occur in the zebra document in the C029-Zebra case as shown in Fig. 1 which gives the gist scores 0.05 and 0.24.

3.4   Uncovering the Underlying Gist via Segment Centroids

Producing a gist embedding over all words can uncover the gist by taking into account all the semantic information however, to capture the gist the importance of individual words is low and can introduce noise. A key principle of FTT states the gist can be encoded at different levels of fuzziness along the fuzzy-to-verbatim continua. Therefore, to investigate further fuzzy gist representations we introduce a method that approximates the gist embedding at a less granular level by taking gist embeddings over centroids of partitioned segments from the text.

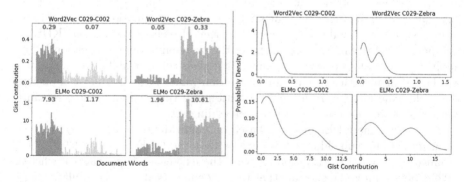

Fig. 3. Gist embedding with score (left) and corresponding KDE (right) with segment size of 50.

Figure 3 displays the effects on the gist embedding and KDE plots with a segmentation size of 50. The relationship between the gist score between highly related classes C029 and C002 becomes less distinguishable in the sense that the difference in the gist score becomes large. However, the KDEs unveil an underlying semantic difference in the distributions. In both KDEs, we see the possible existence of two classes displayed by the unimodal distributions but in both cases C029-C002 there is a higher degree of overlap between the documents displayed by the unevenness of the modes.

4   Gist Score Similarity for N-Shot Document Classification

Determining the semantic similarity between documents via N-shot learning involves solving multiple instances of a decision task given a *support set*, a small set of labelled documents $S = \{S_{C_1}, S_{C_2}, ..., S_{C_i}\}$ where S_{C_i} represents the labelled documents for class i and $|S_{c_i}| = N$ and a *query set*, $Q = \{q_1, q_2, ..., q_n\}$ of n unlabelled document to predict which is equivalent to a test set. We can define a similarity decision instance in the style of a N-shot learning instance or episode as follows:

Similarity Decision Instance: Given a single query document from the query set and a set of support documents, the goal is to match the query document to the most related support document based on some semantic aspect e.g. meaning or topic.

Based on this definition, Algorithms 2 and 3 outline the procedure to perform N-shot document classification using the gist score. Fundamentally, document classification involves determining the semantic similarity between documents which has been argued to fundamentally be a cognitive modelling problem [14]. Therefore, to some extent computational semantic similarity measures should align to some aspect of human judgement which we aim to do by aligning our method towards principals in FTT. As such, we explore the use of two types of gist known as the local and global gist to compute the gist score. It has been proposed that the gist can be differentiated into two types, the global gist which captures the meaning of an entire event as a whole and the local gist which captures the meaning of a more discrete event [17]. To some extent determining the semantic similarity between documents in a few-shot learning instance should involve both the global and local gist, In Algorithm 3 we employ the local gist to capture the discrete pairwise gist between the query and support documents whereas the global gist captures the query document in relation to the entire support set.

Algorithm 2. Gist Score Extraction, $GSE(d_1, d_2, ..., d_n, size)$

Input: Documents set $d_{i:n}$, Segmentation size
Output: Gist score for each input document $d_{i:n}$
1: $text \leftarrow concatenate(d_1, d_2, ..., d_n)$ ▷ join all text together
2: $gistEmbed \leftarrow gistEmbedding(text, size)$
3: **for** i in 1 to n **do**
4:    $score_{d_i} \leftarrow average(gistEmbed[d_i])$ ▷ segment in embedding related to text d_i
5: **return** $score_{d_1}, score_{d_2}, ..., score_{d_n}$

Algorithm 3. Gist Score Similarity N-Shot Instance, $GSS(q, S_{C_1}, S_{C_2}, ..., S_{C_n}, size)$

Input: Query document q, Support documents $S_{C_{1:n}}$, Segment size
Output: Probability of q belonging to each class $C_{1:n}$
1: $global \leftarrow GSE(q, S_{C_1}, S_{C_2}, ..., S_{C_n}, size)$ ▷ consider gist across all support texts
2: **for** i in 1 to n **do**
3:    **for** $document$ in S_{C_i} **do**   ▷ extract pairwise gist similarity
4:        $local_{q, S_{C_i}} \leftarrow GSE(q, document, size)$
5:    $gist_{q, S_{C_i}} \leftarrow average(local_{q, S_{C_i}}, global_{q, S_{C_i}})$
6: **return** $softmax(-gist_q, S_{C_1}, -gist_q, S_{C_1}, ..., -gist_q, S_{C_n})$ ▷ probability of classes

---

5   Experiments

To evaluate our approach to gist extraction and reasoning we perform a series of experiments to analyse the inferencing capabilities of the gist score and baseline algorithms for few-shot learning on large documents, identify the importance of the local and global gists towards inferencing and the effect segments size in our framework has on uncovering the underlying semantic distribution.

5.1   Datasets

Popular benchmark datasets for document classification typically consist of a large number of documents with a low average number of words per document. For our experiments, we use a combination of documents collections typically used as benchmark datasets for topic segmentation[1]. These documents on average have a large number of words but also a mix of small and large documents as shown in Table 1.

Table 1. Statistics for datasets.

	Documents	Minimum words	Maximum words	Average words	Total words
Wiki animal	214	162	15696	3885	831480
Clinical	227	353	14750	2648	601171
Fiction	82	4578	53494	33542	2750472
Physics	33	6325	7956	7155	236127

---

[1] Dataset available at https://github.com/JaronMar/Large-Document-Dataset.

5.2   Baseline Algorithms

For baseline algorithms, we compare both few-shot document classification, distance-based classifiers and traditional document classification algorithms trained only on the N examples of each class. To compare the few-shot learning baseline algorithms we perform N-way N-shot learning with minimal pretraining to evaluate how existing models perform when access to labelled data is restrictive.

WCD: Word Centroid Distances using ELMo embedding which is an approximation of word movers distance (WMD) [13]. We apply WCD as the restrictive time complexity of n^3 to calculate the full WMD is infeasible for large documents.

Centroid: Applies a traditional but effective semantic distance measure using the euclidean distance between ELMo document centroids.

SVM: Support vector machine with linear kernel [11] using term frequency (TF-IDF) features. The penalty parameters were optimised for using grid search.

HAN: Hierarchical Attention Network trained using the same ELMo embeddings as RD$_{WCD}$ [24]. Due to memory constraints, we train 150000 features using 50 sentences per document, 20 words per sentence over 20 epochs.

Proto: Prototypical network is a few-shot method that meta-learns to minimizes the squared Euclidean distance between the centroid of each class to its training examples in a metric/embedding space [23].

MAML: Model-Agnostic Meta-Learning is a few-shot method that meta-learns a prior over model parameters which allows the model to quickly adapt to unseen classes [8] where we set the number of inner steps to 5.

6   Results

We perform two sets of experiments; one performs binary classification on the animal and clinical datasets and the other multiclass classification using all datasets. The results show the average using the same randomly seeded support documents.

Tables 2 and 3 display the results for 1-shot classification with segment size of 50 using GSS. The results show that our proposed gist representation retains the full expressiveness of the centroid classifier and even slightly improves on the accuracy while heavily reducing the number of features. This result suggests we can accurately extract and represent the gist in large text documents. Interestingly, although taking different approaches to judge the semantic distance our result aligns closely to that of the centroid classifier. We also see both SVM and HAN, traditional document classification algorithms are not suitable for one-shot classification and report the two worst results in both cases. As for the few-shot algorithms we see that with minimal pretraining both classifiers are out performed by the unsupervised distance-based classifiers.

Table 2. Binary 1-shot classification results.

	Accuracy	Precision	Recall	F_1
WCD	0.8238	0.7521	0.9811	0.8515
Centroid	0.9807	**0.9890**	0.9724	0.9784
SVM	0.6696	0.6420	0.8097	0.7162
HAN	0.7791	0.8325	0.7796	0.7392
Proto	0.8503	0.7366	**0.9978**	0.8475
MAML	0.4852	0.5351	0.4852	0.4852
GSS_{ELMo}	**0.9814**	0.9709	0.993	**0.9813**
GSS_{W2V}	0.9093	0.8974	0.9322	0.9094
GSS_{GloVe}	0.5961	0.5754	0.7519	0.6434
GSS_{FT}	0.7429	0.7229	0.8	0.7555

Table 3. Multiclass 1-shot classification results.

	Accuracy	Precision	Recall	F_1
WCD	0.8531	0.9041	0.8678	0.8703
Centroid	0.9552	**0.9274**	**0.9718**	**0.9430**
SVM	0.5631	0.6864	0.7200	0.6398
HAN	0.7538,	0.7803	0.7842	0.7295
Proto	0.7803	0.7069	0.8554	0.6938
MAML	0.4010	0.2249	0.2830	0.1987
GSS_{ELMo}	**0.9573**	0.9251	0.9705	0.9406
GSS_{W2V}	0.9385	0.9163	0.9503	0.9258
GSS_{GloVe}	0.9160	0.8998	0.9346	0.9074
GSS_{FT}	0.8950	0.8792	0.9198	0.8819

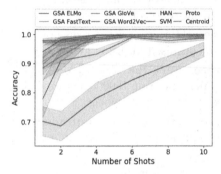

Fig. 4. Few-shot binary accuracy.   **Fig. 5.** Few-shot multiclass accuracy.

When increasing the number of shots (N) from 1 to 10 in Fig. 4 and 5 we expect all classifiers to generally improve. This statement holds true especially for the traditional SVM model that slowly increases the performance with more training data. In general, across all experiments GSS using ELMo performs consistently better compared to GSS with other embedding types suggesting the ELMo embeddings are semantically more meaningful. Our result also suggests for large documents we can achieve high levels of accuracy using just a single example of each class using unsupervised methods in NLP.

6.1 Effects of Segmentation

Section 3.4 shows that quantifying the gist over segment centroids can unveil an underlying semantic distribution. Figure 6 and 7 display the effects segment size has on capturing this underlying distribution based on different embedding types. The results show that segment size can significantly improve that initially under-performing GloVe and FastText models to be more comparable but still not better than ELMo and Word2Vec based embeddings. Interestingly, this aligns with psychological experiments where fuzzier gist-based representations are better from making decisions rather than verbatim representations [1]. In both cases, we see that ELMo embeddings are robust in the sense that the accuracy is not greatly affected when the segment size is changed one again. More significantly, when the segment size is one we still get relatively high accuracy for both ELMo and Word2Vec embeddings. This implies that theses embeddings are semantically more meaningful and it is possible to represent each word embedding as a single real number and still achieve accurate results in large document classification. This is a significant implication as in general nearly all the features in the original embeddings are lost in creating the gist embedding however our results show that we can still capture the semantic similarity between documents. This suggests for certain tasks we can feasible train lower dimensional embeddings thus reducing training time and the memory requirements associated with handling large sets of embeddings.

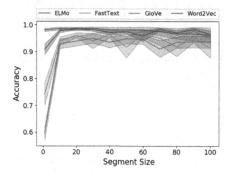

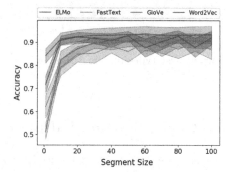

Fig. 6. Segmentation on the binary case.   **Fig. 7.** Segmentation on the multiclass case.

6.2 Importance of Local and Global Gists

In Sect. 4 we introduced the concept of the global and local gists and provided a method to extract both of these gists to create the gist score for a given few-shot classification instance. The results in Fig. 8 and 9 show that generally the local gist is more effective to perform inferencing on over the global gist in both binary and multiclass classification. This makes sense as the local gist captures the discrete differences between two documents which is a more direct measure for classification opposed to the global gist. When naively combining the local and global gists by averaging, in binary classification the combined gist performs within 2–4% better or worse than the local gist whereas in the multiclass case the combined gist performs 2–20% better in all cases. Once again, intuition tells us that when there are more classes to compare the global or contextual comparison becomes more important as reflected in the results. This suggests that as the number of classes or size of the support set increases evaluating the pairwise semantic similarity is not sufficient and global or contextual information about other classes can improve accuracy. From a psychological standpoint based on the fuzzy-preference theory, in general the combined gist is the preferred gist representation along the fuzzy-to-verbatim continua which although isn't that fuzziest representation provides still provide the most information needed for inferencing.

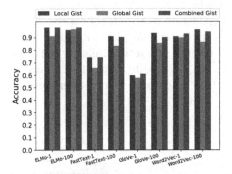 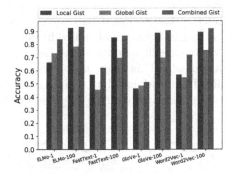

Fig. 8. Gist types on the 1-shot binary case.

Fig. 9. Gist types on the 1-shot multi-class case.

7   Conclusion and Future Work

In this paper, we critically reduce the size of word embeddings from their original size of 300–1000 dimensions each to one dimension to create a gist representation based on psychological notions that successfully encapsulates the essential semantic information for few-shot large document classification. As future work, in this paper we assumed a sequential memory model in which the gist representation is created from the verbatim representation, but it is theorised that the gist and verbatim representations are created in parallel in FTT. It would be interesting to explore a model which learns both the verbatim and gist represents of words simultaneously as our work shows that one-dimensional gist representations for words are sufficient for large document classification and can be created from higher dimensional word embeddings, such a representation would be beneficial for memory constrained environments.

References

1. Abadie, M., Waroquier, L., Terrier, P.: Gist memory in the unconscious-thought effect. Psychol. Sci. **24**(7), 1253–1259 (2013)
2. Blei, D.M., Ng, A.Y., Jordan, M.I.: Latent dirichlet allocation. J. Mach. Learn. Res. **3**, 993–1022 (2003)
3. Bojanowski, P., Grave, E., Joulin, A., Mikolov, T.: Enriching word vectors with subword information. Trans. Assoc. Comput. Linguist. **5**, 135–146 (2017)

4. Brainerd, C.J., Reyna, V.F.: Gist is the grist: fuzzy-trace theory and the new intuitionism. Dev. Rev. **10**(1), 3–47 (1990)
5. Brainerd, C.J., Reyna, V.F.: Fuzzy-trace theory: Dual processes in memory, reasoning, and cognitive neuroscience (2001)
6. Douze, M., Jégou, H., Sandhawalia, H., Amsaleg, L., Schmid, C.: Evaluation of gist descriptors for web-scale image search. In: Proceedings of the ACM International Conference on Image and Video Retrieval, pp. 1–8 (2009)
7. Fei-Fei, L., Fergus, R., Perona, P.: One-shot learning of object categories. IEEE Trans. Pattern Anal. Mach. Intell. **28**(4), 594–611 (2006)
8. Finn, C., Abbeel, P., Levine, S.: Model-agnostic meta-learning for fast adaptation of deep networks. CoRR abs/1703.03400 (2017). http://arxiv.org/abs/1703.03400
9. Griffiths, T.L., Steyvers, M., Tenenbaum, J.B.: Topics in semantic representation. Psychol. Rev. **114**(2), 211 (2007)
10. Hu, S., Leung, C.W., Leung, H.F., Liu, J.: To be big picture thinker or detail-oriented?: utilizing perceived gist information to achieve efficient convention emergence with bilateralism and multilateralism. In: Proceedings of the 18th International Conference on Autonomous Agents and MultiAgent Systems, pp. 2021–2023 (2019)
11. Joachims, T.: Text categorization with support vector machines: learning with many relevant features. In: Nédellec, C., Rouveirol, C. (eds.) ECML 1998. LNCS, vol. 1398, pp. 137–142. Springer, Heidelberg (1998). https://doi.org/10.1007/BFb0026683
12. Jones, K.S.: A statistical interpretation of term specificity and its application in retrieval. J. Doc. **28**, 11–21 (1972)
13. Kusner, M., Sun, Y., Kolkin, N., Weinberger, K.: From word embeddings to document distances. In: International Conference on Machine Learning, pp. 957–966 (2015)
14. Lee, M.D., Pincombe, B., Welsh, M.: A comparison of machine measures of text document similarity with human judgments. In: 27th Annual Meeting of the Cognitive Science Society (CogSci 2005), pp. 1254–1259 (2005)
15. Michael Lampinen, J., Leding, J.K., Reed, K.B., Odegard, T.N.: Global gist extraction in children and adults. Memory **14**(8), 952–964 (2006)
16. Mikolov, T., Chen, K., Corrado, G., Dean, J.: Efficient estimation of word representations in vector space. arXiv preprint arXiv:1301.3781 (2013)
17. Neuschatz, J.S., Lampinen, J.M., Preston, E.L., Hawkins, E.R., Toglia, M.P.: The effect of memory schemata on memory and the phenomenological experience of naturalistic situations. Appl. Cogn. Psychol. Offic. J. Soc. Appl. Res. Memory Cogn. **16**(6), 687–708 (2002)
18. Pardo, T.A.S., Rino, L.H.M., Nunes, M.G.V.: GistSumm: a summarization tool based on a new extractive method. In: Mamede, N.J., Trancoso, I., Baptista, J., das Graças Volpe Nunes, M. (eds.) PROPOR 2003. LNCS (LNAI), vol. 2721, pp. 210–218. Springer, Heidelberg (2003). https://doi.org/10.1007/3-540-45011-4_34
19. Pennington, J., Socher, R., Manning, C.: Glove: global vectors for word representation. In: Proceedings of the 2014 Conference on Empirical Methods in Natural Language Processing (EMNLP), pp. 1532–1543 (2014)
20. Peters, M.E., et al.: Deep contextualized word representations. arXiv preprint arXiv:1802.05365 (2018)
21. Raunak, V.: Simple and effective dimensionality reduction for word embeddings. arXiv preprint arXiv:1708.03629 (2017)

22. Rino, L.H.M., Scott, D.: A discourse model for gist preservation. In: Borges, D.L., Kaestner, C.A.A. (eds.) SBIA 1996. LNCS, vol. 1159, pp. 131–140. Springer, Heidelberg (1996). https://doi.org/10.1007/3-540-61859-7_14
23. Snell, J., Swersky, K., Zemel, R.S.: Prototypical networks for few-shot learning. CoRR abs/1703.05175 (2017). http://arxiv.org/abs/1703.05175
24. Yang, Z., Yang, D., Dyer, C., He, X., Smola, A., Hovy, E.: Hierarchical attention networks for document classification. In: Proceedings of the 2016 Conference of the North American Chapter of the Association for Computational Linguistics: Human Language Technologies, pp. 1480–1489 (2016)
25. Zipf, G.K.: Selected studies of the principle of relative frequency in language (1932)

SGCN: A Graph Sparsifier Based on Graph Convolutional Networks

Jiayu Li[1(✉)], Tianyun Zhang[2], Hao Tian[1], Shengmin Jin[1], Makan Fardad[2], and Reza Zafarani[1]

[1] Data Lab, EECS Department, Syracuse University, Syracuse, NY 13244, USA
{jli221,haotian,shengmin,reza}@data.syr.edu
[2] EECS Department, Syracuse University, Syracuse, NY 13244, USA
{tzhan120,makan}@syr.edu

Abstract. Graphs are ubiquitous across the globe and within science and engineering. With graphs growing in size, *node classification* on large graphs can be space and time consuming, even with powerful classifiers such as Graph Convolutional Networks (GCNs). Hence, some questions are raised, particularly, whether one can keep only some of the edges of a graph while maintaining prediction performance for node classification, or train classifiers on specific subgraphs instead of a whole graph with limited performance loss in node classification. To address these questions, we propose *Sparsified Graph Convolutional Network* (SGCN), a neural network graph sparsifier that sparsifies a graph by pruning some edges. We formulate sparsification as an optimization problem, which we solve by an Alternating Direction Method of Multipliers (ADMM)-based solution. We show that sparsified graphs provided by SGCN can be used as inputs to GCN, leading to better or comparable node classification performance with that of original graphs in GCN, DeepWalk, and GraphSAGE.

Keywords: Graph sparsification · Node classification · Graph convolutional network

1 Introduction

Graphs have become universal and are growing in scale in many domains, especially on the Internet and social media. Addressing graph-based problems with various objectives has been the subject of many recent studies. Examples include studies on link prediction [16] and graph clustering [21], or node classification [2], which is the particular focus of this study.

In node classification, one aims to classify nodes in a network by relying on node attributes and the network structure. There are two main categories of node classification methods: (1) methods that directly use node attributes and structural information as features and use [local] classifiers (e.g., decision trees) to classify nodes, and (2) random walk-based methods (often used in semi-supervised learning), which classify nodes by determining the probability p that

© Springer Nature Switzerland AG 2020
H. W. Lauw et al. (Eds.): PAKDD 2020, LNAI 12084, pp. 275–287, 2020.
https://doi.org/10.1007/978-3-030-47426-3_22

a random walk starting from node $v_i \in V$ with label c will end at a node with the same label c. The performance of random walk-based methods implicitly relies on graph structural properties, e.g., degrees, neighborhoods, and reachabilities.

In recent studies, neural network classifiers [27] are widely used for both types of methods due to their performance and flexibility. A well-established example is the Graph Convolutional Network (GCN) [14], a semi-supervised model that uses the *whole* adjacency matrix as a *filter* in each neural network layer.

However, there is a major difficulty faced by methods that directly use the whole graph to extract structural information: the size of the graph. Unlike node attributes, as a graph with n nodes grows, the size of its adjacency matrix increases at an $O(n^2)$ rate, which introduces an unavoidable space and computational cost to classifiers. One engineering solution is to store the adjacency matrix in a sparse matrix (i.e., save non-zeros); however, the process is still extremely slow and requires massive storage when the graph is dense or large.

The Present Work: Sparsified Graph Convolutional Network (SGCN). To address space and computational challenge in node classification, we explore whether one can just rely on a subgraph instead of the whole graph, or some edges (potentially weighted), to extract structural information. We propose *Sparsified Graph Convolutional Network* (SGCN), a neural network graph sparsifier to prune the input graph to GCN without losing much accuracy in node classification. We formulate graph sparsification as an optimization problem, which we efficiently solve via the Alternating Direction Method of Multipliers (ADMM) [3]. We also introduce a new gradient update method for the pruning process of the adjacency matrices, ensuring updates to the matrices are consistent within SGCN layers.

To evaluate SGCN, we compare its performance with other classical graph sparsifiers on multiple real-world graphs. We demonstrate that within a range of pruning ratios, SGCN provides better sparsified graphs compared to other graph sparsifiers. We also show that node classification performance using these sparsified graphs can be better or comparable to when original graphs are used in GCN, DeepWalk [18], and GraphSAGE [11]. In sum, our contributions can be summarized as:

1. We propose Sparsified Graph Convolutional Network (SGCN), the first neural network graph sparsifier aiming to sparsify graphs for node classification;
2. We design a gradient update method that ensures adjacency matrices in the two SGCN layers are updated consistently;
3. We demonstrate the sparsified graphs from SGCN perform better in node classification that those provided by other graph sparsifiers; and
4. We show that sparsified graphs obtained from SGCN with various pruning ratios, if used as inputs to GCN, lead to classification performances similar to that of GCN, DeepWalk and GraphSAGE using the whole graphs.

The paper is organized as follows. We review related work in Sect. 2. We provide the SGCN problem definition in Sect. 3. Section 4 details the problem formulation, solution, and time complexity of SGCN. We conduct experiments in Sect. 5 and conclude in Sect. 6.

2   Related Work

Graph Neural Networks. Inspired by the major success of convolutional neural networks in computer vision research, new convolutional methods have emerged for solving graph-based problems. There are two main types of graph convolutional networks: *spectral-based* methods and *spatial-based* methods.

Spectral-based methods, which include GCNs [6,14], are based on spectral graph theory. Spectral-based convolutional networks often rely on graph signal processing and are mostly based on normalized graph Laplacian. Other examples include the work of Bhagat et al. [17], which aims to represent a graph by extracting its locally connected components. Another is DUIF, proposed by Geng et al. [9], which uses a hierarchical softmax for forward propagation to maximize modularity. One main drawback of spectral-based methods is the need to perform matrix multiplication on the adjacency matrix, which is costly for large graphs.

Spatial-based methods focus on aggregating the neighborhood for each node. These methods can be grouped into (1) recurrent-based and (2) composition-based methods. Recurrent-based methods update latest node representation using that of their neighbors until convergence [5,20]. Composition-based methods update the nodes' representations by stacking multiple graph convolution layers. For example, Gilmer et al. [10] develop a message passing neural network to embed any existing GCN model into a message passing (the influence of neighbors) and readout pattern. Spatial-based methods are often more flexible and easier to apply to large networks.

Graph Sparsification. For graph sparsification, previous studies have distinct objectives from that of ours. Generally speaking, most graph properties of a dense graph can be approximated from its [sparsified] sparse graph. *Cut sparsifiers* [1,8,13] ensure the total weight of cuts in the sparsified graph approximates that of cuts in the original graph within some bounded distance. Spectral sparsifiers [23,24] ensure sparsified graphs preserve spectral properties of the graph Laplacian. There are various applications for graph sparsification. Some examples include, the work of Serrano et al. [22], which aims to identity the *backbone of a network* that preserves structural and hierarchical information in the original graph; the study by Satuluri et al. [19], which applies local sparsification to preprocess a graph for clustering; the study by Lindner et al. [15], which proposes a local degree sparsifier to preserve nodes surrounding local hub nodes by weighing edges linking to higher degree nodes more; and the work by Wilder and Sukthankar [26], which aims to minimize divergence of stationary distribution of a random walk while sparsifying the graph.

These studies are similar, but with different objectives from that of ours. Instead of preserving graph properties, the neural network sparsifier proposed in this work focuses on node classification, so that the space cost is reduced due to sparsification, while node classification performance is maintained.

3 Problem Definition

Consider an undirected graph $G = (V, E)$, its nodes $V = \{v_1, \ldots, v_n\}$, and its edges $E = \{e_1, \ldots, e_m\}$. Let $n = |V|$ denote the number of nodes and $m = |E|$ denote the number of edges. Given adjacency matrix A of G and features for each node $v : X(v) = [x_1, \ldots, x_k]$, the forward model (i.e., output) of a two-layered graph convolutional network (GCN), as formulated by Kipf and Welling [14], is

$$Z(\hat{A}, W) = \text{softmax}(\hat{A} \ \text{ReLU}(\hat{A}XW^{(0)})W^{(1)}), \tag{1}$$

where $\hat{A} = \tilde{D}^{-\frac{1}{2}} \tilde{A} \tilde{D}^{-\frac{1}{2}}$, $\tilde{D} = \text{diag}(\sum_j \tilde{A}_{ij})$, $\tilde{A} = A + I_N$, X is the matrix of node feature vectors $X(v)$, and $W^{(0)}$ and $W^{(1)}$ are the weights in the first and second layer, respectively. Functions $\text{softmax}(x_i) = \exp(x_i)/\sum_i \exp(x_i)$ and $\text{ReLU}(\cdot) = \max(0, \cdot)$ both perform entry-wise operations on their arguments. Graph sparsification aims to reduce the number of edges $|E|$ in the original graph G to $|E_s|$ in a subgraph G_s, i.e., $|E_s| < |E|$, such that subgraph G_s, when used as input to GCN, results in similar classification performance to that of the original graph G. In pruning, adjacency A is pruned to $A_p = A - B \odot A$, where B is a matrix and $\odot$ is Hadamard product. Thus, the new $\tilde{A}$ is $\tilde{A} = A_p + I_N$ and $\hat{A}$ is the updated filter for A_p. We will explore how the ratio of graph sparsification in this filter affects SGCN performance.

4 SGCN: Sparsified Graph Convolutional Networks

We first illustrate the problem formulation and solution, followed by SGCN algorithm, a new gradient update method, and the SGCN time complexity analysis.

4.1 Problem Formulation and Solution

Problem Formulation. The output of graph convolutional networks in Eq. (1) is a function of $\hat{A}$ and W, but as $\hat{A}$ can be written as a function of A, the output can be stated as $Z(A, W)$. For semi-supervised multiclass classification, loss function of the neural networks is the cross-entropy error over labeled examples:

$$f(A, W) = -\sum_{l \in \mathcal{Y}_L} \sum_f Y_{lf} \ln(Z_{lf}), \tag{2}$$

where $\mathcal{Y}_L$ is the set of node indices that have labels, Y_{lf} is a matrix of labels, and Z_{lf} is the output of the GCN forward model. Our aim is to achieve a sparse graph, with weight matrices being fixed in SGCN. In the following, we will use $f(A)$ to present the loss function and formulate our problem as:

$$\begin{aligned} \underset{A}{\text{minimize}} \quad & f(A), \\ \text{subject to} \quad & \|A\|_0 \leq \eta. \end{aligned} \tag{3}$$

For Eq. (3), we define an indicator function to replace constraint:

$$g(\Lambda) = \begin{cases} 0 & \text{if } \|\Lambda\|_0 \le \eta; \\ +\infty & \text{otherwise.} \end{cases}$$

Therefore, Eq. (3) formulation can be rewritten as

$$\underset{A}{\text{minimize}} \quad f(A) + g(A). \tag{4}$$

Solution. In Eq. (4), the first term $f(\cdot)$ is the differentiable loss function of the GCN, while the second term $g(\cdot)$ is the non-differentiable indicator function; hence, problem (4) cannot be solved directly by gradient descent. To deal with this issue, we propose to use Alternating Direction Method of Multipliers (ADMM) to rewrite problem (4). ADMM is a powerful method for solving convex optimization problems [3]. Recent studies [12,25] have demonstrated that ADMM also works well for some nonconvex problems.

The general form of a problem solvable by ADMM is

$$\underset{\alpha,\ \beta}{\text{minimize}} \quad f(\alpha) + g(\beta),$$
$$\text{subject to} \quad P\alpha + Q\beta = r. \tag{5}$$

The problem can be decomposed to two subproblems via augmented Lagrangian. One subproblem contains $f(\alpha)$ and a quadratic term of α; the other contains $g(\beta)$ and a quadratic term of β. Since the quadratic term is convex and differentiable, the two subproblems can often be efficiently solved. Hence, we rewrite problem (4) as

$$\underset{A}{\text{minimize}} \quad f(A) + g(V),$$
$$\text{subject to} \quad A = V. \tag{6}$$

The augmented Lagrangian [3] of problem (6) is given by

$$L_\rho(A, V, \Lambda) = f(A) + g(V) + \text{Tr}[\Lambda^T(A - V)] + \frac{\rho}{2}\|(A - V)\|_F^2,$$

where Λ is the Lagrangian multiplier (i.e., the dual variable) corresponding to constraint $A = V$, the positive scalar ρ is the penalty parameter, $\text{Tr}(\cdot)$ is the trace, and $\| \cdot \|_F^2$ is the Frobenius norm.

By defining the scaled dual variable $U = (1/\rho)\Lambda$, the augmented Lagrangian can be equivalently expressed in the scaled form:

$$L_\rho(A, V, U) = f(A) + g(V) + \frac{\rho}{2}\|A - V + U\|_F^2 - \frac{\rho}{2}\|U\|_F^2.$$

When we apply ADMM [3] to this problem, we alternately update the variables according to

$$A^{k+1} := \underset{A}{\arg\min} \quad L_\rho(A, V^k, U^k), \tag{7}$$

$$V^{k+1} := \underset{V}{\arg\min} \quad L_\rho(A^{k+1}, V, U^k), \tag{8}$$

$$U^{k+1} := U^k + A^{k+1} - V^{k+1}, \tag{9}$$

until

$$\|A^{k+1} - V^{k+1}\|_F^2 \le \epsilon, \quad \|V^{k+1} - V^k\|_F^2 \le \epsilon. \tag{10}$$

In (7), we solve the first subproblem:

$$\underset{A}{\text{minimize}} \quad f'(A) := f(A) + \frac{\rho}{2}\|A - V^k + U^k\|_F^2 . \tag{11}$$

In the above problem, as the loss function $f(A)$ and the ℓ_2-norm are differentiable, we can use gradient descent to solve it. As $f(A)$ is nonconvex with respect to the variable A, there has been no theoretical guarantee on the convergence, when solving problem (11). We present a method to solve (11) in Sect. 4.3.

In (8), we solve the second subproblem, which is

$$\underset{V}{\text{minimize}} \quad g(V) + \frac{\rho}{2}\|A^{k+1} - V + U^k\|_F^2 . \tag{12}$$

As $g(\cdot)$ is the indicator function, problem (12) can be solved analytically [3], where the solution is

$$V^{k+1} = \mathbf{\Pi_S}(A^{k+1} + U^k), \tag{13}$$

where $\mathbf{\Pi_S}(\cdot)$ is the Euclidean projection onto set $\mathbf{S} = \{A \mid \|A\|_0 \le \eta\}$.

Finally, we update the scaled dual variable U according to (9). This is one ADMM iteration. We update the variables iteratively until condition (10) is satisfied, indicating the convergence of ADMM.

4.2 SGCN Algorithm

In the solution provided in Sect. 4.1, we need to maintain η, the number of nonzero elements. The Euclidean projection in Eq. (13) maintains η elements in $\widetilde{A}^{k+1} + U^k$ with the largest magnitude and sets the rest to zero. This is proved to be the optimal and the analytical solution to subproblem (12) for edge pruning of graphs. In GCN, filters in the loss function in Eq. (2) consist of $\widetilde{D}^{-\frac{1}{2}}\widetilde{A}\widetilde{D}^{-\frac{1}{2}}$, where $\widetilde{A} = A + I_N$ and $\widetilde{D} = \sum_j \widetilde{A}_{ij}$. Variable I_N is the identity matrix and $\widetilde{A}$ is a [modified] adjacency matrix. Variables $\widetilde{A}$ and $\widetilde{D}$ in each layer are fixed and non-trainable in the original GCN. To solve graph sparsification based on GCN and maintain classification performance, variable $\widetilde{A}$ should be trained and updated iteratively. As variable $\widetilde{D}$ depends on $\widetilde{A}$, $\widetilde{A}$ in the original loss function cannot be directly differentiated. Thus, we expand the forward model into:

$$Z(A) = \text{diag}(\sum_j (A + I)_{ij})^{-\frac{1}{2}}(A + I)\text{diag}(\sum_j (A + I)_{ij})^{-\frac{1}{2}}XW. \tag{14}$$

In Eq. (14), no variable depends on $\widetilde{A}$. However, we cannot still train variables A and W simultaneously as the differentiation of A depends on W and vice versa. Hence, we first train weights variable W in SGCN. By fixing variable W in this model, the adjacency matrix A can be regarded as a trainable variable. With ADAptive Moment estimation (ADAM) optimizer, gradients of the variable (adjacency matrix A) can be updated in SGCN. Algorithm 1 provides the SGCN pseudo-code. We use variable A to initialize variable V in each layer using function Initialize() and apply function Zerolike() to V to ensure variable U has the same shape as V with all the zero elements.

Algorithm 1: The SGCN Algorithm

---

input : Adjacency matrix A, feature matrix X, ADMM iterations k, and
        pruning ratio $p\% = \frac{\eta}{|E|} \times 100\%$
output: Pruned adjacency matrix A_p

Train weight matrix W in SGCN;
for $i \leftarrow 1$ **to** *the number of layers* **do**
    $V_i \leftarrow$ Initialize(A_i);
    $U_i \leftarrow$ Zerolike(V_i);

for $k \leftarrow 0$ **to** *ADMM iterations* **do**
    Solve subproblem (11) and update A's in two layers;
    for $i \leftarrow 1$ **to** *the number of layers* **do**
        Update V_i's by performing Euclidean projection (13);
        Update U_i's by performing (9);

Fetch A_1 from the first layer;
Set the smallest $p\%$ of non-zero elements in A_1 to zero;
Obtain a pruned adjacency matrix A_p;

4.3 Adjacency Matrix Training

When training adjacency matrix A in Algorithm 1, we should maintain the adjacency matrices in the first and second layer consistent. To address this issue, we propose a method to update the gradients of the adjacency matrix, when fixing weight matrices W in the two layers. A mask m is defined using the adjacency matrix A. As we use gradient descent, the following equation based on Eqs. (2) and (14) can be applied to update the trainable variable (adjacency matrix A) at each step to solve problem in Eq. (11):

$$A_i^{k+1} = A_i^k - \gamma(m \odot \frac{\partial f'(A_i^k)}{\partial A_i^k}), \tag{15}$$

for $i = 1, \ldots, n$, where γ is the learning rate. In the process of updating A, we keep the gradient matrices of the adjacency matrix symmetric in two layers and gradients are set to zero when there are no edges between nodes. Also, diagonal elements are zero in the gradient matrix as we only update the adjacency matrix and consider no self-loops at each node. To maintain the adjacency matrices in the two layers identical, we compute average gradients for the same edge in the two adjacency matrices. We assign these average gradients to the corresponding edges in the matrices for updating elements of the adjacency matrices.

4.4 Time Complexity Analysis

The GCN training time complexity is $\mathcal{O}(L|A_0|F + LNF^2)$, where L is the number of layers, N is the number of nodes, $|A_0|$ is the number of non-zeros in an adjacency matrix, and F is the number of features [4]. Hence, assuming ADMM takes k iterations, the SGCN time complexity is $\mathcal{O}(kL|A_0|F + kLNF^2)$. Compared to SGCN training time complexity, the time to update variables V and U according to Eqs. (13) and (9) is negligible. In our SGCN, $k = 4$ and $L = 2$. Also, we need only a few iterations to solve subproblem (11), which indicates the training time complexity of SGCN is similar to that of GCN. The time complexity for the forward model in SGCN is $\mathcal{O}(|\Gamma|FC)$, where $|\Gamma|$ is linear in the number of edges and C is the dimension of feature maps. Hence, it is less than that of GCN: $\mathcal{O}(|\epsilon|FC)$, as we have $|\Gamma| \leq |\epsilon|$.

5 Experiments

There are two natural ways to measure the effectiveness of SGCN.

- First, is to compare the node classification performance of sparsified subgraphs obtained using SGCN with that of other sparsifiers. For that, we use GCN for node classification, and compare the node classification performance of SGCN with two well-known sparsifiers: *Random Pruning* (RP) sparsifier and *Spectral Sparsifier* (SS). The RP removes edges uniformly at random from a graph with some probabilities. The SS is the state of the art spectral sparsifier [7], which sparsifies graphs in near linear-time.
- Second, is to compare the node classification performance of the sparsified graphs compared to that of the original graphs. For that, we compare the performance of GCN using sparsified subgraphs provided by SGCN with that of GCN, DeepWalk, and GraphSAGE using original graphs.

5.1 Experimental Setup

Datasets. To evaluate the performance of node classification on sparsified graphs, we conduct our experiments on four attributed graphs. These graphs have been utilized for evaluation in previous studies and are hence used for evaluation. All datasets are available online.[1] Here, we briefly introduce these datasets:

- **CiteSeer:** A citation network of publications classified into six categories. Each publication is attributed by a 0/1-valued word vector indicating the absence/presence of the corresponding word from the dictionary;
- **Cora:** Similar to CiteSeer, a citation network with 7 categories;
- **Terrorists:** This dataset contains information about terrorists and their relationships. Each terrorist is described by a 0/1-valued vector providing features of the individual; and
- **Terrorist Attacks:** The dataset provides information on terrorist attacks classified into 6 different categories, while a 0/1-valued vector provides the absence/presence of a feature.

---

[1] http://linqs.soe.ucsc.edu/data.

Preprocessing. We preprocess the data for existing node classification models [14,28]. We split the data into 10 folds for cross validation. In each training fold, we only select 20 instances for each label as the labeled instances. Other instances remain unlabeled, from which we randomly select 500 instances for validation set, which is used to train our hyper-parameters. We filter and reorder the adjacency matrices and attribute vectors to ensure they are ordered according to training/testing folds.

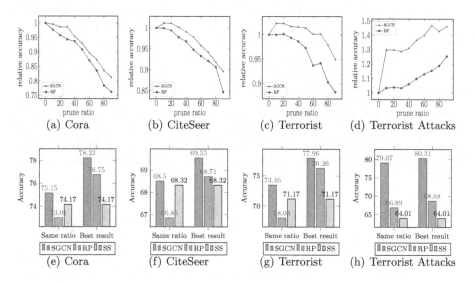

Fig. 1. Performance of GCN using sparsified subgraphs provided by SGCN, RP, and SS sparsifiers. SGCN outperforms all other sparsifiers across datasets. (Color figure online)

Parameter Setup. We vary the pruning ratio (p in Algorithm 1) from 10% to 90% in SGCN and RP. When pruning ratio is 0%, the model is the original GCN. We use the default parameters in GCN, DeepWalk, and GraphSAGE. In RP, we set random seeds from 0 to 9. For SGCN, we set ρ to 0.001 and the training learning rate to 0.001. In SS, we use the default suggested parameters for spectral sparsifier [7]. Due to obtaining 10 folds for each dataset, we run SGCN, RP and SS, in each fold of each dataset to obtain sparsified subgraphs and use these subgraphs as inputs for GCN.

5.2   Results and Performance Analysis

Comparing Sparsifiers. Fig. 1 provides the average performance of GCN with sparsified subgraphs obtained from SGCN and other graph sparsifiers. In Figs. 1(a), (b), (c) and (d), performances are provided in *relative accuracy*, where accuracy is divided by the baseline: accuracy of models from GCN. In Cora dataset, sparsified subgraph provided by SGCN perform better in GCN than those provided by RP, as shown in Fig. 1(a). For CiteSeer dataset, Fig. 1(b) shows that sparsified subgraph provided by SGCN with pruning ratios between 0% and 30%, when used as input to GCN, can yield accurate classification models. In Terrorists datasets, applying subgraphs from SGCN as inputs to GCN can easily obtain a higher accuracy, as shown in Fig. 1(c). Finally, in Fig. 1(d), we observe that GCN performance increases as pruning ratio increase in the Terrorist Attack dataset. Here also SGCN provides better subgraphs than RP does. Figures 1(e), (f), (g) and (h) illustrate the performance of GCN using subgraphs from SGCN, RP, and SS. We compare their best performance, and the performance under the same pruning ratio, as for Spectral Sparsifier (SS) we cannot set pruning ratio. The results show that subgraphs from SGCN perform the best in node classification, and SGCN is more flexible than SS as SGCN allows different pruning ratios.

Node Classification Performance. When using sparsified subgraphs provided by SGCN as inputs to GCN, we obtain a node-classification model, which we denote as SGCN-GCN. On all datasets, SGCN-GCN either outperforms other methods or yields comparable performance using much smaller graphs. On Cora

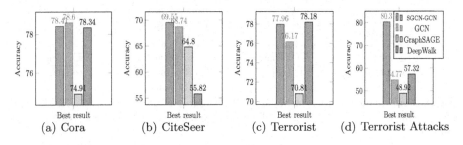

Fig. 2. The performance of SGCN-GCN, GCN, GraphSAGE, and DeepWalk. SGCN-GCN either outperforms or is comparatively accurate, using much smaller graphs. (Color figure online)

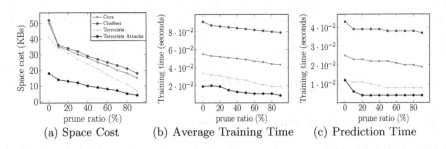

Fig. 3. Space and computational cost using subgraphs from SGCN as inputs to GCN

dataset (Fig. 2(a)), SGCN-GCN outperforms GraphSAGE, and has a comparable performance to DeepWalk and GCN. On other datasets (Figs. 2(b), (c) and (d)), SGCN-GCN outperforms other methods, with the exception of Terrorist dataset (Fig. 2(c)) on which it performs similarly to DeepWalk. Therefore, even though many edges are pruned, subgraphs provided by SGCN when used as inputs to GCN can lead to better or comparable node classification performance over these datasets.

Space and Computational Cost. Here, we feed the subgraphs from SGCN as inputs to GCN and show the actual space and computational cost. The space cost in a graph is $\mathcal{O}(|V| + |E|)$. As SGCN decreases the number of edges $|E|$, the space cost is obviously reduced, as shown in Fig. 3(a). Figure 3(b) and (c) show average training and prediction times in seconds, which have declining trends when the pruning ratio increases. Hence the proposed framework reduces space and computational cost.

6 Conclusion

When a graph is large or dense, node classification often requires massive storage or is computationally expensive. In this paper, we address this issue by proposing the first neural network architecture that can sparsify graphs for node classification. We propose *Sparsified Graph Convolutional Network* (SGCN), a neural network sparsifier. In SGCN, we formulate sparsification as an optimization problem and provide an ADMM-based solution to solve it. Experimental results on real-world datasets demonstrate that the proposed framework can sparsify graphs and its output (sparsified graphs) can be used as inputs to GCN to obtain classification models that are as accurate as using the whole graphs. Hence, SGCN reduces storage and computational cost with a limited loss in classification accuracy.

References

1. Benczúr, A.A., Karger, D.R.: Approximating s-t minimum cuts in $\tilde{O}(n^2)$ time. In: Proceedings of the Twenty-Eighth Annual ACM Symposium on the Theory of Computing, Philadelphia, Pennsylvania, USA, 22–24 May 1996, pp. 47–55 (1996)
2. Bhagat, S., Cormode, G., Muthukrishnan, S.: Node classification in social networks. CoRR abs/1101.3291 (2011)
3. Boyd, S., Parikh, N., Chu, E., Peleato, B., Eckstein, J., et al.: Distributed optimization and statistical learning via the alternating direction method of multipliers. Found. Trends® Mach. Learn. **3**(1), 1–122 (2011)
4. Chiang, W., Liu, X., Si, S., Li, Y., Bengio, S., Hsieh, C.: Cluster-GCN: an efficient algorithm for training deep and large graph convolutional networks. CoRR abs/1905.07953 (2019)
5. Cho, K., et al.: Learning phrase representations using RNN encoder-decoder for statistical machine translation. Comput. Sci. (2014)

6. Defferrard, M., Bresson, X., Vandergheynst, P.: Convolutional neural networks on graphs with fast localized spectral filtering. CoRR abs/1606.09375 (2016)
7. Feng, Z.: Spectral graph sparsification in nearly-linear time leveraging efficient spectral perturbation analysis. In: Proceedings of the 53rd Annual Design Automation Conference, DAC 2016, pp. 57:1–57:6. ACM, New York (2016)
8. Fung, W.S., Hariharan, R., Harvey, N.J., Panigrahi, D.: A general framework for graph sparsification. In: Proceedings of the Forty-third Annual ACM Symposium on Theory of Computing, STOC 2011, pp. 71–80. ACM, New York (2011)
9. Geng, X., Zhang, H., Bian, J., Chua, T.: Learning image and user features for recommendation in social networks. In: IEEE International Conference on Computer Vision (ICCV), pp. 4274–4282, December 2015
10. Gilmer, J., Schoenholz, S.S., Riley, P.F., Vinyals, O., Dahl, G.E.: Neural message passing for quantum chemistry. CoRR abs/1704.01212 (2017)
11. Hamilton, W.L., Ying, R., Leskovec, J.: Inductive representation learning on large graphs. In: NIPS (2017)
12. Hong, M., Luo, Z.Q., Razaviyayn, M.: Convergence analysis of alternating direction method of multipliers for a family of nonconvex problems. SIAM J. Optim. **26**(1), 337–364 (2016)
13. Karger, D.R.: Random sampling in cut, flow, and network design problems. In: Proceedings of the Twenty-Sixth Annual ACM Symposium on Theory of Computing, Montréal, Québec, Canada, 23–25 May 1994, pp. 648–657 (1994)
14. Kipf, T.N., Welling, M.: Semi-supervised classification with graph convolutional networks. CoRR abs/1609.02907 (2016)
15. Lindner, G., Staudt, C.L., Hamann, M., Meyerhenke, H., Wagner, D.: Structure-preserving sparsification of social networks. In: Proceedings of the IEEE/ACM International Conference on Advances in Social Networks Analysis and Mining 2015, ASONAM 2015, pp. 448–454. ACM, New York (2015)
16. Lü, L., Zhou, T.: Link prediction in complex networks: a survey. Physica A **390**(6), 1150–1170 (2011)
17. Niepert, M., Ahmed, M., Kutzkov, K.: Learning convolutional neural networks for graphs. CoRR abs/1605.05273 (2016)
18. Perozzi, B., Al-Rfou, R., Skiena, S.: Deepwalk: online learning of social representations. In: Proceedings of the 20th ACM SIGKDD International Conference on Knowledge Discovery and Data Mining, KDD 2014, pp. 701–710. ACM, New York (2014)
19. Satuluri, V., Parthasarathy, S., Ruan, Y.: Local graph sparsification for scalable clustering. In: Proceedings of the ACM SIGMOD International Conference on Management of Data, SIGMOD 2011, pp. 721–732. ACM, New York (2011)
20. Scarselli, F., Gori, M., Tsoi, A.C., Hagenbuchner, M., Monfardini, G.: The graph neural network model. Trans. Neur. Netw. **20**(1), 61–80 (2009)
21. Schaeffer, S.E.: Survey: graph clustering. Comput. Sci. Rev. **1**(1), 27–64 (2007)
22. Serrano, M.Á., Boguñá, M., Vespignani, A.: Extracting the multiscale backbone of complex weighted networks. Proc. Nat. Acad. Sci. U.S.A. **106**(16), 6483–8 (2009)
23. Spielman, D.A., Srivastava, N.: Graph sparsification by effective resistances. CoRR abs/0803.0929 (2008)
24. Spielman, D.A., Teng, S.: Nearly-linear time algorithms for preconditioning and solving symmetric, diagonally dominant linear systems. CoRR abs/cs/0607105 (2006)
25. Takapoui, R., Moehle, N., Boyd, S., Bemporad, A.: A simple effective heuristic for embedded mixed-integer quadratic programming. Int. J. Control, pp. 1–11 (2017)

26. Wilder, B., Wilder, T.: Sparsification of social networks using random walks 2015 (2015)
27. Wu, Z., Pan, S., Chen, F., Long, G., Zhang, C., Yu, P.S.: A comprehensive survey on graph neural networks. CoRR abs/1901.00596 (2019)
28. Yang, Z., Cohen, W.W., Salakhutdinov, R.: Revisiting semi-supervised learning with graph embeddings. In: Proceedings of the 33rd International Conference on International Conference on Machine Learning, ICML 2016, vol. 48, pp. 40–48. JMLR.org (2016)

Clustering

Fast Community Detection with Graph Sparsification

Jesse Laeuchli$^{(\boxtimes)}$ (iD)

Cyber Security Research and Innovation Centre, Deakin University,
Geelong, Australia
j.laeuchli@deakin.edu.au

Abstract. A popular model for detecting community structure in large graphs is the Stochastic Block Model (SBM). The exact parameters to recover the community structure of a SBM has been well studied, and many methods have been proposed to recover a nodes' community membership. A popular approach is to use spectral methods where the Graph Laplacian L of the given graph is created, and the Fiedler vector of the graph is found. This vector is then used to cluster nodes in the same community. While a robust method, it can be expensive to compute the Fiedler vector exactly. In this paper we examine the types of errors that can be tolerated using spectral methods while still recovering the communities. The two sources of error considered are: (i) dropping edges using different sparsification strategies; and (ii) inaccurately computing the eigenvectors. In this way, spectral clustering algorithms can be tuned to be far more efficient at detecting community structure for these community models.

Keywords: Clustering · Graph sparsification · Stopping criteria

1 Background and Motivation

Stochastic Block Models. Detecting communities through clustering is an important problem in a wide variety of network applications characterized by graphs [1,3]. However, it can be difficult to study the accuracy of clustering on arbitrary graphs. To aid network analysis, generative models are frequently introduced. One popular model is the Stochastic Block Model (SBM) [2]. In this model a number of nodes n with community memberships are given, and the connectivity of vertices p and q within (and between) the communities are also specified. For a given graph with parameters $G(n, p, q)$, we define $a = pn$, $b = qn$. It has been shown that the community structure can only be recovered when $(a - b)^2 > 2(a + b)$ [14]. While models of more than two communities are sometimes studied, in this paper we restrict our attention to the case where the number of communities is fixed at two. There are two reasons for this. The first is that there is more theory available to work with. The second is that in practice it is often the custom when seeking communities in a graph to recursively cluster

© Springer Nature Switzerland AG 2020
H. W. Lauw et al. (Eds.): PAKDD 2020, LNAI 12084, pp. 291–304, 2020.
https://doi.org/10.1007/978-3-030-47426-3_23

the nodes into two groups and then continue recursively, since this approach lends itself to high performance computing [4]. A two community model is therefore relevant to real-world approaches and worthy of study. Our goal in this paper is to discuss the question of how we can recover the communities of a SBM faster, by applying graph sparsification and inaccurate eigenvector computation, without harming the accuracy of our recovery methods. Additionally, we show how we can leverage recent research on nearly linear-time solvers to capitalize on the sparser graphs we obtain.

Spectral Sparsification. A popular approach to clustering is to find the Fiedler vector of the graph Laplacian L [4]. This is faster the sparser L is. Given a matrix L, we say that matrix $\tilde{L}$ is similar iff for all x,

$$x'Lx(1 - \epsilon) \leq x'\tilde{L}x \leq x'Lx(1 + \epsilon). \tag{1}$$

Matrices that are similar to each other by the criteria of Eq. (1) share similar eigenvectors and eigenvalues [5]. While fast methods exist for computing such similar matrices through sparsification [5], it is unclear how errors in eigenvector approximation translate into errors in the communities recovered. Answering this question is a key contribution of this paper.

Spectrum of SBM Matrices. Since we will make extensive use of the spectrum of the different matrix representations of a Stochastic Block Model (SBM), we review the known results here, and provide some new ones.

First we consider the spectrum of a two community adjacency matrix. Define $a = np$, $b = nq$, where p is the probability of a connection between nodes inside the community, and q is the probability of a connection between nodes in different communities. Then the average instance of a SBM model with these parameters can be represented in the form,

$$<\mathbf{A}> = \frac{1}{2}(a + b)\mathbf{11}^T + \frac{1}{2}(a - b)\mathbf{uu}^T \tag{2}$$

where $\mathbf{1} = (1, 1, 1, \ldots, 1)/\sqrt{n}$ and $\mathbf{u} = (1, 1 \ldots, -1, -1, \ldots)/\sqrt{n}$. Any particular instance $\mathbf{A}$ of a SBM drawn from this distribution of matrices can be represented as $\mathbf{A} = <\mathbf{A}> + \mathbf{X}$, where $\mathbf{X}$ is a random Wigner matrix. Because the eigenvalues of $\mathbf{X}$ follow the famous semicircle law, the spectrum of A also follows such a distribution [14], with the exception of the two largest eigenvalues. The distribution of the bulk of the eigenvalues follows the equation,

$$\rho(z) = \frac{n}{\pi} \frac{\sqrt{2(a + b) - z^2}}{a + b}. \tag{3}$$

The radius of the bulk of the spectrum of $\mathbf{A}$ is given as below, with the center of the semi-circle being at 0.

$$r_{\mathbf{A}} = \sqrt{(2(a + b))} \tag{4}$$

Finally we also have the two largest eigenvalues of $\mathbf{A}$ given as below.

$$\lambda_n = \frac{1}{2}(a+b) + 1, \lambda_{n-1} = \frac{1}{2}(a-b) + \frac{a+b}{a-b} \tag{5}$$

We note that the eigenvectors of $\mathbf{A}$ are randomly distributed vectors on the unit sphere except for the top two eigenvectors. The top two eigenvectors are perturbed versions of the vectors of $< \mathbf{A} >$ [14].

We will also be interested in the spectrum and the eigenvectors of the scaled Laplacian $\mathcal{L}$ of instances of our SBM. The bulk of the spectrum of $\mathcal{L}$ is also known to follow a semi-circle distribution [11]. If we denote the average degree of the SBM as $\bar{d}$, then the distribution of the bulk of the eigenvalues follows the equation,

$$\rho(z) = \frac{2n}{\pi} \frac{\sqrt{\frac{2(a+b)}{\bar{d}^2} - z^2}}{\frac{2(a+b)}{\bar{d}^2}}. \tag{6}$$

The radius of the bulk of the spectrum are as below, with the center of the semi-circle being at 1.

$$r_{\mathcal{L}} = \frac{\sqrt{(2(a+b))}}{\bar{d}} \tag{7}$$

Avrachenkov et. al [11] states that the other non-trivial eigenvalue of $\mathcal{L}$ remains to be characterized, so we briefly show that the eigenvalues outside the semi-circle are as below and bound their deviation from this mean, since our algorithms will make use of this information.

$$\lambda_1 = 0, \lambda_2 = 1 - \frac{\frac{1}{2}(a-b) + \frac{a+b}{a-b}}{\bar{d}} \tag{8}$$

We have $\lambda_1 = 0$, since $\mathcal{L}$ is a Laplacian. If $\mathbf{A}$ is a regular graph, then the value for λ_2 is directly computable from the eigenvalues of $\mathbf{A}$, as above. Since SMBs are close to regular, with each node having the same average degree of $a+b$, we need to show that the deviation from the mean is small and with high probability will not change the result. From Lutzeyer and Walden [16] we have that the error of applying this linear transform of the eigenvalues of A, in order to obtain the eigenvalues of $\mathcal{L}$, is $3\frac{d_{max}-d_{min}}{d_{max}+d_{min}}$. We can then use the Chernoff concentration bounds to show that this error goes to zero with high probability.

The elements of the rows of $\mathbf{A}$ are drawn from a binomial distribution, with $n/2$ of them with probability p, and $n/2$ of them with probability q. For each diagonal element of $\mathcal{L}$, we then have,

$$\Pr(|\mathcal{L}_{ii} - \bar{d}| > \sqrt{n}\sqrt{\log(n^2)}) < 2e^{-log(n^2)} = \frac{2}{n^2}. \tag{9}$$

Since we have n diagonal elements, the probability that none exceed this bound can be computed as,

$$\lim_{n \to \infty} (1 - \frac{1}{n^2})^n = 1 \tag{10}$$

The error in our approximation for λ_2 is then

$$
3\frac{d_{max} - d_{min}}{d_{max} + d_{min}} = 3\frac{\bar{d} + \sqrt{n}\sqrt{\log(n^2)} - (\bar{d} - \sqrt{n}\sqrt{\log(n^2)})}{\bar{d} + \sqrt{n}\sqrt{\log(n^2)} + \bar{d} - \sqrt{n}\sqrt{\log(n^2)}}
$$
$$
= 3\frac{2\sqrt{n}\sqrt{\log(n^2)}}{2\bar{d}} = 3\frac{2\sqrt{n}\sqrt{\log(n^2)}}{n(p+q)} \tag{11}
$$

Taking the limit as n increases we then have,

$$
\lim_{n\to\infty} 3\frac{2\sqrt{n}\sqrt{\log(n^2)}}{n(p+q)} = 0. \tag{12}
$$

Finally, we state two properties of $\mathcal{L}$ that we will make use of later. We can write $\mathcal{L} = D^{-1/2}\mathbf{A}D^{-1/2} = D^{-1/2}\mathbf{X}D^{-1/2} + D^{-1/2} < \mathbf{A} > D^{-1/2}$. Recall that the eigenvectors of $\mathbf{X}$ are randomly distributed on the unit sphere. Then for any $e_i, e_j \in \mathbf{I}$

$$
E[e_i D^{-1/2}\mathbf{X}D^{-1/2}e_i] = E[e_i D^{-1/2}\sum_{j=1}^{n}\lambda_j x_j x_j' D^{-1/2}e_i]
$$
$$
E[e_i D^{-1/2}\sum_{j=1}^{n}\lambda_j x_j x_j' D^{-1/2}e_i] = E[\sum_{j=1}^{n}\frac{1}{d_i}\lambda_i x_i x_i' = \sum_{j=1}^{n}\frac{1}{d_i}\lambda_i\frac{1}{n}] \tag{13}
$$

Alternatively, we have

$$
E[e_i D^{-1/2}\mathbf{X}D^{-1/2}e_j] = E[e_i D^{-1/2}\sum_{j=1}^{n}\lambda_j x_j x_j' D^{-1/2}e_j]
$$
$$
E[e_i D^{-1/2}\sum_{j=1}^{n}\lambda_j x_j x_j' D^{-1/2}e_j] = E[\sum_{j=1}^{n}\frac{1}{d_i}\lambda_i x_i x_j'] = 0 \tag{14}
$$

Overall Approach. We now outline our overall problem. We would like to accelerate spectral algorithms for Stochastic Block Models (SBMs) while still recovering the communities accurately. Our main approach is to analyze the impact of two different types of error on SBM algorithms. The first is 'edge dropping'. We investigate two strategies for dropping edges which allow us to recover the communities despite, in some cases, having significantly fewer edges than the original problem. While the idea of sparsifying graphs in order to more efficiently recover communities is not new, our contribution is to determine the level of sparsification that can take place while still recovering communities.

Our second approach is to stop convergence of the eigensolver early. We analyze 'power iteration', and show that for many SBM instances the solver does not need to be run to convergence. We choose power iteration both because the analysis is simple, and because in conjunction with nearly linear-time solvers, and the dropping strategy previously mentioned, we can design extremely efficient algorithms.

This is because power iteration based on these solvers are $O(m)$ complexity. In some cases we can reduce the number of edges by orders of magnitude, making these solvers very attractive.

The foundation of both these methods is a careful use of the model parameters and the known results for the spectra of SBM models.

2   Methods and Technical Solutions

Sampling with Effective Resistance. The main idea is that for a given Stochastic Block Model (SBM) we know when we can recover the communities based on the parameters a, b of the model. While it is sometimes assumed that these parameters are known, Mossel et al. [7] gives Eq. (15) for recovering the parameters of an unknown SBM, where $|E|$ is the number of edges in the graph, $k_n = \lfloor log^{1/4}(n) \rfloor$, and X_{k_n} is the number of cycles of length k_n in the graph. While X_{k_n} is difficult to compute, Mossel et al. shows that this can be well approximated by counting the number of non-backtracking walks in the graph that can be made in $O(n)$ time. They then obtain a linear-time algorithm for estimating a, b by showing that $a \approx \hat{d}_n + \hat{f}_n$, and $b \approx \hat{d}_n - \hat{f}_n$ where,

$$\hat{d}_n = \frac{2|E|}{n}$$

$$\hat{f}_n = (2k_n X_{k_n} - \hat{d}^{k_n})^{1/k_n}. \tag{15}$$

Once we obtain an estimate for a, b then we can estimate how much we should sparsify the graph to ensure that $(a - b)^2 > 2(a + b)$, while still dropping edges to obtain a much sparser matrix, for which we can obtain the Fiedler Vector much faster. We can also estimate the percentage of the nodes we will recover using the equation $\alpha^2 = \frac{(a-b)^2 - 2(a-b)}{(a-b)^2}$, $\frac{1}{2}[1 + \mathrm{erf}(\sqrt{\alpha^2/2(1 - \alpha^2)})$ [14] .

In order to understand the percentage of the edges of the graph that we should sample we need to consider what the odds are they we will sample an edge connecting two nodes inside a community, against the odds that they will sample an inter-community edge. Ideally we would only sample edges inside the communities, since this would make the communities trivial to detect. Unfortunately, it has been shown by Luxburg et al. [9,10] that for SBM as $n \to \infty$, the effective resistance of a given edge (i, j) in the graph tends toward $\frac{1}{d_i} + \frac{1}{d_j}$. Since the degrees of the nodes in this model are $O(n)$, the variation between effective resistances will be small, and will in any case not reflect the community structure of the graph. At this point our spectral sparsifier will be selecting edges essentially at random. While Luxburg et al. state that theoretical results suggest that the effective resistances could degenerate only for very large graphs, their experimental results show that this behaviour arises even for small communities of $1,000$ vertices.

$$\mathbb{E}(E) = 2q(\frac{n}{2})^2 + 2p(\frac{n}{2})^2 \tag{16}$$

$$p_{intra} = \frac{(2p(\frac{n}{2})^2)}{\mathbb{E}(E)} \quad q_{inter} = \frac{(2q(\frac{n}{2})^2)}{\mathbb{E}(E)} \tag{17}$$

$$\hat{p} = \frac{Sp_{intra}}{2(\frac{n}{2})^2} \quad \hat{q} = \frac{Sp_{inter}}{2(\frac{n}{2})^2} \tag{18}$$

While in some sense this is a drawback, since this result is telling us we may as well sample randomly, our algorithm can still function, and we can save the cost of computing the effective resistances. For $(a-b)^2 > 2(a+b)$ to hold true, there must be significantly more intra-community edges than inter-community ones. If we are sampling randomly with spectral sparsification, we should still sample more of the desired edge type, since more of this type exist and we are sampling each edge with roughly the same probability. If we have probabilities p, q, and number of nodes n, then the expected value for the number of edges is shown in Eq. (16). We can then compute the probability of sampling an intra-community or inter-community edge as in Eq. (17). If we take S samples, Eq. (18) shows the estimated $\hat{p}, \hat{q}$ for our sparsified graph. We then have $\hat{a} = \hat{p}n$, $\hat{b} = \hat{q}n$, which can be used to decide if the communities can be recovered.

Correcting Effective Resistance. While Luxburg et al. [10] show that as $n \to \infty$ the effective resistance $\mathbf{eff}_{a,b}$ for a SBM degenerates to $(1/d_i + 1/d_j)$ for two nodes i, j, there are various methods known for correcting this. One of these is to multiply by the sum of the degrees. While this does not correct the issue in and of itself, since the effective resistance between every pair of nodes converges to two, the variance around two may be meaningful. Using these "scaled" effective resistances captures the community structure of a SBM, and sparsifying by these resistances can cause us to find the community structure of an SBM very quickly. These scaled effective resistances can be obtained by taking the scaled Laplacian $\mathcal{L}$ of our SBM, and applying the same algorithm that is used to estimate the effective resistance of L.

Given the constants a, b, we can calculate the average difference in scaled effective resistance between edges both inside the communities and outside. This is useful because it allows us to predict on average how much we should sample to ensure $(a - b)^2 > 2(a + b)$, given the increased chance of sampling inter-community edges.

Recall that $\mathbf{eff}_{a,b} = e_a \mathcal{L}^{\dagger} e_a + e_b \mathcal{L}^{\dagger} e_b - 2e_a \mathcal{L} e_b$. Using our knowledge of the spectrum of $\mathcal{L}$, we can compute the average values of these terms.

$$E[\mathcal{L}_{aa}^{\dagger}] = E[\mathcal{L}_{bb}^{\dagger}] = E[e_a D^{-1/2} \mathbf{X}^{-1} D^{-1/2} e_a] + E[e_a D^{-1/2} \mathbf{A}^{-1} D^{-1/2} e_a]$$

$$E[e_a D^{-1/2} \mathbf{X}^{-1} D^{-1/2} e_a] = \frac{1}{n} \sum \lambda \text{ by Eq. (13)}$$

$$E[\mathcal{L}_{aa}^{\dagger}] = \frac{1}{n} \int_{1-r_{\mathcal{L}}}^{1+r_{\mathcal{L}}} \frac{1}{z} \rho(z) dz = 1$$

$$E[\mathcal{L}_{ab}^{\dagger}] = E[e_a D^{1/2} X^{-1} D^{1/2} e_b] + E[e_a D^{1/2} A^{-1} D^{1/2} e_b] \tag{19}$$

$$E[e_a D^{1/2} X^{-1} D^{1/2} e_b] = 0 \text{ by Eq. (14) so}$$

$$E[\mathcal{L}_{ab}^{\dagger}] = E[e_a D^{1/2} A^{-1} D^{1/2} e_b] = e_a \frac{1}{\lambda_2} \mathbf{u}\mathbf{u}^T e_b$$

$$e_a \frac{1}{\lambda_2} \mathbf{u}\mathbf{u}^T e_b = \frac{1}{\lambda_2} (-1)^x, x = 0 \text{ if } a, b \in G \text{ and } x = 1 \text{ if } a, b \notin G.$$

We see that the effective resistance inside the group on average is $e_a \mathcal{L}^{\dagger} e_a + e_b \mathcal{L}^{\dagger} e_b - 2e_a \mathcal{L} e_b = 1 + 1 - 2\frac{1}{\lambda_2}$ and $e_a \mathcal{L}^{\dagger} e_a + e_b \mathcal{L}^{\dagger} e_b - 2e_a \mathcal{L} e_b = 1 + 1 + 2\frac{1}{\lambda_2}$ otherwise. This allows us to amend our estimates for $\hat{a}$ and $\hat{b}$. If we let r' be the ratio between the effective resistance of the two links, then Eq. (21) gives the scaled $\hat{p}'$, $\hat{q}'$.

$$p'_{intra} = \frac{p_{intra}}{p_{intra} + r' q_{intra}} \tag{20}$$

$$q'_{inter} = 1 - p'_{intra};$$

$$\hat{p}' = \frac{S p'_{intra}}{2(\frac{n}{2})^2} \quad \hat{q}' = \frac{S p'_{inter}}{2(\frac{n}{2})^2} \tag{21}$$

We note that our method above does have a potential drawback for very small graphs. This is because we need to sample $\Theta(n \log(n))$ edges to avoid the graph being disconnected [12]. As graphs become large this should be a non-issue because we have $\lim_{n \to \infty} \frac{(pn-qn)^2 - 2(pn+qn)}{n \log n} = \infty$, which indicates that our sampling criteria will require more edges than needed to ensure connectivity.

Computing the Eigenvector Using Inverse Power Iteration. One of the challenges of spectral methods is computing the eigenvectors needed for clustering, since this can be expensive. Given a nearly linear-time solver, one can compute the eigenvectors of a scaled graph Lapalcian in nearly time in the order of the number of elements of $\mathcal{L}$ [6], by using Inverse Power Iteration. This is attractive given our edge dropping strategy, where we may reduce the number of edges by several orders of magnitude for favourable graphs.

An additional feature is that it is possible to calculate a stopping criteria for the eigensolver that will allow us to recover the communities, even though the eigenvector has not fully converged. This is a desirable property, since full convergence can be slow. While the bound for our stopping criteria is not tight, it nevertheless is significantly faster than would otherwise be the case for full convergence.

Recall that for the power iteration we have an initial state $c_1\lambda_1 v_1 + \ldots c_n\lambda_n v_n$. On average the c_i terms will be of approximately the same size. We are attempting to compute the eigenvector $\mathbf{u} = (1, 1\ldots, -1, -1, \ldots)/\sqrt{n}$. After each iteration of the power method we have a resultant vector which consists of the desired eigenvector $\mathbf{u}$, and some sum of the other eigenvectors. We need to compute the likely contribution from the other eigenvectors. Once these contributions are smaller than $O(\frac{1}{\sqrt{n}})$ with high probability, we can stop the iteration, because the signal from the desired eigenvector will dominate the calculation, and allow for the correct community assignment.

We need to compute the average contribution from the remaining eigenvectors at each iteration. We begin by computing the average size for each component of the other eigenvectors. Assuming all the c_i are equal, we have $\lambda_2(\mathbf{u} + \sum \frac{\lambda_i}{\lambda_2}^k \mathbf{v})$. The eigenvectors $\mathbf{v}$ are randomly distributed around the unit sphere, as in Wigner matrices. We know from O'Rourke and Wang [17], that the elements of these eigenvectors are normally distributed variables, $N(0, \frac{1}{n})$.

Multiplying $N(0, \frac{1}{n})$ by $\frac{\lambda_i}{\lambda_2}^k$ we have $N(0, (\frac{\lambda_n}{\lambda_2})^{2k}\frac{1}{n})$ after k iterations. We then have that each component of the sum of the eigenvectors $\mathbf{v}$ are normal variables $N(0, \Sigma(\frac{\lambda_n}{\lambda_2})^{2k}\frac{1}{n})$.

We can now use Chebyshev's inequality to compute the probability that a component of the sum of the eigenvectors $\mathbf{v}$ is greater than $\frac{1}{\sqrt{n}}$, the size of the components of the dominant eigenvector $\mathbf{u}$ as follows,

$$Pr(|X - E[X]| \geq a) \leq \frac{Var[X]}{a^2}$$
$$Pr(|X| \geq \frac{1}{\sqrt{n}}) \leq \frac{Var[X]}{(\frac{1}{\sqrt{n}})^2}$$
$$Pr(|X| \geq \frac{1}{\sqrt{n}}) \leq \frac{\Sigma\frac{\lambda_n}{\lambda_2}^{2k}\frac{1}{n}}{(\frac{1}{\sqrt{n}})^2} \tag{22}$$
$$Pr(|X| \geq \frac{1}{\sqrt{n}}) \leq \Sigma(\frac{\lambda_n}{\lambda_2})^{2k}.$$

Using our knowledge of the density of the spectrum of $\mathcal{L}$, we can compute the probability in Eq. (22), for $\mathcal{L}^\dagger$ as follows,

$$\Sigma(\frac{\lambda_n}{\lambda_2})^{2k} = \int_{1-r_\mathcal{L}}^{1+r_\mathcal{L}} (\frac{\frac{1}{z}}{\lambda_2})^{2k}\rho(z)dz. \tag{23}$$

Once we know the probability of a single component of the eigenvector being greater than the $\frac{1}{\sqrt{n}}$, we can use this in a binomial distribution to calculate how many elements we are likely to incorrectly classify. We can, either stop when k is large enough to imply this is close to zero, or when the number is the same order as the error introduced by the perturbation of the main eigenvector from the addition of the random eigenvectors to $< \mathbf{A} >$, as given in [13].

Regularized Spectral Clustering. While spectral clustering is robust for matrices with high average degrees (*cf.* Saade et al. [8]), for very sparse matrices that have low degree entries the technique may struggle to recover the communities when the graph approaches the theoretical limits of community detection. This issue is exacerbated by the fact that we are dropping edges, and thus may create such problematic cases. To combat this we use the method of regularized spectral clustering method given in Saade et al. [8]. Given a regularization parameter τ, and the matrix $\mathbf{J}$ with constant entries $\frac{1}{n}$, the authors first define the regularized adjacency matrix $\mathbf{A}_\tau$ as,

$$\mathbf{A}_\tau = \mathbf{A} + \tau \mathbf{J} \tag{24}$$

Similarly they define the regularized diagonal as D_τ as,

$$\mathbf{D}_\tau = \mathbf{D} + \mathbf{I}\tau \tag{25}$$

Then the regularized scaled Laplacian is given as,

$$\mathcal{L}_\tau = \mathbf{D}_\tau^{-1/2}\mathbf{A} + \tau \mathbf{J}\mathbf{D}_\tau^{-1/2} \tag{26}$$

We note that the Fiedler vector of this matrix can be computed using the power method using nearly linear-time sparse solvers. $\mathbf{D}_\tau^{-1/2}\mathbf{A}\mathbf{D}_\tau^{-1/2}$ is symmetric and diagonally dominate so we can make use of nearly linear-time solvers to compute $(\mathbf{D}_\tau^{-1/2}\mathbf{A}\mathbf{D}_\tau^{-1/2})^{-1}x$. Then, since $\mathbf{D}_\tau^{-1/2}\tau \mathbf{J}\mathbf{D}_\tau^{-1/2}$ is a rank one matrix $\tau \mathbf{D}_\tau^{-1/2}j\mathbf{D}_\tau^{-1/2}j^T = \mathbf{D}_\tau^{-1/2}\tau \mathbf{J}\mathbf{D}_\tau^{-1/2}$, we can compute $\mathcal{L}_\tau^{-1}$ using the Sherman-Morrison formula which allows us to solve $\mathcal{L}_\tau^{-1}$ in terms of $\mathbf{D}_\tau^{-1/2}\mathbf{A}\mathbf{D}_\tau^{-1/2}$.

$$(\mathbf{D}_\tau^{-1/2}\mathbf{A}\mathbf{D}_\tau^{-1/2})^{-1} = \mathcal{A}^{-1}, \mathbf{S} = \frac{\mathcal{A}^{-1}\mathbf{D}_\tau^{-1/2}j\mathbf{D}_\tau^{-1/2}j^T\mathcal{A}^{-1}}{1 + \mathbf{D}_\tau^{-1/2}j^T\mathcal{A}^{-1}\mathbf{D}_\tau^{-1/2}j} \rightarrow$$
$$\mathcal{L}_\tau^{-1} = (\mathbf{D}_\tau^{-1/2}\mathbf{A}\mathbf{D}_\tau^{-1/2} + \mathbf{D}_\tau^{-1/2}j\mathbf{D}_\tau^{-1/2}j^T)^{-1} = (\mathbf{D}_\tau^{-1/2}\mathbf{A}\mathbf{D}_\tau^{-1/2})^{-1} - \mathbf{S} \tag{27}$$

Using Eq. (27) we can then proceed to compute the Fielder vector using power iteration. In order to determine when to stop the power iteration we proceed in the same way as in **Computing the Eigenvector Using Inverse Power Iteration** by determining the spectrum $\mathcal{L}_\tau$. We begin by noting that $\mathcal{L}_\tau$ has the same spectrum as $D_\tau^{1/2}AD_\tau^{1/2}$, except that the top eigenvalue is increased by the rank one update $\mathbf{D}_\tau^{-1/2}\tau \mathbf{J}\mathbf{D}_\tau^{-1/2}$, as discussed in Ding and Zhou [15]. Since we will project out this eigenvector when performing power iteration, we then only need to consider the density function of $\mathbf{D}_\tau^{-1/2}\tau \mathbf{A}\mathbf{D}_\tau^{-1/2}$. By the same argument that we used Eq. (12), we can show that as n increases, *whp* this density function is given by,

$$\rho(z) = \frac{2n}{\pi} \frac{\sqrt{\frac{2(a+b)}{(d+\tau)^2} - z^2}}{\frac{2(a+b)}{(d+\tau)^2}} \tag{28}$$

Our Algorithm. We now present our algorithm. We first obtain (or the user provides) an estimate for the Stochastic Block Model (SBM) parameters. We then obtain the scaled effective resistances **eff** of the elements of the scaled Laplacian $\mathcal{L}$, which we then use to create a probability density function. We note that we modify the probability density function to sample the edges that have a low effective resistance over those that have a high resistance, since these are the edges that make up our community. This approach is slightly different from the standard algorithm of Spielman and Srivastava [5], which seeks to sample the highest resistance edges.

Next we compute the estimated p, q we will obtain after sparsification, using either Eq. (18) or (21), depending on our sampling strategy, and based on this we decide how much sparsification we can safely apply. After creating our new matrix, we then obtain the relevant eigenvector, depending on whether we are using the Laplacian or the Regularized Laplacian from Eq. (26).

Algorithm 1. RecursivePartition

INPUT: adj matrix A, boolean S for using scaled effective resistance (**eff**), regularization parameter τ

RETURN: partition p

[p,q]=EstParam(A) { Est param using eqn. (15)}

if $S ==$ True **then**

    $\mathcal{L}$ = CreateScaledLap(A);

    eff = EstResistance($\mathcal{L}$) { Est resistance using Spielman and Srivastava [5]}

    $pdf = \frac{(\mathbf{eff}-min(\mathbf{eff}))}{\sum((\mathbf{eff}-min(\mathbf{eff})))}$ {Normalize distribution}

    $pdf = 1 - pdf$ {Sample the low resistance nodes}

    S=0 {Init. number of samples}

    while $(\hat{a}' - \hat{b}')^2 - 2(\hat{a}' + \hat{b}') \leq 0$ **do**

        Increase S

        $[\hat{a}' \ \hat{b}']$= EstSparseAB(p,q,S) {est $\hat{a}' \ \hat{b}'$ using eqn. (21)}

    end while

    [i j]= find(A)

    [ni nj]= randsample(S,pdf); {Sample S with pdf}

else

    [i j]= find(A)

    [ni nj]= randsample(S); {Sample S with uniform distribution}

end if

A=sparse(i(ni), j(nj),1, size(A,1), size(A,2)) {Create the Sparsified Adjacency Matrix}

D_τ = CreateDiag(A)+τ {Create Degree Matrix }

$\mathcal{L}_\tau = D_\tau^{-1/2} A D_\tau^{-1/2}$

[v e]=powermethod($\mathcal{L}_\tau$); {Get eigenvector}

[i p]= sort(v) {Get permutation}

return p

A Comment on Complexity. While the best performance we obtained was by using the scaled effective resistance, depending on what solver is available, this may not always be the most effective strategy. This is because obtaining the scaled effective resistances using the method of Spielman and Srivastava [5], requires us to solve a number of linear systems. If a nearly linear time solver is available, this will take $O(m)$ time, where m is the number of edges before our dropping strategy. This will dominate the cost of the computation, and we will not get significant speed-up from using power iteration, which is of order $O(m')$, where m' again is the number of sparsified edges. In the case of our examples this is clearly sub-optimal, since we can reduce m several orders of magnitude and still recover the communities, even when we are dropping edges randomly. In this case it makes sense <u>not</u> to use the scaled effective resistance. On the other hand, in practice, we may wish to use a different eigensolver, since the code for these may be more mature. In this case, the cost of the eigensolver may dominate, especially since the cost of applicable solvers (such as Lanczos-based solvers), does not entirely depend on m. In this case the use of scaled effective resistance sampling may be more effective.

3   Empirical Evaluation

We now present some experimental results. We first examine the difference between effective-resistance and scaled-effective resistance, and how closely they follow the predicted percentage of recovery. Additionally, we investigate the time needed to compute the eigenvectors of the sparsified versus the unsparsified matrix, and our convergence criteria for the Fiedler Vector.

Recovery of Communities. We now examine the success of our method in recovering the communities with the given sparsification. In Figs. 1a we see that using the Regularized Laplacian we can quickly recover almost all the nodes correctly, at around the sparsification level, predicted by Eqs. (18) and (21). This also highlights the impact of using the scaled effective resistance for sampling, with the method converging faster, and following the prediction of Eq. (21) more closely. We note that for both sampling methods the percent of edges we preserve is very small, of the order of 10^{-3} of the original graph for the Scaled Effective Resistance method.

In Fig. 1b, we try the real-world example of Saade et al. [8], where the authors attempt to partition two blogging communities by their political alignment. This is an interesting example because the communities are difficult to recover, requiring the use of regularization techniques, and because the graph structure is not exactly captured by the SBM model. Further this graph is quite small with only 1, 222 nodes, meaning that the graph may be disconnected, as discussed earlier in Sect. 2. Despite these difficulties, we are still able to recover the communities even after a significant amount of sparsification is applied, at the point that our criteria indicate we should be successful.

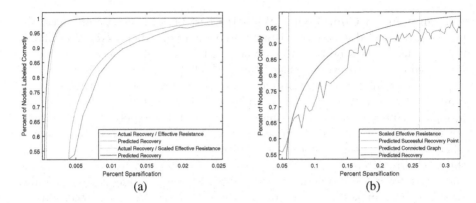

Fig. 1. (a) Results of recovering the communities using regularization after sparsification SBM $(10000, 0.5, 0.3)$. Shows the results for Effective resistance and Scaled Effective Resistance as well as predicted recovery. (b) Results of recovering the communities using regularization after sparsification for the political blog example. This example shows the effect of sparsification on a small graph, where there is an interval between the sparsification criteria, and the point at which the graph is connected.

Time Saved in Eigenvector Calculation. One of the main motivations of this work is to obtain the correct community labels while spending less time computing the require eigenvectors. Since we are able to recover the communities, despite applying large amounts of sparsification, we would expect our eigensolver to converge faster. Exactly how fast depends on the solver. For the eigensolver shown in Spielman and Teng [6], built on top of their nearly linear-time solver and constructed solely to find the Fiedler vector of the Laplacian, our time to compute the eigenvector would depend on the number of elements of our graph. Since we have reduced the number of elements by multiple orders of magnitude when sampling with scaled effective-resistance we would get a multiple order of magnitude speed-up. Unfortunately, these solvers are not available for use in production code, so we do not benchmark them here.

When using the off-the-shelf solver available in Matlab to find the desired eigenvector, with our best method we achieve essentially an order of magnitude speed-up. This is because the solvers used by this method are not optimized for graphs in the way that the solver of Spielman and Teng. The observed speed-up can be seen in Table 1b.

While we do not have a nearly linear-time solver to fairly benchmark our Inverse Power method, we are able to test the number of iterations required to obtain 10^{-8} accuracy vs the number of iterations recommended by our stopping criteria, seen in Table 1a. In all four cases all the community nodes were recovered, even though the sparsification was of the order of $O(10^{-3})$.

Table 1. (a) Speed-up in eigensolver from sparsification for the Regularized Laplacian for SBMs (10000, 0.5, 0.3) and (10000, 0.5, 0.2) respectively, using an off the shelf solver. (b) Number of iterations of the inverse power method required to reach the stopping criteria vs number of iterations to reach 10^{-8} accuracy using the Scaled Laplacian for the SMB (10000, 0.5, 0.3).

SMB.5,.3	Sparse	SMB.5,.2	Sparse
1.168185 sec	0.141 sec	1.05 sec	0.075 sec

(a)

Criteria	To 10^{-8}	Criteria	To 10^{-8}
1.148 sec	0.141 sec	12	102

(b)

4 Conclusion and Future Work

In this paper we explored the use of sparsifying by effective resistance and scaled effective resistances in order to recover sparsify SBMs, as well as effective stopping criteria for eigensolvers used for community detection. The main goal is to obtain faster solutions while still being confident in our ability to recover the communities. We have provided a method that determines the number of samples needed, depending on the type of sampling used. We found that the community structure can be recovered even when the matrix becomes very sparse. Since SBMs are a commonly studied model for clustering, this method is widely applicable. We leave several areas open for future work. While SBMs are widely studied, the model has certain intrinsic limits which prevent it from modeling certain real-world networks well. We would like to provide a similar analysis for more complex community models, in particular models which have a non-constant average degree. We could then apply our model to a larger variety of real-world graphs.

Acknowledgements. We would like to acknowledge the efforts of Professor Peter W. Eklund, who helped make this paper possible.

References

1. Girvan, M., Newman, M.E.J.: Community structure in social and biological networks. Proc. Natl. Acad. Sci. USA **99**, 7821–7826 (2002)
2. Condon, A., Karp, R.M.: Algorithms for graph partitioning on the planted partition model. Random Struct. Algor. **18**, 116–140 (2001)
3. Abbe, E.: Community detection and stochastic block models: recent developments. J. Mach. Learn. Res. **18**(1), 6446–6531 (2017)
4. Pothen, A., Simon, H., Liou, K.: Partitioning sparse matrices with eigenvectors of graphs. SIAM. J. Matrix Anal. Appl. **11**(3), 430–452 (1990)
5. Spielman, D., Srivastava, N.: Graph Sparsification by effective resistances. In: Proceedings of the 40th Annual ACM symposium on Theory of computing, STOC 2008, pp. 563–568 (2008)
6. Spielman, D., Teng, S.: Nearly linear time algorithms for preconditioning and solving symmetric, diagonally dominant linear systems. SIAM J. Matrix Anal. Appl. **35**(3), 835–885 (2014)

7. Mossel, E., Neeman, J., Sly, A.: Reconstruction and estimation in the planted partition model. Probab. Theory Relat. Fields **162**(3), 431–461 (2014). https:// doi.org/10.1007/s00440-014-0576-6
8. Saade, A., Krzakala, F., Zdeborová, L.: Impact of regularization on spectral clustering. Ann. Stat. **44**, 1765–1791 (2016)
9. Luxburg, U., Radl, A., Hein, M.: Getting lost in space: Large sample analysis of the resistance distance. In: Advances in Neural Information Processing Systems, vol. 23 (2010)
10. Luxburg, U., Radl, A., Hein, M.: Hitting and commute times in large random neighborhood graphs. J. Mach. Learn. Res. **15**, 1751–1798 (2014)
11. Avrachenkov, K., Cottatellucci, L., Kadavankandy, A.: Spectral properties of random matrices for stochastic block model. In: WiOpt, pp. 25–29, May 2015
12. Fung, W.S., Hariharan, R., Harvey, N.J., Panigrahi, D.: A general framework for graph sparsification. In: STOC 2011, pp. 71–80, 06–08 June 2011
13. McSherry, F.: Spectral partitioning of random graphs. In: Proceedings 42nd IEEE Symposium on Foundations of Computer Science (2001)
14. Nadakuditi, R.R., Newman, M.E.: Graph spectra and the detectability of community structure in networks. Phys. Rev. Lett. **108**(18), 188701 (2012)
15. Ding, J., Zhou, A.: Eigenvalues of rank-one updated matrices with some applications. Appl. Math. Lett. **20**(12), 1223–1226 (2007)
16. Lutzeyer, J., Walden, A.: Comparing graph spectra of adjacency and Laplacian matrices. arXiv:171203769
17. O'Rourke, S., Vu, V., Wang, K.: Eigenvectors of random matrices: a survey. J. Comb. Theory Ser. A **144**, 361–442 (2016)

Deep Multimodal Clustering with Cross Reconstruction

Xianchao Zhang[1,2], Xiaorui Tang[1,2], Linlin Zong[1,2(✉)], Xinyue Liu[1,2], and Jie Mu[1,2]

[1] School of Software, Dalian University of Technology, Dalian 116620, China
llzong@dlut.edu.cn
[2] Key Laboratory for Ubiquitous Network and Service Software
of Liaoning Province, Dalian 116024, China

Abstract. Recently, there has been surging interests in multimodal clustering. And extracting common features plays a critical role in these methods. However, since the ignorance of the fact that data in different modalities shares similar distributions in feature space, most works did not mining the inter-modal distribution relationships completely, which eventually leads to unacceptable common features. To address this issue, we propose the deep multimodal clustering with cross reconstruction method, which firstly focuses on multimodal feature extraction in an unsupervised way and then clusters these extracted features. The proposed cross reconstruction aims to build latent connections among different modalities, which effectively reduces the distribution differences in feature space. The theoretical analysis shows that the cross reconstruction reduces the Wasserstein distance of multimodal feature distributions. Experimental results on six benchmark datasets demonstrate that our method achieves obviously improvement over several state-of-arts.

Keywords: Deep learning · Unsupervised learning · Multimodal clustering

1 Introduction

Clustering is a vital research topic in data science and machine learning. Multimodal clustering is an important field in clustering and has made great progress. Multimodal clustering aims to divide the multimodal data information into different clusters in an unsupervised manner. The existing works usually are based on spectral clustering [14], subspace clustering [1], deep clustering [23] etc. On account of the amazing performance for feature extraction and dimensionality reduction tasks, deep clustering receives much attention in recent years [12,17,20,23]. For deep multimodal clustering, the most common method extracts common features from different modalities [19] by using multiple deep neural networks (DNN) and clusters on the common features.

This work was supported by National Science Foundation of China (No. 61876028; No. 61632019; No. 61972065; No. 61806034).

H. W. Lauw et al. (Eds.): PAKDD 2020, LNAI 12084, pp. 305–317, 2020.
https://doi.org/10.1007/978-3-030-47426-3_24

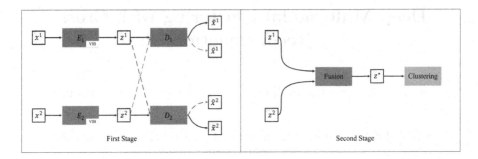

Fig. 1. The two stages of DMCR framework: The left part illustrates the first stage. Two autoencoders extract features from two modalities, VIB is used both in E_1 and E_2. $\tilde{x}^1$ are reconstructed from z^1, $\tilde{x}^2$ are reconstructed from z^2. The dotted lines illustrate the cross reconstruction method, $\hat{x}^1$ are reconstructed from z^2, $\hat{x}^2$ are reconstructed from z^1. The right part illustrates the second stage. The fusion layers fuse the features z^1 and z^2 to common features z^*, which are used for clustering.

So far, the deep neural networks (DNN) based multimodal clustering methods can be divided into three categories: autoencoder based methods [16], Deep Bolzmann Machine (DBM) based methods [19] and deep canonical correlation analysis (DCCA) [3] based methods [21]. The autoencoder based methods use autoencoders to extract common features of different modalities and choose common features that can best reconstruct the input data [16,21]. However, autoencoders do not really discover the similarity of the common feature distributions. The DBM based methods [19] learn a joint representation of different modalities by DBM. But due to the high computational costs in high-dimensional data space [11], the DBM based methods have not been widely studied in recent years. The DCCA based methods [21] learn features that are most correlated from different modalities by canonical correlation analysis (CCA). Like autoencoder based methods, DCCA based methods use autoencoders to extract features from different modalities, called deep canonically correlated autoencoder (DCCAE) [21]. The difference is that DCCAE further optimizes the canonical correlation among features of different modalities. But DCCA based methods lack the analysis of probability theory, which makes it difficult to measure the distribution differences of different modalities. Moreover, data of different modalities contain different numerical characteristics, and may not show obvious correlation. In this case, the depth typical correlation analysis may not be effective.

In this paper, we focus on multimodal clustering by extracting the common features of multimodal data in an unsupervised way, and reduce the distribution differences of different modalities in feature space. Firstly, we apply Variational Information Bottleneck (VIB) [2] to extract features from different modalities. By minimizing mutual information between raw data and the extracted features, VIB can control the amount of information owing through the network when extracting features. And due to the mutual information, VIB also provides explicit probabilistic analysis on feature space. Secondly, we apply cross reconstruction method during extracting features from different modalities, which can effectively reduce the distribution differences of different modalities in feature space. We also provide theoretical analysis to prove the similarity of multimodal distributions. Thirdly, we fuse the extracted features to common features using fusion layers. Finally, we cluster the common features using clustering algorithm. The entire process above constitute our deep multimodal clustering with cross reconstruction (DMCR).

The contributions of this work are summarized as below: (1) We propose a novel deep multimodal clustering algorithm, which can effectively reduce the distribution differences among different modalities in feature space. (2) We provide a theoretical analysis to prove that the proposed cross reconstruction method effectively reduce the distribution difference of different modalities in feature space. (3) Experiments show obviously improvement over state-of-the-art multimodal clustering methods on six benchmark multimodal datasets.

2   Related Work

2.1   Deep Clustering

The existing deep clustering methods are roughly divided into two categories: two-stage methods and end-to-end methods [21].

The two-stage methods first extract features of the data by deep learning method, and finally apply the clustering methods to the features. Tian et al. [20] uses autoencoder to extract the features of graph and finally uses k-means to cluster. Chen [7] applies Deep Belief Network (DBN) to extract features and finally uses non-parametric maximum-margin clustering to cluster the features.

The end-to-end methods jointly optimize the feature extraction and clustering. The joint unsupervised learning (JULE) algorithm [24] uses a recurrent framework for joint unsupervised learning of deep representations and image clustering, which are optimized jointly in training process. The deep embedding clustering (DEC) algorithm [23] clusters a set of data points in a jointly optimized feature space. Based on DEC, the improved deep embedding clustering (IDEC) algorithm [12] jointly optimization and preserve local structure of data generating distribution.

2.2   Multimodal Clustering

Based on the basic algorithms used in the multimodal methods, the existing multimodal clustering are roughly divided into two categories: the traditional clustering based methods [5,6,10,22,25] and deep clustering based methods [3, 16,19,21].

The traditional clustering based methods learn a consensus matrix or minimize the divergence of multiple views simultaneously. For example, the multiview spectral clustering (MMSC) algorithm [5] learns a commonly shared graph Laplacian matrix by unifying different modalities. Gao et al. [10] proposes a novel NMF-based multi-view clustering algorithm by searching for a factorization that gives compatible clustering solutions across multimodal. The diversity-induced multi-view subspace clustering (DIMSC) algorithm [6] extend the existing subspace clustering into the multimodal domain. The low-rank tensor constrained multi-view subspace clustering (LT-MSC) algorithm [25] introduces a low-rank tensor constraint to explore the complementary information from multimodal data. The exclusivity-consistency regularized multi-view subspace clustering (ECMSC) algorithm [22] attempts to harness the complementary information between different representations by introducing a novel position-aware exclusivity term.

Deep clustering based methods firstly jointly learn low-dimensional features from multimodal data, and then cluster the features. Ngiam et al. [16] proposes a series of frameworks for deep multimodal learning based on autoencoders. Srivastava and Salakhutdinov [19] proposes a deep multimodal representation learning framework, which learns a joint representation of different modalities by DBM. The DCCA [3] learns complex nonlinear transformations of two modalities of data such that the resulting representations are highly linearly correlated. The DCCAE [21] add an autoencoder regularization term to DCCA.

3   The Proposed Algorithm

In this section, we introduce our DMCR algorithm in detail. Consider the problem of clustering a set of n points $X = \{x_1, x_2, ..., x_n\}$ into k clusters $\{c_1, c_2, ..., c_k\}$, each data point x_i contains m modalities $x_i = \{x_i^1, x_i^2, ..., x_i^m\}$. These modalities have different dimensions, i.e. $x_i^1 \in R^{d_1}$, $x_i^2 \in R^{d_2}$,..., $x_i^m \in R^{d_m}$. Data in the same modality have the same dimensions. Multimodal clustering patitions data in m modalities into k clusters.

Figure 1 illustrates the framework of DMCR for two modalities. The DMCR has two stages. In the first stage, we extract features from different modalities using VIB and cross reconstruction to constrain encoders, which ensures the extracted features of different modalities sharing similar distributions. In the first stage of Fig. 1, E_1 and D_1 are the encoder and decoder used for the first modality, E_2 and D_2 are the encoder and decoder used for the second modality; z^1 and z^2 are features extracted from x^1 and x^2; VIB in E_1 and E_2 denote the VIB regularization terms; $\tilde{x}^1$ and $\tilde{x}^2$ are data reconstructed from z^1 and z^2; $\hat{x}^1$ and $\hat{x}^2$ are data reconstructed from cross reconstruction; In the second stage, we fuse the features to common features by fusion layers, then we cluster these fused common features. In the second stage of Fig. 1, the fusion layers fuse features from different modalities to common features, z^* is the common features. We describe our algorithm next.

3.1   Multimodal Feature Extraction

Multimodal data contain modality-unique features and modality-common features. It is difficult to extract the modality-common features directly from different modalities with traditional encoders. We first use the Variational Information Bottleneck (VIB) [2] to extract the modality-common features among different modalities. And then apply Cross Reconstruction method to ensure the modality-common features of different modalities satisfy similar distribution.

Multimodal Feature Extraction with VIB. We adopt deep autoencoders as a features extractor. For a given input x^i in the i-th modality, the encoder aims to get a feature z^i in a low-dimensional space, and the decoder aims to reconstruct the input from the latent representation. So, the goal of the deep autoencoder is to get a good reconstruction $\tilde{x}^i$ for input x^i.

But autoencoders cannot control the amount of information contained in extracted features, which makes it difficult to extract modality-common features from each modality.

Given that VIB is able to control the scale of feature information, we use the VIB [2] regularization term in the encoders to eliminate unique features and extract the common features. The loss function of extracting features of the i-th modality is:

$$\min_{\theta^i, \varphi^i} E_{x^i \sim p(x^i)} [-E_{z^i \sim p(z^i|x^i;\theta^i)} [\log q(\tilde{x}^i|z^i;\varphi^i)] + \beta KL(p(z^i|x^i;\theta^i)||q(z^i))], \quad (1)$$

where $p(z^i|x^i;\theta^i)$ denotes the encoder for the i-th modality; θ^i is the parameter of the encoder; $q(x^i|z^i;\varphi^i)$ denotes the decoder for the i-th modality; z^i are generated with reparameterization trick [2,13]; φ^i is the parameter of the decoder; β controls the weight of the VIB regularization term. The first term $-E_{z^i \sim p(z^i|x^i;\theta^i)} [\log q(\tilde{x}^i|z^i;\varphi^i)]$ in Eq. 1 is the reconstruction loss of autoencoder for the i-th modality. The second term in Eq. 1 is the VIB regularization loss for the i-th modality.

Cross Reconstruction. In the last section, we only extract modality-common features from each modality using VIB. In multimodal learning tasks, the basic task is mining the relationships among different modalities. Previous work, such as DCCAE [21] learn complex nonlinear transformations of two modalities of data such that the resulting representations are highly linearly correlated. But data of different modalities have different numerical characteristics, correlation constraints on different modalities may failed to capture the statistical properties of implicit features. Considering the fact that modality-common features of different modalities share similar distributions, we propose a cross reconstruction method to promote the features extraction process.

The dotted lines in Fig. 1 represent the our cross reconstruction process. The decoders D_1 and D_2 both take z^1 and z^2 as inputs simultaneously. Specifically, the green dotted lines in Fig. 1 represent reconstructing x^1 with z^2 using D_1 and the red dotted lines in Fig. 1 represent reconstructing x^2 with z^1 using D_2. The loss function of reconstructing x^j with z^i ($j \neq i$) is:

$$\min_{\theta^i, \varphi^j} E_{x^i \sim p(x^i)} [-E_{z^i \sim p(z^i|x^i;\theta^i)} [\log q(\hat{x}^j|z^i;\varphi^j)]]. \quad (2)$$

where $q(\hat{x}^j|z^i;\varphi^j)$ denotes the decoder used for reconstructing x^j with z^i. Note that, it is also the same decoder for reconstructing x^j with z^j .

As a regularization term, cross reconstruction restrains the similarity of different modalities in distribution, which will analysed later.

The Overall Loss Function. The complete loss function of extracting feature of the i-th modality is:

$$\min E_{x^i\sim p(x^i)}[[-E_{z^i\sim p(z^i|x^i;\theta^i)}[\log q(\tilde{x}^i|z^i;\varphi^i)] + \beta KL(p(z^i|x^i;\theta^i)||q(z^i))$$

$$+\gamma[\sum_{j=1}^{M,j\neq i} -E_{z^i\sim p(z^i|x^i;\theta^i)}[\log q(\hat{x}^j|z^i;\varphi^j)]]], \tag{3}$$

where j represents a modality except the i-th modality; the last term of Eq. 3 is cross reconstruction regularization loss of reconstructing x^j with z^i; γ controls the weight of the cross reconstruction regularization term.

Algorithm 1. Training Process of Deep Multimodal Clustering with Cross Reconstruction.

Input:
    The number of modality m;
    The dataset of n data points for each modality i: $x^i = \{x_1^i, x_2^i, ..., x_n^i\}$, $i \in [1, m]$.
1: **for** number of training iterations **do**
2:     Sampling a minibatch of samples from each modality;
3:     **for** each $i \in [1, m]$ **do**
4:         $\mu(x^i), \sigma(x^i) = E_i(x^i)$;
5:         $z^i = \text{Reparameterization}(\mu(x^i), \sigma(x^i))$;
6:         $\tilde{x}^i = D_i(z^i)$;
7:         **for** each $j \in [1, m]\backslash i$ **do**
8:             $\hat{x}^j = D_j(z^i)$;
9:         **end for**
10:        Training E_i with Eq.3;
11:     **end for**
12: **end for**
13: **for** number of training iterations **do**
14:     Sampling a minibatch of samples from each modality;
15:     **for** each $i \in [1, m]$ **do**
16:         $\mu(x^i), \sigma(x^i) = E_i(x^i)$;
17:         $z^i = \text{Reparameterization}(\mu(x^i), \sigma(x^i))$;
18:     **end for**
19:     $z^* = \text{Fusion}(z^1, z^2, ..., z^m; \eta)$;
20:     Training the fusion layer with Eq.5;
21: **end for**

3.2 Feature Fusion

After extracting features from different modalities, we fuse these features to common features, then cluster on the common features. As shown in the second stage of Fig. 1, we use fusion layers to fuse extracted features. The fusion layers consist of fully connected layers, and z^* is the fused common features:

$$z^* = \text{Fusion}(z^1, ..., z^m; \eta), \tag{4}$$

where η is the parameter of the fusion layers. We use L2 loss between z^* and extracted features of different modalities to train the fusion layers:

$$\min_{\eta} \sum_{i=1}^{m} \left\| z^* - z^i \right\|_2 . \tag{5}$$

3.3 The DMCR Algorithm

In this section, we describe the training process and clustering process of DMCR. The entire training process has two steps: (1) Training the autoencoders with Eq. 3. (2) Training the fusion layers according to Eq. 5. The training process of DMCR is summarized in Algorithm 1.

After training DMCR, we get the common features associated with multimodal data. Then we cluster the common features. Here, we choose k-means as the final clustering algorithm. The clustering process of DMCR is summarized in Algorithm 2.

Algorithm 2. Clustering Process of Deep Multimodal Clustering with Cross Reconstruction.

Input:
    The number of modality m;
    The dataset of n data points for each modality i: $x^i = \{x_1^i, x_2^i, ..., x_n^i\}$, $i \in [1, m]$;
    The number of clusters k.
Output:
    Cluster assignments for n multimodal data points: $C = \{c_1, c_2, ..., c_n\}$, $c_i \in [1, k]$, $i \in [1, n]$.
1: **for** each $i \in [1, m]$ **do**
2:     $\mu(x^i), \sigma(x^i) = E_i(x^i)$;
3:     $z^i = \text{Reparameterization}(\mu(x^i), \sigma(x^i))$;
4: **end for**
5: $z^* = \text{Fusion}(z^1, z^2, ..., z^m; \eta)$;
6: $C = k\text{-means}(z^*, k)$.

---

4 Theoretical Analysis

As mentioned previously, cross reconstruction can build implicit connection among different modalities. In this section, we explore the probability theory of connection among different modalities built by cross reconstruction method. Here we assume $q(\hat{x}^i | z^i; \varphi^i)$ to be a Gaussian distribution in the i-th modality with mean $\mu_i(z^i)$ and variance $\sigma_i^2(z^i)$, $q(\hat{x}^i | z^j; \varphi^i)$ to be a Gaussian distribution in the i-th modality with mean $\mu_j(z^j)$ and variance $\sigma_j^2(z^j)$. And then we can further derive the loss function of cross reconstruction:

$$L_i = E_{x^i \sim p(x^i)}[-E_{z^i \sim p(z^i | x^i; \theta^i)}[\log q(\hat{x}^i | z^i; \varphi^i)]]$$

$$= E_{x^i \sim p(x^i)}[E_{z^i \sim p(z^i | x^i; \theta^i)}[\frac{1}{2} \log 2\pi + \frac{1}{2} \log \sigma_i^2(z^i) + \frac{(x^i - \mu_i(z^i))^2}{2\sigma_i^2(z^i)}]],$$

$$L_j = E_{x^j \sim p(x^j)}[-E_{z^j \sim p(z^j | x^j; \theta^j)}[\log q(\hat{x}^i | z^j; \varphi^i)]]$$

$$= E_{x^j \sim p(x^j)}[E_{z^j \sim p(z^j | x^j; \theta^j)}[\frac{1}{2} \log 2\pi + \frac{1}{2} \log \sigma_j^2(z^j) + \frac{(x^i - \mu_j(z^j))^2}{2\sigma_j^2(z^j)}]],$$

where L_i represents the loss of reconstructing x^i with z^i; L_j represents the loss of reconstructing x^i with z^j.

Combining L_i and L_j, both $\mu_i(z^i)$ and $\mu_j(z^j)$ reduce the difference from x^i, which means that the difference between $\mu_i(z^i)$ and $\mu_j(z^j)$ also decrease. Note that both $\mu_i(z^i)$ and $\mu_j(z^j)$ are outputs of decoder D_i, so the input of D_i, i.e. z^i and z^j are similar. z^i and z^j are generated with reparameterization trick:

$$z^i = \text{Reparameterization}(\mu(x^i), \sigma(x^i)),$$
$$z^j = \text{Reparameterization}(\mu(x^j), \sigma(x^j)),$$

where $\mu(x^i)$ and $\sigma(x^i)$ are the outputs of E_i, $\mu(x^j)$ and $\sigma(x^j)$ are the outputs of E_j; z^i and z^j are randomly sampled from Gaussian distribution $N_i(\mu(x^i), \sigma(x^i))$ and $N_j(\mu(x^j), \sigma(x^j))$ respectively. So the Wasserstein distance [4] between N_i and N_j also decrease:

$$W(N_i, N_j) = inf_{\epsilon \in \sqcap(N_i,N_j)} E_{(z_i,z_j)\sim\epsilon}[\| z_i - z_j \|], \tag{6}$$

where $\sqcap(N_i, N_j)$ denotes the set of all joint distributions where the marginals of $\epsilon(z_i, z_j)$ are N_i and N_j respectively. Therefore, under the constraints of cross reconstruction, these encoders will reduce the distribution differences of multi-modal features. So we prove that the cross reconstruction constrain extracted features to share similar distributions in feature spaces of different modalities.

5 Experiments

5.1 Description of Datasets

We test our model on six multimodal datasets: Digits[1], CNN[2], AwA[3], Cal101[4], LUse-21[5] and Scene-15 [9]: Digits contains three modalities of 2000 samples belonging to 10 clusters. The three modalities respectively have 76, 216 and 240 dimensions. CNN is a news dataset that contains two modalities of 2107 samples belonging to 7 clusters. The first modality consists of text contents, the second modality contains the images of articles. AwA contains three modalities of 5814 samples belonging to 10 clusters. These three modalities are local self-similarity features, SIFT features and SURF features. Cal101, LUse-21 and Scene-15 contain three modalities: we extract LBP, GIST and CENTRIST descriptors from these datasets as three modalities. Cal101 contains 712 samples and these samples belong to 10 clusters. LUse-21 contains 2100 samples belonging to 21 clusters. Scene-15 contains 3000 samples assigned to 15 clusters.

---

[1] https://archive.ics.uci.edu/ml/datasets/Multiple+Features.
[2] https://sites.google.com/site/qianmingjie/home/datasets/cnn-and-fox-news.
[3] https://cvml.ist.ac.at/AwA/.
[4] http://www.vision.caltech.edu/Image_Datasets/Caltech101/.
[5] http://weegee.vision.ucmerced.edu/datasets/landuse.html.

Table 1. Clustering ACC (%)

	DEC	IDEC	JULE	DCCAE	MMSC	RMKMC	LT-MSC	DIMSC	ECMSC	DMC	DMCR
Digits	44.07	46.70	76.36	66.19	54.00	73.30	73.35	52.10	77.40	85.55	**90.75**
CNN	36.96	31.69	40.00	34.27	32.02	34.21	21.26	21.64	25.34	55.52	**66.68**
AwA	16.10	20.08	23.05	24.31	20.28	23.17	24.17	20.79	22.19	26.23	**28.67**
Cal101	35.74	43.54	63.20	62.85	49.02	51.97	61.35	39.47	53.90	62.50	**66.57**
LUse-21	12.34	25.14	27.14	23.72	20.38	27.24	30.86	22.81	25.29	30.14	**31.62**
Scene-15	16.97	25.03	38.10	34.95	18.20	40.03	43.93	23.87	42.70	44.60	**54.00**

5.2 Comparing Methods

We compare the proposed DMCR algorithm with the following baselines: (1) Single modal clustering: DEC [23], IDEC [12] and JULE [24]. We test these methods on each modality data and take the best result as their final result. Multimodal clustering: MMSC [5], RMKMC [10], DIMSC [6], LT-MSC [25], ECMSC [22] and DCCAE [21]. Among these multimodal clustering methods, DCCAE is a two-modal method. In order to extend DCCAE to multimodal clustering task, we combine every two of the multiple modalities, and take the average results as the final result. (3) The simplified DMCR: the DMCR without cross reconstruction regularization term, called DMC.

Table 2. Clustering NMI (%)

	DEC	IDEC	JULE	DCCAE	MMSC	RMKMC	LT-MSC	DIMSC	ECMSC	DMC	DMCR
Digits	35.11	44.46	70.25	67.59	57.21	70.74	70.40	39.25	71.21	74.98	**83.17**
CNN	20.79	13.28	18.44	14.27	11.31	13.07	13.84	12.67	18.87	37.74	**50.93**
AwA	4.10	6.73	8.33	10.13	1.81	9.23	9.24	7.61	7.33	10.20	**12.72**
Cal101	22.63	31.00	54.12	57.96	45.55	50.49	53.41	33.74	51.53	57.51	**64.31**
LUse-21	15.18	28.02	34.99	32.05	26.56	30.55	35.62	21.69	25.93	39.17	**40.39**
Scene-15	16.10	19.92	35.84	37.82	14.44	39.03	41.36	19.39	41.16	40.58	**55.55**

5.3 Model and Parameter Settings

The model and parameter settings of our experiments are follows: (1) We keep these parameter settings of comparing methods as the original papers. During training, we fine-tune the parameters of these methods to get the best performance as the final result. (2) We use three autoencoders to handle three modalities and two autoencoders for two modalities. The encoders and decoders are composed of fully connected layers. We use sigmoid as the activation function in the last layer of decoders, and use ReLU activation in the other layers of encoders and decoders. The parameters of our method are randomly initialized and we set the learning rate of Adam to 0.001. (3) We note that the k-means, which is the final step of DMCR, can be replaced by other clustering algorithms. But considering the interpretation of the Euclidean distance in the feature space as diffusion distance in the input space [8,15,18], we choose k-means as the final clustering algorithm.

5.4 Experiment Results

Clustering Results. We evaluate our approach on three metrics of Accuracy (ACC), Normalized Mutual Information (NMI), and Purity. The experiment results of clustering ACC, NMI and Purity are summarized in Table 1, Table 2 and Table 3. The best results are marked in bold.

Firstly, we compare DMCR with the single modal algorithms DEC, IDEC and JULE. DMCR performs better than DEC and IDEC on each dataset in terms of ACC, NMI and Purity. DMCR outperforms JULE in most cases in terms of ACC, NMI and Purity. As exceptional case, DMCR performs worse than JULE on Cal101 dataset in terms of Purity. The Purity of JULE only increased by 4%, however, the NMI of JULE is decreased by 10%. Generally, it can be seen that DMCR outperforms the single modal algorithms when clustering multimodal data. The results indicate that it is reasonable to ensemble multimodal.

Secondly, we compare DMCR with multi-modal methods MMSC, RMKMC, DIMSC, LT-MSC, ECMSC and DCCAE. DMCR outperforms MMSC, RMKMC, DIMSC and ECMSC on each dataset in terms of ACC, NMI and Purity. DMCR outperforms LT-MSC and DCCAE in most cases. Taking NMI for example, the NMI of DMCR raises 12% on the Digits dataset, 3% on the AwA dataset, 13% on the Cal101 dataset, 10% on the LUse-21 dataset, 14% on the LUse-21 dataset. As exceptional cases, LT-MSC achieves a better Purity on Cal101 which is about 0.1% higher than DMCR, and DCCAE achieves a better Purity on Cal101 which is about 2% higher than DMCR. However, the NMI of LT-MSC is decreased by 10%, and the NMI of DCCAE is decreased by 7%. Generally, DMCR outperforms the other multimodal methods.

Finally, we compare DMCR with DMC, we can find that DMCR outperforms DMC, especially on Digits, CNN and Scene-15, which is more than 5% higher than DMC. That proves that the cross reconstruction regularization is effective for extracting common features of different modalities. From these tables, we can also observe that DMC also demonstrates strong competitiveness compared to other models. That proves that VIB is a effective feature extraction method that is universally applicable to different datasets. Note that DEC and IDEC just use an autoencoder without VIB, and do not perform well on multimodal datasets.

In summary, it can be concluded that our method performs the best on the multimodal datasets. The proposed cross reconstruction regularization improves the results of multimodal clustering, which further proves that it is beneficial to establish a connection among different modalities.

Parameter Setting Results. In Table 4, we explore the effect of the parameters β and γ to clustering performance of DMCR on each dataset. Due to space limitation, we only present the experimental results on the Digits dataset and Cal101 dataset in this paper. Both β and γ vary in the set [0, 0.5, 1] and the best results are marked in bold.

Table 3. Clustering Purity (%)

	DEC	IDEC	JULE	DCCAE	MMSC	RMKMC	LT-MSC	DIMSC	ECMSC	DMC	DMCR
Digits	47.97	49.00	77.44	69.92	58.25	76.40	77.35	53.50	78.13	85.55	**90.75**
CNN	40.84	37.66	40.80	35.19	32.21	34.87	25.63	24.54	25.49	56.95	**61.70**
AwA	17.96	21.87	23.58	25.68	20.64	24.70	27.35	23.89	23.24	27.95	**31.84**
Cal101	37.88	47.19	**68.68**	66.29	54.21	58.85	64.58	47.33	61.94	62.50	64.46
LUse-21	14.29	27.52	30.57	27.49	21.81	29.00	32.24	24.43	28.33	34.43	**35.05**
Scene-15	17.65	26.43	38.97	38.69	18.60	41.40	44.70	25.87	44.80	46.57	**56.60**

Table 4. Parameter Setting results on Digits and Cal101 (%)

	Digits			Cal101		
	ACC	NMI	Purity	ACC	NMI	Purity
$\beta = 0, \gamma = 0$	69.05	68.05	73.55	54.07	47.98	55.76
$\beta = 0.5, \gamma = 0$	81.20	72.84	81.20	57.16	50.39	59.55
$\beta = 1, \gamma = 0$	85.55	74.98	85.55	62.50	57.51	62.50
$\beta = 0, \gamma = 0.5$	81.85	80.53	82.25	60.67	58.51	63.62
$\beta = 0.5, \gamma = 0.5$	90.35	82.46	90.35	63.76	63.68	63.34
$\beta = 1, \gamma = 0.5$	**90.75**	**83.17**	**90.75**	**66.57**	**64.31**	**64.46**
$\beta = 0, \gamma = 1$	80.50	81.85	84.05	58.00	59.88	63.34
$\beta = 0.5, \gamma = 1$	90.25	82.60	90.25	62.92	61.08	59.26
$\beta = 1, \gamma = 1$	90.55	82.02	90.25	58.14	58.57	61.65

The value of β and γ separately reflects how much we want to enforce the cross reconstruction regularization and the VIB regularization. The $\beta = 1$, $\gamma = 0$ stands for DMCR without cross reconstruction regularization, the $\beta = 1$, $\gamma = 0.5$ stands for DMCR without VIB regularization, and the $\beta = 1$, $\gamma = 0$ stands for DMCR without both cross reconstruction regularization and VIB regularization. It can be seen that the performance of DMCR without one regularization is better than that of DMCR without both regularization, but is worse than that of DMCR with both regularization, which proves the validity of the VIB regularization and cross reconstruction regularization. Furthermore, as shown in the tables, we get the best results when $\beta = 1$ and $\gamma = 0.5$.

6   Conclusion

In this paper, we propose a novel deep multimodal clustering framework called DMCR. Firstly, we control the scale of feature using VIB. Secondly, we reduce the distribution differences among multimodal features using cross reconstruction. Thirdly, we fuse the extracted features to common features. Finally, we cluster the common features using k-means. In addition, we prove that the proposed cross reconstruction method effectively reduce the distribution differences of multimodal features. We compare our DMCR algorithm with the state-of-the-art multimodal methods on many multimodal datasets. Experimental results show that our algorithm achieves obviously improvement on multimodal clustering task.

References

1. Agrawal, R., Gehrke, J., Gunopulos, D., Raghavan, P.: Automatic subspace clustering of high dimensional data for data mining applications. In: SIGMOD Conference (1998)
2. Alemi, A.A., Fischer, I., Dillon, J.V., Murphy, K.: Deep variational information bottleneck. ArXiv abs/1612.00410 (2016)
3. Andrew, G., Arora, R., Bilmes, J.A., Livescu, K.: Deep canonical correlation analysis. In: ICML (2013)
4. Arjovsky, M., Chintala, S., Bottou, L.: Wasserstein GAN. ArXiv abs/1701.07875 (2017)
5. Cai, X., Nie, F., Huang, H., Kamangar, F.: Heterogeneous image feature integration via multi-modal spectral clustering. In: CVPR, pp. 1977–1984 (2011)
6. Cao, X., Zhang, C., Fu, H., Liu, S., Zhang, H.: Diversity-induced multi-view subspace clustering. In: CVPR, pp. 586–594 (2015)
7. Chen, G.: Deep learning with nonparametric clustering. ArXiv abs/1501.03084 (2015)
8. Coifman, R.R., Lafon, S.: Diffusion maps. Appl. Comput. Harmonic Anal. **21**, 5–30 (2006)
9. Fei-Fei, L., Perona, P.: A Bayesian hierarchical model for learning natural scene categories. In: CVPR, vol. 2, pp. 524–531 (2005)
10. Gao, J., Han, J., Liu, J., Wang, C.: Multi-view clustering via joint nonnegative matrix factorization. In: SDM (2013)
11. Goodfellow, I.J.: NIPS 2016 tutorial: Generative adversarial networks. ArXiv abs/1701.00160 (2016)
12. Guo, X., Gao, L., Liu, X., Yin, J.: Improved deep embedded clustering with local structure preservation. In: IJCAI (2017)
13. Kingma, D.P., Welling, M.: Auto-encoding variational Bayes. CoRR abs/1312.6114 (2013)
14. von Luxburg, U.: A tutorial on spectral clustering. Stat. Comput. **17**, 395–416 (2007)
15. Nadler, B., Lafon, S., Coifman, R.R., Kevrekidis, I.G.: Diffusion maps, spectral clustering and eigenfunctions of Fokker-Planck operators. In: NIPS (2005)
16. Ngiam, J., Khosla, A., Kim, M., Nam, J., Lee, H., Ng, A.Y.: Multimodal deep learning. In: ICML (2011)
17. Peng, X., Xiao, S., Feng, J., Yau, W.Y., Yi, Z.: Deep subspace clustering with sparsity prior. In: IJCAI (2016)
18. Shaham, U., Stanton, K.P., Li, H., Nadler, B., Basri, R., Kluger, Y.: SpectralNet: spectral clustering using deep neural networks. ArXiv abs/1801.01587 (2018)
19. Srivastava, N., Salakhutdinov, R.: Multimodal learning with deep Boltzmann machines. J. Mach. Learn. Res. **15**, 2949–2980 (2012)
20. Tian, F., Gao, B., Cui, Q., Chen, E., Liu, T.Y.: Learning deep representations for graph clustering. In: AAAI (2014)

21. Wang, W., Arora, R., Livescu, K., Bilmes, J.A.: On deep multi-view representation learning. In: ICML (2015)
22. Wang, X., Guo, X., Lei, Z., Zhang, C., Li, S.Z.: Exclusivity-consistency regularized multi-view subspace clustering. In: CVPR, pp. 1–9 (2017)
23. Xie, J., Girshick, R.B., Farhadi, A.: Unsupervised deep embedding for clustering analysis. In: ICML (2015)
24. Yang, J., Parikh, D., Batra, D.: Joint unsupervised learning of deep representations and image clusters. In: CVPR, pp. 5147–5156 (2016)
25. Zhang, C., Fu, H., Liu, S., Liu, G., Cao, X.: Low-rank tensor constrained multiview subspace clustering. In: ICCV, pp. 1582–1590 (2015)

Deep Multivariate Time Series Embedding Clustering via Attentive-Gated Autoencoder

Dino Ienco[1]([✉]) [iD] and Roberto Interdonato[2] [iD]

[1] INRAE, UMR TETIS, LIRMM, Univ. Montpellier, Montpellier, France
`dino.ienco@irstea.fr`
[2] CIRAD, UMR TETIS, Montpellier, France
`roberto.interdonato@cirad.fr`

Abstract. Nowadays, great quantities of data are produced by a large and diverse family of sensors (e.g., remote sensors, biochemical sensors, wearable devices), which typically measure multiple variables over time, resulting in data streams that can be profitably organized as multivariate time-series. In practical scenarios, the speed at which such information is collected often makes the data labeling task uneasy and too expensive, so that limit the use of supervised approaches. For this reason, unsupervised and exploratory methods represent a fundamental tool to deal with the analysis of multivariate time series. In this paper we propose a deep-learning based framework for clustering multivariate time series data with varying lengths. Our framework, namely DeTSEC (Deep Time Series Embedding Clustering), includes two stages: firstly a recurrent autoencoder exploits attention and gating mechanisms to produce a preliminary embedding representation; then, a clustering refinement stage is introduced to stretch the embedding manifold towards the corresponding clusters. Experimental assessment on six real-world benchmarks coming from different domains has highlighted the effectiveness of our proposal.

1 Introduction

Nowadays, huge amount of data is produced by a large and diverse family of sensors (e.g., remote sensors, biochemical sensors, wearable devices). Modern sensors typically measure multiple variables over time, resulting in streams of data that can be profitably organized as multivariate time-series. While a major part of recent literature about multivariate time-series focuses on tasks such as forecasting [14,19,20] and classification [11,26] of such data objects, the study of multivariate time-series clustering has often been neglected. The development of effective unsupervised clustering techniques is crucial in practical scenarios, where labeling enough data to deploy a supervised process may be too expensive (i.e., in terms of both time and money). Moreover, clustering allows to discover characteristics of multivariate time series data that go beyond the apriori knowledge on a specific domain, serving as tool to support subsequent exploration and analysis processes.

© Springer Nature Switzerland AG 2020
H. W. Lauw et al. (Eds.): PAKDD 2020, LNAI 12084, pp. 318–329, 2020.
https://doi.org/10.1007/978-3-030-47426-3_25

While several methods exist for the clustering of univariate time series [13], the clustering of multivariate time series remains a challenging task. Early approaches have been proposed which were generally based on adaptations of standard clustering techniques to such data, e.g., density based methods [3], methods based on independent component analysis [25] and fuzzy approaches [5,8]. Recently, Hallac et al. [9] proposed a method, namely TICC (Toeplitz inverse covariance-based clustering), that segments multivariate time series and, successively, clusters subsequences through a Markov Random fields based approach. The algorithm leverages an (EM)-like strategy, based on alternating minimization, that iteratively clusters the data and then updates the cluster parameters. Unfortunately, this method does not produce a clustering solution considering the original time series but a data partition where the unit of analysis is the subsequence.

As regards deep learning based clustering, such methods have recent become popular in the context of image and relational data [17,24], but their potential has not yet been fully exploited in the context of the unsupervised analysis of time series data. Tzirakis et al. [24] recently proposed a segmentation/clustering framework based on agglomerative clustering which works on video data (time series of RGB images). The approach firstly extracts a clustering assignment via hierarchical clustering, then performs temporal segmentation and, finally, extracts representation via Convolutional Neural Network (CNN). The clustering assignment is used as pseudo-label information to extract the new representation (training the CNN network) and to perform video segmentation. The proposed approach is specific to RGB video segmentation/clustering and it is not well suited for varying length information. All these factors limit its use to standard multivariate time-series analysis. A method based on Recurrent Neural Networks (RNNs) has also been recently proposed in [23]. The representation provided by the RNN is clustered using a divergence-based clustering loss function in an end-to-end manner. The loss function is designed to consider cluster separability and compactness, cluster orthogonality and closeness of cluster memberships to a simplex corner. The approach requires training and validation data to learn parameters and choose hyperparameter setting, respectively. Finally, the framework is evaluated on a test set indicating that the approach seems not completely unsupervised and, for this reason, not directly exploitable in our scenario.

In this work, we propose a new deep-learning based framework, namely DeTSEC (Deep Time Series Embedding Clustering), to cope with multivariate time-series clustering. Differently from previous approaches, our framework is enough general to deal with time-series coming from different domains, providing a partition at the time-series level as well as manage varying length information. The DeTSEC has two stages: firstly a recurrent autoencoder exploits attention and gating mechanisms to produce a preliminary embedding representation. Then, a clustering refinement stage is introduced to stretch the embedding manifold towards the corresponding clusters. We provide an experimental analysis which includes comparison with five state of the art methods and ablations analysis of the proposed framework on six real-world benchmarks from different domains.

The results of this analysis highlight the effectiveness of the proposed framework as well as the added value of the new learnt representation.

The rest of the paper is structured as follows: in Sect. 2 we introduce the DeT-SEC framework, in Sect. 3 we present our experimental evaluation, and Sect. 4 concludes the work.

2   DeTSEC: Deep Time Series Embedding Clustering

In this section we introduce DeTSEC (Deep Time Series Embedding Clustering via Attentive-Gated Autoencoder). Let $X = \{X_i\}_{i=1}^{n}$ be a multivariate time-series dataset. Each $X_i \in X$ is a time-series where $X_{ij} \in R^d$ is the multi-dimensional vector of the time-series X_i at timestamp j, with $1 \leq j \leq T$, d being the dimensionality of X_{ij} and T the maximum time-series length. We underline that X can contain time-series with different lengths. The goal of DeTSEC is to partition X in a given number of clusters, provided as an input parameter. To this purpose, we propose to deal with the multivariate time-series clustering task by means of recurrent neural networks [1] (RNN), in order to manage at the same time (i) the sequential information exhibited by time-series data and (ii) the multivariate (multi-dimensional) information that characterizes time-series acquired by real-world sensors. Our approach exploits a Gated Recurrent Unit (GRU) [4], a type of RNN, to model the time-series behavior and to encode the original time-series in a new vector embedding representation. DeTSEC has two different stages. In the first one, the GRU based autoencoder is exploited to summarize the time-series information and to produce the new vector embedding representation, obtained by forcing the network to reconstruct the original signal, that integrates the temporal behavior and the multi-dimensional information. Once the autoencoder network has been pretrained, the second stage of our framework refines such representation by taking into account a twofold task, i.e., the reconstruction one and another one devoted to stretch the embedding manifold towards clustering centroids. Such centroids can be derived by applying any centroid-based clustering algorithm (i.e. K-means) on the new data representation. The final clustering assignment is derived by applying the K-means clustering algorithm on the embeddings produced by DeTSEC.

Figure 1 visually depicts the encoder/decoder structure of DeTSEC, consisting of three different components in our network architecture: i) an encoder, ii) a backward decoder and iii) a forward decoder. The encoder is composed by two GRU units that process the multivariate time series: the first one (in red) processes the time-series in reverse order (backward) while the second one (in green) processes the input time-series in the original order (forward). Successively, for each GRU unit, an attention mechanism [2] is applied to combine together the information coming from different timestamps. Attention mechanisms are widely used in automatic signal processing [2] (1D signal or Natural Language Processing) as they allow to merge together the information extracted by the RNN model at different timestamps via a convex combination of the input sources. The attention formulation we used is the following one:

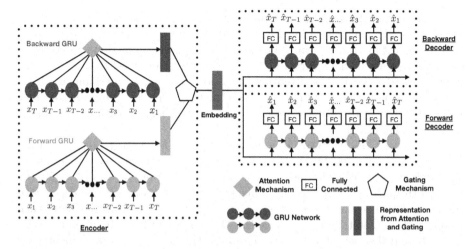

Fig. 1. Encoder/Decoder structure of DeTSEC. The network has three main components: i) an encoder, ii) a forward decoder and iii) a backward decoder. The encoder includes forward/backward GRU networks. For each network an attention mechanism is employed to combine the sequential information. Subsequently, the gating mechanism combines the forward/backward information to produce the embedding representation. The two decoder networks have similar structure: the forward decoder reconstructs the original signal considering its original order (forward - green color) while the backward decoder reconstructs the same signal but in inverse order (backward - red color). (Color figure online)

$$v_a = tanh(H \cdot W_a + b_a) \tag{1}$$

$$\lambda = SoftMax(v_a \odot u_a) \tag{2}$$

$$h^{att} = \sum_{j=1}^{T} \lambda_j \cdot h_{t_j} \tag{3}$$

where $H \in \mathbb{R}^{T,l}$ is a matrix obtained by vertically stacking all feature vectors $h_{t_j} \in \mathbb{R}^l$ learned at T different timestamps by the GRU and l is the hidden state size of the GRU network. Matrix $W_a \in \mathbb{R}^{l,l}$ and vectors $b_a, u_a \in \mathbb{R}^l$ are parameters learned during the process. The $\odot$ symbol indicates element-wise multiplication. The purpose of this procedure is to learn a set of weights $(\lambda_{t_1}, \ldots, \lambda_{t_T})$ that allows to combine the contribution of each timestamp h_{t_j}. The $SoftMax$ function is used to normalize weights λ so that their sum is equal to 1. The results of the attention mechanism for the backward (h^{att}_{back}) and for the forward (h^{att}_{forw}) GRU units are depicted with red and green boxes, respectively, in Fig. 1. Finally, the two sets of features are combined by means of a gating mechanism [18] as follows:

$$embedding = gate(h^{att}_{back}) \odot h^{att}_{back} + gate(h^{att}_{forw}) \odot h^{att}_{forw} \tag{4}$$

$$gate(x) = sigmoid(W' \cdot x + b) \tag{5}$$

where the gating function $gate(\cdot)$ performs a non linear transformation of the input via a sigmoid activation function and a set of parameters (W' and b) that are learnt at training time. The result of the $gate(\cdot)$ function is a vector of elements ranging in the interval $[0, 1]$ that is successively used to modulate the information derived by the attention operation. The gating mechanism adds a further decision level in the fusion between the h_{forw}^{att} and h_{back}^{att} information since it has the ability to select (or retain a part of) the helpful features to support the task at hand [27].

The forward and backward decoder networks are fed with the representation (embedding) generated by the encoder. They deal with the reconstruction of the original signal considering the same order (resp. the reverse order) for the forward (resp. backward) decoder. This means that the autoencoder copes with the sum of two reconstruction tasks (i.e., forward and backward) where each reconstruction task tries to minimize the Mean Squared Error between the original data and the reconstructed one. Formally, the loss function implemented by the autoencoder network is defined as follows:

$$L_{ae} = \frac{1}{|X|} \sum_{i=1}^{|X|} ||X_i - dec(enc(X_i, \Theta_1), \Theta_2)||_2^2 \tag{6}$$

$$+ \frac{1}{|X|} \sum_{i=1}^{|X|} ||rev(X_i) - dec_{back}(enc(X_i, \Theta_1), \Theta_3)||_2^2$$

where $||\,||_2^2$ is the squared L_2 distance, dec (resp. dec_{back}) is the forward (resp. backward) decoder network, enc is the encoder network and $rev(x_i)$ is the time-series x_i in reverse order. Θ_1 are the parameters associated to the encoder while Θ_2 (resp. Θ_3) are the parameters associated to the forward (resp. backward) decoder.

Algorithm 1 depicts the whole procedure implemented by DeTSEC. It takes as input the dataset X, the number of epochs N_EPOCHS and the number of expected clusters $nClust$. The output of the algorithm is the new representation derived by the GRU based attentive-gated autoencoder, named $embeddings$. The first stage of the framework (lines 2–6) trains the autoencoder reported in Fig. 1 for a total of 50 epochs. Successively, the second stage of the framework (lines 8–14) performs a loop considering the remaining number of epochs in which, at each epoch, the current representation is extracted, a K-Means algorithm is executed to obtain the current cluster assignment and the corresponding centroids. Successively, the autoencoder parameters are optimized considering the reconstruction loss L_{ae} plus a third term that has the objective to stretch the data embeddings closer to the corresponding cluster centroids:

$$\frac{1}{|X|} \sum_{i=1}^{|X|} \sum_{l=1}^{nClust} \delta_{il} ||Centroids_l - enc(X_i, \Theta_1)||_2^2 \tag{7}$$

where δ_{il} is a function that is equal to 1 if the data embedding of the time-series x_i belongs to cluster l and 0 elsewhere. $Centroids_l$ is the centroid of cluster l.

Finally, the new data representation (*embeddings*) is extracted (line 15) and returned by the procedure. The final partition is obtained by applying the K-Means clustering algorithm on the new data representation.

Algorithm 1. DeTSEC Optimization

Require: X, N_EPOCHS, $nClust$.
Ensure: *embeddings*.
1: $i = 0$
2: **while** i < 50 **do**
3: Update Θ_1, Θ_2 and Θ_3 by descending the gradient:
4: $\nabla_{\Theta_1,\Theta_2,\Theta_3} \frac{1}{|X|} \sum_{i=1}^{|X|} ||X_i - dec(enc(X_i,\Theta_1),\Theta_2)||_2^2 + \frac{1}{|X|} \sum_{x_i \in X} ||rev(X_i) - dec_{back}(enc(X_i,\Theta_1),\Theta_3)||_2^2$
5:   $i = i + 1$
6: **end while**
7: $i = 0$
8: **while** i < (N_EPOCHS - 50) **do**
9: $embeddings$ = extractEmbedding(Θ_1, X)
10: δ, Centroids = runKMeans(embeddings, nClust)
11: Update Θ_1, Θ_2 and Θ_3 by descending the gradient:
12: $\nabla_{\Theta_1,\Theta_2,\Theta_3} \frac{1}{|X|} \sum_{i=1}^{|X|} ||X_i - dec(enc(X_i,\Theta_1),\Theta_2)||_2^2 + \frac{1}{|X|} \sum_{x_i \in X} ||rev(X_i) - dec_{back}(enc(X_i,\Theta_1),\Theta_3)||_2^2 + \frac{1}{|X|} \sum_{i=1}^{|X|} \sum_{j=1}^{nClust} \delta_{ij} ||Centroids_j - enc(X_i,\Theta_1)||_2^2$

13:   $i = i + 1$
14: **end while**
15: $embeddings$ = extractEmbedding(Θ_1, X)
16: **return** *embeddings*

---

3 Experimental Evaluation

In this section we assess the behavior of DeTSEC considering six real world multivariate time series benchmarks. To evaluate the performance of our proposal, we compare it with several competing and baselines approaches by means of standard clustering evaluation metrics. In addition, we perform a qualitative analysis based on a visual inspection of the embedding representations learnt by our framework and by competing approaches.

3.1 Competitors and Method Ablations

For the comparative study, we consider the following competitors:

- The classic *K-means* algorithm [21] based on euclidean distance.
- The spectral clustering algorithm [15] (*SC*). This approach leverages spectral graph theory to extract a new representation of the original data. K-means method is then applied to obtain the final data partition.

- The Deep Embedding Clustering algorithm [28] (*DEC*) that performs partitional clustering through deep learning. Similarly to K-means, also this approach is suited for data with fixed length. Also in this case we perform zero padding to fit all the time-series lengths to the size of the longest one.
- The Dynamic Time Warping measures [7] (*DTW*) coupled with K-means algorithm. Such distance measure is especially tailored for time-series data with variable length-size.
- The Soft Dynamic Time Warping measures introduced in [6] (*SOFTDTW*). This measure is a differentiable distance measure recently introduced to manage dissimilarity evaluation between multivariate time-series of variable length. We couple such measure with the K-means algorithm.

Note that when using *K-means* and *SC*, due to the fact that multivariate time series can have different lengths, we perform zero padding to fit all the time-series lengths to the longest one. For the *DEC* method, we use the KERAS implementation[1]. For the *DTW* and *SOFTDTW* measures we use their publicly available implementations [22]. With the aim to understand the interplay among the different components of DeTSEC, we also propose an ablation study by taking into account the following variants of our framework:

- A variant of our approach that does not involve the gating mechanism. The information coming from the forward and backward encoder are summed directly without any weighting schema. We name such ablation DeTSEC$_{noGate}$.
- A variant of our approach that only involves the forward encoder/decoder GRU networks disregarding the use of the multivariate time series in reverse order. We name such ablation DeTSEC$_{noBack}$.

3.2   Data and Experimental Settings

Our comparative evaluation has been carried out by performing experiments on six benchmarks characterized by different characteristics in terms of number of samples, number of attributes (dimensions) and time length: *AUSLAN*, *JapVowel*, *ArabicDigits*, *RemSensing*, *BasicM* and *ECG*. All datasets, except *RemSensing* – which was obtained contacting the authors of [10] – are available online[2]. The characteristics of the six datasets are reported in Table 1.

Clustering performances were evaluated by using two evaluation measures: the Normalized Mutual Information (NMI) and Adjusted Rand Index (ARI) [21]. The NMI measure varies in the range $[0, 1]$ while the ARI measure varies in the range $[-1, 1]$. These measures take their maximum value when the clustering partition completely matches the original one, i.e., the partition induced by the available class labels. Due to the non deterministic nature of all the clustering

---

[1] https://github.com/XifengGuo/DEC-keras.

[2] *AUSLAN, JapVowel, ArabicDigits* and *ECG* are available at http://www.mustafabaydogan.com/files/viewcategory/20-data-sets.html; *BasicM* is available at http://www.timeseriesclassification.com/dataset.php.

Table 1. Dataset characteristics

Dataset	# Samples	# Dims	Min/Max length	Avg. length	# Classes
AUSLAN	2 565	22	45/136	57	95
JapVowel	640	12	7/29	15	9
ArabicDigits	8 800	13	4/93	39	10
RemSensing	1 673	16	37/37	37	7
BasicM	80	6	100/100	100	4
ECG	200	2	39/152	89	2

algorithms involved in the evaluation, we run the clustering process 30 times for each configuration, and we report average and standard deviation for each method, benchmark and measure.

DeTSEC is implemented via the Tensorflow python library. For the comparison, we set the size of the hidden units in each of the GRU networks (forward/backward - encoder/decoder) to 64 for *BasicM*, *ECG* benchmarks and 512 for *AUSLAN*, *JapVowel*, *ArabicDigits*, *RemSensing* benchmarks. This difference is due to the fact that the former group includes datasets with limited number of samples that cannot be employed to efficiently learn recurrent neural networks with too many parameters. To train the model, we set the batch size equal to 16, the learning rate to 10^{-4} and we use the ADAM optimizer [12] to learn the parameters of the model. The model are trained for 300 epochs: in the first 50 epochs the autoencoder is pre-trained while in the remaining 250 epochs the model is refined via clustering loss. Experiments are carried out on a workstation equipped with an Intel(R) Xeon(R) E5-2667 v4@3.20 GHz CPU, with 256 GB of RAM and one TITAN X GPU.

3.3   Quantitative Results

Table 2 reports on the performances of DeTSEC and the competing methods in terms of NMI and ARI. We can observe that DeTSEC outperforms all the other methods on five datasets over six. The highest gains in performance are achieved on speech and activity recognition datasetes (i.e., *JapVowel*, *ArabicDigits*, *AUSLAN* and *BasicM*). On such benchmarks, DeTSEC outperforms the best competitors of at least 8 points (*AUSLAN*) with a maximum gap of 45 points on *ArabicDigits*. Regarding the *EGC* dataset, we can note that best performances are obtained by *K-Means* and *DEC*. However, it should be noted that also in this case DeTSEC outperforms the competitors specifically tailored to manage multivariate time-series data (i.e., *DTW* and *SOFTDTW*).

Table 3 reports on the comparison between DeTSEC and its ablations. It can be noted how there is not a clear winner resulting from this analysis. DeTSEC obtains the best performance (in terms of NMI and ARI) on two benchmarks (*ArabicDigits* and *BasicM*), while DeTSEC$_{noGate}$ and DeTSEC$_{noBack}$ appear to be more suitable for other benchmarks (even if the performances of DeTSEC remain always comparable to the best ones). For instance, we can observe that $DeTSEC_{noGate}$ achieves the best performances on ECG. This is probably due to the fact that this ablation requires a lower number of parameters to learn, and this can be beneficial for processing datasets with a limited number of samples, timestamps and dimensions.

Table 2. Results in terms of Normalized Mutual Information and Adjusted Rand Index of the different competing methods on the six considered multivariate time series benchmarks.

	AUSLAN		JapVowel		ArabDigits		RemSens		BasicM		ECG	
	NMI	ARI	NMI	ARI	NMI	ARI	NMI	ARI	NMI	ARI	NMI	ARI
K-means	0.35	0.23	0.16	0.11	0.14	0.06	0.39	0.43	0.25	0.11	0.16	**0.25**
SC	0.29	0.00	0.31	0.08	0.09	0.03	0.51	0.34	0.76	0.59	**0.23**	0.08
DEC	0.47	0.07	0.23	0.11	0.19	0.09	0.48	0.33	0.38	0.20	0.16	**0.25**
DTW	0.71	0.33	0.81	0.71	0.17	0.03	0.60	**0.47**	0.67	0.43	0.06	0.06
SOFTDTW	0.72	0.34	0.75	0.62	0.13	0.05	0.56	0.41	0.14	0.18	0.10	0.05
DeTSEC	**0.80**	**0.47**	**0.96**	**0.89**	**0.64**	**0.53**	**0.61**	0.45	**0.80**	**0.62**	0.12	0.19

Table 3. Results in terms of Normalized Mutual Information and Adjusted Rand Index of the different ablations of the proposed method on the six considered multivariate time series benchmarks.

	AUSLAN		JapVowel		ArabDigits		RemSens		BasicM		ECG	
	NMI	ARI	NMI	ARI	NMI	ARI	NMI	ARI	NMI	ARI	NMI	ARI
$DeTSEC_{noGate}$	**0.83**	**0.52**	**0.96**	0.95	0.63	0.52	**0.61**	0.46	0.79	0.61	**0.16**	**0.25**
$DeTSEC_{noBack}$	0.79	0.46	**0.96**	**0.96**	0.60	0.49	**0.61**	**0.50**	0.79	0.61	0.05	0.1
DeTSEC	0.80	0.47	**0.96**	0.89	**0.64**	**0.53**	**0.61**	0.45	**0.80**	**0.62**	0.12	0.19

3.4   Visual Inspection

To proceed further in the analysis, we visually inspect the new data representation produced by DeTSEC and the best two competing methods (i.e., SC and DTW) by using $BasicM$ as illustrative example. We choose this benchmark since it includes a limited number of samples (i.e., to ease the visualization and avoid possible visual cluttering) and it is characterized by timeseries of fixed length that avoid zero padding transformation. The $BasicM$ benchmark includes examples belonging to four different classes that, in Fig. 2, are depicted with four different colors: red, blue, green and black. Figure 2(a), (b), (c) and (d) show the two-dimensional projections of the original data versus the DTW and SC approaches on such dataset. The two dimensional representation is obtained via the t-distributed stochastic neighbor embedding ($TSNE$) approach [16].

In this evaluation, we clearly observe that DeTSEC recovers the underlying data structure better than the competing approaches. The original data representation (Fig. 2(a)) drastically fails to capture data separability. The *DTW* method (Fig. 2(b)) retrieves the cluster involving the blue points, on the left side of the figure, but it can be noted how all the other classes still remain mixed up. *SC* produces a better representation than the previous two cases but it still exhibits some issue to recover the four cluster structure: the green and black examples are slightly separated but some confusion is still present while the red and blue examples lie in a very close region (a fact that negatively impacts the discrimination between these two classes). Conversely, DeTSEC is able to stretch the data manifold producing embeddings that visually fit the underlying data distribution better than the competing approaches, and distinctly organize the samples according to their inner cluster structure.

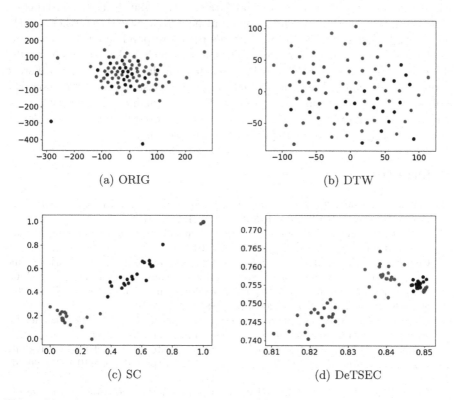

(a) ORIG

(b) DTW

(c) SC

(d) DeTSEC

Fig. 2. Visual projection of the original data (a), the distance matrix induced by Dynamic Time Warping measure (b), the representation generated via the Spectral Clustering method (c) and the embeddings learnt by DeTSEC (d) on the *BasicM* benchmark. (Color figure online)

To sum up, we can underline that explicitly managing the temporal autocorrelation leads to better performances regarding the clustering of multivariate time-series of variable length. Considering the benchmarks involved in this work, DeTSEC exhibits a general better behavior with respect to the competitors when the benchmark contains enough data to learn the model parameters. This is particularly evident when speech or activity recognition tasks are considered. In addition, the visual inspection of the generated embedding representation is in line with the quantitative results and it underlines the quality of the proposed framework.

4 Conclusions

In this paper we have presented DeTSEC, a deep learning based approach to cluster multivariate time series data of variable length. DeTSEC is a two stages framework in which firstly an attentive-gated RNN-based autoencoder is learnt with the aim to reconstruct the original data and, successively, the reconstruction task is complemented with a clustering refinement loss devoted to further stretching the embedding representations towards the corresponding cluster structure.

The evaluation on six real-world time-series benchmarks has demonstrated the effectiveness of DeTSEC and its flexibility on data coming from different application domains. We also showed, through a visual inspection, how the embedding representations generated by DeTSEC highly improve data separability. As future work, we plan to extend the proposed framework considering a semi-supervised and/or constrained clustering setting.

References

1. Bengio, Y., Courville, A.C., Vincent, P.: Representation learning: a review and new perspectives. IEEE TPAMI **35**(8), 1798–1828 (2013)
2. Britz, D., Guan, M.Y., Luong, M.: Efficient attention using a fixed-size memory representation. In: EMNLP, pp. 392–400 (2017)
3. Chandrakala, S., Sekhar, C.C.: A density based method for multivariate time series clustering in kernel feature space. In: Proceedings of the International Joint Conference on Neural Networks, IJCNN 2008, Part of the IEEE WCCI 2008, Hong Kong, China, 1–6 June 2008, pp. 1885–1890 (2008)
4. Cho, K., et al.: Learning phrase representations using RNN encoder-decoder for statistical machine translation. In: EMNLP, pp. 1724–1734 (2014)
5. Coppi, R., D'Urso, P., Giordani, P.: A fuzzy clustering model for multivariate spatial time series. J. Classif. **27**(1), 54–88 (2010). https://doi.org/10.1007/s00357-010-9043-y
6. Cuturi, M., Blondel, M.: Soft-DTW: a differentiable loss function for time-series. In: ICML, pp. 894–903 (2017)
7. Dau, H.A., et al.: Optimizing dynamic time warping's window width for time series data mining applications. Data Min. Knowl. Discov. **32**(4), 1074–1120 (2018). https://doi.org/10.1007/s10618-018-0565-y
8. D'Urso, P., Maharaj, E.A.: Wavelets-based clustering of multivariate time series. Fuzzy Sets Syst. **193**, 33–61 (2012)
9. Hallac, D., Vare, S., Boyd, S.P., Leskovec, J.: Toeplitz inverse covariance-based clustering of multivariate time series data. In: KDD, pp. 215–223 (2017)

10. Interdonato, R., Ienco, D., Gaetano, R., Ose, K.: DuPLO: a dual view point deep learning architecture for time series classification. ISPRS J. Photogramm. Remote Sens. **149**, 91–104 (2019)
11. Karim, F., Majumdar, S., Darabi, H., Harford, S.: Multivariate LSTM-FCNs for time series classification. Neural Netw. **116**, 237–245 (2019)
12. Kingma, D.P., Ba, J.: Adam: a method for stochastic optimization. CoRR abs/1412.6980 (2014)
13. Liao, T.W.: Clustering of time series data - a survey. Pattern Recogn. **38**(11), 1857–1874 (2005)
14. Liu, F., Cai, M., Wang, L., Lu, Y.: An ensemble model based on adaptive noise reducer and over-fitting prevention LSTM for multivariate time series forecasting. IEEE Access **7**, 26102–26115 (2019)
15. von Luxburg, U.: A tutorial on spectral clustering. Stat. Comput. **17**(4), 395–416 (2007). https://doi.org/10.1007/s11222-007-9033-z
16. van der Maaten, L., Hinton, G.: Visualizing data Using t-SNE. J. Mach. Learn. Res. **9**, 2579–2605 (2008)
17. Min, E., Guo, X., Liu, Q., Zhang, G., Cui, J., Long, J.: A survey of clustering with deep learning: from the perspective of network architecture. IEEE Access **6**, 39501–39514 (2018)
18. Ravanelli, M., Brakel, P., Omologo, M., Bengio, Y.: Improving speech recognition by revising gated recurrent units. In: Interspeech, pp. 1308–1312 (2017)
19. Shih, S.-Y., Sun, F.-K., Lee, H.Y.: Temporal pattern attention for multivariate time series forecasting. Mach. Learn. 1421–1441 (2019). https://doi.org/10.1007/s10994-019-05815-0
20. Talavera-Llames, R.L., Pérez-Chacón, R., Troncoso, A., Martínez-Álvarez, F.: MV-KWNN: a novel multivariate and multi-output weighted nearest neighbours algorithm for big data time series forecasting. Neurocomputing **353**, 56–73 (2019)
21. Tan, P.N., Steinbach, M., Kumar, V.: Introduction to Data Mining, 1st edn. Addison-Wesley Longman Publishing Co. Inc., Boston (2005)
22. Tavenard, R.: tslearn: a machine learning toolkit dedicated to time-series data (2017). https://github.com/rtavenar/tslearn
23. Trosten, D.J., Strauman, A.S., Kampffmeyer, M., Jenssen, R.: Recurrent deep divergence-based clustering for simultaneous feature learning and clustering of variable length time series. In: ICASSP, pp. 3257–3261 (2019)
24. Tzirakis, P., Nicolaou, M.A., Schuller, B.W., Zafeiriou, S.: Time-series clustering with jointly learning deep representations, clusters and temporal boundaries. In: ICAFGR, pp. 1–5 (2019)
25. Wu, E.H.C., Yu, P.L.H.: Independent component analysis for clustering multivariate time series data. In: Li, X., Wang, S., Dong, Z.Y. (eds.) ADMA 2005. LNCS (LNAI), vol. 3584, pp. 474–482. Springer, Heidelberg (2005). https://doi.org/10.1007/11527503_57
26. Wu, G., Zhang, H., He, Y., Bao, X., Li, L., Hu, X.: Learning Kullback-Leibler divergence-based gaussian model for multivariate time series classification. IEEE Access **7**, 139580–139591 (2019)
27. Xiao, L., Zhang, H., Chen, W.: Gated multi-task network for text classification. In: NAACL-HLT, pp. 726–731 (2018)
28. Xie, J., Girshick, R.B., Farhadi, A.: Unsupervised deep embedding for clustering analysis. In: ICML, pp. 478–487 (2016)

Spectral Clustering by Subspace Randomization and Graph Fusion for High-Dimensional Data

Xiaosha Cai[1,2], Dong Huang[1,2($\boxtimes$)], Chang-Dong Wang[3], and Chee-Keong Kwoh[4]

[1] College of Mathematics and Informatics, South China Agricultural University, Guangzhou, China
xiaoshacai@hotmail.com, huangdonghere@gmail.com
[2] Guangzhou Key Laboratory of Smart Agriculture, Guangzhou, China
[3] School of Data and Computer Science, Sun Yat-sen University, Guangzhou, China
changdongwang@hotmail.com
[4] School of Computer Science and Engineering, Nanyang Technological University, Singapore, Singapore
asckkwoh@ntu.edu.sg

Abstract. Subspace clustering has been gaining increasing attention in recent years due to its promising ability in dealing with high-dimensional data. However, most of the existing subspace clustering methods tend to only exploit the subspace information to construct a single affinity graph (typically for spectral clustering), which often lack the ability to go beyond a single graph to explore multiple graphs built in various subspaces in high-dimensional space. To address this, this paper presents a new spectral clustering approach based on subspace randomization and graph fusion (SC-SRGF) for high-dimensional data. In particular, a set of random subspaces are first generated by performing random sampling on the original feature space. Then, multiple K-nearest neighbor (K-NN) affinity graphs are constructed to capture the local structures in the generated subspaces. To fuse the multiple affinity graphs from multiple subspaces, an iterative similarity network fusion scheme is utilized to achieve a unified graph for the final spectral clustering. Experiments on twelve real-world high-dimensional datasets demonstrate the superiority of the proposed approach. The MATLAB source code is available at https://www.researchgate.net/publication/338864134.

Keywords: Data clustering · Spectral clustering · Subspace clustering · High-dimensional data · Random subspaces · Graph fusion

1 Introduction

Data clustering is a fundamental yet still very challenging problem in data mining and knowledge discovery [13]. A large number of clustering techniques have been

© Springer Nature Switzerland AG 2020
H. W. Lauw et al. (Eds.): PAKDD 2020, LNAI 12084, pp. 330–342, 2020.
https://doi.org/10.1007/978-3-030-47426-3_26

developed in the past few decades [2–6, 8–12, 14–18, 21–24], out of which the spectral clustering has been a very important category with its effectiveness and robustness in dealing with complex data [3, 6, 14, 18, 22]. In this paper, we focus on the spectral clustering technique, especially for high-dimensional scenarios.

In high-dimensional data, it is often recognized that the cluster structures of data may lie in some low-dimensional subspaces [3]. Starting from this assumption, many efforts have been made to enable the spectral clustering for high-dimensional data by exploiting the subspace information from different technical perspectives [1, 3, 4, 15, 17, 21, 23]. Typically, a new affinity matrix is often learned with the subspace structure taken into consideration, upon which the spectral clustering process is then performed. For example, Liu et al. [17] proposed a low-rank representation (LRR) approach to learn an affinity matrix, whose goal is to segment the data points into their respective subspaces. Chen et al. [1] exploited K-nearest neighbor (K-NN) based sparse representation coefficient vectors to build an affinity matrix for high-dimensional data. He et al. [4] used information theoretic objective functions to combine structured LRRs, where the global structure of data is incorporated. Li et al. [15] presented a subspace clustering approach based on Cauchy loss function (CLF) to alleviate the potential noise in high-dimensional data. Elhamifar and Vidal [3] proposed the sparse subspace clustering (SSC) approach by incorporating the low-dimensional neighborhood information, where each data point is represented by a combination of other points in its own subspace and a new similarity matrix is then constructed. You et al. [23] extended the SSC approach by introducing orthogonal matching pursuit (OMP) to learn a subspace-preserving representation. Wang et al. [21] combined SSC and LRR into a novel low-rank sparse subspace clustering (LRSSC) approach.

Although these methods [1, 3, 4, 15, 17, 21, 23] have made significant progress in exploiting subspace information for enhancing spectral clustering of high-dimensional data, most of them tend to utilize a single affinity graph (associated with a single affinity matrix) by subspace learning, but lack the ability to go beyond a single affinity graph to jointly explore a variety of graph structures in various subspaces in the high-dimensional space. To overcome this limitation, this paper presents a new spectral clustering by subspace randomization and graph fusion (SC-SRGF) approach. Specifically, multiple random subspaces are first produced, based on which we construct multiple K-NN affinity graphs to capture the locality information in various subspaces. Then, the multiple affinity graphs (associated with multiple affinity matrices) are integrated into a unified affinity graph by using an iterative similarity network fusion scheme. With the unified graph obtained, the final spectral clustering result can be obtained by partitioning the this new affinity graph. We conduct experiments on twelve high-dimensional datasets, which have shown the superiority of our approach.

The rest of the paper is organized as follows. The proposed approach is described in Sect. 2. The experimental results are reported in Sect. 3. The paper is concluded in Sect. 4.

2   Proposed Framework

In this section, we describe the overall process of the proposed SC-SRGF approach. The formulation of the clustering problem is given in Sect. 2.1. The construction of multiple K-NN graphs (corresponding to multiple affinity matrices) in a variety of random subspaces is introduced in Sect. 2.2. Finally, the fusion of the multiple graphs into a unified graph and the spectral clustering process are described in Sect. 2.3.

2.1   Problem Formulation

Let $X \in \mathbb{R}^{n \times d}$ be the data matrix, where n is the number of data points and d is the number of features. Let $x_i \in \mathbb{R}^d$ denote the i-th data point, corresponding to the i-row in X. Thus the data matrix can be represented as $X = (x_1, x_2, \cdots, x_n)^{\top}$. Let $f_j \in \mathbb{R}^n$ denote the j-th data feature, corresponding to the j-th column in X. Thus the data matrix can also be represented as $X = (f_1, f_2, \cdots, f_d)$. The purpose of clustering is to group the n data points into a certain number of subsets, each of which is referred to as a cluster.

2.2   Affinity Construction in Random Subspaces

In this work, we aim to enhance the spectral clustering for high-dimensional datasets with the help of the information of various subspaces. Before exploring the subspace information, a set of random subspaces are first generated. Note that each subspace consists of a certain number of features, and thereby corresponds to a certain number of columns in the data matrix X.

Multiple random subspaces are generated by performing random sampling (without replacement) on the data features with a sampling ratio r. Let m denote the number of generated random subspaces. Then the set of random subspaces can be represented as

$$\mathcal{F} = \{F^{(1)}, F^{(2)}, \cdots, F^{(m)}\}, \tag{1}$$

where

$$F^{(i)} = (f_1^{(i)}, f_2^{(i)}, \cdots, f_{d'}^{(i)}) \tag{2}$$

denotes the i-th random subspace, $f_j^{(i)}$ denotes the j-th feature in $F^{(i)}$, and $d' = \lfloor r \cdot d \rfloor$ is the number of features. Each subspace can be viewed as selecting corresponding columns in the original data matrix. Therefore, the data submatrix in a given subspace $F^{(i)}$ can be represented as

$$X^{(i)} = (x_1^{(i)}, x_2^{(i)}, \cdots, x_n^{(i)})^{\top} \tag{3}$$

where $x_j^{(i)} \in \mathbb{R}^{d'}$ denotes the j-th data point in this subspace.

To explore the locality structures in various subspaces, multiple K-NN graphs are constructed. Specifically, given a subspace $F^{(i)}$, its K-NN graph can be defined as

$$G^{(i)} = \{V, E^{(i)}\}, \tag{4}$$

where $V = \{x_1, x_2, \cdots, x_n\}$ is the node set and $E^{(i)}$ is the edge set. The weights of the edges in the graph are computed as

$$E^{(i)} = \{e_{jk}^{(i)}\}_{n \times n}, \tag{5}$$

$$e_{jk}^{(i)} = \begin{cases} \exp(-\dfrac{d(x_j^{(i)}, x_k^{(i)})}{2\sigma}), & \text{if } x_j \in KNN^i(x_k) \text{ or } x_k \in KNN^i(x_j), \\ 0, & \text{otherwise,} \end{cases} \tag{6}$$

where $e_{jk}^{(i)}$ is the edge weight between nodes x_j and x_k in $G^{(i)}$, $d(x_j, x_k)$ is the Euclidean distance between $x_j^{(i)}$ and $x_k^{(i)}$, $KNN^i(x_k)$ is the set of K-NNs of x_k in the i-th subspace, and the kernel parameter σ is set to the average distance between all points.

With the m random subspaces, we can construct m affinity graphs (corresponding to m affinity matrices) as follows:

$$\mathcal{G} = \{G^{(1)}, G^{(2)}, \cdots, G^{(m)}\}. \tag{7}$$

Note that these affinity graphs share the same node set (i.e., the set of all data points), but have different edge weights constructed in different subspaces, which enable them to capture a variety of underlying subspace structure information in high-dimensional space for enhanced clustering performance.

2.3 Fusing Affinity Graphs for Spectral Clustering

In this section, we proceed to fuse multiple affinity graphs (corresponding to multiple affinity matrices) into a unified affinity graph for robust spectral clustering of high-dimensional data.

Specifically, we adopt the similarity network fusion (SNF) [20] scheme to fuse the information of multiple graphs. For simplicity, the set of the affinity matrices for the m graphs is represented as $\mathcal{E} = \{E^{(1)}, E^{(2)}, \cdots, E^{(m)}\}$. The goal here is to merge the m affinity matrices in $\mathcal{E}$ into a unified affinity matrix $\bar{E}$.

By normalizing the rows in the affinity matrix $E^{(i)}$, we have $\bar{E}^{(i)} = \{\bar{e}_{jk}^{(i)}\}_{n \times n} = (D^{(i)})^{-1} E^{(i)}$, where $D^{(i)}$ is the degree matrix of $E^{(i)}$. Then the initial status matrix $P_{t=0}^{(i)}$ can be defined as

$$P_{t=0}^{(i)} = \frac{\bar{E}^{(i)} + (\bar{E}^{(i)})^\top}{2}, \tag{8}$$

And the kernel matrix $S^{(i)} = \{s_{jk}^{(i)}\}_{n \times n}$ can be defined as

$$s_{jk}^{(i)} = \begin{cases} \dfrac{\bar{e}_{jk}^{(i)}}{\sum_{x_l \in KNN(x_j)} \bar{e}_{jl}^{(i)}}, & \text{if } x_k \in KNN(x_j), \\ 0, & \text{otherwise.} \end{cases} \tag{9}$$

With the above two types of matrices defined, we can iteratively update the status matrices by exploiting the information of multiple affinity matrices. Particularly, in each iteration, the i-th status matrix is updated as follows [20]:

$$P_{t+1}^{(i)} = S^{(i)} \times \left(\frac{\sum_{j \neq i} P_t^{(j)}}{m - 1} \right) \times (S^{(i)})^\top, \ i = 1, 2, \cdots, m. \tag{10}$$

After each iteration, $P_{t+1}^{(i)}$ will be normalized by $P_{t+1}^{(i)} = (D_{t+1}^{(i)})^{-1} P_{t+1}^{(i)}$ with $D_{t+1}^{(i)}$ being the degree matrix of $P_{t+1}^{(i)}$.

When the status matrices converge or the maximum number of iterations is reached, the iteration process stops and the fused affinity matrix will be computed as

$$\tilde{E} = \frac{1}{m} \sum_{i=1}^{m} P^{(i)}. \tag{11}$$

Then the unified matrix $\tilde{E}$ will be symmetrized by $\tilde{E} = (\tilde{E} + \tilde{E}^\top)/2$. With the unified affinity matrix $\tilde{E}$ obtained by fusing information of multiple affinity matrices from multiple subspaces, we can proceed to perform spectral clustering on this unified matrix to build the clustering result with a certain number of, say, k', clusters.

Let $\tilde{D}$ be the degree matrix of $\tilde{E}$. Its graph Laplacian can be computed as

$$\tilde{L} = \tilde{D} - \tilde{E}. \tag{12}$$

After that, eigen-decomposition is performed on the graph Laplacian $\tilde{L}$ to obtain the k' eigenvectors that correspond to its first k' eigenvalues. Then the k' eigenvectors are stacked to form a new matrix $\tilde{U} \in \mathbb{R}^{n \times k'}$, where the i-th column corresponds to the i-th eigenvector. Then, by treating each row as a new feature vector for the data point, some discretization techniques like k-means [18] can be performed on the matrix $\tilde{U}$ to achieve the final spectral clustering result.

3 Experiments

In this section, we conduct experiments on a variety of high-dimensional datasets to compare our approach against several other spectral clustering approaches.

3.1 Datasets and Evaluation Measures

In our experiments, twelve real-world high-dimensional datasets are used, namely, *Armstrong-2002-v1* [19], *Chowdary-2006* [19], *Golub-1999-v2* [19], *Alizadeh-2000-v2* [19], *Alizadeh-2000-v3* [19], *Bittner-2000* [19], *Bredel-2005* [19], *Garber-2001* [19], *Khan-2001* [19], *Binary-Alpha* (*BA*) [14], *Coil20* [14], and *Multiple Features* (*MF*) [5]. To simplify the description, the twelve benchmark datasets are abbreviated as *DS-1* to *DS-12*, respectively (as shown in Table 1).

Table 1. Dataset description

Dataset	Abbr.	#Instance	Dimension	#Class
Armstrong-2002-v1	*DS-1*	72	1081	2
Chowdary-2006	*DS-2*	104	182	2
Golub-1999-v2	*DS-3*	72	1868	3
Alizadeh-2000-v2	*DS-4*	62	2093	3
Alizadeh-2000-v3	*DS-5*	62	2093	4
Bittner-2000	*DS-6*	38	2201	2
Bredel-2005	*DS-7*	50	739	3
Garber-2001	*DS-8*	66	4553	4
Khan-2001	*DS-9*	83	1069	4
Binary Alpha	*DS-10*	1404	320	36
Coil20	*DS-11*	1440	1024	20
Multiple Features	*DS-12*	2000	649	10

Table 2. Average NMI over 20 runs by different methods on the benchmark datasets. The best score in each row is in bold.

Dataset	SC	KASP	SSC	SSC-OMP	SC-SRGF
DS-1	$0.366_{\pm0.000}$	$0.263_{\pm0.104}$	$0.366_{\pm0.000}$	$0.351_{\pm0.000}$	$\mathbf{0.546}_{\pm0.117}$
DS-2	$0.081_{\pm0.000}$	$0.171_{\pm0.295}$	$0.764_{\pm0.000}$	$\mathbf{0.860}_{\pm0.000}$	$0.849_{\pm0.022}$
DS-3	$0.596_{\pm0.000}$	$0.404_{\pm0.245}$	$0.690_{\pm0.000}$	$0.700_{\pm0.000}$	$\mathbf{0.801}_{\pm0.049}$
DS-4	$0.605_{\pm0.000}$	$0.851_{\pm0.164}$	$0.734_{\pm0.000}$	$0.620_{\pm0.000}$	$\mathbf{0.913}_{\pm0.000}$
DS-5	$0.560_{\pm0.000}$	$0.614_{\pm0.061}$	$0.442_{\pm0.001}$	$0.441_{\pm0.007}$	$\mathbf{0.626}_{\pm0.002}$
DS-6	$0.032_{\pm0.000}$	$0.032_{\pm0.027}$	$0.035_{\pm0.000}$	$0.035_{\pm0.000}$	$\mathbf{0.053}_{\pm0.003}$
DS-7	$0.249_{\pm0.000}$	$\mathbf{0.367}_{\pm0.089}$	$0.102_{\pm0.000}$	$0.115_{\pm0.000}$	$0.311_{\pm0.075}$
DS-8	$0.082_{\pm0.005}$	$0.139_{\pm0.055}$	$0.086_{\pm0.004}$	$\mathbf{0.172}_{\pm0.011}$	$0.161_{\pm0.024}$
DS-9	$0.604_{\pm0.000}$	$0.328_{\pm0.073}$	$0.835_{\pm0.000}$	$0.533_{\pm0.009}$	$\mathbf{0.881}_{\pm0.014}$
DS-10	$0.503_{\pm0.005}$	$0.591_{\pm0.009}$	$0.580_{\pm0.006}$	$0.260_{\pm0.006}$	$\mathbf{0.613}_{\pm0.007}$
DS-11	$0.780_{\pm0.000}$	$0.860_{\pm0.022}$	$0.864_{\pm0.005}$	$0.517_{\pm0.201}$	$\mathbf{0.888}_{\pm0.001}$
DS-12	$0.655_{\pm0.000}$	$0.866_{\pm0.018}$	$0.824_{\pm0.001}$	$0.556_{\pm0.002}$	$\mathbf{0.871}_{\pm0.030}$
Avg. score	0.425	0.457	0.527	0.430	**0.626**
Avg. rank	3.83	3.17	3.00	3.50	**1.25**

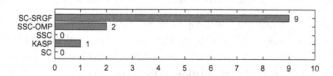

Fig. 1. Number of times being ranked in the first position in Table 2.

To quantitatively evaluate the clustering results of different algorithms, two widely-used evaluation measures are used, namely, normalized mutual information (NMI) [7] and adjusted Rand index (ARI) [7]. Note that larger values of NMI and ARI indicate better clustering results.

In terms of the experimental setting, we use $m = 20$, $K = 5$, and $r = 0.5$ on all the datasets in the experiments. In the following, the robustness of our approach with varying values of the parameters will also be evaluated in Sect. 3.3.

Table 3. Average ARI over 20 runs by different methods on the benchmark datasets. The best score in each row is in bold.

Dataset	SC	KASP	SSC	SSC-OMP	SC-SRGF
DS-1	$0.268_{\pm0.000}$	$0.152_{\pm0.058}$	$0.268_{\pm0.000}$	$0.238_{\pm0.000}$	$\mathbf{0.578}_{\pm0.181}$
DS-2	$0.066_{\pm0.000}$	$0.168_{\pm0.340}$	$0.851_{\pm0.000}$	$\mathbf{0.924}_{\pm0.000}$	$0.916_{\pm0.015}$
DS-3	$0.656_{\pm0.000}$	$0.378_{\pm0.270}$	$0.707_{\pm0.000}$	$0.729_{\pm0.000}$	$\mathbf{0.844}_{\pm0.047}$
DS-4	$0.506_{\pm0.000}$	$0.897_{\pm0.148}$	$0.796_{\pm0.000}$	$0.627_{\pm0.000}$	$\mathbf{0.947}_{\pm0.000}$
DS-5	$0.360_{\pm0.003}$	$\mathbf{0.479}_{\pm0.057}$	$0.261_{\pm0.006}$	$0.289_{\pm0.005}$	$0.427_{\pm0.005}$
DS-6	$0.018_{\pm0.000}$	$0.009_{\pm0.029}$	$0.020_{\pm0.000}$	$0.020_{\pm0.000}$	$\mathbf{0.047}_{\pm0.036}$
DS-7	$0.277_{\pm0.000}$	$0.387_{\pm0.169}$	$0.105_{\pm0.000}$	$0.112_{\pm0.000}$	$\mathbf{0.404}_{\pm0.122}$
DS-8	$0.068_{\pm0.010}$	$0.059_{\pm0.067}$	$0.0004_{\pm0.003}$	$0.103_{\pm0.020}$	$\mathbf{0.128}_{\pm0.024}$
DS-9	$0.466_{\pm0.000}$	$0.206_{\pm0.056}$	$0.826_{\pm0.000}$	$0.433_{\pm0.009}$	$\mathbf{0.860}_{\pm0.011}$
DS-10	$0.210_{\pm0.005}$	$0.291_{\pm0.011}$	$0.300_{\pm0.008}$	$0.051_{\pm0.004}$	$\mathbf{0.327}_{\pm0.008}$
DS-11	$0.638_{\pm0.000}$	$0.682_{\pm0.055}$	$0.701_{\pm0.017}$	$0.260_{\pm0.019}$	$\mathbf{0.744}_{\pm0.002}$
DS-12	$0.559_{\pm0.000}$	$0.818_{\pm0.029}$	$0.754_{\pm0.000}$	$0.445_{\pm0.006}$	$\mathbf{0.826}_{\pm0.056}$
Avg. score	0.341	0.377	0.466	0.353	**0.587**
Avg. rank	3.67	3.42	3.08	3.50	**1.17**

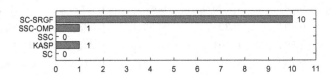

Fig. 2. Number of times being ranked in the first position in Table 3.

3.2 Comparison Against the Baseline Approaches

In this section, we compare the proposed SC-SRGF method against four baseline spectral clustering methods, namely, original spectral clustering (SC) [18], k-means-based approximate spectral clustering (KASP) [22], sparse subspace clustering (SSC) [3], and sparse subspace clustering by orthogonal matching pursuit (SSC-OMP) [23]. The detailed comparison results are reported in Tables 2, 3, and 4, and Figs. 1 and 2.

In terms of NMI, as shown in Table 2, the proposed SC-SRGF method obtains the best scores on the *DS-1*, *DS-3*, *DS-4*, *DS-5*, *DS-6*, *DS-9*, *DS-10*, *DS-11*, and *DS-12* datasets. The average NMI score (across the twelve datasets) of our method is 0.626, which is much higher than the second highest average score of 0.527 (obtained by SSC). The average rank of our method is 1.25, whereas the second best method only achieves an average rank of 3.00. As shown in Fig. 1, our SC-SRGF method yields the best NMI scores on nine out of the twelve datasets in Table 2, whereas the second and third best methods only achieves the best scores on two and one benchmark datasets, respectively.

Table 4. Average time costs (s) by different methods on the benchmark datasets.

Dataset	SC	KASP	SSC	SSC-OMP	SC-SRGF
DS-1	0.197	0.215	0.309	0.229	0.296
DS-2	0.193	0.225	0.316	0.219	0.734
DS-3	0.204	0.217	0.376	0.222	0.770
DS-4	0.203	0.226	0.291	0.221	0.298
DS-5	0.205	0.224	0.295	0.223	0.296
DS-6	0.194	0.216	0.299	0.214	0.290
DS-7	0.200	0.214	0.299	0.215	0.287
DS-8	0.213	0.230	0.727	0.257	0.295
DS-9	0.201	0.217	0.337	0.218	0.295
DS-10	0.681	0.330	7.740	0.640	19.592
DS-11	0.871	0.440	21.571	0.769	20.915
DS-12	1.060	0.489	25.134	0.787	27.666

In terms of ARI, as shown in Table 3, our SC-SRGF method also yields overall better performance than the baseline methods. Specifically, our method achieves an average ARI score (across twelve datasets) of 0.587, whereas the second best score is only 0.466. Our method obtains an average rank of 1.17, whereas the second best average rank is only 3.08. Further, as can be seen in Fig. 2, our method achieves the best ARI score on ten out of the twelve datasets, which also significantly outperforms the other spectral clustering methods.

In terms of time cost, as shown in Table 4, it takes our SC-SRGF method less than 1 s to process the first nine smaller datasets and less than 30 s to process the other three larger datasets, which is comparable to the time costs of the SSC method. Therefore, with the experimental results in Tables 2, 3, and 4 taken into account, it can be observed that our method is able to achieve significantly better clustering results for high-dimensional datasets (as shown in Tables 2 and 3) while exhibiting comparable efficiency with the important baseline of SSC (as shown in Table 4).

All experiments were conducted in MATLAB R2016a on a PC with i5-8400 CPU and 64 GB of RAM.

3.3 Parameter Analysis

In this section, we evaluate the performance of our SC-SRGF approach with three
different parameters, i.e., the number of affinity matrices (or random subspaces)
m, the number of nearest neighbors K, and the sampling ratio r.

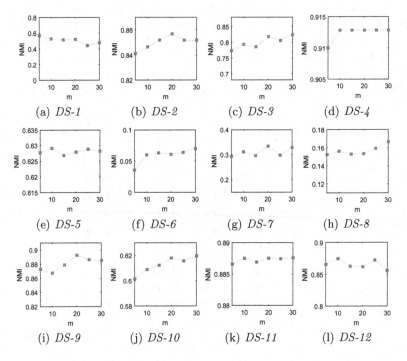

Fig. 3. Average NMI over 20 runs by SC-SRGF with varying number of affinity matrices m.

Influence of the Number of Affinity Matrices m. The parameter m controls the number of random subspaces to be generated, which is also the number
of affinity matrices to be fused in the affinity fusion process. Figure 3 illustrates
the performance (w.r.t. NMI) of our SC-SRGF approach as the number of affinity
matrices goes from 5 to 30 with an interval of 5. As shown in Fig. 3, the performance of SC-SRGF is stable with different values of m. Empirically, a moderate
value of m, say, in the interval of $[10, 30]$, is preferred. In the experiments, we
use $m = 20$ on all of the datasets.

Influence of the Number of Nearest Neighbors K. The parameter K
controls the number of nearest neighbors when constructing the K-NN graphs
for the multiple random subspaces. As can be seen in Fig. 4, a smaller value of
K can be beneficial to the performance, probably due to the fact that the K-NN
graph with a smaller K may better reflect the locality characteristics in a given
subspace. In the experiments, we use $K = 5$ on all of the datasets.

Influence of the Sampling Ratio r. The parameter r controls the sampling ratio when producing the multiple random subspaces from the high-dimensional space. As shown in Fig. 5, a moderate value of r is often preferred on the benchmark datasets. Empirically, it is suggested that the sampling ratio be set in the interval of $[0.2, 0.8]$. In the experiments, we use $r = 0.5$ on all of the datasets.

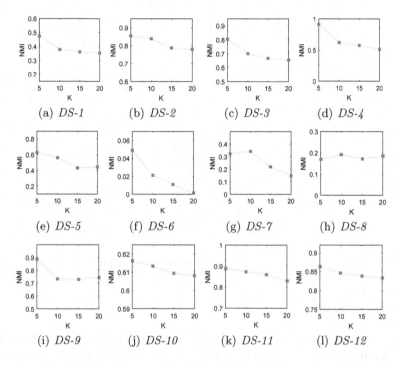

Fig. 4. Average NMI over 20 runs by SC-SRGF with varying number of nearest neighbors K.

Brief Summary. From the above experimental results, we can observe that the proposed SC-SRGF approach exhibits quite good consistency and robustness w.r.t. the three parameters, which do not require any sophisticated parameter tuning and can be safely set to some moderate values across different datasets.

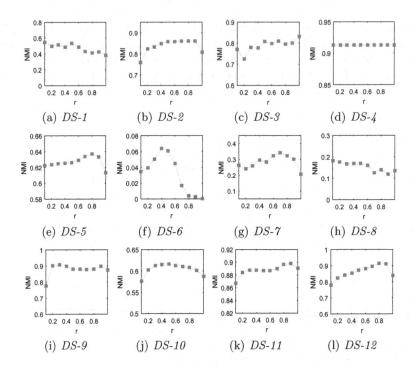

Fig. 5. Average NMI over 20 runs by SC-SRGF with varying sampling ratio r.

4 Conclusion

In this paper, we propose a new spectral clustering approach termed SC-SRGF for high-dimensional data, which is able to explore diversified subspace information inherent in high-dimensional space by means of subspace randomization and affinity graph fusion. In particular, a set of multiple random subspaces are first generated by performing random sampling on the original feature space repeatedly. After that, multiple K-NN graphs are constructed to capture the locality information of the multiple subspaces. Then, we utilize an iterative graph fusion scheme to combine the multiple affinity graphs (i.e., multiple affinity matrices) into a unified affinity graph, based on which the final spectral clustering result can be achieved. We have conducted extensive experiments on twelve real-world high-dimensional datasets, which demonstrate the superiority of our SC-SRGF approach when compared with several baseline spectral clustering approaches.

Acknowledgments. This work was supported by NSFC (61976097 & 61876193) and A*STAR-NTU-SUTD AI Partnership Grant (No. RGANS1905).

References

1. Chen, F., Wang, S., Fang, J.: Spectral clustering of high-dimensional data via k-nearest neighbor based sparse representation coefficients. In: Proceedings of International Joint Conference on Neural Networks (IJCNN), pp. 363–374 (2015)
2. Chen, M.S., Huang, L., Wang, C.D., Huang, D.: Multi-view clustering in latent embedding space. In: Proceedings of AAAI Conference on Artificial Intelligence (2020)
3. Elhamifar, E., Vidal, R.: Sparse subspace clustering: algorithm, theory, and applications. IEEE Trans. Pattern Anal. Mach. Intell. **35**(11), 2765–2781 (2013)
4. He, R., Wang, L., Sun, Z., Zhang, Y., Li, B.: Information theoretic subspace clustering. IEEE Trans. Neural Netw. Learn. Syst. **27**(12), 2643–2655 (2016)
5. Huang, D., Wang, C.D., Lai, J.H.: Locally weighted ensemble clustering. IEEE Trans. Cybern. **48**(5), 1460–1473 (2018)
6. Huang, D., Wang, C.D., Wu, J.S., Lai, J.H., Kwoh, C.K.: Ultra-scalable spectral clustering and ensemble clustering. IEEE Trans. Knowl. Data Eng. (2019). https://doi.org/10.1109/TKDE.2019.2903410
7. Huang, D., Cai, X., Wang, C.D.: Unsupervised feature selection with multi-subspace randomization and collaboration. Knowl.-Based Syst. **182**, 104856 (2019)
8. Huang, D., Lai, J.H., Wang, C.D.: Combining multiple clusterings via crowd agreement estimation and multi-granularity link analysis. Neurocomputing **170**, 240–250 (2015)
9. Huang, D., Lai, J.H., Wang, C.D.: Robust ensemble clustering using probability trajectories. IEEE Trans. Knowl. Data Eng. **28**(5), 1312–1326 (2016)
10. Huang, D., Lai, J.H., Wang, C.D., Yuen, P.C.: Ensembling over-segmentations: from weak evidence to strong segmentation. Neurocomputing **207**, 416–427 (2016)
11. Huang, D., Lai, J., Wang, C.D.: Ensemble clustering using factor graph. Pattern Recognit. **50**, 131–142 (2016)
12. Huang, D., Wang, C.D., Peng, H., Lai, J., Kwoh, C.K.: Enhanced ensemble clustering via fast propagation of cluster-wise similarities. IEEE Trans. Syst. Man Cybern. Syst. (2018). https://doi.org/10.1109/TSMC.2018.2876202
13. Jain, A.K.: Data clustering: 50 years beyond k-means. Pattern Recogn. Lett. **31**(8), 651–666 (2010)
14. Kang, Z., Peng, C., Cheng, Q., Xu, Z.: Unified spectral clustering with optimal graph. In: Proceedings of AAAI Conference on Artificial Intelligence, pp. 3366–3373 (2018)
15. Li, X., Lu, Q., Dong, Y., Tao, D.: Robust subspace clustering by Cauchy loss function. IEEE Trans. Neural Netw. Learn. Syst. **30**(7), 2067–2078 (2019)
16. Liang, Y., Huang, D., Wang, C.D.: Consistency meets inconsistency: a unified graph learning framework for multi-view clustering. In: Proceedings of IEEE International Conference on Data Mining (ICDM) (2019)
17. Liu, G., Lin, Z., Yan, S., Sun, J., Ma, Y., Yu, Y.: Robust recovery of subspace structures by low-rank representation. IEEE Trans. Pattern Anal. Mach. Intell. **35**(1), 171–184 (2013)
18. von Luxburg, U.: A tutorial on spectral clustering. Stat. Comput. **17**(4), 395–416 (2007)
19. de Souto, M.C., Costa, I.G., de Araujo, D.S., Ludermir, T.B., Schliep, A.: Clustering cancer gene expression data: a comparative study. BMC Bioinformatics **9**(1), 497 (2008)

20. Wang, B., et al.: Similarity network fusion for aggregating data types on a genomic scale. Nat. Methods **11**, 333–337 (2014)
21. Wang, Y., Xu, H., Leng, C.: Provable subspace clustering: when LRR meets SSC. IEEE Trans. Inf. Theory **65**(9), 5406–5432 (2019)
22. Yan, D., Huang, L., Jordan, M.I.: Fast approximate spectral clustering. In: Proceedings of ACM SIGKDD International Conference on Knowledge Discovery and Data Mining, pp. 907–916 (2009)
23. You, C., Robinson, D.P., Vidal, R.: Scalable sparse subspace clustering by orthogonal matching pursuit. In: IEEE Conference on Computer Vision and Pattern Recognition (CVPR) (2016)
24. Zhang, G.Y., Zhou, Y.R., He, X.Y., Wang, C.D., Huang, D.: One-step kernel multiview subspace clustering. Knowl.-Based Syst. **189**, 105126 (2020)

Decentralized and Adaptive K-Means Clustering for Non-IID Data Using HyperLogLog Counters

Amira Soliman[1]([✉]), Sarunas Girdzijauskas[1], Mohamed-Rafik Bouguelia[2],
Sepideh Pashami[2], and Slawomir Nowaczyk[2]

[1] RISE SICS, Stockholm, Sweden
{aaeh,sarunasg}@kth.se
[2] Halmstad University, Halmstad, Sweden
{mohamed-rafik.bouguelia,sepideh.pashami,slawomir.nowaczyk}@hh.se

Abstract. The data shared over the Internet tends to originate from ubiquitous and autonomous sources such as mobile phones, fitness trackers, and IoT devices. Centralized and federated machine learning solutions represent the predominant way of providing smart services for users. However, moving data to central location for analysis causes not only many privacy concerns, but also communication overhead. Therefore, in certain situations machine learning models need to be trained in a collaborative and decentralized manner, similar to the way the data is originally generated without requiring any central authority for data or model aggregation. This paper presents a decentralized and adaptive k-means algorithm that clusters data from multiple sources organized in peer-to-peer networks. Our algorithm allows peers to reach an approximation of the global model without sharing any raw data. Most importantly, we address the challenge of decentralized clustering with skewed non-IID data and asynchronous computations by integrating HyperLogLog counters with k-means algorithm. Furthermore, our clustering algorithm allows nodes to individually determine the number of clusters that fits their local data. Results using synthetic and real-world datasets show that our algorithm outperforms state-of-the-art decentralized k-means algorithms achieving accuracy gain that is up-to 36%.

1 Introduction

The predominant way of using machine learning (ML) involves collecting data to a centralized repository often in communication costly and privacy-invasive manner. Therefore, Federated Learning (FL) has been introduced as an alternative distributed and privacy-friendly approach. FL allows users to train models locally on their devices using their sensitive data, and communicate intermediate model updates to a central server without the need to centrally store the data [13]. Specifically, users start by contacting the central server and downloading the learning algorithm and a global model, that is common to all users. The algorithm trains its model locally on each device using user private data and

© Springer Nature Switzerland AG 2020
H. W. Lauw et al. (Eds.): PAKDD 2020, LNAI 12084, pp. 343–355, 2020.
https://doi.org/10.1007/978-3-030-47426-3_27

computes update to the current global model. Afterwards, the new updates on the learning parameters obtained from the algorithm on the device of each user are sent to the central server for aggregation. The server integrates the new learning parameters and sends the aggregated global model back to each user. These interactions with the central server are repeated till reaching convergence. This distributed approach for model computation diminishes the need for central storage of raw data, hence, computation becomes distributed among users and their personal data never leaves their devices.

FL can work very efficiently in many scenarios. The principal advantage of FL is the decoupling of global model training from the need for direct access to the raw data. However, FL has issues that can be related to system and data challenges. Scalability of FL is a major system challenge, especially in use-cases involving a large number of users (e.g., thousands of users) using and improving the global model at the same point. Additionally, data skewness represents one of the main data challenges for FL, since the data is fully distributed and is generated according to behaviours of participating users. Generating a single global model that accumulates all user behaviours might not produce the best model for particular categories of the users. Specifically, global averaging model enforces a bias towards the behavioural patterns provided by the majority of users, while suppressing the patterns of less significant users [20,21].

It is important for distributed ML and FL to ensure that the training data is uniformly distributed (i.e., IID sampling that represents independent and identical random sampling) so that any resulting model represents unbiased estimate of the expected model parameters. However, with a huge number of users participating in the training of a FL model, there is no control over size and statistical properties of training data used at each device. Thus, it is unrealistic to assume that the data produced by many different users will always be IID data. Specifically, data points generated by users can be quite different as data on each node can be driven using different phenomena. Therefore, two randomly selected users are likely to compute very different updates. This leads to a statistical standpoint where assumptions need to be made for non-IID data [13].

Recently, Peer-to-Peer (P2P) systems have been used as underlying communication frameworks to provide decentralized ML algorithms. The overall system can be thought of as a connected undirected graph with n vertices each representing a node. These nodes can be allowed to communicate randomly with any other node in the network, which shapes the underlying topology to a random graph [5,12,18,22]. Also, the communication among nodes can be restricted to enforce a specific underlying graph topology, for example the communication can be only allowed for friendship ties in social networks or among geographically co-located IoT devices [1,20,21].

In this paper, we present a P2P k-means clustering algorithm. The general k-means algorithm takes input as an integer k and a set of m data points with d dimensions in $\mathbb{R}^d$. The goal is to cluster these data points by finding k centers that minimize the sum of the squared distances between each point and the closest center to which it can be assigned to form a cluster [14,15]. Finding an exact solution to the k-means problem is known to be NP-hard, therefore existing algorithms adopt incremental optimization strategies [4,14]. Our proposed algorithm extends the general k-means algorithm and allows nodes having distributed data to cooperate in P2P fashion to reach a clustering consensus using their solitary local data and leverage models from others peers.

Our P2P k-means algorithm executes in iterations, such that in each iteration nodes compute an approximation of the new centroids in a decentralized manner by collaboratively exchanging their local estimations and applying weighted averaging. Updating the centroids using weighted averaging function takes into account the number of data points that a node used to calculate its centroids. The more data points used in calculating a centroid, the higher the weight associated with this centroid while applying the averaging function. Differently form existing FL and general P2P k-means algorithms, our proposed algorithm deals with skewed data distributions as well as asynchronous updates of the cluster centroids. We allow nodes to have different pace in executing the exchange iterations, such that some nodes can be more actively engaged than others.

The active nodes can make the system biased toward the properties of their local data. Additionally, these nodes execute exchanges more often which makes their data to be over-represented when applying the weighted averaging function [8]. Naiive weighted averaging function fails to keep track of unique data points represented by a centroid, consequently it keeps accumulating the number of data points owned by active nodes each time they are engaged in an exchanging round. Therefore, our clustering algorithm employs HyperLogLog counters to correctly approximate the total number of data points used in calculating the centroids [6]. HyperLogLog is a probabilistic data structure, which provides a reasonable approximation of cardinality estimation. We integrate HyperLogLog counters so that nodes can keep track of distinct data points used so far in model training, hence allow our clustering algorithm to correctly approximate the number of data points in the network. Therefore, our clustering algorithm can operate under asynchronous computations and prevent model aggregation from being biased towards peers interacting with high frequency.

Decentralized data generation makes imbalanced data and missing classes imperative. The data is expected to be highly skewed due to the heterogeneous nature of participating nodes. A lot of work has been done for solving class imbalance and missing classes using data resampling, however most of these methods require access to the whole data, which is not applicable in decentralized systems [17]. To address these challenges, our clustering algorithm incorporates two different techniques to allow nodes decide the proper number of clusters that fit their local data. Particularly, when two nodes try to merge their local models represented by their centroids, our merging function applies k-means on centroids to group every pair of centroids that are close to each other. Then, our first approach to adaptively fix the number of cluster applies Bradley, Fayyad and Reina (BFR) algorithm to further merge the closest clusters together [19]. We provide another merging function using MinHash algorithm [3].

Our contributions can be described as follows: 1) We provide a decentralized P2P k-means algorithm that can successfully handle **skewed and non-IID data distribution** among the participating nodes. 2) We provide a computational environment participating nodes to **asynchronously compute clustering consensus** in P2P networks. 3) We provide a novel **adaptive k-means clustering** algorithm that allow nodes to individually determine the number of clusters that fits their local data. 4) We provide experimental evaluation of the proposed decentralized and adaptive k-means algorithm using multiple synthetic as well as real-world dataset. The results show that our algorithm outperforms state-of-the-art decentralized M-Means algorithms achieving accuracy gain that is up to 36%.

The paper is organized as follows: in Sect. 2 and Sect. 3, we present an overview of existing centralized, distributed as well as P2P k-means algorithms. Section 4 introduces our proposed methods for P2P Adaptive k-means clustering algorithm. Section 5 shows the experimental evaluation of our proposed algorithm compared to the state-of-the-art P2P k-means algorithms. Finally, Sect. 6 concludes our paper.

2   Background

Clustering is a technique that is used to partition elements in a dataset such that similar elements are assigned to same cluster while elements with different properties are assigned to different clusters. One of the earliest clustering techniques in the literature is the k-means clustering method [14,15]. Given a set $\mathbf{X} = \{x_1...x_n\}$ of m samples in $\mathbb{R}^d$, the k-means problem is to find the minimum variance clustering of the dataset into k clusters with centroids C, such that the following potential function is minimized,

$$\phi = \frac{1}{m} \sum_{x \in X} \min_{c \in C} \|x - c\|^2 . \tag{1}$$

Identifying these centroids implicitly defines the cluster to which each sample is assigned. Each data point is mapped to the cluster with the nearest mean, serving as a representation of the cluster. As defined, finding an exact solution to the k-means problem even for $k = 2$ is NP-hard [4].

The k-means algorithm starts by randomly choosing k points in the vector representation space of input data, these points serve as the initial centroids of the clusters. Afterwards, all samples are each assigned to the centroid they are closest to. Then, for each cluster a new centroid is computed by averaging the feature vectors of all samples that are assigned to it. The process of assigning samples and recomputing centroids is repeated until the process converges.

3   Related Work

Several distributed k-means algorithms have been proposed to cluster datasets that are distributed over different locations. These algorithms assume that there is a central coordinator that communicates with all other nodes in the distributed system. The clustering goal is to partition the distributed dataset, into k clusters consistent with the global clustering that can be obtained using the centralized algorithm. Some of these algorithms perform the process of computing the centroids of the clusters in a distributed manner using averaging techniques. The main idea is to generate centroids of local data at each computing node, then transmit them to the central coordinator which computes the average [7,23]. Other algorithms generate summaries of local data at each node and send them to the central coordinator to perform the clustering algorithm using the collected summaries [10,11].

Decentralized clustering on distributed data using P2P has been studied recently. Some solutions introduce distributed k-means algorithms that construct a global set of artificial points to act as a proxy for the entire dataset [1,16]. There are some solutions that consider P2P random networks and work in static settings, however they are aimed at computing basic average of centroids. Fellus et al. [5] propose a decentralized k-means algorithm which executes in communication rounds, and in each round nodes compute an approximation of the new centroids in a distributed manner.

It is clear that both distributed and decentralized k-means can be efficiently solved using collaborative averaging as well as summarizing techniques. However, the calculation of local approximation only succeed when the data is not skewed. As aforementioned, our main focus is to provide a decentralized P2P k-means method to handle non-IID data as well as asynchronous computations.

4   Decentralized K-Means

In P2P k-means, we consider a set of n nodes $V = \{v_i, 1 \leq i \leq n\}$ which can communicate randomly with each other. On each node v_i there is a local set of data points $P_i \subseteq \mathbb{R}^d$, and the global dataset is $P = \bigcup_{i=1}^{n} P_i$. The goal is to find a set of k centers which optimize cost function defined in (1) in a decentralized manner while preserving theoretical guarantees for approximating clustering cost without exchanging the local data among nodes.

4.1   General P2P K-Means Algorithms and Their Limitations

In the beginning, we want to emphasize on the limitations of general methods in case of asynchronous scenarios with non-IID data distribution. General P2P k-means methods apply the steps of k-means while using the local data points available at each node after all nodes agree on the set of initial centroids. Then, each node performs the exchange procedure by selecting a random peer form the network to which it sends the computed centroids. We introduce two examples to further explain the consequences of update procedure. First, we consider a P2P network with number of nodes $n = 3$, such that nodes n_1, n_2, and n_3, have data points with sizes equal to 30, 60, 90 data points, respectively. Also, we assume that the number of clusters equals to 3.

Example 1. We assume that every node has data points from the three clusters, where each cluster is represented by one third of the number of points at each node (i.e. n_1 has 10 data points in each cluster, n_2 has 20, etc.). Node n_1 is the only active node to perform exchange iterations. Thus, n_2 and n_3 are going to apply the update operation as described in Algorithm (1). The update function applies simple averaging and treats the centroids generated by n_1 equally with the centroids of other peers, though for example n_3 uses more data points in computing its centroids. Accordingly, if the data owned by n_1 is not representative of the data owned by other peers, n_1 is causing deviation for the general clustering model, though it owns only less than 17% of total data points in the system.

Algorithm 1. Update for k-means at node n_i with centroids from n_j

---

Local centroids $c_k^{(i)}$: $c_1^{(i)}$, $c_2^{(i)}$, ..., $c_k^{(i)}$

Procedure Update($c_k^{(j)}$)

    for $k \leftarrow 1$ **to** K **do**

1        $c_k^{(i)} \leftarrow \frac{1}{2}\left(c_k^{(i)} + c_k^{(j)}\right)$

2   KM-Clustering()

Before illustrating our second example, we want to briefly describe how weighted averaging can be executed in instead of non-weighting averaging. The centroid weight is going to be proportional to the number of data points used to calculate it. In this case, the update function takes an extra input that tells the number of data points belong to each cluster, i.e., nodes exchange the number of data points used to compute each centroid. For further exchange rounds, nodes have to update their counters to keep track of the number of data points used so far in generating the current centroids. Thus, nodes need to continuously accumulate the number of data points used to compute the centroids after every update operation.

Example 2. We assume that n_3 has a missing class, so the data points belong in two clusters not three. However, k-means algorithm splits the points into 3 clusters according to the input $k = 3$. Consider n_3 to be the active node in the first exchange round, so it exchanges its centroids with the number of their associated data points to n_1 and n_2. Then, n_1 and n_2 perform weighted averaging and update their centroids and increase their counters with data points from n_3. In the second exchange round, n_1 and n_2 are engaged together in exchange iteration. Now, when n_1 updates its centroids again using centroids of n_2, number of data points used in weighted averaging is going to reflect what n_3 owns twice, as centroids of n_2 and n_1 both count data points of n_3. Accordingly, data points owned by n_3 are going to be overrepresented, adding to this the fact that its centroids are not correct in representing the three clusters expected in the global model.

4.2   P2P K-Means with HyperLogLog Counters

HyperLogLog (HLL) counters are extremely useful for big data as they dramatically decrease the amount of memory needed to approximate the exact cardinality estimation compared to other data structures [6]. HLL counters hash the input data into a bit sequence, while making sure that the hashing function distributes bits as evenly and uniformly as possible in the hashing space. Then, HLL counters encodes the generated hash representation of the input in their bit sequence. Regardless of how many times a particular value appears in the input, it is going to be hashed to the same value, hence encoded only once in the HLL bit sequence. The cardinality is estimated by calculating the maximum number of leading zeros in the binary representation of the generated bit sequence. If the maximum number of leading zeros observed is n, an estimate for the number of distinct elements in the input set is expected to be 2^n.

Algorithm 2. Generate HyperLogLog function for k-means at node n_i

---

    Procedure GenerateHLL($(hll)_k^{(i)}$)
        foreach $x \in X_i$ **do**
  1          $c \leftarrow clusterID\,(x)$
  2          $hll_c^{(i)}.append\,(x)$
  3   **for** $k \leftarrow 1$ **to** K **do**
  4   **if** $k \neq c$ **then** $hll_k^{(i)}.remove\,(x)$

Interestingly, HLL counters have the property that they can be merged by combining their bit sequences [9], such that generated representation contains the elements encoded in the two HLL counters. In our clustering algorithms we integrate HLL counters to address the limitations of general P2P k-means methods as described in the previous two examples. We start by executing a regular k-means at each node to generate the centroids using the local data. Afterwards, we create a HLL counter per cluster at each node as described in Algorithm (2). The bit sequence of each HLL encodes the hash representation of the data points belonging to that cluster.

When nodes get engaged in an exchange round, they communicate their computed centroids as well as HLL counters representing data seen so for in computing the centroids. We use HLL counters to estimate the number of unique data points for each centroid. The update function executes first a regular k-means to find out the centroids to be merged, as shown in Algorithm (3), lines 1:2. We consider applying k-means instead of directly performing weighted averaging procedure as a first step to handle data skewness, such that two local centroids might be closer to each other and better being merged than combing them with worse options computed by other peers. We perform weighted averaging procedure using the estimated cardinalities as shown in lines 5:9. Lastly, nodes update their previous HLL counters by merging them with the received HLL counters, as described in line 10.

Algorithm 3. HyperLogLog update for k-means at node n_i

Procedure Update$(c_k^{(j)}, (hll)_k^{(j)})$

1    $centroids \leftarrow c_k^{(i)} \cup c_k^{(j)}$; $hll_{all} \leftarrow (hll)_k^{(i)} \cup (hll)_k^{(j)}$

2    $cent\_merge \leftarrow KMeans\,(centroids, k)$ // identify centroid pairs

3    $i \leftarrow 0; a \leftarrow 0 ; b \leftarrow 0$

4   **for** $m \in cent\_merge$ **do**

         /* m is a pair indicating centroids to be merged   */

5        $card_x \leftarrow cardinality\,(hll_{all}[m[0]]); card_y \leftarrow cardinality\,(hll_{all}[m[1]])$

6        $hll_{un} \leftarrow merge\,(hll_{all}[m[0]], hll_{all}[m[1]]); card_{un} \leftarrow cardinality\,(hll_{un})$

7   **if** $card_{un} < (card_x + card_y)$ **then**

8   **if** $card_x > card_y$ **then** $a \leftarrow \frac{card_x}{card_{un}}$; $b \leftarrow 1 - a$

             else $b \leftarrow \frac{card_y}{card_{un}}$; $a \leftarrow 1 - b$

         else $a \leftarrow \frac{card_x}{card_{un}}$; $b \leftarrow \frac{card_y}{card_{un}}$

9        $c_i^{(i)} \leftarrow a \times centroids[m[0]] + b \times centroids[m[1]]$

10       $hll_i^{(i)} \leftarrow hll\_un$; $i \leftarrow i + 1$

11   KM-Clustering()

4.3 Adaptive Number of Clusters at Each Node

In our algorithm we provide two functions to adaptively detect the number of clusters at each node. Our first approach applies merging function using MinHash algorithm [3]. MinHash is widely used to estimate how similar two sets of points are. In our clustering algorithm, we create bit sequences similar to ones of HLL counters that encode data points using the MinHash algorithm. Having such bit sequences per cluster, nodes can evaluate how their data points are similar to data points used in other peers to calculate the centroids before performing the merge function. If there is an overlap in the MinHash bit sequences, then the centroids can be merged, otherwise no overlap indicates the clusters are not similar. Interestingly, this indicates that one of the nodes might not have the correct clustering results due to missing classes, and by adopting the centroids from the other node without changing them it can fix the cluster memberships of its local data.

Our second approach is implemeted using BFR algorithm [19] to further merge the closest clusters together. We use BFR algorithm to computes the sum and sum of squares of each cluster in order to compute the standard deviation of points belonging to this cluster. The criterion for further merges can be determined by the gain in terms of cluster variance (i.e. lower value) after combining the data points in one cluster. The variance of merging the two clusters can still be computed using the sum and sum of squares of individual clusters.

5 Evaluation

We proceed with evaluating the performance of proposed clustering algorithm by comparing it with the state-of-the-art P2P k-means algorithms. We have implemented the competitor algorithms according to implementation provided by the original authors using C++. For each method we have used their default settings for the parameters as introduced by each algorithm. To evaluate the clustering accuracy, we have used the F1 score measure that is computed as harmonic mean of precision and recall. Precision reflects mixing of different ground-truth clusters into the extracted ones. Moreover, recall reflects the goodness of grouping nodes that belong to the same ground-truth cluster.

5.1 K-Means Clustering Algorithms

We use the name **DKM** as an identifier of our P2P k-means clustering algorithm. The first method we use for comparison is **cent** that represents a centralized version of k-means algorithm. Then, we have **fedps** that is implemeted as a distributed version of k-means using FL paradigm, such that there is a dedicated centralized node responsible for model aggregation for other nodes in the system. The third method is **agml**, a dicentralized version of P2P k-means that allows nodes to exchage summaries representing their local data, then apply clustering using generated summaries [5]. Also, we implemented **gdc** as a P2P k-means algothim that that allows nodes to generate and exchange a global set of artificial points to act as a proxy for the entire dataset [16]. Finally, we use **golf** that is a P2P k-means implemented using gossip protocol [2].

5.2 Datasets

We have performed the comparison using some real-world as well as synthetic benchmark datasets available from UCI Machine Learning[1] and Fundamental clustering problem suite[2].

Real-World Datasets: We use *Daily and Sports Activities* as well as *PAMAP2* datasets. These two datasets comprise motion sensor data of some daily and sports activities each performed by different persons in their own style. Our objective is to cluster these activities into 3 categories: 1) low intense activities such as sitting and standing, 2) moderate activities such as walking or running on a treadmill, and 3) intense activities such as rowing and cycling. The first dataset contains 9,120 data points, while the second one contains 27,582 data points. We used 2D representation of the data.

Synthetic Datasets: We use *Energy Time* and *S1* datasets that are generating as Gaussian clusters. The first dataset contains 4,096 data points into 2 Gaussian clusters. The second dataset has 5,000 data points clustered into 15 Gaussian clusters.

---

[1] https://archive.ics.uci.edu/ml/datasets.php?format=&task=clu.
[2] https://www.uni-marburg.de/fb12/arbeitsgruppen/datenbionik/data.

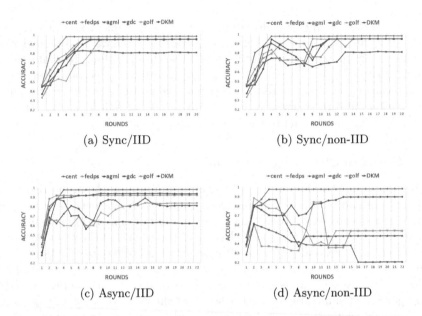

Fig. 1. Evaluation using daily and sports activities dataset.

5.3 Skewed Data and Asynchronous Computations

For the following experiments, we create a P2P network with 100 nodes. Each node has its own local data repository and can communicate with any random subset of peers in the network. For IID test cases, we evenly distribute the training sets among the peers. Also, we distribute the data in non-IID manner, such that allow one third of the nodes to obtain 50% of the data points per each cluster, whereas the remaining data points are distributed randomly among the remaining nodes.

We also create some highly unbalanced distribution, in which one third of the nodes in the network have missing classes among their allocated data points. Additionally, we create asynchronous computation scenario by assign nodes different speed to perform the exchange rounds. We split the network randomly in three parts, the first part remains idle, the second part performs only one exchange per computation round, while the last set are actively participating by performing up to three exchanges in one round.

Figure 1 shows the evaluation of different P2P methods using the first dataset. As show, we report the accuracy in different use-cases: first (a) when we have IID data distribution and synchronous computation when all nodes have the same exchange pace. Then (b) when data becomes non-IID distributed. In (c) and (d) cases, we report the accuracy in case of asynchronous computations when data is distributed in IID and non-IID manner. The results confirm that general P2P methods work when data is uniformly distributed and nodes update their centroids with the same frequencies.

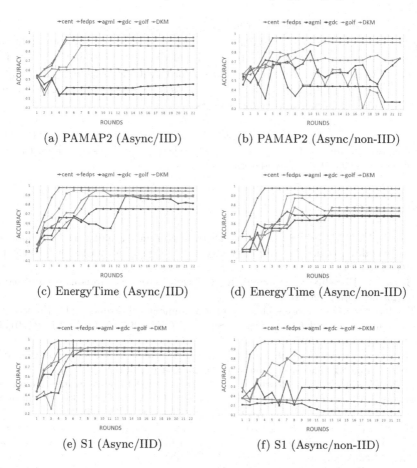

Fig. 2. Evaluation using PAMAP2, EnergyTime, and S1 datasets in the cases of asynchronous computations.

Figure 2 reports the results of the remaining datasets in asynchronous computation scenarios. Results using PAMAP2, EnergyTime, and S1 confirm that our algorithm (DKM) is the only method capable of achieving accuracy comparable to the centralized version when we explore the expected real-world case scenarios of having non-IID data and asynchronous computations, while other methods fail to achieve acceptable accuracy.

6   Conclusion

This paper presents a novel decentralized as well as adaptive k-means clustering algorithm that is highly beneficial for dynamic and fully distributed environments. Our main contribution is to provide a decentralized k-means method for skewed data distribution and asynchronous computations in P2P networks.

We integrate HyperLogLog counters with our k-means algorithm to efficiently handle data skewness in such dynamic execution environment. Furthermore, our clustering algorithm allows nodes to individually determine the number of clusters that fits their local data. Our experimental evaluation confirms the ability of our algorithm to adapt to difficult scenarios in which existing P2P k-means methods fail to generate acceptable results.

Acknowledgements. This research has been conducted within the "BIDAF: A Big Data Analytics Framework for a Smart Society" (http://bidaf.sics.se/) project funded by the Swedish Knowledge Foundation.

References

1. Balcan, M.F., Ehrlich, S., Liang, Y.: Distributed k-means and k-median clustering on general topologies. In: Advances in Neural Information Processing Systems, pp. 1995–2003 (2013)
2. Berta, Á., Hegedűs, I., Ormándi, R.: Lightning fast asynchronous distributed k-means clustering (2014)
3. Broder, A.Z.: On the resemblance and containment of documents. In: Proceedings of Compression and Complexity of SEQUENCES 1997 (Cat. No. 97TB100171), pp. 21–29. IEEE (1997)
4. Drineas, P., Frieze, A., Kannan, R., Vempala, S., Vinay, V.: Clustering large graphs via the singular value decomposition. Mach. Learn. **56**(1–3), 9–33 (2004)
5. Fellus, J, Picard, D., Gosselin, P.-H.: Decentralized k-means using randomized gossip protocols for clustering large datasets. In: 2013 IEEE 13th International Conference on Data Mining Workshops, pp. 599–606. IEEE (2013)
6. Flajolet, P., Fusy, É., Gandouet, O., Meunier, F.: HyperLogLog: the analysis of a near-optimal cardinality estimation algorithm. In: Discrete Mathematics and Theoretical Computer Science, pp. 137–156 (2007)
7. Forman, G., Zhang, B.: Distributed data clustering can be efficient and exact. SIGKDD Explor. **2**(2), 34–38 (2000)
8. Giaretta, L., Girdzijauskas, Š.: Gossip learning: off the beaten path. In: IEEE International Conference on Big Data (IEEE Big Data 2019), Los Angeles, CA, USA, 9–12 December 2019, p. 2019 (2019)
9. Heule, S., Nunkesser, M., Hall, A.: Hyperloglog in practice: algorithmic engineering of a state of the art cardinality estimation algorithm. In: Proceedings of the 16th International Conference on Extending Database Technology, pp. 683–692. ACM (2013)
10. Januzaj, E., Kriegel, H.-P., Pfeifle, M.: Towards effective and efficient distributed clustering. In: Workshop on Clustering Large Data Sets (ICDM 2003) (2003)
11. Kargupta, H., Huang, W., Sivakumar, K., Johnson, E.: Distributed clustering using collective principal component analysis. Knowl. Inf. Syst. **3**(4), 422–448 (2001)
12. Khelghatdoust, M., Girdzijauskas, S.: Short: gossip-based sampling in social overlays. In: Noubir, G., Raynal, M. (eds.) NETYS 2014. LNCS, vol. 8593, pp. 335–340. Springer, Cham (2014). https://doi.org/10.1007/978-3-319-09581-3_26
13. Konečný, J., McMahan, H.B., Ramage, D., Richtárik, P.: Federated optimization: distributed machine learning for on-device intelligence. arXiv preprint arXiv:1610.02527 (2016)

14. Lloyd, S.: Least squares quantization in PCM. IEEE Trans. Inf. Theory **28**(2), 129–137 (1982)
15. MacQueen, J., et al.: Some methods for classification and analysis of multivariate observations. In: Proceedings of the Fifth Berkeley Symposium on Mathematical Statistics and Probability, Oakland, CA, USA, vol. 1, pp. 281–297 (1967)
16. Mashayekhi, H., Habibi, J., Khalafbeigi, T., Voulgaris, S., Van Steen, M.: GDCluster: a general decentralized clustering algorithm. IEEE Trans. Knowl. Data Eng. **27**(7), 1892–1905 (2015)
17. Nguyen, G.H., Bouzerdoum, A., Phung, S.L.: Learning pattern classification tasks with imbalanced data sets. In: Yin, P.-Y. (ed.) Pattern Recognition. IntechOpen, Rijeka (2009)
18. Ormándi, R., Hegedűs, I., Jelasity, M.: Gossip learning with linear models on fully distributed data. Concurrency Comput. Pract. Experience **25**(4), 556–571 (2013)
19. Rajaraman, A., David Ullman, J.: Mining of Massive Datasets. Cambridge University Press, Cambridge (2011)
20. Soliman, A., Bahri, L., Carminati, B., Ferrari, E., Girdzijauskas, S.: DIVa: decentralized identity validation for social networks. In: Proceedings of the 2015 IEEE/ACM International Conference on Advances in Social Networks Analysis and Mining 2015, pp. 383–391. ACM (2015)
21. Soliman, A., Bahri, L., Girdzijauskas, S., Carminati, B., Ferrari, E.: CADIVa: cooperative and adaptive decentralized identity validation model for social networks. Soc. Network Anal. Min. **6**(1), 36 (2016)
22. Soliman, A., Girdzijauskas, S.: DLSAS: distributed large-scale anti-spam framework for decentralized online social networks. In: 2016 IEEE 2nd International Conference on Collaboration and Internet Computing (CIC), pp. 363–372. IEEE (2016)
23. Tasoulis, D.K., Vrahatis, M.N.: Unsupervised distributed clustering. In: Parallel and Distributed Computing and Networks, pp. 347–351 (2004)

Detecting Arbitrarily Oriented Subspace Clusters in Data Streams Using Hough Transform

Felix Borutta$^{(\boxtimes)}$, Daniyal Kazempour, Felix Mathy,
Peer Kröger, and Thomas Seidl

Ludwig-Maximilians-Universität München, Munich, Germany
{borutta,kazempour,kroeger,seidl}@dbs.ifi.lmu.de

Abstract. When facing high-dimensional data streams, clustering algorithms quickly reach the boundaries of their usefulness as most of these methods are not designed to deal with the curse of dimensionality. Due to inherent sparsity in high-dimensional data, distances between objects tend to become meaningless since the distances between any two objects measured in the full dimensional space tend to become the same for all pairs of objects. In this work, we present a novel oriented subspace clustering algorithm that is able to deal with such issues and detects arbitrarily oriented subspace clusters in high-dimensional data streams. Data streams generally implicate the challenge that the data cannot be stored entirely and hence there is a general demand for suitable data handling strategies for clustering algorithms such that the data can be processed within a single scan. We therefore propose the CASHSTREAM algorithm that unites state-of-the-art stream processing techniques and additionally relies on the Hough transform to detect arbitrarily oriented subspace clusters. Our experiments compare CASHSTREAM to its static counterpart and show that the amount of consumed memory is significantly decreased while there is no loss in terms of runtime.

Keywords: Oriented subspace clustering · Stream clustering

1 Introduction

Data clustering, i.e., finding groups of similar objects, is an established and widely used technique for unsupervised problems and/or for explorative data analysis. However, when facing high-dimensional data, particularly clustering algorithms quickly reach the boundaries of their usefulness as most of them are not designed to deal with the problems known by the "curse of dimensionality". Due to inherent sparsity in high-dimensional data, distances between any two objects measured in the full dimensional space tend to become the same for all pairs of objects and, thus, can no longer be used to distinguish similar from dissimilar objects. Furthermore, clusters often appear within different

Electronic supplementary material The online version of this chapter (https://doi.org/10.1007/978-3-030-47426-3_28) contains supplementary material, which is available to authorized users.

H. W. Lauw et al. (Eds.): PAKDD 2020, LNAI 12084, pp. 356–368, 2020.
https://doi.org/10.1007/978-3-030-47426-3_28

lower dimensional subspaces. Therefore, it is usually not useful to search for clusters in the full dimensional data space or apply dimensionality reduction which would only result in one subspace rather than several different ones. To overcome those issues, several subspace clustering algorithms have been developed in the past that simultaneously search for meaningful subspaces and for clusters (within these subspaces). Some of these algorithms, e.g. [4,15,16], assume attribute independence and restrict themselves to the detection of axis-parallel subspace clusters for performance reason. More general, so-called correlation clustering algorithms, e.g. [1,2,7,8], allow arbitrarily oriented subspaces that represent a (usually linear) combination of features, i.e., explicitly allow correlation among features.

Another, yet less considered challenge is subspace clustering in data streams. Nowadays, as data is produced with high velocity, streaming algorithms become more and more important. This also holds for areas where high-dimensional data is produced rapidly, e.g., in industry where large numbers of machine sensors record huge amounts of data within short time periods. In these scenarios, the data can usually no longer be stored entirely and hence there is a general need for suitable data handling strategies for clustering algorithms such that the data can be processed within a single scan. In this work, we tackle this problem and present a novel oriented subspace clustering algorithm that is able to detect arbitrarily oriented subspace clusters in data streams. This method not only reduces the amount of required memory for processing the data significantly, but also compresses entire groups of data that are similar wrt to various combinations of features. The key idea of the proposed method is to load chunks of data into memory, deriving so-called *Concepts* as summary structures and applying a decay mechanism to downgrade the relevance of stale data. Our experimental evaluation demonstrates the usefulness of the presented method and shows that the used heap space is drastically reduced without losses in terms of runtime and accuracy.

2   Related Work

Correlation Clustering. Static algorithms for oriented subspace clustering can be categorized into PCA-based and Hough-based approaches. The PCA-based approaches [2,5,7] rely on decomposing neighborhood sets into Eigensystems that are used to define the corresponding subspaces. The usage of neighborhood sets makes them prone to outliers and noise. In contrast, approaches based on Hough transformations [1,14] rely on parameter space transformations, making them generally more robust. All these methods have been designed for static data and are not applicable in streaming environments.

Stream Clustering. Previously published work on stream clustering can generally be distinguished by the way the algorithms process the incoming data. A large group of algorithms rely on *(clustering) feature vector* (CF) data structures that have originally been proposed for the *BIRCH* algorithm [22]. The idea is to represent a set of data objects by only a few key statistics that sufficiently describe the aggregated data. This approach has been adapted for many other stream clustering approaches, e.g., [3,9,10]. Another compression technique that is widely employed for stream clustering is to only keep track of the cluster representatives. The basic idea is to represent entire chunks of data solely in form of cluster representatives, e.g., cluster centroids, [12,17,23]. Further, but less related, techniques to deal with the challenge of summarizing data streams can be found in [21].

Subspace Clustering in Data Streams. The first method able to cluster high-dimensional data streams properly was *HPStream* [4], a *k*-means based axis-parallel subspace clustering method that uses an adopted form of CF vectors to represent relevant cluster statistics. *IncPreDeCon* [15] is an incremental, axis-parallel subspace clsutering algorithm based on a density-based clustering model that supports incremental updates but lacks supporting any form of aging and hence cannot deal with streaming data directly. *PreDeConStream* [13] and *HDDStream* [16] present density-based (axis-parallel) subspace clustering algorithms that both aggregate incoming data objects within different microcluster structures and retrieve the final clustering by following (slightly different) variants of the density-based clustering scheme proposed in [6]. The *SiblingTree* method [18] is a grid-based axis-parallel subspace clustering approach aiming at detecting all low-dimensional clusters in all subspaces. All these previously mentioned methods are limited to find axis-parallel subspaces. The recently presented *CorrStream* algorithm [8] is a PCA-based approach for arbitrarily-oriented subspace clustering on data streams. As a PCA-based method, it determines subspace clusters derived from neighborhood sets, and hence is prone to outliers. In contrast, our method relies on Hough transformation and hence is able to filter outlier.

3   Correlation Clustering Using Hough Transform

The Hough transformation originally has been introduced for detecting linear segments in image data [19]. The basic idea is to map every object in data space to its corresponding object function in Hough space, and subsequently identify intersections of a specific amount of object functions. If such an intersection exists, the corresponding data objects are located on a line segment in data space. This duality of the

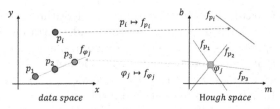

Fig. 1. Left: data space, right: Hough space

Hough transform is shown in Fig. 1. The *CASH* algorithm [1] borrows this idea of parameter space transformation for the sake of oriented subspace clustering. Precisely, they transform objects from data space to Hough space and scan the Hough space for dense areas, i.e., areas where many functions intersect, by subdividing the space into grid cells in a top-down fashion. For a given cell c, if the

Input: Data Stream $\mathcal{S}$, Batch size b
Output: *Clustering*
1: *Clustering* $\leftarrow \emptyset$
2: *batch* $\leftarrow$ empty collection of size b
3: **for** incoming data object o from $\mathcal{S}$ **do**
4:    **if** *batch* is not full **then**
5:       add o to *batch*
6:    **end if**
7:    **if** *batch* is full **then**
8:       currentConcepts $= CASH(batch)$
9:       *Clustering*.add(currentConcepts)
10:      *unifyConcepts(Clustering, ...)*
11:      // see Section 4.4
12:      *batch* $\leftarrow$ empty collection of size b
13:   **end if**
14: **end for**

Algorithm 1. CashStream

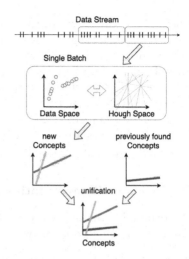

Fig. 2. Workflow

number of object functions intersecting c is greater or equal than a pre-defined *minPts* parameter, c is split into halves according to a predefined order on the axes. The division terminates if a resulting cell is either considered sparse, i.e., the number of object functions intersecting this cell is less than *minPts*, or a maximum number of splits *maxSplit* is reached. A grid cell c that is dense after *maxSplit* divisions represents a cluster: the points corresponding to the functions intersecting c form a cluster within a arbitrarily oriented $(d-1)$-dimensional subspace. However, the cluster (or some of the contained objects) might form an even lower dimensional cluster. Therefore, the object functions that form the $(d-1)$-dimensional cluster are transformed back into the data space and projected onto the orthonormal basis that can be derived from c. To detect subspace clusters of lower dimensions, the *CASH* algorithm is performed on the resulting $(d-1)$-dimensional dataset recursively until no more cluster can be found.

4   CashStream

4.1   Data Processing: Batch Processing

Regarding the facts that data cannot be kept in memory entirely and stale data shall be downgraded within stream applications, the *CASH* algorithm cannot be adjusted straightforwardly. To tackle these challenges, we propose to process incoming data in batches, similar to [12], i.e., loading chunks of data into memory and eventually computing cluster representatives which are kept in memory while the actual data objects are discarded. This data processing scheme has several advantages as it (1) enables the adaptation to concept shifts since processing data batch-wise allows to identify dense grid cells[1], potentially with novel subspaces, during the division steps, (2) caps the amount of consumed memory and (3) even

---

[1] Note that this is not possible with real-time stream processing.

allows the flexibility to adjust to changing data dimensionality as there is no need for defining a static grid. Precisely, our algorithm basically performs an adapted variant of *CASH* on single data chunks and keeps cluster representatives, that we will refer to as *Concepts*, in memory. Since the *Concepts* must be maintained efficiently, they are designed to be additive, such that two similar *Concepts* can conveniently be unified into a single *Concept* (see Fig. 2). Algorithm 1 outlines the main procedure of CASHSTREAM. After defining the *Concept* data structure, we define the similarity between *Concepts* and describe the unification step as well as the aging procedure in the following.

4.2   Cluster Representatives: Concepts

As a suitable summary structure for data objects that are assigned to a cluster, we define a *Concept* as follows.

Definition 1. *A Concept is a data structure used as abstraction of a cluster resulting from CASH. In a data space $\mathcal{D} \in \mathbb{R}^d$, a Concept of dimensionality $l < d$ captures an l-dimensional hyperplane in parameter space $\mathcal{P}$ with aggregated information of the data objects it contained as a result of CASH. A Concept consists of the following attributes:*

- *a set E containing $d - l$ equations in Hessian normal form,*
- *mean μ of all data objects that are assigned to the cluster,*
- *number of data objects N that are assigned to the cluster,*
- *the timestamp t of the last update, and*
- *reference P to parent Concept of dimensionality $l + 1$, if $l < d - 1$.*

The $d - l$ equations in Hessian normal form are the hyperplane equations that define the l-dimensional subspace. These are obviously an essential part of the *Concept* as they describe the subspace, are used for the unification with other *Concepts*, and also are part of the final result of CASHSTREAM. The mean μ is the centroid of the data objects that are assigned to the corresponding cluster and is used for checking whether the *Concept* can be merged with another one. N denotes the number of data objects that are assigned to the cluster. This value and the timestamp t of the last update of this *Concept* are used to calculate an importance score for the *Concept*. The importance scores are used to weight the *Concepts* for the unification of two similar *Concepts*, since a recent *Concept* that represents a large number of data objects should contribute more than a stale *Concept* that does not represent as many objects. Finally, a *Concept* also includes a reference to a parent *Concept*, i.e., a *Concept* representing a higher-dimensional subspace in which the child *Concept* is embedded. This enables CASHSTREAM to retrieve a cluster hierarchy.

On Representing Subspaces in Hessian Normal Form. The Hessian normal form (HNF) [20] has proven to be a well-suited representation for linear correlation cluster models as it contains a normal vector which describes the orientation of the corresponding hyperplane, respectively subspace. This is essential for the unification step as we use the orientations of two subspaces to determine their similarity. By using the HNF, we can formally describe a $(d-1)$-dimensional hyperplane $\mathcal{H}$ as

$$x \cdot n + b \leq \epsilon,$$

with $\cdot$ indicating the scalar product, $x \in \mathbb{R}^d$ denoting a data point lying on the hyperplane, $n \in \mathbb{R}^d$ denoting the unit normal vector and b being the minimum distance between the hyperplane and the origin. Since subspace clusters typically are not perfectly correlated, we allow a certain amount of deviation ϵ and consider every data point x that solves this equation to lie on $\mathcal{H}$. Note that the ϵ parameter is implicitly defined by setting the *maxSplit* parameter, i.e., the parameter that basically defines the size of a grid cell on the lowest split level.

A *Concept* contains $d - l$ of such hyperplane equations as it requires $d - l$ HNF equations for describing a l-dimensional subspace. Intuitively, this can be understood as follows: if $d - l$ $(d - 1)$-dimensional hyperplanes intersect in a d-dimensional space (with $l < d$), the intersection is a l-dimensional hyperplane. Mathematically, this can be seen as solving a simple linear system

$$Ax = b,$$

with A denoting an $m \times d$ matrix, where m is the number of normal vectors. If $d > m$, the linear system is under determined and hence the solution set describes a $(d - m)$-dimensional subspace.

As described in Sect. 3, CASHSTREAM likewise projects the data objects of an i-dimensional cluster onto the corresponding $(i - 1)$-dimensional subspace to find even lower dimensional clusters. In particular, it also produces an i-dimensional normal vector n_i to define an i-dimensional basis B_i from which the $(i - 1)$-dimensional subspace is derived as $B_i \setminus n_i \in \mathbb{R}^{i-1}$ in this step. By doing this iteratively until no lower dimensional subspace can be found, the *CASH* procedure retrieves an ordered set of $d - l$ HNF equations for an l-dimensional subspace, i.e.,

$$n_d \cdot x + r_0 = 0$$
$$n_{d-1} \cdot (B_d \setminus n_d \cdot x) + r_1 = 0$$
$$n_{d-2} \cdot (B_{d-1} \setminus n_{d-1} \cdot (B_d \setminus n_d \cdot x)) + r_2 = 0$$
$$\dots$$

with $n_{d-i} \in \mathbb{R}^{d-i}$, $0 \leq i < l$, denoting the $(d - i)$-dimensional normal vector that defines the $(d - i)$-dimensional basis B_{d-i}, x being a data point associated with the i-dimensional subspace cluster and r_i being the distances between the subspace hyperplane and the origin. $B_{d-i} \setminus n_{d-i}$ is a $(d-i-1) \times (d-i)$ projection matrix that is used to project $(d-i)$-dimensional data objects onto the $(d-i-1)$-dimensional subspace. However, for measuring the similarity between two *Concepts* (cf. Sect. 4.3), the normal vectors have to be d-dimensional. We therefore reconstruct d-dimensional normal vectors from lower-dimensional normal vectors as follows. Let $n_{d-i} \in \mathbb{R}^{d-i}$, with $0 < i < l$, be the $(d - i)$-dimensional normal vector defining the subspace whose basis is denoted as $B_{d-i-1} = B_{d-i} \setminus n_{d-i}$, then the reconstructed d-dimensional normal vector $n'_d \in \mathbb{R}^d$ is

$$n'_d = ((((n_{d-i} \cdot B_{d-i+1} \setminus n_{d-i+1}) \cdot B_{d-i+2} \setminus n_{d-i+2}) \cdot \ldots) \cdot B_d \setminus n_d).$$

Employing this reconstruction strategy to all $(d-i)$-dimensional normal vectors with $0 < i < l$ in addition with the d-dimensional normal vector n_d finally results in the desired set of $d - l$ non-parallel, and hence linearly independent [11], d-dimensional normal vectors that define the $d - l$ hyperplane equations.

4.3 Similarity Between Concepts

Theoretically, there is an infinite number of equation sets describing a single subspace cluster, e.g., a 1-dimensional subspace cluster can be modeled by the intersection of two 2D hyperplanes, the orientation of which is not necessarily important. In terms of *Concept* similarity, this means that two *Concepts* shall be considered similar as long as the intersections of their subspace equations describe approximately the same subspace, regardless the orientations of their subspace equations when considering them individually. Given this observation and the fact that each subspace hyperplane is defined by its normal vectors, we formalize the distance measure based on the following idea: Understanding an intersecting set of hyperplanes as the set of their respective normal vectors, every other normal vector contained in a second set of equations representing the same linear subspace is linearly dependent to the first set. However, since we aim at quantifying the linear dependence of these vectors rather than just determining whether they are linearly dependent or not, we propose the following similarity measure. Given a set of linearly independent normal vectors $V = \{n_1, ..., n_k\}$, we quantify the linear dependence of another vector m wrt V by calculating the singular values $SV(A)$ of matrix $A = (n_1, ..., n_k, m)$ and dividing the smallest value by the largest one. The closer the resulting value

$$L_{dep}\left(\underbrace{v_1, ...v_k, m}_{A}\right) = \frac{\min(SV(A))}{\max(SV(A))}$$

is to zero, the closer the vectors of the matrix are to being linearly dependent due to adding m. Given two *Concepts* C_1 and C_2 with their sets of normal vectors N_1 and N_2 being of cardinality k, and each normal vector representing a $(d-k)$-dimensional subspace, we define the *Singular Value Distance* as follows:

$$SV_{dist}(C_1, C_2) = \max_{n \in N_2}(L_{dep}(N_1, n)).$$

Note that this distance measure only accounts for the orientation of the correlation clusters described by the *Concepts*. However, two *Concepts* that describe different, parallel subspaces would have a singular value distance equal to zero. To avoid an unification of such *Concepts* we introduce the following secondary measure accounting for the actual distance in an Euclidean sense, i.e.,

$$d_{perp}(p, E) = |n_1 p_1 + ... + n_d p_d - r|,$$

with p denoting any data point of a *Concept* C_1, E denoting the HNF equation of a *Concept* C_2 and n being the corresponding normal vector. As the actual data points that defined the subspace are not available due to aggregating the necessary information, we use the centroid of the *Concept* as representative. Thus, we compute the *Equation Shift Distance* between two *Concepts* C_1 and C_2 as

$$d_{shift}(C_1, C_2) = \max_{i=1,\dots,k} d_{perp}(\boldsymbol{\mu}_2, E_{1,i}),$$

with $E_{1,i}$ being the hyperplane equations of C_1 and $\boldsymbol{\mu}_2$ being the mean of all data points forming the subspace captured in C_2.

4.4 Aging and Unification

Aging. Informally, the unification of two *Concepts* is the process of merging two subspace cluster representatives. However, when unifying two *Concepts* it is important to consider the importance of the *Concepts*, as for instance a very recent *Concept* is typically more important than a stale *Concept*, or a *Concept* that represents lots of data objects is more important than a *Concept* that represents only a few. Therefore, we introduce an *importance score* for each *Concept* that we use as weighting factor when merging two *Concepts*. Formally, we define the importance score of a *Concept* C as

$$\mathcal{I}(C) = e^{-\lambda \Delta t} \cdot N_C,$$

with λ being the decay parameter, Δt being the temporal difference between the current timestamp and the timestamp given in C, and N_C being the number of data objects that have been assigned to C. The first part of this equation, i.e., $e^{-\lambda \Delta t}$, is referred to as temporal part and contains the damping factor $\lambda > 0$. A high value of λ means low importance of old data and vice versa. The temporal part is also used to discard very old *Concepts* that are considered irrelevant for an up-to-date subspace clustering model. We therefore introduce a threshold θ that basically models a sliding window approach as a *Concept* whose temporal part falls below the threshold θ is discarded.

Unification. After extracting the new *Concepts* of a batch and recalculating the importance score of all *Concepts* in memory, we perform an unification step for the new *Concepts* and the previously extracted ones. Beginning at dimensionality $d - 1$, we compare all *Concepts* pairwise in terms of similarity and unify two *Concepts* if they are similar enough wrt some similarity threshold. The unification is continued in descending order regarding dimensionality. If two *Concepts* C_1 and C_2 of the same dimensionality can be unified, the following operations are performed to create the resulting *Concept* C^*:

– For each pair of equations $E_{1,i}$ and $E_{2,i}$ with $0 < i < d - l$, we define a new equation E_i^* by using the weighted mean of the normal vectors and the weighted mean of the distances to the origin of the two equations, i.e.,

$$E_i^* = \frac{\mathcal{I}(C_1) \cdot n_{E_{1,i}} + \mathcal{I}(C_2) \cdot n_{E_{2,i}}}{2} \cdot x + \frac{\mathcal{I}(C_1) \cdot r_{E_{1,i}} + \mathcal{I}(C_2) \cdot r_{E_{2,i}}}{2}.$$

This creates a new and possibly slightly shifted set of hyperplane equations.
- The mean representative for C^* is calculated by weighting the respective means from C_1 and C_2 with their importance, i.e.,

$$\mu_{C^*} = \frac{\mathcal{I}(C_1) \cdot \mu_{C_1} + \mathcal{I}(C_2) \cdot \mu_{C_2}}{2}.$$

- The number of data objects represented by C^* is the sum of data objects represented by C_1 and C_2, i.e., $N_{C^*} = N_{C_1} + N_{C_2}$.
- The timestamp of C^* is set to the current timestamp, i.e., the timestamp of the younger *Concept* C_1, such that $t_{C^*} = t_{C_1}$.
- The reference to the parent *Concept* of C^* will be set to the parent *Concept* of C_1. Pointers of *Concepts* having C_1 or C_2 as parent are set to C^*.

As *Concepts* do not have to be identical wrt normal vectors and origin distances in order to trigger the unification, there will be some shifts of the yet found subspace clusters. In some applications it might be useful to record these shifts, e.g., to detect abnormal behaviors. CASHSTREAM enables the tracking of concept shift, since eventual drifts would result in rotations or parallel shifts of one or several plane equations describing the *Concept*. Hence, one simply has to record changes that may result from an unification of an old and a new *Concept* to get a history of changes in the underlying data distribution. However, this comes to the costs of requiring additional memory space.

5   Experiments

We evaluate CASHSTREAM by comparing the proposed streaming algorithm against the static counterpart *CASH* wrt the performance indicators accuracy, throughput and memory consumption. Those measures are important metrics for streaming methods as these methods typically aim at trading some accuracy for a drastically decreased memory consumption, or runtime.

Datasets. We use synthetic and real world datasets throughout this section. The synthetic dataset is a 4-dimensional set of points, containing two 2-dimensional planes of 1000 data points each, and 1000 random noise points. The planes both are jittered, making the data not perfectly correlated within their corresponding subspaces (as it appears in real world applications). The real-world dataset is a slightly manipulated version of the *wages dataset*. The original dataset has also been used in [1], and consists of 534 records each having four different features, i.e., age, years of education, years of experience and salary. However, we enlarge the dataset by copying and shuffling the records such that we have 40000 data points and finally can use the data to simulate a data stream appropriately.

Parameter Settings. We perform grid searches over various parameter settings and report the results for the best settings. Precisely, we range the parameters over the following sets: damping factor $\lambda \in \{.2, .5, .8\}$, temporal threshold $\theta \in \{.5, .8, 1\}$, singular value distance threshold $\tau_{SVdist} \in \{.005, .01, .02, .03\}$, and equation shift distance threshold $\tau_{shift} \in \{.05, .1, .15\}$[2]. The timestamp of a batch is set according to its number, i.e., the i-th batch gets timestamp i. The *minPts* parameter that must be set for *CASH* is set proportionally to the batch size, i.e., $minPts = \tilde{m} \cdot s$, with $\tilde{m}$ being the *minPts* fraction and s being the batch size. The other *CASH* specific parameter *maxSplits* is set according to the dataset at hand and reported for each experiment individually.

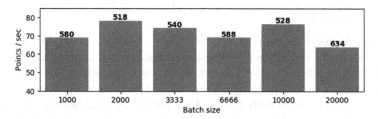

Fig. 3. Throughput for various batch sizes on the wages dataset; values above the bars are the absolute runtimes in sec; $maxSplits = 10$, $\tilde{m} = 0.2$.

Clustering Quality. For measuring the clustering quality of CASHSTREAM, we compare the results to a clustering on the same dataset for several different settings of the batch size parameter, including the batch size for which a single batch contains the entire dataset, which is equivalent to the static *CASH*. In terms of evaluation metrics, we employ the Adjusted Rand Index (*ARI*) and the Adjusted Mutual Information (*AMI*) scores.

Table 1. Results on the synthetic dataset. k is the number of batches, $maxSplits = 9$, $\tilde{m} = 0.3$.

Batch size	k	ARI	AMI
3000	1	0.951	0.922
1500	2	0.943	0.907
1000	3	0.924	0.881
750	4	0.875	0.829

Note that due to the lack of ground truth in the real-world dataset, we restrict ourselves to a synthetic dataset for evaluating the clustering quality. The calculated *ARI* and *AMI* for this dataset can be seen in Table 1. In general, it can be observed that the clustering quality slightly drops when choosing a batch size below 1000. This might indicate that the subsample might not reflect the data distribution sufficiently when choosing the batch size too small, which can be especially problematic in scenarios where correlations are imperfect. Another reason for the decreasing clustering accuracy can be the presence of temporal effects (i.e., slight drifts in the data distribution, increasing amount of noise, etc.).

Runtime/Throughput. We investigate the actual throughput in terms of data points per second. In general, our evaluation of the throughput can be understood as a runtime comparison between the batched algorithm and the static *CASH*. For the throughput experiment, we used the enlarged real-world dataset to demonstrate the scalability of the batched streaming approach. In Fig. 3, we

---

[2] Note that those parameters are application dependent and thus not investigated in further detail.

report the throughput in data points per second and the total runtime in seconds. Each of the reported values is the mean value over three runs. For all those runs, we compared the resulting clustering models (by means of comparing the detected subspaces) with the expected clustering model and selected the parameter setting according to the best result. This experiment shows that the stream processing procedure has no loss in runtime compared to the static variant. In particular, it can be seen that the unification of *Concepts* barely has any effect on the runtime performance. We also observe that the batch size barely affects this performance measure.

Memory. As memory consumption is a critical metric for streaming applications, we show the monitored RAM usage of the batched approach and compare it to the static *CASH*. Precisely, we report the heap space usage profiles for both approaches as the memory usage at runtime is the decisive performance metric. The shown graphs were created using Java ViusalVM 1.4.2, which is included in the Java JDK. To simulate a light-weight system, we cap the maximal available heap space to 2 GB (Fig. 4).

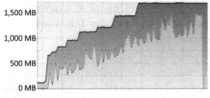 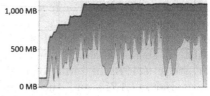

(a) Static approach, processing a single batch of size 20000, max at ≈1500MB.

(b) Streaming approach, processing three batches of size 6666, max at ≈850MB.

Fig. 4. Heap space usage profiles for the wages dataset ($maxSplits = 8$, $\tilde{m} = 0.2$).

For this experiment, we again use the enlarged wages dataset. This time the dataset consists of 20000 data points (augmented the same way as previously). Figure 4a shows the heap usage profile when using a single batch that contains all data points, resp. the static version, and Fig. 4b shows the profile when computing the same experiment with three batches.

For the static approach simulated in the full-sized 20000 points batch, the heap space rises steadily to a maximum level of around 1500 MB. When subdividing the points into 3 batches of 6666 points, we observe two crucial details: Firstly, the peak heap space usage is approx. 850 MB, which is significantly lower than in the static approach. Secondly, the three sequentially processed batches can clearly be identified as three peaks in the heap space profile.

6   Conclusion

In this work, we presented the novel subspace clustering algorithm CASHSTREAM that is able to deal with high-dimensional streaming data efficiently. Precisely,

CASHSTREAM relies on the subspace clustering paradigm that was introduced for the static *CASH* algorithm, i.e., using Hough transformations to identify interesting linear subspaces. However, in contrast to *CASH*, the proposed algorithm uses a batch processing scheme, identifies interesting subspaces within the data batches, and subsequently compresses important information within *Concept* data structures. Our experiments showed that CASHSTREAM is fairly robust against different choices for the batch size and simultaneously reduces the memory consumption significantly compared to the static *CASH* algorithm (less than 50% on the real-world dataset). At the same time the loss in terms of clustering quality is negligible.

Acknowledgement. This work has been funded by the German Federal Ministry of Education and Research (BMBF) under Grant No. 01IS18036A. The authors of this work take full responsibilities for its content.

References

1. Achtert, E., Böhm, C., David, J., Kröger, P., Zimek, A.: Global correlation clustering based on the Hough transform. Stat. Anal. Data Min. **1**(3), 111–127 (2008)
2. Achtert, E., Böhm, C., Kriegel, H.P., Kröger, P., Zimek, A.: On exploring complex relationships of correlation clusters. In: Proceedings of SSDBM, p. 7 (2007)
3. Aggarwal, C.C., Han, J., Wang, J., Yu, P.S.: A framework for clustering evolving data streams. In: Proceedings of VLDB, pp. 81–92 (2003)
4. Aggarwal, C.C., Han, J., Wang, J., Yu, P.S.: A framework for projected clustering of high dimensional data streams. In: Proceedings of VLDB, pp. 852–863 (2004)
5. Aggarwal, C.C., Yu, P.S.: Finding generalized projected clusters in high dimensional spaces, vol. 29 (2000)
6. Böhm, C., Kailing, K., Kriegel, H.P., Kröger, P.: Density connected clustering with local subspace preferences (2004)
7. Böhm, C., Kailing, K., Kröger, P., Zimek, A.: Computing clusters of correlation connected objects. In: Proceedings of SIGMOD, pp. 455–466 (2004)
8. Borutta, F., Kröger, P., Hubauer, T.: A generic summary structure for arbitrarily oriented subspace clustering in data streams. In: Amato, G., Gennaro, C., Oria, V., Radovanović, M. (eds.) SISAP 2019. LNCS, vol. 11807, pp. 203–211. Springer, Cham (2019). https://doi.org/10.1007/978-3-030-32047-8_18
9. Bradley, P.S., Fayyad, U.M., Reina, C., et al.: Scaling clustering algorithms to large databases. In: Proceedings of KDD, vol. 98, pp. 9–15 (1998)
10. Cao, F., Ester, M., Qian, W., Zhou, A.: Density-based clustering over an evolving data stream with noise. In: Proceedings of SDM, vol. 6, pp. 328–339 (2006)
11. Corwin, L.: Multivariable Calculus. Routledge, London (2017)
12. Guha, S., Mishra, N., Motwani, R., o'Callaghan, L.: Clustering data streams. In: Proceedings of FOCS, pp. 359–366 (2000)
13. Hassani, M., Spaus, P., Gaber, M.M., Seidl, T.: Density-based projected clustering of data streams. In: Hüllermeier, E., Link, S., Fober, T., Seeger, B. (eds.) SUM 2012. LNCS (LNAI), vol. 7520, pp. 311–324. Springer, Heidelberg (2012). https://doi.org/10.1007/978-3-642-33362-0_24
14. Kazempour, D., Mauder, M., Kröger, P., Seidl, T.: Detecting global hyperparaboloid correlated clusters: a Hough-transform based multicore algorithm. Distrib. Parallel Databases **39**, 37–72 (2018). https://doi.org/10.1007/s10619-018-7246-0

15. Kriegel, H.P., Kröger, P., Ntoutsi, I., Zimek, A.: Towards subspace clustering on dynamic data: an incremental version of PreDeCon. In: Proceedings of International Workshop on Novel Data Stream Pattern Mining Techniques, pp. 31–38 (2010)
16. Ntoutsi, I., Zimek, A., Palpanas, T., Kröger, P., Kriegel, H.P.: Density-based projected clustering over high dimensional data streams. In: Proceedings of SDM, pp. 987–998 (2012)
17. O'Callaghan, L., Mishra, N., Meyerson, A., Guha, S., Motwani, R.: Streaming-data algorithms for high-quality clustering. In: Proceedings of ICDE, pp. 685–694 (2002)
18. Park, N.H., Lee, W.S.: Grid-based subspace clustering over data streams. In: Proceedings of CIKM, pp. 801–810 (2007)
19. Rosenfeld, A.: Picture processing by computer, vol. 1, pp. 147–176. ACM (1969)
20. Scheid, H., Schwarz, W.: Elemente der linearen Algebra und der Analysis (2009)
21. Silva, J.A., Faria, E.R., Barros, R.C., Hruschka, E.R., De Carvalho, A.C., Gama, J.: Data stream clustering: a survey. ACM Comput. Surv. **46**(1), 13 (2013)
22. Zhang, T., Ramakrishnan, R., Livny, M.: BIRCH: an efficient data clustering method for very large databases. ACM Sigmod Rec. **25**, 103–114 (1996)
23. Zhou, A., Cao, F., Qian, W., Jin, C.: Tracking clusters in evolving data streams over sliding windows. Knowl. Inf. Syst. **15**(2), 181–214 (2008). https://doi.org/10.1007/s10115-007-0070-x

Strong Baselines for Author Name Disambiguation with and Without Neural Networks

Zhenyu Zhang[1,2], Bowen Yu[1,2], Tingwen Liu[1(✉)], and Dong Wang[1,2]

[1] Institute of Information Engineering, Chinese Academy of Sciences, Beijing, China
{zhangzhenyu1996,yubowen,liutingwen,wangdong}@iie.ac.cn
[2] School of Cyber Security, University of Chinese Academy of Sciences,
Beijing, China

Abstract. Author name disambiguation (AND) is one of the most vital problems in scientometrics, which has become a great challenge with the rapid growth of academic digital libraries. Existing approaches for this task substantially rely on complex clustering-like architectures, and they usually assume the number of clusters is known beforehand or predict the number by applying another model, which involve increasingly complex and time-consuming architectures. In this paper, we combine simple neural networks with two sets of heuristic rules to explore strong baselines for the author name disambiguation problem without any priori knowledge or estimation about cluster size, which frees the model from unnecessary complexity. On a popular benchmark dataset AMiner, our solution significantly outperforms several state-of-the-art methods both in performance and efficiency, and it still achieves comparable performance with many complex models when only using a group of rules. Experimental results also indicate that gains from sophisticated deep learning techniques are quite modest in the author name disambiguation problem.

Keywords: Author name disambiguation · Heuristic rules · Clustering problem · Baseline methods

1 Introduction

There has been significant historic and recent interest in the author name disambiguation (AND) problem, which can be defined as the problem of clustering unique authors using the metadata of publication records (title, venue, keyword, author name and affiliation, etc.) [11,19,23]. With the fast growth of scientific literature, the disambiguation problem has become an imminent issue since numerous downstream applications are affected by its preferences, such as information retrieval and bibliographic data analysis [5,13]. But unfortunately, AND is not an elementary problem because distinct authors may share the same name,

H. W. Lauw et al. (Eds.): PAKDD 2020, LNAI 12084, pp. 369–381, 2020.
https://doi.org/10.1007/978-3-030-47426-3_29

which is quite common for Asians, especially Chinese researchers [9], since different Chinese names will be the same when mapped to English (*e.g.*, 王伟 and 汪卫 share the same English name Wei Wang).

The problem of disambiguating *who is who* dates back at least few decades, and it is typically viewed as a clustering problem and solved by various clustering models, such models have to answer two questions inevitably, that is how to quantify the similarity and how to determine cluster size [8]. Many existing literatures mainly focus on answering the first question, such as feature-based methods [12,13] and graph-based methods [3,16,20]. Actually, quite a few of them involve increasingly complex and time-consuming architectures that yield progressively smaller gains over the previous state-of-the-art. When it comes to the second question, most previous approaches assume the number of clusters is known beforehand or predict the number by applying another model [25]. However, there is no doubt that the former is unrealistic in real situations and the latter may lead to error propagation.

Lost in this push, we argue that author name disambiguation is not a typical clustering task. From the source of this problem, we should pay more attention to the precision, followed by recall, since that once two clusters are merged incorrectly, re-splitting them is an almost impossible process. Cast in this light, many existing clustering models are not very suitable for the author name disambiguation problem. Meanwhile, cost-effective blocking technique [1] and lightweight rule-based methods [2,22] are worthy of research as they have been proven to achieve convincing precision in this problem.

In line with an existing research that aims to improve empirical rigor by focusing on insights and knowledge, as opposed to simply "winning" [17], we peel away unnecessary components until we arrive at the simplest model that works well without any priori knowledge about cluster size, which only consists of simple neural networks and some heuristic rules. Furthermore, the hierarchical agglomerative clustering (HAC) algorithm is adopted as the guiding ideology to cluster publications. On the benchmark dataset AMiner [25], we find that our proposed solution achieves significantly better performance than several state-of-the-art methods. Experiments on another public dataset show that such rules conform to the natural law and are applicable to the whole author name disambiguation task rather than just the AMiner dataset. Experimental results also suggest that while complex models do indeed contribute to meaningful advances towards this problem, some of them exhibit unnecessary complexity and rules play a role that cannot be ignored in this task.

2   Problem Definition

Given an author name α and a set of publication records $\mathcal{P} = \{p_1, p_2, ..., p_l\}$ with the name α, the problem of author name disambiguation is to partition the publication records $\mathcal{P}$ into different clusters $\{C_1, C_2, ..., C_K\}$ such that:

- All the records in C_k belong to the same author α_k.
- All the records in $\mathcal{P}$ by α_k are in C_k.

where $\{\alpha_1, ..., \alpha_K\}$ are K different people with the same name α.

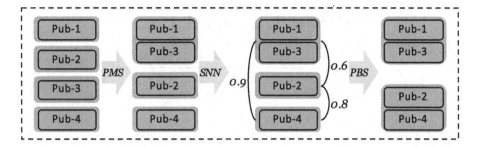

Fig. 1. A concrete process of our proposed approach.

3 Methodology

In this section, we discuss the design and implementation of our solution in detail, whose design philosophy is based on the observation that the interests of researchers usually do not change too frequently, and in particular, he/she would stay in the same institution for a relatively long time [3]. For this purpose, we can infer that researchers usually have relatively stable sets of coauthors, and topics of publications belong to a researcher should be close in the semantic space during a certain period. This is also in line with the law of human social activities in the real world, that is, friends and interests of a person are usually relatively fixed [6].

With this in mind, we first scatter the publication records $\mathcal{P} = \{p_1, p_2, ..., p_l\}$ into l sets, and there is only one unique publication p in each original set. Next, a pre-merging strategy (PMS) is proposed to make preliminary merge decisions according to coauthors. Furthermore, simple neural networks (SNN) are further employed to measure the semantic similarity between two clusters by publication titles, since titles naturally convey the main point of publications. Finally, we introduce a post-blocking strategy (PBS) to determine the final clusters elegantly. Figure 1 shows a concrete process of our proposed approach.

3.1 Pre-merging Strategy

This step aims to merge the initial publication sets preliminarily using the point-to-point and cluster-to-cluster rules. For convenience, we set an identity constraint $\mathcal{M}(i, j) \in \{1, 0\}$ to indicate that i and j will (not) be merged into a cluster, where i and j refer to two publications or clusters (Fig. 2).

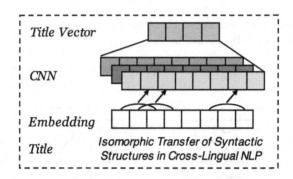

Fig. 2. An illustration of our simple neural networks.

- **Point-to-Point**: Given two publications p_i and p_j, if $|S_n(p_i) \cap S_n(p_j)| > \lambda_1$, or $A_\alpha(p_i) = A_\alpha(p_j)$ & $|S_n(p_i) \cap S_n(p_j)| > 1$, then $\mathcal{M}(p_i, p_j) = 1$. For a publication p_i, $S_n(p_i)$ and $A_\alpha(p_i)$ denote the set of author names and the affiliations of current author name α, respectively.
- **Cluster-to-Cluster**: Given two clusters C_i and C_j, if $\mathcal{O}_n(C_i, C_j) > \lambda_2$, or $\mathcal{O}_a(C_i, C_j) > \lambda_2$, then $\mathcal{M}(C_i, C_j) = 1$, where $\mathcal{O}_x(C_i, C_j)$ denotes the overlap ratio of two clusters in the aspect of x, and $x \in \{n, a\}$ denotes the name or affiliation of authors. We define the overlap ratio $\mathcal{O}_x(C_i, C_j)$ as:

$$\mathcal{O}_x(C_i, C_j) = \frac{\sum_{\bar{x} \in (S_x(C_i) \cap S_x(C_j))} (F_{\bar{x}}(C_i) + F_{\bar{x}}(C_j))}{\min(\sum_{\bar{x} \in S_x(C_i)} F_{\bar{x}}(C_i), \sum_{\bar{x} \in S_x(C_j)} F_{\bar{x}}(C_j))} \tag{1}$$

where $F_{\bar{x}}(C_i)$ is the occurrence number of $\bar{x}$ in the cluster C_i.

Intuitively, the point-to-point stage can be understood as that we regard two publications p_i, p_j belong to the same cluster when the number of coauthors of p_i and p_j exceeds a threshold λ_1, and if the affiliations of current author name α are identical in p_i and p_j, the threshold is relaxed to 1, which means that only one coauthor except α is needed to satisfy the merge condition. For ease of exposition, we take author name as an example here (*i.e.*, $x = n$) to describe the process of cluster-to-cluster stage. To calculate the numerator of overlap ratio $\mathcal{O}_n(C_i, C_j)$, we consider names that appear in the intersection of two name sets $S_n(C_i), S_n(C_j)$, and calculate the total occurrence number of such names in these two clusters. In addition, the minimum of total occurrence number of all author names in $S_n(C_i)$ and $S_n(C_j)$ is defined as the denominator. Considering that the total number of author names in two clusters may vary greatly, such a minimum value selection strategy can effectively avoid the problem that a small cluster cannot be merged with a large cluster.

3.2   Simple Neural Networks

As mentioned above, it is a natural idea to determine whether two publications belong to the same author by their topic similarity, since topic reflects the interest and direction of a researcher. In order to quantify the similarity effectively, we design a simple model based on convolutional neural networks (CNN) to project publications into a low-dimensional latent common space.

We believe that *title* contains enough information to express the topic of a publication, thus we first transform each $p_i \in P$ into a sequence of vectors $[\mathbf{w}_1, ..., \mathbf{w}_n]$, where $\mathbf{w}_j$ is the embedding of j-th word in the title. Note that we employ CBOW [14] to pre-train initial word embeddings, which will be fine-tuned afterwards. Then a standard CNN is utilized to produce the title vector for each publication, in which convolutional operations are performed with m different filters, and the final representation $\mathbf{p}_i \in \mathbb{R}^m$ is computed by a max-pooling layer. Next, we follow the basic idea of [25] to train this representation model. Let (p_i, p_{i_+}, p_{i_-}) be a triplet where p_{i_+} and p_i are publications authored by the same person, while p_{i_-} is a randomly selected negative example belonging to another person. Hence, our training data T consists of a set of triplets and we optimize a margin-based loss function as follows:

$$\mathcal{L} = \frac{1}{|T|} \sum_{i=1}^{|T|} \max(0, \delta - \cos(\mathcal{R}(p_i), \mathcal{R}(p_{i_+}))$$

$$+ \cos(\mathcal{R}(p_i), \mathcal{R}(p_{i_-}))) \tag{2}$$

where $\mathcal{R}(\cdot)$ denotes the representation model and δ is the margin. The intuition behind Eq. 2 is that we want the positive pair (p_i, p_{i_+}) to be more similar to each other than their negative example p_{i_-}, by a margin of at least δ.

For a given cluster C_i containing $|C_i|$ publications, the cluster embedding is defined as $\mathbf{c}_i = \frac{1}{|C_i|} \sum_{j=1}^{|C_i|} \mathcal{R}(p_j)$. We choose the cluster with the highest similarity with C_i as its target merging cluster, denoted as C_j, the similarity between these two clusters is measured by the cosine similarity between $\mathbf{c}_i$ and $\mathbf{c}_j$. Finally, C_i and C_j will be merged with some post-blocking strategies, we will discuss them in the following paragraph.

3.3 Post-blocking Strategy

Based on the learned model $\mathcal{R}(\cdot)$ and cluster embeddings, this step is proposed to determine the final partition. To avoid undesirable mergence caused by only measuring intra-cluster semantic similarity, we introduce Post-Blocking Strategy to take the statistical characteristics of two clusters into consideration. In our design, publication with the largest number of coauthors in C_i is selected as the anchor publication p_i^*, and p_j^* for C_j can be selected similarly. Then, the anchor-to-anchor rule is deployed as follows:

– **Anchor-to-Anchor:** if $S_n(p_i^*) \cap S_n(p_j^*) = \{\alpha\}$ and $S_{a \backslash \alpha}(p_i^*) \cap S_{a \backslash \alpha}(p_j^*) = \emptyset$, then $\mathcal{M}(C_i, C_j) = 0$. For an anchor publication p_i^*, $S_{a \backslash \alpha}(p_i^*)$ denote the set of affiliations except the current author α.

The anchor-to-anchor rule can be interpreted as that, if there is no intersection between the name sets or the affiliation sets of p_i^* and p_j^* except the current author name α and its affiliation, we do not think C_i and C_j belong to the same author. To illustrate this process intuitively, we describe an example in Fig. 1 (the third step). Although the similarity between {Pub-1, Pub-3} and {Pub-4} is the highest, the merge operation is still blocked as the anchor-to-anchor rule is violated.

4   Experiments

4.1   Dataset

We conduct our experiments on a recently widely used public benchmark dataset AMiner introduced in [25][1], which is sampled from a well-labeled academic database. The labeling process of the dataset is based on the publication lists on authors' homepages and the affiliations, e-mails in web databases (*e.g.* Scopus, ACM Digital Library). The training set contains publications of 500 author names, and the test set has 100 author names. For each publication, there are five fields as follows: *title, keywords, venue, author name and corresponding affiliation*. In this paper, we only use title, author name and affiliation to develop our solution. Compared with existing benchmarks for name disambiguation, AMiner is significantly larger (in terms of the number of documents) and more challenging (since each candidate set contains much more clusters) [25].

4.2   Experiment Settings

Following popular choices, we tune our model using five-fold cross validation. For the pre-merging strategy (PMS), we set λ_1 to 2 and λ_2 to 0.5 experimentally. Beyond that, CBOW model [14] with $k = 100$ is employed to learn initial word representations on the training set of AMiner. The simple neural networks (SNN) model is trained using Stochastic Gradient Descent (SGD) algorithm with the initial learning rate of 0.1 and the weight decay of 0.9, the batch size is 50 and the margin is 0.3. At convolutional layer, the number of filter maps is 100 and the window size is 3. Dropout with $p = 0.3$ is used after the input layer.

4.3   Comparison Methods

Following Zhang et al. [25], we compare our model against 5 different methods:

- **Basic Rules** [25]: It constructs linkage graphs by connecting two publications when their co-authors, affiliations or venues are strictly equal. Results are obtained by simply partitioning the graph into connected components.
- **Fan et al.** [3]: For each name, it constructs a graph by collapsing all the co-authors with identical names to one node. The final results are generated by affinity propagation algorithm and the distance between two nodes is measured based on the number of valid paths.

---

[1] https://static.aminer.cn/misc/na-data-kdd18.zip.

– **Louppe et al.** [13]: It trains a pairwise distance function based on carefully designed similarity features, and uses semi-supervised Hierarchical Agglomerative Clustering (HAC) algorithm to determine clusters.
– **Zhang and Al Hasan** [24]: It constructs graphs for each author name based on co-author and document similarity. Embeddings are learned for each name and the final results are also obtained by HAC.

Table 1. Results of author name disambiguation on the AMiner benchmark dataset. † marks results reported in [25].

Model	Precision	Recall	F1 Score
Basic Rules [25]†	44.94	89.30	53.42
Fan et al. [3]†	81.62	40.43	50.23
Louppe et al. [13]†	57.09	**77.22**	63.10
Zhang and Al Hasan [24]†	70.63	59.53	62.81
Zhang et al. [25]†	77.96	63.03	67.79
PMS	**81.86**	55.61	66.23
PMS+SNN	73.90	61.97	67.41
PMS+SNN+PBS (PNP)	76.92	64.54	**70.19**

– **Zhang et al.** [25]: It introduces a representation learning framework by leveraging both global supervision and local contexts, and also uses HAC as clustering method, which is the latest approach on the dataset[2]. Besides, it deploys the recurrent neural networks to estimate the number of cluster.

Our method is indicated by **PNP**. In order to analyze the contribution of each component, we present results at each of the three stages described in Sect. 3.

4.4 Results

Table 1 shows the performances of different methods on the AMiner dataset. Following previous settings [25], we utilize pairwise Precision, Recall, and F1-score to evaluate all methods. Meanwhile, a macro averaged score of each metric is calculated according to all test names.

Louppe et al. [13] use some manual features to learn a pairwise similarity function and achieve competitive performance. Similarly, we hold the view that in the era of deep learning, the feature engineering methods may not be certainly worse than some exquisite neural networks, especially in this task. Moreover, some features can be further abstracted into rules and be used universally in the whole author name disambiguation problem, rather than limited to this dataset, we will discuss this phenomenon in Sect. 5.2. However, the results of Basic Rules

---

[2] https://github.com/neozhangthe1/disambiguation/.

are disappointing and contrary to ours. Since there is no implementation details, we speculate that it might be because the merging rules are too loose. By incorporating both rules and neural networks to model co-authorships, affiliations and titles explicitly, our PNP model outperforms all baselines in terms of F1-score (+3.54% over Zhang et al. [25], +11.75% over Zhang and Al Hasan [24], +11.23% over Louppe et al. [13] and +39.74% over Fan et al. [3] relatively).

Table 2. Runtime and trainable parameter number of different models.

Model	Runtime		Trainable
	Training	Testing	Parameters Number
Zhang el al. [25]	>24 h	~573 s	3,024,193
PMS	-	~31 s	0
SNN	~2 h	-	30,100
PBS	-	~88 s	0
PMS+SNN+PBS (PNP)	~2 h	~119 s	30,100

In the bottom half part of Table 1, some incremental results of our method are presented. Specifically, PMS outperforms most baselines, which indicates the effectiveness of heuristic rules. PMS+SNN with optimal reject threshold (0.8) yields better performance than PMS (+1.78% in terms of F1-score), which suggests the advantage of SNN. PNP outperforms PMS+SNN by +4.12% in terms of F1-score and +4.09% in terms of precision which verifies the incorporation of PBS can greatly enhance the performance. Overall, we attribute these successes to the comprehensive consideration of rules and semantics based on the inherent characteristics of the author name disambiguation problem.

5 Analyses

5.1 Efficiency Analysis

We study the runtime and model size (except word embeddings) of our method as well as the state-of-the-art model [25] using official implementation. For the sake of fairness, we run them on the same GPU server.

From Table 2, we find that Zhang et al. [25] is indeed computationally expensive, which is caused by the complex operations in modeling the local linkage with graph auto-encoder and estimating the number of clusters. Instead, our PNP model is quite simpler and faster because it mainly relies on the heuristic rules to model co-authors rather than embed the local co-authorship into representations. Beyond that, our proposed model removes the need to know or estimate cluster size beforehand, which is unrealistic or time-consuming. Generally, our approach is almost 5 times faster than the state-of-the-art model in test time and has a significant advantage in the model size, which means that training our model requires much fewer computation resources and less time.

5.2   Rule Sensitivity Analysis

As aforementioned, we hold that the optimal parameters (λ_1 and λ_2) can be applicable to the general author name disambiguation task, rather than limited to the AMiner dataset. To validate our opinion, we employ the Open Academic Data Challenge 2018 (OPEDAC 2018) dataset to analyze the parameter sensitivity of rules. OPEDAC 2018 consists of 80,050 publications of 50 authors. Different from AMiner, many publications in OPEDAC 2018 contain hundreds of authors, which means that it is more difficult and closer to reality.

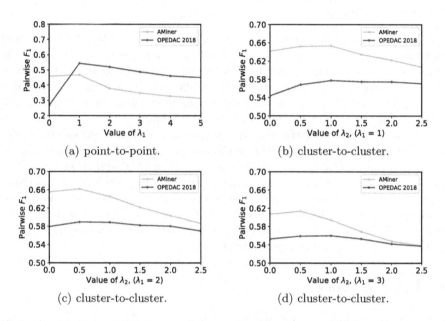

(a) point-to-point.

(b) cluster-to-cluster.

(c) cluster-to-cluster.

(d) cluster-to-cluster.

Fig. 3. The effects of λ_1 and λ_2 to the performance when using different datasets. The subfigure (a) depicts results when only the point-to-point rules are used, while remaining subgraphs show the results of the entire pre-merging strategy.

By varying the value of λ_1 across $\{0, 1, 2, 3, 4, 5\}$, we repeat the experiments and report results in Fig. 3(a). As observed, when λ_1 increases, the F1-score first increases and then decreases, the best performances of both datasets are achieved when $\lambda_1 = 1$. It is intuitive, because a person usually has a fixed partner, such as a mentor or leader. Furthermore, as shown in Fig. 3(b), 3(c) and 3(d), when fixing the value of λ_1 and varying λ_2, the two datasets have the similar trends and achieve the peak at almost the same value of λ_2, which is a strong evidence for our claim that such rules conform to the natural law and the hyperparameters of rules are relatively insensitive to datasets. We hypothesize that this phenomenon is due to the particularity of problem, which is that friends and affiliations of a person are usually relatively fixed.

We also reproduce the state-of-the-art model [25] on the OPEDAC 2018 dataset and achieved the F1-score of 50.4%, and our PNP model outperforms it by a substantial margin (+15.4%), which suggests the generalizability of our model[3]. It is worthy to mention that the results of OPEDAC 2018 in Fig. 3 should not be compared with other competitors in the leaderboard. The reason is that OPEDAC 2018 suffers from the problem of noise in the author list. Actually, when combined with other denoising strategy, our PNP method finally ranks top 3% without any ensemble tricks in the competition.

5.3   Error Analysis

We analyze some of the errors made by our model on the AMiner dataset, and find that the most common error is the incorrect mergence when publications have the same short and incomplete affiliations (*e.g.* Department of Computer Science). In other words, there might be two different people with the same name who happen to work in the department of computer science, but if they do not belong to the same school, things will become trickier.

For this purpose, we perform a supplemental experiment to explore the upper bound of precision, we merge two publications if and only if $S_n(p_i)=S_n(p_j)$ & $S_a(p_i)=S_a(p_j)$, which means that the name set and the affiliation set of two publications are exactly the same. Experimental results show that the precision is just about 95%. When facing the remaining 5%, even humans have no certain confidence to deal with them correctly. In this case, after removing these indistinguishable samples, our pre-merging strategy attains 86% precision, which is quite acceptable for the unsupervised heuristic rules.

6   Related Work

In many applications, author name disambiguation (AND) has been regarded as a challenging problem, which can date back at least few decades. With the growth of scientific literature, it becomes more and more difficult and urgent to solve this problem [4,18,21]. Based on the different scenarios, the author name disambiguation problem can be divided into two subtasks: author name disambiguation from scratch (ANDS) [24,25] and incremental author name disambiguation (IAND) [9,10], the former is generally a clustering problem, while the latter is a classification problem.

In this paper, we focus on the ANDS scenario, which is more challenging and practical than IAND. On the whole, state-of-the-art solutions for the task can be divided into two categories: feature-based and graph-based. Feature-based methods leverage pairwise distance function to measure documents. Huang et al. [7] first uses blocking technique to group candidate documents with similar names

---

[3] Note that we do not report the comparison results on this dataset in Sect. 5.2 because we cannot reproduce other baseline methods without official implementation.

together and employs DBSCAN to cluster documents. Louppe el al. [13] uses a classifier to learn pairwise similarity and performs semi-supervised hierarchical clustering to generate results. Graph-based methods utilize graph topology and aggregate information from neighbors. Fan et al. [3] builds document graph for each name by co-authorship, and uses carefully-designed similarity function and affinity propagation algorithm to generate clustering results. Tang el al. [20] employs Hidden Markov Random Fields to model node and edge features in a unified probabilistic framework. Zhang and Al Hasan [24] learns graph embedding from three constructed graphs based on document similarity and co-authorship. Moreover, Zhang et al. [25] combines the advantages of above two methods by learning a global embedding using supervised metric learning and refining the embedding using local linkage structures. In this push towards complexity, we do not believe that all researchers have adequately explored baseline methods, and thus it is unclear how much various fussy techniques actually help.

7   Conclusion

In this paper, we take heuristic rules that come from real-world observations into consideration and propose a strong baseline for the author name disambiguation problem. The proposed model contains a pre-merging strategy, simple neural networks and a post-blocking strategy, which do not need any extra knowledge about cluster size. Experimental results verify the advantage of our method over state-of-the-art methods, and demonstrate the proposed model is highly efficient and rules can be extended to other datasets, in which many conclusions are consistent with some sociological phenomena. Beyond that, we further explore the upper bound of disambiguation precision and analyze the possible reasons, which will be leaved as our future work. To conclude, we offer all data mining researchers a point of reflection like some previous work [15]: The most important thing is to consider baselines that do not involve complex architectures, simple methods might lead to unexpected performances.

Acknowledgements. This research is supported by the National Key Research and Development Program of China (grant No. 2016YFB0801003) and the Strategic Priority Research Program of Chinese Academy of Sciences (grant No. XDC02040400).

References

1. Backes, T.: The impact of name-matching and blocking on author disambiguation. In: Proceedings of the 27th ACM International Conference on Information and Knowledge Management (CIKM) (2018)
2. Caron, E., van Eck, N.J.: Large scale author name disambiguation using rule-based scoring and clustering. In: Proceedings of the International Conference on Science and Technology Indicators (STI) (2014)
3. Fan, X., Wang, J., Pu, X., Zhou, L., Lv, B.: On graph-based name disambiguation. J. Data Inf. Qual. (2011)

4. Ferreira, A.A., Gonçalves, M.A., Laender, A.H.: A brief survey of automatic methods for author name disambiguation. ACM SIGMOD Record (2012)
5. Han, D., Liu, S., Hu, Y., Wang, B., Sun, Y.: Elm-based name disambiguation in bibliography. World Wide Web (2015)
6. Hirsch, J.E.: An index to quantify an individual's scientific research output that takes into account the effect of multiple coauthorship. Scientometrics **85**, 741–754 (2010)
7. Huang, J., Ertekin, S., Giles, C.L.: Efficient name disambiguation for large-scale databases. In: Proceedings of the European Conference on Machine Learning and Principles and Practice of Knowledge Discovery in Databases (ECML/PKDD) (2006)
8. Hussain, I., Asghar, S.: A survey of author name disambiguation techniques: 2010–2016. Knowl. Eng. Rev. (2017)
9. Hussain, I., Asghar, S.: Incremental author name disambiguation using author profile models and self-citations. Turkish J. Electric. Eng. Comput. Sci. (2019)
10. Kim, K., Rohatgi, S., Giles, C.L.: Hybrid deep pairwise classification for author name disambiguation. In: Proceedings of the 28th ACM International Conference on Information and Knowledge Management (CIKM) (2019)
11. Levin, M., Krawczyk, S., Bethard, S., Jurafsky, D.: Citation-based bootstrapping for large-scale author disambiguation. J. Am. Soc. Inf. Sci. Technol. (2012)
12. Liu, J., Lei, K.H., Liu, J.Y., Wang, C., Han, J.: Ranking-based name matching for author disambiguation in bibliographic data. In: Proceedings of the 2013 KDD Cup 2013 Workshop (2013)
13. Louppe, G., Al-Natsheh, H.T., Susik, M., Maguire, E.J.: Ethnicity sensitive author disambiguation using semi-supervised learning. In: Proceedings of the 7th International Conference on Knowledge Engineering and Semantic Web (KESW) (2016)
14. Mikolov, T., Sutskever, I., Chen, K., Corrado, G.S., Dean, J.: Distributed representations of words and phrases and their compositionality. In: Proceedings of the 27th Annual Conference on Neural Information Processing Systems (NeruIPS) (2013)
15. Mohammed, S., Shi, P., Lin, J.: Strong baselines for simple question answering over knowledge graphs with and without neural networks. In: Proceedings of the 16th Annual Conference of the North American Chapter of the Association for Computational Linguistics (NAACL) (2018)
16. Niu, F., Ré, C., Doan, A., Shavlik, J.: Tuffy: scaling up statistical inference in markov logic networks using an RDBMS. In: Proceedings of the Very Large Data Bases Endowment (VLDB) (2011)
17. Sculley, D., Snoek, J., Wiltschko, A., Rahimi, A.: Winner's curse? on pace, progress, and empirical rigor. In: Workshop on 6th The International Conference on Learning Representations (ICLR) (2018)
18. Shen, Q., Wu, T., Yang, H., Wu, Y., Qu, H., Cui, W.: Nameclarifier: a visual analytics system for author name disambiguation. IEEE Trans. Visual. Comput. Graph. (2016)
19. Smalheiser, N.R., Torvik, V.I.: Author name disambiguation. Annual Rev. Inf. Sci. Technol. (2009)
20. Tang, J., Fong, A.C., Wang, B., Zhang, J.: A unified probabilistic framework for name disambiguation in digital library. IEEE Trans. Knowl. Data Eng. (2012)
21. Tang, J., Zhang, J., Yao, L., Li, J., Zhang, L., Su, Z.: Arnetminer: extraction and mining of academic social networks. In: Proceedings of the 14th ACM International Conference on Knowledge Discovery & Data Mining (KDD) (2008)

22. Veloso, A., Ferreira, A.A., Gonçalves, M.A., Laender, A.H., Meira, W.: Cost-effective on-demand associative author name disambiguation. Inf. Process. Manage. Int. J. (2012)
23. Yoshida, M., Ikeda, M., Ono, S., Sato, I., Nakagawa, H.: Person name disambiguation by bootstrapping. In: Proceedings of the 23rd International ACM SIGIR Conference on Research and Development in Information Retrieval (SIGIR) (2010)
24. Zhang, B., Al Hasan, M.: Name disambiguation in anonymized graphs using network embedding. In: Proceedings of the 26th ACM International Conference on Information and Knowledge Management (CIKM) (2017)
25. Zhang, Y., Zhang, F., Yao, P., Tang, J.: Name disambiguation in aminer: clustering, maintenance, and human in the loop. In: Proceedings of the 24th ACM International Conference on Knowledge Discovery & Data Mining (KDD) (2018)

Mining Social Networks

Retrofitting Embeddings
for Unsupervised User Identity Linkage

Tao Zhou[1]([✉]), Ee-Peng Lim[2], Roy Ka-Wei Lee[3], Feida Zhu[2], and Jiuxin Cao[4]

[1] School of Computer Science and Engineering, Southeast University, Nanjing, China
`zhoutao@seu.edu.cn`
[2] School of Information Systems, Singapore Management University,
Singapore, Singapore
{`eplim,fdzhu`}`@smu.edu.sg`
[3] Department of Computer Science, University of Saskatchewan,
Saskatchewan, Canada
`roylee@cs.usask.ca`
[4] Jiangsu Provincial Key Laboratory of Computer Networking Technology,
School of Cyber Science and Engineering, Southeast University, Nanjing, China
`jx.cao@seu.edu.cn`

Abstract. User Identity Linkage (UIL) is the problem of matching user identities across multiple online social networks (OSNs) which belong to the same person. The solutions to UIL problem facilitate cross-platform research on OSN users and enable many useful applications such as user profiling and recommendation. As the UIL labeled data are often lacking and costly to obtain, learning user embeddings for matching user identities using an unsupervised approach is therefore highly desired. In this paper, we propose a novel unsupervised UIL framework for enhancing existing user embedding-based UIL methods. Our proposed framework incorporates two key ideas, *user-discriminative features* and *retrofitting embedding*. The user-discriminative features enable us to differentiate a specific user identity from other users in its OSN. From the user-discriminative features, we derive pairs of similar user identities across OSNs for retrofitting the base user embeddings of existing UIL methods. Through extensive experiments on three real-world OSN datasets, we show that our framework can leverage user-discriminative features to improve the accuracy of different user embedding-based UIL methods significantly. The quantum of improvement can also be surprisingly good even for existing UIL methods with very poor matching accuracy.

Keywords: User identity linkage · Retrofitting embedding · Discriminative features

Electronic supplementary material The online version of this chapter (https://doi.org/10.1007/978-3-030-47426-3_30) contains supplementary material, which is available to authorized users.

© Springer Nature Switzerland AG 2020
H. W. Lauw et al. (Eds.): PAKDD 2020, LNAI 12084, pp. 385–397, 2020.
https://doi.org/10.1007/978-3-030-47426-3_30

1   Introduction

With rapid development of online social networks (OSNs), the number of OSN platforms increases quickly serving different user needs. The multiplicity of OSNs motivates the problem of User Identity Linkage (UIL), which aims to match user accounts from different OSN platforms belonging to the same persons. UIL addresses the issue of fragmented user information across platforms, which is important to cross-platform user profiling, recommendation applications and research on social networks including information diffusion, community analysis, and influential user modeling.

1.1   Unsupervised User Identity Linkage

We denote an OSN as $G = (U, E)$, where U represents the set of user identities and $E \subseteq U \times U$ represents the set of links between user identities. Each user identity $u_i \in U$ is associated with some attributes, e.g., *name*, *content*, etc.

Given two OSNs G_s and G_t as the source and target platforms respectively, the UIL task is to find for each user identity u_s from U_s a user identity u_t from U_t such that u_s and u_t belong to the same real person. While the problem is defined for a two-platform setting, it can be easily extended to more platforms.

UIL methods can be classified into *supervised*, *semi-supervised* and *unsupervised* approaches. Most of the existing UIL methods adopt the supervised and semi-supervised approaches [19]. These approaches require ground truth labeled user identity pairs for training while the collecting of labeled data suffers from many problems. The unsupervised approach to UIL can avoid the issues from labeled data. It, however, has another set of challenges: 1) Unsupervised UIL method has to cope with multiple attributes with heterogeneity domains, preferably in a unified manner; 2) Discriminative cross-platform attribute similarities are needed to compare the attribute values; 3) The attribute importance need to be incorporated without pre-labeling.

1.2   Objectives and Proposed Framework

Our main research objective is to create unsupervised UIL methods that can cope with the above challenges. With recent advances in embedding techniques, user embeddings techniques have been shown to be effective in solving the UIL problem in the unsupervised approach [21]. The user embedding techniques essentially map every user identity (from any OSN) to a common embedding space. User identities with similar attribute values are expected to be mapped to similar locations. Hence, user embeddings can effectively address the first challenge.

To address the remaining two challenges, we propose a general framework for unsupervised UIL using two main ideas, namely: (a) **user-discriminative features**, and (b) **retrofitting embeddings**. User-discriminative features are ones that are indicative of specific user identities in an OSN. Retrofitting embeddings is a technique, used largely in word embeddings, to modify an existing *base embeddings* of words to incorporate some synonym word-pair knowledge [3].

To the best of our knowledge, this paper is the first that introduce retrofitting to improve user embedding-based UIL techniques.

Our framework is novel in that it can accommodate any unsupervised UIL method as user embeddings. The framework then improves the user embeddings of the existing method using user identity pairs obtained by pairing user identities that are similar based on user-discriminative features.

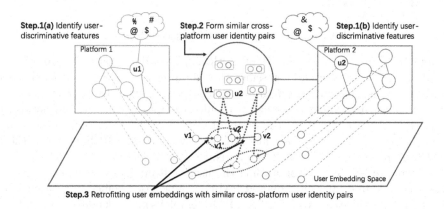

Fig. 1. Proposed User Identity Linkage Framework.

Overview of Proposed Framework. Fig. 1 depicts our proposed UIL framework for two OSN platforms, Platforms 1 and 2. The choice of two platforms is to keep the description simple, as the framework can be easily generalized to handle more OSN platforms. The framework takes an existing user embedding as input, which we call the **base embeddings**. In the figure, user identities $u1$ and $u2$ are from different OSNs, and they are assigned with embeddings vectors $v1$ and $v2$ respectively in the base embedding space. The other user identities are similarly mapped into the same user embeddings space.

In Step 1, the framework identifies user-discriminative features for each user identity in Platform 1, and does the same for Platform 2.

In Step 2, we form a set of cross-platform similar user identity pairs by pairing user identities with some overlapping user-discriminative features.

In Step 3, a set of similar cross-platform user identity pairs are used to retrofit the base user embeddings for final user identity linkage. As only qualified part of user pairs are considered for retrofitting, this process would be highly efficient.

Research Contribution. We summarize our key contributions as follows:

- We propose user-discriminative features to overcome the issues of multiple attributes of heterogeneous domains in different OSN platforms. We introduce a parameter to incorporate the importance of attribute in UIL.
- We propose an unsupervised UIL algorithm based on retrofitting embeddings which take advantage of both base user embeddings and similar user-identity

pairs. To the best of our knowledge, this is the first time retrofitting is used to achieve higher UIL accuracy for different base user embeddings. Moreover, retrofitting is highly efficient compared to the base user embedding learning.

- We conduct extensive experiments on three real-world OSN datasets with many different settings. The results show the effectiveness of our methods.

2   Related Work

2.1   Supervised and Semi-supervised Approaches

There are many UIL methods adopting the supervised approach [5,6,10–12,14–16,22]. They can be broadly classified into those using *classification techniques* and others using *embedding techniques*. The former typically extract features from user attributes (e.g., user name, profile description, content, and network) to train a classifier for predicting pairs of user identities to belong to the same users or not. For example, Zafarani et al. [22] proposed MOBIUS, a UIL method which utilizes username features and a Naive Bayes classifier.

There are few recent works using the user embedding techniques for supervised UIL. Man et al. [10] proposed PALE, a supervised embedding based UIL method that utilizes network features. PALE employs network embeddings incorporating known pairs of matching user identities from different OSNs as anchor links. Mu et al. proposed another supervised method called ULink [12] to map known pairs of matching user identities to a common latent space.

Semi-supervised approach considers both labeled and unlabeled pairs of matching user identities in model learning [1,2,8,13,18,20,23,24]. HYDRA is a semi-supervised framework which models user behaviors and structure consistency [8]. COSNET is a semi-supervised method which utilizes local and global consistency across multiple networks [23]. Unlike the above methods, our proposed model adopts an unsupervised embedding approach to address the UIL problem.

2.2   Unsupervised Approach

There are relatively fewer works on unsupervised UIL [4,7,17,21]. Gao et al. [4] proposed CNL, an unsupervised method, to utilize multiple attributes to perform UIL in an incremental manner. Factoid Embedding [21] is the state-of-art unsupervised approach which utilizes multiple user attributes to learn a user embeddings for UIL. The method first constructs factoids from user attributes and learns user identity latent representation by embedding the factoids. However, the user embedding is learned based on only local information of OSNs. Cross platforms features have been ignored. The UIL results, therefore, could be poor if the local user attribute information is noisy. Our proposed framework addresses this limitation by introducing user-discriminative features. In this paper, we will demonstrate how Factoid Embeddings can be used as input base embeddings so as to achieve improved UIL results.

3 Base User Embeddings and User-Discriminative Features

3.1 Base User Embeddings

Our proposed framework supports different types of base user embeddings. While these embeddings are input to our framework, we would like to introduce two important embeddings techniques: one for matching user identities based on a single user attribute, and another for matching based on multiple user attributes.

Single Attribute-Based User Embeddings. Here we use *username* attribute to illustrate the single attribute-based user embeddings, also known as **name embeddings**. Note that the process could be applied to any other attribute which has similarity measure for two users. We define username similarity using cosine similarity on TF-IDF vectors of n-gram representation of usernames. We first collect all n-grams ($n \in [2, 5]$ in this work) from username of user identities from **all** the OSN platforms. Next, we construct the n-gram TF-IDF vector of every user in $U_s \cup U_t$. Then we define $sim_{username}(u_i, u_j)$ as the cosine similarity between the TF-IDF vectors of users u_i and u_j denoted by w_i and w_j respectively. The username embeddings $\mathbf{v}$ are learnt by minimizing:

$$O_{username} = \sum_{u_i, u_j \in U_s \cup U_t} \left(\mathbf{v}_i^\top \mathbf{v}_j - cosine(w_i, w_j) \right)^2 \tag{1}$$

Factoid Embeddings. It is an embedding UIL method making use of multiple user attributes [21]. Details are in Section A.2 of Supplementary Material.

3.2 User-Discriminative Features

User-discriminative features are ones that help distinguishing a user identity from others in the same OSN. From the discriminative features of user identities, we derive the **cross-platform similar user identity pairs**. Each cross-platform similar user identity pair (u_i, u_j) is assigned a similarity score s_{ij}. The larger the s_{ij}, the higher the likelihood that the u_i and u_j from different OSNs belong to the same user.

As a user identity can have multiple attributes, we derive different types of user-discriminative features and the associated cross-platform similarity score s_{ij}'s as follows. One can derive for other user attributes in a similar manner.

User-Discriminative Name Features. We use n-grams in username to generate discriminative name feature. For each user identity u_i in OSN platform G_s, we collect n-grams ($n \in [2, 5]$) in its username as NG_i^s. Let NG_s be the set of all n-grams of platform $G_s = (U_s, E_s)$, i.e., $\cup_{u_i \in U_s} NG_i$. The set of user-discriminative n-grams is then defined by $DN_s = \{ng | ng \in NG_s, |\{u_i | ng \in NG_i^s\}| < t_n\}$ where t_n is a pre-defined threshold to keep only the ngrams that are not popular among user identities. In a similar way, we define the user-discriminative n-grams for the target OSN as DN_t.

Given user u_i from G_s and user u_j from G_t, we finally define the similarity score s_{ij} by Jaccard Similarity, i.e.:

$$s_{ij} = \frac{DN_i^s \cap DN_j^t}{DN_i^s \cup DN_j^t} \tag{2}$$

where $DN_i^s = NG_i^s \cap DN_s$ and $DN_j^t = NG_j^t \cap DN_t$.

Note that s_{ij} is normalized to $[0,1]$ to avoid the effect of scale difference.

User-Discriminative Content Features. Users may generate different types of content such as text and images. In this paper, we consider textual content attribute only. The calculation is similar with user-discriminative name features except we exchange n-grams with words in user content and use t_c as the threshold for selecting content features not popular among users rather than t_n.

User-Discriminative Network Features. We denote the neighbor set of a user identity u in OSN platform G_s as $N^s(u)$. If the degree of u', a neighbor of u, is large, u' would be less important for identifying u because many user identities have u' as their neighbor. We thus use the degree of user identity to determine user-discriminative neighbors. For $u_i \in U_s$, we define the user-discriminative neighbors of u_i as $DB_i^s = \{u'|u' \in N^s(u_i), degree^s(u') < t_d\}$. t_d is a threshold to determine neighbors who do not have many social connections. Similarly, the user-discriminative neighbors of u_j in OSN G_s, DB_j^t is defined.

Unlike the earlier attributes, it is not possible to expect overlapping neighbors between two OSN platforms. We adopt some base user embeddings to determine pairs of similar discriminative neighbors across platforms. The *similar discriminative neighbor pairs*, denoted as DP_{ij}, according to the base embeddings.

$DP_{ij} = \{(u_{i'}, u_{j'})|u_i' \in DB_i^s, u_j' \in DB_j^t, (1 - cos(\hat{\mathbf{v}}_{i'}, \hat{\mathbf{v}}_{j'})) < t_s\}$ where t_s is the dissimilarity threshold and $\hat{\mathbf{v}}_{\mathbf{k}}$ is u_k's base embedding,

Intuitively, the number of unique user identity pairs in DP_{ij} reflects the cross-platform identity similarity between u_i and u_j. Hence, s_{ij} is defined as:

$$s_{ij} = |\{(u_{i'}, u_{j'}) \in DP_{ij}\}| \tag{3}$$

4   Retrofitting Embedding for UIL

4.1   Retrofitting Embedding

The intuition of our method is to retrofit by pushing cross-platform similar user identity pairs closer in embedding space while keeping the other base user embedding vectors unchanged as much as possible. For each cross-platform user identity pair (u_i, u_j), we would retrofit the affected user embedding vectors according to the cross-platform similarity score s_{ij}. The larger s_{ij}, the closer the retrofitted embedding vectors of u_i and u_j should be.

For a user identity u_i, let $\hat{\mathbf{v}}_i$ denote the base embedding vector of u_i generated using base user embeddings. We use $\mathbf{v}_i$ to denote the retrofitted embedding vector of u_i, which needs to be learned. Let P be the set of cross-platform similar user identity pairs with s_{ij} scores, i.e. $P = \{(u_i, u_j)\} | u_i \in U_s, u_j \in U_t, s_{ij} > 0\}$.

We learn the retrofitted embedding vector $\mathbf{v}$ for all the $u \in U_s \cup U_t$ by minimizing the following objective function:

$$O = \sum_{u_i \in U_s \cup U_t} \left(\varphi\left(\mathbf{v}_i, \hat{\mathbf{v}}_i\right) + \alpha \sum_{(u_i, u_j) \in P} s_{ij} * \varphi\left(\mathbf{v}_i, \mathbf{v}_j\right) \right) \tag{4}$$

where $\varphi\left(\mathbf{a}, \mathbf{b}\right)$ is the cosine distance between vectors $\mathbf{a}$ and $\mathbf{b}$, i.e. $\varphi\left(\mathbf{a}, \mathbf{b}\right) = 1 - cos\left(\mathbf{a}, \mathbf{b}\right)$. α $(0 \leq \alpha \leq 1)$ is the weight to adjust the degree of retrofitting.

4.2 Variants of Retrofitting Embeddings

Stepwise Approach. As we want to use multiple discriminative features to retrofit the base user embedding, we adopt a stepwise approach to retrofit the user embedding iteratively, which is to regard the retrofitted embeddings as new base embeddings when another discriminative feature is applied.

Hierarchical Approach to Generate User-Discriminative Features. To comprehensively capture the similar user identities, we introduce a hierarchical approach to generate the user-discriminative features. We basically select a few thresholds t's, and derive different sets of user-discriminative features based on the thresholds. Each cross-platform user identity pair will then be assigned a set of scores s_{ij}'s, one for each set of user-discriminative features (e.g., name).

4.3 Optimization

With cosine distance, we cannot apply the traditional approach in retrofitting to minimize the objective function. Instead, we use Stochastic Gradient Descent (SGD) for optimization. To apply SGD, we rewrite the objective function in Eq. 4 as following by moving the position of summation:

$$O = \sum_{\{u_i, u_j\} \in P} \left(\varphi\left(\mathbf{v}_i, \hat{\mathbf{v}}_i\right) + \varphi\left(\mathbf{v}_j, \hat{\mathbf{v}}_j\right) + \beta * s_{ij} * \varphi\left(\mathbf{v}_i, \mathbf{v}_j\right) \right) \tag{5}$$

where β is the weight to adjust the degree of retrofitting.

In each iteration, we update the embedding $\mathbf{v}_i$ and $\mathbf{v}_j$ by the following rule:

$$\mathbf{v}_i \leftarrow \mathbf{v}_i - \gamma \frac{\partial O}{\partial \mathbf{v}_i} \qquad \mathbf{v}_j \leftarrow \mathbf{v}_j - \gamma \frac{\partial O}{\partial \mathbf{v}_j} \tag{6}$$

where γ is the learning rate. The detailed optimization is available in Section C of Supplementary Material.

We summarize our retrofitting embedding in Algorithm 1 which excludes hierarchical user-discriminative feature for clarity. Each of the hierarchical features would need one step of retrofitting similar as lines 2–17. The retrofitting algorithm is efficient as only the user pairs with positive score will be used.

Finally, once we have learned the retrofitted embedding vector $\mathbf{v}$ for all the $u \in U_s \cup U_t$, we will compute the cosine similarity between two user's embedding vectors as linkage score for each user pair across platforms. The user pairs with larger scores are more likely to belong to the same underlying natural person.

4.4   Selecting Parameter β

In the optimization objective function, weight β is an important parameter to control the learning of retrofitting embedding. Smaller β indicates the retrofitted embedding preserves more of the base user embedding, while a larger β will give more weight to the user-discriminative features to change the base embedding. Therefore, β should be set larger when the base user embedding has not shown strong ability in performing UIL, and the user-discriminative features should be given more weight to improve UIL. The choice of β for different user-discriminative features would also balance the importance of multiple attributes.

5   Experiments and Results

5.1   Dataset Preparation

We evaluate our proposed framework using three real-world datasets, namely Instagram-Twitter (*IG-TW*), Foursquare-Twitter (*FQ-TW*), and *IG-TW content* datasets. These are social network datasets that are significantly larger than other social networks for UIL research involving. We start from a set of Singapore-based Twitter users and retrieve users who declared their Instagram or Foursquare accounts to construct the multi-platform datasets. From the *IG-TW* dataset, we extracted user identities with post content only into the *IG-TW content* dataset. The statistics of all the datasets are summarized in Table 1.

5.2   Baselines and Retrofitting Embeddings

We compare methods based on the proposed framework with several other unsupervised baseline methods. The baseline methods include:

- **Name embeddings (NE)**: This represents a single attribute-based user embeddings UIL method (see Sect. 3.1).
- **TF-IDF**: User identity is represented by a TF-IDF vector of content words.
- **Content embedding (CE)**: This represents a user identity by content embedding defined as the average of word vectors (obtained through the NLP tool Spacy) of words found in the content attribute [9].

Algorithm 1. Retrofitting Embedding For UIL

Input:
 Source platform user set U_s, target platform user set U_t;
 Base user embedding vectors $\hat{\mathbf{v}}_i$ for each $u_i \in U_s \cup U_t$;
 Attribute set A and user-dicriminative features for each attribute $a_k, k \in [1, |A|]$;
Output:
 Retrofitted embedding vector $\mathbf{v}_i$ for each $u_i \in U_s \cup U_t$;
1: **for** $k \in [1, |A|]$ **do**
2:    # prepare scores of shared discriminative features #
3:    calculate cross-platform similarity scores of s_{ij}^k for each user pair (u_i, u_j) $(u_i \in$ $U_s, u_i \in U_t)$;
4:    create pair set $P^k = \{(u_i, u_j)|u_i \in U_s, u_i \in U_t, s_{ij}^k > 0\}$;
5:    # retrofitting embedding #
6:    **for** each $u_i \in U_s \cup U_t$ **do**
7:       initialize retrofitted embedding vectors $\mathbf{v}_i$ as $\hat{\mathbf{v}}_i$;
8:    **end for**
9:    **repeat**
10:      **for** each $\{u_i, u_j\} \in P^k$ **do**
11:         update $\mathbf{v}_i$ as $\mathbf{v}_i \leftarrow \mathbf{v}_i - \gamma \frac{\partial O}{\partial \mathbf{v}_i}$;
12:         update $\mathbf{v}_j$ as $\mathbf{v}_j \leftarrow \mathbf{v}_j - \gamma \frac{\partial O}{\partial \mathbf{v}_j}$;
13:      **end for**
14:    **until** convergence or reach maximum number of iterations;
15:    **for** each $u_i \in U_s \cup U_t$ **do**
16:      assign $\hat{\mathbf{v}}_i = \mathbf{v}_i$ unless it is the last attribute;
17:    **end for**
18: **end for**
19: **return** $\{\mathbf{v}_i|u_i \in U_s \cup U_t\}$

Table 1. Dataset description (uname: username, sname: screen name, Twitter as target)

Dataset	IG-TW		FQ-TW		IG-TW (content)	
Platform	Instagram	Twitter	Foursquare	Twitter	Instgram	Twitter
#Users	12,109	21,034	17,294	19,796	800	800
#Links	163,403	170,675	262,330	319,635	4,189	3,155
Avail Info	uname, sname, network		sname, network		user post, network	
# GT pairs	1,228		3,482		800	

- **Weighted content embedding (CE_weighted):** This is similar to content embedding except that the user identity is represented by a weighted average of word vectors of words found in the content attribute. The weight of a word is defined by its TF-IDF value in the content.
- **Factoid Embedding (FE):** This is the state-of-art unsupervised method [21]. In our experiment, FE makes use of all attributes in each dataset (FE for

IG-TW content dataset is denoted as $\mathbf{FE}_c$ for differentiation). Name embedding and content embedding are used as the attribute embeddings in FE when applying the name and content attributes respectively.

We evaluate different RE's using our proposed framework with different baselines as their base user embeddings. We use RE_p^q to denote our proposed method with q as base user embeddings and p as the user-discriminative feature(s) used for retrofitting. These proposed methods are $\mathbf{RE}_n^{NE}$, $\mathbf{RE}_{nb}^{NE}$, $\mathbf{RE}_c^{CE}$, $\mathbf{RE}_n^{FE}$, $\mathbf{RE}_{nb}^{FE}$, $\mathbf{RE}_c^{FE_c}$ and $\mathbf{RE}_{cb}^{FE_c}$, where n, b and c denote user-discriminative features for name, network and content respectively. Note that the order of applying user-discriminative features depends on the base embedding. For the sake of showing the usefulness of user-discriminative features, we start retrofitting the more discriminative features before the less discriminative ones.

5.3   Experiment Configuration

When generating user-discriminative features, we need to configure the threshold for each attribute as defined in Sect. 3. In the following experiments, t_n for name attribute is set to 5. For the content attribute, we adopt a hierarchical approach to generate user-discriminative features using multiple thresholds. The details will be elaborated in subsequent sections. Threshold t_d is set to 20 for all the datasets, and t_s in network attribute is set to be 0.4, 0.2 and 0.15 when FE, NE, and CE are used as the base user embedding respectively. The choice of t_s is dependent on the similarity distribution of user pairs cross platforms.

In retrofitting embedding, the parameter β needs to be configured. We set β to 1 when name attribute is used for retrofitting (a special case will be mentioned in later experiment sections). When the content attribute is employed, β is varied for the different settings in a hierarchical approach used to generate the user-discriminative features. For network attribute, β is set to be 15, 10 and 4 respectively for *IG-TW*, *FQ-TW* and *IG-TW content* datasets. The maximum number of iterations for the optimization is set to be 30,000. It is also interesting to note that our optimization process is fast as we only consider pairs of users who have non-zero similarity scores based on their user-discriminative features.

5.4   Experiment Results and Analysis

All the methods are required to rank the ground truth matching identity as high as possible based on the linkage score (cosine similarity of embeddings). We use **HitRate@K** and **Mean Reciprocal Rank(MRR)** to evaluate the ranking.

Experiments with Name and Network Attributes. *IG-TW* and *FQ-TW* datasets both offer username and network attributes. The baselines of **NE**, **FE**, and **RE**s which utilized both username and network attributes are included for comparison. The results of experiments are shown in Tables 2 and 3 respectively.

For *IG-TW* dataset, $\mathbf{RE}_n^{NE}$ slightly outperforms **NE**, indicating that the user-discriminative name features can improve the UIL accuracy even when

Table 2. Results in IG-TW dataset

	H@1	H@3	H@5	H@10	MRR
NE	0.8314	0.8648	0.8787	0.8974	0.8538
RE_n^{NE}	0.8404	0.8689	0.8811	0.8982	0.8603
RE_{nb}^{NE}	0.8893	0.9088	0.9178	0.9283	**0.9023**
FE	0.8265	0.8697	0.8844	0.9088	0.8539
RE_n^{FE}	0.8436	0.8762	0.8909	0.9080	0.8646
RE_{nb}^{FE}	0.9153	0.9349	0.9430	0.9495	**0.9277**

Table 3. Results in FQ-TW dataset

	H@1	H@3	H@5	H@10	MRR
NE	0.5827	0.6789	0.7128	0.7550	0.6430
RE_n^{NE}	0.5827	0.6781	0.7128	0.7550	0.6430
RE_{nb}^{NE}	0.6163	0.7074	0.7361	0.7725	**0.6716**
FE	0.5761	0.6786	0.7134	0.7588	0.6402
RE_n^{FE}	0.5796	0.6789	0.7128	0.7599	0.6419
RE_{nb}^{FE}	0.6551	0.7453	0.7769	0.8139	**0.7108**

NE has already made good use of username attribute in base user embeddings. When the user-discriminative network features are applied, RE_{nb}^{NE} achieves even more improvement over RE_n^{NE} and **NE**. Both RE_{nb}^{NE} and **FE** utilize name and network attributes. RE_{nb}^{NE} significantly outperforms **FE**, demonstrating that retrofitting embedding can effectively use cross-platform similar user identities based on different user-discriminative features. The user-discriminative network features can improve the results more significantly because they are under-explored in the base user embedding. More results are in Supplementary D.4.

For *FQ-TW* dataset, the performances of RE_n^{NE} and **NE** are similar. A possible reason is that *FQ-TW* dataset only contains screen name, and has less useful information that can be used for retrofitting. β has been set to a relatively lower value (0.08) to avoid introducing noise in this specific case. Even though it is difficult to improve using user-discriminative name feature, the retrofitting could still be controlled to retain the base user embedding performance.

On the whole, our proposed methods using the retrofitted embeddings have outperformed the state-of-art embedding based methods. RE_{nb}^{FE}, which combines **FE** with user-discriminative name and network features, obtains the best performance in linking user identities across multiple platforms.

Experiments with Content and Network Attributes. *IG-TW content* dataset contains both content and network attribute information. Thus, the experiment on this dataset involves the baselines **CE**, $\mathbf{FE}_c$, and **RE**s using user-discriminative content and network features. The results of the experiment on *IG-TW content* dataset are shown in Table 4. The first four methods make use of content-only information. Our method RE_c^{CE}, with **CE** as the base user embedding, has significantly outperformed the baselines.

The $\mathbf{FE}_c$ in Table 4 uses **CE** as its attribute embedding. We observe that $\mathbf{FE}_c$ has obtained a significant improvement in performance over **CE** by introducing the network information. However, it is interesting to note that RE_c^{CE} outperforms $\mathbf{FE}_c$, and $\mathrm{RE}_c^{FE_c}$ has even further improved the performance with the use of better base embedding (i.e., $\mathbf{FE}_c$).

$\mathrm{RE}_c^{FE_c}$_**h1** and $\mathrm{RE}_c^{FE_c}$_**h2** are retrofitting embedding methods that utilize hierarchical approach introduced in Sect. 4.2 to generate the user-discriminative content features. $\mathrm{RE}_c^{FE_c}$ uses user-discriminative content features with $t_c = 2$,

Table 4. Results in Instagram-Twitter content dataset

Method	H@1	H@2	H@3	H@4	H@5	H@10	H@30	MRR
TF-IDF	0.1488	0.1675	0.1775	0.1863	0.2000	0.2375	0.3175	0.1805
CE	0.0563	0.0675	0.0825	0.0963	0.1013	0.1425	0.2375	0.0875
CE_weighted	0.0463	0.0625	0.0725	0.0813	0.0825	0.1125	0.1863	0.0732
RE_c^{CE}	0.6238	0.6438	0.6525	0.6550	0.6563	0.6725	0.7000	**0.6428**
FE_c	0.1788	0.2125	0.2275	0.2425	0.2613	0.3313	0.4625	0.2297
$RE_c^{FE_c}$	0.7113	0.7263	0.7350	0.7388	0.7413	0.7488	0.7638	0.7261
$RE_c^{FE_c}$_h1	0.7175	0.7463	0.7588	0.7650	0.7675	0.7750	0.7950	0.7413
$RE_c^{FE_c}$_h2	0.7238	0.7500	0.7638	0.7688	0.7738	0.7813	0.7913	0.7465
$RE_{cb}^{FE_c}$	0.7413	0.7713	0.7800	0.7850	0.7888	0.7938	0.8113	**0.7638**

while $\mathbf{RE}_c^{FE_c}$bf _h1 uses features with $t_c = 2, 5$ and $\mathbf{RE}_c^{FE_c}$_h2 uses features with $t_c = 2, 5, 10$. From the results, we can see the employment of the hierarchical approach to generate user-discriminative content features improve performance. Finally, $\mathbf{RE}_{cb}^{FE_c}$ outperforms the remaining baselines by incorporating the user-discriminative content and network features.

6   Conclusion

In this paper, we propose a novel unsupervised user identity linkage (UIL) framework for enhancing existing UIL methods based on user embeddings techniques. Our proposed framework incorporates two key ideas, *user-discriminative features* and *retrofitting embeddings*. Our framework applies the user-discriminative features to derive pairs of cross-platform similar user identities for retrofitting the base user embeddings. Through extensive experiments on three real-world OSN datasets, we show that our proposed framework can leverage user-discriminative features to effectively improve the accuracy of different base user embeddings. For future work, we will conduct a more in-depth study on the parameters used in our framework, and will design methods to optimize them automatically.

Acknowledgements. This research was supported by the National Research Foundation, Prime Minister's Office, Singapore under its International Research Centres in Singapore Funding Initiative. This work is also supported by National Natural Science Foundation of China under Grants No.61772133, No.61972087, National Social Science Foundation of China under Grants No. 19@ZH014, Jiangsu Provincial Key Project under Grants No.BE2018706, Natural Science Foundation of Jiangsu province under Grants No.SBK2019022870, Jiangsu Provincial Key Laboratory of Computer Networking Technology, Jiangsu Provincial Key Laboratory of Network and Information Security under Grants No. BM2003201, Key Laboratory of Computer Network and Information Integration of Ministry of Education of China under Grants No. 93K-9, and China Scholarship Council.

References

1. Bennacer, N., Jipmo, C.N., Penta, A., Quercini, G.: Matching user profiles across social networks. In: CAiSE (2014)
2. Buccafurri, F., Lax, G., Nocera, A., Ursino, D.: Discovering links among social networks. In: ECML/PKDD (2012)
3. Faruqui, M., Dodge, J., Jauhar, S.K., Dyer, C., Hovy, E.H., Smith, N.A.: Retrofitting word vectors to semantic lexicons. In: NAACL (2015)
4. Gao, M., Lim, E.P., Lo, D., Zhu, F., Prasetyo, P.K., Zhou, A.: CNL: collective network linkage across heterogeneous social platforms. In: ICDM (2015)
5. Goga, O., Lei, H., Parthasarathi, S.H.K., Friedland, G., Sommer, R., Teixeira, R.: Exploiting innocuous activity for correlating users across sites. In: WWW (2013)
6. Iofciu, T., Fankhauser, P., Abel, F., Bischoff, K.: Identifying users across social tagging systems. In: ICWSM (2011)
7. Liu, J., Zhang, F., Song, X., Song, Y.I., Lin, C.Y., Hon, H.W.: What's in a name?: an unsupervised approach to link users across communities. In: WSDM (2013)
8. Liu, S., Wang, S., Zhu, F., Zhang, J., Krishnan, R.: Hydra: Large-scale social identity linkage via heterogeneous behavior modeling. In: SIGMOD (2014)
9. Liu, Y., Liu, Z., Chua, T.S., Sun, M.: Topical word embeddings. In: AAAI. pp. 2418–2424 (2015)
10. Man, T., Shen, H., Liu, S., Jin, X., Cheng, X.: Predict anchor links across social networks via an embedding approach. In: IJCAI (2016)
11. Mu, X., Xie, W., Lee, R.K., Zhu, F., Lim, E.: Ad-link: an adaptive approach for user identity linkage. In: ICBK, pp. 183–190 (2019)
12. Mu, X., Zhu, F., Lim, E.P., Xiao, J., Wang, J., Zhou, Z.H.: User identity linkage by latent user space modelling. In: KDD (2016)
13. Narayanan, A., Shmatikov, V.: De-anonymizing social networks. In: IEEE Symposium on Security and Privacy (2009)
14. Nie, Y., Jia, Y., Li, S., Zhu, X., Li, A., Zhou, B.: Identifying users across social networks based on dynamic core interests. Neurocomputing 210, 107–115 (2016)
15. Peled, O., Fire, M., Rokach, L., Elovici, Y.: Entity matching in online social networks. In: Socialcom (2013)
16. Perito, D., Castelluccia, C., Kaafar, M.A., Manils, P.: How unique and traceable are usernames? In: PETS (2011)
17. Riederer, C., Kim, Y., Chaintreau, A., Korula, N., Lattanzi, S.: Linking users across domains with location data: Theory and validation. In: WWW (2016)
18. Shen, Y., Jin, H.: Controllable information sharing for user accounts linkage across multiple online social networks. In: CIKM (2014)
19. Shu Kai, E.A.: User identity linkage across online social networks: a review. SIGKDD Explorations Newsletter 18(2), 5–17 (2017)
20. Tan, S., Guan, Z., Cai, D., Qin, X., Bu, J., Chen, C.: Mapping users across networks by manifold alignment on hypergraph. AAAI 14, 159–165 (2014)
21. Xie, W., Mu, X., Lee, R.K.W., Zhu, F., Lim, E.P.: Unsupervised user identity linkage via factoid embedding. In: ICDM (2018)
22. Zafarani, R., Liu, H.: Connecting users across social media sites: a behavioral-modeling approach. In: KDD (2013)
23. Zhang, Y., Tang, J., Yang, Z., Pei, J., Yu, P.S.: Cosnet: Connecting heterogeneous social networks with local and global consistency. In: KDD (2015)
24. Zhou, X., Liang, X., Zhang, H., Ma, Y.: Cross-platform identification of anonymous identical users in multiple social media networks. TKDE 28(2), 1 (2016)

Image Analysis Enhanced Event Detection from Geo-Tagged Tweet Streams

Yi Han$^{(\boxtimes)}$ ⓘ, Shanika Karunasekera ⓘ, and Christopher Leckie ⓘ

School of Computing and Information Systems, The University of Melbourne,
Melbourne, Australia
{yi.han,karus,caleckie}@unimelb.edu.au

Abstract. Events detected from social media streams often include early signs of accidents, crimes or disasters. Therefore, they can be used by related parties for timely and efficient response. Although significant progress has been made on event detection from tweet streams, most existing methods have not considered the posted images in tweets, which provide richer information than the text, and potentially can be a reliable indicator of whether an event occurs or not. In this paper, we design an event detection algorithm that combines textual, statistical and image information, following an unsupervised machine learning approach. Specifically, the algorithm starts with semantic and statistical analyses to obtain a list of tweet clusters, each of which corresponds to an event candidate, and then performs image analysis to separate events from non-events—a convolutional autoencoder is trained for each cluster as an anomaly detector, where a part of the images are used as the training data and the remaining images are used as the test instances. Our experiments on multiple datasets verify that when an event occurs, the mean reconstruction errors of the training and test images are much closer, compared with the case where the candidate is a non-event cluster. Based on this finding, the algorithm rejects a candidate if the difference is larger than a threshold. Experimental results over millions of tweets demonstrate that this image analysis enhanced approach can significantly increase the precision with minimum impact on the recall.

Keywords: Event detection · Autoencoder · Tweet stream mining

1 Introduction

While social media, especially Twitter, has gained growing popularity over the past decade, it has also become a new source of news—events detected from social media streams often contain early signs of accidents, crimes or disasters. Therefore, they can provide valuable information for related parties to take timely and efficient responses.

Although event detection from tweet streams has been extensively studied, most existing methods still suffer from relatively high false positive and false

© Springer Nature Switzerland AG 2020
H. W. Lauw et al. (Eds.): PAKDD 2020, LNAI 12084, pp. 398–410, 2020.
https://doi.org/10.1007/978-3-030-47426-3_31

negative rates, especially for unsupervised machine learning approaches. These algorithms normally rely on semantic, spatial, temporal and frequency information. Images, on the other hand, have rarely been considered yet. Compared with text, especially short posts like tweets, images often provide richer information and potentially can help discover the occurrence of an event.

In this paper, we design an unsupervised event detection algorithm that utilises images in addition to textual and statistical information. The core idea is that when an event occurs, the images posted in the surrounding area are likely to be similar/correlated. Therefore, if we use part of them to train an autoencoder, and keep the rest as the test instances, the reconstruction errors of the training and test images should be close. However, when no event happens, the images posted in a certain region are likely to be more diverse, and hence the reconstruction errors of the test instances will be much higher than those of the training instances, as the autoencoder has not seen similar images before. Based on this idea, the algorithm uses the ratio between the mean reconstruction errors of the test and training images as an additional criterion to further decrease the false positive rate for event detection. Note that since image analysis is relatively expensive, it is only performed at the last step, after the semantic and statistical analyses are finished, which follow a similar approach to [9] with several improvements. In addition, considering that the posted images are normally limited, the algorithm randomly generates the same number of crops for each of them, and trains the autoencoder on the snippets.

In summary, the main contributions of this paper include:

- We analyse images posted in both event and non-event tweet clusters based on the reconstruction errors of autoencoders, and demonstrate that when an event occurs, the images are more coherent (Sect. 2.2);
- We utilise this finding and propose an image analysis enhanced event detection algorithm from tweet streams. It should be emphasised that although we integrate image analysis with a specific existing method [9], the analysis is generic and can be incorporated with other event detection schemes as well (Sect. 2.3);
- We conduct experiments on multiple tweet datasets, and demonstrate that this unsupervised, image analysis enhanced approach can significantly increase the precision without any impact on the recall (Sect. 3).

The remainder of this paper is organised as follows: Sect. 2 specifies the event detection problem, and introduces the image analysis enhanced algorithm; Sect. 3 presents the experimental verification; Sect. 4 overviews previous work on event detection; and Sect. 5 concludes the paper and gives directions for future work.

2   Image Analysis Enhanced Event Detection

In this section, we start with a brief definition of the event detection problem from geo-tagged tweet streams, then introduce in detail how image analysis is performed, and how it is integrated with semantic and statistical analyses.

2.1   Autoencoder Based Image Analysis

We study the event detection problem defined as follows: given a tweet stream $T = \{t_1, t_2, ..., t_n\}$ from a certain region, and a query window $W = \{t_{n-m+1}, t_{n-m+2}, ..., t_n\}$ (m is the number of tweets in W) that represents currently observed tweets, the aim is to identify a set of tweets $T_i \subseteq W$ that are associated with an event, e.g., an accident, a disaster or protest, as close to where and when the event occurs as possible.

A common type of solution to the above problem takes the clustering based approach [3,10,12,25–28], which generates a list of event candidates by clustering the tweets according to their semantic, spatial and temporal information, and then removes non-event clusters via supervised or unsupervised methods. In this work, we focus on how image analysis can be used to enhance the second step.

Specifically, suppose that a set of images, $IM = \{im_1, im_2, ..., im_k\}$, are extracted from an event candidate, *i.e.*, a cluster of tweets that are semantically coherent, and geographically and temporally close, IM is divided into two subsets $IM_{train} \subset IM$, $IM_{test} = IM \setminus IM_{train}$, which are the training and test datasets, respectively. For each image $im_i \in IM$, c random crops of the same size are generated, $\{im_{ij}, \ j = 1, 2, ..., c\}$, and $\{im_{ij} \mid im_i \in IM_{train}\}$ are used to train a convolutional autoencoder, while $\{im_{ij} \mid im_i \in IM_{test}\}$ are kept as the test instances.

As mentioned in the introduction, when an event occurs the images in IM are likely to be similar, and hence the reconstruction errors of $\{im_{ij} \mid im_i \in IM_{train}\}$ should be close to those of $\{im_{ij} \mid im_i \in IM_{test}\}$. On the other hand, when there is not any event the difference in the reconstruction errors between the training and test instances should be much larger. Therefore, we propose to quantify the coherence of the images in a cluster, and use that as a metric to detect and remove non-event clusters.

2.2   Quantitative Study

In order to validate the above idea, we collected (part of) the posted images in the following three Twitter datasets:

- Dataset shared by the authors of [28], which includes 9.5 million geo-tagged tweets from New York between 1 August, 2014 and 30 November 2014—617K images are retrieved from it;
- All geo-tagged tweets from Los Angeles between 9 February and 22 February 2019, with a size of 13.2K—20K images are retrieved from it;
- All geo-tagged tweets from Sydney between 12 February and 5 April 2019, with a size of 28.4K—16K images are retrieved from it.

For each dataset, we first perform semantic and statistical analyses using the method in [9] (more details are given in the next subsection) to obtain a list of event candidates. If a candidate contains at least three images, we then (1) randomly generate 500 crops of size 32×32 for each image—there are

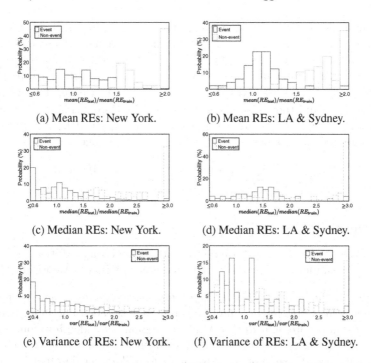

(a) Mean REs: New York.   (b) Mean REs: LA & Sydney.

(c) Median REs: New York.   (d) Median REs: LA & Sydney.

(e) Variance of REs: New York.   (f) Variance of REs: LA & Sydney.

Fig. 1. Probability distributions of $\frac{mean(RE_{test})}{mean(RE_{train})}$, $\frac{median(RE_{test})}{median(RE_{train})}$, and $\frac{var(RE_{test})}{var(RE_{train})}$ for New York, Los Angeles and Sydney. Note that the results for Los Angeles and Sydney are combined due to a relatively smaller amount of data.

normally a limited number of images within each cluster, and they are insufficient for the training of an autoencoder; (2) use two-thirds of the crops to train a convolutional autoencoder, and keep the rest as the test data. Note that all the 500 crops of an image are either in the training or test dataset. In addition, we also notice that if a considerable part of an image is about human beings, the image is often quite different from the rest even if there is an event. For example, during a sports game or a concert, while the focus of most images is the court or the stadium, selfie images are likely to be very different and hence cause false negatives. Therefore, images of this type are excluded in the analysis (see Sect. 3.1 for more details), *i.e.*, each cluster needs to have at least three non-human images in order to be analysed; (3) compare the mean, median and variance of the reconstruction errors (REs, $RE(x) = \|x - x'\|^2$, where x and x' are the input and output of the autoencoder, respectively) for the training and test instances, and calculate the ratios of $\frac{mean(RE_{test})}{mean(RE_{train})}$, $\frac{median(RE_{test})}{median(RE_{train})}$, and $\frac{var(RE_{test})}{var(RE_{train})}$, where RE_{train} and RE_{test} represent the set of training and test REs, respectively.

Figure 1 shows the probability distributions of these three ratios for (manually labelled) event and non-event clusters obtained after the semantic and statistical analyses. Note that the results for Los Angeles and Sydney are combined due to a relatively smaller amount of data. It is clear from these figures that when a candidate corresponds to a non-event, all the three ratios are distinctively higher in general, which indicates the images are more diverse. Specifically, we find that $\frac{mean(RE_{test})}{mean(RE_{train})}$ gives the best performance. Hence, it is selected in our experiment, and the threshold is set to be 1.5. More formally, denoting the reconstruction error of the autoencoder for input im_{ij} by $RE(im_{ij})$, we define the following metric to measure the coherence of the images in IM:

$$R = \frac{\overline{RE_{test}}}{\overline{RE_{train}}} = \frac{\sum_i \sum_{j=1}^c RE(im_{ij}),\ im_i\ \in\ IM_{test}/|IM_{test}|}{\sum_i \sum_{j=1}^c RE(im_{ij}),\ im_i\ \in\ IM_{train}/|IM_{train}|} \tag{1}$$

2.3   Algorithm Description

As mentioned earlier in the above section, for semantic and statistical analyses we adopt the similar method to [9], which works as follows (Algorithm 1):

- *Building a Quad-tree (QT)* [8,17] *for the sliding windows.* The root of QT represents the whole region, and if the number of tweets in the sliding windows is larger than a pre-defined threshold, the region is divided into four equally-sized sub-regions. The process continues until the number of tweets in each leaf node is smaller than or equal to the threshold, or the depth of QT reaches the maximum value. It should be emphasised that once the Quad-tree is built, **the detection will be run at all levels**, in order to mitigate the impact of the arbitrary division of space.
- *Embedding.* Entities and noun phrases from each tweet are extracted using the NLP tool [16] mentioned in [28]. These keywords are then embedded with the fastText algorithm [5], and each tweet is represented by the average value of all its keyword vectors. Note that the temporal and spatial information is not included in the embedding, as the similarities in time and space are ensured by the sliding window and the Quad-tree.
- *Clustering.* The generated vectors are clustered using the algorithm of BIRCH (Balanced Iterative Reducing and Clustering using Hierarchies) [29].
- *Power-law Detection.* The study in [9] finds that when an event occurs, it is much more likely to observe power-law distributions in tweet streams. Based on this finding, we run power-law detection [6,21] within each cluster. Note that the clustering is only done at the root level of QT against all tweets in the sliding windows, but the power-law detection is run at all levels, so that the event can be identified as close to where it occurs as possible. For example, suppose that cluster A is formed at the root level (Level 0), it is divided into A_1, A_2, A_3, A_4 at Level 1, each of which is further divided into four sub-clusters at Level 2 and so on. Power-law detection is done in each of these clusters.
- *Verification.* For each remaining cluster that passes the power-law detection, we collect additional tweets from the verification window, which is set to 5 min in our experiment, and repeat the last three steps. The only difference

is that when vectorising the tweet, the original text is directly embedded to make sure that both the keywords and texts are semantically close within a cluster. Each remaining event candidate is then checked against each cluster found in this step. If any two of them share more than half of the tweets, they are considered as a match. Otherwise the candidate is removed. The verification process is done twice.

While the above steps are similar to [9], we modify and add the following steps (see Fig. 2 for an illustration):

- *Pruning.* We extract all hashtags and mentions for each remaining cluster, and remove a tweet if it contains hashtags and/or mentions, but all of them either (1) only appear once in the cluster, (2) appear only in one tweet, or (3) are excluded keywords—including commonly used stop words, names of the city, state and country for the examined region, etc. Then we identify the top $X(= 5)$ hashtags and mentions, and reject an event candidate if less than half of the remaining tweets contain any of them.
- *Image Analysis.* If a cluster passes all the above tests and has at least three (non-human) images, we perform image analysis as described in Sect. 2.2 for each of them. One point worth noticing is that an image is only considered if it is posted in a tweet that contains at least one of the top $X(= 5)$ hashtags or mentions. It is found in our experiments that this can make the prediction more accurate. Finally, we calculate the ratio R as defined in Eq. (1) and reject a candidate if $R \geq 1.5$.

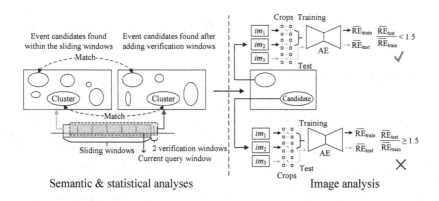

Fig. 2. An illustration of the image analysis enhanced event detection algorithm

3 Experimental Evaluation

In this section, we present the results on the three datasets as described in Sect. 2.2 to test the effectiveness of the image analysis enhanced event detection algorithm.

3.1   Experimental Setup

Baseline Algorithms. The following two methods are chosen as the base-lines: (1) Geoburst [28], a widely cited event detection algorithm that considers temporal, spatial and semantic information. Although improved versions exist (Geoburst+ [26], TrioVec [27]), we do not use them as baselines in this work as they are supervised approaches, while both Geoburst and our method use unsupervised approaches; (2) Power-law advanced [9] that combines fastText, BIRCH, and power-law verification as introduced in the last section. Note that Power-law advanced is unsupervised as well.

Parameters. (1) All the parameters for Geoburst take the default values in the code shared by the author. (2) For Power-law advanced, (i) a pre-trained fastText model is used, and it is re-trained incrementally [15] with the new tweets in the last 24 h. Since the re-training is done in parallel, it does not delay the detection; (ii) the threshold of the cluster radius is the most important parameter in BIRCH. We do not set its value arbitrarily. Instead, we start with a value close to zero, and increase it by a small step size until either less than 5% of all items are in small clusters, *i.e.,* clusters with a size less than 10, or over half of the items are in the largest cluster, whichever occurs first; (iii) the Quad-tree has a maximum depth of 30, and each node can hold up to 50 tweets; (iv) the sliding windows keep the latest six query windows, each of which is 30 min.

In addition, as described in Sect. 2.2, an image is excluded in the image analysis if a considerable part of it is about human beings. In our experiment, we reject an image if a total of 40% of the area is detected as humans, or if a person takes up over 20% of the size. Note that since we are only interested in detecting humans in an image, the pre-trained models provided in [2] can be used directly and do not need to be re-trained. Specifically, "ssdlite_mobilenet_v2_coco" is chosen in our experiment.

3.2   Quantitative Analysis

Figure 3 presents the performance comparison between the three event detection algorithms. The result demonstrates that our image analysis enhanced approach can significantly increase the precision without any impact on the recall. One reason why the recall is not affected is that the detection is run at all levels of the Quad-tree, so even if an event candidate is rejected, the same event can be detected at a different level.

Note that when calculating the precision for Power-law advanced and our image analysis enhanced method, duplicated events—same events that are detected at different levels of the Quad-tree, or in consecutive query windows—are merged together. The precision will be much higher (over 10% higher) if we use the raw data directly.

Note also that since the ground truth of the three datasets are not given, it is difficult to calculate the true recall. Therefore, we adopt a similar approach as in [26,27] and calculate the *pseudo recall* $= N_{true}/N_{total}$, where N_{true} is the number of true events detected by a method, and N_{total} is the number of true

---

Algorithm 1. Image analysis enhanced event detection algorithm

---

    Input   : Geo-tagged tweets in the query window, W; Maximum depth of the Quad-tree (QT), D; Threshold for splitting a node in QT, m_s

    Output : Event list, E

1 **Build Quad-tree**
2   Create an empty Quad-tree QT;
3   **for** *tweet t in W* **do**
4   **if** *child nodes != NULL* **then**
5   Insert t into one of the child nodes based on t's coordinates;
6   **else if** *the number of tweets in the current node $\geq m_s$ && QT's depth $< D$* **then**
7   Split into four nodes; move all tweets into one of them based on coordinates;
8   **else**
9   Insert t into the current node;

10 **Embedding**
11   Extract entities and noun phrases using the NLP tool [16] for each tweet;
12   Call fastText to embed the extracted keywords;

13 **Clustering**
14   Cluster the generated vectors using BIRCH;

15 **Power-law detection**
16   **for** *Cluster C found in the last step* **do**
17          $E \leftarrow$ Power-law detection at different layers of QT;

18 **Verification**
19   **for** $i = 0$; $i < 2$ && E *is not NULL* **do**
20   Call fastText to directly embed the text of each tweet;
21   Cluster the generated vectors using BIRCH;
22   **for** *Cluster C' found in the last step* **do**
23             $E' \leftarrow$ Power-law detection at different layers of QT;
24   **for** *Remaining event candidate $e \in E$* **do**
25   Remove e if there is no match in E';

26 **Pruning**
27   **for** *Remaining event candidate $e \in E$* **do**
28   Remove a tweet if none of its hashtag/mention appears in other tweet, or is not an excluded keyword;
29   Remove e if $\geq 50\%$ tweets does not contain any top $X = 5$ hashtag/mention;

30 **Image analysis**
31   **for** *Remaining event candidate $e \in E$* **do**
32   **if** *e has at least three non-human images* **then**
33   Train an autoencoder with 2/3 of the crops generated from each image;
34   Calculate the ratio R and remove e if $R \geq 1.5$

35 **return** E

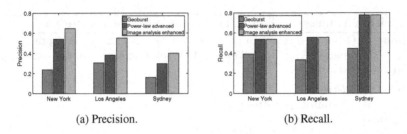

(a) Precision.   (b) Recall.

Fig. 3. Performance comparison of the three event detection algorithms

events detected by all methods, plus the events hand-picked by us that occurred during the query periods within the chosen cities, including protests, ceremonies, sport games, natural disasters, etc.

Discussion on Efficiency. The proposed image analysis mainly contains three parts: using the object detector to remove images of human beings, training a convolutional autoencoder, and feeding all the training and test instances to the autoencoder to obtain the reconstruction errors.

The following approaches are taken to minimise the time for image analysis: (1) it is performed only at the last step after the semantic and statistical analyses are finished. In over 95% of our experiments, less than 10 clusters/event candidates are able to reach the last step in one round of detection; (2) as mentioned in Sect. 2.3, an image is only considered if it is posted in a tweet that contains at least one of the top $X(=5)$ keywords. This largely decreases the number of images to be examined; (3) since the analysis of a cluster is independent of each other, it can be done in parallel.

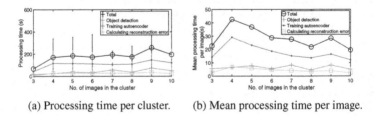

(a) Processing time per cluster.   (b) Mean processing time per image.

Fig. 4. Efficiency of the image analysis.

Figure 4 shows the processing time of the image analysis for around 240 event candidates in the Los Angeles dataset (results on the other two datasets are omitted due to similarity), including the total processing time over the entire cluster, and the time for each of three main operations. We can see that (1) the training of the autoencoder takes up more than half of the time, (2) the total processing time grows rather slowly with the number of images within the cluster, and in the majority cases the image analysis can be finished within 200 seconds. Considering that the detection is run every 30 min, the image analysis for each cluster can be done in parallel, and that GPUs are not used in the experiment, the overhead is acceptable.

4 Related Work

This section briefly reviews the previous work on event detection from social media. We start with the work that has considered images for event detection, and then summarise two types of commonly used algorithms: clustering based and anomaly based [14].

4.1 Fusion of Text and Image for Event Detection

Although images have been used in domains such as event detection from videos and fake news detection, only a limited number of studies have used both text and images for event detection from social media streams. In addition, the image is also used in a very different way from ours. For example, Alqhtani et al. [13] extract three types of features from images, including Histogram of Oriented Gradients descriptors, Grey-Level Co-occurrence Matrix and color histogram, which are then combined with features extracted from text to train a Support Vector Machine for event detection. In another example, Kaneko and Yanai [11] propose a method to select images from tweet streams for detected events. Specifically, the images are clustered based on densely sampled speeded-up robust features (SURF) and 64-dimensional RGB color histograms. Visually coherent images are then selected according to the keywords extracted from the text.

4.2 Clustering Based Event Detection

This type of detection method takes a two-step approach [3,4,10,12,22,23,25–28]. First, tweets are clustered based on their temporal, spatial, semantic, frequency and user information. However, since the generated clusters may correspond to non-events, a second step is taken to eliminate false positives. For example, for each pair of tweets, Geoburst [28] measures their geographical and semantic impact based on the Epanechnikov kernel and the random-walk-with-restart algorithm, respectively. In this way, they obtain a list of clusters that are geographically close and semantically coherent, i.e., event candidates. Finally, these candidates are ranked according to historical activities, and the top K events are returned. In terms of the improved versions: (1) Geoburst+ [26] adopts a supervised approach, and builds a candidate classification module, which learns the latent embeddings of tweets and keywords; then together with the activity timeline, the module extracts spatial unusualness and temporal burstiness to characterise each candidate event; (2) TrioVecEvent [27] learns multimodal embeddings of the location, time and text, and then performs online clustering using a Bayesian mixture model.

4.3   Anomaly Based Event Detection

This type of method [7,18–20,24] aims to identify abnormal observations in word usage, spatial activity and sentiment levels. For example, Vavliakis *et al.* [20] propose event detection for the MediaEval Benchmark 2012 [1] based on Latent Dirichlet Allocation. They detect peaks in the number of photos assigned to each topic, and identify an event for a topic if it receives an unexpectedly high number of photos. Another example is using a Discrete Wavelet Transformation [7] for the detection of peaks in Twitter hashtags, which are likely to correspond to real-world events. Specifically, only the hashtags are used, and all the remaining tweet text is discarded.

5   Conclusions and Future Work

In this paper, we propose an event detection algorithm that combines textual, statistical and image information. It generates a list of tweet clusters after the semantic and statistical analyses, and then performs image analysis to separate events from non-events. Specifically, a convolutional autoencoder is trained for each cluster, where a part of the images are used as the training data and the rest are kept as the test instances. When an event occurs, since the images posted in the surrounding area are more likely to be coherent, the reconstruction errors between test and training images will be closer. The algorithm utilises this as an additional criterion to further remove non-event clusters. Experimental results over multiple datasets demonstrate that the image analysis enhanced approach can significantly increase the precision without any impact on the recall.

For future work, we will improve the effectiveness of the image analysis. For example, currently each crop of an image is feed into the convolutional autoencoder independently, and we intend to find a way that can "stitch" them together. In addition, we will also explore other measurements of the reconstruction errors rather than the mean value to quantify the coherence of the images in a cluster.

Acknowledgements. This research is funded in part by the Defence Science and Technology Group, Edinburgh, South Australia, under contract MyIP:7293.

References

1. MediaEval 2012 (2019). http://www.multimediaeval.org/mediaeval2012/
2. Tensorflow/models (2019). https://github.com/tensorflow/models
3. Abdelhaq, H., Sengstock, C., Gertz, M.: EvenTweet: online localized event detection from twitter. Proc. VLDB Endow. **6**(12), 1326–1329 (2013). https://doi.org/10.14778/2536274.2536307
4. Becker, H., Naaman, M., Gravano, L.: Beyond trending topics: real-world event identification on twitter. In: ICWSM 2011 (2011)
5. Bojanowski, P., Grave, E., Joulin, A., Mikolov, T.: Enriching word vectors with subword information. arXiv:1607.04606 [cs] (2016)

6. Clauset, A., Shalizi, C.R., Newman, M.E.J.: Power-law distributions in empirical data. SIAM Rev. **51**(4), 661–703 (2009)
7. Cordeiro, M., Frias, R.: Twitter event detection: combining wavelet analysis and topic inference summarization. In: Doctoral Symposium on Informatics Engineering, DSIE (2011)
8. Finkel, R.A., Bentley, J.L.: Quad trees a data structure for retrieval on composite keys. Acta Inf. **4**(1), 1–9 (1974). https://doi.org/10.1007/BF00288933
9. Han, Y., Karunasekera, S., Leckie, C., Harwood, A.: Multi-spatial scale event detection from geo-tagged tweet streams via power-law verification. In: Accepted by IEEE Big Data 2019 (2019)
10. Hasan, M., Orgun, M.A., Schwitter, R.: Real-time event detection from the twitter data stream using the TwitterNews+ framework. Inf. Process. Manage. **56**(3), 1146–1165 (2019). https://doi.org/10.1016/j.ipm.2018.03.001
11. Kaneko, T., Yanai, K.: Event photo mining from twitter using keyword bursts and image clustering. Neurocomput. **172**, 143–158 (2016). https://doi.org/10.1016/j.neucom.2015.02.081
12. Li, R., Lei, K.H., Khadiwala, R., Chang, K.C.C.: TEDAS: a Twitter-based event detection and analysis system. In: Proceedings of the 2012 IEEE 28th International Conference on Data Engineering, pp. 1273–1276. ICDE 2012, IEEE Computer Society (2012). DOI: https://doi.org/10.1109/ICDE.2012.125
13. Alqhtani, M., Luo, S., Regan, B.: Fusing text and image for event detection in Twitter. Int. J. Multimedia Appl. **7**(1), 27–35 (2015). https://doi.org/10.5121/ijma.2015.7103
14. Panagiotou, N., Katakis, I., Gunopulos, D.: Detecting events in online social networks: definitions, trends and challenges. In: Michaelis, S., Piatkowski, N., Stolpe, M. (eds.) Solving Large Scale Learning Tasks. Challenges and Algorithms. LNCS (LNAI), vol. 9580, pp. 42–84. Springer, Cham (2016). https://doi.org/10.1007/978-3-319-41706-6_2
15. QinLuo: Library for fast text representation and classification: ericxsun/fastText (2019). https://github.com/ericxsun/fastText
16. Ritter, A.: Twitter NLP tools. contribute to aritter/twitter_nlp development by creating an account on GitHub (2011). https://github.com/aritter/twitter_nlp
17. Samet, H.: The quadtree and related hierarchical data structures. ACM Comput. Surv. **16**(2), 187–260 (1984). https://doi.org/10.1145/356924.356930
18. Valkanas, G., Gunopulos, D.: Event detection from social media data. IEEE Data Eng. Bull. **36**(3), 51–58 (2013)
19. Valkanas, G., Gunopulos, D.: How the live web feels about events. In: Proceedings of the 22nd ACM International Conference on Information & Knowledge Management, pp. 639–648. CIKM 2013, ACM (2013). DOI: https://doi.org/10.1145/2505515.2505572
20. Vavliakis, K.N., Tzima, F.A., Mitkas, P.A.: Event detection via LDA for the MediaEval2012 SED task. In: MediaEval (2012)
21. Virkar, Y., Clauset, A.: Power-law distributions in binned empirical data. Ann. Appl. Stat. **8**(1), 89–119 (2014)
22. Walther, M., Kaisser, M.: Geo-spatial event detection in the Twitter stream. In: Serdyukov, P., et al. (eds.) Adv. Inf. Retrieval, pp. 356–367. Springer, Berlin Heidelberg (2013)

23. Wei, H., Zhou, H., Sankaranarayanan, J., Sengupta, S., Samet, H.: Detecting latest local events from geotagged tweet streams. In: Proceedings of the 26th ACM SIGSPATIAL International Conference on Advances in Geographic Information Systems, pp. 520–523. SIGSPATIAL 2018, ACM (2018). DOI: https://doi.org/10.1145/3274895.3274977

24. Xia, C., Hu, J., Zhu, Y., Naaman, M.: What is new in our city? a framework for event extraction using social media posts. In: Cao, T., Lim, E.-P., Zhou, Z.-H., Ho, T.-B., Cheung, D., Motoda, H. (eds.) PAKDD 2015. LNCS (LNAI), vol. 9077, pp. 16–32. Springer, Cham (2015). https://doi.org/10.1007/978-3-319-18038-0_2

25. Xie, W., Zhu, F., Jiang, J., Lim, E., Wang, K.: TopicSketch: real-time bursty topic detection from Twitter. IEEE Trans. Knowl. Data Eng. **28**(8), 2216–2229 (2016). https://doi.org/10.1109/TKDE.2016.2556661

26. Zhang, C., et al.: GeoBurst+: Effective and real-time local event detection in geo-tagged tweet streams. ACM Trans. Intell. Syst. Technol. **9**(3), 341–3424 (2018). https://doi.org/10.1145/3066166

27. Zhang, C., et al.: TrioVecEvent: embedding-based online local event detection in geo-tagged tweet streams. In: Proceedings of the 23rd ACM SIGKDD International Conference on Knowledge Discovery and Data Mining, pp. 595–604. KDD 2017, ACM (2017). DOI: https://doi.org/10.1145/3097983.3098027

28. Zhang, C., et al.: GeoBurst: real-time local event detection in geo-tagged tweet streams. In: Proceedings of the 39th International ACM SIGIR Conference on Research and Development in Information Retrieval, pp. 513–522. SIGIR 2016, ACM (2016). DOI: https://doi.org/10.1145/2911451.2911519

29. Zhang, T., Ramakrishnan, R., Livny, M.: BIRCH: An efficient data clustering method for very large databases. In: Proceedings of ACM SIGMOD 1996, pp. 103–114. ACM (1996). DOI: https://doi.org/10.1145/233269.233324

Representation Learning and Embedding

TemporalGAT: Attention-Based Dynamic Graph Representation Learning

Ahmed Fathy and Kan Li[(✉)]

School of Computer Science and Technology, Beijing Institute of Technology,
Beijing 10081, China
{ahmedfathy,likan}@bit.edu.cn

Abstract. Learning representations for dynamic graphs is fundamental as it supports numerous graph analytic tasks such as dynamic link prediction, node classification, and visualization. Real-world dynamic graphs are continuously evolved where new nodes and edges are introduced or removed during graph evolution. Most existing dynamic graph representation learning methods focus on modeling dynamic graphs with fixed nodes due to the complexity of modeling dynamic graphs, and therefore, cannot efficiently learn the evolutionary patterns of real-world evolving graphs. Moreover, existing methods generally model the structural information of evolving graphs separately from temporal information. This leads to the loss of important structural and temporal information that could cause the degradation of predictive performance of the model. By employing an innovative neural network architecture based on graph attention networks and temporal convolutions, our framework jointly learns graph representations contemplating evolving graph structure and temporal patterns. We propose a deep attention model to learn low-dimensional feature representations which preserves the graph structure and features among series of graph snapshots over time. Experimental results on multiple real-world dynamic graph datasets show that, our proposed method is competitive against various state-of-the-art methods.

Keywords: Dynamic graph representation learning · Graph attention networks · Temporal convolutional networks

1 Introduction

Many appealing real-world applications involve data streams that cannot be well represented in a planar structure, but exist in irregular domain. This case applies to knowledge bases [35], 3D models [18], social media [22], and biological networks [7] which are usually represented by graphs.

In graph representation learning, the key challenge is to learn a low-dimensional representation of the data that is most informative to preserve the structural information among the nodes in graphs. Through graph embedding, we can represent the nodes in a low-dimensional vector form. This paves the way

© Springer Nature Switzerland AG 2020
H. W. Lauw et al. (Eds.): PAKDD 2020, LNAI 12084, pp. 413–423, 2020.
https://doi.org/10.1007/978-3-030-47426-3_32

to apply machine learning in graph analysis and data mining tasks easily and efficiently such as node classification [11,22], link prediction [7], clustering [4], and visualization [30].

Recently, there has been significant interest in graph representation learning mainly focuses on static graphs [5,7,8,11,22,29] which attracted the attention of researchers due to its extensive usage in numerous real-world applications. However, a wide range of real-world applications are intrinsically dynamic and the underlying graph structure evolves over time and are usually represented as a sequence of graph snapshots over time [14].

Learning dynamic graph representations is challenging due to the time-varying nature of graph structures, where the graph nodes and edges are in continues evolution. New nodes and edges can be introduced or removed in each time step. Consequently, this requires the learned representations not only to preserve structural information of the graphs, but also to efficiently capture the temporal variations over time.

Recently, novel methods for learning dynamic graph representations have been proposed in literature. Some recent work attempts to learn dynamic graph representation such as [10,15,36,37], where they mainly apply a temporally regularized weights to enforce the smoothness of node representations from different adjacent time steps. However, these methods generally fail to learn effective representations when graph nodes exhibit substantially distinct evolutionary behaviors over time [24].

Trivedi et al. [27] handle temporal reasoning problem in multi-relational knowledge graphs through employing a recurrent neural network. However, their learned temporal representations are limited to modeling first-order proximity between nodes, while ignoring the higher-order proximities among neighborhoods which are essential for preventing the graph structure as explained in [25,34].

Recently, the authors in [24] propose dynamic graph embedding approach that leverage self-attention networks to learn node representations. This method focus on learning representations that capture structural properties and temporal evolutionary patterns over time. However, this method cannot effectively capture the structural evolution information over time, since it employs structure attention layers to each time step separately and generate node representations, which is followed by temporal attention layers to capture the variations in generated representations.

Recently, attention mechanisms have achieved great success in NLP and sequential learning tasks [1,31]. Attention mechanisms learn a function that aggregates a variable-sized inputs while focusing on the most relevant sequences of the input to make decisions, which makes them unique. An attention mechanism is commonly referred to as self-attention, when it computes the representation of a single sequence.

Veličković et al. [29] extend the self-attention mechanism and apply it on static graphs by enabling each node to attend over its neighbors. In this paper, we specifically focus on applying graph attention networks (GATs) [29] because of its effectiveness in addressing the shortcomings of prior methods based on graph convolutions such as [8,11]. GATs allow for assigning different weights to nodes of the same neighborhood by applying multi-head self-attention layers, which enables a leap in model capacity. Additionally, the self-attention mechanism is applied to all graph edges, and thus, it does not depend on direct access to the graph structure or its nodes, which was a limitation of many prior dynamic graph representation learning techniques.

Inspired by this recent work, we present a temporal self-attention neural network architecture to learn node representations on dynamic graphs. Specifically, we apply self-attention along structural neighborhoods over temporal dynamics through leveraging temporal convolutional network (TCN) [2,20]. We learn dynamic node representation by considering the neighborhood in each time step during graph evolution by applying a self-attention strategy without violating the ordering of the graph snapshots.

Overall our paper makes the following contributions:

- We present a novel neural architecture named (TemporalGAT) to learn representations on dynamic graphs through integrating GAT, TCN, and a statistical loss function.
- We conduct extensive experiments on real-world dynamic graph datasets and compare with state-of-the-art approaches which validate our method.

2   Problem Formulation

In this work, we aim to solve the problem of dynamic graph representation learning. We represent dynamic graph G as a sequence of graph snapshots, $G_1, G_2, \ldots, G_T$, from timestamps 1 to T. A graph at specific time t is represented by $G_t = (V_t, E_t, F_t)$ where V_t, E_t and F_t represent the nodes, edges and features of the graph respectively. The goal of dynamic graph representation learning is to learn effective latent representations for each node in the graph $v \in V$ at each time step $t = 1, 2, \ldots, T$. The learned node representations should efficiently preserve the graph structure for all node $v \in V$ at any time step t.

3   TemporalGAT Framework

In this section, we present our proposed TemporalGAT framework, as illustrated in Fig. 1. We propose a novel model architecture to learn representations for dynamic graphs through utilizing GATs and TCNs networks to promote the model ability in capturing temporal evolutionary patterns in a dynamic graph. We employ multi-head graph attentions and TCNs as a special recurrent structure to improve model efficiency. TCNs has proven to be stable and powerful for modeling long-range dependencies as discussed in previous studies [2,20]. In addition, this architecture can take a sequence of any length and map it to an output sequence of specific length which can be very effective in dynamic graphs due to varying size of adjacency and feature matrices.

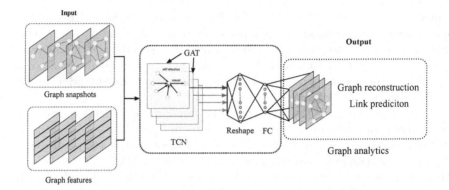

Fig. 1. The framework of TemporalGAT.

The input graph snapshot is applied to GAT layer which has dilated causal convolutions to ensure no information leakage from future to past graph snapshots. Formally, for an input vector $x \in \mathbb{R}^n$ and a filter $f : \{0, \ldots, k-1\} \to \mathbb{R}$, the dilated convolution operation C_d on element u of the vector x is defined as:

$$Conv_d(u) = (x *_d f)(u) = \sum_{i=0}^{k-1} f(i) \cdot x_{u-d \cdot i} \tag{1}$$

where d is the dilation factor, k is the filter size, and $u - d \cdot i$ makes up for the direction of the past information. When using a large dilation factors, the output at the highest level can represent a wider range of inputs, thus effectively expanding the receptive field [32] of convolution networks. For instance, through applying dilated convolution operations, it is possible to aggregate the input features from previous snapshots towards final snapshot.

The inputs to a single GAT layer are graph snapshots (adjacency matrix) and graph feature or 1-hot encoded vectors for each node. The output is node representations across time that capture both local structural and temporal properties. The self-attention layer in GAT attends over the immediate neighbors of each node by employing self-attention over the node features. The proposed GAT layer is a variant of GAT [29], with dilated convolutions applied on each graph snapshot:

$$h_u = \sigma \left(\sum_{v \in N_u} \alpha_{vu} W_d x_v \right) \tag{2}$$

where h_u is the learned hidden representations of node u, σ is a non-linear activation function, N_u represents the immediate neighbors of u, W_d is the shared transformation weight of dilated convolutions, x_v is the input representation vector of node v, and α_{vu} is the coefficient learned by the attention mechanism defined as:

$$\alpha_{vu} = \frac{\exp \left(\sigma \left(A_{vu} \cdot a^T [W_d x_v \| W_d x_u] \right) \right)}{\sum_{w \in N_u} \exp \left(\sigma \left(A_{wu} \cdot a^T [W_d x_w \| W_d x_u] \right) \right)} \tag{3}$$

where A_{vu} is the edge weight of the adjacency matrix between u and v, a^T is a weight vector parameter of the attention function implemented as feed-forward layer and $\|$ is the concatenation operator. α_{vu} is based on softmax function over the neighborhood of each node. This is to indicate the importance of node v to node v at the current snapshot. We use residual connections between GAT layers to avoid vanishing gradients and ensure smooth learning of the deep architecture.

Following, we adopt binary cross-entropy loss function to predict the existence of an edge between a pair of nodes using the learned node representations similar to [24]. The binary cross-entropy loss function for certain node v can be defined as:

$$\mathcal{L}_v = \sum_{t=1}^{\mathcal{T}} \sum_{u \in pos^t} -\log(\sigma(z_u^t \cdot z_v^t)) - W_{neg} \cdot \sum_{g \in neg^t} \log(1 - \sigma(z_v^t \cdot z_g^t)) \tag{4}$$

where $\mathcal{T}$ is the number of training snapshots, pos^t is the set of nodes connected with edges to v at snapshot t, neg^t is the negative sampling distribution for snapshot t, W_{neg} is the negative sampling parameter, σ is the sigmoid function and the dot operator represents the inner product operation between the representations of node pair.

4 Experiments

In this section, we conduct extensive experiments to evaluate the performance of our method via link prediction task. We present experiential results of our proposed method against several baselines.

4.1 Datasets

We use real-world dynamic graph datasets for analysis and performance evaluation. An outline of the datasets we use in our experiments is given in Table 1.

Table 1. Dynamic graph datasets used for performance evaluation.

Dataset	# Nodes	# Edges	# Time steps	Category
Enron	143	2,347	10	Communication
UCI	1,809	16,822	13	
Yelp	6,569	95,361	12	Rating

The detailed dataset descriptions are listed as follows:

- Enron [12] and UCI [21] are online communication network datasets. Enron dataset is constructed by email interactions between employees where the employees represent the nodes and the email communications represent the edges. UCI dataset is an online social network where the messages sent between users represent the edges.

– Yelp[1] is a rating network (Round 11 of the Yelp Dataset Challenge) where the ratings of users and businesses are collected over specific time.

The datasets have multiple graph time steps and were created based on specific interactions in fixed time windows. For more details on the dataset collection and statistics see [24].

4.2 Experimental Setup

We evaluate the performance of different baselines by conducting link prediction experiment. We learn dynamic graph representations on snapshots $S = \{1, 2, \ldots, t-1\}$ and use the links of $t-1$ to predict the links at t graph snapshot. We follow the experiment design by [24] and classify each node pair into linked and non-linked nodes, and use sampling approach to achieve positive and negative node pairs where we randomly sample 25% of each snapshot nodes for training and use the remaining 75% for testing.

4.3 Parameter Settings

For our method, we train the model using Adam optimizer and adopt dropout regularization to avoid model over-fitting. We trained the model for a maximum of 300 epochs and the best performing model on the validation set, is chosen for link perdition evaluation. For the datasets, we use a 4 TCN blocks, with each GAT layer comprising attention heads computing 32 features, and we concatenate the output features. The output low-dimensional embedding size of the last fully-connected layer is set to 128.

4.4 Baseline Algorithms

We evaluate our method against the several baseline algorithms including static graph representation approaches such as: GAT [29], Node2Vec [7], GraphSAGE [8], graph autoencoders [9], GCN-AE and GAT-AE as autoencoders for link prediction [38]. Dynamic graph representation learning including Know-Evolve [27], DynamicTriad [36], DynGEM [10] and DySAT [24].

4.5 Link Prediction

The task of link prediction is to leverage structural and temporal information up to time step t and predict the existence of an edge between a pair of vertices (u, v) at time $t + 1$.

To evaluate the link prediction performance of each baseline model, we train a logistic regression classifier similar to [36]. We use Hadmard operator to compute element-wise product of feature representation for an edge using the connected

---

[1] https://www.yelp.com/dataset/challenge.

Table 2. Link prediction results on Enron, UCI and Yelp datasets.

Algorithm	Enron		UCI		Yelp	
	Micro	Macro	Micro	Macro	Micro	Macro
Node2Vec	83.7 ± 0.7	83.1 ± 1.2	80.0 ± 0.4	80.5 ± 0.6	67.9 ± 0.2	65.34 ± 0.2
G-SAGE	82.5 ± 0.6	81.9 ± 0.5	79.2 ± 0.4	82.9 ± 0.2	61.0 ± 0.1	58.56 ± 0.2
G-SAGE + GAT	72.5 ± 0.4	73.3 ± 0.6	74.0 ± 0.4	79.8 ± 0.2	66.2 ± 0.1	65.1 ± 0.2
GCN-AE	81.6 ± 1.5	81.7 ± 1.5	80.5 ± 0.3	83.5 ± 0.5	66.7 ± 0.2	65.8 ± 0.2
GAT-AE	75.7 ± 1.1	76.0 ± 1.4	80.0 ± 0.2	81.9 ± 0.3	65.9 ± 0.1	65.4 ± 0.1
DynamicTriad	80.3 ± 0.8	79.0 ± 0.9	77.6 ± 0.6	80.3 ± 0.5	63.5 ± 0.3	62.7 ± 0.3
Know-Evolve	61.6 ± 1.1	62.3 ± 1.5	71.2 ± 0.5	80.9 ± 0.2	56.9 ± 0.2	59.7 ± 0.2
DynGEM	67.8 ± 0.6	69.7 ± 1.3	77.5 ± 0.3	79.8 ± 0.5	66.0 ± 0.2	66.0 ± 0.2
DySAT	85.7 ± 0.3	86.6 ± 0.2	81.0 ± 0.2	$\mathbf{85.8 \pm 0.1}$	70.2 ± 0.1	69.9 ± 0.1
TemporalGAT	$\mathbf{86.4 \pm 0.4}$	$\mathbf{86.8 \pm 0.3}$	$\mathbf{82.7 \pm 0.2}$	85.2 ± 0.2	$\mathbf{71.9 \pm 0.3}$	$\mathbf{70.3 \pm 0.2}$

pair of nodes as suggested by [7]. We repeat the experiment for 10 times and report the average of Area Under the ROC Curve (AUC) score.

We evaluate each baseline at each time step t separately, by training the models up to snapshot t and evaluate the performance at $t+1$ for each snapshot up to $\mathcal{T}$ snapshots. We report the averaged micro and macro AUC scores over all time steps for the methods in Table 2 (given in paper [24]).

From the results, we observe that TemporalGAT outperforms state-of-the-art methods in micro and macro AUC scores. Moreover, the results suggest that GAT using TCN architecture with minimal tuning outperforms graph representation methods, which validates the efficient of TCN in capturing the temporal and structural properties of dynamic graph snapshots.

5 Related Work

5.1 Static Graph Representation Learning

Static graph embedding can be observed as dimensionality reduction approach that maps each node into a low dimensional vector space which preserves the vertex neighborhood proximities. Earlier research work for linear (e.g., PCA) and non-linear (e.g., IsoMap) dimensionality reduction methods have been studied extensively in the literature [3,23,26].

To improve large-scale graph embedding scalability, several approaches have been proposed such as [6,7,22], which adopt random walks and skip-gram procedure to learn network representations. Tang et al. [25] designed two loss functions to capture the local and global graph structure.

More recently, network embedding approaches design models that rely on convolutions to achieve good generalizations such as [8,11,19,29]. These methods usually provide performance gains on network analytic tasks such as node classification and link prediction. However, these approaches are unable to efficiency learn representations for dynamic graphs due to evolving nature.

5.2 Dynamic Graph Representation Learning

Methods for dynamic graphs representation learning are often an extension of static methods with an additional component to model the temporal variation. For instance, in matrix factorization approaches such as [3,26] the purpose is to learn node representations that come from eigenvectors of the graph Laplacian matrix decomposition. DANE [16] is based on this idea to update the eigenvectors of graph Laplacian matrix over time series.

For the methods based on random walk such as [7,22], the aim is to model the node transition probabilities of random walks as the normalized inner products of the corresponding node representations. In [33], the authors learn representations through observing the graph changes and incrementally re-sample a few walks in the successive time step.

Another line of works for dynamic graph representation employ temporal regularization that acts as smoothness factor to enforce embedding stability across time steps [36,37]. Recent works learn incremental node representations across time steps [10], where the authors apply an autoencoder approach that minimizes the reconstruction loss with a distance metric between connected nodes in the embedding space. However, this may not guarantee the ability of model to capture long-term proximities.

Another category of dynamic graph representation learning is point processes that are continuous in time [13,17,28]. These approaches model the edge occurrence as a point process and parameterize the intensity function by applying the learned node representations as an input to a neural network.

More recently, [24] proposed an approach that leverage the most relevant historical contexts through self-attention layers to preserve graph structure and temporal evolution patterns. Unlike this approach, our framework captures the most relevant historical information through applying a temporal self-attention architecture using TCN and GAT layers to learn dynamic representations for real-world data.

6 Conclusion

In this paper, we introduce a novel end-to-end dynamic graph representation learning framework named TemporalGAT. Our framework architecture is based on graph attention networks and temporal convolutional network and operates on dynamic graph-structured data through leveraging self-attention layers over time. Our experiments on various real-world dynamic graph datasets show that the proposed framework is superior to existing graph embedding methods as it achieves significant performance gains over several state-of-the-art static and dynamic graph embedding baselines.

There are several challenges for future work. For instance, learning representations for multi-layer dynamic graphs while incorporating structural and feature information is a promising direction.

Acknowledgments. This research was supported by Beijing Natural Science Foundation (No. L181010, 4172054), National Key R & D Program of China (No. 2016 YFB0801100), and National Basic Research Program of China (No. 2013CB329605).

References

1. Bahdanau, D., Cho, K., Bengio, Y.: Neural machine translation by jointly learning to align and translate. In: International Conference on Learning Representations (ICLR) (2015)
2. Bai, S., Kolter, J.Z., Koltun, V.: An empirical evaluation of generic convolutional and recurrent networks for sequence modeling. arXiv preprint arXiv:1803.01271 (2018)
3. Belkin, M., Niyogi, P.: Laplacian Eigenmaps for dimensionality reduction and data representation. Neural Comput. **15**(6), 1373–1396 (2003)
4. Cao, S., Lu, W., Xu, Q.: Deep neural networks for learning graph representations. In: AAAI, pp. 1145–1152 (2016)
5. Chen, J., Ma, T., Xiao, C.: FastGCN: fast learning with graph convolutional networks via importance sampling. arXiv preprint arXiv:1801.10247 (2018)
6. Fathy, A., Li, K.: ComNE: reinforcing network embedding with community learning. In: Gedeon, T., Wong, K.W., Lee, M. (eds.) ICONIP 2019. CCIS, vol. 1142, pp. 397–405. Springer, Cham (2019). https://doi.org/10.1007/978-3-030-36808-1_43
7. Grover, A., Leskovec, J.: node2vec: scalable feature learning for networks. In: Proceedings of the 22nd ACM SIGKDD International Conference on Knowledge Discovery and Data Mining, pp. 855–864. ACM (2016)
8. Hamilton, W., Ying, Z., Leskovec, J.: Inductive representation learning on large graphs. In: Advances in Neural Information Processing Systems, pp. 1024–1034 (2017)
9. Hamilton, W.L., Ying, R., Leskovec, J.: Representation learning on graphs: methods and applications. arXiv preprint arXiv:1709.05584 (2017)
10. Kamra, N., Goyal, P., He, X., Liu, Y.: DynGEM: deep embedding method for dynamic graphs. In: IJCAI International Workshop on Representation Learning for Graphs (ReLiG) (2017)
11. Kipf, T.N., Welling, M.: Semi-supervised classification with graph convolutional networks. arXiv preprint arXiv:1609.02907 (2016)
12. Klimt, B., Yang, Y.: Introducing the Enron corpus. In: CEAS (2004)
13. Kumar, S., Zhang, X., Leskovec, J.: Learning dynamic embeddings from temporal interactions (2018)
14. Leskovec, J., Kleinberg, J., Faloutsos, C.: Graph evolution: densification and shrinking diameters. ACM Trans. Knowl. Discov. Data **1**(1), 2 (2007)
15. Li, J., Dani, H., Hu, X., Tang, J., Chang, Y., Liu, H.: Attributed network embedding for learning in a dynamic environment. In: Proceedings of the 2017 ACM on Conference on Information and Knowledge Management, CIKM 2017, pp. 387–396. ACM, New York (2017). https://doi.org/10.1145/3132847.3132919, http://doi.acm.org/10.1145/3132847.3132919
16. Li, J., Dani, H., Xia, H., Tang, J., Liu, H.: Attributed network embedding for learning in a dynamic environment (2017)
17. Nguyen, G.H., Lee, J.B., Rossi, R.A., Ahmed, N.K., Kim, S.: Continuous-time dynamic network embeddings. In: Companion of the The Web Conference 2018, pp. 969–976 (2018)

18. Nguyen, S.H., Yao, Z., Kolbe, T.H.: Spatio-semantic comparison of large 3D city models in CityGML using a graph database (2017)
19. Niepert, M., Ahmed, M., Kutzkov, K.: Learning convolutional neural networks for graphs. In: International Conference on Machine Learning, pp. 2014–2023 (2016)
20. Oord, A.v.d., et al.: WaveNet: a generative model for raw audio. arXiv preprint arXiv:1609.03499 (2016)
21. Panzarasa, P., Opsahl, T., Carley, K.M.: Patterns and dynamics of users' behavior and interaction: network analysis of an online community. J. Am. Soc. Inform. Sci. Technol. **60**(5), 911–932 (2009)
22. Perozzi, B., Al-Rfou, R., Skiena, S.: DeepWalk: online learning of social representations. In: Proceedings of the 20th ACM SIGKDD International Conference on Knowledge Discovery and Data Mining, pp. 701–710. ACM (2014)
23. Roweis, S.T., Saul, L.K.: Nonlinear dimensionality reduction by locally linear embedding. Science **290**(5500), 2323–2326 (2000)
24. Sankar, A., Wu, Y., Gou, L., Zhang, W., Yang, H.: Dynamic graph representation learning via self-attention networks (2018)
25. Tang, J., Qu, M., Wang, M., Zhang, M., Yan, J., Mei, Q.: Line: large-scale information network embedding. In: Proceedings of the 24th International Conference on World Wide Web, pp. 1067–1077. International World Wide Web Conferences Steering Committee (2015)
26. Tenenbaum, J.B., De Silva, V., Langford, J.C.: A global geometric framework for nonlinear dimensionality reduction. Science **290**(5500), 2319–2323 (2000)
27. Trivedi, R., Dai, H., Wang, Y., Song, L.: Know-evolve: deep temporal reasoning for dynamic knowledge graphs. In: Proceedings of the 34th International Conference on Machine Learning, vol. 70, pp. 3462–3471 (2017). JMLR.org
28. Trivedi, R., Farajtbar, M., Biswal, P., Zha, H.: Representation learning over dynamic graphs (2018)
29. Veličković, P., Cucurull, G., Casanova, A., Romero, A., Liò, P., Bengio, Y.: Graph attention networks. In: International Conference on Learning Representations (2018). https://openreview.net/forum?id=rJXMpikCZ
30. Wang, D., Cui, P., Zhu, W.: Structural deep network embedding. In: Proceedings of the 22nd ACM SIGKDD International Conference on Knowledge Discovery and Data Mining, pp. 1225–1234. ACM (2016)
31. Yu, A., Dohan, D., Luong, M.T., Zhao, R., Chen, K., Le, Q.: QANet: combining local convolution with global self-attention for reading comprehension (2018)
32. Yu, F., Koltun, V.: Multi-scale context aggregation by dilated convolutions. arXiv preprint arXiv:1511.07122 (2015)
33. Yu, W., Cheng, W., Aggarwal, C.C., Zhang, K., Chen, H., Wang, W.: NetWalk: a flexible deep embedding approach for anomaly detection in dynamic networks. In: Proceedings of the 24th ACM SIGKDD International Conference on Knowledge Discovery and Data Mining, KDD 2018, pp. 2672–2681. ACM, New York (2018). https://doi.org/10.1145/3219819.3220024, http://doi.acm.org/10.1145/3219819.3220024
34. Zhang, D., Yin, J., Zhu, X., Zhang, C.: Network representation learning: a survey. arXiv preprint arXiv:1801.05852 (2017)
35. Zhen, W., Zhang, J., Feng, J., Zheng, C.: Knowledge graph embedding by translating on hyperplanes. In: Twenty-Eighth AAAI Conference on Artificial Intelligence (2014)
36. Zhou, L., Yang, Y., Ren, X., Wu, F., Zhuang, Y.: Dynamic network embedding by modeling triadic closure process. In: Thirty-Second AAAI Conference on Artificial Intelligence (2018)

37. Zhu, L., Dong, G., Yin, J., Steeg, G.V., Galstyan, A.: Scalable temporal latent space inference for link prediction in dynamic social networks. IEEE Trans. Knowl. Data Eng. **28**(10), 2765–2777 (2016)
38. Zitnik, M., Agrawal, M., Leskovec, J.: Modeling polypharmacy side effects with graph convolutional networks. Bioinformatics **34**(13), i457–i466 (2018)

MSGE: A Multi-step Gated Model for Knowledge Graph Completion

Chunyang Tan$^{(\boxtimes)}$, Kaijia Yang, Xinyu Dai, Shujian Huang, and Jiajun Chen

National Key Laboratory for Novel Software Technology,
Nanjing University, Nanjing, China
{tancy,yangkj}@smail.nju.edu.cn, {daixinyu,huangsj,chenjj}@nju.edu.cn

Abstract. Knowledge graph embedding models aim to represent entities and relations in continuous low-dimensional vector space, benefiting many research areas such as knowledge graph completion and web searching. However, previous works do not consider controlling information flow, which makes them hard to obtain useful latent information and limits model performance. Specifically, as human beings, predictions are usually made in multiple steps with every step filtering out irrelevant information and targeting at helpful information. In this paper, we first integrate iterative mechanism into knowledge graph embedding and propose a multi-step gated model which utilizes relations as queries to extract useful information from coarse to fine in multiple steps. First gate mechanism is adopted to control information flow by the interaction between entity and relation with multiple steps. Then we repeat the gate cell for several times to refine the information incrementally. Our model achieves state-of-the-art performance on most benchmark datasets compared to strong baselines. Further analyses demonstrate the effectiveness of our model and its scalability on large knowledge graphs.

Keywords: Knowledge graph embedding · Gate mechanism · Multi-step

1 Introduction

Large-scale knowledge graphs(KGs), such as Freebase [1], YAGO3 [2] and DBpedia [3], have attracted extensive interests with progress in artificial intelligence. Real-world facts are stored in KGs with the form of (subject entity, relation, object entity), denoted as (s, r, o), benefiting many applications and research areas such as question answering and semantic searching. Meanwhile, KGs are still far from complete with missing a lot of valid triplets. As a consequence, many researches have been devoted to knowledge graph completion task which aims to predict missing links in knowledge graphs.

Knowledge graph embedding models try to represent entities and relations in low-dimensional continuous vector space. Benefiting from these embedding models, we can do complicated computations on KG facts and better tackle the

© Springer Nature Switzerland AG 2020
H. W. Lauw et al. (Eds.): PAKDD 2020, LNAI 12084, pp. 424–435, 2020.
https://doi.org/10.1007/978-3-030-47426-3_33

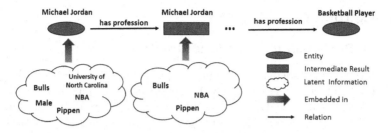

Fig. 1. Example of link prediction in knowledge graph. An entity has much latent information entailed in its embedding, but with a given relation, only part of them are helpful for predicting.

KG completion task. Translation distance based models [4–8] regard predicting a relation between two entities as a translation from subject entity to tail entity with the relation as a media. While plenty of bilinear models [9–13] propose different energy functions representing the score of its validity rather than measure the distance between entities. Apart from these shallow models, recently, deeper models [14,15] are proposed to extract information at deep level.

Though effective, these models do not consider: **1.** Controlling information flow specifically, which means keeping relevant information and filtering out useless ones, as a result restricting the performance of models. **2.** The multi-step reasoning nature of a prediction process. An entity in a knowledge graph contains rich latent information in its representation. As illustrated in Fig. 1, the entity *Michael Jordon* has much latent information embedded in the knowledge graph and will be learned into the representation implicitly. However, when given a relation, not all latent semantics are helpful for the prediction of object entity. Intuitively, it is more reasonable to design a module that can capture useful latent information and filter out useless ones. At the meantime, for a complex graph, an entity may contain much latent information entailed in an entity, one-step predicting is not enough for complicated predictions, while almost all previous models ignore this nature. Multi-step architecture [16,17] allows the model to refine the information from coarse to fine in multiple steps and has been proved to benefit a lot for the feature extraction procedure.

In this paper, we propose a **Multi-Step Gated Embedding** (MSGE) model for link prediction in KGs. During every step, gate mechanism is applied several times, which is used to decide what features are retained and what are excluded at the dimension level, corresponding to the multi-step reasoning procedure. For partial dataset, gate cells are repeated for several times iteratively for more fine-grained information. All parameters are shared among the repeating cells, which allows our model to target the right features in multi-steps with high parameter efficiency. We do link prediction experiments on 6 public available benchmark datasets and achieve better performance compared to strong baselines on most datasets. We further analyse the influence of gate mechanism and the length of steps to demonstrate our motivation.

2   Background

2.1   Link Prediction in Knowledge Graphs

Link prediction in knowledge graphs aims to predict correct object entities given a pair of subject entity and relation. In a knowledge graph, there are a huge amount of entities and relations, which inspires previous work to transform the prediction task as a scoring and ranking task. Given a known pair of subject entity and relation (s, r), a model needs to design a scoring function for a triple (s, r, o), where o belongs to all entities in a knowledge graph. Then model ranks all these triples in order to find the position of the valid one. The goal of a model is to rank all valid triples before the false ones.

2.2   Knowledge Graph Embedding

Knowledge graph embedding models aim to represent entities and relations in knowledge graphs with low-dimensional vectors (e_s, e_r, e_t). TransE [4] is a typical distance-based model with constraint formula $e_s + e_r - e_t \approx 0$. Many other models extend TransE by projecting subject and object entities into relation-specific vector space, such as TransH [5], TransR [6] and TransD [18]. TorusE [7] and RotatE [8] are also extensions of distance-based models. Instead of measuring distance among entities, bilinear models such as RESCAL [9], DistMult [10] and ComplEx [11] are proposed with multiplication operations to score a triplet. Tensor decomposition methods such as SimplE [12], CP-N3 [19] and TuckER [13] can also be seen as bilinear models with extra constraints. Apart from above shallow models, several deeper non-linear models have been proposed to further capture more underlying features. For example, (R-GCNs) [15] applies a specific convolution operator to model locality information in accordance to the topology of knowledge graphs. ConvE [14] first applies 2-D convolution into knowledge graph embedding and achieves competitive performance.

The main idea of our model is to control information flow in a multi-step way. To our best knowledge, the most related work to ours is TransAt [20] which also mentioned the two-step reasoning nature of link prediction. However, in TransAt, the first step is categorizing entities with Kmeans and then it adopts a distance-based scoring function to measure the validity. This architecture is not an end-to-end structure which is not flexible. Besides, error propagation will happen due to the usage of Kmeans algorithm.

3   Methods

3.1   Notations

We denote a knowledge graph as $\mathcal{G} = \{(s, r, o)\} \subseteq \mathcal{E} \times \mathcal{R} \times \mathcal{E}$, where $\mathcal{E}$ and $\mathcal{R}$ are the sets of entities, relations respectively. The number of entities in $\mathcal{G}$ is n_e, the number of relations in $\mathcal{G}$ is n_r and we allocate the same dimension d to entities and relations for simplicity. $E \in \mathbb{R}^{n_e * d}$ is the embedding matrix for

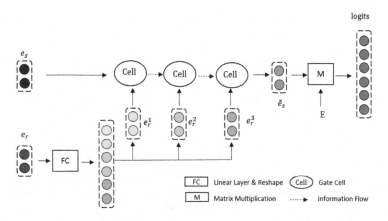

Fig. 2. The schematic diagram of our model with length of step 3. e_s and e_r represent embedding of subject entity and relation respectively. e_r^i means the query relation are fed into the i-th step to refine information. $\tilde{e}_s$ is the final output information, then matrix multiplication is operated between $\tilde{e}_s$ and embedding matrix of entities E. At last, logistic sigmoid function is applied to restrict the final score between 0 and 1.

entities and $R \in \mathbb{R}^{n_r * d}$ is the embedding matrix for relations. e_s, e_r and e_o are used to represent the embedding of subject entity, relation and subject entity respectively. Besides, we denote a gate cell in our model as C.

3.2 Multi-step Gate Mechanism

In order to obtain useful information, we need a specific module to extract needed information from subject entity with respect to the given relation, which can be regarded as a control of information flow guided by the relation. To model this process, we introduce gate mechanism, which is widely used in data mining and natural language processing models to guide the transmission of information, e.g. Long Short-Term Memory (LSTM) [21] and Gated Recurrent Unit (GRU) [22]. Here we adopt gating mechanism at dimension level to control information entailed in the embedding. To make the entity interact with relation specifically, we rewrite the gate cell in multi-steps with two gates as below:

$$z = \sigma(W_z[e_r, e_s] + b_z)$$
$$r = \sigma(W_r[e_r, e_s] + b_r) \qquad (1)$$

Two gates z and r are called update gate and reset gate respectively for controlling the information flow. Reset gate is designed for generating a new e_s' or new information in another saying as follows:

$$e_s' = tanh(W_s[r \odot e_s, e_r] + b) \qquad (2)$$

Update gate aims to decide how much the generated information are kept according to formula (3):

$$\tilde{e}_s = (1 - z) \odot e_s' + z \odot e_s \qquad (3)$$

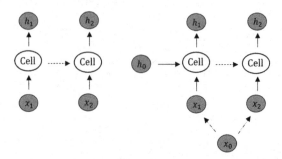

Fig. 3. The differences between traditional RNN-like model and our model. In RNN-like model (left), h_0 is initialized randomly, x represents a sequence. In our model(right), h_0 comes from subject entity and x is transformed from relation x_0.

Hardmard product is performed to control the information at a dimension level. The values of these two gates are generated by the interaction between subject entity and relation. σ-Logistic sigmoid function is performed to project results between 0 and 1. Here 0 means totally excluded while 1 means totally kept, which is the core module to control the flow of information. We denote the gate cell as C.

Besides, to verify the effectiveness of gate mechanism, we also list the formula of a cell that exclude gates as below for ablation study:

$$\tilde{e}_s = tanh(\boldsymbol{W}[\boldsymbol{e_r}, \boldsymbol{e_s}] + \boldsymbol{b}) \tag{4}$$

With the gate cell containing several gating operations, the overall architecture in one gate cell is indeed a multi-step information controlling way.

3.3 Iterative Multi-step Architecture

In fact, a single gate cell can generate useful information since the two gating operations already hold great power for information controlling. However, for a complex dataset, more fine and precise features are needed for prediction. The iterative multi-step architecture allows the model to refine the representations incrementally. During each step, a query is fed into the model to interact with given features from previous step to obtain relevant information for next step. As illustrated in Fig. 2, to generate the sequence as the input for multi-step training, we first feed relation embedding into a fully connected layer:

$$\boldsymbol{e}_r' = \boldsymbol{W}\boldsymbol{e}_r + \boldsymbol{b} \tag{5}$$

We reshape the output as a sequence $[\boldsymbol{e}_r^0, \boldsymbol{e}_r^1, ..., \boldsymbol{e}_r^k] = Reshape(\boldsymbol{e}_r')$ which are named query relations. This projection aims to obtain query relations of different latent aspects such that we can utilize them to extract diverse information across multiple steps. Information of diversity can increase the robustness of a model, which further benefits the performance. Query relations are fed sequentially into the gate cell to interact with subject entity and generate information from coarse to fine. Parameters are shared across all steps so multi-step training are performed in an iterative way indeed.

Our score function for a given triple can be summarized as:

$$\phi = (C^k(e_s, [e_r^0, e_r^1, ..., e_r^k]))e_o \tag{6}$$

where C^k means repeating gate cell for k steps and during each step only the corresponding e_r^i is fed to interact with output information from last step. See Fig. 2 for better understanding. After we extract the final information, it is interacted with object entity with a dot product operation to produce final score.

Differences with RNN-like Model. In previous RNN-like models, a cell is repeated several times to produce information of an input sequence, where the repeating times are decided by the length of the input sequence. Differently, we have two inputs e_s and e_r with totally different properties, which are embeddings of subject entity and relation respectively, which should not be seen as a sequence as usual. As a result, a gate cell is used for capturing interactive information among entities and relations iteratively in our model, rather than extracting information of just one input sequence. See Fig. 3 for differences more clearly.

Training. At last, matrix multiplication is applied between the final output information and embedding matrix E, which can be called 1-N scoring [14] to score all triples in one time for efficiency and better performance. We also add reciprocal triple for every instance in the dataset which means for a given (s, r, t), we add a reverse triple (t, r^{-1}, s) as the previous work. We use binary cross-entropy loss as our loss function:

$$\mathcal{L}(p, y) = -\frac{1}{N} \sum_i (y_i \cdot log(p_i) + (1 - y_i) \cdot log(1 - p_i)) \tag{7}$$

We add batch normalization to regularise our model and dropout is also used after layers. For optimization, we use Adam for a stable and fast training process. Embedding matrices are initialized with xavier normalization. Label smoothing [23] is also used to lessen overfitting.

4   Experiments

In this section we first introduce the benchmark datasets used in this paper, then we report the empirical results to demonstrate the effectiveness of our model. Analyses and ablation study are further reported to strengthen our motivation.

Table 1. Statistics of datasets.

Dataset	#Entity	#Rel	#Train	#Valid	#Test
WN18	40943	18	141442	5000	5000
WN18RR	40943	11	86835	3034	3134
FB15k	14951	1345	483142	50000	59071
FB15k-237	14541	237	212115	17535	20466
UMLS	135	49	5216	652	661
KINSHIP	104	26	8544	1068	1074

4.1 Datasets

Six datasets are used in our experiments:

- **WN18** [4] is extracted from WordNet describing the hierarchical structure of words, consisting relations such as *hyponym* and *hypernym*.
- **WN18RR** [4, 14] is a subset of WN18 which removes inverse relations. Inverse relation pairs are relations such as (*hyponym*, *hypernym*). Inverse relations may cause severe test leakage: a lot of test triples can be obtained from train data simply by inverting them. That means a simple rule-based model can easily figure out the right o given a (s, r), only if it has seen $(o, r^{'}, s)$ in the train data and it knows $r^{'}$ is the reverse of r.
- **FB15k** [4] is extracted from Freebase describing mostly relations about movies, actors, awards, sports and so on.
- **FB15k-237** [24] is a subset of FB15k which removes inverse relations and the triples involved in train, valid and test data.
- **UMLS** [25] comes from biomedicine. Entities in UMLS (Unified Medical Language System) are biomedical concepts such as *disease* and *antibiotic*.
- **Kinship** [25] contains kinship relationships among members of the Alyawarra tribe from Central Australia.

The details of these datasets are reported in Table 1.

4.2 Experiment Setup

The evaluation metric we use in our paper includes Mean Reciprocal Rank(MRR) and Hit@K. MRR represents the reciprocal rank of the right triple, the higher the better of the model. Hit@K reflects the proportion of gold triples ranked in the top K. Here we select K among {1, 3, 10}, consistent with previous work. When Hit@K is higher, the model can be considered as better. All results are reported with 'Filter' setting which removes all gold triples that have existed in train, valid and test data during ranking. We report the test results according to the best performance of MRR on validation data as the same with previous works.

Table 2. Link prediction results on WN18, WN18RR, FB15k and FB15k-237. [†] denotes the results are taken from [14]; - denotes the results are not provided; The results of RotatE [8] are reported without self-adversarial negative sampling, this sampling trick is irrelevant with the model itself; Other results are all taken from the original paper. Best results are in bold. The second best are underlined.

Model	WN18		WN18RR		FB15k		FB15k-237	
	MRR	Hit@10	MRR	Hit@10	MRR	Hit@10	MRR	Hit@10
TransE (2013)	-	0.892	-	-	-	0.471	-	-
DistMult[†] (2015)	0.822	0.936	0.430	0.490	0.654	0.824	0.241	0.419
ComplEx[†] (2016)	0.941	0.947	0.440	0.510	0.692	0.840	0.247	0.428
R-GCN (2017)	0.814	**0.964**	-	-	0.696	0.842	0.248	0.417
TransAt (2018)	-	0.951	-	-	-	0.782	-	-
MINERVA (2018)	-	-	0.448	0.513	-	-	0.293	0.456
ConvE (2018)	0.943	0.956	0.430	0.520	0.657	0.831	0.325	0.501
TorusE (2018)	0.947	0.954	-	-	0.733	0.832	-	-
RotatE (2019)	-	-	-	-	-	-	0.297	0.480
SimplE (2018)	0.942	0.947	-	-	0.727	0.838	-	-
TuckER (2019)	**0.953**	0.958	**0.470**	0.526	0.795	0.892	**0.358**	0.544
MSGE(Ours)	0.951	0.961	0.464	**0.547**	**0.806**	**0.894**	0.357	**0.545**

Table 3. Link prediction results on UMLS and Kinship.

Model	UMLS				Kinship			
	MRR	Hit@10	Hit@3	Hit@1	MRR	Hit@10	Hit@3	Hit@1
ComplEx ◁ (2016)	0.894	**0.995**	0.962	0.824	0.838	0.980	0.910	0.754
ConvE ◁ (2018)	0.933	0.992	0.964	0.894	0.797	0.974	0.886	0.697
NTP (2017)	0.872	0.970	0.906	0.817	0.612	0.777	0.700	0.500
NeuralLP (2017)	0.778	0.962	0.869	0.643	0.619	0.912	0.707	0.475
MINERVA (2018)	0.825	0.968	0.900	0.728	0.720	0.924	0.812	0.605
MSGE(Ours)	**0.946**	0.993	**0.973**	**0.914**	**0.865**	**0.988**	**0.941**	**0.785**

For different datasets, the best setting of the number of iterations varies a lot. For FB15k and UMLS the number at 1 provides the best performance, however for other datasets, iterative mechanism is helpful for boosting the performance. The best number of iterations is set to 5 for WN18, 3 for WN18RR, 8 for FB15k-237 and 2 for Kinship.

4.3 Link Prediction Results

We do link prediction task on 6 benchmark datasets, comparing with several classical baselines such as TransE [4], DistMult [10] and some SOTA strong baselines such as ConvE [14], RotatE [8] and TuckER [13]. For smaller datasets

Table 4. Influence of number of iterations on FB15k-237.

Length	FB15k-237			
	MRR	Hit@10	Hit@3	Hit@1
1	0.349	0.536	0.384	0.255
3	0.354	0.539	0.389	0.261
5	0.354	0.541	0.391	0.261
8	**0.357**	**0.544**	**0.392**	**0.264**
10	0.355	0.540	0.391	0.263

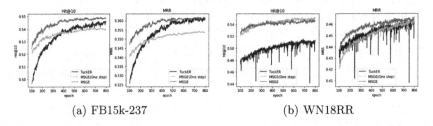

(a) FB15k-237   (b) WN18RR

Fig. 4. Convergence study between TuckER and MSGE(ours) on FB15k-237 and WN18RR.

UMLS and Kinship, we also compare with some non-embedding methods such as NTP [26] and NeuralLP [27] which learn logic rules for predicting, as well as MINERVA [28] which utilizes reinforcement learning for reasoning over paths in knowledge graphs.

The results are reported in Table 2 and Table 3. Overall, from the results we can conclude that our model achieves comparable or better performance than SOTA models on datasets. Even with datasets without inverse relations such as WN18RR, FB15k-237 which are more difficult datasets, our model can still achieve comparable performance.

4.4 Analysis on Number of Iterations

To study the effectiveness of the iterative multi-step architecture, we list the performance of different number of steps on FB15k-237 in Table 4. The model settings are all exactly the same except for length of steps. From the results on FB15k-237 we can conclude that the multi-step mechanism indeed boosts the performance for a complex knowledge graph like FB15k-237, which verify our motivation that refining information for several steps can obtain more helpful information for some complex datasets.

4.5 Convergence Study

We report the convergence process of TuckER and MSGE on FB15k-237 dataset and WN18RR dataset in Fig. 4. We re-run TuckER with exactly the same settings

Table 5. Parameter counts comparison.

Dataset	ConvE	TuckER	MSGE
WN18	10.32M	9.39M	8.48M
WN18RR	10.31M	9.39M	8.84M
FB15k	6.16M	11.53M	3.81M
FB15k-237	5.19M	11.00M	3.57M

Table 6. Ablation study on FB15k-237.

Model	FB15k-237			
	MRR	Hit@10	Hit@3	Hit@1
MSGE	**0.357**	**0.544**	**0.392**	**0.264**
No gate	0.301	0.459	0.327	0.222
Concat	0.349	0.534	0.384	0.256
Replicate	0.351	0.537	0.388	0.257

claimed in the paper. All the results stand for the performance on valid dataset. For MSGE, we also report the result of one step for comparison. It is obvious that MSGE can converge rapidly compared to TuckER with nearly the same or better final performance. From the analysis of model architecture, TuckER needs an extra core tensor W to capture interactive information. While in MSGE, entities and relations are directly interacted with each other through a gate cell. On dataset WN18RR, we can find that the convergence process of TuckER is not as steady as MSGE, which demonstrates the efficiency of our model.

4.6 Efficiency Analysis

In Table 5, we report the parameter counts of ConvE, TuckER and our model for comparison. Our model can achieve better performance on most datasets with much less parameters, which means our model can be more easily migrated to large knowledge graphs. As for TuckER, which is the current SOTA method, the parameter count is mainly due to the core interaction tensor W, whose size is $d_e * d_r * d_e$. As the grow of embedding dimension, this core tensor will lead to a large increasing on parameter size. However, note that our model is an iterative architecture therefore only a very few parameters are needed apart from the embedding, the complexity is $\mathcal{O}(n_e d + n_r d)$. For evaluating time efficiency, we re-run TuckER and our model on Telsa K40c. TuckER needs 29 s/28 s to run an epoch on FB15k-237/WN18RR respectively, MSGE needs 17 s/24 s respectively, which demonstrate the time efficiency due to few operations in our model.

4.7 Ablation Study

To further demonstrate our motivation that gate mechanism and multi-step reasoning are beneficial for extracting information. We do ablation study with the following settings:

- **No gate:** Remove the gates in our model to verify the necessity of controlling information flow.
- **Concat:** Concatenate information extracted in every step together and feed them into a fully connected layer to obtain another kind of final information, which is used to verify that more useful information are produced by the procedure of multi-step.
- **Replicate:** Replicate the relation to gain k same query relations for training. This is to prove that extracting diverse information from multi-view query relations is more helpful than using the same relation for k times.

The experiment results are reported in Table 6. All results demonstrate our motivation that controlling information flow in a multi-step way is beneficial for link prediction task in knowledge graphs. Especially a gated cell is of much benefit for information extraction.

5 Conclusion and Future Work

In this paper, we propose a multi-step gated model MSGE for link prediction task in knowledge graph completion. We utilize gate mechanism to control information flow generated by the interaction between subject entity and relation. Then we repeat gated module to refine information from coarse to fine. It has been proved from the empirical results that utilizing gated module for multiple steps is beneficial for extracting more useful information, which can further boost the performance on link prediction. We also do analysis from different views to demonstrate this conclusion. Note that, all information contained in embeddings are learned across the training procedure implicitly. In future work, we would like to aggregate more information for entities to enhance feature extraction, for example, from the neighbor nodes and relations.

References

1. Bollacker, K.D., Evans, C., Paritosh, P., Sturge, T., Taylor, J.: Freebase: a collaboratively created graph database for structuring human knowledge. In: ACM SIGMOD, pp. 1247–1250 (2008)
2. Mahdisoltani, F., Biega, J., Suchanek, F.M.: Yago3: A knowledge base from multilingual wikipedias (2015)
3. Auer, S., Bizer, C., Kobilarov, G., Lehmann, J., Cyganiak, R., Ives, Z.: DBpedia: a nucleus for a web of open data. In: Aberer, K., et al. (eds.) ASWC/ISWC -2007. LNCS, vol. 4825, pp. 722–735. Springer, Heidelberg (2007). https://doi.org/10.1007/978-3-540-76298-0_52
4. Bordes, A., Usunier, N., Garcia-Duran, A., Weston, J., Yakhnenko, O.: Translating embeddings for modeling multi-relational data. In: NIPS, pp. 2787–2795 (2013)

5. Wang, Z., Zhang, J., Feng, J., Chen, Z.: Knowledge graph embedding by translating on hyperplanes. AAAI **14**, 1112–1119 (2014)
6. Lin, Y., Liu, Z., Sun, M., Liu, Y., Zhu, X.: Learning entity and relation embeddings for knowledge graph completion. AAAI **15**, 2181–2187 (2015)
7. Ebisu, T., Ichise, R.: Knowledge graph embedding on a lie group. In: AAAI, Toruse (2018)
8. Sun, Z., Deng, Z.H., Nie, J.Y.: Rotate: knowledge graph embedding by relational rotation in complex space. In: ICLR (2019)
9. Nickel, M., Tresp, V., Kriegel, H.P.: A three-way model for collective learning on multi-relational data. In: ICML (2011)
10. Yang, B., Yih, W., He, X., Gao, J., Deng, L.: Embedding entities and relations for learning and inference in knowledge bases. In: ICLR (2015)
11. Trouillon, T., Welbl, J., Riedel, S., Gaussier, E., Bouchard, G.: Complex embeddings for simple link prediction. In: ICML, pp. 2071–2080 (2016)
12. Kazemi, S.M., Poole, D.: Simple embedding for link prediction in knowledge graphs. In: NIPS (2018)
13. Balažević, I., Allen, C., Hospedales, T.: Tensor factorization for knowledge graph completion. In: EMNLP (2019)
14. Dettmers, T., Minervini, P., Stenetorp, P., Riedel, S.: Convolutional 2D knowledge graph embeddings. In: AAAI (2018)
15. Schlichtkrull, M., Bloem,T.N., Kipf nd, P., van den Berg, R., Titov, I., Welling, M.: Modeling relational data with graph convolutional networks. In: European Semantic Web Conference (2018)
16. Shen, Y., Huang, P.S., Gao, J. Reasonet: learning to stop reading in machine comprehension. In: ACM SIGKDD (2017)
17. Dhingra, B., Liu, H., Yang, Z.: Gated-attention readers for text comprehension (2016)
18. Ji, G., He, S., Xu, L., Liu, K.: Knowledge graph embedding via dynamic mapping matrix. In: ACL (2015)
19. Lacroix, T., Usunier, N., Obozinski, G.: Canonicaltensor decomposition for knowledge base completion. In: ICML (2018)
20. Qian, W., Fu, C., Zhu, Y., Cai, D., He, X.: Translating embeddings for knowledge graph completion with relation attention mechanism. In: European Semantic Web Conference (2018)
21. Hochreiter, S., Schmidhuber, J.: Long short-term memory. Neural Comput. **9**, 1735–1780 (1997)
22. Cho, K., et al.: Learning phrase representations using RNN encoder-decoder for statistical machine translation. arXiv preprint (2014)
23. Szegedy, C., Vanhoucke, V., Ioffe, S., Shlens, I., Wojna, Z.: Rethinking the inception architecture for computer vision. In: Proceedings of IEEE CVPR, pp. 2818–2826 (2016)
24. Toutanova, K., Chen, D.: Observed versus latent features for knowledge base and text inference. In: Proceedings of the 3rd Workshop on Continuous Vector Space Models and their Compositionality, pp. 57–66 (2015)
25. Kok, S., Domingos, P.: Statistical predicate invention. In: ICML (2007)
26. Rocktaschel, T., Riedel, S.: End-to-end differentiable proving. In: NIPS (2017)
27. Yang, F., Yang, Z., Cohen, W.: Differentiable learning of logical rules for knowledge base reasoning. In: NIPS (2017)
28. Das, R., et al.: Go for a walk and arrive at the answer: reasoning over paths in knowledge bases using reinforcement learning. In: ICLR (2018)

Attention-Based Graph Evolution

Shuangfei Fan$^{(\boxtimes)}$ ⓘ and Bert Huang ⓘ

Virginia Tech, Blacksburg 24060, USA
{sophia23,bhuang}@vt.edu

Abstract. Based on the recent success of deep generative models on continuous data, various new methods are being developed to generate discrete data such as graphs. However, these approaches focus on unconditioned generation, which limits their control over the generating procedure to produce graphs in context, thus limiting the applicability to real-world settings. To address this gap, we introduce an attention-based graph evolution model (AGE). AGE is a conditional graph generator based on the neural attention mechanism that can not only model graph evolution in both space and time, but can also model the transformation between graphs from one state to another. We evaluate AGE on multiple conditional graph-generation tasks, and our results show that it can generate realistic graphs conditioned on source graphs, outperforming existing methods in terms of quality and generality.

Keywords: Conditional graph generation · Attention · Graph evolution

1 Introduction

As a fundamental topic in graph modeling, graph generation has a long history that began as early as the 1950s [6]. However, most traditional methods rely on prior knowledge of the graph topology and are limited in capability of learning generative properties from observations. To solve this problem, researchers have recently been exploring trainable deep models for graph generation based on the effectiveness of graph neural networks—e.g., graph convolutional networks [14]—which have been applied to various kinds of data describing, for example, molecular chemicals for drug design and scientific publications for predicting citations [25, 31]. However, these approaches are unconditional generative models, which limits their control over the generating procedure and makes them unable to produce graphs in context. These limitations restrict the applicability of these approaches to real world settings where graphs transform from one state to another and evolve in dynamic network settings.

Modeling graph evolution is an important task that can be applied to various practical applications. A model of graph evolution would be a powerful tool for both predicting the future and the transformation of networks. For example, a marketer aiming to post an advertisement on an online social network may

© Springer Nature Switzerland AG 2020
H. W. Lauw et al. (Eds.): PAKDD 2020, LNAI 12084, pp. 436–447, 2020.
https://doi.org/10.1007/978-3-030-47426-3_34

only have access to short-hop ego networks around users, but they need to know how the information would spread into the extended network beyond these ego networks. In disease control and prevention, when an infectious disease emerges and starts to spread, it is important to understand how it may spread beyond the visible network. Because graph data represents real-world phenomena that is changing or incompletely observed, there are many other examples of problems that could benefit from new tools for modeling graph evolution. Yet existing methods lack the flexibility of deep generative models or the ability to condition on previous graph states.

To provide this missing capability, we introduce an attention-based graph evolution model (AGE). AGE is a model for conditional graph generation based on the attention mechanism that allows consideration of global information with parallel computation across all graph nodes. AGE adopts the encoder-decoder structure, where the encoder tries to learn the representation of conditioned graphs using a self-attention mechanism, and the decoder tries to generate the representation of the target graphs using the correlation with the conditioned graphs and also with itself. The decoder can thus capture both global and local information. This graph-conditioned generation framework greatly enriches the potential applications for graph generation. AGE can be used to model not only graph evolution in space and in time, but also the transformation between graphs from one state to another. To evaluate how AGE performs on this problem setting, we perform experiments on datasets in various areas. The experiment results in terms of both the evaluation metrics, show that AGE can not only generate extremely realistic graphs, but also has the strong ability to model the evolution of graphs as a powerful conditioned graph generative model.

2 Related Work

Graph generation is one of the core topics in graph analysis. Many methods have been proposed to solve this problem, which can be traced back to at least 1959 when Erdös and Rényi [6] first introduced the Erdös-Rényi (E-R) model for generating random graphs. The model is based on the assumption that each pair of nodes are connected with a fixed pre-defined probability. However, this assumption is not realistic in most real world networks. To mimic the structure of real graphs, Albert and Barabási [2] proposed the preferential attachment model by further customizing the probability of each possible edge to be conditioned on current degrees of nodes. Separately, Airoldi et al. [1] proposed the mixed-membership stochastic block model (MMSB) to generate graphs that have a fixed number of communities based on a probability matrix to determine the possibility of a node pair from two communities been connected. This model is able to learn distributions from observed data, which makes it generate more useful random graphs based on basic assumptions. Other classical graph generative models include exponential random graph models (ERGMs) [21,26], the stochastic block model (SBM) [9], the Watts-Strogatz model [29], the Kronecker graph model [16], and many more. These older approaches have limited ability to learn about graph distributions from collections of graphs.

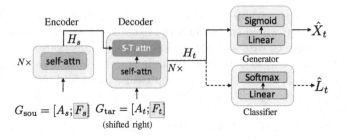

Fig. 1. The model architecture of AGE.

Recently, researchers also have proposed to use deep models to learn distributions for graph generation. These methods can be divided into two categories. Some of them are auto-regressive models, which generate the graph in a sequential manner. Examples of these are the DeepGMG model [18] and the GraphRNN model You et al. [31]. While some other methods are non-auto regressive models [22,25]. Among them, many models are based on generative adversarial networks (GANs) [10], which learn data distributions without explicitly defining a density function [3,5,7]. However, these deep models are either limited to generating small graphs with less than thirty nodes [18,25], or to generating specific types of graphs such as molecular graphs [5,30]. More importantly, the overarching drawback of all these deep generative models is that they are unconditioned, which severely limits their applicability to real-world tasks.

To further strengthen the power of graph generative models, Fan and Huang [7] proposed a conditioned model, which can generate graphs conditioned on discrete labels based on the conditional GAN frameworks [19,20]. However, this approach cannot be applied to circumstances where we want to generate graphs conditioned on another graph, which the motivating case for graph evolution and graph transformation. Also Jin et al. [12] proposed a model with the junction tree encoder-decoder framework for graph to graph transformation. However, they only target the task of molecular optimization. We largely expand the applications of conditioned graph generative model to various interesting problems for graph transformation, such as predicting the graph evolution in space (e.g., how ego-networks would look if expanded to a larger radius) and predicting graph evolution in time (forecasting the changes of dynamic graphs).

3   Attention-Based Graph Evolution Model

We define the prediction of graph evolution as taking an existing *source* graph with nodes (with or without label) as input and predicting, or generating, a transformed version of the graph, or *target* graph. The transformation can represent change over time in a dynamic graph, or expansion in space, such as how ego networks change as we expand out to more steps. Many powerful graph generation models are autoregressive, meaning they generate graphs by sequentially adding new nodes and evaluating relevant possible edges [18,31]. We also adopt this approach and further incorporate an attention-based transformer [27] to process a source graph. We use an attention mechanism instead of a graph convolutional network [14] because attention models can overcome depth limitations of GCNs. Therefore, they can learn more powerful embeddings based on global context.

We model the graph generation procedure as a sequential problem by adding new nodes one-at-a-time. Many other graph generative models such as GraphRNN [31] and DeepGMG [18] also use this same procedural structure; however, they all suffer from efficiency bottlenecks since the sequential procedure prohibits parallelization within instances during the training procedure. This drawback limits their applications on large graphs, especially for DeepGMG, which can only be applied to graphs with less than 30 nodes. To avoid these issues for large graphs with long sequences, we adopt the transformer framework, which instead processes the nodes ordered in a sequence in parallel while using the attention mechanism to incorporate information from all other nodes—even those far away in the sequence. By processing the nodes in parallel, we also significantly shorten the training time, making it much faster than other models.

The architecture of AGE is illustrated in Fig. 1. As in the standard transformer framework, AGE consists of two main components: an encoder E and a decoder D. The encoder learns hidden representations $\boldsymbol{H}_s$ of source graphs through a multi-head attention mechanism (where N is the number of identical layers, we set $N = 6$ in the experiments). The decoder, which is an autoregressive model, then sequentially generates one new node at a time, with possible edges connecting to existing nodes (i.e., the nodes in source graphs and the ones generated previously) and also learns a hidden representations of the target graph $\boldsymbol{H}_t$. In our model, a graph is represented as $G = (\boldsymbol{F}, \boldsymbol{A}, \boldsymbol{L})$ where $\boldsymbol{F}$ is the feature matrix of nodes in source graphs (if one is given), $\boldsymbol{A}$ is the adjacency matrix of source graphs, and $\boldsymbol{L}$ is the label matrix of the nodes in the graph (if labels are available). Among these three components, the adjacency matrix is essential. In some settings, we can leave out the features and labels if we do not have this information. The goal of AGE is therefore to learn a mapping from a source graph G_{sou} to a target graph G_{tar}.

3.1 Self Attention

In AGE, the encoder and the decoder each have their own self-attention block, which is designed to learn high-level node representations based on other nodes within the same graph. In the encoder, the representation of node i in source graphs is updated based on the following rule:

$$h_i^{t+1} = h_i^t + \sigma(\sum_{j=1}^{N_s} a_{i,j}^t \times \boldsymbol{W}_s^s h_j^t), \tag{1}$$

where $a_{i,j}$ is the normalized weights the model learns between node v_i and v_j, h_i is the hidden node feature of node i, N_s is the number of nodes in the source graph, σ is a nonlinear activation and $\boldsymbol{W}_s^s$ is the linear transformation where the weights are learnable parameters separately instantiated for each attention step in the model. The edge weights between two nodes are computed based on the attention mechanism:

$$e_{i,j}^{t+1} = \text{Attention}(\boldsymbol{W}_s \boldsymbol{h}_j^{t+1}, \boldsymbol{W}_s' \boldsymbol{h}_i^{t+1}), \quad a_{i,j}^{t+1} = \frac{\exp(e_{i,j}^{t+1})}{\sum_{k=1}^{N_s} \exp(e_{k,j}^{t+1})}, \qquad (2)$$

where $a_{i,j}$ is the normalized attention weight of $e_{i,j}$, which is the attention weight of edge from node i to node j, $\boldsymbol{W}_s$ and $\boldsymbol{W}_s'$ are linear transformations.

3.2   Source-Target Attention

To learn the correlations between the nodes in source graph and the ones to be generated by decoder, we apply a source-target (S-T) attention block after the self-attention operations. The representation of a predicted node j in generated graph is updated based on the learned embeddings of all nodes in the source graph using the following rule:

$$\boldsymbol{h}_j = \boldsymbol{h}_j + \sigma \left(\sum_{i=1}^{N_s} a_{i,j} \times \boldsymbol{W}_s^t \boldsymbol{h}_i \right), \qquad (3)$$

where σ is a nonlinear activation function, $\boldsymbol{W}_s^t$ is a learnable linear transformation and $a_{i,j}$ is the normalized weights the model learned between node v_i and v_j. The edge weights between two nodes in different graphs are typically calculated in the same way as shown in Eq. 2.

3.3   Encoder

In AGE, the encoder takes in a source graph G_{sou} represented by its initial representations $G_{\text{sou}} = [\boldsymbol{A}_s; \boldsymbol{F}_s]$ (we can leave out $\boldsymbol{F}_s$ if it is not given) and maps it to a high-level embedding. Here $\boldsymbol{A}_s$ and $\boldsymbol{F}_s$ are the adjacency matrix and the feature matrix of the source graph, where the nodes are arranged in a breadth-first-search (BFS) ordering. We concatenate the feature matrix if we have one. When available, we can use features to generate new node features in addition to the graph structure. In our experiments, we focus on undirected, unweighted graphs where the adjacency matrix $\boldsymbol{A}$ is a symmetric binary matrix with each element represents the connectivity of a pair of nodes, but our approach can be easily extended to both directed and weighted graphs.

We use a fixed maximum number of nodes, N_s for the source graph and N_t for the target graph. AGE can learn about and generate structures with various sizes smaller than these maximums by ignoring isolated nodes in the generated graph. We also define a fixed minimum number of nodes for both source and target graphs to ensure that the input graph is not empty, and to ensure that there are some differences between the source and target graphs.

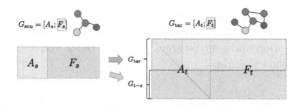

Fig. 2. Data construction for graph evolution in space. The graph and matrix on the left represents the input source graph, which contains a portion of the full target graph on the right. The full target graph contains the adjacency and feature matrices of the source graph in this setting.

3.4 Decoder

The decoder is composed of several stacked attention modules that alternate self-attention and source-target attention layers. The input for the decoder includes two parts: the target graphs G_{tar} and the learned embeddings $\boldsymbol{H}_s$ of the source graph (provided by the encoder). The target graph G_{tar} is represented by the shifted node representations (shifted to the right by one position): $G_{\text{tar}} = [\boldsymbol{A}_t; \boldsymbol{F}_t]$ (leaving out $\boldsymbol{F}_t$ if it is not given), with a start token and an end token filled at the beginning and appended to the end to ensure that the decoder predicts the next node based on the previously generated set. Like the source graph, the nodes in the target graph are also arranged in a breadth-first-search (BFS) ordering at training time, and the model is expected to learn to generate BFS orders.

Given $\boldsymbol{H}_s$, the autoregressive decoder generates an output sequence of nodes one at a time, where each step is also conditioned on the previously generated nodes. The decoder maps the embedding to the space of adjacency matrices and space of label matrices (if the data has label information) to reconstruct the generated graphs. We use a generator which is a combination of a linear transformation and the sigmoid activation function to map $\boldsymbol{H}_t$ to the adjacency matrix $\hat{\boldsymbol{A}}_t$ and we use a classifier which is a combination of a linear transformation and the softmax activation function to map $\boldsymbol{H}_t$ to the label vector $\hat{\boldsymbol{L}}_t$:

$$\hat{\boldsymbol{A}}_t = \text{sigmoid}(\boldsymbol{W}_g \boldsymbol{H}_t); \quad \hat{\boldsymbol{L}}_t = \text{softmax}(\boldsymbol{W}_c \boldsymbol{H}_t). \tag{4}$$

For the predicted adjacency matrix, we use the binary cross-entropy loss function to measure the differences:

$$L_{\text{adj}} = -\sum_{i=1}^{N}\sum_{j=1}^{N} \boldsymbol{A}_{ij} \log(\hat{\boldsymbol{A}}_{ij}) + (1 - \boldsymbol{A}_{ij})\log(1 - (\hat{\boldsymbol{A}}_{ij})). \tag{5}$$

Moreover, if the data has the label information, we also added the loss on labels based on label smoothing using the KL divergence loss.

4 Experiments

In this section, we compare AGE with other graph generation methods on various conditioned graph generation problems to demonstrate its wide applicability.

In the following experiments, we extract 70% of the data as training set, 20% for the validation set and 10% for the test sets. We used six attention layers ($N = 6$) for both self-attention and source-target attention block and within each, we set the number of heads to eight.

Baselines. As we mentioned before, some other methods have been proposed to generate graphs using deep models. However, few of them can condition on existing graphs for general tasks. Therefore, we compare AGE against two categories of other relevant models. The first set consists of methods that can (or can be modified to) generate graphs conditionally, such as the Erdös-Rényi model (E-R) and the Barabási-Albert (B-A) model. These generative models iteratively grow a graph, so they can start from an existing graph. The second set of more recent methods are unconditional graph generation models, such as the mixed-membership stochastic block models (MMSB), DeepGMG and GraphRNN, which include state-of-the-art deep generative models. Notice that due to the computational complexity of the DeepGMG model, we only perform experiments with it on small graphs. In our experiments, we train these models directly on the target graphs without the source graphs.

Evaluation Metrics. We evaluate the generated graphs in two modes. First, we evaluate whether the distribution of generated target graphs is realistic, which captures how well the generative model captures variation in generated graphs. We compute the distances of the distributions of generated graphs and the target graphs using *maximum mean discrepancy* (MMD) [11], following the evaluation procedure used by You et al. [31]. We compute MMD for four graph statistics: degree distribution, clustering coefficient distribution, node-label distribution (if labels are unavailable, the metric "MMD_label" will be listed as N/A), and average orbit count statistics. A model that faithfully captures the conditional distribution over target graphs should have low MMD with the set of true target graphs. Secondly, we compute the similarity between the generated graph and the true target graph for each source graph. This metric evaluates the performance of conditional generation. We calculate the graph similarities using three graph kernels: the shortest path kernel [4] (GK_st), the graphlet sampling kernel [24] (GK_gs), and the SVM-θ kernel [13] (GK_svm). A good conditional graph generator should generate graphs with high similarity to the true target graphs.

4.1   Graph Evolution in Space

Our first evaluation setting considers the graph evolution problem in space. In real-world networks, graph data is collected by subsampling from larger graphs. Due to resource constraints, data collection may not gather as large subsamples as needed. A generative model that can conditionally add nodes in a manner consistent with how graphs grow as one expands the subsample could enable larger analyses of semi-synthetic networks.

Table 1. Comparison of AGE and other generative models on graph evolution in space using MMD evaluation metrics and graph kernel similarities.

	Cora_small							Citeseer						
	Distribution distance				Graph similarity			Distribution distance				Graph similarity		
	Degree	Clustering	Orbit	Label	GK$_{st}$	GK$_{gs}$	GK$_{svm}$	Degree	Clustering	Orbit	Label	GK$_{st}$	GK$_{gs}$	GK$_{svm}$
E-R	0.33	0.53	0.11	N/A	0.77	0.74	0.93	0.66	0.62	0.21	N/A	0.72	0.74	0.96
B-A	0.35	0.40	0.22	N/A	0.71	0.50	0.53	0.14	0.29	0.14	N/A	0.80	0.78	0.91
MMSB	0.09	0.53	0.14	0.16	0.93	**0.85**	0.98	0.24	1.01	0.15	0.09	0.93	0.84	0.98
DeepGMG	0.37	0.54	0.06	N/A	0.88	0.79	0.90	–	–	–	–	–	–	–
GraphRNN	0.08	0.34	0.09	N/A	0.91	0.76	0.94	0.03	0.23	0.03	N/A	0.86	0.81	0.95
AGE	**0.01**	**0.04**	**0.01**	**0.01**	**0.94**	**0.85**	**0.99**	**0.01**	**0.01**	**0.02**	**0.01**	**0.94**	**0.85**	**0.99**

Datasets. We test this problem setting on citation networks. The problem is to predict the expansion of ego networks with farther-hop neighbors. We used the Cora and Citeseer datasets [23]. We evaluated our models with different graph sizes. For small datasets (Cora_small and Citeseer_small), we extract one-hop ($G_{sou} = G_1 = \{V_1, E_1\}$) and two-hop ($G_{tar} = G_2 = \{V_2, E_2\}$) ego networks with $5 \leq |V_1| \leq 20$ and $30 \leq |V_2| \leq 50$ as the source and target graphs. For the large datasets (Cora and Citeseer), we extract two-hop ($G_{sou} = G_2 = \{V_2, E_2\}$) and three-hop ($G_{tar} = G_3 = \{V_3, E_3\}$) ego networks with $10 \leq |V_2| \leq 50$ and $40 \leq |V_3| \leq 170$ as the source and target graphs. Data construction for this problem is illustrated in Fig. 2. The training data consists of graph pairs extracted from the datasets. The source graph G_{sou} is the i-hop ego network where the initial embeddings is constructed by concatenating the adjacency matrix A_s and the feature matrix F_s (if F_s is given). The target graphs G_{tar} are the $(i + 1)$-hop ego networks of the same node v where the initial embeddings is constructed by concatenating the adjacency matrix A_t and the feature matrix F_t.

Results are listed in Table 1. (In all tables, values are rounded to two decimal places.) The metrics indicate that AGE is a strong graph generator in both its ability to mimic graph distributions and match the target graphs. Considering the evaluation of the distance between the distributions of generated graphs and target graphs, AGE achieves the best scores. AGE scores less than 0.1 MMD on all cases, with at least a 30% decrease compared to the second best method, GraphRNN on two datasets with different graph sizes. This result corroborates that, as a graph generative model, AGE can generate realistic graphs that appear to be from the same distribution as the true target graphs. Moreover, considering how well generated graphs match the specific target graphs, we also calculate the graph similarities between the generated graphs and the target graphs. The kernel similarity scores are normalized, so they range from 0 to 1. The graphs AGE generates consistently have the best similarity scores.

4.2 Graph Evolution in Time

Many graph generation methods are designed for static graphs. However in practice, many networks are not static. Instead, they change and evolve over time, with the addition of new nodes and edges, such as in citation networks and collaboration networks, and also with the deletion of existing nodes and edges, such as in computer networks and social networks.

Table 2. Comparison of AGE and other generative models on graph evolution in time using MMD evaluation metrics and graph kernel similarities.

	Facebook-friend							Cit-HepPh						
	Distribution distance				Graph similarity			Distribution distance				Graph similarity		
	Degree	Clustering	Orbit	Label	GK_{st}	GK_{gs}	GK_{svm}	Degree	Clustering	Orbit	Label	GK_{st}	GK_{gs}	GK_{svm}
E-R	0.54	1.25	0.32	–	0.50	0.55	0.98	0.43	1.15	0.27	–	0.55	0.56	0.93
B-A	0.49	1.08	0.34	–	0.78	0.85	0.78	0.43	0.65	0.16	–	0.71	0.85	0.94
MMSB	**0.09**	0.53	**0.14**	–	0.89	0.85	0.98	0.19	1.20	0.14	–	0.84	0.59	0.99
GraphRNN	0.17	0.18	0.21	–	0.76	0.64	0.95	**0.08**	0.81	0.08	–	0.86	0.69	0.92
AGE	**0.09**	**0.01**	0.19	–	**0.93**	**0.88**	**0.99**	0.10	**0.01**	**0.04**	–	**0.94**	**0.89**	**0.99**

	Bitcoin-OTC							Cit-HepTh_small						
	Distribution distance				Graph similarity			Distribution distance				Graph similarity		
	Degree	Clustering	Orbit	Label	GK_{st}	GK_{gs}	GK_{svm}	Degree	Clustering	Orbit	Label	GK_{st}	GK_{gs}	GK_{svm}
E-R	0.63	1.12	0.21	N/A	0.57	0.43	0.98	0.33	0.81	0.22	–	0.64	0.24	0.93
B-A	0.40	0.46	0.14	N/A	0.68	0.90	0.95	0.37	0.71	0.28	–	0.63	0.57	0.86
MMSB	0.30	1.17	0.12	0.15	0.80	0.59	0.98	0.28	0.83	0.42	–	0.82	0.36	0.98
DeepGMG	–	–	–	–	–	–	–	0.12	0.68	0.20	–	0.93	0.56	0.92
GraphRNN	0.16	0.43	0.20	N/A	0.84	0.64	0.94	0.05	0.27	0.07	–	0.96	0.80	0.95
AGE	**0.08**	**0.04**	**0.10**	**0.01**	**0.97**	**0.92**	**0.99**	**0.04**	**0.01**	**0.04**	–	**0.99**	**0.94**	**0.99**

Datasets. For this task, we evaluate AGE on three datasets: the Facebook Friendship Networks [28], the Bitcoin Networks [15], and two citation networks in Physics: cit-HepPh and cit-HepTh [8]. We extract two-hop ($G_2 = \{V_2, E_2\}$) ego networks with $30 \leq |V_2| \leq 120$ (or $20 \leq |V_2| \leq 50$ for _small data) at time t as the source graphs and the two-hop ego networks of the same node at time $t+1$ as the target graphs. Here, we have $G_2^t \in G_2^{t+1}$, and the problem is to model how networks evolve (or grow) with actual time.

We compare AGE with other graph generative models and the results are shown in Table 2. The evaluation results show that AGE can accurately model the graph evolution or growth over time. We compute the distance between the distributions of generated graphs and target graphs, and, as before, AGE achieves the best scores among all the generative models regarding the realism of the generated graphs. Again, this is strong evidence that AGE can generate realistic graphs that appear to be from the same distribution of the target graphs. Considering the graph similarities between the generated graphs by all models and the target graphs, Table 2 shows that among all models, AGE is the only one that can reach similarity 0.9 for all three graph kernels, while the other methods cannot consistently score high across different kernels. This suggests some aspect of graph similarity is not satisfied by these other generation procedures. These results again demonstrate that AGE represents a significant step in our ability to model the evolution of graphs in time.

4.3   Graph Evolution in Time with Deletion

To evaluate the performance of AGE on modeling the evolution of graphs with deletion, study cases where the source graphs evolves with not only addition of new nodes and edges, but also allows the deletion of existing nodes and edges.

Table 3. Comparison of AGE and other generative models on graph evolution in time with deletion using MMD evaluation metrics and graph kernel similarities.

| | Oregon | | | | | | |
| | Distribution distance | | | | Graph similarity | | |
	Degree	Clustering	Orbit	Label	GK_{st}	GK_{gs}	GK_{svm}
E-R	0.51	0.37	0.25	–	0.55	0.63	0.96
B-A	0.11	0.35	0.21	–	0.85	0.98	0.92
MMSB	0.54	0.39	0.29	–	0.71	0.45	0.93
GraphRNN	0.14	0.12	0.20	–	0.91	0.88	0.93
AGE	**0.01**	**0.01**	**0.01**	–	**0.99**	**0.99**	**0.99**

Datasets. We use the Computer Network dataset [17], which is a network describing peering information inferred from Oregon route-views with nine different timestamps in total. We extract two-hop ($G_2 = \{V_2, E_2\}$) ego networks with $30 \leq |V_2| \leq 120$ at the first and last timestamp, respectively, as the source and target graphs. In this experiment, we focus on the more difficult problem of modeling the evolution of graphs with deletion. The difference with the second experiment is that in this case, the condition $G_2^t \subseteq G_2^{t+1}$ does not hold anymore.

We compare AGE with other graph generative models, listing results in Table 3. The evaluation results show that, even for this more complex problem, AGE still maintains a high-level performance compared to the other generative models in terms of both the realism of generated graphs and the similarity to the target ones. Therefore, together with the second experiment, we find that AGE is not only able to learn graph evolution through growth, but also the more complex setting of volatile evolution.

5   Conclusion

In this work, we proposed attention-based graph evolution (AGE), a conditioned generative model for graphs based on the attention mechanism, which can model graph evolution in both space and time. AGE is capable of generating graphs conditioned on existing graphs. Our model can be useful for many applications in various domains, such as for predicting information propagation in social networks, disease control for healthcare, and traffic prediction in road networks. We model graph generation as a sequential problem, yet we are able to train AGE models in parallel by adopting the transformer framework. Our experimental results demonstrate that AGE is a powerful and efficient conditioned graph generative model, which outperforms all the other state-of-the-art deep generative models for graphs. In our several experiments on various datasets, AGE is to be able to adapt to various kinds of evolution or transformations between graphs, and it performs consistently well in terms of both the realism of its generated graphs and the similarity to ground-truth target graphs. Finally, AGE has a flexible structure that can be used to generate graphs with or without features and labels. This flexibility thus enables a wider range of applications by allowing it to model many forms of graph evolution.

References

1. Airoldi, E.M., Blei, D.M., Fienberg, S.E., Xing, E.P.: Mixed membership stochastic blockmodels. J. Mach. Learn. Res. **9**(Sep), 1981–2014 (2008)
2. Albert, R., Barabási, A.L.: Statistical mechanics of complex networks. Rev. Mod. Phys. **74**(1), 47 (2002)
3. Bojchevski, A., Shchur, O., Zügner, D., Günnemann, S.: NetGAN: generating graphs via random walks. In: International Conference on Learning Representations (2018)
4. Borgwardt, K.M., Kriegel, H.P.: Shortest-path kernels on graphs. In: Fifth IEEE International Conference on Data Mining, pp. 8–pp, IEEE (2005)
5. De Cao, N., Kipf, T.: MolGAN: an implicit generative model for small molecular graphs. arXiv preprint arXiv:1805.11973 (2018)
6. Erdös, P., Rényi, A.: On random graphs I. Publicationes Math. Debrecen **6**, 290–297 (1959)
7. Fan, S., Huang, B.: Labeled graph generative adversarial networks. arXiv preprint arXiv:1906.03220 (2019)
8. Gehrke, J., Ginsparg, P., Kleinberg, J.: Overview of the 2003 KDD cup. ACM SIGKDD Explor. Newsl. **5**(2), 149–151 (2003)
9. Goldenberg, A., Zheng, A.X., Fienberg, S.E., Airoldi, E.M.: A survey of statistical network models. Found. Trends Mach. Learn. **2**(2), 129–233 (2010)
10. Goodfellow, I., et al.: Generative adversarial nets. In: Advances in Neural Information Processing Systems, pp. 2672–2680 (2014)
11. Gretton, A., Borgwardt, K.M., Rasch, M.J., Schölkopf, B., Smola, A.: A kernel two-sample test. J. Mach. Learn. Res. **13**(Mar), 723–773 (2012)
12. Jin, W., Yang, K., Barzilay, R., Jaakkola, T.: Learning multimodal graph-to-graph translation for molecular optimization. In: International Conference on Learning Representations (2019)
13. Johansson, F., Jethava, V., Dubhashi, D., Bhattacharyya, C.: Global graph kernels using geometric embeddings. In: Proceedings of the International Conference on Machine Learning (2014)
14. Kipf, T.N., Welling, M.: Semi-supervised classification with graph convolutional networks. In: International Conference on Learning Representations (ICLR) (2017)
15. Kumar, S., Hooi, B., Makhija, D., Kumar, M., Faloutsos, C., Subrahmanian, V.: REV2: fraudulent user prediction in rating platforms. In: Proceedings of the ACM International Conferene on Web Search and Data Mining, pp. 333–341 (2018)

16. Leskovec, J., Chakrabarti, D., Kleinberg, J., Faloutsos, C., Ghahramani, Z.: Kronecker graphs: an approach to modeling networks. J. Mach. Learn. Res. **11**(Feb), 985–1042 (2010)
17. Leskovec, J., Kleinberg, J., Faloutsos, C.: Graphs over time: densification laws, shrinking diameters and possible explanations. In: Proceedings of the Eleventh ACM SIGKDD International Conference on Knowledge Discovery in Data Mining, pp. 177–187. ACM (2005)
18. Li, Y., Vinyals, O., Dyer, C., Pascanu, R., Battaglia, P.: Learning deep generative models of graphs. arXiv preprint arXiv:1803.03324 (2018)
19. Mirza, M., Osindero, S.: Conditional generative adversarial nets. ArXiv abs/1411.1784 (2014)
20. Odena, A., Olah, C., Shlens, J.: Conditional image synthesis with auxiliary classifier GANs. In: Proceedings of the International Conference on Machine Learning, pp. 2642–2651 (2017)
21. Robins, G., Pattison, P., Kalish, Y., Lusher, D.: An introduction to exponential random graph (p*) models for social networks. Soc. Netw. **29**(2), 173–191 (2007)
22. Samanta, B., De, A., Ganguly, N., Gomez-Rodriguez, M.: Designing random graph models using variational autoencoders with applications to chemical design. arXiv preprint arXiv:1802.05283 (2018)
23. Sen, P., Namata, G., Bilgic, M., Getoor, L., Galligher, B., Eliassi-Rad, T.: Collective classification in network data. AI Mag. **29**(3), 93 (2008)
24. Shervashidze, N., Vishwanathan, S., Petri, T., Mehlhorn, K., Borgwardt, K.: Efficient graphlet kernels for large graph comparison. In: Artificial Intelligence and Statistics, pp. 488–495 (2009)
25. Simonovsky, M., Komodakis, N.: GraphVAE: towards generation of small graphs using variational autoencoders. arXiv preprint arXiv:1802.03480 (2018)
26. Snijders, T.A., Pattison, P.E., Robins, G.L., Handcock, M.S.: New specifications for exponential random graph models. Sociol. Methodol. **36**(1), 99–153 (2006)
27. Vaswani, A., et al.: Attention is all you need. In: Advances in neural information processing systems, pp. 5998–6008 (2017)
28. Viswanath, B., Mislove, A., Cha, M., Gummadi, K.P.: On the evolution of user interaction in Facebook. In: Proceedings of the Workshop on Online Social Networks, pp. 37–42 (2009)
29. Watts, D.J., Strogatz, S.H.: Collective dynamics of small-world networks. Nature **393**(6684), 440 (1998)
30. You, J., Liu, B., Ying, R., Pande, V., Leskovec, J.: Graph convolutional policy network for goal-directed molecular graph generation. In: Advances in Neural Information Processing Systems (2018)
31. You, J., Ying, R., Ren, X., Hamilton, W., Leskovec, J.: GraphRNN: generating realistic graphs with deep auto-regressive models. In: International Conference on Machine Learning, pp. 5694–5703 (2018)

Quality-Aware Streaming Network Embedding with Memory Refreshing

Hsi-Wen Chen[1], Hong-Han Shuai[2], Sheng-De Wang[1], and De-Nian Yang[3,4(✉)]

[1] Department of Electrical Engineering, National Taiwan University, Taipei, Taiwan
{r06921045,sdwang}@ntu.edu.tw
[2] Department of Electrical and Computer Engineering,
National Chiao Tung University, Hsinchu, Taiwan
hhshuai@nctu.edu.tw
[3] Institute of Information Science, Academia Sinica, Taipei, Taiwan
dnyang@iis.sinica.edu.tw
[4] Research Center for Information Technology Innovation (CITI), Academia Sinica,
Taipei, Taiwan

Abstract. Static network embedding has been widely studied to convert sparse structure information into a dense latent space. However, the majority of real networks are continuously evolving, and deriving the whole embedding for every snapshot is computationally intensive. To avoid recomputing the embedding over time, we explore streaming network embedding for two reasons: 1) to efficiently identify the nodes required to update the embeddings under multi-type network changes, and 2) to carefully revise the embeddings to maintain transduction over different parts of the network. Specifically, we propose a new representation learning framework, named *Graph Memory Refreshing (GMR)*, to preserve both global types of structural information efficiently. We prove that GMR maintains the consistency of embeddings (crucial for network analysis) for isomorphic structures better than existing approaches. Experimental results demonstrate that GMR outperforms the baselines with much smaller time.

Keywords: Network embedding · Streaming data mining

1 Introduction

Low-dimensional vector representation of nodes in large-scale networks has been widely applied to a variety of domains, such as social media [13], molecular structure [7], and transportation [9]. Previous approaches, e.g., DeepWalk [13], LINE [16], and SDNE [20], are designed to reduce the sparse structure information to a dense latent space for node classification [13], link prediction [16], and network visualization [21]. However, the above embedding schemes were not designed for evolutionary networks. Current popular networks tend to evolve with time, e.g., the average number of friends increases from 155 in 2016 and to

© Springer Nature Switzerland AG 2020
H. W. Lauw et al. (Eds.): PAKDD 2020, LNAI 12084, pp. 448–461, 2020.
https://doi.org/10.1007/978-3-030-47426-3_35

338 in 2018 [8]. Ephemeral social networks, like Snapchat for short-term conversations, may disappear within weeks. However, retraining the whole embedding for each snapshot is computationally intensive for a massive network. Therefore, streaming network embedding is a desirable option to quickly update and generate new embeddings in a minimum amount of time.

Different from dynamic network embeddings [12,21] that analyze a sequence of networks to capture the temporal patterns, *streaming network embedding*[1] aims to update the network embedding from the changed part of the network to find the new embedding. Efficient streaming network embedding has the following four main challenges. 1) *Multi-type change.* Dynamic changes of networks with insertions and deletions of nodes and edges are usually frequent and complex. It is thus important to derive the new embedding in minimum time to timely reflect the new network status. 2) *Evaluation of affected nodes.* Updating the embeddings of only the nodes neighboring to the changed part ignores the ripple effect on the remaining nodes. It is crucial to identify the nodes required to update the embeddings and ensure that the nodes with similar structures share similar embeddings. 3) *Transduction.* When a network significantly changes, it is difficult to keep the local proximity between the changed part and the remaining part of the network. It is also important to reflect the change in the global structure. 4) *Quality guarantee.* For streaming embeddings based on neural networks (usually regarded as a black box), it is challenging to provide theoretical guarantees about the embedding quality.

To effectively address the above challenges, this paper proposes a new representation learning approach, named *Graph Memory Refreshing (GMR)*. GMR first derives the new embedding of the changed part by decomposing the loss function of Skip-Gram to support multi-type changes. It carefully evaluates the ripple-effect area and ensures the correctness by proposing a globally structure-aware selecting strategy, named *hierarchical addressing*, to efficiently identify and update those affected nodes with beam search to avoid the overfitting problem. To effectively support streaming data, our idea is to interpret the update of embeddings as the memory networks with two controllers, a *refreshing gate* and *percolation gate*, to tailor the embeddings from the structural aspect and maintain the transduction. GMR then updates the embeddings according to the streaming information of the new network and the stored features (i.e., memory) of the current network to avoid recomputing the embedding of the whole network. Moreover, GMR aims to both preserve the global structural information and maintain the embeddings of isomorphic structures, i.e., ensuring that the nodes with similar local structures share similar embeddings. This property is essential to ensure the correctness of network analysis based on network embeddings [18]. We theoretically prove that GMR preserves the consistency of embeddings for isomorphic structures better than that of the existing approaches. The contributions of this paper are summarized as follows.

---

[1] In *streaming* data mining [10], the incoming data stream, instead of the whole dataset, is employed to update the previous mining results efficiently.

- GMR explores streaming network embedding with quality guarantees. The hierarchical addressing, refreshing gate, and percolation gate efficiently find and update the affected nodes under multi-type changes.
- We prove that GMR embedding preserves isomorphic structures better than the existing approaches. According to our literature review, this is the first theoretical analysis for streaming network embedding.
- Experimental results show that GMR outperforms the baselines by at least 10.5% for link prediction and node classification with a much shorter time.

2   Related Work

Static network embedding has attracted a wide range of attention. Laplacian Eigenmaps [1] and IsoMaps [17] first constructed the adjacency matrix and then solved the matrix factorization, but the adjacency matrix was not scalable for massive networks. After Skip-Gram [11] was demonstrated to be powerful for representation learning, DeepWalk [13] and node2vec [5] employed random walks to learn network embedding, while LINE [16] and SDNE [20] were able to preserve the first-order and second-order proximity. GraphSAGE [6] and GAT [19] generated node representations in an inductive manner, by mapping and aggregating node features from the neighborhood.

In addition, a recent line of research proposed to learn the embeddings from a sequence of networks over time for finding temporal behaviors [12,21]. However, these approaches focused on capturing the temporal changes rather than the efficiency since they recomputed the embeddings of the whole network, instead of updating only the changed part. Another line of recent research studied the dynamic embedding without retraining. However, the SVD-based approach [22] was more difficult to support large-scale networks according to [5]. Besides, [10] only supported the edge insertion and ignored edge deletion, whereas the consistency of the embeddings for globally isomorphic structures was not ensured. Compared with the above research and [3], the proposed GMR is the only one that provides a theoretical guarantee on the embedding quality (detailed later). It also more accurately preserves both the global structural information and the consistency of the embeddings.

3   Problem Formulation

In this section, we present the definitions for streaming network embeddings.

Definition 1 (*Streaming Networks*). A dynamic network $\mathcal{G}$ is a sequence of networks $\mathcal{G} = \{G_1, \cdots, G_T\}$ over time, where $G_t = (V_t, E_t)$ is the network snapshot at timestamp t. $\Delta G_t = (\Delta V_t, \Delta E_t)$ represents the streaming network with the changed part ΔV_t and ΔE_t as the sets of vertices and edges inserted or deleted between t and $t + 1$.

Definition 2 (*Streaming Network Embeddings*). Let $z_{i,t}$ denote the streaming network embedding that preserves the structural property of $v_i \in G_t$ at timestamp t. The streaming network embeddings are derived by $\Phi^s = (\phi_1^s, \cdots, \phi_{t+1}^s, \cdots, \phi_T^s)$, where ϕ_{t+1}^s updates the node embedding $z_{i,t+1}$ at timestamp $t+1$ according to $\mathbf{z}_t$ and ΔG_t, i.e., $z_{i,t+1} = \phi_{t+1}^s(\mathbf{z}_t, \Delta G_t)$, where $\mathbf{z}_t = \{z_{i,t} | \forall v_i \in V_t\}$.

In other words, the inputs of the streaming network function are the embedding in the current time and the changed part of the network. In contrast, for [12,21], given a dynamic network $\mathcal{G}$, the embedding is derived by a sequence of functions $\Phi = (\phi_1, \cdots, \phi_{t+1}, \cdots, \phi_T)$, where ϕ_{t+1} maps the node v_i to the d-dimensional embedding $z_{i,t+1}$ at timestamp $t+1$, i.e., $z_{i,t+1} = \phi_{t+1}(v_i, G_{t+1})$. Therefore, the inputs are the whole networks in the current and next time. In the following, we present the problem studied in this paper.

Definition 3 (*Quality-aware Multi-type Streaming Network Embeddings*). Given a streaming network with ΔV_t and ΔE_t as the sets of the vertices and edges inserted or deleted between t and $t+1$, the goal is to find the streaming network embedding and derive the corresponding embedding quality to ensure that the nodes with similar structures share similar embeddings.

Later in Sect. 5, we formally present and theoretically analyze the quality of the embedding with a new metric, named *isomorphic retaining score*. Moreover, we prove that the proposed GMR better preserves the structures than other state-of-the-art methods in Theorems 1.

4   Graph Memory Refreshing

In this section, we propose Graph Memory Refreshing (GMR) to support multi-type embedding updates, to identify the affected nodes required to update the embeddings by hierarchical addressing, and to ensure that the nodes with similar structures share similar embeddings. To effectively support streaming data, we leverage the controllers (refreshing and percolation gates) of *memory networks* [4] to refresh the memory (update the embedding) according to the current state (the current embedding) and new input (streaming network).

4.1   Multi-type Embedding Updating

For each node v_i, the Skip-Gram model predicts the context nodes $v_j \in N(v_i)$ and maximizes the log probability,

$$\sum_{v_i \in V} \sum_{v_j \in N(v_i)} \log p(v_j | v_i). \tag{4.1}$$

However, it is computationally intensive to derive the above probabilities for all nodes. Therefore, the probabilities are approximated by negative sampling [11],

$$\sum_{(v_i, v_j) \in E} \sigma(z_i^T z_j) + \sum_{v_i \in V} \mathbb{E}_{v_j \sim P_N(v_i)}[\sigma(-z_i^T z_j)], \tag{4.2}$$

where $\sigma(x) = 1/(1 + e^{-x})$ is the sigmoid function, z_i and z_j are respectively the embedding vectors of v_i and v_j, and $P_N(v_i)$ is the noise distribution for negative sampling. The two terms respectively model the observed neighborhoods and the negative samples (i.e., node pairs without an edge) drawn from distribution $P_N(v_i)$. However, Eq. (4.2) focuses on only the edge insertion. To support the edge deletion, the second part in Eq. (4.2) is revised to consider unpaired negative samples and the deletion as follows,

$$\sum_{(v_i,v_j)\in E} \sigma(z_i^T z_j) + \sum_{v_i \in V} \mathbb{E}_{v_j \sim P_N(v_i)}[\sigma(-z_i^T z_j)] + \alpha \sum_{(v_i,v_j)\in D} \sigma(-z_i^T z_j), \quad (4.3)$$

where D is the set of deleted edges, and α is required to be set greater than 1 because the samples from D usually provide more information than the unpaired negative samples $P(v_i)$.[2] Note that node deletion is handled by removing all incident edges of a node, while adding a node with new edges is regarded as the edge insertion.[3]

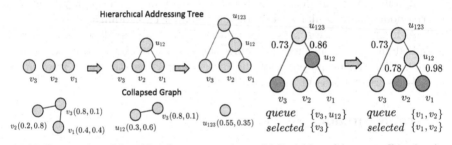

(a) Construction of the addressing tree, $t = 1$.   (b) Searching of the most affected nodes for v_4 on the addressing tree, $t = 2$.

Fig. 1. Example of hierarchical addressing.

4.2   Hierarchical Addressing

For streaming network embedding, previous computationally intensive approaches [4] find the embeddings of *all nodes* by global addressing. A more efficient way is updating only the *neighboring nodes* of the changed part with local addressing [10]. However, the ripple-effect area usually has an arbitrary shape (i.e., including not only the neighboring nodes). Therefore, instead of extracting the neighboring nodes with heuristics, *hierarchical addressing* systematically transforms the original network into a search tree that is aware of the global

---

[2] Equation (4.3) is introduced as the general form for the Skip-Gram model under the multi-type change, and GMR only samples the insertions/deletions from streaming network ΔG_t at time stamp t for updating the embeddings.

[3] The new node embedding is initialized by the average of its neighborhood [10] and then updated by maximizing Eq.(4.3).

structure for the efficient identification of the affected nodes to update their embeddings.

Hierarchical addressing has the following advantages: 1) *Efficient.* It can be regarded as a series of binary classifications (on a tree), whereas global addressing and local addressing belong to multi-class classification (on the candidate list). Therefore, the time complexity to consider each node in ΔV_t is reduced from $O(|V_t|)$ (i.e., pairwise comparison) to $O(k \log(|V_t|))$, where k is the number of search beams (explained later). 2) *Topology-aware.* It carefully examines the graph structure to evaluate the proximity and maintain the isomorphic structure, i.e., ensuring that the nodes with similar structures share similar embeddings. This property is essential for the correctness of network analysis with network embeddings [18].

Specifically, hierarchical addressing first exploits graph coarsening to build an addressing tree for the efficient search of the affected nodes. Graph coarsening includes both first-hop and second-hop collapsing: first-hop collapsing preserves the first-order proximity by merging two adjacent nodes into a supernode; second-hop collapsing aggregates the nodes with a common neighbor into a supernode, where the embedding of the supernode is averaged from its child nodes [2]. Second-hop collapsing is prioritized because it can effectively compress the network into a smaller tree.

The network is accordingly transformed into an addressing tree with each node $v \in V_t$ as a leaf node. Afterward, for each node $v_i \in \Delta V_t$, we search for the node $v_j \in V_t$ sharing the highest similarity with v_i as the first affected node for v_i by comparing their cosine similarity [4] along the addressing tree. For each node in the tree, if the left child node shares a greater similarity to v_i, the search continues on the left subtree; otherwise, it searches the right subtree. The similarity search ends when it reaches the leaf node with the highest similarity to v_i, and any node in V_t (not only the neighbors of v_i) is thereby allowed to be extracted. In other words, hierarchical addressing enables GMR to extract the affected nodes located in different locations of the network (not necessary to be close to v_i), whereas previous approaches [3,10,21] update only the neighboring nodes of v_i. Afterward, hierarchical addressing extracts the top-1 result for all nodes in ΔV_t as the initially affected nodes (more will be included later), where the nodes with the similarity smaller than a threshold h are filtered. To prevent over-fitting in a local minimum, hierarchical addressing can also extract the top-k results at each iteration with the beam search.[4]

Figure 1 presents an example of hierarchical addressing with the dimension of embeddings as 2. At timestamp $t = 1$ (Fig. 1(a)), we construct the addressing tree by first merging nodes v_1 and v_2 into supernode u_{12} through second-hop collapsing. The embedding of u_{12} is $0.5 \cdot (0.4, 0.4) + 0.5 \cdot (0.2, 0.8) = (0.3, 0.6)$. Afterward, v_3 merges u_{12} into u_{123} through first-hop collapsing, and u_{123} is the root of the tree. At $t = 2$ (Fig. 1(b)), if a new node v_4 is linked to v_1 with the

---

[4] For each node, the k search beams iteratively examine their child nodes (e.g., total $2k$ nodes) and maintain only the top-k child nodes with the highest similarity in a queue. Any leaf node reached by a beam will be included in the top-k results.

embedding as $(0.3, 0.2)$, we identify the affected nodes with bream search $(k = 2)$ and start from the root u_{123}. First, we insert v_3 and u_{12} into the search queue with the size as 2 since $k = 2$, to compare the similarity of v_4 with that of v_3 and u_{12}. Both u_{12} and v_3 are then popped out from the queue because v_1 and v_2 have higher similarity i.e., the top-2 results (0.78 and 0.98), compared with 0.73 for v_3.

4.3   Refresh and Percolate

After identifying the nodes required to update the embeddings by hierarchical addressing, a simple approach is to update the embeddings of those affected nodes with a constant shift [6,20]. However, a streaming network with a topology change on only a subset of nodes usually leads to different shifts for the nodes in distinct locations. Moreover, updating only the nodes extracted from hierarchical addressing is insufficient to ensure consistency of embeddings for the nodes with similar structures when the embeddings are tailored independently.

To effectively support streaming data, inspired by the gating mechanism in GRU [4], we parameterize the update of the embedding according to the current embedding and incoming streaming network. Specifically, GMR decomposes the update procedure into two controller gates: a *refreshing gate* g_r and *percolation gate* g_p. For each node v_j selected in hierarchical addressing for each $v_i \in \Delta V_t$, the refreshing gate first updates the embedding of v_j according the new embedding of v_i, and the percolation gate then updates the embedding for every neighbor v_k of v_j from the new embedding of v_j. The refreshing gate quantifies the embedding update for v_j from an incoming stream (i.e., one-to-one update), while the percolation gate transduces the embedding of v_j to its neighborhoods (i.e., one-to-many update) to preserve better local structure. The two gates are the cornerstones to maintain isomorphic structure, as proved later in the Theorem 1.

To update the embeddings of v_j, i.e., updating $z_{j,t+1}$ from $z_{j,t}$, we first define a shared function a_r to find the refreshing coefficient ρ_r, which represents the correlation between the embedding of v_j and the new embedding of v_i, i.e., $\rho_r = a_r(z_{i,t+1}, z_{j,t})$. The refreshing gate selects the correlation function [19] as the shared function a_r to extract the residual relation [19] between the two embeddings, instead of directly adopting a constant shift as was done in previous work. Here $a_r \in \mathbb{R}^{2d}$ is a shift projection, and ρ_r is derived by $a_r^T[z_{i,t+1}||z_{j,t}]$, where $||$ is the vector concatenation operation. After this, we regulate refreshing coefficient ρ_r into $[0, 1]$ by a sigmoid function $g_r = \sigma(\rho_r)$ to provide a non-linear transformation. Therefore, g_r quantifies the extent that $z_{i,t+1}$ affects $z_{j,t}$,

$$z_{j,t+1} \leftarrow g_r z_{i,t+1} + (1 - g_r) z_{j,t}. \tag{4.4}$$

Thereafter, the percolation gate revises the embedding of the neighbor nodes of v_j to ensure the consistency of the embeddings for the nodes with similar structures. The percolation gate learns another sharable vector $a_p \in \mathbb{R}^{2d}$ and

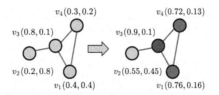

Fig. 2. Example of percolation gate.

finds the percolation coefficient $\rho_p = a_p^T[z_{j,t+1}||z_{k,t}]$, to quantify the extent that v_j affects v_k. Similarly, we regulate ρ_p by $g_p = \sigma(\rho_p)$ to update $z_{k,t}$ as follows,

$$z_{k,t+1} \leftarrow g_p z_{j,t+1} + (1 - g_p)z_{k,t}. \tag{4.5}$$

Therefore, when the refreshing and percolation gates are 0, the streaming network is ignored. In contrast, when both gates become 1, the previous snapshot embedding is dropped accordingly. In summary, the refreshing and percolation gates act as decision makers to learn the impact of the streaming network on different nodes. For the percolation gate, when node v_j is updated, the percolation gate tailors the embedding of each $v_k \in N_1(v_j)$,[5] by evaluating the similarity of v_j and v_k according to the embeddings z_k and z_j. If v_j and v_k share many common neighbors, the percolation value of (v_j, v_k) will increase to draw z_k and z_j closer to each other. The idea is similar for the refreshing gate. Note that a_r and a_p are both differentiable and can be trained in an unsupervised setting by maximize the objective Eq. (4.3). The unsupervised loss can also be replaced or augmented by a task-oriented objective (e.g., cross-entropy loss) when labels are provided. We alternatively update the embeddings (i.e., $z_{i,t}$ and $z_{j,t}$) and the correlation parameters (i.e., a_r and a_p) to achieve better convergence.

Figure 2 illustrates an example of updating the node v_3. After the embedding of v_3 updated from $(0.8, 0.1)$ to $(0.9, 0.1)$, GMR uses the percolation gate to transduce the embedding to the neighborhood nodes (i.e., v_1, v_2, and v_4) to preserve the local structure. Since v_1 shares more common neighbors (v_4) with v_3 than v_2 (none), the values of percolation gate for v_1 and v_2 are 0.8 and 0.5, respectively. The embeddings of node v_1 and v_2 become $(0.76, 0.16) = 0.2 \cdot (0.4, 0.4) + 0.8 \cdot (0.9, 0.1)$ and $(0.55, 0.45) = 0.5 \cdot (0.2, 0.8) + 0.5 \cdot (0.9, 0.1)$ through the percolation gate from v_3, respectively. Therefore, relative distance between $\|z_3 - z_2\|$ and $\|z_3 - z_1\|$ can be maintained.

5   Theoretical Analysis

The quality of network embedding can be empirically evaluated from the experiment of network analysis, e.g., link prediction [16] and node classification [13], since the network embedding algorithm is unsupervised learning without knowing the ground truth. In contrast, when the network analysis task is unknown

---

[5] $N_1(.)$ represents the set of first-hop neighborhoods.

a priori, it is important to theoretically analyze the quality of network embedding. To achieve this goal, we first define the isomorphic pairs and prove that the embeddings of isomorphic pairs are the same in GMR. This property has been regarded as a very important criterion to evaluate the quality of network embedding [18], because the nodes with similar structures are necessary to share similar embeddings. Moreover, the experimental results in Sect. 6 manifest that a higher quality leads to better performance on task-oriented metrics.

Definition 4 (*Isomorphic Pair*). Any two different nodes v_i and v_j form an isomorphic pair if the sets of their first-hop neighbors $N_1(.)$ are the same.

Lemma 1 *If (v_i, v_j) and (v_j, v_k) are both isomorphic pairs, (v_i, v_k) is also an isomorphic pair.*

Proof: According to Definition 4, (v_i, v_j) and (v_j, v_k) are both isomorphic pairs, indicating that $N_1(v_i) = N_1(v_j)$ and $N_1(v_j) = N_1(v_k)$. Therefore, $N_1(v_i)$ is equal to $N_1(v_j)$, and thus (v_i, v_k) is also an isomorphic pair. □

Lemma 2. *The embeddings z_i and z_j are the same after GMR converges if and only if (v_i, v_j) is an isomorphic pair.*

Proof: We first prove the sufficient condition. If (v_i, v_j) is an isomorphic pair with $z_i \neq z_j$, the probability of v_i to predict the context nodes is not to equal to that of v_j (Eq. (4.1)). Therefore, there exists a better solution that makes z_i and z_j be equal, contradicting the condition that the algorithm has converged. For the necessary condition, if $z_i = z_j$ but (v_i, v_j) is not an isomorphic pair, since the probabilities are equal and the algorithm has converged, $N(v_i)$ should be identical to $N(v_j)$ for Eq. (4.1), contradicting that (v_i, v_j) is not an isomorphic pair. The lemma follows. □

As proved in [14], the network embedding algorithms can be unified into the factorization of the affinity matrix. Therefore, nodes with the same first-hop neighborhood have the same embedding when the decomposition ends.

Based on Lemma 2, we define the isomorphic retaining score as follows.

Definition 5 (*Isomorphic Retaining Score*). The isomorphic retaining score, denoted as S_t, is the summation of the cosine similarity over every isomorphic pair in G_t, $S_t \in [-1, 1]$. Specifically,

$$S_t = \frac{1}{|\xi_t|} \sum_{(v_i, v_j) \in \xi_t} s_{ij,t}, \qquad (5.1)$$

where $s_{ij,t}$ is the cosine similarity between $z_{i,t}$ and $z_{j,t}$, and ξ_t is the set of isomorphic pairs in G_t. In other words, the embeddings of any two nodes v_i and v_j with the same structure are more consistent to each other if $s_{ij,t}$ is close to 1 [18]. Experiment results in the next section show that higher isomorphic retaining scores lead to better performance of 1) the AUC score for link prediction and 2) the Macro-F1 score for node classification.

The following theorem proves that GMR retains the isomorphic structure better than other Skip-Gram-based approaches, e.g., [5,13,16], under edge insertion. Afterward, the time complexity analysis is presented.

Theorem 1. *GMR outperforms other Skip-Gram-based models regarding the isomorphic retaining score under edge insertion after each update by gradient descent.*

Proof: Due to the space constraint, Theorem 1 is proved in the online version.[6]

□

Time Complexity. In GMR, the initialization of the addressing tree involves $O(|V_1|)$ time. For each t, GMR first updates the embeddings of ΔV_t in $O(|\Delta V_t| \log(|\Delta V_t|))$ time. After this, hierarchical addressing takes $O(k|\Delta V_t| \log(|V_t|))$ time to identify the affected nodes. Notice that it requires $O(|\Delta V_t| \log(|V_t|))$ time to update the addressing tree. To update the affected nodes, the refreshing and percolation respectively involve $O(1)$ and $O(d_{max})$ time for one affected node, where d_{max} is the maximum node degree of the network. Therefore, updating all the affected nodes requires $O(kd_{max}|\Delta V_t|)$. Therefore, the overall time complexity of GMR is $O(kd_{max}|\Delta V_t| + k|\Delta V_t| \log(|V_t|))$, while retraining the whole network requires $O(|V_t| \log(|V_t|))$ time at each timestamp. Since k is a small constant, $d_{max} \ll |V_t|$, and $|\Delta V_t| \ll |V_t|$, GMR is faster than retraining.

6 Experiments

To evaluate the effectiveness and efficiency of GMR, we compare GMR with the state-of-the-art methods on two tasks, i.e., link prediction and node classification. For the baselines, we compare GMR with 1) FULL, which updates the whole network with DeepWalk [13]; 2) CHANGE [3], which only takes the changed part as the samples with DeepWalk;[7] 3) GraphSAGE [6], which derives the embeddings from graph inductive learning; 4) SDNE [20], which extends the auto-encoder model to generate the embeddings of new nodes from the embeddings of neighbors; 5) CTDNE [12], which performs the biased random walk on the dynamic network;[8] and 6) DNE [3], which updates only one affected node; 7) SLA [10], which handles only node/edge insertion; 8) DHPE [22], which is an SVD method based on matrix perturbation theory. The default α, h, k, d, batch size, and learning rate are 1, 0.8, 3, 64, 16, and 0.001, respectively. Stochastic gradient descent (SGD) with Adagrad is adopted to optimize the loss function.

---

[6] The online version is presented in https://bit.ly/2UUeO7B.

[7] The setting follows OpenNE: https://github.com/thunlp/OpenNE.

[8] For fair comparison, SDNE only takes the adjacency matrix of current stream as the input feature. CTDNE only samples from the latest 50 streams instead of the whole network.

6.1   Link Prediction

For link prediction, three real datasets [15] for streaming networks are evaluated: *Facebook* (63,731 nodes, 1,269,502 edges, and 736,675 timestamps), *Yahoo* (100,001 nodes, 3,179,718 edges, and 1,498,868 timestamps), and *Epinions* (131,828 nodes, 841,372 edges, and 939 timestamps).[9] The concatenated embedding $[z_i \| z_j]$ of pair (v_i, v_j) is employed as the feature to predict the link by logistic regression.[10]

Table 1. Experiment results of link prediction.

	Facebook			Yahoo			Epinions		
	AUC	S	sec	AUC	S	sec	AUC	S	sec
GMR	0.7943	0.94	3325	0.7674	0.93	3456	0.9294	0.92	3507
FULL	0.8004	0 95	66412	0.7641	0.95	72197	0.9512	0.96	61133
CHANGE	0.6926	0.79	2488	0.6326	0.82	2721	0.8233	0.84	2429
GraphSAGE	0.6569	0.77	4094	0.6441	0.79	5117	0.8158	0.85	4588
SDNE	0.6712	0.81	7078	0.6585	0.83	7622	0.8456	0.88	6799
CTDNE	0.7091	0.85	4322	0.6799	0.84	5136	0.8398	0.90	5097
DNE	0.7294	0.87	2699	0.6892	0.86	2843	0.8648	0.92	2613
SLA	0.7148	0.86	2398	0.6910	0.86	2438	0.8598	0.91	2569
DHPE	0.7350	0.88	3571	0.7102	0.88	3543	0.8458	0.90	3913

Table 1 reports the AUC [5], isomorphic retaining score S in Eq. (5.1), and running time of different methods.[11] The results show that the proposed GMR achieves the best AUC among all streaming network embedding algorithms. Compared with other state-of-the-art baselines, GMR outperforms other three baselines in terms of AUC by at least 17.1%, 15.7% and 11.3% on *Facebook*, *Yahoo* and *Epinions*, respectively. Besides, GMR is close to that of FULL(1.7% less on *Facebook*, 0.6% more on *Yahoo* and 2.2% less on *Epinions*), but the running time is only 4.7%. Moreover, GraphSAGE has relatively weak performance since it cannot preserve the structural information without node features. The running time of SDNE is 2.1× greater than that of GMR due to the processing of the deep structure, while the AUC of SDNE is at least 12.5% less than that of GMR on all datasets.

---

[9] *Facebook* and *Epinions* contain both the edge insertion and deletion, represented by "i j -1 t" for removing edge (i, j) at timestamp t. *Yahoo* lacks deletion since it is a message network.

[10] For link prediction, at time t, we predict the new edges for time $t + 1$ (excluding the edges incident to the nodes arriving at time $t + 1$).

[11] For FULL, due to high computational complexity in retraining the networks for all timestamps, we partition all timestamps into 50 parts [23] with the network changes aggregated in each part.

Compared to other streaming network embedding methods (e.g., DNE, SLA, and DHPE), GMR achieves at least 10.8% of improvement because the embeddings of other methods are updated without considering the global topology. In contrast, GMR selects the affected nodes by globally structure-aware hierarchical addressing, and the selected nodes are not restricted to the nearby nodes. Furthermore, GMR outperforms baselines regarding the isomorphic retraining score since it percolates the embeddings to preserve the structural information. Note that the isomorphic retaining score S is highly related to the AUC with a correlation coefficient of 0.92, demonstrating that it is indeed crucial to ensure the embedding consistency for the nodes with similar structures.

6.2 Node Classification

For node classification, we compare different approaches on *BlogCatalog* [16] (10,132 nodes, 333,983 edges, and 39 classes), *Wiki* [5] (2,405 nodes, 17,981 edges, and 19 classes), and *DBLP* [22] (101,253 nodes, 223,810 edges, 48 timestamps, and 4 classes). *DBLP* is a real streaming network by extracting the paper citation network of four research areas from 1970 to 2017. *BlogCatalog* and *Wiki* are adopted in previous research [3] to generate the streaming networks.[12] The learned embeddings are employed to classify the nodes according to the labels. Cross-entropy is adopted in the loss function for classification with logistic regression. We randomly sample 20% of labels for training and 80% of

Table 2. Experiment results of node classification.

	BlogCatalog			Wiki			DBLP		
	F1	S	sec	F1	S	sec	F1	S	sec
GMR	0.2059	0.90	1998	0.4945	0.92	199	0.7619	0.93	7638
FULL	0.2214	0.91	37214	0.5288	0.93	3811	0.7727	0.94	149451
CHANGE	0.1651	0.71	1237	0.3597	0.79	122	0.6841	0.86	5976
GraphSAGE	0.1558	0.81	2494	0.3419	0.82	173	0.6766	0.86	11410
SDNE	0.1723	0.83	2795	0.3438	0.84	266	0.6914	0.87	16847
CTDNE	0.1808	0.84	2923	0.4013	0.85	301	0.7171	0.88	9115
DNE	0.1848	0.86	1547	0.4187	0.86	141	0.7302	0.90	6521
SLA	0.1899	0.87	1399	0.3998	0.85	149	0.7110	0.88	6193
DHPE	0.1877	0.87	2047	0.4204	0.86	215	0.7311	0.90	8159

---

[12] The streaming network $\mathcal{G} = \{G_1, ..., G_T\}$ is generated from the original network by first sampling half of the original network as G_1. For each timestamp t, ΔG_t is constructed by sampling 200 edges (not in G_{t-1}) from the original network and adding them (and the corresponding terminal nodes) to G_{t-1}, whereas 100 edges of G_{t-1} are deleted.

labels for testing, and the average results from 50 runs are reported.[13] Table 2 demonstrates that GMR outperforms CHANGE by 27.1% regarding Macro-F1 [13], and it is close to FULL but with 20.7× speed-up. The Macro-F1 scores of GraphSAGE and SDNE are at least 40% worse than that of GMR, indicating that GraphSAGE and SDNE cannot adequately handle multi-type changes in dynamic networks. Moreover, GMR achieves better improvement on *BlogCatalog* than on *DBLP*, because the density (i.e., the average degree) of *BlogCatalog* is larger, enabling hierarchical addressing of GMR to exploit more structural information for updating multiple nodes. For *DBLP*, GMR also achieves the performance close to FULL.

It is worth noting that the isomorphic retaining score S is also positively related to Macro-F1. We further investigate the percentages of isomorphic pairs with the same label on different datasets. The results manifest that 88%, 92% and 97% of isomorphic pairs share the same labels on *BlogCatalog*, *Wiki*, and *DBLP*, respectively. Therefore, it is crucial to maintain the consistency between isomorphic pairs since similar embeddings of isomorphic pairs are inclined to be classified with the same labels.

7 Conclusion

In this paper, we propose GMR for streaming network embeddings featuring the hierarchical addressing, refreshing gate, and percolation gate to preserve the structural information and consistency. We also prove that the embeddings generated by GMR are more consistent than the current network embedding schemes under insertion. The experiment results demonstrate that GMR outperforms the state-of-the-art methods in link prediction and node classification. Moreover, multi-type updates with the beam search improve GMR in both task-oriented scores and the isomorphic retaining score. Our future work will extend GMR to support multi-relations in knowledge graphs.

References

1. Belkin, M., Niyogi, P.: Laplacian eigenmaps and spectral techniques for embedding and clustering. In: Advances in NIPS, pp. 585–591 (2002)
2. Chen, H., Perozzi, B., Hu, Y., Skiena, S.: HARP: hierarchical representation learning for networks. In: Thirty-Second AAAI (2018)
3. Du, L., Wang, Y., Song, G., Lu, Z., Wang, J.: Dynamic network embedding: an extended approach for skip-gram based network embedding. In: IJCAI, pp. 2086–2092 (2018)
4. Graves, A., Wayne, G., Danihelka, I.: Neural turing machines. arXiv preprint arXiv:1410.5401 (2014)
5. Grover, A., Leskovec, J.: node2vec: scalable feature learning for networks. In: Proceedings of the 22nd ACM SIGKDD, pp. 855–864 (2016)

---

[13] For a new node, only its embedding derived after the arrival is employed in the testing.

6. Hamilton, W., Ying, Z., Leskovec, J.: Inductive representation learning on large graphs. In: Advances in NIPS, pp. 1024–1034 (2017)
7. Jaeger, S., Fulle, S., Turk, S.: Mol2vec: unsupervised machine learning approach with chemical intuition. J. Chem. Inf. Model. **58**(1), 27–35 (2018)
8. Leskovec, J., Krevl, A.: SNAP datasets: Stanford large network dataset collection, June 2014
9. Li, J., Chen, C., Tong, H., Liu, H.: Multi-layered network embedding. In: Proceedings of the 2018 SIAM ICDM, pp. 684–692 (2018)
10. Liu, X., Hsieh, P.C., Duffield, N., Chen, R., Xie, M., Wen, X.: Real-time streaming graph embedding through local actions. In: Proceedings of the WWW, pp. 285–293 (2019)
11. Mikolov, T., Sutskever, I., Chen, K., Corrado, G.S., Dean, J.: Distributed representations of words and phrases and their compositionality. In: Advances in NIPS, pp. 3111–3119 (2013)
12. Nguyen, G.H., Lee, J.B., Rossi, R.A., Ahmed, N.K., Koh, E., Kim, S.: Continuous-time dynamic network embeddings. In: Proceedings of the WWW, pp. 969–976 (2018)
13. Perozzi, B., Al-Rfou, R., Skiena, S.: DeepWalk: online learning of social representations. In: Proceedings of the 20th ACM SIGKDD, pp. 701–710 (2014)
14. Qiu, J., Dong, Y., Ma, H., Li, J., Wang, K., Tang, J.: Network embedding as matrix factorization: unifying DeepWalk, LINE, PTE, and node2vec. In: Proceedings of the WSDM, pp. 459–467 (2018)
15. Rossi, R., Ahmed, N.: The network data repository with interactive graph analytics and visualization. In: Twenty-Ninth AAAI (2015)
16. Tang, J., Qu, M., Wang, M., Zhang, M., Yan, J., Mei, Q.: LINE: large-scale information network embedding. In: Proceedings of the WWW, pp. 1067–1077 (2015)
17. Tenenbaum, J.B., De Silva, V., Langford, J.C.: A global geometric framework for nonlinear dimensionality reduction. Science **290**(5500), 2319–2323 (2000)
18. Tsitsulin, A., Mottin, D., Karras, P., Müller, E.: VERSE: versatile graph embeddings from similarity measures. In: Proceedings of the the WWW, pp. 539–548 (2018)
19. Veličković, P., Cucurull, G., Casanova, A., Romero, A., Lio, P., Bengio, Y.: Graph attention networks. arXiv preprint arXiv:1710.10903 (2017)
20. Wang, D., Cui, P., Zhu, W.: Structural deep network embedding. In: Proceedings of the 22nd ACM SIGKDD, pp. 1225–1234 (2016)
21. Zhou, L., Yang, Y., Ren, X., Wu, F., Zhuang, Y.: Dynamic network embedding by modeling triadic closure process. In: Thirty-Second AAAI (2018)
22. Zhu, D., Cui, P., Zhang, Z., Pei, J., Zhu, W.: High-order proximity preserved embedding for dynamic networks. Trans. Knowl. Data Eng. **30**, 2134–2144 (2018)
23. Zoghi, M., Tunys, T., Ghavamzadeh, M., Kveton, B., Szepesvari, C., Wen, Z.: Online learning to rank in stochastic click models. In: Proceedings of the ICML, pp. 4199–4208 (2017)

Correlation Matters: Multi-scale Fine-Grained Contextual Information Extraction for Hepatic Tumor Segmentation

Shuchao Pang[1(✉)], Anan Du[2], Zhenmei Yu[3], and Mehmet A. Orgun[1]

[1] Department of Computing, Macquarie University, Sydney, NSW 2109, Australia
pangshuchao1212@sina.com, mehmet.orgun@mq.edu.au
[2] School of Electrical and Data Engineering, University of Technology Sydney, Ultimo, NSW 2007, Australia
anan.du@student.uts.edu.au
[3] School of Data and Computer Science, Shandong Women's University, Jinan 250014, China
zhenmei_yu@sdwu.edu.cn

Abstract. Automatic tumor segmentation has been used as a diagnostic aid in the identification of diseases such as tumors from liver CT scans, and their treatment. Owing to their success in computer vision tasks, the state-of-the-art Fully Convolutional Networks (FCNs) or U-Net based models have often been employed in many recent studies for automatic tumor segmentation to learn numerous weight-shared convolutional kernels and extract various semantic features. However, the correlation between different tumor regions in feature maps cannot be easily captured due to the lack of contextual dependencies, which in turn limits the representative capability of the adopted models and thus affects the accuracy of tumor segmentation results. To resolve this issue, we propose a novel framework for segmentation of tumors in liver CT scans, which can explicitly extract multi-scale fine-grained contextual information by adaptively aggregating local features with their global dependencies. The proposed multi-scale framework features a light model with a very few additional parameters, and also its visualization capability significantly boosts networks' interpretability. Experimental results on a real-world liver tumor CT dataset illustrate that the proposed framework achieves the state-of-the-art performance in terms of a number of widely used evaluation criteria for the hepatic tumor segmentation task.

Keywords: Hepatic tumor segmentation · Contextual information · Visualization · FCNs

1 Introduction

According to the latest liver cancer statistics from World Cancer Research Fund International and American Institute for Cancer Research, liver cancer was the sixth most common cancer worldwide in 2018 [1]. In particular, it is the ninth most commonly occurring cancer in women, but the fifth most common cancer in men. Furthermore, there were more than a total of 840,000 new cases diagnosed in 2018 which was 1.074

H. W. Lauw et al. (Eds.): PAKDD 2020, LNAI 12084, pp. 462–474, 2020.
https://doi.org/10.1007/978-3-030-47426-3_36

times more than that in 2012 [2, 3]. Besides having a healthy diet and being physically active, an early detection and intervention is also critical in mitigating the risk of liver cancer. Currently, with the rapid development of medical imaging technology, CT and MRI medical imaging examinations have been widely used in clinical applications to monitor the liver structure and state for diagnosis and treatment of liver cancer [4]. However, manually analyzing detected imaging slices is really a time-consuming and error-prone task to conduct for physicians and radiologists alike and there often exist some inter-observer variations for this kind of pixel-level labelling tasks [5]. Therefore, an accurate and automatic hepatic lesions/tumors localization and segmentation approach is urgently required as a diagnostic aid for early liver cancer detection.

However, in medical tumor segmentation tasks from liver scans, there still exist several hard challenges, with hepatic tumors as an example, such as low tissue contrast, large variability in tumor shape, size and number among inter-patient CT scans and intra-patient slices, and the vague boundary problem between diseased and healthy regions in the whole liver. In recent years, Fully Convolutional Networks (FCNs) [6] and U-Net [7] based deep neural networks have been widely utilized in biomedical and medical image segmentation tasks with an outstanding success [9, 11, 12]. Both types of network architectures utilize skip connections to integrate shallow feature maps and high semantic feature maps from different scales, which can generate more precise pixel-level recognition by fusing detailed positional information from shallow layers. Still, it should be noted that the range of contextual information obtained from those models is heavily limited by the depth of networks and the size of kernels used. Several recent works [13] modify these basic architectures by introducing multi-scale context fusion motivated by the Inception-ResNet-V2 model, where a large reception field can extract more abstract features for large objects, while a small reception field is better for small objects. Even though fusing multi-scale contextual information can capture different size objects, it cannot leverage the correlation between different objects in a global context, which is very important for medical tumor segmentation, in particular, segmenting common multiple tumors in a liver. To further exploit contextual dependencies, U-Net variants based on Recurrent Neutral Networks (RNNs) have been proposed to aggregate the context over local features from output feature maps of top layers of pre-trained CNN models [16]. Despite the enhancement of their representative capability, the implicitly captured global dependencies heavily rely on the learning outcome of the long-term memorization [17].

Different from these contextual extraction modules, in this paper, we propose a multi-scale contextual dependency framework inspired by attention mechanisms in machine translation tasks [14] to capture fine-grained contexts for inter- and intra-tumor regions and enhance the discriminability of learned features, and thus improve the performance in the hepatic tumor segmentation task, as shown in Fig. 1. More specifically, we first construct a new U-shape model motivated by CE-Net [13], where the pre-trained ResNet model and different size context aggregation with dilated convolutions and a multi-kernel pyramid pooling are fused into an encoder-decoder architecture. Then, we place the multi-scale context extraction model on all the skip connections to capture fine-grained contextual information by adaptively aggregating local features with their global dependencies from different scale feature maps, respectively. Finally, for a context extraction block on each skip connection, we model the semantic context interdependencies over all the local features from both the spatial and the channel dimensions. In this way, the spatial contextual relationship can avoid the effect of the position distance between tumor regions in 2D feature maps and meanwhile, aggregate tumor features at each location by summing a global dependency on all the related tumor features. Furthermore, a global interdependent channel affinity map is also computed to exploit and emphasize the correlation among different feature categories along the channel dimensionality. By adding the two-level extracted contextual information element-by-element, the explicit fine-grained contexts can be learnt to produce more precise predictions for hepatic tumor segmentation, especially for small tumors. Moreover, with the guidance of the learned multi-scale contextual dependencies, the false-positive results are also significantly reduced, which is quite important for early cancer detection due to the existence of small lesions or tumor regions in the early stages. Furthermore, the interpretability of the proposed networks has also been greatly improved for hepatic tumor segmentation.

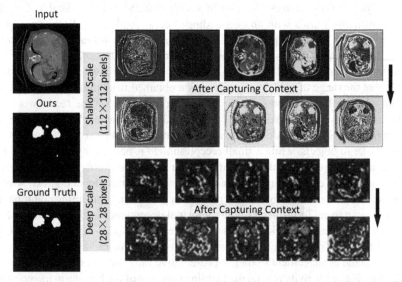

Fig. 1. A test example with our segmentation result and internal learned feature visualization comparison before and after using our multi-scale contextual dependency framework. Several feature map pairs corresponding to two scale contextual operations are respectively given and each learned feature map is enlarged for clarity. Note that the width and height of input image is set to 448 × 448 pixels in our networks.

Contributions of this study can be summarized as follows:

• We propose a novel framework to explicitly aggregate contextual relationships between hepatic tumors in different scale feature maps, which can successfully address various complex and hard challenges in medical tumor segmentation. The proposed framework is also an important improvement over the current automatic segmentation methods. Moreover, parts or all of the proposed framework can be integrated into any FCNs or U-Net based architectures seamlessly.

- Our proposed global dependency extraction module operates on all skip connections to capture multi-scale fine-grained hepatic tumor contextual information, where two types of context aggregations are embedded into each skip connection for exploiting long-range contextual dependencies from both tumor spatial and channel dimensionalities. In addition, the explicit context aggregation with feature visualization noticeably boosts model's interpretability.
- The proposed medical tumor segmentation framework has been evaluated on real-world hepatic tumor data. The results show that multi-scale contextual dependencies over feature spatial regions and channel maps have significantly improved tumor segmentation performance, while reducing false positive and false negative rates of hepatic tumors on CT slices, and they have also enhanced the discriminative ability of learned representations in medical tumor segmentation.

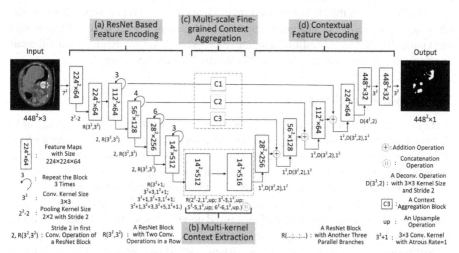

Fig. 2. Our multi-scale fine-grained contextual dependency framework for hepatic tumor segmentation, which consists of several main functional modules: (a) a ResNet-34 based feature encoding module, (b) a multi-kernel context extraction module, (c) a multi-scale fine-grained contextual aggregation module and (d) a contextual feature decoding module. An example with its prediction from the proposed algorithm is illustrated end-to-end in the whole workflow.

2   The Proposed Multi-scale Framework

2.1   Overview

In this paper, we propose a multi-scale fine-grained contextual information extraction framework to model long-range contextual dependencies over CT imaging regions for improving hepatic tumor segmentation performance. The proposed network framework can perform global context aggregation over locally connected feature maps and then embed their global dependencies into local features, which can further increase the correlations between tumor regions and enhance their representative capability for medical tumor segmentation. By explicitly passing similar local contexts regardless of positional distances like in an undirected graph operation, the correlation and interaction of contextual dependencies from both the spatial and the channel dimensions is explicitly propagated and encoded into subsequent feature maps. Moreover, the characteristics of small-size tumor/lesion regions can also be inferred better after they are perfectly contextualized by utilizing this multi-scale contextual design, which noticeably reduces false positive cases as well as giving clear boundary predictions.

In order to take the full advantage of its effectiveness, the proposed multi-scale context framework is fused into a new U-shape context encoder network, which gives a significant improvement for the backbone and its variants, and really differentiates them in the aspect of context aggregation. Moreover, our proposed multi-scale framework requires a very few additional parameters, which only increases by 0.37% over that of the backbone networks. Experimental results show that our proposed multi-scale framework performs better than the state-of-the-art methods for medical tumor segmentation. The whole architecture of our designed networks is shown in Fig. 2, which includes four main parts: ResNet based feature encoding, multi-kernel context extraction, multi-scale fine-grained contextual aggregation and contextual feature decoding.

2.2 Spatial Context Extractor

There is a spatial context extractor for modeling the 2D contextual dependencies and a channel context extractor for modeling the 3D contextual dependencies on each of the three-dimensional feature map groups (where W × H × C refers to width, height and channel numbers of the learned features for each input image).

Subsequently, we introduce the spatial context extractor in detail and discuss the process of adaptively aggregating the 2D contextual dependencies. First, an input image with 448 × 448 × 3 size on the left in Fig. 2 is fed into the ResNet based feature encoding subnetwork for extracting its high-level semantic features. We assume that the learned 3D feature maps are a W × H × C tensor, where each 2D feature map is W × H pixels, the channel number is C and the batch size is set to 1 for clarity, like the input data $X \in \mathbb{R}^{28 \times 28 \times 256}$ shown on the left side of Fig. 3. $V = \{v_i\}_{i=1:N}$ is the vertex set for each local contextual feature v_i at all 2D positions and N = W × H (also N = 784 in this example from Fig. 3). Then, in order to obtain the spatial contextual map among all the global spatial positions, two new feature maps $Q \in \mathbb{R}^{28 \times 28 \times 32}$ and $K \in \mathbb{R}^{28 \times 28 \times 32}$ are respectively generated with two single convolutional operations by 1 × 1 kernels, which is based on the fed feature map, as calculated by the following equations:

$$Q^{(v_i)} = f\left(w_1 X^{(v_i)} + b_1\right); \quad K^{(v_i)} = f\left(w_2 X^{(v_i)} + b_2\right), \tag{1}$$

where these two operations can further encode each local positional context feature v_i and also reduce the parameters by reducing the channel dimensionality from 256 to 32, and f is a non-linear activation function and w_1, b_1, w_2, b_2 are network parameters. After reshaping them into $Q' \in \mathbb{R}^{(28 \cdot 28) \times 32}$ and $K' \in \mathbb{R}^{(28 \cdot 28) \times 32}$, we perform a 2D matrix multiplication between the K' and the transposed Q^t, which aims to calculate the mutual similarity of any two local contextual features $v_i \in K'$ and $v_j \in Q^t$. In this way, the spatial context map M with global knowledge is generated, which represents the interdependency of local features from any two positions in a 2D spatial context. By applying a softmax operation to it as shown below, the updated context map M_{ij} can indicate a greater correlation between the two positions if their similarity value is larger.

$$M_{ij} = e^{v_i \cdot v_j} / \sum\nolimits_{j=1}^{N} e^{v_i \cdot v_j}. \tag{2}$$

Later, for aggregating all positional local contextual information with global context dependencies for fine-grained spatial context extraction, another new feature map $F' \in \mathbb{R}^{(28 \cdot 28) \times 256}$ is also produced by performing a convolutional layer on the original fed feature map X without a channel dimensionality reduction and a reshaped operation successively. After that, a context aggregation operation is performed to generate the aggregated feature map $X' \in \mathbb{R}^{(28 \cdot 28) \times 256}$ by a matrix multiplication operation between M and F', where each position in X' represents its corresponding weighted summarization of features across all the positions. The aggregated feature map X' is then reshaped into a new $X' \in \mathbb{R}^{28 \times 28 \times 256}$. Finally, local contextual features at each position from the original input feature map X are fused with their global contextual dependencies X' by an addition operation as in the following equation.

$$X^s = \alpha X' + X \tag{3}$$

where X^s is the selectively aggregated contextual features by fusing local contexts and global contexts and α is a learnable scale parameter. Overall, the spatial context extraction as shown in Fig. 3(1) is completed in the whole 2D spatial positions, where the fine-grained context features can further improve intra-class compact and semantic consistency and contribute to enhancing hepatic tumor segmentation performance.

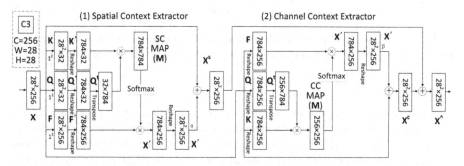

Fig. 3. A fine-grained contextual information aggregation block, taking C3 in Fig. 2 as an example. The details of the spatial context extractor and those of the channel context extractor for capturing rich contextual dependencies are illustrated in (1) and (2), respectively. Note that the operation $\otimes$ indicates matrix multiplication.

2.3 Channel Context Extractor

We observe that above context process just considers the 2D spatial positions by lever-aging each local context v_i where v_i is a C dimensionality vector, which means that the interdependency and the correlation between different channels is not fully exploited. However, the 3D channel context information is essential to extract robust hepatic tumor knowledge. Therefore, this subsection discusses the extraction of channel contextual information. Different channel feature maps usually represent different image feature types and semantic information. Furthermore, semantic information from different chan-nels are usually associated with each other, which can improve the representative capa-bility of feature maps if we exploit them in global knowledge. So, in order to explicitly model the interdependencies between the channel maps, we respectively build a channel context extractor for each contextual information aggregation block from our proposed multi-scale fine-grained context extraction framework.

As illustrated in Fig. 3(2), a light channel context model is utilized to achieve fewer parameters in the process. When the input original feature maps $X \in \mathbb{R}^{28 \times 28 \times 256}$ are fed into the spatial context extractor, we also deliver them into the channel context extractor in the meantime. Different from the former step, X is directly reshaped into $Q, K, F \in \mathbb{R}^{(28 \cdot 28) \times 256}$ without any convolutional operation. Besides, $V = \{v_i\}_{i=1:C}$ is the channel set for each channel contextual feature $v_i \in \mathbb{R}^{28 \cdot 28}$ at the third dimension. Then, we perform a matrix multiplication between the transposed Q^t and K to calculate the channel similarity of any two channel maps over all the spatial positions. Later, the generated channel context map M is applied by a softmax layer to normalize them for satisfying the properties of probability. In addition, the global contextual dependency extraction X' for each channel map is obtained by a matrix multiplication along the channel dimension. To this end, the following equations are used.

$$M = Q^t K; M_{ij} = e^{v_i \cdot v_j} / \sum_{j=1}^{C} e^{v_i \cdot v_j}, v_i \in Q^t, v_j \in K. \tag{4}$$

$$X' = FM. \tag{5}$$

Finally, the obtained global contextual aggregation result X' with a parameter β is added into each original channel feature map from X along the channel dimension.

$$X^c = \beta X' + X. \tag{6}$$

Overall, the final feature of each channel X^c is constructed by fusing a weighted sum of all the channel feature maps and the original single feature map in each channel space, which successfully models the long-range context semantic dependencies among the channel maps to boost their representative ability for medical tumor segmentation. Based on an addition operation from both of these context extraction steps, each context aggregation block can fully exploit contextual information in a global view from the spatial and the channel perspectives, as shown in Fig. 3.

$$X^\wedge = X^s + X^c. \tag{7}$$

3 Experiments and Analysis

3.1 Data and Implementation Details

Evaluation Dataset and Metrics. Tumor segmentation is a more difficult task than general body organ segmentation tasks due to vague boundaries between diseased and healthy tissues. For this task, a new and challenging hepatic tumor dataset [5] is used to show hepatic tumor segmentation performance for all the methods considered. This dataset consists of 131 abdominal 3D CT scans acquired from 131 subjects with different types of liver tumor diseases, e.g., primary tumor diseases and secondary liver tumors. These medical data were collected from clinical sites in the world with different CT scanners and acquisition protocols. Here, we can extract 7190 CT slices with tumor annotations. For comprehensive comparisons between different segmentation methods, a number of widely used evaluation metrics are utilized in our study, including Dice similarity coefficient, Hausdorff distance, Jaccard index, precision (also called positive predictive value), recall (also called sensitivity coefficient or true positive rate), specificity coefficient (also called true negative rate) and F1 score. Except Hausdorff distance, the others indicate that the larger results are better.

Parameter Setting. 2 NVIDIA CUDA cores with 4 logical GPUs, and 1 Intel Haswell E5-2670v3 CPU are used to train our proposed multi-scale segmentation framework. The batch size for each forward pass is 8 CT slices and the initial learning rate is set to 0.0002, which could be dynamically changed during the training process under the guidance of the variations of errors. If there is no reduction of errors in the next 10 epochs, then the learning rate would be cut in half. Meanwhile, we set the maximum training epoch to 400 with an early stopping strategy. When the generated error is no longer reduced in the next 20 epochs or the learning rate drops below 5e-7, the training process is finished. And the training data and test data are randomly split into 4:1 from all raw data with tumor annotations. In addition, some widely used data augmentation techniques are also used dynamically during our training process [13]. Only the basic and plain cross entropy loss is employed for better demonstrating the robustness of our model. The Adam optimizer is employed to optimize and update all the network parameters in our segmentation network. The compared state-of-the-art methods are also trained on our dataset according to their original papers.

Compared Methods. The nine state-of-the-art segmentation methods are chosen in our experiments based on several representative models, as baseline methods for comparison: (1) *U-Net Based Model*: U-Net [7] is a highly cited architecture; Attention UNet [9] adds a spatial attention scheme; Nested UNet [12] employs hot dense skip pathways. (2) *Context Based Model*: R2U-Net [11] utilizes recurrent and residual networks; CE-Net [13] embeds a multi-kernel context encoding mechanism like Inception architecture; Self-attention [8, 10] exploits spatial context information. And (3) *Attention Based Model*: SENet [15] uses channel attention mechanism; both DANet [17] and CS-Net [18] place self-attention schemes on the top of encoder stage, but with different network architectures. (4) *Fused Model*: Attention UNet [9] and Self-attention [8, 10].

3.2 Quantitative Analysis

For quantitative analysis, all the ten representative segmentation methods are evaluated on the test dataset, as shown in Table 1. The pioneering U-shape network, U-Net [7] can be used to predict hepatic tumor regions on CT slices but with an unsatisfactory performance (e.g., 73.62% in Dice) as well as its variant Nested UNet [12] (e.g., 73.58% in Dice), while the attention based variant Attention UNet [9] is better by around 5% than the original U-Net under different segmentation criteria. This is because Attention UNet can give a further refinement for learned features from the spatial dimension to highlight the salient features and suppress useless ones. Similarly, SENet [15] also improves the segmentation performance by embedding squeeze-and-excitation blocks after skip connections as a channel attention mechanism, in spite of a slight decline compared to Attention UNet. Then, we compare popular context based models for medical tumor segmentation. R2U-Net [11] only outperforms its backbone model (U-Net) by about 1% in segmentation accuracies by employing RNNs and residual connections to extract feature context features. By contrast, multi-kernel context encoder networks CE-Net [13] can achieve relatively better performance (such as 78.41% in Dice, 33.78 pixels in HD, 72.92% in Precision and 89.33% in Recall) with different evaluation measures like Attention UNet [9], where pretrained network parameters can also provide some help in improving segmentation performance together with multiple kernel contextual feature extraction.

Table 1. Comparison results of the state-of-the-art segmentation methods with widely used evaluation metrics for hepatic tumor segmentation. The numbers in bold represent the best results. Note that Hausdorff distance uses pixel units and others %.

Methods/Metrics	Dice	Hausdorff distance	Jaccard	Precision	Recall	Specificity	F1
U-Net [7]	73.62	52.65	63.67	67.46	86.70	99.76	75.88
Attention UNet [9]	78.70	37.13	69.32	72.93	89.65	99.83	80.43
R2U-Net [11]	74.55	46.04	64.46	68.38	87.27	99.77	76.68
Nested UNet [12]	73.58	46.89	63.55	67.39	86.95	99.76	75.93
CE-Net [13]	78.41	33.78	69.09	72.92	89.33	99.82	80.30
SENet [15]	77.88	39.09	68.55	72.39	89.16	99.82	79.90
Self-attention [8, 10]	76.49	38.78	66.80	70.82	88.72	99.79	78.76
DANet [17]	79.97	30.94	71.00	74.50	90.38	99.84	81.67
CS-Net [18]	78.90	32.90	69.45	73.03	90.03	99.83	80.64
Ours	**82.16**	**30.01**	**73.46**	**76.96**	**91.18**	**99.86**	**83.37**
Average Gain ($\nearrow$)	*5.26*	*9.79*	*6.14*	*5.87*	*2.49*	*0.058*	*4.46*

For comparison with recent self-attention and non-local models [8, 10], we have integrated their original spatial context extraction module into our backbone networks in lieu of ours. As we can see from Table 1, the Self-attention model [8, 10] drops two percentage points over multi-kernel context encoder networks [13]. Very recently, both DANet [17] and CS-Net [18] have exploited two types of self-attention models acting on the top of a feature encoder path from different pretrained network architectures with better performance than Attention UNet [9] and CE-Net [13], for example, 79.97% vs 78.90% in Dice, 30.94 pixels vs 32.90 pixels in HD, 74.50% vs 73.03% in Precision and 90.38% vs 90.03% in Recall. Moreover, these good segmentation results also illustrate that diverse self-attention strategies can further boost the feature representative capability of a model for accurate tumor localization and segmentation.

More importantly, our proposed multi-scale framework performs the best under all the evaluation metrics while outperforming nine compared state-of-the-art methods by an average of 5.26% in Dice coefficient, ranging from 2.19% to 8.58%. In terms of Jaccard index and Precision coefficient, our model also shows an average gain of 6.14% ranging from 2.46% to 9.91%, and 5.87% ranging from 2.46% to 9.57%, repectively. In addition, the true positive rate (TPR, also Recall coefficient) from our method is also significantly better with an average 2.49%. While Specificity coefficient with 0.058% increase, also called true negative rate (TNR), is also slightly better than all the other methods due to a small percentage of tumor regions in CT slices; F1 score of our model noticeably outperforms all the baseline methods by an average of 4.46% by leveraging Precision and Recall results. Last but not the least, our multi-scale context aggregation method exhibits an average reduction in Hausdorff distance of 9.79 pixels, which means that the boundaries from our segmentation results can better coincide with their corresponding ground truths from radiologists than those of the nine state-of-the-art methods. Overall, our proposed segmentation method can outperform those nine state-of-the-art segmentation methods because our multi-scale context guided information aggregation process can better encode global knowledge into local features with fine-grained representations from spatial and channel dimensions and other important modules in our networks also boost segmentation performance of our framework.

3.3 Qualitative Analysis

As shown in Fig. 4, several segmentation results from randomly chosen CT imaging slices are visualized to provide a qualitative comparison of different models. Both our proposed method and DANet [17] perform well on the first sample, but others falsely consider healthy regions as hepatic tumors. This is similar in the second sample, except that Attention UNet [9] also works well. However, from the third sample, we see that DANet [17] has difficulty to differentiate hepatic tumors from surrounding tissues. As a whole, in cases Fig. 4(3–5), the false positive rates of the state-of-the-art methods are really high, resulting in many mis-segmented regions. This would negatively affect an accurate diagnosis for patients with hepatopathy, especially for early stage patients. On the other hand, in the sixth sample, the compared models just give partial predictions for tumor regions with some undiagnosed cases, which means a high false negative rate from their models. More importantly, in some challenging cases (e.g., Fig. 4(7)), all the baseline methods completely fail. Overall, all these misdiagnoses generated from the state-of-the-art automatic segmentation methods could be due to a lack of effective context extraction for accurate hepatic tumor segmentation. By contrast, our proposed multi-scale segmentation framework can extract fine-grained global context dependencies from spatial and channel dimensions and then aggregate them together with local features to generate more precise segmentation results, as depicted in Fig. 4.

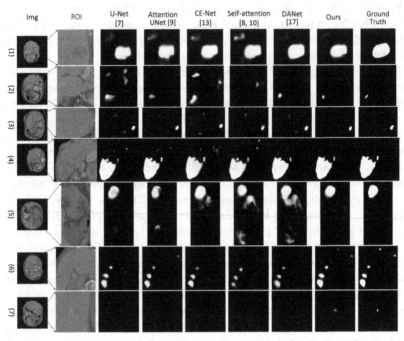

Fig. 4. Seven randomly selected samples with their segmentation results from the state-of-the-art methods. For clarity, we only report the regions of interest (ROI) of some of the compared methods due to space limitations.

4 Conclusions

In this paper, we have proposed a multi-scale contextual dependency framework to explicitly capture fine-grained context correlations between tumor regions and enhance the discriminability of the learned features and hence to improve segmentation performance for hepatic tumors. In particular, we have modeled the semantic context dependencies over all the local features from both the spatial and channel dimensions. To be specific, the spatial contextual relationship can aggregate tumor features at each spatial location by summing a global dependency on all related tumor features, which can lessen the effect of the position distance of local features in feature maps. On the other hand, a global interdependent channel affinity map is also computed to emphasize the correlation among different feature categories along the channel dimensionality. In addition, feature visualization analysis and comparison significantly improves the interpretability of our proposed automatic segmentation networks. Extensive experiments conducted on a real-life liver tumor dataset also demonstrate that our model outperforms nine compared state-of-the-art segmentation methods. In the future, we plan to extend this framework into further clinical applications.

Acknowledgment. This work is supported in part by an International Macquarie University Research Excellence Scholarship (iMQRES: 2018150) and partially supported by the National Natural Science Foundation of China (No. 61472416).

References

1. Liver Cancer Statistics. https://www.wcrf.org/dietandcancer/cancer-trends/liver-cancer-statistics. Accessed 11 Dec 2019
2. Liver Cancer. https://www.wcrf.org/dietandcancer/liver-cancer. Accessed 11 Dec 2019
3. Bray, F., Ferlay, J., Soerjomataram, I., Siegel, R.L., Torre, L.A., Jemal, A.: Global cancer statistics 2018: GLOBOCAN estimates of incidence and mortality worldwide for 36 cancers in 185 countries. CA Cancer J. Clin. **68**(6), 394–424 (2018)
4. Budak, Ü., Guo, Y., Tanyildizi, E., Şengür, A.: Cascaded deep convolutional encoder-decoder neural networks for efficient liver tumor segmentation. Med. Hypotheses **134**, 109431 (2020)
5. Bilic, P., et al.: The liver tumor segmentation benchmark (LiTS). arXiv preprint arXiv:1901. 04056 (2019)
6. Long, J., Shelhamer, E., Darrell, T.: Fully convolutional networks for semantic segmentation. In: Proceedings of the IEEE Conference on Computer Vision and Pattern Recognition, pp. 3431–3440 (2015)
7. Ronneberger, O., Fischer, P., Brox, T.: U-Net: convolutional networks for biomedical image segmentation. In: Navab, N., Hornegger, J., Wells, W.M., Frangi, Alejandro F. (eds.) MICCAI 2015. LNCS, vol. 9351, pp. 234–241. Springer, Cham (2015). https://doi.org/10.1007/978-3-319-24574-4_28
8. Zhang, H., Goodfellow, I., Metaxas, D., Odena, A.: Self-attention generative adversarial networks. arXiv preprint arXiv:1805.08318 (2018)
9. Schlemper, J., et al.: Attention gated networks: learning to leverage salient regions in medical images. Med. Image Anal. **53**, 197–207 (2019)
10. Wang, X., Girshick, R., Gupta, A., He, K.: Non-local neural networks. In: Proceedings of the IEEE Conference on Computer Vision and Pattern Recognition, pp. 7794–7803 (2018)
11. Alom, M.Z., Yakopcic, C., Hasan, M., Taha, T.M., Asari, V.K.: Recurrent residual U-Net for medical image segmentation. J. Med. Imaging **6**(1), 014006 (2019)
12. Zhou, Z., Rahman Siddiquee, M.M., Tajbakhsh, N., Liang, J.: UNet++: a nested U-Net architecture for medical image segmentation. In: Stoyanov, D., et al. (eds.) DLMIA/ML-CDS-2018. LNCS, vol. 11045, pp. 3–11. Springer, Cham (2018). https://doi.org/10.1007/978-3-030-00889-5_1
13. Gu, Z., et al.: CE-Net: context encoder network for 2D medical image segmentation. IEEE Trans. Med. Imaging **38**, 2281–2292 (2019)
14. Vaswani, A., et al.: Attention is all you need. In: Advances in Neural Information Processing Systems, pp. 5998–6008 (2017)
15. Hu, J., Shen, L., Sun, G.: Squeeze-and-excitation networks. In: Proceedings of the IEEE Conference on Computer Vision and Pattern Recognition, pp. 7132–7141 (2018)
16. Shuai, B., Zuo, Z., Wang, B., Wang, G.: Scene segmentation with dag-recurrent neural networks. IEEE Trans. Pattern Anal. Mach. Intell. **40**(6), 1480–1493 (2017)

17. Fu, J., et al.: Dual attention network for scene segmentation. In: Proceedings of the IEEE Conference on Computer Vision and Pattern Recognition, pp. 3146–3154 (2019)
18. Mou, L., et al.: CS-Net: channel and spatial attention network for curvilinear structure segmentation. In: Shen, D., et al. (eds.) MICCAI 2019. LNCS, vol. 11764, pp. 721–730. Springer, Cham (2019). https://doi.org/10.1007/978-3-030-32239-7_80

Context-Aware Latent Dirichlet Allocation for Topic Segmentation

Wenbo Li[1]([✉]), Tetsu Matsukawa[1], Hiroto Saigo[1], and Einoshin Suzuki[1,2]

[1] Graduate School and Faculty of Information Science and Electrical Engineering,
Kyushu University, Fukuoka, Japan
liwenbo_923@hotmail.com, {matsukawa,saigo,suzuki}@inf.kyushu-u.ac.jp
[2] Graduate School of Systems Life Sciences, Kyushu University, Fukuoka, Japan

Abstract. We propose a new generative model for topic segmentation based on Latent Dirichlet Allocation. The task is to divide a document into a sequence of topically coherent segments, while preserving long topic change-points (coherency) and keeping short topic segments from getting merged (saliency). Most of the existing models either fuse topic segments by keywords or focus on modeling word co-occurrence patterns without merging. They can hardly achieve both coherency and saliency since many words have high uncertainties in topic assignments due to their polysemous nature. To solve this problem, we introduce topic-specific co-occurrence of word pairs within contexts in modeling, to generate more coherent segments and alleviate the influence of irrelevant words on topic assignment. We also design an optimization algorithm to eliminate redundant items in the generated topic segments. Experimental results show that our proposal produces significant improvements in both topic coherence and topic segmentation.

1 Introduction

Topic segmentation is the task of dividing a document into a sequence of topically coherent segments [19]. Specifically, besides the topic distribution, the order of topic segments is also an essential part of document semantic information [18]. Even with the same topic distribution, different orders might represent different or even opposite standpoints. For example, a commentary at the end often determines the guidance of the public opinion, such as the coverage of politics, in particular, election campaigns [6,12]. The challenge of this task is to ensure both the coherency and the saliency of the topic segments, where the coherency refers to keeping long topic segments without being split, while the saliency reserving short topic segments without being absorbed with longer ones.

Conventional topic modeling, such as Latent Dirichlet Allocation (LDA) [5], has made significant progress in various specific applications by handling sparse

A part of this work is supported by Grant-in-Aid for Scientific Research JP18H03290 from the Japan Society for the Promotion of Science (JSPS) and the State Scholarship Fund of China Scholarship Council (grant 201706680067).

© Springer Nature Switzerland AG 2020
H. W. Lauw et al. (Eds.): PAKDD 2020, LNAI 12084, pp. 475–486, 2020.
https://doi.org/10.1007/978-3-030-47426-3_37

high dimensional features and finding latent semantic relationships [14,27]. Nevertheless, the "bag of words" based models are unable to capture the order of topics within each document. A simple solution is to consider the physical structure [2] (e.g., sentences and paragraphs) of each document and use a Hidden Markov Model (HMM) structure [4,9,21,23,24] or predefine a common canonical topic ordering to model the order of topics [8]. However, in recent decades, massive document data are continuously generated in various forms (e.g., news and postings) and from multiple modes (e.g., voice and video). The above models cannot handle these documents with no physical structure information.

Another way is to use high-frequency words as keywords of topics [22]. Detecting and utilizing keywords on the topic assignments improve the coherency of topic segments, especially in documents with well-proportioned topic distribution and sufficient keywords. However, relying heavily on extracted keywords limits the saliency of topic segments. For example, for a document with an uneven topic distribution, extracting enough keywords for all the segments is difficult. As a result, less proportionate topic segments are likely to be absorbed by topic segments with higher proportions, due to insufficient keywords.

The fundamental reason for the limited saliency and coherency is that the topic assignment of each word is highly uncertain. Most words can represent multiple topics, due to their polysemy. The distributional hypothesis [20], which states that words in similar contexts have similar meanings, is one of the primary theories used to quantify the meaning of words according to their context (e.g., Word2vec [11]). Inspired by it, we assume that the topic of each word in a document is related to its context, that is, similar contexts correspond to similar topics. Intuitively, even if a word can be assigned to multiple topics, given its context, we can assign a corresponding topic more certainly. For example, the word "Liverpool" can belong to a topic of sports, geography or art, etc. However, if we combine it to the words in its context (e.g., "Liverpool" & "football" or "Liverpool" & "Beatles"), the assignment is much clearer.

In this paper, we propose a new generative model, Context-Aware Latent Dirichlet Allocation (C-LDA), for document segmentation. In the topic assignment, we consider both the topic distributions and the topic-specific occurrence of word pairs in contexts. Our model enjoys two substantial merits over the state-of-the-art methods: (1) a word is generated by both the document-specific topic distribution and the topic distribution associated with each word and its context; (2) it is independent of physical structures.

2 Related Work

Document segmentation has long been studied in various topic models [4,8,9,21, 23,24], such as segHMM [4] and Bayesseg [9]. The traditional methods mainly rely on the document physical structure, which refers to the text-spans in each document, such as sentences or paragraphs [2]. They basically assume that words in the same text-span share the same topic or topic distribution. They conduct segmentation by introducing HMM structure in their topic models and modeling dependencies between consecutive text-spans. However, these approaches are unable to handle data with no structural information, which significantly limits their applicability. Moreover, in most cases, topics might evolve in long paragraphs or sections, and thus a text-span might contain multiple topics.

Recent studies have been focusing on physical structure-independent segmentation [1,7,22,25]. Topic Keyword Model (TKM) [22] is a topic model based on keywords and their contexts. Its main weakness lies in handling short topic segments, which are likely to be absorbed by long topic segments due to their small number of keywords. Biterm Topic Model (BTM) [7] learns topics by modeling the generation of word co-occurrence patterns, which improves the sensitivity of the discovery of phrases in short text data. On the basis of the former, Bursty Biterm Topic Model (BBTM) introduces a new variable to discover bursty topics[1] [25]. These phrase-level topic modeling methods can achieve good results in discovering word co-occurrence patterns in individual short documents and require no physical structure information. However, high-frequency phrases only make up a tiny proportion of the corpus, which limits their ability to generate coherent topics in topic segmentation tasks. The main difference from our model is that they consider all distinct word pairs of each fixed-size window, while we focus on the topic-specific word pairs, which only concern the target word in the corresponding context. Copula LDA with Segmentation (SegLDA) [1] is an LDA-based model which automatically segments documents into topically coherent sequences of words. SegLDA predefines segments for each document before modeling. For each word in a segment, a topic is assigned either from the segment-specific topic distribution or the document-specific topic distribution. These distributions differentiate the main topics of a document from potential segment-specific topics, which improves the saliency of short segments. However, the two distributions are independent. Specifically, in the former distribution, a topic assignment depends only on the words within the segment, which leads to a loss of much context information in the original document.

In addition, context information is also utilized in other topic models to solve various specific problems in document semantic analysis [16,26], such as Contextual Topic Model (CTM) [26] and Contextual Latent Dirichlet Allocation (Contextual-LDA) [16]. CTM considers the dependencies of topics between each sentence in document summarization while Contextual-LDA uses the topic position of each physical structure-based segment for key information detection. Different from them, we focus on solving the problem of topic segmentation by considering topic-specific word pairs in contexts.

3 Context-Aware Topic Modeling

3.1 Context Word Pairs-Topic Distribution

For conventional LDA and its extended models, topic assignment for each word mostly relies on topic distribution and word distribution. Although the constraints

---

[1] In their study [25], a topic is considered to be bursty in a time slice if it is heavily discussed, but not in most of the other slices.

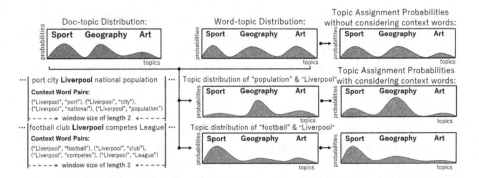

Fig. 1. Schematic illustration of topic assignment for word "Liverpool" with and without considering its context words (respectively labeled by red and blue). We see that if "Liverpool" co-occurs with word "football" in the same context, it is more likely to be assigned to the topic of "sports", while "geography" if co-occurs with "population". (Color figure online)

of topic distribution can alleviate the uncertainty in the topic assignment, it is still insufficient to handle documents containing multiple main topics. For example, a document on the study of modern football and the geographical distribution of England, should at least belong to two topics (geography and sports). We study the topic assignment of the word "Liverpool" in a specific location and consider its 3 related topics: sports, geography, and art. As shown in Fig. 1, for traditional topic models, although the topic distribution reduces the probability of being assigned to the topic of "art", there is still a large uncertainty between "sports" and "geography". However, by considering the frequency of co-occurrence of context words on various topics, this uncertainty can be further reduced, which also coincides with the distributional hypothesis.

Therefore, in our model, we give each word w a context window of length L and define a set of words within the window as context words c_w. For the topic assignment of w, we consider the topics of word pairs $\boldsymbol{b}_w$ which consist of w and c_w. $\boldsymbol{b}_w$ is defined as:

$$\boldsymbol{b}_w \triangleq \{(w, w')|w' \in c_w\}.$$

Following LDA [5], we also assume that the topic distribution $\boldsymbol{\lambda}_w$ of all the sets of word pairs follows a Dirichlet distribution and name it Context Word Pairs-Topic Distribution (CWTD):

$$\boldsymbol{\lambda}_w \sim Dir(\boldsymbol{\gamma}).$$

$\boldsymbol{\lambda}_w$ depends on the topic distribution of the word pairs of $\boldsymbol{b}_w$ in all other documents. By the definition of Dirichlet distribution [15], the expectation can be calculated as:

$$E_{Dir(\gamma)}(\lambda_{w,k}) = \frac{n_{k,-(d,l)}^{b_w} + \gamma_k}{\sum_{s=1}^{K}(n_{s,-(d,l)}^{b_w} + \gamma_s)}, \tag{1}$$

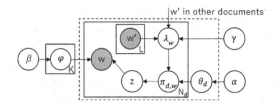

Fig. 2. Graphical model for Context-Aware LDA.

where $n^{b_w}_{s,-(d,l)}$ is the total number of word pairs which are in b_w and belong to topic k in all documents without containing the lth word of document d. In topic assignment, we reorganize the topic distribution θ_d of a document based on the context of each word and name the reorganized topic distribution as Context-Aware Topic Distribution (CTD), denoted by $\pi_{d,w}$. Therefore, the topic $Z_{d,w}$ for word w in d follows a Categorical distribution which is from the Dirichlet distribution $\pi_{d,w}$ with the prior of both the topic distribution θ_d and the CWTD λ_w:

$$\pi_{d,w} \sim Dir(\theta_d + \lambda_w), Z_{d,w} \sim Cat(\pi_{d,w}).$$

3.2 Context-Aware Latent Dirichlet Allocation

As Fig. 2 shows, we introduce four variables $\pi_{d,w}$, λ_w, w' and γ based on traditional LDA, where $\pi_{d,w}$ represents the CTD for word w in document d, λ_w is the corresponding CWTD with prior of γ and w' refers to a context word of w. Besides, θ_d represents the topic distribution of document d with prior α and ϕ_k is the word distribution of topic k with prior β. For a dataset of D documents with a vocabulary of size V and latent topics indexed in $\{1, ..., K\}$, C-LDA is associated to the following generative model.

1. Generate the word-topic distribution ϕ_k for each topic k: $\phi_k \sim Dir(\beta)$.
2. For each document d:
   (a) Generate the topic-word distribution θ_d of document d: $\theta_d \sim Dir(\alpha)$.
   (b) For each word w in d (index by l):
      i. Get context word pairs b_w and generate the CWTD λ_w based on Eq. (1): $\lambda_w \sim Dir(\gamma)$.
      ii. Generate the CTD $\pi_{d,w}$ of word w according to θ_d and λ_w: $\pi_{d,w} \sim Dir(\lambda_w + \theta_d)$.
      iii. Choose a topic $Z_{d,l}$ assignment according to $\pi_{d,w}$: $Z_{d,l} \sim Cat(\pi_{d,w})$.
      iv. Generate $w_{d,l}$ based on the topic $Z_{d,l}$ and ϕ_k: $w_{d,l} \sim Cat(\phi_{Z_{d,l}})$.

The topic distribution and the context words are combined to further reduce the uncertainty of the topic assignment. As we explain in Sect. 3.4, this reduction ensures a high probability that consecutive words are assigned to the same topic.

Algorithm 1: Gibbs sampling algorithm

Input: A set D of documents with length N_d ($d \in D$); number of iterations N_{iter}; number of topics K

Output: For each document $d \in D$, topic distribution θ_d; for each topic k, word distribution ϕ_k ($1 \leq k \leq K$); word co-occurrence matrix Λ

1 Initialize topic assignments randomly for all words in D
2 **for** *iteration = 1 to N_{iter}* **do**
3   **for** *d = 1 to $|D|$* **do**
4   **for** *l = 1 to N_d* **do**
5   Generate a topic $Z_{d,l}$ from $P_{d,l}$ according to Eq. (2).
6   Update θ_d, ϕ_k and Λ

7 **return** ϕ_k for each topic k, θ_d for each document d and Λ.

3.3 Parameter Estimation

We use Gibbs sampling [10] to estimate parameters. In our sampling procedure, we need to calculate the conditional probability of topic assignment $P_{d,l,k} = P(Z_{d,l} = k|W_{d,l}, Z_{d,-(d,l)}, W'_{d,l}, \alpha, \beta, \gamma)$ for each word, where $W_{d,l}$ represents the lth word in d. $Z_{d,-(d,l)}$ refers to the topic assignments for all words in d except for word $W_{d,l}$. $W'_{d,l}$ are the context words of $W_{d,l}$. The result of $P_{d,l,k}$ is computed as follow (See Appendix A in Supplementary for detailed derivation):

$$P_{d,l,k} \propto \left[(n^{b_w}_{k,-(d,i)} + \gamma_t) + (n_{d,k,-(d,l)} + \alpha_k) \right] \frac{n^t_{k,-(d,l)} + \beta_t}{\sum_{f=1}^{V}(n^f_{k,-(d,l)} + \beta_f)}, \quad (2)$$

where $n_{d,k,-(d,l)}$ is the number of words in d which belongs to topic k without $W_{d,l}$, $n^t_{k,-(d,l)}$ represents the number of word t of topic k without $W_{d,l}$. Compared with the conditional probability of traditional topic models, such as LDA (as Eq. (3)), we see the difference is the probability of topic k for each word, which is affected by the frequency of its context word pairs on topic k in other documents.

$$P'_{d,l,k} \propto (n_{d,k,-(d,l)} + \alpha_k) \frac{n^t_{k,-(d,l)} + \beta_t}{\sum_{f=1}^{V}(n^f_{k,-(d,l)} + \beta_f)}. \quad (3)$$

According to Eq. (2), we obtain the conditional probabilities of topic assignment $P_{d,l,k}$ of each word in document d, so as to compute their corresponding topic distribution $P_{d,l}$. Our sampling algorithm is shown in Algorithm 1. The word co-occurrence matrix Λ recording the number of word pairs in each topic is utilized to compute λ, where the first two dimensions of Λ are all the unique words and the third dimension records the accumulated shared topic counts.

3.4 Topic Coherency Ratio

To further study how C-LDA affects the coherency and saliency in modeling, we calculate the joint probability of consecutive words which share the same topic in two cases: with and without considering context word pairs. For consecutive words $\boldsymbol{W}_{d,i:j}$ from W_i to W_j in document d, we denote the joint probability of sharing topic k by $P(\boldsymbol{W}_{d,i:j}, k)$ in the former case and the one in the latter case by $P'(\boldsymbol{W}_{d,i:j}, k)$. Taking their logarithms and computing their ratios as well as removing constant terms, we obtain the result as shown in Eq. (4). We retain the fraction of the right-hand side and name it Topic Coherency Ratio (TCR) as Eq. (5), denoted by R_t (See Appendix B in Supplementary for detailed derivation).

$$\frac{\log P(\boldsymbol{W}_{d,i:j}, k)}{\log P'(\boldsymbol{W}_{d,i:j}, k)} \propto 1 + \frac{\sum_{w \in \boldsymbol{W}_{d,i:j}} \log n_{k,-\boldsymbol{W}_{d,i:j}}^{b_w}}{\sum_{w \in \boldsymbol{W}_{d,i:j}} \log n_{k,-\boldsymbol{W}_{d,i:j}}^{w}} \tag{4}$$

$$R_t(\boldsymbol{W}_{d,i:j}, k) \triangleq \frac{\sum_{w \in \boldsymbol{W}_{d,i:j}} \log n_{k,-\boldsymbol{W}_{d,i:j}}^{b_w}}{\sum_{w \in \boldsymbol{W}_{d,i:j}} \log n_{k,-\boldsymbol{W}_{d,i:j}}^{w}}. \tag{5}$$

For a set of consecutive words, the TCR is a ratio of occurrence number in the same topic between the context word pairs and words. The ratio ranges from $[0, 1]$ and reflects the intensity of coherency for a set of consecutive words[2]. A higher ratio corresponds to a stronger coherency. By Eq. (4), we see $P(\boldsymbol{W}_{d,i:j}, k)$ is always greater than $P'(\boldsymbol{W}_{d,i:j}, k)$, which proves that C-LDA is more likely to generate coherent topic segments than other conventional topic models, including LDA and most of its extended versions[3]. For short segments consisting of a tiny proportion of words in a document, they can still be assigned to the topic k with a higher probability than others if they contain frequent word pairs in topic k. Thus C-LDA ensures both better coherency and saliency in topic segmentation.

Since the number K of topics is a given empirical value, it is inevitable to generate redundant topic segments in each document. Although we might be able to specify a good K value beforehand, the difference in the number of topics contained in each document also leads to the inevitability of generating redundant segments. Therefore, merging redundant segments with frequent ones is indispensable, where the key is to judge whether the resulting segment has a higher coherency than the original ones. The TCR is a coherency measurement based on the ratio of word pairs and words instead of relying solely on their frequencies. This property ensures the coherency of segments are independent of their lengths; thus, we design a TCR based Redundant Topic Merging (RTM) algorithm to optimize the generated topic segments. The steps of RTM are: for each topic segment, we consider three cases: (1) merging with the previous segment; (2) merging with the next segment; (3) non-merging. For these three cases, the TCRs are calculated separately and the case with the highest ratio is selected. We repeat the above steps until the number of segments stays unchanged.

---

[2] For the words in $\boldsymbol{W}_{d,i:j}$ belonging to topic k, if and only if they all occur as context word pairs of topic k in all the documents, the TCR gets the maximum value 1, while it gets the minimum value 0 if and only if none of them occurs in a context.

[3] The fraction on the right-hand side is always positive.

4 Experiments

We evaluate our model by a series of experiments. Results were obtained with eight-fold cross-validation on a machine with Intel i9 processor and 128 GB memory. The hyper-parameters (α, β, γ) were all fixed to 0.05.

We tested our model on three standard datasets[4] (**Wikicities** (Wici), **Cellphones Reviews** (Cell) and **Wikielements** (Wiel)) and three extended datasets based on the former three. **Wikicities** contains Wikipedia articles about the world 100 largest cities by population, **Cellphones Reviews** contains 100 cellphone reviews and **Wikielements** contains 118 English Wikipedia articles about chemical elements. Labeled topic segments of the 3 standard datasets are all of the similar lengths (about 3000 words per document) and uniformly distributed; thus, to simulate the cases of more diverse topic structures, we increase their original total number of documents to 2000 and generated various sizes of topic segments for each document. The detailed generating steps for a document are: (1) select the number of segments based on a uniform distribution from 10 to 50; (2) for each segment, set its length from a uniform distribution of 10 to 100 and randomly assign it to a topic from the topic labels; (3) choose sentences of the corresponding assigned topics from the labeled documents to fill the segments until all segments are loaded.

We compare C-LDA (available on Github[5]) against four topic models: LDA [5], BTM [7], TKM [22] and SegLDA [1]. BTM is a topic model based on word co-occurrence modeling. TKM is a method to generate coherent topics by considering the influence of keywords on their contexts. SegLDA is a LDA-extended model for topic segmentation by introducing an independent topic distribution for each predefined segment.

We use Normalized Point-wise Mutual Information (NPMI)[6] to measure the topic coherence scores [17]. It assumes that a topic is more coherent if the most probable words in the topic co-occur more frequently in the corpus [13]. NPMI scores are in $[-1, 1]$ and a higher value indicates that the topic distributions are semantically more coherent. The performances of topic segmentation is evaluated with two metrics: PK[7] and Window Diff (WD)[8]. They both refer to error rates which are calculated by comparing the inferred segmentation with the gold-standard (ground truth) for each window based on moving a sliding window over the document. Lower scores refer to better segmentation performance.

---

[4] http://groups.csail.mit.edu/rbg/code/mallows/.

[5] https://github.com/liliverpool/C-LDA.git.

[6] $\text{NPMI}(k) = \sum_{1 \leq i < j \leq T} \frac{1}{-\log P(w_i, w_j)} \log \frac{P(w_i, w_j)}{P(w_i)P(w_j)}$, where $P(w_i, w_j)$ and $P(w_i)$ are the occurrence probabilities of word pair (w_i, w_j) and word w_i, respectively.

[7] $P_k(\text{ref}, \text{hyp}) = P(\text{false}|\text{refer}, \text{hyp}, \text{same}, k)P(\text{same}|\text{refer}, k) + P(\text{miss}|\text{refer}, \text{hyp}, \text{diff}, k)$ $P(\text{diff}|\text{refer}, k)$, where "refer" is the ground truth and "hyp" is the generated segments. k is usually the half of the average gold-standard segment size ($k = 15$ in our experiments). More details are in [3].

[8] $WD(\text{ref}, \text{hyp}) = \frac{1}{N-k} \sum_{i=1}^{N-k} (|b(\text{ref}_i, \text{ref}_{i+k}) - b(\text{hyp}_i, \text{hyp}_{i+k})| > 0)$, where $b(i, j)$ represents the number of boundaries between positions i and j in the text and N is the number of sentences in the document [17].

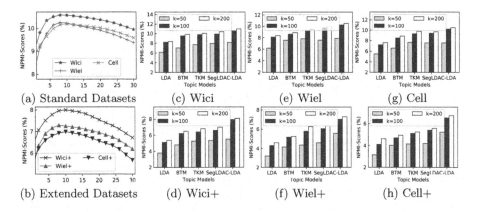

Fig. 3. NPMIs of different L values (a–b) and different topic numbers k (c–h).

4.1 Topic Coherence

Firstly, we calculated NPMIs of C-LDA under different window sizes L (from 1 to 30) with topic number $K = 100$. The results are shown in Fig. 3(a–b). We see that, in both standard and extended datasets, NPMIs increase sharply until around $L = 10$ then begin to decline. Moreover, we see there is a sharp decline in the extended datasets when $L > 15$. This might be because of their more complex topic structures and longer window sizes are more likely to contain irrelevant content. Therefore, we set $L = 10$ in the rest of our experiments.

The results of NPMIs (with $K = 50, 100, 200$) for all baseline models are shown in Fig. 3(c–h). We see that C-LDA shows the best results on all six datasets and more significant improvements in data sets with more complex topic structures (Wici+, Wile+, Cell+), which proves the validity of our model for generating coherent topics. A possible reason is that C-LDA combines the frequency of context word pairs for each topic in modeling, while the other models (such as TKM) either consider only the words frequency in each topic or the frequency of all word pairs in individual documents (such as BTM). Moreover, semantic expressions in a document are usually coherent and segmented, e.g., paragraphs and sections, thus, considering the context in a topic assignment can clarify the semantics of the word, so as to reduce the risk of splitting a coherent semantic segment.

4.2 Topic Segmentation

The results in topics of $K = 50$ and $K = 100$ are shown in Table 1, where the C-LDA-R is the C-LDA with RTM optimization algorithm. We see that C-LDA and C-LDA-R perform the best in all cases of $K = 100$ and dominate in most cases when $K = 50$, which validates their performance for coherency and saliency of different segments in topic segmentation tasks.

BTM aims to generate all the distinct word pairs within a fixed window given a topic. Therefore, its effect on the topic coherency is achieved by increasing the

Table 1. Topic segmentation results. PK and WD scores are in %. Bold fonts indicate best scores yielded by models except for C-LDA-R and * indicates the best scores among all the models.

K	Models	PK						WindowDiff						Time Cost (hours)					
		Wici.	Wiel.	Cell.	Wici+	Wiel+	Cell+	Wici.	Wiel.	Cell.	Wici+	Wiel+	Cell+	Wici.	Wiel.	Cell.	Wici+	Wiel+	Cell+
50	BTM	35.9	33.6	41.2	42.2	38.7	47.1	38.2	34.5	41.0	45.6	42.1	49.8	9.2	7.2	7.7	4.9	4.2	4.2
	TKM	28.6	23.9	37.8	33.8	28.5	43.2	28.7	33.4	38.7	35.8	31.8	46.4	1.1*	0.7*	0.8*	0.4*	0.3*	0.3*
	SegLDA	26.1	22.7	**35.2**	30.5	27.2	38.9	**27.1***	25.6	35.8	**33.4***	28.3	39.3	4.5	3.1	3.3	1.7	1.4	1.5
	C-LDA	**25.3**	**22.2**	35.3	**29.9***	**26.3**	**37.6**	27.7	25.7	**34.1***	33.7	**28.2**	**38.1***	1.9	1.2	1.5	0.9	0.8	0.8
	C-LDA-R	24.8*	20.6*	34.9*	30.3	26.2*	37.5*	27.3	24.8*	33.5	33.8	27.9*	38.5	2.0	1.3	1.6	1.0	0.9	0.9
100	BTM	32.5	30.2	37.5	40.1	36.5	44.3	35.7	33.4	40.2	41.4	39.8	45.7	15.7	12.6	11.5	8.6	8.2	8.5
	TKM	26.7	21.2	30.6	31.3	27.4	37.2	29.9	24.6	36.6	32.8	29.8	41.7	2.1*	1.5*	1.7*	0.9*	0.7*	0.8*
	SegLDA	23.2	20.4	31.3	27.4	24.1	34.8	28.5	23.9	33.5	29.8	24.6	36.3	8.8	6.5	7.6	3.1	2.4	2.6
	C-LDA	**22.1**	**19.7**	**29.8**	**25.8**	**23.2**	**31.7**	**27.5**	**22.6**	**32.2**	**27.4**	**24.5**	**33.9**	4.2	3.2	3.8	2.4	2.3	2.4
	C-LDA-R	21.9*	19.2*	27.6*	24.5*	22.6*	30.4*	25.2*	21.6*	30.7*	26.8*	23.7*	32.4*	4.3	3.3	3.9	2.5	2.4	2.5

joint probability of each word pair and topics. The high frequent word pairs in a corpus are of high joint probabilities. However, in a corpus, the majority are ordinary words but not word pairs, and their topic assignments are still of high uncertainty. Besides, the computation of all distinct word pairs significantly increases its training time. TKM improves the coherency of topic segmentation by considering the influence of keywords on the topic assignment of surrounding words and cost the least time. However, short topic segments with insufficient keywords are likely to be absorbed by long topic segments, which is a possible reason of its low performance. In some cases of insufficient topic number ($K = 50$), SegLDA outperforms other methods. However, as K increased from 50 to 100, its performance growth is inferior to C-LDA. For SegLDA, the topics for words in a segment can be assigned from the segment-specific topic distribution, which improves the saliency of topic segments. However, assigning topics without considering the original document can lead to a loss of context information and degrade the accuracy of topic modeling. That is, a word is possibly assigned to an incorrect topic even if it is not absorbed by others. C-LDA considers both the contextual word pairs and topic distribution. Based on the reorganized topic distribution CTD, it reduces the uncertainty of the topic assignment and increases the joint probability of consecutive words sharing the same topic at the expense of increasing time consumption. Moreover, comparing the results of the original and their extended datasets, we see our method has stronger robustness to more complex topic structures, which also leads to better applicability.

For C-LDA-R, we see that the effect of the RTM algorithm is limited in the case when $K = 50$ since it is insufficient to cover all the occurred topics. When $K = 100$, RTM effectively improves the performance of topic segmentation. To further study the effect of RTM, we calculated the changes of PK and WindowDiff with different numbers K of topics (from 25 to 200). The experiments were conducted on the 3 extended datasets and the results are shown in Fig. 4. We see the measures of both C-LDA and C-LDA-R decrease quickly with the increase in length of K until $K = 100$. For C-LDA, the performance starts to

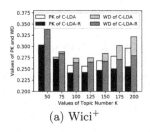 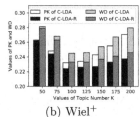 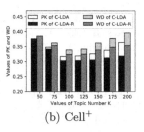

(a) Wici⁺   (b) Wiel⁺   (b) Cell⁺

Fig. 4. PK and WindowDiff scores with the increase of the number K of topics in (a) Wikicities⁺, (b) Wikielements⁺ and (c) CellphoneReviews⁺. The stacked part above each bar is the improvement from RTM algorithm.

decrease around $K = 150$, while for C-LDA-R, it tends to saturate as K keeps on increasing. The improvement by RTM becomes increasingly remarkable with the increase of K, which also proves the robustness of C-LDA-R for redundant topics. In addition, the time complexity of RTM for each document is $O(L \sum_{S' \in S} |S'|)$, where L is the context window size, S is the list of segments for a document and $|S'|$ represents the length of each segment S' in S. The time consumption of the RTM is acceptable, since L is set less than 30. Besides, the optimization process of each document is independent, which is easy for parallelization.

5 Conclusion

We proposed a new generative model for topic segmentation. By combining topic distribution and context word pairs-topic distribution, our model improves the certainty of the topic assignment and ensures high coherency and saliency in topic segmentation. Besides, we designed an optimization algorithm to merge redundant topic segments for each document. Our experiments show that our proposal outperforms baseline models, in terms of the segmentation scores of PK and WD in topic segmentation. In future work, we will further optimize the parameter estimation steps, such as reducing the size of the word co-occurrence matrix, and use more efficient estimation methods (e.g., Variational Inference).

References

1. Amoualian, H., Lu, W., Gaussier, M.: Topical coherence in LDA-based models through induced segmentation. In: Proceedings of ACL, vol. 1, pp. 1799–1809 (2017)
2. Balikas, G., Amoualian, H., Clausel, M., Gaussier, E., Amini, M.R.: Modeling topic dependencies in semantically coherent text spans with copulas. In: Proceedings of COLING, pp. 1767–1776 (2016)
3. Beeferman, D., Berger, A., Lafferty, J.: Statistical models for text segmentation. Mach. Learn. **34**(1–3), 177–210 (1999)
4. Blei, D.M., Moreno, P.J.: Topic segmentation with an aspect hidden Markov model. In: Proceedings of SIGIR, pp. 343–348 (2001)

5. Blei, D.M., Ng, A.Y., Jordan, M.I.: Latent Dirichlet allocation. J. Mach. Learn. Res. **3**, 993–1022 (2003)
6. Cappella, J.N., Jamieson, K.H.: Spiral of Cynicism: The Press and the PublicGood. Oxford University Press, New York (1997)
7. Cheng, X., Yan, X., Lan, Y., Guo, J.: BTM: topic modeling over short texts. IEEE TKDE **26**(12), 2928–2941 (2014)
8. Du, L., Pate, J.K., Johnson, M.: Topic segmentation with an ordering-based topic model. In: Proceedings of AAAI (2015)
9. Eisenstein, J., Barzilay, R.: Bayesian unsupervised topic segmentation. In: Proceedings of EMNLP, pp. 334–343 (2008)
10. Geman, S., Geman, D.: Stochastic relaxation, Gibbs distributions, and the Bayesian restoration of images. IEEE Trans. PAMI **6**(6), 721–741 (2009)
11. Goldberg, Y., Levy, O.: Word2vec explained: deriving Mikolov et al'.s negative-sampling word-embedding method. arXiv preprint arXiv:1402.3722 (2014)
12. Jenks, J.W.: The guidance of public opinion. Am. J. Sociol. **1**(2), 158–169 (1895)
13. Lamprier, S., Amghar, T., Levrat, B., Saubion, F.: On evaluation methodologies for text segmentation algorithms. In: Proceedings of ICTAI, vol. 2, pp. 19–26 (2007)
14. Liang, S., Ren, Z., Yilmaz, E., Kanoulas, E.: Collaborative user clustering for short text streams. In: Proceedings of AAAI, pp. 3504–3510 (2017)
15. Ng, K.W., Tian, G.L., Tang, M.L.: Dirichlet and Related Distributions: Theory, Methods and Applications, vol. 888. Wiley, Oxford (2011)
16. Peng, D., Guilan, D., Yong, Z.: Contextual-LDA: a context coherent latent topic model for mining large corpora. In: Proceedings of BigMM, pp. 420–425. IEEE (2016)
17. Pevzner, L., Hearst, M.A.: A critique and improvement of an evaluation metric for text segmentation. Comput. Linguist. **28**(1), 19–36 (2002)
18. Purver, M.: Topic Segmentation. Spoken Language Understanding: Systems for Extracting Semantic Information from Speech, pp. 291–317 (2011)
19. Reynar, J.C.: Topic segmentation: algorithms and applications. Ph.D. thesis, Institute for Research in Cognitive Science Technical, University of Pennsylvania (1998)
20. Sahlgren, M.: The distributional hypothesis. Ital. J. Disabil. Stud. **20**, 33–53 (2008)
21. Sauper, C., Haghighi, A., Barzilay, R.: Content models with attitude. In: Proceedings of ACL, pp. 350–358 (2011)
22. Schneider, J., Vlachos, M.: Topic modeling based on keywords and context. In: Proceedings of ICDM, pp. 369–377 (2018)
23. Wang, H., Zhang, D., Zhai, C.: Structural topic model for latent topical structure analysis. In: Proceedings of ACL, pp. 1526–1535 (2011)
24. Wang, X., McCallum, A., Wei, X.: Topical n-grams: phrase and topic discovery, with an application to information retrieval. In: Proceedings of ICDM, pp. 697–702 (2007)
25. Yan, X., Guo, J., Lan, Y., Xu, J., Cheng, X.: A probabilistic model for bursty topic discovery in microblogs. In: Proceedings of AAAI (2015)
26. Yang, G., Wen, D., Chen, N.S., Sutinen, E., et al.: A novel contextual topic model for multi-document summarization. Expert Syst. Appl. **42**(3), 1340–1352 (2015)
27. Yin, J., Wang, J.: A Dirichlet multinomial mixture model-based approach for short text clustering. In: Proceedings of SIGKDD, pp. 233–242 (2014)

SubRank: Subgraph Embeddings via a Subgraph Proximity Measure

Oana Balalau[1(✉)] and Sagar Goyal[2]

[1] Inria and École Polytechnique, Palaiseau, France
oana.balalau@inria.fr
[2] Microsoft, Vancouver, Canada
sagoya@microsoft.com

Abstract. Representation learning for graph data has gained a lot of attention in recent years. However, state-of-the-art research is focused mostly on node embeddings, with little effort dedicated to the closely related task of computing subgraph embeddings. Subgraph embeddings have many applications, such as community detection, cascade prediction, and question answering. In this work, we propose a subgraph to subgraph proximity measure as a building block for a subgraph embedding framework. Experiments on real-world datasets show that our approach, SUBRANK, outperforms state-of-the-art methods on several important data mining tasks.

Keywords: Subgraph embeddings · Personalized PageRank

1 Introduction

In recent years we have witnessed the success of graph representation learning in many tasks such as community detection [8,19], link prediction [10,20], graph classification [3], and cascade growth prediction [13]. A large body of work has focused on node embeddings, techniques that represent nodes as dense vectors that preserve the properties of nodes in the original graph [5,9]. Representation learning of larger structures has generally been associated with embedding collections of graphs [3]. *Paths, subgraphs and communities embeddings* have received far less attention despite their importance in graphs. In homogeneous graphs, subgraph embeddings have been used in community prediction [1,8], and cascade growth prediction [6,13]. In heterogeneous graphs, subgraphs embedding have tackled tasks such as semantic user search [14] and question answering [4].

Nevertheless, the techniques proposed in the literature for computing subgraph embeddings have at least one of the following two drawbacks: *i*) they are supervised techniques and such they are dependent on annotated data and do not generalize to other tasks; *ii*) they can tackle only a specific type of subgraph.

O. Balalau and S. Goyal—Part of this work was done while the authors were at Max Planck Institute for Informatics, Germany.

H. W. Lauw et al. (Eds.): PAKDD 2020, LNAI 12084, pp. 487–498, 2020.
https://doi.org/10.1007/978-3-030-47426-3_38

488   O. Balalau and S. Goyal

Approach. In this work, we tackle the problem of computing subgraph embeddings in an unsupervised setting, where embeddings are trained for one task and will be tested on different tasks. We propose a *subgraph embedding method based on a novel subgraph proximity measure*. Our measure is inspired by the random walk proximity measure Personalized PageRank [11]. We show that our subgraph embeddings are *comprehensive* and achieve competitive performance on three important data mining tasks: community detection, link prediction, and cascade growth prediction.

Contributions. Our salient contributions in this work are:

- We define a novel subgraph to subgraph proximity measure;
- We introduce a framework that learns comprehensive subgraphs embeddings;
- In a thorough experimental evaluation, we highlight the potential of our method on a variety of data mining tasks.

2   Related Work

Node Embeddings. Methods for computing node embeddings aim to represent nodes as low-dimensional vectors that summarize properties of nodes, such as their neighborhood. The numerous embedding techniques differ in the computational model and in what properties of nodes are conserved. For example, in matrix factorization approaches, the goal is to perform dimension reduction on a matrix that encodes the pairwise proximity of nodes, where proximity is defined as adjacency [2], k-step transitions [7], or Katz centrality [16]. Random walk approaches have been inspired by the important progress achieved in the NLP community in computing word embeddings [15]. These techniques optimize node embeddings such that nodes co-occurring in short random walks in the graph have similar embeddings [10,18]. Another successful technique is to take as input a node and an embedding similarity distribution and minimizes the KL-divergence between the two distributions [19,20].

Subgraph Embeddings. A natural follow-up question is how to compute embeddings for larger structures in the graph, such as paths, arbitrary subgraphs, motifs or communities. In [1], the authors propose a method inspired by ParagraphVector [12], where each subgraph is represented as a collection of random walks. Subgraph and node embeddings are learned such that given a subgraph and a random walk, we can predict the next node in the walk using the subgraph embedding and the node embeddings. The approach is tested on link prediction and on community detection, using ego-networks to represent nodes. In [13], the authors present an end-to-end neural framework that given in input the cascade graph, predicts the future growth of the cascade for a given time period. A cascade graph is sampled for a set of random walks, which are given as input to a gated neural network to predict the future size of the cascade. [6] is similarly an end-to-end neural framework for cascade prediction, but based on the Hawkes process. The method transforms the cascade into diffusion paths, where each path describes the process of information propagation within the observation time-frame. Another very important type of subgraph is a community and in [8] community embeddings are represented as multivariate Gaussian distributions.

Graph Embeddings. Given a collection of graphs, a graph embedding technique will learn representations for each graph. In [3], the authors propose an inductive framework for computing graph embeddings, based on training an attention network to predict a graph proximity measure, such as graph edit distance. Graph embeddings are closely related to graph kernels, functions that measure the similarity between pairs of graphs [21]. Graph kernels are used together with kernel methods such as SVM to perform graph classification [22].

3   Feature Learning Framework

Preliminaries. PageRank [17] is the stationary distribution of a random walk in which, at a given step, with a probability α, a surfer teleports to a random node and with probability $1 - \alpha$, moves along a randomly chosen outgoing edge of the current node. In Personalized PageRank (PPR) [11], instead of teleporting to a random node with probability α, the surfer teleports to a randomly chosen node from a set of predefined seed nodes. Let $Pr(u)$ be the PageRank of node u and $PPR(u, v)$ be the PageRank score of node v personalized for seed node u.

Problem Statement. Given a directed graph $G = (V, E)$, a set of subgraphs $S_1, S_2, \cdots, S_k$ of G and an integer d, compute the d-dimensional embeddings of the subgraphs.

3.1   Subgraph Proximity Measure

We define a subgraph proximity measure inspired by Personalized PageRank. Let S_i and S_j be two subgraphs in a directed graph G. Their proximity in the graph is:

$$px(S_i, S_j) = \sum_{v_i \in S_i} PR_{S_i}(v_i) \sum_{v_j \in S_j} PR_{S_j}(v_j) \cdot PPR(v_i, v_j), \tag{1}$$

where $PR_{S_i}(v_i)$ represents the PageRank of node v_i in the subgraph S_i, and $PPR(v_i, v_j)$ the PageRank of node v_j personalized for node v_i in the graph G.

When considering how to define proximity between subgraphs, our intuition is as follows: important nodes in subgraph S_i should be close to important nodes in subgraph S_j. This condition is fulfilled as PageRank will give high scores to important nodes in the subgraphs and Personalized PageRank will give high scores to nodes that are "close" or "similar". We note that our measure is a similarity measure, hence subgraphs that are similar will receive a high proximity score. We choose the term *proximity* to emphasis that our measure relates to nearness in the graph, as it is computed using random walks.

We can interpret Eq. 1 using random walks, as follows: Alice is a random surfer in the subgraph S_i, Bob is a random surfer in the subgraph S_j, and Carol is a random surfer in graph G. Alice decides to send a message to Bob via Carol. Carol starts from the current node Alice is visiting $(PR_{S_i}(v_i))$ and she will reach a node $v_j \in S_j$ with probability $PPR(v_i, v_j)$. Bob will be there to receive the message with probability $PR_{S_j}(v_j)$.

Normalized Proximity. Given a collection of subgraphs $S = \{S_1, S_2, \cdots S_k\}$, we normalize the proximity $px(S_i, S_j), \forall j \in 1, k$ such that it can be interpreted as a probability distribution. The normalized proximity for a subgraph S_i is:

$$\hat{px}(S_i, S_j) = \frac{px(S_i, S_j)}{\sum_{S_k \in S} px(S_i, S_k)} \qquad (2)$$

Rank of a Subgraph. Similarly to PageRank, our proximity can inform us of the importance of a subgraph. The normalized proximity given a collection of subgraphs $S_1, S_2, \cdots S_k$ can be expressed as a stochastic matrix, where each row i encodes the normalized proximity given subgraph S_i. The importance of subgraph S_i can be computed by summing up the elements of column i.

Sampling According to the Proximity Measure. Given a subgraph S_i in input, we present a procedure for efficiently sampling $px(S_i, \cdot)$ introduced in Eq. 1. We suppose that all the Pagerank vectors of the subgraphs $\{S_1, S_2, \cdots S_k\}$ have been precomputed. We first select a node n_i in S_i according to distribution PR_{S_i}. Secondly, we start a random walk from n_i in the graph G and we select n_j, the last node in the walk before the teleportation. Lastly, node n_j may belong to several subgraphs $S_1^j, S_2^j \cdots$. We return a subgraph S_j according to the normalized distribution $PR_{S_1^j}(n_j), PR_{S_2^j}(n_j), \cdots$. The procedure doesn't require computing the Personalized Pagerank vectors, which saves us $O(n^2)$ space. We shall use this procedure for computing embeddings, thus avoiding computing and storing the full proximity measure px.

3.2   Subgraph Embeddings via SubRank

Given a graph $G = (V, E)$ and set of subgraphs of G, $S = \{S_1, S_2, \cdots, S_k\}$, we learn their representations as dense vectors, i.e. as embeddings. We extend the framework in [20] proposed for computing node embeddings to an approach for subgraph embeddings. In [20], the authors propose to learn node embeddings such that the embeddings preserve an input similarity distribution between nodes. The similarities of a node v to any other node in the graph are represented by the similarity distribution sim_G, where $\sum_{w \in V} sim_G(v, w) = 1$. The corresponding embedding similarity distribution is sim_E. The optimization function of the learning algorithm minimizes the Kullback-Leibler (KL) divergence between the two proximity distributions:

$$\sum_{v \in V} KL(sim_G(v, \cdot), sim_E(v, \cdot))$$

The authors propose several options for instantiating sim_G, such as Personalized PageRank and adjacency similarity. The similarity between embeddings, sim_E, is the normalized dot product of the vectors.

In order to adapt this approach to our case, we define the subgraph-to-subgraph proximity sim_G to be the normalized proximity presented in Eq. 2. The embedding similarity sim_E is computed in the same manner and the optimization function now minimizes the divergence between distributions defined on our input subgraphs, i.e. $sim_G, sim_E : S \times S \mapsto [0,1]$. In our experimental evaluation we use this method, which we refer to as **SubRank**. We note that sim_G will not be fully computed, but approximated using the sampling procedure presented in Sect. 3.1.

3.3   Applications

Proximity of Ego-Networks. Two very important tasks in graph mining are community detection and link prediction. Suppose Alice is a computer scientist and she joins Twitter. She starts following the updates of Andrew Ng, but also the updates of her friends, Diana and John. Bob is also a computer scientist on Twitter and he follows Andrew Ng, Jure Leskovec and his friend Julia. As shown in Fig. 1, there is no path in the directed graph between Alice and Bob. A path-based similarity measure between nodes Alice and Bob, such as Personalized PageRank, will return similarity 0, while it will return high values between Alice and Andrew Ng and between Bob and Andrew Ng. An optimization algorithm for computing node embeddings will have to address this trade-off, with a potential loss in the quality of the representations. Thus, we might miss that both Alice and Bob are computer scientists. To address this issue we capture the information stored in the neighbors of the nodes by considering ego-networks. Therefore in our work, we represent a *node v as its ego network* of size k (the nodes reachable from v in k steps). In Sect. 4, we perform quantitative analysis to validate our intuition.

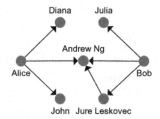

Fig. 1. Illustrative example for ego-network proximity.

Proximity of Cascade Subgraphs. In a graph, an information cascade can be modeled as a directed tree, where the root represents the original content creator, and the remaining nodes represent the content reshares. When considering the task of predicting the future size of the cascade, the nodes already in the cascade are important, as it very likely their neighbors will be affected by the information propagation. However, nodes that have reshared more recently the information are more visible to their neighbors. When running PageRank on a directed tree, we observe that nodes on the same level have the same score, and the score of nodes increases as we increase the depth. Hence, two cascade trees will have a high proximity score $\hat{px}$ if nodes that have joined later the cascades (i.e. are on lower levels in the trees) are "close" or "similar" according to Personalized Pagerank. In Sect. 5, we perform quantitative analysis and we show that our approach gives better results than a method that gives equal importance to all nodes in the cascade.

4   Feature Learning for Ego-Networks

Datasets. We perform experiments on five real-world graphs, described below. We report their characteristics in Table 1.

- Citeseer[1] is a citation network created from the CiteSeer digital library. Nodes are publications and edges denote citations. The node labels represent fields in computer science.
- Cora (see footnote 1) is also a citation network and the node labels represent subfields in machine learning.
- Polblogs[2] is a directed network of hyperlinks between political blogs discussing US politics. The labels correspond to republican and democrat blogs.
- Cithep[3] is a directed network of citations in high energy physics phenomenology. The network does not have ground-truth communities.
- DBLP (see footnote 3) is a co-authorship network where two authors are connected if they published at least one paper together. The communities are conferences in which the authors have published.

Table 1. Dataset description: type, vertices V, edges E, node labels L.

Dataset	Type	$|V|$	$|E|$	$|L|$
Citeseer	Citation	3.3K	4.7K	6
Cora	Citation	2.7K	5.4K	7
Polblogs	Hyperlink	1.4K	19K	2
Cithep	Citation	34K	421k	1
DBLP	Co-authorship	66K	542K	20

---

[1] https://linqs.soe.ucsc.edu/data.
[2] http://networkrepository.com/polblogs.php.
[3] https://snap.stanford.edu/data.

Competitors. We evaluate our method, SUBRANK, against several state-of-the-art methods for node and subgraph embedding computation. For each method, we used the code provided by the authors. We compare with:

- DEEPWALK [18] learns node embeddings by sampling random walks, and then applying the SkipGram model. The parameters are set to the recommended values, i.e. walk length $t = 80$, $\gamma = 80$, and window size $w = 10$.
- NODE2VEC [10] is a hyperparameter-supervised approach that extends DEEP-WALK. We fine-tuned the hyperparameters p and q on each dataset and task. In addition, $r = 10, l = 80, k = 10$, and the optimization is run for an epoch.
- LINE [19] proposes two proximity measures for computing two d-dimensional vectors for each node. In our experiments, we use the second-order proximity, as it can be used for both directed and undirected graphs. We run experiments with $T = 1000$ samples and $s = 5$ negative samples, as described in the paper.
- VERSE [20] learns node embeddings that preserve the proximity of nodes in the graph. We use Personalized PageRank as a proximity measure, the default option proposed in the paper. We run the learning algorithm for 10^5 iterations.
- VERSEAVG is a adaption of VERSE, in which the embedding of a node is the average of the VERSE embeddings of the nodes in its ego network.
- SUB2VEC [1] computes subgraph embeddings and for the experimental evaluation, we compute the embeddings of the ego networks. Using the guidelines of the authors, for Cora, Citeseer and Polblogs we select ego networks of size 2 and for the denser networks Cithep and DBLP, ego networks of size 1.

For the first four methods, node embeddings are used to represent nodes. For SUB2VEC, SUBRANK and VERSEAVG, the ego network embedding is the node representation. The embeddings are used as node features for community detection and link prediction. We compute 128 dimensional embeddings.

Parameter Setting for SubRank. We represent each node by its ego network of size 1. We run the learning algorithm for 10^5 iterations. **Our code is public.**[4]

Running Time SubRank. In the interest of space, we report only the time required by SUBRANK for computing ego network embeddings. We run the experiments on a Intel Xeon CPU E5-2667 v4 @ 3.20 GHz, using 40 threads. The running times are as follows: 1 m 40 s Citeseer, 1 m 26 s Cora, 49 s Polblogs, 19 m 39 s for Cithep and 39 m 45 s for DBLP.

4.1 Node Clustering

We assess the quality of the embeddings in terms of their ability to capture communities in a graph. For this, we use the k-means algorithm to cluster the nodes embedded in the d-dimensional space. In Table 2 we report the Normalized Mutual Information (NMI) with respect to the original label distribution. On Polblogs, SUBRANK has a low NMI, while on Citeseer and Cora it outperforms the other methods. On DBLP it has a comparative performance with VERSE.

---

[4] https://github.com/nyxpho/subrank

Table 2. Normalized Mutual Information (NMI) for node clustering.

Method	Dataset			
	Citeseer	Cora	Polblogs	DBLP
DEEPWALK	0.015	0.018	0.013	0.314
NODE2VEC	0.023	0.100	0.013	0.336
LINE	0.084	0.208	**0.448**	0.284
VERSE	0.103	0.257	0.024	**0.363**
VERSEAVG	0.125	0.310	0.318	0.360
SUB2VEC	0.007	0.004	0.001	0.001
SUBRANK	**0.179**	**0.347**	0.021	0.357

4.2 Node Classification

Node classification is the task of predicting the correct node labels in a graph. For each dataset, we try several configurations by varying the percentage of nodes used in training. We evaluate the methods using the micro and macro $F1$ score, and we report the micro $F1$, as both measures present similar trends. The results are presented in Table 3. On Citeseer and Cora SUBRANK significantly outperforms the other methods. On Polblogs, SUBRANK performs similarly to the other baselines, even though the embeddings achieved a low NMI score. On DBLP, SUBRANK is the second best method.

4.3 Link Prediction

To create training data for link prediction, we randomly remove 10% of edges, ensuring that each node retains at least one neighbor. This set represents the ground truth in the test set, while we take the remaining graph as the training set. In addition, we randomly sample an equal number of node pairs that have no edge connecting them as negative samples in our test set. We then learn embeddings on the graph without the 10% edges. Next, for each edge (u, v) in the training or the test set, we obtain the edge features by computing the Hadamard product of the embeddings for u and v. The Hadamard product has shown a better performance than other operators for this task [10,20]. We report the accuracy of the link prediction task in Table 4. Our method achieves the best performance on 4 out of 5 datasets.

5   Feature Learning for Information Cascades

Given in input: i) a social network $G = (V, E)$, captured at a time t_0, ii) a set of information cascades C that appear in G after the timestamp t_0, and that are captured after t_1 duration from their creation, iii) a time window t_2, our goal is to predict the growth of a cascade, i.e. the number of new nodes a

Table 3. $F1$ micro score for the classification task.

% of labelled nodes

Method	1%	5%	10%	20%
DEEPWALK	20.95	19.98	22.26	26.90
NODE2VEC	31.20	31.11	28.24	30.15
LINE	30.81	33.58	44.81	53.62
VERSE	24.48	31.61	41.52	51.66
VERSEAVG	29.46	38.51	46.12	55.77
SUB2VEC	18.23	20.17	22.04	22.79
SUBRANK	**40.46**	**48.52**	**55.75**	**61.66**

(a) $F1$ micro score for classification in Citeseer

% of labelled nodes

Method	1%	5%	10%	20%
DEEPWALK	46.40	45.82	47.53	50.25
NODE2VEC	46.40	44.26	46.55	50.16
LINE	44.46	46.28	57.54	61.74
VERSE	46.77	50.48	58.57	65.25
VERSEAVG	53.11	57.83	65.75	70.14
SUB2VEC	25.55	46.38	46.42	46.42
SUBRANK	**65.08**	**71.78**	**73.66**	**76.83**

(b) $F1$ micro score for classification in Cora

% of labelled nodes

Method	1%	5%	10%	20%
DEEPWALK	83.19	87.78	89.63	89.68
NODE2VEC	85.83	**88.91**	**89.93**	**90.52**
LINE	73.50	87.50	89.70	89.34
VERSE	81.30	86.86	87.77	87.75
VERSEAVG	**87.12**	88.77	86.26	88.42
SUB2VEC	51.55	51.20	51.23	51.42
SUBRANK	85.70	88.94	88.59	88.33

(c) $F1$ micro score for classification in Polblogs

% of labelled nodes

Method	1%	5%	10%	20%
DEEPWALK	41.43	46.79	50.77	54.09
NODE2VEC	42.61	48.00	51.51	54.92
LINE	25.02	33.93	37.96	41.31
VERSE	44.22	48.21	51.14	54.81
VERSEAVG	45.41	**51.69**	**55.22**	**58.46**
SUB2VEC	6.00	7.71	8.85	9.60
SUBRANK	**45.67**	50.84	54.70	57.06

(d) $F1$ micro score for classification in DBLP

cascade acquires, at $t_1 + t_2$ time from its creation. Note that given a cascade $c = (V_c, E_c) \in C$, we know that the nodes V_c are present in V, however c can contain new edges not present in E.

Datasets. We select for evaluation two datasets from the literature:

- AMiner [13] represents cascades of scientific citations. We use the simplified version made available by the authors[5]. The dataset contains a global citation graph and the cascades graphs. A node in a graph represents an author and an edge from a_1 to a_2 represents the citation of a_2 in an article of a_1. A cascade shows all the citations of a given paper. There are 9860 nodes in the global graph and 560 cascade graphs that are split into training, test and validation sets. The global network is based on citations between 1992 and 2002, while the training set consists of papers published from 2003 to 2007. Papers published in 2008 and 2009 are used for validation and testing. The cascade graphs are captured at the end of 1 year and we predict the increase in citations after 1 and 2 years.

---

[5] https://github.com/chengli-um/DeepCas.

Table 4. Accuracy for link prediction.

Method	Dataset				
	Cora	Citeseer	Polblogs	Cithep	DBLP
DEEPWALK	67.42	50.75	81.93	72.24	97.83
NODE2VEC	67.04	59.54	82.76	75.58	98.56
LINE	71.49	61.48	83.72	84.85	98.26
VERSE	70.17	67.16	**85.83**	92.18	**99.27**
SUB2VEC	52.46	50.32	53.30	51.08	50.28
SUBRANK	**80.10**	**82.10**	82.70	**94.10**	**99.30**

- Sina Weibo [6] consists of retweet cascades occurring on June 1, 2016 on the social network. Each node in the graph represent a Sina Weibo user, and an edge between u_1 and u_2 represent a retweet of u_2 by u_1. Each cascade corresponds to the retweets of one message. The global network is constructed by the union of the cascades occurring in the first half of the day, while the training, test and validation cascades are taken from the second half of the day. The cascades are captured after 1 h from the initial post timestamp and we predict the increase in retweets in 1 h, 2 h and by the end of the day.

Table 5. Mean squared error (MSE) for predicted increase in cascade size.

	AMiner		Sina Weibo		
Time period	1 year	2 years	1 h	2 h	1 day
DEEPCAS	2.764	2.946	6.978	9.544	13.284
DEEPHAWKES	2.088	**1.790**	**2.403**	**2.368**	**3.714**
VERSE	2.313	2.181	3.580	4.243	5.862
SUBRANK	**1.984**	1.809	3.354	3.797	4.818

Competitors. We compare SUBRANK with the following state-of-the-art methods for the task of predicting the future size of cascades:

- DEEPCAS [13] is an end-to-end neural network framework that given in input the cascade graph, predicts the future growth of the cascade for a given period. The parameters are set to the values specified in the paper: $k = 200$, $T = 10$, mini-batch size is 5 and $\alpha = 0.01$.
- DEEPHAWKES [6] is similarly an end-to-end deep learning framework for cascade prediction based on the Hawkes process. We set the parameters to the default given by the authors: the learning rate for user embeddings is 5×10^{-4} and the learning rate for other variables is 5×10^{-3}.

- In addition, we consider the node embedding method VERSE [20], as one of the top-performing baseline in the previous section. The node embeddings are learned on the original graph and a cascade is represented as the average of the embeddings of the nodes it contains. We then train a multi-layer perceptron (MLP) regressor to predict the growth of the cascade.

Parameter Setting for SubRank. We recall that our subgraph proximity measure requires the computation of PPR of nodes in the graph and the PR of nodes in the subgraphs. For this task, we consider the PPR of nodes in the global graph and the PR of nodes in the cascades. We obtain the cascade embeddings which are then used to train an MLP regressor. For both VERSE and SUBRANK we perform a grid search for the optimal parameters of the regressor.

We report the mean squared error (MSE) on the logarithm of the cascade growth value, as done in previous work on cascade prediction [6,13] in Table 5. We observe that SUBRANK out-performs VERSE thus corroborating our intuition that nodes appearing later in a cascade should be given more importance. The best MSE overall is obtained by the end-to-end framework DEEPHAWKES which is expected as the method is tailored for the task. We note, however, that SUBRANK achieves the best results on AMiner.

6 Conclusion

In this work, we introduce a new measure of proximity for subgraphs and a framework for computing subgraph embeddings. In a departure from previous work, we focus on general-purpose embeddings, and we shed light on why our method is suited for several data mining tasks. Our experimental evaluation shows that the subgraph embeddings achieve competitive performance on three downstream applications: community detection, link prediction, and cascade prediction.

References

1. Adhikari, B., Zhang, Y., Ramakrishnan, N., Prakash, B.A.: Sub2Vec: feature learning for subgraphs. In: Phung, D., Tseng, V.S., Webb, G.I., Ho, B., Ganji, M., Rashidi, L. (eds.) PAKDD 2018. LNCS (LNAI), vol. 10938, pp. 170–182. Springer, Cham (2018). https://doi.org/10.1007/978-3-319-93037-4_14
2. Ahmed, A., Shervashidze, N., Narayanamurthy, S., Josifovski, V., Smola, A.J.: Distributed large-scale natural graph factorization. In: Proceedings of the 22nd International Conference on World Wide Web, pp. 37–48. ACM (2013)
3. Bai, Y., et al.: Unsupervised inductive graph-level representation learning via graph-graph proximity (2019)
4. Bordes, A., Chopra, S., Weston, J.: Question answering with subgraph embeddings. arXiv preprint arXiv:1406.3676 (2014)
5. Cai, H., Zheng, V.W., Chang, K.C.C.: A comprehensive survey of graph embedding: problems, techniques, and applications. IEEE Trans. Knowl. Data Eng. **30**(9), 1616–1637 (2018)

6. Cao, Q., Shen, H., Cen, K., Ouyang, W., Cheng, X.: DeepHawkes: bridging the gap between prediction and understanding of information cascades. In: Proceedings of the 2017 ACM on Conference on Information and Knowledge Management, pp. 1149–1158. ACM (2017)

7. Cao, S., Lu, W., Xu, Q.: GraRep: learning graph representations with global structural information. In: Proceedings of the 24th ACM International on Conference on Information and Knowledge Management, pp. 891–900. ACM (2015)

8. Cavallari, S., Zheng, V.W., Cai, H., Chang, K.C.C., Cambria, E.: Learning community embedding with community detection and node embedding on graphs. In: Proceedings of the 2017 ACM on Conference on Information and Knowledge Management, pp. 377–386. ACM (2017)

9. Goyal, P., Ferrara, E.: Graph embedding techniques, applications, and performance: a survey. Knowl. Based Syst. **151**, 78–94 (2018)

10. Grover, A., Leskovec, J.: node2vec: scalable feature learning for networks. In: Proceedings of the 22nd ACM SIGKDD International Conference on Knowledge Discovery and Data Mining, pp. 855–864. ACM (2016)

11. Haveliwala, T.H.: Topic-sensitive PageRank: a context-sensitive ranking algorithm for Web search. TKDE **15**(4), 784–796 (2003)

12. Le, Q., Mikolov, T.: Distributed representations of sentences and documents. In: International Conference on Machine Learning, pp. 1188–1196 (2014)

13. Li, C., Ma, J., Guo, X., Mei, Q.: DeepCas: an end-to-end predictor of information cascades. In: Proceedings of the 26th International Conference on World Wide Web, pp. 577–586 (2017)

14. Liu, Z., et al.: Subgraph-augmented path embedding for semantic user search on heterogeneous social network. In: Proceedings of the 2018 World Wide Web Conference, pp. 1613–1622 (2018)

15. Mikolov, T., Sutskever, I., Chen, K., Corrado, G.S., Dean, J.: Distributed representations of words and phrases and their compositionality. In: Advances in Neural Information Processing Systems, pp. 3111–3119 (2013)

16. Ou, M., Cui, P., Pei, J., Zhang, Z., Zhu, W.: Asymmetric transitivity preserving graph embedding. In: Proceedings of the 22nd ACM SIGKDD International Conference on Knowledge Discovery and Data Mining, pp. 1105–1114. ACM (2016)

17. Page, L., Brin, S., Motwani, R., Winograd, T.: The PageRank citation ranking: bringing order to the Web. Technical report, Stanford InfoLab (1999)

18. Perozzi, B., Al-Rfou, R., Skiena, S.: DeepWalk: online learning of social representations. In: Proceedings of the 20th ACM SIGKDD International Conference on Knowledge Discovery and Data Mining, pp. 701–710. ACM (2014)

19. Tang, J., Qu, M., Wang, M., Zhang, M., Yan, J., Mei, Q.: Line: large-scale information network embedding. In: Proceedings of the 24th International Conference on World Wide Web, pp. 1067–1077 (2015)

20. Tsitsulin, A., Mottin, D., Karras, P., Müller, E.: Verse: versatile graph embeddings from similarity measures. In: Proceedings of the 2018 World Wide Web Conference, pp. 539–548 (2018)

21. Vishwanathan, S.V.N., Schraudolph, N.N., Kondor, R., Borgwardt, K.M.: Graph kernels. J. Mach. Learn. Res. **11**, 1201–1242 (2010)

22. Zhang, Z., Wang, M., Xiang, Y., Huang, Y., Nehorai, A.: RetGK: graph kernels based on return probabilities of random walks. In: Advances in Neural Information Processing Systems, pp. 3964–3974 (2018)

Self-supervised Learning
for Semi-supervised Time Series
Classification

Shayan Jawed[(✉)], Josif Grabocka, and Lars Schmidt-Thieme

Information Systems and Machine Learning Lab, University of Hildesheim,
Hildesheim, Germany
{shayan,josif,schmidt-thieme}@ismll.uni-hildesheim.de

Abstract. Self-supervised learning is a promising new technique for learning representative features in the absence of manual annotations. It is particularly efficient in cases where labeling the training data is expensive and tedious, naturally linking it to the semi-supervised learning paradigm. In this work, we propose a new semi-supervised time series classification model that leverages features learned from the self-supervised task on unlabeled data. The idea is to exploit the unlabeled training data with a forecasting task which provides a strong surrogate supervision signal for feature learning. We draw from established multi-task learning approaches and model forecasting as an auxiliary task to be optimized jointly with the main task of classification. We evaluate our proposed method on benchmark time series classification datasets in semi-supervised setting and are able to show that it significantly outperforms the state-of-the-art baselines.

Keywords: Self-supervised features · Semi-supervised classification · Auxiliary tasks · Convolutional Neural Networks

1 Introduction

Modern deep learning architectures have taken the fields of Computer Vision, Natural Language Processing and Recommender Systems by storm. Time series Classification is no stranger to Recurrent Neural Networks and Convolutional Neural Networks (ConvNets) too [6,19]. Although proven to learn high level features across a broad domain of time series classification problems, the success of ConvNets hinges on the availability of large amounts of labeled training data. In reality, however, there is a high cost associated in acquiring such labeled data. As a result, there have been efforts to utilize semi-supervised learning algorithms catered especially for time series classification [2,9,12,17,21,22]. The idea behind semi-supervised learning is to exploit unlabeled data for training purpose in the presence of only few labeled instances. The applicability of this learning paradigm naturally extends to time series data as plentiful of it can be acquired trivially. For example, a single polysomnography (sleep study) can generate up to

© Springer Nature Switzerland AG 2020
H. W. Lauw et al. (Eds.): PAKDD 2020, LNAI 12084, pp. 499–511, 2020.
https://doi.org/10.1007/978-3-030-47426-3_39

40,000 heartbeats but it takes the time and expertise of a cardiologist to annotate individual heartbeats [2]. Hence, effective methods for semi-supervised learning can lead to mining vast amounts of time series data for which only comparatively few labels might be available.

A related stream of works has been dedicated to learning high level ConvNets based representations that do not require any manual annotation of data. Self-supervised learning has emerged as a prominent learning paradigm among such, where the idea is to define an annotation-free pretext task that is inherent in the data itself. The task stands to provide a surrogate supervision signal for feature learning. Example tasks include classifying image rotations [7], colorizing images [23] solving Jigsaw puzzles [15] to learn transferable representations for high-level tasks such as object detection and semantic segmentation. Until so far, applications have been limited to the Computer Vision domain.

In the same spirit of learning generalizable representations, we now introduce Multi-task learning. Multi-task learning is an important paradigm in machine learning which builds upon the idea of sharing knowledge between different tasks [1]. A set of tasks is learned in parallel, aiming to improve performance over each task compared with learning one of these tasks in isolation. A multi-task learning problem can also be formulated with respect to main and auxiliary tasks. Auxiliary tasks are motivated by the intuition that for most problem settings, performance over one particular task is of primary importance. However, in order to still reap the benefits of multi-task learning, related tasks could be modeled as auxiliary tasks [16]. These exist solely for the purpose of learning an enriched representation that could increase prediction accuracy over the main tasks.

In our work, we bring together ideas from these high-impact research ideas of self-supervised learning and multi-task learning to propose an auxiliary forecasting task that is inherent in labeled and unlabeled time series data both. This auxiliary task stands to provide a strong surrogate supervision signal for feature learning which when learned in parallel with the main task of classification of time series boosts the performance of the classifier especially in semi-supervised setting. More specifically, we first define a sliding window function parametrized by hyper-parameters of stride and horizon to be forecasted. Next, we augment the training set with generated samples for the forecasting task by providing labeled and unlabeled samples as input to this function. The ConvNet model is trained jointly to classify the labeled samples and forecast future series values. This exploitation of the unlabeled samples leads to learning representations that help boost the classification accuracy. The intuition is that these unlabeled samples come from the same distribution and if the model learns the complex task of forecasting series values accurately, then the same latent representations could be leveraged for classification. In our experiments we show that is indeed the case and our proposed method excels in semi-supervised setting where only a few labeled instances might be available for the model to learn from.

To recap, our contributions are:

- A novel self-supervised task that is intuitive, requires close to no changes in the base network structure and provides a strong surrogate supervisory signal for feature learning in the realm of time series classification.
- A multi-task network which enables the forecasting and classification task to share latent representations and learns high-order interactions automatically.
- Extensive experimental evaluation of our self-supervised method in the domain of semi-supervised learning for time series classification and show that it outperforms state-of-the-art baselines.

2 Related Work

The problem of learning with both labeled and unlabeled data is of central importance in machine learning [25]. We specifically review works that have focused on time series classification. We note the seminal work in the field from Wei et al. [21]. They proposed a self-training approach based on a nearest neighbor classifier. The work from [2] later improved the method significantly by proposing a new meta-feature based distance. In [14] a clustering approach was proposed combined with self-training. Another SSL algorithm in [12] also is in essence a clustering based method. The authors of [22] proposed a graph theoretic SSL algorithm that constructs graphs relating all samples based on different distance functions and consequently propagates labels. The current state-of-the-art method in the field [17] is based on shapelet learning [8] on both labeled and unlabeled time series data.

On the other hand, we note recent works [4,5,7,15,23] which showed that strong supervision could be leveraged by describing a task that is inherent in the data itself (requires no manual annotation). We consider the pioneering work by [4] which leveraged spatial context in an image for self-supervised learning by predicting relative location of one sampled patch to another. Similar self-supervised tasks were image colorization [23], solving jigsaw puzzles [15] and classifying image rotations [7]. More closely related to our work is a multi-task self-supervised network [5]. The work firstly tries to compare how the representations learned from recent proposed self-supervised approaches like above compare with each other, and then shows that combining these tasks even in a bare-bones multi-task network without catering for any controlled parameter sharing lifted the accuracy compared with the single-task networks compared before. Moreover, we also note the works that cater for temporal structure. Such temporal structure is inherent in video data, work in [13] proposed a sequential verification task to determine whether a sequence of frames was in correct order. It was shown that with this simple but intuitive task, the ConvNet captures temporally varying information such as human poses and ultimately lifted the accuracy on benchmark action recognition datasets. Another closely related example is [20] where the task was to recognize whether the video is playing forwards or backwards.

With motivations behind our method set from the literature review, we now draw the following insights: firstly there exist semi-supervised learning approaches similar to ours that learn from unlabeled data, most notably current state-of-the-art shapelet learning approach [17] if we consider shapelets to be similar to convolutional filters. However, with our work we exploit deep learning based methods which solve an auxiliary self-supervised task of forecasting which forces the network to learn filters to solve this particular complex task. Secondly, there have been a plethora of works that proposed novel self-supervised tasks, however to the best of our knowledge, there are no examples for the time series domain and neither that cast a self-supervised task as an auxiliary task.

3   Method

Our aim is to learn a ConvNet model that can estimate a forecasting function $f(.)$ and a classification function $g(.)$ jointly. To put it in concrete terms, we have a set of univariate time series samples $X = \{X_1, X_2, ..., X_n\}$ with their respective labels $Y = \{Y_1, Y_2, ..., Y_n\}$. We randomly split X to artificially construct $X^U = \{X_1^U, X_2^U, ..., X_k^U\}$ a set of unlabeled samples, and a labeled set comprising of $X^L = \{X_1^L, X_2^L, ..., X_l^L\}$ and $Y^L = \{Y_1^L, Y_2^L, ..., Y_l^L\}$. Note that $k + l = n$ and total series length is T. Furthermore, we define a sliding window function $w(.)$ which is parametrized by a stride s and horizon h. This function takes as input time series from X, and segments each in forecasting samples for e.g., $X_{11}^F = \{x_{1,t=p}^1, x_{1,t=p+1}^1, ..., x_{1,t=p+h}^1\}$ and $Y_{11}^F = \{y_{1,t=p+h+1}^1, y_{1,t=p+h+2}^1, ..., y_{1,t=p+2h}^1\}$ which denote the first sample i.e X_1's first window. The next sample is chosen with regard to $p = p + s$ and complete set of forecasting samples is given by $X^F = \{X_{11}^F, X_{12}^F, ..., X_{nm}^F\}$ and $Y^F = \{Y_1^F, Y_2^F, ..., Y_{nm}^F\}$. It is worth noting that these windows have a total length of $2h < T$ of which the later half consists of targets to be forecasted. And, the total number of forecasting samples, $m = n \times \lfloor (2 \times h + 1)/s \rfloor$ where $s > 0$. To fix ideas, our objectives are $Y^F = f(X^F)$ and $Y^L = g(X^L)$. The loss function for the objective with respect to $f(.)$:

$$L_f(X^F, \theta_f) = \frac{1}{n \times m \times h} \sum_i^n \sum_j^m \sum_t^h (y_{jt}^i - \hat{y}_{jt}^i)^2 \tag{1}$$

Specifically, we wish to learn the set of parameters θ_f that minimize the loss with respect to predictions, $\hat{Y}^F$. The model does multi-step predictions for the horizon h and the loss stated above captures this with the outer sum.

Moreover, for the classification task, the model outputs a probability distribution over all possible classes, C. In contrast to the forecasting samples, the input corresponds to the complete length, T. We also emphasize here the difference in parameters by denoting θ_c as the classification task parameters. The loss to be minimized with respect to predicting classes C for samples X^L:

$$L_c(X^L, \theta_c) = -\frac{1}{l} \sum_i^l \log \left(\frac{e^{\hat{y}_{i=c}}}{\sum_j^C e^{\hat{y}_i}} \right) \tag{2}$$

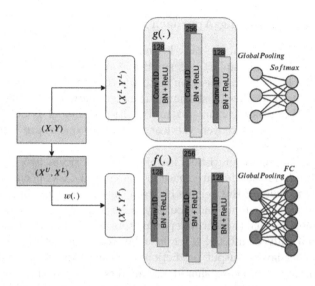

Fig. 1. The proposed multi-task model for joint forecasting and classification of time series. We adopt this architecture from [19] where it was shown to outperform variety of baselines on a majority of datasets. We reuse the same parameters for $f(.)$ up-to the last convolutional block, from where a dedicated linearly fully connected layer denoted by FC outputs for the horizon.

3.1 Forecasting as a Self-supervised Task

The core intuition to model forecasting as an auxiliary task is to force the ConvNet model to learn a set of rich hidden state representations from unlabeled but structured data. In the case of only few labeled instances being available as in semi-supervised setting, a fully-supervised approach can overfit on the training instances by learning a poor set of features which can hardly distinguish different classes. However, since training proceeds, by using the same set of features repeatedly the model can be more assuming of its predictions which would decrease the training loss in turn. In order to avoid this, a self-supervised task on unlabeled data could be leveraged that can learn comparatively more discriminative features for training and ultimately lead to a significant lift in accuracy on unseen data.

Additionally, forecasting is well-studied and easily formulated, but at the same time is complex enough which does not open any doors for cheating, as there are no trivial shortcuts for the model to exploit for solving the task [7]. Moreover, the task allows us flexibility in terms of data generation. By configuring the different values of the horizon and stride, h and s respectively, one could control the number of samples needed to configure an optimal balance between the classification and forecasting task samples.

3.2   Multi-task Learning Approach

Central to the theory of multi-task learning is the leveraging of hidden state representations from multiple tasks simultaneously in order to create a more robust model. This begs the question as to whether there exist tasks that could mutually benefit each other by sharing parameters between. Naturally, forecasting fits well with a classification task in a multi-task model as both tasks share the same input space. Moreover, the learned feature spaces are expected to be correlated in turn also [1].

However, designing a multi-task learning network poses two key challenges. Firstly, how to divide the feature space in shared and task-specific feature sets. Secondly, how to balance the weights between the different loss functions so as to distinguish between the main and auxiliary tasks. We rely on the hard-parameter sharing scheme, in which the learning parameters are all shared between the tasks up to the final fully connected layer in a layered architecture. From thereon, task-specific final layers output predictions for each task. This is illustrated in the Fig. 1 where we indicate shared parameters between the two tasks with same colored space. On the other hand, by adopting task specific weights we aim to cast the forecasting as an auxiliary task. We formulate the multi-task learning approach as an optimization process over the weighted sum of the two loss functions.

$$L_{MTL}(X^F, \theta_f, X^L, \theta_c) = L_c(X^L, \theta_c) + \lambda L_f(X^F, \theta_f) \tag{3}$$

λ is a hyper-parameter that controls parameter updates of the network relative to forecasting loss. It is thus crucial to tune for λ as too high of a value could bias the network weights for the forecasting task. On the other hand, if it is set too low, then the network would not learn for the forecasting task at all [1,10].

So far we have not drawn a link between the two feature sets of the tasks. In order to do so, consider that in a multi-task setting, the model is able to accurately forecast an unlabeled sample. The intuition is, if this unlabeled sample belongs to the same class as the very labeled sample the model is now trying to classify, and hence both are similar, then the latent features that were activated for the unlabeled sample could be leveraged to classify. Additionally, since the model is trained end-to-end, we also hypothesize that the model automatically learns to share latent representations between tasks and their corresponding high-order interactions based on this latent space.

4   Experiments

We compare our proposed multi-task model to multiple baselines on 13 real-world public time series datasets [3]. Since the data generating processes are completely different[1], the proposed method's performance can be judged without bias to similar data generating processes. Previously proposed methods were

---

[1] With exception to Lightning datasets.

compared on the same in [17]. A summary of the datasets is given in Table 1. All experiments were run with PyTorch and code[2] is published online to encourage reproducibility.

Table 1. Summary statistics of 13 real-world datasets from [3,17].

	Coffee	CBF	ECG	Face-Four	OSULf	Italy-Power	Light.2	Light.7	Gun-Point	Trace	Word-Syn	Olive-Oil	Star-Light
#	56	930	200	112	442	1096	121	143	200	200	905	60	9236
C	2	3	2	4	6	2	2	7	2	4	25	4	3
T	286	128	96	350	427	24	637	319	150	275	270	570	1024

4.1 Baselines

Wei's method [21] is based on self-training through which the classifier iteratively augments the labeled set by adding a sample from the unlabeled set. The choice as to which sample to add is based on the (nearest neighbour) classifier's prediction of which sample was the closest to any of its labeled counterpart in euclidean distance. The newly added sample is then given the same class as its closest neighbour.

DTW-D [2] is a meta-feature based distance. This distance was defined as the ratio of DTW to the euclidean distance. The intuition is to exploit the difference between the two distance's performance mainly the benefit of choosing DTW over the euclidean distance. Self-training is then carried out based on this distance.

SUCCESS [12] does constrained hierarchical clustering of the complete set of training samples, irrespective of labels. The distance metric utilized is DTW and all unlabeled samples are given the top-level seed's label.

Xu's method [22] is a graph theoretic SSL algorithm that constructs graphs relating all samples based on different distance functions such as DTW or Wavelet Transform. A probabilistic method optimally combines these various graphs after which a well studied harmonic Gaussian field based method [24] is adopted for label propagation.

Bag-of-words [18] leverages a sliding window procedure to generate local segments from time series data. These local segments are used to create histograms to train an SVM model for classification. It is worth noting that this method differs from above as it uses only labeled samples.

---

[2] https://github.com/super-shayan/semi-super-ts-clf.

SSSL [17] is the current state-of-the-art method in the field. It uses shapelets to classify unlabeled samples thereby producing pseudo-labels. A coordinate descent solver wraps the optimization process by iteratively solving for the classification of labeled samples, pseudo-labels and shapelets respectively.

Base [19] is a single-task variant of our proposed method that is only trained on the labeled samples to do classification.

Π-*Model* [11] is well-known semi-supervised learning method for image classification task. The basic idea is rooted in incorporating stronger regularization via ensembling. The method relies on dropout and asks the network being trained to output consistent labels for the same input. The input albeit goes through different dropout conditions leading to stochastic outputs. This makes it a well-defined task to exploit especially for unlabeled data. As the training proceeds, it is expected for the network's self-ensembled predictions to converge to the same labels for both labeled and unlabeled data. We sandwiched dropout layers after the batch-normalization layers and trained with dropout values of 20% and 40%.

Transfer Learning is common in the regime of self-supervised learning based methods [4,7]. Following these works, we train a non-linear classifier on top of each of a network's layers trained particularly for forecasting the datasets under consideration. The forecasting network in question is composed of stacking 6 convolutional layers in successive order with filter numbers 8, 16, 32, 64, 128, 256 respectively. Moreover, we sandwich maxpooling layers between halving the input in temporal dimension after each convolutional layer. Next, flattening and training 2 non-linear fully connected layers with dimensions 200 and 100. The very final layer's dimensionality corresponds to the horizon. This network is the result of an extensive grid search over multiple forecasting tasks from concurrent work. As we motivated, this network is geared towards forecasting in sharp contrast to the network in Fig. 1 adopted for the classification task. We trained this network with a grid search in $s \times h$ where, $s \in \{0.05, 0.1, 0.2\}$ and $h \in \{0.1, 0.2\}^3$, and used the configuration resulting with the least loss in Eq. 1.
This baseline serves to evaluate the self-supervised learned features from the forecasting task, by measuring classification accuracy that they achieve when we train a classifier on top of them without any fine-tuning [7]. This classifier has two non-linear layers corresponding to dimensions of 200 and 100 respectively. We hypothesize that if the features do correlate between the classification and forecasting task, then this non-linear classifier is expected to perform well.

5   Results

We begin this section by shedding light on the evaluation protocol. We randomly split each dataset into train and test splits with 80% and 20% of the samples.

---

[3] We overload the notation, and use s and h as percentages of the series length T.

Secondly, we split the train split further into labeled and unlabeled sets by randomly discarding 90% of the labels. This evaluation protocol is kept in line with the previous published methods, so as to report a direct fair comparison. The metric of evaluation is classification accuracy throughout the experiments. Given that the initial splits can bias the maximum achievable accuracy, similar to the works before ours, we report the maximum achieved accuracy on the test split by running the experiments 10 times with different hyper-parameters altogether.

Table 2 shows the comparison of accuracies for the proposed method and the baselines. The results are also stated for the best performing transfer learning scheme and the Π-model. A number of interesting observations can be drawn from these results. Firstly, we observe that our proposed method is able to outperform all other methods by a wide margin across almost all benchmark datasets considered. This is only made possible because of the exploitation of the unlabeled data better than other methods. Given that we consider here only 10% labeled samples, the difference between the performance of the methods boils down to how these cater for the unlabeled samples. By leveraging the forecasting task, the model is able to pick up useful representations that directly effect the final accuracy.

We observe that the proposed model fails to correctly model the underlying distribution of the *WordSynonyms* dataset. Firstly, we observe that in contrast to other datasets, the number of classes is the highest and hence we hypothesize that due to intra-class variances the model simply needs more labeled samples to model the underlying distribution. Moreover, we plot samples from the dataset together with our forecasts for last window of each of these samples in Fig. 2. Our second intuition is that given the dataset is based on handwriting, it can be a difficult task to forecast it correctly. The mean squared error that we achieve also hints in this direction, though exceptionally for these handwriting samples it does not convey explicit meaning.

Perhaps surprisingly, the Base method, is able to come at a close second. With exception to *WordSynonyms* and the *Lightning7* datasets, it is able to beat the current state-of-the-art by a considerable margin. We posit that this relates to the powerful non-linear modeling of the ConvNet in contrast to other algorithms. Also worth considering is that this architecture is the result of an extensive search over a wide variety of benchmark datasets as evident in [19]. Hence because of these reasons, even with few labeled samples available it is able to lead over rest of the baselines.

Additionally, we notice that the Π-model does not lead to fruitful results. Although the underlying architecture is the same as in *Base* model, we observed that the model was unfortunately not able to properly cater for the consistency regularization term for the unlabeled data. As a result, the multi-task loss it optimizes for diverges resulting in poor performance over the test splits not outperforming the *base* model. Despite initially considering to orthogonally integrate the Π-model with our proposed multi-task model, we refrained because of poor performance for this standard configuration.

We also summarize the results for the transfer learning based approach which serves to quantify the usefulness of features learned purely for the self-supervised forecasting task. We can see that without any fine-tuning, by learning a non-linear classifier on top of the layers provides useful results. Although, results reported here are generalized over the layers, by reporting only the maximum possible accuracy regardless of the layer, it still serves as a validation of our initial hypothesis that feature spaces correlate heavily among the forecasting and classification tasks.

To point out the effect of hyper-parameters on our proposed multi-task model, we state the results with respect to different stride and horizon values in Table 3. It can be noted that for a subset of datasets the search was fruitful. Indeed, we find out that performance varies considerably with respect to the size of forecasting samples generated with particular stride and horizon, as it has direct effect on the learned representations.

We also wish to highlight further observations here though briefly. We observed that the final forecasting loss (Eq. 1) was consistent across s and h configurations albeit least at the extremities of stride and horizon values i.e those that lead to maximum possible forecasting samples. Also, we observed that network was robust to the different values of λ altogether. More importantly, as we posited earlier, the network performance was indeed biased to labeled samples resulted from random splits.

Table 2. The proposed method vs. baselines.

Datasets	Results verbatim from table in [17]						Proposed			
	Wei.	DTW-D	SUC.	Xu.	BoW	SSSL	Base	Π	Tr.	MTL
Coffee	0.571	0.601	0.632	0.588	0.620	0.792	**1.0**	**1.0**	**1.0**	**1.0**
CBF	0.995	0.833	0.997	0.921	0.873	**1.0**	**1.0**	**1.0**	0.784	**1.0**
cre ECG	0.763	0.953	0.775	0.819	0.955	0.793	0.9	0.875	0.9	**0.975**
FaceFour	0.818	0.782	0.800	0.833	0.744	0.851	0.913	0.913	0.739	**0.957**
OSULf	0.468	0.701	0.534	0.642	0.685	0.835	0.977	0.977	0.460	**0.978**
ItalyPower	0.934	0.664	0.924	0.772	0.813	0.941	0.986	0.986	0.959	**0.991**
Light.2	0.658	0.641	0.683	0.698	0.721	0.813	0.92	0.84	0.88	**0.92**
Light.7	0.464	0.503	0.471	0.511	0.677	0.796	0.758	0.689	0.482	**0.828**
GunPoint	0.925	0.711	0.955	0.729	0.925	0.824	**1.0**	**1.0**	0.825	**1.0**
Trace	0.950	0.801	**1.0**	0.788	**1.0**	**1.0**	**1.0**	**1.0**	**1.0**	**1.0**
WordSyn	0.590	0.863	0.618	0.639	0.795	**0.875**	0.497	0.491	0.342	0.519
OliveOil	0.633	0.732	0.617	0.639	0.766	0.776	0.916	**1.0**	0.833	**1.0**
StarLight	0.860	0.743	0.800	0.755	0.851	0.872	0.982	0.983	**1.0**	0.991

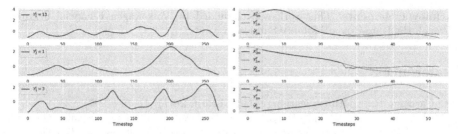

(a) First 3 samples from WordSynonyms   (b) Predictions for last window

Fig. 2. We plot here the qualitative results for the forecasting task. We observe that the network is able to model the underlying distribution, albeit not perfectly.

Table 3. This table reports maximum accuracy for our proposed approach when marginalizing out horizon and stride from all runs and possible λ values.

Datasets	s: 0.05		0.1		0.2	
	h: 0.1	0.2	0.1	0.2	0.1	0.2
Coffee	**1.0**	**1.0**	**1.0**	**1.0**	**1.0**	**1.0**
CBF	**1.0**	**1.0**	**1.0**	**1.0**	**1.0**	**1.0**
ECG	0.950	0.9	0.925	0.9	**0.975**	0.875
FaceFr.	0.913	0.913	0.870	**0.957**	**0.957**	0.913
OSULf.	0.966	0.966	**0.978**	0.955	**0.978**	0.955
ItalyPower	0.986	**0.991**	0.986	0.986	0.982	**0.991**
Light.2	0.840	**0.920**	0.840	0.880	0.880	0.880
Light.7	**0.828**	**0.828**	0.759	0.759	0.793	0.759
GunPoint	**1.0**	**1.0**	**1.0**	**1.0**	**1.0**	**1.0**
Trace	**1.0**	**1.0**	**1.0**	**1.0**	**1.0**	**1.0**
WordSyn.	0.497	**0.519**	0.508	0.497	0.503	0.508
OliveOil	**1.0**	**1.0**	**1.0**	**1.0**	**1.0**	**1.0**
StarLight	0.983	0.983	0.99	0.97	0.983	**0.991**

5.1 Conclusion

We proposed a novel semi-supervised learning algorithm for time series classification based on a self-supervised feature learning task. We trained a ConvNet model that jointly classified and did auxiliary forecasting by sharing latent representations and learning high-order interactions end-to-end. As a result of exploiting the unlabeled data more effectively, our method was able to outperform state-of-the-art baselines. Future work includes extending our method to multivariate time series and researching additional ways to incorporate consistency regularization, which might yield better performance.

Acknowledgements. This work was co-funded by Volkswagen Financial Services through the Data-driven Mobility Services project.

References

1. Caruana, R.: Multitask learning. Mach. Learn. **28**(1), 41–75 (1997)
2. Chen, Y., Hu, B., Keogh, E., Batista, G.E.: DTW-D: time series semi-supervised learning from a single example. In: Proceedings of the 19th ACM SIGKDD, pp. 383–391. ACM (2013)
3. Chen, Y., et al.: The UCR time series classification archive (2015)
4. Doersch, C., Gupta, A., Efros, A.A.: Unsupervised visual representation learning by context prediction. In: Proceedings of the IEEE ICCV, pp. 1422–1430 (2015)
5. Doersch, C., Zisserman, A.: Multi-task self-supervised visual learning. In: Proceedings of the IEEE ICCV, pp. 2051–2060 (2017)
6. Ismail Fawaz, H., Forestier, G., Weber, J., Idoumghar, L., Muller, P.-A.: Deep learning for time series classification: a review. Data Min. Knowl. Disc. **33**(4), 917–963 (2019). https://doi.org/10.1007/s10618-019-00619-1
7. Gidaris, S., Singh, P., Komodakis, N.: Unsupervised representation learning by predicting image rotations. arXiv preprint arXiv:1803.07728 (2018)
8. Grabocka, J., Schilling, N., Wistuba, M., Schmidt-Thieme, L.: Learning time-series shapelets. In: Proceedings of the 20th ACM SIGKDD, pp. 392–401. ACM (2014)
9. Grabocka, Josif, Schmidt-Thieme, Lars: Invariant time-series factorization. Data Min. Knowl. Disc. **28**(5), 1455–1479 (2014). https://doi.org/10.1007/s10618-014-0364-z
10. Kendall, A., Gal, Y., Cipolla, R.: Multi-task learning using uncertainty to weigh losses for scene geometry and semantics. In: Proceedings of the IEEE CVPR, pp. 7482–7491 (2018)
11. Laine, S., Aila, T.: Temporal ensembling for semi-supervised learning. arXiv preprint arXiv:1610.02242 (2016)
12. Marussy, K., Buza, K.: SUCCESS: a new approach for semi-supervised classification of time-series. In: Rutkowski, L., Korytkowski, M., Scherer, R., Tadeusiewicz, R., Zadeh, L.A., Zurada, J.M. (eds.) ICAISC 2013, Part I. LNCS (LNAI), vol. 7894, pp. 437–447. Springer, Heidelberg (2013). https://doi.org/10.1007/978-3-642-38658-9_39
13. Misra, I., Zitnick, C.L., Hebert, M.: Shuffle and learn: unsupervised learning using temporal order verification. In: Leibe, B., Matas, J., Sebe, N., Welling, M. (eds.) ECCV 2016, Part I. LNCS, vol. 9905, pp. 527–544. Springer, Cham (2016). https://doi.org/10.1007/978-3-319-46448-0_32
14. Nguyen, M.N., Li, X.L., Ng, S.K.: Positive unlabeled learning for time series classification. In: Twenty-Second International Joint Conference on Artificial Intelligence (2011)
15. Noroozi, M., Favaro, P.: Unsupervised learning of visual representations by solving jigsaw puzzles. In: Leibe, B., Matas, J., Sebe, N., Welling, M. (eds.) ECCV 2016, Part VI. LNCS, vol. 9910, pp. 69–84. Springer, Cham (2016). https://doi.org/10.1007/978-3-319-46466-4_5
16. Ruder, S.: An overview of multi-task learning in deep neural networks. arXiv preprint arXiv:1706.05098 (2017)
17. Wang, H., Zhang, Q., Wu, J., Pan, S., Chen, Y.: Time series feature learning with labeled and unlabeled data. Pattern Recogn. **89**, 55–66 (2019)

18. Wang, J., Liu, P., She, M.F., Nahavandi, S., Kouzani, A.: Bag-of-words representation for biomedical time series classification. Biomed. Signal Process. Control **8**(6), 634–644 (2013)
19. Wang, Z., Yan, W., Oates, T.: Time series classification from scratch with deep neural networks: a strong baseline. In: 2017 international joint conference on neural networks (IJCNN), pp. 1578–1585. IEEE (2017)
20. Wei, D., Lim, J.J., Zisserman, A., Freeman, W.T.: Learning and using the arrow of time. In: Proceedings of the IEEE CVPR, pp. 8052–8060 (2018)
21. Wei, L., Keogh, E.: Semi-supervised time series classification. In: Proceedings of the 12th ACM SIGKDD, pp. 748–753. ACM (2006)
22. Xu, Z., Funaya, K.: Time series analysis with graph-based semi-supervised learning. In: 2015 IEEE International Conference on Data Science and Advanced Analytics (DSAA), pp. 1–6. IEEE (2015)
23. Zhang, R., Isola, P., Efros, A.A.: Colorful image colorization. In: Leibe, B., Matas, J., Sebe, N., Welling, M. (eds.) ECCV 2016, Part III. LNCS, vol. 9907, pp. 649–666. Springer, Cham (2016). https://doi.org/10.1007/978-3-319-46487-9_40
24. Zhu, X., Ghahramani, Z., Lafferty, J.D.: Semi-supervised learning using gaussian fields and harmonic functions. In: Proceedings of the 20th International conference on Machine learning (ICML-2003), pp. 912–919 (2003)
25. Zhu, X.J.: Semi-supervised learning literature survey. University of Wisconsin-Madison Department of Computer Sciences, Technical report (2005)

SLGAT: Soft Labels Guided Graph Attention Networks

Yubin Wang[1,2], Zhenyu Zhang[1,2], Tingwen Liu[1,2(✉)], and Li Guo[1,2]

[1] Institute of Information Engineering, Chinese Academy of Sciences, Beijing, China
{wangyubin,zhangzhenyu1996,liutingwen,guoli}@iie.ac.cn
[2] School of Cyber Security, University of Chinese Academy of Sciences,
Beijing, China

Abstract. Graph convolutional neural networks have been widely studied for semi-supervised classification on graph-structured data in recent years. They usually learn node representations by transforming, propagating, aggregating node features and minimizing the prediction loss on labeled nodes. However, the pseudo labels generated on unlabeled nodes are usually overlooked during the learning process. In this paper, we propose a soft labels guided graph attention network (SLGAT) to improve the performance of node representation learning by leveraging generated pseudo labels. Unlike the prior graph attention networks, our SLGAT uses soft labels as guidance to learn different weights for neighboring nodes, which allows SLGAT to pay more attention to the features closely related to the central node labels during the feature aggregation process. We further propose a self-training based optimization method to train SLGAT on both labeled and pseudo labeled nodes. Specifically, we first pre-train SLGAT on labeled nodes and generate pseudo labels for unlabeled nodes. Next, for each iteration, we train SLGAT on the combination of labeled and pseudo labeled nodes, and then generate new pseudo labels for further training. Experimental results on semi-supervised node classification show that SLGAT achieves state-of-the-art performance.

Keywords: Graph neural networks · Attention mechanism · Self-training · Soft labels · Semi-supervised classification

1 Introduction

In recent years, graph convolutional neural networks (GCNs) [26], which can learn from graph-structured data, have attracted much attention. The general approach with GCNs is to learn node representations by passing, transforming, and aggregating node features across the graph. The generated node representations can then be used as input to a prediction layer for various downstream tasks, such as node classification [12], graph classification [30], link prediction [17] and social recommendation [19].

Graph attention networks (GAT) [23], which is one of the most representative GCNs, learns the weights for neighborhood aggregation via self-attention mechanism [22] and achieves promising performance on semi-supervised node

© Springer Nature Switzerland AG 2020
H. W. Lauw et al. (Eds.): PAKDD 2020, LNAI 12084, pp. 512–523, 2020.
https://doi.org/10.1007/978-3-030-47426-3_40

classification problem. The model is expected to learn to pay more attention to the important neighbors. It calculates important scores between connected nodes based solely on the node representations. However, the label information of nodes is usually overlooked. Besides, the cluster assumption [3] for semi-supervised learning states that the decision boundary should lie in regions of low density. It means aggregating the features from the nodes with different classes could reduce the generalization performance of the model. This motivates us to introduce label information to improve the performance of node classification in the following two aspects: (1) We introduce soft labels to guide the feature aggregation for generating discriminative node embeddings for classification. (2) We use SLGAT to predict pseudo labels for unlabeled nodes and further train SLGAT on the composition of labeled and pseudo labeled nodes. In this way, SLGAT can benefit from unlabeled data.

In this paper, we propose soft labels guided attention networks (SLGAT) for semi-supervised node representation learning. The learning process consists of two main steps. First, SLGAT aggregates the features of neighbors using convolutional networks and predicts soft labels for each node based on the learned embeddings. And then, it uses soft labels to guide the feature aggregation via attention mechanism. Unlike the prior graph attention networks, SLGAT allows paying more attention to the features closely related to the central node labels. The weights for neighborhood aggregation learned by a feedforward neural network based on both label information of central nodes and features of neighboring nodes, which can lead to learning more discriminative node representations for classification.

We further propose a self-training based optimization method to improve the generalization performance of SLGAT using unlabeled data. Specifically, we first pre-train SLGAT on labeled nodes using standard cross-entropy loss. Then we generate pseudo labels for unlabeled nodes using SLGAT. Next, for each iteration, we train SLGAT using a combined cross-entropy loss on both labeled nodes and pseudo labeled nodes, and then generate new pseudo labels for further training. In this way, SLGAT can benefit from unlabeled data by minimizing the entropy of predictions on unlabeled nodes.

We conduct extensive experiments on semi-supervised node classification to evaluate our proposed model. And experimental results on several datasets show that SLGAT achieves state-of-the-art performance. The source code of this paper can be obtained from https://github.com/jadbin/SLGAT.

2   Related Work

Graph-Based Semi-supervised Learning. A large number of methods for semi-supervised learning using graph representations have been proposed in recent years, most of which can be divided into two categories: graph regularization-based methods and graph embedding-based methods. Different graph regularization-based approaches can have different variants of the regularization term. And graph Laplacian regularizer is most commonly used in previous studies including label propagation [32], local and global consistency regularization [31], manifold regularization [1] and deep semi-supervised embedding [25]. Recently, graph embedding-based methods inspired by the skip-gram model [14] has attracted much attention. DeepWalk [16] samples node sequences via uniform random walks on the network, and then learns embeddings via the prediction of the local neighborhood of nodes. Afterward, a large number of works including LINE [21] and node2vec [8] extend DeepWalk with more sophisticated random walk schemes. For such embedding based methods, a two-step pipeline including embedding learning and semi-supervised training is required where each step has to be optimized separately. Planetoid [29] alleviates this by incorporating label information into the process of learning embeddings.

Graph Convolutional Neural Networks. Recently, graph convolutional neural networks (GCNs) [26] have been successfully applied in many applications. Existing GCNs are often categorized as spectral methods and non-spectral methods. Spectral methods define graph convolution based on the spectral graph theory. The early studies [2,10] developed convolution operation based graph Fourier transformation. Defferrard et al. [4] used polynomial spectral filters to reduce the computational cost. Kipf & Welling [12] then simplified the previous method by using a linear filter to operate one-hop neighboring nodes. Wu et al. [27] used graph wavelet to implement localized convolution. Xu et al. [27] used a heat kernel to enhance low-frequency filters and enforce smoothness in the signal variation on the graph. Along with spectral graph convolution, define the graph convolution in the spatial domain was also investigated by many researchers. GraphSAGE [9] performs various aggregators such as mean-pooling over a fixed-size neighborhood of each node. Monti et al. [15] provided a unified framework that generalized various GCNs. GraphsGAN [5] generates fake samples and trains generator-classifier networks in the adversarial learning setting. Instead of fixed weight for aggregation, graph attention networks (GAT) [23] adopts attention mechanisms to learn the relative weights between two connected nodes. Wang et al. [24] generalized GAT to learn representations of heterogeneous networks using meta-paths. Shortest Path Graph Attention Network (SPAGAN) to explore high-order path-based attentions.

Our method is based on spatial graph convolution. Unlike the existing graph attention networks, we introduce soft labels to guide the feature aggregation of neighboring nodes. And experiments show that this can further improve the semi-supervised classification performance.

3   Problem Definition

In this paper, we focus on the problem of semi-supervised node classification. Many other applications can be reformulated into this fundamental problem. Let $G = (V, E)$ be a graph, in which V is a set of nodes, E is a set of edges. Each node $u \in V$ has a attribute vector $\mathbf{x}_u$. Given a few labeled nodes $V_L \in V$, where each node $u \in V_L$ is associated with a label $\mathbf{y}_u \in Y$, the goal is to predict the labels for the remaining unlabeled nodes $V_U = V \setminus V_L$.

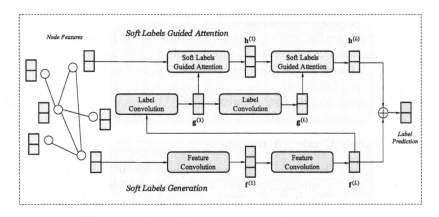

Fig. 1. The overall architecture of SLGAT.

4 Proposed Model: SLGAT

In this section, we will give more details of SLGAT. The overall structure of SLGAT is shown in Fig. 1. The learning process of our method consists of two main steps. We first use a multi-layer graph convolution network to generate soft labels for each node based on nodes features. We then leverage the soft labels to guide the feature aggregation via attention mechanism to learn better representations of nodes. Furthermore, we develop a self-training based optimization method to train SLGAT on the combination of labeled nodes and pseudo labeled nodes. This enforces SLGAT can further benefit from the unlabeled data under the semi-supervised learning setting.

4.1 Soft Labels Generation

In the initial phase, we need to first predict the pseudo labels for each node based on node features **x**. The pseudo labels can be soft (a continuous distribution) or hard (a one-hot distribution). In practice, we observe that soft labels are usually more stable than hard labels, especially when the model has low prediction accuracy. Since the labels predicted by the model are not absolutely correct, the error from hard labels may propagate to the inference on other labels and hurt the performance. While using soft labels can alleviate this problem.

We use a multi-layer graph convolutional network [12] to aggregate the features of neighboring nodes. The layer-wise propagation rule of feature convolution is as follows:

$$\mathbf{f}^{(l+1)} = \sigma\left(\widetilde{D}^{-\frac{1}{2}}\widetilde{A}\widetilde{D}^{-\frac{1}{2}}\mathbf{f}^{(l)}W_f^{(l)}\right) \tag{1}$$

Here, $\widetilde{A} = A + I$ is the adjacency matrix with added self-connections. I is the identity matrix, $\widetilde{D}_{ii} = \sum_j \widetilde{A}_{ij}$ and $W_f^{(l)} \in \mathbb{R}^{d_f^{(l)} \times d_f^{(l+1)}}$ is a layer-specific trainable transformation matrix. $\sigma\left(\cdot\right)$ denotes an activation function such as $\text{ReLU}(\cdot) = \max(0, \cdot)$. $\mathbf{f}^{(l)} \in \mathbb{R}^{|V| \times d_f^{(l)}}$ denotes the hidden representations of nodes in the lth layer. The representations of nodes $\mathbf{f}^{(l+1)}$ are obtained by aggregating information from the features of their neighborhoods $\mathbf{f}^{(l)}$. Initially, $\mathbf{f}^{(0)} = \mathbf{x}$.

After going through L layers of feature convolution, we predict the soft labels for each node u based on the output embeddings of nodes:

$$\widehat{\mathbf{y}}_u = \text{softmax}\left(\mathbf{f}_u^{(L)}\right) \tag{2}$$

4.2   Soft Labels Guided Attention

Now we will present how to leverage the previous generated soft labels for each node to guide the feature aggregation via attention mechanism. The attention network consists of several stacked layers. In each layer, we first aggregate the label information of neighboring nodes. Then we learn the weights for neighborhood aggregation based on both aggregated label information of central nodes and feature embeddings of neighboring nodes.

We use a label convolution unit to aggregate the label information of neighboring nodes, and the layer-wise propagation rule is as follows:

$$\mathbf{g}^{(l+1)} = \sigma\left(\widetilde{D}^{-\frac{1}{2}}\widetilde{A}\widetilde{D}^{-\frac{1}{2}}\mathbf{g}^{(l)}W_g^{(l)}\right) \tag{3}$$

where $W_g^{(l)} \in \mathbb{R}^{d_g^{(l)} \times d_g^{(l+1)}}$ is a layer-specific trainable transformation matrix, and $\mathbf{g}^{(l)} \in \mathbb{R}^{|V| \times d_g^{(l)}}$ denotes the hidden representations the label information of nodes. The label information $\mathbf{g}^{(l+1)}$ are obtained by aggregating from the label information $\mathbf{g}^{(l)}$ of neighboring nodes. Initially, $\mathbf{g}^{(0)} = \text{softmax}\left(\mathbf{f}^{(L)}\right)$ according to Eq. 2.

Then we use the aggregated label information to guide the feature aggregation via attention mechanism. Unlike the prior graph attention networks [23,28], we use label information as guidance to learn the weights of neighboring nodes for feature aggregation. We enforce the model to pay more attention to the features closely related to the labels of the central nodes.

A single-layer feedforward neural network is applied to calculate the attention scores between connected nodes based on the central node label information $\mathbf{g}^{(l+1)}$ and the neighboring node features $\mathbf{h}^{(l)}$:

$$a_{ij} = \tanh\left(\mathbf{a}^{(l)\top}\left[W_t^{(l)}\mathbf{g}_i^{(l+1)}\|W_h^{(l)}\mathbf{h}_j^{(l)}\right]\right) \tag{4}$$

where $\mathbf{a}^{(l)} \in \mathbb{R}^{2d_h^{(l+1)}}$ is a layer-specific attention vector, $W_t^{(l)} \in \mathbb{R}^{d_h^{(l+1)} \times d_g^{(l+1)}}$ and $W_h^{(l)} \in \mathbb{R}^{d_h^{(l+1)} \times d_h^{(l)}}$ are layer-specific trainable transformation matrices, $\mathbf{h}^{(l)} \in \mathbb{R}^{|V| \times d_h^{(l)}}$ denotes the hidden representations of node features. $\cdot^\top$ represents transposition and $\|$ is the concatenation operation. Then we obtain the attention weights by normalizing the attention scores with the softmax function:

$$\alpha_{ij} = \frac{\exp\left(a_{ij}\right)}{\sum_{k \in N_i} \exp\left(a_{ik}\right)} \tag{5}$$

where N_i is the neighborhood of node i in the graph. Then, the embedding of node i can be aggregated by the projected features of neighbors with the corresponding coefficients as follows:

$$\mathbf{h}_i^{(l+1)} = \sigma \left(\sum_{j \in N_i} \alpha_{ij} W_h^{(l)} \mathbf{h}_j^{(l)} \right) \tag{6}$$

Finally, we can achieve better predictions for the labels of each node u by replacing the Eq. 2 as follows:

$$\widehat{\mathbf{y}}_u = \text{softmax} \left(\mathbf{f}_u^{(L)} \oplus \mathbf{h}_u^{(L)} \right) \tag{7}$$

where $\oplus$ is the mean-pooling aggregator.

4.3 Self-training Based Optimization

Grandvalet & Bengio [7] argued that adding an extra loss to minimize the entropy of predictions on unlabeled data can further improve the generalization performance for semi-supervised learning. Thus we estimate pseudo labels for unlabeled nodes based on the learned node representations, and develop a self-training based optimization method to train SLGAT on both labeled and pseudo labeled nodes. Int this way, SLGAT can further benefit from the unlabeled data.

For semi-supervised node classification, we can minimize the cross-entropy loss over all labeled nodes between the ground-truth and the prediction:

$$\mathcal{L}_{sup} = -\frac{1}{|V_L|} \sum_{i \in V_L} \sum_{j=1}^{C} \mathbf{y}_{ij} \cdot \log \widehat{\mathbf{y}}_{ij} \tag{8}$$

where C is the number of classes.

To achieve training on the composition of labeled and unlabeled nodes, we first estimate the labels of unlabeled nodes using the learned node embeddings as follows:

$$\widetilde{\mathbf{y}}_u = \text{softmax} \left(\frac{\mathbf{f}_u^{(L)} \oplus \mathbf{h}_u^{(L)}}{\tau} \right) \tag{9}$$

where τ is an annealing parameter. We can set τ to a small value (e.g. 0.1) to further reduce the entropy of pseudo labels. Then the loss for minimizing the entropy of predictions on unlabeled data can be defined as:

$$\mathcal{L}_{unsup} = -\frac{1}{|V_U|} \sum_{i \in V_U} \sum_{j=1}^{C} \widetilde{\mathbf{y}}_{ij} \cdot \log \widehat{\mathbf{y}}_{ij} \tag{10}$$

The joint objective function is defined as a weighted linear combination of the loss on labeled nodes and unlabeled nodes:

$$\mathcal{L} = \mathcal{L}_{sup} + \lambda \mathcal{L}_{unsup} \tag{11}$$

where λ is a weight balance factor.

Algorithm 1: Optimization Algorithm

Input: A graph G, the features of each node $\{\mathbf{x}_u : u \in V\}$ and the labels
$\qquad \{\mathbf{y}_u : u \in V_L\}$ of some nodes
Output: Labels $\{\widehat{\mathbf{y}}_u : u \in V_U\}$ for unlabeld nodes
Pre-train the model with $\{\mathbf{x}_u : u \in V\}$ and $\{\mathbf{y}_u : u \in V_L\}$ according to Eq. 8.
while not converge **do**
$\qquad$ Generate pseudo labels $\{\widetilde{\mathbf{y}}_u : u \in V_U\}$ on unlabeled nodes based on Eq. 9.
$\qquad$ Predict $\{\widehat{\mathbf{y}}_u : u \in V\}$ based on Eq. 7
$\qquad$ Update parameters with $\{\mathbf{y}_u : u \in V_L\}$, $\{\widetilde{\mathbf{y}}_u : u \in V_U\}$ and $\{\widehat{\mathbf{y}}_u : u \in V\}$
$\qquad$ based on Eq. 8, Eq. 10 and Eq. 11.
end
Predict $\{\widehat{\mathbf{y}}_u : u \in V_U\}$ based on Eq. 7

We give a self-training based method to train SLGAT which is listed in Algorithm. 1. The inputs to the algorithm are both labeled and unlabeled nodes. We first use labeled nodes to pre-train the model using cross-entropy loss. Then we use the model to generate pseudo labels on unlabeled nodes. Afterward, we train the model by minimizing the combined cross-entropy loss on both labeled and unlabeled nodes. Finally, we iteratively generate new pseudo labels and further train the model.

5   Experiments

In this section, we evaluate our proposed SLGAT on semi-supervised node classification task using several standard benchmarks. We also conduct an ablation study on SLGAT to investigate the contribution of various components to performance improvements.

5.1   Datasets

We follow existing studies [12,23,29] and use three standard citation network benchmark datasets for evaluation, including Cora, Citeseer and Pubmed. In all these datasets, the nodes represent documents and edges are citation links. Node features correspond to elements of a bag-of-words representation of a document. Class labels correspond to research areas and each node has a class label. In each dataset, 20 nodes from each class are treated as labeled data. The statistics of datasets are summarized in Table 1.

5.2   Baselines

We compare against several traditional graph-based semi-supervised classification methods, including manifold regularization (ManiReg) [1], semi-supervised embedding (SemiEmb) [25], label propagation (LP) [32], graph embeddings (DeepWalk) [16], iterative classification algorithm (ICA) [13] and Planetoid [29].

Table 1. The Statistics of Datasets.

Dataset	Nodes	Edges	Features	Classes	Training	Validation	Test
Cora	2,708	5,429	1,433	7	140	500	1,000
Citeseer	3,327	4,732	3,703	6	120	500	1,000
Pubmed	19,717	44,338	500	3	60	500	1,000

Furthermore, since graph neural networks are proved to be effective for semi-supervised classification, we also compare with several state-of-arts graph neural networks including ChebyNet [4], MoNet [15], graph convolutional networks (GCN) [12], graph attention networks (GAT) [23], graph wavelet neural network (GWNN) [27], shortest path graph attention network (SPAGAN) [28] and graph convolutional networks using heat kernel (GraphHeat) [27].

5.3 Experimental Settings

We train a two-layer SLGAT model for semi-supervised node classification and evaluate the performance using prediction accuracy. The partition of datasets is the same as the previous studies [12,23,29] with an additional validation set of 500 labeled samples to determine hyper-parameters.

Weights are initialized following Glorot and Bengio [6]. We adopt the Adam optimizer [11] for parameter optimization with initial learning rate as 0.05 and weight decay as 0.0005. We set the hidden layer size of features as 32 for Cora and Citeseer and 16 for Pubmed. We set the hidden layer size of soft labels as 16 for Cora and Citeseer and 8 for Pubmed. We apply dropout [20] with $p = 0.5$ to both layers inputs, as well as to the normalized attention coefficients. The proper setting of λ in Eq. 11 affects the semi-supervised classification performance. If λ is too large, it disturbs training for labeled nodes. Whereas if λ is too small, we cannot benefit from unlabeled data. In our experiments, we set $\lambda = 1$. We anticipate the results can be further improved by using sophisticated scheduling strategies such as deterministic annealing [7], and we leave it as future work. Furthermore, inspired by dropout [20], we ignore the loss in Eq. 10 with $p = 0.5$ during training to prevent overfitting on pseudo labeled nodes.

5.4 Semi-supervised Node Classification

We now validate the effectiveness of SLGAT on semi-supervised node classification task. Following the previous studies [12,23,29], we use the classification accuracy metric for quantitative evaluation. Experimental results are summarized in Table 2. We present the mean classification accuracy (with standard deviation) of our method over 100 runs. And we reuse the results already reported in [5,12,23,27,28] for baselines.

We can observe that our SLGAT achieves consistently better performance than all baselines. When directly compared to GAT, SLGAT gains 1.0%, 2.3%

Table 2. Semi-supervised node classification accuracies (%).

Method	Cora	Citeseer	Pubmed
MLP	55.1	46.5	71.4
ManiReg [1]	59.5	60.1	70.7
SemiEmb [25]	59.0	59.6	71.7
LP [32]	68.0	45.3	63.0
DeepWalk [16]	67.2	43.2	65.3
ICA [13]	75.1	69.1	73.9
Planetoid [29]	75.7	64.7	77.2
ChebyNet [4]	81.2	69.8	74.4
GCN [12]	81.5	70.3	79.0
MoNet [15]	81.7 ± 0.5	–	78.8 ± 0.3
GAT [23]	83.0 ± 0.7	72.5 ± 0.7	79.0 ± 0.3
SPAGAN [28]	83.6 ± 0.5	73.0 ± 0.4	79.6 ± 0.4
GraphHeat [27]	83.7	72.5	80.5
SLGAT (ours)	$\mathbf{84.0 \pm 0.6}$	$\mathbf{74.8 \pm 0.6}$	$\mathbf{82.2 \pm 0.5}$

and 3.2% improvements for Cora, Citeseer and Pubmed respectively. The performance gain is from two folds. First, SLGAT uses soft labels to guide the feature aggregation of neighboring nodes. This indeed leads to more discriminative node representations. Second, SLGAT is trained on both labeled and pseudo labeled nodes using our proposed self-training based optimization method. SLGAT benefits from unlabeled data by minimizing the entropy of predictions on unlabeled nodes.

5.5   Classification Results on Random Data Splits

Following Shchur et al. [18], we also further validate the effectiveness and robustness of SLGAT on random data splits. We created 10 random splits of the Cora, Citeseer, Pubmed with the same size of training, validation, test sets as the standard split from Yang et al. [29]. We compare SLGAT with other most related competitive baselines including GCN [12] and GAT [23] on those random data splits.[1] We run each method with 10 random seeds on each data split and report the overall mean accuracy in Table 3. We can observe that SLGAT consistently outperforms GCN and GAT on all datasets. This proves the effectiveness and robustness of SLGAT.

---

[1] Note that we do not report results of SPAGAN and GraphHeat in this experiment, because we cannot reproduce these two methods without official implementation.

Table 3. Classification results on random data splits (%).

Method	Cora	Citeseer	Pubmed
GCN [12]	79.5	69.1	80.0
GAT [23]	79.7	68.8	79.2
SLGAT (ours)	**82.9**	**72.5**	**80.6**

Table 4. Ablation study results of node classification (%).

Method	Cora	Citeseer	Pubmed
SLGAT	**84.0**	**74.8**	**82.2**
SLGAT without soft labels guided attention	83.7	74.1	**82.2**
SLGAT without self-training	83.6	72.9	81.1
SLGAT without attention & Self-training	82.3	71.7	80.5

5.6 Ablation Study

In this section, we conduct an ablation study to investigate the effectiveness of our proposed soft label guided attention mechanism and the self-training based optimization method for SLGAT. We compare several variants of SLGAT on node classification, and the results are reported in Table 4.

We observe that SLGAT has better performance than the methods without soft labels guided attention in most cases. This demonstrates that using soft labels to guide the neighboring nodes aggregation is effective for generating better node embeddings. Note that attention mechanism seems has little contribution to performance on Pubmed when using self-training. The reason behind such phenomenon is still under investigation, we presume that it is due to the label sparsity of Pubmed.[2] The similar phenomenon is reported in [23] that GAT has little improvement on Pubmed compared to GCN.

We also observe that SLGAT significantly outperforms all the methods without self-training. This indicates that our proposed self-training based optimization method is much effective to improve the generalization performance of the model for semi-supervised classification.

6 Conclusion

In this work, we propose SLGAT for semi-supervised node representation learning. SLGAT uses soft labels to guide the feature aggregation of neighboring nodes for generating discriminative node representations. A self-training based optimization method is proposed to train SLGAT on both labeled data and pseudo labeled data, which is effective to improve the generalization performance of

---

[2] The label rate of Cora, Citeseer and Pubmed are 0.052, 0.036 and 0.003 respectively.

SLGAT. Experimental results demonstrate that our SLGAT achieves state-of-the-art performance on several semi-supervised node classification benchmarks. One direction of the future work is to make SLGAT going deeper to capture the features of long-range neighbors. This perhaps helps to improve performance on the dataset with sparse labels.

Acknowledgment. This work is supported by the National Key Research and Development Program of China (grant No. 2016YFB0801003) and the Strategic Priority Research Program of Chinese Academy of Sciences (grant No. XDC02040400).

References

1. Belkin, M., Niyogi, P., Sindhwani, V.: Manifold regularization: a geometric framework for learning from labeled and unlabeled examples. J. Mach. Learn. Res. **7**, 2399–2434 (2006)
2. Bruna, J., Zaremba, W., Szlam, A., LeCun, Y.: Spectral networks and locally connected networks on graphs. In: International Conference on Learning Representations (ICLR) (2013)
3. Chapelle, O., Weston, J., Schölkopf, B.: Cluster kernels for semi-supervised learning. In: Advances in Neural Information Processing Systems, pp. 601–608 (2003)
4. Defferrard, M., Bresson, X., Vandergheynst, P.: Convolutional neural networks on graphs with fast localized spectral filtering. In: Proceedings of the 30th International Conference on Neural Information Processing Systems, pp. 3844–3852 (2016)
5. Ding, M., Tang, J., Zhang, J.: Semi-supervised learning on graphs with generative adversarial nets. In: Proceedings of the 27th ACM International Conference on Information and Knowledge Management, pp. 913–922 (2018)
6. Glorot, X., Bengio, Y.: Understanding the difficulty of training deep feed for leveraging graph wavelet transform to address the short-comings of previous spectral graphrd neural networks. In: AISTATS, pp. 249–256 (2010)
7. Grandvalet, Y., Bengio, Y.: Semi-supervised learning by entropy minimization. In: Advances in Neural Information Processing Systems, pp. 529–536 (2005)
8. Grover, A., Leskovec, J.: node2vec: scalable feature learning for networks. In: Proceedings of the 22nd ACM SIGKDD International Conference on Knowledge Discovery and Data Mining, pp. 855–864 (2016)
9. Hamilton, W., Ying, Z., Leskovec, J.: Inductive representation learning on large graphs. In: Advances in Neural Information Processing Systems, pp. 1024–1034 (2017)
10. Henaff, M., Bruna, J., LeCun, Y.: Deep convolutional networks on graph-structured data. arXiv preprint arXiv:1506.05163 (2015)
11. Kingma, D.P., Ba, J.: Adam: a method for stochastic optimization. arXiv preprint arXiv:1412.6980 (2014)
12. Kipf, T.N., Welling, M.: Semi-supervised classification with graph convolutional networks. In: International Conference on Learning Representations (ICLR) (2017)
13. Lu, Q., Getoor, L.: Link-based classification. In: Proceedings of the 20th International Conference on Machine Learning, pp. 496–503 (2003)
14. Mikolov, T., Chen, K., Corrado, G.S., Dean, J.: Efficient estimation of word representations in vector space. In: ICLR Workshop (2013)

15. Monti, F., Boscaini, D., Masci, J., Rodola, E., Svoboda, J., Bronstein, M.M.: Geometric deep learning on graphs and manifolds using mixture model CNNS. In: IEEE Conference on Computer Vision and Pattern Recognition (CVPR), pp. 5425–5434 (2017)
16. Perozzi, B., Al-Rfou, R., Skiena, S.: Deepwalk: online learning of social representations. In: Proceedings of the 20th ACM SIGKDD International Conference on Knowledge Discovery and Data Mining, pp. 701–710 (2014)
17. Schütt, K., Kindermans, P.J., Felix, H.E.S., Chmiela, S., Tkatchenko, A., Müller, K.R.: Schnet: a continuous-filter convolutional neural network for modeling quantum interactions. In: Advances in Neural Information Processing Systems, pp. 991–1001 (2017)
18. Shchur, O., Mumme, M., Bojchevski, A., Günnemann, S.: Pitfalls of graph neural network evaluation. arXiv preprint arXiv:1811.05868 (2018)
19. Shi, C., et al.: Deep collaborative filtering with multi-aspect information in heterogeneous networks. IEEE Trans. Knowl. Data Eng. 1 (2019)
20. Srivastava, N., Hinton, G., Krizhevsky, A., Sutskever, I., Salakhutdinov, R.: Dropout: a simple way to prevent neural networks from overfitting. J. Mach. Learn. Res. 15(1), 1929–1958 (2014)
21. Tang, J., Qu, M., Wang, M., Zhang, M., Yan, J., Mei, Q.: Line: large-scale information network embedding. In: Proceedings of the 24th International Conference on World Wide Web, pp. 1067–1077 (2015)
22. Vaswani, A., et al.: Attention is all you need. In: Advances in Neural Information Processing Systems, pp. 5998–6008 (2017)
23. Velikovi, P., Cucurull, G., Casanova, A., Romero, A., Lió, P., Bengio, Y.: Graph attention networks. In: International Conference on Learning Representations (ICLR) (2018)
24. Wang, X., et al.: Heterogeneous graph attention network. In: The World Wide Web Conference, pp. 2022–2032 (2019)
25. Weston, J., Ratle, F., Mobahi, H., Collobert, R.: Deep learning via semi-supervised embedding. In: Montavon, G., Orr, G.B., Müller, K.-R. (eds.) Neural Networks: Tricks of the Trade. LNCS, vol. 7700, pp. 639–655. Springer, Heidelberg (2012). https://doi.org/10.1007/978-3-642-35289-8_34
26. Wu, Z., Pan, S., Chen, F., Long, G., Zhang, C., Yu, P.S.: A comprehensive survey on graph neural networks. arXiv preprint arXiv:1901.00596 (2019)
27. Xu, B., Shen, H., Cao, Q., Qiu, Y., Cheng, X.: Graph wavelet neural network. In: International Conference on Learning Representations (ICLR) (2019)
28. Yang, Y., Wang, X., Song, M., Yuan, J., Tao, D.: SPAGAN: shortest path graph attention network. In: Proceedings of the 28th International Joint Conference on Artificial Intelligence, pp. 4099–4105 (2019)
29. Yang, Z., Cohen, W.W., Salakhutdinov, R.: Revisiting semi-supervised learning with graph embeddings. In: Proceedings of the 33rd International Conference on International Conference on Machine Learning, pp. 40–48 (2016)
30. Zhang, M., Cui, Z., Neumann, M., Chen, Y.: An end-to-end deep learning architecture for graph classification. In: Thirty-Second AAAI Conference on Artificial Intelligence (2018)
31. Zhou, D., Bousquet, O., Lal, T.N., Weston, J., Schölkopf, B.: Learning with local and global consistency. In: Advances in Neural Information Processing Systems, pp. 321–328 (2004)
32. Zhu, X., Ghahramani, Z., Lafferty, J.: Semi-supervised learning using Gaussian fields and harmonic functions. In: Proceedings of the 20th International Conference on International Conference on Machine Learning, pp. 912–919 (2003)

Learning Multigraph Node Embeddings Using Guided Lévy Flights

Aman Roy[1]([⊠]), Vinayak Kumar[1], Debdoot Mukherjee[2],
and Tanmoy Chakraborty[1]

[1] Department of CSE, IIIT-Delhi, New Delhi, India
{aman16011,vinayakk,tanmoy}@iiitd.ac.in
[2] ShareChat, Bengaluru, India
debdoot@sharechat.co

Abstract. Learning efficient representation of graphs has recently been studied extensively for simple networks to facilitate various downstream applications. In this paper, we deal with a more generalized graph structure, called *multigraph* (multiple edges of different types connecting a pair of nodes) and propose Multigraph2Vec, a random walk based framework for learning multigraph network representation. Multigraph2Vec samples a heterogeneous neighborhood structure for each node by preserving the inter-layer interactions. It employs *Lévy flight random walk strategy*, which allows the random walker to travel across multiple layers and reach far-off nodes in a single step. The transition probabilities are learned in a supervised fashion as a function of node attributes (metadata based and/or network structure based). We compare Multigraph2Vec with four state-of-the-art baselines after suitably adopting to our setting on four datasets. Multigraph2Vec outperforms others in the task of link prediction, by beating the best baseline with 5.977% higher AUC score; while in the multi-class node classification task, it beats the best baseline with 5.28% higher accuracy. We also deployed Multigraph2Vec for friend recommendation on Hike Messenger.

Keywords: Representation learning · Social networks · Guided Lévy flight

1 Introduction

Representation learning of networks has gained considerable attention in recent times [6,7,10,13,18,19,21,22]. The goal of this body of research is to learn a low dimensional, dense representation for each node in a network while preserving structural information about the neighborhood of the node. These embeddings

The research was done when A. Roy and D. Mukherjee were a part of Hike Messenger (https://hike.in). The project was partially supported by SERB (Ramanujan fellowship and ECR/2017/001691) and the Infosys Centre of AI, IIIT Delhi, India.
A. Roy and V. Kumar—Equal Contribution.

H. W. Lauw et al. (Eds.): PAKDD 2020, LNAI 12084, pp. 524–537, 2020.
https://doi.org/10.1007/978-3-030-47426-3_41

can then be used in a variety of downstream social network tasks such as link prediction, node clustering, multi-label classification of nodes, etc.

Majority of the research in network embedding are on networks where nodes share a single form of relationship. However, most real-world networks are *multi-graphs* as multifaceted relationships are quite common between nodes. This is known as the *multiplexity* property [23] in social networks. For instance, a pair of users on a social network can be related through friendship, messaging, etc. In a scientific network, researchers can share a link by virtue of being co-authors on a paper or by citing each other's works. A high quality representation of a node in a multigraph should not only capture information about its neighboring nodes but also encode the relationships that exist with its neighbors. Hence, network embedding methods built for homogeneous networks must be extended to characterize the rich context present in multiple types of edges.

In this paper, we propose a novel method, called Multigraph2Vec which is a random walk based node embedding method for multigraph. It employs a novel context sampling strategy, followed by the Skip-gram model to generate node embeddings. The employed random walker uses a novel strategy, called Lévy flight [8] to traverse through any node (without requiring an edge to traverse between nodes) in a single step, with its transition probabilities learned in a supervised fashion. Multigraph2Vec preserves multi-relational interaction among nodes via generating an (edge-)heterogeneous context.

We show the efficiency of Multigraph2Vec via two downstream tasks - *link prediction* and *multi-class node classification*. In the former task, Multigraph2Vec outperforms several baselines – it beats the best baseline by 5.977% higher AUC score (averaged over all datasets and all layers). In the latter task, Multigraph2Vec outperforms the best baseline by 5.28% higher classification accuracy. We also deployed Multigraph2Vec for friend recommendation on Hike app.

In short, our major contributions are threefold:

- We propose Multigraph2Vec, a novel multigraph embedding technique that samples the neighborhood for each node via a "Lévy flight" random walk strategy, and learns the random walk transition probabilities in a supervised fashion, rather than treating them as hyperparameters.
- We perform a comprehensive analysis to show the superiority of Multigraph2Vec.
- We deployed Multigraph2Vec on a real-world system for friend recommendation.

For the purpose of reproducible research, we have made the codes and the datasets public at [20].

2   Related Work

In this section, we present a brief literature survey of the embedding methods developed for different types of networks.

Homogeneous Network Embedding: Representation learning for homogeneous networks has been studied extensively. DeepWalk [18] follows Skip-gram model [15], a two phase algorithm for learning node embedding. Node2Vec [7] employs a second order random walk governed by two parameters that control the breadth first search and depth first search nature of the random walker. LINE [21] learns the node embedding by preserving a certain measure of proximity among the nodes. Matrix factorization approaches such as spectral clustering [22] perform eigen decomposition on the normalized Laplacian matrix of a graph. Another body of work is built on Graph Convolutional Networks (GCN). [4] developed a variant of GCN based on spectral graph theory. [9] performed convolution in graph domain by aggregating information of neighboring nodes. [1] parameterized the context distribution function and used softmax attention to learn the importance of kth hop neighbors. Graph generative networks, on the other hand, aim to generate structures from data.

Heterogeneous Network Embedding: A heterogeneous information network (HIN) consists of multiple types of edges and nodes with only one edge connecting any two nodes. Metapath2vec [6] samples a heterogeneous context for a node using random walks guided by the predefined metapaths (a path consisting of a specific sequence of relationships/edge-types). [5] used the content and the link structure to generate important cues for creating a unified feature representation of the underlying network.

Multidimensional Network Embedding: Despite its profound relevance in real-world scenario, limited attempts have been made to address multi-layer/multidimensional embedding, compared to the vast amount of literature on simple graphs. MNE [25] generates a d-dimensional layer-specific embedding for each node by combining its d-dimensional base embedding (which remains common across layers), a transformation matrix (which is learned for each layer) and an s-dimensional auxiliary layer-specific embedding ($s \ll d$). [14] considered all the immediate neighbors (in each layer) of a node as its context and then employed a specific Skip-gram with a softmax taking into consideration node categories and layer information to obtain the embeddings for each node. PMNE [13] extends Node2Vec by introducing another parameter that allows the random walker to traverse across layers while sampling the context for each node. It does not learn this parameter, rather tunes it manually.

3   Problem Statement

Definition 1 (Multigraph). *It is defined as a directed graph (directed, for the sake of generalization) $G = (V, E, L)$, where V is the set of vertices, L is the set of edge types and E is the set of triplets (v_i, v_j, l) representing an edge of type l directed from node v_i to v_j, where $v_i, v_j \in V$ and $l \in L$. There can be multiple edges of different types between any two vertices.*

Figure 1(a) shows a toy example of a multigraph. Nodes are assumed to be of same type. For the sake of better representation, we unfold a multigraph to a *multidimensional network* as shown in Fig. 1(b).

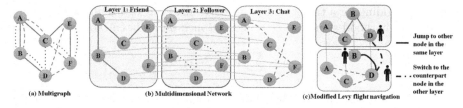

Fig. 1. (a) A toy example of a multigraph representing a social network (e.g, Facebook) where nodes are users, and they are connected via at most three types of edges (red: friend, blue: follower, green: chat). It is not necessary that all pairs of nodes are always connected by three different edges. For example, nodes C and E are connected by only friendship link. But they do not follow each other and do not chat. (b) Each edge type mentioned in Fig (a) forms a layer/dimension in the corresponding multidimensional network. Node set remains same across layers, and each layer is homogeneous in terms of the edge type. (c) Illustration of the modified Lévy flight strategy on a multidimensional network. The figure shows the different elementary steps that the random walker can adopt. (Color figure onilne)

Definition 2 (Multidimensional Network). *It can be defined as a multilayer network*[1] *$G = (V, E, L)$ having $|L|$ layers or dimensions. V denotes a set of N unique nodes. A node $v_i \in V$ in layer $l \in L$ is denoted by v_i^l, $1 \le i \le N$; $1 \le l \le |L|$. Each edge $E_{i,j}^l \in E$ is a tuple (v_i, v_j, l) representing an edge of type l emanating from node v_i^l to node v_j^l, where $v_i, v_j \in V$. Essentially, G consists of a total of $|V| \times |L|$ number of nodes. For simplicity, we assume that all nodes in V are present in all the layers. If a node is absent in a layer (i.e. no edge of type l connects to that node), we add the node as an isolated node in that layer.*

Definition 3 (Problem Statement). *Given a multigraph $G = (V, E, L)$, our aim is to learn a low dimensional representation (embedding) for each node $v_i \in V$, i.e., $X_i \in R^D$, where $D \ll |V|$.*

4   Multigraph2Vec

We propose Multigraph2Vec, which is essentially a Skip-gram model with a novel neighborhood (context) sampling strategy for multigraphs. Algorithm 1 shows the pseudocode of Multigraph2Vec.

4.1   Skip-Gram Model

Skip-gram [16] has been utilised for learning node embeddings in multiple studies [6,7,25] by treating networks as documents and nodes as words. In order to

---

[1] Multilayer network is a stacked representation of multiple single layers. Multidimensional network is a special type of multilayer network which is edge-homogeneous i.e., each layer represents a particular type of relationship among nodes.

obtain embedding for a target node v_i, it maximizes the log likelihood of observing its neighborhood structure $N(v_i)$ conditioned on its latent node embedding vector X_i, i.e.,

$$\arg\max_X \sum_{v_i \in V} \log p(N(v_i)|X_i) \tag{1}$$

where, X_i represents the ith row (D dimensional embedding vector for node v_i) of an $N \times D$ embedding matrix X. The neighborhood structure $N(v_i)$ for v_i is the result of a specific neighborhood sampling strategy, and its member nodes are the context nodes for v_i. The likelihood of observing neighborhood structure $N(v_i)$ for node v_i can be expressed as follows,

$$p(N(v_i)|X_i) = \prod_{n_j \in N(v_i)} p(n_j|X_i) = \prod_{n_j \in N(v_i)} \frac{e^{(X_j \cdot X_i)}}{\sum_{n=1}^{N} e^{(X_n \cdot X_i)}} \tag{2}$$

The log likelihood of Eq. 2 becomes

$$\log(p(n_j|X_i)) = \log(e^{(X_j \cdot X_i)}) - \log(\sum_{n=1}^{N} e^{X_n \cdot X_i}) \tag{3}$$

The second term in Eq. 3 is computationally expensive for large networks and is thus approximated using negative sampling [16].

$$\log(p(n_j|X_i)) = \log(\sigma(X_j \cdot X_i)) + \sum_{m=1}^{M} \log(\sigma(-X_m \cdot X_i)) \tag{4}$$

where, $\sigma(x) = \frac{1}{1+\exp(-x)}$, and M is the negative sample size. After plugging in this approximation, the final objective function takes the following form:

$$\arg\max_X \sum_{v_i \in V} \sum_{n_j \in N(v_i)} (\log(\sigma(X_j \cdot X_i)) + \sum_{m=1}^{M} \log(\sigma(-X_m \cdot X_i))) \tag{5}$$

The above objective function can be optimized using Stochastic Gradient Descent (SGD) algorithm.

4.2   Neighborhood Sampling in Multigraph2Vec

We propose a novel neighborhood sampling strategy. We allow our random walker to jump to nodes that can be separated by any number of hops from the current node. We employ a random walk process, called 'Lévy flight' [8]. It does not require a direct edge between current and target nodes; thus it can hop over very large distance and visit far-off nodes effectively taking a 'flight' rather than a 'walk' within a single hop. Moreover, its ability to switch across layers preserves inter-layer interactions and thus produces an (edge-)heterogeneous context (see Fig. 1(c)).

Such a random walker, if used in an unsupervised fashion (for example, by letting it hop to any node from the current node with equal probability), can generate arbitrary contexts. This can be detrimental for the downstream prediction tasks. Thus, it is necessary to guide it in a principled fashion. In order to do this, *we make its transition probabilities as a function of linear weighted combination of node attributes* (which can be metadata/network-property based or a combination of two) and learn these weights subject to certain constraints, essentially converting the random walk guidance problem into a constrained optimization problem.

Random Walk in Multigraph2Vec: We modify the Lévy flight strategy in two ways. Firstly, our random walker at any step has only two possible steps to adopt as shown in Fig. 1(c). Secondly, the transition probabilities are a parameterized function of node attributes. It is calculated by taking inner product of weight vector with node-pair feature vector and then passing it through a nonlinear function (in our case, sigmoid function), which maps it between 0 and 1. Formally, Lévy flight random walk strategy for multidimensional networks can be defined as follows.

Given that the random walker is currently at node $c_t = v_i^l$, the probability of hopping to node $c_{t+1} = v_j^{l'}$ is given by:

$$P(c_{t+1} = v_j^{l'} | c_t = v_i^l) = \begin{cases} \frac{f(\phi_l^{i,j})}{Z} & l = l', i \neq j \\ \frac{f(\phi_{ll'}^i)}{Z} & l \neq l', i = j \\ 0 & l \neq l', i \neq j \end{cases}$$

where, $\phi_l^{i,j} = \beta_l^{\mathsf{T}} \psi_{v_i^l v_j^l}$ and $\phi_{ll'}^i = \beta_{ll'}^{\mathsf{T}} \psi_{v_i^l v_i^{l'}}$.

- $f(x)$ is a strength function, defined as a function of a linear weighted combination of node-pair features (obtained by combining the attributes of the corresponding nodes in the node-pair). $f(x)$ must be non-negative and differentiable. We choose it to be a sigmoid function.
- Z is a normalization constant.
- $\psi_{v_i^l v_j^l}$ is a node-pair feature vector obtained by combining the attributes of corresponding nodes v_i and v_j in layer l. It is utilized for hopping to nodes within the same layer. The node attributes can be derived from metadata (e.g., number of papers published by an author in different research areas) or from the network structure at layer l (e.g., degree, clustering coefficient, etc. at layer l). The difference between the attribute vectors of the two nodes can form the node-pair feature vector $\psi_{v_i^l v_j^l}$.
- $\psi_{v_i^l v_i^{l'}}$ is a node-pair feature vector obtained by concatenating together some centrality measure (like degree) of node v_i in layers l and l'. It is utilized for hopping to same node in different layers.
- β^l is a weight vector corresponding to transition probabilities in layer l.
- $\beta^{ll'}$ is a weight vector corresponding to probability of switching from layer l to l'.

Learning the Transition Probability: Multigraph2Vec learns the weight parameters β such that the random walker has a higher probability of hopping to one of the "high priority nodes" (set H) than the "low priority nodes" (set L) from the current node [3]. This hopping behavior is enforced on the random walker w.r.t. a subset of nodes, referred to as S; each $s \in S$ represents a source node. S contains equal number of nodes from each layer sampled from the degree distribution at the corresponding layer. The learned weights are expected to generalize the behavior of the random walk for all the nodes in the network.

There can be multiple ways of constructing H and L sets for a given source node s, denoted by H_s and L_s respectively. Multigraph2Vec constructs H_s by considering proximity and attribute similarity. Considering s to be a source node from layer l, a node v_i satisfying at least one of the following three conditions w.r.t. s is eligible to be included in H_s: (i) the distance between v_i and s is less than or equal to k in layer l, (ii) the attribute similarity between s and v_i (based on cosine similarity) is more than a certain threshold τ in layer l, (iii) if it is an alias of s in any layer. Remaining nodes in the layer to which s belongs, comprise the L_s set.

We use personalized PageRank scores to enforce this behavior on the random walker. The objective function becomes:

$$\arg\min_{\beta} ||\beta||^2 + \lambda_1 \sum_{s \in S} \sum_{h_s \in H_s, l_s \in L_s} h(p_{l_s} - p_{h_s}) \tag{6}$$

where, h is a loss function which penalizes the objective function if PageRank score of nodes in H_s becomes smaller than that of nodes in L_s. The loss function must be continuous and differentiable. We choose it to be Wilcoxon-Mann-Whitney (WMW) loss with width b.[2]

$$h(x) = \frac{1}{1 + \exp(-x/b)}$$

The PageRank scores are obtained from the following eigenvector equation: $p^\mathsf{T} = p^\mathsf{T} Q$, where, Q represents the random walk transition matrix and p represents the PageRank vector.

Upon Incorporating the restart probability, each element (u, v) of Q becomes:

$$P'(c_{t+1} = v | c_t = u) = (1 - \alpha) P(c_{t+1} = v | c_t = u) + \alpha \mathbf{1} \tag{7}$$

where, α is the restart probability, i.e., the probability of hopping back to s from any current node u. The cost function in Eq. 6 is optimized using L-BFGS algorithm [12]. The learned weights β are chosen such that the random walker at any current node v_i hops to nodes matching the traits of nodes in H_{v_i}, with a higher probability than the nodes matching the traits of L_{v_i}.

Finally, multiple walks are simulated starting from each node in each layer for neighborhood sampling. While doing this, restart probabilities are not incorporated i.e., the transition probabilities $P(c_{t+1} | c_t)$ are used (and not $P'(c_{t+1} | c_t)$).

---

[2] Wilcoxon-Mann-Whitney loss is usually used when AUC (Area Under the ROC curve) is maximized [24].

Brief Description of the Pseudocode: Algorithm 1 takes the graph G and node attributes as inputs and returns the embedding matrix X. The function LEARN_WEIGHTS (Line 13) takes the multigraph G and number of source nodes per layer s_l as input. It first samples equal number of source nodes from each layer uniformly at random and then constructs the H and L sets corresponding to each source node. Finally it optimizes the objective function (Eq. 6) and returns the parameter vector β. Then, the learned parameter vector β and the graph G along with all the node-pair feature vectors for each layer are taken as the input by the function BUILD_FINAL_TRANSITION_MATRIX (Line 27), and the final transition matrix Q to be used for generating the random walks is returned. The function RANDOM_WALKS (Line 37) takes in the final transition matrix Q along with number of walks and walk length as input and returns multiple random walks of fixed length starting from each node in each layer. The generated random walks are then passed into the SKIP_GRAM (Line 12) function that optimizes the objective function (Eq. 5) and returns the final learned D dimensional continuous embedding matrix X, which can further be used for any downstream tasks.

Complexity Analysis: Learning β is the most expensive task in Multigraph2Vec. To compute the loss (Eq. 6), for a source node we need to obtain personalized PageRank scores for each node in its corresponding H and L sets. We use power iteration method [3] for the same. In theory, PageRank computation takes $\mathcal{O}(N^3)$. However, in practice, it takes 5–6 iterations to get the personalized PageRank vector. Since we perform this operation for all the source nodes S, the overall time complexity per iteration becomes $\mathcal{O}(|S|N^3)$. We observed that L-BFGS takes 15–20 iterations to converge and returns the optimal β.

5   Evaluation

We show the efficiency of Multigraph2Vec via two tasks – link prediction and multi-class node classification.

5.1   Experimental Setup

We set the similarity threshold hyper-parameter τ to 90%. A low similarity threshold value introduces a large number of common nodes in the set H of each source node, thereby reducing the uniqueness of set H (high priority node set) of each source node. All the baselines we consider uses logistic regression classifier. So, in order to maintain a fair ground for comparison we use logistic regression classifier as well. Table 1 describes the datasets used in this study.

5.2   Link Prediction

We evaluate the ability of Multigraph2Vec to predict the presence of a specific type of link between any two nodes given all other links between them. We pose

Table 1. Summary of the datasets.

Dataset	# of nodes	Layer (# edges)	Metadata	Description
EU	1319	FP7 (114845) H2020 (75013)	Yes	Nodes are Organization, Relations are based upon projects funded under FP7 and H2020 program
Hike	1230	Contact Book (2605) Friend (4666)	Yes	Nodes are users of the network, Two type of relations are based upon whether two users have each other in their contact book or are friends
Lazega	71	Co-work (892) Friendship (575) Advice (1104)	No	Nodes are partners and associates of a corporate partnership Relations are directed which are based upon whether two nodes have worked with each other or has taken advice or are friends
Publication	1180	Co-citation (530) Co-author (170000)	No	Nodes are authors, Relations are based upon whether they have cited each other or are co-author of a paper. We used papers after 2009 in this study

Table 2. Layer-specific performance of different competing methods in the task of link prediction on four datasets. The AUC score is reported after averaging the performance across 50 iterations. The results are reported with network-property based attributes, and the dimension of the embedding vector is set to 128.

Method	EU		Hike		Publication		Lazega		
	Layer1	Layer2	Layer1	Layer2	Layer1	Layer2	Layer1	Layer2	Layer3
Jaccard coefficient	0.7587	0.7573	0.6152	0.6298	0.6883	0.7243	0.6487	0.6363	0.6641
Adamic-Aard	0.7157	0.6860	0.6364	0.6206	0.6756	0.7145	0.6317	0.6437	0.6302
Common neighbor	0.6697	0.6580	0.6159	0.6271	0.6457	0.6256	0.6170	0.6008	0.6267
Node2Vec	0.6209	0.6367	0.6481	0.6576	0.6893	0.7478	0.5883	0.5839	0.6022
LINE	0.7113	0.7207	0.6423	0.6369	0.7006	0.7306	0.6521	0.6456	0.6568
MNE	0.7601	0.7773	0.6782	0.6734	0.7261	0.7563	0.6673	0.6563	0.6850
PMNE	0.7264	0.7345	0.6629	0.6786	0.7046	0.7456	0.6408	0.6376	0.6678
Multigraph2Vec	**0.8032**	**0.8192**	**0.7135**	**0.7156**	**0.7561**	**0.7886**	**0.7143**	**0.7071**	**0.7281**

it as a binary classification problem. Let us assume that we wish to evaluate the performance for layer l. We then proceed by splitting $tr\%$ (training) and $ts\%$ (testing) of the edges (set as 75% and 25%, respectively in our experiments) in layer l into training set tr_{pos} and test set ts_{pos} respectively, thereby obtaining positive class samples for training and testing. Similarly, we split the 'no edge/absent edges' in layer l into training set tr_{neg} and test set ts_{neg}, thereby obtaining negative class samples for training and testing, respectively. We then learn the node embeddings on the training set $tr = tr_{pos} \cup tr_{neg}$.

Once the node embeddings are learned, a d-dimensional edge representation for each edge in training and test sets is obtained by averaging the corresponding node embeddings. Due to real-world networks being sparse, the training set is

---

Algorithm 1. `Multigraph2vec`

1: **Input** : $G, Node\_attributes$
2: **Output** : X
3: **Initialize:**
4:     $s_l \leftarrow 100$ ▷ Number of source nodes from each layer
5:     $\tau \leftarrow 0.9$ ▷ Similarity Threshold
6:     $n\_walks \leftarrow 10$ ▷ Number of walks
7:     $walk\_len \leftarrow 80$ ▷ Walk Length
8:     $\psi : \psi_{v_i^l v_j^l}' \vee 1 \leq i,j \leq N; 1 \leq l \leq |L|$ ▷ node pair features
9: $\beta = \text{LEARN\_WEIGHTS}(G, s_l)$
10: $Q = \text{BUILD\_FINAL\_TRANSITION\_MATRIX}(G, \beta, \psi)$
11: $walks = \text{RANDOM\_WALKS}(Q, walk\_len, n\_walks)$
12: $X = \text{SKIP\_GRAM}(walks)$

13: **function** LEARN_WEIGHTS(G, s_l)
14:     $S \leftarrow [\,]$
15:     **for** l in L **do**
16:         $S.extend(Sample(G_l, s_l))$
17:     **end for**
18:     **for** s in S **do**
19:         $H_s \leftarrow [\,]$
20:         $L_s \leftarrow [\,]$
21:         $H_s \leftarrow neighbor(s, k) \cup sim\_node(s, \tau) \cup alias(s, G)$
22:         $L_s \leftarrow G_l - H_s$
23:     **end for**
24:     $\beta \leftarrow L - BFGS(minObj[6], H_s, L_s, S, \Psi)$
25:     **return** β
26: **end function**
27: **function** BUILD_TRANSITION_MATRIX(G, β, ψ)
28:     $Q \leftarrow [\,]$
29:     **for** $\psi_{v_i^l, v_j^l}$ in ψ **do**
30:         $Q[v_i^l, v_j^l] \leftarrow \beta^T \psi_{v_i^l, v_j^l}$
31:     **end for**
32:     **for** $\psi_{v_i^l, v_i^{l'}}$ in ψ **do**
33:         $Q[v_i^l, v_i^{l'}] \leftarrow \beta^T \psi_{v_i^l, v_i^{l'}}$
34:     **end for**
35:     **return** Q
36: **end function**
37: **function** RANDOM_WALKS$(Q, walk\_len, n\_walks)$
38:     $walks = [\,]$
39:     **for** l in L **do**
40:         **for** v_j^l in G_l **do**
41:             $walks.extend(Walk(Q, n\_walks, walk\_len, v_j^l))$
42:         **end for**
43:     **end for**
44:     **return** $walks$
45: **end function**

---

highly imbalanced. It contains an overwhelming proportion of negative samples (no-edge) compared to that of positive samples. To remove class imbalance, we undersample the negative class by taking similar number of samples as that present in the positive class. We then train a logistic regression model on the training set (formed after removing class imbalance) and test the performance of the model on the test set. We repeat the experiments 50 times and report the average AUC score.

534 A. Roy et al.

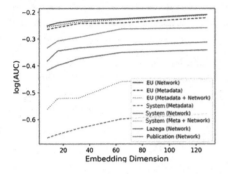 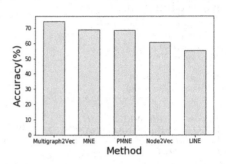

Fig. 2. Variation in the performance of Multigraph2Vec w.r.t. the increasing dimension of embedding and node attributes (metadata based or network-structure based) on link prediction. AUC scores averaged across layers are plotted on a log scale to elucidates mall differences in AUC values. Note that Lazega network does not have any metadata information of nodes.

Fig. 3. Accuracy obtained with different competing methods in multiclass node classification task on the Publication dataset. The accuracy is reported after averaging the performance across 50 iterations. The results are reported with network-property based attributes, and the dimension of the embedding vector is set to 128.

Baseline Methods: We compare Multigraph2Vec with single-layer methods, namely Node2Vec [7], LINE [21], and multi-layer methods, namely PMNE [13] and MNE [25]. We also compare against non-embedding methods like Jaccard Coefficient (JC) [11], Adamic-Adar (AA) [2], and common neighbor (CN) [17] based link prediction approaches.

Single-layer methods are not straightforwardly applicable to multidimensional networks and are also unable to capture multi-relation/interlayer interactions in the learned embeddings. For these methods, in order to obtain embeddings while evaluating for layer l, we only consider the training edges of layer l. Multi-layer methods (PMNE and MNE) are straightforward to apply in our setting, apart from the fact that these methods do not handle isolated nodes. For this, we terminate the random walk if it starts from or reaches an isolated node.

Parameter Sensitivity: We examine how different choices of embedding dimensions and node attributes (metadata based, network structure based and combination) affect the performance of Multigraph2Vec for link prediction. Figure 2 shows that with the increase of embedding dimension d, Multigraph2Vec performs consistently better. However, it performs the best if only network structure based attributes are used, rather than metadata based or their combination. Table 2 shows the performance of Multigraph2Vec with network structure based attributes keeping $d = 128$.

Comparative Analysis: Table 2 shows the performance of different embedding methods on four datasets (layer-wise). As expected, multilayer embedding methods (Multigraph2Vec, PMNE and MNE) outperform single-layer embedding methods (Node2Vec, LINE). The reason is that multilayer methods can capture the useful multi-relational interactions among nodes, while single-layer networks cannot. MNE turns out to be the best baseline. However, Multigraph2Vec outperforms MNE by 5.53%, 5.73%, 6.66% and 5.21% higher AUC (relative) on EU, Hike, Lazega and Publication datasets, respectively (averaged over the layers). From Fig. 2 it can be seen that when only network attributes are used AUC values are always higher than when either metadata attributes or both metadata and network attributes are used. This is because metadata features are redundant when combined with network properties, Hence together these features are actually losing information instead of gaining one. To support the fact we perform correlation analysis between every metadata and network properties features. We compute both linear (Pearson) as well as non linear (Spearman) coefficient on EU and System dataset because only they had metadata attributes. The mean linear correlation comes out to be 0.82 and 0.92 while the mean non linear correlation is 0.78 and 0.86 respectively on EU and Hike dataset. These values support the fact that network properties along with metadata properties causes redundancy which decreases the AUC-ROC score and hence network attributes alone gives best result.

5.3   Node Classification

In this setting, each node is assigned a label from a label set. The entire multigraph is used for unsupervised feature learning i.e., for learning the embedding of each node. Once the embeddings are learned, 75% nodes represented by their corresponding embeddings are used for training a multi-class classifier (here we use Logistic Regression classifier with one v/s rest approach). The remaining 25% nodes are used as test set. Multi-class node classification experiments are performed on the **publication dataset only**, since other datasets do not have node labels.

Baseline Methods: We learn the embeddings using single-layer baseline methods – Node2Vec, LINE, on an aggregated network. A pair of nodes are connected if they have at least one edge between them in the original multigraph. Multilayer baseline methods (PMNE and MNE) are trained on the entire multigraph itself.

Comparative Analysis: Figure 3 shows the performance of different embedding methods on the publication dataset. Multigraph2Vec with an accuracy of 74.28% outperforms other multi-layer embedding methods, MNE (accuracy of 69%) and PMNE (accuracy of 68.53%); whereas, single-layer methods, Node2Vec and LINE could only achieve an accuracy of 60.54% and 55.31%, respectively.

6   Conclusion

In this paper, we proposed Multigraph2Vec, a novel multigraph embedding generation method, which allowed flights instead of walks and learns transition probabilities while concurrently preserving multi-relation interactions among nodes,

in a principled fashion. We compared Multigraph2Vec with four state-of-the-art
network embedding methods on four real-world datasets for the task of link prediction and multi-class node classification and observed significant improvement
over these baselines. We also deployed Multigraph2Vec on Hike app for friend
recommendation.

References

1. Abu-El-Haija, S., Perozzi, B., Al-Rfou, R., Alemi, A.: Watch your step: learning
   graph embeddings through attention. CoRR abs/1710.09599 (2017)
2. Adamic, L.A., Adar, E.: Friends and neighbors on the web. Soc. Netw. **25**, 211–230
   (2001)
3. Backstrom, L., Leskovec, J.: Supervised random walks: predicting and recommending links in social networks. In: WSDM, pp. 635–644 (2011)
4. Bruna, J., Zaremba, W., Szlam, A., LeCun, Y.: Spectral networks and locally
   connected networks on graphs. CoRR abs/1312.6203 (2013)
5. Chang, S., Han, W., Tang, J., Qi, G.J., Aggarwal, C.C., Huang, T.S.: Heterogeneous network embedding via deep architectures. In: ACM SIGKDD, pp. 119–128
   (2015)
6. Dong, Y., Chawla, N.V., Swami, A.: Metapath2vec: scalable representation learning for heterogeneous networks. In: ACM SIGKDD, pp. 135–144 (2017)
7. Grover, A., Leskovec, J.: Node2vec: scalable feature learning for networks. In: ACM
   SIGKDD, pp. 855–864. New York, NY (2016)
8. Guo, Q., Cozzo, E., Zheng, Z., Moreno, Y.: Lévy random walks on multiplex networks. Sci. Rep. **6**, 1–11 (2016)
9. Hamilton, W.L., Ying, R., Leskovec, J.: Inductive representation learning on large
   graphs. CoRR abs/1706.02216 (2017)
10. Hong, S., Chakraborty, T., Ahn, S., Husari, G., Park, N.: SENA: preserving social
    structure for network embedding. In: 28th ACM Conference on Hypertext and
    Social Media, pp. 235–244 (2017)
11. Liben-Nowell, D., Kleinberg, J.: The link-prediction problem for social networks.
    JASIST **58**(7), 1019–1031 (2007)
12. Liu, D.C., Nocedal, J.: On the limited memory bfgs method for large scale optimiza-
    tion. Math. Program. **45**(3), 503–528 (1989). https://doi.org/10.1007/BF01589116
13. Liu, W., Chen, P.Y., Yeung, S., Suzumura, T., Chen, L.: Principled multilayer
    network embedding. In: ICDMW, pp. 134–141 (2017)
14. Ma, Y., Ren, Z., Jiang, Z., Tang, J., Yin, D.: Multi-dimensional network embedding
    with hierarchical structure. In: WSDM, pp. 387–395 (2018)
15. Mikolov, T., Chen, K., Corrado, G., Dean, J.: Efficient estimation of word repre-
    sentations in vector space. CoRR abs/1301.3781 (2013)
16. Mikolov, T., Sutskever, I., Chen, K., Corrado, G., Dean, J.: Distributed represen-
    tations of words and phrases and their compositionality. In: NIPS, pp. 3111–3119
    (2013)
17. Newman, M.E.J.: Clustering and preferential attachment in growing networks.
    Phys. Rev. E **64**, 025102 (2001)
18. Perozzi, B., Al-Rfou, R., Skiena, S.: DeepWalk: online learning of social represen-
    tations. In: ACM SIGKDD, New York, NY, USA, pp. 701–710 (2014)
19. Shi, C., Hu, B., Zhao, W.X., Philip, S.Y.: Heterogeneous information network
    embedding for recommendation. IEEE TKDE **31**(2), 357–370 (2019)

20. Supplementary, I.: Multigraph2Vec: code & data (2019). https://tinyurl.com/y5goe7vx
21. Tang, J., Qu, M., Wang, M., Zhang, M., Yan, J., Mei, Q.: Line: Large-scale information network embedding. In: WWW, pp. 1067–1077 (2015)
22. Tang, L., Liu, H.: Leveraging social media networks for classification. Data Min. Knowl. Disc. **23**, 447–478 (2010). https://doi.org/10.1007/s10618-010-0210-x
23. Verbrugge, L.M.: Multiplexity in adult friendships. Soc. Forces **57**(4), 1286–1309 (1979)
24. Yan, L., Dodier, R., Mozer, M.C., Wolniewicz, R.: Optimizing classifier performance via an approximation to the wilcoxon-mann-whitney statistic. In: ICML, pp. 848–855 (2003)
25. Zhang, H., Qiu, L., Yi, L., Song, Y.: Scalable multiplex network embedding. In: IJCAI, pp. 3082–3088, July 2018

Mining Behavioral Data

Mobility Irregularity Detection
with Smart Transit Card Data

Xuesong Wang[1]([✉]), Lina Yao[1], Wei Liu[1,2], Can Li[1], Lei Bai[1],
and S. Travis Waller[2]

[1] Computer Science and Engineering, University of New South Wales,
Sydney, Australia
{xuesong.wang1,lina.yao,Wei.Liu,can.li4}@unsw.edu.au,
baisanshi@gmail.com
[2] Civil and Environmental Engineering, University of New South Wales,
Sydney, Australia
s.waller@unsw.edu.au

Abstract. Identifying patterns and detecting irregularities regarding individual mobility in public transport system is crucial for transport planning and law enforcement applications (e.g., fraudulent behavior). In this context, most of recent approaches exploit similarity learning through comparing spatial-temporal patterns between normal and irregular records. However, they are limited in utilizing passenger-level information. First, all passenger transits are fused in a certain region at a timestamp whereas each passenger has own repetitive stops and time slots. Second, these differences in passenger profile result in high intra-class variance of normal records and blur the decision boundaries. To tackle these problems, we propose a modelling framework to extract passenger-level spatial-temporal profile and present a personalised similarity learning for irregular behavior detection. Specifically, a route-to-stop embedding is proposed to extract spatial correlations between transit stops and routes. Then attentive fusion is adopted to uncover spatial repetitive and time invariant patterns. Finally, a personalised similarity function is learned to evaluate the historical and recent mobility patterns. Experimental results on a large-scale dataset demonstrate that our model outperforms the state-of-the-art methods on recall, F1 score and accuracy. Raw features and the extracted patterns are visualized and illustrate the learned deviation between the normal and the irregular records.

Keywords: Irregular pattern detection · Spatial-temporal profiling ·
Similarity learning

1 Introduction

Smart public transit card is now widely used in cities all over the world. It brings massive convenience for both passengers and transit operators in daily lives.

© Springer Nature Switzerland AG 2020
H. W. Lauw et al. (Eds.): PAKDD 2020, LNAI 12084, pp. 541–552, 2020.
https://doi.org/10.1007/978-3-030-47426-3_42

Online recharging and fare calculation can be automatically achieved with minimum labour cost involved. In this context, large volume of transit smart card data is continuously generated, which provides an unprecedented opportunity to profile passenger mobility patterns [8]. For example, the Opal card in the Greater Sydney area involves millions of users and records travel patterns of them on a daily basis. Uncovering recurrent patterns, and systematic variations, and irregular behavior patterns from these large datasets can aid in future transit route and stop planning or refinement, bus or train scheduling. Moreover, detecting irregular behavior patterns may also help alleviate or limit potential fraudulent behavior with smart transit card and subsequent loss.

The repetitiveness or regularity of travel patterns indeed allow planners and operators to optimally design public transport systems. However, in recent years, with a growing availability of individual mobility data, detecting irregularities regarding individual mobility in public transport system and quantifying the impacts of these become increasingly important, which can help the system operator and planner to more proactively accommodate both systematic behavior variations and stochasticity related to travel in public transit systems. At the same time, discovering and preventing potential fraudulent behavior with smart transit cards is also important in many cities. For example, the public transit card in cities such as Sydney, Melbourne, and Hong Kong is often linked to users' credit cards. Moreover, public transit cards in some cities (e.g., Octopus card in Hong Kong) can also be used to purchase daily goods from a variety of shops. Detecting irregular and potential fraudulent behavior with smart transit cards at early stages may help avoid considerable loss of travelers who lose their smart transit cards.

In order to address the problem of detecting irregular or fraudulent behavior in smart transit data, recent efforts have been made in spatial-temporal profile extraction and pattern comparison. First, convolutional-based or graph-based methods are adopted for describing spatial connections and layout for different stops [1,5,14]. Then a sequential layer is applied to model temporal correlations among historical transits. In this way, the model is able to predict a traffic-related value for a location at a timestamp. Finally, similarity-based algorithms are used to compare different passenger patterns. The similarity function can either be measured by a statistical distance metric between the normal and fraud data, or defined by a reconstruction error derived from an encoder-decoder structure [6,13,16]. Therefore, a reference passenger pattern can be discriminated from a potential irregular/fraudulent pattern.

Despite promising success in excavating spatial-temporal profile based on morphological layout or traffic flow, passenger level information is often fused within a certain region, which is inadequate when distinguishing fine-grained passenger profile since everyone has their own mobility patterns. Besides, most of the existing fraud or irregularity detection methods only consider all passenger data in an aggregate manner and learn a decision boundary for common outlier patterns. However, these methods tend to fail when normal data has high intra-class variance, meaning that normal data is not compacted and the boundary between the normal and fraud data is blurry, or reconstructed errors are high even for normal data. This is exactly the case of mobility pattern where one passenger's normal record can be another one's abnormal data and totally confuses the aforementioned methods, thus calling for a personalised fraudulent behavior detection method.

In this paper, we build a deep learning framework to detect irregu-lar/fraudulent behavior with respect to smart transit card (note that we may simply use "fraud" or "fraudulent" to refer to "irregular" behaviors later on). We managed to extract passenger level spatial-temporal profile and present a personalised similarity learning for detection. More specifically, a route-to-stop embedding is first proposed to extract spatial correlations between different tran-sit stops and routes for each passenger. Then attentive fusion is adopted to find spatial repetitive and time invariant pattern. Finally, a personalised similarity function is learned to evaluate the historical and recent mobility patterns. To summarize, this paper makes the following major contributions.

- We propose a novel route-to-stop embedding to explore spatial correlations between routes and transit stops. It does not need to compute tens of thou-sands of global nodes in a graph. Instead, it only focuses on personalised nodes for each passenger, meanwhile maintain the ability to abstract node and edge correlations.
- We propose a learnable similarity function to measure the distance between repetitive invariant mobility pattern and recency pattern. Instead of integrat-ing all the passenger data with high intra-class variance, the function directly applies to each passenger and makes personalised decision.
- We conduct experiments on a large-scale real-world dataset. Results demon-strated that using 20% of the total fraudulent data can achieve state-of-the art performance. With overall data, our model gains significant improvements on F1 and accuracy.

2   Related Works

Recently a host of studies have investigated to extract spatial-temporal profile for a passenger. One typical approach is to use convolutional layers over a spatial map and to use recurrent layers over a time sequence. Lan et al. [7] and Chen et al. [3] adopted convolutional layers on the morphological layout of a city and LSTM to estimate travel time and predict urban air quality index. Recently convolutional graph networks have drawn more attention in helping discover non-linearity correlation between nodes and edges in a graph [5,17]. Each node is represented by a vector while connections of each node are represented by an adjacency matrix or by fixed edge features. Nevertheless, most of existing approaches [1,14] fuse passenger features in a node, while features on the same node can be dynamic for different passengers, since two passengers on the same stop may have different time slot preference. Also, usually nodes were built by segmenting city layout into hundreds of grids so as to compute adjacency matrix. However, in our scenario nodes are tens of thousands of transit stops, demanding highly expensive computation to build a traditional graph.

In order to distinguish unique passenger profile from potential irregular or fraudulent behavior, distance-based and reconstruction-based detection methods have been widely used. The distance-based approaches assume that normal data are compact in distribution and far from sparse fraud. Conventional methods include isolation Forest [9], and One-Class Support Vector Machine. Present deep learning-based models try to learn a distinguished density space between the normal and fraud data [10,11,15]. DevNet [10] defines a deviation loss based on z-score of a prior Gaussian distribution and squeezes the outliers to the tail of the distribution. Perera et al. [11] present a compactness and a descriptiveness loss for one-class learning. Yoon et al. [15] propose a learnable scoring matrix to detecting incongruity between news headline and body text. The reconstruction based methods adopt encoder-decoder structures and claim that fraud can not be well-reconstructed through the structure. Cao et al. [2] and Xu et al. [13] propose variation-auto-encoder based models with extensive experiments. Zhang et al. [16] detect fraud on reconstructed residual correlation matrix. LSTM-NDT [6] and OmniAnomaly [12] adopt dynamic thresholding on reconstructed feature errors. Despite great effectiveness, these approaches tend to underperform in our task due to high intra-class variance of normal data, where one passenger's normal records can be irregular/fraudulent for others.

Summary. The proposed method in this paper is fundamentally different from the literature in the following aspects. Firstly, the proposed route-to-stop embedding does not need to compute tens of thousands of node features in a graph. Instead, it only concentrates on personalised nodes for each passenger, meanwhile maintaining the ability of abstracting node and edge correlations. Furthermore, this study directly applies a personalised similarity function to learn the discrepancy between historical and new records for each passenger. In this way, the variance of data can be reduced by only focusing records of the same passenger. Therefore, the high intra-class variance problem of some existing approaches is avoided.

3   Proposed Approach

3.1   Data Characteristics

Data Description. We use public transit card of the Greater Sydney area (Opal card) in the case study. In total 187,000 passenger records were collected from April 1st to 30th, 2017. Each record is characterized with transit stop features and route features. Transit stop features consist of tap on/off time, longitude/latitude and postcode of stops, stop id and whether the tap is a transfer from another vehicle. Transit route features include vehicle type, vehicle id, duration, distance bands, journey costs and run direction. In this way, every record can be described as a starting stop to an ending stop through a route, and a passenger can be represented as a sequence of such records. As demonstrated in Fig. 1, there are four transit stops marked as red and three connecting routes for this passenger. Each stop has one or more records, representing the passenger pattern such as visiting frequency.

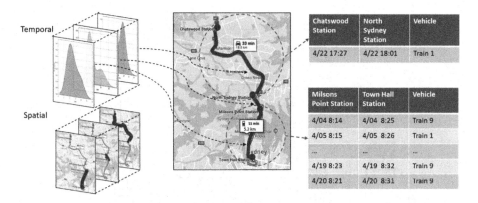

Fig. 1. Passenger spatial-temporal profile.

From Fig. 1, it is able to profile a passenger through spatial-temporal pattern. For instance, a route is made from Milsons Point Station to Town Hall Station nearly every weekday morning, indicating home/office location and potential occupation of the passenger. These repetitive stops together with less visiting stops, each with their own time invariant pattern, profile a unique passenger. We hereby aim to leverage this profile by excavating spatial correlations between transit stops and temporal preferences for each route, named "personalised spatial-temporal profile" for short. We expect to learn discriminative passenger profile, which can not only help transit operators provide more customised service, but can also alert passengers when irregular/fraudulent behavior occurs.

3.2   Problem Statement

Given a set of historical records $X = \{x_1, x_2, ..., x_N\}$ with $x_i \in \mathbb{R}^D$ and a recent record x_{N+1} for a passenger, each record $x_i = (s_{i1}, s_{i2}, r_i)$ can be viewed as a route r_i from a stop s_{i1} to a stop s_{i2} where $(.,.)$ denotes concatenation. The goal is to learn a personalised similarity function $\phi : (x_{N+1}, X) \mapsto \mathbb{R}^2$ in a way that x_{N+1} is similar to X if $\phi(x_{N+1}, X)_1 > \phi(x_{N+1}, X)_2$. Otherwise, it is a irregular/fraudulent behavior.

3.3   The Proposed Framework

Figure 2 presents the overall framework of the personalised spatial-temporal similarity learning network. Historical pattern u_N and the latest pattern u_{N+1} are extracted and compared from the corresponding data $\{x_1, x_2, ..., x_N\}$ and x_{N+1} to detect a irregular/fraudulent behavior. There are four major components in the framework: a route-to-stop embedding to describe the spatial mapping function from routes to stops, an attentive fusion to capture repetitive and time invariant pattern, a fully connected layer to extract recent pattern, and a similarity function to learn the discrepancy between the historical and recent patterns.

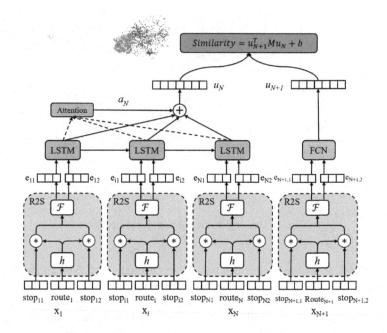

Fig. 2. The framework of personalised spatial-temporal similarity learning.

Route-to-Stop Embedding (R2S). As mentioned before, every record is featured by two transit stops and a route. Instead of directly input raw features $x_i = (s_{i1}, s_{i2}, r_i)$ into the model, we want to map two stop features s_{i1}, s_{i2} into the same space since starting and ending stops share the same raw input space. Also, stop and route features (s_i, r_i) have strong dependency correlations, for example, in Fig. 1, given route features like vehicle id, time duration and cost and starting stop features like tap on time and location, it is possible to speculate corresponding ending stop features. Hence, route features should also be projected to the same space as transit stops. Inspired by [4], a route-to-stop(R2S) embedding that is generalizable for each passenger is proposed to represent spatial correlation: {route r_i: starting stop $s_{i1} \mapsto$ ending stop s_{i2} }:

$$e_i = \mathcal{E}(s_{i1}, s_{i2}, r_i) = (\mathcal{F}[h(r_i) \odot s_{i1}], \mathcal{F}[h(r_i) \odot s_{i2}]) \tag{1}$$

where e_i is the embedding of the i-th record. $\mathcal{F}$ and h denote neural networks. $h(r_i)$ has the same dimension as s_{i1} and s_{i2}, and $\odot$ denotes element-wise multiplication. What R2S has achieved is to use h to project route features into stop space and to share a projection $\mathcal{F}$ between two stops.

The advantage of R2S layers lies in the ability to draw a customized spatial profile for each passenger. Different weights $h(r_i)$ are assigned to stops. The starting and ending stops are treated equally with $\mathcal{F}$. In this way, two passengers who share the same starting stop will have distinguished weights on that stop during to other factors like duration or costs.

Repetitive and Time Invariant Pattern. A unique passenger profile lies in repetitive visiting stops and invariant transit time slot preference observed from historical records. To capture such repetitive and time invariant pattern u_N, an LSTM layer followed by an attentive fusion is adopted:

$$u_i = LSTM(e_i, u_{i-1}), \quad \text{s.t.} \quad 2 \leq i \leq N, u_1 = \mathbf{0}$$
$$a = softmax(\mathbf{u} * W^u) \in \mathbb{R}^{N \times 1}, \qquad u_N = \sum_{i=0}^{N} a_i u_i \qquad (2)$$

where u_i is the hidden layer of the i-th record defined by the R2S embedding e_i and the hidden layer of the last timestamp u_{i-1}. Then, an attentive probability a_i is calculated for each u_i through attention matrix W^u. The attention matrix is learned to focus on repetitive and time invariant stops so that the extracted pattern u_N is distinguished from irregular/fraudulent behavior pattern.

Recency Mobility Pattern. For the latest record, the spatial profile e_{N+1} is directly fed into a fully-connected layer to get recency mobility pattern u_{N+1}:

$$u_{N+1} = FCN(e_{N+1}) \qquad (3)$$

The structure of hidden layers were chosen as same as the lstm hidden layers in order to learn a homogeneous projection as the historical pattern.

Personalised Similarity Learning. Given historical and recent record patterns u_N and u_{N+1}, A similarity function is modified from [15] aiming to provide personalised discrepancy decision:

$$P_{fraud} = (u_{N+1})^T M_1 u_N + b_1$$
$$P_{normal} = (u_{N+1})^T M_2 u_N + b_2 \qquad (4)$$
$$P(u_{N+1}, u_N) = softmax([p_{fraud}, p_{normal}])$$

where M_1, b_1, M_2, b_2 are learnable parameters. If $p_{fraud} > p_{normal}$, then it is irregular/fraudulent behavior. Using $u^T M u$ instead of directly adopting inner product $u^T u$ introduces a learnable matrix that can diminish differences between normal and historical data meanwhile enlarge the distributional gap between historical and fraud data. Hence, during training process, a pair of three records, i.e., (normal, irregular/fraudulent, historical) is built intentionally. The loss function is defined as:

$$\mathcal{L}(u_{N+1}, u_N) = -\mathbb{E}_{u_{N+1} \sim u_N} \log[P(u_{N+1}, u_N)] - \mathbb{E}_{u_{N+1} \not\sim u_N} \log[1 - P(u_{N+1}, u_N)] \qquad (5)$$

$u_{N+1} \sim u_N$ refers to normal data and $u_{N+1} \not\sim u_N$ refers to fraud data. The reason why the problem is designed in a supervised manner is that a limited number of labeled anomalies can always provide critical prior knowledge for an unsupervised model [10]. However, in many real-world applications it is unable to collect massive labels. In order to address this issue, we generate labels based on the intuition that u_{N+1} is a normal record if it comes from the same passenger as the historical records and it is an irregular record if it comes from other passengers. In this way, hand-crafted labels are not necessary.

4   Experiments

4.1   Experimental Settings

For the data set, records of 175,000 and 12,000 passengers were used as training and testing data. For each passenger, the number of historical records N is set to be 20. Embedding was adopted for categorical features. The overall dimension after the embedding is 322, with the dimension of stop1, stop2 and route features equalling 105, 105 and 112 respectively. For the R2S embedding $\mathcal{E}$, hidden units of the neural network h is the same as the stop dimension 105, and the number of hidden units of $\mathcal{F}$ is 50. The hidden states and output dimensions of LSTM are set to be 50 and 30. The hidden units of the FCN are 50 and 30.

4.2   Experimental Results

Baseline Methods. We choose three fraud detection methods on general data: OCSVM, iForest and DevNet, and two fraud detection methods on time series data: LSTM-NDT, MSCRED as baseline models. Also, two variants of our method are compared to test efficiency.

- OCSVM. The One-Class Support-Vector-Machine profiles normal data distribution boundary and claims x_{N+1} a fraud if it is outside the frontier.
- iForest [9]. The isolation Forest finds anomalies far from distributed-dense data. Each passenger data (x_{N+1}, X) is fit with an iForest model and a score of x_{N+1} is given.
- DevNet [10]. A new deviation loss based on z-score is proposed for anomaly detection. The objective is to squeeze normal data into a small range and deviate outliers from this range using a network. Since it does not have sequential layers, all historical as well as the latest features were stacked to prevent input information loss.
- LSTM-NDT [6]. The LSTM with the Nonparametric Dynamic Thresholding uses LSTM for multivariate time series prediction and defines a reconstructed error threshold based on historical error mean and variance.
- MSCRED [16]. The Multi-Scale Convolutional Recurrent Encoder-Decoder encodes the correlation matrix for multivariate time series and uses the residual reconstructed matrix to detect a fraud.
- Conv-Sim. A variant of our approach that replaces R2S embedding with 1d convolution layers. A 1×1 kernel whose channel equals to input dimension slides over the 20 historical data. The motivation is that all historical data should share the same kernel.

- R2S-Net. A variant of our approach whose similarity function is a fully connected neural network. The input of the function is the concatenation of historical and recent data representation, and the output is irregular/fraudulent score.

Each experiment is given 10 runs and the mean and deviation values of the metrics are displayed in Table 1. The general fraud detection methods (OCSVM, DevNet) outperforms the sequential methods (LSTM-DNT and MSCRED). This is probably due to high intra-variance of the normal data, whereas a binary decision for a general method is easier to make than generating reconstructed data for a sequential model.

Overall, R2S-Sim as well as two variants significantly improves the state-of-the-art algorithms and is robust on different runs. It achieves high performance on all of the metrics other than a skewed precision. It gains 0.11 and 15.6% improvements on F1 and accuracy over DevNet. Conv-Sim is the closest to our method since attentive fusion compensates for the lack of temporal layers in 1d-convolution. The accuracy of R2S-Sim is around 2% higher than R2S-Net, verifying the effectiveness of the learned similarity function.

Table 1. Performance comparison

Method	Precision (Std.Dev.)	Recall (Std.Dev.)	F1 (Std.Dev.)	Acc (Std.Dev.)
OCSVM	**0.984 (0)**	0.286 (0)	0.443 (0)	0.641 (0)
iForest [9]	0.562 (0.002)	0.873 (0.006)	0.684 (0.003)	0.596 (0.004)
DevNet [10]	0.668 (0.028)	**0.900 (0.042)**	0.765 (0.006)	0.724 (0.018)
LSTM-NDT [6]	0.700 (0.003)	0.485 (0.006)	0.573 (0.005)	0.638(0.003)
MSCRED [16]	0.484 (0.010)	0.888 (0.078)	0.626 (0.028)	0.473 (0.017)
Conv-Sim	0.866 (0.007)	0.879 (0.007)	0.873 (0.002)	0.872 (0.002)
R2S-Net	0.847 (0.005)	0.880 (0.008)	0.863 (0.003)	0.861 (0.003)
R2S-Sim(ours)	0.868 (0.005)	**0.895 (0.005)**	**0.881 (0.003)**	**0.880 (0.003)**

4.3 Ablation Study

Injection of fraud data. The original ratio of normal to fraudulent data is 1:1. We try to decrease the proportion of fraud training data. If 0% fraud data is injected, then it becomes a completely unsupervised problem. Hence, we use different proportion of fraud training data: $\{1\%, 5\%, 10\%, 20\%, 50\%, 70\%, 90\%, 100\%\}$ to validate the performance. The ratio of test data is still 1:1 to keep consistency. Therefore if all the test data is treated as normal, the accuracy is 0.5 and the recall 1.0.

Different Historical Window Size. Default window size is 20 in the setting. We assume that a passenger tap a card twice a day, then 20 is approximately a collection of weekly data. Different window sizes including $\{5, 10, 15\}$ were tested to see if passenger profile can be captured within a shorter time span.

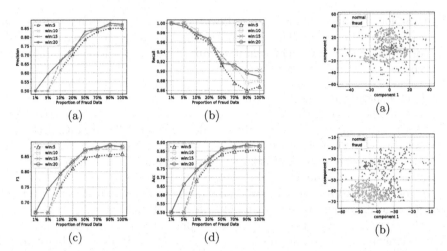

Fig. 3. Performance w.r.t. fraud data ratio and window size. (a) Precision. (b) Recall. (c) F1. (d) Accuracy.

Fig. 4. t-sne visualization on (a) raw features. (b) learned features.

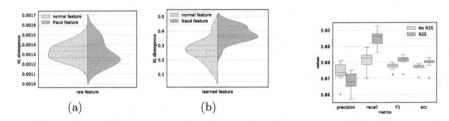

Fig. 5. KL divergence between normal and fraud on (a) raw features. (b) learned features.

Fig. 6. Performance with/ without R2S embedding.

Figure 3 demonstrates the metrics with respect to data proportion and window size. All test data was regarded as normal using 1% fraud data. However, with 5% data, the performance of the model using a 20-time-step sequence begins to improve. A pattern is observed that the longer the sequence, the less training data is needed for better performance. With 20% of the overall fraud data, all models can achieve the state-of-the-art accuracy of 0.7.

Remove R2S Embedding. Route-to-Stop embedding is removed and raw input features are input to attentive fusion. From Fig. 6, we can observe that except for precision, all the other metrics are improved with the embedding. Also, due to the reduced dimension of the input for the later LSTM layer, the overall training time is shorter than using raw features even with the added embedding.

4.4 Visualization on the Passenger Pattern

In order to test if distinguishable patterns were learnt, a subset of the test data is visualized on raw features and learned features u_N, u_{N+1} (see Fig. 4). A t-sne model is trained with the pair (historical, normal, fraudulent). The relative vectors $\mathbf{v}_{historical} - \mathbf{v}_{fraudulent}, \mathbf{v}_{historical} - \mathbf{v}_{normal}$ are displayed rather than $\mathbf{v}_{historical}, \mathbf{v}_{fraudulent}, \mathbf{v}_{normal}$. In this way, each data point in the plot is the difference between the historical and the latest representation of every passenger. Besides, test data was split into 40 groups and KL divergence was compared. Specifically, $KL(normal\|historical)$ and $KL(fraudulent\|historical)$ were compared and the violin plot is given in Fig. 5.

It is observed from Fig. 4(a) that the center of both normal and fraud cluster is around (0,0), meaning that the distribution of historical, normal and irregular/fraudulent raw data are homogeneous. This can also be concluded from Fig. 5(a) where difference between $KL(normal\|historical)$ and $KL(fraud\|historical)$ is negligible. After passenger pattern extraction, both differences are enlarged in Fig. 4(b) and Fig. 5(b), indicating that the model is pushing recent data away from historical one yet push irregular/fraudulent data harder so as to be distinctive. Also, there is a clear boundary between irregular/fraudulent and normal data.

5 Conclusions

In this study, we build a deep learning framework to detect irregular or fraudulent behavior with respect to smart transit card usage. We managed to extract passenger-level spatial-temporal profile and present a personalised similarity learning for detection. More specifically, a route-to-stop embedding is first proposed to exploit spatial correlations between different transit stops and routes. Then attentive fusion is adopted to find spatial repetitive and time invariant pattern. Finally, a personalised similarity function is learned to discriminate the historical and recent mobility patterns. Experimental results on a large-scale dataset demonstrate that the proposed model outperforms baseline methods in terms of recall, F1 score, and accuracy. Moreover, with 20% of the total fraud/irregular data, we can achieve state-of-the-art performance. Visualization on learned patterns reveals that the method can learn distinctive features among the irregularity/fraud and the normal records.

References

1. Bai, L., Yao, L., Kanhere, S., Wang, X., Sheng, Q., et al.: Stg2Seq: spatial-temporal graph to sequence model for multi-step passenger demand forecasting. In: Proceedings of the 28th International Joint Conference on Artificial Intelligence (IJCAI), pp. 1981–1987 (2019)
2. Cao, V.L., Nicolau, M., McDermott, J.: Learning neural representations for network anomaly detection. IEEE Trans. Cybern. **49**(8), 3074–3087 (2019)

3. Chen, L., Ding, Y., Lyu, D., Liu, X., Long, H.: Deep multi-task learning based urban air quality index modelling. Proc. ACM Interact. Mob. Wearable Ubiquit. Technol. **3**(1), 2 (2019)

4. Gilmer, J., Schoenholz, S.S., Riley, P.F., Vinyals, O., Dahl, G.E.: Neural message passing for quantum chemistry. In: Proceedings of the 34th International Conference on Machine Learning-Volume 70, pp. 1263–1272. JMLR. org (2017)

5. Guo, S., Lin, Y., Feng, N., Song, C., Wan, H.: Attention based spatial-temporal graph convolutional networks for traffic flow forecasting. In: Proceedings of the AAAI Conference on Artificial Intelligence, 33, pp. 922–929 (2019)

6. Hundman, K., Constantinou, V., Laporte, C., Colwell, I., Soderstrom, T.: Detecting spacecraft anomalies using LSTMs and nonparametric dynamic thresholding. In: Proceedings of the 24th ACM SIGKDD International Conference on Knowledge Discovery & Data Mining, pp. 387–395. ACM (2018)

7. Lan, W., Xu, Y., Zhao, B.: Travel time estimation without road networks: an urban morphological layout representation approach. In: Proceedings of the 28th International Joint Conference on Artificial Intelligence (IJCAI), pp. 1772–1778 (2019)

8. Li, C., Bai, L., Liu, W., Yao, L., Waller, S.T.: Passenger demographic attributes prediction for human-centered public transport. In: Gedeon, T., Wong, K.W., Lee, M. (eds.) ICONIP 2019. CCIS, vol. 1142, pp. 486–494. Springer, Cham (2019). https://doi.org/10.1007/978-3-030-36808-1_53

9. Liu, F.T., Ting, K.M., Zhou, Z.H.: Isolation forest. In: 2008 Eighth IEEE International Conference on Data Mining, pp. 413–422. IEEE (2008)

10. Pang, G., Shen, C., van den Hengel, A.: Deep anomaly detection with deviation networks. In: Proceedings of the 25th ACM SIGKDD International Conference on Knowledge Discovery & Data Mining, pp. 353–362. ACM (2019)

11. Perera, P., Patel, V.M.: Learning deep features for one-class classification. IEEE Trans. Image Process. **28**(11), 5450–5463 (2019)

12. Su, Y., Zhao, Y., Niu, C., Liu, R., Sun, W., Pei, D.: Robust anomaly detection for multivariate time series through stochastic recurrent neural network. In: Proceedings of the 25th ACM SIGKDD International Conference on Knowledge Discovery & Data Mining, pp. 2828–2837. ACM (2019)

13. Xu, H., et al.: Unsupervised anomaly detection via variational auto-encoder for seasonal KPIs in web applications. In: Proceedings of the 2018 World Wide Web Conference, pp. 187–196. International World Wide Web Conferences Steering Committee (2018)

14. Yao, H., Tang, X., Wei, H., Zheng, G., Li, Z.: Revisiting spatial-temporal similarity: a deep learning framework for traffic prediction. In: AAAI Conference on Artificial Intelligence (2019)

15. Yoon, S., et al.: Detecting incongruity between news headline and body text via a deep hierarchical encoder. In: Proceedings of the AAAI Conference on Artificial Intelligence, vol. 33, pp. 791–800 (2019)

16. Zhang, C., et al.: A deep neural network for unsupervised anomaly detection and diagnosis in multivariate time series data. In: Proceedings of the AAAI Conference on Artificial Intelligence, vol. 33, pp. 1409–1416 (2019)

17. Zheng, L., Li, Z., Li, J., Li, Z., Gao, J.: AddGraph: anomaly detection in dynamic graph using attention-based temporal GCN. In: Proceedings of the 28th International Joint Conference on Artificial Intelligence, pp. 4419–4425 (2019)

BRUNCH: Branching Structure Inference of Hybrid Multivariate Hawkes Processes with Application to Social Media

Hui Li[1($\boxtimes$)], Hui Li[2], and Sourav S. Bhowmick[1]

[1] School of Computer Science and Engineering, Nanyang Technological University,
Singapore, Singapore
HLI019@e.ntu.edu.sg, assourav@ntu.edu.sg
[2] School of Cyber Engineering, Xidian University, Xi'an, China
hli@xidian.edu.cn

Abstract. Multivariate Hawkes processes (MHPs) are a class of point processes where an arrival in one dimension can affect the future arrivals in all dimensions. Existing MHPs are associated with *homogeneous link functions*. However, in reality, different dimensions may exhibit different temporal characteristics. In this paper, we augment MHPs by incorporating *heterogeneous link functions*, referred to as *hybrid MHPs*, to capture the temporal characteristics in different dimensions. Since the *branching structure* can be utilized to equivalently represent MHPs, we propose a novel model called BRUNCH via *intensity-driven Chinese Restaurant Processes* (intCRP) to identify the optimal branching structure of hybrid MHPs. Furthermore, we relax the constraint on the shapes of triggering kernels in MHPs. We develop a *Monte Carlo-based inference* algorithm called MEDIA to infer the branching structure. Experiments on real-world datasets demonstrate the superior performance of BRUNCH and its usefulness in social media applications.

Keywords: Branching structure · Hawkes process · Heterogeneous link functions · Social media

1 Introduction

Multivariate Hawkes processes (MHPs) are a class of point processes with mutually exciting components to model sequences of discrete events in continuous time, where an arrival in one dimension can affect future arrivals in all dimensions [5,6]. Recently, MHPs have emerged in multiple fields to capture mutual excitation between dimensions, including high frequency trading [1], social influence analysis [16] and computational biology [13]. However, these MHPs are limited to a specific scenario where a past arrival can only excite the occurrence of future arrivals, and the corresponding *link functions*[1] are linear (*i.e.,* linear MHPs). However, in reality, inhibitory arrivals and non-additive aggregation of

---

[1] *Link functions* describe the dynamics of the comprehensive effects from previous events.

© Springer Nature Switzerland AG 2020
H. W. Lauw et al. (Eds.): PAKDD 2020, LNAI 12084, pp. 553–566, 2020.
https://doi.org/10.1007/978-3-030-47426-3_43

effects from past arrivals are present in several application domains [10]. For instance, negative feedbacks of online consumers may inhibit others' purchasing behaviours. Consequently, MHPs associated with nonlinear link functions, namely *nonlinear MHPs* [10], have been proposed where effects from past events encompass *both* excitation and inhibition.

Prior work on MHPs also assume that all dimensions take the *same* link function *i.e.,* either linear or nonlinear MHPs (*homogeneous* MHPs). That is, all dimensions follow roughly the same temporal characteristics. Note that a dimension may record actions of a user (*e.g.,* tweet, retweet, comment, share) in social media, behavior of a customer (*e.g.,* purchase, comment, return) in online shopping websites, and so on. In reality, different dimensions may exhibit different temporal characteristics. For example, in *Twitter*, one individual (*i.e.,* dimension) may be extremely interested in a popular topic and interact with her followers frequently whereas another individual may take little interest in that topic and seldom respond to his followers. In such scenario, the cumulative influence from recent events on the former individual is clearly different from the one on the latter. Hence, *homogeneous MHPs are insufficient to capture such diverse temporal characteristics*. To address this problem, in this paper we augment MHPs by incorporating *heterogeneous* link functions, referred to as *hybrid MHPs*, allowing us to cope with diverse impact of past events on future events in different dimensions.

The *cluster Poisson process interpretation* [7] of MHPs separates the events into two categories, namely, *immigrants* and *offspring*. The offspring events are triggered by past events, while the immigrants arrive independently and thus do not have a existing parent event. Offsprings are structured into *clusters* associated with each immigrant event. This is called the *branching structure* [8], which is an useful representation of MHPs in various applications. For example, in social influence analysis it can construct the narrative of information diffusion to pave the way for strategies to encourage or limit individual behaviors [14]. Additionally, the branching structure is widely utilized as a strategy in the maximum likelihood estimation of MHPs [16]. Unfortunately, such cluster Poisson process representation can only be applied to linear MHPs due to the mutually exciting assumption. Nonlinear MHPs cover both mutual excitation and mutual inhibition stochastically. Consequently, existing approaches based on the cluster Poisson process representation cannot be adopted to infer the branching structure of hybrid MHPs. In this paper, we *infer* the *branching structure* of hybrid MHPs regardless of the shapes of the *triggering kernel functions*[2].

We propose a novel probabilistic model called BRUNCH (**B**ranching st**RU**cture i**N**fere**C**e of **H**ybrid multivariate Hawkes processes) to reveal the branching structure of hybrid MHPs *without assuming homogeneity of link functions or shapes of triggering kernel functions* (Sect. 3). It is important for our probabilistic model to emphasize the following two features mirrored by the

---

[2] *Triggering kernel functions* describe the dynamics of how previous events trigger future events and may vary widely across different applications, *e.g.,* the triggering patterns in social media can be very different from the ones in high frequency trading.

Table 1. Key notations.

Notation	Definition	Notation	Definition
$\mathbf{X}$	Event sequences	t_{ik}	k-th arrival in i-th dimension
X_i	i-th event sequence	$N_i(t)$	Event number until t in i-th dimension
$\mathcal{B}$	Collection of event links	$t_{il} \to t_{ik}$	Event link from event t_{il} to event t_{ik}
$\mathcal{C}$	Collection of cluster links	$s \to g$	Cluster link from cluster s to cluster g
P_{ik}	Events triggered by t_{ik}	$\mathcal{I}(\mathcal{B}, \mathcal{C})$	Collection of cascades
Z_{ik}	Parent event of t_{ik}	$\mathcal{Z}_{ik}$	The cascade the event t_{ik} belongs to

event sequences in MHPs: (a) the chronological order of events is nonexchangeable; and (b) the triggering relations could distribute within or across dimensions stochastically. To this end, we propose *intensity-driven Chinese Restaurant Process* (intCRP), a novel extension of classical CRP [3] in which the random seating assignment of the customers depends on the triggering kernels between them. In particular, intCRP has a nested structure – *inner* intCRP to explore the possible triggering relations among events occurring in one dimension (*i.e.*, *event links*), and *outer* intCRP to identify the collection of triggering relations between all events and their parents (if any) across dimensions (*i.e.*, *cluster links*). Obviously, the changes to the triggering relations within and across dimensions are highly coupled, *i.e.*, the inner intCRP and outer outCRP are strongly interlaced. Since there are countably infinite sets of triggering relations, we propose a novel inference approach called MEDIA (MontE Carlo-baseD Inference Approach) that leverages the triggering nature of MHPs to sample event links and cluster links alternatively (Sect. 4). Finally, we apply BRUNCH on real-world social media datasets, and the experimental study in Sect. 5 demonstrates its superior performance and usefulness. Formal algorithms and proofs of theorems and lemmas appear in [9]. List of key symbols used in this paper is given in Table 1.

2 Preliminaries

In this section, we introduce relevant concepts for understanding this paper.

2.1 Multivariate Hawkes Processes (MHPs)

The conditional intensity function of the i-th dimension for an M-dimensional MHP takes the following form [10]:

$$\lambda_i(t) = \mathcal{F}_i\big(\mu_i + \sum\nolimits_{j=1}^{M} \sum\nolimits_{t_{jl} < t} \alpha_{ij}\phi_{ij}(t - t_{jl})\big) \tag{2.1}$$

where $\mu_i > 0$ is the base intensity capturing the arrival rate of exogenous events independent of historical events. The term $\sum_{j=1}^{M} \sum_{t_{jl}<t} \alpha_{ij}\phi_{ij}(t-t_{jl})$ represents the accumulation of endogenous intensity caused by history [4]. The coefficient

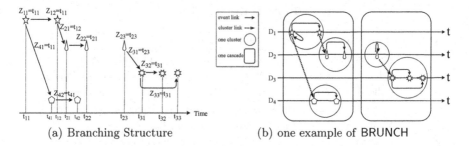

(a) Branching Structure   (b) one example of BRUNCH

Fig. 1. (a) An example of branching structure of MHPs and the events on the time axis; (b) Branching structure construction using BRUNCH.

α_{ij} measures the influence from the j-th dimension to the i-th dimension, allowing mutual excitation ($\alpha_{ij} > 0$) and mutual inhibition ($\alpha_{ij} < 0$). The *triggering kernel function* $\phi_{ij}(t - t_{jl})$ quantifies the triggering effect from the event t_{jl} (*i.e.*, t_{jl} denotes the l-th arrival occurring in the j-th dimension) to the occurrence rate of the i-th dimension. Most of the existing work use predefined kernel functions with unknown parameters, such as the exponential kernels [16] and the power-law kernels [15]. The *link function* $\mathcal{F}_i : \mathcal{R} \to \mathcal{R}^+$, recognizes the triggering pattern of the i-th dimension over the historical events. The linear MHPs [6] is the case $\mathcal{F}_i(x) = x$ with nonnegative α_{ij} for each dimension, while nonlinear MHPs apply various $\mathcal{F}_i(x)$ to guarantee the positive intensities. In *hybrid* MHPs, we allow each dimension to take a *personalized* link function to capture diverse temporal characteristics in real-world scenarios.

2.2 Branching Structure

Recall that the events in MHPs are classified as either *immigrants* or *offsprings*. An immigrant event arrives independently of other events, while an offspring event is triggered by a previous event. In the sequel, we refer to an immigrant together with its offsprings as a *cascade*. The collection of triggering relations in cascades is called the *branching structure* [8]. The cluster Poisson processes [7] could equivalently represent the branching structure of linear MHPs. Briefly, each immigrant starts one cascade, which consists of offspring events of the $1^{st}, 2^{nd}, 3^{rd}, \cdots$ generations, controlled by the endogenous intensity in Eq. 2.1 [11]. Due to the non-linear link functions, the above branching structure representation based on the cluster Poisson processes is inapplicable for nonlinear MHPs and hybrid MHPs.

Suppose that $X_i = \{t_{ik}\}_{k=1}^{N_i(t)}$ denotes the i-th event sequence during a time window $[0, t]$. Then $\mathbf{X} = \{X_i\}_{i \in [M]}$ is the collection of events from M dimensions during $[0, t]$. While modeling the sequences $\mathbf{X}$ via hybrid MHPs, the corresponding *branching structure* could be represented by the variable set $\mathcal{K} = \{\{(Z_{ik}, P_{ik})\}_{k=1}^{N_i(t)}\}_{i \in [M]}$ mathematically, such that

- $Z_{ik} = t_{ik}$ if t_{ik} is an immigrant; and $Z_{ik} = t_{jl}$ if event t_{jl} triggers t_{ik}; and
- $P_{ik} = \{t_{hm}, t_{rs}, \ldots\}$ if there are some events $\{t_{hm}, t_{rs}\}$ triggered by t_{ik}; otherwise, $P_{ik} = \varnothing$.

Our objective is to infer (Z_{ik}, P_{ik}) for each event. Consider Fig. 1(a). Directed links sketch an example of branching structure. $Z_{11} = t_{11}$ indicates the event t_{11} is an immigrant, and $Z_{12} = t_{11}$ shows t_{11} triggers t_{12}. $Z_{32} = t_{31}$ and $Z_{33} = t_{31}$ leads to $P_{31} = \{t_{32}, t_{33}\}$, denoting that t_{31} triggers t_{32} and t_{33} successively.

3   The BRUNCH Model

While modeling the asynchronous time-stamped event sequences via hybrid MHPs, we aim to reveal the underlying branching structure. Although the traditional Chinese Restaurant Process (CRP) [3] provides a flexible class of distributions that is amenable for modeling dependencies between elements, the exchangeability assumption here is problematic for elements with temporal dependencies. This is because events in MHPs occur at different time points, and are nonexchangeable. In addition, in our problem setting the influence that determines the pairwise dependencies between events is not homogeneous within and across different sequences. Intuitively, it is natural to quantify the influence via the triggering kernels in Eq. 2.1. In order to tackle these issues, we present the BRUNCH model, which is based on *intensity-driven Chinese restaurant processes* (intCRP), a new variant of CRP that allows a number of intensity-driven distributions as priors on triggering relations between events.

The events in one cascade could stem from different dimensions. So, beyond the triggering relations obtained from single-sequence intCRP, we need to capture the cross-sequence triggering relations among events. To this end, BRUNCH allows us to identify the possible dependencies among multi-dimensional event sequences in hybrid MHPs. Specifically, it presents a class of prior distributions over branching structure according to intCRP, which has nested structure, *inner* intCRP and *outer* intCRP. Briefly, the inner intCRP identifies the possible triggering relations in each sequence independently, which are referred to as **event links**. Linked events in each sequence form one cluster. Subsequently, *outer* intCRP captures the potential cross-sequence triggering relations, referred to as **cluster links**, which connects parent events with children from cross-sequence *clusters*.

We resort to the Chinese Restaurant metaphor to describe the generative process of event links and cluster links in BRUNCH. Imagine a collection of event sequences as a collection of restaurants, and the events in each sequence as customers entering a restaurant. The linked events in each sequence compose one cluster, and such clusters correspond to tables. Figure 1(b) illustrates the process. Note that in traditional CRP, the probability of a customer sitting at a table is computed from the number of other customers already sitting at that table.

3.1   Event Link Construction

In each sequence, if one event is an immigrant, there exists one self-link with itself; otherwise, there exists a triggering dependency for the event. That is, if event t_{il} generates event t_{ik}, the link from t_{il} to t_{ik} is created spontaneously. The inner intCRP assigns event link $t_{il} \rightarrow t_{ik}$ in a biased way, according to the following cluster-specific distribution:

$$\Pr(t_{il} \rightarrow t_{ik}|\rho_i, A^i) \propto \begin{cases} A^i_{lk} & t_{ik} > t_{il} \\ \rho_i & t_{ik} = t_{il} \end{cases} \quad (3.1)$$

where self-affinity $\rho_i = \mu_i$ yields new immigrant events, and larger self-affinity favors more cascades. A^i_{lk} describes how the affinity between a pair of events affects the probability for t_{il} triggering t_{ik}. In accordance with the propagation characteristics described by hybrid MHPs, child events tend to be generated by preceding events with stronger triggering effect. We define A^i_{lk} as the product of two parts: $f^w(t_{il}, t_{ik})$ and $f^d(t_{il}, t_{ik})$. For a window size W, we set the decay function $f^w(t_{il}, t_{ik})$ such that for $t_{ik} - t_{il} < W$, $f^w(t_{il}, t_{ik}) = 1$, and zero otherwise. It determines the probability to link with events that are at most W timespan away, and disregards the historical events as time progresses. Intuitively, the possible links existing between events that are far away from each other are negligibly rare. For $f^d(t_{il}, t_{ik})$, we apply the self-triggering kernel $f^d(t_{il}, t_{ik}) = \alpha_{ii}\phi_{ii}(t_{ik} - t_{il})$ which decays the probability of connecting events along with the timespan to the current one. Consequently, the event links $B_i = \{t_{il} \rightarrow t_{ik}|k = 1, 2, \cdots, N_i(t), l \in \{1, 2, \cdots, k\}\}$ in i-th dimensional sequence assign events into clusters, where two events are assigned to the same cluster if one is reachable from the other by traversing the directed links. Once the event link $t_{il} \rightarrow t_{ik}$ is confirmed, we can obtain the branching structure $Z_{ik} = t_{il}$ within sequences.

3.2   Cluster Link Construction

Accordingly, the collection of event links $\mathcal{B} = \{B_1, B_2, \cdots, B_M\}$ will divide the event sequences $\mathbf{X}$ into clusters, denoted by $\mathcal{C}(\mathcal{B})$. By involving the mutual-triggering kernels, we could measure the pairwise affinity between cross-sequence events. Hence, given two clusters, s and g, the outer intCRP assigns the cluster link $s \rightarrow g$ according to the following cascade-specific distribution:

$$\Pr(s \rightarrow g|\mathcal{B}) \propto \max_{t_{ik} \in s, t_{ik} < t_{je}} \left(|\alpha_{ij}|\phi_{ij}(t_{je} - t_{ik}) \right) \quad g \neq s \quad (3.2)$$

where $t_{je} = \min\{t_{jl}|t_{jl} \in g\}$. Only if one event (i.e., t_{ik}) in cluster s generates the earliest event in cluster g, there exists a cluster link $s \rightarrow g$. In particular, self-loop cluster link is non-existent. Once the cluster link $s \rightarrow g$ is determined, we could construct the equivalent branching structure $P_{ik} = P_{ik} \bigcup \{t_{je}\}$. In summary, we construct the complete branching structure $\mathcal{K} = \{(Z_{ik}, P_{ik})\}$ via scanning the obtained event links $\mathcal{B}$ and cluster links $\mathcal{C}$.

Intuitively, a collection of cluster links will divide clusters into cascades. We represent one cascade as one set of events. Let $\mathcal{Z}_{ik}$ denote the cascade associated with event t_{ik}, and $\mathcal{Z} = \{\mathcal{Z}_{ik}|i = 1, 2, \cdots, M; k = 1, 2, \cdots, N_i\}$ records the final cascade assignments. Notice that events t_{ik} and t_{jl} belong to one cascade (i.e., $\mathcal{Z}_{ik} = \mathcal{Z}_{jl}$) if and only if they are reachable via combinations of event links and cluster links. Given the collection of event links $\mathcal{B}$ and cluster links $\mathcal{C}$, we denote $\mathcal{I}(\mathcal{B}, \mathcal{C})$ as the final collection of cascades. We initialize the Hawkes likelihood parameters $\Theta^{1:M} = \{\mu_i, \alpha_{ij}, \phi_{ij}\}_{i,j \in [M]} \sim \pi(\gamma)$ where γ are the hyper-parameters, and $\pi(\gamma)$ is the collection of distributions.

The central goal of BRUNCH is to infer the posterior distribution of the latent links $(\mathcal{B}, \mathcal{C})$, given a collection of time-stamped events. It places a prior distribution over a combinatorial number of possible event links and cluster links, according to inner intCRP (Eq. 3.1) and outer intCRP (Eq. 3.2), respectively. Intuitively, applying Bayes's Theorem, the posterior distribution takes the form $\Pr(\mathcal{B}, \mathcal{C} | \mathbf{X}) = \frac{\Pr(\mathbf{X}, \mathcal{B}, \mathcal{C})}{\Pr(\mathbf{X})}$. Unfortunately, we cannot compute $\Pr(\mathbf{X})$. Hence, the posterior inference of links is intractable. To address this, in the following section we present a strategy that approximately infers the posterior distribution.

4 Model Inference

As the number of event links and cluster links varies with the observed events, we need to undertake Bayesian inference over a link set of unknown cardinality. Moreover, changes over event links may induce subsequent changes to other event links and current cluster links. To this end, we propose the Monte Carlo-based inference approach (MEDIA) that leverages the triggering nature of hybrid MHPs to sample event links and cluster links.

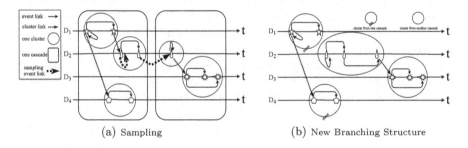

(a) Sampling   (b) New Branching Structure

Fig. 2. Sampling event links in Panel (a) leads a chain of changes to current branching structure, and constructs new one in Panel (b).

We aim to construct a Markov chain whose stationary distribution is the target posterior distribution $\Pr(\mathcal{B}, \mathcal{C} | \mathbf{X})$. The state of the chain is represented by $(\mathcal{B}, \mathcal{C})$, a collection of links over event sequences. Furthermore, event links $\mathcal{B}$ and cluster links $\mathcal{C}$ are strongly coupled, that is, sampling event links could trigger a chain of merges and splits to the current structure, as shown in Fig. 2. In view of this, we design the Monte Carlo-based inference approach, which involves two key phases: (a) sampling event links $\mathcal{B}$ via a Metropolis-Hastings rule, which could possibly bring changes to current cluster links $\mathcal{C}$, and then (b) update cluster links $\mathcal{C}$ via a Gibbs sampler. We elaborate on them in turn.

Sampling Event Links. Let current links be $(\mathcal{B}, \mathcal{C})$. After sampling one event link, the reconstructed links are denoted as $(\tilde{\mathcal{B}}, \tilde{\mathcal{C}})$. The iterative procedure runs until approaching the stationary distribution as follows:

1. Using the current links $\mathcal{B}$, sample a candidate link set $\tilde{\mathcal{B}}$ from the transition probability $q(\tilde{\mathcal{B}}, \tilde{\mathcal{C}}|\mathbf{X}, \mathcal{B}, \mathcal{C})$;
2. Sampled $\tilde{\mathcal{B}}$ leads to cluster links $\tilde{\mathcal{C}}$. Calculate the acceptance probability $\eta(\tilde{\mathcal{B}}, \tilde{\mathcal{C}}|\mathbf{X}, \mathcal{B}, \mathcal{C})$ for the candidate set $\tilde{\mathcal{B}}$,

$$\eta(\tilde{\mathcal{B}}, \tilde{\mathcal{C}}|\mathbf{X}, \mathcal{B}, \mathcal{C}) = \min\Big\{ \frac{\Pr(\mathbf{X}, \tilde{\mathcal{B}}, \tilde{\mathcal{C}})q(\mathcal{B}, \mathcal{C}|\mathbf{X}, \tilde{\mathcal{B}}, \tilde{\mathcal{C}})}{\Pr(\mathbf{X}, \mathcal{B}, \mathcal{C})q(\tilde{\mathcal{B}}, \tilde{\mathcal{C}}|\mathbf{X}, \mathcal{B}, \mathcal{C})}, 1 \Big\}$$

Notice that we are considering the ratio of $\Pr(\mathcal{B}, \mathcal{C}|\mathbf{X})$ under two different structures, so the denominator $\Pr(\mathbf{X})$ is eliminated.

Theorem 4.1 *The above Metropolis-Hastings rule satisfies detailed balance.*

Based on Theorem 4.1, we can guarantee the resulting Markov chain converges to a stationary distribution uniquely [2]. BRUNCH provides a joint distribution for a collection of events and current links as following:

$$\Pr(\mathbf{X}, \mathcal{B}, \mathcal{C}) = \Pr(\mathcal{B})\Pr(\mathcal{C}|\mathcal{B})\Pr(\mathbf{X}|\mathcal{B}, \mathcal{C}) \tag{4.1}$$

If one event is an offspring, it has only one parent event. So once the affinity functions in inner intCRP are predefined, the generated event links are conditionally independent. Furthermore, event links divide all events into clusters. Hence, once the event links and the affinity functions in outer intCRP are predefined, the generated cluster links are conditionally independent. That is to say, event links $\mathcal{B}$ are conditionally independent given $(\rho_{1:M}, A^{1:M})$, and cluster links $\mathcal{C}$ are conditionally independent given $\mathcal{B}$, thereby causing the independent cascades. As a consequence, the joint distribution on events and links equals to:

$$\Pr(\mathbf{X}, \mathcal{B}, \mathcal{C}|\rho_{1:M}, A^{1:M}, \gamma) = \prod_{I \in \mathcal{I}(\mathcal{B}, \mathcal{C})} \Pr(t_{\mathcal{Z}=I}|\gamma) \prod_{i=1}^{M} \prod_{k=1}^{N_i} \prod_{l=1}^{k} \Pr(t_{il} \to t_{ik}|\rho_i, A^i) \prod_{t_{ik} \in g}^{s \in \mathcal{C}(\mathcal{B})} \Pr(s \to g|\mathcal{B}) \tag{4.2}$$

The activities belonging to cascade I are represented as $t_{\mathcal{Z}=I}$, hence,

$$\Pr(t_{\mathcal{Z}=I}|\gamma) = \int \prod_{\mathcal{Z}_{ik}=I} \Pr(t_{ik}|\Theta^{1:M})d\pi(\Theta^{1:M}|\gamma) \tag{4.3}$$

where the parameter set Θ could be drawn from pre-determined distributions associated with the hyper-parameters γ. Hence, the above integral is tractable. Based on the hybrid MHPs associated with conditional intensity (Eq. 2.1), we derive the conditional probability density [8] that an event occurs at time t_{ik} is:

$$\Pr(t_{ik}|\mathcal{Z}_{ik}=I, \Theta^{1:M}) = \lambda_i(t_{ik}|\mathcal{Z}_{ik}=I, \Theta^{1:M}) \cdot \exp\Big(-\int_0^{t_{ik}} \lambda_i(s|\Theta^{1:M})ds\Big) \tag{4.4}$$

where the integral $\int_0^{t_{ik}} \lambda_i(s|\Theta^{1:M})ds$ is not always analytically integrable w.r.t. various link functions of hybrid MHPs. To address the issue, we propose the approximation: $\int_0^t \lambda_i(s|\Theta^{1:M})ds = \sum_{m=1}^n (t_m - t_{m-1})\lambda_i(t_m)$.

We describe how replacing an event link affects the current links $(\mathcal{B}, \mathcal{C})$, and there are four cases:

1. Split. If adding event link $t_{ik} \to t_{ik}$ breaks the existing link $t_{il} \to t_{ik}$ and divides t_{ik} and t_{il} into two clusters, it shows that event t_{ik} is an offspring. Moreover, there are no existing clusters to be merged after sampling event link $t_{ik} \to t_{il'}$. Thus, the new cluster including t_{il} has the same incoming cluster links as the previous cluster containing both t_{ik} and t_{il}. We assume that the incoming links are independently linked to the new cluster with equal probability. New cluster s including t_{ik} collects its outgoing cluster links $\mathcal{C}_s$ according to the distribution $\Pr(\mathcal{C}_s|\mathbf{X}, \tilde{\mathcal{B}}, \mathcal{C}_{-s})$ where $\mathcal{C}_{-s}$ represents the set of cluster links excluding the ones $s \to g, g \in \mathcal{C}(\tilde{\mathcal{B}})$. Then, the transition probability is:

$$q_1(\tilde{\mathcal{B}}, \tilde{\mathcal{C}}|\mathbf{X}, \mathcal{B}, \mathcal{C}) = \Pr(t_{ik} \to t_{il'}|\rho^i, A^i) \cdot 0.5^{|\mathcal{C}_{t_{ik}} \cup \mathcal{C}_{t_{il}}|} \Pr(\mathcal{C}_s|\mathbf{X}, \tilde{\mathcal{B}}, \mathcal{C}_{-s}) \quad (4.5)$$

where $|\mathcal{C}_{t_{ik}} \cup \mathcal{C}_{t_{il}}|$ records the number of incoming cluster links for the old cluster containing both t_{ik} and t_{il}. Calculate $\Pr(t_{ik} \to t_{il'}|\rho^i, A^i)$ according to Eq. 3.1.

2. Split and Merge. Adding event link $t_{ik} \to t_{ik}$ breaks existing link $t_{il} \to t_{ik}$. Moreover, the cluster including event t_{ik} and the cluster including event $t_{il'}$ are merged after sampling event link $t_{ik} \to t_{il'}$. Thus, the outgoing cluster links of new cluster retain the outgoing cluster links of the old cluster including $t_{il'}$, and the incoming cluster links of new cluster combine the incoming cluster links connecting to the cluster including t_{ik} and the cluster including $t_{il'}$. The transition probability is:

$$q_2(\tilde{\mathcal{B}}, \tilde{\mathcal{C}}|\mathbf{X}, \mathcal{B}, \mathcal{C}) = q(t_{ik} \to t_{il'}) \cdot 0.5^{|\mathcal{C}_{t_{ik}} \cup \mathcal{C}_{t_{il}}|} \quad (4.6)$$

Also, the incoming cluster links are assumed to be assigned to the new merged cluster equally. When the sampling link $t_{ik} \to t_{il'}$ merges two clusters from one cascade, $q(t_{ik} \to t_{il'}) = \Pr(t_{ik} \to t_{il'}|\rho^i, A^i)$. Otherwise, when $t_{ik} \to t_{il'}$ merges two clusters from different cascades, it combines the two cascades. Hence,

$$q(t_{ik} \to t_{il'}) = \Pr(t_{ik} \to t_{il'}|\rho^i, A^i) \cdot \frac{\Pr(\mathbf{X}_{\mathcal{Z}^1 = \mathcal{Z}_{ik}} \cup \mathbf{X}_{\mathcal{Z}^2 = \mathcal{Z}_{il'}}|\mathcal{Z}_{ik} \neq \mathcal{Z}_{il'}, \gamma)}{W_1 \cdot W_2} \quad (4.7)$$

wherein $W_1 = \Pr(\mathbf{X}_{\mathcal{Z}^1 = \mathcal{Z}_{ik}}|\mathcal{Z}_{ik} \neq \mathcal{Z}_{il'}, \gamma)$, and $\mathbf{X}_{\mathcal{Z}^1 = \mathcal{Z}_{ik}}$ represents the events in the cascade $\mathcal{Z}_{ik}$ excluding the events in the cascade $\mathcal{Z}_{il'}$. Similarly, $W_2 = \Pr(\mathbf{X}_{\mathcal{Z}^2 = \mathcal{Z}_{il'}}|\mathcal{Z}_{ik} \neq \mathcal{Z}_{il'}, \gamma)$, and $\mathbf{X}_{\mathcal{Z}^2 = \mathcal{Z}_{il'}}$ denotes the events in the cascade $\mathcal{Z}_{il'}$ excluding the events in the cascade $\mathcal{Z}_{ik}$.

3. Merge. After adding event link $t_{ik} \to t_{ik}$, if there is no new cluster to appear, it shows that event t_{ik} is an immigrant. Moreover, sampling event link $t_{ik} \to t_{il'}$ causes two existing clusters to be merged. Hence, the transition probability is:

$$q_3(\tilde{\mathcal{B}}, \tilde{\mathcal{C}}|\mathbf{X}, \mathcal{B}, \mathcal{C}) = q(t_{ik} \to t_{il'}) \quad (4.8)$$

Considering the two merged clusters come from one cascade or two cascades, $q(t_{ik} \rightarrow t_{il'})$ is analogous to the analysis of $q_2(\tilde{\mathcal{B}}, \tilde{\mathcal{C}} | \mathbf{X}, \mathcal{B}, \mathcal{C})$.

4. No Change. There is no new cluster after setting $t_{ik} \rightarrow t_{ik}$, and also no merge after sampling event link $t_{ik} \rightarrow t_{il'}$. In this case, the corresponding transition probability is: $q_4(\tilde{\mathcal{B}}, \tilde{\mathcal{C}} | \mathbf{X}, \mathcal{B}, \mathcal{C}) = \Pr(t_{ik} \rightarrow t_{il'} | \rho^i, A^i)$.

Obviously, after sampling each event link, the resulting split (*i.e.*, case 1) and merge (*i.e.*, case 3) are inverse of each other, meanwhile, the other two cases (*i.e.*, split and merge vs. no change) are inverse transform. Accordingly, by taking the inverse pairs, we derive the corresponding acceptance ratios $\eta(\tilde{\mathcal{B}}, \tilde{\mathcal{C}} | \mathbf{X}, \mathcal{B}, \mathcal{C}) = \min\{\tau, 1\}$, where the Hastings ratio $\tau = \frac{\Pr(\mathbf{X}, \tilde{\mathcal{B}}, \tilde{\mathcal{C}}) q(\mathcal{B}, \mathcal{C} | \mathbf{X}, \tilde{\mathcal{B}}, \tilde{\mathcal{C}})}{\Pr(\mathbf{X}, \mathcal{B}, \mathcal{C}) q(\tilde{\mathcal{B}}, \tilde{\mathcal{C}} | \mathbf{X}, \mathcal{B}, \mathcal{C})}$.

As aforementioned, sampling an event link may lead four possible changes to current links $(\mathcal{B}, \mathcal{C})$. Hence, the corresponding Hastings ratio is:

- A single offspring event becomes an immigrant and the previous cluster is split into two clusters. Thus the candidate partition structure $(\tilde{\mathcal{B}}, \tilde{\mathcal{C}})$ is generated. The transitions corresponding to q_1 and q_3 are the inverse of each other. Substituting Eq. 4.1, 4.5 and 4.8, the Hastings ratio works out to be

$$\tau_1 = \frac{\Pr(\mathbf{X}, \tilde{\mathcal{B}}, \tilde{\mathcal{C}}) q_3(\mathcal{B}, \mathcal{C} | \mathbf{X}, \tilde{\mathcal{B}}, \tilde{\mathcal{C}})}{\Pr(\mathbf{X}, \mathcal{B}, \mathcal{C}) q_1(\tilde{\mathcal{B}}, \tilde{\mathcal{C}} | \mathbf{X}, \mathcal{B}, \mathcal{C})} = \frac{1}{0.5^{|\mathcal{C}_{t_{ik}} \cup \mathcal{C}_{t_{il}}|}} \frac{\Pr(\mathcal{C}_{-s} | \tilde{\mathcal{B}})}{\Pr(\mathcal{C} | \mathcal{B})} \frac{\Pr(\mathbf{X} | \tilde{\mathcal{B}}, \mathcal{C}_{-s})}{\Pr(\mathbf{X} | \mathcal{B}, \mathcal{C})} \tag{4.9}$$

When the offspring event changes its parent event from one cluster to another cluster under the condition that the two clusters locate in different cascades, the reverse transition q_3 leads to the merger of two cascades. Consequently, the transition probability is:

$$q_3(\mathcal{B}, \mathcal{C} | \mathbf{X}, \tilde{\mathcal{B}}, \tilde{\mathcal{C}}) = \Pr(t_{ik} \rightarrow t_{il'} | \rho^i, A^i) \cdot \frac{\Pr(\mathbf{X}_{\mathcal{Z}^1 = \mathcal{Z}_{ik}} \cup \mathbf{X}_{\mathcal{Z}^2 = \mathcal{Z}_{il'}} | \mathcal{C}_{t_{ik}} \neq \mathcal{C}_{t_{il'}}, \gamma)}{W_1 \cdot W_2}$$

$$W_1 = \Pr(\mathbf{X}_{\mathcal{Z}^1 = \mathcal{Z}_{ik}} | \mathcal{Z}_{ik} \neq \mathcal{Z}_{il'}, \gamma) \qquad W_2 = \Pr(\mathbf{X}_{\mathcal{Z}^2 = \mathcal{Z}_{il'}} | \mathcal{Z}_{ik} \neq \mathcal{Z}_{il'}, \gamma)$$

Similarly,
$$q_1(\tilde{\mathcal{B}}, \tilde{\mathcal{C}} | \mathbf{X}, \mathcal{B}, \mathcal{C}) = \Pr(t_{ik} \rightarrow t_{il'} | \rho^i, A^i) \cdot 0.5^{|\mathcal{C}_{t_{ik}} \cup \mathcal{C}_{t_{il}}|} \Pr(\mathcal{C}_s | \mathbf{X}, \tilde{\mathcal{B}}, \mathcal{C}_{-s}, \rho).$$
The corresponding transition probability becomes: $\tau_1 = \frac{1}{0.5^{|\mathcal{C}_{t_{ik}} \cup \mathcal{C}_{t_{il}}|}} \frac{\Pr(\mathcal{C}_{-s} | \tilde{\mathcal{B}})}{\Pr(\mathcal{C} | \mathcal{B})}$

- A single offspring event switches to an immigrant, and sampling a new event link leads to the combination of two local clusters. In this case, the transitions corresponding to q_2 and q_4 are the inverse of each other. If the two merged clusters come from one cascade,

$$\tau_2 = \frac{\Pr(\mathbf{X}, \tilde{\mathcal{B}}, \tilde{\mathcal{C}}) q_4(\mathcal{B}, \mathcal{C} | \mathbf{X}, \tilde{\mathcal{B}}, \tilde{\mathcal{C}})}{\Pr(\mathbf{X}, \mathcal{B}, \mathcal{C}) q_2(\tilde{\mathcal{B}}, \tilde{\mathcal{C}} | \mathbf{X}, \mathcal{B}, \mathcal{C})} = \frac{1}{0.5^{|\mathcal{C}_{t_{ik}} \cup \mathcal{C}_{t_{il}}|}} \frac{\Pr(\tilde{\mathcal{C}} | \tilde{\mathcal{B}})}{\Pr(\mathcal{C} | \mathcal{B})} \frac{\Pr(\mathbf{X} | \tilde{\mathcal{B}}, \tilde{\mathcal{C}})}{\Pr(\mathbf{X} | \mathcal{B}, \mathcal{C})} \tag{4.10}$$

If the sampling new event link causes two cascades to be merged, we obtain $\tau_2 = \frac{1}{0.5^{|\mathcal{C}_{t_{ik}} \cup \mathcal{C}_{t_{il}}|}} \frac{\Pr(\tilde{\mathcal{C}} | \tilde{\mathcal{B}})}{\Pr(\mathcal{C} | \mathcal{B})}$.

- Sampling $\mathcal{C}_{t_{il'}} = t_{ik}$ leads the immigrant event t_{ik} to trigger new offspring. Similar to τ_1, we can calculate the Hastings ratios: $\tau_3 = \frac{\Pr(\mathbf{X}, \tilde{\mathcal{B}}, \tilde{\mathcal{C}}) q_1(\mathcal{B}, \mathcal{C} | \mathbf{X}, \tilde{\mathcal{B}}, \tilde{\mathcal{C}})}{\Pr(\mathbf{X}, \mathcal{B}, \mathcal{C}) q_3(\tilde{\mathcal{B}}, \tilde{\mathcal{C}} | \mathbf{X}, \mathcal{B}, \mathcal{C})}$.

- Samplings which change event links but cause no change to the cluster links always have $\tau_4 = 1$.

Sampling Cluster Links. Once the event links $\mathcal{B}$ are sampled via the aforementioned Metropolis-Hasting rule, we update the cluster links $\mathcal{C}$ again via Gibbs sampler as follows: [i)] Scan each cluster $s \in \mathbf{C}(\mathcal{B})$; [ii)] Draw $\mathcal{C}_s \sim \Pr(\mathcal{C}_s | \mathbf{X}, \mathcal{B}, \mathcal{C}_{-s})$. Repeat the above steps until convergence. $\mathcal{C}_s$ represents the outgoing cluster links for cluster s, and $\mathcal{C}_{-s}$ records the set of cluster links excluding the ones $s \to g, g \in \mathcal{C}(\mathcal{B})$. We calculate $\Pr(\mathcal{C}_s | \mathbf{X}, \mathcal{B}, \mathcal{C}_{-s})$ according to Eq. 3.2.

We keep all event links in an adjacency matrix $S \in R^{n \times n}(n = \sum_{i=1}^{M} N_i(t))$, wherein rows and columns are indexed by ordered events from all sequences, value 1 or 0 is recorded in entry (t_{ik}, t_{jl}) according to whether t_{ik} triggers t_{jl} or not. The formal description of MEDIA, is given in [9]. The time complexity of MEDIA is $\mathcal{O}(LM^3 n_a^2 n_c)$ [9].

5   Experiments

In this section, we investigate the performance of our model and inference algorithm and report the key results. All experiments are performed on a machine with 16 GB RAM with Intel(R) Core(TM) E5-1620V2 CPU@3.70 GHz processor running on Windows 8.1 Pro.

Competitors. Recall that there is no existing work that infers the branching structure of nonlinear MHPs. Hence, we are confined to compare our proposed frameworks to techniques that infer the branching structure of linear MHPs in [12,17]. In particular, we consider the following strategies for our study. (a) Cluster-L: Based on the alternative representation of the linear Hawkes process in terms of cluster Poisson processes, [12,17] propose the cluster-based method. (b) MEDIA-L: Use MEDIA to infer the branching structure of linear MHPs. (c) MEDIA-E: Apply MEDIA to infer the branching structure of exponential MHPs (*i.e.*, the corresponding link function $\mathcal{F}_i(x) = e^x$). (d) MEDIA-H: The odd dimensions of MHPs take linear link function, and the even dimensions adopt exponential one. Then we use MEDIA to infer the branching structure of hybrid MHPs.

As mentioned earlier, BRUNCH is not sensitive to shapes of the triggering kernel functions in hybrid MHPs. Hence, we adopt an exponential kernel function $\phi_{ij}(t) = \exp(-\beta_{ij}t)(\beta_{ij} > 0)$ in the experiments (see [9] for the performance associated with other kernel functions). For each dimension, the hyper-parameter γ is sampled by a uniform distribution $\mathcal{U}(0, 10)$. The base intensity μ is set varying over dimensions and is sampled from $\mathcal{U}(0, \gamma)$, then the coefficient α_{ij} is sampled from $\mathcal{N}(0, \gamma^2)$, and the decay parameter β_{ij} has the form of $\beta_{ij} = c * \alpha_{ij}$ where c is sampled from $\mathcal{U}(0, \gamma)$. The initial parameters $\Theta^{1:M} = (\mu, \alpha, \phi)$ need satisfy the stability and uniqueness conditions (see details in [9]). Additionally, we set the time window size to $W = 12\,\text{h}$.

Datasets and Ground Truth. We fit the aforementioned models on two real-world social media datasets: (1) *Facebook* (Fa): $43, 679, 231$ events from $109, 211$

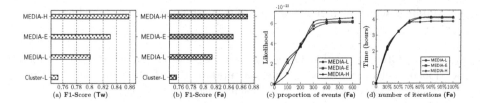

Fig. 3. Experimental results.

individuals during March 2018 to May 2018; (2) *Twitter* (Tw): $51,622,139$ events from $123,972$ individuals from March 2018 to May 2018. While crawling the triggering relations of events (*i.e.*, which event triggers which events) as ground truth via Facebook Graph API and Twitter Streaming API, we crawl the social network structure in advance. For each immigrant event in each individual's sequence, we grab the triggered events (*i.e.*, offsprings) starting from the individual's followers via a depth-first search algorithm. Then, while modeling the observed timestamped events via MHPs, we aim to infer the branching structure *without* the knowledge of social network structure.

Inferring Branching Structure. We convert the branching structure to a binary matrix S as mentioned in Sect. 4. Given the estimated links $(\tilde{\mathcal{B}}, \tilde{\mathcal{C}})$, we update $\tilde{S}$ according to $\tilde{\mathcal{B}}$, and then derive the across-dimensional branching structure $\mathcal{K}$ from $\tilde{\mathcal{C}}$ before filling in the final $\tilde{S}$. Afterwards, comparing the estimated matrix $\tilde{S}$ with the ground truth S, we evaluate the effectiveness for all the aforementioned strategies in terms of *F1-Score*.

Figures 3(a) and 3(b) plot the results. Clearly, our proposed model BRUNCH with MEDIA outperforms the baseline Cluster-L, obtaining higher inference *F1-Score*. That is, the triggering relations among events (*i.e.*, branching structure of MHPs) identified by the MEDIA approach are more reliable. While applying the same inferring procedure MEDIA, hybrid MHPs (mixing exponential MHPs and linear MHPs) show superior inference performance compared to other alternatives. In particular, MEDIA-H is superior to MEDIA-L and MEDIA-E. This further verifies the justifiability of our proposed hybrid MHPs.

Convergence. We compare the convergence rate of our proposed techniques in Fig. 3(c) on *Facebook* data. The results on *Twitter* are qualitatively similar (see [9]). Clearly, MEDIA-H is of higher likelihood than MEDIA-L and MEDIA-E. This further validates the usefulness of our hybrid MHPs.

Scalability. Figures 3(d) plots the scalability of our algorithms with increasing events on *Facebook* data. The results are qualitatively similar on *Twitter* (see [9]). We run the inference methods on different sizes of datasets (*i.e.*, slice different percentages of events in datasets as input data for BRUNCH). Observe that the average inference time of MEDIA stabilizes with increasing number of events. Since the number of event links and cluster links grows significantly as events increases, we expect the average runtime of MEDIA becomes relatively stable when more than 70% input data are utilized.

6   Conclusions

In this paper, we propose a novel probabilistic model called **BRUNCH** to infer the branching structure of hybrid MHPs. It bridges a significant chasm between hybrid MHPs (nonlinear MHPs as well) and branching structure inference. We handle the inferencing procedure via the **MEDIA** method, which provides a heuristic to make coordinated changes to both event links within clusters and cluster links within cascades. Empirically, our model demonstrates good performance and application potential in the real world.

Acknowledgments. This work is partly supported by the National Natural Science Foundation of China (No. 61672408, 61972309) and National Engineering Laboratory of China for Public Safety Risk Perception and Control by Big Data (PSRPC).

References

1. Bacry, E., Muzy, J.F.: Hawkes model for price and trades high-frequency dynamics. Quant. Finance **14**, 1147–1166 (2014)
2. Bishop, C.M.: Pattern Recognition and Machine Learning. Springer, Heidelberg (2006)
3. Blei, D.M., Frazier, P.I.: Distance dependent Chinese restaurant processes. JMLR **12**, 2461–2488 (2011)
4. Farajtabar, M., Du, N., Rodriguez, M.G., Valera, I., Zha, H., Song, L.: Shaping social activity by incentivizing users. In: NIPS (2014)
5. Hawkes, A.G.: Point spectra of some mutually exciting point processes. J. Roy. Stat. Soc.: Ser. B (Methodol.) **33**, 438–443 (1971)
6. Hawkes, A.G.: Spectra of some self-exciting and mutually exciting point processes. Biometrika **58**, 83–90 (1971)
7. Hawkes, A.G., Oakes, D.: A cluster process representation of a self-exciting process. J. Appl. Probab. **11**, 493–503 (1974)
8. Lee, Y., Lim, K.W., Ong, C.S.: Hawkes processes with stochastic excitations. In: ICML (2016)
9. Li, H., Li, H., Bhowmick, S.S.: Brunch: branching structure inference of hybrid multivariate Hawkes processes with application to social media. Technical report http://www.ntu.edu.sg/home/assourav/TechReports/BRUNCH-TR.pdf
10. Mei, H., Eisner, J.M.: The neural Hawkes process: A neurally self-modulating multivariate point process. In: NIPS (2017)
11. Møller, J., Rasmussen, J.G.: Perfect simulation of Hawkes processes. Adv. Appl. Probab. **37**, 629–646 (2005)
12. Rasmussen, J.G.: Bayesian inference for Hawkes processes. Methodol. Comput. Appl. Probab. **15**, 623–642 (2013). https://doi.org/10.1007/s11009-011-9272-5
13. Reynaud-Bouret, P., Rivoirard, V., Grammont, F., Tuleau-Malot, C.: Goodness-of-fit tests and nonparametric adaptive estimation for spike train analysis. J. Math. Neurosci. (JMN) **4**(1), 1–41 (2014). https://doi.org/10.1186/2190-8567-4-3
14. Wang, Y., Theodorou, E., Verma, A., Song, L.: A stochastic differential equation framework for guiding online user activities in closed loop. In: AISTATS (2018)
15. Zhang, C.: Modeling high frequency data using hawkes processes with power-law kernels. Procedia Comput. Sci. **80**, 762–771 (2016)

16. Zhou, K., Zha, H., Song, L.: Learning social infectivity in sparse low-rank networks using multi-dimensional Hawkes processes. In: AISTATS (2013)
17. Zhou, K., Zha, H., Song, L.: Learning triggering kernels for multi-dimensional Hawkes processes. In: ICML (2013)

Student Academic Performance Prediction Using Deep Multi-source Behavior Sequential Network

Xiang Li[1], Xinning Zhu[1(✉)], Xiaoying Zhu[2], Yang Ji[1], and Xiaosheng Tang[1]

[1] Key Laboratory of Universal Wireless Communications, Ministry of Education,
Beijing University of Posts and Telecommunications, Beijing, China
{lixiang14,zhuxn,jiyang,txs}@bupt.edu.cn
[2] Information Technology Center, Beijing University of Posts and Telecommunications,
Beijing, China
zhuxy@bupt.edu.cn

Abstract. Online education is becoming increasingly popular and often combined with traditional place-based study to improve learning efficiency for university students. Since students have left a large amount of online learning data, it provides an effective way to predict students' academic performance and enable pre-intervention for at-risk students. Current data sources used to predict students' performance are limited to data just from the corresponding learning platform, from which only learning behaviors on that course can be observed. However, students' academic performance will be related to other behavioral factors, especially the patterns of using Internet. In this paper, we utilize two types of datasets from 505 university students, i.e., online learning records for a project-based course, and network logs of university campus network. A deep learning framework: Sequential Prediction based on Deep Network (SPDN) is proposed to predict students' performance in the course. SPDN models students' online behavioral sequences by utilizing multi-source fusion CNN technique, and incorporates static information based on bidirectional LSTM. Experiments demonstrate that the proposed SPDN model outperforms the baselines and has a significant improvement on early-warning. Furthermore, it can be learned that Internet access patterns even have a greater impact on students' academic performance than online learning activities.

Keywords: Educational data mining · Multi-source online behaviors · Student performance prediction · Student clustering

1 Introduction

Since online learning can generate large amounts of records in students' learning process, it provides an effective way to get deep understanding of students' learning behaviors and predict their academic performance. Due to the benefits of online learning, more and more universities combine traditional place-based courses with online education to achieve better teaching results. For this kind of course, it is feasible to give early predictions of

© Springer Nature Switzerland AG 2020
H. W. Lauw et al. (Eds.): PAKDD 2020, LNAI 12084, pp. 567–579, 2020.
https://doi.org/10.1007/978-3-030-47426-3_44

the students' final performance through the student's online learning records, so that a timely pre-intervention could be carried out for at-risk students.

In this paper, we conduct research on university students' academic performance prediction for a course which combines the online learning and traditional place-based learning. While current researches generally focus on the learning behaviors records collected from the corresponding learning management system, but ignoring other factors that may be potentially relevant to students' academic performance. As indicated in [15], internet access activities were discovered to be a major factor affecting students' academic performance. Both users' online behaviors which can be clustered into several distinct pattern [14] and students' static information [5] have impacts on the academic performance prediction. In this study, two types of data are collected from 505 anonymous students to predict at-risk students in a university project-based course. One dataset records the students' online learning activities of the course which provides a learning platform for self-study. The other collects Internet access activity data from the campus network logs, from which the students' behavioral patterns of accessing the Internet can be explored. Combining these two datasets will obtain deep insights into students' learning behaviors and the correlation with their academic performance.

The remaining part of this paper is organized as follows. Section 2 reviews the related work on the EDM techniques for predicting student's performance and feature learning from time series. Section 3 mentioned two types experimental datasets used in detail. Section 4 presents the proposed SPDN model. Experimental results are described in Sect. 5 and finally Sect. 6 concludes this work and discusses future avenues of research.

2   Related Work

2.1   Related Methods of Education Data Mining

There has been a large amount of relevant work about the student performance prediction. The current methods of EDM are generally divided into two categories. The first traditional method relies on machine learning methods for binary classification prediction. In [1, 3, 4, 13], each machine learning model considers different types of predictive features extracted from raw online learning activity records to predict whether students can graduate on time. Also generalized linear model is used to predict students' dropout by extracting features from the original learning website log files such as page click rate, forums and so on [2, 10]. The second emerging approach involves the exploration of neural networks (NN). Because deep learning achieves better performance than traditional machine learning in many respects, work has been done to predict students' dropout in MOOC through deep neural network (DNN) models [10] and recurrent neural network (RNN) models [6]. Different from all current methods which still rely on feature engineering to reduce the input dimension and limit the development of larger NN models, Kim et al. [11] propose GritNet which extracts the original learning behavior sequence from network log as raw input of the RNN model. It outperforms the standard logistic-regression based method without complex feature engineering.

2.2 CNN for Behavioral Feature Learning of Time Series

The method of learning a time series feature is to represent a sequence of behaviors within a time window as a low-dimensional vector. KimCNN [12] is a typical CNN structure, which applies the convolution operation with several different size kernels on every possible location of the activity vector matrix, and use max-pooling to get the most prominent feature. In this way, it can automatically extract the features of the behavior sequence, and the model can be easily transferred to other datasets. KimCNN has been used in news recommendation to fuse semantic-level and knowledge-level representations of news [17]. Wang et al. proposed knowledge-aware CNN (KCNN) to treat words and entities as multiple channels instead of simple concatenating, and explicitly keeps their alignment relationship during convolution. In this way, it is suitable to connect words and associated entities and convolute them together in a single vector space. In this paper, we implement this structure to fuse student Internet access activities and learning activities and learning student behavioral representation in MFCNN component.

3 Dataset Description and Insight

The analysis in this work is based on two datasets from 505 anonymous students. One of the datasets is website log of a university project-based course for freshmen which involves students' online learning activities. The other one is the campus network logging record which reflects students' Internet access activities.

In this section, we will introduce and describe the details of online learning activities with the university project-based course and Internet access activities. Then, we investigate four distinct online behavior patterns by clustering.

3.1 Online Learning Activity

Students' online learning activities are extracted from the online learning website log of a university project-based course which spans over 13 weeks from 2018.9.28 to 2018.12.27. This course aims to help freshmen students get started in communication engineering and its greatest characteristics is implementing the online education combining with traditional class. The course is taught by teachers every Friday and students can learn on course's wiki and forum messages from the online learning website, also create their own wiki post or participate in the forum. Meanwhile, all online learning activities of students will be recorded in the website log as online learning activity sequence. Table 1 lists statistics of actions in this dataset which involves two categories of activities such as viewing and writing. Each category involves six activities and we have a more detailed distinction between different types of web pages for each activity.

In addition, there is a weekly quiz on each Wednesday which are scored by the teachers. And the students are grouped to do the final innovation project which are scored by the teachers. The final performance of students consists of two parts: average score of weekly quiz and the final innovation project score. In this paper, we judge the at-risk students based on the course results. Specifically, students are considered at-risk

Table 1. Statistics of learning behavior dataset of the Introductory course

Category	Activity	#Type
View	# Learning the theoretical basics from course's wiki (i.e. wiki)	4724
	# Learning the requirements of project (i.e. project)	806
	# Files and images in the post (i.e. attachment)	15
	# Viewing the questions raised in the forum (i.e. question)	211
	# Viewing the answer in the forum (i.e. answer)	94
	# Other pages (i.e. other)	32
Write/Create	# Adding terms to the wiki (i.e. w_wiki)	4650
	# Creating a post to introduce the own project (i.e. w_project)	195
	# Asking a question in the forum (i.e. w_question)	103
	# Answering a question in forum (i.e. w_answer)	91
	# Editing the post of project (i.e. w_revision)	4021
	# Uploading the files or images (i.e. w_attachment)	3942

students whether their average score of quizzes or innovation project scores is at the last 25% of the whole grade. Because he or she is lacking in theory or practice. In our dataset, there are 202 at-risk students in total.

3.2 Internet Access Activity

The campus network can record the students' internet access activities in the log file which contains the categories of URLs and corresponding timestamp. There are 11 categories of internet access activities, namely: 'News', 'Game', 'Music', 'Download', 'File transfer', 'Search engine', 'Video', 'Shopping', 'Living tools', 'Instant messaging' and 'Non-instant messaging'. The log file holds a total of 22 million records for 505 students during the semester of the project-based course.

In order to build a complete student online activity sequence, we converge the students' online learning activities with current Internet access activities based on the students' anonymous IDs. We rename the all online learning activities to a new category of internet access activity, 'Learning', and merge them with the original internet access activities in chronological order as the new internet access activities. In order to ensure that the online learning activity sequence and the Internet access activity sequence are aligned in the time dimension, we use zero padding to complete the online learning activity sequence.

3.3 Distinct Behavior Patterns and Static Information

To investigate the different online habits, we conducted a cluster analysis and feed the normalized frequency counts of each action of all students into Ward's hierarchical cluster algorithm [7]. The number of clusters is set to 4 based on Calinski-Harabasz

(CH) index [16] on the data. Table 2 shows the students' number and at-risk rate of four clusters. It illustrates that cluster 1 and cluster 2 have low at-risk rate and high proportion, while nearly a quarter of the student in cluster 3 and cluster 4 are at-risk.

Table 2. Statistics of four clusters

	Cluster 1	Cluster 2	Cluster 3	Cluster 4
Total #student	276	111	74	44
At-risk rate	0.18	0.14	0.28	0.25

Specifically, Fig. 1 illustrates the proportion of occurrence frequency of each activity in different clustering patterns. The proportion is calculated by the frequency of the particular activity divided by the count of all activities for each case. And in each cluster, we calculated the average of the above proportions across all the cases which are assigned to the particular cluster. In the x-axis, we list different actions of original internet access activities and online learning activities. It can be seen that there are obvious differences between clusters. The overall access internet frequency of students in cluster 1 is very low, so they may prefer offline learning. Students in Cluster 2 often use search engines, which may be related to learning. Conversely, Cluster 3's students prefer to watch videos and use life tool applications which may not be educational. On the learning website, they ask and answer questions in the forum relatively frequently, but there are few viewing actions. Cluster 4 has the fewest numbers, but is extremely focused on online games and rarely involves other types of online activities. On the learning website, their learning behavior is relatively inactive, which may also be the reason why the student's at-risk rate is high in the cluster.

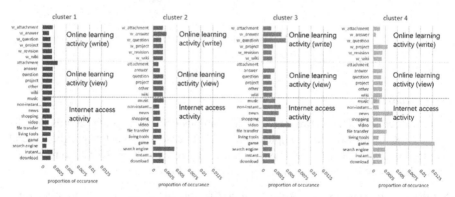

Fig. 1. The four cluster interaction patterns

In addition, students experiment in a group and always learn together in a group. So students in the same group will have a high probability of having the same academic status and the grouping information has important impact on prediction. For the reason above, we take the student's group id and cluster patterns as static information and joint them into the framework to model the prediction of student performance.

4 Framework of Sequential Prediction Based on Deep Network

The overall framework of sequential prediction based on deep network (SPDN) is shown in Fig. 2 and can be divided into four parts roughly. In this section, we first introduce the process of constructing and embedding the complete input sequence in input representation component. Then we will discuss the details of Multi-source fusion CNN (MFCNN) which represents the student's multiple activity sequences in weeks. After that, we will present the process of joining static information with students' behavioural representation and feed them into bi-LSTM model for prediction. Let us begin with a formulation of the problem we are going to address.

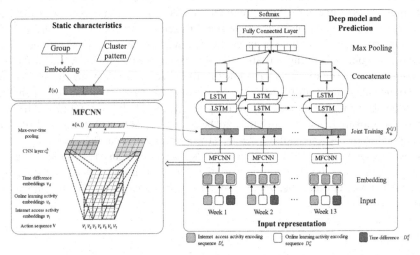

Fig. 2. The architecture of SPDN

4.1 Formulation

As introduced in Sect. 3.2, we converge the campus network logging records and the course's website log to build a complete student u's Internet access activity sequence, and complement the online learning activity sequence by zero padding. In order to formulate the problem more precisely, we first introduce the following definitions.

Definition 1. Internet Access Activity. Let I denote the set of Internet access activities. The complete student u's Internet access activity sequence can be formulated into $\hat{I}(u) = i_{1:M} = [i_1, i_2, \ldots, i_M]$, where M is the length of weekly Internet access activity sequence. Each element i_t is defined as a paired tuple of (a_t^i, d_t), where a^i represents the Internet access activities such as "Game", "Music" or "Learning" and d_t is the corresponding timestamp at time t.

Definition 2. Online Learning Activity. Let O denote the set of online learning activities. Student u's zero-padding online learning activity sequence which can be formulated into $\widehat{O}(u) = o_{1:N} = [o_1, o_2, \ldots, o_N](N = M)$, where N is the length of weekly online learning activity sequence. Each element o_t is defined as a paired tuple of $\left(a_t^o, d_t\right)$ which a_t^o is the online learning activity with zero-padding at time t. If a_t^i is "Learning", $a_t^o \in O$, otherwise, $a_t^o = 0$.

Definition 3. Static Characteristics. Static information comprises student u's group id Z_g and cluster pattern Z_p. These characteristics do not vary over time and can be concatenated and represented by a vector $Z(u)$.

Definition 4. Time Difference. Since directly employing each timestamp d_t will increase the input space too fast, we define the discretised time difference between adjacent events as:

$$\Delta d_t = d_{t+1} - d_t \tag{1}$$

In this way, each activity sequence will be accompanied by a time difference sequence as $\widehat{T}(u) = [\Delta d_1, \Delta d_2, \ldots, \Delta d_N](N = M)$.

Problem Formulation. With these definitions, our task of predicting student performance can be expressed as a sequential event prediction problem: given student u's Internet access activity $\widehat{I}(u)$, online learning activity $\widehat{O}(u)$ in first $j(j \leq 13)$ weeks of the semester, as well as static characteristics $Z(u)$, our goal is to predict whether u will be at-risk in the course. More precisely, let y(u) $\in \{0, 1\}$ denotes the ground truth of whether u is at-risk, y(u) is positive if and only if u is at-risk in the course. Then our task is to learn a function:

$$f : \left(\widehat{I}(u), \widehat{O}(u), \widehat{T}(u), Z(u),\right) \to \text{y(u)} \tag{2}$$

4.2 Input Representation

In order to feed students' activity sequence into the SPDN, we transform each online learning activity a_t^o, Internet access activity a_t^i and time difference Δd_t into one-hot encoded feature vector $1\left(a_t^o\right) \in \{0, 1\}^{L_o}, 1\left(a_t^i\right) \in \{0, 1\}^{L_i}, 1(\Delta d_t) \in \{0, 1\}^{L_d}$, where L_o, L_i and L_d respectively are the number of online learning activity unique types, Internet access activity unique types and hours of the week. The student u's encoding vectors are represented by $D_u^o = \left[1\left(a_1^o\right), 1\left(a_2^o\right), \ldots, 1\left(a_M^o\right)\right] \in R^{M \times L_o}$, $D_u^i = \left[1\left(a_1^i\right), 1\left(a_2^i\right), \ldots, 1\left(a_M^i\right)\right] \in R^{M \times L_i}$ and $D_u^d = [1(\Delta d_1), 1(\Delta d_2), \ldots, 1(\Delta d_M)] \in R^{M \times L_d}$.

Then each one-hot vector is converted to a dense vector through an embedding layer. That means to learn three embedding matrixes $E_o \in R^{e \times L_o}$, $E_i \in R^{e \times L_i}$, and

$E_d \in R^{e \times L_d}$, where e is the embedding dimension. The low-dimensional embedding vectors of online learning activity, Internet access activity and time difference are defined as:

$$
\begin{cases}
v_o = E_o \cdot 1(a_t^o) \\
v_i = E_i \cdot 1(a_t^i) \\
v_d = E_d \cdot 1(\Delta d_t)
\end{cases}
\tag{3}
$$

The dimensions of the various embedded vectors are the same and similar events appear to be closer in the embedding event space.

4.3 Multi-source Fusion CNN (MFCNN)

Following the process used in Sect. 4.2, the next step is multi-source fusion. We employ the MFCNN component which is multi-channel and multiple-activities-aligned to compress the representation of the student's three types of embedding activity sequences per week. They can be regarded as representations of multiple different channels of the same action. We align and stack the three vector matrices $V = [[v_{o1}\ v_{i1}\ v_{d1}][v_{o2}\ v_{i2}\ v_{d2}]...[v_{oM}\ v_{iM}\ v_{dM}]] \in R^{e \times M \times 3}$. Then similar to KimCNN [12] introduced in Sect. 2.2, we use multiple convolution kernels $h \in R^{e \times k \times 3}$ to extract a particular local pattern in the action sequence, while $k(k \leq M)$ is window size. The local activation of the submatrix $V_{n:n+k-1}$ with respect to the convolution kernel h can be recorded as:

$$
c_n^h = f(h * V_{n:n+k-1} + b)(0 \leq n \leq M - k + 1),
\tag{4}
$$

where f is the nonlinear function and $*$ is the convolution operator and b is the bias.

Then we use the max pooling operation on the feature map of the output as:

$$
\tilde{c}^h = \max\left\{c_1^h, c_2^h, \ldots, c_{M-k+1}^h\right\}
\tag{5}
$$

All the features are concatenated together to form the final representation $a(u, j)$ of the student u's online behavior in $j^{th} (0 \leq j \leq 13)$ week $a(u, j) = [\tilde{c}^{h_1}\tilde{c}^{h_2}...\tilde{c}^{h_m}]$, where m is the number of kernels. The weekly online behavioral representation will be passed into the bi-LSTM with static information.

4.4 Static Characteristics Component

This component builds a simple effective strategy to incorporate group id Z_g and cluster pattern Z_p into SPDN. Since these characteristics are categorical values, we model them into one-hot vectors as $1(Z_g) \in \{0, 1\}^{L_g}$ and $1(Z_p) \in \{0, 1\}^{L_p}$, where L_g is the number of students learning group and L_p is the cluster pattern types. And embed the group encoding vector $1(Z_g)$ and convert it into a low-dimensional embedding vector $v_{Z_g} \in R^{e_g}$, where e_g is the dimension of the embedding vector. The student u's static characteristics can be represented by $\widehat{Z}(u) = [v_{Z_g} \oplus 1(Z_p)] \in R^{e_g + L_p}$. Then we join the same static feature vectors $\widehat{Z}(u)$ with students' weekly behavioural representation

$a(u, j)$ as shown in Fig. 2. Let $\widehat{X} = \widehat{X}_u^{(1)} \oplus \widehat{X}_u^{(2)} \oplus \ldots \oplus \widehat{X}_u^{(j)}$ represents the augmented feature vector, where each $\widehat{X}_u^{(j)} \in R^{e_g + L_p + k}$ is a fused feature group which consists of student u's weekly online behavioural representation $a(u, j)$ and his or her static characteristics: $\widehat{X}_u^{(j)} = \left[a(u, j) \oplus \widehat{Z}(u) \right]$.

4.5 Bi-LSTM and Prediction

The fused feature groups of each week are passed into bi-LSTM [8] and the output vectors are formed by concatenating each forward and backward direction outputs. The purpose of bi-LSTM is to make full use of context information and prevent gradient explosion. Then a max pooling layer is added to learn the most relevant part of the event embedding sequence and the output is fed into a fully connected layer and a Softmax layer sequentially to estimate the student's at-risk probability $\hat{y}(u) \in [0, 1]$.

The parameters to be updated in the whole framework SPDN mainly come from four parts, 1) embedding layers parameters. 2) CNN parameters. 3) bi-LSTM parameters and 4) fully connected layer parameters. All the parameters can be learned by minimizing the follow binary cross entropy objective function:

$$L(\theta) = -\sum_{u \in U} \left[y(u) \log(\hat{y}(u)) + (1 - y(u))\log(1 - \hat{y}(u)) \right], \qquad (6)$$

where θ denotes the set of model parameters, $\hat{y}(u)$ is the probability of student at risk, $y(u)$ is the corresponding ground truth, U is the set of the whole students.

5 Experiments

We conduct various experiments to evaluate the effectiveness of SPDN on the online action datasets of 505 anonymous students and adopt Adam to optimize the model.

5.1 Setting

In our experiments, we divide all behaviour sequences into 13 weeks and encode respectively as input series. The inter-event time interval is an hour. The embedding dimensions of Internet access activity, online learning activity and time difference are 100 while the dimension of embedding group id is 50 and the cluster patterns are one-hot encoding. In the MFCNN, we use 64 different kernels which the window size of kernel is 1. The bi-LSTM with forward and backward LSTM layers containing 64 cell dimensions per direction is used. In addition, batch normalization layer [9] is applied to the bi-LSTM output and fully connected layer output. It can avoid gradient disappearance problems and speed up the training with a mini-batch size of 64. We divide 64% of the data set into a training set, 16% is a validation set, and 20% is a test set.

All the parameters above are the best group in all experiments with the grid search. Since the true binary target label is imbalanced, the evaluation metrics include Accuracy, Area Under the ROC Curve (AUC) and F1 Score (F1).

5.2 Baseline Models

In order to assess how much added value is brought by the SPDN, we set several baseline models to compare.

To compare with the universal deep learning method, we take the **BLSTM_MA** (Bidirectional Long Short-Term Memory with Multiple Activity) as a baseline model. We encode and embed the activities in the same way as SPDN, however, in order to show the effect of MFCNN, we align and stack the Internet access activity embeddings, online learning activity embeddings and time difference embeddings vector matrices in multi-channel and use the max pooling operation to get the features on each dimension instead of extracting the features by CNN. In addition, other parameters are consistent with the experimental parameters of SPDN.

For other baseline models **LR** (logistic regression model), **NB** (Naive Bayesian), **DT** (Decision Tree) and **RF** (random forest), we use the bag of words (BoW) model to represent each student's past event sequence. After transforming all students' activities into a BoW model, we count the number of each unique activity appearing in weekly sequence as the part of input. The group id and cluster pattern are other parts of input. The purpose of these experiments is to demonstrate the effectiveness of deep learning.

5.3 Prediction Performance

Table 3 presents the results on the test set for all comparison methods. Overall, SPDN gets the best performance on the dataset. Furthermore, BLSTM_MA and SPDN have the clearly better performance than other traditional machine learning algorithms, that means deep learning models can automatically get more effective information from the activity sequence. Moreover, as the F1 score is a weighted average of both precision and recall, thus it provides more comprehensive evaluation of the model. In our problem, the higher F1 of positive sample is excepted. As can be observed clearly, SPDN gets higher F1 score of positive samples than BLSTM_MA, so it shows that extracting features through MFCNN can provide advantages for predicting positive samples.

Table 3. Overall results

Approaches	Accuracy (%)	AUC (%)	F1	
			Positive	Negative
SPDN	**73.51**	**79.67**	**0.65**	**0.78**
BLSTM_MA	70.30	76.31	0.57	0.76
LR	52.48	52.20	0.41	0.59
NB	53.27	58.09	0.49	0.57
RF	61.78	54.64.	0.32	0.73
DT	65.15	60.09	0.51	0.72

In order to identify the importance of different kinds of engagement activities in this task, we conduct feature ablation experiments for three parts of input, i.e. online learning activity, Internet access activity and static characteristics. Specially, we first input three parts of input to the SPDN, then remove every type of activity one by one to observe the variety of performance.

The results are shown in Table 4. We can observe that all three inputs are useful in this task, especially static information. Because when it is removed, the experimental result of AUC steeply drops to 0.7419. Furthermore, Internet access activity play a more important role, while the student's online learning activity is sparser than Internet access activity, so it is less important.

Table 4. Contribution analysis for different engagement activities

Removed feature	Accuracy	AUC	F1	
			Positive	Negative
Total	0.7129	0.7911	0.66	0.74
Online learning activity	0.7364	0.7831	0.654	0.78
Internet access activity	0.6908	0.7771	0.644	0.728
Static characteristic	0.7128	0.7419	0.62	0.77

5.4 Early Prediction

As shown in the Fig. 3, with the accumulation of activity sequences, the performance of the SPDN and baseline models gradually improve from the perspective of AUC. But it can be clearly seen that the deep learning model always has a higher AUC than the general machine learning model (Fig. 3 only shows one of machine learning baseline models, RF, and others have the similar trend). Meanwhile, one of deep models BLSTM_MA

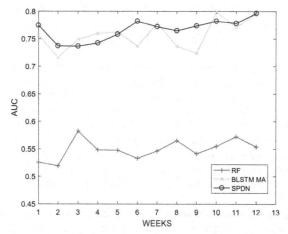

Fig. 3. Comparisons of the SPDN and baseline models in terms of mean AUC for early prediction

requires 11 weeks of student data to achieve the same performance as SPDN is able to achieve significant prediction-quality improvements within the first seven weeks of the semester. It illustrates that MFCNN can form the suitable weekly representation vector of user behaviour and extract features from a long behaviour sequence. In this way, SPDN can be used to early prediction and it can promote early intervention by teachers.

6 Conclusion

In this paper, we propose the model named SPDN, which fully uses online learning activities and Internet access activities and joins the static information to predict the performance of the students based on bi-LSTM. Through the experiments on the dataset of a university project-based course and the anonymous student's network logging records, the results show that SPDN gets the best performance and can achieve results close to the final value within the early weeks to find the at-risk students in time. Meanwhile, Internet access activities have a greater impact on students' academic performance prediction. In the future, we can combine more courses information into the model to make it more scalable.

Acknowledgements. This work is supported by the project "Virtual Simulation Experiment of Engineering Cognition and Innovation Diathesis Cultivation for Freshmen".

References

1. Tamhane, A., Ikbal, S., Sengupta, B., Duggirala, M., Appleton, J.: Predicting student risks through longitudinal analysis. In: Proceedings of the 20th ACM SIGKDD International Conference on Knowledge Discovery and Data Mining, KDD 2014, pp. 1544–1552. ACM, New York (2014)
2. Bailey, J., Zhang, R., Rubinstein, B., et al.: Identifying at-risk students in massive open online courses. In: AAAI (2015)
3. Aguiar, E., Lakkaraju, H., Bhanpuri, N., Miller, D., Yuhas, B., Addison, K.: Who, when, and why: a machine learning approach to prioritizing students at risk of not graduating high school on time. In: Proceedings of the 5th Learning Analytics and Knowledge Conference. ACM (2015)
4. Er, E.: Identifying at-risk students using machine learning techniques: a case study with is 100. Int. J. Mach. Learn. Comput. 2(4), 279 (2012)
5. Feng, W., Tang, J., Liu, T.X.: Understanding dropouts in MOOCs. In: AAAI, 2019 (2019)
6. Mi, F., Yeung, D.-Y.: Temporal models for predicting student dropout in massive open online courses. In: Proceedings of 15th IEEE International Conference on Data Mining Workshop (ICDMW 2015), Atlantic City, New Jersey, pp. 256–263 (2015)
7. Murtagh, F., Legendre, P.: Ward's hierarchical agglomerative clustering method: which algorithms implement ward's criterion? J. Classif. 31(3), 274–295 (2014)
8. Hochreiter, S., Schmidhuber, J.: Long short-term memory. Neural Comput. 9(8), 1735–1780 (1997)
9. Ioffe, S., Szegedy, C.: Batch normalization: accelerating deep network training by reducing internal covariate shift. In: International Conference on International Conference on Machine Learning. JMLR.org (2015)

10. Whitehill, J., Mohan, K., Seaton, D., Rosen, Y., Tingley, D.: Delving deeper into mooc student dropout prediction. arXiv preprint arXiv:1702.06404 (2017)
11. Kim, B.H., Vizitei, E., Ganapathi, V.: GritNet: student performance prediction with deep learning (2018)
12. KIMY: Convolutional neural networks for sentence classification. In: EMNLP. [S.l.]: [s.n.] (2014)
13. Lakkaraju, H.: A machine learning framework to identify students at risk of adverse academic outcomes. In: KDD (2015)
14. Lee, S.Y., Chae, H.S., Natriello, G.: Identifying user engagement patterns in an online video discussion platform. In: (Education Data Mining) EDM (2018)
15. Shahiri, A.M., Husain, W., Rashid, N.A.: A review on predicting student's performance using data mining techniques. Proc. Comput. Sci. **72**, 414–422 (2015)
16. Calinski, T., Harabasz, J.: A dendrite method for cluster analysis. Commun. Stat. - Theory Methods **3**(1), 1–27 (1974)
17. Wang, H., Zhang, F., Xie, X., et al.: DKN: deep knowledge-aware network for news recommendation (2018)

FCP Filter: A Dynamic Clustering-Prediction Framework for Customer Behavior

Yuanzhe Zhang[1]([✉]), Ling Luo[2], Yang Wang[3], and Zhiyong Wang[1]

[1] The University of Sydney, Sydney, NSW 2006, Australia
yzha9691@uni.sydney.edu.au, zhiyong.wang@sydney.edu.au
[2] The University of Melbourne, Melbourne, VIC 3010, Australia
ling.luo@unimelb.edu.au
[3] University of Technology Sydney, Sydney, NSW 2007, Australia
Yang.Wang@uts.edu.au

Abstract. Customer purchase behavior prediction plays an important role in modern retailing, but the performance of this task is often limited by the randomness of individual historic transaction data. In the meanwhile, Fragmentation and Coagulation Process (FCP), a stochastic partition model, has recently been proposed for identifying dynamic customer groups and modeling their purchase behavior. However, FCP is not able to forecast the purchase behavior because such a data-driven method requires transaction observations to conduct clustering. To tackle this challenge, we propose FCP filter, a clustering-prediction framework based on FCP, which can forecast purchase behavior and filter random noise of individual transaction data. In our model, FCP clusters customers into groups by their temporal interests to filter random noise of individual transaction data. Then a predictor is built on grouped data. The predicted results are also fed to FCP to adjust the parameter for prior knowledge at the next time step. Our model is superior in capturing temporal dynamics and having flexible number of groups. We conduct experiments on both synthetic and real-world datasets, demonstrating that our model is able to discover the latent group of individual customers and provides accurate predictions for dynamic purchase behavior.

Keywords: Dynamic clustering · Customer behavior · Prediction

1 Introduction

In modern retailing, accurate prediction on the quantity that customers are going to purchase over items helps retailers to design effective marketing and warehousing strategies. However, the purchase behavior of individual customer is often random, limiting the accuracy of prediction. For example, Tom normally purchases 1 bottle of milk in his weekly visit to supermarket, but may buy 2 bottles occasionally. The observation of purchase intensity on transaction data

© Springer Nature Switzerland AG 2020
H. W. Lauw et al. (Eds.): PAKDD 2020, LNAI 12084, pp. 580–591, 2020.
https://doi.org/10.1007/978-3-030-47426-3_45

is 1 or 2 but the real purchase intensity could be 1.2, so the observational noise is 0.2 and 0.8 for those two observations. In the above example, we can see that the purchase behavior of individual customer is not stable. To address this problem, we propose to cluster customers into groups by their historic transaction data because the purchase intensity of customer group is more stable and can represent the real purchase intensity of individuals. The random purchase noise of a customer can be filtered if his latent group could be accurately found.

For clustering customers into groups, a dynamic and flexible clustering model, Fragmentation and Coagulation Process (FCP) [7], has been recently proposed. FCP is a data-driven clustering model, with scalable number of customer groups, which does not need to be predefined, and can evolve with the data. This property enables FCP to capture the dynamic purchase behavior of customers accurately. However, FCP clustering can only be conducted when customer purchase data is given, which makes it hard to forecast the behavior of customer groups in the future. The significance of FCP in real-world applications is limited by the unavailability of future transaction data. For retailers, forecasting the behavior of customer groups is more important than just grouping customers in the past time.

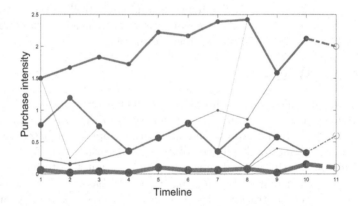

Fig. 1. The purchase intensities of customer groups evolve with time. Each bubble implies a customer group and the size of bubbles implies the size of groups. The line connecting two bubbles represents customers shifting between groups.

In order to reduce the purchase random noise of individual customers as well as to enable FCP to forecast group purchase intensity, we propose our FCP filter based on FCP to predict purchase intensity at group level instead of individual customer. For example, as shown in Fig. 1, there are 3 groups at $t = 10$. We aim to predict the purchase intensity of these 3 groups at $t = 11$ and use the predicted value of each group as the purchase intensity of its members. The purchase intensity of individual customer changes rapidly and randomly, but the group-based purchase intensity is more stable and easier to discover regular patterns. We can take the group-level purchase intensity as the actual state of its members, while taking the individual customer purchase intensity as the observation of group purchase intensity. By predicting over actual states instead of observations, the individual randomness can be filtered.

Also, in our model, not only the clustering results influence prediction but also the prediction results influence FCP clustering. In traditional FCP clustering, there is a hyperparameter to represent the prior knowledge of group purchase intensity. Since our FCP filter can get the prediction of group purchase intensity, we propose to update this parameter in a time-evolving manner instead of using a predefined value. This parameter can be calculated from prediction results and influence FCP clustering at the next time step. Theoretically, an accurate prediction leads to better clustering fitness than fixing the parameter.

In summary, we construct a dynamical clustering-prediction framework for modeling customer behavior. The main contributions of our model are (1) from **prediction perspective**, this framework helps to filter individual random purchase noise, (2) from **clustering perspective**, we enable FCP, a data-driven clustering model, to forecast group purchase intensity. The flexibility and dynamics of our FCP filter are appropriate for modeling customer behavior. It is *flexible* that the number of groups do not need to be predefined but estimated from customer transaction data. It is *dynamic* that the customer membership and group number can change with time. The hyperparameter controlling the priori knowledge of group purchase intensity is also updated dynamically so that the group purchase intensity can be estimated more accurately.

2   Related Works

Clustering on customers is also known as customer segmentation, which aims to identify the customers whose purchase behavior is in the same manner [10]. In order to identify customer groups, the data-driven approaches based on clustering analysis are formal and reliable solution [3]. Decision tree [5] was used to segment customers using their demographic information. Clustering models like K-means [4] for static clustering and mixture model based on Non-homogenous Poisson process [6] for tracking dynamic group interests were also proposed. However, the preferences and interests of customers may also change over time. In order to track the customers' temporal shifting across groups, a novel Bayesian non-parametric customer segmentation model FC-CSM [7] based on a random partition process, Fragmentation and Coagulation Process (FCP) [1], was proposed. It achieves high accuracy in fitting individual purchase frequency. Besides modeling the dynamics of segmentation, another advantage of FC-CSM is the flexibility. There is no need to set the number of customer groups manually, which can be learned automatically from data directly. However, the FC-CSM relies on the observed transaction data, so that the clustering can only be conducted for the past time. It is more meaningful to forecast the purchase behavior of groups instead of only analyzing past data. In this way, we propose to build prediction on FCP. Due to the efficiency of FCP to identify latent groups and model purchase behavior, the prediction could be more accurate than individual prediction.

3   Methodology

Our problem can be formally described as follows. Given the transaction data of a product, a matrix $\mathbf{X}^{U \times T}$ is generated to record the transaction quantity, for U customers during T time steps. Each entry x_{it} in $\mathbf{X}^{U \times T}$ refers to the purchase quantity of customer i at time step t. The task is to forecast the purchase quantities of customers at the next time step $T + 1$, i.e. $\hat{\mathbf{\Lambda}}_{T+1}^{U \times 1}$ in which $\hat{\lambda}_{i(T+1)}$ means the predicted purchase quantity of customer i at time $T + 1$.

Overall, our model has three main components: (1) **customer segmentation** based on FCP; (2) **tracking model** to track group purchase intensity trajectory and (3) **predictor** to forecast group purchase intensity at next time step.

3.1   Customer Segmentation

We adopt Fragmentation and Coagulation Process (FCP)[1,7], a dynamic random partition model, to segment customers and capture dynamic interests of customers. The schematic diagram of FCP from time step t to $t+1$ is illustrated in Fig. 2. FCP contains two procedures: fragmentation and coagulation. Given the initial customer partition π_t, at the fragmentation step, each customer group can remain the same or be split into several subgroups, forming the intermediate partition π'_t. Then, at the following coagulation step, a group can remain the same or be merged with other groups, forming the new partition π_{t+1}. In this way, FCP can capture the evolution of customer segmentation from t to $t + 1$. Theoretically, FCP is flexible to model any change of segmentation, which means that the new segmentation can be totally different from the previous one.

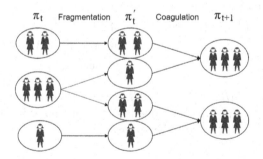

Fig. 2. Illustration of customer segmentation using FCP

Priori Probability of Customer Segmentation. FCP defines the priori transition probability from partition π_t to π_{t+1}. Formally, at $t = 1$, we adopt a random partition process Chinese Restaurant Process (CRP) [8] to model the initial partition of customers, and the probability of customer i in group g is:

$$P\left(\pi_1(i) = g | \pi_1^{-i}\right) = \begin{cases} |M_g| / (|U| - 1 + \rho) & \text{if } M_g \in \pi_t^{-i} \\ \rho / (|U| - 1 + \rho) & \text{if } M_g = \phi \end{cases} \tag{1}$$

where the hyperparameter ρ is to control the probability that the customer starts a new group, and M_g denotes the set of customer members in group g. π_t^{-i} is the partition of customers except for customer i at t, which assumes customer i is the last one who needs to allocate. In CRP model, the larger groups of a partition tends to attract more members and becomes larger.

Given partition and allocation at previous time step, for customer i, the transition probability from group g in the current partition to group g' in *fragmentation* step is defined as:

$$P\left(\pi_t'(i) = g'|\pi_t(i) = g, \pi_t^{-i}, \pi_t'^{-i}\right)$$

$$= \begin{cases} 1, & \text{if } M_g = M_{g'} = \phi \\ \delta \left|F_t\left(M_g\right)\right|/\left|M_g\right|, & \text{if } M_g \in \pi_t^{-i}, M_{g'} = \phi \\ \left(\left|M_{g'}\right| - \delta\right)/\left|M_g\right|, & \text{if } M_g \in \pi_t^{-i}, M_{g'} \in F_t\left(M_g\right) \\ 0, & \text{otherwise} \end{cases} \quad (2)$$

where $F_t\left(M_g\right)$ is formally defined as $\left\{B|B \in \pi_t'^{-i}, B \subseteq M_g, B \neq \phi\right\}$, which refers to the groups splitting from M_g. Equation (2) shows that a customer is more likely to join large groups splitting from M_g. The hyperparameter δ controls the probability that customer i starts a new group not existing in the previous group $\pi_t(i)$, which is also the temporal dependency of partitions between consecutive time steps.

Similarly, in the *coagulation* step, the transition probability of customer i joining group l from the intermediate group g' is:

$$P\left(\pi_{t+1}(i) = l|\pi_t'(i) = g', \pi_{t+1}^{-i}, \pi_t'^{-i}\right)$$

$$= \begin{cases} \rho/\left(\rho + \delta\left|\pi_t'^{-i}\right|\right), & \text{if } M_l = M_{g'} = \phi \\ \delta\left|C_t\left(M_l\right)\right|/\left(\rho + \delta\left|\pi_t'^{-i}\right|\right), & \text{if } M_l \in \pi_{t+1}^{-i}, M_{g'} = \phi \\ 1, & \text{if } M_l \in \pi_{t+1}^{-i}, M_{g'} \in C_t\left(M_l\right) \\ 0, & \text{otherwise} \end{cases} \quad (3)$$

where $C_t\left(M_l\right) = \left\{B|B \in \pi_{t+1}'^{-i}, B \subseteq M_l, B \neq \phi\right\}$ denotes the set of subgroups merged into M_l. The priori knowledge is that a customer is more likely to join the group that merged by more subgroups.

Likelihood of Observations. The individual purchase quantity is modeled by Poisson distribution. Given the purchase quantity of customer i at time step t, x_{it}, the likelihood of customer i belonging to group g at t is represented as follows:

$$P\left(x_{it}|\pi_t(i) = g\right) = \frac{\lambda_g^{x_{it}} e^{-\lambda_g}}{x_{it}!} \quad (4)$$

where the purchase intensity for customer group g is λ_g.

The purchase intensity has Gamma distribution as its prior, due to the conjugacy of Poisson and Gamma distributions. Therefore, we have the Maximum A Posteriori (MAP) of λ_g as follows:

$$\lambda_g = \begin{cases} \dfrac{\sum\limits_{j \in M_g} x_{jt} + \alpha_t - 1}{|M_g| + \beta^{-1}} & \text{if } M_g \in \pi_t^{-i} \\[4mm] \dfrac{\sum\limits_{j \in U \setminus \{i\}} x_{jt} + \alpha_t - 1}{|U| - 1 + \beta^{-1}} & \text{if } M_g = \phi \end{cases} \tag{5}$$

where the purchase intensity of a group can be interpreted as the average purchase quantities of its members, and impacted by the hyperparameters of α_t (i.e. shape parameter) and β (i.e. scale parameter) of the Gamma prior.

3.2   Tracking Purchase Intensity

For each customer i, we need to determine the purchase intensity trajectory $\{\lambda_{it}\}_1^T$ in order to predict for the future. An intuitive idea is to use the purchase intensity of the group that customer i belongs to along the time as the trajectory of purchase intensity, i.e. $\lambda_{it} = \lambda_{\pi_t(i)}$ for any t. However, the customer interests are evolving with time that the groups from the past may not fit the customers' current interests, and those $\lambda_{\pi_{T-n}(i)}$ may demonstrate misleading trends for prediction.

Therefore, we propose to predict their purchase intensity $\hat{\lambda}_{i(T+1)}$ only considering the current group membership, $\pi_T(i)$ and *backtrack the intensities of this group* in the past time steps, instead of using the actual groups the customers belonged to. The difficulty for tracking the purchase intensity of group $\pi_t(i)$ is that the group members could be totally different in consecutive time steps i.e. $M_{\pi_t(i)} \neq M_{\pi_{t-1}(i)}$. To address this problem, we build a *backward tracking model* to get the series of purchase intensities for the current group $M_{\pi_T(i)}$ in partition π_T.

Assume the group we are going to track is denoted as $g_{tracking}$ and the members of $g_{tracking}$ as $M_{g_{tracking}}$. The group $g_{tracking}$ is initialized as $\pi_T(i)$ for current time step $t = T$. If there exists $g \in \pi_{t-1}$ satisfying tracking rules (Eq. (6)), we update the group g as the new group to be tracked.

$$g_{tracking} \Leftarrow g : \frac{|M_g \cap M_{g_{tracking}}|}{|M_{g_{tracking}}|} > \eta_1 \text{ and } \frac{|M_g \cap M_{g_{tracking}}|}{|M_g|} > \eta_2 \tag{6}$$

In the tracking rules (Eq. (6)), we require that the majority of group g has shifted to group $g_{tracking}$ and the majority of group $g_{tracking}$ come from group g. The hyperparameter η_1 and η_2 are generally set as >0.5, so there could only be at most one or no tracked group. If there is no group $g \in \pi_{t-1}$ satisfying the tracking rules, $g_{tracking}$ remains the same:

$$M_{g_{tracking}} = \begin{cases} M_g, & \text{if } \exists \, g \in \pi_{t-1}, s.t. \, g_{tracking} \Leftarrow g \\ M_{g_{tracking}}, & \text{otherwise} \end{cases} \tag{7}$$

As to the individual purchase intensity, it is defined as follows based on whether there is a group g found:

$$\lambda_{i(t-1)} = \begin{cases} \lambda_g, & \text{if } \exists \, g \in \pi_{t-1}, s.t. \, g_{tracking} \Leftarrow g \\ \dfrac{\sum_{j \in M_{g_{tracking}}} \lambda_{\pi_{t-1}(j)}}{|M_{g_{tracking}}|}, & \text{otherwise} \end{cases} \quad (8)$$

If there is no tracked group g found, we use the average purchase intensity at $t-1$ of all members of group $g_{tracking}$ to represent tracked group intensity.

By computing backwards from $t = T$ to $t = 1$, we can finally get the trajectory of group purchase intensity $\{\lambda_{it}\}_1^T$ for customer i.

3.3   Predicting Purchase Intensity

Finally, the prediction model can be applied on the tracked purchase intensity trajectory $\{\lambda_{it}\}_1^T$ of customer i.

$$\hat{\lambda}_{i(T+1)} = Pred(\lambda_{i(T)}, \lambda_{i(T-1)}, \ldots, \lambda_{i1}) \quad (9)$$

In traditional FCP, the priori distribution of group purchase intensity is modeled by Gamma distribution with static predefined hyperparameter α_t and β in Eq. (5). Since our FCP filter can get the prediction of group purchase intensity, we propose to update this prior hyperparameter with the prediction results so that the priori knowledge of group purchase intensity could be more accurate. For Gamma distribution, we estimate the parameter α_{T+1} by Maximum Likelihood Estimation (MLE), taking the predicted group purchase intensity $\hat{\lambda}_g$ at time step $T+1$ as observations, and we have:

$$\alpha_{T+1} = \frac{\sum_{g \in \pi_T} \hat{\lambda}_g}{|\pi_T|\beta} \quad (10)$$

where $|\pi_T|$ is the total number of groups in the partition.

Our framework does not restrict the prediction models to use, and we have tested the performance of using the framework with various models including linear regressions and Long Short Term Memory (LSTM) in our experiments.

3.4   Graphical Model of the Framework

The generative graphical model of our FCP filter is shown in Fig. 3. The initial partition π_1 is sampled based on CRP rules and the partitions in following time steps obey FCP rules as described in Sect. 3.1. Given customer i belonging to group $\pi_t(i)$ at time t, the individual purchase intensity x_{it} is drawn from Poisson distribution with parameter $\lambda_{\pi_t(i)}$, which is the purchase intensity of the group he belongs to. The group purchase intensity $\lambda_{\pi_t(i)}$ at time t is drawn from Gamma distribution with hyperparameters α_t (i.e. shape parameter) and β (i.e. scale parameter). It is worth noting that α_t is dynamic, which means that different α_t at different time step t, that is different from original FCP. The parameter α_t is computed by using MLE of Gamma distribution with the predicted group purchase intensity $\hat{\lambda}_t$ and the scale parameter β as shown in Sect. 3.3.

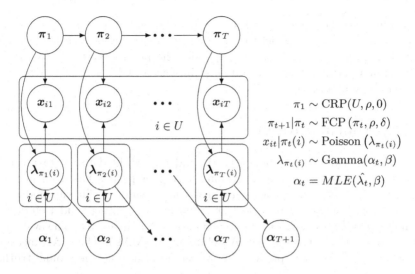

$$\pi_1 \sim \text{CRP}(U, \rho, 0)$$
$$\pi_{t+1}|\pi_t \sim \text{FCP}\,(\pi_t, \rho, \delta)$$
$$x_{it}|\pi_t(i) \sim \text{Poisson}\left(\lambda_{\pi_t(i)}\right)$$
$$\lambda_{\pi_t(i)} \sim \text{Gamma}(\alpha_t, \beta)$$
$$\alpha_t = MLE(\hat{\lambda}_t, \beta)$$

Fig. 3. The generative graphical model of our FCP filter

3.5   Inference

The customer partition and allocation are inferred by sampling using the posterior transition probabilities, computed by Eqs. (11) and (12) based on the priori transition probabilities and the observation likelihood terms.

For the customer segmentation component, we use Gibbs sampler to infer the group membership of each customer over time $\pi_t(i)$. In more detail, since the FCP is exchangeable and projective [9], we assume that customer i is the last customer to be sampled, which means that we can allocate customer i given the allocation of all the other customers. According to Bayesian theorem, the sampling posterior transition probabilities for split and merge steps are defined respectively as:

$$P\left(\pi'_t(i) = g'|\pi_t(i) = g, \mathbf{x}_i, \left\{\pi_\tau^{-i}\right\}_1^T, \left\{\pi_\tau'^{-i}\right\}_1^{T-1}\right)$$
$$\propto P\left(\pi'_t(i) = g'|\pi_t(i) = g, \pi_t^{-i}, \pi_t'^{-i}\right) \tag{11}$$
$$\times P\left(\{x_{i\tau}\}_{t+1}^T |\pi'_t(i) = g', \left\{\pi_\tau^{-i}\right\}_t^T, \left\{\pi_\tau'^{-i}\right\}_t^{T-1}\right)$$

$$P\left(\pi_{t+1}(i) = l|\pi'_t(i) = g', \mathbf{x}_i, \left\{\pi_\tau^{-i}\right\}_1^T, \left\{\pi_\tau'^{-i}\right\}_1^{T-1}\right)$$
$$\propto P\left(\pi_{t+1}(i) = l|\pi'_t(i) = g', \pi_{t+1}^{-i}, \pi_t'^{-i}\right) P\left(x_{i(t+1)}|\pi_{t+1}(i) = l\right) \tag{12}$$
$$\times P\left(\{x_{i\tau}\}_{t+2}^T |\pi_{t+1}(i) = l, \left\{\pi_\tau^{-i}\right\}_{t+1}^T, \left\{\pi_\tau'^{-i}\right\}_{t+1}^{T-1}\right)$$

where the priori terms in the equations above can be calculated based on Eqs. (2) and (3) by forward and backward algorithm as used in Hidden Markov Model [2], with the likelihood terms given in Eq. (4).

In summary, the dynamic customer segmentation is firstly modeled by FCP. Then we build tracking model to get intensity trajectory of each latent group. After that, predictor can be used to predict the purchase intensity of tracked groups. Finally, the predicted results also influence FCP clustering at the next time step by updating α_t.

4   Experimental Results

We conducted experiments on synthetic and real-world datasets to illustrate that our model can (1) identify dynamic customer groups based on purchase behavior, (2) achieve more accurate prediction results by filtering individual random noise. The hyperparameters are empirically set using validation dataset as follows: $\rho = 0.8$, $\delta = 0.4$, $\eta_1 = \eta_2 = 0.65$, $\alpha_1 = 2$ and $\beta = 0.5$. The evaluation metrics in our study is the Mean Absolute Error (MAE). The MAE measures the average error between predicted purchase intensity and the ground truth.

4.1   Synthetic Dataset

We generate a synthetic dataset to demonstrate our model's capability to identify the latent group and customer shifting over groups. There are 40 products in the synthetic dataset. For each product, we generate purchase quantity $X^{100 \times 10}$ of 100 customers from 3 latent groups with 10 time steps.

Specifically, we firstly generate the group purchase intensity of those 3 groups at the first 5 time steps randomly $\Lambda^{3 \times 5}$. At each time step, we sort the group-level purchase intensities from large to small values, so that those 3 groups can show relevant purchase patterns continuously. To fill in the intensity matrix $\Lambda^{3 \times 10}$ of 10 time steps, λ_{gt} from $t = 6$ to $t = 10$ is generated by linear regression of 3 orders: $\lambda_{gt} = \sum_{n=1}^{3} a_n * \lambda_{g(t-n)} + b$. Then all customers are allocated into those 3 groups randomly at $t = 1$. We assume that a customer changes group membership over time with probability of 0.1, which means that the customers have 10% of chance shifting into another group. Finally, we generate customer purchase quantities using Poisson distribution with parameter $\lambda = \lambda_{\pi_t(i)}$ based on their allocation.

We test the predicting performance using FCP filter model and using individual records. As the purchase intensity of each group in our synthetic data evolves according to the rule of linear regression of 3 orders, the same regression predictor is used for both cases. Accurate prediction results could demonstrate the capability of our model to identify latent groups for customers. The results are shown in Fig. 4 comparing these two models. We can see that our FCP filter achieves lower MAE on almost all products. The average MAE over 40 products of individual prediction and our FCP filter are 5.58 and 3.34, respectively. This means that FCP filter successfully tracked the evolving purchase intensity of latent groups in this dynamic dataset and predicted accurately.

To illustrate the flexibility of FCP filter, we also compared the average MAE using prediction models built on static K-means clustering with different number

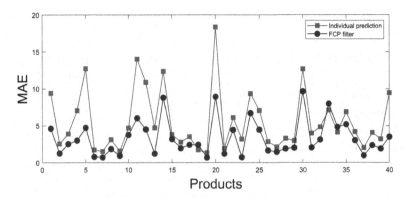

Fig. 4. Comparison of prediction results (MAE) using FCP filter and individual records on 40 synthetic products

of clusters (k). The average MAE results of K-means are *3.93* and *4.76* for $K = 3$ and $K = 5$, respectively, which are higher than FCP filter result (*3.34*). Our model outperformed static K-means clustering with $K = 3$ or 5, even when the ground truth for the number of clusters is 3. It shows that the importance of dynamics and flexibility of FCP filter in capturing the evolution of the purchase intensities. Moreover, there is no need to pre-define the number of clusters in our model.

4.2   Real-World Dataset

In this section, we use a real-world supermarket dataset[1] to illustrate our model's capability of filtering random purchase noise of individuals to get accurate prediction and usage of various predictors. The dataset contains 2,595,732 transaction records of 2,500 frequent customers on 2,383 products in 711 days (about two years). The transaction data is sparse in the first several months, so that we use the transaction data from 141 days to 420 days (40 weeks) for experiments. We divide 40 weeks into 10 time steps with 4 weeks in each time step. We select 24 popular products, which had the largest number of records and common in our daily life for experiments such as milk, cereal, eggs and so on. For each product, we discard customers who never bought that product and who ranked at the top 5 % based on purchase quantities as outliers. We randomly sample 100 customers for computational convenience and the purchase frequency is defined as the quantity purchased by a customer at one time step (4 weeks).

Several predictors are applied in our experiments to show FCP filter can generally achieve better prediction accuracy. They are LSTM network, 1-order and 3-order linear regressions, and a last-step predictor which takes the value at last time step as predicted value $\lambda_{i(T+1)} = \lambda_{\pi_T(i)}$. The average MAE is shown in Table 1. Similar to the results on the synthetic data, our FCP filter achieves the

---

[1] https://www.dunnhumby.com/careers/engineering/sourcefiles.

Table 1. Average MAE for FCP filter, individual and static K-means with different predictors

Average MAE	LSTM	Last-step predictor	Regression (1-order)	Regression (3-order)
Individual	1.05	1.06	1.16	2.27
K-means (K = 3)	1.18	1.04	1.10	1.77
K-means (K = 5)	1.16	1.02	1.10	4.29
FCP filter	**0.98**	**1.00**	**1.07**	**1.53**

best prediction accuracy with all the predictors. It is mainly because our dynamic model is suitable for modeling customers' dynamic interests and identifies the latent groups covered by random individual purchase behavior. We notice that the 3-order regression is not accurate and stable, and the possible reason could be that it is sensitive to the input purchase intensity series data.

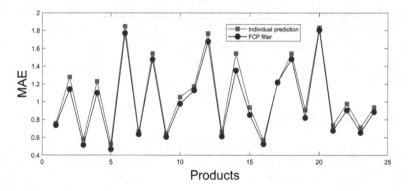

Fig. 5. Comparison of MAE for FCP filter and individual model with the last-step predictor on all products

Specially, Fig. 5 shows the prediction results of our model and individual model with the simple last-step predictor on all products. Our FCP filter gets higher prediction accuracy than individual prediction for every product. Since the predictor is quite simple, this result implies that the evolving customer purchase intensity is closer to group purchase intensity than individual one, and our FCP filter is able to find the latent group of customers and filter the noise in the individual records to produce accurate prediction results.

5   Conclusion

We build a dynamic and flexible clustering-prediction framework FCP filter to predict customer purchase intensity regardless of the random noise of individual customer behavior. Our model segments customers by FCP and then predict customer purchase intensity on the tracked group purchase intensity. After that, the prediction result adjusts priori knowledge of clustering at next time step. We conduct experiments on both synthetic and real-world datasets, and show that FCP filter model is able to (1) identify the latent group and track purchase intensity evolving trends of groups; (2) improve the accuracy of customer purchase intensity prediction. Our framework is scalable with the datasets, without the needs of defining the number of clusters and is flexible to work with different predictors. Generally, our proposed model is not restricted to the domain of customer behavior modeling. It is also useful for other sequential data containing subjects that shifting among latent groups. In our future work, our model will be built on other domains with sequential data to improve prediction accuracy.

References

1. Bertoin, J.: Random Fragmentation and Coagulation Processes. vol. 102. Cambridge University Press, Cambridge (2006)
2. Bishop, C.M.: Pattern Recognition and Machine Learning. Springer, Heidelberg (2006)
3. Carnein, M., Trautmann, H.: Customer segmentation based on transactional data using stream clustering. In: Yang, Q., Zhou, Z.-H., Gong, Z., Zhang, M.-L., Huang, S.-J. (eds.) PAKDD 2019. LNCS (LNAI), vol. 11439, pp. 280–292. Springer, Cham (2019). https://doi.org/10.1007/978-3-030-16148-4_22
4. Dennis, C., Marsland, D., Cockett, T.: Data mining for shopping centres-customer knowledge-management framework. J. Knowl. Manage. 5(4), 368–374 (2001)
5. Kim, S.Y., Jung, T.S., Suh, E.H., Hwang, H.S.: Customer segmentation and strategy development based on customer lifetime value: a case study. Exp. Syst. Appl. 31(1), 101–107 (2006)
6. Luo, L., Li, B., Koprinska, I., Berkovsky, S., Chen, F.: Discovering temporal purchase patterns with different responses to promotions. In: International on Conference on Information and Knowledge Management (2016)
7. Luo, L., Li, B., Koprinska, I., Berkovsky, S., Chen, F.: Tracking the evolution of customer purchase behavior segmentation via a fragmentation-coagulation process. In: International Joint Conference on Artificial Intelligence (2017)
8. Pitman, J.: Combinatorial stochastic processes. Technical Report (2002)
9. Teh, Y.W., Blundell, C., Elliott, L., Gatsby, T.: Modelling genetic variations with fragmentation-coagulation processes. In: Advances in Neural Information Processing Systems (2011)
10. Tuma, M.N., Decker, R., Scholz, S.W.: A survey of the challenges and pifalls of cluster analysis application in market segmentation. Int. J. Mark. Res. 53(3), 391–414 (2011)

CrowdQM: Learning Aspect-Level User Reliability and Comment Trustworthiness in Discussion Forums

Alex Morales, Kanika Narang[✉], Hari Sundaram, and Chengxiang Zhai

University of Illinois at Urbana-Champaign, Urbana, IL, USA
{amorale4,knarang2,hs1,czhai}@illinois.edu

Abstract. Community discussion forums are increasingly used to seek advice; however, they often contain conflicting and unreliable information. Truth discovery models estimate source reliability and infer information trustworthiness simultaneously in a mutual reinforcement manner, and can be used to distinguish trustworthy comments with no supervision. However, they do not capture the diversity of word expressions and learn a single reliability score for the user. CrowdQM addresses these limitations by modeling the fine-grained aspect-level reliability of users and incorporate semantic similarity between words to learn a latent trustworthy comment embedding. We apply our latent trustworthy comment for comment ranking for three diverse communities in Reddit and show consistent improvement over non-aspect based approaches. We also show qualitative results on learned reliability scores and word embeddings by our model.

1 Introduction

Users are increasingly turning to community discussion forums to solicit domain expertise, such as querying about inscrutable political events on history forums or posting a health-related issue to seek medical suggestions or diagnosis. While these forums may be useful, due to almost no regulations on post requirements or user background, most responses contain conflicting and unreliable information [10]. This misinformation could lead to severe consequences, especially in health-related forums, that outweigh the positive benefits of these communities. Currently, most of the forums either employ moderators to curate the content or use community voting. However, both of these methods are not scalable [8]. This creates a dire need for an automated mechanism to estimate the trustworthiness of the responses in the online forums.

In general, the answers written by reliable users tend to be more trustworthy, while the users who have written trustworthy answers are more likely to be reliable. This mutual reinforcement, also referred to as the truth discovery principle, is leveraged by previous works that attempt to learn information trustworthiness

---

A. Morales and K. Narang—Equal Contribution.

H. W. Lauw et al. (Eds.): PAKDD 2020, LNAI 12084, pp. 592–605, 2020.
https://doi.org/10.1007/978-3-030-47426-3_46

in the presence of noisy information sources with promising results [6,7,26,28]. This data-driven principle particularly works for community forums as they tend to be of large scale and exhibit redundancy in the posts and comments.

Community discussion forums usually encompass various topics or aspects. A significant deficiency of previous work is the lack of aspect-level modeling of a user's reliability. This heterogeneity is especially true for discussion forums, like Reddit, with communities catering to broad themes; while within each community, questions span a diverse range of sub-topics. Intuitively, a user's reliability will be limited to only a few topics, for instance, in a science forum, a biologist could be highly knowledgeable, and in turn reliable, when she answers biology or chemistry-related questions but may not be competent enough for linguistic queries.

Another challenge is the diversity of word expressions in the responses. Truth discovery based approaches treat each response as categorical data. However, in discussion forums, users' text responses can include contextually correlated comments [27]. For instance, in the *context* of a post describing symptoms like "headache" and "fever", either of the related responses of a viral fever or an allergic reaction can be a correct diagnosis. On the other hand, unrelated comments in the post should be unreliable; for instance, a comment giving a diagnosis of "bone fracture" for the above symptoms.

CrowdQM addresses both limitations by jointly modeling the aspect-level user reliability and latent trustworthy comment in an optimization framework. In particular, 1) CrowdQM learns user reliability over fine-grained topics discussed in the forum. 2) Our model captures the semantic meaning of comments and posts through word embeddings. We learn a trustworthy comment embedding for each post, such that it is semantically similar to comments of reliable users on the post and also similar to the post's context. Contrary to the earlier approaches [1,2,18], we propose an *unsupervised model* for comment trustworthiness that does not need labeled training data.

We verified our proposed model on the comment ranking task based on trustworthiness for three Ask* *subreddit communities*. Our model outperforms state-of-the-art baselines in identifying the most trustworthy responses, deemed by community experts and community consensus. We also show the effectiveness of our aspect-based user reliability estimation and word embeddings qualitatively. Further, our improved model of reliability enables us to identify reliable users per aspect discussed in the community.

2   Methodology

A challenge in applying truth discovery to discussion forums is capturing the variation in user's reliability and the diversity of word usage in the answers. To address it, we model aspect-level user reliability and use semantic representations for the comments.

2.1   Problem Formulation

Each *submission* is a post, i.e., question, which starts a discussion thread while a *comment* is a response to a submission post. Formally, each submission post, m, is associated with a set of terms, c_m. A user, n, may reply with a comment on submission m, with a set of terms $w_{m,n}$. $\mathcal{V}$ is the vocabulary set comprising of all terms present in our dataset i.e. all submissions and comments. Each term, $\omega \in \mathcal{V}$ has a corresponding word-vector representation, or word embedding, $v_\omega \in \mathbb{R}^D$. Thus, we can represent a *post embeddings* in terms of its constituent terms, $\{v_c\}, \forall c \in c_m$. To capture the semantic meaning, we represent each comment as the mean word-vector representation of their constituent terms[1]. Formally, we represent the comment given on the post m by user n as the *comment embeddings*, $a_{m,n} = |w_{m,n}|^{-1} \sum_{\omega \in w_{m,n}} v_\omega$. Our model treats the post embeddings as static and learns the comment word embeddings. The set of posts user n has commented on is denoted by $\mathcal{M}_n$ and the set of users who have posted on submission m is denoted as $\mathcal{N}_m$.

There are K aspects or topics discussed in the forum, and each post and comment can be composed of multiple *aspects*. We denote submission m's distribution over these aspects as the *post-aspect distribution*, $p_m \in \mathbb{R}^K$. Similarly, we also compute, *user-aspect distribution*, $u_n \in \mathbb{R}^K$, learned over all the comments posted by the user n in the forum. This distribution captures familiarity (or frequency) of user n with each aspect based on their activity in the forum. Each user n also has a *user reliability* vector defined over K aspects, $r_n \in \mathbb{R}^K$. The reliability captures the likelihood of the user providing a trustworthy comment about a specific aspect. Note high familiarity in an aspect does not always imply high reliability in the same aspect.

For each submission post m associated with a set of responses $\{a_{m,n}\}$, our goal is to estimate the real-valued vector representations, or *latent trustworthy comment* embeddings, $a_m^* \in \mathbb{R}^D$. We also simultaneously infer the *user reliability* vector $\{r_n\}$ and update the word embeddings $\{v_\omega\}$. The latent trustworthy comment embeddings, a_m^*, can be used to rank current comments on the post.

2.2   Proposed Method

Our model follows the truth discovery principle: trustworthy comment is supported by many reliable users and vice-versa. In other words, the weighted error between the trustworthy comment and the given comments on the post is minimum, where user reliabilities provide the weight. We extend the approach to use an aspect-level user reliability and compute a post-specific reliability weight. We further compute the error in terms of the *embeddings* of posts and comments to capture their semantic meaning.

In particular, we minimize the *embedding error*, $E_{m,n} = ||a_m^* - a_{m,n}||^2$, i.e., mean squared error between learned *trustworthy comment* embeddings, a_m^*

---

[1] Sentence, and furthermore document representation is a complex problem. In our work, we explore a simple aggregation method for comment semantic composition [23].

and comment embeddings, $a_{m,n}$, on the post m. This error ensures that the trustworthy comment is semantically similar to the comments given for the post.

Next, to ensure context similarity of the comments with the post, we compute the *context error*, $Q_{m,n} = |c_m|^{-1} \sum_{c \in c_m} ||a_{m,n} - v_c||^2$, reducing the difference between the *comment embeddings* and *post embeddings*. The key idea is similar to that of the distributional hypothesis that if two comments co-occur a lot in similar posts, they should be closer in the embedding space.

Further, these errors are weighted by the aspect-level reliability of the user providing the comment. We estimate the reliability of user n for the specific post m through the *user-post reliability* score, $R_{m,n} = r_n \odot s(u_n, p_m) = \sum_k r_n^{(k)} \cdot (u_n^{(k)} \cdot p_m^{(k)})$. The $\odot$ symbol represents the Hadamard product. This scores computes the magnitude of *user reliability* vector, r_n, weighted by the similarity function $s(.)$. The similarity function $s(u_n, p_m)$ captures user familiarity with post's context by computing the product of the aspect distribution of user n and post m. Thus, to get a high *user-post reliability* score, $R_{m,n}$, the user should both be reliable and familiar to the aspects discussed in the post.

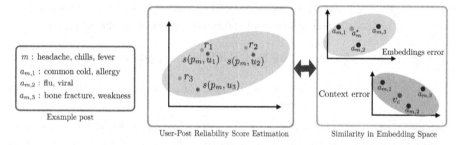

Fig. 1. An illustrative toy example detailing our model components. The left-hand side details the user-post reliability score estimation, $R_{m,n}$, that is a function of similarity function $s(.)$ between the user and post aspect distributions and user aspect reliabilities, r_n. In the right-hand, we learn trustworthy comment embedding, a_m^*, such that it is similar to user comments, $a_{m,n}$ which are, in turn, similar to the post context v_c.

Finally, these errors are aggregated over all the users and their comments. Thus, we define our objective function as follows,

$$\min_{\{a_m^*\},\{v_\omega\},\{r_n\}} \sum_{n=1}^{N} \sum_{m \in \mathcal{M}_n} \underbrace{R_{m,n}}_{\text{user-post reliability}} \left(\underbrace{E_{m,n}}_{\text{embedding error}} + \beta \odot \underbrace{Q_{m,n}}_{\text{context error}} \right)$$

$$\text{s.t.} \sum_{n=1}^{N} e^{-r_n^{(k)}} = 1; \forall k \tag{1}$$

where N is the number of users. $R_{m,n} \cdot E_{m,n}$ ensures that the latent trustworthy comment embeddings are most similar to comment embeddings of *reliable* users for post m. While $R_{m,n} \cdot Q_{m,n}$ ensures trust aware learning of contextualized comment embeddings. The hyperparameter β controls the importance of context error in our method. The exponential regularization constraint, $\sum_{n=1}^{N} e^{-r_n^{(k)}} = 1$ for each k, ensures that the reliability across users are nonzero. Figure 1 shows the overview of our model using a toy example of a post in a medical forum with flu-like symptoms. The commenters describing flu-related diagnoses are deemed more reliable for this post.

2.3   Solving the Optimization Problem

We use coordinate descent [3] to solve our optimization problem. In particular, we solve the equation for each variable while keeping the rest fixed.

Case 1: Fixing $\{r_n\}$ and $\{v_\omega\}$, we have the following update equation for $\{a_m^*\}$:

$$a_m^* = \frac{\sum_{n \in \mathcal{N}_m} R_{m,n} a_{m,n}}{\sum_{n \in \mathcal{N}_m} R_{m,n}} \tag{2}$$

Thus, the latent *trustworthy comment* is a weighted combination of comments where weights are provided by the *user-post reliability* score $R_{m,n}$. Alternatively, it can also be interpreted as a reliable summarization of all the comments.

Case 2: Fixing $\{a_m^*\}$, $\{v_\omega\}$, we have the following update equation for $\{r_n^{(k)}\}$:

$$r_n^{(k)} \propto -\ln \sum_{m \in \mathcal{M}_n} s(u_n^{(k)}, p_m^{(k)}) (E_{m,n} + \beta Q_{m,n}) \tag{3}$$

Reliability of a user in aspect k is inversely proportional to the errors with respect to the latent trustworthy comment a_m^* ($E_{m,n}$) and submission's context v_c ($Q_{m,n}$) over all of her posted comments ($\mathcal{M}_n$). The embedding error ensures that if there is a large difference between the user's comment and the trustworthy comment, her reliability becomes lower. The context error ensures that non-relevant comments to the post's context are penalized heavily. In other words, a reliable user should give trustworthy and contextualized responses to posts.

This error is further weighed by the similarity score, $s(.)$, capturing familiarity of the user with the post's context. Thus, familiar users are penalized higher for their mistakes as compared to unfamiliar users.

Case 3: Fixing $\{a_m^*\}$, $\{r_n^{(k)}\}$, we have the following update equation for $\{v_\omega\}$:

$$v_\omega = \frac{\sum_{<m,n> \in D_\omega} R_{m,n} (a_m^* + \beta |c_m|^{-1} \sum_{c \in c_m} v_c) - R_{m,n}(\beta + 1)|c_m|^{-1} a_{m,n}^{-\omega}}{\sum_{<m,n> \in D_\omega} R_{m,n}(\beta + 1)} \tag{4}$$

where $< m, n > \in D_\omega = \{(m,n)|\omega \in w_{m,n}\}$ and $a_{m,n}^{-\omega} = |w_{m,n}|^{-1} \sum_{\omega' \in w_{m,n} \setminus \{\omega\}} v_{\omega'}$. To update v_ω, we only consider those comment and submission pairs, D_ω, in which the particular word appears. The update of the embeddings depend on the submission context v_c, latent trustworthy comment embedding, a_m^* as well as *user-post reliability* score, $R_{m,n}$. Thus, word embeddings are updated in a trust-aware manner such that reliable user's comments weigh more than those of unreliable users as they can contain noisy text. Note that there is also some negative dependency on the contribution of other terms in the comments.

Implementation Details: We used popular Latent Dirichlet Allocation (LDA) [4] to estimate aspects of the posts in our dataset[2]. Specifically, we combined the title and body text to represent each post. We applied topic model inference to all comments of user n to compute its combined aspect distribution, u_n. We randomly initialized the user reliability, r_n. We initialized the word embeddings, v_ω, via word2vec [19] trained on our dataset. We used both unigrams and bigrams in our model. We fixed β to 0.15.[3] The model converges after only about six iterations indicating quick approximation. In general, the computational complexity is $O(|\mathcal{V}|NM)$; however, we leverage the data sparsity in the comment-word usage and user-posts for efficient implementation.

3   Experiments

In this section, we first discuss our novel dataset, followed by experiments on the outputs learned by our model. In particular, we evaluate the trustworthy comment embeddings on the comment ranking task while we qualitatively evaluate user reliabilities and word embeddings. For brevity, we focus the qualitative analysis on our largest subreddit, askscience.

3.1   Dataset

We evaluate our model on a widely popular discussion forum Reddit. Reddit covers diverse topics of discussion and is challenging due to the prevalence of noisy responses. We specifically tested on *Ask** subreddits as they are primarily used to seek answers to a variety of topics from mundane issues to serious medical concerns. In particular, we crawled data from three subreddits, /r/askscience, /r/AskHistorians, and /r/AskDocs from their inception until October 2017[4]. While these subreddits share the same platform, the communities differ vastly, see Table 1. We preprocessed the data by removing uninformative comments and posts with either less than ten characters or containing only URLs or with a missing title or author information. We removed users who have posted less than two comments and also submissions with three or fewer comments. To handle sparsity, we treated all users with a single comment as "UNK".

For each submission post, there is an associated flair text denoting the *category* of the post, referred to as the *submission flair* that is either Moderator added or self-annotated,e.g., Physics, Chemistry, Biology. Similarly, users have *author flairs* attributed next to their user-name describing their educational

---

[2] We ran LDA with 50 topics for all experiments and examined its sensitivity in Sect. 3.2.

[3] We did not find a significant change in results for different values of β.

[4] praw.readthedocs.io/en/latest/.

Table 1. Dataset statistics for the subreddit communities. N and M denotes total users and posts respectively; N_e: number of experts; $|a_{m,e}|$: number of posts with at least one expert comment; $|w_{m,n}|$: average comment word length.

Dataset	Created	N	N_e	M	$|a_{m,e}|$	$|w_{m,n}|$
*Docs	07/13	3,334	286	17,342	10,389	53.5
*Science	04/10	73,463	2,195	100,237	70,108	74.0
*Historians	08/11	27,264	296	45,650	30,268	103.4

background, e.g., Astrophysicist, Bioengineering. Only users verified by the moderator have *author flairs*, and we denote them as experts in the rest of the paper. AskDocs does not have submission flairs as it is a smaller community. For both subreddits, we observed that around 80% of the users comment on posts from more than two categories.

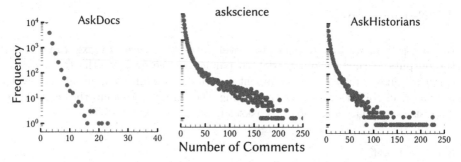

Fig. 2. Frequency plot (log scale) of number of comments per post for three subreddits. A post on AskDocs tend to have fewer comments than the other two communities.

Experts are highly active in the community answering around 60–70% of the posts (Table 1). askscience and AskHistorians have significantly higher (Fig. 2) and more detailed comments ($|w_{m,n}|$ in Table 1) per post than AskDocs. Due to the prevalence of a large number of comments, manual curation is very expensive, thus necessitating the need for an automatic tool to infer comments trustworthiness.

3.2   Trustworthy Comment Embedding Analysis

We evaluate latent trustworthy comment learned by our model on a trustworthy comment ranking task. That is, given a submission post, our goal is to rank the posted comment based on their trustworthiness. For this experiment, we treat expert users' comment as the most trustworthy comment of the post.[5] Besides, we also report results using the highest upvoted comment as the gold standard.

---

[5] While human judgment would be the most precise; it is also the most challenging to collect. For instance, in askscience we would need experts in over 35 science fields, reading up to 250 comments for a single post.

Highest upvoted comments represent community consensus on the most trustworthy response for the post [16]. In particular, we rank comments for each post m, in the order of descending cosine similarity between their embedding, $a_{m,n}$, and the latent trustworthy comment embeddings, a_m^*. We then report average Precison@k values over all the posts, where k denotes the position in the output ranked list of comments.

Baselines: We compare our model with state-of-the-art truth discovery methods proposed for continuous and text data and non-aspect version of our model[6].

Mean Bag of Answers (MBoA): In this baseline, we represent the trustworthy comment for a post as the mean comment embedding and thus assume uniform user reliability.

CRH: is a popular truth discovery-based model for numerical data [12]. CRH minimizes the weighted deviation of the trustworthy comment embedding from the individual comment embeddings with user reliabilities providing the weights.

CATD: is an extension of CRH that learns a confidence interval over user reliabilities to handle data skewness [11]. For both the above models, we represent each comment as the average word embeddings of its constituent terms.

TrustAnswer: Li et al. [14] modeled semantic similarity between comments by representing each comment with embeddings of its key phrase.

CrowdQM-no-aspect: In this baseline, we condense the user's aspect reliabilities to a single r_n. This model acts as a control to gauge the performance of our proposed model.

Results: Table 2a reports the Precision@1 results using expert's comments as the gold standard. MBoA, with uniform source reliability, outperforms the CRH method that estimates reliability for each user separately. Thus, simple mean embeddings provide a robust representation for the trustworthy comment.

We also observe that CrowdQM-no-aspect performs consistently better than TrustAnswer. Note that both approaches do not model aspect-level user reliability but use semantic representations of comments. However, while TrustAnswer assigns a single reliability score for each comment, CrowdQM-no-aspect additionally takes into account the user's familiarity with the post's context (*similarity* function, $s(.)$) to compute her reliability for the post. Finally, CrowdQM consistently outperforms both the models, indicating that aspect modeling is beneficial.

CATD uses a confidence-aware approach to handle data skewness and performs the best among the baselines. This skewness is especially helpful in Reddit as experts are the most active users (Table 1); and, CATD likely assigns them high reliability. Our model achieves competitive precision as CATD for AskDocs while outperforming for the others. This indicates that our data-driven model works better for communities which are less sparse (Sect. 3.1 and Fig. 2).

---

[6] Note that there is no label information used, so we cannot compare to other supervised CQA models [1,21,24] which need this supervision. Our *unsupervised model* is complementary to these approaches, and thus, a rigorous comparison is impossible.

Table 2. Precision@1 for all three Ask* subreddits, with (2a) the experts' comments and (2b) upvotes used to identify trustworthy comments.

(a)   (b)

Model	*Docs	*Science	*Historians
MBoA	0.592	0.633	0.602
CRH [12]	0.585	0.597	0.556
CATD [11]	**0.635**	0.700	0.669
TrustAnswer [14]	0.501	0.657	0.637
CrowdQM-no-aspect	0.509	0.666	0.640
CrowdQM	0.617	**0.734**	**0.753**

Model	*Docs	*Science	*Historians
MBoA	**0.434**	0.302	0.257
CRH [12]	0.386	0.234	0.183
CATD [11]	0.405	0.291	0.257
TrustAnswer [14]	0.386	0.373	0.449
CrowdQM-no-aspect	0.388	0.368	0.450
CrowdQM	0.426	**0.402**	**0.493**

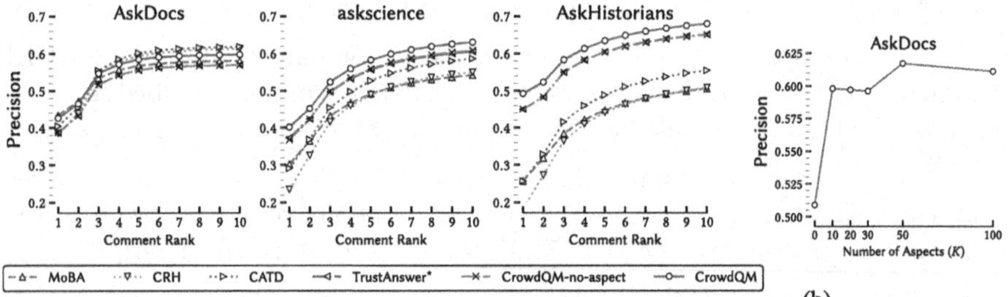

Fig. 3. Precision of our model (a) vs. comment rank computed by user's upvotes and (b) vs. number of aspects. Our model outperforms the baselines for askscience and AskHistorians while performs similarly for AskDocs. Value of K does not have much impact on the precision value.

Table 2b reports Precision@1 results using community upvoted comments as the gold standard, while Fig. 3a plots the precision values against the size of the output ranked comment list. In general, there is a drop in performance for all models on this metric because it is harder to predict upvotes as they are inherently noisy [8]. TrustAnswer and CrowdQM-no-aspect perform best among the baselines indicating that modeling semantic representation is essential for forums. CrowdQM again consistently outperforms the non-aspect based models verifying that aspect modeling is needed to identify trustworthy comments in forums. CrowdQM remains competitive in the smaller AskDocs dataset, where the best performing model is MoBA. Thus, for AskDocs, the comment summarizing all other comments tends to get the highest votes.

Parameter Sensitivity. In Fig. 3b, we plot our model's precision with varying number of aspects. Although there is an optimal range around 50 aspects, the precision remains relatively stable indicating that our model is not sensitive to aspects.[7] We also did similar analysis with β and did not find any significant changes to the Precision.

---

[7] We also observed similar results for the other datasets and omitted those figures for lack of space.

3.3 Aspect Reliability Analysis

We evaluate learned user reliabilities through users commenting on a post with a *submission flair*. Note that a submission flair is manually curated and denotes post's category, and this information is not used in our model. Specifically, for each post m, we compute the *user-post reliability* score, $R_{m,n}$, for every user n who commented on the post. We then ranked these scores for each category and report top *author flairs* for few categories in Table 3. The top *author flairs* for each category are domain experts.

Table 3. Top author flairs with their corresponding post categories.

Post Category: Computing	Post Category:Linguistics
Embedded Systems, Software Engineering, Robotics	Linguistics, Hispanic Sociolinguistics
Computer Science	Comparative Political Behaviour
Quantum Optics, Singular Optics	Historical Linguistics, Language Documentation
Robotics, Machine Learning, Computer Vision, Manipulators	Linguistics, Hispanic Sociolinguistics
Computer Science	Historical Linguistics, Language Documentation
Biomechanical Engineering, Biomaterials	Nanostructured Materials, Heterogeneous Catalysis
Post Category: Biology	**Post Category: Psychology**
Animal Cognition	Clinical Psychology, Psychotherapy, Behavior Analysis
Cell and Developmental Biology	International Relations, Comparative Politics
Biochemistry, Molecular Biology, Enzymology	Neuropsychology
Genetics, Cell biology, Bioengineering	Psychology, PTSD, Trauma, and Resilience
Computational Physics, Biological Physics	Cognitive Neuroscience, Neuroimaging, fMRI
Aquatic Ecology and Evolution, Active Acoustics	Psychology, Legal psychology, Eyewitness testimonies

For instance, for the Computing category highly reliable users have author flairs like Software Engineering and Machine Learning, while for Linguistics authors with flairs Hispanic Sociolinguistics and Language Documentation rank high. These results align with our hypothesis that in-domain experts should have higher reliabilities. We also observe out of domain authors with flairs like Comparative Political Behavior and Nanostructured Materials in the Linguistic category. This diversity could be due to the interdisciplinary nature of the domain. Our model, thus, can be used by the moderators of the discussion forum to identify and recommend potential reliable users to respond to new submission posts of a particular category.

(a) Health   (b) Cosmos   (c) Oceanography

Fig. 4. Top words for highly correlated aspects between user reliability and user karma.

To further analyze the user reliability, we qualitatively examine the aspects with the largest reliability value of highly upvoted users in a post category. First,

we identify users deemed reliable by the community for a category through a
karma score. Category-specific user *karma* is given by the average upvotes the
user's comments have received in the category. We then correlate the category-
specific user *karma* with her reliability score in each $k \in K$ aspect, $r_n^{(k)}$ to identify
aspects relevant for that category. Figure 4 shows the top words of the highest
correlated aspects for some categories. The identified words are topically relevant
thus our model associates aspect level user reliability coherently. Interestingly,
the aspects themselves tend to encompass several themes, for example, in the
Health category, the themes are software and health.

3.4   Word Embedding Analysis

The CrowdQM model updates word embeddings to better model semantic meaning of the comments. For each category, we identify the frequent terms and find
its most similar keywords using cosine distance between the learned word embeddings.

Table 4. Similar words using embeddings learned using CrowdQM for askscience.

Liquid		Cancer		Quantum		Life	
Initial	CrowdQM	Initial	CrowdQM	Initial	CrowdQM	Initial	CrowdQM
unimaginably	gas	mg	disease	search results	model	molaison	species
bigger so	chemical	curie	white	sis	energy	around	natural
two lenses	solid	wobbly	cell	shallower water	particle	machos	nature
orbiting around	air	subject	food	starts rolling	mechanics	brain	production
fire itself	material	"yes" then	complete	antimatter galaxies	mathematical	"dark" matter	size

The left column for each term in Table 4 are the most similar terms returned
by the initial embeddings while the right column reports the results from updated
embeddings $\{v_\omega\}$ from our CrowdQM model. We observe that there is a lot of
noise in words returned by the initial model as they are just co-occurrence based
while words returned by our model are semantically similar and describe similar
concepts. This improvement is because our model updates word embeddings in
a trust aware manner such that they are similar to terms used in responses from
reliable users.

4   Related Work

Our work is related to two main themes of research, truth discovery and community question answering (CQA).

Truth Discovery: Truth discovery has attracted much attention recently. Different approaches have been proposed to address different scenarios [13,20,29].
Most of the truth discovery approaches are tailored to categorical data and thus
assume there is a single objective truth that can be derived from the claims of
different sources [15]. Faitcrowd [17] assumes an objective truth in the answer set
and uses a probabilistic generative model to perform fine-grained truth discovery. On the other hand, Wan et al. [22] propose trustworthy *opinion* discovery

where the true value of an entity is modeled as a random variable with a probability density function instead of a single value. However, it still fails to capture the semantic similarity between the textual responses. Some truth discovery approaches also leverage text data to identify correct responses effectively. Li et al. [14] proposed a model for capturing semantic meanings of crowd provided diagnosis in a Chinese medical forum. Zhang et al. [27] also leveraged semantic representation of answers and proposed a Bayesian approach to capture the multifactorial property of text answers. These approaches only use certain keywords to represent each answer and are thus, limited in their scope. Also, they learn a scalar user reliability score. To the best of our knowledge, there has been no work that models both fine-grained user reliability with semantic representations of the text to discover trustworthy comments from community responses.

Community Question Answering: Typically CQA is framed as a classification problem to predict correct responses for a post. Most of the previous work can be categorized into feature-based or text relevance-based approaches. Feature-driven models [1,5,9] extract content or user based features that are fed into classifiers to identify the best comment. CQARank leverages voting information as well as user history and estimates user interests and expertise on different topics [25]. Barron-Cedeno et al. [2] also look at the relationship between the answers, measuring textual and structural similarities between them to classify useful and relevant answers. Text-based deep learning models learn an optimal representation of question and answer pairs to identify the most relevant answer [24]. In SemEval 2017 task on CQA, Nakov et al. [21] developed a task to recommend related answers to a new question in the forum. SemEval 2019 further extends this line of work by proposing fact checking in community question answering [18]. It is not only expensive to curate each reply manually to train these models, but also unsustainable. On the contrary, CrowdQM is an unsupervised method and thus does not require any labeled data. Also, we estimate the comments' *trustworthiness* that implicitly assumes relevance to the post (modeled by these works).

5   Conclusion

We proposed an unsupervised model to learn a trustworthy comment embedding from all the given comments for each post in a discussion forum. The learned embedding can be further used to rank the comments for that post. We explored Reddit, a novel community discussion forum dataset for this task. Reddit is challenging as posts typically receive a large number of responses from a diverse set of users and each user engages in a wide range of topics. Our model estimates aspect-level user reliability and semantic representation of each comment simultaneously. Experiments show that modeling aspect level user reliability improves the prediction performance compared to the non-aspect version of our model. We also show that the estimated user-post reliability can be used to identify trustworthy users for particular post categories.

References

1. Agichtein, E., Castillo, C., Donato, D., Gionis, A., Mishne, G.: Finding high-quality content in social media. In: WSDM (2008)
2. Barrón-Cedeno, A., et al.: Thread-level information for comment classification in community question answering. In: ACL (2015)
3. Bertsekas, D.P.: Nonlinear Programming. Athena scientific, Belmont (1999)
4. Blei, D.M., Ng, A.Y., Jordan, M.I.: Latent Dirichlet allocation. JMLR **3**(Jan), 993–1022 (2003)
5. Burel, G., Mulholland, P., Alani, H.: Structural normalisation methods for improving best answer identification in question answering communities. In: WWW (2016)
6. Dong, X.L., Berti-Equille, L., Srivastava, D.: Integrating conflicting data: the role of source dependence. Proc. VLDB Endow. **2**(1), 550–561 (2009)
7. Galland, A., Abiteboul, S., Marian, A., Senellart, P.: Corroborating information from disagreeing views. In: WSDM (2010)
8. Gilbert, E.: Widespread underprovision on reddit. In: CSCW (2013)
9. Jenders, M., Krestel, R., Naumann, F.: Which answer is best?: Predicting accepted answers in MOOC forums. In: International Conference on World Wide Web (2016)
10. Li, G., Wang, J., Zheng, Y., Franklin, M.: Crowdsourced data management: a survey. In: IEEE ICDE (2017)
11. Li, Q., et al.: A confidence-aware approach for truth discovery on long-tail data. VLDB **8**(4), 425–436 (2014)
12. Li, Q., Li, Y., Gao, J., Zhao, B., Fan, W., Han, J.: Resolving conflicts in heterogeneous data by truth discovery and source reliability estimation. In: ACM SIGMOD (2014)
13. Li, Q., Ma, F., Gao, J., Su, L., Quinn, C.J.: Crowdsourcing high quality labels with a tight budget. In: WSDM (2016)
14. Li, Y., et al.: Reliable medical diagnosis from crowdsourcing: discover trustworthy answers from non-experts. In: WSDM (2017)
15. Li, Y., et al.: A survey on truth discovery. ACM Sigkdd Explor. Newslett. **17**(2), 1–16 (2016)
16. Lyu, S., Ouyang, W., Wang, Y., Shen, H., Cheng, X.: What we vote for? Answer selection from user expertise view in community question answering. In: WWW (2019)
17. Ma, F., et al.: Faitcrowd: fine grained truth discovery for crowdsourced data aggregation. In: KDD (2015)
18. Mihaylova, T., Karadzhov, G., Atanasova, P., Baly, R., Mohtarami, M., Nakov, P.: Semeval-2019 task 8: fact checking in community question answering. In: International Workshop on Semantic Evaluation (2019)
19. Mikolov, T., Sutskever, I., Chen, K., Corrado, G.S., Dean, J.: Distributed representations of words and phrases and their compositionality. In: NIPS (2013)
20. Mukherjee, T., Parajuli, B., Kumar, P., Pasiliao, E.: Truthcore: Non-parametric estimation of truth from a collection of authoritative sources. In: IEEE BigData (2016)
21. Nakov, P., et al.: Semeval-2017 task 3: community question answering. In: International Workshop on Semantic Evaluation (2017)
22. Wan, M., Chen, X., Kaplan, L., Han, J., Gao, J., Zhao, B.: From truth discovery to trustworthy opinion discovery: an uncertainty-aware quantitative modeling approach. In: KDD (2016)

23. Wang, Z., Mi, H., Ittycheriah, A.: Sentence similarity learning by lexical decomposition and composition. arXiv preprint (2016)
24. Wen, J., Ma, J., Feng, Y., Zhong, M.: Hybrid attentive answer selection in cqa with deep users modelling. In: AAAI Conference on Artificial Intelligence (2018)
25. Yang, L., et al.: Cqarank: jointly model topics and expertise in community question answering. In: CIKM (2013)
26. Yin, X., Han, J., Yu, P.S.: Truth discovery with multiple conflicting information providers on the web. In: KDD (2007)
27. Zhang, H., Li, Y., Ma, F., Gao, J., Su, L.: Texttruth: an unsupervised approach to discover trustworthy information from multi-sourced text data. In: KDD (2018)
28. Zhao, B., Han, J.: A probabilistic model for estimating real-valued truth from conflicting sources. In: Proceedings of QDB (2012)
29. Zheng, Y., Li, G., Li, Y., Shan, C., Cheng, R.: Truth inference in crowdsourcing: is the problem solved? Proc. VLDB Endow. $10(5)$, 541–552 (2017)

Deep Learning

6GCVAE: Gated Convolutional Variational Autoencoder for IPv6 Target Generation

Tianyu Cui[1,2], Gaopeng Gou[1,2(✉)], and Gang Xiong[1,2]

[1] Institute of Information Engineering, Chinese Academy of Sciences, Beijing, China
{cuitianyu,gougaopeng,xionggang}@iie.ac.cn
[2] School of Cyber Security, University of Chinese Academy of Sciences,
Beijing, China

Abstract. IPv6 scanning has always been a challenge for researchers in the field of network measurement. Due to the considerable IPv6 address space, while recent network speed and computational power have been improved, using a brute-force approach to probe the entire network space of IPv6 is almost impossible. Systems are required an algorithmic approach to generate more possible active target candidate sets to probe. In this paper, we first try to use deep learning to design such IPv6 target generation algorithms. The model effectively learns the address structure by stacking the gated convolutional layer to construct Variational Autoencoder (VAE). We also introduce two address classification methods to improve the model effect of the target generation. Experiments indicate that our approach 6GCVAE outperformed the conventional VAE models and the state of the art target generation algorithm in two active address datasets.

Keywords: IPv6 target generation · Deep learning · Data mining · Network scanning · Unsupervised clustering

1 Introduction

In the network measurement task, in order to discover the active hosts in the network and judge their active state, the researchers usually use the network scanning method to actively detect all the hosts existing in the network space. Systems confirm that the host is active by sending the request packets and waiting until receiving the response packets from the host. However, IPv6 [4] contains a considerable address space. The current scanner [5] cannot complete the entire IPv6 network space scanning.

The state of the art approach to solving this problem is using IPv6 target generation technology [6,10,16]. The technology requires a set of active IPv6 seed addresses as the input and learns the structure of the seed addresses to generate possible active IPv6 target candidate sets. Due to the semantics of the

© Springer Nature Switzerland AG 2020
H. W. Lauw et al. (Eds.): PAKDD 2020, LNAI 12084, pp. 609–622, 2020.
https://doi.org/10.1007/978-3-030-47426-3_47

IPv6 address is opaque, it is difficult to infer the IPv6 address structure of a real host or perform effective analysis of the addressing schemes.

The representative algorithms of IPv6 target generation technology include Entropy/IP [6] which trained the Bayesian network to generate active candidate sets. However, the approach requires assuming that address segments exist dependency. The confirmed model determined by experience and assumption may be influenced in various datasets, thus leading to quite different effects [6]. In addition, because of the characteristics of such algorithms, they will consume a long time under a large dataset.

Deep neural network architectures are used for the batch processing of big data tasks. Models are able to automatically adapt to seed datasets by training, thus usually performing well in a variety of large datasets. Variational Autoencoder (VAE) [9] is a typical generative model in deep neural networks. The model samples the latent vector and finally reconstructs the text or image that is similar to the original. The encoding idea may contribute to deeply mine the potential relationship between addresses and active hosts. The gated convolutional network was proposed by Dauphin et al. [3] The convolution and gating mechanism of the model effectively learn the text structure while understanding the relevance of the text, which can help models learn the key features of IPv6 addresses.

In this paper, we use a deep neural network architecture for the first time to accomplish the IPv6 target generation task. Our contribution can be summarized as follows:

- We first propose using deep learning architecture to achieve IPv6 target generation. Our work achieves a new model 6GCVAE that stacks the gated convolutional layer to construct VAE model.
- We use two methods of seed classification, which contributes to explore the IPv6 addressing schemes to effectively improve the effect of the model.
- Our model demonstrates better results on both two datasets than conventional VAE models (FNN VAE, Convolutional VAE, RNN VAE, LSTM VAE, and GRU VAE) and the state of the art target generation technology Entropy/IP.

The organizational structure for the rest of the paper is as follows. Section 2 introduces the related work of IPv6 target generation. Section 3 introduces the background and considerations of this task. 6GCVAE architecture and seed classification methods are shown in Sect. 4. Section 5 evaluates our work and Sect. 6 summarizes the paper.

2   Related Work

In previous work, researchers have found there are certain patterns in active IPv6 address sets. Planka and Berger [13] first explored the potential patterns of IPv6 active addresses in time and space. They used Multi-Resolution Aggregate plots to quantify the correlation of each portion of an address to grouping addresses together into dense address space regions. Czyz et al. [2] found 80% of the routes and 22% of the server addresses have only non-zero addresses in the lowest 16 bits of the address. Gasser et al. [7] used entropy clustering to classify the hitlist into different addressing schemes. We adopt their methods by performing seed classification to help neural networks improve model performance.

	Human-readable Text Format	Commonly Used Address Format
Fixed IID	2001:0db8:0020:0003:**0000:0000:0000:0321**	2001:db8:20:3::**321**
Low 64-bit Subnet	2001:0db8:0156:1109:**0000:0000:0020:0901**	2001:db8:156:3322::**20:901**
SLAAC EUI-64	2001:0db8:0000:2fcd:**032f:e4ff:fec0:21bd**	2001:db8:0:2fcd:**32f:e4ff:fec0:21bd**
SLAAC Privacy	2001:0db8:5263:90e7:**2071:f467:ddee:5c6a**	2001:db8:5263:90e7:**2071:f467:ddee:5c6a**

Fig. 1. Sample IPv6 addresses in presentation format with the low 64 bits shown bold.

Ullrich et al. [16] used a recursive algorithm for the first attempt to address generation. They iteratively searched for the largest match between each bit of the address and the current address range until the undetermined bits were left, which is used to generate a range of addresses to be scanned. Murdock et al. [10] introduced 6Gen, which generates the densest address range cluster by combining the closest Hamming distance addresses in each iteration. Foremski et al. [6] used Entropy/IP for efficient address generation. The algorithm models the entropy of address bits in the seed set and divides the bits into segments according to the entropy values. Then they used a Bayesian network to model the statistical dependence between the values of different segments. This learned statistical model can then generate target addresses for scanning. Different from these work, we use the neural network to construct the generated model and mainly compare it with Entropy/IP.

Researchers have extensively studied the VAE models in many fields, including text generation [15] and image generation [14]. Recently, gated convolutional networks have made outstanding progress on many Natural Language Processing (NLP) tasks due to their parallel computing advantages. Dauphin et al. [3] first proposed the model and called its key modules Gated Linear Units (GLU). Their approach achieves state-of-the-art performance on the WikiText-103 benchmark. Gehring et al. [8] simplified the gradient propagation using GLU and made a breakthrough on the WMT'14 English-German and WMT'14 English-French translation. To the best of our knowledge, we are using a gated convolutional network for the first time to construct a VAE model and to overcome the challenge of the IPv6 target generation task.

3   IPv6 Target Generation

In this section, we provide a brief description of IPv6 addressing background and our consideration of target generation tasks. We refer the reader to RFC 2460 [4] for a detailed description of the protocol.

3.1 IPv6 Addressing Background

An IPv6 address consists of a global network identifier (network prefix, e.g./32 prefix), subnet prefix, and an interface identifier (IID) [1]. It is composed of 128-bit binary digits, which are usually represented in human-readable text format, using 8 groups of 4 hexadecimal digits and separating them by colons, as shown in Fig. 1. Each of the hexadecimal digits is called a nybble. Since IPv6 addresses usually use "::" to replace groups of consecutive zero values and omit the first zero value in each group, a commonly used address format representation for IPv6 is also shown in Fig. 1.

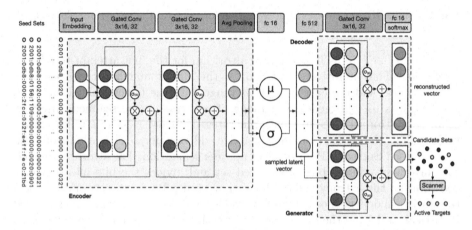

Fig. 2. The overall architecture of 6GCVAE. The model requires seed sets removed the colon as input and learns the address structure distribution through the encoder. The decoder reconstructs the latent vector after sampling. After training, the generator produces considerable candidates sets waited for probing by a scanner, which can finally discover the active targets.

There are many IPv6 addressing schemes and network operators are reminded to treat interface identifiers as semantically opaque [1]. Administrators have the option to use various standards to customize the address types. In addition, some IPv6 addresses have SLAAC [12] address format that the 64-bit IID usually embeds the MAC address according to the EUI-64 standard [12] or is set completely pseudo-random [11]. Consider the sample addresses in Fig. 1. In increasing order of complexity, these addresses appear to be:

- an address with fixed IID value (::321).
- an address with a structured value in the low 64 bits (perhaps a subnet distinguished by ::20).
- a SLAAC address with EUI-64 Ethernet-MAC-based IID (ff:fe flag).
- a SLAAC privacy address with a pseudorandom IID.

3.2   Considerations

Due to the semantic opacity of IPv6 addresses and the hybridization of multiple addressing schemes, the deep learning model may have difficulty in effectively training when learning the address structure. An address of the SLAAC format also has a highly randomized address structure, which is bound to pose a challenge to the generation task. However, to ensure that each addressing scheme can be included in the generation set, the selected seed set must contain all address patterns. Therefore, the target generation task requires the model to be able to effectively extract the underlying semantic information of IPv6 addresses. In addition, since the mixture of multiple structures, certain classification work on the seed set will alleviate the pressure on the model.

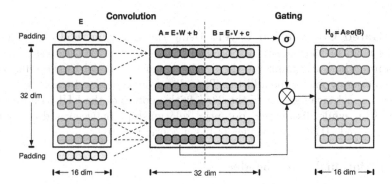

Fig. 3. Structure of the gated convolutional layer for IPv6 target generation. After convolution, the output of the vector A is controlled by the sigmoid value of vector B, which is used as an output gate to select the address vector.

4   Approach

In this section, we will introduce our approach and two seed classification methods for IPv6 target generation.

6GCVAE relies on stacked gated convolutional layers to form a Variational Autoencoder. The detailed model architecture is shown in Fig. 2. We remove the colon in each address and leave the 32-bit hexadecimal as a sample input (e.g., 20010db80020000300000000000000301). Since each nybble may be one of **0-f** characters, the alphabet size is 16 and we can arrive at a final input representation with a dimension of 32×16 after input embedding.

Our training model expects the generated address to be constantly approaching the input address to produce a new possible active target. To achieve the goal, the model is required to learn the distribution of the input by an encoder, sample latent vector and reconstruct the new generation by a decoder.

4.1 Gated Convolution Layer

The gated convolutional network enables to complete sequence tasks by adding a gating mechanism to the convolution. The structure is shown in Fig. 3.

We define the input embedding as $E = [D_0, ..., D_i, ..., D_{31}]$, where D_i represents the vector representation of the i-th nybble of the address. We use 32 3×16 convolution kernels to convolve the input E to obtain a 32×32-dimensional output vector which is divided equally to vector A and vector B. Finally, we take the sigmoid function as the gate for the vector B in the second half to control the output of the vector A. The approach to compute the hidden layers H_i can be summarized as

$$H_i = A \otimes \sigma B \tag{1}$$

where σ is the sigmoid function and $\otimes$ is the element-wise product between matrices.

Why Gated Convolution Layer. Using the gating method can effectively help us monitor the importance of each nybble of an IPv6 address. The convolution method also improves the sensitivity of the model to the relationship between each nybble of the address. This allows our model to be able to focus on address importance flags (e.g., the 23rd–26th nybbles of the EUI-64 address are always **fffe**) while discovering potential relationships between address nybbles (e.g., the fixed IID address typically has a contiguous 0).

4.2 Variational Autoencoder

In VAE models, a deterministic internal representation z (provided by the encoder) of an input x is usually replaced with a posterior distribution $q(z|x)$. Inputs are then reconstructed by sampling z from this posterior and passing them through a decoder. After training, the model will mass-produce text or images by a generator. In this section, we will introduce the encoder, decoder, and generator structure in our approach.

Encoder. In our model, we use two gated convolutional layers and an average pooling layer stack as the encoder for the model. In order to maintain the memory of the original input, we used a residual connection between each gated convolutional layer.

According to the principle of VAE, we use two fully connected layers to train the mean μ and the log variance $log\sigma^2$ to learn the distribution of the input x.

Decoder. To ensure that we can sample from any point of the latent space and still generate valid and diverse outputs, the posterior $q(z|x)$ is regularized with its KL divergence from a prior distribution $p(z)$. The prior is typically chosen to be a Gaussian with zero mean and unit variance. Then the latent vector z can be computed as

$$z = \mu + \epsilon * \sigma \tag{2}$$

where ϵ is sampled from the prior.

The decoder consists of a gated convolutional layer, fully connected layers, and a softmax activation. After sampling the latent vector z. We use the fully connected layer and adjust it to 32×16 dimensions as the input to the gated convolutional layer. Finally, the reconstructed address vector can be obtained through the fully connected layer and softmax activation function.

Our model loss consists of two parts, including the cross-entropy loss J_{xent} and the KL divergence $KL(q(z|x)||p(z))$. The cross-entropy loss expects the smallest reconstruction error between the reconstructed vector y and the input seed x. The KL divergence constraint model samples from the standard normal distribution:

$$J_{xent} = -(x \cdot log(y) + (1 - x) \cdot log(1 - y)) \tag{3}$$

$$KL(q(z|x)||p(z)) = -\frac{1}{2} \cdot (1 + log\ \sigma^2 - \mu^2 - \sigma^2) \tag{4}$$

$$J_{vae} = J_{xent} + KL(q(z|x)||p(z)) \tag{5}$$

Generator. After training, we use the trained decoder as a generator for batch generation of addresses. By sampling the 16-dimensional vector as a sample input in a standard normal distribution, the final generator outputs our ideal scan candidate. We set the sampling time N to control the number of targets we expect to generate.

4.3   Seed Classification

Since IPv6 addresses include multiple addressing schemes, they are often inter-mixed in the seed set. Early classification of seeds with different structural patterns can help to improve the learning effect of the model on each structure of the address. The model then can generate addresses closer to the real structural pattern, which has greater possible activity. In this section, we will introduce two methods of seed classification that we used, including manual classification and unsupervised clustering.

Manual Classification. In Sect. 3.1, we discussed the possible structural composition of the address. In this paper, we divide the address into four categories in Fig. 1, including fixed IID, low 64-bit subnet, SLAAC EUI-64, and SLAAC Privacy. We perform feature matching on the active seed set to estimate the address category to which the seed belongs:

- **Fixed IID.** The last 16 nybbles have a unique consecutive 0 in the address. It is speculated that the last 16 nybbles may consist of the fixed IID.
- **Low 64-bit subnet.** The last 16 nybbles of the address have two or more consecutive 0 segments. It is speculated that it may consist of a subnet identifier and an IID.
- **SLAAC EUI-64.** The 23rd-26th nybbles of the address are **fffe**.

– **SLAAC privacy**. After the statistics, the character appearance randomness of the last 16 nybbles is calculated, it is presumed to be a pseudo-random IID if the address has a high entropy value. We consider an address as SLAAC privacy if it has a greater entropy value than 0.8 (the highest is 1).

Unsupervised Clustering. We perform an entropy clustering method on the seed set, which was proposed by Gasser et al. [7]. We applied the idea to the target generation algorithm for the first time.

In an address set S, we define the probability $P(x_i)$ for the character x_i of the i-th nybble in an address, where $x \in \Omega = \{0, 1, ..., f\}$. Then by calculating the entropy value $H(X_i)$ for each nybble, we can get a fingerprint F_b^a of the address set S:

$$F_b^a = (H(X_a), ..., H(X_i), ..., H(X_b)) \tag{6}$$

$$H(X_i) = -\frac{1}{4} \sum_{x \in \Omega} P(x_i) \cdot log \ P(x_i) \tag{7}$$

where a and b are the first and the last considered nybble, respectively. Since /32 prefix is a large prefix that administrators usually use, which containing enough active addresses, we extract F_{32}^9 for each /32 prefix network address set (all addresses have the same first 8 nybbles in each network address set) and use the k-means algorithm to cluster each network fingerprint to find similar entropy fingerprint categories.

5   Evaluation

In this section, we evaluate 6GCVAE effects. We will introduce the datasets used in the paper, the evaluation method, and our comparative experiment results.

5.1   Dataset

Our experimental datasets are mainly from two parts, a daily updated public dataset IPv6 Hitlist and a measurement dataset CERN IPv6 2018. Table 1 summarizes the datasets used in this paper. The public dataset IPv6 Hitlist is from the data scanning the IPv6 public list for daily active addresses, which is provided by Gasser et al. [7]. In addition, we passively collected address sets under the China Education and Research Network from March to July 2018. We continued to scan and track the IPs that are still active until October 14, 2019 as our measurement dataset.

Table 1. The detail of the two active address datasets we used in the paper.

Dataset	Seeds	Period	Collection Method
IPv6 Hitlist	3,157,675	October 14, 2019	Public
CERN IPv6 2018	90,010	March 2018 - July 2018	Passive measurement

5.2 Evaluation Method

Scanning Method. To evaluate the activity of the generated address, we use the Zmapv6 tool [7] to perform ICMPv6, TCP/80, TCP/443, UDP/53, UDP/443 scans on the generated address. When the query sent by any scanning method gets a response, we will determine the address as active. Due to the difference in activity between hosts at different times, we maintain continuous scanning of the host for 3 days to ensure the accuracy of our method.

Evaluation Metric. Since IPv6 target generation is different from text generation tasks, we need to define a new evaluation metric for the address generative model. In the case of a given seed set, $N_{candidate}$ represents the number of the generated candidate set, N_{hit} represents the number of generated active addresses, N_{new} represents the generated address that is active and not in the seed set. Then the active hit rate r_{hit} and active generation rate r_{gen} of the model can be computed as

$$r_{hit} = \frac{N_{hit}}{N_{candidate}} \times 100\% \qquad r_{gen} = \frac{N_{new}}{N_{candidate}} \times 100\% \qquad (8)$$

We consider that r_{hit} can represent the learning ability to learn from the seed set. r_{gen} highlights the generation ability to generate new active addresses.

5.3 Result of Seed Classification

First, we summarize our seed classification. After manual classification, the seed will be classified into four categories. Table 2 shows the classification details on the IPv6 Hitlist dataset.

For the unsupervised clustering, we use the elbow method to find the number of clusters, k, plotting the sum of squared errors (SSE) for $k = \{1, ..., 20\}$. We selected the value $k = 6$ for the point where increasing k does not yield a relatively large reduction in SSE. Figure 4 shows the results of the clustering.

Table 2. The detail of manual classification on the IPv6 Hitlist dataset.

Category	Feature	Seeds	Percentage
Fixed IID	The last 16 nybbles have a consecutive 0	1,208,117	38.26%
Low 64-bit Subnet	The last 16 nybbles have more consecutive 0	1,062,093	33.64%
SLAAC EUI-64	The 23–26th nybbles is fffe	279,458	8.85%
SLAAC Privacy	Entropy value of the last 16 nybbles > 0.8	608,007	19.25%
Total	-	3,157,675	100%

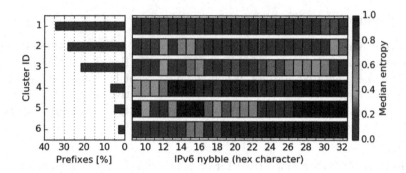

Fig. 4. The detail of unsupervised entropy clustering on the IPv6 Hitlist dataset. We obtained 6 clusters of all /32 prefix networks and the nybble distribution of each cluster.

It is worth noting that there is a certain relationship between the seed classification results. We know that the closer the $H(X_i)$ is to 0, the more likely the nybble is to be constant. The closer the $H(X_i)$ is to 1, the more random the nybble is. Therefore, in Fig. 4, Cluster 1–3 may be fixed IID or a low 64-bit subnet addresses. Cluster 5 is likely to be SLAAC EUI-64 addresses with the **fffe** flag. Cluster 4 and Cluster 6 are likely to be SLAAC privacy addresses because of the high entropy value of most of the nybbles.

After seed classification, we trained 6GCVAE with each category of seed sets. Table 3 shows the effect of the model without seed classification, with manual classification and with unsupervised clustering on the IPv6 Hitlist dataset.

The model is trained by using the dataset or each category of seeds as a seed set and uses the generator to generate candidate targets after 1,000,000 samplings. We remove duplicate candidate targets and ultimately get a valid candidate set. The results show that seed classification can actually improve

Table 3. Model effect with 3 types of seed processing, including none of the seed classification, manual classification, and unsupervised clustering.

Seed classification	Category	$N_{candidate}$	N_{hit}	N_{new}	r_{hit}	r_{gen}
None	IPv6 Hitlist	756,658	14,894	9,685	1.97%	1.28%
Manual classification	Fixed IID	412,181	32,589	**17,933**	7.91%	**4.35%**
	Low 64-bit Subnet	901,222	7,092	5,450	0.79%	0.61%
	SLAAC EUI-64	981,204	1,299	1,263	0.13%	0.13%
	SLAAC Privacy	999,920	13,351	13,351	1.34%	1.34%
Unsupervised clustering	Cluster 1	526,542	25,235	12,364	4.79%	2.35%
	Cluster 2	450,919	57,245	**35,508**	12.70%	**7.87%**
	Cluster 3	759,617	5,273	2,404	0.69%	0.32%
	Cluster 4	985,390	6,605	6,309	0.67%	0.64%
	Cluster 5	832,917	1,748	845	0.21%	0.10%
	Cluster 6	968,178	1,193	994	0.12%	0.10%

the performance of the model. Among them, the most generated addresses are manually classified Fixed IID and unsupervised clustered Cluster 2 respectively in the two methods. However, Low 64-bit subnet, SLAAC EUI-64, and Cluster 3–6 show a lower r_{gen} due to the complex address structure or lack of training samples. In addition, the model has a characteristic on the generation of SLAAC privacy addresses. All generated hits are new active targets. Because of the high randomness of this kind of address, the model may learn a high random structure, resulting in the generated addresses which are without duplicates.

Table 4. The comparative experiments result by comparing with 5 conventional VAE models and Entropy/IP. Results show that unsupervised clustering reached the best performance in our experiments.

Model	$N_{candidate}$	N_{hit}	N_{new}	r_{hit}	r_{gen}
FNN VAE	1,000,000	68	68	0.007%	0.007%
RNN VAE	498,509	3,009	2,085	0.604%	0.418%
Convolutional VAE	595,475	4,432	2,856	0.744%	0.480%
LSTM VAE	478,660	4,464	3,203	0.933%	0.669%
GRU VAE	525,134	5,694	4,548	1.084%	0.866%
Entropy/IP	593,795	15,244	5,402	2.570%	0.910%
6GCVAE	756,658	14,894	9,685	1.970%	1.280%
6GCVAE with Manual classification	557,653	28,957	15,870	5.193%	2.846%
6GCVAE with Unsupervised clustering	571,330	54,915	**31,376**	9.611%	**5.492%**

5.4   Comparing with Conventional VAE Models

In order to verify the superiority of 6GCVAE, we built the baseline of the conventional VAE models by replacing the key components gated convolutional layer of 6GCVAE and compared them with our model. We also use the generator for 1,000,000 samples after training the model with the IPv6 Hitlist dataset. Table 4 summarizes the results of the comparative experiments. The results show that due to the inability of feedforward neural networks to well capture semantic information, the FNN VAE displays a difficulty to complete the IPv6 target generation task. RNN VAE and Convolutional VAE only focus on sequence relationships or structure information, thus causing lower hits. By promoting the simple RNN layer to LSTM or GRU, the VAE model gets better performance than RNN VAE. Finally, 6GCVAE performs best under this task because of learning both the key segment structure and segment relationship information of an address.

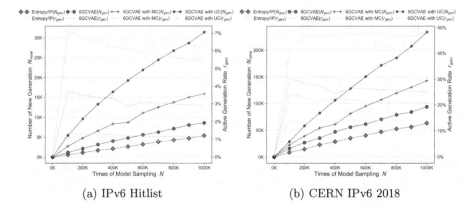

(a) IPv6 Hitlist   (b) CERN IPv6 2018

Fig. 5. The comparative experiments result by comparing with Entropy/IP on the two datasets. N_{new} and r_{gen} are evaluated under the different sampling times N.

5.5 Comparing with Entropy/IP

Entropy/IP [6] is the current state of the art address generation tool that can also efficiently generate active IPv6 targets. We compare the effects of 6GCVAE with Entropy/IP by training model and sampling 1,000,000 times for target generation as usual. As shown in Table 4, the experimental results show that our model outperformed Entropy/IP under the IPv6 Hitlist dataset. Although the r_{hit} of Entropy/IP is higher, its lower r_{gen} indicates that it generates more addresses that are duplicated in the dataset.

For representing the final effect of each seed classification method, we control the generation ratio of each type of address through r_{gen} to maximum the generation of new active target N_{new}. The ratio can be represented as $(r_{gen_1} : r_{gen_2} : ... : r_{gen_i})$, where i represents the category id of a seed classification method. Finally, we set the total sampling number N in each round of experiments and control the generation number of each category of seed set through the ratio. We then reached the best experimental results in Table 4. 6GCVAE has been greatly improved with seed classification.

In addition, in Fig. 5, we evaluated N_{new} and r_{gen} by changing the sampling times N on the two datasets, which can prove the general generation ability of the models. Results indicate that our approach reaches a better performance than Entropy/IP. 6GCVAE found 1.60–1.79 times more hits than Entropy/IP. Under manual classification (MC) and unsupervised clustering (UC), the N_{new} of 6GCVAE has been improved 1.52–1.85 and 2.50–3.67 times respectively. The seed classification methods have a higher r_{gen} than all other approaches. Unsupervised clustering reached the best performance in our experiments.

6 Conclusion

In this paper, we explored the challenges of IPv6 target generation tasks. Our work achieved a new model 6GCVAE by constructing a gated convolutional Variational Autoencoder. In addition, we introduce two kinds of seed classification techniques, which effectively improve the address generation performance of the deep learning model. The results show that 6GCVAE is superior to the previous conventional VAE models. The address generation quality of 6GCVAE is better than the state of the art target generation algorithm Entropy/IP.

Acknowledgements. This work is supported by The National Key Research and Development Program of China (No. 2016QY05X1000) and The National Natural Science Foundation of China (No. U1636217) and Key research and Development Program for Guangdong Province under grant No. 2019B010137003.

References

1. Carpenter, B., Jiang, S.: Significance of IPv6 interface identifiers. In: Internet Engineering Task Force, pp. 1–10 (2014)
2. Czyz, J., Luckie, M.J., Allman, M., Bailey, M.: Don't forget to lock the back door! a characterization of IPv6 network security policy. In: NDSS (2016)
3. Dauphin, Y.N., Fan, A., Auli, M., Grangier, D.: Language modeling with gated convolutional networks. In: Proceedings of the 34th International Conference on Machine Learning - Volume 70, pp. 933–941. JMLR. org (2017)
4. Deering, S., Hinden, R.: Internet protocol, version 6 (ipv6) specification (1998)
5. Durumeric, Z., Wustrow, E., Halderman, J.A.: ZMAP: fast internet-wide scanning and its security applications. In: Presented as part of the 22nd {USENIX} security symposium ({USENIX} security 13), pp. 605–620 (2013)
6. Foremski, P., Plonka, D., Berger, A.: Entropy/IP: uncovering structure in ipv6 addresses. In: Proceedings of the 2016 Internet Measurement Conference, pp. 167–181. ACM (2016)
7. Gasser, O., et al.: Clusters in the expanse: understanding and unbiasing IPv6 hitlists. In: Proceedings of the Internet Measurement Conference 2018, pp. 364–378. ACM (2018)
8. Gehring, J., Auli, M., Grangier, D., Yarats, D., Dauphin, Y.N.: Convolutional sequence to sequence learning. In: Proceedings of the 34th International Conference on Machine Learning-Volume 70, pp. 1243–1252. JMLR. org (2017)
9. Kingma, D.P., Welling, M.: Auto-encoding variational Bayes. arXiv preprint arXiv:1312.6114 (2013)
10. Murdock, A., Li, F., Bramsen, P., Durumeric, Z., Paxson, V.: Target generation for internet-wide IPv6 scanning. In: Proceedings of the 2017 Internet Measurement Conference, pp. 242–253. ACM (2017)
11. Narten, T.: Rfc3041: Privacy extensions for stateless address autoconfiguration in IPv6. RFC (2001)
12. Narten, T., Thomson, S., Jinmei, T.: IPv6 stateless address autoconfiguration (2007)
13. Plonka, D., Berger, A.: Temporal and spatial classification of active ipv6 addresses. In: Proceedings of the 2015 Internet Measurement Conference, pp. 509–522. ACM (2015)

14. Pu, Y., et al.: Variational autoencoder for deep learning of images, labels and captions. In: Advances in Neural Information Processing Systems, pp. 2352–2360 (2016)
15. Semeniuta, S., Severyn, A., Barth, E.: A hybrid convolutional variational autoencoder for text generation. arXiv preprint arXiv:1702.02390 (2017)
16. Ullrich, J., Kieseberg, P., Krombholz, K., Weippl, E.: On reconnaissance with IPv6: a pattern-based scanning approach. In: 2015 10th International Conference on Availability, Reliability and Security, pp. 186–192. IEEE (2015)

DELAFO: An Efficient Portfolio Optimization Using Deep Neural Networks

Hieu K. Cao[1,3], Han K. Cao[2], and Binh T. Nguyen[1,2,4,5(✉)]

[1] AISIA Research Lab, Ho Chi Minh City, Vietnam
[2] Inspectorio Research Lab, Ho Chi Minh City, Vietnam
[3] John Von Neumann Institute, Ho Chi Minh City, Vietnam
[4] University of Science, Ho Chi Minh City, Vietnam
ngtbinh@hcmus.edu.vn
[5] Vietnam National University in Ho Chi Minh City, Ho Chi Minh City, Vietnam

Abstract. Portfolio optimization has been broadly investigated during the last decades and had a lot of applications in finance and economics. In this paper, we study the portfolio optimization problem in the Vietnamese stock market by using deep-learning methodologies and one dataset collected from the Ho Chi Minh City Stock Exchange (VN-HOSE) from the beginning of the year 2013 to the middle of the year 2019. We aim to construct an efficient algorithm that can find the portfolio having the highest Sharpe ratio in the next coming weeks. To overcome this challenge, we propose a novel loss function and transform the original problem into a supervised problem. The input data can be determined as a 3D tensor, while the predicted output is the unnormalized weighted proportion for each ticker in the portfolio to maximize the daily return Y of the stock market after a given number of days. We compare different deep learning models, including Residual Networks (ResNet), Long short-term memory (LSTM), Gated Recurrent Unit (GRU), Self-Attention (SA), Additive Attention (AA), and various combinations: SA + LSTM, SA + GRU, AA + LSTM, and AA + GRU. The experimental results show that the AA + GRU outperforms the rest of the methods on the Sharpe ratio and provides promising results for the portfolio optimization problem not only in Vietnam but also in other countries.

Keywords: Portfolio optimization · Self-attention · Addictive attention · Residual Network · LSTM

1 Introduction

Using historical stock data for portfolio optimization has been one of the most exciting and challenging topics for investors in the financial market during the

Electronic supplementary material The online version of this chapter (https://doi.org/10.1007/978-3-030-47426-3_48) contains supplementary material, which is available to authorized users.

last decades [1, 2]. Many factors have different influences on the stock price, and it is essential to extract a list of crucial factors from both historical stock prices and other data sources. As there is no such thing as a free lunch, investors have to find an efficient strategy for a trade-off between getting more profits and reducing the investment risk. Sometimes, they need to invest multiple assets for diversifying the portfolio.

Traditionally, one can use statistical methods for predicting a financial time series problem. There are popular techniques, including autoregressive moving average (ARMA) [3], autoregressive conditional heteroscedastic (ARCH) [4], and autoregressive integrated moving average (ARIMA) [5]. Importantly, these statistical methods usually consider the stock time series as a linear process and then model the generation process for a latent time series to foresee future stock prices. Practically, a stock time series is generally a nonlinear dynamic process. There are many different approaches, including artificial neural networks (ANN), support vector machines (SVM), and other ensemble methods [6] to capture nonlinear characters from a given dataset without knowing any prior information. Especially, deep neural networks such as e.g. convolutional neural networks (CNN) and recurrent neural networks (RNN) have been proven to work well in many applications and multi-variable time series data.

The future price represents the future growth of each company in the stock market. Typically, the stock price of each company listed in a stock market can vary whenever one puts a sell or buy order, and the corresponding transaction completes. Many factors have influenced the stock price of one company, for example, such as the company's net profit, demand stability, competitive strength in the market, new technology used, and production volume. Also, the macro-economic condition can play a unique role in the stock market as well as the currency exchange rate and the change of the government's policies. After boasting increased macro-economic stability and improving the pro-business financial environment, Vietnam has become one of the world's most attractive markets for international investors. With the population of nearly 100 million people and most of whom are young people (under the age of 35), Vietnam can provide a young, motivated, highly skilled, and educated workforce to multiple international startups and enterprises with a competitive cost. At the moment, Vietnam's stock exchange is considered as one of the most promising and prospective market in the Southeast Asia. Especially, the Ho Chi Minh Stock Exchange (HOSE)[1] is becoming one of the largest securities firms in terms of both capital and size. Since launching in 2002, it has been performing strongly and more and more investors continue exhibiting a special interest in both Vietnam stock market. HOSE is currently predicted to be upgraded to an emerging market in 2021.

Up to now, there have existed a large number of useful applications using machine learning techniques in different aspects of daily life. Duy and co-workers combine deep neural networks and Gaussian mixture models for extracting brain tissues from high-resolution magnetic resonance images [7]. Deep neural networks

---

[1] https://www.hsx.vn/.

can also be applied to automatic music generation [8], food recognition [9], and portfolio optimization problem [10–12]. In this paper, we aim at investigating a portfolio optimization problem in which by using historical stock data of different tickers, one wants to find the equally weighted portfolio having the highest Sharpe ratio [13] in the future. This is one of the winning solutions in a well-known data science competition using the HOSE stock data in 2019. In this competition, one can use one training dataset, including all volume and prices of different tickers appearing in the Vietnam stock market from the beginning of the year 2013 to the middle of the year 2019 (July 2019), for learning an appropriate model of the portfolio optimization problem. It is worth noting that the Sharpe ratio is often used as a measure of the health of a portfolio. One usually expects that the higher the Sharpe ratio of one portfolio is in the past, the larger its Sharpe ratio is in the future. In this work, we assume that there are no new tickers joining the stock market during the testing period.

We study the portfolio optimization problem by assuming that there are N tickers in the stock market, only using the historical stock data during the last M days for training or updating the proposed model, and then doing prediction for the equally weighted portfolio having the highest Sharpe ratio during the next K days. Different from other approaches using statistical methods or time series algorithms, we transform the input data into a 3D tensor and then consider each input data as an image. As a result, we have a chance to apply different state-of-the-art methods such as e.g. Residual Networks (ResNet) [14], Long-short term memory(LSTM) [15], Gate Recurrent Unit [16], Self-Attention (SA) [17], and Additive Attention (AA) [18] for extracting important features as well as learning an appropriate model. Also, we compare them with different combinations of these techniques (SA + LSTM, SA + GRU, AA + LSTM, and AA + GRU) and measure the actual performance in the testing dataset. The experimental results show that the AA + LSTM outperforms other techniques in terms of achieving a much better value of the Sharpe ratio and a comparably smaller value of the corresponding standard deviation.

2   DELAFO: A New DeEp Learning Approach for portFolio Optimization

In this section, we present our methods to solve the portfolio optimization using the VN-HOSE dataset and deep neural networks.

2.1   Problem Formulation

We consider a dataset collected from the Vietnamese stock market from the beginning date D_0 and the ending date D_1 and N is the number of tickers appearing during that period of time. We denote $T = \{T_1, T_2, .., T_N\}$ as the list of all tickers in the market during the time window. For a given ticker T_i , $v_{i,j}$ and $p_{i,j}$ are the corresponding volume and price on the day d_j, consecutively. Moreover, we assume that all investors aim to determine the list of potential tickers in their portfolio for the next K days without putting any weight for different tickers (or equally weighted, such as e.g. $1/N$). It is important to note that all the investors usually do not want their portfolios to have a few tickers or "put all the eggs in one bucket" or lack of diversity. Having too many tickers may cost a lot of management time and fee as well. As a consequence, the outcome of the problem can be regarded as an N-binary vector (N is the number of tickers), where a one-valued entry means the corresponding ticker is chosen; otherwise, it is not selected. There are two main constraints in this problem: a) Having the same proportion for each tickers in portfolios; (b) The maximum numbers of tickers selected is 50.

The *daily return*, $R_{i,j}$, of the ticker T_i at the day d_j can be defined as $R_{i,j} = p_{i,j}/p_{i,j-1} - 1$ for all $i = 1, \ldots, N$ [13]. The daily return of portfolio can be computed by $R = \sum_1^N w_i * R_i$, where $\sum_{i=1}^N w_i = 1$. In the equally weighted portfolio optimization problem, one can assume that $w_i = \frac{1}{N}$, and therefore, the "Sharpe ratio" can be determined as [13]:

$$\text{Sharpe Ratio} = \sqrt{n} * \frac{\mathbb{E}[R - R_f]}{\sqrt{var[R - R_f]}}, \tag{1}$$

where n is an annualization factor of period (e.g, n= 252 for trading date in one year) and R_f is the risk-free rate, the expected return of any portfolio with no risk. In this work, we choose $R_f = 0$. Combining with $\mu = \frac{\sum_i^n R_i}{n}$ and $Q = \frac{\sum_i^n (R_i - \mu)^2}{n-1}$, the Sharpe ratio is calculated as:

$$\text{Sharpe Ratio} = \sqrt{n} * \frac{\mathbb{E}[R]}{\sqrt{var[R]}} = \sqrt{n} * \frac{\hat{w}^T \mu}{\sqrt{\hat{w}^T Q \hat{w}}}, \tag{2}$$

where $\hat{w}$ is an estimated preference vector for the list of all tickers. Typically, the equally weighted portfolio optimization problem can be formulated as follows:

$$\text{minimize } f(w) = -\frac{w^T \mu}{\sqrt{w^T Q w}},$$
$$\text{subject to: } g(w) = \mathbf{1}^T.w \le N_0,$$
$$w_i \in \{0, 1\}, \forall i = 1, \ldots, N. \tag{3}$$

Here, N_0 is the maximum number of tickers selected in the optimal portfolio ($N_0 = 50$ in our initial assumption). The main goal in our work is to estimate the optimal solution w^{opt} for the portfolio optimization problem (3) in order to obtain the maximum Sharpe ratio during the next K days.

To study a deep learning model for the portfolio optimization problem, we aim at only using the historical stock data during the last M days for training and then predict the optimal equally weighted portfolio having the highest Sharpe ratio during the next K days. To solve the optimization problem in (3), we represent each input data as a 3D tensor of size $N \times M \times 2$ that includes all stock data (both the volume and the price) of N different tickers during the

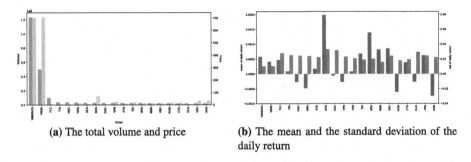

(a) The total volume and price

(b) The mean and the standard deviation of the daily return

Fig. 1. Top 20 tickers in VN-HOSE.

last M consecutive days and the corresponding output of the deep network is a vector $\hat{w} = (\hat{w}_1, \hat{w}_2, \ldots, \hat{w}_N)$ of size $N \times 1$, where $\hat{w}_i \in [0, 1]$ $(i = 1, \ldots, N)$ is the estimated preference rate of the i-th ticker in the list of all N tickers in the stock market. Finally, the optimal portfolio can be determined by the corresponding estimated solution w^{opt}, where the i-th ticker can be chosen if the corresponding preference $\hat{w}_i \geq \theta$ (or $w_i^{opt} = 1$); otherwise, it is not selected.

2.2 A New Loss Function for the Sharpe-Ratio Maximization

Traditionally, one can estimate the maximum value of the Sharpe ratio by solving the following optimization problem [19] :

$$\hat{w} = \operatorname{argmin} \left(w^T Q w - \lambda w^T \mu\right) / \left(w^T w\right). \tag{4}$$

Although it does not directly optimize the Sharpe ratio as shown in Eq. (2), one can use the stochastic gradient descent method for approximating the optimal $\hat{w}$ [20]. In this paper, we propose the following new loss function for the equally weighted portfolio optimization problem:

$$L(\hat{w}) = -\left(\hat{w}^T \mu\right) / \sqrt{\hat{w}^T \mathbf{Q} \hat{w}} + \lambda (C.\mathbb{1} - \hat{w})^T.\hat{w}, \tag{5}$$

where $\lambda > 0$ and $C > 1$ are two hyper parameters. One can find more details of how we can derive the loss function $L(\hat{w})$ in the section Supplementary Material. After that, by implementing an appropriate deep neural network to estimate the optimal solution $\hat{w} = (\hat{w}_1, \hat{w}_2, \ldots, \hat{w}_N)$ in Eq. (5), we can derive the final optimal vector w^{opt} in Eq. (3) by the following rules:

$$w_i^{opt} = 1, \text{ if } \hat{w}_i \geq \theta, w_i^{opt} = 0, \text{ if } \hat{w}_i < \theta, \forall i = 1, \ldots, N. \tag{6}$$

In our experiments, we choose $\theta = 0.5$.

2.3 Our Proposed Models for the Portfolio Optimization

To estimate the output vector $\hat{w}$, we consider different deep learning approaches for solving the portfolio optimization problem based on the proposed loss function in Eq. (5). We select both Long-short term memory(LSTM) [15] and Gate

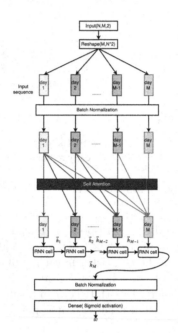

Fig. 2. Our proposed Self Attention + LSTM/GRU.

Recurrent Unit [16] architectures as two baseline models. Especially, by converting the input data into an $N \times M \times 2$ tensor as an "image", we construct a new ResNet architecture for the problem and create four other combinations of deep neural networks. They are SA + LSTM (Self-Attention model and LSTM), SA + GRU (Self-Attention model and GRU), AA + LSTM (Additional Attention and LSTM), and AA + GRU (Additional Attention and GRU). The architecture of RNN, GRU, and LSTM cells can be found more details at [15, 16, 21].

ResNet. ResNet architecture has been proven to become one of the most efficient deep learning models in computer vision, whose the first version was proposed by He et al. [22]. After that, these authors later released the second update for ResNet [14]. By using residual blocks inside its architecture, ResNet can help us to overcome the gradient vanishing problem and then well learn deep features without using too many parameters. In this work, we apply ResNet for estimating the optimal value for the vector $\hat{w}$ in the loss function (5). To the best of our knowledge, this is the first time ResNet is used for the Sharpe ratio maximization and our proposed ResNet architecture can be described in Fig. 4.

SA/AA + LSTM/GRU. The attention mechanism is currently one of the state-of-the-art algorithms, which are ubiquitously used in many NLP problems. There are many types of attention models, including Bahdanau attention [18], Luong Attention [21], and Self Attention [17]. Although the attention mechanism has been applying for the stock price prediction [23], there is few attention scheme used for maximizing the Sharpe ratio in the portfolio optimization problem. In this paper, we exploit two mechanisms, which are Self-Attention and Bahdanau attention (Additive Attention). The corresponding architecture of our four proposed models (SA + LSTM, SA + GRU, AA + LSTM, AA + GRU) can be visualized in Figs. 2 and 3.

3   Experiments

In this section, we present our experiments and the corresponding implementation of each proposed model. All tests are performed on a computer with Intel(R) Core(TM) i9-7900X CPU, running at 3.6 GHz with 128 GB of RAM, and two GPUs RTX-2080Ti (2×12 GB of RAM). We collect all stock data from the VN-HOSE stock exchange over six years (from January 1, 2013, to July 31, 2019) for measuring the performance of different models. There are 438 tickers appearing in the Vietnam stock market during this period. However, 57 tickers disappeared in the stock market at the end of 31/07/2019. For this reason, we only consider 381 remaining tickers for training and testing models. In Fig. 1(a) and 1(b), we visualize the mean values of both volume and price of the top 20 highest volume tickers in HOSE as well as the corresponding average value and the standard deviation of the daily return.

3.1   Model Configuration

In our experiments, all proposed models use the Adam optimizer [24] with the optimal learning rate $\alpha = 0.0762$, $\beta_1 = 0.9$, and $\beta_2 = 0.999$. The learning rate

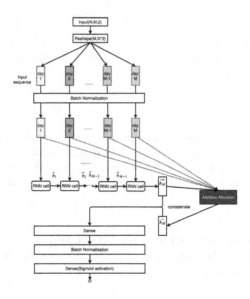

Fig. 3. Our proposed Additive Attention + LSTM/GRU.

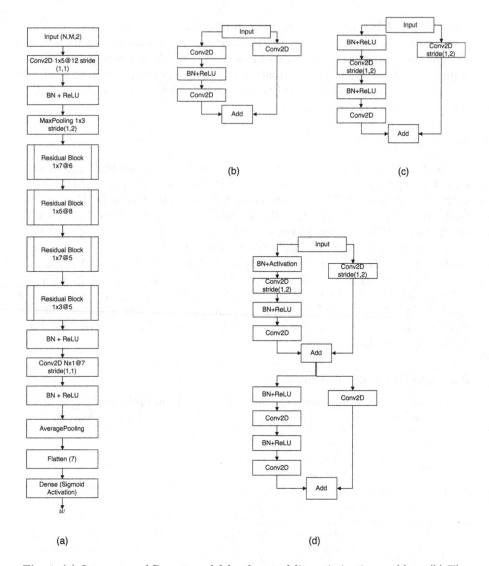

Fig. 4. (a) Our proposed Resnet model for the portfolio optimization problem. (b) The first residual block. (c) The second and the third residual block (d) The final residual block. Here, "BN" denotes "Batch Normalization", N is the number of tickers, and M is the number of days to extract the input data. In our experiments, $N = 381$ and $M = 64$.

and L2 regularization are tuned by using 141 random samples from the training set. We use the library Hyperas[2] for automatically tuning all hyper-parameters of the proposed models.

---

[2] https://github.com/maxpumperla/hyperas.

For two base line models (LSTM and GRU), we use 32 hidden units in which the L_2-regularization term is 0.0473. As shown in Fig. 4, our proposed ResNet model has the input data of the size $(381, 64, 2)$ passing to the first convolution layer where the kernel size is (1×5) and the L_2-regularization is 0.0932. After that, the data continue going through four different residual blocks, whose corresponding kernel sizes are (1×7),(1×5), (1×7), and (1×3), respectively, and all kernels have the L_2-regularization as 10^{-4}. Using these kernels, we aim at capturing the time dependency from the input data. The last convolution layer in our ResNet model has the kernel size $(381, 1)$ and the L_2-regularization as 0.0372 for estimating the correlation among all tickers. Its output data continue going through an average pooling layer before passing the final fully connected layer with the Sigmoid activation function to compute the vector $\hat{w}$. The last Dense layer has L2 regularization 0.099 and the learning rate of our ResNet model is 0.0256.

For four proposed models (SA/AA + LSTM/GRU), both Self-Attention and Additive Attention have 32 hidden units and the L_2-regularization term is 0.01. Both GRU and LSTM cells use 32 hidden units, the Sigmoid activation function, and the L_2-regularization as 0.0473. Two last fully connected layers have 32 hidden unites and the corresponding L_2-regularization is 0.0727. In our experiments, we choose $\theta = 0.5$, $\lambda = 0.003$, and $C = 1.6$, where θ, λ, and C are hyper-parameters of our proposed loss function.

3.2 Data Preparation

As there are only 381 tickers ($N = 381$) in the market at the end of the month July, 2019, we use the time windows of M consecutive days for extracting the input data of proposed models. On each day, we collect the information of both "price" and "volume" of these 381 tickers and $\mathbf{y}$, the daily return on the market in the next K days ($K = 19$). Consequently, the input data has the shape $(381, 64, 2)$ and we move the time window during the studying period of time (from January 1, 2013, to July 31, 2019) to obtain 1415 samples.

To deal with new tickers appeared, we fill all missing values by 0. For these missing data, our model may not learn anything from these data. Meanwhile, for the daily return in the next K days, we fill all missing values by -100. That is, as those tickers have been not disappeared yet, we set its daily return as a negative number so as to ensure chosen portfolios containing these tickers can get a negative Sharpe ratio. During training proposed models, we believe that the optimizer can learn well and avoid selecting these tickers from portfolios as much as possible.

3.3 Experimental Results

We evaluate each model by using 10-fold cross-validation or forward chaining validation in time series data. As shown in Fig. 5, while measuring the performance of each proposed model, we create the training data by moving the selected time window (64 days) during the investigating period (from January 2013 to July

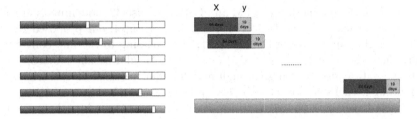

Fig. 5. The 10- Fold cross validation in our experiments. The blue blocks contain the training data and the red blocks contain the testing data. In experiments, we just use from Fold 5 to Fold 10 for evaluating the Sharpe ratio due to the lack of data for training models. At each fold, we train our deep models using 200 epochs. (Color figure online)

2019) and consider the corresponding sequence of daily returns in the next coming 19 days. It is crucial to make sure all training samples are independent of the testing samples.

The experiment results show that the Additive Attention + GRU model outperforms with the others. One of the possible reasons is Additive Attention + GRU can retain the information from the input sequence, which may loose from RNN cells when dealing with a very long sequence. Models using Self Attention can also get good results; however, as the outputs of the Self-Attention module still go to the RNN cell, without keeping any information from the sequence input. For this reason, the mean value of the Sharpe ratio of SA + GRU (0.9047) is a bit lower than AA + GRU (1.1056). Interestingly, the mean value of the Sharpe ratio of SA + LSTM (1.0206) is better than AA + LSTM (0.9235). Although not getting a high Sharpe ration in comparison with SA/AA + LSTM/GRU, the ResNet model has a quite short training time. In our experiments, the total time for its running 10-Fold Cross Validation is only 40 min, while taking over two hours for all SA/AA + LSTM/GRU models. In Fig. 6, our best-proposed model, AA + GRU, has a better performance than both VN30[3] and VNINDEX[4] in terms of the Sharpe ratio values. These experimental results show that our proposed techniques can achieve promising results and possibly apply not only in the Vietnamese stock market but also in other countries (Table 1).

---

[3] VN30 is the bucket of 30 companies having highest market capitalization and highest volume in six months for all the companies listed on the Ho Chi Minh City Stock Exchange. They also have the free float larger than 5%: https://iboard.ssi.com.vn/bang-gia/vn30.

[4] VN-Index is a capitalization-weighted index of all the companies listed on the Ho Chi Minh City Stock Exchange: https://www.bloomberg.com/quote/VNINDEX:IND.

Table 1. The performance of different models by the Sharpe ratio

Model	Number of learning parameters	mean (Sharpe ratio)	std (Sharpe ratio)
Resnet	66,967	0.8309	0.3391
LSTM	114,333	0,77057	0.2972
GRU	88,893	0.750	0.3182
SA + LSTM	164,689	1.0206	0.2976
SA + GRU	139,249	0.9047	0.3574
AA + LSTM	166,865	0.9235	0.2718
AA + GRU	141,425	**1.1056**	**0.2188**

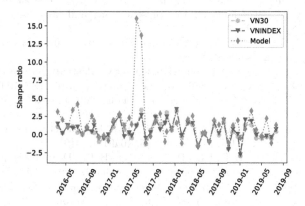

Fig. 6. The performance of our AA + GRU model with the VN30 and VNINDEX in terms of the Sharpe ratio in the testing dataset.

4   Conclusion and Further Work

We have proposed a novel approach for a portfolio optimization problem with N tickers by using the historical stock data during the last M days to compute an optimal portfolio that maximizes the Sharpe ratio of the daily returns during the next K days. We have also presented a new loss function for the Sharpe ratio maximization problem and transform the input data into a $N \times M \times 2$ tensor, and apply seven different deep learning methods (LSTM, GRU, SA + GRU, SA + LSTM, AA + LSTM, AA + GRU, and ResNet) for investigating the problem. To learning a suitable deep learning model for the problem, we collect the stock data in VN-HOSE during the period from January 2013 to July 2019. The experimental results show that the AA + GRU model outperforms with the other techniques and also achieves a better performance in terms of the Sharpe ratio for two popular indexes VN30 and VNINDEX.

In future works, we will extend our approaches to similar problems in other countries and continue improving our algorithms. Our project, including datasets and implementation details, will be publicly available[5].

Acknowledgement. We would like to thank The National Foundation for Science and Technology Development (NAFOSTED), University of Science, Inspectorio Research Lab, and AISIA Research Lab for supporting us throughout this paper.

References

1. Fernández, A., Gómez, S.: Portfolio selection using neural networks. Comput. Oper. Res. **34**(4), 1177–1191 (2007)
2. Chong, E., Han, C., Park, F.C.: Deep learning networks for stock market analysis and prediction: methodology, data representations, and case studies. Expert Syst. Appl. **83**, 187–205 (2017)
3. Box, G.E.P., Jenkins, G.: Time Series Analysis, Forecasting and Control. Holden-Day Inc, San Francisco (1990)
4. Engle, R.F.: Autoregressive conditional heteroscedasticity with estimates of the variance of United Kingdom inflation. Econometrica **50**(4), 987–1007 (1982)
5. Mills, T.C.: Time Series Techniques for Economists. Cambridge University Press, Cambridge (1990)
6. Nguyen, B.T., Nguyen, D.M., Ho, L.S.T., Dinh, V.: An active learning framework for set inversion. Knowl. Based Syst. **185**, 104917 (2019)
7. Nguyen, D.M.H., Vu, H.T., Ung, H.Q., Nguyen, B.T.: 3D-brain segmentation using deep neural network and gaussian mixture model. In: 2017 IEEE Winter Conference on Applications of Computer Vision (WACV), pp. 815–824, March 2017
8. Cao, H.K., Ly, D.T., Nguyen, D.M., Nguyen, B.T.: Automatically generate hymns using variational attention models. In: Lu, H., Tang, H., Wang, Z. (eds.) ISNN 2019, Part II. LNCS, vol. 11555, pp. 317–327. Springer, Cham (2019). https://doi.org/10.1007/978-3-030-22808-8_32
9. Nguyen, B.T., Dang-Nguyen, D.-T., Dang, T. X., Phat, T., Gurrin, C.: A deep learning based food recognition system for lifelog images. In: Proceedings of the 7th International Conference on Pattern Recognition Applications and Methods - Volume 1: INDEED, pp. 657–664. INSTICC, SciTePress (2018)
10. Liu, Q., Dang, C., Huang, T.: A one-layer recurrent neural network for real-time portfolio optimization with probability criterion. IEEE Trans. Cybern. **43**(1), 14–23 (2012)
11. Ding, X., Zhang, Y., Liu, T., Duan, J.: Deep learning for event-driven stock prediction. In: Twenty-Fourth International Joint Conference on Artificial Intelligence (2015)
12. Liu, J., Chao, F., Lin, Y.-C., Lin, C.-M.: Stock prices prediction using deep learning models, arXiv preprint arXiv:1909.12227 (2019)
13. Sharpe, W.F.: The sharpe ratio. J. Portfolio Manag. **21**(1), 49–58 (1994)
14. He, K., Zhang, X., Ren, S., Sun, J.: Identity mappings in deep residual networks. In: Leibe, B., Matas, J., Sebe, N., Welling, M. (eds.) ECCV 2016, Part IV. LNCS, vol. 9908, pp. 630–645. Springer, Cham (2016). https://doi.org/10.1007/978-3-319-46493-0_38

---

[5] https://github.com/caokyhieu/DELAFO-DeEp-Learning-Approach-for-portFolio-Optimization.

15. Hochreiter, S., Schmidhuber, J.: Long short-term memory. Neural Comput. **9**, 1735–1780 (1997)
16. Cho, K., et al.: Learning phrase representations using rnn encoder-decoder for statistical machine translation, arXiv preprint arXiv:1406.1078 (2014)
17. Vaswani, A., et al.: Attention is all you need. In: Advances in Neural Information Processing Systems, pp. 5998–6008 (2017)
18. Bahdanau, D., Cho, K., Bengio, Y.: Neural machine translation by jointly learning to align and translate (2014)
19. Markowitz, H.: Portfolio selection. J. Finan. **7**(1), 77–91 (1952)
20. Kopman, L., Liu, S.: Maximizing the sharpe ratio, June 2009. In: MSCI Barra Research Paper, no. 2009–22 (2009)
21. Luong, M.-T., Pham, H., Manning, C.D.: Effective approaches to attention-based neural machine translation, arXiv preprint arXiv:1508.04025 (2015)
22. He, K., Zhang, X., Ren, S., Sun, J.: Deep residual learning for image recognition. In: 2016 IEEE Conference on Computer Vision and Pattern Recognition (CVPR), June 2016
23. Li, H., Shen, Y., Zhu, Y.: Stock price prediction using attention-based multi-input LSTM. In: Asian Conference on Machine Learning, pp. 454–469 (2018)
24. Kingma, D.P., Ba, J.: Adam: a method for stochastic optimization, arXiv preprint arXiv:1412.6980 (2014)

CACRNN: A Context-Aware Attention-Based Convolutional Recurrent Neural Network for Fine-Grained Taxi Demand Prediction

Wenbin Wu[1], Tong Liu[1,2,3(✉)], and Jiahao Yang[1]

[1] School of Computer Engineering and Science, Shanghai University, Shanghai, China
{wenbinw,tong_liu,Jiahao_Yang}@shu.edu.cn
[2] Shanghai Engineering Research Center of Intelligent Computing System,
Shanghai University, Shanghai, China
[3] Shanghai Institute for Advanced Communication and Data Science,
Shanghai University, Shanghai, China

Abstract. As taxis are primary public transport in metropolises, accurately predicting fine-grained taxi demands of passengers in real time is important for guiding drivers to plan their routes and reducing the waiting time of passengers. Many efforts have been paid to provide accurate taxi demand prediction, and deep neural networks are leveraged recently. However, existing works are limited in properly incorporating multi-view taxi demand predictions together, by simply assigning fixed weights learned by training to the predictions of each region. To solve this problem, we apply the attention mechanism for leveraging contextual information to assist prediction, and a context-aware attention-based convolutional recurrent neural network (CACRNN) is proposed. Specially, we forecast fine-grained taxi demands with considering multi-view features, including spatial correlations among adjacent regions, short-term periodicity, long-term periodicity, and impacts of external factors. Local convolutional (LC) layers and gated recurrent units (GRUs) are utilized to extract the features from historical records. Moreover, a context-aware attention module is employed to incorporate the predictions of each region with considering different features, which is our novel attempt. This module assigns different weights to the predictions of a region according to its contextual information such as weather, index of time slots, and region function. We conduct comprehensive experiments based on a large-scale real-world dataset from New York City, and the results show that our method outperforms state-of-the-art baselines.

Keywords: Taxi demand prediction · Convolutional recurrent neural networks · Attention mechanism · Multi-view spatial-temporal feature extraction

© Springer Nature Switzerland AG 2020
H. W. Lauw et al. (Eds.): PAKDD 2020, LNAI 12084, pp. 636–648, 2020.
https://doi.org/10.1007/978-3-030-47426-3_49

1   Introduction

Taxis play an important role in public transportation systems, providing comfortable and convenient services to a larger amount of passengers every day, especially in metropolises like New York City. According to a survey conducted in 2016, the number of taxis is over 13,000 in New York City, and about 420,000 orders on average are completed per day. However, a major problem exists in taxi service is that the spatial-temporal imbalance between supply of drivers and demand of passengers. For example, some drivers steer empty taxis on some streets, while some passengers cannot take taxis even after a long wait on other streets. This problem leads to the increase of waiting time of passengers and the decrease of incomes of drivers.

Predicting fine-grained taxi demands in future is of great significance to solve the problem. Extracting spatial-temporal patterns from historical taxi trip records can help prediction. However, there exist several challenges to make accurate prediction. *Firstly*, taxi demands are highly dynamic, i.e., varying rapidly and randomly over time, which are determined by passengers. On the other hand, certain periodic patterns exist objectively, like high taxi demands in rush hours on weekdays. *Secondly*, the variations of taxi demands in different functional regions of a city are unlike, e.g., central business districts and residential areas. In addition, the taxi demand of a region has high correlations with other regions, especially its adjacent regions, due to the flows of passengers. *Thirdly*, taxi demands are greatly influenced by some external factors, such as weather condition, holidays and weekends. For example, many people take taxis in the early morning on the New Year's Day because of celebratory activity, which does not occur in ordinary days.

There has been a long line of studies in taxi demand prediction. Model-based methods are widely developed in the earlier works. For instance, autoregressive integrated moving average (ARIMA) and its improvements are used [6,8], via modeling taxi demand prediction problem as a time series prediction problem. Recently, deep neural networks (DNN) are introduced to predict taxi demands, in which complicated spatial-temporal correlations are extracted and external factors are used to assist prediction. For example, Xu et al. [11] propose a sequential learning framework based on long short-term memory (LSTM) network, in which instant temporal dependencies are leveraged. Convolution operation is integrated with LSTM by Yao et al. [12], and spatial correlations and temporal dependencies are both extracted. External factors are further leveraged in [2] to improve the prediction accuracy. However, these works are limited in properly incorporating multi-view features of taxi demands and external factors together, by simply assigning them fixed weights learned by training.

In this work, we propose a convolutional recurrent network model for taxi demand prediction. We first divide time into time slots and partition an urban area into regions, based on which fine-grained taxi demands are defined. Then, multi-view spatial-temporal features of taxi demands are used to perform prediction. Specially, for each region, three predictions are obtained, considering the spatial correlations and temporal dependencies among adjacent regions in successive time slots, and the short-term and long-term periodicity with the impacts of external factors respectively. Local convolutional layers and gated recurrent units are employed in our network model. Finally, we develop a novel context-aware attention mechanism to incorporate the predictions of each region. Contextual factors are input into fully-connected layers to learn the weight assigned to each prediction, and the final prediction is calculated as the weighted sum.

The main contributions of this paper can be summarized as follows.

- We propose a convolutional recurrent network model for fine-grained taxi demand prediction. Multi-view features of taxi demands, including the spatial correlations among adjacent regions, short-term and long-term periodicity, and the impacts of external factors, are considered to perform prediction.
- We also develop a context-aware attention mechanism to incorporate the predictions of each region, by assigning them different notice. Contextual information, such as weather condition, index of time slots, and region function, are taken into account in our attention network.
- We conduct comprehensive experiments based on real-world datasets from New York City. The results show that our proposed network outperforms state-of-the-art methods.

The rest of this paper is organized as follows. Section 2 describes some key definitions and our problem formulation. The details of our designed neural network is illustrated in Sect. 3. Section 4 presents the experimental results of our model and several baselines. We review related work and conclude our paper in Sect. 5 and Sect. 6, respectively.

2   Problem Formulation

In this section, we first present some key definitions, and then formally formulate the taxi demand prediction problem.

Definition 1 (Road Network). *A road network of an urban area is composed of a set of road segments. Each road segment is associated with two terminal points (i.e., intersections of crossroads), and connects with other road segments by sharing the same terminals. All road segments compose the road network in the format of a graph.*

To formally describe fine-grained taxi demands in spatial and temporal dimensions, we discretize time into a set of equal-interval time slots, denoted by $\mathcal{T} = \{t_1, t_2, \cdots, t_\tau, \cdots\}$, where t_τ represents the current time slot. We also divide the whole urban area into disjoint regions based on its road network, by leveraging the map segmentation method in [14]. Each region is an irregular polygon, encompassed by several road segments. The set of regions is represented by $\mathcal{R} = \{r_1, r_2, \cdots, r_N\}$, where N represents the number of regions. Based on the definitions of time slots and regions, we further present the formal definition of fine-grained taxi demands as follows.

Definition 2 (Taxi Demands). *We use $X_{n,\tau}$ to represent the number of passengers with the demand of taking a taxi in region $r_n \in \mathcal{R}$ at time slot $t_\tau \in \mathcal{T}$. Then, the taxi demands at time slot t_τ are defined as $\mathbf{X}_\tau = [X_{1,\tau}, X_{2,\tau}, \cdots, X_{N,\tau}]$.*

Definition 3 (Taxi Tripping Records). *We denote $\{tr\}$ is a set of historical taxi tripping records. Each record tr contains locations and timestamps of picking up and dropping off a passenger, which can be denoted by a tuple $tr = (tr.pl, tr.pt, tr.dl, tr.dt)$. Here, pick-up location $tr.pl$ and drop-off location $tr.dl$ are given by their latitudes and longitudes, while pick-up timestamp $tr.pt$ and drop-off timestamp $tr.dt$ are given by their dates, hours and minutes.*

To predict taxi demands in future, we first dig fine-grained taxi demands in past time slots from historical taxi tripping records as defined in Definition 3. Given a dataset of taxi tripping records in an urban area, historical taxi demands in region r_n at time slot t_τ can be approximated by the number of passengers have taken a taxi, which is derived as

$$X_{n,\tau} = |\{tr|tr.pl \in r_n \wedge tr.pt \in t_\tau\}|, \tag{1}$$

where $tr.pl \in r_n$ and $tr.pt \in t_\tau$ mean that the pick-up location of record tr is in region r_n, and the pick-up timestamp is within time slot t_τ, respectively. Function $|\cdot|$ denotes the cardinality of a set.

Definition 4 (POI). *A point of interest (POI) is a venue in an urban area like a shopping mall. Each POI is associated with a location and a category.*

Information contained in POIs indicates the function of regions (e.g., central business districts) as well as the flows of passengers. We define a *function vector* for each region, denoted by $r_n.func$, in which each element is the number of POIs of a specific category. In addition, we also define a set of neighbours for each region composed of its adjacent regions, denoted by $r_n.neig$.

We now formulate the problem of predicting fine-grained taxi demands in the next time slot as follows.

Definition 5 (Taxi Demand Prediction Problem). *Consider an urban area is divided into disjoint regions $\mathcal{R}$ by the road network. Given fine-grained taxi demands in the past time slots $\{\mathbf{X}_t|t = 1, 2, \cdots, \tau\}$ extracted from historical taxi tripping records, we try to predict fine-grained taxi demands at the next time slot. The prediction is denoted as $\hat{\mathbf{X}}_{\tau+1} = [\hat{X}_{1,\tau+1}, \hat{X}_{2,\tau+1}, \cdots, \hat{X}_{N,\tau+1}]$.*

3   Methodology

3.1   Overview of CACRNN Model

Figure 1 provides an overview of our proposed deep neural network model, which comprises of four modules.

Instant Spatial-Temporal Module. This module is composed of a series of local convolutional (LC) layers and a gated recurrent unit (GRU), which are employed to extract spatial and temporal dependencies of taxi demands in a close period. Specially, it takes the taxi demands in o successive time slots as its input, denoted by $\mathbf{Y}^i = [\mathbf{X}_{\tau+1-o}, \mathbf{X}_{\tau+2-o}, \cdots, \mathbf{X}_\tau] \in \mathbb{R}^{o \times N}$, and outputs a prediction of taxi demands in the next time slot $\mathbf{f}^i \in \mathbb{R}^{1 \times N}$.

Short-Term Periodic Module. This module considers the existence of short-term (e.g., a few days) periodicity in taxi demands to perform the prediction. We employ a GRU to learn the short-term periodicity, which takes a sequence of taxi demands in p periodic time slots with interval Δ_s as the input, i.e., $\mathbf{Y}^s = [\mathbf{X}_{\tau+1-p\Delta_s}, \mathbf{X}_{\tau+1-(p-1)\Delta_s}, \cdots, \mathbf{X}_{\tau+1-\Delta_s}] \in \mathbb{R}^{p \times N}$. Besides, the influence of some external factors (like weather and holidays) to the periodicity is also considered in this module. We represent the features of external factors in t_τ as a vector $\mathbf{u}_\tau \in \mathbb{R}^{1 \times \omega}$, and concatenate it with taxi demands as the input of the GRU. Then, a prediction of taxi demands $\mathbf{f}^s \in \mathbb{R}^{1 \times N}$ is obtained.

Long-Term Periodic Module. This module draws the long-term (e.g., a few weeks) periodic pattern of taxi demands. Similar with the last module, a sequence of taxi demands $\mathbf{Y}^l = [\mathbf{X}_{\tau+1-q\Delta_l}, \mathbf{X}_{\tau+1-(q-1)\Delta_l}, \cdots, \mathbf{X}_{\tau+1-\Delta_l}] \in \mathbb{R}^{q \times N}$ combined with features of external factors is fed to a GRU, and a prediction of taxi demands at time slot $t_{\tau+1}$ is output, denoted by $\mathbf{f}^l \in \mathbb{R}^{1 \times N}$.

Context-Aware Attention Module. We leverage an attention module to incorporate the outputs of the above modules into the final taxi demand prediction $\hat{\mathbf{X}}_{\tau+1}$, which is a novel attempt. Especially, our attention model can be interpreted as assigning different weights to the predictions of each region, according to contextual information like weather condition, index of time slots, and region function.

In the following, we provide details of each module respectively. Main notations and descriptions are summarized in Table 1, where '#' represents 'number'.

3.2   Instant Spatial-Temporal Module

The structure of this module is built based on local convolutional layers and a GRU, to extract the latent spatial correlations in adjacent regions and the temporal dependencies in a close period.

A sequence of taxi demands $\mathbf{Y}^i$ is first fed to the LC layers. In each layer, local convolutional operation is conducted, and k convolution kernels are used to extract high-dimensional spatial features. Specially, we take the l-th ($2 \le l \le L$) LC layer as an example to illustrate the details. We denote the input of this

Table 1. Main notations

o	# of time slots in instant spatial-temporal module
k	# of convolution kernels
L	# of LC layers
p	# of time slots in short-term periodic module
Δ_s	Interval in short-term periodic module
q	# of time slots in long-term periodic module
Δ_l	Interval in long-term periodic module

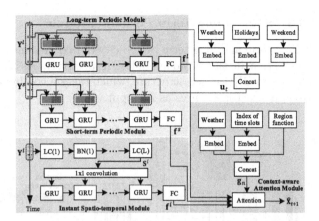

Fig. 1. Framework of our CACRNN model

layer as $\mathbf{Y}_l^i \in \mathbb{R}^{k \times o \times N}$, which also is the output of the $(l-1)$-th LC layer. *Firstly*, for each region r_n, we construct a *sub-matrix* $\mathbf{Y}_{l,n}^i$ by rearranging some columns of $\mathbf{Y}_l^i$. Specially, we define $M = \max_{\forall n} \{|r_n.neig|\}$ and thus define $\mathbf{Y}_{l,n}^i \in \mathbb{R}^{k \times o \times (M+1)}$. For region r_n, the columns in $\mathbf{Y}_l^i$ corresponding to its neighbouring regions are chosen to be a part of $\mathbf{Y}_{l,n}^i$, as shown in Fig. 2. Besides, we pad the left vacant columns by duplicating the column in $\mathbf{Y}_l^i$ corresponding to r_n $(M+1-|r_n.neig|)$ times. *Secondly*, we conduct a convolutional operation on each $\mathbf{Y}_{l,n}^i$, respectively. Convolution kernels with size equal to $1 \times (M+1)$ are used to scan each row of $\mathbf{Y}_{l,n}^i$, and a $o \times 1$ vector is output by each kernel for r_n. We also add batch normalization (BN) after each LC layer to accelerate the training speed. By concatenating the outputs of k kernels for all regions, we get the output of the l-th LC layer, $\mathbf{Y}_{l+1}^i \in \mathbb{R}^{k \times o \times N}$, which is also the input of the $(l+1)$-th LC layer. After L LC layers, a 1×1 convolutional operation is applied to compress high-dimensional spatial features, and a high-level representation is obtained, denoted by $\mathbf{S}^i \in \mathbb{R}^{o \times N}$.

Next, the high-level representation is fed to a GRU proposed by [3]. Specially, each row of $\mathbf{S}^i$ (denoted by $\mathbf{S}_t^i$), containing high-level spatial features at time slot $t \in [t_{\tau+1-o}, t_\tau]$, is fed to the GRU in order. The computations of this component can be represented as

$$\mathbf{h}_\tau^i = GRU(\mathbf{S}_{\tau+1-o}^i, \mathbf{S}_{\tau+2-o}^i, \cdots, \mathbf{S}_\tau^i), \tag{2}$$

where $\mathbf{h}_\tau^i \in \mathbb{R}^{1 \times \kappa}$ is a high-level representation containing temporal dependencies of taxi demands among o successive time slots. Here, κ is a tunable parameter in the GRU, representing how many hidden nodes are used. Finally, a prediction of taxi demands at next time slot $t_{\tau+1}$, denoted by $\mathbf{f}^i = [f_1^i, f_2^i, \cdots, f_N^i]$, is output by a fully-connected (FC) layer with input $\mathbf{h}_\tau^i$. Overall, the prediction is obtained based on recent taxi demands, considering spatial correlations among adjacent regions and temporal dependencies among successive time slots.

3.3 Short/Long-Term Periodic Module

Short-term and long-term periodicity of taxi demands are considered to perform prediction in these two modules, respectively. As shown in Fig. 1, they share the same GRU-based structure, which takes a combination of taxi demands and external factor features as its input.

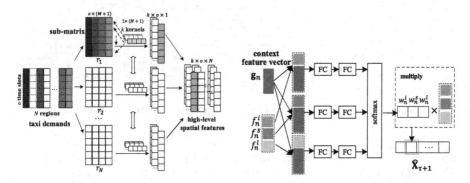

Fig. 2. Structure of a LC layer   **Fig. 3.** Structure of attention network

External factors in temporal dimension, like weather condition and holidays/weekends, have great impact on the periodicity of taxi demands. For example, we find that the hourly variation of taxi demands in weekends or holidays is significantly different from weekdays. Besides, the peak durations of taxi demands in a rainy day and a sunny day are also different. To capture the features of external factors, we employ an embedding method [5] to transform the values of these factors at each time slot to an *external feature vector*, denoted by $\mathbf{u}_t$. This embedding method is widely used to map categorical values into a low-dimensional vector.

Then, we concatenate the sequences of taxi demands with the external feature vectors in the corresponding time slots as the input of a GRU, and the output is transformed to a prediction of taxi demands at the next time slot by a FC layer. The computations of the short-term periodic module are defined as follows,

$$\mathbf{f}^s = FC(GRU(\mathbf{X}_{\tau+1-p\Delta_s} \oplus \mathbf{u}_{\tau+1-p\Delta_s}, \cdots, \mathbf{X}_{\tau+1-\Delta_s} \oplus \mathbf{u}_{\tau+1-\Delta_s})), \quad (3)$$

where $\oplus$ denotes the concatenation operation, and $\mathbf{f}^s = [f_1^s, f_2^s, \cdots, f_N^s]$. Similarly, the prediction output by the long-term periodic module can be computed as

$$\mathbf{f}^l = FC(GRU(\mathbf{X}_{\tau+1-q\Delta_l} \oplus \mathbf{u}_{\tau+1-q\Delta_l}, \cdots, \mathbf{X}_{\tau+1-\Delta_l} \oplus \mathbf{u}_{\tau+1-\Delta_l})), \quad (4)$$

where $\mathbf{f}^l = [f_1^l, f_2^l, \cdots, f_N^l]$.

3.4   Context-Aware Attention Module

Three predictions (i.e., $\mathbf{f}^i, \mathbf{f}^s$, and $\mathbf{f}^l$) have been output by the previous modules. In this subsection, we leverage attention mechanism to incorporate the three predictions by considering context information which is our first attempt. In what follows, we first introduce how to extract context features, and then explain our context-aware attention network structure.

As shown in Fig. 3, we construct a *context feature vector* for each region r_n at time slot $t_{\tau+1}$, denoted by $\mathbf{g}_n$. Here, we consider three main context factors, including weather condition at $t_{\tau+1}$, index of time slots $t_{\tau+1}$, and function of region r_n, which make a difference to taxi demands. Specially, we use the same method in feature extraction of external factors, to embed the index of time slots into a low-dimensional vector, and concatenate it with the vectors of weather condition and region function.

Next, we construct a perceptron to learn the attention should be paid to the three predictions of each region. Figure 3 presents the detailed structure of the perceptron, which is composed of two FC layers and a softmax operation. It takes the context feature vector and taxi demand predictions of region r_n at $t_{\tau+1}$ and outputs a 1×3 vector, denoted by $\mathbf{w}_n = [w_n^i, w_n^s, w_n^l]$. The three elements of the vector can be interpreted as the weights assigned to the predictions of r_n. Thus, we can obtain the final taxi demand prediction of r_n at $t_{\tau+1}$ by computing the weighted sum of its three predictions, i.e.,

$$\hat{X}_{n,\tau+1} = w_n^i \cdot f_n^i + w_n^s \cdot f_n^s + w_n^l \cdot f_n^l. \tag{5}$$

Note that the weights indicate that to what extent the predictions should be noticed.

3.5   Learning

Since the taxi demand prediction is a regression problem, we adopt mean square error as our loss function, and train our network model by minimizing the error between prediction $\hat{\mathbf{X}}_{\tau+1}$ and ground truth $\mathbf{X}_{\tau+1}$, i.e.,

$$L_{loss}(\Omega) = ||\mathbf{X}_{\tau+1} - \hat{\mathbf{X}}_{\tau+1}||_2^2, \tag{6}$$

where Ω is the set of all learnable parameters in our network model.

4   Experiments

4.1   Datasets

We first introduce the real-world datasets from New York City (NYC) used in our experiments. **Road Network Data.** The road network of NYC consists of 87,898 intersections and 91,649 road segments. In this paper, we partition NYC into 972 regions by road segments, as shown in Fig. 4 (The averaged number of taxi demands on weekdays are plotted, in which deeper color indicates more taxi demands). **Taxi Tripping Data.** An open dataset of taxi tripping records in NYC [1], which contains the detailed driving information like the pick-up and drop-off locations and timestamps of each trip. The taxi tripping data from Jan. 1, 2016 to Jun. 30, 2016 (130 weekdays and 52 weekends) are used, containing 87,866,988 trips. **POI Data.** We use a POI dataset with 670,916 POIs in NYC, classified into 16 different categories. **Meteorological and Holiday Data.** A dataset of meteorological records from Jan. 1, 2016 to Jun. 30, 2016 is also used in our work, containing weather condition (e.g., sunny and rainy), temperature, wind speed, and humidity information recorded every six hours. We also consider 10 statutory holidays in the United States.

4.2   Compared Methods

We compare our proposed model with the following baselines.

– **Historical Average (HA):** predicts taxi demands at the next time slot in each region by averaging the historical taxi demands at the same time slot.
– **Autoregressive Integrated Moving Average (ARIMA):** is a widely-used method for time-series prediction problems, which model the temporal dependencies by combining moving averages and autoregressive components.
– **Long Short Term Memory (LSTM):** is a variant of recurrent neural networks, which can effectively learn underlying dependencies in long and short term from a sequence data.
– **Diffusion Convolution Recurrent Neural Network (DCRNN)** [7]: integrates graph convolution into gated recurrent units to predict traffic flows on the road network. In this model, bidirectional graph random walk operation is employed, to extract the spatial dynamics of the traffic flows, and the temporal dynamics are captured by RNN.
– **Spatial-Temporal Graph Convolutional Networks (STGCN)** [13]: consists of several ST-Conv blocks, which are built with entirely convolutional layers, to tackle traffic prediction tasks. Specifically, each block is composed of graph convolution and gated temporal convolution, which jointly process graph-structured time series.

We also analyze the performance achieved by different modules of our model, to study their effectiveness in taxi demand prediction.

– **Instant Spatial-Temporal Module (ISTM):** we only use the instant spatial-temporal module, which includes LC layers and a GRU.
– **Short/Long-Term Periodic Module and Context-Aware Attention Module(PM+CAAM):** we only use two periodic modules with considering short-term and long-term periods. The outputs of the two modules are fused by the context-aware attention module.
– **Instant Module w/o LC, Short/Long-Term Periodic Module, and Context-Aware Attention Module (IM+PM+CAAM):** we use the instant spatial-temporal module without LC layers and the periodic modules to predict taxi demands respectively. The outputs of the three modules are fused by the context-aware attention module.

- **Instant Spatial-Temporal Module and Short/Long-Term Periodic Module (ISTM+PM):** we only use the instant spatial-temporal module and the periodic modules, and their outputs are fused by a weight tensor which is learned during network training.

4.3 Default Setting

The default values of parameters in our experiments are set up as follows. We set a time slot as 15 min. In the instant spatial-temporal module, six successive time slots are used, i.e., $o = 6$. In addition, we set $k = 16$, $M = 14$, and $L = 3$ in the default setting. In the short-term and long-term periodic modules, 4 and 2 periodic time slots are employed respectively, with intervals $\Delta_s = 96$ (a day) and $\Delta_l = 96 \times 7$ (a week). We embed weather condition, holiday condition, and weekend into a 1×3 vector, respectively. The numbers of hidden nodes in GRUs in the three modules are all set as 512. In the context-aware attention module, we embed index of time slots into a 1×5 vector.

We use the historical records during Jun. 2016 as testing data, and the rest records as training data. The performance achieved by each method is evaluated by root mean square error (RMSE) and mean absolute error (MAE). Besides, we adopt Adam optimization algorithm for training parameters. The learning rate of Adam is set as 10^{-4}, and the batch size during training is 64. We also employ early stop in our experiments, in which the number of rounds and the maximal epoch are set as 6 and 100, respectively. All experiments are conducted on a NVIDIA RTX2070 graphics card, and experimental results are the average of five runs under the same setting with different random seeds.

4.4 Experimental Results

Comparison with Baselines. Table 2 shows the performance achieved by our proposed model and the baselines under the default setting. We can easily find that our model achieves the lowest RMSE (3.209) and MAE (1.119), compared with all the baselines. Specifically, HA and ARIMA perform the poorest, which achieves 81.8% (46.1%) and 196.9% (145.0%) higher RMSE (MAE) than our proposed model, respectively. It demonstrates that deep neural networks (e.g., LSTM) can work effectively in urban data prediction. Furthermore, LSTM achieves worse performance than our model, as it only models the temporal dependencies in taxi demands. In the baselines, STGCN and DCRNN achieve good performance, which capture both spatial and temporal correlations. Compared with STGCN and DCRNN, our model achieves 8.4% (10.8%) and 9.0% (11.8%) lower RMSE (MAE), respectively.

Evaluation of Modules. We also evaluate the effectiveness of different modules in our model, which is shown in Table 3. It can be easily found that each module in our model works in terms of achieving better prediction performance. Specially, by comparing the results of ISTM and ISTM+PM, we confirm that the periodic modules work. As PM+CAAC achieves worse performance than our model, we can know that the instant spatial-temporal module is useful. The effectiveness of LC layers, which extract spatial correlations of taxi demands in different regions, is verified by comparing the results of IM+PM+CAAM and our model. Moreover, our model achieves better performance than ISTM+PM, which confirms the usefulness of the context-aware attention module.

5   Related Work

Model-Based Methods. Some model-based prediction methods are provided in the earlier works [6,8,9,15], to capture the intrinsic patterns of historical taxi demands. For example, Li et al. [6] model taxi demand prediction as a time series prediction problem, and an improved ARIMA method is developed to predict taxi demands by leveraging the temporal dependencies. Tong et al. [9] propose a unified linear regression model with high-dimensional features to predict taxi demands for each region. Due to a lack of nonlinear modeling capabilities, these methods usually have low prediction accuracy.

Fig. 4. Regions

Table 2. Performance comparison

Methods	RMSE	MAE
HA	5.835	1.635
ARIMA	9.530	2.742
LSTM	3.650	1.286
DCRNN	3.497	1.251
STGCN	3.479	1.240
CACRNN	**3.209**	**1.119**

Table 3. Evaluation of different components

Methods	RMSE	MAE
ISTM	3.464	1.280
PM+CAAM	3.974	1.302
IM+PM+CAAM	3.485	1.186
ISTM+PM	3.354	1.213
CACRNN	**3.209**	**1.119**

DNN-Based Methods. Recently, deep neural networks, such as convolutional neural networks (CNN) and recurrent neural networks (RNN), are widely used in taxi demand prediction, to capture spatial and temporal features. Fully-connected layers and residual networks are employed in [10] to automatically learn features to assist taxi demand prediction. Xu et al. [11] propose a LSTM-based sequential learning framework to model temporal dependencies of taxi demand in recent moments. Furthermore, Yao et al. [12] adopt CNN and LSTM to extract the spatial correlations among adjacent regions and temporal dependencies in a close period, respectively. External factors are further leveraged in [2] to improve the prediction accuracy. Chu et al. [4] try to incorporate the spatial-temporal dependencies and external factors by using fixed parameter matrixes learned during model training. However, all the above existing works are limited in incorporating different spatial-temporal features and external factors together, since fixed notice is paid to them without considering the impacts of contextual information.

6   Conclusion

In this paper, we propose a context-aware attention-based convolutional recurrent neural network to predict fine-grained taxi demands. We capture multi-view features, i.e., spatial correlations among adjacent regions, short-term periodicity, long-term periodicity, and impacts of external factors, by adopting the LC layers and GRUs. More important, we develop a context-aware attention network to incorporate the predictions of each region, by assigning them different weights according to contextual information. The weights indicate that to what extent the predictions should be noticed. Finally, comprehensive experiments are conducted based on real-world multi-source datasets. The results show that our method achieves 8.4% (10.8%) and 9.0% (11.8%) improvement in RMSE (MAE) over two state-of-the-art methods, STGCN and DCRNN.

Acknowledgment. This research is supported by National Natural Science Foundation of China (NSFC) under Grant No. 61802245 and the Shanghai Sailing Program under Grant No. 18YF1408200. This work is also supported by Science and Technology Commission Shanghai Municipality (STCSM) (No. 19511121002).

References

1. New York taxi dataset. https://www1.nyc.gov/site/tlc/about/tlc-trip-record-data.page
2. Bai, L., Yao, L., Kanhere, S.S., Yang, Z., Chu, J., Wang, X.: Passenger demand forecasting with multi-task convolutional recurrent neural networks. In: Yang, Q., Zhou, Z.-H., Gong, Z., Zhang, M.-L., Huang, S.-J. (eds.) PAKDD 2019. LNCS (LNAI), vol. 11440, pp. 29–42. Springer, Cham (2019). https://doi.org/10.1007/978-3-030-16145-3_3
3. Cho, K., et al.: Learning phrase representations using RNN encoder-decoder for statistical machine translation. In: Proceedings of the 2014 Conference on Empirical Methods in Natural Language Processing (EMNLP), pp. 1724–1734 (2014)
4. Chu, J., et al.: Passenger demand prediction with cellular footprints. In: 2018 15th Annual IEEE International Conference on Sensing, Communication, and Networking (SECON), pp. 1–9. IEEE (2018)
5. Gal, Y., Ghahramani, Z.: A theoretically grounded application of dropout in recurrent neural networks. In: Advances in Neural Information Processing Systems, pp. 1019–1027 (2016)
6. Li, X., et al.: Prediction of urban human mobility using large-scale taxi traces and its applications. Frontiers Comput. Sci. **6**(1), 111–121 (2012)
7. Li, Y., Yu, R., Shahabi, C., Liu, Y.: Diffusion convolutional recurrent neural network: data-driven traffic forecasting. In: International Conference on Learning Representations, ICLR 2018 (2018)

8. Moreira-Matias, L., Gama, J., Ferreira, M., Damas, L.: A predictive model for the passenger demand on a taxi network. In: 2012 15th International IEEE Conference on Intelligent Transportation Systems, pp. 1014–1019. IEEE (2012)
9. Tong, Y., et al.: The simpler the better: a unified approach to predicting original taxi demands based on large-scale online platforms. In: Proceedings of the 23rd ACM SIGKDD International Conference on Knowledge Discovery and Data Mining, pp. 1653–1662. ACM (2017)
10. Wang, D., Cao, W., Li, J., Ye, J.: DeepSD: supply-demand prediction for online car-hailing services using deep neural networks. In: 2017 IEEE 33rd International Conference on Data Engineering (ICDE), pp. 243–254. IEEE (2017)
11. Xu, J., Rahmatizadeh, R., Bölöni, L., Turgut, D.: Real-time prediction of taxi demand using recurrent neural networks. IEEE Trans. Intell. Transp. Syst. **19**(8), 2572–2581 (2017)
12. Yao, H., et al.: Deep multi-view spatial-temporal network for taxi demand prediction. In: Thirty-Second AAAI Conference on Artificial Intelligence (2018)
13. Yu, B., Yin, H., Zhu, Z.: Spatio-temporal graph convolutional networks: a deep learning framework for traffic forecasting. In: Proceedings of the 27th International Joint Conference on Artificial Intelligence, pp. 3634–3640. AAAI Press (2018)
14. Yuan, N.J., Zheng, Y., Xie, X.: Segmentation of urban areas using road networks. MSR-TR-2012-65, Technical report (2012)
15. Zhang, L., Chen, C., Wang, Y., Guan, X.: Exploiting taxi demand hotspots based on vehicular big data analytics. In: 2016 IEEE 84th Vehicular Technology Conference, VTC-Fall, pp. 1–5. IEEE (2016)

Prototype Similarity Learning
for Activity Recognition

Lei Bai[1]([✉]), Lina Yao[1], Xianzhi Wang[2], Salil S. Kanhere[1], and Yang Xiao[3]

[1] University of New South Wales, Sydney, Australia
baisanshi@gmail.com, {lina.yao,salil.kanhere}@unsw.edu.au
[2] University of Technology Sydney, Sydney, Australia
xianzhi.wang@uts.edu.au
[3] Xidian University, Xi'an, China
yxiao_052126@stu.xidian.edu.cn

Abstract. Human Activity Recognition (HAR) plays an irreplaceable role in various applications such as security, gaming, and assisted living. Recent studies introduce deep learning to mitigate the manual feature extraction (i.e., data representation) efforts and achieve high accuracy. However, there are still challenges in learning accurate representations for sensory data due to the weakness of representation modules and the subject variances. We propose a scheme called Distance-based HAR from Ensembled spatial-temporal Representations (DHARER) to address above challenges. The idea behind DHARER is straightforward—the same activities should have similar representations. We first learn representations of the input sensory segments and latent prototype representations of each class, using a Convolution Neural Network (CNN)-based dual-stream representation module; then the learned representations are projected to activity types by measuring their similarity to the learned prototypes. We have conducted extensive experiments under a strict subject-independent setting on three large-scale datasets to evaluate the proposed scheme, and our experimental results demonstrate superior performance of DHARER to several state-of-the-art methods.

Keywords: Activity recognition · Deep learning · Similarity comparison · Spatial-temporal correlations

1 Introduction

Human activity recognition (HAR) is a significant step towards human computer interaction and enables a series of promising applications such as assistant living, skills training, health monitoring, and robotics [6]. Existing HAR techniques are either video- or sensor-based. In particular, sensor-based HAR aims at inferring human activities from a set of sensors (e.g., accelerometer, gyroscope, and magnetometer), which generate data streams over time. This approach is generally known to have several advantages over video-based HAR including: ease of deployment, low cost and less invasive from a privacy perspective [7].

© Springer Nature Switzerland AG 2020
H. W. Lauw et al. (Eds.): PAKDD 2020, LNAI 12084, pp. 649–661, 2020.
https://doi.org/10.1007/978-3-030-47426-3_50

Previous studies on sensor-based HAR focus on designing powerful hand-crafted features in time (e.g., mean, variance) and frequency domain (e.g., power spectral density) to represent segments of raw sensory streams [9]. Traditional machine learning models such as Support Vector Machine (SVM) and Random Forest are employed to project the feature vector to activity labels [2]. The performance of these methods normally depends on the effectiveness of the extracted features where are heuristic, task-independent, and not specially designed for HAR [12]. Since designing powerful task-specific features require significant domain knowledge, and are labour intensive and time consuming, recent research introduces deep learning methods, which have exceptional data representation ability to expedite feature extraction. These works utilize deep neural networks, such as Convolution Neural Networks (CNN) [5,16] and Long-Short Term Memory (LSTM) [8,11], as feature extractors to learn the representation of the input sensory segments automatically, and then map the representation to labels using another neural network (normally a basic fully-connected layer).

Although deep learning methods have achieved significant progress, it is still difficult to learn accurate representations for the input segments due to the complex spatial correlations among sensors and temporal correlations between time periods. Considering the sensitivity of neural networks to noise, the biases in the representations further prevent neural network-based classifiers from making correct activity classification. In addition, subject variances inherently exist in HAR, where people tend to perform activities that are heavily influenced by personal characteristics, such as gender, height, weight, and strength. For example, men usually perform activities at a larger magnitude than women. Such divergence introduces deviations to the representations among subjects and thus prevent the model from getting accurate classification for new subjects (haven't appeared in the training set).

We propose to solve this problem from three perspectives: 1) Representation Stage: It is necessary to jointly capture the spatial and temporal correlations to achieve more accurate feature extraction. 2) Classification Stage: Intuitively, representations of the same activities should be similar. Therefore, using a distance metric which can infer the type of an input segment from labels of the most similar prototype is likely to make the classification module less susceptible to the preciseness of the data representations (compared to neural network based classification). 3) Training Stage: the subject variance can be explicitly modeled and minimized in the training stage to enhance the generalization ability of the approach.

The main contributions of this work are as follows:

- We propose a novel end-to-end deep learning framework for HAR to deal with the bias and deviations in the representations due to inaccurate learning and subject-variances.
- We design a dual-stream CNN network to jointly capture the spatial and temporal correlations in the multivariate sensory data, which can achieve more accurate representation and decrease the bias.

- We introduce a distance-based classification module to classify the segments by comparing their similarity to the learned prototypes of each class in the representation space, which is less susceptible to representation bias. We also introduce a cross-subject training strategy to train the module for minimizing the deviation caused by subject-variance.
- We conduct extensive experiments on three large-scale datasets under a strict subject-independent setting and demonstrate the superior performance of our model in new subjects. Our method consistently outperforms state-of-the-art methods by at least 3%.

2   Related Works

The recent work in HAR has moved towards designing deep learning models for more accurate recognition, given the exceptional representation ability of deep learning techniques. Most deep learning-based HAR methods focus on capturing the temporal correlations in the sensory streams. Jian Bo et al. [16] tackle the problem with convolutional neural networks, in which the convolution and pooling filters are designed along the temporal dimensions to process the readings of all sensors. Their work can capture long-term temporal correlation by stacking multiple CNN layers. Ordóñez et al. [12] further extend this model to Deep-ConvLSTM by integrating LSTM after CNN layers. The proposed DeepConvLSTM framework contains four CNN layers and two LSTM layers to capture the short-term and long-term temporal correlations, separately. One drawback of the DeepConvLSTM is that it potentially assumes the signals in all time steps are relevant and contribute equally to the target activity, which may not true. Murahari et al. [11] propose to solve the problem by integrating the temporal attention module to DeepConvLSTM. The attention module aligns the output vector at the last time step with other vectors at earlier steps to learn a relative importance score for each previous time step. Different from these methods, Guan et al. [8] propose to achieve more robust data representation ability with the ensemble method. They employ the Epoch-wise Bagging scheme in the training procedure and select multiple LSTMs in different training epochs as basic learners to form a powerful model. However, these methods neglect the spatial correlations among the different sensors, which cannot represent the sensory data precisely. Besides, they directly classify the learned representations to activity type with basic NN-based classifier, which could lead to misguided result due to the learning deviation and subject variances in the representations.

3   Problem Definition

The typical scenario for sensor-based HAR involves multiple devices attached to different parts of the human body. Each device carries multiples sensors, e.g., an inertial measurement unit (IMU) typically contains nine sensors: 3-axis accelerometer, 3-axis gyroscope, and 3-axis magnetometer. In this work,

652   L. Bai et al.

we consider each 3-axis device as three sensors for capturing spatial correlations, e.g., 3-axis accelerometer contains x-accelerometer, y-accelerometer, and z-accelerometer. Thus, an IMU with 3-axis accelerometer, 3-axis gyroscope, and 3-axis magnetometer contains nine sensors. Let M be the total number of sensors embedded in multiple body-worn devices, and s_i ($1 \leq i \leq M$) be the reading from the i_{th} sensor. Then, at each time point, the sensors, together, generate a vector of readings: $s = [s_1, s_2, ... , s_M]^T$. Thus, a segment with the sliding window size T can be represented by $Seg = [s_1, s_2, ... , s_T]$.

Let there be N potential activities to be recognized, $\mathcal{C} = \{c_1, c_2, ... , c_N\}$, HAR aims to learn a function, $\mathcal{F}(Seg, \bullet)$, to infer the correct activity label for the given segment, where $\bullet$ represents all learnable parameters.

4   Methodology

In this section, we elaborate our proposed methods for more accurate HAR, which contains three components: a dual-stream representation module to learn more accurate representations of the input segment, a distance-based classification module to recognize human activities, and a cross-subject training strategy to minimizing the subject-divergence.

4.1   Dual-Stream Representation Module

We first introduce the CNN-based dual-stream representation module (DARM) (shown in Fig. 1), which contains a spatial CNN network and a temporal CNN network. The two CNN networks learn two sub-representations capturing the spatial correlations and temporal correlations within the input segment, respectively, which can be regarded as an image of $M \times T$ (as denoted in Sect. 3). Then the two sub-representations are merged by summing to get the final joint representation of the input segment. Compared to the previous data representation models, the dual-stream representation module is more accurate by encapsulating both spatial and temporal correlations jointly. Besides, it is more light-weight and easy-to-train compared to LSTM-based approaches [8,11,12].

As shown in Fig. 1, the overall architectures of the temporal CNN and spatial CNN are the same. Both of them contain three consecutive CNN blocks to extract prominent patterns in the segment from different perspectives. The difference between the temporal CNN and spatial CNN mainly lays in the size of CNN kernels. More specifically, the temporal CNN applies the CNN kernels with size $1 \times k_T^l$ in the l_{th} T-CNN block, which operate the data along the time axis to capture the temporal correlations between different time points. As a contrast, the spatial CNN applies the CNN kernels with size $k_S^l \times k_S^l$ in the l_{th} S-CNN block to capture the spatial correlations between different sensor series. Besides the kernel size, either of the T-CNN block and the S-CNN block comprises a convolutional layer with a rectified linear units (ReLu) activation function, a max-pooling layer, and a batch-normalization layer. The convolutional layer performs the main function of pattern extraction, which employs several kernels

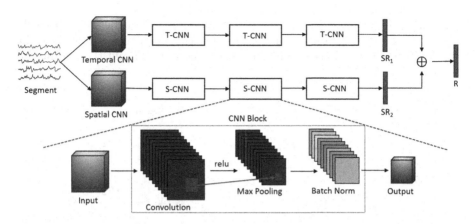

Fig. 1. The proposed dual-stream data representation module based on CNN networks

of the same shape to filter the input data X and extract meaningful patterns. We calculate a convolution layer with the ReLu activation function as follows:

$$X_j^{l+1} = \sigma(\sum_{i=1}^{i=F^l} W_{i,j} \times X_i^l + b_j^l)$$ (1)

where X_i^l is the i_{th} channel of the input for the l_{th} convolutional layer, F^l is the feature map (channel) numbers, $W_{i,j}$ is the j_{th} kernel, b_j^l is the bias and $\sigma(\cdot)$ is the ReLu function defined as: $\sigma(X^{l+1}) = max(0, X^{l+1})$. Then, the max pooling layer is employed as the sampling method to down-sampling the extracted representations while keeping the most protrusive patterns. We further integrate the batch-normalization layer to the CNN block to achieve faster and more stable training. The batch-normalization layer normalizes the layer's input with batch mean and batch variance to force the input of every layer to have approximately the same distribution [10].

4.2   Distance-Based Classification Module

Based on the representation module, we then propose to learn to recognition human activities by distance based classification module (DCAM) (Fig. 2), which is based on the Prototypical Networks [14]. Different from the general HAR process, which first learns a representation for the input segment and then maps the representation to the corresponding activity with classifiers, DCAM first learns a representation for the input segment and a latent prototype representation (a vector) for each class together. The prototypes are used to represent the embedding of each class. Then, DCAM recognizes the segment representation by comparing its similarity with the prototypes, which follows the same idea with the nearest neighbour methods. For clarity, we denote the data used to learning the prototypes as the support set and the segments to be recognized as queries (see Fig. 2). In the training period, both support set and queries come from the training dataset. In the testing phase, we extract the support set from the training dataset and the queries from the testing dataset to avoid the information leakage.

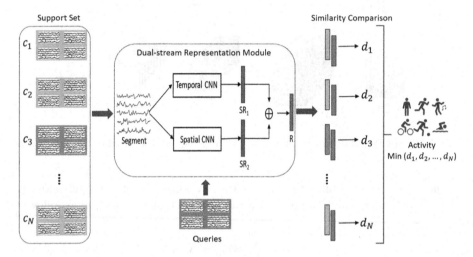

Fig. 2. The proposed distanced-based classification module

To learn the prototypes, we randomly select N_s samples from each class to form the support set for a batch of queries. Then, these support samples are fed into our dual-stream representation module to get their representations. The prototype of each class is the mean vector of the learned representations in the support set belonging to the corresponding class. Take $f(\cdot)$ denote the transformation of representation module, X_i^j as the i_{th} support sample in the j_{th} class, then the prototype of class j can be calculated as:

$$C_j = \frac{1}{N_s} \sum_{i=1}^{N_s} f(X_i^j) \tag{2}$$

Similarly, the query instances are also mapped to the embedding space by our representation module. DCAM can then learn a distribution of a query x over classes based on the softmax of its distances to the learned prototypes $\{C_1, C_2, ..., C_N\}$ in the representation space [14]:

$$p_f(y = c_j|x) = \frac{exp(-d(f(x), C_j)}{\sum_{j'=1}^{N} exp(-d(f(x), C_{j'}))} \tag{3}$$

where $d(\cdot, \cdot)$ is a distance function to measure the similarity of two given vectors. There are multiple widely used choices for calculating distance in the literature, such as the Cosine distance, Mahalanobis distance, Euclidean distance and so on.

In this work, we employ the squared Euclidean distance as the distance function as it is proved to be more effective than others in [14].

The whole model can be easily trained in an end-to-end manner by minimizing the negative log-probability $-log(p_f(y = c_j|x))$ according to the true label c_j of the query segment x via back-propagation strategy. Thus, We define the loss function as follows:

$$\mathcal{L}_x = d(f(x), C_j) + log(\sum_{j'=1}^{N} exp(-d(f(x), C_{j'}))) \tag{4}$$

4.3 Cross-Subject Training

We further propose the cross-subject training strategy to alleviate the influence of subject variances to the representations. Instead of random sampling support samples and queries from the training set, our cross-subject training strategy intentionally select queries from one subject and support set from other subjects for each batch during the training process. Thus, we can decrease the divergence between different subjects in the representation space through training iteration by minimizing the distance between queries representations and prototypes, which are learned from different subjects separately. Besides, the cross-subject training strategy also harmonizes the training stage and testing stage under the subject-independent setting, where the support set from the training dataset and queries from the testing dataset come from different subject inherently. Algorithm 1 describes the method's overall training procedure.

Algorithm 1. Training and Optimization

Require: the training dataset $L = \{(X, Y, U)\}$ (U is the subjects set in training), number of samples in queries N_q, number of samples in the support set for each class N_s, maximum training iteration $Iter$.

1: random initialize the network parameters
2: **for** $iter = 0$; $iter < Iter$ **do**
3:     randomly choose query subjects u_i from U
4:     load N_q query samples from subject u_i as $\mathcal{Q}$
5:     load N_s support samples for each class from $U - u_i$ as support set $\mathcal{S}$
6:     calculate representations of the queries and support samples with DARM
7:     **for** c_i in $\{c_1, c_2, ..., c_n\}$ **do**
8:         calculate prototype C_i of class c_i according to Equation 2 with represented $\mathcal{S}$
9:     **end for**
10:     Init loss $\mathcal{L} = 0$
11:     **for** x, y in represented $\mathcal{Q}$ **do**
12:         calculate loss $\mathcal{L}_x$ with Equation 4
13:         update loss with $\mathcal{L} = \mathcal{L} + \mathcal{L}_x$
14:     **end for**
15:     Back-propagate $\mathcal{L}$ and update the network parameters
16: **end for**

Table 1. Statistics of datasets (# denotes the "number").

Dataset	Subject#	Activity#	Frequency	Window	Devices#	Sensors#	Sample#
MHEALTH	10	12	50 Hz	20 (0.4 s)	3	23	34 097
PAMAP2	8	12	100 Hz	20 (0.2 s)	3	36	191 309
UCIDSADS	8	19	25 Hz	20 (0.8 s)	5	45	113 848

5 Experiments

5.1 Datasets

While several datasets are publicly available for HAR, many of them are limited in the scale of subjects (e.g. the Skoda dataset [15] only has one subject) or activities (e.g. the UCI dataset [1] only contains six activities). To evaluate the performance of our method in classifying activities and dealing with subject divergence more comprehensively, we select the following three datasets with relatively more activities and subjects:

MHEALTH Dataset. This dataset [3] contains body motion and vital signs for ten volunteers of diverse profiles. Each subject performed 12 activities in an out-of-lab environment with no constraints.

PAMAP2 Dataset. The PAMAP2 dataset [13] was designed to benchmark daily physical activities. It contains data collected from nine subjects related to 18 daily activities such as vacuum cleaning, ironing, and rope jumping.

UCIDSADS Dataset. The UCIDSADS dataset [4] was specially designed for daily and sports activities. It comprises motion sensor data of 19 sports activities such as walking on a treadmill and exercising on a stepper. Each activity was performed by eight subjects for 5 min without constraints.

Data Pre-processing. For the MHEALTH and UCIDSADS dataset, we use all the data from all subjects for experiments. For the PAMAP2 dataset, we remove six activities (watching TV, computer work, car driving, folding laundry, house cleaning, and playing soccer) as they are only executed by one subject. As a result, 12 activities from eight subjects are kept for our experiments in PAMAP2. Only the basic data segmentation and normalization methods are applied to the dataset. More specially, we first divide the raw sensory data streams into small segments with a fixed-sized sling window and an overlap of 50% for all the three dataset. Each window contains 20 time points, resulting the window lengths for MHEALTH, PAMAP2, and UCIDSADS are 0.4 s, 0.2 s, and 0.8 s, respectively. Then, we normalize the segments with the standard normalization methods. Table 1 gives the statistics of the three datasets.

5.2 Evaluation Settings

The main parameters in our evaluation includes network parameters and training parameters. For the temporal CNN part, we use 128 kernels in all three layers shaped $(1 \times 5) \rightarrow (1 \times 5) \rightarrow (1 \times 2)$ respectively. For the spatial CNN part, we user 128 kernels in all three layers shaped $(6 \times 5) \rightarrow (6 \times 5) \rightarrow (2 \times 2)$, $(5 \times 5) \rightarrow (5 \times 5) \rightarrow (5 \times 2)$, and $(6 \times 5) \rightarrow (7 \times 5) \rightarrow (5 \times 2)$ for MHEALTH, PAMAP2 and UCIDSADS respectively. In learning the queries representations, we set the Batch_size (N_q) to 240 to accelerate the training speed and the length of the learned segment representations is 64. For learning the prototypes, we sample five samples from each class (N_s) as the support set in each iteration. We initialize the network parameters with Xavier Normal initialization and optimize them by Adam optimizer at the learning rate of 0.0005 for all three datasets.

To thoroughly evaluate the performance of our proposed model, we assess it iteratively with LOSO protocol on every subject separately. In each experiment, we train the model from scratch and test the model with one subject's data. Finally, we will get $subject_{number}$ results for each model. Considering the space limitation, we mainly report the mean result, worst result, and best result of all subjects as $mean[worst, best]$, which reflects both the overall performance and the generalization ability of a model. Besides, the weighted Precision (P_w) and weighted F_{score} (F_w) are used as the performance metrics for comparison.

5.3 Overall Comparison

To verify the overall performance of the proposed model, we compare our method with the following baseline and SOTAs: 1) the support vector machine (SVM), 2) MC-CNN [16], 3) b-LSTM-S [9], 4) ConvLSTM [12], 5) Ensem-LSTM [8], 6) AttConvLSTM [11], 7) Multi-Agent [5]. These SOTAs vary from CNN-based, LSTM-based to CNN-LSTM hybrid model and also include ensemble and attention methods. We replicated each method with the same settings as introduced in the original papers, except for the data pre-processing steps, where we use the same window size and overlap as ours. We also evaluate them with the LOSO evaluation protocol iteratively to achieve a fair and thorough comparison.

Table 2 shows the experimental results, from which we can observe the following points: 1) all the SOTAs deep learning models perform better than SVM, showing the superior ability of deep learning models in extracting complex nonlinear temporal patterns in the sensory streams. 2) the MC-CNN model outperforms LSTM-based methods in the MHEALTH dataset and PAMAP2 dataset, but fails in the UCIDSADS dataset. Recall the window length of each dataset, we interpret the results as the admirable ability of temporal CNN in capturing accurate temporal correlations with only a short time period of data. As a contrast, LSTM-based methods need data from longer period of time. 3) the complex reinforcement learning-based Multi-agent model does not work very well as reported in [5], where only six basic activities are selected for experiments. The result indicates the difficulty of selecting important modalities for numerous and more complex activities. 4) Last but not the least, our method consistently beats all the comparison models on three datasets with a significant margin. The mean recognition F_{score} achieves 4.52%, 4.78%, and 3.17% absolute improvements over the best SOTA in the MHEALTH, PAMAP2 and UCIDSADS datasets, respectively. The comparison demonstrates the effectiveness of our proposed model.

Table 2. Overall comparison with SOTAs on three datasets. Each cell consists of the mean score of a method in one evaluation metric, followed by the corresponding minimum and maximum scores in brackets. The best performance values are in bold.

MHEALTH	Method	SVM	MC-CNN	Bi-LSTM-S	ConvLSTM
	P_w	79.53 [65.29, 94.47]	93.51 [84.11, 98.18]	87.16 [76.51, 95.41]	89.37 [81.48, 99.21]
	F_w	76.73 [59.33, 92.80]	92.17 [85.34, 97.98]	87.90 [79.01, 94.85]	89.89 [81.49, 99.22]
	Method	Ensem_LSTM	AttConvLSTM	Multi-Agent	DHARER
	P_w	84.81 [74.57, 98.59]	89.96 [78.30, 98.21]	91.87 [80.51, 98.06]	**97.05** **[94.31, 99.59]**
	F_w	84.64 [70.32, 98.55]	90.75 [80.36, 98.17]	91.20 [81.12, 98.01]	**96.69** **[93.55, 99.58]**
PAMAP2	Method	SVM	MC-CNN	Bi-LSTM-S	ConvLSTM
	P_w	70.77 [41.69, 88.76]	80.64 [57.65, 93.82]	71.12 [29.01, 92.21]	73.04 [36.42, 92.95]
	F_w	68.11 [36.72, 86.68]	78.05 [52.09, 93.37]	68.65 [32.34, 91.94]	72.36 [41.67, 92.65]
	Method	Ensem_LSTM	AttConvLSTM	Multi-Agent	DHARER
	P_w	73.90 [36.88, 90.93]	73.92 [50.40, 85.02]	73.35 [36.22, 89.88]	**83.32** **[60.25, 94.38]**
	F_w	71.98 [42.09, 88.84]	71.83 [44.79, 86.58]	71.39 [31.70, 87.14]	**82.83** **[56.09, 94.32]**
UCIDSADS	Method	SVM	MC-CNN	Bi-LSTM-S	ConvLSTM
	P_w	70.60 [63.19, 78.84]	87.18 [64.01, 95.42]	89.72 [74.29, 95.25]	89.58 [79.88, 95.27]
	F_w	67.74 [60.25, 78.33]	85.52 [66.57, 94.53]	87.73 [75.36, 93.28]	88.42 [77.95, 94.08]
	Method	Ensem_LSTM	AttConvLSTM	Multi-Agent	DHARER
	P_w	84.06 [72.65, 93.51]	88.24 [74.57, 94.78]	87.45 [79.48, 92.91]	**93.72** **[89.71, 96.59]**
	F_w	81.09 [71.48, 90.19]	86.75 [74.64, 94.22]	84.26 [73.03, 90.70]	**91.59** **[82.77, 96.22]**

5.4   Ablation and Case Study

We further conduct an ablation study to evaluate the performance of the basic modules in our method. Figure 3 gives the weighted F_{score} of the spatial CNN module with two-layer MLP as classifier (S-CNN), temporal CNN module with two-layer MLP as classifier(T-CNN), our dual-stream representation module with two-layer MLP as classifier (Dual-CNN), and our dual-stream representation module with distance-based classification module (DHARER) on three datasets. We can observe that the dual-CNN is better than both S-CNN and T-CNN, indicating that ensembling T-CNN and S-CNN to capture both spatial and temporal correlations is useful. Besides, our DHARER further improves the dual-CNN significantly, which demonstrates the effectiveness of our distance-based classification module and the cross-subject training strategy.

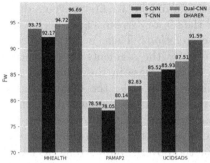
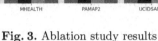
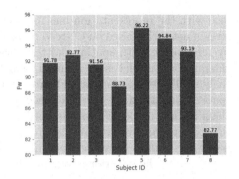

Fig. 3. Ablation study results

Fig. 4. Results of all subjects on UCIDSADS dataset

Considering the space limitation, we only shows the case study results on the UCIDSADS dataset in Fig. 4 and Fig. 5, which present the testing weighted F_{score} for each subject and the confusion matrix of subject 5 (achieve best performance among UCIDSADS) and subject 8 (achieve worst performance). As we can see, the results of different subjects and different activities vary seriously. Our method can achieve impressive performance on some subjects and most of the activities. But there still exist some hard-to-distinguish subjects and hard-to-distinguish activities (e.g. activity 7 which represents standing in an elevator still). In our future work, we will focus on improving the model's performance on these hard-to-distinguish subjects/activities.

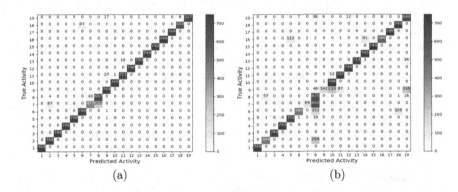

(a)   (b)

Fig. 5. Confusion Matrix of subject 5 (a) and subject 8 (b) from UCIDSADS dataset

6   Conclusion

In this work, we propose DHARER – a novel human activity recognition scheme based on similarity comparison and ensembled convolutional neural networks to deal with the representation bias and deviation problem. We first design a dual-stream networks based on CNN to represent the sensory streams more accurately by integrating both spatial and temporal correlations. Then, a distance-based classification model is introduced, which classify the segments by comparing their similarity to the learned prototypes of each class in the representation space. Comparing to the NN-based classification module, the distance-based classification model is less susceptible to the bias in the segment representations. Moreover, we propose the cross-subject training strategy to deal with the deviations caused by subject-variance. Extensive experiments on three datasets demonstrate the superior of our proposed method over several strong SOTAs.

Acknowledgements. This research was partially supported by grant ONRG NICOPN 2909-19-1-2009.

References

1. Anguita, D., et al.: A public domain dataset for human activity recognition using smartphones. In: ESANN (2013)
2. Bai, L., et al.: Automatic device classification from network traffic streams of internet of things. In: IEEE 43rd Conference on Local Computer Networks (LCN). IEEE (2018)
3. Banos, O., et al.: mHealthDroid: a novel framework for agile development of mobile health applications. In: Pecchia, L., Chen, L.L., Nugent, C., Bravo, J. (eds.) IWAAL 2014. LNCS, vol. 8868, pp. 91–98. Springer, Cham (2014). https://doi.org/10.1007/978-3-319-13105-4_14
4. Barshan, B., Yüksek, M.C.: Recognizing daily and sports activities in two open source machine learning environments using body-worn sensor units. Comput. J. **57**(11), 1649–1667 (2014)
5. Chen, K., et al.: Multi-agent attention activity recognition. In: IJCAI (2019)
6. Chen, K., et al.: Deep learning for sensor-based human activity recognition: overview, challenges and opportunities. arXiv preprint arXiv:2001.07416 (2020)
7. Davoudi, H., Li, X.-L., Nhut, N.M., Krishnaswamy, S.P.: Activity recognition using a few label samples. In: Tseng, V.S., Ho, T.B., Zhou, Z.-H., Chen, A.L.P., Kao, H.-Y. (eds.) PAKDD 2014. LNCS (LNAI), vol. 8443, pp. 521–532. Springer, Cham (2014). https://doi.org/10.1007/978-3-319-06608-0_43
8. Guan, Y., Plötz, T.: Ensembles of deep LSTM learners for activity recognition using wearables. Proc. ACM Interact. Mob. Wearable Ubiquit. Technol. **1**(2), 11 (2017)
9. Hammerla, N.Y., et al.: Deep, convolutional, and recurrent models for human activity recognition using wearables. In: IJCAI, pp. 1533–1540. AAAI Press (2016)
10. Ioffe, S., Szegedy, C.: Batch normalization: accelerating deep network training by reducing internal covariate shift. In: ICML, pp. 448–456 (2015)
11. Murahari, V.S., Plötz, T.: On attention models for human activity recognition. In: The 2018 ACM International Symposium on Wearable Computers. ACM (2018)
12. Ordóñez, F., Roggen, D.: Deep convolutional and LSTM recurrent neural networks for multimodal wearable activity recognition. Sensors **16**(1), 115 (2016)
13. Reiss, A., Stricker, D.: Introducing a new benchmarked dataset for activity monitoring. In: 16th International Symposium on Wearable Computers. IEEE (2012)

14. Snell, J., et al.: Prototypical networks for few-shot learning. In: NIPS. pp. 4077–4087 (2017)
15. Stiefmeier, T., et al.: Wearable activity tracking in car manufacturing. IEEE Pervasive Comput. **2**, 42–50 (2008)
16. Yang, J., et al.: Deep convolutional neural networks on multichannel time series for human activity recognition. In: IJCAI (2015)

Case-Sensitive Neural Machine Translation

Xuewen Shi[1,2], Heyan Huang[1,2], Ping Jian[1,2(✉)], and Yi-Kun Tang[1,2]

[1] School of Computer Science and Technology, Beijing Institute of Technology,
Beijing 100081, China
{xwshi,hhy63,pjian,tangyk}@bit.edu.cn
[2] Beijing Engineering Research Center of High Volume Language Information
Processing and Cloud Computing Applications, Beijing, China

Abstract. Even as an important lexical information for Latin languages, word case is often ignored in machine translation. According to observations, the translation performance drops significantly when we introduce case-sensitive evaluation metrics. In this paper, we introduce two types of case-sensitive neural machine translation (NMT) approaches to alleviate the above problems: i) adding case tokens into the decoding sequence, and ii) adopting case prediction to the conventional NMT. Our proposed approaches incorporate case information to the NMT decoder by jointly learning target word generation and word case prediction. We compare our approaches with multiple kinds of baselines including NMT with naive case-restoration methods and analyze the impacts of various setups on our approaches. Experimental results on three typical translation tasks (Zh-En, En-Fr, En-De) show that our proposed methods lead to the improvements up to 2.5, 1.0 and 0.5 in case-sensitive BLEU scores respectively. Further analyses also illustrate the inherent reasons why our approaches lead to different improvements on different translation tasks.

Keywords: Natural language processing · Neural machine translation · Case-sensitive

1 Introduction

In the real world, many of the natural language texts that are written in Latin language are case sensitive, such as English, French, German, etc. For many natural language processing (NLP) tasks, case information is an important feature for algorithms to distinguish sentence structures, identify the part-of-speech of a word, and recognize named entities. However, most existing machine translation approaches pay little attention to the capitalization correctness of the generated words, which does not meet the needs of practical requirements and may introduce noise to downstream NLP applications [9,20].

In fact, there is a contradiction in the training corpus preprocessing process: using lowercased corpus can reduce the expansion of the vocabulary but neglecting some morphology information, while keeping the original morphological form

H. W. Lauw et al. (Eds.): PAKDD 2020, LNAI 12084, pp. 662–674, 2020.
https://doi.org/10.1007/978-3-030-47426-3_51

Chinese (pinyin)	English
zhè shì yī kē pígguǒ.	This is an **apple**.
zhè shì yī kuài pígguǒ shǒubiǎo.	This is an **Apple** Watch.

Fig. 1. Two example of Zh-En translation. The Chinese side is presented in pinyin. "*pígguǒ*" and "**apple**" are aligned words pair, which are same in the source side but written in different case in the target side in our examples. The contradiction is that using lowercased "apple" in the second example will lose the information of a proper noun, while using a individual word "**Apple**" will lose the semantic connection with the parallel pair (*"pígguǒ"* "apple").

Table 1. Case insensitive/sensitive BLEU scores on Zh-En translation. Δ represents the reduced BLEU scores compared to the "insensitive". *NRC* is a rule-based case restoring method and more experiment setup details are described in Sect. 5.2.

Models	Insensitive	Sensitive (Δ)
Regular case	43.23	**41.45 (−1.78)**
True-case	43.08	40.02 (−3.06)
True-case + *NRC*	43.08	41.22 (−1.86)
Lowercase	**43.49**	28.49 (−15.00)
Lowercase + *NRC*	**43.49**	30.02 (−12.49)

will increase the vocabulary and lose its connection with the lowercase form of the word. Figure 1 gives an example to illustrate this contradiction. Using true-cased corpus seems to balance the unnecessary increasing vocabulary and the missing morphology information of word case. However, re-storing cases from true-cased corpus is not as easy as the reverse process. Table 1 shows that using corpus in lowercase and regular case gets the highest case-insensitive and case-sensitive BLEU scores respectively, which reflects the difficulty of case restoration.

In this paper, we introduce case-sensitive neural machine translation (NMT) approaches to alleviate the above problems. In our approaches, we apply lower-cased vocabulary to both the source input and target output side in the NMT model, and the model is trained to jointly learn to generate translation and distinguish the capitalization of the generated words. During the decoding step, the model predicts the case of the output word while generating the translation.

Specifically, we proposed two kinds of methods to this extent: i) mixing case tokens into lowercased corpus to indicate the real case of the adjacent word; ii) expanding NMT model architecture with an additional network layer that performances case prediction. We evaluate on pairs of linguistically disparate corpora in three translation tasks: Chinese-English (Zh-En), English-German (En-De) and English-French (En-Fr), and observe that the proposed techniques improve translation quality on case-sensitive BLEU [16]. We also study the model performances on case-restoration tasks and experimental results show that our proposed methods lead to improvements on P, R and F_1 scores.

2   Related Work

Recently, neural machine translation (NMT) with encoder-decoder framework [6] has shown promising results on many language pairs [8,21], and incorporating linguistic knowledge into neural machine translation has been extensively studied [7,12,17]. However, the procedure of NMT decoding rarely considers the case correctness of the generated words, and there are approaches performing case restoration on the machine generated texts [9,20].

Recent efforts have demonstrated that incorporating linguistic information can be useful in NMT [7,12,15,17,22,23]. Since the source sentence is definitive and easy to attach extra information, it is a straightforward way to improve the translation performance by using the source side features [12,17]. For example, Sennrich and Haddow incorporate linguistic features to improve the NMT performance by appending feature vectors to word embeddings [17], and the source side hierarchical syntax structures are also used for achieving promising improvement [7,12]. It is uncertain to leverage target syntactic information for NMT as target words in the real decoding process. Niehues and Cho apply multi-task learning where the encoder of the NMT model is trained to produce multiple tasks such as POS tagging and named-entity recognition into NMT models [15]. There are also works that directly model the syntax of the target sentence during decoding [22–24].

Word case information is a kind of lexical morphology which is definitive and easy to be obtained without any additional annotation and parsing of the training corpus. Recently, a joint decoder is proposed for predicting words as well as their cases synchronously [25], which shares a similar spirit with a part of our approaches (see Sect. 4.2). The main distinction of our approaches is that we propose two series of case-sensitive NMT and study various model setups.

3   Neural Machine Translation

Given a source sentence $x = \{x_1, x_2, ..., x_{T_x}\}$ and a target sentence $y = \{y_1, y_2, ..., y_{T_y}\}$, most of popular neural machine translation approaches [3,8,21] directly model the conditional probability:

$$p(y|x; \theta) = \prod_{t=1}^{T} p(y_t|y_{<t}, x; \theta),$$ (1)

where $y_{<t}$ is the partial translation before decoding step t and θ is a set of parameters of the NMT model.

In this paper, the proposed approaches make scarcely assumptions about the specific NMT model, and it can be applied to any popular encoder-decoder based NMT model architecture [8,21]. To simplify the experiment and highlight our contributions, we take the Transformer [21], one of the popular state-of-the-art NMT models, as the specific implementation of the baseline NMT model. Specifically, the encoder contains a stack of six identical layers. Each layer consists of two sub-layers: i) a multi-head self-attention mechanism, and ii) a position-wise fully connected feed-forward network. A residual connection is applied around each of the two sub-layers, followed by layer normalization [2]. The decoder is also composed of a stack of six identical layers. Besides the two sub-layers stated above, a third sub-layer is inserted in each layer that performs multi-head attention over the output of the encoder. The implementations of our approaches are all based on the above model architecture. Following the base model setups of the Transformer [21], we use 8 attention heads, 512-dimensional output vectors for each layer, and 2048-dimensional inner-layer of the feed-forward network.

4 Approaches

4.1 Adding Case Token

The technique of adding artificial tokens is a straightforward and practical way to incorporate additional knowledge to NMT [4,18], since it hardly modifies the model architecture or increases the model parameters.

In our approach, we add two artificial tokens "<ca>" and "<ab>" to indicate capital words and abbreviation words in a sequence, respectively. This special token can be insert to the left (LCT) or the right (RCT) side of the capital word. For the target sequence, LCT represents to predict the case of word previously and then generate general target language word and the case is opposite for applying RCT.

For the corpus segmented by subword units [11,19], we insert the LCT to the left side of the first subword unit of a capital word and insert RCT to the right side of the last subword unit of a capital word. For instance, Fig. 2 shows the modified sentences by adding LCT and RCT given the original sentence and the sentence encoded by subword units.

Original	Executive Committee of FIFA also announced some reform measures .
LCT	<ca> executive <ca> committee of <ab> fifa also announced some reform measures .
RCT	executive <ca> committee <ca> of fifa <ab> also announced some reform measures .
Subword	_Executive _Committee _of _FIFA _also _announc ed _some _reform _measures _.
Subword+LCT	_ <ca> _executive _ <ca> _committee _of _ <ab> _fifa _also _an- nounc ed _some _reform _measures _.
Subword+RCT	_executive _ <ca> _committee _ <ca> _of _fifa _ <ab> _also _an- nounc ed _some _reform _measures _.

Fig. 2. Examples of modifying original sentence (or sentence encoded by subwords) by LCT and RCT. "<ca>" and "<ab>" are two additional artificial tokens for indicating capital words and abbreviation words.

4.2   NMT Jointly Learning Case Prediction

In this approach, we add an additional case prediction output to the decoder of the encoder-decoder based NMT model on each decoding step. Given a source sentence: $x = \{x_1, x_2, ..., x_{T_x}\}$, its target translation: $y = \{y_1, y_2, .., y_{T_y}\}$, and the case category sequence of the target language: $c = \{c_1, c_2, ..., c_{T_c}\}$, the goal of the extension is to enable NMT model to compute the joint probability $P(y, c|x)$. The overall joint model can be computed as:

$$P(y, c|x) = \prod_{t=1}^{T_y} p(y_t|y_{<t}, c_{<t}, x)p(c_t|y_{<t}, c_{<t}, x). \qquad (2)$$

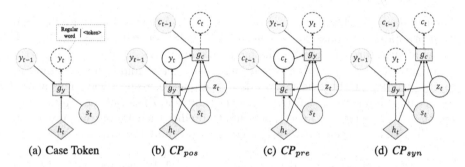

(a) Case Token   (b) CP_{pos} (c) CP_{pre} (d) CP_{syn}

Fig. 3. The graphical illustrations of the proposed approaches. The hollow circle with black dashed lines represents the next word/case to be generated. (a) represents adding case token without modifying the decoder (see Sect. 4.1 for more details); (b), (c) and (d) are three kinds of implementations for joint predicting word and its cases (see Sect. 4.2 for more details).

Intuitively, there are three assumptions about joint predicting c_t at time step t: i) predicting c_t before generating the word y_t (CP_{pre}), ii) predicting c_t after the word y_t generated (CP_{pos}), and iii) predicting the probability of c_t and y_t synchronously (CP_{syn}).

CP_{pos}: At the time step t, the model first predict y_t and then predict the case c_t for the known word y_t, which is consistent with most of the case restoration process (as shown in Fig. 3(b)). Under this assumption, the conditional probabilities in Eq. (2) can be computed as:

$$p(y_t|y_{<t}, c_{<t}, x) = g_y(y_{t-1}, z_t, s_t, h_t) \qquad (3)$$

and

$$p(c_t|y_{\leq t}, c_{<t}, x) = g_c(y_t, c_{t-1}, z_t, s_t, h_t), \qquad (4)$$

respectively, where s_t and z_t are self-attention based context vectors of previous generated $y_{<t}$ and $c_{<t}$. h_t is the output of the encoder. $g_y(\cdot)$ is the output layer

of the Transformer [21] decoder, and $g_c(\cdot)$ is the additional output layer that performs case prediction. z_t and $g_c(\cdot)$ compose an additional 1-layer Transformer-based decoder with one attention head, 32-dimensional output vectors and inner-layer of the feed-forward network, which works parallel with the original NMT decoder.

CP_{pre}: For the case of CP_{pre}, the decoder first estimates the categories of the probable word for narrowing the selection of the vocabulary and then further confirms the output words (as shown in Fig. 3(c)). Under this assumption, the conditional probabilities in Eq. (2) can be computed as:

$$p(c_t|\boldsymbol{y}_{<t}, \boldsymbol{c}_{<t}, \boldsymbol{x}) = g_c(c_{t-1}, z_t, s_t, h_t) \tag{5}$$

and

$$p(y_t|\boldsymbol{y}_{<t}, \boldsymbol{c}_{\leq t}, \boldsymbol{x}) = g_y(y_{t-1}, c_t, z_t, s_t, h_t). \tag{6}$$

CP_{syn}: Under this assumption, the two generation processes are simultaneous and independent to each other (as shown in Fig. 3(d)), then, the decoder predicting the probability of c_t and y_t synchronously. The conditional probabilities in Eq. (2) can be computed as:

$$p(c_t|\boldsymbol{y}_{<t}, \boldsymbol{c}_{<t}, \boldsymbol{x}) = g_c(c_{t-1}, z_t, s_t, h_t) \tag{7}$$

and

$$p(y_t|\boldsymbol{y}_{<t}, \boldsymbol{c}_{<t}, \boldsymbol{x}) = g_y(y_{t-1}, z_t, s_t, h_t). \tag{8}$$

4.3   Adaptive Scaling Algorithm

In training corpus, capitalized words account for a small percentage of the vocabulary, which leads to class inequality problem for training case classification model. Reported results indicate that simply applying standard classification paradigm to class inequality tasks will result in deficient performance [1,13]. To alleviate this problem, we apply Adaptive Scaling (AS) [13] to the case prediction training.

We refer words with uppercase letters as the positive instances and regard lowercased words as the negative instances. Formally, given P positive training instances $\mathcal{P}$ and N negative instances $\mathcal{N}$, $TP(\theta)$ and $TN(\theta)$ are the number of correctly predicted positive instances and the number of correctly predicted negative instances on training data with respect to θ-parameterized model. Then, taking the loss of CP_{pre} as the example, the loss function is modified as:

$$\mathcal{L}_{AS}(\theta) = - \sum_{(c_j,y_j)\in\mathcal{P}} \log p(c_j|y_j;\theta) - \sum_{(c_j,y_j)\in\mathcal{N}} w(\theta) \cdot \log p(c_j|y_j;\theta), \tag{9}$$

where

$$w(\theta) = \frac{TP(\theta)}{P + N - TN(\theta)}. \tag{10}$$

Batch-wise Adaptive Scaling Algorithm. In practice, most NMT models are trained with batch-wise gradient based algorithm, so we apply the batch-wise version of the adaptive scaling algorithm [13] in our work. Let $\mathcal{P}^B$ represents P^B positive instances and $\mathcal{N}^B$ denotes N^B negative instances in a batch, TP^B and TN^B is estimated as:

$$TP^B(\theta) = \sum_{(c_i, y_i) \in \mathcal{P}^B} p(c_i | y_i; \theta) \tag{11}$$

and

$$TN^B(\theta) = \sum_{(c_i, y_i) \in \mathcal{N}^B} p(c_i | y_i; \theta). \tag{12}$$

Then $w(\theta)^B$ is estimated as:

$$w(\theta) = \frac{TP^B(\theta)}{P^B + N^B - TN^B(\theta)}. \tag{13}$$

5 Experiment

5.1 Datasets and Setups

To verify the effectiveness of the proposed methods, we evaluate the proposed approaches on three typical translation tasks: Chinese-English (Zh-En), English-French (En-Fr) and English-German (En-De). The above three language pair translation tasks represent three typical application scenarios: i) the source language does not share any word capitalization information with the target language (Zh-En); ii) the word capitalizing rules of the source language and the target language are approximate (En-Fr); iii) the words capitalizing rules for the source language and the target language are not the same (En-De). Those typical translation tasks will be helpful to study the effects of word cases on NMT performances.

Chinese-English. For Chinese-English translation, our training data are extracted from three LDC corpora[1]. The training set contains about 1.3M parallel sentence pairs. For preprocessing, the Chinese part for both training sets and testing sets is segmented by the LTP Chinese word segmentor [5]. With the encoding of unigram language model [11], we get a Chinese vocabulary of about 39K tokens, and an English vocabulary of about 40K words. We use NIST02 as our validation set and use NIST2003–NIST2005 datasets as our test sets.

English-German and English-French. For English-German and English-French translation, we conduct our experiments on the publicly available corpora of WMT'14 dataset. This data set contains 4.5M sentence pairs and 18M sentence pairs for En-De translation task and the significantly larger En-Fr dataset consisting of 18M sentences pairs. We encode the corpora with unigram language

---

[1] LDC2005T10, LDC2003E14, LDC2004T08 and LDC2002E18. LDC2003E14 is a document alignment comparable and parallel sentence pairs are extracted by Champollion tools [14].

model [11], and both source and target vocabulary contain about 37K tokens and 30K tokens for En-De and En-Fr translation tasks, respectively. We report results on newstest2014, and the newstest2013 is used as validation.

For all translation tasks, we tokenize all corpora with the Moses tokenizer[2] before applying subword units, and sentences longer than 200 words are discarded.

Evaluation. Following [21], we report the result of a single model obtained by averaging the 5 checkpoints around the best model selected on the development set. We apply beam search during decoding with the beam size of 6. The translation results in this paper are measured in both case-insensitive and case-sensitive BLEU scores [16] evaluated by the multi-bleu.perl script (See footnote 2). We also analyze the model performances on word case restoration tasks and evaluate the results on P, R and F_1 scores.

5.2 Baselines

Regular Case (RC) and Lowercase (LC). RC and LC represent using original corpus in regular case and lowercasing all training corpus, respectively.

Table 2. "Case-insensitive/case-sensitive" BLEU scores on Zh-En, En-Fr and En-De translation tasks. For the column of "Models", **bold** and *italic* represents target words cases and performed methods, respectively.

#	Models	Zh-En			En-Fr	En-De
		NIST2003	NIST2004	NIST2005	newstest2014	newstest2014
1	**RC**	44.42/42.74	42.86/41.37	41.51/39.72	39.61/38.70	26.88/26.40
2	**TC** + *NRC*	42.42/40.63	43.61/42.00	41.97/40.58	39.63/38.65	26.87/26.32
3	**LC** + *NRC*	43.11/37.03	44.02/38.92	42.12/36.67	39.94/35.43	26.91/23.49
4	**LC** + *JPM* [25]	43.48/41.72	43.97/42.73	42.81/41.12	40.01/39.11	26.77/26.37
5	**LC** + *LCT*	42.70/40.83	44.10/42.45	41.66/40.31	39.71/38.89	26.48/25.66
6	**LC** + *RCT*	41.71/39.72	43.18/41.53	41.36/39.92	39.84/39.05	26.38/25.57
7	**LC** + CP_{pre}	**44.53**/42.88	44.84/43.37	42.95/41.72	**40.85**/39.70	26.94/26.58
8	**LC** + CP_{pos}	43.64/42.10	44.36/43.39	42.84/41.55	40.72/39.69	26.72/26.45
9	**LC** + CP_{syn}	43.62/42.74	44.53/42.98	43.01/41.92	40.02/38.78	26.78/26.54
10	**LC** + CP_{pre} + *AS*	44.52/**43.04**	**45.01**/**43.97**	42.91/42.05	40.70/**39.75**	**27.02**/**26.87**
11	**LC** + CP_{pos} + *AS*	43.76/42.87	44.75/43.81	42.92/41.86	40.59/39.60	26.89/26.56
12	**LC** + CP_{syn} + *AS*	43.57/42.82	44.66/43.56	**43.01**/**42.07**	40.61/39.67	26.93/26.64

Truecase (TC). We truecase the target language part of the corpora using Moses [10] script truecase.perl (See footnote 2). It tries to keep words in their natural case, and only changes the words at the beginning of their sentence to their most frequent form.

---

[2] The related Moses [10] scripts are available at: https://github.com/moses-smt/mosesdecoder/blob/master/scripts/.

Naive Re-case (*NRC*). For comparative research, we also apply rule-based methods that restore model outputs into regular case. We first build a capitalized words dictionary based on the target side of the translation corpus. The dictionary counts the words that usually appear in capitalized form (the frequency of occurrence in capitalized form is greater than 50%).

Joint Prediction Model (*JPM*) [25]. This work shares similar motivation with our approach. It proposes an NMT model that jointly predicts English words and their cases by employing two outputs layers on one decoder.

5.3   Main Results

Table 2 shows the experimental results on the three translation tasks. The results of baseline methods are listed in rows of #1–#4 and from #5 to #12 are results of our proposed methods. From Table 2 we can observe that for each experimental setup, model gains higher case-insensitive BLEU score than the case-sensitive version. The reduction in case-sensitive BLEU is more pronounced in Zh-En translation, since the source language does not provide any relevant morphological information. For En-Fr translation, since the target language shares similar capitalization rules with the source input, the case-sensitive performance reduces less. The phenomenon is not very prominent in En-De translation, probably because the writing rules of German are different from the other two languages (En and Fr).

The results show that our proposed *CP* methods obtain better performances than multiple baseline setups on the three translation tasks, but the translation quality of *LCT* and *RCT* decrease in some cases. The reason for the negative results on "Adding case token" approaches may be: i) the additional case tokens

Table 3. Case restoration results on Zh-En, En-Fr and En-De translation tasks. For the column of "Models", **bold** and *italic* represents target words cases and performed methods, respectively.

#	Methods	Zh-En			En-Fr			En-De		
		P	R	F_1	P	R	F_1	P	R	F_1
1	**RC**	74.19	63.15	68.23	75.62	81.23	78.32	58.39	58.12	58.25
2	**TC**+*NRC*	73.98	63.58	68.39	75.41	81.33	78.25	57.86	58.24	58.05
3	**LC**+*NRC*	74.70	17.07	27.79	75.56	24.15	36.60	57.25	51.07	53.99
4	**LC**+*JPM* [25]	73.10	64.87	68.74	74.91	82.68	78.60	57.37	58.46	57.91
5	**LC**+*LCT*	71.22	65.29	68.13	73.46	83.67	78.23	56.05	58.53	57.26
6	**LC**+*RCT*	69.53	65.59	67.50	72.84	83.01	78.03	56.22	58.35	57.26
7	**LC** + CP_{pre}	73.67	65.43	69.31	74.89	83.20	78.82	57.74	58.54	58.13
8	**LC** + CP_{pos}	73.26	64.87	68.81	75.07	82.12	78.43	57.31	58.42	57.85
9	**LC** + CP_{syn}	73.71	64.24	68.65	74.65	83.09	78.64	57.40	58.65	58.01
10	**LC** + CP_{pre} + *AS*	73.73	66.39	69.87	75.42	83.44	79.22	58.09	58.23	58.15
11	**LC** + CP_{pos} + *AS*	73.65	66.17	69.71	75.08	83.30	78.97	57.93	58.76	58.34
12	**LC** + CP_{syn} + *AS*	73.68	66.20	69.74	75.13	83.25	78.98	58.20	58.29	58.24

increase the average length of the generated sequences by more than 5 words; ii) decoding with case tokens inside the sequence may dilute the impacts of previous generated words. On the contrast, CP methods use relatively independent decoders and the case information performs as additional feature inputs for NMT decoding.

One of the interesting findings in the overall results is that LCT and CP_{pre} usually gains better BLEU scores than RCT and CP_{pos}. In our approaches, LCT and CP_{pre} predict case label before generate target word while RCT and CP_{pos} follow the reverse order. We suspect that the possible reason for experimental results is that the generated label can reduce the search space of the target words. CP_{pos} and CP_{syn} also achieve improvements on baseline methods. We also study the impact of applying adaptive scaling algorithm [13] and the results are listed in rows from #10 to #12 in Table 2. The experimental results show that the proposed methods with scaling algorithm (AS) performs better under case-sensitive measurements, which indicates that applying AS can enhance the prediction of the word cases.

5.4   Case Restoration

In this section, we analyze the impact of different methods on case restoration tasks. We conduct the experiments on three testsets: NIST2003–NIST2005 (Zh-En), newstest2014 and newstest2015 (En-Fr and En-de). Experimental results are evaluated on P, R and F_1[3] scores as shown in Table 3. From Table 3, we can see that our proposed CP methods gains higher F_1 scores for most model setups. Comparing with adding case token, CP approaches separate case prediction from word prediction and introduce an additional network block to handle this task. Since the separated case prediction decoder learns more about lexical information, it leads to improvements on case-restoration tasks. As shown in rows #10–#12, applying adaptive scaling algorithm [13] is also effective for case prediction tasks, which can adaptively scale the influence of negative instances in loss function.

Comparing the three translation tasks, P, R and F_1 performances on En-Fr are significantly better than other languages. As mentioned above, French shares similar capitalization rules with English, so the decoder can capture more lexical information from the source side. The NRC method works much better on En-De translation tasks than the others, since the capitalization rules for German words are relatively fixed.

5.5   Decoding Efficiency

We analyze the decoding time of our method compared with the baseline approach on NIST2002 Zh-En valid set with one NVIDIA GeForce GTX 1080Ti GPU and a batch size of 32 sentences. Table 4 shows that the proposed methods

---

[3] We regard a word sequence as a collection without considering the word orders in the generated sequence for calculating P, R and F_1 scores.

has lower decoding efficiency than the baseline method. For NMT with CP methods, the additional decoder creates extra decoding overhead. Especially, CP_{pre} and CP_{pos} require additional autoregressive steps to predict word case, which reduces decoding efficiency. For the approach of adding case token, although it does not increase the parameters number of NMT model, the additional tokens increase the length of generated target sequence.

Table 4. Comparison of model parameters and decoding efficiency. "#parameters" represents the free parameters number of the NMT model. "Speed" means the decoding speed (sentences per second) which are evaluated on NIST2002 Zh-En valid set.

Methods	#parameters	Speed (sents/s)
Transformer [21]	65×10^6	5.88
+ case token	65×10^6	5.06
+ CP_{syn}	66×10^6	3.64
+ $CP_{pre}/ + CP_{pos}$	66×10^6	2.85

6   Conclusion

Word case information, as one of linguistics features, is definitive and easily obtainable. Incorporating case information into machine translation also meets the needs of practical applications. In this paper, we propose two types of approaches to perform case-sensitive neural machine translation: i) directly adding a case token into the word sequence to indicate the case information of the nearby word; ii) applying additional decoder to the conventional NMT model performing case prediction along with generating translation. We test our approaches on multiple setups and three typical translation tasks (Zh-En, En-Fr, En-De). Experimental results show that our approaches outperform baseline approaches on case-sensitive BLEU score. Specifically, adding case token is easy to apply to any NMT models without modifying the network architecture but lose some accuracy, while applying case prediction decoder will offer more reliable results but increasing model parameters. In the future, we will apply our approaches to other natural language generation relatively tasks such as dialogue generation, text generation and automatic speech recognition.

Acknowledgments. We thank all anonymous reviewers for their valuable comments. This work is supported by the National Key Research and Development Program of China (Grant No. 2017YFB1002103) and the National Natural Science Foundation of China (No. 61732005).

References

1. Anand, R., Mehrotra, K.G., Mohan, C.K., Ranka, S.: An improved algorithm for neural network classification of imbalanced training sets. IEEE Trans. Neural Netw. 4(6), 962–969 (1993)

2. Ba, L.J., Kiros, R., Hinton, G.E.: Layer normalization. CoRR abs/1607.06450 (2016)
3. Bahdanau, D., Cho, K., Bengio, Y.: Neural machine translation by jointly learning to align and translate. In: 3rd International Conference on Learning Representations, ICLR 2015, San Diego, CA, USA, 7–9 May 2015, Conference Track Proceedings (2015)
4. Britz, D., Le, Q., Pryzant, R.: Effective domain mixing for neural machine translation. In: Proceedings of the Second Conference on Machine Translation, pp. 118–126 (2017)
5. Che, W., Li, Z., Liu, T.: LTP: a Chinese language technology platform. In: COLING 2010, 23rd International Conference on Computational Linguistics, Demonstrations Volume, Beijing, China, 23–27 August 2010, pp. 13–16 (2010)
6. Cho, K., et al.: Learning phrase representations using RNN encoder-decoder for statistical machine translation. In: Proceedings of the 2014 Conference on Empirical Methods in Natural Language Processing, EMNLP 2014, Doha, Qatar, 25–29 October 2014, A Meeting of SIGDAT, a Special Interest Group of the ACL, pp. 1724–1734 (2014)
7. Eriguchi, A., Hashimoto, K., Tsuruoka, Y.: Tree-to-sequence attentional neural machine translation. In: Proceedings of the 54th Annual Meeting of the Association for Computational Linguistics, ACL 2016, Berlin, Germany, 7–12 August 2016, Long Papers, vol. 1, pp. 823–833 (2016)
8. Gehring, J., Auli, M., Grangier, D., Yarats, D., Dauphin, Y.N.: Convolutional sequence to sequence learning. In: Proceedings of the 34th International Conference on Machine Learning, ICML 2017, Sydney, NSW, Australia, 6–11 August 2017, pp. 1243–1252 (2017)
9. Han, B., Cook, P., Baldwin, T.: Lexical normalization for social media text. ACM Trans. Intell. Syst. Technol. 4(1), 5:1–5:27 (2013)
10. Koehn, P., et al.: Moses: open source toolkit for statistical machine translation. In: Proceedings of the 45th Annual Meeting of the Association for Computational Linguistics Companion Volume Proceedings of the Demo and Poster Sessions, pp. 177–180 (2007)
11. Kudo, T.: Subword regularization: improving neural network translation models with multiple subword candidates. In: Proceedings of the 56th Annual Meeting of the Association for Computational Linguistics, ACL 2018, Melbourne, Australia, 15–20 July 2018, Long Papers, vol. 1, pp. 66–75 (2018)
12. Li, J., Xiong, D., Tu, Z., Zhu, M., Zhang, M., Zhou, G.: Modeling source syntax for neural machine translation. In: Proceedings of the 55th Annual Meeting of the Association for Computational Linguistics, ACL 2017, Vancouver, Canada, 30 July–4 August, Long Papers, vol. 1, pp. 688–697 (2017)
13. Lin, H., Lu, Y., Han, X., Sun, L.: Adaptive scaling for sparse detection in information extraction. In: Proceedings of the 56th Annual Meeting of the Association for Computational Linguistics, ACL 2018, Melbourne, Australia, 15–20 July 2018, Long Papers, vol. 1, pp. 1033–1043 (2018)
14. Ma, X.: Champollion: a robust parallel text sentence aligner. In: Proceedings of the Fifth International Conference on Language Resources and Evaluation, LREC 2006, Genoa, Italy, 22–28 May 2006, pp. 489–492 (2006)
15. Niehues, J., Cho, E.: Exploiting linguistic resources for neural machine translation using multi-task learning. In: Proceedings of the Second Conference on Machine Translation, WMT 2017, Copenhagen, Denmark, 7–8 September 2017, pp. 80–89 (2017)

16. Papineni, K., Roukos, S., Ward, T., Zhu, W.: Bleu: a method for automatic evaluation of machine translation. In: Proceedings of the 40th Annual Meeting of the Association for Computational Linguistics, Philadelphia, PA, USA, 6–12 July 2002, pp. 311–318 (2002)
17. Sennrich, R., Haddow, B.: Linguistic input features improve neural machine translation. In: Proceedings of the First Conference on Machine Translation, WMT 2016, colocated with ACL 2016, 11–12 August, Berlin, Germany, pp. 83–91 (2016)
18. Sennrich, R., Haddow, B., Birch, A.: Controlling politeness in neural machine translation via side constraints. In: Proceedings of the 2016 Conference of the North American Chapter of the Association for Computational Linguistics: Human Language Technologies, pp. 35–40 (2016)
19. Sennrich, R., Haddow, B., Birch, A.: Neural machine translation of rare words with subword units. In: Proceedings of the 54th Annual Meeting of the Association for Computational Linguistics, Long Papers, vol. 1, pp. 1715–1725 (2016)
20. Susanto, R.H., Chieu, H.L., Lu, W.: Learning to capitalize with character-level recurrent neural networks: an empirical study. In: Proceedings of the 2016 Conference on Empirical Methods in Natural Language Processing, EMNLP 2016, Austin, Texas, USA, 1–4 November 2016, pp. 2090–2095 (2016)
21. Vaswani, A., et al.: Attention is all you need. In: Advances in Neural Information Processing Systems 30: Annual Conference on Neural Information Processing Systems 2017, Long Beach, CA, USA, 4–9 December 2017, pp. 6000–6010 (2017)
22. Wang, X., Pham, H., Yin, P., Neubig, G.: A tree-based decoder for neural machine translation. In: Proceedings of the 2018 Conference on Empirical Methods in Natural Language Processing, Brussels, Belgium, 31 October–4 November 2018, pp. 4772–4777 (2018)
23. Wu, S., Zhang, D., Yang, N., Li, M., Zhou, M.: Sequence-to-dependency neural machine translation. In: Proceedings of the 55th Annual Meeting of the Association for Computational Linguistics, ACL 2017, Vancouver, Canada, 30 July–4 August, Long Papers, vol. 1, pp. 698–707 (2017)
24. Yang, X., Liu, Y., Xie, D., Wang, X., Balasubramanian, N.: Latent part-of-speech sequences for neural machine translation. CoRR abs/1908.11782 (2019)
25. Zhang, N., Li, X., Jin, X., Chen, W.: Joint prediction model of English words and their cases in neural machine translation. J. Chin. Inf. Process. **33**(3), 52–58 (2019)

Attribute-Driven Capsule Network for Entity Relation Prediction

Jiayin Chen[1], Xiaolong Gong[1,2], Xi Chen[1(✉)], and Zhiyi Ma[1,3]

[1] Advanced Institute of Information Technology, Peking University, Hangzhou, China
{jychen,xlgong,xchen,mazhiyi}@aiit.org.cn
[2] Department of Computer Science, Shanghai Jiao Tong University, Shanghai, China
[3] School of Electronics Engineering and Computer Science,
Peking University, Beijing, China

Abstract. Multi-attribute entity relation prediction is a novel data mining application about designing an intelligent system that supports inferencing across attributes information. However, most existing deep learning methods capture the inner structural information between different attributes are far more limited. In this paper, we propose an attribute-driven approach for entity relation prediction task based on capsule networks that have been shown to demonstrate good performance on relation mining. We develop a self-attention routing method to encapsulate multiple attributes semantic representation into relational semantic capsules and using dynamic routing method to generate class capsules for predicting relations. Due to the lack of multi-attribute entity relation data is a major obstacle in this task, we construct a new real-world multi-attribute entity relation dataset in this work. Experimental results show significant superiority of our model, as compared with other baselines.

Keywords: Entity relation prediction · Capsule networks ·
Self-attention routing

1 Introduction

Learning to predict relationship between the entities plays a vital role in recommendation system, knowledge base population and question answering system, etc. In the big data era, we aim to know the relation between two homogeneous or heterogeneous entities through the latent knowledge behind the data. Take an example in business mining field, we attempt to predict what the relationship between the two companies is, which can help an enterprise to search his potential customers or providers. The *relation prediction* (RP) task is different from *relation extraction* (RE) task, the entity pairs in RP task does not appear in the same semantic sentence and sometimes they may consist of many common attributes. For instance, there exists many common multiple attributes information in a pair of companies such as *company name, company address,*

© Springer Nature Switzerland AG 2020
H. W. Lauw et al. (Eds.): PAKDD 2020, LNAI 12084, pp. 675–686, 2020.
https://doi.org/10.1007/978-3-030-47426-3_52

company profile, business scope, etc. Hence, a demanding requirement for promoting RP is to develop a novel model that can support the entity relation for those multi-attribute data.

On RP task, most traditional methods are kernel-based method [1–4] that they need to do complicated feature engineering. Moreover, those methods limit to capture latent semantic information and they cannot extract some new effective features from relation examples easily. In recent years, a variety of neural network models [5–15] have been widely applied to relation prediction and achieved remarkable success. Those models are mainly based on an architecture of distributed representation, which learns a scalar-output to represent entity relation. All these methods can be divided into three categories: the CNN-based method [10,11], the RNN-based method [12,13] and the Transformer-based method [14,15]. Although above methods can capture latent semantic information due to the deep learning way, some disadvantages remain: 1) they heavily rely on the quality of entity semantic representation. Using one scalar-output to represent entity relation is limited because attribute information is abundant and diverse. 2) Above methods fail to retain the precise spatial relationships between high-level parts. The structural relationships such as the homogeneous information in all attributes are valuable. To address above problems, the capsule network methods have been proposed [16–18], which encapsulate multiple attributes into groups of neurons and replaces the scalar-output feature detectors with vector-output capsules to preserve additional information such as position and correlation [19]. Recently, capsule networks have achieved competitive results in classification tasks [18,20,21], relation extraction [22], especially for those structural information learning tasks [19,23]. In RP task, the entity relationship is usually correlate with their multiple attributes information. The capsule networks could represent those multiple attributes of entities as individual capsules, preserving the structural, correlation, relationship information between multiple attributes to drive entity relation prediction.

In this paper, we propose a novel Attribute-driven Capsule Network (**ACNet**) for entity relation prediction task, which retains the structural and correlation information by using capsule networks. Our **ACNet** makes attribute capsules generate relation capsules by developing a self-attention routing method, which assign weights to different attribute capsules and improve relation prediction performance. Furthermore, we adopt k-max pooling method to improve robust representation and training efficiency. The major contributions of this paper are briefly summarized as follows.

1. We propose a novel entity relation prediction approach based on capsule networks with self-attention routing method for those multi-attribute entity datasets. To the best of our knowledge, this is the first work that capsule network has been empirically apply on multi-attribute entity relation prediction.
2. We devise self-attention routing method between the attribute capsule layer and the relation capsule layer to improve the ability to capture relational semantic information. We conduct extensive experiments on a new real-world scenario CompanyRelationCollection (CRC) dataset that we constructed

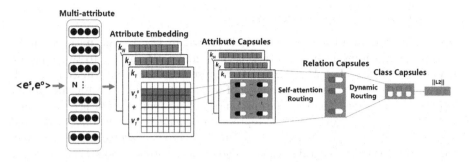

Fig. 1. The whole framework of **ACNet** method. It consists of four layers: 1) **Attribute Embedding Layer** converts each of common attributes into *attribute-key* and *attribute-value* vectors; 2) **Attribute Capsule** extracts feature from *attribute-value* vector and generates attribute capsules; 3) **Relation Capsule** uses self-attention routing method to aggregate attribute capsules and *attribute-key* vectors into a set of relation feature capsules; 4) **Class Capsule** produces classification capsules to represent each relation category.

from web and one public BlurbGenreCollection (BGC) dataset. The results demonstrate our **ACNet** consistently outperforms the state-of-the-art baselines.

The rest of the paper is organized as follows: Sect. 2 describes the proposed our model; Sect. 3 evaluates the approach; Sect. 4 concludes the paper.

2 Model

2.1 Definitions

Definition 1 (Relation prediction). *Let $D=\{e^1, e^2, ... e^n\}$ represent a set of entities, where $|D| = n$. The ordered pair $<e^s, e^o>$ in D denotes two entities has a relevant link represented by $r<e^s, e^o>$, which is called relation. The learning task is to improve the target predictive function for relation $f_r<e^s, e^o>$.*

Definition 2 (Attribute information). *Let $e^s = \{k_1 : v_1^s, ..., k_N : v_N^s\}$ represent multi-attribute entity information, where $|e^s| = N$ means that there exists N attributes for each entity. And multi-attribute in the form of key-value $(k : v)$ pairs to indicate their information. We utilize E^k (attribute-key) and E^v (attribute-value) to represent the key and value information of one attribute, respectively.*

2.2   Attribute Embedding Layer

The whole framework of our method is shown in Fig. 1. The purpose of the attribute embedding layer is to turn each common attribute into two separate embedding vectors. Let $M^E \in \mathbb{R}^{d_w \times |V|}$ represent attribute information embedding matrix, where d_w is the dimension of word vectors and $|V|$ is the vocabulary size. Here, the embedding for information of j-th attribute can be separated into two vectors, using $E^{k_j} \in \mathbb{R}^{1 \times d_w}$ to represent *attribute-key* embedding vector and $E^{v_j} = \{x_1, ..., x_i, ..., x_L\} \in \mathbb{R}^{L \times d_w}$ to represent *attribute-value* embedding vector, where x_i is the i-th word in the *attribute-value* sentence and L is the sentence length. For a relation pair $<e^s, e^o>$, due to the relationship is strongly related to their common attributes information, we concatenate their *attribute-value* vectors for each attribute and they can be formulated as $<e^s, e^o> = \{E^{k_1} : E^{v_1^s} + E^{v_1^o}, ..., E^{k_N} : E^{v_N^s} + E^{v_N^o}\} = \{E^{k_1} : E^{v_1}, ..., E^{k_N} : E^{v_N}\}$.

2.3   Attribute Capsule Layer

This layer aims to use multiple convolution operations to extract n-gram features from the *attribute-value embedding*, which contain local semantic information about the *attribute-key* in a fixed window. In general, let $x_{i:i+j}$ refers to the concatenation of words $x_i, x_{i+1}, ..., x_{i+j}$. Multiple convolution operations involves a kernel group $F \in \mathbb{R}^{d_p \times (d_w \times h)}$, which is applied to a window with h words to generate multiple h-gram features. $d_w \times h$ is the size of one convolutional kernel, h is the n-gram size and d_p is the dimension of one attribute capsule. For a j-th attribute, a feature c_i is produced from a window of words $x_{i:i+h-1}$ by

$$c_i = F \odot E^{v_j}_{i:i+h-1} + b \tag{1}$$

where $\odot$ denotes the component-wise multiplication and $b \in \mathbb{R}$ is a bias term. Thus, we can get a set of attribute capsules $c \in \mathbb{R}^{d_p \times (L-h+1)}$, which encapsulates n-gram features and extracts from the whole textual information of an *attribute-value*.

In fact, different kernel groups F can capture different categories of semantic meaning. We repeat the above procedure B times with different kernel groups, and get multiple channels of features to represent B categories of semantic meaning. The final output of this layer is arranged as $C \in \mathbb{R}^{B \times d_p \times (L-h+1)}$, where $C = [c_1, c_2, ... c_B]$.

2.4   Relation Capsule Layer

Self-Attention Routing Approach. For a common attribute, different n-gram features are extracted from the *attribute-value* and they have different effects on the *attribute-key*. What's more, n-gram features contain different semantic information of entity relation. To alleviate aforementioned problem, and following self-attention mechanism [24,25], we propose a novel attention routing approach to compute the weight for the n-gram features of h-size window in E^{v_j}.

First, we apply a fusing convolution operation to the embedding E^{v_j} with a kernel $V_s \in \mathbb{R}^{d_w \times h}$, and getting a set of feature vectors $F_s \in \mathbb{R}^{1 \times (L-h+1)}$. Second, we let E^{k_j} as our query input, a simple linear projection is used to construct the query $Q = E^{k_j} W^q$, and the key $K = F_s W^k$. Then, we use the query Q to perform a scaled dot-product attention over K. The returned scalars can be put through a softmax function to produce a set of weights.

$$a_i = softmax \left(\frac{E^{k_j} W^q (F_s W^k)^T}{\sqrt{d_w}} \right) \tag{2}$$

where $a_i \in \mathbb{R}^{1 \times (L-h+1)}$, $W^q \in \mathbb{R}^{d_w \times u}$ and $W^k \in \mathbb{R}^{(L-h+1) \times u}$ represent weighted parameter matrices. The generate attention weight $a_i \in [0, 1]$ contains information with respect to *attribute-value*. It controls how much information in current n-gram feature can be transmitted to the next layer. If a_i is zero, the feature capsule would be totally blocked. Since produced B different channels of attribute capsules in above layer, we repeat the above computational process B times to get the whole attention routing weights $A \in \mathbb{R}^{B \times 1 \times (L-h+1)}$, where $A = [a_1, a_2, ..., a_B]$. Finally, the attribute capsules are routed using these weights:

$$S = C \odot A \tag{3}$$

where $S \in \mathbb{R}^{B \times d_p \times (L-h+1)}$ is the attribute-customized feature capsules, and $\odot$ denotes element-wise multiplication.

Relation Capsule Generation. The above generated S is transformed from attribute capsules. Though encoding key-related information, there are still many unrelated capsules in S. Moreover, the large number of capsules in S may prevent the next layer from learning robust representations. If using a method similar to the max pooling, it will lead to lose some capsules about the structural or position information. Hence, we adopt a compromise method, k-max method in S to aggregate all attribute capsules in the third channel horizontally.

$$P = max(k, [S_1, S_2, .., S_{L-h+1}]) \tag{4}$$

where $P \in \mathbb{R}^{B \times k \times d_p}$, k is a constant that meaning to preserve top k capsules and max is a descending sort operation. Through Eq. 4, the network can filter out many unimportant capsules and obtain more relation capsules.

From Eq. 1 to Eq. 4, a attribute can generate a set of capsules P and we loop N attributes in the same way to get a set of all attributes capsules u. Then we combine all attributes capsules together to produce relation capsules:

$$u = [P_1, P_2, ..., P_N] \tag{5}$$

where $u \in \mathbb{R}^{(B \times K \times N) \times d_p}$. Then, we use the non-linear "squash" function [16], using the length of each relation feature capsule u_i to represent the probability that u_i's feature meaning is present in the current input.

$$u_i \leftarrow \frac{\|u_i\|^2}{1 + \|u_i\|^2} \frac{u_i}{\|u_i\|} \tag{6}$$

Algorithm 1. Dynamic Routing Algorithm

1: **Procedure** ROUTING($\hat{u}_{j|i}, r, l$) ;
2: for all capsule i in layer l and capsule j in layer (l+1):$b_{ij} \leftarrow 0$.
3: **for** r iterations **do**
4:     for all capsule i in layer l: $c_i \leftarrow softmax(b_i)$
5:     for all capsule j in layer (l+1): $s_j \leftarrow \sum_i c_{ij}\hat{u}_{j|i}$
6:     for all capsule j in layer (l+1): $v_j \leftarrow squash(s_j)$
7:     for all capsule i in layer l and capsule j in layer (l+1): $b_{ij} \leftarrow b_{ij} + \hat{u}_{j|i}.v_j$
8: **end forreturn** v_j;

2.5 Class Capsules Layer

In the capsule network, it uses class capsules to represent entity relation categories that means the number of relation capsules to be consistent with categories of entity relations. Let the number of relation categories be m, and there are m relation capsules learned in this layer. Each relation capsule is used for calculating the classification probability of each relation in entity prediction task. Hence each class capsule should have its own routing weights to adaptively aggregate relation capsules from the previous layer.

A capsule's prediction vector $\tilde{u}_{j|i}$ is generated by multiplying the output u_i by a weight matrix W_{ij}, where $W_{ij} \in \mathbb{R}^{d_r \times d_p}$ is a weight matrix, d_r and d_p are the dimensions of class capsule j and relation capsule i, u_i is the vector representation of relation capsule i.

$$\hat{u}_{j|i} = W_{ij}u_i \tag{7}$$

Then all prediction vectors generated by relation capsules are summed up with weights c_{ij} to obtain the vector representation s_j of class capsule j:

$$\mathbf{s_j} = \sum_i c_{ij}\tilde{u}_{j|i} \tag{8}$$

where c_{ij} is a coupling coefficient that determine the contribution of each relation capsule's output to a class capsule are calculated using a dynamic routing heuristic [16] and defined by a "routing softmax":

$$c_{ij} = \frac{exp(b_{ij})}{\sum_k exp(b_{ik})} \tag{9}$$

where each b_{ij} is the log prior probability that a relation capsule i should pass to a class capsule j. It is computed using a dynamic routing approach which is written in Algorithm 1 [16].

After that, we apply the non-linear "squash" function again to $\mathbf{s_j}$ in Eq. 6 to get a final representation $\mathbf{v_j}$ for class capsule j.

$$\mathbf{v_j} = squash(\mathbf{s_j}) \tag{10}$$

2.6 Margin Loss

We use the length of a class vector to represent the probability of the relationship between entities. The capsule length of the active relation should be larger than others. We adopt a separate margin loss L_j for each class capsule j in our task:

$$L_j = T_j max(0, m^+ - \|\mathbf{v_j}\|)^2 + \lambda(1 - T_j)max(0, \|\mathbf{v_j}\| - m^-)^2 \qquad (11)$$

where $T_j = 1$ if the entity relation is present in class capsule j. We set m^+=0.9, and $m^- = 0.1$, $\lambda = 0.5$ following in the research [16]. The total loss is simply the sum of the losses of all class capsules, $L_T = \sum_{j=1}^{J} L_j$.

3 Experiments

3.1 Datasets

We evaluate our model on two datasets[1]: **CompanyRelationCollection (CRC)** refers to company entities and **BlurbGenreCollection (BGC)** refers to book entities. The **CRC** is a Chinese company entity dataset that collected from the Internet. It consists of 58,013 company entities and there are 6 common attributes for each company entity, which includes *company_name, company_address, company_type, industry_category, business_scope* and *abstract*. For a pair of company entities, there exists three major links content, which includes customer (C), provider (P), rival (R). Figure 2 gives an example of a relationship in **CRC** dataset, which demonstrates *Entity_O* is a customer of *Entity_S*. In our task, we retain only one relationship between two company entities. The **BGC** is an English public dataset [23]. It includes 91,892 book entities and each entity has 3 common attributes. We define three kinds of link according to book categories, which includes similar(S), presumably-similar(P), dissimilar(D). Table 1 lists some important quantitative characteristics of both datasets.

Fig. 2. An example of one relationship in CRC dataset.

Table 1. Quantitative characteristics of both datasets

	CRC	BGC
Number of entities	58,013	91,892
Number of attributes per entity	6	3
Total number of relationships	3(C,P,R)	3(S,P,D)
Number of relational pairs	61,441	918,920
Train set	43,009	735,136
Validation set	9216	91,892
Test set	9216	91,892

3.2 Experimental Setting

Due to different text lengths of *attribute-values*, we fix text length of all *attribute-values* equals to 200. We train words embedding [26] in two dataset respectively.

For all the experiments below, we set some parameters: $d_w = 200$ for word embedding dimensionality, $d_p = 16$ and $d_r = 24$ for the dimension of a relation capsule and a class capsule, respectively. We tune some parameters of our models by grid searching on the validation dataset and grid search is utilized to select optimal learning rate λ for Adam optimizer, we final set our λ equal to 0.001 and filters number B equals to 64. The significant parameter k with 12 different values in our experiment and detailed discussion is presented in Sect. 3.5. Table 2 shows that hyper-parameters of the optimum model were selected by the evaluation results on the validation dataset. For other parameters, we use empirical settings because they make few influence on performance of our model. Three widespread used evaluation metrics are applied in the experiments, which includes the precision, recall and F1. We select F1 as our final main evaluation indicator.

3.3 Baselines

To demonstrate the superiority of **ACNet** on relation prediction task between multi-attribute entities, we compare it with following six baselines: **CNN** proposes a convolutional deep neural network model for entity relation mining. **PCNN** puts forward a piecewise CNN model for distant supervision for relation mining. **BLSTM** proposes a bidirectional LSTM model for relation mining. **ATT-BLSTM** is a bidirectional LSTM model with attention mechanism. **BERT** is a pre-training bidirectional transformer model for relation mining. All above methods are based on the idea of classification and they are suitable for our relation prediction tasks. **Basic-Caps** is the original capsule network model without self-attention routing mechanism.

Table 2. List of hyper-parameters

Hyper-parameter	Value
Word embedding size (d_w)	200
Dimension of attribute capsule (d_p)	16
convolutional kernel size (h)	2
Number of convolution kernels (B)	64
Self-attention matrix parameter (u)	100
Number of reserved top capsules (k)	10
Dimension of class capsule (d_r)	24
Learning rate (λ)	0.001

Table 3. The results of Comparison of different methods. Best scores are in bold.

Method	CRC			BGC		
	Precision	Recall	F1	Precision	Recall	F1
CNN [10]	0.7706	0.7012	0.7343	0.8420	0.8265	0.8342
PCNN [11]	0.7825	0.7103	0.7447	0.8578	0.8299	0.8436
BLSTM [12]	0.7682	0.7066	0.7361	0.85378	0.8122	0.8324
BERT [27]	**0.8067**	0.6936	0.7459	**0.8628**	0.8345	0.8484
Basic-Caps	0.7528	0.7331	0.7428	0.8534	0.8304	0.8417
ACNet	0.7662	**0.7405**	**0.7531**	0.8612	**0.8405**	**0.8507**

3.4   Main Results

We conduct experiments on the seven methods mentioned above. The comparison results of all models are shown in Table 3. It is clear that our attribute-driven capsule network achieves the highest F1 scores, outperforming the other deep network-based methods, simultaneously in terms of recall. Our **ACNnet** has the smallest fluctuation between precision and recall on two datasets. Both situations demonstrate that our method is superior to other models on relation prediction between multi-attribute entities and RP task learning is more robust.

The results of **ACNet** significantly outperform the **Basic-Caps** and others on the F1 indicator show that the self-attention routing approach is effective, which indicates that our approach could capture more relational semantic information and enhance the ability to represent class capsules by self-attention mechanism. Moreover, capsule networks have shown to identify and combine relational information with common attributes more accurately than the baselines.

BERT performs the best result on precision indicator among all baselines except our model, which demonstrates that the powerful pre-training model can achieve richful representation information. We also can observe that the self-attention routing approach beneficial to improve relation prediction between multi-attribute entity. Among CNN-based methods, **PCNN** achieves higher performance than **CNN** since it uses dynamic max pooling method and preserves some level of information about attributes. However, **BLSTM** is better than **ATT-BLSTM** beyond our expectations. **ATT-BLSTM** performs the worst among all others, as maybe its based attention model can not extract more effective attribute features.

3.5   Parameter Analysis

Stability of Training. In order to investigate the difference between our model and other models in training process, we conduct a statistical analysis on training loss where we set epochs equal to 10 and select the lowest training loss at each epoch for comparison. The results are shown in Fig. 3. We can observe that the capsule networks convergence much faster than other methods, getting a stable training process and achieve less fluctuation. The reason behind this situation should be that capsule network discard pooling and retain all the feature information.

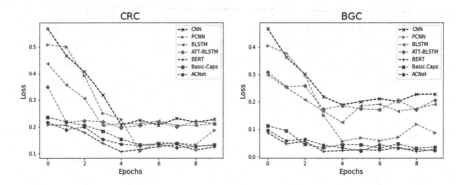

Fig. 3. The result of training loss from all models on two datasets.

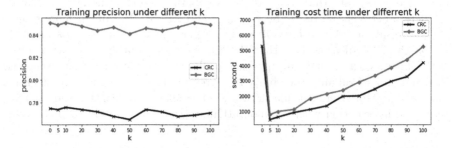

Fig. 4. Training results under different k values

k-max Pooling. To explore whether the capsule networks discard many features by the pooling way will have an impact on the prediction results, we use k-max pooling method in **ACNnet** to test it. We set 12 different k values and $k = 0$ means without using pooling. The results are shown in Fig. 4. The test results show that k-max pooling method does not decrease the precision of entity relationship prediction. Conversely, using a smaller k can greatly reduce training time and increase training efficiency. This also illustrates that it is effective to retain the main attribute capsules and filter out many unimportant capsules.

4 Conclusion

We present attribute-driven capsule network model for relation prediction between multi-attribute entities in this work. In order to capture relational information from common attributes and improve relation prediction, we develop self-attention routing method based on capsule networks to generate relational capsules and link with class capsules. The experimental results demonstrate the effectiveness of our model on RP task. Our future work includes: (i) to enrich the representation of the capsule network with more attributes, (ii) to consider entity relation prediction with different attributes, (iii) to apply some methods of the recommended domain on entity relation prediction.

Acknowledgments. This work is supported by the National Natural Science Foundation of China (No. 61672046). We thank all the anonymous reviewers for their insightful comments.

References

1. Mooney, R.J., Bunescu, R.C.: Subsequence kernels for relation extraction (2005)
2. Bunescu, R.C., Mooney, R.J.: A shortest path dependency kernel for relation extraction (2005)
3. Yu, K., Chu, W., Yu, S., Tresp, V., Xu, Z.: Stochastic relational models for discriminative link prediction. In: Advances in Neural Information Processing Systems 19, Proceedings of the Twentieth Annual Conference on Neural Information Processing Systems, Vancouver, British Columbia, Canada, 4–7 December 2006 (2006)
4. Li, J., Zhang, Z., Li, X., Chen, H.: Kernel-based learning for biomedical relation extraction. J. Am. Soc. Inf. Sci. Technol. **59**(5), 756–769 (2008)
5. Nguyen, T.H., Grishman, R.: Relation extraction: perspective from convolutional neural networks. In: Proceedings of the 1st Workshop on Vector Space Modeling for Natural Language Processing, pp. 39–48 (2015)
6. Li, Z., Ding, N., Liu, Z., Zheng, H., Shen, Y.: Chinese relation extraction with multi-grained information and external linguistic knowledge. In: Proceedings of the 57th Annual Meeting of the Association for Computational Linguistics, pp. 4377–4386 (2019)
7. Sahu, S.K., Christopoulou, F., Miwa, M., Ananiadou, S.: Inter-sentence relation extraction with document-level graph convolutional neural network. arXiv preprint arXiv:1906.04684 (2019)

8. Miwa, M., Bansal, M.: End-to-end relation extraction using LSTMs on sequences and tree structures. arXiv preprint arXiv:1601.00770 (2016)
9. Lin, Y., Shen, S., Liu, Z., Luan, H., Sun, M.: Neural relation extraction with selective attention over instances. In: Proceedings of the 54th Annual Meeting of the Association for Computational Linguistics (Volume 1: Long Papers), pp. 2124–2133 (2016)
10. Zeng, D., Liu, K., Lai, S., Zhou, G., Zhao, J., et al.: Relation classification via convolutional deep neural network (2014)
11. Zeng, D., Liu, K., Chen, Y., Zhao, J.: Distant supervision for relation extraction via piecewise convolutional neural networks. In: Proceedings of the 2015 Conference on Empirical Methods in Natural Language Processing, pp. 1753–1762 (2015)
12. Zhang, D., Wang, D.: Relation classification via recurrent neural network. arXiv preprint arXiv:1508.01006 (2015)
13. Zhou, P., et al.: Attention-based bidirectional long short-term memory networks for relation classification. In: Proceedings of the 54th Annual Meeting of the Association for Computational Linguistics (Volume 2: Short Papers), pp. 207–212 (2016)
14. Papanikolaou, Y., Roberts, I., Pierleoni, A.: Deep bidirectional transformers for relation extraction without supervision. arXiv preprint arXiv:1911.00313 (2019)
15. Wang, H., et al.: Extracting multiple-relations in one-pass with pre-trained transformers. arXiv preprint arXiv:1902.01030 (2019)
16. Sabour, S., Frosst, N., Hinton, G.E.: Dynamic routing between capsules. In: Advances in Neural Information Processing Systems, pp. 3856–3866 (2017)
17. Hinton, G.E., Sabour, S., Frosst, N.: Matrix capsules with EM routing (2018)
18. Zhao, W., Ye, J., Yang, M., Lei, Z., Zhang, S., Zhao, Z.: Investigating capsule networks with dynamic routing for text classification. arXiv preprint arXiv:1804.00538 (2018)
19. Chen, Z., Qian, T.: Transfer capsule network for aspect level sentiment classification. In: Proceedings of the 57th Annual Meeting of the Association for Computational Linguistics, pp. 547–556 (2019)
20. Xi, E., Bing, S., Jin, Y.: Capsule network performance on complex data. arXiv preprint arXiv:1712.03480 (2017)
21. Kim, J., Jang, S., Park, E., Choi, S.: Text classification using capsules. Neurocomputing **376**, 214–221 (2020)
22. Zhang, N., Deng, S., Sun, Z., Chen, X., Zhang, W., Chen, H.: Attention-based capsule networks with dynamic routing for relation extraction. arXiv preprint arXiv:1812.11321 (2018)
23. Aly, R., Remus, S., Biemann, C.: Hierarchical multi-label classification of text with capsule networks. In: Proceedings of the 57th Annual Meeting of the Association for Computational Linguistics: Student Research Workshop, pp. 323–330 (2019)
24. Vaswani, A., et al.: Attention is all you need. In: Advances in Neural Information Processing Systems, pp. 5998–6008 (2017)
25. Santoro, A., et al.: Relational recurrent neural networks. In: Advances in Neural Information Processing Systems, pp. 7299–7310 (2018)
26. Mikolov, T., Sutskever, I., Chen, K., Corrado, G.S., Dean, J.: Distributed representations of words and phrases and their compositionality. In: Advances in Neural Information Processing Systems, pp. 3111–3119 (2013)
27. Devlin, J., Chang, M.-W., Lee, K., Toutanova, K.: BERT: pre-training of deep bidirectional transformers for language understanding. arXiv preprint arXiv:1810.04805 (2018)

Estimation of Conditional Mixture Weibull Distribution with Right Censored Data Using Neural Network for Time-to-Event Analysis

Achraf Bennis[(✉)], Sandrine Mouysset[(✉)], and Mathieu Serrurier[(✉)]

I.R.I.T - Université Toulouse III Paul Sabatier, 31330 Toulouse, France
{achraf.bennis,sandrine.mouysset,mathieu.serrurier}@irit.fr,
bennis.achraf@outlook.fr

Abstract. In this paper, we consider survival analysis with right-censored data which is a common situation in predictive maintenance and health field. We propose a model based on the estimation of two-parameter Weibull distribution conditionally to the features. To achieve this result, we describe a neural network architecture and the associated loss functions that takes into account the right-censored data. We extend the approach to a finite mixture of two-parameter Weibull distributions. We first validate that our model is able to precisely estimate the right parameters of the conditional Weibull distribution on synthetic datasets. In numerical experiments on two real-word datasets (METABRIC and SEER), our model outperforms the state-of-the-art methods. We also demonstrate that our approach can consider any survival time horizon.

Keywords: Survival analysis · Weibull distribution · Neural network

1 Introduction

Time-to-event analysis, also called survival analysis, is needed in many areas. This branch of statistics which emerged in the 20th century is heavily used in engineering, economics and finance, insurance, marketing, health field and many more application areas. Most previous works and diverse literature approach time-to-event analysis by dealing with time until occurrence of an event of interest; e.g. cardiovascular death after some treatment intervention, tumor recurrence, failure of an aircraft air system, etc. The time of the event may nevertheless not be observed within the relevant time period, and could potentially occur after this recorded time, producing so called right-censored data. The main objective of survival analysis is to identify the relationship between the distribution of the time-to-event distribution and the covariates of the observations, such as the features of a given patient, the characteristics of an electronic device

Supported by Smart Occitania, ADEME and ENEDIS.

© Springer Nature Switzerland AG 2020
H. W. Lauw et al. (Eds.): PAKDD 2020, LNAI 12084, pp. 687–698, 2020.
https://doi.org/10.1007/978-3-030-47426-3_53

or a mechanical system with some informations concerning the environment in which it must operate. The Weibull distribution could be used as lifetime distributions in survival analysis where the goal would be to estimate its parameters taking account the right-censored data. Several previous works focused on the estimation of a Weibull distribution with right-censored data (see Bacha and Celeux [1], Ferreira and Silva [2] and Wu [3]).

Among the first estimators widely used in this field is the Kaplan-Meier estimator [4] that may be useful to estimate the probability that an event of interest occurs at a given point in time. However, it is limited in its ability to estimate this probability adjusted for covariates; i.e. it doesn't incorporate observations' covariates. The semi-parametric Cox proportional hazards (CPH) [5] is used to estimate covariate-adjusted survival, but it assumes that the subject's risk is a linear function of their covariates which may be too simplistic for many real world data. Since neural networks can learn nonlinear functions, many researchers tried to model the relationship between the covariates and the times that passes before some event occurs, including Faraggi-Simon network [6] who proposed a simple feed-forward as the basis for a non-linear proportional hazards model to model this relationship. After that, several works focused on combining neural networks and survival analysis, notably DeepSurv [7] whose architecture is deeper than Faraggi-Simon's one and minimizes the negative log Cox partial likelihood with a risk not necessarily linear. These models use multilayer perceptron that is capable to learn non-linear models, but it is sensitive to feature scaling which is necessary in data preprocessing step and has limitations when we use unstructured data (e.g. images). There is a number of other models that approach survival analysis with right-censored data using machine learning, namely RandomForest Survival [8], dependent logistic regressors [9] and Liao's model [10] who are capable of incorporating the individual observation's covariates. This paper proposes a novel approach to survival analysis: we assume that the survival times distribution are modeled according to a finite Mixture of Weibull distributions (at least one), whose parameters depends on the covariates of a given observations with right-censored data. As Luck [11], we propose a deep learning model that learns the survival function, but we will do this by estimating the Weibull's parameters. Unlike DeepHit [12] whose model consists on discretizing the time considering a predefined maximum time horizon. Here, as we try to estimate the parameters, we can model a continuous survival function, and thus, estimate the risk at any given survival time horizon. For this purpose, we construct a deep neural network model considering that the survival times follow a finite mixture of two-parameter Weibull distributions. This model, which we call **DeepWeiSurv** tries to estimate the parameters that maximize the likelihood of the distribution. To prove the usefulness of our method, we compare its predictive performance with that of state-of-the art methods using two real-world datasets. DeepWeiSurv outperforms the previous state-of-the-art methods.

2   Weibull Mixture Distribution for Survival Analysis

2.1   Survival Analysis with Right-Censored Data

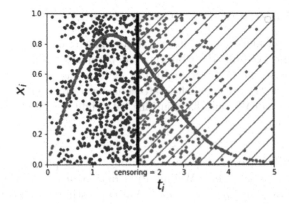

Fig. 1. Weibull distribution right-censored at $t_c = 2$ with $x \in [0,1]$ uniformly distributed. In this figure, the parameters of the law are independent with regard to x. (Color figure online)

Let $X = \{(x_i, t_i, \delta_i) | i \leq n\}$ be a set of observations with $x_i \in \mathbb{R}^d$, the ith observation of the baseline data (covariates), $t_i \in \mathbb{R}$ its survival time associated, and δ_i indicates if the ith observation is censored ($\delta_i = 0$) or not ($\delta_i = 1$). As can be seen in Fig. 1, a blue point represents an uncensored observation $(x_i, t_i, \delta_i = 1)$ and a red point represents a censored observation $(x_i, t_i, \delta_i = 0)$. In order to characterize the distribution of the survival times $T = (t_i | x_i)_{i \leq n}$, the aim is to estimate, for each observation, the probability that the event occurs after or at a certain survival time horizon t_{STH} defined by:

$$S(t_i | x_i) = P(t_i \geq t_{STH} | x_i). \tag{1}$$

Note that, t_{STH} may be different to the censoring threshold time t_c. An alternative characterization of the distribution of T is given by the hazard function $\lambda(t)$ that is defined as the event rate at time t conditional on survival at time t or beyond. Literature has shown that $\lambda(t)$ can be expressed as follows: $\lambda(t) = \frac{f(t)}{S(t)}$, $f(t)$ being the density function.

Instead of estimating the $S(t_i | x_i)$, it is common to estimate directly the survival time $\hat{t}_i$. In this case, we can measure the quality of estimations with the concordance index [13] defined as follows:

$$C_{index} = \frac{\sum_{i,j} \mathbb{1}_{t_i > t_j} \cdot \mathbb{1}_{\hat{t}_i > \hat{t}_j} \cdot \delta_j}{\sum_{i,j} \mathbb{1}_{t_i > t_j} \cdot \delta_j}. \tag{2}$$

C_{index} is designed to calculate the number of concordant pairs of observations among all the comparable pairs (i, j) such that $\delta_i = \delta_j = 1$. It estimates the probability $\mathbb{P}(\hat{t}_i > \hat{t}_j | t_i > t_j)$ that compares the rankings of two independent pairs of survival times t_i, t_j and associated predictions $\hat{t}_i$, $\hat{t}_j$.

2.2 Weibull Distribution for Censored Data

From now, we consider that T follows a finite mixture of two-parameter Weibull (at least a single Weibull) distributions independently from x_i (i.e. $S(t_i|x_i) = S(t_i)$). In this case, we have the analytical expressions of S and λ with respect to the mixture parameters. This leads to consider a problem of parameters estimation of mixture of Weibull distributions with right-censored observations. Let $y = (y_i)_i = (t_i, \delta_i)_i$.

Single Weibull Case. Here, we are dealing with a particular case where T follows a single two-parameter Weibull distribution, $\mathscr{W}(\beta, \eta)$, whose parameters are $\beta > 0$ (*shape*) and $\eta > 0$ (*scale*). We can estimate these parameters by solving the following likelihood optimization problem:

$$\hat{\beta}, \hat{\eta} = \underset{\beta, \eta}{\operatorname{argmax}} \{\mathcal{LL}(\beta, \eta | y) = \sum_{i=1}^{n} \delta_i log[(S_{\beta, \eta}.\lambda_{\beta, \eta})(t_i)] + (1 - \delta_i)log[S_{\beta, \eta}(t_c)] \quad (3)$$

where:

$$S_{\beta, \eta}(t) = exp[-(\frac{t}{\eta})^{\beta}],$$
$$\lambda_{\beta, \eta}(t) = (\frac{\beta}{\eta})(\frac{t}{\eta})^{\beta - 1} \quad (4)$$

and t_c being the censoring threshold time. $\mathcal{LL}$ is the log-likelihood of Weibull distribution with right-censored data. To be sure that the $\mathcal{LL}$ is concave, we make a choice to consider that the shape parameter β is greater than 1 ($\beta \geq 1$).

Mixture Case. Now, we suppose that T follows $\mathcal{W}_p = [(\mathscr{W}(\beta_k, \eta_k)), (\alpha_k)]_{k=1..p}$ a mixture of p Weibull distributions with its weighting coefficients ($\sum_k \alpha_k = 1$, $\alpha_k \geq 0$). In statistics, the density associated is defined by:

$$f_{\mathcal{W}_p} = \sum_k \alpha_k f_{\beta_k, \eta_k} = \sum_k \alpha_k S_{\beta_k, \eta_k} \lambda_{\beta_k, \eta_k}. \quad (5)$$

Thus, the log-likelihood of $\mathcal{W}_p$ can be written as follows:

$$\mathcal{LL}(\beta, \eta, \alpha | y) = \sum_{i=1}^{n} \delta_i log \left[\sum_k \alpha_k (S_{\beta_k, \eta_k}.\lambda_{\beta_k, \eta_k})(t_i) \right]$$
$$+ (1 - \delta_i)log \left[\sum_k \alpha_k S_{\beta_k, \eta_k}(t_c) \right]. \quad (6)$$

In addition to the mixture's parameters $(\beta_k, \eta_k)_{k=1...p}$, we need to estimate the weighting coefficients (α_k) considered as probabilities. Therefore, we estimate the tuple (α, β, η) by solving the following problem:

$$(\hat{\beta}, \hat{\eta}, \hat{\alpha}) = \underset{\beta,\eta,\alpha}{\operatorname{argmax}}\{\mathcal{LL}(\beta, \eta, \alpha|(t_i, \delta_i)_i)\} \tag{7}$$

Knowing Weibull's mean formula μ and given that the mean of a mixture is a weighted combination of the means of the distributions that form this mixture (more precisely, $\mu = \sum_k \alpha_k \mu_k$), the mean lifetime can thus be estimated as follows:

$$\mu = \hat{\alpha}.diag(\hat{\eta}).\Gamma(1 + \frac{1}{\beta})^T \tag{8}$$

where Γ is the Gamma function. μ can be used as the survival time estimation for the computation of the concordance index (with $\hat{t}_i = \mu_i = \mu$ when the parameters of the distribution are independent from x_i).

3 Neural Network for Estimating Conditional Weibull Mixture

We now consider that the Weibull mixture's parameters depend on the covariates $x = (x_i)$. We propose to use a neural network to model this dependence.

3.1 Model Description

We name g_p the function that models the relationship between x_i and the parameters of the conditional Weibull mixture:

$$\begin{aligned} g_p : \mathbb{R}^d &\rightarrow \quad \mathbb{R}^{p \times 3} \\ x_i &\mapsto (\alpha, \beta, \eta) \end{aligned} \tag{9}$$

where $\alpha = (\alpha_1, ..\alpha_p)$ and $(\beta, \eta) = ((\beta_1, .., \beta_p), (\eta_1, .., \eta_p))$. Note that, when $p = 1$, it is no more required to estimate α. This function is represented by the network named DeepWeiSurv described in Fig. 2. Hence, our goal is to train the network to learn g_p and thus $(\hat{\beta}, \hat{\eta})$ the vector of parameters that maximize the likelihood of the time-to-event distribution ($\hat{\alpha}$ as well if $p > 1$). DeepWeiSurv is therefore a multi-task network. It consists of a common sub-network, a classification sub-network (*clf*) and a regression sub-network (*reg*). The shared sub-network takes as an input the baseline data **x** of size n and compute a latent representation of the data z. When $p > 1$, *clf* and *reg* take z as an input towards producing $\hat{\alpha}$ and $(\hat{\beta}, \hat{\eta})$ respectively. For *reg* sub-network, we use ELU (with its constant $= 1$) as an activation function for both output layers. We use this function to be sure that we have enough gradient to learn the parameters thanks to the fact that it becomes smooth slowly unlike ReLU function. However the codomain of ELU is $]-1, \infty[$, which is problematic given the constraints on the parameters mentioned in the previous section ($\beta \geq 1$ and $\eta > 0$). To get around this problem, the network

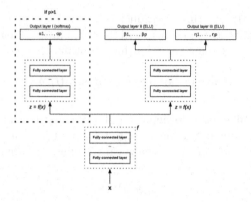

Fig. 2. The architecture of DeepWeiSurv

will learn $\hat{\beta}_{off} = \hat{\beta} + 2$ and $\hat{\eta}_{off} = \hat{\eta} + 1 + \epsilon$. The offset is then applied in the opposite direction to recover the parameters concerned. For the classification part we need to learn $\alpha \in \mathbb{R}^p$. To ensure that $\sum_k \alpha_k = 1$ and $\alpha_k \in [0, 1]$, we use a *softmax* activation in the output layer of *clf*. For each $1 \le k \le p$, *clf* produces, $\alpha_k = (\alpha_{1k}, ...\alpha_{nk})$ where α_{ik} is such that: $\hat{P}(\{Y = t_i\}) = \alpha_{ik}$ with $Y \sim \mathscr{W}(\beta_k, \eta_k)$ and $\hat{P}$ a probability estimate, whereas *reg* outputs $\beta_k = (\beta_{1k}, ..\beta_{nk})$ and $\eta_k = (\eta_{1k}, ...\eta_{nk})$. Otherwise, i.e. $p = 1$, we have $\alpha_1 = 1$, thus we don't need to train *clf*.

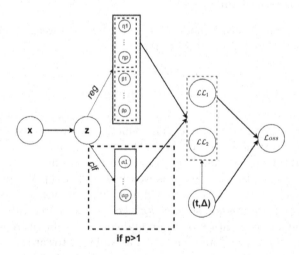

Fig. 3. Computational graph of $\mathcal{L}oss$

To train DeepWeiSurv, we minimize the following loss function:

$$\mathcal{L}oss = -\mathcal{LL}(\beta, \eta, \alpha|y) \underset{(6)}{=} \mathcal{LL}_1.\Delta^T + \mathcal{LL}_2.(\mathbf{1}_{\mathbb{R}^n} - \Delta)^T \qquad (10)$$

where Δ is the vector of event indicators and:

$$\mathcal{LL}_1 = log[\hat{\alpha}.S\Lambda_{\hat{\beta},\hat{\eta}}(T)] \text{ and } \mathcal{LL}_2 = log[\hat{\alpha}.S_{\hat{\beta},\hat{\eta}}(t_c)] \tag{11}$$

with:

$$S\Lambda_{\hat{\beta},\hat{\eta}}(t) = \begin{pmatrix} (S_{\beta_1,\eta_1}.\lambda_{\beta_1,\eta_1})(t_1) & \cdots & (S_{\beta_1,\eta_1}.\lambda_{\beta_1,\eta_1})(t_n) \\ \cdots & \cdots & \cdots \\ (S_{\beta_p,\eta_p}.\lambda_{\beta_p,\eta_p})(t_1) & \cdots & (S_{\beta_p,\eta_p}.\lambda_{\beta_p,\eta_p})(t_n) \end{pmatrix} \tag{12}$$

and

$$S_{\hat{\beta},\hat{\eta}}(t_c) = \begin{pmatrix} S_{\beta_1,\eta_1}(t_c) \\ \cdots \\ S_{\beta_p,\eta_p}(t_c) \end{pmatrix} \tag{13}$$

$\mathcal{LL}_1$ exploits uncensored data, whereas $\mathcal{LL}_2$ exploits censored observations by extracting the knowledge that the event will occur after the given censoring threshold time t_c. Figure 3 is an illustration of the computational graph of our training loss: the inputs are the covariates x, the real values of time and event indicator (t, Δ) and the outputs are the estimates $(\hat{\alpha}, \hat{\beta}, \hat{\eta})$.

3.2 Experiment on SYNTHETIC Dataset

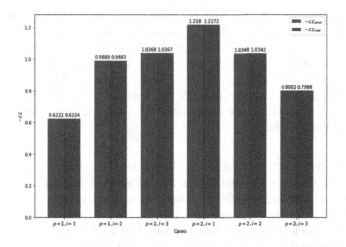

Fig. 4. $-\mathcal{LL}_{pred}$ and $-\mathcal{LL}_{real}$ values for each studied case

The main objective in this section is to validate mathematically Deep-WeiSurv, that is, to show that this latter is able to estimate the parameters. For this purpose, we perform an experiment on a simulated data. In this experiment, we treat the case of a *single* Weibull distribution ($\alpha_{p=1} = 1$) and a *mixture* of 2 Weibull distributions ($\alpha_{p=2} = (0.7, 0.3)$) using three different functions: f_1 (*linear*), f_2 (*quadratic*), f_3 (*cubic*). For each function f_i we generate $T_{p=1}^i$

$\sim \mathcal{W}(\beta_1^i, \eta_1^i)$ and $T_{p=2}^i \sim \mathcal{W}_{p=2}(\beta_{0.7}^i, \eta_{0.7}^i, \beta_{0.3}^i, \eta_{0.3}^i)$. We compare the predicted likelihood with the real, and optimal one. These two likelihoods are equal when the estimated parameters correspond to the real ones. Let X be a vector of 10000 observations generated from an uniform distribution $\mathcal{U}_{[0,1]}$. Here we select 50% of observations to be right censored at the median of survival times t_m ($\delta_i = 0$ if $t_i > t_m$). We set the parameters to be the following functions:

$$\begin{pmatrix} \beta_1^1 \\ \eta_1^1 \\ \beta_{0.7}^1 \\ \eta_{0.7}^1 \\ \beta_{0.3}^1 \\ \eta_{0.3}^1 \end{pmatrix} = \begin{pmatrix} 3 & 2 \\ 2 & 1 \\ 2 & 1 \\ 1 & 2 \\ 1 & 2 \\ 3 & 1 \end{pmatrix} \cdot \begin{pmatrix} X \\ 1 \end{pmatrix} \quad \begin{pmatrix} \beta_1^2 \\ \eta_1^2 \\ \beta_{0.7}^2 \\ \eta_{0.7}^2 \\ \beta_{0.3}^2 \\ \eta_{0.3}^2 \end{pmatrix} = \begin{pmatrix} 2 & 1 & 1 \\ 1 & 2 & 1 \\ 2 & 2 & 1 \\ 1 & 3 & 1 \\ 1 & 1 & 2 \\ 1 & 0 & 2 \end{pmatrix} \cdot \begin{pmatrix} X^2 \\ X \\ 1 \end{pmatrix} \quad \begin{pmatrix} \beta_1^3 \\ \eta_1^3 \\ \beta_{0.7}^3 \\ \eta_{0.7}^3 \\ \beta_{0.3}^3 \\ \eta_{0.3}^3 \end{pmatrix} = \begin{pmatrix} 2 & 0 & 1 & 1 \\ 1 & 1 & 0 & 1 \\ 2 & 0 & 1 & 1 \\ 1 & 1 & 0 & 1 \\ 1 & 2 & 0 & 1 \\ 3 & 2 & 0 & 1 \end{pmatrix} \cdot \begin{pmatrix} X^3 \\ X^2 \\ X \\ 1 \end{pmatrix}$$

The bar plot in Fig. 4 displays the predicted likelihood $-\mathcal{LL}_{pred}$ of each distribution and their real one $-\mathcal{LL}_{real}$. We notice that the real value and predicted one of each case are very close to each other which means that the model can identify very precisely the parameters of the conditional distributions. Now, we test DeepWeisurv on the real-world datasets.

4   Experiments

We perform two sets of experiments based on real survival data: METABRIC and SEER. We give a brief descriptions of the datasets below; Table 1 gives an overview on some descriptive statistics of both real-word datasets. We train DeepWeiSurv on real survival datasets. We compare the predictive performance of DeepWeiSurv with that of CPH [5] which is the most-widely used model in the medical field and DeepHit [12] that seems to achieve outperformance over previous methods. These models are also tested in the same experimental protocol as DeepWeiSurv.

METABLNCSRIC. METABRIC (Molecular Taxonomy of Breast Cancer International Consortium) dataset is for a Canada-UK project that aims to classify breast tumours into further subcategories. It contains gene expressions profiles and clinical features used for this purpose. In this data, we have 1981 patients, of which 44.8% were died during the study and 55.2% were right-censored. We used 21 clinical variables including tumor size, age at diagnosis, Progesterone Receptor (PR) status etc. (see Bilal et al. [14]).

SEER. The Surveillance, Epidemiology, and End Results (SEER[1]) [15] Program provides information on cancer statistics during 1975–2016. We focused on the patients (in total 33387) recorded between 1998 and 2002 who died from a breast cancer BC (42.8%) or a heart disease HD (49.6%), or who were right-censored

---

[1] https://seer.cancer.gov.

(57.2% and 50.4% respectively). We extracted 30 covariates including gender, race, tumor size, number of malignant of benign tumors, Estrogen Receptor status (ER), PR status, etc. For evaluation we separated the data into two datasets with respect of the death's cause (BC & HD) while keeping censored patients in both of them.

Table 1. Descriptive statistics of real-world datasets

Datasets	No. uncensored	No. censored	No. features	
			Qualitative	Quantitative
METABRIC	888 (44.8%)	1093 (55.2%)	15	6
SEER BC	9152(42.8%)	12221 (57.2%)	23	11
SEER HD	12014 (49.6%)	12221 (50.4%)		

4.1 Network Configuration

DeepWeiSurv is consisted of three blocks: the shared sub-network which is a 4-layer network, 3 of which are fully connected layers (128, 64, 32 nodes respectively) and the remain is a batch normalization layer, the second and the third block (*reg, clf* respectively) consisted of 2 fully connected layers (16, 8 nodes) and 1 batch normalization layer. Added to that, the network finishes by one softmax layer and two ELU layers as outputs. The hidden layers are activated by ReLU function. DeepWeiSurv is trained via Adam optimizer and learning rate of 10^{-4}. DeepWeiSurv is implemented in a PyTorch environment.

4.2 Experimental Protocol

We applied 5-fold cross validation: the data is randomly splitted into training set (80% and 20% of which is reserved for validation) and test set (20%). We use the predicted values of the parameters to calculate the mean lifetime μ and then C_{index} defined by Eq. (2). This latter is calculated on the validation set. We tested DeepWeiSurv with $p = 1$ and $p = 2$ (we tested higher values of p, but without better performance).

4.3 Results

Table 2 displays the C_{index} results of the experiments realized on SEER and METABRIC datasets. We can observe that, for METABRIC, DeepWeiSurv's performances exceed by far that of DeepHit and CPH. For the SEER data, Deep-WeiSurv with $p = 1$ outperfoms CPH (in BC and HD cases) and has a slight improvement over DeepHit especially for SEER HD data but without a significant difference (their confidence intervals did overlap). However, the improvement

Table 2. Comparison of C_{index} performance tested on METABRIC and SEER (mean and 95% confidence interval)

Algorithms	Datasets		
	METABRIC	SEER BC	SEER HD
CPH	0.658 (0.646−0.671)	0.833 (0.829−0.838)	0.784 (0.779−0.788)
DeepHit	0.651 (0.641−0.661)	0.875 (0.867−0.883)	0.846 (0.842−0.851)
DeepWeiSurv ($p=1$)	0.805 (0.782−0.829)	0.877 (0.864−0.891)	0.857 (0.85−0.866)
DeepWeiSurv ($p=2$)	**0.819 (0.812−0.837)**	**0.908 (0.906−0.909)**	**0.863 (0.86−0.868)**

of DeepWeiSurv with $p = 2$ over all the other methods is highly statistically significant. We suspect that the good performances of DeepWeiSurv comes from its ability to learn implicitly the relationship between the covariates and the parameters without making any restrictive assumption.

4.4   Censoring Threshold Sensitivity

In the previous experiments the survival time horizon and the censoring threshold coincide, but it is not always the case. Since DeepWeiSurv predicts the conditional Weibull distributions with respect to the covariates, it is able to consider any survival time horizon given a censoring threshold. We add another experiment on METABRIC[2] dataset where we assess DeepWeiSurv ($p = 2$) performance with respect to censoring threshold time t_c. The aim of this experiment, is to check if DeepWeiSurv can handle data in highly censored setting for different survival time horizons. For this purpose, we apply the same experimental protocol as before, but changing the censoring threshold. We do this for some values of t_c far below than that used in the previous experiment ($t_c = t_{METABRIC} = 8940$). This values, expressed in quantiles[3], are carefully selected in order to have a significant added portion (compared to that of the adjacent value that precedes) of censored observations. As an observation may change from a censored status to an uncensored status by changing the threshold of censorship and vice versa, for each value of censoring threshold time t_c we therefore have a new set of observed events $OE_{t_c} = \{(t_i, \delta_i) \| \delta_i = 1 \text{ if } t_i < t_c \text{ else } 0\}$ (i.e. comparable events, and this contributes to the calculation of C_{index}). The training set, as it is selected, contains $ref = 866$ censored observations. Table 3 gives the number of censored and uncensored observations of each selected value of t_c. For each value of t_c, we apply the 5-fold cross validation and then calculate the average C_{index} for every survival time horizons t_{STH}. The results are displayed in Fig. 5.

---

[2] We have chosen METABRIC dataset because of its small size compared to that of SEER dataset in order to avoid long calculations.

[3] We choose this values by using the quantiles of the survival times vector T.

Table 3. Distribution of training set's observations (censored/uncensored) for each selected censoring threshold.

t_c	No. censored	No. uncensored	Added portion (w.r.t ref)
$q_{0.5}$	1026	558	160
$q_{0.45}$	1127	457	261
$q_{0.35}$	1248	336	382
$q_{0.25}$	1338	246	472

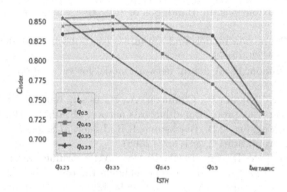

Fig. 5. The average of C_{index} w.r.t survival time horizon t_{STH} for every selected threshold t_c.

Each curve in Fig. 5 represents the scores calculated for a given censoring threshold t_c in different survival time horizons t_{STH} in x-axis. We can notice that the average score decreases when t_c decreases which is expected because we have less and less of uncensored data which means that it becomes more and more difficult to model the distribution of survival times. However, DeepWeiSurv still performing well in highly censored setting.

5 Conclusion

In this paper, we described a new approach, DeepWeiSurv, to the survival analysis. The key role of DeepWeiSurv is to predict the parameters of a mixture of Weibull distributions with respect to the covariates in presence of right-censored data. In addition to the fact that Weibull distributions are known to be a good representation for this kind of problem, it also permits to consider any survival time horizon given a censoring threshold. Experiments on generated databases show that DeepWeiSurv converges to the real parameters when the survival time data follows a mixture of Weibull distributions whose parameters are a simple function of the covariates. On real datasets, DeepWeiSurv clearly outperforms the state-of-the-art approaches and demonstrates its ability to consider any survival time horizon.

References

1. Bacha, M., Celeux, G.: Bayesian estimation of a Weibull distribution in a highly censored and small sample setting. INRIA (1996)
2. Ferreira, L.A., Silva, J.L.: Parameter estimation for Weibull distribution with right censored data using EM algorithm. Eksploatacja i Niezawodność **19**, 310–315 (2017)
3. Wu, S.-J.: Estimations of the parameters of the Weibull distribution with progressively censored data. J. Jpn. Stat. Soc. **32**, 155–163 (2002)
4. Marin, J.-M., Mengersen, K., Robert, C.P.: Bayesian modelling and inference on mixtures of distributions. In: Handbook of Statistics, vol. 25, pp. 459–507. Elsevier (2005)
5. Cox, D.R.: Regression models and life tables (with discussion). J. Roy. Stat. Soc. Ser. B. **34**, 187–220 (1972)
6. Faraggi, D., Simon, R.: A neural network model for survival data. Stat. Med. **14**, 73–82 (1995)
7. Katzman, J.L., Shaham, U., Cloninger, A., Bates, J., Jiang, T., Kluger, Y.: Deep survival: a deep Cox proportional hazards network. Statistics **1050**, 2 (2016)
8. Ishwaran, H., Kogalur, U.B., Blackstone, E.H., Lauer, M.S., et al.: Random survival forests. Ann. Appl. Stat. **2**, 841–860 (2008)
9. Yu, C.-N., Greiner, R., Lin, H.-C., Baracos, V.: Learning patient-specific cancer survival distributions as a sequence of dependent regressors. In: Advances in Neural Information Processing Systems 24, pp. 1845–1853. Curran Associates Inc. (2011)
10. Liao, L., Ahn, H.-I.: Combining deep learning and survival analysis for asset health management. Int. J. Progn. Health Manag. (2016)
11. Luck, M., Sylvain, T., Cardinal, H., Lodi, A., Bengio, Y.: Deep learning for patient-specific kidney graft survival analysis. arXiv preprint arXiv:1705.10245 (2017)
12. Lee, C., Zame, W.R., Yoon, J., van der Schaar, M.: DeepHit: a deep learning approach to survival analysis with competing risks. In: Thirty-Second AAAI Conference on Artificial Intelligence (2018)
13. Harrell, F.E., Califf, R.M., Pryor, D.B., Lee, K.L., Rosati, R.A.: Evaluating the yield of medical tests. JAMA **247**(18), 2543–2546 (1982)
14. Bilal, E., et al.: Improving breast cancer survival analysis through competition-based multidimensional modeling. PLoS Comput. Biol. **9**, e1003047 (2013)
15. National Cancer Institute, DCCPS, Surveillance Research Program: Surveillance, Epidemiology, and End Results (SEER) Program. www.seer.cancer.gov. SEER*Stat Database: Incidence - SEER 18 Regs Research Data + Hurricane Katrina Impacted Louisiana Cases, November 2018 Submission (1975–2016 varying). Linked To County Attributes - Total U.S., 1969–2017 Counties, Released April 2019, Based on the November 2018 Submission

Dual-Component Deep Domain Adaptation: A New Approach for Cross Project Software Vulnerability Detection

Van Nguyen[1($\boxtimes$)], Trung Le[1($\boxtimes$)], Olivier de Vel[2($\boxtimes$)], Paul Montague[2($\boxtimes$)], John Grundy[1($\boxtimes$)], and Dinh Phung[1($\boxtimes$)]

[1] Monash University, Clayton, Australia
{van.nk,trunglm,john.grundy,dinh.phung}@monash.edu
[2] Defence Science and Technology Group, Canberra, Australia
{Olivier.DeVel,Paul.Montague}@dst.defence.gov.au

Abstract. Owing to the ubiquity of computer software, software vulnerability detection (SVD) has become an important problem in the software industry and computer security. One of the most crucial issues in SVD is coping with the scarcity of labeled vulnerabilities in projects that require the laborious manual labeling of code by software security experts. One possible solution is to employ deep domain adaptation (DA) which has recently witnessed enormous success in transferring learning from structural labeled to unlabeled data sources. Generative adversarial network (GAN) is a technique that attempts to bridge the gap between source and target data in the joint space and emerges as a building block to develop deep DA approaches with state-of-the-art performance. However, deep DA approaches using the GAN principle to close the gap are subject to the mode collapsing problem that negatively impacts the predictive performance. Our aim in this paper is to propose Dual Generator-Discriminator Deep Code Domain Adaptation Network (Dual-GD-DDAN) for tackling the problem of transfer learning from labeled to unlabeled software projects in SVD to resolve the mode collapsing problem faced in previous approaches. The experimental results on real-world software projects show that our method outperforms state-of-the-art baselines by a wide margin.

Keywords: Domain adaptation · Cyber security · Software vulnerability detection · Machine learning · Deep learning

1 Introduction

In the software industry, software vulnerabilities relate to specific flaws or oversights in software programs which allow attackers to expose or alter sensitive information, disrupt or destroy a system, or take control of a program or computer system. The software vulnerability detection problem has become an important issue in the software industry and in the field of computer security. Computer software development employs of a vast variety of technologies and different software development methodologies, and much computer software contains vulnerabilities.

© Springer Nature Switzerland AG 2020
H. W. Lauw et al. (Eds.): PAKDD 2020, LNAI 12084, pp. 699–711, 2020.
https://doi.org/10.1007/978-3-030-47426-3_54

This has necessitated the development of automated advanced techniques and tools that can efficiently and effectively detect software vulnerabilities with a minimal level of human intervention. To respond to this demand, many vulnerability detection systems and methods, ranging from open source to commercial tools, and from manual to automatic methods have been proposed and implemented. Most of the previous works in software vulnerability detection (SVD) [1, 8] have been developed based on handcrafted features which are manually chosen by knowledgeable domain experts who may have outdated experience and underlying biases. In many situations, handcrafted features normally do not generalize well. For example, features that work well in a certain software project may not perform well in other projects. To alleviate the dependency on handcrafted features, the use of automatic features in SVD has been studied recently [11–13]. These works have shown the advantages of automatic features over handcrafted features in the context of software vulnerability detection.

However, most of these approaches lead to another crucial issue in SVD research, namely the scarcity of labeled projects. Labelled vulnerable code is needed to train these models, and the process of labeling vulnerable source code is very tedious, time-consuming, error-prone, and challenging even for domain experts. This has led to few labeled projects compared with the vast volume of unlabeled ones. A viable solution is to apply transfer learning or domain adaptation which aims to devise automated methods that make it possible to transfer a learned model from the source domain with labels to the target domains without labels. Studies in domain adaptation can be broadly categorized into two themes: shallow [6] and deep domain adaptations [3, 14, 18]. These recent studies have shown the advantages of deep over shallow domain adaptation (i.e., higher predictive performance and capacity to tackle structural data). Deep domain adaptation encourages the learning of new representations for both source and target data in order to minimize the divergence between them [3, 14, 18]. The general idea is to map source and target data to a joint feature space via a generator, where the discrepancy between the source and target distributions is reduced. Notably, the work of [3, 18] employed generative adversarial networks (GANs) [4] to close the gap between source and target data in the joint space. However, most of aforementioned works mainly focus on transfer learning in the computer vision domain. The work of [16] is the first work which applies deep domain adaptation to SVD with promising predictive performance on real-world source code projects. The underlying idea is to employ the GAN to close the gap between the source and target domains in the joint space and enforce the clustering assumption [2] to utilize the information carried in the unlabeled target samples in a semi-supervised context.

GANs are known to be affected by the mode collapsing problem [5, 7, 10, 17]. In particular, the study in [17] recently studied the mode collapsing problem and further classified this into the missing mode problem i.e., the generated samples miss some modes in the true data, and the boundary distortion problem i.e., the generated samples can only partly recover some modes in the true data. It is certain that deep domain adaptation approaches that use the GAN principle will inherently encounter both the missing mode and boundary distortion problems. Last but not least, deep domain adaptation approaches using the GAN principle also face the data distortion problem. The representations of source and target examples in the joint feature space degenerate to very small regions that cannot preserve the manifold/clustering structure in the original space.

Our aim in this paper is to address not only deep domain adaptation mode collapsing problems but also boundary distortion problems when employing the GAN as a principle in order to close the gap between source and target data in the joint feature space. Our two approaches are: i) apply manifold regularization for enabling the preservation of manifold/clustering structures in the joint feature space, hence avoiding the degeneration of source and target data in this space; and ii) invoke dual discriminators in an elegant way to reduce the negative impacts of the missing mode and boundary distortion problems in deep domain adaptation using the GAN principle as mentioned before. We name our mechanism when applied to SVD as *Dual Generator-Discriminator Deep Code Domain Adaptation Network* (Dual-GD-DDAN). We empirically demonstrate that our Dual-GD-DDAN can overcome the missing mode and boundary distortion problems which is likely to happen as in Deep Code Domain Adaptation (DDAN) [16] in which the GAN was solely applied to close the gap between the source and target domains in the joint space (see the discussion in Sects. 2.3 and 3.3, and the visualization in Fig. 3). In addition, we incorporate the relevant approaches – minimizing the conditional entropy and manifold regularization with spectral graph – proposed in [16] to enforce the clustering assumption [2] and arrive at a new model named *Dual Generator-Discriminator Semi-supervised Deep Code Domain Adaptation Network* (Dual-GD-SDDAN). We further demonstrate that our Dual-GD-SDDAN can overcome the mode collapsing problem better than SCDAN in [16], hence obtaining better predictive performance.

We conducted experiments using the data sets collected by [13], that consist of five real-world software projects: FFmpeg, LibTIFF, LibPNG, VLC and Pidgin to compare our proposed Dual-GD-DDAN and Dual-GD-SDDAN with the baselines. The baselines consider to include VULD (i.e., the model proposed in [12] without domain adaptation), MMD, DIRT-T, DDAN and SCDAN as mentioned [16] and D2GAN [15] (a variant of the GAN using dual-discriminator to reduce the mode collapse for which we apply this mechanism in the joint feature space). Our experimental results show that our proposed methods are able to overcome the negative impact of the missing mode and boundary distortion problems inherent in deep domain adaptation approaches when solely using the GAN principle as in DDAN and SCDAN [16]. In addition, our method outperforms the rival baselines in terms of predictive performance by a wide margin.

2 Deep Code Domain Adaptation with GAN

2.1 Problem Statement

A source domain data set $S = \{(x_1^S, y_1), \ldots, (x_{N_S}^S, y_{N_S})\}$ where $y_i \in \{-1, 1\}$ (i.e., 1: vulnerable code and -1: non-vulnerable code) and $x_i^S = [x_{i1}^S, \ldots, x_{iL}^S]$ is a sequence of L embedding vectors, and the target domain data set $T = \{x_1^T, \ldots, x_{N_T}^T\}$ where $x_i^T = [x_{i1}^T, \ldots, x_{iL}^T]$ is also a sequence of L embedding vectors. We wish to bridge the gap between the source and target domains in the joint feature space. This allows us to transfer a classifier trained on the source domain to predict well on the target domain.

2.2 Deep Code Domain Adaptation with a Bidirectional RNN

To handle sequential data in the context of domain adaptation of software vulnerability detection, the work of [16] proposed an architecture referred to as the Code Domain Adaptation Network (CDAN). This network architecture recruits a Bidirectional RNN to process the sequential input from both source and target domains (i.e., $x_i^S = [x_{i1}^S, \ldots, x_{iL}^S]$ and $x_i^T = [x_{i1}^T, \ldots, x_{iL}^T]$). A fully connected layer is then employed to connect the output layer of the Bidirectional RNN with the joint feature layer while bridging the gap between the source and target domains. Furthermore, inspired by the Deep Domain Adaptation approach [3], the authors employ the source classifier C to classify the source samples, the domain discriminator D to distinguish the source and target samples and propose Deep Code Domain Adaptation (DDAN) whose objective function is as follows:

$$\mathcal{J}(G,D,C) = \frac{1}{N_S}\sum_{i=1}^{N_S}\ell(C(G(x_i^S)),y_i) + \lambda(\frac{1}{N_S}\sum_{i=1}^{N_S}\log D(G(x_i^S)) + \frac{1}{N_T}\sum_{i=1}^{N_T}\log[1 - D(G(x_i^T))])$$

2.3 The Shortcomings of DDAN

We observe that DDAN suffers from several shortcomings. First, the *data distortion* problem (i.e., the source and target data in the joint space might collapse into small regions) may occur since there is no mechanism in DDAN to circumvent this. Second, since DDAN is based on the GAN approach, DDAN might suffer from the mode collapsing problem [5,17]. In particular, [17] has recently studied the mode collapsing problem of GANs and discovered that they are also subject to i) the *missing mode* problem (i.e., in the joint space, either the target data misses some modes in the source data or vice versa) and ii) the *boundary distortion* problem (i.e., in the joint space either the target data partly covers the source data or vice versa), which makes the target distribution significantly diverge from the source distribution. As shown in Fig. 1, both the missing mode and boundary distortion problems simultaneously happen since the target distribution misses source mode 2, while the source distribution can only partly cover the target mode 2 in the target distribution and the target distribution can only partly cover the source mode 1 in the source distribution.

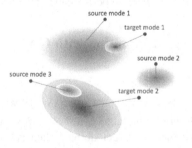

Fig. 1. An illustration of the missing mode and boundary distortion problems of DDAN. In the joint space, the target distribution misses source mode 2, while the source distribution can only partly cover the target mode 2 in the target distribution and the target distribution can only partly cover the source mode 1 in the source distribution.

3 Dual Generator-Discriminator Deep Code Domain Adaptation

3.1 Key Idea of Our Approach

We employ two discriminators (namely, D_S and D_T) to classify the source and target examples and vice versa and two separate generators (namely, G_S and G_T) to map the source and target examples to the joint space respectively. In particular, D_S produces high values on the source examples in the joint space (i.e., $G_S(x^S)$) and low values on the target examples in the joint space (i.e., $G_T(x^T)$), while D_T produces high values on the target examples in the joint space (i.e., $G_T(x^T)$) and low values on the source examples (i.e., $G_S(x^S)$). The generator G_S is trained to push $G_S(x^S)$ to the high value region of D_T and the generator G_T is trained to push $G_T(x^T)$ to the high value region of D_S. Eventually, both $D_S(G_S(x^S))$ and $D_S(G_T(x^T))$ are possibly high and both $D_T(G_S(x^S))$ and $D_T(G_T(x^T))$ are possibly high. This helps to mitigate the issues of missing mode and boundary distortion since as in Fig. 1, if the target mode 1 can only partly cover the source mode 1, then D_T cannot receive large values from source mode 1. Another important aspect of our approach is to maintain the cluster/manifold structure of source and target data in the joint space via the manifold regularization to avoid the data distortion problem.

3.2 Dual Generator-Discriminator Deep Code Domain Adaptation Network

To address the two inherent problems in the DDAN mentioned in Sect. 2.3, we employ two different generators G_S and G_T to map source and target domain examples to the joint space and two discriminators D_S and D_T to distinguish source examples against target examples and vice versa together with the source classifier C which is used to classify the source examples with labels as shown in Fig. 2. We name our proposed model as Dual Generator-Discriminator Deep Code Domain Adaptation Network (Dual-GD-DDAN).

Updating the Discriminators. The two discriminators D_S and D_T are trained to distinguish the source examples against the target examples and vice versa as follows:

$$\min_{D_S} \left(\frac{(1+\theta)}{N_S} \sum_{i=1}^{N_S} [-\log D_S(G_S(x_i^S))] + \frac{1}{N_T} \sum_{i=1}^{N_T} [-\log[1 - D_S(G_T(x_i^T))]] \right) \tag{1}$$

$$\min_{D_T} \left(\frac{1}{N_S} \sum_{i=1}^{N_S} [-\log[1 - D_T(G_S(x_i^S))]] + \frac{(1+\theta)}{N_T} \sum_{i=1}^{N_T} [-\log D_T(G_T(x_i^T))] \right) \tag{2}$$

where $\theta > 0$. Note that a high value of θ encourages D_S and D_T place higher values on $G_S(x^S)$ and $G_T(x^T)$ respectively.

Updating the Source Classifier. The source classifier is employed to classify the source examples with labels as: $\min_C \frac{1}{N_S} \sum_{i=1}^{N_S} \ell(C(G_S(x_i^S)), y_i)$, where ℓ specifies the cross-entropy loss function for the binary classification (e.g., using cross-entropy).

Updating the Generators. The two generators G_S and G_T are trained to i) maintain the manifold/cluster structures of source and target data in their original spaces to avoid the data distortion problem and ii) move the target samples toward the source samples in the joint space and resolve the missing mode and boundary distortion problems in the joint space.

To maintain the manifold/cluster structures of source and target data in their original spaces, we propose minimizing the manifold regularization term as: $\min_G \mathcal{M}(G_S, G_T)$ where $\mathcal{M}(G_S, G_T)$ is formulated as:

$$\mathcal{M}(G_S, G_T) = \sum_{i,j=1}^{N_S} \mu_{ij} \|G_S(x_i^S) - G_S(x_j^S)\|^2 + \sum_{i,j=1}^{N_T} \mu_{ij} \|G_T(x_i^T) - G_T(x_j^T)\|^2$$

in which the weights are defined as $\mu_{ij} = \exp\{-\|h(x_i) - h(x_j)\|^2 / (2\sigma^2)\}$ with $h(x) = \text{concat}(\overleftarrow{h_L}(x), \overrightarrow{h_L}(x))$ where $\overrightarrow{h_L}(x)$ and $\overleftarrow{h_L}(x)$ are the last hidden states of the bidirectional RNN with input x.

To move the target samples toward the source samples and resolve the missing mode and boundary distortion problems in the joint space, we propose minimizing the following objective function: $\min_D \mathcal{K}(G_S, G_T)$ where $\mathcal{K}(G_S, G_T)$ is defined as:

$$\mathcal{K}(G_S, G_T) = \frac{1}{N_S} \sum_{i=1}^{N_S} [-\log D_T(G_S(x_i^S))] + \frac{1}{N_T} \sum_{i=1}^{N_T} [-\log D_S(G_T(x_i^T))] \tag{3}$$

Moreover, the source generator G_S has to work out the representation that is suitable for the source classifier, hence we need to minimize the following objective function:

$$\min_{G_S} \frac{1}{N_S} \sum_{i=1}^{N_S} \ell(C(G_S(x_i^S)), y_i)$$

Finally, to update G_S and G_T, we need to minimize the following objective function:

$$\frac{1}{N_S} \sum_{i=1}^{N_S} \ell(C(G_S(x_i^S)), y_i) + \alpha \mathcal{M}(G_S, G_T) + \beta \mathcal{K}(G_S, G_T)$$

where $\alpha, \beta > 0$ are two non-negative parameters.

3.3 The Rationale for Our Dual Generator-Discriminator Deep Code Domain Adaptation Network Approach

Below we explain why our proposed Dual-GD-DDAN is able to resolve the two critical problems that occur with the DDAN approach. First, if x_i^S and x_j^S are proximal to each other and are located in the same cluster, then their representations $h(x_i^S)$ and $h(x_j^S)$ are close and hence, the weight μ_{ij} is large. This implies $G_S(x_i^S)$ and $G_S(x_j^S)$ are encouraged to be close in the joint space because we are minimizing $\mu_{ij} \|G_S(x_i^S) - G_S(x_j^S)\|^2$. This increases the chance of the two representations residing in the same cluster in the joint space. Therefore, Dual-GD-DDAN is able to preserve the clustering structure of the source data in the joint space. By using the same argument, we reach the same conclusion for the target domain.

Second, following Eqs. (1, 2), the discriminator D_S is trained to encourage large values for the source modes (i.e., $G_S(x^S)$), while the discriminator D_T is trained to produce large values for the target modes (i.e., $G_T(x^T)$). Moreover, as in Eq. (3), G_s is trained to move the source domain examples x^S to the high-valued region of D_T (i.e., the target modes or $G_T(x^T)$) and G_T is trained to move the target examples x^T to the high-valued region of D_S (i.e., the source modes or $G_S(x^S)$). As a consequence, eventually, the source modes (i.e., $G_S(x^S)$) and target modes (i.e., $G_T(x^T)$) overlap, while D_S and D_T place large values on both source (i.e., $G_S(x^S)$) and target (i.e., $G_T(x^T)$) modes. The mode missing problem is less likely to happen since, as shown in Fig. 1, if the target data misses source mode 2, then D_T cannot receive large values from source mode 2. Similarly, the boundary distortion problem is also less likely to happen since as in Fig. 1, if the target mode 1 can only partly cover the source mode 1, then D_T cannot receive large values from source mode 1. Therefore, Dual-GD-DDAN allows us to reduce the impact of the missing mode and boundary distortion problems, hence making the target distribution more identical to the source distribution in the joint space.

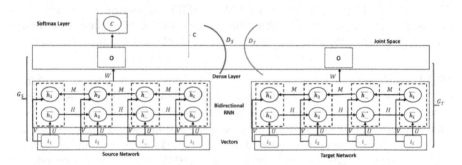

Fig. 2. The architecture of our Dual-GD-DDAN. The generators G_S and G_T take the sequential code tokens of the source domain and target domain in vectorial form respectively and map this sequence to the joint layer (i.e., the joint space). The vector representation of each statement x in source code is denoted by **i**. The discriminators D_S and D_T are invoked to discriminate the source and target data. The source classifier C is trained on the source domain with labels. We note that the source and target networks do not share parameters and are not identical.

3.4 Dual Generator-Discriminator Semi-supervised Deep Code Domain Adaptation Network

Our proposed model can be incorporated with minimizing the conditional entropy and using the spectral graph to inspire the smoothness to enforce the clustering assumption [2] proposed in [16] to form Dual Generator-Discriminator Semi-supervised Deep Code Domain Adaptation Network (Dual-GD-SDDAN). Please read our Supplementary Material for more technical details, available at https://app.box.com/s/aijcavbcp.

4   Experiments

In this section, firstly, we compare our proposed Dual-GD-DDAN with VulDeePecker without domain adaptation, MMD, D2GAN, DIRT-T and DDAN using the architecture CDAN proposed in [16]. Secondly, we do Boundary Distortion Analysis to further demonstrate the efficiency of our proposed Dual-GD-DDAN in alleviating the boundary distortion problem caused by using the GAN principle. Finally, we compare our Dual-GD-SDDAN and SCDAN introduced in [16].

4.1   Experimental Setup

Experimental Data Set. We use the real-world data sets collected by [13], which contain the source code of vulnerable and non-vulnerable functions obtained from five real-world software projects, namely FFmpeg (#vul-funcs: 187, #non-vul-funcs: 5,427), LibTIFF (#vul-funcs: 81, #non-vul-funcs: 695), LibPNG (#vul-funcs: 43, #non-vul-funcs: 551), VLC (#vul-funcs: 25, #non-vul-funcs: 5,548) and Pidgin (#vul-funcs: 42, #non-vul-funcs: 8,268) where #vul-funcs and #non-vul-funcs is the number of vulnerable and non-vulnerable functions respectively. The data sets contain both multimedia (FFmpeg, VLC, Pidgin) and image (LibPNG, LibTIFF) application categories. In our experiment, data sets from the multimedia category were used as the source domain whilst data sets from the image category were used as the target domain (see Table 1).

Model Configuration. For training the eight methods – VulDeePecker, MMD, D2GAN, DIRT-T, DDAN, Dual-GD-DDAN, SCDAN and Dual-GD-SDDAN – we use one-layer bidirectional recurrent neural networks with LSTM cells where the size of hidden states is in $\{128, 256\}$ for the generators. For the source classifier and discriminators, we use deep feed-forward neural networks with two hidden layers in which the size of each hidden layer is in $\{200, 300\}$. We embed the opcode and statement information in the $\{150, 150\}$ dimensional embedding spaces respectively (see our Supplementary Material for Data Processing and Embedding, available at https://app.box.com/s/aijcavbcp). We employ the Adam optimizer with an initial learning rate in $\{10^{-3}, 10^{-4}\}$. The mini-batch size is 64. The trade-off parameters $\alpha, \beta, \gamma, \lambda$ are in $\{10^{-1}, 10^{-2}, 10^{-3}\}$, θ is in $\{0, 1\}$ and $1/(2\sigma^2)$ is in $\{2^{-10}, 2^{-9}\}$.

We split the data of the source domain into two random partitions containing 80% for training and 20% for validation. We also split the data of the target domain into two random partitions. The first partition contains 80% for training the models of VulDeePecker, MMD, D2GAN, DIRT-T, DDAN, Dual-GD-DDAN, SCDAN and Dual-GD-SDDAN without using any label information while the second partition contains 20% for testing the models. We additionally apply gradient clipping regularization to prevent over-fitting in the training process of each model. We implement eight mentioned methods in Python using Tensorflow which is an open-source software library for Machine Intelligence developed by the Google Brain Team.

Table 1. Performance results in terms of false negative rate (FNR), false positive rate (FPR), Recall, Precision and F1-measure of VulDeePecker (VULD), MMD, D2GAN, DIRT-T, DDAN and Dual-GD-DDAN for predicting vulnerable and non-vulnerable code functions on the testing set of the target domain (Best performance in **bold**).

Source → Target	Methods	FNR	FPR	Recall	Precision	F1-measure
Pidgin → LibPNG	VULD	42.86%	1.08%	57.14%	80%	66.67%
	MMD	37.50%	**0%**	62.50%	**100%**	76.92%
	D2GAN	**33.33%**	1.06%	**66.67%**	80%	72.73%
	DIRT-T	**33.33%**	1.06%	**66.67%**	80%	72.73%
	DDAN	37.50%	**0%**	62.50%	**100%**	76.92%
	Dual-GD-DDAN	**33.33%**	**0%**	**66.67%**	**100%**	**80%**
FFmpeg → LibTIFF	VULD	43.75%	**6.72%**	56.25%	50%	52.94%
	MMD	28.57%	12.79%	71.43%	47.62%	57.14%
	D2GAN	30.77%	6.97%	69.23%	**64.29%**	66.67%
	DIRT-T	25%	9.09%	75%	52.94%	62.07%
	DDAN	35.71%	6.98%	64.29%	60%	62.07%
	Dual-GD-DDAN	**12.5%**	8.2%	**87.5%**	56%	**68.29%**
FFmpeg → LibPNG	VULD	25%	**2.17%**	75%	75%	75%
	MMD	12.5%	3.26%	87.5%	70%	77.78%
	D2GAN	14.29%	**2.17%**	85.71%	75%	80%
	DIRT-T	15.11%	2.2%	84.89%	**80%**	84.21%
	DDAN	**0%**	3.26%	**100%**	72.73%	84.21%
	Dual-GD-DDAN	**0%**	**2.17%**	**100%**	80%	**88.89%**
VLC → LibPNG	VULD	57.14%	**1.08%**	42.86%	75%	54.55%
	MMD	45%	4.35%	55%	60%	66.67%
	D2GAN	28.57%	4.3%	71.43%	55.56%	62.5%
	DIRT-T	50%	1.09%	50%	**80%**	61.54%
	DDAN	33.33%	2.20%	66.67%	75%	70.59%
	Dual-GD-DDAN	**28.57%**	2.15%	**71.43%**	71.43%	**71.43%**
Pidgin → LibTIFF	VULD	35.29%	8.27%	64.71%	50%	56.41%
	MMD	30.18%	12.35%	69.82%	50%	58.27%
	D2GAN	40%	7.95%	60%	**60%**	60%
	DIRT-T	38.46%	8.05%	61.54%	53.33%	57.14%
	DDAN	**27.27%**	8.99%	**72.73%**	50%	59.26%
	Dual-GD-DDAN	29.41%	**6.76%**	70.59%	57.14%	**63.16%**

4.2   Experimental Results

Code Domain Adaptation for a Fully Non-labeled Target Project. We investigate the performance of our proposed Dual-GD-DDAN compared with other methods including VulDeePecker (VULD) without domain adaptation [12], DDAN [16], MMD [14], D2GAN [15] and DIRT-T [18] with VAP applied in the joint feature layer using the architecture CDAN introduced in [16]. The VulDeePecker method is only trained on the source data and then tested on the target data, while the MMD, D2GAN, DIRT-T, DDAN and Dual-GD-DDAN methods employ the target data without using any label information for domain adaptation.

In Table 1, the experimental results *show that our proposed Dual-GD-DDAN achieves a higher performance for detecting vulnerable and non-vulnerable functions for most performance measures,* including FNR, FPR, Recall, Precision and F1-measure in almost cases of the source and target domains, especially for F1-measure. Particularly, our Dual-GD-DDAN always obtains the highest F1-measure in all cases. For example, for the case of the source domain (FFmpeg) and target domain (LibPNG), Dual-GD-DDAN achieves an F1-measure of 88.89% compared with an F1-measure of 84.21%, 84.21%, 80%, 77.78% and 75% obtained with DDAN, DIRT-T, D2GAN, MMD and VulDeePecker respectively.

Boundary Distortion Analysis

Quantitative Results. To quantitatively demonstrate the efficiency of our proposed Dual-GD-DDAN in alleviating the boundary distortion problem caused by using the GAN principle, we reuse the experimental setting in Sect. 5.2 [17]. The basic idea is, given two data sets S_1 and S_2, to quantify the degree of cover of these two data sets. We train a classifier C_1 on S_1, then test on S_2 and another classifier C_2 on S_2, then test on S_1. If these two data sets cover each other well with reduced boundary distortion, we expect that if C_1 predicts well on S_1, then it should predict well on S_2 and vice versa if C_2 predicts well on S_2, then it should predict well on S_1. This would seem reasonable since if boundary distortion occurs (i.e., assume that S_2 partly covers S_1), then C_2 trained on S_2 would struggle to predict S_1 well which is much larger and possibly more complex. Therefore, we can utilize the magnitude of the accuracies and the accuracy gap of C_1 and C_2 when predicting their training and testing sets to assess the severity of the boundary distortion problem.

Table 2. Accuracies obtained by the DDAN and Dual-GD-DDAN methods when predicting vulnerable and non-vulnerable code functions on the source and target domains. Note that tr src, ts tar, tr tar, ts src, and acc gap are the shorthands of train source, test target, train target, test source, and accuracy gap respectively. For the accuracy gap, a smaller value is better.

Source → Target	Methods	Accuracy			Accuracy		
		Tr src/Ts tar/acc gap			Tr tar/Ts src/ acc gap		
Pidgin → LibPNG	DDAN	98.8%	96%	2.8%	97%	92%	5%
	Dual-GD-DDAN	99%	97%	**2%**	97%	95%	**2%**
FFmpeg → LibPNG	Methods	Accuracy			Accuracy		
		Tr src/Ts tar/acc gap			Tr tar/Te src/acc gap		
	DDAN	95.9%	92%	3.9%	91%	83.3%	7.7%
	Dual-GD-DDAN	97%	96%	**1%**	98%	95.6%	**2.4%**

Inspired by this observation, we compare our Dual-GD-DDAN with DDAN using the representations of the source and target samples in the joint feature space corresponding to their best models. In particular, for a given pair of source and target data sets and for comparing each method, we train a neural network classifier on the best representations of the source data set in the joint space, then predict on the source and target data set and do the same but swap the role of the source and target data sets. We then measure the difference of the corresponding accuracies as a means of measuring the severity of the boundary distortion. We choose to conduct such a boundary distortion analysis for two pairs of the source (FFmpeg and Pidgin) and target (LibPNG) domains. As shown in Table 2, *all gaps obtained by our Dual-GD-DDAN are always smaller than those obtained by DDAN*, while the accuracies obtained by our proposed method are always larger. We can therefore conclude that our Dual-GD-DDAN method produces a better representation for source and target samples in the joint space and is less susceptible to boundary distortion compared with the DDAN method.

Visualization. We further demonstrate the efficiency of our proposed Dual-GD-DDAN in alleviating the boundary distortion problem caused by using the GAN principle. Using a t-SNE [9] projection, with perplexity equal to 30, we visualize the feature distributions of the source and target domains in the joint space. Specifically, we project the source and target data in the joint space (i.e., $G(x)$) into a 2D space with domain adaptation (DDAN) and with dual-domain adaptation (Dual-GD-DDAN). In Fig. 3, we observe these cases when performing domain adaptation from a software project (FFmpeg) to another (LibPNG). As shown in Fig. 3, with undertaking domain adaptation (DDAN, the left figure) and dual-domain adaptation (Dual-GD-DDAN, the right figure), *the source and target data sampled are intermingled especially for Dual-GD-DDAN*. However, it can be observed that DDAN when solely applying the GAN is seriously vulnerable to the boundary distortion issue. In particular, in the clusters/data modes 2, 3 and 4 (the left figure), the boundary distortion issue occurs since the blue data only partly cover the corresponding red ones (i.e., the source and target data do not totally mix up). Meanwhile, for our Dual-GD-DDAN, *the boundary distortion issue is much less vulnerable*, and the mixing-up level of source and target data is significantly higher in each cluster/data mode.

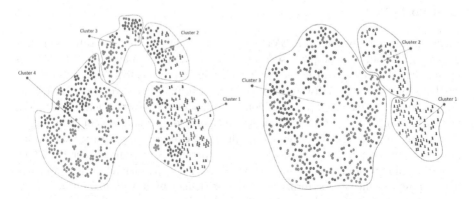

Fig. 3. A 2D t-SNE projection for the case of the FFmpeg → LibPNG domain adaptation. The blue and red points represent the source and target domains in the joint space respectively. In both cases of the source and target domains, data points labeled 0 stand for non-vulnerable samples and data points labeled 1 stand for vulnerable samples. (Color figure online)

Quantitative Results of Dual Generator-Discriminator Semi-supervised Deep Code Domain Adaptation. In this section, we compare the performance of our Dual-GD-SDDAN with Semi-supervised Deep Code Domain Adaptation (SCDAN) [16] on four pairs of the source and target domains. In Table 3, *the experimental results show that our Dual-GD-SDDAN achieves a higher performance than SCDAN for detecting vulnerable and non-vulnerable functions* in terms of FPR, Precision and F1-measure in almost cases of the source and target domains, especially for F1-measure. For example, to the case of the source domain (VLC) and target domain (LibPNG), our Dual-GD-SDDAN achieves an F1-measure of 76.19% compared with an F1-measure of 72.73% obtained with SCDAN. These results further demonstrate the ability of our Dual-GD-SDDAN for dealing with the mode collapsing problem better than SCDAN [16], hence obtaining better predictive performance in the context of software domain adaptation.

Table 3. Performance results in terms of false negative rate (FNR), false positive rate (FPR), Recall, Precision and F1-measure of SCDAN and Dual-GD-SDDAN for predicting vulnerable/non-vulnerable code functions on the testing set of the target domain (Best performance in **bold**).

Source → Target	Methods	FPR	FNR	Recall	Precision	F1-measure
FFmpeg → LibTIFF	SCDAN	5.38%	**14.29%**	**85.71%**	57.14%	68.57%
	Dual-GD-SDDAN	**3.01%**	35.29%	64.71%	**73.33%**	**68.75%**
FFmpeg → LibPNG	SCDAN	1.08%	**12.5%**	**87.5%**	87.5%	87.5%
	Dual-GD-SDDAN	**0%**	17.5%	82.5%	**100%**	**90.41%**
VLC→ LibPNG	SCDAN	**1.06%**	33.33%	66.67%	**80%**	72.73%
	Dual-GD-SDDAN	4.39%	**11.11%**	**88.89%**	66.67%	**76.19%**
Pidgin → LibTIFF	SCDAN	5.56%	**30%**	**70%**	58.33%	63.64%
	Dual-GD-SDDAN	**2.98%**	37.5%	62.5%	**71.43%**	**66.67%**

5 Conclusion

Software vulnerability detection (SVD) is an important problem in the software industry and in the field of computer security. One of the most crucial issues in SVD is to cope with the scarcity of labeled vulnerabilities in projects that require the laborious labeling of code by software security experts. In this paper, we propose the Dual Generator-Discriminator Deep Code Domain Adaptation Network (Dual-GD-DDAN) method to deal with the missing mode and boundary distortion problems which arise from the use of the GAN principle when reducing the discrepancy between source and target data in the joint space. We conducted experiments to compare our Dual-GD-DDAN method with the state-of-the-art baselines. The experimental results show that our proposed method outperforms these rival baselines by a wide margin in term of predictive performances.

Acknowledgement. This research was supported under the Defence Science and Technology Group's Next Generation Technologies Program.

References

1. Almorsy, M., Grundy, J., Ibrahim, A.: Supporting automated vulnerability analysis using formalized vulnerability signatures. In: Proceedings of the 27th IEEE/ACM International Conference on Automated Software Engineering, ASE, pp. 100–109. ACM (2012)
2. Chapelle, O., Zien, A.: Semi-supervised classification by low density separation. In: AISTATS, pp. 57–64. Citeseer (2005)
3. Ganin, Y., Lempitsky, V.: Unsupervised domain adaptation by backpropagation. In: Proceedings of the 32nd International Conference on Machine Learning, vol. 37, pp. 1180–1189. ICML (2015)
4. Goodfellow, I., et al.: Generative adversarial nets. In: Advances in Neural Information Processing Systems, pp. 2672–2680 (2014)
5. Goodfellow, I.: Nips 2016 tutorial: Generative adversarial networks. arXiv preprint arXiv:1701.00160 (2016)
6. Gopalan, R., Ruonan, L., Chellappa, R.: Domain adaptation for object recognition: an unsupervised approach. In: Proceedings of the 2011 International Conference on Computer Vision, pp. 999–1006. ICCV (2011)
7. Hoang, Q., Nguyen, T.D., Le, T., Phung, D.: MGAN: training generative adversarial nets with multiple generators. In: International Conference on Learning Representation (2018)
8. Kim, S., Woo, S., Lee, H., Oh, H.: VUDDY: a scalable approach for vulnerable code clone discovery. In: IEEE Symposium on Security and Privacy, pp. 595–614. IEEE Computer Society (2017)
9. Laurens, V.M., Geoffrey, H.: Visualizing data using t-SNE. J. Mach. Learn. Res. **9**, 2579–2605 (2008)
10. Le, T., Hoang, Q., Vu, H., Nguyen, T.D., Bui, H., Phung, D.: Learning generative adversarial networks from multiple data sources. In: 2019 International Joint Conference on Artificial Intelligence (2019)
11. Le, T., et al.: Maximal divergence sequential autoencoder for binary software vulnerability detection. In: International Conference on Learning Representations (2019)
12. Li, Z., et al.: VulDeePecker: a deep learning-based system for vulnerability detection. CoRR abs/1801.01681 (2018)
13. Lin, G., et al.: Cross-project transfer representation learning for vulnerable function discovery. IEEE Trans. Industr. Inform. **14**, 3289–3297 (2018)
14. Long, M., Cao, Y., Wang, J., Jordan, M.: Learning transferable features with deep adaptation networks. In: Bach, F., Blei, D. (eds.) Proceedings of the 32nd International Conference on Machine Learning. Proceedings of Machine Learning Research, Lille, France, vol. 37, pp. 97–105 (2015)
15. Nguyen, T.D., Le, T., Vu, H., Phung, D.: Dual discriminator generative adversarial nets. In: Advances in Neural Information Processing (2017)
16. Nguyen, V., et al.: Deep domain adaptation for vulnerable code function identification. In: The International Joint Conference on Neural Networks (IJCNN) (2019)
17. Santurkar, S., Schmidt, L., Madry, A.: A classification-based study of covariate shift in GAN distributions. In: Proceedings of the 35th International Conference on Machine Learning. Proceedings of Machine Learning Research, vol. 80, pp. 4480–4489. PMLR (2018)
18. Shu, R., Bui, H., Narui, H., Ermon, S.: A DIRT-t approach to unsupervised domain adaptation. In: International Conference on Learning Representations (2018)

Code Action Network for Binary Function Scope Identification

Van Nguyen[1]([✉]), Trung Le[1]([✉]), Tue Le[2]([✉]), Khanh Nguyen[2]([✉]),
Olivier de Vel[3]([✉]), Paul Montague[3]([✉]), John Grundy[1]([✉]), and Dinh Phung[1]([✉])

[1] Monash University, Clayton, Australia
{van.nk,trunglm,john.grundy,dinh.phung}@monash.edu
[2] AI Research Lab, Trusting Social, Melbourne, Australia
tue.le.ict@jvn.edu.vn, khanh@trustingsocial.com
[3] Defence Science and Technology Group, Canberra, Australia
{Olivier.DeVel,Paul.Montague}@dst.defence.gov.au

Abstract. Function identification is a preliminary step in binary analysis for many applications from malware detection, common vulnerability detection and binary instrumentation to name a few. In this paper, we propose the Code Action Network (CAN) whose key idea is to encode the task of function scope identification to a sequence of three action states NI (i.e., next inclusion), NE (i.e., next exclusion), and FE (i.e., function end) to efficiently and effectively tackle function scope identification, the hardest and most crucial task in function identification. A bidirectional Recurrent Neural Network is trained to match binary programs with their sequence of action states. To work out function scopes in a binary, this binary is first fed to a trained CAN to output its sequence of action states which can be further decoded to know the function scopes in the binary. We undertake extensive experiments to compare our proposed method with other state-of-the-art baselines. Experimental results demonstrate that our proposed method outperforms the state-of-the-art baselines in terms of predictive performance on real-world datasets which include binaries from well-known libraries.

Keywords: Cyber security · Function scope identification · Machine learning · Deep learning

1 Introduction

In computer security, we often encounter situations where source code is not available or impossible to access and only binaries are accessible. In these situations, binary analysis is an essential tool enabling many applications such as malware detection, common vulnerability detection [9], and etc. Function identification is usually the first step in many binary analysis methods. This aims to specify function scopes in a binary and is a building block to a diverse range of application domains including binary instrumentation [5], vulnerability research [10] and binary protection structures with Control-Flow Integrity. In both binary

H. W. Lauw et al. (Eds.): PAKDD 2020, LNAI 12084, pp. 712–725, 2020.
https://doi.org/10.1007/978-3-030-47426-3_55

analysis and function identification, tackling the loss of high-level semantic structures in binaries which results from compilers during the process of compilation is likely the most challenging problem.

There have been many effective methods for dealing with the function identification problem from heuristic solutions (statistical methods for binary analysis) to complicated approaches employing machine learning or deep learning techniques. In an early work, Kruegel et al. [4] through his research which leveraged statistical methods with control flow graphs concluded that the task of function start identification can be trivially solved for regular binaries. However, later research in [14] argued that this task is non-trivial and complex in some specific cases wherein it is too challenging for heuristics-based methods to discover all function boundaries. Other influential works and tools that rely on signature database and structural graphs include IDA Pro, Dyninst, (Binary Analysis Platform) BAP, and Nucleus [1]. Andriesse et al. [1] has recently proposed a new signature-less approach to function detection for stripped binaries named Nucleus which is based on structural Control Flow Graph analysis. More specifically, Nucleus identifies functions in the intraprocedural control flow graph (ICFG) by analyzing the control flow between basic blocks, based on the observation that intraprocedural control flow tends to use different types and patterns of control flow instructions than inter-procedural control flow.

Machine learning has been applied to binary analysis and function identification in particular. The seminal work of [11] modeled function start identification as a Conditional Random Field (CRF) in which binary offsets and a number of selected patterns appear in the CRF. Since the inference on a CRF is very expensive, though feature selection and approximate inference were adopted to speed up this model, its computational complexity is still very high. ByteWeight [2] is another successful machine learning based method for function identification aiming to learn signatures for function starts using a weighted prefix tree, and recognizes function starts by matching binary fragments with the signatures. Each node in the tree corresponds to either a byte or an instruction, with the path from the root node to any given node representing a possible sequence of bytes or instructions. Although ByteWeight significantly outperformed disassembler approaches such as IDA Pro, Dyninst and Binary Analysis Platform (BAP), it is not scalable enough for even medium-sized datasets [12].

Deep learning has undergone a renaissance in the past few years, achieving breakthrough results in multiple application domains such as visual object recognition [3], language modeling [13], and software vulnerability detection [6–8]. The study in [12] is the first work which applied a deep learning technique for the function identification problem. In particular, a bidirectional Recurrent Neural Network (Bidirectional RNN) was used to identify whether a byte is a start point (or end point) of a function or not. This method was proven to outperform ByteWeight [2] while requiring much less training time. However, to address the boundary identification problem with [12], a simple heuristic to pair adjacent function starts and function ends was used (see Section 5.3 in that paper). Consequently, this approach is not able to efficiently utilize the context information of consecutive bytes and machine instructions in a function and the pairing procedure might lead to inconsistency since the networks for function start and end were trained independently. Furthermore, this method cannot address the function scope identification problem, the hardest and most essential sub problem in function identification, wherein the scope (i.e., the addresses of all machine instructions in a function) of each function must be specified.

Inspired from the idea of a Turing machine, we imagine a memory tape consisting of many cells on which machine instructions of a binary are stored. The head is first pointed to the first machine instruction located in the first cell. Each machine instruction is assigned to an action state in the action state set {NI, NE, FE} depending on its nature. After reading the current machine instruction and assigning the corresponding action state to it, the head is moved to the next cell and this procedure is halted as we reach the last cell in the tape (see Sect. 3.1). Eventually, the sequence of machine instructions in a given binary is translated to the corresponding sequence of action states. Based on this incentive, in this paper, we propose a novel method named the *Code Action Network* (CAN) whose underlying idea is to equivalently transform the task of function scope identification to learning a sequence of action states. A bidirectional Recurrent Neural Network is trained to match binary programs with their corresponding sequences of action states. To predict function scopes in any binary, the binary is first fed to a trained CAN to output its corresponding sequence of action states on which we can then work out function scopes in the binary. The proposed CAN can tackle binaries for which there exist external gaps between functions and internal gaps inside functions wherein each internal gap in a function does not contain instructions from other functions. By default, our CAN named as CAN-B operates at the byte level and can cope with all binaries that satisfy the aforementioned condition. However, for the binaries that can be further disassembled into machine instructions, another variant named as CAN-M is able to operate at the machine instruction level. CAN-M can efficiently exploit the semantic relationship among bytes in an instruction and instructions in a function as well as requiring much shorter sequence length compared with the Bidirectional RNN in [12] which also works at the byte level. In addition, our proposed CAN-B and CAN-M can directly address the function scope identification task, hence inherently offering the solution for other simpler tasks including the function start/end/boundary identifications.

We undertake extensive experiments to compare our proposed CAN-B and CAN-M with state-of-the-art methods including IDA, the Bidirectional RNN, ByteWeight no-RFCR and ByteWeight on the dataset used in [2,12]. The experimental results show that our proposed CAN-B and CAN-M outperform the baselines on function start, function end and function boundary identification tasks as well as achieving very good performance on function scope identification and also surpass the Nucleus [1] on this task. Our proposed methods slightly outperform the Bidirectional RNN proposed in [12] on the function start and end identification tasks, but significantly surpass this method on the function boundary identification task – the more important task. This demonstrates the capacity of our methods in efficiently utilizing the contextual relationship carried in consecutive machine instructions or bytes to properly match the function start and end entries for this task. As expected, our CAN-M obtains the best predictive performances on most experiments and is much faster than the Bidirectional RNN proposed in [12]. Particularly, CAN-M takes about 1 hour for training with 20,000 iterations which is nearly 4 times faster than the Bidirectional RNN proposed in [12] using the same number of iterations for training and the same number of bytes for handling input. This is due to the fact that CAN-M operates at the machine instruction level, while the Bidirectional RNN proposed in [12] operates at the byte level.

We also do error analysis to qualitatively compare our CAN-M and CAN-B with the baselines. We observe that there are a variety of instruction styles for the function start and function end (e.g., in the experimental dataset, there are a thousand different function start styles and function end styles). In their error analyses, Shin et al. [12] and Bao et al. [2] mentioned that for functions which encompass several function start styles or function end styles, their proposed methods tend to make mistakes in predicting the function start or end bytes with many false positives and negatives. However, it is not the case for our proposed methods, since we further observe that for the functions which contain more than one function start style or function end style which account for 98.38% and 28% of the testing set respectively, our proposed CAN-M has 0.24% and 1.09% false positive rates respectively.

2 The Function Identification Problem

This section discusses the function identification problem. We begin with definitions of the sub problems in the function identification problem, followed by an example of source code in the C language and its binaries compiled with optimization levels O1 using *gcc* on the Linux platform for the x86-64 architecture.

2.1 Problem Definitions

Given a binary program P, our task is to identify the necessary information (e.g., function starts, function ends) in its n functions $\{f_1, ..., f_n\}$ which is initially unknown. Depending on the nature of information we need from $\{f_1, ..., f_n\}$, we can categorize the task of function identification into the following such problems.

Function Start/End/boundary Identification. In the first problem, we need to specify the set $S = \{s_1, ..., s_n\}$ which contains the start instruction byte for each of the corresponding functions in $\{f_1, ..., f_n\}$. If a function (e.g. f_i) has multiple start points, s_i will be the first start instruction byte for f_i. In the second problem, we need to identify the set $E = \{e_1, ..., e_n\}$ which contains the end instruction byte for each of the corresponding functions in $\{f_1, ..., f_n\}$. If a function (e.g. f_i) has multiple exit points, e_i will be the last end instruction byte for f_i. In the last problem, we have to point out the set of (start, end) pairs $SE = \{(s_1, e_1), ..., (s_n, e_n)\}$ which contains the pairs of the function start and the function end for each of the corresponding functions in $\{f_1, ..., f_n\}$.

Function Scope Identification. This is the hardest problem in the function identification task. In this problem, we need to find out the set $\{(f_{1,s_1}, ..., f_{1,e_1}), ..., (f_{n,s_n}, ..., f_{n,e_n})\}$ which specifies the instruction bytes in each function $f_1, ..., f_n$ in the given binary program P. Here we note that because functions may be not contiguous, the instruction bytes $(f_{i,s_i}, ..., f_{i,e_i})$ may also be not contiguous. It is apparent that the solution of this problem covers the three aforementioned problems. Since our proposed CAN addresses this problem, it inherently offers solutions for the other problems.

2.2 Running Example

In Fig. 1, we show an example of a short source code fragment for a function in the C programming language, the corresponding assembly code in the machine instruction and corresponding hexadecimal mode of the binary code respectively, which was compiled using *gcc* with the optimization level O1 for the x86-64 architecture on the Linux platform. We further observe that in real binary code, the patterns for the entry point vary over a wide range and can start with *push*, *mov*, *movsx*, *inc*, *cmp*, *or*, *and*, etc. In the example, the assembly code corresponding with the optimization level O1 on Linux has three *ret* statements. Furthermore, in real binary code, the ending point of a function can vary in pattern beside the *ret* pattern. These make the task of function identification very challenging. For the challenges of the function scope identification task, we refer the readers to [2,12] and the discussions therein.

```c
int bubbleSort(int arr[], int n)
{
  if (n <= 1)
    return 1;

   int i, j, temp;
   for (i = 0; i < n-1; i++)

       for (j = 0; j < n-i-1; j++)
           if (arr[j] > arr[j+1])
           {
               int temp = arr[j];
               arr[j] = arr[j+1];
               arr[j+1] = temp;
           }
  return 0;
}
```

```
0x4ed bubbleSort:
0x4ed:  cmp esi, 1
0x4f0:  jle 0x52c
0x4f2:  lea r8d, dword ptr [rsi - 1]
0x4f6:  test    r8d, r8d
...
0x4fb:  jmp 0x51d
0x4fd:  mov edx, dword ptr [rdi + rax*4]
0x500:  mov ecx, dword ptr [rdi + rax*4 + 4]
0x504:  cmp edx, ecx
0x506:  jle 0x50f
0x508:  mov dword ptr [rdi + rax*4], ecx
...
0x523:  jle 0x517
0x525:  mov eax, 0
0x52a:  jmp 0x4fd
0x52c:  mov eax, 1
0x531:  ret
0x532:  mov eax, 0
0x537:  ret
0x538:  mov eax, 0
0x53d:  ret
```

```
0x4ed bubbleSort:
0x4ed:  83fe01
0x4f0:  7e3a
0x4f2:  448d46ff
0x4f6:  4585c0
...
0x4fb:  eb20
0x4fd:  8b1487
0x500:  8b4c8704
0x504:  39ca
0x506:  7e07
0x508:  890c87
...
0x523:  7ef2
0x525:  b800000000
0x52a:  ebd1
0x52c:  b801000000
0x531:  c3
0x532:  b800000000
0x537:  c3
0x538:  b800000000
0x53d:  c3
```

Fig. 1. Example source code of a function in the C language programming (Left), the corresponding assembly code (Middle) with some parts omitted for brevity and the corresponding hexadecimal mode of the binary code (Right).

3 Code Action Network for the Function Identification Problem

3.1 Key Idea

In what follows, we present the key idea of our CAN. In a binary, there are external gaps between functions as well as internal gaps inside a non-contiguous function. The external gaps might contain data, jump tables or padding-instruction bytes which do not belong to any function (e.g., additional instructions generated by a compiler such as *nop, int3*). The internal gaps in general might contain data, jump tables or instructions from other functions (e.g., nested functions). We further assume that the internal gaps do not contain any instruction from other functions. It means that if there exist functions nested in a function, our CAN ignores these internal functions. However, we believe that the nested functions are extremely rare in real-world binaries. For example, in the experimental dataset, we observe that there are only 506 nested functions over the total of 757,125 functions (i.e., the occurrence rate is 0.067%).

The key idea of CAN is to encode the task of function scope identification to a sequence of three action states NI (i.e., next inclusion), NE (i.e., next exclusion), and FE (i.e., function end). With the aforementioned assumption, the binaries of interest consist of several functions and the functions in a binary do not intermingle, that is, each function only contains its machine instructions, data, or jump-tables and do not contain any machine instruction of other functions. Each function can be therefore viewed as a collection of bytes where each byte is from a machine instruction of this function (i.e., instruction byte) or data/jump-tables inside this function (i.e., non-instruction byte). To clarify how to proceed over a binary function given a sequence of action states, let us imagine this

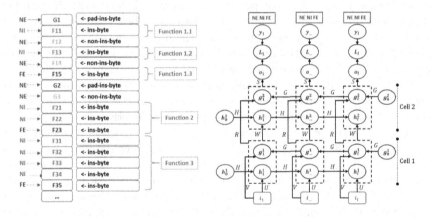

Fig. 2. (The left-hand figure) The key idea of Code Action Network. Assume that we have a sequence of instruction bytes in three functions where the functions may not be contiguous and there exist gaps between the functions. The Code Action Network transforms this sequence of instruction bytes to those of action states (i.e., NI, NE, and FE). (The right-hand figure) The architecture of the Code Action Network. Each output value takes one of three action states *NI*, *NE*, or *FE*. The Code Action Network will learn to map the input sequences of items $(i_1, i_2, ..., i_l)$ to the target output sequence $(\mathbf{y}_1, \mathbf{y}_2, ..., \mathbf{y}_l)$ with the loss L_i at each time step t. The h represents for the forward-propagated hidden state (toward the right) while the g stands for the backward-propagated hidden state (toward the left). At each time step t, the predicted output $\mathbf{o}_t$ can benefit from the relevant information of the past from its h and the future from its g.

binary program including many instruction and non-instruction bytes as a tape of many cells wherein each cell contains a instruction or non-instruction byte and a pointer firstly points to the first cell in the tape. The action state NI includes the current instruction or non-instruction byte in the current cell to the current function and moves the pointer to the next cell (i.e., the next instruction or non-instruction byte). The action state NE excludes the current instruction or non-instruction byte in the current cell from the current function and moves the pointer to the next cell. The action state FE counts the current instruction or non-instruction byte in the current cell, ends the current function, starts reading a new function, and moves the pointer to the next cell.

To further explain how to transform a binary program to a sequence of action states, we consider an example binary code depicted in Fig. 2 (the left-hand figure). Assume that we have a sequence of instruction and non-instruction bytes, which belong to *Function 1*, *Function 2* and *Function 3*, respectively where the functions may be not contiguous and there exist gaps between the functions (e.g., the gap between *Function 1* and *Function 2* includes the padding-instruction byte (pad-ins-byte) G2 and the non-instruction (non-ins-byte) byte G3). The pointer of CAN firstly points to G1, labels this padding-instruction byte (pad-ins-byte) as NE since G1 does not belong to any function, and moves to the instruction byte F11. The instruction byte F11 is labeled as NI since it belongs to the function *Function 1*. The pointer then moves to the non-instruction byte F12 which can come from a jump-table or data and labels it as NE because F12 does not belong to any function. After that, the pointer moves to the instruction byte F13 and the non-instruction byte F14 subsequently. F13 and F14 are then labeled as NI and NE respectively since F13 belong to the function *Function 1* while F14 does not belong to any function, and the pointer moves to the instruction byte F15 and labels it as FE since it is the end of the function *Function 1* and we need to start reading the new function (i.e., the function *Function 2*). The pointer subsequently moves to the instruction byte G2 and the non-instruction G3 which can come from a jump-table or data and labels them as NE since they do not belong to any function. The pointer then traverses across the instruction bytes F21, F22, F23 and labels them as NI, NI, FE. The pointer now starts reading the new function (i.e., the function *Function 3*). This process is repeated until the pointer reaches the last instruction or non-instruction byte and we eventually identify all functions.

It is worth noting that if binaries can be disassembled and a function in these binaries can be thus viewed as a collection of instructions and non-instructions, we can perform the aforementioned idea at the machine instruction level wherein each cell in the tape represents an instruction or non-instruction of a binary. The advantages of performing the task of function identification at the machine instruction level include: i) the sequence length of the bidirectional RNN is significantly reduced and ii) the semantic relationship among bytes in a machine instruction and machine instructions can be further exploited. As a consequence, the gradient exploding and vanishing which often occur with long RNNs can be avoided and the model is easier to train while obtaining higher predictive performance and much shorter training times as shown in our experiments.

3.2   Preprocess Input Statement

Byte Level and Machine Instruction Level. To process data for the byte level, we simply take the raw bytes in the text segment of the given binary and input them to CAN-B. To process data for the machine instruction level, we first use Capstone[1] to disassemble the binaries and preprocess the machine instructions obtained from the text segment of a binary before inputting them to CAN-M. This preprocessing step aims to work out fixed length inputs from machine instructions. For each machine instruction, we employ Capstone to detect entire machine instructions, then eliminate redundant prefixes to obtain core parts that contain the opcode and other significant information (see our Supplementary Material for details, available at https://app.box.com/s/iq9u8r).

3.3   Code Action Network Architecture

Training Procedure. The Code Action Network (CAN) is a multicell bidirectional RNN whose architecture is depicted in Fig. 2 (the right-hand figure) where we assume the number of cells over the input is 2. Our CAN takes a binary program $\mathbf{B} = (\mathbf{i}_1, \mathbf{i}_2, \ldots, \mathbf{i}_l)$ including l instructions (non-instructions) for CAN-M or instruction bytes (non-instruction bytes) for CAN-B and learns to output the corresponding sequence of action states $\mathbf{Y} = (\mathbf{y}_1, \mathbf{y}_2, \ldots, \mathbf{y}_l)$ where each $\mathbf{y}_k$ takes one of three action states NI (i.e., $\mathbf{y}_k = 1$), NE (i.e., $\mathbf{y}_k = 2$), or FE (i.e., $\mathbf{y}_k = 3$). The computational process of CAN is as follows:

$$\mathbf{h}_k^1 = \tanh(H^\top \mathbf{h}_{k-1}^1 + U^\top \mathbf{i}_k); \ \mathbf{g}_k^1 = \tanh(G^\top \mathbf{g}_{k+1}^1 + V^\top \mathbf{i}_k); \ \mathbf{h}_k^2 = \tanh(H^\top \mathbf{h}_{k-1}^2 + W^\top [\begin{smallmatrix} \mathbf{h}_k^1 \\ \mathbf{g}_k^1 \end{smallmatrix}])$$

$$\mathbf{g}_k^2 = \tanh(G^\top \mathbf{g}_{k+1}^2 + R^\top [\begin{smallmatrix} \mathbf{h}_k^1 \\ \mathbf{g}_k^1 \end{smallmatrix}]); \ \mathbf{o}_k = S^\top [\begin{smallmatrix} \mathbf{h}_k^2 \\ \mathbf{g}_k^2 \end{smallmatrix}]; \ \mathbf{p}_k = \text{softmax}(\mathbf{o}_k)$$

where $k = 1, \ldots l$, $\mathbf{h}_0^1$, $\mathbf{h}_0^2$, $\mathbf{g}_{l+1}^1 = \mathbf{g}_0^1$, $\mathbf{g}_{l+1}^2 = \mathbf{g}_0^2$ are initial hidden states and $\theta = (U, V, W, H, G, R, S)$ is the model. We further note that $\mathbf{p}_k$, $k = 1, \ldots, l$ is a *discrete* distribution over the three labels NI, NE, and FE.

To find the best model θ^*, we need to solve the following optimization problem:

$$\max_\theta \sum_{(\mathbf{B}, \mathbf{Y}) \in \mathcal{D}} \log p(\mathbf{Y} \mid \mathbf{B}) \tag{1}$$

where $\mathcal{D}$ is the training set including pairs $(\mathbf{B}, \mathbf{Y})$ of the binaries and their corresponding sequence of action states.

Because o_k is a function (lossy summary) of $\mathbf{i}_{1:l}$, we further derive $\log p(\mathbf{Y} \mid \mathbf{B})$ as:

$$\log p(\mathbf{Y} \mid \mathbf{B}) = \sum_{k=1}^{l} \log p(\mathbf{y}_k \mid \mathbf{y}_{1:k-1}, \mathbf{i}_{1:l}) = \sum_{k=1}^{l} \log p(\mathbf{y}_k \mid \mathbf{o}_k)$$

---

[1] www.capstone-engine.org.

Substituting back to the optimization problem in Eq. (1), we arrive the following optimization problem:

$$\max_\theta \sum_{(\mathbf{B},\mathbf{Y})\in\mathcal{D}} \sum_{k=1}^{l} \log p\left(\mathbf{y}_k \mid \mathbf{o}_k\right)$$

where $p(\mathbf{y}_k \mid \mathbf{o}_k)$ is the $\mathbf{y}_k$-th element of the discrete distribution $\mathbf{p}_k$ or in other words, we have $p(\mathbf{y}_k \mid \mathbf{o}_k) = \mathbf{p}_{k,\mathbf{y}_k}$.

Testing Procedure. In what follows, we present how to work out the function scopes in a binary using a trained CAN. The machine instructions/non-instructions for CAN-M or instruction/non-instruction bytes for CAN-B in the testing binary are fed to the trained model to work out the predicted sequence of action states. This predicted sequence of action states is then decoded to the function scopes inside the binary. As shown in Fig. 3, the binary in Fig. 2 when inputted to the trained CAN outputs the sequence of action states NE, NI, ..., NI, FE and is later decoded to the scopes of the functions *Function 1, Function 2* and *Function 3*.

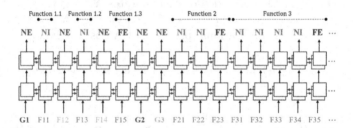

Fig. 3. The testing procedure of our Code Action Network. The sequence of machine instructions/non-instructions or instruction bytes/non-instruction bytes in a binary program is fed to the trained Code Action Network to work out the sequence of action states. Subsequently, the sequence of action states is decoded to the set of functions in this binary.

4   Experiments

In this section, firstly, we present the experimental results of our proposed Code Action Network for the machine instruction level (CAN-M) and the byte level (CAN-B) compared with other baselines including IDA, ByteWeight (BW) no-RFCR, ByteWeight (BW) [2], the Bidirectional RNN (BRNN) [12] and Nucleus [1]. Secondly, we perform error analysis to qualitatively investigate our proposed methods. We also investigate the model behaviour of our CAN-M with various RNN cells and with different size for hidden states (see in our Supplementary Material, available at https://app.box.com/s/iq9u8r).

4.1 Experimental Dataset

We used the dataset from [2,12], which consists of 2,200 different binaries including 2,064 binaries obtained from the *findutils*, *binutils*, and *coreutils* packages and compiled with both *icc* and *gcc* for Linux at four optimization levels O0, O1, O2, and O3. The remaining binaries for Windows are from various well-known open-source projects which were compiled with Microsoft Visual Studio for the x86 (32 bit) and the x86-64 (64 bit) architectures at four optimization levels Od, O1, O2, and Ox.

4.2 Experimental Setting

We divided the binaries into three random parts; the first part contains 80% of the binaries used for training, the second part contains 10% of the binaries used for testing, and the third part contains 10% of the binaries for validation. For CAN-M, we used a sequence of 250 hidden states for the x86 architecture and 125 hidden states for the x86-64 architecture where the size of hidden states is 256. For CAN-B, akin to the Bidirectional RNN in [12], we used a sequence length of 1,000 hidden states for the x86 and x86-64 architectures. We employed the Adam optimizer with the default learning rate 0.001 and the mini-batch size of 32. In addition, we applied gradient clipping regularization to prevent the over-fitting problem when training the model. We implemented the Code Action Networks in Python using Tensorflow, an open-source software library for Machine Intelligence developed by the Google Brain Team.

4.3 Experimental Results

Code Action Network Versus Baselines. We compared our CAN-M and CAN-B using the Long Short Term Memory (LSTM) cell and the hidden size of 256 with IDA, the Bidirectional RNN (BRNN), ByteWeight (BW) no-RFCR and ByteWeight (BW) in the task of function start, function end, function boundary and function scope identification. For the well-known tool IDA as well as the Bidirectional RNN, ByteWeight no-RFCR, and ByteWeight methods, we reported the experimental results presented in [2] and [12]. Obviously, the task of function scope identification wherein we need to specify addresses of machine instructions in each function is harder than that of function boundary identification. To compute the function scope results, given a predicted function by CAN variants, we considered their start and end instructions for CAN-M and start and end bytes for CAN-B, and then evaluated measures (e.g., Precision, Recall, and F1 score) based on this pair. In addition, in the function scope identification task, a pair is counted as a correct pair if all predicted bytes or machine instructions accompanied with this pair forms a function that exactly matches to a valid function in the ground truth. In contrast, in the function boundary identification task, we only require the start and end positions of this pair to be correct.

The experimental results in Table 1 show that our proposed CAN-M and CAN-B achieved better predictive performances (i.e., Recall, Precision, and F1 score) compared with the baselines in most cases (PE x86, PE x86-64, ELF x86 and ELF x86-64). For the function boundary identification task, our CAN-B and CAN-M significantly outperformed the baselines in all measures, especially for CAN-M. Interestingly, the predictive performance of our proposed methods on the harder task of function scope identification was higher or comparable with that of the baselines on the easier task of function boundary identification. In comparison with the Bidirectional RNN proposed in [12], our proposed methods slightly outperform it on the function start and function end identification tasks, but significantly surpass this method on the function boundary identification task - the more important task. This result demonstrates the capacity of our methods in efficiently utilizing the contextual relationship carried in consecutive machine instructions or bytes to properly match the function start and end entries for this task. Regarding the amount of time taken for training, our CAN-M took approximately 3,490 s for training in 20,000 iterations, while our CAN-B and the Bidirectional RNN using the same number of iterations with the sequence length 1,000 took about 12,030 seconds (i.e., roughly four times slower). This is due to a much smaller sequence length of CAN-M compared with CAN-B and the Bidirectional RNN.

Code Action Network Versus Bidirectional RNN, ByteWeight and Nucleus. We also compared the average predictive performance for case by case including the function start, function bound and function scope identifications of our CAN-M and CAN-B using the hidden size of 256 and LSTM cell with the Bidirectional RNN, ByteWeight, and Nucleus in both Linux and Windows platforms. For Nucleus [1], we reported the experimental results reported in that paper. The experimental results in Table 2 indicate that our CAN-M and CAN-B again outperformed the baselines, while CAN-M obtained the highest predictive performances in all measures (Recall, Precision and F1 score).

4.4   Error Analysis

For a qualitative assessment, we performed error analysis of our CAN-M and CAN-B for all cases including PEx86, PEx64, ELFx86 and ELFx64.

At the machine instruction level, we observed that there are *4,714, 4,464, 3,320* and *8,147* different types of machine instructions for function start while there are *1,926, 5,523, 9,082* and *11,421* different types of machine instructions for function end in the PEx86, PEx64, ELFx86 and ELFx64 datasets respectively. At byte level, we found that there are *91, 49, 41* and *53* different types of instruction bytes for function start while there are *166, 125, 133* and *126* different types of bytes for function end in the PEx86, PEx64, ELFx86 and ELFx64 datasets respectively. Obviously, these diverse ranges in the function start and function styles make the task of function identification really challenging. In all four cases (PEx86, PEx64, ELFx86 and ELFx64), the compilers in use often add padding between functions such as *nop, int3*.

We summarize some observations for our methods performance as follows:

- Shin et al. [12] and Bao et al. [2] commonly mentioned that for the functions that contain either several function start or function end styles inside, their models tend to confuse in determining the true start or end points, hence offering many false positives. This is due to a high level of ambiguity in the start or end entries for these functions. However, it is not the case for our proposed CAN-M and CAN-B. For example, at the machine instruction level with PE x86, we found that the functions which contain more than one function start style or function end style account for 98.38% and 28.00% of the testing set and when predicting these functions, our proposed CAN-M has 0.28% false negative rate and 0.24% false positive rate as well as 1.56% false negative rate and 1.09% false positive rate.

- Our proposed methods also share the same behavior as the method in [12] in predicting some first and last items in an input sequence, that is, the CAN-M and CAN-B sometimes offer false positives and negatives when predicting some first and last instructions or bytes in an input sequence. More specifically, if an input sequence involves several functions, the start of the first function and the end of the last function are more likely to be predicted incorrectly. This is possibly due to the scarcity of context before or after them. For example, at the machine instruction level with PE x86, we record that there is about 2.39% of input sequences which contain function ends at some first and last input items. When predicting these function end entries, our proposed CAN-M obtains 21.21% false positive rate and 27.27% false negative rate.

Table 1. Comparison of our Code Action Network and baselines (Best in **bold**, second best in underline). Noting that f.s, f.e, f.b and f.sc stand for func. start, func. end, func. boundary and func. scope while R, P, and F1 represent Recall, Precision and F1 score respectively.

Task	Architectures Methods	ELF x86			ELF x86-64			PE x86			PE x86-64		
		R	P	F1	R	P	F1	R	P	F1	R	P	F1
(f.s)	IDA	58.34%	70.97%	64.04%	55.50%	74.20%	63.50%	87.80%	94.67%	91.11%	93.34%	98.22%	95.72%
	BW no-RFCR	96.17%	98.36%	97.25%	97.57%	99.11%	98.33%	92.13%	96.75%	94.38%	96.22%	97.74%	96.97%
	BW	97.94%	98.41%	98.17%	**98.47%**	99.14%	98.80%	95.37%	93.78%	94.57%	97.98%	97.88%	97.93%
	BRNN	99.06%	_99.56%_	99.31%	97.80%	98.80%	98.30%	98.46%	99.01%	98.73%	_99.09%_	_99.52%_	_99.30%_
	CAN-B	_99.23%_	99.41%	_99.32%_	_98.19%_	_99.05%_	_98.62%_	_98.95%_	_99.53%_	_99.24%_	**99.20%**	99.46%	**99.33%**
	CAN-M	**99.35%**	**99.61%**	**99.48%**	98.02%	**99.34%**	**98.68%**	**99.52%**	**99.67%**	**99.59%**	99.05%	**99.53%**	99.29%
(f.e)	BRNN	97.87%	98.69%	98.28%	95.03%	97.45%	96.22%	98.35%	99.24%	98.79%	**99.20%**	99.28%	**99.24%**
	CAN-B	_99.16%_	_99.38%_	_99.27%_	**98.34%**	_99.20%_	**98.77%**	_98.82%_	_99.39%_	_99.10%_	_99.15%_	_99.30%_	_99.22%_
	CAN-M	**99.30%**	**99.56%**	**99.43%**	_97.97%_	**99.29%**	_98.63%_	**99.56%**	**99.71%**	**99.64%**	99.12%	**99.31%**	99.21%
(f.b)	IDA	56.53%	70.63%	62.80%	53.46%	72.84%	61.66%	87.10%	93.93%	90.39%	93.24%	98.11%	95.61%
	BW no-RFCR	90.58%	92.85%	91.70%	91.59%	93.17%	92.37%	90.48%	95.03%	92.70%	91.35%	92.87%	92.10%
	BW	92.29%	92.78%	92.53%	92.52%	93.22%	92.87%	93.91%	92.30%	93.10%	93.13%	93.04%	93.08%
	BRNN	95.34%	97.75%	96.53%	89.91%	94.85%	92.31%	95.27%	97.53%	96.39%	97.33%	**98.43%**	97.88%
	CAN-B	_98.08%_	_98.29%_	_98.18%_	**96.45%**	_97.24%_	**96.84%**	_97.81%_	_98.36%_	_98.08%_	**97.89%**	98.27%	**98.08%**
	CAN-M	**98.43%**	**98.68%**	**98.55%**	_96.13%_	**97.34%**	_96.73%_	**98.99%**	**99.14%**	**99.06%**	_97.63%_	_98.39%_	_98.01%_
(f.sc)	CAN-B	_98.03%_	_98.25%_	_98.14%_	**96.28%**	_97.10%_	**96.69%**	_97.75%_	_98.31%_	_98.03%_	**97.83%**	_98.22%_	**98.02%**
	CAN-M	**98.40%**	**98.65%**	**98.52%**	_95.94%_	**97.21%**	_96.57%_	**98.97%**	**99.12%**	**99.05%**	_97.52%_	**98.28%**	_97.90%_

Table 2. Comparison with the baselines (the Bidirectional RNN, ByteWeight and Nucleus) using average scores for all architectures (x86 and x86-64) for both Linux and Windows of our Code Action Network. The experimental results for Nucleus are from the original paper using the same dataset (Best performance in **bold**, second best in underline).

Tasks	Function Start			Function Bound			Function Scope		
Methods	Recall	Precision	F1	Recall	Precision	F1	Recall	Precision	F1
Nucleus	94%	96%	94.99%	88%	96%	91.83%	88%	96%	91.83%
ByteWeight	97.44%	97.30%	97.37%	92.96%	92.84%	92.90%	-	-	-
Bidirectional RNN	98.60%	99.22%	98.92%	94.46%	97.14%	95.78%	-	-	-
CAN-B	*98.89%*	*99.36%*	*99.12%*	*97.56%*	*98.04%*	*97.80%*	*97.47%*	*97.97%*	*97.72%*
CAN-M	**98.99%**	**99.54%**	**99.26%**	**97.80%**	**98.39%**	**98.09%**	**97.71%**	**98.32%**	**98.01%**

5 Conclusion

In this paper, we have proposed the novel Code Action Network (CAN) for dealing with the function identification problem, a preliminary and significant step in binary analysis for many security applications such as malware detection, common vulnerability detection and binary instrumentation. Specifically, the CAN leverages the underlying idea of a multicell bidirectional recurrent neural network with the idea of encoding the task of function scope identification to a sequence of three action states NI (i.e., next inclusion), NE (i.e., next exclusion), and FE (i.e., function end) in order to tackle function scope identification, the hardest and most crucial task in function identification. The experimental results show that the CAN can achieve state-of-the-art performance in terms of efficiency and efficacy.

Acknowledgement. This research was supported under the Defence Science and Technology Group's Next Generation Technologies Program.

References

1. Andriesse, D., Slowinska, A., Bos, H.: Compiler-agnostic function detection in binaries. In: IEEE European Symposium on Security and Privacy (EuroS&P) (2017)
2. Bao, T., Burket, J., Woo, M.: Byteweight: learning to recognize functions in binary code. In: 23rd USENIX Security Symposium (USENIX Security 2014) (2014)
3. Krizhevsky, A., Sutskever, I., Hinton, G.E.: Imagenet classification with deep convolutional neural networks. In: Advances in Neural Information Processing Systems 25 (2012)
4. Kruegel, C., Robertson, W., Valeur, F., Vigna, G.: Static disassembly of obfuscated binaries. In: Proceedings of Conference on USENIX Security Symposium (2004)
5. Laurenzano, M.A., Tikir, M.M., Carrington, L., Snavely, A.: PEBIL: efficient static binary instrumentation for Linux. In: International Symposium on Performance Analysis of Systems and Software (ISPASS) (2010)
6. Le, T., et al.: Maximal divergence sequential autoencoder for binary software vulnerability detection. In: International Conference on Learning Representations (2019)

7. Nguyen, T., et al.: Deep cost-sensitive kernel machine for binary software vulnerability detection. In: Pacific-Asia Conference on Knowledge Discovery and Data Mining (2020)
8. Nguyen, V., et al.: Deep domain adaptation for vulnerable code function identification. In: International Joint Conference on Neural Networks (2019)
9. Perkins, J.H., et al.: Automatically patching errors in deployed software. In: Proceedings of the ACM SIGOPS 22nd Symposium on Operating Systems Principles (2009)
10. Pewny, J., Garmany, B., Gawlik, R., Rossow, C., Holz, T.: Cross-architecture bug search in binary executables. In: Proceedings of IEEE Symposium on Security and Privacy (2015)
11. Rosenblum, N.E., Zhu, X., Miller, B.P., Hunt, K.: Learning to analyze binary computer code. In: AAAI, pp. 798–804 (2008)
12. Shin, E.C.R., Song, D., Moazzezi, R.: Recognizing functions in binaries with neural networks. In: 24th USENIX Security Symposium (USENIX Security 2015) (2015)
13. Sutskever, I., Vinyals, O., Le, Q.V.: Sequence to sequence learning with neural networks. In: Proceedings of the 27th International Conference on Neural Information Processing Systems, vol. 2 (2014)
14. Zhang, M., Sekar, R.: Control flow integrity for COTS binaries. In: Proceedings of the 22nd USENIX Conference on Security (2013)

Multi-level Memory Network with CRFs for Keyphrase Extraction

Tao Zhou, Yuxiang Zhang$^{(\boxtimes)}$, and Haoxiang Zhu

College of Computer Science and Technology, Civil Aviation University of China,
Tianjin, China
{zhou.tao1,zhu.hx}@outlook.com, yxzhang@cauc.edu.cn

Abstract. Keyphrase, that concisely describe the high-level topics discussed in a document, are very useful for a wide range of natural language processing (NLP) tasks. Current popular supervised methods for keyphrase extraction commonly cannot effectively utilize the long-range contextual information in text. In this paper, we focus on how to effectively exploit the long-range contextual information to improve the keyphrase extraction performance. Specifically, we propose a multi-level memory network with the conditional random fields (CRFs), which allows to have unrestricted access to the long-range and local contextual information in text. We first design the multi-level memory network with sentence level and document level to enhance the text representation. Then, we integrate the multi-level memory network with the CRFs, which has an advantage in modeling the local contextual information. Compared with the recent state-of-the-art methods, our model can achieve better results through experiments on two datasets.

Keywords: Keyphrase extraction · Sequence labeling · Memory network

1 Introduction

Automatic keyphrase extraction is to recommend a set of representative phrases that are related to the main topics discussed in a document. Since keyphrases can provide a high-level topic description of a document, they are beneficial for a wide range of natural language processing tasks such as information extraction, text summarization and question answering [21]. However, the performance of existing methods is still far from being satisfactory [10]. The main reason is that it is very challenging to determine whether a phrase or sets of phrases can accurately capture main topics that are presented in the document.

Existing methods for keyphrase extraction can be broadly divided into unsupervised and supervised methods. Specifically, unsupervised approaches directly treat keyphrase extraction as a ranking problem, scoring each word using various measures such as TF-IDF (term frequency-inverse document frequency) and graph-based ranking scores (*e.g.*, degree centrality or PageRank score) [7,8,22,27].

© Springer Nature Switzerland AG 2020
H. W. Lauw et al. (Eds.): PAKDD 2020, LNAI 12084, pp. 726–738, 2020.
https://doi.org/10.1007/978-3-030-47426-3_56

Supervised methods usually treat the keyphrase extraction as a binary classification task, in which a classifier is trained on the features of labeled keyphrases to determine whether a candidate phrase is a keyphrase [9,10,19]. Compared with unsupervised methods, supervised approaches can yield good results given sufficient training samples.

Recently, EK-CRF [9] employed the CRFs to extract keyphrases from scientific research articles, which was trained on token-based features incorporating linguistic, document structure information, and expert knowledge. This work achieved better performance on keyphrase extraction task and was shown to be state-of-the-art in previous traditional supervised methods. However, if we can not consider the features used in EK-CRF, CRFs only capture local structural dependencies. In addition, EK-CRF mainly relies on manual feature engineering, which may require considerable effort and domain-specific knowledge.

In this work, we aim to capture the long-range contextual information hidden in the text sequence and remove the need of manual feature engineering to extract keyphrases form scientific papers. Specifically, we formulate the keyphrase extraction as a sequence labeling task. We first use the memory network [23] to capture the long-range contextual information hidden in text data. Note that although plain recurrent neural networks (RNNs) can encode the sequential text and their variants such as long short-term memory (LSTM) models can further capture non-local patterns, they still exhibit a significant local bias in practice [14]. In order to make full use of the effective information hidden in text sequence, we extend the input memory of the memory network with two different levels: sentence level and document level. Secondly, we use the CRF model to capture the dependencies between adjacent words in text sequence and determine whether a candidate phrase is a keyphrase. Finally, we conduct comprehensive experiments over two publicly available datasets (KDD and WWW) in Computer Science area. Experimental results show that the proposed approach outperforms several state-of-the-art supervised methods.

The remainder of this paper is organized as follows. We firstly summarize related works on keyphrase extraction and memory networks in Sect. 2. Secondly, the proposed model for keyphrase extraction is described in Sect. 3. Then, the datasets, experimental results and discussions are illustrated in Sect. 4. Finally, we conclude this paper in Sect. 5.

2 Related Work

In this section, we firstly review the related works on keyphrase extraction and then summarize the existing works on the memory network.

2.1 Keyphrase Extraction

As mentioned in Sect. 1, existing approaches for keyphrase extraction can be broadly divided into unsupervised and supervised methods. This work is mainly related to supervised methods which have been proven to be effective in the keyphrase extraction task. Research on supervised methods has focused on two issues: classifier selection and feature design. Current state-of-the-art classifiers typically include Naïve Bayes [3,24], decision trees [19], CRFs [9], deep recurrent neural networks (RNN) [16], *etc.* The features used to represent an instance can be broadly divided into three categories: statistical features, structural features and syntactic features [10].

Zhang *et al.* [26] is the first to use the CRFs extracting keyphrases, which provides a way to explore the local contextual information in text sequence and traditional features, to identify each candidate word by sequence labeling. Bhaskar *et al.* [2] employed CRFs trained mainly on linguistic features such as part-of-speech (POS), chunking and named-entity tags for keyphrase extraction. Gollapalli *et al.* [9] also utilized CRFs to extract keyphrases from research papers, which was trained on token-based features incorporating linguistic, document-structure information and expert knowledge. CopyRNN [16] is the first to employ the sequence-to-sequence (Seq2Seq) deep learning model to predict keyphrases for documents. Following CopyRNN, a few extensions have been proposed to help better generate keyphrases [4,28]. In addition, Alzaidy *et al.* [1] integrated the CRF with the bidirectional long short term memory networks (LSTMs) to extract keyphrases from research papers. However, this method didn't capture the long-range contextual dependencies between words in text. We extend the memory network with stronger storage capacity to jointly maintain local structural information provided by RNNs with long-range dependencies in the long text.

2.2   Memory Network

Despite of the success of the RNNs on various text modeling tasks, simple RNNs still exhibit a significant local bias in practice [25]. Memory network [23] enhances the long-term memory capability of deep network by augmenting the internal memory with a series of extra memory components, and provides a general approach for modeling long-range dependencies and making multi-hop reasoning, which has advanced many NLP tasks such as question answering [20] and reading documents [17]. Sukhbaatar *et al.* [20] proposed the end-to-end memory network, which can be trained end-to-end without any intervention. Kumar *et al.* [12] proposed the dynamic memory network, which uses a sentence-level attention mechanism to update its internal memory during multi-hop inference. Miller *et al.* [17] encoded prior knowledge by introducing a key memory structure which stores facts to address to the relevant memory value. Taking inspiration from these works, we design the multi-level memory network with CRFs to extract keyphrases from research papers.

3   Methodology

In this section, we first present the problem definition in Subsect. 3.1. We then explain the overview of our proposed model in Subsect. 3.2, followed by the details of each component of the model from Subsect. 3.3 to 3.4.

3.1   Problem Definition

Keyphrase extraction is formulated as a task of sequence labeling, predicting a label for each word in the input text sequence. More specifically, we denote the input source document as a sequence $\mathbf{x} = \{x_1, x_2, ..., x_l\}$, where x_t represents t-th input word and l is the length of the sequence. The goal of the model is to predict a sequence of labels $\mathbf{y} = \{y_1, y_2, ..., y_l\}$, where each label y_t corresponding to the input word x_t represents whether x_t is a keyphrase word or not keyphrase word.

3.2   Model Overview

Figure 1 illustrates the overview of the Multi-Level Memory network with CRFs (**MLM-CRF**) for keyphrase extraction. This model includes two main parts: the memory layer, capturing long-range dependencies using the deep memory network; and the CRF layer, capturing local dependencies and labeling each word of input text sequence with five different labels (detailed in Subsect. 4.3).

The memory layer can be divided into two parallel modules at different levels: sentence level memory and document level memory. Each module further includes three components similar to the works [15, 20]: (1) the input memory vector m_t, which captures the information from the word embedding layer of the text sequence; (2) the current input embedding u_t, which is the representation of the current word; and (3) the output vector c_t, which is similar to the input memory m_t.

In addition, the output memory representation of the memory layer o, summarizing the long-range semantic and structure information from the input text sequence without distance limitation, is calculated by a weighted sum over the output representations, in which the attention weights are determined by measuring the similarity between the input memory vector and the current input embedding. Finally, the output of the memory layer o is fed into the CRF layer to predict keyphrases for documents using sequence labelling model CRF. In the remainder of this section, we will present the MLM-CRF in detail.

3.3   Memory Layer

Input Memory Representation. At first, the word embedding look-up table, trained by GloVe [18], is applied to map each word x_t in the text sequence into an embedding vector x_t. Although we can directly use this embedding vector as the input memory representation in the context of the memory network, in order to tackle the drawback of insensitivity to temporal information between memory cells [15], we obtain the input memory representation m_t by adopting the bidirectional gate recurrent unit (GRU) [5] to encode the word embedding vectors x_t:

$$\overrightarrow{m}_t = \overrightarrow{\mathbf{GRU}}(x_t, \overrightarrow{m}_{t-1}) \tag{1}$$

$$\overleftarrow{m}_t = \overleftarrow{\mathbf{GRU}}(x_t, \overleftarrow{m}_{t+1}) \tag{2}$$

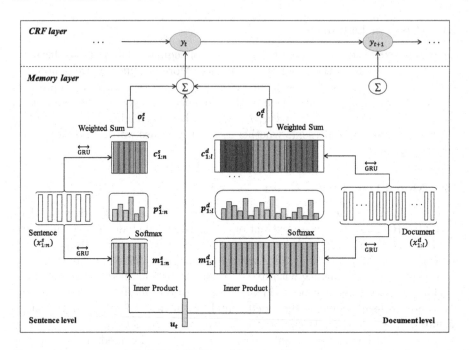

Fig. 1. An overview of the MLM-CRF model for keyphrase extraction. It is shown only as a single hop.

$$m_t = \tanh(\overrightarrow{W}_m \overrightarrow{m}_t + \overleftarrow{W}_m \overleftarrow{m}_t + b_m) \tag{3}$$

where $\overrightarrow{W}_m$, $\overleftarrow{W}_m$ and b_m are three trainable parameters to adjust the input memory representation m_t.

Current Input Representation. In order to calculate the attention weight of each element in the input memory, we enforce the current input to be in the same space as the input memory. More specifically, we use the obtained m_t to represent the current input representation u_t, *i.e.*, $u_t = m_t$. Note that as illustrated in Fig. 1, the current input u_t in the sentence level and the document level is set to the same. We will detail it in the subsection Extensions.

Attention Weight Calculation. We compute the attention weight of each element in the input memory by measuring the relevance between the current input u_t and each element of the input memory m_i with a softmax function:

$$p_{t,i} = \mathrm{softmax}(u_t^T m_i) \tag{4}$$

where $softmax(x_i) = \frac{e^{x_i}}{\sum_j e^{x_j}}$.

Output Memory Representation. Similar to the input memory vector m_t, the output vector c_i is also the contextual representation vector which is used to capture the contextual semantic information of the text sequence. The output vector is also encoded by bidirectional GRU, but with different parameters in the GRUs function and tanh layers of Eq. (1), (2) and (3).

The output vector is used to generate the final output memory of the memory layer o_t, which is the weighted sum over the attention weight and the output vector, as:

$$o_t = \sum_i p_{t,i} c_i. \tag{5}$$

The output memory allows the model to have unrestricted access to elements in previous steps as opposed to a single hidden state in RNNs, which will helps the CRF fully utilize the long-range dependencies in the text sequence to better predict keyphrases for documents.

Extensions. Many existing works [6,17] discussed the influence of the different lengths covered by the attention mechanism in the memory network. Inspired by these works, we explore the different length of the input memory at two different levels: the sentence level and document level.

In the sentence level, the attention mechanism covers just the sentence containing the current word, and the corresponding attention weight is calculated as:

$$p_{t,i}^s = \mathtt{softmax}(u_t^T m_i^s) \tag{6}$$

where $i \in [1,n]$ and n is the length of the sentence.

In the document level, the whole document is covered by the attention mechanism and the attention weight as computed as:

$$p_{t,i}^d = \mathtt{softmax}(u_t^T m_i^d) \tag{7}$$

where $i \in [1,l]$ and l is the length of the document. The current input u_t used in both the sentence level and the document level is set to the same.

Then we calculate the final output memory of the memory layer as:

$$o_t = \lambda \sum_i p_{t,i}^d c_i^d + (1 - \lambda) \sum_i p_{t,i}^s c_i^s \tag{8}$$

where λ is a hyper-parameter, which is set to adjust weight from the different levels. Thus we replace Eq. (4) and (5) with Eq. (6), (7) and (8). The output memory of the memory layer can capture the information from not only the local but also the long-distance context by using the two-level output vectors.

We can further extend the model by stacking multiple memory hops for capturing multiple fact from the memory, which stacks hops between the current input u_t and the k-th hop o_t^k to be the input to the $(k+1)$-th hop:

$$u_t^{k+1} = u_t^k + o_t^k \tag{9}$$

In our model, we simply limit the hop to only 1.

3.4   CRF Layer

In this section, we feed the output of the memory layer into the CRF layer for extracting keyphrases. CRF [13] has been proven to be effective for sequence labeling tasks. We use CRF jointly with the memory network to predict the sequence of labels for the keyphrase extraction task.

Given the input text sequence $\mathbf{x} = \{x_1, x_2, ..., x_l\}$ and the sequence of output labels $\mathbf{y} = \{y_1, y_2, ..., y_l\}$, the score is computed as:

$$s(\mathbf{x}, \mathbf{y}) = \sum_{t=0}^{l} \boldsymbol{A}_{y_t, y_{t+1}} + \sum_{t=1}^{l} \boldsymbol{P}_{t, y_t}, \tag{10}$$

where $\boldsymbol{P}$ is the linearly transformed matrix from the output matrix of memory network $\boldsymbol{U}$ such that $\boldsymbol{P} = \boldsymbol{U}\boldsymbol{W}$. The size of $\boldsymbol{U}$ is $l \times d$, where d is the size of the output vector $\boldsymbol{u}$. The size of $\boldsymbol{W}$ is the weight matrix with the size of $d \times k$, where k is the number of labels. Thus, the size of P is $l \times k$, where $p_{i,j}$ represents the score of the j-th label of the i-th word of the input sequence. In addition, $\boldsymbol{A}$ is the matrix of transition scores, in which $a_{i,j}$ represents the score of a transition from the label i to label j.

The probability of the label sequence $\mathbf{y}$ can be calculated by the softmax function as follow:

$$p(\mathbf{y}|\mathbf{x}) = \frac{\exp(s(\mathbf{x}, \mathbf{y}))}{\sum_{\tilde{\mathbf{y}} \in \mathbf{Y}_\mathbf{x}} \exp(s(\mathbf{x}, \tilde{\mathbf{y}}))}, \tag{11}$$

where $\mathbf{Y}_\mathbf{x}$ represents all possible label sequences given a input sequence $\mathbf{x}$. In the training procedure, we maximize the log-probability of the correct label sequence:

$$\mathcal{L} = \log(p(\mathbf{y}|\mathbf{x})) = s(\mathbf{x}, \mathbf{y}) - \log\left(\sum_{\tilde{\mathbf{y}} \in \mathbf{Y}_\mathbf{x}} \exp(s(\mathbf{x}, \tilde{\mathbf{y}})) \right). \tag{12}$$

This objective function and its gradients can be efficiently computed by dynamic programming algorithm. In order to find the best sequence of labels during decoding, the Viterbi algorithm is employed to decode the label sequence efficiently by maximizing the score $s(\mathbf{x}, \tilde{\mathbf{y}})$:

$$y^* = \arg\max_{\tilde{\mathbf{y}} \in \mathbf{Y}_\mathbf{x}} s(\mathbf{x}, \tilde{\mathbf{y}}). \tag{13}$$

4   Experiments

4.1   Datasets

To analyze the effectiveness of our model for keyphrase extraction, we conduct comparative experiments on two scientific publication datasets provided by Caragea et al. [3], which are from two top-tier machine learning conferences: ACM Knowledge Discovery and Data Mining (KDD) and ACM World Wide

Web (WWW). Each dataset consists of the research paper titles, abstracts and corresponding author manually labeled keyphrases (gold standard).

A detail description of datasets is summarized in Table 1, containing the total number of abstracts and keyphrases in the original dataset (#Abs/#KPs(All)), the number of abstracts for which at least one author-labeled keyphrase could be located and the total number of keyphrases located (#Abs/#KPs(Locatable)), the percentage of keyphrases not present in the abstracts (MissingKPs), the average number of keyphrase per paper (AvgKPs), and the number of keyphrases with one, two, three and more than three tokens found in these abstracts.

4.2 Evaluation Metrics

Almost all previous works on keyphrase extraction use precision (P), recall (R) and F1-score $(F1)$ to evaluate the results. Hence, we also keep our evaluation metric consistent. P, R and $F1$ are defined as follows:

$$P = \frac{\#_c}{\#_e}, R = \frac{\#_c}{\#_s}, F1 = \frac{2PR}{P + R} \qquad (14)$$

where $\#_c$ is the number of correctly extracted keyphrases predicted by model, $\#_e$ is the total number of keyphrases predicted by model and $\#_s$ is the total number of standard keyphrases labeled by author.

In our experiments, we partition the dataset into three groups using tenfold cross-validation: Onefold is used as the testing data; Onefold is used as the validating data; the remaining eightfolds are used as the training data. We report the average results of tenfold cross-validation.

Table 1. Statistics of the two benchmark datasets.

Dataset	#Abs/ #Kps (All)	#Abs/ #Kps (Loc.)	MissingKPs (%)	#AvgKPs	#unigrams	#bigrams	#trigrams	#> trigrams
KDD	365/1471	315/719	51.12	4.03	363	853	189	66
WWW	425/2073	388/904	56.39	4.87	680	1036	247	110

4.3 Implementation Details

In the experiment, we divide keyphrases into two categories: simple keyphrase (1-gram, referred to as SK) and complicated keyphrase (n-grams ($n > 1$), that is composed by two or more than two words, referred to as CK). Each word in dataset is labeled with non-keyphrase (O), simple keyphrase (SK) or complicated keyphrase (CK). For the complicated keyphrase, B-CK, M-CK and E-CK correspond to the beginning, middle and end word of CK, respectively. Thus, the number of labels is set to $k = 5$.

In order to eliminate the negative effects of different text formats, we convert the input text to lowercase in data pre-processing and employ two binary lexical features: whether the word contains digits or punctuation, which is similar to the works [11,15], We use the 50-dimensional embeddings pre-trained by GloVe[1] [18] on two corpora: Wikipedia2014[2] and Gigaword5[3]. In addition, some parameters of model are empirically set as follows: the hyper-parameter in Eq. (8) $\lambda = 0.6$, and the trainable parameters in Eq. (3) $\overrightarrow{W}_m$ and $\overleftarrow{W}_m \in \mathbb{R}^{50 \times 50}$, $b_m \in \mathbb{R}^{50}$. Dropout is applied to all GRU recurrent units on the input and output connections to avoid over-fitting, with a keep rate of 0.6 in the training procedure.

4.4 Comparative Methods

To evaluate the performance of our method, we compare our method with four state-of-the-art keyphrase extraction methods, as follows:

- **KEA** [24], which employs a supervised Naïve Bayes classifier to extract keyphrases using only two features: TF-IDF (*i.e.*, term frequency-inverse document frequency) of a phrase and the distance of a phrase from the beginning of a document (*i.e.*, its relative position).
- **CeKE** [3], which also uses a Naïve Bayes classifier for extracting keyphrases from research papers embedded in citation networks. This work designs some novel features for keyphrase extraction based on citation context information and uses them in conjunction with traditional features which have been widely used in the previous supervised works of keyphrase extraction.
- **EK-CRF** [9], which is the state-of-the-art traditional supervised method, and uses the CRF algorithm based on sequence labeling to extract keyphrases from research papers. This method incorporates the expert-knowledge and domain-specific hints.
- **CopyRNN** [16], which is the first to employ sequence-to-sequence (Seq2Seq) framework with attention and copy mechanisms to generate keyphrases. This method is able to predict absent keyphrases that do not appear in the target document.
- **M-CRF**^{s}, which is the simplified model of our complete model MLM-CRF. M-CRF^s only uses the attention at sentence level. That is, the coverage of attention mechanism in memory network only depends on the length of the sentence, which the current word belongs to. In this model, the output memory vector and attention weight are calculated by the Eq. (5) and (6), respectively.
- **M-CRF**^{d}, which is the another simplified model of our complete model MLM-CRF. M-CRF^d only calculates attention weight between the current word and the whole input document. In this model, the output memory vector and attention weight are computed by the Eq. (5) and (7), respectively.

4.5 Comparison with Supervised Prediction Methods

Table 2 shows the comparison of results of our model with other state-of-the-art supervised approaches. From Table 2, we can see that the overall results of KDD

---

[1] http://nlp.stanford.edu/projects/glove/.

[2] https://code.google.com/archive/p/word2vec/.

[3] https://catalog.ldc.upenn.edu/LDC2011T07.

dataset is better than those of WWW, which is consistent with percentage of keyphrases not present in the abstracts (MissingKPs) in given research papers (MissingKPs = 51.12% on KDD, 56.39% on WWW), as given in Table 1. The benefit is that the experiment can reflect real application environment.

We first conduct experiments to compare the MLM-CRF with its two simplified models M-CRF^s and M-CRF^d. As the results given in Table 2, MLM-CRF gets the best results in terms of performance measures, and M-CRF^d achieves better results than M-CRF^s. These results indicate that long-range and more contextual information is more conducive to keyphrase extraction. More specifically, the contextual information captured by M-CRF^d is longer than by M-CRF^s, and MLM-CRF can capture the contextual information in the sentence level and document level.

Secondly, we discuss the comparison of our model MLM-CRF with other comparative keyphrase prediction methods, including KEA, CeKE, EK-CRF and CopyRNN. As given in Table 2, MLM-CRF outperforms all comparative methods on two datasets, and even the M-CRF^d has a margin over the best performing extraction method CRF on the two test datasets. It is also worth mentioning that CeKE includes features based on the document-citation network, EK-CRF designs complex features integrating expert-knowledge and domain-specific hints during keyphrase extraction, and CopyRNN can generate absent keyphrases, whereas our model does not need to use extra knowledge, design complex features, and can not predict absent keyphrases.

In conclusion, the MLM-CRF can capture automatically much useful information from the source text for keyphrase extraction. Thus, our model gets the best results in terms of the performance measures, indicating that our method indeed outperforms the other approaches on all two datasets.

Table 2. Comparison of the proposed models with other approaches

Method	KDD			WWW		
	Precision	Recall	F1-score	Precision	Recall	F1-score
KEA [24]	0.1551	0.3278	0.2105	0.1549	0.3182	0.2084
CeKE [3]	0.2174	0.3905	0.2793	0.2251	0.2519	0.2377
EK-CRF [9]	0.4068	0.2162	0.2823	0.3689	0.194	0.2547
CopyRNN@5 [16]	0.2221	0.4926	0.3062	0.1907	0.3993	0.2581
M-CRF^s	0.3438	0.2354	0.2794	0.3276	0.2059	0.2528
M-CRF^d	0.3597	0.2542	0.2979	0.3551	0.2129	0.2662
MLM-CRF	**0.3787**	**0.2771**	**0.32**	**0.3251**	**0.2417**	**0.2773**

4.6   Comparison in Different Types of Keyphrases

We compare our different models in two different types of keyphrases: SK (including only single word, *i.e.*, 1-gram) and CK (including several consecutive words, *i.e.*, n-gram, $n \geq 2$). We first compare the MLM-CRF with its two simplified models M-CRF^s and M-CRF^d in SK and CK on both KDD and WWW datasets, respectively. As the results given in Table 3, both in SK and in CK, MLM-CRF gets the best results in terms of the performance measures, and M-CRF^d achieves better results than M-CRF^s on two datasets. These results indicate that long-range and more contextual information is more conducive to keyphrase extraction.

Table 3. Comparison of our different models in different type keyphrases.

Methods	KDD						WWW					
	SK			CK			SK			CK		
	P	R	$F1$	P	R	$F1$	P	R	$F1$	P	R	$F1$
M-CRF^s	0.3679	0.1235	0.1849	0.3382	0.3059	0.3212	0.3534	0.1868	0.2444	0.3092	0.2247	0.2603
M-CRF^d	0.3180	0.1444	0.1986	0.3734	0.3235	0.3466	0.3659	0.2009	0.2594	0.3460	0.2247	0.2725
MLM-CRF	0.4589	0.1843	0.2630	0.3720	0.3520	0.3617	0.3453	0.2283	0.2749	0.3090	0.2548	0.2793

Secondly, we compare the growth performance from the simplified method M-CRF^s to MLM-CRF in SK and CK. From Table 3, we can see that the growth of F1-score is 0.0781 for SK and 0.0450 for CK on KDD, and is 0.0305 for SK and 0.0190 for CK on WWW. It is obvious enough that the growth of F1-score in SK is more than that in CK on both KDD and WWW datasets. We can obtain the similar growth trends of Precision and Recall in SK and CK on two datasets. These results show that the 1-gram keyphrases have a stronger long-distance dependencies in text sequence than the n-gram ($n \geq 2$) keyphrases, which are more dependent on the local structural information. The experimental setup might be able to explain the main reason for these results. More specifically, for identifying keyphrases labeled by CK using the CRF model, different labels of CK are restricted, while for identifying keyphrases labeled by SK, the single SK label is totally unrestricted. For example, the B-CK label must be followed by the M-CK or E-CK label in the experiments.

Finally, we discuss the performance of our models in different types of keyphrases SK and CK. As the results given in Table 3, we can see that our models can obtain better performance in CK than that in SK. The main reason may be that the percentage of 1-gram keyphrases in all keyphrases is significantly less than the percentage of n-gram ($n \geq 2$) keyphrases.

5   Conclusions

In this paper, we proposed a multi-level memory network with CRFs named MLM-CRF for extracting keyphrases from scientific research papers. In particular, we first extended the input memory of the memory network with two different levels (*i.e.*, sentence level and document level) to capture the long-range contextual information hidden in text data. We then employed the CRF model to capture the structural dependencies between adjacent words in text sequence and determine whether a candidate phrase is a keyphrase. Our experimental results have shown that the proposed model MLM-CRF can significantly outperform the state-of-the-art supervised prediction approaches (including three extraction methods and one generation method) on both WWW and KDD datasets. In future, we plan to explore the more effective attention mechanism for taking much less computing costs in encoding the long document.

Acknowledgements. This work was partially supported by grants from the National Natural Science Foundation of China (Nos. U1933114, 61573231) and Open Project Foundation of Intelligent Information Processing Key Laboratory of Shanxi Province (No. CICIP2018004).

References

1. Alzaidy, R., Caragea, C., Giles, C.L.: Bi-LSTM-CRF sequence labeling for keyphrase extraction from scholarly documents. In: Proceedings of WWW, pp. 2551–2557 (2019)
2. Bhaskar, P., Nongmeikapam, K., Bandyopadhyay, S.: Keyphrase extraction in scientific articles: a supervised approach. In: Proceedings of COLING, pp. 17–24 (2012)
3. Caragea, C., Bulgarov, F., Godea, A., Das Gollapalli, S.: Citation-enhanced keyphrase extraction from research papers: a supervised approach. In: Proceedings of EMNLP, pp. 1435–1446 (2014)
4. Chen, W., Gao, Y., Zhang, J., King, I., Lyu, M.R.: Title-guided encoding for keyphrase generation. In: Proceedings of AAAI, pp. 6268–6275 (2019)
5. Chung, J., Gulcehre, C., Cho, K., Bengio, Y.: Empirical evaluation of gated recurrent neural networks on sequence modeling. In: Proceedings of NIPS (2014)
6. Dai, Z., et al.: Transformer-XL: attentive language models beyond a fixed-length context. In: Proceedings of ACL, pp. 2978–2988 (2019)
7. Florescu, C., Caragea, C.: Positionrank: an unsupervised approach to keyphrase extraction from scholarly documents. In: Proceedings of ACL, pp. 1105–1115 (2017)
8. Gollapalli, S.D., Caragea, C.: Extracting keyphrases from research papers using citation networks. In: Proceedings of AAAI, pp. 1629–1635 (2014)
9. Gollapalli, S.D., Li, X.L., Yang, P.: Incorporating expert knowledge into keyphrase extraction. In: Proceedings of AAAI, pp. 3180–3187 (2017)
10. Hasan, K.S., Ng, V.: Automatic keyphrase extraction: a survey of the state of the art. In: Proceedings of ACL, pp. 1262–1273 (2014)
11. Huang, Z., Xu, W., Yu, K.: Bidirectional LSTM-CRF models for sequence tagging. arXiv preprint arXiv:1508.01991 (2015)
12. Kumar, A., et al.: Ask me anything: dynamic memory networks for natural language processing. In: Proceedings of ICML, pp. 1378–1387 (2016)
13. Lafferty, J., McCallum, A., Pereira, F.C.: Conditional random fields: probabilistic models for segmenting and labeling sequence data. In: Proceedings of ICML, pp. 282–289 (2001)
14. Linzen, T., Dupoux, E., Goldberg, Y.: Assessing the ability of LSTMs to learn syntax-sensitive dependencies. In: Transactions of ACL, pp. 521–535 (2016)

15. Liu, F., Baldwin, T., Cohn, T.: Capturing long-range contextual dependencies with memory-enhanced conditional random fields. In: Proceedings of IJCNLP, pp. 555–565 (2017)
16. Meng, R., Zhao, S., Han, S., He, D., Brusilovsky, P., Chi, Y.: Deep keyphrase generation. In: Proceedings of ACL, pp. 582–592 (2017)
17. Miller, A., Fisch, A., Dodge, J., Karimi, A.H., Weston, J.: Key-value memory networks for directly reading documents. In: Proceedings of EMNLP, pp. 1400–1409 (2016)
18. Pennington, J., Socher, R., Manning, C.: Glove: global vectors for word representation. In: Proceedings of EMNLP, pp. 1532–1543 (2014)
19. Sterckx, L., Caragea, C., Demeester, T., Develder, C.: Supervised keyphrase extraction as positive unlabeled learning. In: Proceedings of EMNLP, pp. 1924–1929 (2016)
20. Sukhbaatar, S., Szlam, A., Weston, J., Fergus, R.: End-to-end memory networks. In: Proceedings of NIPS, pp. 2440–2448 (2015)
21. Tang, Y., et al.: Qalink: enriching text documents with relevant Q&A site contents. In: Proceedings of CIKM, pp. 1359–1368 (2017)
22. Wang, F., Wang, Z., Wang, S., Li, Z.: Exploiting description knowledge for keyphrase extraction. In: Proceedings of PRICAI, pp. 130–142 (2014)
23. Weston, J., Chopra, S., Bordes, A.: Memory networks. In: Proceedings of ICLR (2015)
24. Witten, I.H., Paynter, G.W., Frank, E., Gutwin, C., Nevill-Manning, C.G.: Kea: practical automated keyphrase extraction. In: Proceedings of ACM DL, pp. 254–255 (1999)
25. Yang, D., Wang, S., Li, Z.: Ensemble neural relation extraction with adaptive boosting. In: Proceedings of IJCAI, pp. 4532–4538 (2018)
26. Zhang, C., Wang, H., Liu, Y., Wu, D., Liao, Y., Wang, B.: Automatic keyword extraction from documents using conditional random fields. J. Comput. Inf. Syst. **4**(3), 1169–1180 (2008)
27. Zhang, Y., Chang, Y., Liu, X., Gollapalli, S.D., Li, X.: Mike: keyphrase extraction by integrating multidimensional information. In: Proceedings of CIKM, pp. 1349–1358 (2017)
28. Zhao, J., Zhang, Y.: Incorporating linguistic constraints into keyphrase generation. In: Proceedings of ACL, pp. 5224–5233 (2019)

Inter-sentence and Implicit Causality Extraction from Chinese Corpus

Xianxian Jin[1], Xinzhi Wang[1(✉)], Xiangfeng Luo[1(✉)], Subin Huang[1,2],
and Shengwei Gu[1,3]

[1] School of Computer Engineering and Science, Shanghai Institute for Advanced
Communication and Data Science, Shanghai University, Shanghai 200444, China
{xianxianjin,wxz2017,luoxf,huangsubin,gushengwei}@shu.edu.cn
[2] School of Computer and Information, Anhui Polytechnic University,
Wuhu 241000, China
[3] School of Computer and Information Engineering, Chuzhou University,
Chuzhou 213000, China

Abstract. Automatically extracting causal relations from texts is a challenging task in Natural Language Processing (NLP). Most existing methods focus on extracting intra-sentence or explicit causality, while neglecting the causal relations that expressed implicitly or hidden in inter-sentences. In this paper, we propose Cascaded multi-Structure Neural Network (CSNN), a novel and unified model that extract inter-sentence or implicit causal relations from Chinese Corpus, without relying on external knowledge. The model employs Convolutional Neural Network (CNN) to capture important features as well as causal structural pattern. Self-attention mechanism is designed to mine semantic and relevant characteristics between different features. The output of CNN and self-attention structure are concatenated as higher-level phrase representations. Then Conditional Random Field (CRF) layer is employed to calculate the label of each word in inter-sentence or implicit causal relation sentences, which improves the performance of inter-sentence or implicit causality extraction. Experimental results show that the proposed model achieves state-of-the-art results, improved on three datasets, when compared with other methods.

Keywords: Causality extraction · Causality · Event extraction

1 Introduction

In recent years, the automatic extraction of causal relation in the field of NLP has attracted increasing attention of researchers. Most existing methods focus on extracting intra-sentence or explicit causality, while neglecting the causality that expressed implicitly or hidden in inter-sentences. In this paper we focus on mining causality in text, and make effect to improve the result of extracting implicitly or inter-sentence causality by building deep learning model.

© Springer Nature Switzerland AG 2020
H. W. Lauw et al. (Eds.): PAKDD 2020, LNAI 12084, pp. 739–751, 2020.
https://doi.org/10.1007/978-3-030-47426-3_57

Causality of text is defined as the relationship between cause and effect, which may be linear or undirected. Causal relation of text exists in many scenario, such as product or social event reviews. The causality can be formalized as the relationship between event e_1 and event e_2, where the event e_2 is considered as a result of the event e_1 [17]. The representation of causal relations can be concluded into four forms: explicit causal relation whose sentence contains explicit causal connective such as "lead to", implicit causal relation whose sentence does not contain causal connective, intra-sentence causal relation whose cause-effect are distributed in short text between two adjacent punctuations, and inter-sentence causal relation whose cause-effect is broken by punctuations. Examples of the four forms are shown in Table 1. Automatic extraction of causality from texts plays an important role in natural language processing application, such as providing event basis for question answer system [19].

Table 1. The forms of causal relation.

Forms	Sentence	Causal-effect
Intra-sentence or explicit	Rising food prices will led to CPI continue to rise	"Rising food prices" → "CPI continue to rise"
Inter-sentence or explicit	RMB appreciation, result in surrounding house prices rise	"RMB appreciation" → "house prices rise"
Intra-sentence or implicit	Reduced food production, falling prices of gold and silver	"Reduced food production" → "falling prices of gold and silver"
Inter-sentence or implicit	According to analysis, loss of controlling interest, many companies are affected, appear passive overweight	"Loss of controlling interest" → "appear passive overweight"

Rule-based [9] methods or traditional machine learning methods [1] contribute a lot on causality mining. However, there are still many drawbacks. More specifically, rule-based methods heavily depend on manually designed language patterns, such as lexical-syntactic patterns [11]. Recently, deep learning methods are widely used in NLP tasks including causality extraction. Some researchers [3] focused on finding language expression of causality and extracting causal triplets from explicit causality sentences. In Table 1, for sentence like the first line, phrase "lead to" indicate the causality blocked by adjacent punctuation explicitly. For sentence like the second line, explicit cause and effect distribute in two adjacent blocks. For sentence like the third line, the cause "Reduced food production" and the effect "falling prices of gold and silver" are hidden implicitly. As being distributed in nonadjacent sentient blocks or lacking of causality indicators, mining inter-sentence or implicit causality is harder when compared with that of intra-sentence and explicit causality. Regardless of implicit causality in nonadjacent sentence blocks like the last line.

This paper proposes model CSNN a novel and unified inter-sentence or implicit causality extraction model. The CSNN model can be described in three steps. Firstly, CNN [2] captures local important features from different blocks of sentences. Secondly, fully considering the extracted advanced features correlation, we cluster the extracted advanced features, and establish semantic relevant characteristics between different features using self-attention. Thirdly and finally, BiLSTM [5] is employed to capture long dependencies between cause and effect using the extracted feature before extracting implicit causal relations or inter-sentence causal relations.

The main contributions of this paper are summarized as follows:

1. We propose a novel and unified model, which can automatic extract inter-sentence or implicit causal relations from Chinese corpus and does not rely on other external knowledge.
2. The model can not only capture local important features from different blocks of sentences, but also obtain long dependencies between cause and effect hidden in different sentence blocks.
3. Experiment results on three differenitemt datasets demonstrate that our model achieves state-of-the-art F1-score (F) in the task for extracting inter-sentence or implicit causal relations.

The paper is organized as follows: the related works on causal relation extraction is shown in Sect. 2. Details of the proposed causal relation extraction model is introduced in Sect. 3. Experimental and results are presented in Sect. 4. Finally, conclusion is given in Sect. 5.

2   Related Work

As complex structure and diverse forms, the extraction of causality in text is still a challenging task. Existing extraction of causality from nature language texts mainly considered two different methods: statistical methods and non-statistical methods.

Non-statistical Approaches: Numerous rule-based [9] methods have been dedicated on causality mining. Kontos and Sidiropoulou [13] used causal language patterns and hand-crafted causal relation templates to detect causal relations which hidden in contexts. Garcia [4] produced a system COATIS, which explorate the rules through contextual and linguistic features to extract causal relations from French texts.

Early work in this area heavily relied on hand-crafted rules and linguistic features. Which limit greatly on flexibility and hard to scale to others corpus. Due to the complexity of causal relation expressions in texts, the precision and recall are also dramatically low.

Statistical Approaches: In recent years, statistical methods have shown promising results in extracting causality from texts. Fu et al. [10], turned the causality extraction problems into sequence labeling problems for the first time.

They extracted causality from Chinese text with two-layer conditional random field. Dasgupta [3] focused on finding language expression of causal relation and proposed a method that combine word-level embedding with other linguistic features to extract causality from sentences. Li and Mao [16] extracted a method named Knowledge-oriented Convolutional Neural Network (KCNN) to extract causal relation. Li et al. [15] proposed a neural causality extractor named SCIFI, which can directly extract causal triplets from explicit causal relation sentences. The methods focused on intra-sentence or explicit causality. Such as "Attrition of associates will affect scheduled release of product causing high business impact." [3]. For sentence like the last line of Table 1, implicit causality in nonadjacent sentence blocks, only considered the dependencies between causal words is not enough.

Our work attempts to extract important features as well as causal structural pattern automatically, combine semantic and relevant characteristics between different features as higher-level phrase representations, to improve the result of inter-sentence or implicit causal relation extraction.

3   Cascaded Multi-structure Neural Network

In this section, our proposed inter-sentence or implicit causality extraction model is presented in detail. The overview model CSNN is shown in Fig. 1.

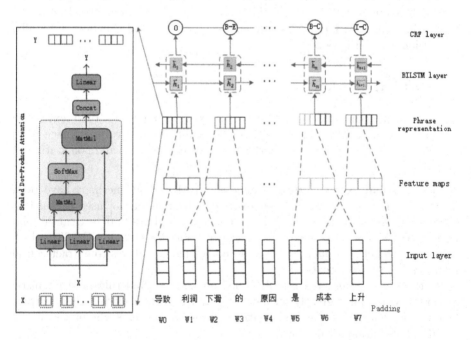

Fig. 1. Overview of the CSNN model for Cause-Effect relation extraction. Left: Semantic and relevant characteristics extraction process.

3.1   Model Architecture

In this subsection, we mainly explain how CSNN is employed to extract inter-sentence or implicit causality from Chinese corpus. The model is composed of two modules: 1) CNN is designed to capture important features within the windows of causality. Self-attention mechanism is designed to mine semantic and relevant characteristics among different features. 2) Long dependencies between cause and effect using BiLSTM [5] are established, which obtain deeper contextual semantic information.

In addition, CSNN expresses sentence as vector embedding. In this regard, a sentence is expressed as a vector $S \in R^{l \times e}$, where l is the number of words in sentences and e is embedding size. Besides, x_i is a vector standing for an e-dimentional word embedding of the i-th word in sentences.

$$S = (x_1, x_2, x_3, ..., x_l) \tag{1}$$

Convolution Layer: CNN [2] utilizes max-pooling to extract data features. However, max-pooling often produces poor results in causality extraction due to loss of information. More specifically, max-pooling only maintains the feature with the highest activation, which discarding all other features even though they seem to be useful. Therefore, all the features after convolution are used as windows features in causality extraction task.

The convolution layer is aimed to capture important features within the windows of causality, and compress these important cues into feature map. In general, let $w \in R^{h \times e}$ be the filter for convolution operation, where h is the number of words to generate a new feature. For example:

$$C_i = f(w \cdot x_{i:i+h-1} + b) \tag{2}$$

Where $b \times R^n$ is a hyper-parameter and f is a nonlinear function such as sigmoid, ReLU etc. In addition, ReLU [6] is used as the nonlinear function. The CSNN model employ multiple filters in convolution to generate multiple feature maps. For example, generated features for each window i-th can be expressed as:

$$W = [C_1, C_2, C_3, ..., C_m] \tag{3}$$

Where C_i is the feature map generated with the i-th filter. W_i is the feature representation generated from m filters for the window vector at position i and stride adopted 1.

In learning process, although each eigenvalue represents the overall characteristics of a window, the internal tendencies of each part of the feature is different. The internal semantic correlations between different features play a crucial role in the extraction of causal relations. Then, these features are grouped and self-attention mechanism is used to mine semantic and relevant characteristics between different features. Number of group is and each of group features is $d = m/t$.

Self-attention Layer: Self-attention is a special attention mechanism according to a sequence to compute its representation and has been successfully applied in many tasks, such as machine translation [20] and language understanding [21].

In our model, the multi-head attention mechanism [23] is employed to mine internal related information between features. As depicted in the left part of Fig. 1, the scaled dot-product attention is used as attention function to compute the attention sources by following Eq. 4. The input consists of query matrix $Q \in R^{t \times d}$, keys $K \in R^{t \times d}$, values $V \in R^{t \times d}$ and d is the number of features in a group.

$$Attention(Q, K, V) = softmax(\frac{QK^T}{\sqrt{d}})V \qquad (4)$$

The multi-head attention mechanism captures semantic relevant information from different features subspaces at different positions. First, we utilized h times different linear projections to get the queries, keys and values matrices, whose dimension is d/h. Then we perform the attention in parallel and concatenate the output values of h heads. The mathematical formulation is shown below:

$$H_i = Attention(QW_i^Q, KW_i^K, KW_i^V) \qquad (5)$$

$$HHead = Concat(H_1, H_2, ..., H_h)W \qquad (6)$$

Where the parameter matrices of i-th linear projections $W_i^Q \in R^{n \times (\frac{d}{h})}$, $W_i^K \in R^{n \times (\frac{d}{h})}$, $W_i^V \in R^{n \times (\frac{d}{h})}$. In addition, the outputs of CNN and self-attention structure are concatenated as higher-level phrase representations and fed into BiLSTM.

BiLSTM Layer: Causality sentence combines a positive relationship between cause-effect and a reverse relationship between effect-cause. Since the information loss is very serious in the long-distance transmission, LSTM [24] is not suitable for modeling causality. Given a sequence of input features $\{f_t\}$, the relation between the cause and the effect can be obtained through forward LSTM and can be enhanced through back LSTM:

$$\overleftarrow{h_t} = \overleftarrow{LSTM}(\overleftarrow{f_t}, \overleftarrow{h_{t+1}}) \qquad (7)$$

$$\overrightarrow{h_t} = \overrightarrow{LSTM}(\overrightarrow{f_t}, \overrightarrow{h_{t-1}}) \qquad (8)$$

$$h_t = [\overrightarrow{h_t}, \overleftarrow{h_t}] \qquad (9)$$

Then, the probabilistic matrix $P = \{p_1, p_2, p_3, ..., p_n\}$ is generated, whose size is $m*n$, n is the number of words while m is the number of tags.

Finally, the conditional random field [14] is used to adjust the previously predicted tag sequence, taking into account the interaction between adjacent tags. In the model, we obtained the last hidden layer to predict the score of the word with each possible label, and the weight matrix is used to learn the conversion probability between different tags. Given a prediction sequence $y = \{y_1, y_2, y_3, ..., y_n\}$, the CRF score can be calculated as:

$$score(x,y) = \sum_{i=1}^{n+1} A_{y_{i-1},y_i} + \sum_{i=1}^{n} P_{i,y_i} \qquad (10)$$

P_{i,y_i} is the prediction that the i-th word is the y_i label probability in a sentence. In addition, the likelihood of transitioning from label y_{i-1} to label y_i can be expressed as A_{y_{i-1},y_i}.

Viterbi algorithm is used to output the valid sequence of labels with the largest $score(x,y)$. The loss function minimizes the scores of other sequences, while maximizing the score of the correct tag sequence. The mathematical formulation is shown below:

$$E = log \sum_{y \in Y} exp^{s(y)} - score(x,y) \qquad (11)$$

Where Y is the set of all possible label sequences for a sentence.

4 Experiments and Results

4.1 Datasets

Chinese encyclopedias in the web, such as Jinrongjie[1] and Hexun[2], which contain a large number of financial datasets with variety of causal relations, from which programmed datasets are extracted. Finally, 11568 web pages were crawled from Jinrongjie and 11742 web pages were crawled from Hexun. 1486 inter-sentence causality sentences and 500 implicit sentences was annotated as our datasets.

Chinese Emergency Corpus (CEC)[3] is an event ontology corpus developed by Semantic Intelligence Laboratory of Shanghai University. It has 332 articles including five categories: earthquake, fire, traffic accident, terrorist attack and intoxication of food, which are derived from Internet and processed by several steps. Finally, 966 inter-sentence causality sentences and 609 implicit causality sentences are extracted.

Financial Event Evolutionary Graph[4] is an event logical knowledge which was published by Harbin Institute of Social Computing and Information Retrieval Research Center (HIT-SCIR). It mainly contains two kinds of relationships, one is causal relation, and the other is a similar relation. Besides, it also contains relationship context sentence information. We obtain 556 intra-sentence causality sentences based on the context information of the datasets.

The above three datasets are used to develop and validate the effectiveness of proposed model generated from the web, the CEC and SCIR datasets. We are willing to share financial datasets with the community.

---

[1] http://www.jrj.com.cn.
[2] http://www.hexun.com.
[3] https://github.com/shijiebei2009/CEC-Corpus.
[4] http://eeg.8wss.com.

Besides, the advice of two experts is followed to annotate the data. First, determine whether a given sentence contains a causal event. Second, annotate which parts are the cause or an effect. The annotated dataset such as "China Wine Network has been <Cause> in a state of loss for a long time </Cause>, which has <Effect> great impact </Effect> on the performance of Qingqing Liquor.". Finally, BIO was used to mark the sentences ("B-X" represents the beginning of the Cause or Effect, "I-X" represents the middle and end of the Cause or Effect, "O" means not belonging to Cause or Effect).

4.2   Experiment Settings

During the experimental pretreatment process, Hanlp[5] is used as a tool for word segmentation. Word2vec is used to train these financial datasets. Skip-Gram algorithm [18,25] is used to get pre-trained 100-dimensional word embedding vectors on financial datasets instead of initialized randomly. Random vectors (All of the random vectors are sampled from a uniform distribution in the range of $[-0.5, 0.5]$) are used to express the words that did not occur in the embedding vocabulary.

Dropout [7] is applied to the last layer to avoid overfitting, which can reduce the coadaptation of hidden units by randomly dropping out a proportion of the hidden units during the training process. Moreover, different filters are adopted within CSNN model in different datasets for causal relation extraction from Chinese. The filter size is 5 in CEC, 3 in SCIR and financial datasets. The number of feature map is 100. The model is fit over 200 epochs, where the batch size is 16. The unit number of LSTM is chosen to be 100 hidden layers, the dropout is 0.2. Adam [12] is used with the learning rate of 0.006 for optimization.

4.3   Results and Analyses

To prevent the impact of uneven data distribution on the experimental results, the averaged F1 score is used to calculate from 10-fold cross validation for evaluation. In addition, the datasets are divided into 66% training set, 18% test set and 16% verification set. We perform a number of different classical experiments to verify the effectiveness of the proposed model.

IDCNN-Softmax: By increasing the width of the filter, this method obtains data on a wider input matrix, which makes up for the shortcomings of the last layer of neurons in the original CNN convolution to obtain only a small piece of information in the original input data. Then each tag is predicted using the Softmax classifier.

IDCNN-CRF [22]: Taking into account the interaction between adjacent tags, the model uses a CRF classifier to maximize the score of the correct tag sequence to obtain the best output sequence.

CNN: Peng Fei [16] firstly bases on this model, by adding human prior knowledge to capture the linguistic clues of causality extraction.

---

[5] https://github.com/hankcs/HanLP

Table 2. Average F-scores (%) of the cause/effect extraction by six extraction models namely, IDCNN-Softmax, IDCNN-CRF, BiLSTM-Softmax, BiLSTM-CRF, CNN-BiLSTM-CRF and CSNN on CEC, SCIR and Financial Chinese datasets.

Model	CEC		Financial		SCIR	
	Cause	Effect.	Cause	Effect.	Cause	Effect.
IDCNN-Softmax	62.96	54.74	50.97	57.65	66.15	60.02
IDCNN-CRF	66.01	59.56	53.65	60.18	76.05	68.24
BiLSTM-Softmax	69.29	66.81	54.51	61.07	79.87	67.53
BiLSTM-CRF	73.87	70.98	58.68	64.61	81.11	70.09
CNN-BiLSTM-CRF	74.55	70.79	59.56	65.85	80.86	72.55
CSNN	**75.40**	**72.72**	**62.24**	**66.70**	**82.27**	**75.34**

BiLSTM-Softmax: Dasgupta [3] uses the bi-directional LSTM model to extract explicit causal relationships automatically, using additional language features and Softmax classifiers to independently predict causal labels.

The above two methods [3,16] are based on knowledge. Due to the lack of Chinese knowledge and the inability to add additional language features, model-based and adding CRF are used as our baseline, such as BiLSTM-CRF [8].

CNN-BiLSTM-CRF: The model uses CNN to recode the input vector bi-directional LSTM to capture longer dependencies and learn the semantic representation of causality.

The experimental results are shown in Table 2, we can easily find that the BiLSTM-based approach is superior to the CNN-based approach. The reason may be that the BiLSTM layer can capture semantic features and establish long dependencies between causal relationships more efficiently. Besides, BiLSTM layer can understand the relationship between causal features and effect characteristics through forward LSTM, and enhance the relationship between effects and causes through reverse LSTM. In addition, we find that the combination of CNN and BiLSTM approach captures more local feature information using CNN, and BiLSTM enhances connections to longer dependencies, yielding better results for causal relation extraction (Fig. 2).

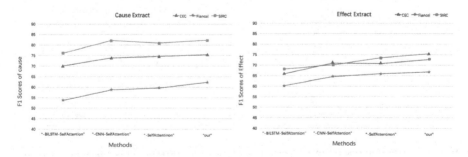

Fig. 2. Ablation analysis of our proposed framework CSNN. "Our" denotes the complete CSNN framework, while "-" denotes removing the component from the CSNN.

For best verifying whether our self-attention mechanism can learn semantics and relevant characteristics between different features, we demonstrate the effectiveness of the causal extraction task. Specifically, through ablation experiment can find that the self-attention mechanism provides significant improvements in the causal extraction task. These results are consistent with our hypothesis that the CSNN model can automatically learn semantics and related features between different features, which is useful for inter-sentence or implicit causality extraction. Besides, we also find that BiLSTM plays an important role in capturing dependencies between causal relationships, thereby improving the accuracy and recall of causality extraction.

Moreover, the result shows the role of self-attention in causality extraction task. The convolutional layer is aimed to capture important features within the windows of causality, but lacks internal correlation learning of important features. For example, in the sentence "the important reason for the repurchase is that Chengdian Medical Star's performance is not up to standard", the reason is "Performance is not up to standard" and the result is "for the repurchase". When the sliding window is 3, the model can learn the overall characteristics of the words "performance", "not" and "up to standard", but the relationship between "not "and" up to standard" can not be learned. Experiments show that in the causality extraction task, self-attention helps to define the cause or result boundary by learning the characteristics of internal words, and makes the

methods	a-Causal-Effect	b-Causal-Effect
Sentence	母公司产品受市场影响，毛利率下降。 "The parent company's products are **affected by the market** and *the gross profit margin is declined.*"	原材料价格下跌，这是产品价格下跌的主要原因。**The price of raw materials fell**, which is the main reason for *the decline in product prices.*
CSNN	**受市场影响** 毛利率下降 **affected by the market** *the gross profit margin is declined*	原材料价格下跌 产品价格下跌 **the price of raw materials fell** *the decline in product prices*
CNN-BILSTM-CRF	**市场** 毛利率下降 **market** *the gross profit margin is declined*	原材料价格下跌 价格下跌 **the price of raw materials fell** *decline prices*
BILSTM-CRF	None 毛利率下降 None *the gross profit margin is declined*	原材料价格下跌 价格下跌 **the price of raw materials fell** *decline prices*
IDCNN-CRF	**市场** 下降 **market** *declined*	**价格下跌** 价格下跌 **decline prices** *decline prices*

Fig. 3. Extraction results by different models, where words are bold represent "Cause", italicize represent "Effect".

cause or result more closely connected in a window. Thus, the effect of causality extraction is improved.

Figure 3 shows some typical cases of inter-sentence or implicit causal extraction to show the advantages and disadvantages of our proposed model compared with other methods. Figure 3a is an example of an implicit causal relationship. Only CSNN captures the relationship between them internally and accurately extracts the causal-effect description. For the causality extraction model, learning the intrinsic relationship of causality is very helpful in defining the boundary.

Due to ambiguity of the boundary in Chinese causal relation, an event may be a cause or effect in different contexts. When the cause and effect are similar, it will lead to mistakes. As shown in Fig. 3b, in this regard, precision and recall can be promoted based on context information and background knowledge.

5 Conclusions

In recent years, automatic extraction of causal relation from texts has attracted increasing attention of researchers. Existing methods mainly focus on mining intra-sentence or explicit causality, while neglecting the causal relations that expressed implicitly or hidden in inter-sentences. In this paper, we proposed a new method named Cascaded multi-Structure Neural Network (CSNN) for the task of inter-sentence or implicit causality extraction. In the proposed model, Convolutional Neural Network (CNN), Long Short-Term Memory (LSTM) with self-attention mechanism, and CRF layer are employed to capture semantic relevant characteristics. The output of CNN and self-attention are concatenated as high-level phrase representations, which improves the performance of inter-sentence or implicit causality extraction. The output of CRF layer is the label of each word in inter-sentence or implicit causal relation sentences. In the experiment, we created three annotation datasets on a wide range of public data, which will be released to facilitate ongoing research. The results shown that our model achieved stat-of-the-art performs by improving the F1-scores of causal extraction up to 82.27% and F1-scores of effect extraction up to 75.34% on the created datasets.

Acknowledgments. The research reported in this paper is supported in part by the National Natural Science Foundation of China under the grant No. 91746203, 61991415, 61625304 and the Ant Financial Services Group.

References

1. Blanco, E., Castell, N., Moldovan, D.: Causal relation extraction (2008)
2. Collobert, R., Weston, J., Bottou, L., Karlen, M., Kavukcuoglu, K., Kuksa, P.: Natural language processing (almost) from scratch. J. Mach. Learn. Res. **12**(1), 2493–2537 (2011)
3. Dasgupta, T., Saha, R., Dey, L., Naskar, A.: Automatic extraction of causal relations from text using linguistically informed deep neural networks, pp. 306–316 (2018). https://doi.org/10.18653/v1/W18-5035

4. Garcia, D.: COATIS, an NLP system to locate expressions of actions connected by causality links. In: Plaza, E., Benjamins, R. (eds.) EKAW 1997. LNCS, vol. 1319, pp. 347–352. Springer, Heidelberg (1997). https://doi.org/10.1007/BFb0026799
5. Graves, A.: Supervised Sequence Labelling. Springer, Heidelberg (2012). https://doi.org/10.1007/978-3-642-24797-2
6. Hinton, G.E.: Rectified linear units improve restricted Boltzmann machines Vinod Nair, pp. 807–814 (2010)
7. Hinton, G.E., Srivastava, N., Krizhevsky, A., Sutskever, I., Salakhutdinov, R.R.: Improving neural networks by preventing co-adaptation of feature detectors. arXiv preprint arXiv:1207.0580 (2012)
8. Huang, Z., Xu, W., Yu, K.: Bidirectional LSTM-CRF models for sequence tagging (2015)
9. Ittoo, A., Bouma, G.: Extracting explicit and implicit causal relations from sparse, domain-specific texts. In: Muñoz, R., Montoyo, A., Métais, E. (eds.) NLDB 2011. LNCS, vol. 6716, pp. 52–63. Springer, Heidelberg (2011). https://doi.org/10.1007/978-3-642-22327-3_6
10. Fu, J.-F., Liu, Z.-T., Liu, W., L., Zhou, W.: Event causal relation extraction based on cascaded conditional random fields. Pattern Recogn. Artif. Intell. 24(4), 567–573 (2011)
11. Khoo, C., Chan, S., Niu, Y.: Extracting causal knowledge from a medical database using graphical patterns. In: Proceedings of 38th Annual Meeting of the ACL, Hong Kong (2002)
12. Kingma, D.P., Ba, J.: Adam: a method for stochastic optimization. arXiv preprint arXiv:1412.6980 (2014)
13. Kontos, J., Sidiropoulou, M.: On the acquisition of causal knowledge from scientific texts with attribute grammars. Literary Linguist. Comput. 4(1), 31–48 (1991)
14. Lafferty, J., Mccallum, A., Pereira, F.: Conditional random fields: probabilistic models for segmenting and labeling sequence data. In: Proceedings of the ICML, January 2002
15. Li, Z., Li, Q., Zou, X., Ren, J.: Causality extraction based on self-attentive BiLSTM-CRF with transferred embeddings (2019)
16. Li, P., Mao, K.: Knowledge-oriented convolutional neural network for causal relation extraction from natural language texts. Pattern Recogn. Artif. Intell. 115, 512–523 (2019)
17. Mackie, J.: The cement of the universe: a study of causation, vol. 42, no. 3, pp. 7930–7946 (1974)
18. Mikolov, T., Sutskever, I., Chen, K., Corrado, G., Dean, J.: Distributed representations of words and phrases and their compositionality. In: Advances in Neural Information Processing Systems, vol. 6 (2013)
19. Oh, J.H., Torisawa, K., Hashimoto, C., Sano, M., De Saeger, S., Ohtake, K.: Why-question answering using intra- and inter-sentential causal relations. In: Proceedings of the 51st Annual Meeting of the Association for Computational Linguistics, Long Papers. vol. 1, pp. 1733–1743. Association for Computational Linguistics, Sofia, Bulgaria, August 2013
20. Paulus, R., Xiong, C., Socher, R.: A deep reinforced model for abstractive summarization (2017)
21. Shen, T., Zhou, T., Long, G., Jiang, J., Pan, S., Zhang, C.: Disan: directional self-attention network for RNN/CNN-free language understanding (2018)
22. Strubell, E., Verga, P., Belanger, D., McCallum, A.: Fast and accurate entity recognition with iterated dilated convolutions (2017)

23. Vaswani, A., et al.: Attention is all you need, pp. 5998–6008 (2017)
24. Wang, X., Yuan, S., Zhang, H., Liu, Y.: Estimation of inter-sentiment correlations employing deep neural network models (2018)
25. Xinzhi Wang, Hui Zhang, Y.L.: Sentence vector model based on implicit word vector expression. IEEE Access p. 17455–17463 (2018)

Accelerating Hyperparameter Optimization of Deep Neural Network via Progressive Multi-Fidelity Evaluation

Guanghui Zhu[✉] and Ruancheng Zhu

National Key Laboratory for Novel Software Technology,
Nanjing University, Nanjing 210023, China
{guanghui.zhu,zrc}@smail.nju.edu.cn

Abstract. Deep neural networks usually require careful tuning of hyperparameters to show their best performance. However, with the size of state-of-the-art neural networks growing larger, the evaluation cost of the traditional Bayesian optimization has become unacceptable in most cases. Moreover, most practical problems usually require good hyperparameter configurations within a limited time budget. To speed up the hyperparameter optimization, the successive halving technique is used to stop poorly-performed configurations as early as possible. In this paper, we propose a novel hyperparameter optimization method FastHO, which combines the progressive multi-fidelity technique with successive halving under a multi-armed bandit framework. Furthermore, we employ Bayesian optimization to guide the selection of initial configurations and an efficient data subsampling based method to warm start the surrogate model of Bayesian optimization. Extensive empirical evaluation on a broad range of neural networks and datasets shows that FastHO is not only effective to speed up hyperparameter optimization but also can achieve better anytime performance and final performance than the state-of-the-art hyperparameter optimization methods.

Keywords: Hyperparameter optimization · Deep neural network · Multi-fidelity optimization

1 Introduction

In recent years, deep learning has achieved great success on a variety of machine learning problems such as computer vision and natural language processing. However, deep neural networks (DNNs) are with too many hyperparameters and the learning performance depends seriously on the careful tuning of them [8]. The correct setting of hyperparameters for DNNs often needs a tedious endeavor, and typically requires considerable expert knowledge and experience. As a result, both researchers and practitioners desire to set hyperparameters automatically without any human intervention.

Unlike traditional machine learning models, hyperparameter optimization for DNNs is more challenging. Since the architecture of DNNs is getting more

© Springer Nature Switzerland AG 2020
H. W. Lauw et al. (Eds.): PAKDD 2020, LNAI 12084, pp. 752–763, 2020.
https://doi.org/10.1007/978-3-030-47426-3_58

and more complex, training large DNNs is more computationally expensive. For example, state-of-the-art neural networks often require days or even weeks to train. Thus, the well-known Bayesian optimization [1,2,10,18,20] methods that view the performance as a black-box function suffer low computational efficiency due to the expensive evaluation of hyperparameters. On the other hand, most practical problems usually require a good hyperparameter configuration within a limited time budget. Besides the strong final performance given a larger budget, practical hyperparameter optimization methods should also achieve strong anytime performance in the case of a small budget.

To speed up the hyperparameter optimization of DNNs, Hyperband [15] uses the successive halving (SH) technique [11] to stop poorly-performed configurations as early as possible and dynamically allocate more resources (i.e., the number of iterations) to well-performed configurations. Another popular method is the multi-fidelity optimization [9,12,13,19]. Generally, the fidelity indicates the sampling ratio of the full dataset. Multi-fidelity optimization uses many cheap low-fidelity evaluations instead of expensive high-fidelity evaluations to extrapolate the performance of hyperparameter configurations on the full dataset.

In this paper, we propose a novel hyperparameter optimization method FastHO to further accelerate the hyperparameter optimization of DNNs, while achieving good anytime performance and final performance. FastHO combines the progressive multi-fidelity technique with successive halving under a multi-armed bandit framework. Each hyperparameter configuration is viewed as an arm. At first, we aggressively evaluate each arm with fewer resources (i.e., small iteration budget and low fidelity). The poorly-performed arms are discarded and more resources are dynamically allocated to the promising configurations. The process is repeated until the maximum iteration budget and the highest fidelity are reached. Furthermore, we employ Bayesian optimization to guide the selection of initial configurations. Additionally, an efficient warmup method based on data subsampling is proposed to initialize the surrogate model of Bayesian optimization. Extensive empirical evaluation on different neural networks and datasets shows that FastHO outperforms the existing hyperparameter optimization methods. FastHO is not only effective to speed up hyperparameter optimization but also can achieve robust and better final performance.

2 Related Work

Given a machine learning algorithm A having hyperparameters $\lambda_1; \ldots; \lambda_n$ with respective domains $\delta_1; \ldots; \delta_n$, we define its hyperparameter space as $\delta = \delta_1 \times \ldots \times \delta_n$. For each hyperparameter setting λ, we use A_λ to denote the learning algorithm A using this configuration. We further use $l(\lambda) = L(A_\lambda; D_{train}; D_{valid})$ to denote the validation loss (e.g., error rate) that A_λ achieves on data D_{valid} when trained on D_{train}. The hyperparameter optimization problem is then to find λ minimizing $l(\lambda)$.

Bayesian optimization (BO) is the most popular hyperparameter optimization method [2,18,20]. BO models the conditional probability $p(y|\lambda)$ of a configuration's performance on an evaluation metric y, given a set of hyperparameters λ.

The commonly-used probabilistic model in BO is Gaussian process (GP), but GP does not typically scale well to high dimensions and exhibits cubic complexity in the number of data points. Another model-based Bayesian optimization method is SMAC [10], which uses random forest as the surrogate model. SMAC can perform well in high-dimensional categorical spaces. TPE [1] is a non-standard Bayesian optimization algorithm based on tree-structured Parzen density estimators. Due to the nature of kernel density estimators, TPE easily supports mixed continuous and discrete spaces. The above three BO methods are well-established and successful, but they are inefficient for the hyperparameter optimization of DNNs due to the huge evaluation cost.

Unlike the model-based Bayesian optimization, the bandit-based strategy Hyperband [15] formulates hyperparameter optimization as a pure-exploration problem by addressing how to allocate resources among randomly-sampled hyperparameter configurations. Besides, it uses successive halving to early stop the poorly-performed configurations. Compared to Bayesian optimization, Hyperband shows strong anytime performance, but it may lead to poor final performance because the initial hyperparameter configurations are selected randomly. BOHB [4] takes advantage of both Bayesian optimization and Hyperband and thus achieves the state-of-the-art anytime performance and final performance.

Another efficient method for the tuning of hyperparameters is multi-fidelity optimization, which uses cheap approximations to the function of interest to speed up the overall optimization process. Generally, the fidelity can be represented by the sampling ratio of the full dataset. Multi-fidelity Bayesian optimization that ranges from a finite number of approximations to continuous approximations has been well studied [12,13,19]. Furthermore, a general multi-fidelity framework based on the black-box optimization methods was proposed [9].

However, due to the huge training cost of DNNs, the existing hyperparameter optimization methods are inefficient and time-consuming for DNNs. Even for the state-of-the-art method BOHB, it still requires 33 GPU days for optimizing the hyperparameters of a medium-sized residual network [4]. In this paper, we combine the successive halving technique with multi-fidelity optimization to accelerate the hyperparameter optimization of DNNs.

3   Method

In this section, we propose a novel early-stopping mechanism to speed up the hyperparameter optimization of DNNs by taking the number of iterations and multi-fidelity into account at the same time. We first analyze the low-fidelity evaluation bias of DNNs, which motivates to progressively increase the fidelity. Then, we introduce the IF-SH (Iteration-and-Fidelity Based Successive Halving) method in detail. Moreover, we propose an efficient warmup technique for Bayesian optimization to further improve the performance, especially the anytime performance of hyperparameter optimization.

3.1 Low-Fidelity Evaluation Bias

Multi-fidelity optimization uses many cheap low-fidelity approximations instead of the expensive high-fidelity evaluations to speed up the overall optimization process. The lower the fidelity is, the cheaper the evaluation will be. However, it is intuitive that the evaluation on a part of the dataset is badly biased because it provides less accurate information about the target function. The experimental results of multi-fidelity optimization on LightGBM [14] show that the hyperparameter configurations chosen by low-fidelity evaluations usually perform poorly on the test dataset. We have tried to apply BOHB to find the best hyperparameter configuration of a convolutional neural network LeNet (with two convolutional layers, a full-connection layer, and a softmax layer) on the MNIST and CIFAR-10 datasets. We evaluated the hyperparameter configurations chosen on the data subset (i.e., 10%) and the whole dataset, and then compared the test error rate. The results are shown in Table 1.

It turns out as expected that the configuration chosen by high-fidelity evaluations is superior to those selected by low-fidelity evaluations. Additionally, we note that the main difference between the hyperparameter configurations chosen by the high-fidelity and low-fidelity evaluations is the regularization hyperparameters such as weight decay and dropout rate. It makes sense because the neural networks trained on the data subset usually require more regularization to deal with overfitting.

Table 1. Test error rate (%) of LeNet on MNIST and CIFAR-10, using hyperparameter configurations chosen by BOHB with different fidelity evaluations. CIFAR-10+ means CIFAR-10 with standard data augmentation. Results are the average over 5 runs.

Data	MNIST	CIFAR-10	CIFAR-10+
The whole dataset	0.6 ± 0.05	20.68 ± 0.68	16.32 ± 0.54
10% data subset	0.76 ± 0.13	23.81 ± 1.17	17.94 ± 0.78

As shown in Table 1, the evaluation performance on the data subset is biased in different cases. Therefore, it is necessary to develop a new method to balance the low-fidelity and high-fidelity evaluations. To address this issue, we propose a progressive multi-fidelity evaluation technique. We further combine this technique with the existing successive halving optimization. The configurations are first evaluated with a small number of epochs and low fidelity. After filtering the poorly-performed configurations as early as possible, we dynamically increase the number of epochs and fidelity simultaneously for the remaining configurations. The process is repeated until the maximum number of epochs and the maximum fidelity (i.e., the full dataset) are used. We call this procedure IF-SH (Iteration-and-Fidelity Based Successive Halving).

3.2   Progressive Multi-Fidelity Evaluation

Multi-armed bandit based methods such as Hyperband and BOHB view each hyperparameter configuration as an arm and dynamically allocate resources to different arms. The existing successive halving method can ensure that the poorly-performed configurations are discarded as early as possible and those promising hyperparameter configurations will get more resources overtime automatically. For the hyperparameter optimization of DNNs, the resource means the number of iterations (i.e., epochs). Since using evaluation on fewer iterations as criteria in HyperBand is feasible, it is worth a try that we use evaluation on both fewer iterations and lower fidelity to judge a hyperparameter configuration, which will remarkably reduce the overall time cost.

Thus, we propose a progressive multi-fidelity evaluation method IF-SH and dynamically allocate multiple resources including iteration budget and fidelity. Specifically, IF-SH usually begins with a small iteration budget on data subsets instead of the whole dataset. Then, IF-SH ranks the configurations by the validation performance and select the top η^{-1} to continue running with an iteration budget η times larger and a fidelity θ times larger. This process is repeated until it runs with the largest iteration budget on the whole dataset.

Another problem of the multi-armed bandit based hyperparameter optimization is how to set the number of initial configurations n. Similar to Hyperband, we consider several possible values of n to balance exploration and exploitation. Associated with each value of n is a minimum iteration budget b_{min} that is allocated to all configurations. A larger value of n corresponds to a smaller b_{min} and hence means more aggressive early stopping.

Algorithm 1. Iteration-and-Fidelity Based Successive Halving

Input: Iteration budget b_{min} and $b_{\mathrm{max}}, \eta, \theta$

1: $s_{\mathrm{max}} = \log_\eta \frac{b_{\mathrm{max}}}{b_{\mathrm{min}}}$
2: **for** s in $\{s_{\mathrm{max}}; s_{\mathrm{max}} - 1; \ldots; 0\}$ **do**
3:     $n = \frac{s_{\mathrm{max}}+1}{s+1} * \eta^s$
4:     T = get hyperparameter configurations(n) using Bayesian optimization
5:     $b_{\mathrm{min}} = b_{\mathrm{max}} * \eta^{-s}$
6:     $f_{\mathrm{min}} = \theta^{-s}$
       //begin the SH inner loop
7:     **for** i in $\{0; \ldots; s\}$ **do**
8:         $n_i = n * \eta^{-i}$
9:         $b_i = b_{\mathrm{min}} * \eta^i$
10:        $f_i = f_{\mathrm{min}} * \theta^i$
11:        D_{sub} = sample f_i data from the training dataset D_{train}
12:        $L = \{$ run on D_{sub} then return validation loss$(t, b_i): t$ in $T\}$
13:        $T = top_k(T, L, n_i/\eta)$
14:    **end for**
15: **end for**
16: **return** *Configuration with the smallest intermediate loss seen so far*

Algorithm 1 shows the process of IF-SH, which requires the following inputs: (1) $[b_{min}, b_{max}]$ that determines the iteration budget space (2) η, an input that controls the proportion of configurations discarded and the number of iterations in each round of SH. Also, η determines the minimum number of iterations of the next round (3) θ, an input that controls the size of fidelity in each round of SH. θ also determines the minimum fidelity of the next round.

This algorithm balances between very aggressive evaluations with many configurations on the minimum resource, and very conservative runs that are directly evaluated on the maximum resource. Table 2 displays the resources allocated within each round of SH in IF-SH. The size of data subsampling is controlled by θ. In practice, the difference caused by various θ settings is not so notable. We will discuss it in Sect. 4.1.

Table 2. The values of n_i, b_i and f_i in IF-SH corresponding to various values of s, when $b_{\min} = 1, b_{\max} = 27, \eta = 3, \theta = 3$

i	$s = 3$			$s = 2$			$s = 1$			$s = 0$		
	n_i	b_i	f_i	n_i	b_i	f_i	n_i	b_i	f_i	n_i	b_i	f_i
0	27	1	1/27	9	3	1/9	6	9	1/3	4	27	1
1	9	3	1/9	3	9	1/3	2	27	1			
2	3	9	1/3	1	27	1						
3	1	27	1									

3.3 Surrogate Model Warmup

Hyperparameter configurations within each round of SH is selected by Bayesian optimization (Line 4 in Algorithm 1). It is well known that all model-based optimization methods including Bayesian optimization need initial observations to build the surrogate model. The most commonly-used startup is to choose random hyperparameter configurations, which is not efficient and robust. When the randomly-sampled configurations perform poorly, the surrogate model will be slow to work, causing a negative influence on anytime performance. A lot of previous work [5,16,21] focuses on meta-learning to handle this issue, but they require historical data or pre-trained models.

Obviously, the data subset contains part information of the whole dataset. As discussed in Sect. 3.1, the difference between configurations chosen by the data subset and the whole dataset is not too remarkable. Thus, using the sampling data to warm start the surrogate model is a feasible way. The configurations chosen by low-fidelity evaluations probably exceed the randomly-sampled configurations, although their final performance may not be so satisfying. To improve the efficiency of the warmup phase, we just run one round of SH. We first sample data from the training dataset with the sampling percent r. Then, we run SH on the sampling data D_r and select the top-k configurations to warm up the surrogate model. In Sect. 4.1, we will evaluate the effect of r, subsampling percent of the warmup phase. In fact, by selecting more promising hyperparameters rather than random selection, the warmup phase is helpful for improving the final performance of hyperparameter optimization.

4   Experiments

In this section, we evaluated the empirical performance of our proposed method FastHO on different neural networks including CNN, Fully-Connected neural network, ResNet18 [7], and ResNet with Shake-Shake [6] and Cutout [3] regularization. The datasets include MNIST, CIFAR-10, and CIFAR-100. We compared the anytime performance and final performance of FastHO with TPE [1], Hyperband [15], and BOHB [4]. BOHB is the state-of-the-art hyperparameter optimization method that combines TPE and Hyperband (HB). We set $\eta = 3$, $\theta = 3$, $r = 0.1$ as default and explore how to set suitable θ and r. If not stated otherwise, for all methods we report the average error rate on the test dataset.

4.1   Convolutional Neural Network

We first evaluated FastHO on a CNN with two convolutional layers, a full-connection layer, and a softmax output layer. We optimized the hyperparameters including learning rate, momentum, weight decay, dropout rate, batch size, the number of full-connection units, kernel size, and weight initialization mode. For this network, we set $b_{min} = 2$ and $b_{max} = 60$ for successive halving. The budget indicates the number of epochs. The IF-SH process contains 4 rounds of successive halving, resulting in 240 epochs in total.

CIFAR-10: The CIFAR-10 dataset contains 50000 training and 10000 test RGB images with 32×32 pixels. The standard data augmentation techniques (i.e., random crop and horizontal flip) are used. To perform hyperparameter optimization, we split off 10000 training images as a validation set. Figure 1 shows the average test error of FastHO with and without the warmup phase. We also compared FastHO with TPE, Hyperband, and BOHB. The total iteration budget is 16 resource units and each resource unit represents 240 epochs. As a result, the complete FastHO process includes 16 runs of IF-SH.

From Fig. 1, we can see that the traditional Bayesian optimization method TPE does not work well and has the worst anytime performance. HB improves the efficiency of hyperparameter optimization with successive halving and thus achieves better anytime performance than TPE. However, its convergence to the global optimal value is limited by its reliance on randomly-drawn configurations. Thus, the final performance of HB is not very strong. BOHB performs well with limited resources and at the same time can achieve better final performance.

In contrast, FastHO outperforms BOHB on anytime performance by combining the progressive multi-fidelity optimization with SH. Furthermore, the

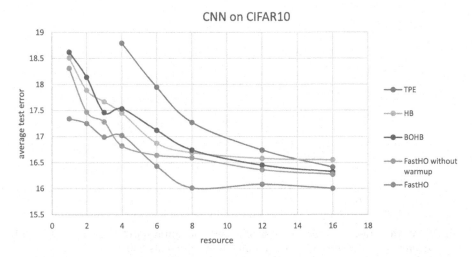

Fig. 1. Average test error of the best-observed configuration of CNN on CIFAR-10. One resource unit represents 240 epochs.

warmup technique can improve both anytime performance and final performance, while its time cost is negligible compared to the following hyperparameter optimization phase. More importantly, it can help FastHO to reach the best performance with much fewer resources. For instance, FastHO gets the best test error rate within 8 units of resources (8*240 epochs in total), about half of the resources consumed by other methods. Additionally, for the wall clock time, BOHB takes 31 h for hyperparameter optimization within 16 resource units. In contrast, FastHO takes only 19 h which is 63% faster than BOHB.

Evaluation of the θ and r Setting. We also evaluated two key parameters of FastHO: the proportion of θ that controls the size of fidelity in each round of successive halving, and the subsampling percent r in the warmup phase.

Intuitively, setting θ to a smaller value leads to a larger fidelity. If θ is set to 1, we will evaluate all configurations on the entire dataset. However, this disobeys our purpose to accelerate the evaluation procedure. In contrast, it should not be set to a very large value, because we aim to differentiate between configurations even when they are evaluated on the smallest data subset. Therefore, we set θ to be 2, 3 (default) and 4, and then compared their performance in Fig. 2(a).

As shown in Fig. 2(a), the difference caused by various θ settings is not so notable. The reason is that the three values are all appropriate ones that guarantee the discrimination of configurations on the smallest data subset. Besides, even if the evaluation bias exists on the low fidelity, the final evaluation is performed on the full dataset, which weakens this bias to some extent. Thus, FastHO is insensitive to the θ setting.

Next, we discuss the setting of r in the warmup phase. If r is set to a larger value, the data subset contains more information, leading to good hyperparameter configurations to warm start the Bayesian surrogate model. Nevertheless,

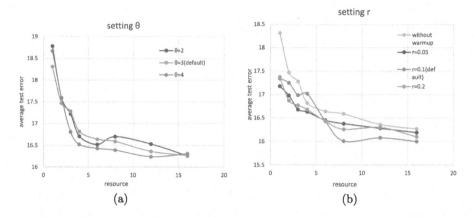

Fig. 2. Average test error of the best-observed configuration of CNN on CIFAR-10 with different θ and r settings. One resource unit represents 240 epochs.

the time cost of the warmup procedure will become larger. We chose 0.05, 0.1, and 0.2 for r, and then compared their performance in Fig. 2(b). Note that the warmup technique can improve the performance of FastHO no matter which value to choose. Meanwhile, none of these values is remarkably superior to other ones. The performance difference is acceptable due to the randomness in the data subsampling and hyperparameter optimization phases. Thus, we can infer that r makes little difference.

4.2   Fully-Connected Neural Network

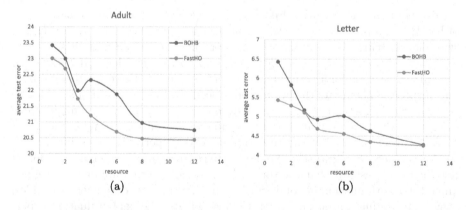

Fig. 3. Average test error of the best-observed configuration of FC network on Adult and Letter. One resource unit represents 90 epochs.

We optimized 6 hyperparameters that control the training procedure (learning rate, batch size, dropout rate, and weight decay). We also optimized the architecture hyperparameters (number of layers, number of units per layer, weight initialization mode, and activation function) of a full-connected neural network. We selected two datasets: Adult and Letter, and set $b_{min} = 3, b_{max} = 30$. Since BOHB outperforms TPE and HB in most cases, we compared FastHO only with BOHB in the following experiments. In both Fig. 3(a) and Fig. 3(b), FastHO outperforms BOHB with not only the better anytime performance but also the better final performance. Moreover, the warmup technique is helpful for converging to optimum faster.

4.3 Large Convolutional Neural Network: ResNet

Next, we optimized the hyperparameters of large and widely-used neural networks including ResNet18 [7] and ResNet with Shake-Shake [6] and Cutout [3] regularization on the CIFAR-10 and CIFAR-100 datasets. We used standard data augmentation techniques (i.e., random crop and horizontal flip) and Nesterov momentum SGD optimizer with a cosine learning decay [17].

ResNet18: We tuned 4 hyperparameters including learning rate, momentum, weight decay, and batch size on the CIFAR-10 and CIFAR-100 datasets. CIFAR-100 shares similar input images to CIFAR-10. The only difference is that CIFAR-100 has 100 classes. We split the training dataset into 80% training data and 20% validation data. We set $b_{min} = 7$ and $b_{max} = 200$. As shown in Fig. 4, the performance improvement of FastHO is more significant, which indicates that FastHO is more effective for the hyperparameter optimization of larger neural networks. Moreover, FastHO is 67% faster than BOHB in terms of the total evaluation time cost.

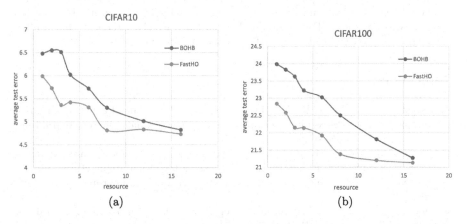

Fig. 4. Average test error of the best-observed configuration of ResNet18 on CIFAR-10 and CIFAR-100. One resource unit represents 800 epochs.

ResNet with Shake-Shake and Cutout Regularization: Next, we used the ResNet with Shake-Shake and Cutout regularization. For this network, we set $b_{min} = 22$ and $b_{max} = 600$ and optimized learning rate, momentum, weight decay, and batch size. In this case, we just trained and evaluated the network with the best configuration after the complete hyperparameter optimization process (i.e., 16 runs of IF-SH). We ran the complete process 3 times and get a test error of $2.81\% \pm 0.07\%$, which is slightly larger than that reported in [4] ($2.78\% \pm 0.09\%$). However, regardless of the differences in training details or the search space setting, FastHO requires only 19 GPU days, while BOHB needs 33 GPU days. Moreover, as shown in Fig. 4, FastHO outperforms BOHB with much better anytime performance.

5   Conclusion and Future Work

In this paper, we presented a novel method to accelerate the hyperparameter optimization of DNNs by combining the progressive multi-fidelity technique with successive halving under a multi-armed bandit framework. Also, we proposed an efficient warmup method for the surrogate model of Bayesian optimization. Extensive empirical evaluation on a broad range of neural networks and datasets shows that FastHO is not only effective to speed up hyperparameter optimization but also can achieve better anytime performance and final performance than other state-of-the-art methods.

Future work includes taking feature subsampling into account to further accelerate hyperparameter optimization.

Acknowledgments. We thank Rong Gu, Chunfeng Yuan, and Yihua Huang for helpful advice. This work was supported by the National Natural Science Foundation of China (U1811461, 61702254), National Key R&D Program of China (2019YFC1711000), Jiangsu Province Science and Technology Program (BE2017155), National Natural Science Foundation of Jiangsu Province (BK20170651), and Collaborative Innovation Center of Novel Software Technology and Industrialization.

References

1. Bergstra, J., Bardenet, R., Bengio, Y., Kégl, B.: Algorithms for hyper-parameter optimization. In: Proceedings of the 24th International Conference on Neural Information Processing Systems, pp. 2546–2554 (2011)
2. Bergstra, J., Yamins, D., Cox, D.D.: Making a science of model search: hyperparameter optimization in hundreds of dimensions for vision architectures. In: Proceedings of the 30th International Conference on Machine Learning, pp. 115–123 (2013)
3. Devries, T., Taylor, G.W.: Improved regularization of convolutional neural networks with cutout. CoRR abs/1708.04552 (2017)
4. Falkner, S., Klein, A., Hutter, F.: BOHB: robust and efficient hyperparameter optimization at scale. In: Proceedings of the 35th International Conference on Machine Learning, pp. 1436–1445 (2018)
5. Feurer, M., Springenberg, J.T., Hutter, F.: Initializing bayesian hyperparameter optimization via meta-learning. In: Proceedings of the 29th AAAI Conference on Artificial Intelligence, pp. 1128–1135 (2015)

6. Gastaldi, X.: Shake-shake regularization. CoRR abs/1705.07485 (2017)
7. He, K., Zhang, X., Ren, S., Sun, J.: Identity mappings in deep residual networks. In: Leibe, B., Matas, J., Sebe, N., Welling, M. (eds.) ECCV 2016. LNCS, vol. 9908, pp. 630–645. Springer, Cham (2016). https://doi.org/10.1007/978-3-319-46493-0_38
8. Henderson, P., Islam, R., Bachman, P., Pineau, J., Precup, D., Meger, D.: Deep reinforcement learning that matters. In: Proceedings of the 32rd AAAI Conference on Artificial Intelligence, pp. 3207–3214 (2018)
9. Hu, Y., Yu, Y., Tu, W., Yang, Q., Chen, Y., Dai, W.: Multi-fidelity automatic hyper-parameter tuning via transfer series expansion. In: Proceedings of the 33rd AAAI Conference on Artificial Intelligence, pp. 3846–3853 (2019)
10. Hutter, F., Hoos, H.H., Leyton-Brown, K.: Sequential model-based optimization for general algorithm configuration. In: Coello, C.A.C. (ed.) LION 2011. LNCS, vol. 6683, pp. 507–523. Springer, Heidelberg (2011). https://doi.org/10.1007/978-3-642-25566-3_40
11. Jamieson, K.G., Talwalkar, A.: Non-stochastic best arm identification and hyper-parameter optimization. In: Proceedings of the 19th International Conference on Artificial Intelligence and Statistic, pp. 240–248 (2016)
12. Kandasamy, K., Dasarathy, G., Oliva, J.B., Schneider, J.G., Póczos, B.: Gaussian process bandit optimisation with multi-fidelity evaluations. In: Proceedings of the 30th International Conference on Neural Information Processing Systems, pp. 1000–1008 (2016)
13. Kandasamy, K., Dasarathy, G., Schneider, J.G., Póczos, B.: Multi-fidelity bayesian optimisation with continuous approximations. In: Proceedings of the 34th International Conference on Machine Learning, pp. 1799–1808 (2017)
14. Ke, G., et al.: LightGBM: a highly efficient gradient boosting decision tree. In: Proceedings of the 31st International Conference on Neural Information Processing Systems, pp. 3149–3157 (2017)
15. Li, L., Jamieson, K., DeSalvo, G., Rostamizadeh, A., Talwalkar, A.: Hyperband: bandit-based configuration evaluation for hyperparameter optimization. J. Mach. Learn. Res. **18**(1), 6765–6816 (2017)
16. Lindauer, M., Hutter, F.: Warmstarting of model-based algorithm configuration. In: Proceedings of the 32rd AAAI Conference on Artificial Intelligence, pp. 1355–1362 (2018)
17. Loshchilov, I., Hutter, F.: SGDR: stochastic gradient descent with warm restarts. In: Proceedings of the 5th International Conference on Learning Representations (2017)
18. Mendoza, H., Klein, A., Feurer, M., Springenberg, J.T., Hutter, F.: Towards automatically-tuned neural networks. In: Proceedings of the Workshop on Automatic Machine Learning, pp. 58–65 (2016)
19. Sen, R., Kandasamy, K., Shakkottai, S.: Multi-fidelity black-box optimization with hierarchical partitions. In: Proceedings of the 35th International Conference on Machine Learning, pp. 4545–4554 (2018)
20. Snoek, J., Larochelle, H., Adams, R.P.: Practical bayesian optimization of machine learning algorithms. In: Proceedings of the 25th International Conference on Neural Information Processing Systems, vol. 2, pp. 2951–2959 (2012)
21. Springenberg, J.T., Klein, A., Falkner, S., Hutter, F.: Bayesian optimization with robust bayesian neural networks. In: Proceedings of the 30th International Conference on Neural Information Processing Systems, pp. 4141–4149 (2016)

Curiosity-Driven Variational Autoencoder for Deep Q Network

Gao-Jie Han, Xiao-Fang Zhang$^{(\boxtimes)}$, Hao Wang, and Chen-Guang Mao

School of Computer Science and Technology, Soochow University, Suzhou, China
xfzhang@suda.edu.cn

Abstract. In recent years, deep reinforcement learning (DRL) has achieved tremendous success in high-dimensional and large-scale space control and sequential decision-making tasks. However, the current model-free DRL methods suffer from low sample efficiency, which is a bottleneck that limits their performance. To alleviate this problem, some researchers used the generative model for modeling the environment. But the generative model may become inaccurate or even collapse if the state has not been sufficiently explored. In this paper, we introduce a model called Curiosity-driven Variational Autoencoder (CVAE), which combines variational autoencoder and curiosity-driven exploration. During the training process, the CVAE model can improve sample efficiency while curiosity-driven exploration can make sufficient exploration in a complex environment. Then, a CVAE-based algorithm is proposed, namely DQN-CVAE, that scales CVAE to higher dimensional environments. Finally, the performance of our algorithm is evaluated through several Atari 2600 games, and the experimental results show that the DQN-CVAE achieves better performance in terms of average reward per episode on these games.

Keywords: Reinforcement learning · Deep Q learning · Exploration · Variational autoencoder

1 Introduction

Reinforcement learning (RL) [17] is a popular area of current research across various fields. The goal of the RL algorithm is achieving the target task by maximizing the expected rewards provided by the environment. Recently, Mnih et al. proposed Deep Q learning (DQN) [3,13,14], which combines deep learning (DL) [12] and RL, achieving a remarkable result in classic games such as Atari 2600 games.

Although DQN and its extensions have tremendous success in Atari 2600 environment, at the beginning of the training process, the current DQN algorithms require millions of training samples based on the random policy before any optimal policy is trained, and insufficient sample diversity will result in the slow training speed. However, in many scenarios, the training sample may be difficult or time-consuming to obtain. Thus, some researchers attempt to represent

© Springer Nature Switzerland AG 2020
H. W. Lauw et al. (Eds.): PAKDD 2020, LNAI 12084, pp. 764–775, 2020.
https://doi.org/10.1007/978-3-030-47426-3_59

the actual environment by using a generative model [1,6,8] to improve sample efficiency. When the generative model is sufficiently trained, the DRL algorithm can be trained without interacts with the actual environment. In [1,2,6,8], it is confirmed that the agent can learn the optimal policy only use generate training samples. However, these generative models may become inaccurate and even collapse where the state-action pair insufficient explored [1,2,6].

Moreover, inadequate exploration of the environment may also result in slow learning speed. In traditional model-free DRL algorithms, they rely on simple heuristics exploration strategies such as ϵ-greedy. However, these exploration strategies are often trapped in local minima of the state space, which leads to the state space may be partially observed in the high-dimensional environment. Curiosity-driven exploration uses an extra reward signal that inspired the agent to explore the state that has not been sufficiently explored before. It tends to seek out the unexplored regions more efficiently in the same amount of time.

In this paper, we propose a new algorithm called Curiosity-driven Variational Autoencoder (CVAE), which uses a CVAE to model the environment in latent space to improve sample efficacy while curiosity-driven exploration to make a sufficient exploration. Then we apply the CVAE to DQN and its variants denoted as DQN-CVAE. In addition, we provide experimental results on several Atari 2600 games. Experimental results show that the DQN-CVAE algorithm can improve the exploration and performance of the agent.

The remainder of the paper is organized as follows. Section 2 discusses related work. Section 3 elaborates on the DQN and VAE algorithms. Section 4 offers an overview of our approach, then describes DQN-CVAE algorithm in detail. Section 5 provides our experimental setup and results. Section 6 concludes.

2   Related Work

Recently, some researchers attempt to model the environment by using a generative model to improve sample efficiency. The notion of modeling the environment in latent space may trace back to [8], which proposed DARLA, an architecture for modeling the environment with β-Variational Autoencoder, and have applied the latent features for transfer learning across multiple environments. In [6], Ha et al. proposed World Model, an architecture for modeling the environment using a VAE model and a recurrent neural network (RNN) model, which shows that the agent can learn the optimal policy only use generate training samples. Similarly, Anderson et al. [1] proposed Dreaming Variational Autoencoder, an architecture for modeling the environment using VAE and RNN, which uses the real trajectories from the actual environment to imitate the behavior of the actual environment. Conversely, Anderson et al. [2] found that in high-dimensional tasks, simple heuristics exploration are often trapped in local minima of the state space, which may cause the generative model to become inaccurate or even collapse.

Previous research on exploration technique may solve the problem that the agent achieves a sufficient exploration in the high-dimensional task. Many researchers focus on using the intrinsic reward to drive the agent to make an efficient exploration. Kulkarni et al. [11] suggested a hierarchical DRL model in which the agent receives the extrinsic reward and the intrinsic reward at different temporal scales. Stadie et al. [16] introduced incentivizing exploration, which use extra reward signal to encourage the agent to visit the state-action pairs that it has not sufficiently explored. Pathak et al. [5,15] proposed an exploration method called curiosity-driven exploration method. The main idea of curiosity-driven exploration is to attempt to use the intrinsic reward to drive an agent to explore trajectories that it has not visited frequently. Hoothooft et al. [9] suggested a curiosity-driven based method called Variational Information Maximizing Exploration, which uses the information gain as an intrinsic reward and achieves a better performance than heuristic exploration methods across various continuous control tasks.

3   Background

3.1   Deep Q Network

DQN combines Q learning and DL, which use the experience replay mechanism and target network mechanism are used to alleviate learning instability [13,14]. The experience replay mechanism is sampling a fixed number of training samples from experience replay pool D uniformly at random. At each discrete time step t, agent receives a state s_t, and selects an action a_t based on ϵ-greedy policy with respect to the action values. As a feedback, agent gets a reward r_t and receives next state s_{t+1}, then (s_t, a_t, r_t, s_{t+1}) is stored as a sequence in experience replay pool D, and a fixed number of samples are taken from the training process as a network input.

DQN uses two independent deep networks, the current value network $Q(s, a; \theta)$ with parameters θ and the target value network $Q(s, a; \theta^-)$ with parameters θ^-, where DQN learns the parameters of the network $Q(s, a; \theta)$ online, and the parameters θ^- is periodically copied by θ. The loss function is determined by the mean square error of the target value function and the current value function. The corresponding formula is shown in Eq. (1):

$$\mathcal{L}(\theta) = \mathbb{E}_{s,a,r,s'}[(r + \gamma \, max_{a'} Q(s', a'; \theta^-) - Q(s, a; \theta))^2] \tag{1}$$

In order to solve the minimized loss function, the parameter θ is derived in Eq. (1). The gradient update is shown in Eq. (2):

$$\nabla_\theta \mathcal{L}(\theta) = \mathbb{E}_{s,a,r,s'}[(r + \gamma \, max_{a'} Q(s', a'; \theta^-) - Q(s, a; \theta))^2] \nabla_\theta Q(s, a; \theta) \tag{2}$$

3.2   Variational Autoencoder

VAE is a generative model capable of learning unsupervised latent representations of complex high-dimensional data [10]. The VAE model consists of two parts: encoder $q_\phi(z|x)$ and decoder $p_\theta(x|z)$. The encoder consumes the sample x, yielding the input in latent space z, then z is fed into decoder to predict sample x. The key idea of the VAE is to learn the marginal likelihood of a sample

x from a distribution parametrized by generative factors z. Thus, $q_\phi(z|x)$ is the variational approximation for the true posterior $p_\theta(z|x)$. The marginal likelihood of a data point x can take following form:

$$\log p_\theta(x) = \mathcal{L}(x; \theta, \phi) + D_{KL}(q_\phi(z|x)||p_\theta(z|x)) \tag{3}$$

Since the true data likelihood is usually intractable, instead, the VAE optimizes an evidence lower bound (ELBO) which is a valid lower bound of the true data log likelihood, denoted as:

$$\mathcal{L}(x; \theta, \phi) = \mathbb{E}_{q_\phi}[\log p_\theta(x|z)] - D_{KL}(q_\phi(z|x)||p(z)) \tag{4}$$

$\mathcal{L}(x; \theta, \phi)$ consists of two terms: the first term can be considered as reconstruction loss, and the second term is approximated posterior $q_\phi(z|x)$ from prior $p(z)$ via KL-divergence. In practice, q_ϕ and p_θ are implemented via deep neural networks, and prior $p(z)$ usually sets to follow Gaussian distribution $N(0, 1)$.

4 Curiosity-Driven Variational Autoencoder

We propose the Curiosity-driven Variational Autoencoder (CVAE), which combines curiosity-driven exploration with the VAE model. The CVAE model uses the prediction error as an intrinsic reward to drive the agent to make a sufficient exploration, which can improve the quality of the generate training samples.

The DQN-CVAE model is consists of two components: the DQN reinforcement learning method and the CVAE model. The structure of DQN-CVAE is presented in Fig. 1(a). Since we use a CVAE model to generate training samples, an additional experience replay pool D_g is used to store up the training samples generated by the CVAE model.

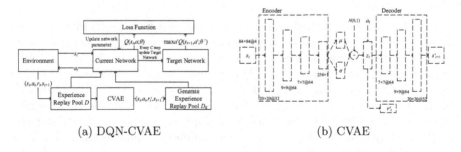

(a) DQN-CVAE   (b) CVAE

Fig. 1. Illustration of the DQN-CVAE model.

The structure of CVAE model is shown in Fig. 1(b). During the training process, the model consumes state s_t, yielding the input encoded in latent space $h_t = [\mu, \sigma]$, which represents a concatenated form of the mean μ and the standard deviation σ, then the h_t is reparametrized into a posterior variable z_t. Then inject the action a_t to the z_t, latent parameter z_t element-wise addition with a_t is fed into the decoder network to predict the next state s'_{t+1}. The predict next state s'_{t+1} is compared with the real state s_{t+1} given by the environment after the action a_t is taken.

To improve the generate sample quality. At time step t we consider a training sample $x_t = (s_t, a_t, r_t, s_{t+1})$ from D. We feed the state s_t and action a_t into encoder as an input, and predict the reward r_t and next state s_{t+1}. In this case, we divided the training sample x_t into two pairs as follows:

$$x_t = [(s_t, a_t), (s_{t+1}, r_t)] \tag{5}$$

where (s_t, a_t) represents the current state-action pair, and (s_{t+1}, r_t) represents the next state pair, which obtains from the agent interacts with the environment. Then, we focused on (s_{t+1}, r_t), we use the KL divergence as prediction error as follows:

$$e_t = D_{KL}((s_{t+1}, r_t)||(s'_{t+1}, r'_t)) \tag{6}$$

Moreover, we use curiosity-driven exploration to improve the efficiency of exploration. An intrinsic reward associated with e_t drives the agent to make a sufficient exploration, the reward function is modified as follows:

$$r'_t = r'_t + \beta e_t \tag{7}$$

where β is the weighted variables.

According to Eq. (4), the loss function of the VAE model consists of two parts: reconstruction loss and latent space loss. Thus, different from the Eq. (4), we use the prediction error e_t as reconstruction error, the loss function is computed by the following formula:

$$\mathcal{L}_{cvae} = e_t - D_{KL}(q_\phi(z_t|s_t)||N(0,1)) \tag{8}$$

The DQN-CVAE algorithm is presented in Algorithm (1). During the learning process, the agent collects the training samples (s_t, a_t, r_t, s_{t+1}) from many episode, and accumulates it as a experience replay pool D. The VAE model is trained using the real training sample in D and generates a new training sample $(s_t, a_t, r'_t, s'_{t+1})$. At the same time, the prediction error e_t is used to predict the intrinsic reward. Then, add the generate sample to D_g, which is an experience replay pool follow the First-in First-out principle to store generate training samples. Next, turn to the DQN part, a fixed number of samples from D and D_g are selected as a minibatch according to the proportion factor g and provided to the agent for training the action-value function and learning the optimal strategy. Besides, during the training process, the VAE model continues to generate training samples and add them to D_g to speed up the learning speed. Although the CVAE model increases the size of the parameter of the neural network, the CVAE model is in parallel with the agent, which does not significantly increase the time complexity of the algorithm, but speed up the learning speed.

Algorithm 1. DQN-CVAE

Initialize replay memory D with capacity N, generate replay memory D_g with capacity N_g, minibatch size M, proportion factor g

Initialize the action-value function Q with random weight θ

Initialize the target action-value function Q with weight θ^-

for episode=1, I **do**

    Observe state s_0

    for t=1,T **do**

        Choose an action a_t based on ϵ-greedy policy

        Observe transition(s_t, a_t, r_t, s_{t+1})

        Store transition(s_t, a_t, r_t, s_{t+1}) in D

        /*CVAE part*/

        Sample random minibatch of transition (s_t, a_t, r_t, s_{t+1}) from D

        Generate transition $(s_t, a_t, r'_t, s'_{t+1})$

        Compute the prediction error e_t

        Store transition $(s_t, a_t, r'_t + \beta e_t, s'_{t+1})$ in D_g

        /*DQN part*/

        Random sample $M \times (1 - g)$ of transition (s_j, a_j, r_j, s_{j+1}) from D

        Random sample $M \times g$ of transition (s_j, a_j, r_j, s_{j+1}) from D_g

        Set

$$y_j = \begin{cases} r_j & \text{if episode terminates at step } j+1 \\ r_j + \gamma max_{a'}Q(s_{j+1}, a'; \theta^-) & \text{otherwise} \end{cases}$$

        Perform a gradient descent step on $(y - Q(s, a; \theta))^2$ with respect to the network parameters θ

        Every C step update $\theta^- = \theta$

    end for

end for

---

5 Experiments

5.1 Research Questions

In these experiments, there are several research questions (RQ) that we consider. For starters, we wish to know whether our algorithm leads to improved DQN. Then, we also want to know whether our algorithm can apply in other DQN extensions. Finally, we investigate how the proportion factor of g affects the performance of our algorithm.

RQ1: Does the DQN-CVAE improve the performance of the DQN?

RQ2: Does the DQN-CVAE improve the performance of other DQN variants?

RQ3: How does the proportion factor g affect the performance of the DQN-CVAE?

5.2   Experimental Environment and Setup

Experimental Environment. We use the Atari 2600 game environment in the OpenAI gym [4] as the experimental environment to evaluate the performance of our proposed algorithm. OpenAI gym is an open-source toolkit that provides a wide variety of Atari 2600 game interfaces. Five games were used in our experiments. A brief introduction to these games is presented in Table 1.

Table 1. A brief introduction of some Atari games

Game	Action number	Introduction
Alien	18	Agent avoids enmenies and reach the target point
BeamRider	9	Agent avoids bullets and hits moving enemies
Kangroo	18	Agent climbs through stairs and avoids obstacles
Seaquest	18	Agent evades obstacles and attacks enemies under water
SpaceInvaders	6	Agent evades and attacks the enemies

Experimental Setup. In order to compare the performance of different algorithms, all algorithms use the same network architecture and hyperparameters settings. The main hyperparameter settings are shown in Table 2.

Table 2. Main hyperparameters and their values

Hyperparameter	Value
Minibatch size	32
Discount factor	0.99
Learning rate	2.5×10^{-4}
Initial exploration factor	0.96
Final exploration factor	0.1
Replay start size	500000
Target network update frequency	1×10^4
Experience replay pool size	1×10^6
Generate experience replay pool size	1×10^5
RMSprop momentum coefficient	0.95
Frame skip rate	4

The DQN-CVAE algorithm consists of two parts: the DQN model and the CVAE model. The network architecture used in DQN and DDQN is the same as the study of Mnih et al. [14] and Hasselt et al. [7]. There are 3 convolutional layers, 2 full-connected layers and 3 deconvolutional layers in CVAE model. The structure used in CVAE is shown in Fig. 1(b).

Evaluation Criteria And Comparison Algorithms. In the Atari environment, we use the average rewards per episode as the evaluation criteria and uses 200 epoch as the training periods, in which 50,000 steps were used to train the network parameters, a total of 100,000,000 steps are trained.

In these experiments, we compare the training performance of two original network (DQN and DDQN) and three networks with DQN-CVAE(DQN-CVAE, DQN-VAE, CDQN), we denote these algorithms as follows:

(1) DQN and DDQN are deep Q learning [13,14] and double deep Q learning [7], which are benchmark comparison algorithms;
(2) CDQN and CDDQN are DQN or DDQN based on curiosity-driven exploration [5,15];
(3) DQN-VAE and DDQN-VAE add a VAE structure to DQN or DDQN, which only uses the VAE model to alleviate insufficient sample diversity;
(4) DQN-CVAE and DDQN-CVAE are our proposed algorithms that combine (2) and (3). It was different from (3) in that we use curiosity-driven exploration to improve the efficiency of exploration.

5.3 Experimental Result

RQ1 asks whether the DQN-CVAE algorithm can improve the performance of DQN. To answer this question, we first compared the performance of DQN, CDQN, DQN-VAE, and DQN-CVAE during each epoch of training. The results are presented in Fig. 2. The x-axis represents the training epoch, and the y-axis represents the average rewards per episode.

As expected, it can be observed that the average rewards per episode of DQN-CVAE are obviously higher than other algorithms. For models with curiosity-driven exploration (DQN-CVAE, CDQN), the performance is significantly improved than DQN. It is indicated that insufficient exploration has existed in some Atari games, which confirms the contribution of the curiosity-driven exploration. For model with VAE (DQN-CVAE, DQN-VAE), we have found that the DQN-CVAE has a better performance than DQN-VAE. It is illustrated that CVAE improves the sample efficiency can improve the generative model performance. However, in some scenarios, it can be seen that the performance of DQN-VAE has dropped below the DQN. It is not surprising, as DQN-VAE would be inaccurate if the state space is sufficiently explored.

To confirm that DQN-CVAE can perform well after training, we compared the performance of DQN, CDQN, DQN-VAE, and DQN-CVAE on five games after training. For each game, the training completed model will be tested 100 times. Each test will receive a score that represents the average reward per episode. The result in terms of the average reward per episode is reported in Table 3. The result demonstrated that the performance of DQN-CVAE is more effective than DQN in the testing process. It is indicated that DQN-CVAE can improve the performance of DQN.

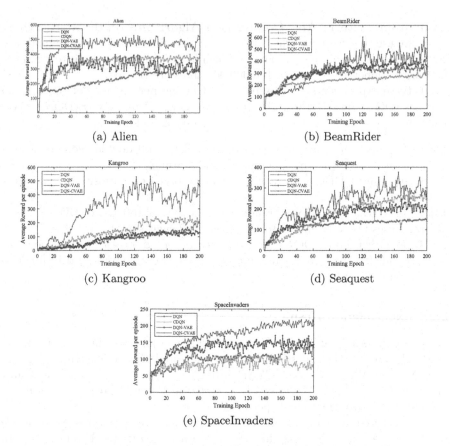

Fig. 2. Comparisons of DQN, CDQN, DQN-VAE and DQN-CVAE

RQ2 asks whether the DQN-CVAE algorithm can improve the performance of other DQN variants. In these experiments, we keep all these settings as in RQ1, but adopt DDQN [7] instead of DQN as the original network, and compares the performance of DDQN, CDDQN, DDQN-VAE and DDQN-CVAE on 5 Atari 2600 games. Figure 3 shows the performance of each algorithm. The x-axis represents the training epoch, and the y-axis represents the average reward per episode.

As shown in Fig. 3, similar to the result of Fig. 2, the performance of the DDQN-CVAE is better than other algorithms. So, we can confirm that DQN-CVAE can perform well in the training process when it applies to DQN and its extensions. Then, we also compared the performance of DDQN, CDDQN, DDQN-VAE, and DDQN-CVAE on 5 Atari 2600 games after training. Table 3 lists the results of these four algorithms for DDQN.

Overall, these results indicated that, in the Atari environment, DQN-CVAE outperforms than DQN in the training and testing process. It is indicated that DQN-CVAE uses the CVAE to model the environment that can improve the performance of the DQN. Besides, DQN-CVAE can successfully apply to other DQN variants, which demonstrates that the DQN-CVAE is a simple extension that can be easily integrated with other DQN variants.

Table 3. Average score after training

Game	DQN		DQN-VAE		CDQN		DQN-CVAE	
	DQN	DDQN	DQN	DDQN	DQN	DDQN	DQN	DDQN
Alien	896	965	945	1104	1052	1142	1087	**1164**
BeamRider	1435	1642	1726	1942	1652	1820	1955	**1974**
Kangroo	2744	2582	2862	2647	2665	2674	**3353**	3287
Seaquest	1215	1285	1326	1426	1462	1508	1527	**1683**
SpaceInvaders	457	559	463	482	342	361	563	**575**

* the best results are highlighted in bold.

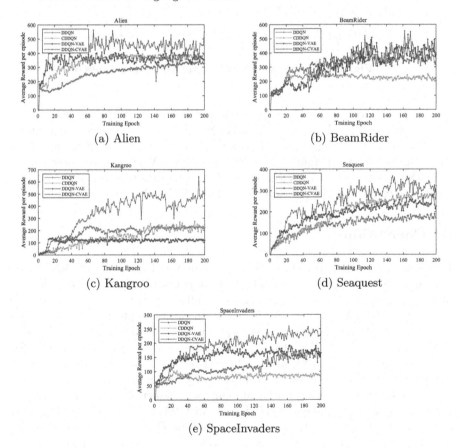

(a) Alien   (b) BeamRider

(c) Kangroo   (d) Seaquest

(e) SpaceInvaders

Fig. 3. Comparisons of DDQN, CDDQN, DDQN-VAE and DDQN-CVAE

RQ3 asks how the proportion factor g affects the performance of the DQN-CVAE algorithm. We investigate the performance of DQN-CVAE with different values of g, which is $g = 0, 0.25, 0.5, 0.75, 1$, respectively. Figure 4 presents the result of DQN-CVAE with various g. It can be seen that the performance of DQN-CVAE becomes better with the increasing of the value of g. However, we also can observe that, in some scenarios like Fig. 4(b), the average reward per episode has a large fluctuation while g is greater than 0.75. So, in these experiments, it is recommended that $g = 0.5$.

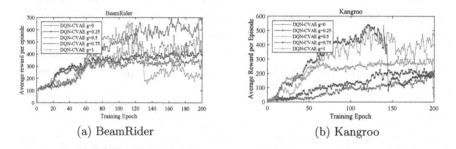

(a) BeamRider   (b) Kangroo

Fig. 4. Comparisons of various g value for Atari games

After conducting three sets of experiments, we confirm that DQN-CVAE can achieve better performance than DQN in the Atari environment during the training and testing process. Besides, we confirm that CVAE model can be easily applied in other model-free DRL algorithms. Moreover, the performance of DQN-CVAE is affected by the value of the proportion factor of g. With the increasing value of g, the performance of DQN-CVAE become better in general.

6   Conclusion

In this paper, we introduce the CVAE algorithm, which combines the VAE model and curiosity-driven exploration. The VAE model can improve sample efficiency, and curiosity-driven exploration can make a sufficient exploration to improve the accuracy of the VAE model. CVAE algorithm can be applied in the traditional model-free DRL algorithm, such as DQN and DDQN. The experiment results show that the DQN-CVAE algorithm can improve the exploration and performance of the agent, and we also confirm that the CVAE algorithm is flexible since it can be easily integrated with other DQN variants.

In future work, more experiments can be conducted on other Atari 2600 games to conform to the generalization of our CVAE algorithm. Besides, a priority can be used to select to generate samples from D_g based on intrinsic reward. Another direction is to make g become a dynamic learnable parameter with the use of neural networks.

Acknowledgments. This work was supported in part of the National Natural Science Foundation of China (61772355, 61876119), Suzhou Technology Development Plan (SYG201807), and the Priority Academic Program Development of Jiangsu Higher Education Institutions.

References

1. Andersen, P.-A., Goodwin, M., Granmo, O.-C.: The dreaming variational autoencoder for reinforcement learning environments. In: Bramer, M., Petridis, M. (eds.) SGAI 2018. LNCS (LNAI), vol. 11311, pp. 143–155. Springer, Cham (2018). https://doi.org/10.1007/978-3-030-04191-5_11
2. Andersen, P.A., Goodwin, M., Granmo, O.C.: Towards model-based reinforcement learning for industry-near environments. arXiv preprint arXiv:1907.11971 (2019)
3. Arulkumaran, K., Deisenroth, P.M., Brundage, M., Bharath, A.A.: Deep reinforcement learning: a brief survey. IEEE Signal Process. Mag. **34**(6), 26–38 (2017)
4. Brockman, G., Cheung, V., Pettersson, L., et al.: Openai gym. arXiv preprint arXiv:1606.01540 (2016)
5. Burda, Y., Edwards, H., Pathak, D., et al.: Large-scale study of curiosity-driven learning. arXiv preprint arXiv:1808.04355 (2018)
6. Ha, D., Schmidhuber, J.: World models. arXiv preprint arXiv:1803.10122 (2018)
7. Hasselt, V.H., Guez, A., Silver, D.: Deep reinforcement learning with double q-learning. In: Proceedings of the 30th AAAI Conference on Artificial Intelligence (AAAI-16), pp. 2094–2100 (2016)
8. Higgins, I., Pal, A., Rusu, A.A., et al.: DARLA: improving zero-shot transfer in reinforcement learning. In: Proceedings of the 34th International Conference on Machine Learning, vol. 70, pp. 1480–1490. JMLR. org (2017)
9. Houthooft, R., Chen, X., Duan, Y., et al.: VIME: variational information maximizing exploration. In: Advances in Neural Information Processing Systems, vol. 29, pp. 1109–1117. Curran Associates, Inc. (2016)
10. Kingma, P.D., Welling, M.: Auto-encoding variational bayes. arXiv preprint arXiv:1312.6114 (2013)
11. Kulkarni, D.T., Narasimhan, R.K., Saeedi, A., Joshua, T.B.: Hierarchical deep reinforcement learning: integrating temporal abstraction and intrinsic motivation. In: Advances in Neural Information Processing Systems, pp. 3675–3683 (2016)
12. LeCun, Y., Bengio, Y., Hinton, G.: Deep learning. Nature **521**(7553), 436 (2015)
13. Mnih, V., Kavukcuoglu, K., Silver, D., et al.: Playing atari with deep reinforcement learning. In: NIPS Deep Learning Workshop (2013)
14. Mnih, V., Kavukcuoglu, K., Silver, D., et al.: Human-level control through deep reinforcement learning. Nature **518**(7540), 529 (2015)
15. Pathak, D., Agrawal, P., Efros, A.A., Darrell, T.: Curiosity-driven exploration by self-supervised prediction. In: Proceedings of the IEEE Conference on Computer Vision and Pattern Recognition Workshops, pp. 16–17 (2017)
16. Stadie, C.B., Levine, S., Abbeel, P.: Incentivizing exploration in reinforcement learning with deep predictive models. arXiv preprint arXiv:1507.00814 (2015)
17. Sutton, R.S., Barto, A.G.: Reinforcement Learning: An Introduction. MIT Press, Cambridge (2018)

Feature Extraction and Selection

Estimating Descriptors for Large Graphs

Zohair Raza Hassan[1], Mudassir Shabbir[1], Imdadullah Khan[2(✉)],
and Waseem Abbas[3]

[1] Information Technology University of the Punjab, Lahore, Pakistan
{zohair.raza,mudassir.shabbir}@itu.edu.pk
[2] Lahore University of Management Sciences, Lahore, Pakistan
imdad.khan@lums.edu.pk
[3] Vanderbilt University, Nashville, USA
waseem.abbas@vanderbilt.edu

Abstract. Embedding networks into a fixed dimensional feature space, while preserving its essential structural properties is a fundamental task in graph analytics. These feature vectors (graph descriptors) are used to measure the pairwise similarity between graphs. This enables applying data mining algorithms (e.g classification, clustering, or anomaly detection) on graph-structured data which have numerous applications in multiple domains. State-of-the-art algorithms for computing descriptors require the entire graph to be in memory, entailing a huge memory footprint, and thus do not scale well to increasing sizes of real-world networks. In this work, we propose streaming algorithms to efficiently approximate descriptors by estimating counts of sub-graphs of order $k \leq 4$, and thereby devise extensions of two existing graph comparison paradigms: the Graphlet Kernel and NetSimile. Our algorithms require a single scan over the edge stream, have space complexity that is a fraction of the input size, and approximate embeddings via a simple sampling scheme. Our design exploits the trade-off between available memory and estimation accuracy to provide a method that works well for limited memory requirements. We perform extensive experiments on real-world networks and demonstrate that our algorithms scale well to massive graphs.

Keywords: Graph descriptor · Edge stream · Graph classification

1 Introduction

Evaluating similarity or distance between a pair of graphs is a building block of many fundamental data analysis tasks on graphs such as classification and clustering. These tasks have numerous applications in social network analysis,

The first two authors have been supported by the grant received to establish CIPL and the third author has been supported the grant received to establish SEIL, both associated with the National Center in Big Data and Cloud Computing, funded by the Planning Commission of Pakistan.

H. W. Lauw et al. (Eds.): PAKDD 2020, LNAI 12084, pp. 779–791, 2020.
https://doi.org/10.1007/978-3-030-47426-3_60

bioinformatics, computational chemistry, and graph theory in general. Unfortunately, large orders (number of vertices) and massive sizes (number of edges) prove to be challenging when applying general-purpose data mining techniques on graphs. Moreover, in many real-world scenarios, graphs in a dataset have varying orders and sizes, hindering the application of data mining algorithms devised for vector spaces. Thus, devising a framework to compare graphs with different orders and sizes would allow for rich analysis and knowledge discovery in many practical domains.

However, graph comparison is a difficult task; the best-known solution for determining whether two graphs are structurally the same takes quasi-polynomial time [1], and determining the minimum number of steps to convert one graph to another is NP-HARD [16]. In a more practical approach, graphs are first mapped into fixed dimensional feature vectors, where vector space-based algorithms are then employed. In a supervised setting, these feature vectors are learned through neural networks [14,25,26]. In unsupervised settings, the feature vectors are descriptive statistics of the graph such as average degree, the eigenspectrum, or spectra of sub-graphs of order at most k contained in the graph [7,11,17,18,22,23].

The runtimes and memory costs of these methods depend directly on the magnitude (order and size) of the graphs and the dimensionality (dependent on the number of statistics) of the feature-space. While computing a larger number of statistics would result in richer representations, these algorithms do not scale well to the increasing magnitudes of a real-world graphs [9].

A promising approach is to process graphs as streams - one edge at a time, without storing the whole graph in memory. In this setting, the graph descriptors are approximated from a representative sample achieving practical time and space complexity [6,15,19–21].

In this work we propose GABE (Graphlet Amounts via Budgeted Estimates), and MAEVE (Moments of Attributes Estimated on Vertices Efficiently), stream-based extensions of the Graphlet Kernel [17], and NetSimile [3], respectively. Our contributions can be summarised as follows:

- We propose two simple and intuitive descriptors for graph comparisons that run in the streaming setting.
- We provide analytical bounds on the time and space complexity of our feature vectors generation; for a fixed budget, the runtime and space cost of our algorithms are linear.
- We perform extensive empirical analysis on benchmark graph classification datasets of varying magnitudes. We demonstrate that GABE and MAEVE are comparable to the state-of-the-art in terms of classification accuracy, and scale to networks with millions of nodes and edges.

The rest of the paper is organized as follows. We discuss the related work in Sect. 2. Section 3 discusses all preliminaries required to read the text. We present GABE and MAEVE in Sect. 4. We report our experimental findings in Sect. 5 and finally conclude the paper in Sect. 6.

2   Related Work

Methods for comparing a pair of graphs can broadly be categorized into *direct approaches, kernel methods, descriptors*, and *neural models*. Direct approaches for evaluating the similarity/distance between a pair of graphs preserve the entire structure of both graphs. The most prominent method under this approach is the *Graph Edit Distance* (GED), which counts the number of edit operations (insertion/deletion of vertices/edges) required to convert a given graph to another [16]. Although intuitive, GED is stymied by its computational intractability. Computing distance based on the vertex permutation that minimizes the "error" between the adjacency representations of two graphs is a difficult task [1], and proposed relaxations of these distances are not robust to permutation [2]. An efficient algorithm for large network comparison DELTACON, is proposed in [9] but it is only feasible when there is a valid one-to-one correspondence between vertices of the two graphs.

In the kernel-based approach, graphs are mapped to a fixed dimensional vector space based on various substructures in the graphs. A kernel function is then defined, which serves as a pairwise similarity measure that takes as input a pair of graphs and outputs a non-negative real number. Typically, the kernel value is the inner-product between two feature vectors corresponding to the two graphs. This so-called kernel trick has been used successfully to evaluate pairwise of other structures such as images and sequences [4,10,12]. Several graph kernels based on sub-structural patterns have been proposed, such as the Shortest-Path [5] and Graphlet [17] kernels. More recently, a hierarchical kernel based on propagating spectral information within the graph [11] was introduced. The WL-Kernel [18] that is based on the Weisfeller-Lehman isomorphism test has been shown to provide excellent results for classification and is used as a benchmark in the graph representation learning literature. Kernels require expensive computation and typically necessitate storing the adjacency matrices, making them infeasible for massive graphs.

Graph Neural Networks (GNNs) learn graph level embeddings by aggregating node representations learned via convolving neighborhood information throughout the neural network's layers. This idea has been the basis of many popular neural networks and is as powerful as WL-Kernels for classification [14,26]. We refer interested readers to a comprehensive survey of these models [25]. Unfortunately, these models also require expensive computation and storing large matrices, hindering scalability to real-world graphs.

Graph descriptors, like the above two paradigms, attempt to map graphs to a vector space such that similar graphs are mapped to closely in the Euclidean space. Generally, the dimensionality of these vectors is small, allowing efficient algorithms for graph embeddings. NetSimile [3] describes graphs by computing moments of vertex features, while SGE [7] uses random walks and hashing to capture the presence of different sub-structures in a graph. State of the art descriptors are based on spectral information; [23] proposed a family of graph spectral distances and embedding the information as histograms on the multiset of distances in a graph, and NetLSD [22] computes the heat (or wave) trace over the eigenvalues of a graph's normalized Laplacian to construct embeddings.

The fundamental limitation of all the above approaches is the requirement that the entire graph is available in memory. This limits the applicability of the methods to a graph of small magnitude. To the best of our knowledge, this work is the first graph comparison method that does not assume this.

Streaming algorithms assume an online setting; the input is streamed one element at a time, and the amount of space we are allowed is limited. This allows one to design scalable approximation algorithms to solve the underlying problems. There has been extensive work on estimating triangles (cycles of length three) in graphs [19,21], butterflies (cycles of length four) in bipartite graphs [15], and anomaly detection [8] when the graph is input as a stream of edges. A framework for estimating the number of connected induced sub-graphs on three and four vertices is presented in [6].

3   Preliminaries and Problem Definition

3.1   Notation and Terminology

Let $G = (V_G, E_G)$ be an undirected, unweighted, simple graph, where V_G is the set of vertices and E_G is the set of edges.

For $v \in V_G$, let $N_G(v) = \{u : (u, v) \in E_G\}$ be the set of neighbors of v, and $d_G^v := |N_G(v)|$ the degree of v. A graph is connected if and only if there exists a path between all pairs in V_G.

A sub-graph of G is a graph, $G' = (V_{G'}, E_{G'})$, such that $V_{G'} \subseteq V_G$ and $E_{G'}$ is a subset of edges in E_G that are incident only on the vertices present in $V_{G'}$, i.e. $E_{G'} \subseteq \{(u, v) : (u, v) \in E_G \wedge u, v \in V_{G'}\}$. If equality holds ($E_{G'}$ contains all edges from the original graph), then G' is called an induced sub-graph of G.

Two graphs, G_1 and G_2, are isomorphic if and only if there exists a permutation $\pi : V_{G_2} \to V_{G_1}$ such that $E_{G_1} = \{(\pi(u), \pi(v)) : (u, v) \in E_{G_2}\}$. For a graph $F = (V_F, E_F)$, let H_G^F (resp. $\widehat{H}_G^F$) be the set of sub-graphs (resp. induced sub-graphs) of G that are isomorphic to F.

We assume vertices in V_G are denoted by integers in the range $[0, |V_G| - 1]$. Let $S = e_1, e_2, \ldots, e_{|E_G|}$ be a sequence of edges in an arbitrary but fixed order, i.e. $e_t = (u_t, v_t)$ is the tth edge. Let b be the maximum number of edges (budget) one can store in our sample, referred to as $\widetilde{E_G}$.

3.2   Problem Definition

We now formally define the graph descriptor problem:

Problem 1 (Constructing Graph Descriptors). Let $\mathcal{G}$ be the set of all possible undirected, unweighted, simple graphs. We wish to find a function, $\varphi : \mathcal{G} \to \mathbb{R}^d$, that can map any given graph to a d-dimensional vector.

Existing work [3,22] on graph descriptors asserts that the underlying algorithms should be able to run on any graph, regardless of order or size, and should output the same representation for different vertex permutations. Moreover, the descriptors should capture features that can be compared across graphs of varying orders; directly comparing sub-graph counts is illogical as bigger graphs will naturally have more sub-graphs. The descriptors we propose are based on graph comparison methods that meet these requirements due to their graph-theoretic nature and feature scaling based on the graph's magnitude. We consider an online setting and model the input graph as a stream of edges. We impose the following constraints on our algorithms:

C1: Single Pass: The algorithm is only allowed to receive the stream once.
C2: Limited Space: The algorithm can store a maximum of b edges at once.
C3: Linear Complexity: Space and time complexity of the algorithms should be linear (for fixed b) with respect to the order and size of the graph.

3.3 Estimating Connected Sub-graph Counts on Streams

Problem 2 (Connected Sub-graph Estimation on Streams). Let S be a stream of edges, $e_1, e_2, \ldots, e_{|E_G|}$ for some graph $G = (V_G, E_G)$. Let $F = (V_F, E_F)$ be a small connected graph such that $|V_F| \ll |V_G|$. Produce an estimate, N_G^F, of $|H_G^F|$ while storing a maximum of b edges at any given instant.

Based on previous works on sub-graph estimation [6, 19–21] the underlying recipe for algorithms that solve Problem 2 consists of the following steps:

- For each edge $e_t \in S$, counting the instances of F incident on e_t. For example, if F is a triangle, then it amounts to counting the number of triangles an edge e_t is part of.
- A sampling scheme through which we can compute the probability of detecting F in our sample, denoted by p_t^F, at the arrival of the tth edge.

At the arrival of e_t, we increment our estimate of $|H_G^F|$ by $1/p_t^F$ for all instances of F in our sample $\widetilde{E_G}$ that e_t belongs to. The pseudocode is provided in Algorithm 1. This simple methodology allows one to compute estimates whose expected values are equal to $|H_G^F|$:

Theorem 1. *Algorithm 1 provides unbiased estimates:* $\mathbb{E}[N_G^F] = |H_G^F|$.

Proof. For a sub-graph $h \in H_F^G$, let X_h be a random variable such that $X_h = 1/p_t^F$ if h is detected at the arrival of its last edge in the stream e_t, and 0 otherwise. Clearly, $N_G^F = \sum_{h \in H_G^F} X_h$, and $\mathbb{E}[X_h] = (1/p_t^F) \times p_t^F = 1$. Therefore,

$$\mathbb{E}\left[N_G^F\right] = \mathbb{E}\left[\sum_{h \in H_G^F} X_h\right] = \sum_{h \in H_G^F} \mathbb{E}[X_h] = \sum_{h \in H_G^F} 1 = |H_G^F|.$$

At the arrival of e_t, counting only the sub-graphs that e_t belongs to ensures that we do count the same sub-graph twice. In this work, we employ reservoir sampling [24], which has been shown to be effective for sub-graph estimation [6, 20, 21]. Using reservoir sampling, the probability of detecting an F that e_t belongs

---

Algorithm 1: Sub-graph Estimation on Streams

Input : Stream of edges $S = e_1, e_2, \ldots, e_{|E_G|}$, budget b, and a graph F
Output: N_G^F (estimate of $|H_G^F|$)
$\widetilde{E_G} \leftarrow \emptyset$, $N_G^F \leftarrow 0$ /* Initialize sample of edges, and estimate */
for $e_t \in S$ **do**
> Find all instances of F that e_t belongs to in $\widetilde{E_G} \cup \{e_t\}$
> Increment N_G^F by $1/p_t^F$ for each F detected
> Sample e_t in $\widetilde{E_G}$, based on b

end

---

to at the arrival of e_t is equivalent to the probability that $|E_F|-1$ particular edges are present in the sample after $t-1$ time-steps: $p_t^F = \min\left(1, \prod_{i=0}^{|E_F|-2} \frac{b-i}{t-1-i}\right)$.

We now derive an upper bound for the variance. Note that while the bound is loose, it is sufficient to show that we obtain better results with greater b, and applies to any connected graph, F.

Theorem 2. *When using reservoir sampling, the variance of N_G^F in Algorithm 1 is bounded as follows:* $\mathrm{Var}[N_G^F] \leq |H_G^F|^2 \prod_{i=0}^{|E_F|-2} \frac{|E_G|-i}{b-i}$.

Proof. The theorem is trivially true when $b \geq |E_G| - 1$. We now explore the case when $b < |E_G| - 1$. Let X_h be a random variable as defined in the proof for Theorem 1. Note that $p_t^F \geq p_{|E_G|}^F$, and $\mathrm{Var}[X_h] = \mathbb{E}[X_h^2] - \mathbb{E}[X_h]^2 = 1/p_t^F - 1 \leq 1/p_{|E_G|}^F$. We bound the total variance using the Cauchy-Schwarz inequality:

$$\mathrm{Var}[N_G^F] = \sum_{h \in H_G^F} \sum_{h' \in H_G^F} \mathrm{Cov}[X_h, X_{h'}] \leq \sum_{h \in H_G^F} \sum_{h' \in H_G^F} \sqrt{\mathrm{Var}[X_h]\mathrm{Var}[X_{h'}]}$$

$$\leq \sum_{h \in H_G^F} \sum_{h' \in H_G^F} \frac{1}{p_{|E_G|}^F} = |H_G^F|^2 \prod_{i=0}^{|E_F|-2} \frac{|E_G| - 1 - i}{b - i}.$$

Note that this methodology is also applicable for estimating the number of sub-graphs that each vertex is incident in, and simple modifications to the proofs for Theorems 1 and 2 will prove the same results for estimations on vertex counts.

4 GABE and MAEVE

In this section discuss our two proposed descriptors: Graphlet Amounts via Budgeted Estimates (GABE), which is based on the Graphlet Kernel, and Moments of Attributes Estimated on Vertices Efficiently (MAEVE), based on NetSimile.

4.1 Graphlet Amounts via Budgeted Estimates

Let $\mathcal{F}_k$ be the set of graphs with order k. For two given graphs, G_1 and G_2, Shervashidze et al. [17] propose counting all graphlets (induced sub-graphs) of

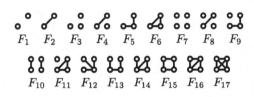

Fig. 1. The graphs counted by GABE, and their corresponding overlap matrix $\mathcal{O}$ (best viewed when zoomed in). Zeros have been omitted for readability.

order k in both graphs, and computing similarity based on the inner product $\langle \phi_k(G_1), \phi_k(G_2) \rangle$, where, for a given k, and graphs $F_i \in \mathcal{F}_k$:

$$\phi_k(G) := \frac{1}{\binom{|V_G|}{k}} \left[\left| \widehat{H}_G^{F_1} \right| \left| \widehat{H}_G^{F_2} \right| \left| \widehat{H}_G^{F_3} \right| \cdots \left| \widehat{H}_G^{F_{|\mathcal{F}_k|-1}} \right| \left| \widehat{H}_G^{F_{|\mathcal{F}_k|}} \right| \right]^{\mathsf{T}}$$

Their algorithm runs in $O(|V_G|d^{k-1})$ ($d = \max_{v \in V_G} d_G^v$) for $k \in \{3, 4, 5\}$, and uses adjacency matrices. We use the methodology of [6], to estimate the sub-graph counts as in Sect. 3.3, then compute induced sub-graph counts based on the overlap of graphs of the same order. We follow this procedure for estimating sub-graph counts of order $k \in \{2, 3, 4\}$, then concatenate the resultant $\phi_k(G)$'s into a vector. The 17 graphs we enumerate are shown in Fig. 1. Note that unlike [6], we also estimate the counts of disconnected induced sub-graphs.

Induced Sub-graph Counts. Let $\mathcal{F} = \{F_1, F_2, \ldots, F_{17}\}$ be the set of graphs we enumerate. Let $\mathcal{H}_G^{\mathcal{F}}$ (resp. $\widehat{\mathcal{H}}_G^{\mathcal{F}}$) be a vector such that i^{th} entry corresponds to $|H_G^{F_i}|$ (resp. $|\widehat{H}_G^{F_i}|$). Let $\mathcal{O}$ be a $|\mathcal{F}| \times |\mathcal{F}|$ matrix such that $O(i,j)$ is the number of sub-graphs of F_j, isomorphic to F_i, when $|V_{F_i}| = |V_{F_j}|$, and 0 otherwise. One can clearly see that $\mathcal{H}_G^{\mathcal{F}} = \mathcal{O}\widehat{\mathcal{H}}_G^{\mathcal{F}}$, as we account for the sub-graph counts that are disregarded when only considering induced sub-graphs. Since $\mathcal{O}$ is an upper triangular matrix, it is invertible. Thereby, given $\mathcal{H}_G^{\mathcal{F}}$, one can retrieve the induced sub-graph counts by computing $\mathcal{O}^{-1}\mathcal{H}_G^{\mathcal{F}}$. By linearity of expectation, Theorem 1 implies that the induced sub-graph counts are unbiased as well.

While processing the stream, we store the degree of each vertex, by incrementing the degree for u_t, v_t when $e_t = (u_t, v_t)$ arrives. We use edge-centric algorithms (as described in Sect. 3.3) to compute estimates for $F_6, F_{13}, \ldots, F_{17}$, and use intuitive combinatorial formulas, listed in Table 1, to compute the remaining 11 sub-graphs. We can compute $|E_G|$ and $|V_G|$ by keeping track of how many edges have been received, and the maximum vertex label received, respectively.

Time and Space Complexity. An array of size $|V_G|$ is used to store degrees, which can be accessed in $O(1)$ time, and hence the counts for F_5 and F_{12} can be incremented each time an edge arrives in $O(1)$. Let G' denote the graph represented by $\widetilde{E}_G$, stored as an adjacency list. Determining if two vertices are adjacent takes $O(\log b)$ time when using a tree data-structure within the stored

Table 1. Graphs and their corresponding sub-graph count formulas.

Graph	Formula	Graph	Formula	Graph	Formula
	$\binom{|V_G|}{2}$		$\binom{|V_G|}{3}$		$\binom{|V_G|}{4}$
	$|E_G|$		$|E_G|(|V_G|-2)$		$|E_G|\binom{|V_G|-2}{2}$
	$\binom{|E_G|}{2} - |H_G^{F_5}|$		$\sum_{v \in V_G}\binom{d_G^v}{2}$		$\sum_{v \in V_G}\binom{d_G^v}{3}$
	$|H_G^{F_5}|(|V_G|-3)$		$|H_G^{F_6}|(|V_G|-3)$	-	-

Table 2. Features extracted for each vertex, $v \in V_G$ for MAEVE, their formulae, and a figure highlighting the relevant edges. The filled in vertex depicts v.

Degree	Clustering Coefficient	Avg. Degree of $N_G(v)$	Edges in $I_G(v)$	Edges leaving $I_G(v)$
d_G^v	$|T_G(v)|/\binom{d_G^v}{2}$	$1 + |P_G(v)|/d_G^v$	$d_G^v + |T_G(v)|$	$|P_G(v)| - 2|T_G(v)|$

adjacency list. At the arrival of $e_t = (u_t, v_t)$, we need to visit only the vertices two hops away from u_t (resp. v_t), then perform at most three adjacency checks. Thereby, we perform $2\left(\sum_{w \in N_{G'}(u_t)} d_{G'}^w + \sum_{w \in N_{G'}(v_t)} d_{G'}^w\right) \times 3\log b = O(b\log b)$ operations for one edge, and $O(b\log b|E_G|)$ in total. Storing an adjacency list with b edges, and an array for degrees takes $O(b + |V_G|)$ space.

4.2 Moments of Attributes Estimated on Vertices Efficiently

NetSimile [3] propose extracting features for each vertex and aggregating them by taking moments over their distribution. Similarly, we propose extracting a subset of those features, listed in Table 2, and computing four moments for each feature: mean, standard deviation, skewness, and kurtosis.

Extracting Vertex Features. For a graph G, and a vertex $v \in V_G$, we use $I_G(v)$ to denote the induced sub-graph of G formed by v and its neighbors. Let $T_G(v)$ be the set of triangles that v belongs to, and $P_G(v)$ be the set of three-paths (paths on three vertices) where v is an end-point. We compute the features in Table 2 by using their formulas on estimates of $|T_G(v)|$, $|P_G(v)|$, and d_G^v computed for each $v \in V$ as in Sects. 3.3 and 4.1.

Theorem 3. *For a vertex $v \in V_G$, all vertex features used in* MAEVE *can be expressed in terms of d_G^v, $|T_G(v)|$, and $|P_G(v)|$.*

Proof. The first two are already expressed in terms of d_G^v and $|T_G(v)|$.

Average Degree of Neighbors: For each $u \in N_G(v)$, there is exactly one edge connected to v, accounting for d_G^v edges. The remaining edges are part of three-paths on which v is an end-point. Therefore, $\sum_{u \in N_G(v)} d_G^u = d_G^v + |P_G(v)|$.

Edges in $I_G(v)$: There are two types of edges in $E_{I_G(v)}$: (1) edges incident on v, of which there are d_G^v, and (2) edges not incident on v. The latter must belong to a pair of vertices which form a triangle with v. For each such edge, there is exactly one triangle. Therefore, $\left|E_{I_G(v)}\right| = d_G^v + |T_G(v)|$.

Edges leaving $I_G(v)$: Consider a sub-graph $h \in P_G(v)$. Let u be the other end-point of h, and w be the center vertex. When $u \notin N_G(v)$, it belongs to a three-path that is not in $N_G(v)$, and is thereby an edge leaving the induced sub-graph of v. Now, consider $u \in N_G(v)$. Clearly, the edge (u, w) forms a triangle, and is incident in exactly two three-paths: $\{(v, u), (u, w)\}$ and $\{(v, w), (u, w)\}$. Therefore, if we account for the three-paths that lie within $N_G(v)$, we can formulate the number of edges leaving $I_G(v)$ as $|P_G(v)| - 2|T_G(v)|$.

Time and Space Complexity. As in Sect. 4.1, we assume an adjacency list with an underlying tree structure and refer to the sampled graph as G'. At the arrival of an edge $e_t = (u_t, v_t)$, one can traverse the neighborhoods to obtain the triangle and three-path count in $(N_{G'}(u_t) + N_{G'}(v_t)) + N_{G'}(u_t) + N_{G'}(v_t) = O(b)$ time. We store three arrays of size $|V_G|$ to store degrees, triangle counts, and three-path counts. We can compute the moments in at most two passes over these arrays, giving us a total of $O(b|E_G| + |V_G|)$ time. Storing an adjacency list of size b and arrays of size $|V_G|$ gives us $O(b + |V_G|)$ space.

Improving Estimation Quality with Multiple Workers. Multiple worker machines can be used in parallel to independently estimate triangle counts before aggregating them [20]. Using W worker machines decreases the variances by a factor of $1/W$. Their methodology can be adopted *mutatis mutandis* in our algorithms to improve the estimation quality.

5 Experimental Evaluation

In this section, we perform experiments to show how the approximation quality changes with respect to b, explore how the descriptors perform on classification tasks, and showcase the scalability of the algorithms. As in [3], from extensive experiments, we found that Canberra distance $\left(d(\boldsymbol{x}, \boldsymbol{y}) := \sum_{i=1}^{d} \frac{|x_i - y_i|}{|x_i| + |y_i|}\right)$ performs best when comparing the descriptors. We refer to the approximation error as the distance between the true vectors and their approximations.

Implementation. All experiments were performed on a machine with 48 Intel Xeon E5-2680 v3 @ 2.50GHz Processors, and 125 GB RAM. The algorithms are implemented[1] in C++ using MPICH 3.2 on the base code provided by the authors of Tri-Fly [20]. We use 25 processes to simulate 1 Master and 24 workers. Each descriptor is computed exactly once under this setting.

Datasets. We evaluate our models on randomly sampled REDDIT graphs[2], five benchmark classification datasets with large graphs: D&D, COLLAB, REDDIT-BINARY, REDDIT-MULTI-5K, and REDDIT-MULTI-12K [27] (Table 3), and

---

[1] Code: https://github.com/zohair-raza/estimating-graph-descriptors/.
[2] https://dynamics.cs.washington.edu/data.html.

Table 3. Details of classification datasets. The number of graphs, classes, and minimum/maximum number of vertices/edges in a graph have been provided.

Dataset	$|\mathcal{G}|$	Classes	max $|V_G|$	max $|E_G|$
D&D	1,178	2	5,748	14,267
COLLAB	5,000	3	492	40,120
REDDIT-BINARY	2,000	2	3,782	4,071
REDDIT-MULTI-5K	4,999	5	3,648	4,783
REDDIT-MULTI-12K	11,929	11	3,782	5,171

Table 4. Massive networks with their order, size, and what they represent.

Graph	$|V_G|$	$|E_G|$	Network type
Patent	3,774,768	16,518,937	Citation
Flickr	2,302,925	22,838,276	Friendship
Full USA	23,947,347	28,854,312	Road
UK Domain 2002	18,483,186	261,787,258	Hyperlink

Table 5. Classification accuracy on the datasets described in Table 3. Results within 1% of the best have been boldfaced.

Descriptor	DD	COLLAB	RDT-2	RDT-5	RDT-12
NetLSD [22]	**70.36%**	**74.27%**	82.85%	**41.23%**	30.9%
GABE ($b = 1/4|E_G|$)	65.23%	63.62%	84.65%	**41.1%**	32.18%
GABE ($b = 1/2|E_G|$)	69.08%	65.23%	**85.35%**	40.63%	**32.96%**
MAEVE ($b = 1/4|E_G|$)	59.44%	68.42%	85.04%	41.15%	32.57%
MAEVE ($b = 1/2|E_G|$)	61.26%	70.95%	**86.15%**	**41.53%**	**33.69%**

massive networks from KONECT [13] (Table 4). For each graph, we remove duplicated edges and self-loops, convert to edge-list format with vertex labels in the range $[0, |V_G| - 1]$, and randomly shuffle the list.

5.1   Approximation Quality

We uniformly sampled 1000 graphs of size 10,000 to 50,000 from REDDIT, representing interactions in various "sub-reddits". In Fig. 2(a) we show how the average approximation error taken over all the sampled graphs decreases as b (a fraction of the number of edges) increases.

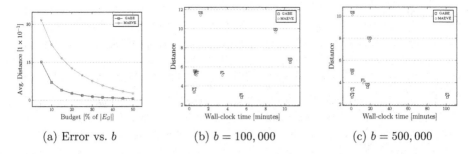

(a) Error vs. b (b) $b = 100,000$ (c) $b = 500,000$

Fig. 2. Approximation error and runtime of GABE and MAEVE (best viewed in color).

5.2 Graph Classification

We computed descriptors for graphs in Table 3 from samples of 25% and 50% of all the edges and examined their classification accuracy. We used the state-of-the-art descriptor, NetLSD [22], as a benchmark, despite the fact that our models have no direct competitors. As in [22], we used a simple 1-Nearest Neighbour classifier. We performed 10-fold cross-validation for 10 different random splits of the dataset (i.e. 100 different folds are tested on), and report the average accuracy in Table 5. Note that despite using only a fraction of edges, GABE and MAEVE give results competitive to the state of the art.

5.3 Scaling to Large Real-World Networks

We run our algorithms on massive networks (Table 4) and estimated descriptors by setting b to $100,000$ and $500,000$. In Figs. 2(b) and (c), we show the scatter plots for wall-clock time taken vs. the distance between the real vectors and their approximations (values nearer to the origin are better). We are able to process a graph with ≈260 million edges under 20 min, with relatively low error. Note that when $b = 500,000$, GABE takes 102 min to compute the descriptor for Flickr, implying that we must take the density of the graph into account for efficient computation when setting the value of b.

6 Conclusion

In this work, we present single-pass streaming algorithms to construct graph descriptors using a fixed amount of memory. We show that these descriptors provide better approximations with increasing b, are comparable with the state-of-the-art known descriptors in terms of classification accuracy, and scale well to networks with millions of vertices and edges.

References

1. Babai, L.: Graph isomorphism in quasipolynomial time. In: STOC, pp. 684–697 (2016)
2. Bento, J., Ioannidis, S.: A family of tractable graph distances. In: SDM, pp. 333–341 (2018)
3. Berlingerio, M., Koutra, D., Eliassi-Rad, T., Faloutsos, C.: Network similarity via multiple social theories. In: ASONAM, pp. 1439–1440 (2013)
4. Bo, L., Ren, X., Fox, D.: Kernel descriptors for visual recognition. In: NIPS, pp. 244–252 (2010)
5. Borgwardt, K., Kriegel, H.: Shortest-path kernels on graphs. In: ICDM, pp. 74–81 (2005)
6. Chen, X., Lui, J.: A unified framework to estimate global and local graphlet counts for streaming graphs. In: ASONAM, pp. 131–138 (2017)
7. Dutta, A., Sahbi, H.: Stochastic graphlet embedding. IEEE Trans. Neural Netw. Learn. Syst. **30**(8), 2369–2382 (2019)
8. Eswaran, D., Faloutsos, C.: SedanSpot: detecting anomalies in edge streams. In: ICDM, pp. 953–958 (2018)
9. Faloutsos, C., Koutra, D., Vogelstein, J.: DeltaCon: a principled massive-graph similarity function. In: SDM, pp. 162–170 (2013)
10. Farhan, M., Tariq, J., Zaman, A., Shabbir, M., Khan, I.: Efficient approximation algorithms for strings kernel based sequence classification. In: NIPS, pp. 6935–6945 (2017)
11. Kondor, R., Pan, H.: The multiscale laplacian graph kernel. In: NeurIPS, pp. 2982–2990 (2016)
12. Kuksa, P., Khan, I., Pavlovic, V.: Generalized similarity kernels for efficient sequence classification. In: SDM, pp. 873–882 (2012)
13. Kunegis, J.: KONECT: the Koblenz network collection. In: WWW, pp. 1343–1350 (2013)
14. Morris, C., et al.: Weisfeiler and Leman go neural: higher-order graph neural networks. In: AAAI, pp. 4602–4609 (2019)
15. Sanei-Mehri, S., Zhang, Y., Sariyüce, A.E., Tirthapura, S.: FLEET: butterfly estimation from a bipartite graph stream. In: CIKM, pp. 1201–1210 (2019)
16. Sanfeliu, A., Fu, K.: A distance measure between attributed relational graphs for pattern recognition. IEEE Trans. Syst. Man Cybern. **13**(3), 353–362 (1983)
17. Shervashidze, N., Vishwanathan, S., Petri, T., Mehlhorn, K., Borgwardt, K.: Efficient graphlet kernels for large graph comparison. In: AISTATS, pp. 488–495 (2009)
18. Shervashidze, N., et al.: Weisfeiler-Lehman graph kernels. J. Mach. Learn. Res. **12**, 2539–2561 (2011)
19. Shin, K.: WRS: waiting room sampling for accurate triangle counting in real graph streams. In: ICDM, pp. 1087–1092 (2017)
20. Shin, K., et al.: Tri-fly: distributed estimation of global and local triangle counts in graph streams. In: PAKDD, pp. 651–663 (2018)
21. Stefani, L.D., et al.: TRIÈST: counting local and global triangles in fully dynamic streams with fixed memory size. TKDD **11**(4), 43:1–43:50 (2017)
22. Tsitsulin, A., Mottin, D., Karras, P., Bronstein, A.M., Müller, E.: NetLSD: hearing the shape of a graph. In: KDD, pp. 2347–2356 (2018)
23. Verma, S., Zhang, Z.: Hunt for the unique, stable, sparse and fast feature learning on graphs. In: NeurIPS, pp. 88–98 (2017)

24. Vitter, J.S.: Random sampling with a reservoir. ACM Trans. Math. Softw. **11**(1), 37–57 (1985)
25. Wu, Z., Pan, S., Chen, F., Long, G., Zhang, C., Yu, P.S.: A comprehensive survey on graph neural networks. CoRR abs/1901.00596 (2019)
26. Xu, K., Hu, W., Leskovec, J., Jegelka, S.: How powerful are graph neural networks? In: ICLR (2019)
27. Yanardag, P., Vishwanathan, S.: Deep graph kernels. In: KDD, pp. 1365–1374 (2015)

A Framework for Feature Selection to Exploit Feature Group Structures

Kushani Perera[1]([✉]), Jeffrey Chan[2], and Shanika Karunasekera[1]

[1] University of Melbourne, Melbourne, VIC 3010, Australia
bperera@student.unimelb.edu.au, karus@unimelb.edu.au
[2] RMIT University, Melbourne, VIC 3000, Australia
jeffrey.chan@rmit.edu.au

Abstract. Filter feature selection methods play an important role in machine learning tasks when low computational costs, classifier independence or simplicity is important. Existing filter methods predominantly focus only on the input data and do not take advantage of the external sources of correlations within feature groups to improve the classification accuracy. We propose a framework which facilitates supervised filter feature selection methods to exploit feature group information from external sources of knowledge and use this framework to incorporate feature group information into minimum Redundancy Maximum Relevance (mRMR) algorithm, resulting in *GroupMRMR* algorithm. We show that *GroupMRMR* achieves high accuracy gains over mRMR (up to ~35%) and other popular filter methods (up to ~50%). *GroupMRMR* has same computational complexity as that of mRMR, therefore, does not incur additional computational costs. Proposed method has many real world applications, particularly the ones that use genomic, text and image data whose features demonstrate strong group structures.

Keywords: Filter feature selection · Feature groups · Squared $L_{0,2}$ norm minimisation

1 Introduction

Feature selection is proven to be an effective method in preparing high dimensional data for machine learning tasks such as classification. The benefits of feature selection include increasing the prediction accuracy, reducing the computational costs and producing more comprehensible data and models. Among the three main feature selection methods, filter methods are preferred to wrapper and embedded methods in applications where the computational efficiency, classifier independence, simplicity, ease of use and the stability of the results are required. Therefore, filter feature selection remains an interesting topic in many recent research areas such as biomarker identification for cancer prediction and drugs discovery, text classification and predicting defective software [3–5,10,11,16,18] and has growing interest in big data applications [19]; according to the Google

© Springer Nature Switzerland AG 2020
H. W. Lauw et al. (Eds.): PAKDD 2020, LNAI 12084, pp. 792–804, 2020.
https://doi.org/10.1007/978-3-030-47426-3_61

Scholar search results, the number of research papers published related to filter methods in year 2018 is ~1,800 of which ~170 are in gene selection area.

Most of the existing filter methods perform feature selection based on the instance-feature data alone [7]. However, in real world datasets, there are external sources of correlations within feature groups which can improve the usefulness of feature selection. For example, the genes in genomic data can be grouped based on the Gene Ontology terms they are annotated with [2] to improve bio-marker identification for the tasks such as disease prediction and drugs discovery. The words in documents can be grouped according to their semantics to select more significant words which are useful in document analysis [14]. The nearby pixels in images can be grouped together based on their spatial locality to improve selection of pixels for image classification. In software data, software metrics can be grouped according to their granularity in the code to improve the prediction of defective software [11,18]. In Sect. 4, using a text dataset as a concrete example, we demonstrate the importance of feature group information for filter feature selection to achieve good classification accuracy.

Although feature group information have been used to improve feature selection in wrapper and embedded approaches [8,12], group information is only rarely used to improve the feature selection accuracy in filter methods. Yu et al. [19] proposes a group based filter method, GroupSAOLA (GSAOLA), yet being an online method, it achieves poor accuracy, which we show experimentally. The common method used by embedded methods to exploit feature group information is minimising the L_1 and L_2 norms of the feature weight matrix, while minimising the classification error. Depending on whether the features are encouraged from the same group [8] or different groups [12], L_1 norm is used to cause inter group or intra group sparsity. Selecting features from different groups is shown to be more effective than selecting features from the same group [12].

Motivated by these approaches, we show that squared $L_{0,2}$ norm minimization of the feature weight matrix can be used to encourage features from different feature groups in filter feature selection. We propose a generic framework which combines existing filter feature ranking methods with feature weight matrix norm minimisation and use this framework to incorporate feature group information in to mRMR objective [7] because mRMR algorithm achieves high accuracy and efficiency at the same time, compared to other filter methods [3,4]. However, the proposed framework can be used to improve any other filter method, such as information gain based methods. As L_0 norm minimization is an NP-hard problem, we propose a greedy feature selection algorithm, *GroupMRMR*, to achieve the feature selection objective, which *has the same computational complexity as the mRMR algorithm. We experimentally show that for the datasets with feature group structures, GroupMRMR obtains significantly higher classification accuracy than the existing filter methods.* Our main contributions are as follows.

- We propose a framework which supports the filter feature selection methods to utilise feature group information to improve their classification accuracy.
- Using the proposed framework, we integrate feature group information into mRMR algorithm and propose a novel feature selection algorithm.

– Through extensive experiments we show that our algorithm obtains significantly higher classification accuracy than the mRMR and existing filter feature selection algorithms for no additional computational costs.

2   Related Work

Utilization of feature group information to improve prediction accuracy has been popular in embedded feature selection [8,12,17]. Among them, algorithms such as GroupLasso [8] encourage features from the same group while algorithms such as Uncorrelated GroupLasso [12] encourage features from different groups. We select the second approach as it is proven to be more effective for real data [12]. Filter feature selection is preferred over wrapper and embedded methods due to their classifier independence, computational efficiency and simplicity, yet have comparatively low prediction accuracy. However, most filter methods select the features based on the instance-feature data alone, which are coded in the data matrix, using information theoretic measures [7,13,15]. Some methods [20] use the feature group concept, yet the groups are also formed using instance-feature data to reduce feature redundancy. None of these methods take advantage of the external sources of knowledge about feature group structures. GSAOLA [19] is an online filter method which exploits feature groups, however we experimentally show that our method significantly outperforms it in terms of accuracy.

3   Preliminaries

In this section and Table 1, we introduce the terms used later in the paper. Let C be the class variable of a dataset, D, and f_i, f_j any two feature variables.

Definition 1. *Given that X and Y are two feature variables in D, with feature values x and y respectively, mutual information between X and Y, is given by* $I(X;Y) = \sum_{x \in X} \sum_{y \in Y} p(x,y) log \frac{p(x,y)}{p(x)p(y)}$.

Definition 2. *The relevancy of $f_i = Rel(f_i) = I(f_i; C)$.*

Definition 3. *The redundancy between f_i and $f_j = Red(f_i, f_j) = I(f_i; f_j)$.*

Given that $W \in \mathbb{R}^{M \times N}$, W_i is the ith row of W, W_{ij} is the jth element in W_i, the squared $L_{0,2}$ norm of W is defined as $\|W\|_{0,2}^2 = \sum_{i=1}^{M} (\|W_i\|_0)^2 = \sum_{i=1}^{M} N_i^2$ where $N_i = \|W_i\|_0 = \# (j|W_{ij} \neq 0)$. For the scenarios in which the rows of W have different importance levels, we define $\|W\|_{0,2}^2 = \sum_{i=1}^{M} \epsilon_i (\|W_i\|_0)^2 = \sum_{i=1}^{M} N_i^2 \epsilon_i$. ϵ_i is the weight of W_i. k is the required number of features.

Table 1. Frequently used definitions

F	Set of all features	I	Set of all feature group indices
S	Selected feature subset, $S \subseteq F$	G_i	Set of features in i^{th} feature group
G	Set of all feature groups	α_i	The weight of the ith feature group

4   Motivation and Background

Ignoring the external sources of correlations within feature groups may result in poor classification accuracy for the datasets whose features show a group behaviour. We demonstrate this using mRMR algorithm as a concrete example, a filter method which otherwise achieves good accuracy.

mRMR Algorithm: mRMR objective for selecting a feature subset $S \subseteq F$ of size k is as follows.

$$\max_S \sum_{f \in S} Rel(f) - \frac{1}{|S|} \sum_{f_i, f_j \in S} Red(f_i, f_j) \text{ subject to } |S| = k, k \in \mathbb{Z}^+ \quad (1)$$

To achieve the above objective, mRMR *selects one feature at a time* to maximise the relevancy of the new feature x with the class variable and to minimise its redundancy with the already selected feature set, as shown in Eq. (2).

$$\max_x Rel(x) - \frac{1}{|S|} \sum_{f \in S} Red(x, f) \quad (2)$$

Example 1: Consider selecting two features from the dataset in Fig. 1. In this dataset, each document is classified into one of the four types: Botany, Zoology, Physics or Agriculture. The rows represent the feature vector, the words which have occurred in the documents. 1 means the word has occurred within the document (or has occurred with high frequency) and 0 means otherwise.

The relevancies of the features, Apple, Rice, Cow and Sheep are 0.549, 0.443, 0.311 and 0.311, respectively. mRMR first selects **Apple**, which has the highest relevancy. The redundancies of Rice, Cow and Sheep with respect to Apple are 0.07, 0.017 and 0.016, respectively. Therefore, mRMR next selects **Rice**, the feature with the highest relevancy redundancy difference, 0.373 (0.443 - 0.07). Global mRMR optimisation approaches [15] also select {Apple, Rice}.

	d_1	d_2	d_3	d_4	d_5	d_6	d_7	d_8	d_9	d_{10}	d_{11}	d_{12}	d_{13}	d_{14}	d_{15}	d_{16}
Apple	1	1	1	0	0	0	0	0	0	0	0	0	1	1	1	0
Rice	0	1	1	1	0	0	0	0	0	0	0	0	0	0	1	1
Cow	0	0	0	0	1	1	0	0	0	0	0	0	0	0	1	1
Sheep	0	0	0	0	0	0	1	1	0	0	0	0	1	1	0	0
Class	**B**	**B**	**B**	**B**	**Z**	**Z**	**Z**	**Z**	**P**	**P**	**P**	**P**	**A**	**A**	**A**	**A**

Fig. 1. Example text document dataset. Column (d_i): a document/instance, Row: a word/feature, Class: document type, 1/0: Occurrence of a word, B: Botany, Z: Zoology, P: Physics, A: Agriculture

mRMR Algorithm {Apple, Rice}					Different Feature Groups {Apple, Sheep}				
Pattern	B	Z	P	A	**Class**	**Pattern**	B	Z	P	A	**Class**
(a=1, r=0)	25%	0%	0%	50%	**A**	(a=1, s=0)	75%	0%	0%	25%	**B**
(a=0, r=1)	25%	0%	0%	25%	**A, B**	(a=0, s=1)	0%	50%	0%	0%	**Z**
(a=0, r=0)	0%	100%	100%	0%	**P, Z**	(a=0, s=0)	25%	50%	100%	25%	**P**
(a=1, r=1)	50%	0%	0%	25%	**B**	(a=1, s=1)	0%	0%	0%	50%	**A**

Fig. 2. Value pattern probabilities created by different feature subsets in each class, A: Agriculture, B: Botany, P: Physics, Z: Zoology, Class: The class assigned to the value pattern, %: $\frac{\#(x,y)\text{value patterns in class } c}{\#\text{instances in class } c} \times 100$; $x, y \in \{0,1\}$, a: Apple, r: Rice, s: Sheep

Exploiting Feature Group Semantics: Figure 2 shows the value pattern distribution of {Apple, Sheep} and {Apple, Rice} pairs within each class. In {Apple, Sheep}, the highest probability value pattern in each class is different from one another. Therefore, each value pattern is associated with a different class, which helps distinguishing all the document types from one another. In {Apple, Rice}, there is no such distinctive relationship between the value patterns and classes. Using the value pattern distribution, the classification algorithm cannot distinguish between the Zoology and Physics documents and between Agriculture and Botany documents. *This shows that features from different groups have achieved better class discrimination.*

The reason behind the suboptimal result of the mRMR algorithm is its ignorance about the high level feature group structures. The words Apple and Rice form a group as they are plant names. Cow and Sheep form another group as they are animal names. The documents are classified according to whether they contain plant names or/and animal names, regardless of the exact plant or animal name they contain. Botany documents (d_1–d_4) contain plant names (Apple or Rice) and no animal names. Zoology documents (d_5–d_8) contain animal names (Cow or Sheep) and no plant names. This high level insight is not captured by the instance-feature data alone. Using feature group information as an external source of knowledge and encouraging features from different feature groups help solving this problem.

5   Proposed Method: GroupMRMR

We propose a framework which facilitates filter feature selection methods to exploit feature group information to achieve better classification accuracy. Using this framework, we extend mRMR algorithm into *GroupMRMR* algorithm, which encourages features from different groups to bring in different semantics which help selecting a more balanced set of features. We select mRMR algorithm for extension because it has proven good classification accuracy with low computation costs, compared to other filter feature selection methods. The feature groups are assigned weights (α_i) to represent their importance levels, and *GroupMRMR* selects more features from the groups with higher importance. Group weights may be decided according to factors such as group size and group quality. For this paper, we assume that the feature groups do not overlap but plan to investigate overlapping groups in the future.

5.1   Feature Selection Objective

Our feature selection objective includes both the filter feature selection objective and encouraging features from different feature groups. To encourage features from different groups, we minimise $\|W\|_{0,2}^2$ of the feature weight matrix, W. Using L_0 norm at intra group level enforces intra group sparsity, discouraging features to be selected from the same group. Using L_2 norm at inter group level encourages features from different feature groups [12].

Let $W \in \mathbb{R}^{|G| \times |F|}$ be a feature weight matrix such that $W_{ij} = 1$ if $f_j \in S$ and $f_j \in G_i$. Otherwise, $W_{ij} = 0$. Given that $g(W)$ is any maximisation quantity used in an existing filter feature selection objective which can be expressed a function of W and λ is a user defined parameter, our objective is to select $S \subseteq F$ to maximise the following subject to $|S| = k$, $k \in \mathbb{Z}^+$:

$$\max_S h(S) = g(W) - \lambda \|W\|_{0,2}^2 \tag{3}$$

Given that $R1 \in \mathbb{R}^{|F| \times |F|}$ is a diagonal matrix in which $R1_{jj} = Rel(f_j)$ and $R2 \in \mathbb{R}^{|F| \times |F|}$ such that $R2_{ij} = Red(f_i, f_j)$ for $i \neq j$ $R1_{ij} = 0$ for $i = j$, it can be shown that $\|WR1W^T\|_{1,1} - \frac{1}{2|S|}\|WR2W^T\|_{1,1} = \sum_{f \in S} Rel(f) - \frac{1}{|S|} \sum_{f_i, f_j \in S} Red(f_i, f_j)$, where W^T is the transpose of W. That is, the maximisation quantity in mRMR objective in Eq. (1) is a function of W. Consequently, $g(W)$ in Eq. (3) can be replaced with the mRMR objective as shown in Eq. (4).

$$\max_S h(S) = \sum_{f \in S} Rel(f) - \frac{1}{|S|} \sum_{f_i, f_j \in S} Red(f_i, f_j) - \lambda \|W\|_{0,2}^2 \tag{4}$$

Definition 4. *Given that S and G_i are as defined in Table 1, $n_i = |S \cap G_i| =$ No. of features in S and G_i.*

Given n_i is as defined in Definition 4, according to Sect. 3, $\|W\|_{0,2}^2 = \sum_{i=1}^{|G|} n_i^2$. When the feature groups have different weights, the rows of W also have different importance levels. In such scenarios, $\|W\|_{0,2}^2 = \sum_{i=1}^{|G|} n_i^2 \epsilon_i$, where $\epsilon_i = \frac{1}{\alpha_i}$ where $\alpha_i > 0$. Consequently, we can rewrite the objective in Eq. (4) as in Eq. (5) subject to $|S| = k$, $k \in \mathbb{Z}^+$. As the feature groups do not overlap, $\sum_{i=1}^{|G|} n_i = |S|$. Using Eq. (5), we present Theorem 1 that shows minimising $\|W\|_{0,2}^2$ is equivalent to encouraging features from different groups in to S.

$$\max_S h(S) = \sum_{f \in S} Rel(f) - \frac{1}{|S|} \sum_{f_i, f_j \in S} Red(f_i, f_j) - \lambda \sum_{i=1}^{|G|} \frac{n_i^2}{\alpha_i} \tag{5}$$

Theorem 1. *Given $\sum_{i=1}^{|G|} n_i = |S| = k$, minimum $\sum_{i=1}^{|G|} \frac{n_i^2}{\alpha_i}$ is obtained when $\frac{n_i}{\alpha_i} = \frac{n_j}{\alpha_j}$, $\forall i, j \in I$, where $k \in \mathbb{Z}^+$ is a constant.*

Algorithm 1. GroupMRMR algorithm

---
input : Dataset (D), Required feature count (r), Group weights $(\alpha_1 \cdots \alpha_{|G|})$
output: Selected feature subset (S)

1 $U \leftarrow F$ in D; $feaCount \leftarrow 0$; $n_1 \cdots n_{|G|} \leftarrow 0$;

2 **while** $feaCount < r$ **do**
3 $\quad$ **for** $x \in U$ **do**
4 $\quad\quad$ $p \leftarrow$ Group index of G_p where $x \in G_p$;
5 $\quad\quad$ $score_x \leftarrow Rel(x)$ - $\frac{1}{|S|} \sum_{f \in S} Red(x; f)$ - $\lambda \frac{2n_p+1}{\alpha_p}$;
6 $\quad$ **end**
7 $\quad$ $f_{max} \leftarrow \text{argmax}_{x \in U} \; score_x$;
8 $\quad$ $S \leftarrow S + f_{max}$; $U \leftarrow U$ - f_{max};
9 $\quad$ $j \leftarrow$ Group index of G_j where $f_{max} \in G_j$;
10 $\quad$ n_j++; $feaCount$++;
11 **end**
12 **return** S;

Proof. Using Lagrange multipliers method, we show minimum $\sum_{i=1}^{|G|} \frac{n_i^2}{\alpha_i}$ is achieved when $\frac{n_1}{\alpha_1} = \frac{n_2}{\alpha_2} = \cdots = \frac{n_{|G|}}{\alpha_{|G|}}$. Please refer to this link[1] for the detailed proof.

5.2   Iterative Feature Selection

As $L_{0,2}^2$ minimisation is NP-hard, we propose a heuristic algorithm to achieve the objective in Eq. (4). The algorithm selects a feature, f_t, at each iteration t to maximise the difference between $h(S_t)$ and $h(S_{t-1})$, where S_t and S_{t-1} are the feature subsets selected after Iteration t and $t-1$ respectively and $h(.)$ is as defined in Eq. (5). As there are datasets with millions of features *we seek an algorithm to select f_t with linear complexity.* Theorem 2 shows that $h(S_t)$ - $h(S_{t-1})$ can be maximised by adding the term, $\lambda \frac{2n_p+1}{\alpha_p}$ to the mRMR algorithm in Eq. (2). p is the feature group of the evaluated feature (f_x), n_p is the number of features already selected from p before Iteration t and α_p is the weight of p.

Theorem 2. *Given that S_t, S_{t-1}, $h(S_t)$, $h(S_{t-1})$, p, n_p, α_p as defined above and S'_{t-1} is the unselected feature subset after Iteration $t-1$,* $\text{argmax}_{f_x \in S'_{t-1}}$

$$h(S_t) \text{ - } h(S_{t-1}) = \text{argmax}_{f_x \in S'_{t-1}} \; Rel(f_x; c) \text{ - } \frac{1}{|S_{t-1}|} \sum_{f_i \in S_{t-1}} Red(f_x; f_i) \text{ - } \lambda \left(\frac{2n_p+1}{\alpha_p} \right).$$

Proof. To prove this, we use the fact that $|S_t|$ and $|S_{t-1}|$ are constants at a given iteration. Please refer to this link (see footnote 1) for the detailed proof.

---

[1] https://sites.google.com/view/kushani/publications.

Table 2. Dataset description. m: # features, n: # instances, c: # classes

Dataset	m	n	c	Type	Dataset	m	n	c	Type
Multi-Tissue (MT) [1]	1,000	103	4	Genomic	CNS [1]	989	42	5	Genomic
Leukemia (LK) [1]	999	38	3	Genomic	Yale [6]	1,024	165	15	Image
Multi-A [1]	5,565	103	4	Genomic	BBC [9]	9,635	2,225	5	Text
Groovy (GRV) [18]	65	757	2	Software					

Based on Theorem 2, we propose *GroupMRMR* algorithm. At each iteration, the feature score of each feature in U is computed as shown in Line 5 of Algorithm 1. The feature with the highest score is removed from U and added to S (Line 7–10 in Algorithm 1). The algorithm can be modified to encourage the features from the same group as well by setting $\lambda < 0$.

Example 1 Revisited: Next, we apply *GroupMRMR* for Example 1. We assume $\lambda = 1$ and $\alpha_i = \alpha_j = 1$, $\forall\, i, j \in I$. *GroupMRMR* first selects Apple, the feature with highest relevancy (0.549). In Iteration 2, n_p value for Rice, Cow, and Sheep are 1, 0 and 0, respectively and $\frac{2n_p+1}{\alpha_p}$ are 3, 0 and 0, respectively. The redundancies of each feature with Apple are same as computed in Sect. 4. The feature scores for Rice, Cow and Sheep are -2.627 (0.443-0.07-3), 0.294 (0.311-0.017-0) and 0.295 (0.311-0.016-0), respectively and *GroupMRMR* selects Sheep, the feature with the highest feature score. Therefore, *GroupMRMR* selects {Apple, Sheep}, the optimal feature subset, as discussed in Sect. 4.

Computation Complexity: The computational complexity of *GroupMRMR* is the same as that of mRMR, which is $O(|S||F|)$. $|S|$ and $|F|$ are the cardinalities of the selected feature subset and the complete feature set, respectively. As $|S| << |F|$, *GroupMRMR* is effectively linear with $|F|$.

6 Experiments

This section discusses the experimental results for *GroupMRMR* for real datasets.

Datasets: We evaluate *GroupMRMR*, using real datasets, which are benchmark datasets used to test group based feature selection. Table 2 shows a summary of them. Images in Yale have a 32×32 pixel map. GRV is a JIRA software defect dataset whose features are code quality metrics.

Grouping Features: The pixel map of the images are partitioned into $m \times m$ non overlapping squares such that each square is a feature group. This introduces spatial locality information, not available from just the data (instance-feature)

Table 3. Comparison of accuracies achieved by different algorithms. Row 1: The maximum accuracy (in AVGF) gained by each algorithm in each dataset. The highest maximum AVGF for each dataset is in bold letters. Row 2 (x): the number of features at which the highest AVGF is achieved. Row 3 (%): The average accuracy gain of *GroupMRMR* over the baseline. +: *GroupMRMR* wins, −: *GroupMRMR* losses

	MT	CNS	LK	Multi-A	Yale	BBC	GRV
GroupMRMR	**1**	**0.9**	**1**	**1**	**0.85**	**0.95**	**0.66**
	(110)	(90)	(20)	(90)	(500)	(800)	(10)
MRMR	0.98	0.88	0.94	0.95	0.83	0.93	0.57
	(70)	(180)	(40)	(110)	(450)	(400)	(30)
	+4%	+11%	+4%	+5%	+7%	0%	+4%
GSAOLA	0.95	0.86	1	0.95	0.84	0.93	0.56
	(60)	(50)	(50)	(170)	(600)	(1000)	(25)
	+1%	+2%	+2%	+3%	+17%	+3%	+3%
SPECCMI	0.9	0.71	1	0.95	0.80	0.93	0.61
	(90)	(180)	(190)	(190)	(500)	(1000)	(30)
	+12%	+16%	+17%	+8%	+14%	+7%	−1%
CMIM	0.95	0.83	0.88	0.93	0.8	0.92	0.61
	(200)	(160)	(90)	(80)	(600)	(800)	(25)
	+10%	+19%	+32%	+9%	+13%	+8%	−1%
ReliefF	0.95	0.83	1	**1**	0.8	0.93	0.52
	(60)	(170)	(80)	(80)	(450)	(1000)	(25)
	+2%	+6%	+3%	−1%	+12%	+2%	+6%

itself. The genes in genomic data are clustered based on the Gene Ontology term annotations as described in [2]. The number of groups is set to 0.04 of the original feature set, based on the previous findings for MT dataset [2]. Words in BBC dataset are clustered using k-means algorithm, based on the semantics available from Word2Vec [14]. We use only 2,411 features, only the words available in the Brown's corpus. Number of word groups is 50, which is selected by cross validation results on the training data. The code metrics in software defect data are grouped into five groups based on their granularity in the code [18].

Baselines: We compare *GroupMRMR* with existing filter methods which have proven high accuracy. mRMR algorithm, of which the *GroupMRMR* is an extension, is a greedy approach to achieve mRMR objective while SPECCMI [15] is a global optimisation algorithm to achieve the same. Conditional Mutual Information (CMIM) [15] is a mutual information based filter method not belonging to the mRMR family. ReliefF [13] is a distance based filter method. GSAOLA [19] is an online filter method which utilises feature group information.

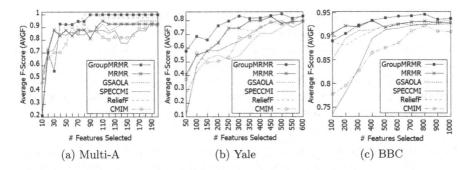

Fig. 3. Classification accuracy variation with the number of selected features

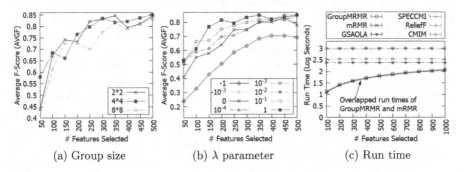

Fig. 4. Accuracy and runtime variations for Yale and BBC datasets (a) Accuracy variation with the group size (Yale) (b) Accuracy variation with λ (Yale) (c) Average run time variation (in log scale) of the algorithms (BBC). 95% confidence interval error bars are too small to be visible due to the high precision (standard deviations $\sim$2 s)

Evaluation Method: The classifier's prediction accuracy on the test dataset with selected features is considered as the prediction accuracy of the feature selection algorithm. It is measured in terms of the Macro-F1, the average of the F1-scores for each class (AVGF). Average accuracy is the average of AVGFs for all the selected feature numbers up to the point algorithm accuracies converge. The log value of the average run time (measured in seconds) is reported.

Experimental Setup: We split each dataset, 60% instances for training set and 40% for test set, using stratified random sampling method. Feature selection is performed on the training set and the classifier is trained on the training set with the selected features. The classifier is then used to predict the labels of the test set. Due to the small sample size of the datasets we do not use a separate validation set for tuning λ. Instead, we select $\lambda \in [0, 2]$, which gives the highest classification accuracy on the training set. The classifier used is the Support Vector Machine. For image data, default $m = 4$. For genomic data, $\alpha_i = 1, \forall i$. For other datasets, $\alpha_i = \frac{|G_i|}{|F|}$ (G_i, F are defined in Table 1).

Experiment 1: Measures the classification accuracy obtained for the datasets with selected features. *Experiment 2:* Performs feature selection for image datasets with different feature group sizes: $m \times m$ ($m = 2,4,8$). This tests the *effect of the group size* on the classification accuracy. *Experiment 3:* Runs *GroupMRMR* for different $\lambda \in [-1, 1]$. This tests the *effect of* λ on the classification accuracy. *Experiment 4:* Executes each feature selection algorithm 20 times and compute the average run time to evaluate *algorithm efficiency.*

Experimental Results: Table 3 shows that *GroupMRMR achieves the highest AVGF in all datasets over baselines.* In LK dataset, the 100% accuracy is achieved with a lower number of features than baselines. *GroupMRMR* achieves higher or same average accuracy compared to baselines in 32 out of 35 cases. Figure 3 shows that, despite the slightly low average accuracy compared to ReliefF, *GroupMRMR* maintains a higher accuracy than baselines in Multi-A for most of the selected feature numbers. Other datasets also show similar results, yet we show only three graphs due to the space limitations. Please refer to this link (see footnote 1) to see all the results graphs. The maximum accuracy gain of *GroupMRMR* over the accuracy gained by the complete feature set is 2%, 10%, 2%, 2%, 1% and 6% for MT, CNS, Multi-A, Yale, BBC and GRV datasets, respectively. The maximum accuracy gain of *GroupMRMR* is 50% over SPECCMI in Yale dataset at 50 selected features. The highest accuracy gain of *GroupMRMR* over mRMR is 35% in CNS dataset at 70 selected features. Figure 4a shows that the classification accuracy of *GroupMRMR* for 8×8 image partitions is less than for 4×4 and 2×2 partitions. Figure 4b shows that the *classification accuracy is not much sensitive to* λ in the $[10^{-3}, 1]$ range, yet degrades to a large extent when $\lambda < 0$. Figure 4c shows that the *runtime of GroupMRMR is almost the same as the run time of mRMR algorithm and lower than most of the other baseline methods* ($\sim$10 times lower than SPECCMI and CMIM for BBC dataset).

Evaluation Insights: *GroupMRMR consistently shows good classification accuracy compared to baselines* for all the datasets (highest average accuracy and highest maximum accuracy in almost all datasets). The equal run times of *GroupMRMR* and mRMR show that the *accuracy gain is obtained for no additional costs* and supports the time complexity analysis in Sect. 5. Better prediction accuracy is obtained for small groups because large feature groups resemble the original feature set with no groupings. This shows the importance of feature group information to gain high feature selection accuracy. The *accuracy is lower when the features are encouraged from the same group* ($\lambda < 0$) *instead from different groups* ($\lambda > 0$), which supports our hypothesis. The classification accuracy is less sensitive to $\lambda \geq 10^{-3}$, therefore *parameter tuning is less required.*

7 Conclusion

We propose a framework which facilitates filter feature selection methods to exploit feature group information as an external source of information. Using this framework, we incorporate feature group information into mRMR algorithm, resulting in *GroupMRMR* algorithm. We show that compared to baselines, *GroupMRMR* achieves high classification accuracy for the datasets with feature group structures. The run time of *GroupMRMR* is same as the run time of mRMR, which is lower than many existing feature selection algorithms. Our future work include experimenting the proposed framework for other filter methods and detecting whether a dataset contains feature group structures.

Acknowledgements. This work is supported by the Australian Government.

References

1. Cancer program datasets. http://portals.broadinstitute.org/cgi-bin/cancer/data sets.cgi. Accessed Nov 2019
2. Acharya, S., Saha, S., Nikhil, N.: Unsupervised gene selection using biological knowledge: application in sample clustering. BMC Bioinform. **18**(1), 513 (2017)
3. Alirezanejad, M., Enayatifar, R., Motameni, H., et al.: Heuristic filter feature selection methods for medical datasets. Genomics (2019). https://doi.org/10.1016/j.ygeno.2019.07.002
4. Bolón-Canedo, V., Rego-Fernández, D., Peteiro-Barral, D., Alonso-Betanzos, A., Guijarro-Berdiñas, B., Sánchez-Maroño, N.: On the scalability of feature selection methods on high-dimensional data. Knowl. Inf. Syst. **56**(2), 395–442 (2017). https://doi.org/10.1007/s10115-017-1140-3
5. Bommert, A., Sun, X., Bischl, B., et al.: Benchmark for filter methods for feature selection in high-dimensional classification data. CSDA **143**, 106839 (2020)
6. Cai, D., He, X., Hu, Y., et al.: Learning a spatially smooth subspace for face recognition. In: Proceedings of IEEE CVPR 2007, pp. 1–7 (2007)
7. Ding, C., Peng, H.: Minimum redundancy feature selection from microarray gene expression data. JBCB **3**(02), 185–205 (2005)
8. Friedman, J., Hastie, T., Tibshirani, R.: A note on the group lasso and a sparse group lasso. arXiv preprint arXiv:1001.0736 (2010)
9. Greene, D., Cunningham, P.: Practical solutions to the problem of diagonal dominance in kernel document clustering. In: Proceedings of the 23rd ICML, pp. 377–384 (2006). https://doi.org/10.1145/1143844.1143892
10. Hancer, E., Xue, B., Zhang, M.: Differential evolution for filter feature selection based on information theory and feature ranking. Knowl.-Based Syst. **140**, 103–119 (2018). https://doi.org/10.1016/j.knosys.2017.10.028
11. Jiarpakdee, J., Tantithamthavorn, C., Treude, C.: Autospearman: Automatically mitigating correlated metrics for interpreting defect models. arXiv preprint arXiv:1806.09791 (2018)
12. Kong, D., Liu, J., Liu, B., et al.: Uncorrelated group lasso. In: AAAI, pp. 1765–1771 (2016)
13. Kononenko, I.: Estimating attributes: analysis and extensions of RELIEF. In: Bergadano, F., De Raedt, L. (eds.) ECML 1994. LNCS, vol. 784, pp. 171–182. Springer, Heidelberg (1994). https://doi.org/10.1007/3-540-57868-4_57

14. Lilleberg, J., Zhu, Y., Zhang, Y.: Support vector machines and word2vec for text classification with semantic features. In: Proceedings of the 14th IEEE ICCI* CC, pp. 136–140 (2015). https://doi.org/10.1109/ICCI-CC.2015.7259377
15. Nguyen, X.V., Chan, J., Romano, S., et al.: Effective global approaches for mutual information based feature selection. In: Proceedings of the 20th ACM SIGKDD, pp. 512–521 (2014). https://doi.org/10.1145/2623330.2623611
16. Uysal, A.K., Gunal, S.: A novel probabilistic feature selection method for text classification. Knowl.-Based Syst. **36**, 226–235 (2012)
17. Wang, J., Wang, M., Li, P., et al.: Online feature selection with group structure analysis. IEEE TKDE **27**(11), 3029–3041 (2015)
18. Yatish, S., Jiarpakdee, J., Thongtanunam, P., et al.: Mining software defects: should we consider affected releases? In: Proceedings of the 41st International Conference on Software Engineering, pp. 654–665. IEEE Press (2019)
19. Yu, K., Wu, X., Ding, W., et al.: Scalable and accurate online feature selection for big data. ACM TKDD **11**(2), 16 (2016). https://doi.org/10.1145/2976744
20. Yu, L., Ding, C., Loscalzo, S.: Stable feature selection via dense feature groups. In: Proceedings of the 14th ACM SIGKDD, pp. 803–811 (2008). https://doi.org/10.1145/1401890.1401986

Group Based Unsupervised Feature Selection

Kushani Perera[1]([✉]), Jeffrey Chan[2], and Shanika Karunasekera[1]

[1] University of Melbourne, Melbourne, VIC 3010, Australia
bperera@student.unimelb.edu.au, karus@unimelb.edu.au
[2] RMIT University, Melbourne, VIC 3000, Australia
jeffrey.chan@rmit.edu.au

Abstract. Unsupervised feature selection is an important task in machine learning applications, yet challenging due to the unavailability of class labels. Although a few unsupervised methods take advantage of external sources of correlations within feature groups in feature selection, they are limited to genomic data, and suffer poor accuracy because they ignore input data or encourage features from the same group. We propose a framework which facilitates unsupervised filter feature selection methods to exploit input data and feature group information simultaneously, encouraging features from different groups. We use this framework to incorporate feature group information into Laplace Score algorithm. Our method achieves high accuracy compared to other popular unsupervised feature selection methods ($\sim$30% maximum improvement of Normalized Mutual Information (NMI)) with low computational costs ($\sim$50 times lower than embedded methods on average). It has many real world applications, particularly the ones that use image, text and genomic data, whose features demonstrate strong group structures.

Keywords: Unsupervised feature selection · Feature groups · $L_{1,1}$ norm minimisation.

1 Introduction

Feature selection is an important task in preparing high dimensional data for machine learning tasks. It improves the prediction accuracy and simplicity of the learning models and reduces the computational costs. Unlike deep learning methods, feature selection identifies the important features that can be interpreted by the humans when explaining AI decisions (E.g.: genes related to certain diseases [12]). Feature selection methods are of two types, supervised and unsupervised, based on the availability of class labels in data. Among them, unsupervised feature selection has wide applicability because data in most real world scenarios are unlabelled. For example, there is a vast amount of text and image data in the web, yet the label information, such as the subject of a tweet, the topic of an image is only rarely available. Due to the unavailability of labels,

H. W. Lauw et al. (Eds.): PAKDD 2020, LNAI 12084, pp. 805–817, 2020.
https://doi.org/10.1007/978-3-030-47426-3_62

unsupervised approach is more challenging than the supervised approach and achieving good accuracy remains a challenge.

Many unsupervised feature selection methods evaluate features using instance-feature data alone, which is available in the form of the data matrix [9, 14]. In contrast, recent work shows that features can be grouped according to various criteria and this group information can improve the usefulness of the feature selection [17]. For example, the nearby pixels in images can be grouped together considering the spatial locality to improve selection of pixels for image analysis. The words in document datasets can be grouped according to their semantics [13] to improve selection of words for document analysis. Genes in genomic data can be grouped using Gene Ontology information [3] to improve bio-marker identification for disease prediction and drug discovery. We show that considering this group structure can enable selection of a better feature subset in real world applications. In Sect. 4, we illustrate this using a concrete text data example.

In contrast to supervised feature selection [11], little work exist in unsupervised feature selection which exploits feature group information. The existing ones are limited to genomic data in which feature selection is limited to simple methods such as selecting the centroids of feature groups [3]. They do not use group information in combination with instance-feature data, which is also useful for feature selection. Hierarchical Unsupervised Feature Selection (HUFS) [17] uses feature group information together with instance-feature data to improve feature selection accuracy and is applicable for different data types. Like many state of the art feature selection methods, HUFS is also an embedded approach, yet embedded methods do not have a significant advantage in unsupervised feature selection due to the unavailability of class labels. Compared to embedded methods, filter methods are fast and produce more generic solutions [15]. Consequently, they are still popular in applications such as bio-marker identification [12] and have growing interest in big data applications [7,16,20].

We propose a framework which helps incorporating feature group information into unsupervised filter feature selection methods. To demonstrate the usefulness of our approach, we incorporate feature group information into Laplace Score (LS) algorithm [9], a well established feature selection method which achieves good accuracy with very low computational costs. We mathematically show that the proposed feature selection objective can be represented as a standard quadratic optimisation problem, such that standard optimisation algorithms can be used to solve the optimisation problem. However, quadratic programming optimisation algorithms are slow and cannot scale to larger problems which are typically encountered, hence we also propose a greedy optimisation method, *Group Laplace Score (GLS)*, which is faster than quadratic optimisation algorithms, yet show comparable performance. *Through extensive experiments we show that GLS achieves high clustering performance with low computational costs*, compared to existing feature selection methods. Our main contributions are as follows.

- We propose a framework which facilitates unsupervised filter feature selection methods to exploit the knowledge about feature groups to achieve higher clustering performance.
- We use the proposed framework to incorporate feature group information into LS algorithm and propose a new feature selection algorithm, *GLS*.
- We experimentally show that *GLS* obtains significantly higher clustering performance than the existing feature selection algorithms.

2   Related Work

Many unsupervised feature selection methods, both similarity preserving (filter) [9,19] and embedded [6,8,10,14] methods, are based on input data alone and rarely take the advantage of the external sources of knowledge about feature group structures. The feature groups used by some feature selection methods are also formed with input data [15,18]. Some domain specific unsupervised methods [3] are proposed for selecting genes from different gene groups, yet they do not combine group based feature selection with instance-feature data which is also useful for feature selection. In contrast, HUFS uses feature group information to improve the instance-feature data based feature selection and is applicable for different data types. However, HUFS encourages features from the same group which is not effective in most real world applications [11]. In contrast, our method encourages features from different groups and we experimentally show that our method outperforms HUFS in terms of accuracy and efficiency. Compared to HUFS, our method requires less parameter tuning too.

3   Preliminaries

This section discusses some frequently used definitions and terms in the paper. $X \in \mathbb{R}^{n \times m}$ is the input data matrix, where n is the number of instances and m is the number of features in X. F is the set of all features in X, $S \subseteq F$ is the selected feature subset, $f_i \in F$ the ith feature in X and k is the number of features to be selected. G_i is the set of features in i^{th} feature group and r is number of groups. Given a matrix $A \in \mathbb{R}^{n \times m}$, $a_{i,j}$, is its element in i^{th} row and j^{th} column. $L_{1,1}$ norm of A, $\|A\|_{1,1} = \sum_{i=1}^{n} \sum_{j=1}^{m} |a_{i,j}|$.

Definition 1. *The feature indicator matrix, $U \in \mathbb{R}^{m \times m}$, is a diagonal matrix whose i^{th} diagonal entry, $u_{i,i} = u_i = 1$ if the ith feature in X is selected into S and $u_{i,i} = u_i = 0$ otherwise. $u_{i,j} = 0$ $(\forall\ i \neq j)$.*

Definition 2. *Given that S is the selected feature subset and G_i is the set of features in i^{th} feature group, $w_i = \frac{No.\ of\ features\ in\ S\ and\ G_i}{No.\ of\ features\ in\ S} = \frac{|S \cap G_i|}{|S|}$.*

	d_1	d_2	d_3	d_4	d_5	d_6
Bank	**13**	**10**	0	0	0	**1**
Patient	0	0	**20**	0	0	0
Cell	0	0	0	**16**	0	0
Google	0	**1**	0	0	**13**	0
Class	**B**	**B**	**H**	**H**	**T**	**T**

(a) Example text dataset. Column
(d_i): a document/instance, Row:
a word/feature, Class: document
type, B: Business, H: Health, T:
Technical

(b) Cluster results for {Bank, Patient, Google}

(c) Cluster results for {Bank, Patient, Cell}

Fig. 1. Feature selection in the text dataset in Example 1

4   Motivation and Background

In this section, we demonstrate the importance of external feature group information for feature selection accuracy, using Reuters (RT) text dataset [1] as a concrete example. As the complete dataset is too large, we select only some instances and feature values which are helpful for the discussion.

Example 1: Figure 1a shows a part of the RT dataset in which the words are the features and documents (d_i) are the instances. Feature values represent the occurrence frequency of each word in each document. Each document is one of the three types: Business, Health, Technical, but in the unsupervised feature selection, the algorithm is not provided this. The feature selection problem is to select three features which achieves the best clustering performance.

The features which result in small distances between the same class instances and large distances between different class instances help the same class instances to get clustered together. For example, with respect to "Bank", business documents have lower distances between each other and large distances with the rest (Manhattan distance of 3 between d_1 and d_2 and 13 between d_1 and d_5). Therefore, "Bank" discriminates business documents from the rest. Similarly, "Google" and "Patient" discriminate some technical (d_5) and health (d_3) documents. {Bank, Patient, Google} collectively discriminate between different class instances from one another. Figure 1b shows the k-means (k = 3) cluster assignments for this feature subset. Only d_4 is assigned to a wrong cluster and cluster purities are 1,1, and 0.67. Clustering performance in terms of NMI [9] is 0.74.

In contrast, no feature in {Bank, Patient, Cell} discriminates between business and technical documents and "Patient" and "Cell" cause large distances between the health documents, the same class instances, leading to poor clustering performance. Figure 1c shows that d_4, d_5, d_6 are assigned to wrong clusters, resulting in impure clusters (cluster purities of 1, 1, and 0.5) compared to the previous case. Clustering performance in terms of NMI is 0.65. Therefore, {Bank, Patient, Google} is better compared to {Bank, Patient, Cell}. However, "Cell"

$$
\begin{array}{c}
\;d_1\;d_2\;d_3\;d_4\;d_5\;d_6 \\
\begin{array}{c} d_1 \\ d_2 \\ d_3 \\ d_4 \\ d_5 \\ d_6 \end{array}
\left[
\begin{array}{cccccc}
1 & -1 & 0 & 0 & 0 & 0 \\
-1 & 2 & 0 & 0 & 0 & -1 \\
0 & 0 & 1 & 0 & 0 & -1 \\
0 & 0 & 0 & 1 & 0 & -1 \\
0 & 0 & 0 & 0 & 1 & -1 \\
0 & -1 & -1 & -1 & -1 & 4
\end{array}
\right]
\end{array}
$$

(a) Laplace Matrix (L)

$$
\begin{array}{c}
\;b\;p\;c\;g \\
\begin{array}{c} b \\ p \\ c \\ g \end{array}
\left[
\begin{array}{cccc}
0 & 0 & 0 & 0 \\
0 & 0 & 1 & 0 \\
0 & 1 & 0 & 0 \\
0 & 0 & 0 & 0
\end{array}
\right]
\end{array}
$$

(b) G

$$
\begin{array}{c}
\;b\;p\;c\;g \\
\begin{array}{c} b \\ p \\ c \\ g \end{array}
\left[
\begin{array}{cccc}
1 & 0 & 0 & 0 \\
0 & 1 & 0 & 0 \\
0 & 0 & 1 & 0 \\
0 & 0 & 0 & 0
\end{array}
\right]
\end{array}
$$

(c) U for {Bank, Patient, Cell}

$$
\begin{array}{c}
\;b\;p\;c\;g \\
\begin{array}{c} b \\ p \\ c \\ g \end{array}
\left[
\begin{array}{cccc}
0 & 0 & 0 & 0 \\
0 & 0 & 1 & 0 \\
0 & 1 & 0 & 0 \\
0 & 0 & 0 & 0
\end{array}
\right]
\end{array}
$$

(d) G' for {Bank, Patient, Cell}

Fig. 2. Matrices for the dataset in Example 1. b: Bank, p: Patient, c: Cell, g: Google

and "Google" have very similar feature value distributions, and class labels are not available for feature selection. Therefore, "Cell" and "Google" cannot be differentiated from one another using instance feature data alone. We show this using LS algorithm, which selects the features which best preserve the locality structure of the instances, as a concrete example.

LS Algorithm: Given that A is the adjacency matrix between the instances, D is the degree matrix and L is the Laplace matrix such that $L = D - A$, the Laplace score of a feature f, $l_f = \frac{\tilde{f}^T L \tilde{f}}{\tilde{f}^T D \tilde{f}}$, where $\tilde{f} = f - \mu_f$ and μ_f is the mean of f. LS objective for selecting k features is shown in Eq. (1). LS algorithm achieves this by selecting the features with k minimum Laplace scores. Figure 2a shows L for RT dataset, assuming a 1-Nearest Neighbour A. Laplace scores for "Bank", "Cell", "Patient" and "Google" are 0.39, 1.06, 1.06 and 1.1, respectively. The selected feature subset is therefore {Bank, Cell, Patient}, which is not optimal.

$$
\min_{S} \sum_{\tilde{f} \in S} \frac{\tilde{f}^T L \tilde{f}}{\tilde{f}^T D \tilde{f}} \text{ subject to } |S| = k \tag{1}
$$

Using Feature Group Information: Consider using Wordnet [13] as an external source of knowledge for Example 1. Wordnet shows a high semantic similarity (0.7) between "Cell" and "Patient", and low similarity between other feature pairs (0.1 between "Google" and "Bank"). Three feature groups can be created based on semantic similarity. Group 1: {Bank}, Group 2: {Patient, Cell}, Group 3: {Google}. Encouraging features from different groups results in {Bank, Patient, Google}, which is optimal. This is because *semantically similar words tend to occur in similar types of documents*. Consequently, words from different groups discriminate different types of documents from one another and result in lower distances between the same type of documents. For example, given "Patient", selecting "Google" (from a different group), results in a lower distance between d_3 and d_4 than selecting "Cell" (from the same group). Opposed to "Cell", "Google" also discriminates between business and technical documents.

5   Proposed Method

We propose a framework which facilitates the unsupervised filter feature selection methods to encourage features from different groups and use this framework to incorporate feature group information into LS algorithm. When the feature groups have different importance levels based on factors such as group size and group quality, more features are encouraged from the groups with higher importance. Proposed feature selection objective can be solved using quadratic optimisation methods, but we also propose a greedy approach, GLS, which achieves the same performance faster. In this paper, we focus on non-overlapped groups, yet the proposed method can easily be extended to overlapped groups as well.

Modelling Feature Group Information: We define $G \in \mathbb{R}^{m \times m}$, the feature group matrix. If f_i, $f_j \in F$ are in the same group, $g_{i,j} = g_{j,i} = 1$. Otherwise $g_{i,j} = g_{j,i} = 0$. $\forall i = 1, \ldots, m$, $g_{i,i} = 0$. G for Example 1 is shown in Fig. 2b. Multiplying G by U twice makes the rows and columns of G corresponding to the unselected features all zeros. This results in $G' = UGU \in \mathbb{R}^{m \times m}$, feature group matrix of the features in S. The number of zeros in G' increases when the features in S are from different feature groups and all the elements in G' ≥ 0. Therefore, given that k features are to be selected, to encourage features from different feature groups, our objective is to select U to minimise $\|UGU\|_{1,1}$ subject to $\|U\|_{1,1} = k$.

Figure 2c and d show U and G' when $S = \{$Bank, Patient, Cell$\}$, for which $\|G'\|_{1,1} = 2$. When $S = \{$Bank, Patient, Google$\}$ U is a diagonal matrix where $diag(U) = [1, 1, 0, 1]$, $G' \in \mathbb{R}^{4 \times 4}$ is a matrix of all zeros and $\|G'\|_{1,1} = 0$. This shows that $\|UGU\|_{1,1}$ is minimal when the features are selected from different groups. When the feature groups have different importance levels, to encourage more features from the groups with higher importance, we set $g_{i,j} = g_{j,i} = \frac{1}{\alpha_i}$ (instead of 1), where α_i *is the weight of* G_i.

Input Data Based Feature Selection: We next propose a common framework to combine group based feature selection with any unsupervised filter feature ranking method. Let Q be a diagonal matrix, where, $q_{i,i} = l_i$, where l_i is the feature score of f_i, in terms of its capability to preserve the sample similarity. $Q' = UQU$ is the feature score matrix for selected features in S. Q' is a diagonal matrix in which $q'_{i,i} = l_i$ if $f_i \in S$ and $q'_{i,i} = 0$ otherwise. Given that $l_i \geq 0, \forall i$, the feature selection objective is to select U to minimise or maximise $\|UQU\|_{1,1}$ subject to $\|U\|_{1,1} = k$. Minimisation or maximisation is decided based on the algorithm used to compute l_i.

Theorem 1 shows that Laplace score is always non-negative and eligible for Q. Consequently, Eq. (1) can be reformulated as minimising $\|UQU\|_{1,1}$ subject to $\|U\|_{1,1} = k$, where $l_i =$ Laplace score of f_i. For example, in Example 1, $diag(Q)$ $= [0.39, 1.06, 1.06, 1.1]$. When $S = \{$Bank, Patient, Cell$\}$, $diag(Q') = [0.39, 1.06, 1.06, 0]$ and $\|Q'\|_{1,1} = 2.51$. When $S = \{$Bank, Patient, Google$\}$, $diag(Q') = [0.39, 1.06, 0, 1.1]$ and $\|Q'\|_{1,1} = 2.55$. Therefore, minimal $\|UQU\|_{1,1}$ is achieved for {Bank, Patient, Cell}, the same feature subset selected by LS algorithm. For the rest of the paper, we assume l_i is computed using Laplace score, therefore minimise $\|UQU\|_{1,1}$. Maximisation is equivalent to minimising $-\|UQU\|_{1,1}$.

Theorem 1. *Given that l_i is the Laplace score of $f_i \in F$, $l_i \geq 0$, $\forall\, i = 1, \cdots, m$.*

Proof. Because L and D are positive definite. Refer to this link[1] for the proof.

Feature Selection Objective: The feature selection objective which combines both group based feature selection and input data based feature selection is shown in Eq. (2). λ is a user defined parameter. In this paper, we assign a fixed value for λ. In future, we plan to itcratively decide λ value for each feature selected. Based on Theorem 2, we reformulate Eq. (2) into Eq. (3).

$$\min_{U} \|UQU\|_{1,1} + \lambda\|UGU\|_{1,1} \text{ subject to } \|U\|_{1,1} = k \tag{2}$$

$$\min_{U} \|U(Q + \lambda G)U\|_{1,1} \text{ subject to } \|U\|_{1,1} = k \tag{3}$$

Theorem 2. *Given $\lambda \geq 0$, $\|UQU\|_{1,1} + \lambda\|UGU\|_{1,1} = \|U(Q + \lambda G)U\|_{1,1}$*

Proof. Because $u_{i,j}$, $q_{i,j}$, $g_{i,j} \geq 0\ \forall\, i,j$. Refer to this link (See footnote 1) for the proof.

Given $u = [u_1, \cdots, u_m]^T$, where u_i is the ith diagonal element of U, Theorem 3 shows that $\|U(Q + \lambda G)U\|_{1,1}$ can be reformulated as a quadratic function of u. Therefore, to solve Eq. (3), we use two approaches: (1) Standard Quadratic Programming (QP) methods (2) Greedy method (GLS algorithm). As the QP method, we use the MATLAB inbuilt "fmincon" function with "interior point" method, but omitted the details due to space limitations. Please refer to this link (See footnote 1) for details. The greedy method showed comparable accuracy to QP method, yet faster. Therefore, in this paper, we focus on the greedy method.

Theorem 3. *Given that $H = Q + \lambda G$, and u as defined above, $\|UHU\|_{1,1} = u^T H u = h(u)$, that is $\|UHU\|_{1,1}$ is a quadratic function of u.*

Proof. Please refer to this link (See footnote 1) for the proof.

Greedy Method: As discussed, $\|U(Q + \lambda G)U\|_{1,1} = \|UHU\|_{1,1} = h(u)$. At each Iteration t, GLS selects a feature, f_t, such that $f_t = \operatorname{argmin}_{f_x \in S'_{t-1}} h(u_t) - h(u_{t-1})$, where u_{t-1} and u_t are the selected feature indicator vectors (u) after Iteration $(t-1)$ and t, respectively and S'_{t-1} is the unselected feature subset after Iteration $t-1$. According to Theorem 4, this is equivalent to selecting $f_t = \operatorname{argmin}_{f_x \in S'_{t-1}} l_x + \lambda \frac{w_i}{\alpha_i}$, where f_x is any feature in S'_{t-1}, l_x is the Laplace score of f_x, G_i the feature group of f_x, α_i is the weight of G_i, $w_i = \frac{|S_{t-1} \cap G_i|}{S_{t-1}}$ and S_{t-1} is the selected feature subset after Iteration $t-1$. Therefore, as shown in Algorithm 1, GLS selects f_x to minimise this quantity (Line 5), which *avoids complex matrix multiplication operations.*

---

[1] https://sites.google.com/view/kushani/publications.

Algorithm 1: GLS algorithm

---

input : Dataset (X), Requested feature count (k), Group weights $(\alpha_1 \cdots \alpha_r)$
output: Selected feature subset (S)

1 $S' \leftarrow F$ in X; $S \leftarrow \emptyset$; $fCount \leftarrow 0$; $n_1 \cdots n_r \leftarrow 0$;

2 **while** $fCount < k$ **do**
3 $\quad$ **for** $x \in S'$ **do**
4 $\quad\quad$ $i \leftarrow$ Group index of G_i where $x \in G_i$;
5 $\quad\quad$ $score_x \leftarrow l_x + \lambda \frac{w_i}{\alpha_i}$;
6 $\quad$ **end**
7 $\quad$ $f_{min} \leftarrow \mathrm{argmin}_{x \in S'}\ score_x$;
8 $\quad$ $S \leftarrow S + f_{min}$; $S' \leftarrow S' - f_{min}$;
9 $\quad$ $j \leftarrow$ Group index of G_j where $f_{min} \in G_j$;
10 $\quad$ $n_j{+}{+}$; $w_j \leftarrow \frac{n_j}{|S|}$; $fCount{+}{+}$;

11 **end**
12 **return** S;

Theorem 4. *Given that S_{t-1}, S'_{t-1}, u_{t-1}, u_t, $f_x \in S'_{t-1}$, l_x, w_i and α_i are as defined above, $\mathrm{argmin}_{f_x \in S'_{t-1}} h(u_t) - h(u_{t-1}) = \mathrm{argmin}_{f_x \in S'_{t-1}} l_x + \lambda \frac{w_i}{\alpha_i}$.*

Proof. Refer to this link (See footnote 1) for the proof.

Example 1 Revisited: We apply *GLS* for Example 1, given the feature groups created in Sect. 4. $\lambda = 1$, $\alpha_i = 1\ \forall = i$. *GLS* first selects "Bank" which has the minimum Laplace score (0.39). In Iteration 2, for all remaining features, $w_i = 0$. Therefore, *GLS* selects "Patient" or "Cell", which has next minimum Laplace score (1.06). Assume it selects "Patient". In Iteration 3, for "Cell" and "Google", $w_i = 0.5$ and 0, respectively and $l_i + \lambda \frac{w_i}{\alpha_i} = 1.56$ and 1.1, respectively. *GLS* selects "Google" which has minimal feature score. Therefore, the selected feature subset is {Bank, Patient, Google}, which is optimal according to Sect. 4.

Computation Complexity Analysis: Given F and S are as defined in Sect. 3, time complexity for computing the Laplace score is $O(|F|)$. The complexity of the iterative group based feature selection (Line 2–11 in Algorithm 1), is $O(|S||F|)$. As $|S| << |F|$, the time complexity of *GLS* is linear to $|F|$.

6 Experimental Evaluation

In this section, we discuss the experimental results obtained by *GLS* algorithm.

Datasets: We evaluate *GLS*, using real datasets, which are benchmark datasets used to test group based feature selection. Table 1 shows a summary of them. Yale, ORL and COIL20 have a 32×32 pixel map and USPS a 16×16 pixel map.

Feature Grouping: To introduce spatial locality information, which is not available from the input data matrix alone, we partition the pixel map of an image into $p \times p$ non overlapping squares. Each square is a feature group. Default p for USPS is 2 and 4 for other image datasets. In text data, pairwise semantic similarities between the words are found using WordNet [13] and words are clustered based on the similarity values, using spectral clustering. We use only 2,468 words, available in WordNet. Genes in genomic data are clustered based on Gene Ontology information as discussed in [3]. Number of groups is set to 0.04 of the original feature set based on the previous findings for MT dataset [3].

Table 1. Dataset description. m: # features, n: # instances, c: # classes

Dataset	m	n	c	Type	Dataset	m	n	c	Type
Multi-Tissue (MT) [2]	1,000	103	4	Genomic	Yale [5]	1,024	165	15	Image
CNS [2]	989	42	5	Genomic	ORL [5]	1,024	400	40	Image
DLBCL-B [2]	661	180	3	Genomic	COIL20 [4]	1,024	1,440	20	Image
Multi-B [2]	5,565	32	4	Genomic	USPS [4]	256	9,298	10	Image
Reuters (RT) [1]	3,068	294	6	Text					

Baselines: As baselines, we use LS algorithm and Spectral Feature Selection SPEC [19] as similarity preserving methods and Multi Cluster Feature Selection (MCFS) [6], Robust Unsupervised Feature Selection (RUFS) [14] and HUFS as embedded methods. RUFS has proven high performance compared to many existing embedded methods and HUFS uses feature group information similar to our method. RUFS and MCFS use two different approaches to control feature redundancy ($L_{2,1}$ norm vs. L_1 norm). k-medoid (KM) [3] is specific for genomic datasets, therefore, we use it with genomic data only. For HUFS, we consider the complete pixel hierarchy as described in [17].

Evaluation Criteria: We consider the clustering performance as the measure of feature selection accuracy and evaluate it in terms of NMI [9]. k-means is the cluster method used. It is run 20 times and we report the average *NMI*. SD is the standard deviation of NMI obtained for the 20 iterations. *Average accuracy of an algorithm in a dataset* is the average of the NMIs obtained for all the selected feature numbers in that dataset. We select features up to the point all algorithm accuracies converge. Algorithm run times are measured in seconds.

Experimental Setup: We split each dataset, 60% instances for training set and 40% for test test, using stratified random sampling method and remove the class labels from both. We perform feature selection on the training dataset and evaluate the clustering performance of the test set, using only the selected feature subset. By default, $\alpha_i = 1$ for all feature groups and $\lambda = 1$.

Table 2. Comparison of the clustering performances of different algorithms. Row 1: maximum NMI of each algorithm for each dataset. The highest maximum NMI for each dataset is in bold letters. Row 2 (±): SD corresponding to maximum NMI. Row 3 (x): the number of features at which the maximum NMI is achieved. Row 4: Algorithm rankings in terms of average accuracy (1 corresponds to the highest average accuracy)

	Yale	ORL	COIL20	USPS	RT	MT	CNS	DLBCL-B	Multi-B
GLS	**0.69**	**0.82**	**0.78**	0.62	**0.34**	**0.76**	**0.71**	0.49	**0.74**
	±0.01	±0.01	±0.01	±0.00	±0.03	±0.00	±0.04	±0.02	±0.00
	(400)	(450)	(200)	(200)	(40)	(20)	(15)	(200)	(40)
	1	1	1	1	1	1	1	1	1
LS	0.67	0.82	0.78	**0.63**	0.31	0.64	0.62	**0.5**	0.69
	±0.02	±0.01	±0.01	±0.01	±0.04	±0.00	±0.07	±0.02	±0.00
	(300)	(900)	(850)	(150)	(35)	(120)	(120)	(180)	(50)
	3	5	5	2	2	5	5	4	3
SPEC	0.67	0.82	0.78	0.62	0.31	0.68	0.59	0.48	0.42
	±0.02	±0.01	±0.01	±0.00	±0.03	±0.03	±0.06	±0.03	±0.00
	(900)	(850)	(750)	(240)	(40)	(100)	(50)	(180)	(10)
	2	6	4	6	3	6	6	2	7
MCFS	0.67	0.82	0.78	0.62	0.32	0.76	0.66	0.27	0.71
	±0.01	±0.01	±0.01	±0.00	±0.04	±0.00	±0.04	±0.04	±0.01
	(750)	(750)	(450)	(240)	(85)	(60)	(130)	(180)	(15)
	4	3	3	3	4	2	3	3	2
RUFS	0.67	0.82	0.78	0.62	0.22	0.74	0.69	0.37	0.66
	±0.02	±0.01	±0.01	±0.00	±0.01	±0.05	±0.05	±0.07	±0.00
	(1000)	(700)	(350)	(240)	(5)	(30)	(10)	(300)	(50)
	6	2	2	5	6	4	2	7	4
HUFS	0.67	0.81	0.77	0.62	0.28	0.63	0.58	0.34	0.57
	±0.02	±0.01	±0.01	±0.00	±0.04	±0.00	±0.03	±0.07	±0.00
	(1000)	(650)	(900)	(240)	(90)	(140)	(110)	(240)	(55)
	5	4	6	4	5	3	4	5	6
KM	-	-	-	-	-	0.68	0.41	0.17	0.57
						±0.02	±0.02	±0.05	±0.02
						(30)	(20)	(280)	(75)
						7	7	6	5

Experiment 1 evaluates the clustering performance of different algorithms for different numbers of selected features. **Experiment 2** evaluates the clustering performance of *GLS* in text and genomic data, for $\alpha_i = \frac{|G_i|}{|F|}$ and $\alpha_i = 1 \ \forall \ i$. This tests the *effect of group weights* on clustering performance. **Experiment 3** executes each feature selection algorithm 100 times and reports the log value of the average run time to evaluate the *algorithm efficiency*. **Experiment 4**

performs feature selection in image datasets for $p = 2, 4, 8, 16$. This tests the *effect of the group size* on the clustering performance. **Experiment 5** runs *GLS* for $\lambda \in$ [-1, 3]. This tests the *effect of λ* on the clustering performance.

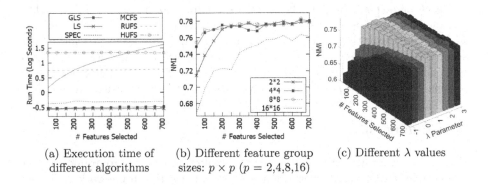

(a) Execution time of different algorithms

(b) Different feature group sizes: $p \times p$ (p = 2,4,8,16)

(c) Different λ values

Fig. 3. *GLS* execution time and accuracy variation for different settings for COIL20

Experimental Results: Table 2 shows that *GLS achieves the highest NMI over baselines* in 7 out of 9 datasets. In ORL and COIL20, *GLS* achieves the highest NMI with a smaller number of features than baselines. *In all datasets, GLS has the highest average accuracy* (rank 1), yet the rankings of baselines vary across the datasets. *GLS*'s average NMI gain over SPEC in Multi-B dataset is ∼30%, which is its maximum NMI gain over baselines. Maximum NMI gain of *GLS* over the NMI obtained by the complete feature set is 3%, 1%, 1%, 2%, 10%, 11%, 4%, 12% and 24% for Yale, ORL, COIL20, USPS, RT, MT, CNS, DLBCL-B and Multi-B respectively. *GLS*'s average accuracy gains for $\alpha_i = \frac{|G_i|}{|F|}$ over $\alpha_i = 1$ are 0.3% and 3% in RT and DLBCL-B datasets, respectively. Due to space limitations, we omit the results graphs for Experiment 1 and 2. Please refer to this link (See footnote 1) to see all the results graphs. *GLS also has the lowest SD for clustering performance* for 7 out of 9 datasets. Figure 3a shows that *GLS has only little increase of run time than LS, which is significantly low compared to embedded methods*. For COIL20 dataset, the run time of *GLS* is ∼50, ∼20 and ∼70 times lower than the run time of MCFS, RUFS and HUFS. Figure 3b shows that compared to large and small feature groups (p = 2, 16), *GLS* performance for medium sized groups (p = 4, 8) is high. According to Fig. 3c, *clustering performance is less sensitive to λ for $\lambda > 0$*, yet significantly low for $\lambda \leq 0$.

Evaluation Insights: Compared to baselines, *GLS consistently shows high clustering performance* for all the datasets (highest average accuracy in all datasets and maximum accuracy in 7 out of 9 datasets), *with low computational costs* (∼50 times lower run time than embedded methods on average). *In*

*all datasets, GLS achieves higher accuracy than using the complete feature set,
with a comparatively smaller number of features.* Higher accuracy obtained by
weighted feature groups show that in some cases, knowledge about the importance level of different feature groups improves the accuracy of *GLS.* Low SD
values for NMI show that *GLS produces more stable clusters and more precise performance results* than the baselines. Medium sized groups achieve higher
accuracy because large and small groups more resemble the case of no groupings.
This demonstrates the contribution of feature group information to achieve high
accuracy. Low accuracy for $\lambda \leq 0$ supports our hypothesis that *selecting features
from the same group is less effective than selecting from different groups. Less
parameter tuning is required* for *GLS* as its accuracy is less sensitive to λ (> 0).

7   Conclusion

We propose a framework which facilitates exploiting feature group information
by unsupervised feature selection methods and use this framework to incorporate feature group information into LS algorithm. We show that compared
to baselines, the proposed method achieves high clustering performance for the
datasets with feature group structures with low computational costs and requires
less parameter tuning. Our future work includes using the proposed framework
for unsupervised feature selection methods other than the LS algorithm.

Acknowledgements. This work is supported by the Australian Government.

References

1. 3 sources. http://mlg.ucd.ie/datasets/3sources.html. Accessed Nov 2019
2. Cancer program datasets. http://portals.broadinstitute.org/cgi-bin/cancer/
   datasets.cgi. Accessed Nov 2019
3. Acharya, S., Saha, S., Nikhil, N.: Unsupervised gene selection using biological
   knowledge: application in sample clustering. BMC Bioinform. **18**(1), 513 (2017)
4. Cai, D., He, X., Han, J.: Speed up kernel discriminant analysis. VLDB J. **20**(1),
   21–33 (2011). https://doi.org/10.1007/s00778-010-0189-3
5. Cai, D., He, X., Hu, Y., et al.: Learning a spatially smooth subspace for face
   recognition. In: Proceedings of IEEE CVPR 2007, pp. 1–7 (2007)
6. Cai, D., Zhang, C., He, X.: Unsupervised feature selection for multi-cluster data.
   In: Proceedings of the 16th ACM SIGKDD, pp. 333–342. ACM (2010)
7. Cai, J., Luo, J., Wang, S., et al.: Feature selection in machine learning: a new
   perspective. Neurocomputing **300**, 70–79 (2018)
8. Guo, J., Zhu, W.: Dependence guided unsupervised feature selection. In: 32nd
   AAAI (2018)
9. He, X., Cai, D., Niyogi, P.: Laplacian score for feature selection. In: NIPS, pp.
   507–514 (2006)
10. Hou, C., Nie, F., Li, X., et al.: Joint embedding learning and sparse regression: a
    framework for unsupervised feature selection. IEEE Trans. Cybern. **44**(6), 793–804
    (2014). https://doi.org/10.1109/TCYB.2013.2272642

11. Kong, D., Fujimaki, R., Liu, J., et al.: Exclusive feature learning on arbitrary structures via $l_{1,2}$-norm. In: NIPS, pp. 1655–1663 (2014)
12. Lazar, C., Taminau, J., Meganck, S., et al.: A survey on filter techniques for feature selection in gene expression microarray analysis. IEEE/ACM TCBB **9**(4), 1106–1119 (2012). https://doi.org/10.1109/TCBB.2012.33
13. Miller, G.A.: WordNet: a lexical database for English. Commun. ACM **38**(11), 39–41 (1995). https://doi.org/10.1145/219717.219748
14. Qian, M., Zhai, C.: Robust unsupervised feature selection. In: IJCAI, pp. 1621–1627 (2013)
15. Sahu, B., Dehuri, S., Jagadev, A.K.: Feature selection model based on clustering and ranking in pipeline for microarray data. Inform. Med. Unlocked IMU **9**, 107–122 (2017)
16. Wang, L., Wang, Y., Chang, Q.: Feature selection methods for big data bioinformatics: a survey from the search perspective. Methods **111**, 21–31 (2016)
17. Wang, S., Wang, Y., Tang, J., et al.: Exploiting hierarchical structures for unsupervised feature selection. In: Proceedings of the 2017 SDM, pp. 507–515. SIAM (2017). https://doi.org/10.1137/1.9781611974973.57
18. Zaharieva, M., Breiteneder, C., Hudec, M.: Unsupervised group feature selection for media classification. Int. J. Multimed. Inf. Retr. **6**(3), 233–249 (2017). https://doi.org/10.1007/s13735-017-0126-y
19. Zhao, Z., Liu, H.: Spectral feature selection for supervised and unsupervised learning. In: Proceedings of the 24th ICML, pp. 1151–1157. ACM (2007)
20. Zou, Q., Zeng, J., Cao, L., et al.: A novel features ranking metric with application to scalable visual and bioinformatics data classification. Neurocomputing **173**, 346–354 (2016). https://doi.org/10.1016/j.neucom.2014.12.123

Cross-data Automatic Feature Engineering via Meta-learning and Reinforcement Learning

Jianyu Zhang[1](✉), Jianye Hao[1], and Françoise Fogelman-Soulié[2]

[1] College of Intelligence and Computing, Tianjin University, Tianjin, China
{edzhang,jianye.hao}@tju.edu.cn
[2] Hub France IA, Paris, France
francoise.soulie@hub-franceia.fr

Abstract. Feature Engineering (FE) is one of the most beneficial, yet most difficult and time-consuming tasks of machine learning projects, and requires strong expert knowledge. It is thus significant to design generalized ways to perform FE. The primary difficulties arise from the multiform information to consider, the potentially infinite number of possible features and the high computational cost of feature generation and evaluation. We present a framework called *Cross-data Automatic Feature Engineering Machine* (CAFEM), which formalizes the FE problem as an optimization problem over a *Feature Transformation Graph* (FTG). CAFEM contains two components: a FE learner (FeL) that learns finegrained FE strategies on one single dataset by Double Deep Q-learning (DDQN) and a Cross-data Component (CdC) that speeds up FE learning on an unseen dataset by the generalized FE policies learned by Meta-Learning on a collection of datasets. We compare the performance of FeL with several existing state-of-the-art automatic FE techniques on a large collection of datasets. It shows that FeL outperforms existing approaches and is robust on the selection of learning algorithms. Further experiments also show that CdC can not only speed up FE learning but also increase learning performance.

1 Introduction

As machine learning becomes more and more widespread, it has been recognized that feature engineering (FE) is the most critical factor for models performance [1]. Various researchers have demonstrated the benefit of using additional features [11]. FE aims at reducing the model error and making learning easier by deriving, through mathematical functions (operators), new features from the original ones. Normally a data scientist combines feature generation, selection and model evaluation iteratively, generating a long sequence of decisions before obtaining the "optimal" set of derived features. This process heavily relies on expert domain knowledge, intuition and technical expertise to handle the complex feedbacks and make best decisions. As a result, the process is difficult, time-consuming and hard to automate.

© Springer Nature Switzerland AG 2020
H. W. Lauw et al. (Eds.): PAKDD 2020, LNAI 12084, pp. 818–829, 2020.
https://doi.org/10.1007/978-3-030-47426-3_63

Most of existing methods of automatic FE either generate a large set of possible features by predefined transformation operators followed by feature selection [3,7,15] or apply simple supervised learning (simple algorithm and/or simple meta-features derived from FE process) to recommend a potentially useful feature [4,5,9]. The former makes the process computationally expensive, which is even worse for complex features, while the latter significantly limits the performance boost.

A recently proposed FE approach [5] is based on Reinforcement Learning (RL). It treats all features in the dataset as a union, then applies traditional Q-learning [14] on FE-augmented examples to learn a strategy for automating FE under a given computing budget. RL is more promising in providing general FE solutions. However, this work uses Q-learning with linear approximation and 12 simple manual features, which limits the ability of automatic FE. Furthermore, it ignores the differences between features and applies a transformation operator on all of them at each step. Because of this nondiscrimination of different features, it is computation expensive, especially for large datasets and complex transformation operators.

To address the above limitations, in this work, we propose FeL (*Feature Engineering Learner*) and CAFEM (*Cross-data Automatic Feature Engineering Machine*). The former is a novel approach for automatic FE for one particular dataset based on off-policy Deep Reinforcement Learning (DRL). In order to speed up the FE process and take advantage of the FE knowledge learned from a large set of datasets, the latter extends FeL to cross-data level by Meta-Learning.

We define a *Feature Transformation Graph* (FTG), a directed graph representing relationships between different transformed versions of features, to organize the FE process. FeL sequentially trains an agent for each feature by DRL algorithms to learn the strategy for feature engineering on one dataset and corresponding FTG representation. We thus view the goal of FE as maximizing model accuracy by searching through a set of features F_+ to generate and a set of features F_- to eliminate. CAFEM extends this process to cross-data by training one agent on a large set of datasets to enable the learned policy to perform well on unseen datasets.

2 Background and Problem Formulation

In this section we review the Reinforcement Learning (RL) [10] background and describe the problem formulation.

2.1 Reinforcement Learning

RL is a family of algorithms that formalizes the interaction of an agent $\mathbb{A}$ with her environment using a Markov Decision Process (MDP) and allows it to devise an optimal sequence of actions. An MDP is defined by a tuple $\langle \mathcal{S}, \mathcal{A}, \mathcal{T}, \mathcal{R}, \gamma \rangle$, where $\mathcal{S}$ is a set of states, $\mathcal{A}$ a set of actions, $\mathcal{T} : \mathcal{S} \times \mathcal{A} \to \Delta(\mathcal{S})$ a transition function that maps each state-action pair to a probability distribution over the possible successor states, $\mathcal{R} : \mathcal{S} \times \mathcal{A} \times \mathcal{S} \rightarrow \mathbb{R}$ a reward function and $\gamma \in [0,1]$ a discount factor for controlling the importance of future rewards. A policy $\pi : \mathcal{S} \rightarrow \mathcal{A}$ is a mapping from states to actions. At every time step t, an agent in state s_t produces an action $a_t = \pi(s_t)$. Based on transition function $\mathcal{T}$ the agent gets into next state s_{t+1} with probability $\mathcal{T}(s_t, a_t)$ and obtains immediate reward $r_t = \mathcal{R}(s_t, a_t, s_{t+1})$. The goal of an agent is to find an optimal policy π^* maximizing her expected discounted cumulated reward $\mathbb{E}[R_0|s_0]$, where $R_t = \sum_{i=t}^{\infty} \gamma^{i-t} r_i$ is the discounted sum of future rewards.

Q-learning is a well-known model-free RL algorithm for finding an optimal policy π^* for any finite MDP. In Q-learning we define the Q-function or action-value function as $Q(s_t, a_t) = \mathbb{E}[R_t|s_t, a_t]$.

Given an optimal policy π^*, we are interested in the optimal function $Q^{\pi^*}(s, a)$, or $Q^*(s, a)$ for short, where $\forall \pi, s \in \mathcal{S}, a \in \mathcal{A}, Q^{\pi^*}(s, a) \geq Q^{\pi}(s, a)$. As a result, Q^* satisfies the following equation:

$$Q^*(s_t, a_t) = r_t + \mathop{\mathbb{E}}_{s_{t+1} \sim \mathcal{T}(s_t, a_t)} [\gamma \max_a Q(s_{t+1}, a)] \tag{1}$$

Double Deep Q-network (DDQN) [12] is a model-free RL algorithm, which estimates the state-action value approximately through a deep neural network with parameters θ. It uses an ϵ-greedy policy to get the next action.

During training, the tuples $\langle s_t, a_t, r_t, s_{t+1} \rangle$ generated by the ϵ-greedy policy are stored in R, the so-called *replay buffer*. Then the neural network is trained by sampling from the *replay buffer*, using mini-batch, and performing gradient descent on loss $\mathcal{L} = \mathbb{E}((Q(s_t, a_t) - y_t)^2)$, where $y_t = r_t + \gamma \max_a Q(s_{t+1}, a)$, $Q(s, t)$ is approximated by the network g with parameter θ.

2.2 Meta-learning

The goal of meta-learning is to quickly train a model for a new task with the help of data from many other similar tasks.

Model-Agnostic Meta-Learning (MAML) [2] is one of the best meta-learning algorithms that were trained by gradient descent. We denote $\{T\}$ as a set of tasks. MAML performs one step gradient descent for a task T_i on loss $\mathcal{L}$ with network g and network parameters θ and gains θ_i' as Equation (2). Then it performs a second gradient descent $\bigtriangledown_\theta$ step on loss $\mathcal{L}$ with network parameters θ_i' as Equation (3). Finally, MAML finds parameters θ that are close to the optimal parameters of every task.

$$\theta_i' = \theta - \alpha \bigtriangledown_\theta \mathcal{L}_{T_i}(g_\theta) \tag{2}$$

where α is the learning rate of each task T_i.

$$\theta = \theta - \beta \bigtriangledown_\theta \sum_{T_i \in \{T\}} \mathcal{L}_{T_i}(g_{\theta_i'}) \tag{3}$$

where β is the meta step size.

2.3 Problem Formulation

We consider a collection of typical supervised learning tasks (binary classification or regression) $T = \{T_1, T_2, ..., T_N\}$ and each task T_i can be represented as $T_i = \langle D, L, m \rangle$, where $D = \langle F, y \rangle$ is a dataset with a set of features $F = \{f_1, f_2, ..., f_n\}$ and a corresponding target variable y, L is a learning algorithm (e.g. Random Forest, Logistic Regression, Neural Network) to be applied on dataset D and m is an evaluation measure (e.g. log-loss, relevant absolute error, f1-score) to measure the performance.

We use $P_L^m(F, y)$ or $P(D)$ to denote the cross-validation performance of learning algorithm L and evaluation measure m on dataset D. The goal of each task is to maximize $P(D)$.

A transformation operator τ in FE is a function that is applied on a set of features to generate a new feature $f_+ = \tau(\{f_i\})$ where the order of the operator follows the number of features in $\{f_i\}$. We denote the set of derived features as F_+. For instance, a *product* transformation applied on two features (Order-2) generates a new feature $f_+ = product(f_i, f_j)$. We use $\mathbb{T}$ to denote the set of all transformation operators.

Feature engineering aims at constructing a subset of features $F^* = F_o \bigcup F_+ - F_-$, where F_o is the set of original features in dataset D, F_+ the set of derived features and $F_- \subseteq F_o$ the set of features that we decide to drop out from original features. For a given dataset D, a feature engineering strategy π specifies a derived feature set $F^* = \pi(D)$, where $F^* = F_o \bigcup F_+ - F_-$. The goal of feature engineering is to find a good policy π^* that maximizes the model performance for a given algorithm L and measure m on a dataset D.

$$\pi^* = \arg\max_{\pi} P_C^m(\pi(D), y) \qquad (4)$$

3 Method

In this section, we present a new framework called *Cross-data Automatic Feature Engineering Machine* (CAFEM). In order to highlight the differences between features and integrate *feature generation* and *feature selection* effectively, we propose a *Feature Transformation Graph* (FTG) to represent the FE process at feature level. Based on FTG, CAFEM can perform feature engineering for each particular feature based on the information related with it. Thus, it avoids the drawback of generating a large set of features at each step in [5], especially for complex features and large number of features. One component of CAFEM called FE Learner (FeL) uses Reinforcement Learning to find the optimal feature set F^* for each feature iteratively, instead of using expensive graph search algorithm [6]. FeL focus on one particular supervised learning task which gives FeL the ability to dig deeply into that task. However, it loses the opportunity to learn and integrate useful experiments from other tasks which can speed up FE process on a similar task. In order to balance performance and speed, another component of CAFEM called Cross-data Component (CdC) applies a Model-Agnostic

Meta-Learning (MAML) [2] method, which is originally designed for supervised learning and on-policy reinforcement learning algorithms, on off-policy reinforcement learning algorithms to speed up FE learning on one particular dataset by integrating the FE knowledges from a set of datasets.

3.1   Feature Transformation Graph

We propose a structure called *Feature Transformation Graph* (FTG) G, which is a directed acyclic dynamic graph, to represent the FE process. Each node f in FTG corresponds to either one original feature in F_o or one feature derived from original features. An edge from node f_i to f_j, $j > i > 0$, with label τ indicates that feature f_j is transformed from feature f_i by transformation operator τ, e.g. $f_{n+2} = square(f_{n+1})$ or transformed partially from f_i by τ, e.g. $f_{n+8} = product(f_{n+4}, f_{n+6})$. At the start of FE, G contains n nodes which correspond to n original features $\{f_1, f_2, ..., f_n\}$. As FE process goes, FTG dynamically grows up (adds more nodes and edges). So we denote FTG at time step t as G_t. An illustrating example is given in Fig. 1.

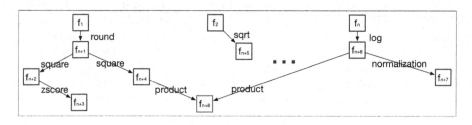

Fig. 1. *Example of FTG*

3.2   MDP Formulation

So far, we have introduced the representation of FE with FTG in our automatic FE framework. After that, what we need to do is to find a suitable strategy to control the growth of FTG. An important property is that FTG is not designed for any particular strategy, but to be a general representation of an FE process. As a result, we can apply many different strategies on the FTG to control it, such as graph search or RL. In this paper, we choose RL to learn a strategy that can make a sequence of decisions on top of FTG, due to its efficiency.

Consider the FE process with FTG on one dataset D as an MDP problem defined as a tuple $\langle \mathcal{S}, \mathcal{A}, \mathcal{T}, \mathcal{R}, \gamma \rangle$. At each time step t, a state $s_t \in \mathcal{S}$ consists of the Feature Transformation graph G_t and the features $\{f_t\}$ we are working on. Due to the complexity of transformation operators, $\{f_t\}$ could contain one or more features. For example, $\{f_t\}$ contains one feature for Order-1 operators (e.g. $log, square$), two features for Order-2 operators (e.g. $product, sum$).

An action $a_t \in \mathcal{A} = \mathcal{A}_G \bigcup \mathcal{A}_S$ comes from the following two groups of actions:

- $\mathcal{A}_G$ is a set of actions for *feature generation*, which apply a transformation $\tau \in \mathbb{T}$ on current features $\{f_t\}$ to derive one new feature.
- $\mathcal{A}_S$ contains one action for *feature selection* by RL, which drops current feature f_t and moves back to the previous feature. One special case is that current feature $f_t \in \{f_1, f_2, .., f_n\}$ belongs to original features. In this case, *feature selection* action drops it and stops current FE process.

The learning objective here is to find a state s_i with feature set F^* in FTG that maximizes the model accuracy $P_C^m(F^*, y)$. The trajectory from original feature to a new feature f_i indicates the final feature engineering strategy for f_i.

Since the target of FE is to maximize the performance $P(D)$, the reward r_t of this FE problem in FTG at time step t is set as:

$$r_t = P_L^m(D_{t+1}) - P_L^m(D_t) \tag{5}$$

3.3 CAFEM Framework

Until now, we have introduced the organization of FE process and the MDP formulation of FE problem. The most critical part is the algorithm to find a good strategy of FE. We introduce CAFEM framework which mainly contains two parts: 1) an algorithm called FeL that can apply an off-policy DRL algorithm $\mathbb{A}$ (such as DQN [8], Double DQN [12]) on FTG for one particular dataset to perform automatic FE; 2) an extended version of model-agnostic meta-learning [2] algorithm on off-policy DRL to speed up FE learning by taking advantage of the generalized FE strategies learned from a set of datasets. It is called off-policy, since the policy being learned can be different from the policy being executed.

In the following sub-section, we will introduce the details of these two parts.

Feature Engineering Learner (FeL): Although FeL works as a component of CAFEM in this paper, it is also a complete algorithm that sequentially optimizes FE strategies for each feature on one particular dataset. The details of FeL algorithm are shown in Algorithm 1. Given a supervised learning task T with n features $F = \{f_1, f_2, ..., f_n\}$, n off-policy DRL agents $\{\mathbb{A}_i\}$, FeL sequentially optimizes a FE policy for each feature (line 2 in Algorithm 1). As traditional training stage of off-policy RL algorithms, FeL starts with performing M episodes of FE process by ϵ-greedy and stores corresponding transitions in replay buffer (line 3–10). In this process, FeL either generates a new feature $\hat{f}$ from feature f by action a_t ($a_t \in \mathcal{A}_G$) or drops current feature f and moves back to previous feature $\hat{f}$ ($a_t \in \mathcal{A}_S$). Then FeL trains the corresponding agent $\mathbb{A}_i$ by performing gradient descent on a mini-batch sampled from *replay buffer* R_i (line 11–14). During test stage the same FE method as Algorithm 1 with $\epsilon = 0$ is used to perform FE for each feature sequentially. Note that the operators in transformation operators set $\mathbb{T}$ are not of the same complexity level. For example, some unary features (e.g. $log(f_i), square(f_i)$) are less complex than binary features (e.g. $product(f_i, f_j), sum(f_i, f_j)$).

As in [15], we introduce features along feature complexity, driving simple features first (e.g. unary features) then complex features (e.g. binary features).

Algorithm 1. FeL

---

input: An dataset $D = \langle F, y \rangle$ with n features $F = \{f_0, ...f_n\}$, n replay buffer $\{R_i, ..., R_n\}$ for each features, n off-policy DRL agents $\{\mathbb{A}_i\}$, number of epochs and episodes E, M, batches to train N

1: **while** epoch $= 1, E$ **do**
2:     **for** f_i in F **do**
3:         **for** episode $= 1, M$ **do**
4:             Get initial state s_0
5:             **while** not terminal **do**
6:                 Get an action a_t by ϵ-greedy and execute a_t on f: $\hat{f} = a_t(f)$
7:                 Obtain reward r_t and next state s_{t+1}
8:                 Store transition (s_t, a_t, r_t, s_{t+1}) in R_i and reset current feature: $f \leftarrow \hat{f}$
9:             **end while**
10:        **end for**
11:        **for** $t = 1, N$ **do**
12:            Sample a mini-batch from replay buffer R_i
13:            Perform one optimization step on $\mathbb{A}_i$
14:        **end for**
15:    **end for**
16:    Reset dataset $D = \langle \{f_i, ..., f_n\}, y \rangle$
17: **end while**

Cross-data Component: In order to speed up FE process and take advantage of a large set of datasets, we apply Model-agnostic Meta-Learning [2] on off-policy RL to perform cross-data level automatic feature engineering. The details of the Cross-data Component (CdC) are shown in Algorithm 2. Given a set of datasets $\{D = \langle F, y \rangle\}$ and an off-policy RL agent $\mathbb{A}$ (we use DDQN here as it can gain relevant a good performance in many tasks [12]) represented by g_θ, Cross-data Component samples a batch of features $\{f_i\}$ and corresponding dataset $\{D_{f_i}\}$ and constructs a batch of supervised learning tasks $\{T_i = \langle D_{f_i}, P, m \rangle\}$ (line 2). For each task $T_i \in \{T_i\}$, CdC uses the RL agent $\mathbb{A}$ together with ϵ-greedy exploration to perform M episodes for T_i and stores the corresponding transitions in *replay buffer* R_i (line 4–5). Then CdC samples K transitions from R_i and computes one step gradient descent as Algorithm 2 (line 7–8) where the loss $\mathcal{L}$ is the same as Algorithm 1. Finally, we sample a batch of transitions and perform meta-update (line 9–11).

Network Design: Until now, we have discussed the details of FeL algorithm and cross-data component. One remaining part is the structure of the neural network that can approximate the Q-values of DDQN in FeL algorithm. In this project, instead of building one approximation function with parameter θ for each action a [5], we use one union function that is approximated by a neural network, for all actions. Thus, we only need to train one DRL model.

As we discussed in Sect. 4.2, the state s_t at time t indicates the FTG G_t and the features $\{f_t\}$ it is working on at time t. In order to cover these two parts of information in the representation of each state s_t, we use the following features to represent s_t:

Algorithm 2. CrossDataComponent

---

input: a set of tasks $\{T\}$, an off-policy DRL agent represented by g_θ, number of epochs and episodes E, M

1: Randomly initialize θ
2: **while** epoch $= 1, E$ **do**
3:     Sample batch of tasks $\{T_i\}$ from $\{T\}$
4:     **for** all $\{T_i\}$ **do**
5:         Perform M episodes on task T_i with ϵ-greedy
6:         Store all transitions in R_i
7:         Sample K transitions T from R_i
8:         Compute adapted parameters with gradient descent: $\theta_i^{'} = \theta - \alpha \bigtriangledown_\theta \mathcal{L}_{T_i}(f_\theta)$
9:         Sample transitions $\mathcal{T}_i^{'}$ from R_i for meta-update
10:     **end for**
11:     Update $\theta = \theta - \beta \bigtriangledown_\theta \sum_{T_i \sim \{T\}} \mathcal{L}_{T_i}(f_{\theta_i^{'}})$ using each $\mathcal{T}_i^{'}$ and $\mathcal{L}_{T_i}$ in Equation 3
12: **end while**

---

1. Extended Quantile Sketch Array (ExQSA) representation of features. Quantile Sketch Array (QSA) uses *quantile* data sketch [13] to represent feature values associated with a class label. For each feature f and binary target y, QSA builds equi-width bins for f with target $y = 0$ and $y = 1$ separately. For regression problems, we extend QSA (ExQSA) by building equi-width bins for f with numeric target $y > median(y)$ and $y < median(y)$ separately.
2. Previous N-step FE history on FTG.
3. The number of each transformation operators used in G_t.
4. The number of next node visited for each action.
5. The number of each operator used from $\{f_t\}$ to its root.
6. Node depth of a feature in HTG.
7. Average performance improvement of each action.

Totally, we use 293 features to represent each state. A neural network with three fully connected hidden layers (128-128-64 neurons) and ReLU activation function is used to approximate Q-values.

4 Experiments

This section describes our experimental results. First, we introduce our experimental settings as well as our training procedure. Then we use F1-score (for classification) and 1 - Relevant Absolute Error (1-RAE) (for regression) criteria to compare the performance of FeL algorithm with several state-of-the-art automatic FE techniques. After that, we evaluate the robustness of our algorithm with respect to different learning algorithms (Random Forest, Logistic Regression). Finally, we show the efficiency of CAFEM on different supervised learning tasks by comparing it with FeL. To our surprise, CAFEM can help improving the prediction performance. Source codes are posted on Github (https://github.com/TjuJianyu/CAFEM.git).

4.1 Experimental Settings

We randomly collect 120 binary classification or regression datasets, which do not contain missing values and too many features and instances, from OpenML. We randomly split them into 100 datasets for training and the other 20 datasets for testing. Following [5,9], we choose 13 transformation operators (set $\mathbb{T}$) including Order-1: *Log, Round, Sigmoid, Tanh, Square, Square Root, ZScore, Min-Max-Normalization* and Order-2: *Sum, Difference, Product, Division*. Following [9], we choose Random Forest and Logistic Regression (Lasso for regression) (from Scikit-learn http://scikit-learn.org) as our learning algorithm and use F1-score/1-RAE to measure the performance. A 5-fold cross validation (same seed for all experiments) using random stratified sampling is used to measure the average performance. FeL is performed on 20 testing datasets directly, while CAFEM is trained on the 100 training datasets by meta-learning. For Order-2 operators, as the number of candidate features is very large, FeL randomly sample a small batch (100) at each step.

To showcase the ability of different FE algorithms, we compare the performance of FeL with the following approaches:

- **Baseline:** applies learning algorithm on original dataset (features) directly.
- **Random-FeL (RS):** is an algorithm where we apply random strategy on FTG rather than the strategy learned by RL like CAFEM to find a set of features that can maximize $P(D)$. This shows the effect of FTG without RL and Meta-learning. This algorithm can be seen as random graph search method on FTG. As some graph search algorithms, such as depth-first search (DFS) or breadth-search algorithm (BFS), are extremely time consuming [5], we do not compare FeL with DFS or BFS in this paper.
- **Brute-force (BF):** is inspired by DSM [3], OneBM [7] and [15]. It applies all transformation operators to all original features and performs feature selection on the augmented dataset. (top-down approach).
- **LFE** [9]: uses QSA to generate the representation of each feature in classification problems. Following [9], a neural network with one hidden layer, $L2$ regularization and dropout is used to predict whether a feature with a transformation operator will gain 1% model performance improvement.
- **FERL:** organizes the FE problem into a Transformation Graph, where each node is either the original dataset D or a dataset transformed from D. Then it uses Q-learning with linear approximation. We use the same setting as [5]. For Order-2 transformation operators, native FERL is extremely computation expensive since the number of new features is very large. During training stage, we prune the branches in Transformation Graph that would generate more than 10,000 new features next to make it trainable.

As the source codes of all these methods are not publicly available and some experiments details are not provided (such as, the random seed of learning algorithm and train-test dataset splitting), we implemented ourselves all the benchmarks. For all the FE approaches except Baseline, we evaluate the performance for Order-1 and (Order-1 & Order-2) transformation operators to compare the ability of handling simple and complex transformation operators.

Table 1. Comparing Performance by F1-score/1-RAE, Random Forest and 5-fold Cross-validation (- indicates cannot finish within 36 h, x indicates the algorithm can not handle corresponding dataset).

Datasets	#Row	#Feature	Baseline	Order-1					Order-1 & 2				
				FeL	BF	LFE	RS	FERL	FeL	BF	LFE	RS	FERL
Balance_scale	625	5	88.2%	88.3%	86.4%	88.2%	88.2%	**88.6%**	95.0%	**97.0%**	95.1%	92.7%	-
Boston	506	21	88.2%	**90.2%**	86.7%	89.2%	89.5%	88.7%	**89.9%**	85.6%	88.2%	89.8%	-
ClimateModel	540	21	95.5%	**96.0%**	95.6%	95.5%	95.7%	95.9%	**96.1%**	95.5%	95.5%	**96.1%**	-
Cpu_small	8,192	13	86.3%	**87.1%**	84.5%	85.8%	86.6%	86.8%	**87.1%**	86.2%	86.3%	87.0%	-
Credit card	14,240	31	50.5%	**68.7%**	64.8%	50.5%	63.8%	64.0%	**71.4%**	65.1%	65.1%	64.6%	-
Disclosure_x	662	4	44.8%	**51.7%**	46.6%	46.8%	49.7%	49.8%	51.4%	46.4%	46.4%	51.4%	**51.8%**
Disclosure_z	662	4	53.8%	**57.7%**	55.6%	53.1%	55.6%	57.0%	**57.0%**	53.8%	55.0%	56.7%	56.9%
fri_c1_1000_25	1,000	26	84.9%	87.7%	85.8%	85.8%	86.7%	**88.0%**	**87.1%**	77.9%	82.1%	**87.1%**	-
Fri_c2_100_10	1,000	11	86.3%	**89.7%**	85.8%	86.8%	88.6%	89.3%	**91.0%**	87.2%	86.7%	89.3%	-
Fri_c3_100_5	1,000	6	88.2%	89.2%	88.5%	88.2%	88.4%	**89.4%**	**90.7%**	87.3%	87.1%	89.3%	-
fri_c3_1000_50	1,000	51	79.7%	83.7%	**88.5%**	80.9%	80.7%	87.8%	83.1%	**88.4%**	78.3%	80.8%	-
Gina_agnostic	3,468	971	92.3%	92.8%	78.9%	92.3%	92.8%	**93.5%**	92.8%	-	92.5%	92.8%	-
Hill-valley	1,212	101	57.5%	**61.7%**	59.2%	57.5%	60.8%	61.1%	100%	100%	57.5%	99.9%	-
Ilpd	583	11	41.3%	**45.7%**	38.7%	38.9%	43.6%	44.9%	**45.9%**	**45.9%**	42.4%	44.8%	-
Kc1	2,109	22	40.4%	**44.5%**	35.3%	38.9%	42.0%	42.7%	**44.4%**	39.9%	38.8%	43.4%	-
openml_589	1,000	25	66.9%	67.7%	55.0%	X	67.2%	**72.6%**	75.0%	**76.9%**	X	68.1%	-
Pc4	1,458	38	47.7%	57.0%	36.2%	45.3%	53.8%	**58.4%**	**58.1%**	50.1%	55.1%	56.5%	-
Pc3+C14	1,563	38	25.9%	**33.4%**	27.9%	23.0%	30.3%	32.0%	**33.3%**	24.6%	27.4%	31.6%	-
Spectrometer	531	103	77.3%	**83.9%**	80.0%	75.2%	80.4%	83.0%	82.7%	**90.8%**	73.2%	81.8%	-
Strikes	625	7	96.6%	**99.5%**	98.7%	97.8%	99.1%	98.9%	**99.5%**	97.8%	93.4%	99.4%	98.9%

Fig. 2. *CAFEM vs FeL over 4 different datasets*

4.2 Performance Comparison of FeL

Table 1 compares the model performance of our automatic FE approach FeL to other state-of-the-art FE approaches on 20 datasets. The first four columns in this table report the dataset, the number of instances (rows) and original features, the baseline performance (F1-score/1-RAE of 5-fold cross validation) of the datasets. The number of instances ranges from 506 to 14,240 and for features, it ranges from 4 to 971. In the middle five columns, we compare different automatic FE approaches with Order-1 transformation operators, and in the last five columns, the performance with Order-1 & Order-2 transformation operators.

In Order-1 transformation operators, FeL outperforms all approaches on most datasets. On average, FeL improves performance by 4.2% on test datasets. In the best two cases, Credit card and Pc4, FeL even improves baseline performance by 18.2% and 9.3%. One interesting phenomenon is that the Random method (random graph search on FTG) can obtain a relevant higher performance on some datasets. This indicates that FTG represents the FE process in an effective way and significantly contributes further strategy learning of FE.

On Order-1 & Order-2 transformation operators, the complexity of FE increases significantly. Thus, it is expected that an inefficient method would easily run out of time, memory space or even would not work. FeL improves performance by 6.9% on average compared with existing approaches. In the best two cases, Pc4 and Ilpd, it improves by 42.5% and 20.9%. As we mentioned above, some FE approaches would be strongly limited as the complexity of transformation operators increasing. Comparing the performance of each approaches on Order-1 & Order-2 with that on Order-1, we found that LFE and Brute-force approaches get a worse performance (-1.54% in average) on half of the datasets, while FeL does not get any performance decrease. FERL approach is really computation expensive here: most of the datasets run out of time (36 h).

4.3   Robustness of FeL on Different Learning Algorithms

In order to showcase the robustness of FeL, we evaluate the performance of FeL with two learning algorithms: Random Forest (tree-based ensemble learning algorithm) and Logistic Regression (Lasso for regression) (general linear algorithm) on 20 test datasets. FeL gains 10.8% and 4.2% performance increase on average with Logistic regression and Random Forest, respectively. The performance of FeL with Logistic regression ranges from 0.2% to 25.8%. For Random Forest, the performance of FeL ranges from 0% to 18.2%. It shows that our algorithm is robust with respect to different learning algorithms.

4.4   Performance of Cross-data Component

One main aim of Cross-data Component is to speed up FE learning. We evaluate FeL and CAFEM on the test datasets and randomly show the comparison on 4 datasets due to the space limitation. Figure 2 shows that CAFEM can increase model performance more rapidly (gain a high score within the first epoch, outperform the best of FeL within around ten epochs). To our surprise, CAFEM can gain a better final model performance than FeL in most of the cases. We hypothesize the reason of this phenomena as that CAFEM learnt some general FE rules from a large set of datasets to help the agent quickly learn a new dataset and regularize its behavior.

5   Conclusion

In this paper, we present a novel framework called CAFEM to perform automatic feature engineering (FE) and transfer FE experiences from a set of datasets to a particular one. It contains a feature transformation graph (FTG) that organized the process of FE, a Single-data FE learner and a Cross-data component. In most datasets, the framework outperforms state-of-the-art automatic FE approaches for both simple and complex transformation operators. With the help of cross-data component, CAFEM can speed up FE and increase FE performance. Moveover, the framework is robust to the choice of different learning algorithms.

Acknowledgments. The work is supported by the National Natural Science Foundation of China (Grant Nos.: 61702362, U1836214).

References

1. Domingos, P.: A few useful things to know about machine learning. Commun. ACM **55**(10), 78–87 (2012)
2. Finn, C., Abbeel, P., Levine, S.: Model-agnostic meta-learning for fast adaptation of deep networks. In: Proceedings of the 34th International Conference on Machine Learning, vol. 70, pp. 1126–1135 (2017). JMLR.org
3. Kanter, J.M., Veeramachaneni, K.: Deep feature synthesis: towards automating data science endeavors. In: IEEE International Conference on Data Science and Advanced Analytics (DSAA), vol. 36678, pp. 1–10. IEEE (2015)
4. Katz, G., Shin, E.C.R., Song, D.: Explorekit: automatic feature generation and selection. In: Proceedings of the IEEE 16th International Conference on Data Mining ICDM 2016, pp. 979–984. IEEE (2016)
5. Khurana, U., Samulowitz, H., Turaga, D.: Feature engineering for predictive modeling using reinforcement learning. In: Thirty-Second AAAI Conference on Artificial Intelligence (2018)
6. Khurana, U., Turaga, D., Samulowitz, H., Parthasrathy, S.: Cognito: automated feature engineering for supervised learning. In: Proceedings of the IEEE 16th International Conference on Data Mining Workshops ICDMW 2016, pp. 1304–1307. IEEE (2016)
7. Lam, H.T., Thiebaut, J.-M., Sinn, M., Chen, B., Mai, T., Alkan, O.: One button machine for automating feature engineering in relational databases. arXiv preprint arXiv:1706.00327 (2017)
8. Mnih, V., et al.: Human-level control through deep reinforcement learning. Nature **518**(7540), 529 (2015)
9. Nargesian, F., Samulowitz, H., Khurana, U., Khalil, E.B., Turaga, D.: Learning feature engineering for classification. In: Proceedings of the 26th International Joint Conference on Artificial Intelligence, IJCAI, vol. 17, pp. 2529–2535 (2017)
10. Sutton, R.S., Barto, A.G., et al.: Reinforcement Learning: An Introduction. MIT Press, Cambridge (1998)
11. Töscher, A., Jahrer, M., Bell, R.M.: The BigChaos solution to the Netflix grand prize. Netflix prize documentation, pp. 1–52 (2009)
12. Van Hasselt, H., Guez, A., Silver, D.: Deep reinforcement learning with double Q-learning. In: AAAI, Phoenix, AZ, vol. 2, p. 5 (2016)
13. Wang, L., Luo, G., Yi, K., Cormode, G.: Quantiles over data streams: an experimental study. In: Proceedings of the 2013 ACM SIGMOD International Conference on Management of Data, pp. 737–748. ACM (2013)
14. Watkins, C.J., Dayan, P.: Q-learning. Mach. Learn. **8**(3–4), 279–292 (1992)
15. Zhang, J., Fogelman-Soulié, F., Largeron, C.: Towards automatic complex feature engineering. In: Hacid, H., Cellary, W., Wang, H., Paik, H.-Y., Zhou, R. (eds.) WISE 2018. LNCS, vol. 11234, pp. 312–322. Springer, Cham (2018). https://doi.org/10.1007/978-3-030-02925-8_22

Discretization and Feature Selection Based on Bias Corrected Mutual Information Considering High-Order Dependencies

Puloma Roy[1(✉)], Sadia Sharmin[2], Amin Ahsan Ali[3], and Mohammad Shoyaib[1]

[1] Institute of Information Technology, University of Dhaka, Dhaka, Bangladesh
pulomaa92@gmail.com, shoyaib@du.ac.bd
[2] Department of CSE, Islamic University of Technology, Gazipur City, Bangladesh
sharmin@iut-dhaka.edu
[3] Department of CSE, Independent University of Bangladesh, Dhaka, Bangladesh
aminali@iub.edu.bd

Abstract. Mutual Information (MI) based feature selection methods are popular due to their ability to capture the nonlinear relationship among variables. However, existing works rarely address the error (bias) that occurs due to the use of finite samples during the estimation of MI. To the best of our knowledge, none of the existing methods address the bias issue for the high-order interaction term which is essential for better approximation of joint MI. In this paper, we first calculate the amount of bias of this term. Moreover, to select features using χ^2 based search, we also show that this term follows χ^2 distribution. Based on these two theoretical results, we propose Discretization and feature Selection based on bias corrected Mutual information (DSbM). DSbM is extended by adding simultaneous forward selection and backward elimination (DSbM$_{fb}$). We demonstrate the superiority of DSbM over four state-of-the-art methods in terms of accuracy and the number of selected features on twenty benchmark datasets. Experimental results also demonstrate that DSbM outperforms the existing methods in terms of accuracy, Pareto Optimality and Friedman test. We also observe that compared to DSbM, in some dataset DSbM$_{fb}$ selects fewer features and increases accuracy.

Keywords: Feature selection · Mutual information · Interaction · Bias correction

1 Introduction

In classification tasks, the objective of feature selection (FS) process is to choose the most useful features that contribute to the prediction of class variable. Usually, all the features of a dataset do not have equal importance, rather some may

Electronic supplementary material The online version of this chapter (https://doi.org/10.1007/978-3-030-47426-3_64) contains supplementary material, which is available to authorized users.

create noise or be redundant. FS methods are used to remove such irrelevant and redundant features and can be divided into three broad categories namely Wrapper [14,18], Embedded [20], and Filter methods [13,15,16]. Among these, filter methods do not depend on a classifier to select a feature. It thus works faster, which is preferable for handling large feature sets [12].

Again, Mutual information (MI) is usually popular in filter based methods. MI can capture non-linear relationships among features and class variable, can be computed for both categorical and numerical data, and can deal with multiple classes [7]. For these reasons, in this paper, we focus on MI based filter methods.

In MI based filter methods, the main goal is to select a subset of features S from the original feature set, $F = \{f_1, f_2, f_3, ..., f_n\}$ in such a way that it will maximize joint MI ($I(S; C)$) with the class variable, C as showed in Eq. 1.

$$I(S; C) = I(f_1, f_2, ..., f_k; C)$$
$$= \sum_{f_1, f_2, ..., f_k} \sum_C P(f_1, f_2, ..., f_k; C) \log \frac{P(f_1, f_2, ..., f_k; C)}{P(f_1, f_2, ..., f_k)P(C)} \quad (1)$$

However, the computation of $I(S; C)$ is a NP-hard problem [7]. To overcome this problem, different approximations such as MIFS [1], mRMR [10], JMI [19], RelaxMRMR [17] have been proposed over the last decades. In these methods, MI terms such as feature relevancy(R), redundancy(r), conditional redundancy(c) and interaction(i) are considered in order to achieve a better approximation. However, none of the aforementioned methods correct "bias" due to finite samples in calculating MI terms. In a recent method mDSM [16], it is shown that incorporating bias correction for R, r, and c terms improves the classification performance. However, the interaction term is not considered in mDSM which needs to be addressed for better approximation [17].

Apart from the evaluation criteria, searching is an important step in the FS methods to find out the combination of feature subset that performs well. Most popular searching techniques are forward selection, backward elimination, genetic algorithms (GA) based search [11]. Forward selection and backward elimination are greedy searching strategy that select/delete a feature one at a time. The limitation of these approaches are after selecting/deleting a feature, it cannot be deleted/re-selected later which may add redundant features [6]. On the other hand, GA based methods are computationally expensive and for a dataset with large number of features, it is not feasible to apply. Convex based Relaxation Approximation (COBRA) is proposed in [7] which provides a global solution for MI based FS. Another search strategy is introduced in mDSM where a small subset of features is selected using χ^2 based forward selection that uses dynamic discretization. However, it cannot deselect a feature once it is already selected and do not show whether it is possible to use χ^2 based search for interaction term. Considering the aforementioned issues, we propose a method called Discretization and feature Selection based on bias corrected MI (DSbM) and make the following major contribution: First, we calculate bias for the interaction terms and propose to use it for FS. Second, we show that the interaction terms follow χ^2 distribution and proposed to use it in χ^2 based search. Third, to obtain reduced number of feature, keeping similar performances with DSbM we propose a new method for simultaneous forward selection and backward elimination (DSbM$_{fb}$).

2   Information Theoretic Feature Selection Methods

The main objective of MI based features selection methods is to determine a subset of features that have maximum dependency with the given class as shown in Eq. 1. Alternatively, this problem can be formulated for incremental feature selection that is to add one feature at a time in the selected subset to maximize $I(S; C)$. From a given set F with n number of features, a new feature f_m is added to the selected set, $S = \{f_1, f_2, \ldots, f_{m-1}\}$, that maximizes the score for a feature f_m:

$$J(f_m) = I(f_m \cup S; C) = I(S; C) + I(f_m; C \mid S) \tag{2}$$

Since $I(S; C)$ remains constant with respect to f_m, we choose f_m that maximizes $I(f_m; C \mid S)$. Using MI identities, this term can be expressed as

$$I(f_m; C|S) = I(f_m; C) - I(f_m; S) + I(f_m; S|C) \tag{3}$$

here, the terms $I(f_m; C)$, $I(f_m; S)$ and $I(f_m; S|C)$ represent feature relevancy, redundancy and conditional redundancy respectively [2]. Hence the score $J(f_m)$ increases if the relevancy of the feature f_m is large and redundancy with the existing features is low. However, the score also increases if the conditional redundancy is higher than the redundancy term. Hence, there is a trade-off, and the overall score is what needs to be maximized. Brown *et al.* in [2] further shows under the assumption that (a) the selected features in S are independent given the feature f_m and (b) the selected features are class-conditionally independent given the feature f_m and removing terms that have no effect on the choice of f_m one can obtain the following equivalent score function:

$$J(f_m) = I(f_m; C) - \beta \sum_{f_i \in S} I(f_m; f_i) + \gamma \sum_{f_i \in S} I(f_m; f_i|C) \tag{4}$$

with $\beta = 1$ and $\gamma = 1$, this is what we call the Rrc criterion. It can then be easily shown that the incremental FS criterion or score function of well known MI based method such as MIFS [1], mRMR [10], Extended mRMR [9], JMI [19], and MIM [5] can be derived from this parameterized version of the score function. For example, JMI [19] criteria can be derived setting the value of $\beta = \gamma = \frac{1}{|S|}$.

In [17], the authors propose a new criterion by relaxing the the first assumption. They show under the relaxed assumption that the selected features are conditionally independent given the f_m and another feature f_i in S, the redundancy term can be approximated as the following

$$I(f_m; S) = I(f_m; f_i) + \sum_{f_j \in S, i \neq j} I(f_m; f_j|f_i) + \Omega \tag{5}$$

where Ω is not dependent on f_m. Instead of finding a feature f_i to condition on, they propose to average the right-hand side over all $f_i \in S$, resulting in the following score function

$$J_{rMRMR}(f_m) = I(f_m; C) - \frac{1}{|S|} \sum_{f_i \in S} I(f_m; f_i) + \frac{1}{|S|} \sum_{f_i \in S} I(f_m; f_i \mid C)$$
$$- \frac{1}{|S||S-1|} \sum_{f_i \in S} \sum_{f_j \in S; i \neq j} I(f_m; f_j \mid f_i) \quad (6)$$

here, the $I(f_m; f_j \mid f_i)$ terms are the second order interaction term between the features. It should be noted that sum of the second order terms is normalized by $\frac{1}{|S||S-1|}$ instead of $\frac{1}{|S|}$. The authors note that this is to prevent this sum to out-weight other terms. It can be seen that one can approximate the redundancy term using 3rd or higher order interaction terms by further relaxing the assumption. However, it is shown that the joint MI is more influenced by lower-order interaction terms in case of forward selection methods [4].

Practically, all aforementioned MI terms that have been used for the approximation need bias correction due to the finite number of samples. To solve this issue, a recent method namely, mDSM [16] is proposed where bias corrected MI has been used for calculating relevancy, redundancy and complementary term. They show incorporating bias correction improves the accuracy of classification. Also, it is theoretically shown that these three terms follow χ^2 distributions.

$$J_{mDSM}(f_m) = I(f_m; C) - \frac{(\mathcal{M}-1)(\mathcal{K}-1)}{2N \ln 2} + \frac{1}{|S|} \sum_{f_i \in S} (I(f_m; f_i \mid C) -$$
$$\frac{(\mathcal{M}-1)(\mathcal{I}-1)\mathcal{K}}{2N \ln 2} - I(f_m; f_i) + \frac{(\mathcal{M}-1)(\mathcal{I}-1)}{2N \ln 2}) \quad (7)$$

here, $\mathcal{M}$ and $\mathcal{I}$ are the number of intervals in feature f_m and f_i respectively. $\mathcal{K}$ is number of class and N is total number of samples. The limitation of mDSM is that it does not consider the interaction term while proposing bias corrected MI to calculate the feature score which is necessary for better approximation of joint MI.

3   Proposed Method

In this paper, we propose Discretization and feature Selection based on bias corrected MI (DSbM) which incorporates bias correction for MI based selection criteria. DSbM also uses dynamic discretization and greedy χ^2 based forward selection. Moreover, a simultaneous forward selection and backward elimination is also proposed. These are described in the following subsections.

3.1   Discretization and Feature Selection Based on Bias Corrected Mutual Information (DSbM)

DSbM incorporates the bias correction for all four terms mentioned in Eq. 6 as it is necessary for better approximation of joint MI. The bias for the first three terms are given in Eq. 7. Theorem 1 shows the amount of bias for the interaction term and Theorem 2 shows that this term follows χ^2 distribution. Proof of the theorems are given as supplementary materials due to page limitation.

Theorem 1. *Bias is $\frac{(\mathcal{M}-1)(\mathcal{J}-1)\mathcal{I}}{2N\ln 2}$ for Interaction $I(f_m; f_j \mid f_i)$ among the features f_m and f_j given feature f_i, where $\mathcal{I}$, $\mathcal{J}$ and $\mathcal{M}$ are the number of intervals in feature f_i , f_j and f_m respectively.*

Incorporating this bias corrected Interaction term with Eq. 7, DSbM uses the following criteria for discretization and feature selection.

$$
\begin{aligned}
J_{DSbM}(f_m) = I(f_m; C) - \frac{(\mathcal{M}-1)(\mathcal{K}-1)}{2N\ln 2} + \frac{1}{|S|} \sum_{f_i \in S} (I(f_m; f_i \mid C) - \\
\frac{(\mathcal{M}-1)(\mathcal{I}-1)\mathcal{K}}{2N\ln 2} - I(f_m; f_i) + \frac{(\mathcal{M}-1)(\mathcal{I}-1)}{2N\ln 2}) - \\
\frac{1}{|S||S-1|} \sum_{f_i \in S} \sum_{f_j \in S; i \neq j} (I(f_m; f_j \mid f_i) - \frac{(\mathcal{M}-1)(\mathcal{J}-1)\mathcal{I}}{2N\ln 2})
\end{aligned}
\tag{8}
$$

Theorem 2. *$I(f_m; f_j \mid f_i)$ follows χ^2 distribution with $(\mathcal{M}-1)(\mathcal{J}-1)\mathcal{I}$ degrees of freedom if f_m, f_i and f_j are statistically independent.*

Based on Theorem 2, the critical value of the *Interaction* term will be as Eq. 9

$$
\chi^2_{(i)} = 2N\ln(2) * I(f_m; f_j \mid f_i)
\tag{9}
$$

As the other three terms of Eq. 6 also follows χ^2 distribution, we can use their critical values (shown in [16]) for selecting a new feature.

The overall process of DSbM is given in Algorithm 1. First, each feature $f_m \in F$ is discretized with minimum number of intervals (d_m) for which its relevancy with the class variable $(J_{rel}(f_m) = I(f_m; C) - \frac{(\mathcal{M}-1)(\mathcal{K}-1)}{2N\ln 2})$ is significant. If the feature is not significant even with some predefined maximum number of intervals (d_{max}), it is dropped. The selected candidate features (F_c) are then sorted according to their relevance J_c in descending order (line 2–12 in Algorithm 1). The first feature f_1 is then included to the final selected feature set S. The remaining features of F_c are evaluated incrementally maximizing the *Rrci* criteria. The score of J_{DSbM} (Eq. 8) is compared (in line 15) with its' critical value $(\chi^2_{(Rrci)})$, to select a new feature f_m if it is not significantly redundant. Otherwise, f_m is discarded considering that it does not contribute to the score significantly. While selecting a new feature, its discretization level is also shifted by a small value δ from its original value (as selected previously based on J_{rel} as shown in line 16–21). This process helps to select the discretization level of features dynamically considering its dependency with other feature. In this way, all the features are discretized and selected simultaneously.

3.2   DSbM with Simultaneous Forward Selection and Backward Elimination (DSbM$_{fb}$)

DSbM follows χ^2 based forward searching strategy where a feature can not be discarded once it is added to the selected subset S. When a candidate feature f_m

---

Algorithm 1 : DSbM

Input: Set of n features, F, Maximum discretization level d_{max}, Class C

Output: Selected set of features, $S = \{f_1, f_2, \cdots, f_k\}$ with discretization, $D = \{d_1, d_2, \cdots, d_k\}$

1: Subset of r candidate features, $F_c \leftarrow \emptyset$
2: **for each** $f_m \in F$ **do**
3:     **for all** $l = 2$ to d_{max} **do**
4:         Discretize f_m with l interval
5:         Calculate J_{rel} for feature f_m
6:         **if** $J_{rel}(f_m) > \chi^2_{(R)}$ **then**
7:             $F_c \Leftarrow F_c \cup f_m$; $D_c \Leftarrow D_c \cup l$; $J_c \Leftarrow J_c \cup J_{rel}(f_m)$;
8:             **break**
9:         **end if**
10:     **end for**
11: **end for**
12: Sort F_c with corresponding D_c in decreasing order based on their J_c values
13: select f_1 with its' corresponding d_1
14: $S \Leftarrow S \cup f_1$; $D \Leftarrow D \cup d_1$; $F_c \Leftarrow F_c \setminus f_1$;
15: **for each** $f_m \in F_c$ **do**
16:     **for all** $l = d_m - \delta$ to $l = d_m + \delta$ **do**
17:         Discretize f_m with l interval
18:         **if** $J_{DSbM}(f_m) > \chi^2_{(Rrci)}$ **then**
19:             $d_m \Leftarrow l$; $J_m \Leftarrow J_{DSbM}(f_m)$; $T \Leftarrow \chi^2_{(Rrci)}$;
20:         **end if**
21:     **end for**
22:     **if** $J_{DSbM} > T$ **then**
23:         $S \Leftarrow S \cup f_m$; $D \Leftarrow D \cup d_m$;
24:     **end if**
25:     $F_c \Leftarrow F_c \setminus f_m$;
26: **end for**
27: **Return** S and their respective D

---

is found redundant with respect to the selected features from S, DSbM does not consider f_m for selection. However, it may happen that f_m is more important and contains extra information compared to the already selected features. In this case, removing the redundant features from S is more appropriate. Therefore, we modify DSbM by including backward elimination and propose DSbM$_{fb}$ where simultaneous selection and elimination is incorporated.

The process of backward elimination is described in Algorithm 2. Here, the redundant candidate feature f_m is rechecked based on its interaction value to decide whether this feature f_m is able to replace some features from S. This checking can be done by several ways such as considering all possible combination of three way interaction of f_m with f_i and f_j and selecting the feature pair whose replacement can increase the J_{DSbM} score significantly. However, it is computationally expensive to check all possible combination pairs of features. Hence, we consider the pair for which we obtain the highest interaction value

---

Algorithm 2 : DSbM$_{fb}$

Input: Set of n features, F, Maximum discretization level d_{max}, Class C
Output: Selected set of features, $S = \{f_1, f_2, \cdots, f_k\}$ with discretization, $D = \{d_1, d_2, \cdots, d_k\}$

1: Line (1-14) from Algorithm 1
2: **for each** $f_m \in F_c$ **do**
3:     Line (16-21) from Algorithm 1
4:     **if** $J_{DSbM} > T$ **then**
5:         $S \Leftarrow S \cup f_m; D \Leftarrow D \cup d_m;$
6:     **else**
7:         Set of interaction values, $E \Leftarrow \emptyset$
8:         **if** $|S| >= 4$ **then**
9:             **for all** $i = 1$ to $|S|$ **do**
10:                **for all** $j = 1$ to $|S|$ and $i \neq j$ **do**
11:                   Calculate Interaction, $I(f_m; f_j \mid f_i)$ among feature f_m, f_i, f_j
12:                   $e_{ij} = I(f_m; f_j \mid f_i)$
13:                **end for**
14:             **end for**
15:             Select feature f_i, f_j with highest interaction value e_{ij} from E
16:             $S' \Leftarrow S \setminus \{f_i, f_j\}$
17:             **if** $J_{DSbM}(f_m)$ on $S' > \chi^2_{(Rrci)}$ && $J_{DSbM}(f_m)$ on $S' > J_{DSbM}(f_m)$ on
      S **then**
18:                $S \Leftarrow S \cup f_m; S \leftarrow S'; D \Leftarrow D \cup d_m; D \Leftarrow D \setminus \{d_i, d_j\};$
19:             **end if**
20:         **end if**
21:     **end if**
22:     $F_c \Leftarrow F_c \setminus f_m;$
23: **end for**
24: **Return** S and their respective D

(line 9–15) and replace that feature pair with f_m if their removal from S passes the χ^2 value and increases the total score (line 17–18). As a result, DSbM$_{fb}$ obtains a smaller subset of features compared to DSbM.

4   Experimental Result

In this section, the experimental setup and evaluation process of different methods along with the proposed ones is presented. Furthermore, a number of experiments are performed to highlight the effectiveness of the proposed contributions.

4.1   Dataset Description and Implementation Details

In this experiment, twenty benchmark datasets collected from UCI Machine Learning Repository [3] are used as they are also employed in [16] and [19]. The description of these datasets are given in Table 1. For classification, we use SVM and KNN, and conduct 10-fold cross-validation on each dataset.

We compare DSbM with four state-of-the-art methods namely mDSM, JMI, JMI with COBRA search (JC) and RelaxMRMR. Here, DSbM, mDSM and JC are feature selection method, however, JMI and RelaxMRMR are feature ranking method. Hence, the number of selected feature obtained in DSbM are used to generate the results for these two methods. For JMI and RelaxMRMR, we use forward selection whereas, JC performs COBRA search and mDSM uses χ^2 based search. For comparing the methods we use three metrics namely accuracy, Score (defined in Eq. 10) and Pareto Optimality(PO). PO returns a set of non-dominant candidate solutions.

$$Score = \frac{\sum_{i=1}^{n} w_i * \alpha_i}{\sum_{i=1}^{n} w_i} \tag{10}$$

here, α_i and w_i indicates the performance evaluation criteria and weights respectively. For our method α_1 and α_2 indicates the percentage accuracy, and $\alpha_2 = (N_t - N_s)/N_t$ is the percentage of reduction features. Here, N_t is the total number of features in a dataset and N_s is the number of selected features. We use equal weights. To calculate PO, we use α_1 and α_2 and to perform Friedman test we use Score to incorporate the joint impact of number of selected features and the corresponding accuracy. We also calculate Win/Tie/Loss which indicates the number of datasets for which comparing method performs better/equally-well/worse than other methods unless otherwise stated. To determine whether the wins are statistically significant we perform t-test at 0.05 significance level.

4.2 Results and Discussion

Here, we first discuss how DSbM performs compared to other methods and then we compare the performance of DSbM with DSbM_fb.

Comparison of DSbM with Other Methods. To investigate the impact of high-order term for approximating joint MI in DSbM, let us first consider Table 2. For this table, win/tie/loss is calculated using the accuracies given in Table 3. RelaxMRMR performs slightly better than JMI due to the incorporation of interaction term. Whereas, mDSM outperforms RelaxMRMR even though mDSM does not consider high-order term. It is due to the bias correction, dynamic discretization and χ^2 based search. This indicates that mDSM with high-order term might perform well which is the proposed DSbM. mDSM also performs better than JC. Table 3 compares DSbM with mDSM, JC, JMI and RelaxMRMR. The number inside the parenthesis represents the number of selected feature. For example, DSbM achieves 96% accuracy using SVM with 2 selected features for Iris dataset.

It is evident from Table 3 that DSbM outperforms all the four state-of-the-art methods. The second last and the last row of Table 3 represent the pair wise win/tie/loss and significant win/loss of DSbM with the existing methods respectively. Even though DSbM wins in thirteen datasets among the twenty compared to mDSM for SVM classifier, the differences in accuracies are not

Table 1. Dataset description

Index	Dataset	Dimension	Instance	Class	Index	Dataset	Dimension	Instance	Class
1	Iris	4	150	3	11	Parkinson	22	197	2
2	Pima	8	768	2	12	Steel	27	1941	7
3	Yeast	8	1484	10	13	Breast	30	569	2
4	Glass	9	214	6	14	Dermatology	34	366	6
5	Wine	13	178	3	15	Spambase	57	4601	2
6	Heart	13	270	2	16	Sonar	60	208	2
7	Australian	14	690	2	17	Liver	6	345	2
8	Segment	17	2310	7	18	Breast Tissue	9	106	6
9	Cardio	21	2126	10	19	Arrhythmia	279	452	16
10	Waveform	21	5000	3	20	Semeion	256	1593	10

Table 2. Comparison of different methods (Win/Tie/Loss)

	RelaxMRMR vs. JMI	mDSM vs. RelaxMRMR	**mDSM vs. JC**
SVM	7/7/6	13/1/6	14/0/6
KNN	14/1/5	14/0/6	16/0/4

significant in most of the cases. DSbM wins significantly only for three datasets and losses for one. However, DSbM selects less number of features than other feature selection methods as it considers the bias corrected interaction term for which some redundant features are discarded. For example, in Wine dataset the accuracy of SVM is 96.84% for both DSbM and mDSM. However, DSbM selects only 9 features whereas mDSM selects 12. But in some cases mDSM selects less feature than DSbM. This is due to the greedy nature of forward selection and difference in the score functions. DSbM and mDSM may select different features in any iteration due to the inclusion of interaction term in DSbM, This may results in DSMb selecting a larger number of features compared to mDSM (for example, in case of Spambase and Sonar).

To understand the joint impact of accuracy and number of selected features, let us consider Table 4, where the ranking of the above mentioned methods is shown according to their frequency in the PO set and Friedman test. In both cases, DSbM achieves the highest rank. In Friedman test, after rejecting the null hypothesis that all the methods perform equivalently, a post-hoc test called Nemenyi test [8] is used to determine the which method performs significantly better than the others. The test indicates that DSbM significantly (at 95% confidence level) outperforms the four other methods both for SVM and KNN.

Impact of DSbM$_{fb}$ over DSbM. To understand the impact of simultaneous forward selection and backward elimination using DSbM$_{fb}$, let us consider Fig. 1a and Fig. 1b. We observe, in most of the cases DSbM$_{fb}$ selects less features than DSbM (number of selected features is given on the top of each bar and on the x-axis the index of datasets are given according to their order in Table 1). These figures also illustrate that when the total number of features for a dataset

Table 3. Comparison among different methods based on its accuracy. (∗) and (○) represents that DSbM wins and loses significantly from that method respectively and bold values represent the overall win among all methods.

	SVM(accuracy in %)					KNN(accuracy in %)				
	DSbM	mDSM	JC	JMI	Relax MRMR	DSbM	mDSM	JC	JMI	Relax MRMR
Iris	**96.00**(2)	94.67(2)	91.30(2)*	93.33	93.33	**91.33**	86.00*	83.30*	87.32	87.33
Pima	**74.94**(5)	74.29(7)	73.60(8)	73.12	73.12	**64.03**	61.69	58.70*	48.83*	48.84*
Yeast	**54.44**(7)	53.46(7)	50.00(7)*	51.83	51.50*	**38.43**	37.45	30.30*	33.33*	32.55*
Glass	**57.59**(4)	50.00(5)*	51.70(7)	54.35	54.35	**55.23**	54.35	51.30	50.00	51.00
Wine	**96.84**(9)	**96.84**(12)	91.60(9)*	94.21	95.79	91.58	91.58	84.20*	**96.32**	94.74
Heart	80.74(9)	80.00(10)	81.10(10)	**83.33**	82.22	72.22	72.59	71.90	**81.11**°	75.93
Australian	**87.71**(10)	**87.71**(10)	68.30(11)*	87.14	87.57	**82.43**	81.14	59.30*	77.43*	75.23*
Segment	**95.51**(14)	94.06(16)	88.80(12)*	89.26*	89.26*	90.43	**91.60**	86.90*	87.45*	87.47*
Cardio	**77.66**(14)	76.88(16)	63.30(13)*	68.99*	68.95*	**72.80**	71.15	61.90*	68.21*	67.02*
Waveform	84.35(19)	**85.29**(19)	80.80(13)*	83.97	83.97	75.87	**76.71**	70.30*	74.81	74.83
Parkinson	**84.50**(10)	83.00(17)	84.50(14)	84.50	84.00	87.00	87.00	92.00	91.50	84.50
Steel	65.61(9)	**72.02**(26)°	69.60(20)°	51.56*	63.79	68.54	**69.39**	69.30	21.01*	62.42*
Breast	93.79(7)	**96.38**(26)	95.70(20)	93.62	95.17	91.21	**94.66**°	92.20	72.93*	89.66
Dermatology	96.00(28)	95.50(33)	95.30(23)	**96.75**	96.50	**96.25**	96.00	93.50*	92.75*	92.75*
Spambase	**93.90**(50)	93.06(47)*	73.30(41)*	74.51*	74.71*	**93.32**	92.62	67.30*	68.31*	68.31*
Sonar	**81.36**(36)	75.91(21)	72.70(60)*	70.45*	73.64*	85.00	83.64	**88.60**	87.27	84.55
Liver	57.14(2)	57.14(2)	**59.43**(6)	57.14	57.14	46.29	46.27	**52.00**°	43.14	43.14
Breast Tissue	60.71(3)	**61.43**(4)	55.00(6)	57.81	56.43	**54.29**	53.57	51.43	52.14	49.29
Arrhythmia	72.79(107)	66.28(118)*	70.70(253)*	72.56	74.19	65.12	65.35	58.60*	64.65	**69.30**
Semeion	**93.23**(253)	92.93(255)	93.20(254)	93.17	93.17	**91.41**	90.73	91.20	91.40	**91.41**
Win/Tie/Loss		13/3/4	15/1/4	16/2/2	15/1/4		12/2/6	15/0/5	16/0/4	16/1/3
Sig. Win/Loss		3/1	9/1	5/0	5/0		1/1	11/1	9/1	8/0

Table 4. Ranking of existing feature selection criteria.

	Frequency in Pareto optimal set				
SVM	DSbM(12)	JC(8)	mDSM(6)	JMI(2)	RelaxMRMR(2)
KNN	DSbM(13)	JC(10)	mDSM(6)	JMI(4)	RelaxMRMR(1)
	Average rank from Friedman test				
SVM	DSbM(1.70)	RelaxMRMR(2.73)	JMI(2.85)	mDSM(3.78)	JC(3.95)
KNN	DSbM(1.68)	RelaxMRMR(2.75)	JMI(2.83)	mDSM(3.80)	JC(3.95)

is comparatively small then the performance of both DSbM and DSbM$_{fb}$ are similar in terms of number of selected features and accuracy (e.g., Iris, Yeast, Glass etc.). Note that in some cases such as in Cardio, Arrhythmia etc., DSbM$_{fb}$ selects fewer features with higher accuracy.

Furthermore, a limitation of mDSM is that, the set of selected features might contain a subset for which better accuracy can be found. DSbM also has similar problem which can be observed in Fig. 2a. This issue is resolved to some extent in DSbM$_{fb}$. Here, we get 74.19% accuracy with 84 selected features (see Fig. 2b) while DSbM obtains an accuracy of 72.79% with 107 features.

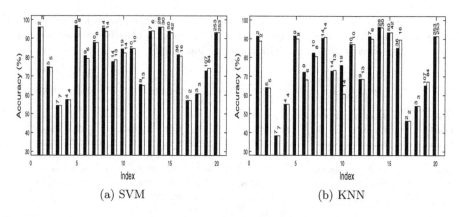

(a) SVM   (b) KNN

Fig. 1. DSbM(black bar) vs. DSbM$_{fb}$(white bar)

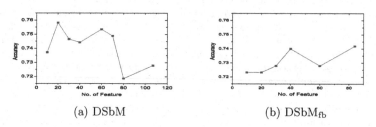

(a) DSbM   (b) DSbM$_{fb}$

Fig. 2. Accuracy (SVM) vs. Number of features for Arrhythmia dataset

5   Conclusion

In this paper, we propose a method DSbM which includes bias correction for high-order dependencies among features and use χ^2 based search that also consider high-order dependencies. Results over a large amount of dataset demonstrate that DSbM outperforms current state-of-the-art methods. Beside this, a χ^2 based simultaneous forward and backward search is also proposed here that shows similar performances with DSbM with less number of features. This method can be applied for different applications such as activity recognition and cancer classification for gene expression data. Incorporation of further high-order terms might improve the overall performance which require further theoretical analysis and experimentation with global feature selection which will be addressed in future work.

Acknowledgement. This research is supported by ICT Division, Ministry of Posts, Telecommunications and Information Technology, Bangladesh. 56.00.0000.028.33.093. 19-427, 20-11-2019.

References

1. Battiti, R.: Using mutual information for selecting features in supervised neural net learning. IEEE Trans. Neural Netw **5**(4), 537–550 (1994)
2. Brown, G., Pocock, A., Zhao, M.J., Luján, M.: Conditional likelihood maximisation: a unifying framework for information theoretic feature selection. J. Mach. Learn. Res. **13**(1), 27–66 (2012)
3. Dua, D., Graff, C.: UCI machine learning repository (2017)
4. Lee, J., Kim, D.W.: Mutual information-based multi-label feature selection using interaction information. Exp. Syst. Appl. **42**(4), 2013–2025 (2015)
5. Lewis, D.D.: Feature selection and feature extraction for text categorization. In: Proceedings of the Workshop on Speech and Natural Language, pp. 212–217 (1992)
6. Mao, K.Z.: Orthogonal forward selection and backward elimination algorithms for feature subset selection. IEEE Trans. Syst. Man Cybern. Part B **34**(1), 629–634 (2004)
7. Naghibi, T., Hoffmann, S., Pfister, B.: A semidefinite programming based search strategy for feature selection with mutual information measure. IEEE Trans. Pattern Anal. Mach. Intell. **37**(8), 1529–1541 (2014)
8. Nemenyi, P.: Distribution-free multiple comparisons. Ph.D. thesis, Princeton University (1963)
9. Nguyen, X.V., Chan, J., Romano, S., Bailey, J.: Effective global approaches for mutual information based feature selection. In: ACM SIGKDD, pp. 512–521 (2014)
10. Peng, H., Long, F., Ding, C.: Feature selection based on mutual information: criteria of max-dependency, max-relevance, and min-redundancy. IEEE Trans. Pattern Anal. Mach. Intell. **8**, 1226–1238 (2005)
11. Saidi, R., Bouaguel, W., Essoussi, N.: Hybrid feature selection method based on the genetic algorithm and pearson correlation coefficient. In: Hassanien, A.E. (ed.) Machine Learning Paradigms: Theory and Application. SCI, vol. 801, pp. 3–24. Springer, Cham (2019). https://doi.org/10.1007/978-3-030-02357-7_1
12. Senawi, A., Wei, H.L., Billings, S.A.: A new maximum relevance-minimum multicollinearity (MRmMC) method for feature selection and ranking. Pattern Recogn. **67**, 47–61 (2017)
13. Sharmin, S., Aktar, F., Ali, A.A., Khan, M.A.H., Shoyaib, M.: BFSp: a feature selection method for bug severity classification. In: R10-HTC, pp. 750–754 (2017)
14. Sharmin, S., Arefin, M.R., Wadud, M.A., Nower, N., Shoyaib, M.: SAL: an effective method for software defect prediction. In: 18th ICCIT, pp. 184–189 (2015)
15. Sharmin, S., Ali, A.A., Khan, M.A.H., Shoyaib, M.: Feature selection and discretization based on mutual information. In: icIVPR, pp. 1–6. IEEE (2017)
16. Sharmin, S., Shoyaib, M., Ali, A.A., Khan, M.A.H., Chae, O.: Simultaneous feature selection and discretization based on mutual information. Pattern Recogn. **91**, 162–174 (2019)
17. Vinh, N.X., Zhou, S., Chan, J., Bailey, J.: Can high-order dependencies improve mutual information based feature selection? Pattern Recogn. **53**, 46–58 (2016)
18. Wanderley, M.F.B., Gardeux, V., Natowicz, R., de Pádua Braga, A.: GA-KDE-Bayes: an evolutionary wrapper method based on non-parametric density estimation applied to bioinformatics problems. In: 21st ESANN, pp. 155–160 (2013)

19. Yang, H., Moody, J.: Feature selection based on joint mutual information. In: Proceedings of International ICSC Symposium on Advances in Intelligent Data Analysis, pp. 22–25. Citeseer (1999)
20. Yuan, G.X., Chang, K.W., Hsieh, C.J., Lin, C.J.: A comparison of optimization methods and software for large-scale L1-regularized linear classification. J. Mach. Learn. Res. **11**, 3183–3234 (2010)

Human, Domain, Organizational and Social Factors in Data Mining

JarKA: Modeling Attribute Interactions for Cross-lingual Knowledge Alignment

Bo Chen[1,2], Jing Zhang[1,2(✉)], Xiaobin Tang[1,2], Hong Chen[1,2],
and Cuiping Li[1,2]

[1] Key Laboratory of Data Engineering and Knowledge Engineering
of Ministry of Education, Renmin University of China, Beijing, China
[2] Information School, Renmin University of China, Beijing, China
{bochen,zhang-jing,txb,chong,licuiping}@ruc.edu.cn

Abstract. Cross-lingual knowledge alignment is the cornerstone in building a comprehensive knowledge graph (KG), which can benefit various knowledge-driven applications. As the structures of KGs are usually sparse, attributes of entities may play an important role in aligning the entities. However, the heterogeneity of the attributes across KGs prevents from accurately embedding and comparing entities. To deal with the issue, we propose to model the interactions between attributes, instead of globally embedding an entity with all the attributes. We further propose a joint framework to merge the alignments inferred from the attributes and the structures. Experimental results show that the proposed model outperforms the state-of-art baselines by up to 38.48% HitRatio@1. The results also demonstrate that our model can infer the alignments between attributes, relationships and values, in addition to entities.

1 Introduction

DBpedia, Freebase, YAGO and so on have been published as noteworthy large and freely available knowledge graphs (KGs), which can benefit many knowledge-driven applications. However, the knowledge embedded in different languages is extremely unbalanced. For example, DBpedia contains about 2.6 billion triplets in English, but only 889 million and 278 million triplets in French and Chinese respectively. Creating the linkages between cross-lingual KGs can reduce the gap of acquiring knowledge across multiple languages and benefit many applications such as machine translation, cross-lingual QA and cross-lingual IR.

Recently, much attention has been paid to leveraging the embedding techniques to align entities between two KGs. Some of them only leverage the structures of the KGs, i.e., the relationship triplets in the form of ⟨entity, relationship, entity⟩ to learn the structure embeddings of entities [3,6,10]. However, the structures of some KGs are sparse, making it difficult to learn the structure embeddings accurately. Other efforts are made to incorporate the attribute triplets in the form of ⟨entity, attribute, value⟩ to learn the attribute embeddings of entities [9,11,12,15]. For example, JAPE [9] embeds attributes via attributes'

© Springer Nature Switzerland AG 2020
H. W. Lauw et al. (Eds.): PAKDD 2020, LNAI 12084, pp. 845–856, 2020.
https://doi.org/10.1007/978-3-030-47426-3_65

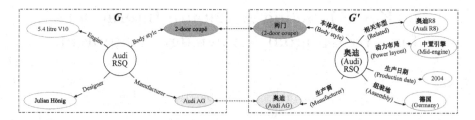

Fig. 1. Illustration of different attributes of same entities in two cross-lingual knowledge graphs from wikipedia.

concurrence. Wang et al. [12] adopt GCNs to embed entities with the one-hot representations of the attributes. Trsedya et al. [11] and MultiKE [15] embed the literal values of the attributes. Despite the existing studies on incorporating the attribute triplets to align entities, there are still unsolved challenges.

Challenge 1: Heterogeneity of Attributes. Different KGs may hold heterogeneous attributes, resulting in the difficulty of aligning entities. For example, in Fig. 1, two entities from cross-lingual KGs named "Audi RSQ" are the same entity. Although the attributes "Manufacturer" and "Body style" and their values in English correspond to certain attribute triplets in Chinese, there are still many attribute such as "Designer" and "Engine" in English that cannot find any counterpart in Chinese. However, if we embed an entity by all its attribute triplets and then compare two entities by their attribute embeddings [11,15], the effects of the same attribute triplets will be diluted by other different ones.

Challenge 2: Multi-view Combination. To combine the effects from attributes and structures, existing works usually learn a combined embedding for each entity, based on which they infer the alignments. For example, JAPE [9] and AttrE [11] refine the structure embeddings by the closeness of the corresponding attribute embeddings. MultiKE [15] map the attribute and structure embeddings into a unified space. However, the issue of the missing attributes or relationships triplets may result in the inaccurate attribute or structure embeddings, which will propagate the errors to the combined embeddings.

Besides the above two challenges, most of the existing works [3,9,15] only focus on aligning entities, or at most relationships, but ignore attributes and values. However, the alignment of different objects influence each other. A unified way to align all of these objects simultaneously is worth studying.

Solution. To deal with the above challenges, we propose a joint model—JarKA to Jointly model the attributes interactions and relationships for cross-lingual Knowledge Alignment. The two views are carefully merged to reinforce the training performance iteratively. The contributions can be summarized as:

- We comprehensively formalize cross-lingual knowledge alignment as linking entities, relationships, attributes and values across cross-lingual KGs.
- To tackle the first challenge, we propose an interaction-based attribute model to capture the attribute-level interactions between two entities instead of

globally representing the two entities. A matrix-based strategy is further proposed to accelerate the similarity estimation.

- To deal with the second challenge, we propose a joint framework to combine the alignments inferred by the attribute model and relationship model respectively instead of learning a combined embedding. Three different merge strategies are proposed to solve the conflicting alignments.
- Experimental results on several datasets of cross-lingual KGs demonstrate that JarKA significantly outperforms state-of-the-art comparison methods (improving 2.35–38.48% in terms of Hit Ratio@1).

2 Problem Definition

Definition 1. *Knowledge Graph: We denote the KG as union of the **relationship triplets** and the **attribute triplets**, i.e., $G = \{(h, r, t)\} \cup \{(h, a, v)\}$, where (h, r, t) is a relationship triplet consisting of a head entity h, a relationship r, and a tail entity t, and (h, a, v) is an attribute triplet consisting of a head entity h, an attribute a and its value v. We also use e to denote entity.*

We distinguish the two kinds of triplets as they are independent views that can take different effects on alignment.

Problem 1. **Cross-lingual Knowledge Alignment:** Given two cross-lingual KGs G and G', and the seed set I of the aligned entities, relationships, attributes, and values, i.e., $I = \{(e \sim e')\} \cup \{(r \sim r')\} \cup \{(a \sim a')\} \cup \{(v \sim v')\}^1$, the goal is to augment I by the inferred new alignments between G and G'.

3 JarKA Model

We propose an interaction-based attribute model to leverage the (h, a, v) triplets, an embedding-based relationship model to leverage the $\{(h, r, t)\}$ triplets, and then incorporate the two models by a carefully designed joint framework.

3.1 Interaction-Based Attribute Model

Existing methods represent an entity globally by all its associated (h, a, v) and then compare the entity embedding between entities [11,15]. However, as shown in Fig. 1, two entities from cross-lingual KGs may have heterogeneous attribute. The irrelevant attribute triplets between two entities may dilute the effects of their similar attribute triplets if globally embedding the entities.

To deal with the above issue, we propose an interaction-based attribute model to directly estimate the similarity of two entities by capturing the interactions between their attributes and values. The model mimics the process that humans solve the problem. The humans usually align two entities if they have many

---

[1] Please refer to Sect. 4 for how to obtain I.

same attributes with same values. Following this, we firstly find all the aligned attribute pairs of two entities, and then compare its values. Since the number of the attributes are far smaller than that of the values in KGs, we initialize the aligned attributes by the attribute seed pairs and gradually extend them by our joint framework, which will be introduced in the following section. To compare the large number of cross-lingual values, we train a machine translation model and use it to estimate the BLEU score [8] of two cross-lingual values as their similarity. Unfortunately, following the idea, we need to enumerate and invoke the translation model for maximal M attribute pairs for each entity pair, resulting in $O(N \times N' \times M)$ time complexity when there are N and N' entities in G and G' respectively, which is too inefficient to finish within available time. To accelerate the similarity estimation, we represent each knowledge graph as a 3-dimension value embedding matrix and then perform an efficient matrix-based strategy to calculate entity similarities. Figure 2 illustrates the whole process of the proposed attribute model. In the following part, we will explain the details.

Embed Cross-lingual Attribute Values. We build an neural machine translation model (NMT) [2] to capture semantic similarities between cross-lingual values. We pretrain NMT based on the value seeds[2]. Since the seeds are limited, we will update NMT by the newly discovered value seeds iteratively.

Then we use NMT to project cross-lingual values into the same vector space. Specifically, for each attribute of each entity in G, we first invoke NMT to predict the translated value given its original value, and then look up the word embedding for each word in the translated value. While for each attribute of each entity in G', we directly look up the word embedding for each word in its original value. With the help of NMT, the embeddings of the cross-lingual values can be unified in the same space. Then we average all the word embeddings in the value as its value embedding. The dimension is denoted as D_v.

Estimate Entity Similarities by Matrix-Based Strategy. We construct a 3-dimension value embedding matrix $\mathbf{V} \in \mathbb{R}^{N \times M \times D_v}$ for G and a similar matrix $\mathbf{V}' \in \mathbb{R}^{N' \times M \times D_v}$ for G', where each element $\mathbf{V}_{mi}$ indicates the i-th value embedding of the m-th entity. Then we use the einsum operation

$$\text{einsum}(NMD_v, N'MD_v \rightarrow NN'MM), \tag{1}$$

i.e., Einstein summation convention [1], to make a multi-dimensional matrix product of $\mathbf{V}$ and $\mathbf{V}'$ to obtain the value similarity matrix $\widetilde{\mathbf{V}} \in \mathbb{R}^{N \times N' \times M \times M}$.

What's more, it is unnecessary to compare the values of different attributes. For example, although the attributes "birthplace" and "deathplace" have the same value "New York", they cannot reflect the similarity of two entities. So, we build an attribute mask matrix $\widetilde{\mathbf{A}}$ to limit the computation within the values of the aligned attributes. Specifically, we prepare a 3-dimension attribute identification matrix $\mathbf{A} \in \mathbb{R}^{N \times M \times K}$ for G and $\mathbf{A}' \in \mathbb{R}^{N' \times M \times K}$ for G', where K denotes the number of the united frequent attributes in G and G'. Each row in $\mathbf{A}$ or $\mathbf{A}'$ is an one-hot vector, with an element $A_{mik} = 1$ if the i-th value of the

---

[2] In the future, external cross-lingual corpus can be easily used to pre-train the model.

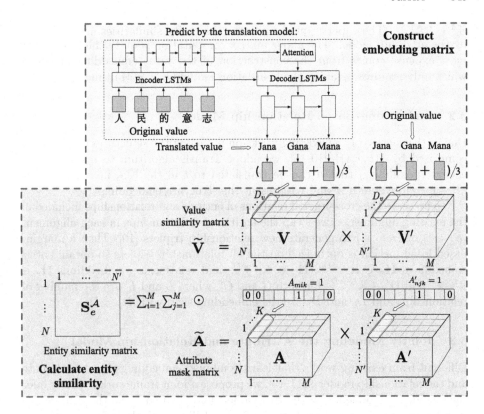

Fig. 2. Illustration of the proposed attribute model. V and V' are the value embedding matrices, and A and A' are the attribute identification matrices for G and G' respectively. The figure can be read from left to right and top to bottom.

m-th entity belongs to the k-th attribute, and $A_{mik} = 0$ otherwise. Note the one-hot identification vector depends on the existing aligned attributes, which will be gradually extended with the joint model iteratively. Whenever two attributes are discovered to be aligned, we will unify their identification. For example, when the k-th attribute in G and the t-th attribute in G' are aligned, we replace the identification k with t, i.e., any row with $A_{mik} = 1$ will be changed to $A_{mit} = 1$. Then we multiply $\mathbf{A}$ and $\mathbf{A}'$ in the same way as Eq. (1) to obtain an attribute mask matrix $\widetilde{\mathbf{A}} \in \mathbb{R}^{N \times N' \times M \times M}$, where each element $\widetilde{A}_{mnij} = 1$ if the i-th value of the m-th entity in G corresponds to the same attribute of the j-th value of the n-th entity in G', and $\widetilde{A}_{mnij} = 0$ otherwise. Then we calculate the element-wise product of $\widetilde{\mathbf{V}}$ and $\widetilde{\mathbf{A}}$, i.e., $\widetilde{\mathbf{V}} \odot \widetilde{\mathbf{A}}$, to get the masked value similarity matrix. Finally, we summarize the similarities of all the M^2 attribute pairs for each entity pair to obtain an entity similarity matrix:

$$\mathbf{S}_e^{\mathcal{A}} = \sum_i^M \sum_j^M \widetilde{V}_{\cdot,\cdot,i,j} \odot \widetilde{A}_{\cdot,\cdot,i,j}, \tag{2}$$

$\mathbf{S}_e^{\mathcal{A}} \in \mathbb{R}^{N \times N'}$. The superscript $^{\mathcal{A}}$ indicates the entity similarities are estimated by the attribute model. The above matrix computation is quite efficient, as the most expense comes from the construction of the value embedding matrices, which only requires invoking the translation model $O(N \times M)$ times.

3.2   Embedding-Based Relationship Model

Due to the success of the existing works on modeling the structures of the graph comprised by $\{(h, r, t)\}$ [10,15], we adopt TransE algorithm to maximize the energy (possibility) that h can be translated to t in the KG, i.e., $E(h, r, t) = \|\mathbf{h} + \mathbf{r} - \mathbf{t}\|$, where $\mathbf{h}$, $\mathbf{r}$ and $\mathbf{t}$ represent the structure embeddings.

To preserve the cross-lingual relations of entities and relationships included in the existing alignments, we swap the entities or relationships in each alignment $(e \sim e')$ or $(r \sim r')$ to generate new relationship triplets [10]. Then a margin-based loss function is optimized on the all relationship triplets to obtain entity embeddings $\mathbf{H}_e \in \mathbb{R}^{N \times D_e}$, $\mathbf{H}_e' \in \mathbb{R}^{N' \times D_e}$ and relationship embeddings $\mathbf{H}_r \in \mathbb{R}^{L \times D_r}$ and $\mathbf{H}_r' \in \mathbb{R}^{L' \times D_r}$ for both G and G', where L and L' are the number of relationships and D_e and D_r are the embedding sizes with $D_e = D_r$.

3.3   Jointly Modeling the Attribute and Relationship Model

Different from existing works that learn combined embeddings by the attribute and the relationship model [9,11,15], we propose a joint framework to firstly infer the confident alignments by the two models and then combine their inferences by three different merge strategies. Algorithm 1 illustrates the whole process. At each iteration, for modeling the attribute triplets, we first train the translation model based on the seed set of the aligned values (Line 3). Then we construct the value embedding matrices by the translation model (Line 4) and meanwhile construct the mask matrices by the existing aligned attributes (Line 5), based on which we perform an efficient matrix-based strategy to calculate the entity similarities (Line 6) and finally infer the new alignments of entities, attributes, and values based on the estimated similarities and existing alignments (Line 7). For modeling the relationship triplets, we train the entity and relationship embeddings based on the swapped relationship triplets between two graphs (Line 8), then we infer the new alignments of entities and relationships (Line 9). Finally, we merge the new aligned entity seeds from the attribute and the relationship model (Line 10) and augment the seed set by all the new alignments (Line 11 and 12). The framework bootstraps the two models iteratively by the extended alignments. Note we remove the new alignments from the candidate pairs at each iteration to avoid duplicate inference (Line 13).

Infer Alignments by the Attribute Model. We select an entity pair $(e_m \sim e_n')$ from all the $N \times N'$ candidate entity pairs into the new aligned set of entities $I_e^{\mathcal{A}}$ if their similarity $S_e^{\mathcal{A}}[m, n]$ is larger than a threshold $\tau_e^{\mathcal{A}}$:

$$I_e^{\mathcal{A}} \leftarrow (e_m \sim e_n'), \text{ if } S_e^{\mathcal{A}}[m, n] > \tau_e^{\mathcal{A}}. \tag{3}$$

Algorithm 1. JarKA

Input: G, G' and the seed alignments
$\qquad I = \{(e \sim e')\} \cup \{(r \sim r')\} \cup \{(a \sim a')\} \cup \{(v \sim v')\}$.
Output: The augmented alignments I.

1   $C = $ all the candidate pairs except the seed pairs in I;
2   **repeat**
       `/* Attribute model`   `*/`
3   Train a translation model on $\{(v \sim v')\}$;
4   Construct the value embedding matrices $\mathbf{V}$ and $\mathbf{V}'$ by the translation model;
5   Construct the mask matrices $\mathbf{A}$ and $\mathbf{A}'$ by $\{(a \sim a')\}$;
6   Calculate entity similarities $\mathbf{S}_e^{\mathcal{A}}$ by Eq. (2);
7   Infer new alignments $I_e^{\mathcal{A}}$, I_a, I_v from C by Eq. (3),(4),(5);
       `/* Relationship model`   `*/`
8   Train the relationship model on $\{(h, r, t)\}$, $\{(h', r', t')\}$, $\{(e \sim e')\}$ and $\{(r \sim r')\}$ to obtain $\mathbf{H}_e$, $\mathbf{H}'_e$, $\mathbf{H}_r$ and $\mathbf{H}'_r$;
9   Infer new alignments $I_e^{\mathcal{R}}$ and I_r from C by Eq. (6);
       `/* Merge new alignments`   `*/`
10      $I_e \leftarrow \text{merge}(I_e^{\mathcal{A}}, I_e^{\mathcal{R}})$;
11      $\triangle I \leftarrow (I_e, I_r, I_a, I_v)$;
12      $I = I + \triangle I$;
13      $C = C - \triangle I$;
14 **until** $\triangle I = \emptyset$;

The candidates of the aligned attributes and values depend on the aligned entities. Specifically, for each aligned entity pair $(e_m \sim e'_n)$, if the similarity of a value pair $\widetilde{V}_{m,n,i,j}$ is larger than a threshold τ_v, we select their corresponding attribute pair $(a_i \sim a'_j)$ into the new aligned attribute set I_a:

$$I_a \leftarrow (a_i \sim a'_j), \forall (e_m \sim e'_n) \in I, \text{ if } \widetilde{V}_{m,n,i,j} > \tau_v. \tag{4}$$

Then for each pair of attribute triplets $(e_m, a_i, v_i) \in G$ and $(e'_n, a'_j, v'_j) \in G'$, if the entities and the attributes are both aligned, we select their corresponding value pairs $(v_i \sim v'_j)$ into the new aligned value set I_v:

$$I_v \leftarrow (v_i \sim v'_j), \forall (e_m, a_i, v_i) \in G \ \& \ (e'_n, a'_j, v'_j) \in G', \tag{5}$$
$$\text{if} (e_m \sim e'_n) \in I \ \& \ (a_i \sim a'_j) \in I.$$

Infer Alignments by the Relationship Model. We calculate the similarity matrix $\mathbf{S}_e^{\mathcal{R}}$ as the dot product of the entity embeddings where the superscript $^{\mathcal{R}}$ indicates the entity similarities are estimated by the relationship model. Then we select an entity pair $(e_m \sim e'_n)$ into the new aligned entity set $I_e^{\mathcal{R}}$ if their similarity $S_e^{\mathcal{R}}[m,n]$ is larger than a threshold $\tau_e^{\mathcal{R}}$:

$$I_e^{\mathcal{R}} \leftarrow (e_m \sim e'_n), \text{ if } S_e^{\mathcal{R}}[m,n] > \tau_e^{\mathcal{R}}. \tag{6}$$

The new aligned relationships are inferred in the same way but with a different threshold τ_r.

Merge Alignments of the Two models. We propose three strategies to merge $I_e^{\mathcal{A}}$ and $I_e^{\mathcal{R}}$ into I_e.

Standard Multi-view Merge Strategy. Following the standard co-training algorithm, we firstly infer $I_e^{\mathcal{A}}$ from candidate entity pairs C_e by Eq. (3). Then we remove $I_e^{\mathcal{A}}$ from C_e, and then infer $I_e^{\mathcal{R}}$ from the remaining candidates $C_e - I_e^{\mathcal{A}}$.

Score-Based Merge Strategy. Due to the missing attributes and relationships, the labels inferred from the two views may have conflicts. For all the conflicting counterparts of an entity e_m, i.e., $\mathcal{C}_m = \{e_n' | (e_m \sim e_n') \in I_e^{\mathcal{A}} \cup I_e^{\mathcal{R}}\}$, we select the counterpart with the maximal score $S_e[m, n] = S_e^{\mathcal{A}}[m, n] + S_e^{\mathcal{R}}[m, n]$ into the final new alignments. The strategy assumes that the alignments discovered by more views will be more confident:

$$I_e \leftarrow (e_m \sim e_n'), e_n' = \mathrm{argmax}_{e_n' \in \mathcal{C}_m} S_e[m, n]. \tag{7}$$

Rank-Based Merge Strategy. Directly comparing the similarities estimated by the two models may suffer from the different scales of scores. Thus, we compare the normalize ranking indexes of the conflicting alignments. Specifically, for all the conflicting counterparts $\mathcal{C}_m$ of e_m, we select the counterpart with the minimal ranking ratio $R[m, n]$ into the final new alignments:

$$I_e \leftarrow (e_m \sim e_n'), e_n' = \mathrm{argmin}_{e_n' \in \mathcal{C}_m} R[m, n],$$

$$R[m, n] = \begin{cases} r^{\mathcal{A}}[m, n]/|I_e^{\mathcal{A}}|, & \text{if } (e_m \sim e_n') \in I_e^{\mathcal{A}}; \\ r^{\mathcal{R}}[m, n]/|I_e^{\mathcal{R}}|, & \text{if } (e_m \sim e_n') \in I_e^{\mathcal{R}}. \end{cases}$$

where $r^{\mathcal{A}}[m, n]$, $r^{\mathcal{R}}[m, n]$ denote the ranking index of the alignment $(e_m \sim e_n')$ in $I_e^{\mathcal{A}}$ and $I_e^{\mathcal{R}}$ respectively, and $R[m, n]$ denotes the normalized ranking index.

Table 1. Data statistics. Notation #Rt denotes the number of the relationship triplets, #Ar denotes the number of the attribute triplets.

Dataset	#Ent.	#Rel.	#Attr.	#Rt	#At
ZH-EN	164,594	5,147	15,286	391,603	947,439
JA-EN	161,424	4,139	11,948	397,692	851,849
FR-EN	172,747	3,588	10,969	470,781	1,105,208

4   Experiments

4.1   Experimental Settings

Dataset. We evaluate the proposed model on DBP15K[3], a well-known public dataset for KG alignment. DBP15K contains 3 pairs of cross-lingual KGs, each of which contains 15,000 inter-lingual links (ILLs). The proportion of the ILLs for training, validating and testing is 4:1:10. Table 1 shows the data statistics.

---

[3] https://github.com/nju-websoft/JAPE.

Baseline Methods. We compare several existing methods:

MuGNN [3]: Learns the structure embeddings by a multi-channel GNNs.

BootEA [10]: Is a bootstrap method that finds new alignments by performing a maximal matching between the structure embeddings of the entities.

JAPE [9]: Leverages the attributes and the type of values to refine the structure embeddings.

GCNs [12]: Learns the structure embeddings by GCNs and use the one-hot representation of all the attributes as the initial input of an entity.

MultiKE [15]: Learns a global attribute embedding for each entity and combines it with the structure embedding. Since it is to solve monolingual entity alignment, for a fair comparison, we translate all the words into English by Google's translator and then applies MultiKE.

JarKA: Is our model. The variant JarKA-r removes the relationship model and JarKA-a removes the attribute model, the bootstrap strategy is still adopted.

As KDCoE [4] and Yang et al. [14] leverage the descriptions of entities, and Xu et al. [13] adopts external cross-lingual corpus to train embeddings, we do not compare with them and leave the studies with these resources in the future.

Evaluation Metrics. In the test set, for each entity in G, we rank all the entities in G' by either $\mathbf{S}_e^{\mathcal{A}}$ or $\mathbf{S}_e^{\mathcal{R}}$, and evaluate the ranking results by HitRatio@K (HRK), i.e., the percentage of entities with the rightly aligned entities ranked before top K, and Mean Reciprocal Rank (MRR), i.e., the average of the reciprocal ranks of the rightly aligned entities.

Implementation Details. In the attribute model, the value embedding size D_v is 100, the maximal number of attributes M is 20, and the frequent attributes are those occurred more than 50 times in $\{(h, a, v)\}$. In the relationship model, the entity/relationship embedding size D_e or D_r is 75, and $\gamma = 1.0$. The thresholds τ_e^A and τ_e^R for selecting the aligned entities are set as the values when the best HR1 is obtained on the validation set. τ_v for selecting the aligned attributes is 0.8, and τ_r for selecting the aligned relationships is 0.9.

Initial Seeds Construction. The existing ILLs can be viewed as the entity seed alignments. Some relationships or attributes in cross-lingual knowledge graphs are both represented in English. So we can easily treat a pair of relationships or attributes with the same name[4] as a relationship or attribute seed alignment. Finally, the corresponding values of the aligned attributes for any aligned entity pairs are added into the seed set of the aligned values.

4.2 Experimental Results

Overall Alignment Performance. Table 2 shows the overall performance of entity alignment. MuGNN and BootEA only leverage relationship triplets.

---

[4] Attributes and relationships are less ambiguous than entities. The sampled 500 pairs of attributes and relationships present that about 95% of them can be safely aligned only based on the same names.

Table 2. Overall performance of entity alignment (%).

Model	DBP15K$_\text{ZH-EN}$			DBP15K$_\text{JA-EN}$			DBP15K$_\text{FR-EN}$		
	HR1	HR10	MRR	HR1	HR10	MRR	HR1	HR10	MRR
MuGNN	49.40	84.40	61.10	50.10	85.70	62.10	49.50	87.00	62.10
BootEA	62.94	84.75	70.30	62.23	85.39	70.10	65.30	87.44	73.10
JAPE	41.18	74.46	49.00	36.25	68.50	47.60	32.39	66.68	43.00
GCNs	41.25	74.38	55.80	39.91	74.46	55.20	37.29	74.49	53.40
MultiKE	50.87	57.61	53.20	39.30	48.85	42.60	63.94	71.19	66.50
JarKA-r	57.18	70.44	61.80	50.63	60.36	54.30	53.92	60.40	56.30
JarKA-a	58.64	83.89	67.10	55.74	83.23	65.10	59.25	85.74	68.60
JarKA(M1)	68.59	86.56	74.90	62.65	82.79	69.70	68.43	87.86	75.10
JarKA(M2)	69.32	87.37	75.50	63.01	83.37	70.00	**70.87**	87.05	76.50
JarKA(M3)	**70.58**	**87.81**	**76.60**	**64.58**	**85.50**	**70.80**	70.41	**88.81**	**76.80**
JarKA-IT	66.39	87.29	73.40	60.08	84.45	68.20	68.31	88.33	75.40

BootEA bootstraps the alignments iteratively and performs better than MuGNN. Although JAPE and GCN additionally consider the attribute triplets, they perform much worse than BootEA, as they only leverage the attributes but ignore their corresponding values. MultiKE utilizes the values and performs better than JAPE and GCN. However, it learns and compares the global embeddings of entities, which may bring in additional noises by the irrelevant attribute triplets.

JarKA proposes an interaction-based attribute model which directly compares the values of the aligned attributes, thus it clearly performs better than others (+2.35-38.48% in HR1). JarKA also outperforms the variant JarKA-r and JarKA-a. Specifically, JarKA-r is comparable to JarKA-a in HR1 but underperforms in HR10 and MRR. Because in JarKA-r, we set a strict threshold (Cf. Fig. 3(a)) to obtain high-qualified alignments, which makes the translation model not easy to include the difficult alignments into the training data, i.e., the seemingly irrelevant value pairs which in fact indicate the same things.

The Effect of Different Merge Strategies. We compare the effects of the proposed three merge strategies and show the results of JarKA(M1), (M2) and (M3) in Table 2. We can see that the standard multi-view merge strategy (M1) performs worst, as it does not solve the conflicts from the two views. The score-based merge strategy (M2) and the rank-based merge strategy (M3) solve the conflicts, thus perform better than M1 (+1.26-2.43% in HR1). M3 avoids comparing the scores of different scales, thus performs better than M2 in most of the metrics. Later, JarKA indicates the proposed model with M3.

The Effect of Iteratively Update the Translation Model. We validate the effect of iteratively updating the translation model (IT) during the joint modeling process. Specifically, we compare JarKA with the translation model being trained only once at the beginning, which is denoted as JarKA-IT. From Table 2, we can see that JarKA-IT performs worse JarKA by 2.56-4.50% in HR1, which indicates that the newly discovered value alignments by our model can boost the performance of the translation model.

The Effect of τ_v **and** τ_r. We verify how the new aligned attributes can benefit the entity alignment. Specifically, we vary the threshold τ_v from 0.6 to 1.0 with interval 0.1 and show the results of JarKA-r on DBP15K-1 FR-EN in Fig. 3(a). It is shown that when $\tau_v = 1.0$, i.e., #new aligned attributes is 0, the accuracy of entity alignment is significantly hurt. When $\tau_v < 1.0$, with the increase of #new aligned attributes, the accuracy improves and approaches the best when $\tau_v = 0.8$, as the quantity and the quality of the new aligned attributes are well balanced. The threshold τ_r for finding the new aligned relationships is set in the same way.

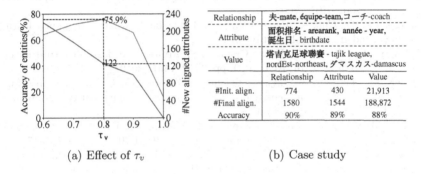

Relationship	夫-mate, équipe-team, コーチ-coach		
Attribute	面积排名 - arearank, année - year, 誕生日 - birthdate		
Value	塔吉克足球聯賽 - tajik league, nordEst-northeast, ダマスカス-damascus		
	Relationship	Attribute	Value
#Init. align.	774	430	21,913
#Final align.	1580	1544	188,872
Accuracy	90%	89%	88%

(a) Effect of τ_v (b) Case study

Fig. 3. Parameter analysis and case study.

Case Study. We present several cases of the new aligned relationships, attributes and values in different languages by JarKA on DBP15K in Fig. 3(b). We also show the number of initial and the finally discovered alignments on DBP15K ZH-EN. Most of the newly discovered alignments are high-frequent attributes or relationships. The low-frequent attributes or relationships are difficult to be aligned by the current method and will be studied in the future. We randomly sample 100 final alignments and manually evaluate the accuracy, as their ground truth is not available. The results demonstrate the effectiveness of our model. The whole alignments together with the codes are available online[5].

5   Conclusions and Future Work

We present the first attempt to formalize the problem of cross-lingual knowledge alignment as comprehensively linking entities, relationships, attributes and values. We propose an interaction-based attribute model to compare the aligned

---

[5] https://github.com/BoChen-Daniel/PAKDD-20-JarKA.

attributes of entities instead of globally embedding entities. A matrix-based strategy is adopted to accelerate the comparing process. Then we propose a joint framework together with three merge strategies to solve the conflicts of the alignments inferred from the attribute model and the relationship model. The experimental results demonstrate the effectiveness of the proposed model. In the future, we plan to incorporate the descriptions of entities and the pre-trained cross-lingual language model to enhance our model's performance.

Acknowledgements. This work is supported by National Key R&D Program of China (No. 2018YFB1004401) and NSFC under the grant No. 61532021, 61772537, 61772536, 61702522.

References

1. Ahlander, K.: Einstein summation for multidimensional arrays. Comput. Math. Appl. **44**, 1007–1017 (2002)
2. Bahdanau, D., Cho, K., Bengio, Y.: Neural machine translation by jointly learning to align and translate. In ICLR 2015 (2015)
3. Cao, Y., Liu, Z., Li, C., Li, J., Chua, T.-S.: Multi-channel graph neural network for entity alignment. In: ACL 2019, pp. 1452–1461 (2019)
4. Chen, M., Tian, Y., Chang, K., Skiena, S., Zaniolo, C.: Co-training embeddings of knowledge graphs and entity descriptions for cross-lingual entity alignment. In: IJCAI 2018, pp. 3998–4004 (2018)
5. Chen, M., Tian, Y., Yang, M., Zaniolo, C.: Multilingual knowledge graph embeddings for cross-lingual knowledge alignment. In: IJCAI 2017, pp. 1511–1517 (2017)
6. Hao, Y., Zhang, Y., He, S., Liu, K., Zhao, J.: A joint embedding method for entity alignment of knowledge bases. In: Chen, H., Ji, H., Sun, L., Wang, H., Qian, T., Ruan, T. (eds.) CCKS 2016. CCIS, vol. 650, pp. 3–14. Springer, Singapore (2016). https://doi.org/10.1007/978-981-10-3168-7_1
7. Li, S., Li, X., Ye, R., Wang, M., Su, H., Ou, Y.: Non-translational alignment for multi-relational networks. In: IJCAI 2018 (2018)
8. Papineni, K., Roukos, S., Ward, T., Zhu, W.-J.: Bleu: a method for automatic evaluation of machine translation. In: ACL 2002, pp. 311–318 (2002)
9. Sun, Z., Hu, W., Li, C.: Cross-lingual entity alignment via joint attribute-preserving embedding. In: ISWC 2017, pp. 628–644 (2017)
10. Sun, Z., Hu, W., Zhang, Q., Qu, Y.: Bootstrapping entity alignment with knowledge graph embedding. In: IJCAI 2018, pp. 4396–4402 (2018)
11. Trsedya, B.D., Qi, J., Zhang, R.: Entity alignment between knowledge graphs using attribute embeddings. In: AAAI 2019 (2019)
12. Wang, Z., Lv, Q., Lan, X., Zhang, Y.: Cross-lingual knowledge graph alignment via graph convolutional networks. In: EMNLP 2018, pp. 349–357 (2018)
13. Xu, K., et al.: Cross-lingual knowledge graph alignment via graph matching neural network. In: ACL 2019, pp. 1452–1461 (2019)
14. Yang, H.-W., Zou, Y., Shi, P., Lu, W., Lin, J., Xu, S.: Aligning cross-lingual entities with multi-aspect information. In EMNLP 2019, pp. 4422–4432 (2019)
15. Zhang, Q., Sun, Z., Hu, W., Chen, M., Guo, L., Qu, Y.: Multi-view knowledge graph embedding for entity alignment. In: AAAI 2019 (2019)
16. Zhu, H., Xie, R., Liu, Z., Sun, M.: Iterative entity alignment via joint knowledge embeddings. In: IJCAI 2017, pp. 4258–4264 (2017)

Multiple Demographic Attributes Prediction in Mobile and Sensor Devices

Yiwen Jiang[1,2,3], Wei Tang[1,2,3], Neng Gao[1,2], Ji Xiang[2], Chenyang Tu[1,2(✉)], and Min Li[1,2]

[1] State Key Laboratory of Information Security, Chinese Academy
of Sciences, Beijing, China
[2] Institute of Information Engineering, Chinese Academy
of Sciences, Beijing, China
{jiangyiwen,tangwei,gaoneng,xiangji,tuchenyang,minli}@iie.ac.cn
[3] School of Cyber Security, University of Chinese Academy
of Sciences, Beijing, China

Abstract. Users' real demographic attributes is impressively useful for intelligent marketing, automatic advertising and human-computer interaction. Traditional method on attribute prediction make great effort on the study of social network data, but ignore massive volumes of disparate, dynamic, and temporal data derived from ubiquitous mobile and sensor devices. For example, daily walking step counts produced by pedometer. Multiple demographic prediction on temporal data have two problems. First one is that differential effectiveness of different time period data for prediction is unclear. And another one is how to effectively learn the complementary correlations between different attributes. To address the above problem, we propose a novel model named Correlation-Aware Neural Embedding with Attention (CANEA), which first directly separates different attribute oriented feature using separated embedding layer, and use attention mechanism to assign a higher weight to dominant time point. Then it captures informative correlations using correlation learning layer. Finally we obtain the refined task-specific representations with optimal correlation information for predicting certain attributes. Experimental results show the effectiveness of our method.

Keywords: Demographic prediction · Pedometer data · Correlation learning

1 Introduction

Knowing users' real demographic attributes is extremely significant for the applications of intelligent marketing, automatic advertising and human-computer interaction. Conventional applications of demographic prediction tend to pay attention to users' behavior in social networks, and few people pay attention to mobile and sensor devices. However, sensor data for demographic prediction has it's own unique applications. For example, it's hard to use online speech to infer the age and gender of a person who rarely speaks on social networks, but it's

© Springer Nature Switzerland AG 2020
H. W. Lauw et al. (Eds.): PAKDD 2020, LNAI 12084, pp. 857–868, 2020.
https://doi.org/10.1007/978-3-030-47426-3_66

easier to infer such attribute via his or her pedometer records, as the walking is a daily stable behavior. Besides, the attributes predicted through sensor data could be directly used to enable human-computer interaction more humanized and friendly in smart home system. For example, when a young lady go home from outside, the air conditioning and audio could select a gender/age-aware response (air conditioning temperature and music) from many possible candidates to make the user more comfortable [10].

Most of earlier studies on attribute prediction are primarily involve analysis of the user-generated public data on the network, especially logs, comments as well as videos. They mostly come from Facebook [12], Twitters [2,13], microblogs [17], YouTube [4], web search queries [6], social networking chats [11], and forum posts [3]. And little work is put into the management of sensor data. Besides, traditional demographic prediction model can not fully learn the complementary correlations between different attributes. Existing work usually infer users' different attributes separately without taking account of correlation learning or infer all the attributes together using shared embedding at the bottom of model. For example, wang et al. [16] proposed a Structured Neural Embedding (SNE) model that use shared embedding to leverages the potential correlations for multi-task learning by concatenating structured label. However, the concatenated formalization makes the prediction task more difficult than separated tasks since the output space for each task becomes much larger. Raehyun et al. [8] proposed an Embedding Transformation Network (ETN) model that shares user representations at the bottom and converts them to task-specific representations using a linear transformation. But this model does not take any steps to explicitly learn the complementary relationship between different task-specific features.

To tackle the above problem, we make effort on the reasonable utilize of pedometer data and go a further step to present a new model named Correlation-Aware Neural Embedding with Attention (CANEA) for multiple demographic attributes prediction. In CANEA, we first leverage a separated embedding layer with attention based on RNN branches to extract task-specific features, and obtain explicit day weight for better prediction. Then, to well learn complementary correlations between different tasks, we design a correlation learning layer with full connection neural pipelines to capture correlation features. Moreover, we enhance the user representation with correlation features using bilinear model. The final user representations are fed into multi-task prediction layer for multiple demographic attributes prediction.

We conduct extensive experiments on a real world pedometer dataset to test our method. Several state-of-the-art baselines are taken into comparison. And we also test our model in traditional application scenario of demographic prediction on transaction data. The experimental results prove the effectiveness of our model. Overall, our contributions are as follows:

(1) We extend our sight to the ubiquitous mobile and sensor devices to bridge the gap between pedometer data and users' demographic attributes.
(2) A new model named Embedding Separation and Correlation Learning with Attention (CANEA) is proposed for multiple demographic prediction, which has strong ability to learn the complementary correlations between tasks.

In addition, we explicitly analyze different days' effect of pedometer records on demographic prediction.

(3) Extensive experiments are conducted on a real world pedometer dataset as well as a public transaction dataset, which all demonstrate the effectiveness of the proposed method.

The rest of this paper is organized as follows. Section 2 gives the problem formalization of multi-task demographic prediction. Section 3 discusses our model Architecture in detail, and Sect. 4 presents the experimental results and analysis. And finally, in Sect. 5, we conclude our work and present future work.

2 Problem Formalization

In our application scenario, we aim to predict demographic attributes based on pedometer data. Specifically, the profile of each user is represented as a sequence of daily step counts, which could be presented as follow:

$$S : [[s_1], [s_2], ..., [s_n]]$$

where S denotes the pedometer record of a certain user, s_i is his/her step count on the i-th day, and n is the total days.

Typically, our work is a multi-task prediction problem. Here, the attributes we are interested in are gender and age, and the attributes can be various if necessary in other applications. The values of gender are male and female regardless of non-traditional gender, and the values of age include young, adult, middle age and old [16]. Therefore, the prediction problem $\mathcal{T}$ could be summarized as:

$$\mathcal{T} : S \rightarrow \{y_1, y_2, ... y_t\}$$

where y_i is the attribute class of i-th task, and t is the total number of the tasks. The objective of our work is to train an effective end-to-end model to simultaneously predict demographic attributes for new users.

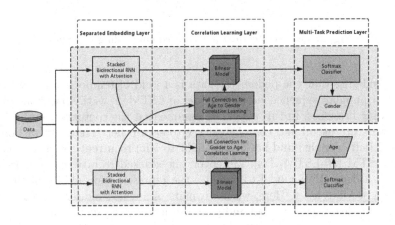

Fig. 1. The architecture of CANEA.

3   Model Architecture

In this section, we present the details of the CANEA. An overview of our framework is illustrated in Fig. 1. We leverage separated embedding layer to extract task-specific representations. And a correlation learning layer is used to learn the hidden correlations between different tasks. Finally, the multi-task prediction layer make the prediction of all tasks simultaneously.

3.1   Separated Embedding Layer

We use separated embedding branches showed in Fig. 2 to learn task-specific representations. Different from mapping user profiles to a shared representation at the bottom of model that ignores the interferences among multiple tasks, the separated embedding branches eliminate these interferences and produce a relatively pure task-specific representations directly. We have to admit that shared embedding retain informative correlations among multiple attributes, and separated embedding method seems to ignore these correlations. But this shared embedding lacks explanations for correlation extraction. And in the next section, we will introduce correlation learning layer to learn these correlations in a more interpretable way.

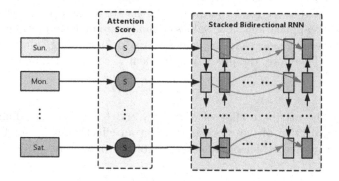

Fig. 2. The architecture of separated embedding branches.

Considering that the pedometer data is a kind of temporal data, we adopt the most popular sequence learning model of LSTM [5] as the backbone of each embedding branches. In this paper, we assume that the contexts from both past and future are useful and complementary to each other. Therefore we combine forward (left to right) and backward (right to left) recurrent to build a bidirectional LSTM (Bi-LSTM) [14]. Moreover, the stacked recurrent layers are used to build a deep RNN model to enhance the representation ability of the separated embedding layer. Here, we use a pairs of stacked bidirectional LSTM to respectively learn age oriented and gender oriented representations.

Note that the different days in each week play differential roles in tasks. For example, in our intuition, female are more likely to go shopping than male on weekends. That means users' step counts on weekend is more important than weekday for gender inference. From this point of view, we adopt attention mechanism [1] to give the significant days higher scores. Thus, the separated embedding branches could be presented as:

$$\mathbf{w}_i = softmax(tanh(\mathbf{v}_i\mathbf{x} + \mathbf{b}_i))$$

$$\mathbf{E}_i = \mathcal{L}_{\theta_i}(\mathbf{w}_i\mathbf{x})$$

where $\mathcal{L}$ is the trainable model of Bi-LSTM, θ_i is the trainable parameters of embedding branches for i-th task, $\mathbf{x}$ is the input sequence, and $\mathbf{E}_i$ is the output task-specific feature for i-th task. Additionally, $\mathbf{v}_i$ and $\mathbf{b}_i$ are trainable parameters of the attention model in i-th branch, $\mathbf{w}_i$ is the attention weights describing the importance assigned to each element of the input.

3.2 Correlation Learning Layer

As we mentioned before, the separated embedding layer eliminate the interferences among multiple tasks, but the informative correlations between different tasks have been ignored. In this situation, we design a correlation learning layer to learn hidden correlation features. The key components of this correlation learning pipelines are a full connection network and a bilinear mixer (presented in Fig. 3).

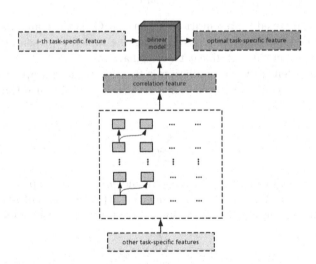

Fig. 3. Architecture of the key component in correlation learning piplines.

Full connection network are widely used in hidden representation learning on account of their excellent learning ability and desirable scalability. The correlation representation for i-th task is presented as:

$$\mathbf{C}_i = \mathcal{F}_{\phi_i}(\mathbf{w}_i \bar{\mathbf{E}}_i)$$

where $\mathcal{F}$ is the trainable model of full connection network, ϕ_i is the trainable parameters, C_i represents correlation feature for i-th task, $\bar{\mathbf{E}}_i$ is the concatenation of other task-specific features.

We combine the separation feature and correlation feature in a bilinear model. The bilinear model is a two-factor model with mathematical property of separability: their outputs are linear in either factor when the others held constant, which has been demonstrated that the influences of two factors can be efficiently separated and combined in a flexible representation [15]. The combination function can be formulated as:

$$\mathbf{M}_i = \mathbf{E}_i \mathbf{W}_i \mathbf{C}_i$$

where $\mathbf{W}_i$ is the tensor of trainable parameters, $\mathbf{E}_i$ denotes separation representation of i-th task , and $\mathbf{C}_i$ is the correlation representation for i-th task.

3.3   Multi-task Prediction Layer

With the separation representation and correlation representation obtained by the previous two layers, we obtain the prediction probability for the demographic attribute of a given user by:

$$p(y_i|S) = softmax(\mathbf{O}_i \mathbf{M}_i)$$

where $\mathbf{M}_i$ is the mixed representation of user and $\mathbf{O}_i$ is the trainable parameter. The parameter is responsible for converting the mixed representation for each task into prediction through linear transformation.

The goal of demographic prediction is to infer all demographic attribute of users from their pedometer profiles. For i-th task, we minimize the sum of the negative log-likelihoods defined as:

$$Loss_i = -\sum_{j=1}^{m} log p(y_{i,j}|S_j)$$

where m is the total number of users. S_j and $y_{i,j}$ are the input of j-th user's daily step count sequence and his/her inferred attribute class of i-th task.

Combining all these task-specific losses, the total multi-task loss function is:

$$Loss = \sum_{i=1}^{t} \lambda_i Loss_i$$

where the hyper-parameter λ controls the trade-off between all of t task-specific losses. Considering that all tasks are equal important in our experiments, we set all λ to be 1.

4 Experiments

In this section, we present the details of our experiments and analyze the effectiveness of our approach.

4.1 Dataset

We build a large-scale real world pedometer dataset came from WeChat, a famous mobile application in China. WeChat develops a subfunction called WeChat Sport that collects and ranks users' as well as their net friends' daily step counts online based on the pedometers embedded in mobile phones, and we crawl the data at the chance. Our dataset contains 39,246 users' 300-days step counts during the period from 2018.6.11 to 2019.4.6. All of the users are annotated with gender and age. To guarantee the reliability of the data, we removed those unsuitable users who have more than 150 days of zero step count records. The distribution of users' attributes are listed in Table 1. In experiment, we use 60% and 20% of the data for training and test, and leave the rest 20% as a validation set for tuning.

Table 1. Distribution of users' attributes.

Attributes	Value	Users	Distribution
Gender	Male	22134	56%
	Female	17112	44%
Age	Young	8635	22%
	Adult	19230	49%
	Middle age	7064	18%
	Old	4317	11%

4.2 Evaluation Metrics

We employ F-measure to evaluate our model. F1-measure is a widely used measure method as a complement for accuracy, and it is the most popular evaluation metrics for demographic prediction. Specifically, F1 score is calculated as the harmonic mean of precision and recall. Note that, in our experiment, we use the weighted precision (wP), recall (wR) and F1 $(wF1)$ score as the evaluation metrics since we consider all classes to be equal important. The weighted F1 is calculated as follows:

$$wP = \sum_{y \in Y} \left(\frac{\sum_{i=1}^{u} I(y_i^* = \hat{y}_i \& y = \hat{y}_i)}{\sum_{i=1}^{u} I(y = \hat{y}_i)} * weight \right)$$

$$wR = \sum_{y \in Y} \left(\frac{\sum_{i=1}^{u} I(y_i^* = \hat{y}_i \& y = \hat{y}_i)}{\sum_{i=1}^{u} I(y = y_i^*)} * weight \right)$$

$$wF1 = 2 \times \frac{wP \times wR}{wP + wR}$$

where $I(\cdot)$ is an indicator function, u denotes the total number of new users, Y is the set of all label combinations to be predicted, y_i^* denotes the ground truth of attributes for the i-th new user, $\hat{y}_i$ denotes the predicted attributes, and $weight = \frac{1}{u}\sum_{i=1}^{u} I(y = y_i)$. The weighted F1 assigns a high weight to the large classes to account for label imbalance.

4.3   Baseline Models

We compare our models with several baselines on demographic prediction. The description of these baselines are listed below:

POP. POP is a naive method that always predicts the given sample as the majority classes. In previous work [8,16], POP is used as a baseline model which ignores characteristics of users.

JNE. Joint Neural Embedding [16] maps users' all walking histories into latent vectors. These vectors are processed by average pooling and then fed into a linear prediction layer for each task.

SNE. Structured Neural Embedding [16] has similar structure with JNE. The only difference between SNE and JNE is that the loss of SNE is computed via a log-bilinear model with structured predictions.

ETN. Embedding Transformation Network [8] uses a shared embedding just as SNE. The shared embedding is fed into an embedding transformation layer to obtain the transformed representation. Then the transformed representation is directly fed into the prediction layer.

ETNA. Embedding Transformation Network with Attention [8] is an improved version of ETN. The transformed representation produced by embedding transformed layer is fed to a task-specific attention layer to take into account the importance of each element in users' profile.

4.4   Experimental Settings

Considering that the recurrent units maintain activation for each time-step which have already make the network to be extremely deep, we use only one layer of bidirectional RNN with 128 LSTM units in each separated embedding branch. And the full connection networks in correlation learning layer is set to be the shallow architectures using only 3 hidden layer with 256 sigmoid units. We use random values drawn from the Gaussian distribution with 0 mean and 0.01 standard deviation to initialize the weight matrices in LSTM, full connected layer, and prediction layer. Learning from [7], the forget gate bias are initialized to be 5 to let the forget gate close to 1, namely no forgetting. Thus, long-range

Table 2. Performance comparison of different models.

Model name	Results		
	wP	wR	wF1
POP [8]	0.137	0.354	0.198
JNE [16]	0.609	0.643	0.626
SNE [16]	0.615	0.648	0.631
ETN [8]	0.634	0.679	0.656
ETNA [8]	0.641	0.688	0.660
CANEA[a]	0.496	0.513	0.504
CANEA[b]	0.681	0.726	0.703
CANEA	**0.695**	**0.741**	**0.717**

[a]abandon correlation learning layer.
[b]abandon attention mechanism.

dependencies can be better learned at the beginning of training. All other bias, the cell as well as hidden states of LSTMs in our work are initialized at 0. Adam [9] is used as the optimization algorithm and the mini-batch size is 128. The learning rate is set to be $1e^{-5}$. After each epoch, we shuffle the training data to make different mini-batches.

4.5   Comparison with Baselines

Table 2 shows the experimental results of our model and the baseline models. Based on these results, we have the following findings:

(1) If we abandon correlation learning layer, our model will degenerate into a parallel integration of multiple RNNs, CANEA[a]. Note that CANEA is much better than CANEA[a], this result proves that the correlation learning layer plays an important role in our models. Furthermore, CANEA[a] is far behind JNE, SNE, ETN and ETNA, because it ignores the informative correlations among multiple tasks. According to this result, it could be demonstrated that capturing such correlations has great significance in multi-task prediction.

(2) As we emphasized in this paper, the ability to learn correlations between different tasks is important in multi-task learning. JNE, SNE, ETN and ETNA use the shared embedding that implicitly leverage these correlations, but ignore the interferences among multiple tasks. We first use the separated embedding to avoid such interference, and then employ the correlation learning to obtain the correlations. Although we use the most simple architectures of our models for baseline comparison (see Sect. 4.4), which still outperform all the baselines with a significant gap.

(3) The attention mechanism is helpful for separation embedding. As shown in Table 2, the CANEA is obviously better than the CANEA[b]. As aforementioned, they have the similar architecture, except that the former model introduces the attention mechanism into separated Embedding layer to

weaken unimportant factors and highlight the important factors of the input. The results are a strong proof that the step count records of different days in week play differential roles in gender and age prediction.

4.6   Visualization of Attention

To further analyze the effectiveness of attention mechanism in separated embedding layer, we provide visualization of attention scores. We pick example that provide insights for users' pedometer records from Sunday to Saturday during 10 weeks with the average attention scores in each task. Based on the attention scores from our model, we draw heatmap in Fig. 4.

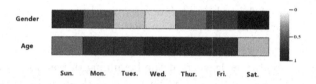

Fig. 4. Comparison of attention weights calculated by separated embedding layer.

Noting that Saturday and Sunday obtain highest attention in gender prediction task. Exactly, in our intuition, women prefer to go shopping on the weekends, which fits the gap between male and female in Fig. 5-(Gender).

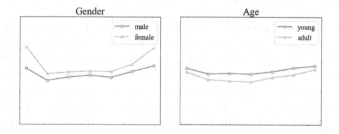

Fig. 5. Mean value (y-axis) of attention scores from Sunday to Saturday (x-axis).

For age prediction, our model give relatively higher attention scores to weekdays but lower scores to weekends. Intuitively, young people are more energetic and active, and most adults tend to stay at their desks on weekdays. But on the weekends, parents and children may go out to play together. Figure 5-(Age) empirically demonstrates the reasonability of this intuition from a statistical point of view, as the gap between adult and young is relatively large on weekdays but small on the weekends.

4.7 Experiments on Transaction Data

We also conduct experiments on transaction dataset used in [8]. This dataset is the first public dataset containing both transaction records and demographic information. It consists of purchasing histories of 56,028 users and contains the gender, age, and marital status of all the users. And this dataset support two types of different prediction applications: partial label prediction and new user prediction. Table 3 reports the experimental results. Results show that CANEA also outperforms all baseline models with impressive improvement on transaction data, which also proves the strong generalization ability of our model.

Table 3. Results on transaction data.

Model name	Partial label			New user		
	wP	wR	wF1	wP	wR	wF1
POP	0.289	0.514	0.370	0.086	0.294	0.134
JNE	0.518	0.563	0.539	0.321	0.348	0.334
SNE	0.521	0.563	0.542	0.295	0.351	0.321
ETN	0.540	0.576	0.557	0.310	0.368	0.336
ETNA	0.554	0.584	0.569	0.339	0.382	0.360
CANEA	**0.568**	**0.596**	**0.582**	**0.356**	**0.401**	**0.377**

5 Conclusion and Future Work

In this paper, we introduce the Correlation-Aware Neural Embedding with Attention (CANEA) model for demographic prediction. Different from previous method using shared embedding to retain hidden correlations between multiple tasks, our approach leverages separated embedding to eliminate the interferences between multiple tasks and then propose correlation learning to obtain the correlations between multiple tasks. Furthermore, we further analyze different effects on gender and age prediction of different days in week, and take advantage of this phenomenon to optimize our model.

In the future, we would like to verify the effectiveness of our approach in a larger number of tasks, which need more annotations. More advanced models are expected as some shortcomings are still existed in current methods, such as lack of external knowledge and excessive reliance on large amounts of training data.

References

1. Bahdanau, D., Cho, K., Bengio, Y.: Neural machine translation by jointly learning to align and translate. In: 3rd International Conference on Learning Representations, ICLR 2015, Conference Track Proceedings, San Diego, CA, USA, 7–9 May 2015 (2015). http://arxiv.org/abs/1409.0473

2. Burger, J.D., Henderson, J., Kim, G., Zarrella, G.: Discriminating gender on twitter. In: Conference on Empirical Methods in Natural Language Processing, pp. 1301–1309 (2011)

3. Dong, N., Smith, N.A.: Author age prediction from text using linear regression. In: ACL-HLT Workshop on Language Technology for Cultural Heritage, Social Sciences, and Humanities, pp. 115–123 (2011)

4. Filippova, K.: User demographics and language in an implicit social network. In: Joint Conference on Empirical Methods in Natural Language Processing and Computational Natural Language Learning, pp. 1478–1488 (2012)

5. Hochreiter, S., Schmidhuber, J.: Long short-term memory. Neural Comput. **9**(8), 1735–1780 (1997). https://doi.org/10.1162/neco.1997.9.8.1735

6. Jones, R., Kumar, R., Pang, B., Tomkins, A.: "I know what you did last summer": query logs and user privacy. In: Sixteenth ACM Conference on Conference on Information and Knowledge Management, pp. 909–914 (2007)

7. Józefowicz, R., Zaremba, W., Sutskever, I.: An empirical exploration of recurrent network architectures. In: Proceedings of the 32nd International Conference on Machine Learning, ICML 2015, Lille, France, 6–11 July 2015. pp. 2342–2350 (2015). http://jmlr.org/proceedings/papers/v37/jozefowicz15.html

8. Kim, R., Kim, H., Lee, J., Kang, J.: Predicting multiple demographic attributes with task specific embedding transformation and attention network. CoRR abs/1903.10144 (2019). http://arxiv.org/abs/1903.10144

9. Kingma, D.P., Ba, J.: Adam: a method for stochastic optimization. CoRR abs/1412.6980 (2014). http://arxiv.org/abs/1412.6980

10. Li, S., Wang, J., Zhou, G., Shi, H.: Interactive gender inference with integer linear programming. In: Proceedings of the Twenty-Fourth International Joint Conference on Artificial Intelligence, IJCAI 2015, Buenos Aires, Argentina, 25–31 July 2015. pp. 2341–2347 (2015). http://ijcai.org/Abstract/15/331

11. Peersman, C., Daelemans, W., Vaerenbergh, L.V.: Predicting age and gender in online social networks. In: International Workshop on Search and Mining User-Generated Contents, pp. 37–44 (2011)

12. Quercia, D., Lambiotte, R., Stillwell, D., Kosinski, M., Crowcroft, J.: The personality of popular facebook users. In: ACM Conference on Computer Supported Cooperative Work, pp. 955–964 (2012)

13. Rao, D., Yarowsky, D., Shreevats, A., Gupta, M.: Classifying latent user attributes in twitter. In: International Workshop on Search and Mining User-Generated Contents, pp. 37–44 (2010)

14. Schuster, M., Paliwal, K.K.: Bidirectional recurrent neural networks. IEEE Trans. Signal Process. **45**(11), 2673–2681 (1997). https://doi.org/10.1109/78.650093

15. Tenenbaum, J.B., Freeman, W.T.: Separating style and content. In: Advances in Neural Information Processing Systems 9, NIPS, Denver, CO, USA, 2–5 December 1996. pp. 662–668 (1996). http://papers.nips.cc/paper/1290-separating-style-and-content

16. Wang, P., Guo, J., Lan, Y., Xu, J., Cheng, X.: Your cart tells you: inferring demographic attributes from purchase data. In: WSDM, pp. 173–182 (2016)

17. Zhang, L., Huang, X., Liu, T., Li, A., Chen, Z., Zhu, T.: Using linguistic features to estimate suicide probability of Chinese microblog users. In: Zu, Q., Hu, B., Gu, N., Seng, S. (eds.) HCC 2014. LNCS, vol. 8944, pp. 549–559. Springer, Cham (2015). https://doi.org/10.1007/978-3-319-15554-8_45

Human Activity Recognition Using Semi-supervised Multi-modal DEC for Instagram Data

Dongmin Kim[(⊠)], Sumin Han, Heesuk Son, and Dongman Lee

School of Computing, Korea Advanced Institute of Science and Technology,
Daejeon, Republic of Korea
{dmkim25,suminhan,heesuk.son,dlee}@kaist.ac.kr

Abstract. *Human Activity Recognition (HAR)* using social media provides a solid basis for a variety of context-aware applications. Existing HAR approaches have adopted supervised machine learning algorithms using texts and their meta-data such as time, venue, and keywords. However, their recognition accuracy may decrease when applied to image-sharing social media where users mostly describe their daily activities and thoughts using both texts and images. In this paper, we propose a semi-supervised multi-modal deep embedding clustering method to recognize human activities on Instagram. Our proposed method learns multi-modal feature representations by alternating a supervised learning phase and an unsupervised learning phase. By utilizing a large number of unlabeled data, it learns a more generalized feature distribution for each HAR class and avoids overfitting to limited labeled data. Evaluation results show that leveraging multi-modality and unlabeled data is effective for HAR and our method outperforms existing approaches.

Keywords: Human activity recognition · Social media · Multi-modal · Deep learning · Deep embedded clustering · Semi-supervised learning

1 Introduction

Social media has been an ambient data platform on which people share their activities of daily living and memorable experience. Using the embedded behavioral patterns in the shared data, *Human Activity Recognition (HAR)* provides a solid basis for a variety of applications such as context-aware recommendation systems and health-care services [9–11]. To achieve better HAR performance using popular image-sharing social media such as *Instagram* and *Yelp*, various machine learning models have been presented [1–3]. Since these social media allow users to put their geolocation features when uploading the posts, human activities extracted from them have high potential to enhance awareness of real world dynamics.

Existing HAR approaches [1–3] leverage supervised machine learning models (e.g., SVM, LSTM) which take texts and meta-data of social media posts for

© Springer Nature Switzerland AG 2020
H. W. Lauw et al. (Eds.): PAKDD 2020, LNAI 12084, pp. 869–880, 2020.
https://doi.org/10.1007/978-3-030-47426-3_67

learning important patterns with respect to human activities. However, its use of uni-modal textual features cannot capture enough patterns of human activities shared on the social media because users mostly describe their daily activities and thoughts using both texts and images. Such a limitation can be relieved by incorporating the inherent multi-modality of social media into the learning process as in [4,5]. These multi-modal approaches adopt an early fusion technique which leverages concatenated features of text and image to their proposed classifiers. However, none of them has investigated applicability to HAR and it is not trivial to construct a labeled dataset which is large enough to train their multi-modal supervised methods; to the best of our knowledge, no such dataset has been published yet for multi-modal HAR using social media.

In this paper, we present a semi-supervised method for HAR using multi-modal Instagram data, that is, both image and text, which achieves a high recognition accuracy while using only a limited amount of labeled data. On social media, the number of unlabeled data exponentially increases every day while only a few labeled data for a specific task exists. In such a domain, *semi-supervised learning* methods which leverage a small amount of labeled data and a much larger set of unlabeled data together are effective alternatives to improve learning performance [13]. To devise a semi-supervised learning method for HAR, we adopt the state-of-the-art clustering method, *MultiDEC* [7], which can learn deep embedded feature representations of social media image and text, respectively and extend it into a semi-supervised model which incorporates a small portion of labeled data into its training procedure. The proposed method minimizes both cross-entropy loss and Kullback-Leibler divergence loss. This enables the proposed model to learn more generalized feature distribution by leveraging the feature distribution of a large unlabeled dataset while optimizing the learning results to the labeled features. Evaluation results show that our method achieves 71.58% of recognition accuracy which outperforms the best accuracy of the existing HAR methods (maximum 64.15%).

2   Related Work

2.1   Human Activity Recognition Using Social Media

In general, previous HAR methods using social media incorporate text features with metadata such as timestamps, venues, and keywords into their supervised machine learning models. Zack et al. [1,2] leverage linear SVM for their human activity classifier and train the model using the text features from *Twitter* and *Instagram* data which they have collected and labeled using crowd-sourcing. Besides, Gong et al. [3] leverage *Yelp* data for HAR: They split each caption of a Yelp post into word tokens and create a sequence of embedded Word2Vec features. In addition to the extracted features, they use keyword dictionary knowledge embedding and temporal information encoding (e.g., date and week) for training a Long Short-Term Memory (LSTM) model to classify Yelp posts to human activity classes based on Yelp taxonomy[1].

---

[1] https://www.yelp.com/developers/documentation/v3/all_category_list.

To improve the recognition performance of the existing methods, multi-modal features (i.e., image and caption) of social media posts can be leveraged; there have been several approaches published already. Roy et al. [4] concatenate image features from a CNN model and text features from a Doc2Vec model and use them together to train a fully connected neural networks to identify social media posts related to illicit drugs. Schifanella et al. [5] use visual semantics from a CNN model and text features from an NLP network model together to train traditional models, SVM and DNN, respectively. After that, they leverage the trained models to detect sarcastic social media posts.

2.2 Deep Embedding Clustering and Semi-supervised Learning

Deep embedded clustering (DEC) [6] is an unsupervised method which simultaneously learns optimal feature representations and cluster assignments of unlabeled data by iteratively optimizing clustering objective. During the training process, DEC minimizes the KL divergence between the cluster soft assignment probability and the proposed target distribution so that its embedding network can learn feature representation. MultiDEC [7] is an extended version of DEC to deal with multi-modal data such as image-caption pairs. While DEC has a single embedding network, MultiDEC is composed of two embedding networks which are jointly trained to simultaneously learn image and text representations having similar distributions.

While DEC and MultiDEC are powerful methods, they cannot be directly used for HAR because they are clustering algorithms. To leverage their proven effectiveness for dealing with classification tasks, a semi-supervised DEC, *SSLDEC* [8], has been recently presented. SSLDEC learns the target distribution of labeled data, iteratively estimates the class probability distribution of unlabeled data by measuring its feature distances from the clusters of labeled data and optimizes them during training. Thus, SSLDEC is a transductive learning method that retains recognition performance even with a relatively small amount of labeled dataset. However, the supervision mechanism of SSLDEC may fail to maximize the HAR performance when the labeled data cannot represent the target distribution correctly or its distribution cannot accommodate that of unlabeled data. Especially, when applied to social media data where such characteristics are evident, the applicability of SSLDEC may drastically decrease.

3 Proposed Method: Semi-supervised Multi-modal DEC

3.1 Overview

The proposed method aims to predict human activity classes of multi-modal Instagram posts while training the optimal embedding network. More specifically, models in the proposed method should be well trained by means of a large number of unlabeled data where a limited number of labeled data is available.

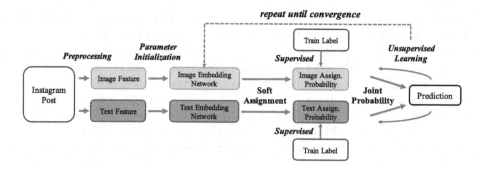

Fig. 1. An overview of our proposed semi-supervised multi-modal DEC

Figure 1 illustrates an overview of our proposed semi-supervised multi-modal DEC method to fulfill the key requirement. When multi-modal Instagram posts are given as a training dataset, our method preprocesses them to extract image and text features. Then, two embedding networks with parameters θ and θ' are initialized for learning deep representations of the image and text features, respectively. These networks are intended to embed image data, X, and text data, X', into the corresponding latent spaces, Z and Z'. Our method trains the embedding networks by alternating a supervised learning phase and an unsupervised learning phase. In the supervised learning phase, labeled multi-modal data is utilized for learning a class assignment. In the unsupervised learning phase, we leverage rich unlabeled data for computing cluster assignment probabilities for both features. After that, we compare them to the target joint probability distribution for adjusting cluster centroids, μ and μ', and eventually improving the cluster purity. This semi-supervised method helps us to learn the optimal representations of image and text features and apply Multi-modal DEC to HAR.

3.2 Multi-modal Data Pre-processing

Instagram data consists of image-text pairs where text is given as a mixture of a caption and multiple hashtags. For image preprocessing, we extract the 2048-dimensional feature representations of ResNet-50 [17] pretrained on ImageNet dataset [18]. We use this embedding method for image data because these features are known to be effective in image clustering as well as classification [19]. We compress the extracted 2048-dimensional features once again into 300-dimensions using Principal Component Analysis (PCA) [20]. For text preprocessing, we split a text into separate words using a Korean tokenizer [14], and embed them onto 300-dimensions of Doc2Vec [15] Skip-gram feature space. It is verified that Doc2vec trained in a large corpora can produce robust vector representations for long text paragraphs [16].

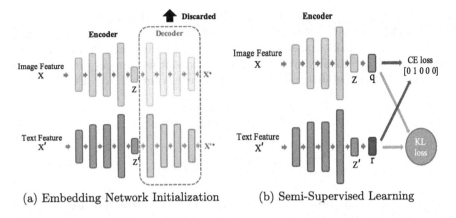

(a) Embedding Network Initialization   (b) Semi-Supervised Learning

Fig. 2. Core components of semi-supervised multi-modal DEC

3.3 Embedding Network Initialization

Once the preprocessed image and text data points, X and X', are given, two embedding networks with initial parameters, θ and θ', are created as in the original MultiDEC [7]. For the embedding networks, we train two symmetric stacked autoencoders which contain encoding and decoding layers; since the networks are symmetric, we describe only one embedding network for image data hereafter, supposing that text data embedding is gone through the same procedure, simultaneously. The stacked autoencoder with parameter θ compresses the input data X into a latent space Z in the encoder of stacked DNN layers and regenerates X^* from Z in the decoder with the minimized mean square error loss between X and X^*. To leverage the embedded features for HAR with j human activity classes, we apply the K-means algorithm to Z where k equals to j and generate j initial clusters with centroids μ. Then, to associate the generated j clusters with the most relevant human activity classes, we generate a $j \times j$ confusion matrix. The (m, n) element of this matrix indicates how many data with the mth class label is contained in the nth cluster. We create a cost matrix by subtracting the maximum value of the confusion matrix from the value of each cell and find the class assignment that minimizes the cost by applying the Hungarian algorithm. Finally, we rearrange the centroids μ to follow the assignment we find (Fig. 2).

3.4 Supervised Learning

When the latent features are ready to be associated with the label-oriented supervision, we initiate the supervised learning phase. In this phase, we optimize the model by minimizing the cross-entropy between the soft assignment probabilities, q_{ij} and r_{ij}, of the image and text samples, x_i and x'_i, from the labeled training set $\mathcal{L}$ and the given class label indicators, y_{ij}, respectively. y_{ij} is a binary indicator and it is assigned by 1 if a data point x_i is assigned to the cluster of its correct class label j and closely located to its centroid, otherwise 0.

Soft Assignment. We calculate the image soft assignment probability, q_{ij}, which is the similarity between the image embedding, z_i, and the image cluster centroid, μ_j, by making use of the Student's t-distribution [22] on 1 degree of freedom (Eq. 1). Similarly, we calculate the text soft assignment probability, r_{ij}, using the text embedding, z'_i, and the text cluster centroid, μ'_j, (Eq. 2).

$$q_{ij} = \frac{(1 + ||z_i - \mu_j||^2)^{-1}}{\sum_{j'}(1 + ||z_i - \mu_{j'}||^2)^{-1}} \tag{1}$$

$$r_{ij} = \frac{(1 + ||z'_i - \mu'_j||^2)^{-1}}{\sum_{j'}(1 + ||z'_i - \mu'_{j'}||^2)^{-1}} \tag{2}$$

Cross Entropy Minimization. The supervised loss functions for image and text models are defined by a sum of cross-entropy values between the calculated soft assignment probability and the given class label indicator of each sample $x_i \in \mathcal{L}$ as follows:

$$SL_{img} = \sum_{x_i \in \mathcal{L}} H(\mathbf{y}_i, \mathbf{q}_i) = -\sum_{x_i \in \mathcal{L}} \sum_j y_{ij} log(q_{ij}) \tag{3}$$

$$SL_{txt} = \sum_{x_i \in \mathcal{L}} H(\mathbf{y}_i, \mathbf{r}_i) = -\sum_{x_i \in \mathcal{L}} \sum_j y_{ij} log(r_{ij}) \tag{4}$$

During the supervised learning phase, our model learns to locate the embedded feature z_i of the labeled data points $x_i \in \mathcal{L}$ as close as possible to the centroid μ_j of each labeled class j.

3.5   Unsupervised Learning

In the unsupervised learning phase, our model is trained by using deep embedded clustering both on the unlabeled and labeled datasets, $\mathcal{U} \cup \mathcal{L}$. This learning proceeds by minimizing the KL-divergence of $\mathbf{q}$ and $\mathbf{r}$ against the generated target probability distribution $\mathbf{p}$.

Joint Target Distribution. The target distribution p_{ij} is computed using q_{ij} and r_{ij} jointly. We apply the second power distribution to q_{ij} and r_{ij}, respectively, in order to improve cluster purity and give more emphasis on data points assigned with high confidence as proposed in the DEC [6]. We take the mean distribution of them to calculate both q_{ij} and r_{ij} evenly (i.e., late fusion), following the MultiDEC [7].

$$p_{ij} = \frac{1}{2}\left(\frac{q_{ij}^2/f_j}{\sum_{j'} q_{ij'}^2/f_{j'}} + \frac{r_{ij}^2/g_j}{\sum_{j'} r_{ij'}^2/g_{j'}}\right) \tag{5}$$

KL Divergence Minimization. Once the joint target distribution is computed, we train our model by minimizing KL divergence with the unsupervised loss functions defined in Eq. 6 and 7. In addition to KL divergence minimization among $\mathbf{p}$, $\mathbf{q}$ and $\mathbf{r}$, DEC models can be trained by introducing extra losses between the mean $\mathbf{h}$ of the target probability distribution $\mathbf{p}$ and the prior knowledge $\mathbf{w}$ of the class distribution [7]. Here, our prior knowledge is obtained from the class distribution of $\mathcal{L}$.

$$UL_{img} = KL(\mathbf{p}\|\mathbf{q}) + KL(\mathbf{h}\|\mathbf{w}) \tag{6}$$

$$UL_{txt} = KL(\mathbf{p}\|\mathbf{r}) + KL(\mathbf{h}\|\mathbf{w}) \tag{7}$$

where $h_j = \sum_i p_{ij}/N$ and $w_j = \sum_i y_{ij}/N$.

Algorithm 1. Semi-Supervised Multi-Modal DEC

Require: models $M = (M_{img}, M_{txt})$, labeled set $\mathcal{L} = (\mathcal{L}_{img}, \mathcal{L}_{txt})$, unlabeled set $\mathcal{U} = (\mathcal{U}_{img}, \mathcal{U}_{txt})$, supervised learning rate η_s, unsupervised learning rate η_u.
Initialization:
$M_{img} \leftarrow$ encoder(autoencoder($\mathcal{L}_{img} \cup \mathcal{U}_{img}$))
$M_{txt} \leftarrow$ encoder(autoencoder($\mathcal{L}_{txt} \cup \mathcal{U}_{txt}$))
repeat
    Supervised Learning:
    $Q_1 \leftarrow$ predictions $(M_{img}, \mathcal{L}_{img})$ ▷ defined in (1)
    $R_1 \leftarrow$ predictions $(M_{txt}, \mathcal{L}_{txt})$ ▷ defined in (2)
    $M_{img} \leftarrow$ supervised_training $(\mathcal{L}_{img}, Q_1)$ ▷ based on loss defined in (3)
    $M_{txt} \leftarrow$ supervised_training $(\mathcal{L}_{txt}, R_1)$ ▷ based on loss defined in (4)
    Unsupervised Learning:
    $Q_2 \leftarrow$ predictions $(M_{img}, \mathcal{L}_{img} \cup \mathcal{U}_{img})$ ▷ defined in (1)
    $R_2 \leftarrow$ predictions $(M_{txt}, \mathcal{L}_{txt} \cup \mathcal{U}_{txt})$ ▷ defined in (2)
    $P \leftarrow$ target_distribution (Q_2, R_2) ▷ defined in (5)
    $M_{img} \leftarrow$ train_model (P, Q_2) ▷ based on loss defined in (6)
    $M_{txt} \leftarrow$ train_model (P, R_2) ▷ based on loss defined in (7)
until *end condition is met;*

In this phase, we set a learning rate, η_u, smaller than that in the supervised learning phase, η_s, so that $Z_{\mathcal{L}}$ is not affected too much by $\mathcal{U}$; in this work, we use $\eta_u = \kappa \times \eta_s$, where κ is an input parameter. Our learning method leverages the feature distributions of $\mathcal{U}$ and $\mathcal{L}$ together to make our model learn more generalized parameters, θ and μ, and prevent the trained model from being overfitted to $\mathcal{L}$. Algorithm 1 presents how the presented algorithms are used together through the entire procedure.

4 Evaluation

4.1 Dataset Construction

For dataset construction, we have collected geo-tagged Instagram posts containing various human activities in urban places nearby 25 stations on subway line 2 in Seoul from January 2015 to December 2018. Our collection is limited to Korean Instagram posts with non-empty captions. We have refined the captions by removing URLs, numbers, email addresses, or emoticons. We filtered out spam posts created multiple times by the same author, with the same caption, or at the same location. If a single post has more than one image, we take only the first image. Eventually, we constructed a dataset of 967,598 image-text pairs.

Table 1. The number of labeled Instagram posts for each human activity classes

Class label	Count	Class label	Count
Eating & Drinking*	5,013	Educational Activities*	256
Arts & Entertainment*	2,721	No Activity	102
Socializing & Communicating*	2,609	Caring for HH Members	87
Traveling*	1,651	Household Activities	35
Personal Care*	1,114	Unknown	27
Relaxing & Leisure*	926	Telephone Calls	19
Sports, Exercise, Recreation*	465	Volunteer Activities	15
Consumer Purchases*	456	Religious & Spiritual Activities	8
Work-Related Activities*	409	Government Services	6
Advertisement	339	Caring for NonHH Members	6
Attending or Hosting Social Events*	337	Household Services	2
Professional & Personal Services*	291	**Total**	**16,894**

For data labeling, we use major human activity classes in *American Time Use Survey (ATUS) taxonomy* [12] which has been widely-used for HAR. To establish a qualified dataset with a consensus mechanism, we first gathered 27 participants and divided them into three groups. Then, each group is given the same set of Instagram posts and asked to annotate the most likely human activity that each post represents. We use only posts that more than two participants agreed on the same human activity class label.

Table 1 shows 23 human activity class labels and their corresponding counts. Out of 17 ATUS classes, *Socializing, Relaxing, and Leisure* class appears too frequently in social media. We divide its Instagram posts into their sub-classes, *Socializing & Communicating, Attending or Hosting Social Events, Relaxing & Leisure, and Arts & Entertainment (other than sports)*, defined in ATUS taxonomy. Additionally, we add *Advertisement* and *Unknown* classes for filtering out spam and ambiguous posts. Eventually, we establish an HAR dataset of 16,894 labeled posts. From the dataset, we use 16,248 posts of 12 most frequently appearing classes for this evaluation, where they are marked as asterisks.

4.2   Evaluation Setup

For evaluation metric, we adopt accuracy score, macro f1 score, and Normalized Mutual Information (NMI). Accuracy score indicates the straightforward recognition performance, macro f1 score is a normalized HAR performance metric, and NMI indicates similarity between the probability distributions of the actual classes of the test set and the probability distributions of the predicted classes.

With these three standard metrics, we perform five-fold cross-testing and measure the average of the results. For training our model, we use unlabeled data with the training set of labeled data. In addition, we use the stochastic gradient descent (SGD) optimizer with a batch size of 256 and a learning rate of 0.01 (η_s). For training the stacked autoencoders in our model, we use the same configurations (i.e., layer structure and hyper-parameters) as in the original DEC model [6].

For a comparative evaluation, we implement baseline models with different data modalities. For text-only baseline models, we implement a linear SVM with a TF-IDF text input vector (TF-IDF+SVM) [1], an LSTM with a text Word2Vec input (Word2Vec+LSTM) [3], and an LSTM with dictionary embedding and a Word2Vec input (Word2Vec+LSTM+DE). For image-only baseline models, we implement a ResNet50 model which is pre-trained on ImageNet. This model is known to be robust to image classification [21] but no empirical results has been presented on HAR using social media data yet. To evaluate whether our proposed model utilizes the multi-modality of image-sharing social media data effectively and enhances the HAR performance, we also implement semi-supervised DEC models using uni-modality (i.e., text or image only) and compare their performance with that of the multi-modal one.

4.3 Evaluation Results

Evaluation results are summarized in Table 2. Above all, we find that our proposed model (Semi-supervised multi DEC) performs the best for HAR in all evaluation metrics. For example, in terms of accuracy score, its performance is 7.43% and 11.89% higher than the best performance of the text-only and image-only models, respectively. In terms of a normalized metric, macro f1 score, our proposed model performs 5.69% and 21.41% better than the text-only and image-only models. The higher NMI of our proposed model indicates that the semi-supervised multi-modal method is more effective for achieving an optimal clustering to the correct distribution than the baseline approaches. Considering that the semi-supervised uni-modal DEC performs worse than the baseline models in text-only case, we can deduce that our proposed model's achievement of the high accuracy is not attributed to the DEC component. In addition, by comparing the semi-supervised models with multi-modality and uni-modality, we can clearly find that incorporating multi-modal data helps to improve the HAR performance.

In order to verify the effect of semi-supervised learning using unlabeled samples, we measure the accuracy improvement as raising the number of unlabeled data while fixing the number of labeled data. Since our model generalizes itself by learning the feature distribution of the unlabeled data and avoids overfitting issue, its recognition accuracy is supposed to increase as the number of unlabeled data does. We fix the number of labeled data to 12,998 (i.e., 5-fold training data) and raise the number of unlabeled data $n(\mathcal{U})$ from 0 to 951,350.

Table 2. The result across different modals

Modality	Model	ACC	Macro F1	NMI
Text only	TF-IDF + SVM	0.6335	0.5283	0.3589
	Word2Vec + LSTM	0.6385	0.5372	0.3815
	Word2Vec + LSTM + DE	0.6415	0.5453	0.3804
	Semi-supervised text DEC	0.5939	0.5205	0.3394
Image only	ResNet50	0.5969	0.3881	0.3149
	Semi-supervised image DEC	0.5984	0.4484	0.3384
Text+Image	Semi-supervised multi DEC	**0.7158**	**0.6022**	**0.4790**

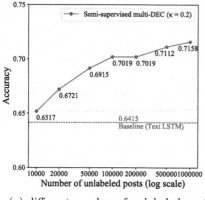

(a) different number of unlabeled posts

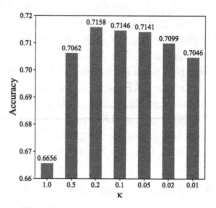

(b) different value of κ ($n(\mathcal{U}) = 1\text{M}$)

Fig. 3. The result of semi-supervised multi-DEC accuracy

From the results in Fig. 3(a), we observe that the accuracy increases logarithmically as the number of unlabeled data does in general. Compared to the accuracy with no unlabeled data given, we achieve about 8.9% of the performance gain when we use all unlabeled data. The accuracy increases very rapidly up to 100K unlabeled data, but the improvement speed slows down when the number of unlabeled data is from 100K to 200K. This means that at least 100K to 200K unlabeled data is required to generalize the feature distribution of 12K labeled data based on our data set. Hence, we conclude that incorporation of unlabeled data into the model training is helpful to improve HAR performance and our proposed model is capable of taking the advantage effectively.

When we set the supervised learning rate and the unsupervised learning rate to the same value ($\kappa = 1$), the performance is 66.56%, which is 2.41% higher than that of the baseline model. We conduct a further experiment here by putting κ, an input parameter that adjusts the unsupervised learning rate, so that supervised learning is not overly influenced by unsupervised learning. As a result, our model shows the highest performance of 71.58% when κ is 0.2 on our dataset when the number of unlabeled data is one million. This result assures that we can control the generalization effect of unsupervised learning with κ. We note that the value of κ varies according to the characteristics of the data such as the number of unlabeled data, the type of dataset, ambiguity among classes, etc. and we leave it for our future research.

5 Conclusion

In this paper, we present a semi-supervised multi-modal deep embedded clustering method for human activity recognition using social media. We adopt MultiDEC to leverage both image and text modalities and extend it into a semi-supervised learning method. By leveraging both labeled and unlabeled data, our model learns generalized feature representations and avoids being overfitted to the labeled features. Our proposed model achieves an improved HAR accuracy, compared to those of existing uni-modal approaches. In addition, we find that the incorporation of unlabeled data into the training procedure is helpful to improve HAR performance and our proposed model is capable of taking the advantage effectively.

Acknowledgement. This work was supported by Institute of Information & communications Technology Planning & Evaluation (IITP) grant funded by the Korea government (MSIT) (No. 2019-0-01126, Self-learning based Autonomic IoT Edge Computing).

References

1. Zhu, Z., Blanke, U., Calatroni, A., Tröster, G.: Human activity recognition using social media data. In: Proceedings of the 12th International Conference on Mobile and Ubiquitous Multimedia, p. 21. ACM (2013)
2. Zhu, Z., Blanke, U., Tröster, G.: Recognizing composite daily activities from crowd-labelled social media data. Pervasive Mob. Comput. **26**, 103–120 (2016)
3. Gong, J., Li, R., Yao, H., Kang, X., Li, S.: Recognizing human daily activity using social media sensors and deep learning. Int. J. Environ. Res. Public Health **16**(20), 3955 (2019)
4. Roy, A., Paul, A., Pirsiavash, H., Pan, S.: Automated detection of substance use-related social media posts based on image and text analysis. In: 2017 IEEE 29th International Conference on Tools with Artificial Intelligence (ICTAI), pp. 772–779. IEEE (2017)
5. Schifanella, R., de Juan, P., Tetreault, J., Cao, L.: Detecting sarcasm in multimodal social platforms. In: Proceedings of the 24th ACM International Conference on Multimedia, pp. 1136–1145. ACM (2016)
6. Xie, J., Girshick, R., Farhadi, A.: Unsupervised deep embedding for clustering analysis. In: International Conference on Machine Learning, pp. 478–487 (2016)
7. Yang, S., Huang, K.H., Howe, B.: MultiDEC: multi-modal clustering of image-caption pairs. arXiv preprint arXiv:1901.01860 (2019)
8. Enguehard, J., O'Halloran, P., Gholipour, A.: Semi-supervised learning with deep embedded clustering for image classification and segmentation. IEEE Access **7**, 11093–11104 (2019)

9. Cain, J.: Social media in health care: the case for organizational policy and employee education. Am. J. Health-Syst. Pharm. **68**(11), 1036–1040 (2011)
10. Mittal, R., Sinha, V.: A personalized time-bound activity recommendation system. In: 2017 IEEE 7th Annual Computing and Communication Workshop and Conference (CCWC), pp. 1–7. IEEE (2017)
11. Wei, Y., Zhu, Y., Leung, C.W.K., Song, Y., Yang, Q.: Instilling social to physical: co-regularized heterogeneous transfer learning. In: Thirtieth AAAI Conference on Artificial Intelligence (2016)
12. Shelley, K.J.: Developing the American time use survey activity classification system. Monthly Lab. Rev. **128**, 3 (2005)
13. Zhu, X., Goldberg, A.B.: Introduction to Semi-Supervised Learning. Synthesis Lectures on Artificial Intelligence and Machine Learning, vol. 3, no. 1, pp. 1–130 (2009)
14. Park, E.L., Cho, S.: KoNLPy: Korean natural language processing in Python. In: Proceedings of the 26th Annual Conference on Human & Cognitive Language Technology, vol. 6 (2014)
15. Le, Q., Mikolov, T.: Distributed representations of sentences and documents. In: International Conference on Machine Learning, pp. 1188–1196 (2014)
16. Lau, J.H., Baldwin, T.: An empirical evaluation of doc2vec with practical insights into document embedding generation. arXiv preprint arXiv:1607.05368 (2016)
17. He, K., Zhang, X., Ren, S., Sun, J.: Deep residual learning for image recognition. In: Proceedings of the IEEE Conference on Computer Vision and Pattern Recognition, pp. 770–778 (2016)
18. Deng, J., Dong, W., Socher, R., Li, L.J., Li, K., Fei-Fei, L.: ImageNet: a large-scale hierarchical image database. In: 2009 IEEE Conference on Computer Vision and Pattern Recognition, pp. 248–255. IEEE (2009)
19. Guérin, J., Gibaru, O., Thiery, S., Nyiri, E.: CNN features are also great at unsupervised classification. arXiv preprint arXiv:1707.01700 (2017)
20. Jolliffe, I.T., Cadima, J.: Principal component analysis: a review and recent developments. Philos. Trans. R. Soc. A Math. Phys. Eng. Sci. **374**(2065), 20150202 (2016)
21. Su, D., Zhang, H., Chen, H., Yi, J., Chen, P.Y., Gao, Y.: Is robustness the cost of accuracy?-A comprehensive study on the robustness of 18 deep image classification models. In: Proceedings of the European Conference on Computer Vision (ECCV), pp. 631–648 (2018)
22. van der Maaten, L., Hinton, G.: Visualizing data using t-SNE. J. Mach. Learn. Res. **9**, 2579–2605 (2008)

Author Index

Printed in the United States
By Bookmasters